W9-AQD-573

Main Cities
of Europe

2017

Contents

DEAR READER 4

OUR COMMITMENTS 5

HOW TO USE THIS GUIDE 6

THE SYMBOLS 8
 Classification & Awards 8
 Facilities & Services 10

PRICES 10

CITY PLAN KEY 11

EUROPE IN MAPS AND NUMBERS 927
 Eurozone 928
 Schengen Countries 929
 Driving in Europe 930
 Distances 932
 Time Zones 934
 Telephone Codes Rear flap

COUNTRIES

21 AUSTRIA
Vienna — 22
Salzburg — 46

61 BELGIUM
Brussels — 62
Antwerp — 94

109 CZECH REPUBLIC
Prague — 110

129 DENMARK
Copenhagen — 130
Aarhus — 150

159 FINLAND
Helsinki — 160

171 FRANCE
Paris — 172
Lyons — 256
Strasbourg — 274

285 GERMANY
Berlin — 286
Cologne — 312
Frankfurt — 328
Hamburg — 344
Munich — 364

385 GREECE
Athens — 386

397 HUNGARY
Budapest — 398

413 IRELAND
Dublin — 414

429 ITALY
Rome — 430
Florence — 454
Milan — 472
Turin — 496

509 LUXEMBOURG
Luxembourg — 510

519 NETHERLANDS
Amsterdam — 520
Hague (The) — 544
Rotterdam — 556

567 NORWAY
Oslo — 568

581 POLAND
Warsaw — 582
Cracow — 594

607 PORTUGAL
Lisbon — 608

623 SPAIN
Madrid — 624
Barcelona — 656
Valencia — 684

697 SWEDEN
Stockholm — 698
Gothenburg — 718
Malmö — 730

739 SWITZERLAND
Bern — 740
Geneva — 748
Zurich — 766

785 UNITED KINGDOM
London — 786
Birmingham — 894
Edinburgh — 902
Glasgow — 916

Dear Reader,

Welcome to the 36th edition of the 'Main Cities of Europe' guide.

This guide is aimed primarily at international business travellers who regularly journey throughout Europe but it is equally ideal for those wishing to discover the delights of some of Europe's most romantic and culturally stimulating cities for a short break or special occasion.

Entry into the MICHELIN guide is completely free of charge and it continues to be compiled by our professionally trained teams of full-time inspectors from across Europe, who make their assessments anonymously in order to ensure complete impartiality and independence. Their mission is to check the quality and consistency of the amenities and services provided by the hotels and restaurants throughout the year and our listings are updated annually in order to ensure the most up-to-date information.

Most of the establishments featured have been hand-picked from our other national guides and therefore our European selection is, effectively, a best-of-the-best listing.

In addition to its user-friendly layout, the guide contains practical and cultural information on each country and each city; suggestions on when to go, what to see and what to eat; and keywords which succinctly convey the style of each establishment.

Thank you for your support and please continue to send us your comments. We hope you will enjoy travelling with the 'Main Cities of Europe' guide 2017.

Consult the MICHELIN guide at:
www.ViaMichelin.com
and write to us at:
themichelinguide-europe@uk.michelin.com

Our Commitments:
Experienced in quality!

Whether they are in Japan, the USA, China or Europe, our inspectors use the same criteria to judge the quality of each and every hotel and restaurant that they visit. The MICHELIN guide commands a worldwide reputation thanks to the commitments we make to our readers - and we reiterate these below:

Anonymous inspections – Our inspectors make regular and anonymous visits to hotels and restaurants to gauge the quality of products and services offered to an ordinary customer. They settle their own bill and may then introduce themselves and ask for more information about the establishment. Our readers' comments are also a valuable source of information, which we can follow up with a visit of our own.

Independence – To remain totally objective for our readers, the selection is made with complete independence. Entry into the guide is free. All decisions are discussed with the Editor and our highest awards are considered at a European level.

Selection and choice – The guide offers a selection of the best hotels and restaurants in every category of comfort and price. This is only possible because all the inspectors rigorously apply the same methods.

Annual updates – All the practical information, classifications and awards are revised and updated every year to give the most reliable information possible.

Consistency – The criteria for the classifications are the same in every country covered by the MICHELIN guide.

The sole intention of Michelin is to make your travels safe and enjoyable.

How to use this Guide

LOCATION

The country, the town, the district and the map.

RESTAURANTS

XxXxX to X
Red: Our most delightful places.

STARS

❀❀❀
Exceptional cuisine, worth a special journey!

❀❀
Excellent cooking, worth a detour!

❀
High quality cooking, worth a stop!

BIB GOURMAND

🅑
Good quality, good value cooking.

RESTAURANTS & HOTELS

The country is indicated by the coloured strip down the side of the page: light for restaurants, dark for hotels.

HOTELS

🏠🏠🏠 to 🏠
Red: Our most delightful places.

PARIS
PARIS
Population 2 243 833

CHAMPS-ÉLYSÉES, ÉTOILE, PAL

Le Petit Four (Martin)
2 rue François 1ᵉʳ (1st) Ⓜ Palais-Royal – ℰ 01 12 9
– www.petit.four.fr – Closed Sunday dinner
Menu 75 €, 185/215 € – Carte 112/170 € (book
→ Foie gras chaud au vinaigre de cidre. Saint
rôti au miel.
• Luxury • Inventive •
In the gardens of the Palais-Royal, sumptuc
rated with splendid "pictures under glass"
worthy of this historic monument.

Au Pied de Porc
15 bd Voltaire (11th) Ⓜ République – ℰ 01
– www.Pieddeporc.org – Closed in July an
Menu 9 €, 32/72 € – Carte 37/61 €
• Classic • Trendy •
Pigs trotters are the speciality of this re
late into the night since opened in 19
fruits designs.

ÉTOILE – CHAMPS-ÉLYSÉES
Rond-point des Champs-É

Palazzo Panthéon Ⓜ Franklin-F
2 rue Montaigne (8th) – www.palazzoc
– ℰ 01 45 12 24 24 – 🛏 – ‡ 250/350 € ‡‡ 400/5
145 rm
❀❀ **La Terrasse** – See restaura
• Palace • Stylish •
Classic style in the luxuriously rec
gallery, stunning designer bar:
ming, green-filled terrace, ensh
when the weather turns nice, i

Le Faubourg St-Thomas
15 r. des Ecuries (7th) Ⓜ St-Fra
– www.faubourgsainthomas
174 rm 🛏20 € – ‡ 250 € ‡‡
❀ **Café Honoré** – See res
• Business • Moder
This "Faubourg" branch of
tech rooms, 1930-style ba
decor, restful indoor gard

Élysée Hotel Ⓜ
112 rue Copernic (8th) – C
– www.elyseehotel.fr – C
29 rm – ‡ 90/120 € ‡‡
• Family • Cosy •
Peninsula family hote

LOCATING
THE ESTABLISHMENT

Use the coordinates to locate the establishment on the city plan.

PRACTICAL & TOURIST
INFORMATION

Pages with practical information on every city: tourist sites, cultural attractions, annual events, public transport... and local cuisine!

FACILITIES
& SERVICES

See also page 10.

ADDRESS & PRICES

All the information you need to make a reservation and find the establishment.
Prices: see also page 10.

DESCRIPTION OF
THE ESTABLISHMENT

Atmosphere, style, character...

DISTRICT

See corresponding plan number.

KEY WORDS

If you are looking for a specific type of establishment, these key words will help you make your choice more quickly.
→ For hotels, the first word explains the establishment type (chain, business, luxury, etc); the second one describes the décor (modern, stylish, design, etc) and sometimes a third will be used to complete the picture.
→ For restaurants, the first word relates to the type of cuisine and the second to the atmosphere.

7

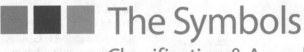

The Symbols
Classification & Awards

CATEGORIES OF COMFORT

The MICHELIN Guide selection lists the best hotels and restaurants in each category of comfort and price. The establishments we choose are classified according to their levels of comfort and, within each category, are listed in order of preference.

🏨 ☓☓☓☓☓ Hotels and restaurants, classified by their comfort, from 5 to 1

🏠 Other recommended accommodation

⚐ Hotel with a restaurant

🛏 Restaurant with bedrooms

| 🍺 | Pubs serving good food |
| 🍴 | Tapas bars |

THE AWARDS

To help you make the best choice, some exceptional establishments have been given an award in this year's guide. They are highlighted with Stars ❀ (One, Two or Three) or a Bib Gourmand 😋.

THE BEST CUISINE

Michelin Stars are awarded to establishments serving cuisine, of whatever style, which is of the highest quality. The cuisine is judged on the quality of the ingredients, the skill in their preparation, the combination of flavours, the levels of creativity, the value for money and the consistency of culinary standards.

For every restaurant awarded a Star we include 3 specialities that are typical of their cooking style. These specific dishes may not always be available.

❀❀❀ **Three Stars: Exceptional cuisine, worth a special journey!**
Our highest award is given for the superlative cooking of chefs at the peak of their profession. The ingredients are exemplary, the cooking is elevated to an art form and their dishes are often destined to become classics.

❀❀ **Two Stars: Excellent cooking, worth a detour!**
The personality and talent of the chef and their team is evident in the expertly crafted dishes, which are refined, inspired and sometimes original.

❀ **One Star: High quality cooking, worth a stop!**
Using top quality ingredients, dishes with distinct flavours are carefully prepared to a consistently high standard.

GOOD FOOD AT MODERATE PRICES

☞   **Bib Gourmand: Good quality, good value cooking**
'Bibs' are awarded for simple yet skilful cooking.

PLEASANT HOTELS AND RESTAURANTS

Symbols shown in red indicate particularly pleasant or restful establishments: the character of the building, its décor, the setting, the welcome and services offered may all contribute to this special appeal.

🏠 to 🏠🏠🏠🏠   **The most delightful hotels**
✒ to ✒✒✒✒   **The most delightful restaurants**

OTHER SPECIAL FEATURES

As well as the categories and awards given to the establishment, Michelin inspectors also make special note of other criteria which can be important when choosing an establishment.

LOCATION

If you are looking for a particularly restful establishment, or one with a special view, look out for the following symbols:

₽   **Peaceful establishment**
≼   **Great view**

WINE LIST

If you are looking for an establishment with an excellent wine list, look out for the following symbol:

🍷   **Particularly interesting wine list**
This symbol might cover the list presented by a sommelier in a luxury restaurant or that of a simple restaurant where the owner has a passion for wine. The two lists will offer something exceptional but very different, so beware of comparing them by each other's standards.

The Symbols
Facilities & Services

Ⓜ	Nearest metro / underground station
🍴	Outside dining available
🌳	Garden or park
Spa	Spa
⌇ ⌇	Outdoor / Indoor swimming pool
🏋	Exercise room
♨	Sauna
✗	Tennis court
♿	Wheelchair access
AK	Air conditioning
⚡	Some facilities reserved for non-smokers
♧	Private dining room
🏛	Conference room
🍲	Vegetarian menus (UK and Ireland)
☕	Restaurant offering lower priced theatre menus
🚘	Valet parking
🚗	Garage
🅿	Parking
🚫	Credit cards not accepted

Prices

The prices are given in the currency of the country in question. Valid for 2017 the rates shown should only vary if the cost of living changes to any great extent.

MEALS

Menu 40/56	Fixed price menu - Lowest / highest price
Carte 65/78	À la carte menu - Lowest / highest price
🍷	House wine included

HOTEL

30 rm	Number of rooms
86 rm - 🛉 650/750	Lowest and highest price for a single
🛉🛉 750/890	and for a double room
28 rm ☕ **-** 🛉 100 🛉🛉 180	Bed & breakfast rate
☕ 20	Price of breakfast where not included in rate

City Plan Key

- ● Hotels
- ● Restaurants

SIGHTS

▬	Place of interest	🏛	Interesting place of worship

ROADS

═══	Motorway	❶	Junctions: complete
═══	Dual carriageway	❶	Junctions: limited
▬	Pedestrian street	🚉	Station and railway

VARIOUS SIGNS

🄸	Tourist Information Centre	✈	Airport
▣▣	Mosque	✚	Hospital
▨▨	Synagogue	✉	Covered market
✿✿	Ruins	▭	Public buildings:
▬	Garden, Park, Wood	H	Town Hall
🚌	Coach station	R	Town Hall (Germany)
Ⓜ	Metro station	M	Museum
⊖	Underground station (UK)	U	University

11

MICHELIN IS CONTINUALLY INNOVATING FOR SAFER, CLEANER, MORE ECONOMICAL, BETTER CONNECTED... ALL-ROUND MOBILITY.

Tyres wear more quickly on short urban journeys.

TRUE!

You tend to accelerate and brake more often when driving around town so your tyres work harder!
If you are stuck in traffic, keep calm and drive slowly.

Tyre pressure only affects your car's safety.

FALSE!

Driving with underinflated tyres (0.5 bar below recommended pressure) doesn't just impact handling and fuel consumption, it will shave 8,000 km off tyre lifespan.
Make sure you check tyre pressure about once a month and before you go on holiday or a long journey.

Fitting **2 winter tyres** on my car guarantees maximum safety.

FALSE!

In the winter, especially when temperatures drop below 7°C, to ensure better road holding, all four tyres should be identical and fitted at the same time.

2 WINTER TYRES ONLY = risk of compromised road holding.

4 WINTER TYRES = **safer handling** when cornering, driving downhill and braking.

If you regularly encounter rain, snow or black ice, choose a **MICHELIN Alpin tyre**. This range offers you sharp handling plus a comfortable ride to safely face the challenge of winter driving.

MICHELIN IS COMMITTED

▶ MICHELIN IS **GLOBAL LEADER IN FUEL-EFFICIENT TYRES** FOR LIGHT VEHICLES.

▶ **TO EDUCATE YOUNGSTERS IN ROAD SAFETY,** INCLUDING CYCLING, MICHELIN ROAD SAFETY CAMPAIGNS WERE RUN IN **16 COUNTRIES** IN 2015.

QUIZ

1 TYRES ARE BLACK SO WHY IS THE MICHELIN MAN WHITE?

Back in 1898 when the Michelin Man
was first created from a stack of tyres,
they were made of natural rubber, cotton
and sulphur and were therefore
light-coloured. The composition of tyres
did not change until after the First World War
when carbon black was introduced.
But the Michelin Man kept his colour!

2 HOW LONG HAS MICHELIN BEEN GUIDING TRAVELLERS?

Since 1900. When the MICHELIN guide was first
published at the turn of the century, it was claimed
that it would last for a hundred years. It's still
around today, with new editions published every
year, along with online restaurant listings.

3 WHEN WAS THE "BIB GOURMAND" INTRODUCED IN THE MICHELIN GUIDE?

The symbol was created in 1997 but as early as 1954
the MICHELIN guide was recommending "good food
at moderate prices". Today, it also features on the
ViaMichelin website and on the Michelin Restaurants app.

If you want to enjoy a fun day out and find out more about Michelin,
why not visit the l'Aventure Michelin museum and shop
in Clermont-Ferrand, France:
www.laventuremichelin.com

Selection by Country

AUSTRIA
ÖSTERREICH

VIENNA ●

● Salzburg

→ **AREA:**
83 878 km²
(32 376 sq mi).

→ **POPULATION:**
8 588 443 inhabitants.
Density = 102 per km².

→ **CAPITAL:**
Vienna.

→ **CURRENCY:**
Euro (€).

→ **GOVERNMENT:**
Parliamentary republic and federal state (since 1955). Member of European Union since 1995.

→ **LANGUAGE:**
German.

→ **PUBLIC HOLIDAYS:**
New Years' Day (1 Jan); Epiphany (6 Jan); Easter Monday (late Mar/Apr); Labor Day (1 May); Ascension Day (May); Whit Monday (late May/June); Corpus Christi (late May/June); Assumption of the Virgin Mary (15 Aug); National Day (26 Oct); All Saints' Day (1 Nov); Immaculate Conception (8 Dec); Christmas Day (25 Dec); St Stephen's Day (26 Dec).

→ **LOCAL TIME:**
GMT+1 hour in winter and GMT+2 hours in summer.

→ **CLIMATE:**
Temperate continental with cold winters - high snow levels - and warm summers (Vienna: January 0°C; July 20°C).

→ **EMERGENCY:**
Police: ✆ **133**;
Medical Assistance: ✆ **144**;
Fire Brigade: ✆ **122**.
(Dialling **112** within any EU country will redirect your call and contact the emergency services.)

→ **ELECTRICITY:**
230 volts AC, 50Hz; 2 round pin sockets.

→ **FORMALITIES:**
Travellers from the European Union (EU), Switzerland, Iceland and the main countries of North and South America need a national identity card or passport (America: passport required) to visit Austria for less than three months (tourism or business purpose).
For visitors from other countries a visa may be required, in addition to a passport, especially for those wishing to stay for longer than three months. We advise you to check with your embassy before travelling.

VIENNA
WIEN

Population: 1 781 105

ReSeandra/Fotolia.com

Beethoven, Brahms, Mozart, Haydn, Strauss…not a bad list of former residents, by any stretch of the imagination. One and all, they succumbed to the opulent aura of Vienna, a city where an appreciation of the arts is as conspicuous as its famed cakes. Sumptuous architecture and a refined air reflect the city's historic position as the seat of the powerful Habsburg dynasty and former epicentre of the Austro-Hungarian Empire. Despite its grand image, Vienna has propelled itself into the 21C with a handful of innovative hotspots, most notably the MuseumsQuartier cultural complex, a stone's throw from the mighty Hofburg Imperial Palace. This is not a big city, although its vivid image gives that impression. The compact centre teems with elegant shops, fashionable coffee-houses and grand avenues, and the empire's awesome 19C remnants keep visitors' eyes fixed forever upwards. Many towns and cities are defined by their ring roads, but Vienna can boast a truly upmarket version: the Ringstrasse, a showpiece boulevard that cradles the inner city and the riches that lie therein. Just outside, to the southwest are the districts of Neubau and Spittelberg, both of which have taken on a quirky, modernistic feel. To the east lies Prater, the green lung of Vienna and further out lies the suburban area enhanced by the grandeur of the Schönbrunn palace.

VIENNA IN...

➜ **ONE DAY**
A tram ride round the Ringstrasse, St Stephen's Cathedral, a section of the Hofburg Palace, cakes in a café.

➜ **TWO DAYS**
MuseumsQuartier, Spittelberg, Hundertwasserhaus, Prater.

➜ **THREE DAYS**
A day at the Belvedere, a night at the opera.

PRACTICAL INFORMATION

ARRIVAL-DEPARTURE

✈ Wien-Schwechat Airport is 19km from the city centre.

The City Airport Express train to Wien Mitte takes 16min and leaves every 30min. A taxi will take around 30min.

GETTING AROUND

The city's buses, trams and metro are renowned for their impressive efficiency. You can purchase Rover tickets for 24hr or 72hr. There are around eighty bus routes in the city. Night buses run every half-hour; trams run every 5-10min and there are timetables at every stop. The Vienna Card, which allows unlimited travel on the whole of the city's public transport network for 24, 48 or 72hr and offers a discount to sights, cafes, restaurants and shops, can be bought from the Tourist Office, at your hotel or from ticket offices of the Vienna Transport Authority.

CALENDAR HIGHLIGHTS

January
New Year's Concert of the Vienna Philharmonic.

February
Opera Ball.

April
Vienna City Marathon.

June
Donau Island Festival.
Life Ball.

October
Viennale Film Festival, Long Night of the Museums.
Literature Festival.

November
Vienna Jazz Floor Festival.

EATING OUT

Vienna is the spiritual home of the café and Austrians drink nearly twice as much coffee as beer. It is also a city with a sweet tooth: cream cakes enhance the window displays of most eateries and is there a visitor to Vienna who hasn't succumbed to the sponge of the Sachertorte? Viennese food is essentially the food of Bohemia, which means that meat has a strong presence on the plate. Expect beef, veal and pork, alongside potatoes, dumplings or cabbage - be sure to try traditional boiled beef and the ubiquitous Wiener Schnitzel (deep-fried breaded veal). Also worth experiencing are the Heurigen, traditional Austrian wine taverns which are found in Grinzing, Heiligenstadt, Neustift and Nussdorf. You'll find plenty of snug cafés and bars too. If you want to snack, the place to go is Naschmarkt, Vienna's best market, where the stalls spill over into the vibrant little restaurants. When it comes to tipping, if you're in the more relaxed, local pubs and wine taverns, just round up the bill, otherwise add on ten per cent.

AUSTRIA - VIENNA

Palais Coburg Residenz   ☆ ⇦ 🏠 🔲 🕭 🗛 🚇 🚗

Coburgbastei 4 ✉ *1010 –* Ⓜ *Stubentor –* ℰ *(01)*   Plan: E2
51 81 80 – www.palais-coburg.com
34 suites 🔲 – ♦695/2695 € ♦♦695/2695 €
• Grand Luxury • Historic • Contemporary •
This magnificent, classic building was built in 1840. It offers guests an imposing
hotel setting that is more than matched by the luxurious, largely duplex suites
and the excellent service. The Clementine restaurant serves international fare,
has a winter garden feel and boasts an attractive terrace.
❀❀ **Silvio Nickol Gourmet Restaurant** – See restaurant listing

Sacher   🗲 🕭 🏠 🕭 🗛 🚇 🚗

Philharmonikerstr. 4 ✉ *1010 –* Ⓜ *Karlsplatz –* ℰ *(01)*   Plan: D3
51 45 60 – www.sacher.com
149 rm – ♦555/960 € ♦♦555/960 € – 🖵 41 € – 16 suites
• Grand Luxury • Classic • Personalised •
The rooms in this hotel that dates back to 1876 are elegant, modern and equipped with the latest technology. The traditional feel is still here, as is the attentive
service. The suites and rooms on the top floor enjoy a wonderful roof terrace
and an exclusive spa. Don't forget to visit the famous Café Sacher.
Anna Sacher • Rote Bar – See restaurant listing

Imperial   ☆ 🗲 🏠 🕭 🗛 🚇

Kärntner Ring 16 ✉ *1015 –* Ⓜ *Karlsplatz –* ℰ *(01)*   Plan: E3
50 11 00 – www.imperialvienna.com
138 rm – ♦399/819 € ♦♦399/819 € – 🖵 41 € – 35 suites
• Palace • Grand Luxury • Historic •
This grand hotel was opened in 1873 to celebrate Vienna's World Expo, and still
promises all the majesty of the Austrian Empire in its splendid interior. The
lobby is stylish, the rooms and suites are lavish and elegant. Don't miss the fascinating 'Course of History'. The restaurant is decidedly upmarket and the Café
Imperial is a classic Viennese coffee house.
❀ **OPUS** – See restaurant listing

Park Hyatt   🗲 🕭 🏠 🔲 🕭 🚇 🚗

Am Hof 2 ✉ *1010 –* Ⓜ *Herrengasse –* ℰ *(01)*   Plan: D2
2 27 40 12 34 – www.parkhyattvienna.com
143 rm – ♦425/520 € ♦♦425/520 € – 🖵 35 € – 35 suites
• Historic • Luxury • Elegant •
Dating back to 1915, this former bank combines stylish period architecture,
modern design and the latest technology. This creates an impressive luxury
hotel with an upmarket Arany Spa – the old vaults now house a gold-plated
pool!
The Bank – See restaurant listing

The Ritz-Carlton   ☆ 🗲 🕭 🏠 🔲 🕭 🗛 🚇 🚗

Schubertring 5 ✉ *1010 –* Ⓜ *Karlsplatz –* ℰ *(01) 3 11 88*   Plan: E3
– www.ritzcarlton.com/vienna
202 rm – ♦365/625 € ♦♦365/625 € – 🖵 36 € – 21 suites
• Business • Grand Luxury • Contemporary •
This luxury hotel is created from four individual buildings and set right on Vienna's Ringstraße. It offers a restrained and tasteful modern interior that is never
ostentatious and has lots of period detail (the comfortable lobby was once a
bank vault). There is an exclusive Guerlain Spa and impeccable service of the
sort you would expect in a Ritz-Carlton. The Distrikt restaurant serves international cuisine and various cuts of steak.

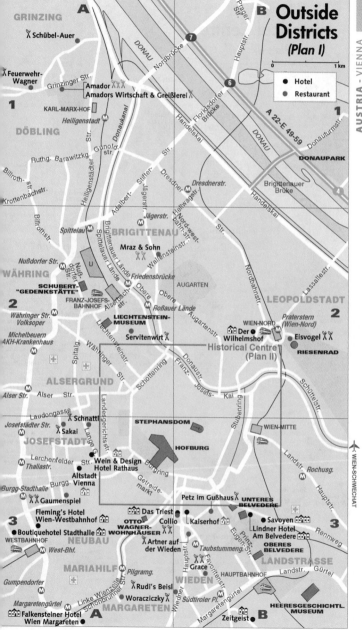

Outside Districts (Plan I)

GRINZING

Schübel-Auer

Feuerwehr-Wagner

Grinzinger Str.

Amador
Amadors Wirtschaft & Greißlerei

KARL-MARX-HOF

Heiligenstadt

DÖBLING

Ruthg. Barawitzkg.

Billroth-str.

Krottenbachstr.

Gunold. str.

Heiligenstädter Str.

Adalbert-

Stifter-

Jägerstr.

Dresdner-

Dresdnerstr.

Nordbahnbrücke

DONAU

Nordwestbahnstr.

Handelskai

Florisdorfer Brücke

Prager Str.

A 22-E 49-59

Donauturmstr.

DONAUPARK

Brigittenauer Brücke

Handelskai

DONAU

0 — 1 km

● Hotel
● Restaurant

Spittelau

Brigittenauer Lände

Spittelauer Lände

Nußdorfer Str.

WÄHRING

Nußdorfer Str.

SCHUBERT-"GEDENKSTÄTTE"

FRANZ-JOSEFS-BAHNHOF

BRIGITTENAU

Mraz & Sohn

Walfensteinstr.

Friedensbrücke

Obere

Obere

AUGARTEN

Roßauer Lände

Augartenstr.

Nordbahnstr.

Lassallestr.

LEOPOLDSTADT

Währinger Str.
Volksoper

LIECHTENSTEIN-MUSEUM

Servitenwirt

Liechtensteinstr.

WIEN-NORD

Der ●
Wilhelmshof

Praterstern
(Wien-Nord)

Eisvogel

RIESENRAD

Michelbeuern
AKH-Krankenhaus

ALSERGRUND

Spitalg.

Währinger Str.

Landesgerichtsstr.

Historical Centre
(Plan II)

Donaustr.

Franz-Josefs-Kai

Schottenring

Alser Str.   Alser   Str.

Laudongasse

Schnattl

Josefstädter Str.

Sakai

JOSEFSTADT

Lange

Stuberting

WIEN-MITTE

WIEN-SCHWECHAT

Lerchenfelder   Str.
Thaliastr.

Burgg.

Burgg-Stadthalle

Gaumenspiel

Wein & Design
Hotel Rathaus

Altstadt
Vienna

STEPHANSDOM

HOFBURG

Landstr. Rochusg.

Haupt str.

Fleming's Hotel
Wien-Westbahnhof

WESTBAHNHOF

Boutiquehotel Stadthalle

West-Bhf.

OTTO
WAGNER-WOHNHÄUSER

Das Triest

Collio

Kaiserhof

Petz im Gußhaus   UNTERES
BELVEDERE

Savoyen

Lindner Hotel
Am Belvedere

OBERES
BELVEDERE

LANDSTRASSE

Rennweg

Getreidemarkt

Ringstr.

NEUBAU

MARIAHILF

Gumpendorfer

Margaretengürtel

Falkensteiner Hotel
Wien Margareten

Artner auf
der Wieden

Prinz-Eugen-Str.

Pilgramg.

Linke Wienzeile

Schönbrunner Str.

MARGARETEN

Rudi's Beisl

Woracziczky

Grace

Taubstummeng.

Favoritenstr.

HAUPTBAHNHOF

Wiedner

Südtiroler Pl.

WIEDEN

Margaretengürtel

Landstr.   Gürtel

HEERESGESCHICHTL.
MUSEUM

Zeitgeist

A   B

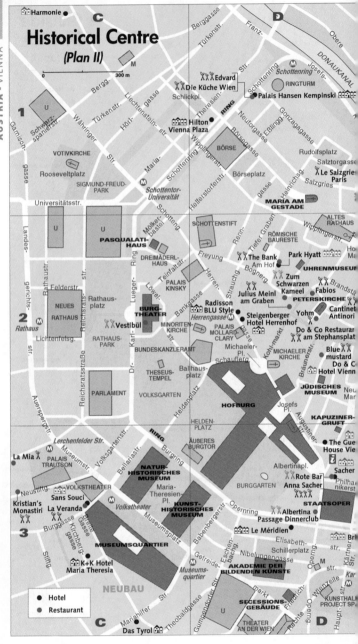

Historical Centre
(Plan II)

0   300 m

Harmonie ●
M

C

D

Berggasse
Türkenstr.
Franz-
Obere
DONAUKANAL

Edvard
Die Küche Wien
Schlickpl.
RING
Schottenring
RINGTURM
Palais Hansen Kempinski

Schwarz-
spanierstr.
Gamison-
gasse
Währinger Str.
Liechtenstein-gasse
Hörl-
Theresien-
Schottenring
Wippinngerstr.
Bösendferg.
Neutorgasse
Eßlinggasse
Gonzagagasse

VOTIVKIRCHE
Roosveltplatz
SIGMUND-FREUD-PARK
Universitätsstr.
M
Schottentor-Universität
Maria-
Schottenring
Helferstorferstr.

Hilton
Vienna Plaza
BÖRSE
Börsegasse
Börseplatz

Rudolfsplatz
Salztorgasse
Le Salzgrie
Paris
Salzgries
Heinrichsg.

MARIA AM
GESTADE

Landes-
gerichts-
str.
Bathaustr.
Felderstr.
NEUES
RATHAUS
M
Rathaus
Lichtenfelsg.
RATHAUS-PARK
PARLAMENT
Reichsratsstraße
Dr.-Karl-Lueger-Ring

PASQUALATI-HAUS
DREIMÄDERL-HAUS
Teinfaltstr.
PALAIS KINSKY
BURG-THEATER
Vestibül
Bankgasse
MINORITEN-KIRCHE
BUNDESKANZLERAMT
THESEUS-TEMPEL
Ballhaus-platz
VOLKSGARTEN
Löwel-
Herren-
Freyung
Renn-
Strauchg.
Bognerg.

SCHOTTENSTIFT
Tiefer Graben
Am Hof
The Bank
Julius Meinl
am Graben
Radisson
BLU Style
Herrengasse
M
Steigenberger
Hotel Herrenhof
PALAIS
MOLLARD-
CLARY
Michaeler-
Pl.
Schauflerg.
MICHAELER-KIRCHE
Kohlmarkt
Bräunerstr.

RÖMISCHE
BAURESTE
Park Hyatt
UHRENMUSEUM
Zum
Schwarzen
Kameel
Fabios
PETERSKIRCHE
Yohm
Cantinet
Antinori
Do & Co Restauran
am Stephansplat
Blue
mustard
Do & C
Hotel Vienn

ALTES
RATHAUS
Wipplinggerstr.
Brandstä

JÜDISCHES
MUSEUM
Neu
Mar
KAPUZINER-GRUFT

HOFBURG
Josefs-Pl.
Augustiner-

HELDEN-PLATZ
ÄUSSERES
BURGTOR
RING
Burgring

Lerchenfelder Str.
La Mia
PALAIS
TRAUTSON
Museumstr.
Volksgartenstr.
Bellariastr.

NATUR-
HISTORISCHES
MUSEUM
Maria-
Theresien-Pl.
KUNST-
HISTORISCHES
MUSEUM
Museumsplatz

Neustiftg.
Kristian's
Monastiri
VOLKSTHEATER
Sans Souci
La Veranda
M
Volkstheater
Burggasse
Breite Gasse
Kirchberg-
gasse
Stiftg.

Albertinapl.
BURGGARTEN
Rote Bar
Anna Sacher
Albertina
Passage Dinnerclub
Le Méridien
Elisabeth-
Schillerplatz
AKADEMIE DER
BILDENDEN KÜNSTE
SECESSIONS-GEBÄUDE

The Gue
House Vie
Sacher
Philha
nikerst
STAATSOPER
Opernring
Opernring
Babenbergerstr.
Nibelungengasse
Eschen-
bachg.

Bri
str.
Kärtner
Str.
M
str.
Kar

K+K Hotel
Maria Theresia
MUSEUMSQUARTIER
Museums-quartier
Getreide-
Gumpendorfer Str.

NEUBAU

Mariahilfer Str.
Theobaldgasse
Das Tyrol
THEATER
AN DER WIEN

U
markt
Friedrich
Wienzeile
Rechte
Haupt-
Opern
KUNSTHALL
PROJECT SP

● Hotel
● Restaurant

C

D

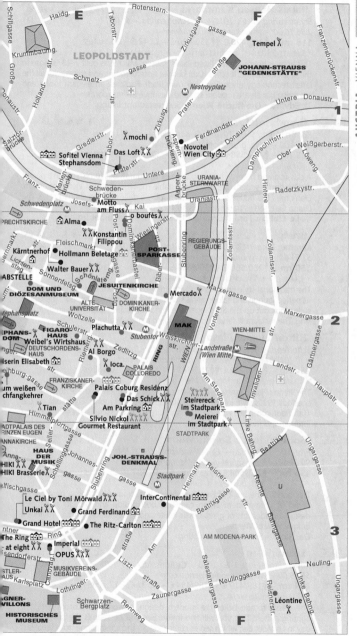

LEOPOLDSTADT

Tempel

JOHANN-STRAUSS
"GEDENKSTÄTTE"

Nestroyplatz

Untere Donaustr.

mochi

Das Loft

Sofitel Vienna
Stephansdom

Novotel
Wien City

URANIA-
STERNWARTE

Motto
am Fluss

o boufés

Uraniastr.

Alma

Konstantin
Filippou

REGIERUNGS-
GEBÄUDE

Kärntnerhof

Fleischmarkt

Hollmann Beletage

POST-
SPARKASSE

Walter Bauer

JESUITENKIRCHE

Mercado

DOM UND
DIÖZESANMUSEUM

ALTE
UNIVERSITÄT

DOMINIKANER-
KIRCHE

MAK

Marxergasse

WIEN-MITTE

Plachutta

FIGARO-
HAUS

Weibel's Wirtshaus

DEUTSCHORDENS-
HAUS

Al Borgo

Stubentor

Landstraße
(Wien Mitte)

Ioca.

PALAIS
COLLOREDO

iserin Elisabeth

FRANZISKANER-
KIRCHE

Palais Coburg Residenz

Das Schick

um weißen
chfangkehrer

Tian

Am Parkring

Steirereck
im Stadtpark

Silvio Nickol

Meierei
im Stadtpark

Gourmet Restaurant

STADTPARK

ADTPALAIS DES
RINZEN EUGEN

ANNAKIRCHE

HAUS
DER
MUSIK

JOH.-STRAUSS-
DENKMAL

HIKI

HIKI Brasserie

Stadtpark

InterContinental

Le Ciel by Toni Mörwald

Unkai

Grand Ferdinand

Grand Hotel

The Ritz-Carlton

The Ring

- at eight

Imperial

OPUS

AM MODENA-PARK

STLER-
AUS

Karlsplatz

MUSIKVEREINS-
GEBÄUDE

Léontine

GNER-
VILLONS

HISTORISCHES
MUSEUM

27

AUSTRIA - VIENNA

Palais Hansen Kempinski

Schottenring 24 ⊠ 1010 – Ⓜ Schottenring – 𝒞 (01)   Plan: **D1**
2 36 10 00 – www.kempinski.com/wien
116 rm – †350/420 € ††350/420 € – ☑ 42 € – 36 suites
• Grand Luxury • Historic • Elegant •
This hotel is housed in the listed Palais Hansen, which was built in 1873 close to the stock exchange. It offers luxurious yet tasteful rooms and suites with all the latest technology (including your own iPad). Facilities: an elegant lobby and attractive bar area, a modern spa and exclusive events rooms.
✿ **Edvard • Die Küche Wien** – See restaurant listing

Grand Hotel

Kärntner Ring 9 ⊠ 1010 – Ⓜ Karlsplatz – 𝒞 (01)   Plan: **E3**
51 58 00 – www.grandhotelwien.com
205 rm – †459/558 € ††459/558 € – ☑ 34 € – 11 suites
• Grand Luxury • Classic •
A classic grand hotel with an imposing lobby, sumptuous furnishings in a period setting and a superb spa. The comfortable rooms exude real Viennese charm. Don't miss the house speciality: 'Guglhupf' – a delicious ring-shaped cake. The Grand Café serves traditional cuisine. Nice pavement terrace.
✿ **Le Ciel by Toni Mörwald • Unkai** – See restaurant listing

Bristol

Kärntner Ring 1 ⊠ 1010 – Ⓜ Karlsplatz – 𝒞 (01)   Plan: **D3**
51 51 60 – www.bristolvienna.com
150 rm – †280/560 € ††300/600 € – ☑ 36 € – 16 suites
• Luxury • Traditional • Classic •
The traditional style Bristol is run with great commitment and Viennese charm. Its period lounge and saloon areas set the tone for the lovely interior. The Opera suites look out on the Staatsoper; the Prince of Wales suite is genuinely imposing. The restaurant serves both classic and regional cuisine.

Hilton Vienna Plaza

Schottenring 11 ⊠ 1010 – Ⓜ Schottentor-Universität   Plan: **D1**
– 𝒞 (01) 31 39 00 – www.vienna-plaza.hilton.com
254 rm – †165/229 € ††165/249 € – ☑ 22 € – 10 suites
• Business • Luxury • Design •
The Vienna Plaza combines a convenient, central location on the Schottenring, a spacious 1920s style lobby, and comfortable, timeless rooms. Try a suite on the 10th floor complete with balcony and city view. Brasserie serves French and international fare.

Sofitel Vienna Stephansdom

Praterstr. 1 ⊠ 1020 – Ⓜ Schwedenplatz – 𝒞 (01)   Plan: **E1**
90 61 60 – www.sofitel-vienna-stephansdom.com
156 rm – †231/564 € ††231/564 € – ☑ 32 € – 26 suites
• Luxury • Business • Design •
This hotel is the work of French architect Jean Nouvel. It offers a harmonious blend of ultra-modern urban elements both inside and out. Its minimalist design includes lots of glass, classic whites, greys and blacks, and it provides a unique view of Vienna.
Das Loft – See restaurant listing

Le Méridien

Robert-Stolz-Platz 1 ⊠ 1010 – Ⓜ Karlsplatz – 𝒞 (01)   Plan: **D3**
58 89 00 – www.lemeridienvienna.com
294 rm – †189/419 € ††189/434 € – ☑ 32 € – 17 suites
• Chain • Design •
The classic façade belies the modern design, artwork and custom-designed lighting system that you will find inside. See and be seen is the order of the day in Le Moët bar, which serves choice snacks and champagne from breakfast to dinner. The YOU restaurant offers a small selection of sharing plates and an evening DJ.

InterContinental

Johannesgasse 28 ✉ *1030* – Ⓜ *Stadtpark* – ✆ *(01)* Plan: **E3**
71 12 20 – *www.vienna.intercontinental.com*
459 rm – 👤199/499 € 👥199/499 € – ⬜ 33 € – 15 suites
• Chain • Business • Classic •

This business hotel on the edge of the Stadtpark boasts a tasteful, elegant lobby and a wide range of conference facilities. If you are looking for something special, the Presidential Suite on the 12th floor promises 140m² of luxury with a view over the city thrown in! Champagne brunch every Sunday.

Savoyen

Rennweg 16 ✉ *1030* – Ⓜ *Karlsplatz* – ✆ *(01) 20 63 30* Plan I: **B3**
– *www.austria-trend.at*
309 rm ⬜ – 👤150/190 € 👥170/210 € – 43 suites
• Luxury • Contemporary •

The most imposing building of the former government printing works. An impressive atrium-style lobby and good conference facilities (including the largest venue in Vienna at 1 100 m²), provide modern style in a historic setting. The rooms on the seventh and eighth floors have balconies. International cuisine.

Sans Souci

Burggasse 2 ✉ *1070* – Ⓜ *Volkstheater* – ✆ *(01)* Plan: **C3**
5 22 25 20 – *www.sanssouci-wien.com*
60 rm ⬜ – 👤264/339 € 👥294/369 € – 3 suites
• Townhouse • Traditional • Personalised •

High class boutique hotel in the Spittelberg artists' quarter. This epitome of urban lifestyle is located opposite the Volkstheater and nearby the major museums. Artwork includes originals by Roy Lichtenstein, Allen Jones and Steve Kaufman.
La Veranda – See restaurant listing

The Ring

Kärntner Ring 8 ✉ *1010* – Ⓜ *Karlsplatz* – ✆ *(01)* Plan: **E3**
2 21 22 – *www.theringhotel.com*
68 rm ⬜ – 👤130/450 € 👥200/500 € – 2 suites
• Townhouse • Contemporary •

This modern, well-run business hotel is housed in a historic townhouse. It has a luxurious touch and a pleasant, informal atmosphere. The heritage protected lift is not to be missed.
at eight – See restaurant listing

Steigenberger Hotel Herrenhof

Herrengasse 10 ✉ *1010* – Ⓜ *Herrengasse* – ✆ *(01)* Plan: **D2**
53 40 41 00 – *www.herrenhof-wien.steigenberger.at*
196 rm – 👤175/410 € 👥175/410 € – ⬜ 29 € – 9 suites
• Townhouse • Historic • Contemporary •

This comfortable hotel set in a lovely historical building and located in the heart of Vienna is popular with business guests and tourists alike. The attractive rooms and suites are decorated in fresh, warm colours and the restaurant serves a mix of international cuisine and regional classics.

Das Triest

Wiedner Hauptstr. 12 ✉ *1040* – Ⓜ *Karlsplatz* – ✆ *(01)* Plan I: **B3**
58 91 80 – *www.dastriest.at*
72 rm – 👤269 € 👥269 € – ⬜ 26 € – 2 suites
• Business • Design •

The light, simple and elegant decor in this designer hotel is the work of Sir Terence Conran. Something of a home-from-home for its many regulars, it was once a posting house on the Vienna-Trieste route. It also has a smart bar.
Collio – See restaurant listing

AUSTRIA - VIENNA

Radisson BLU Style

☆ ⓕ ⓧ 🕭 ⅍ ⅏ ⅏

Herrengasse 12 ✉ *1010 –* Ⓜ *Herrengasse –* ☏ *(01)* Plan: **D2**
22 78 00 – www.radissonblu.com/stylehotel-vienna
78 rm – 👤149/499 € 👥👤169/499 € – ⌷ 24 €
• Townhouse • Historic • Design •

A cosmopolitan style and high quality materials right up into the eaves characterise this former bank building. Even the old vault doors in the gym have been retained! If you like international cuisine, try the Sapori restaurant.

Lindner Hotel Am Belvedere

☆ ⓕ ⓧ 🕭 ⅍ ⅏

Rennweg 12 ✉ *1030 –* Ⓜ *Karlsplatz –* ☏ *(01) 79 47 70* Plan I: **B3**
– www.lindner.de
219 rm – 👤99/439 € 👥👤119/459 € – ⌷ 23 € – 1 suite
• Business • Contemporary •

The Lindner offers a harmonious mix of contemporary style, quality and the latest technology. If you like things private, the Wellness Suite has its own sauna, while the leisure area on the seventh floor offers a view of Schloss Belvedere. The rustically modern Heuriger Am Belvedere serves regional fare. Good transport connections into the city.

Do & Co Hotel Vienna

◁ 🕭 ⓧ 🕭 ⅍

Stephansplatz 12 ✉ *1010 –* Ⓜ *Stephansplatz –* ☏ *(01)* Plan: **D2**
2 41 88 – www.doco.com
43 rm – 👤249/299 € 👥👤249/299 € – ⌷ 29 € – 2 suites
• Business • Design • Grand luxury •

The ultra-modern exterior of this hotel provides a real contrast to the other buildings around St Stephen's Cathedral. A very special designer hotel - fashionable and upmarket. The smokers' bar serves Euro-Asian fusion food from the show kitchen before transforming itself into a trendy club in the evening!
Do & Co Restaurant am Stephansplatz – See restaurant listing

The Guest House Vienna

☆ ⓧ 🕭

Führichgasse 10 ✉ *1010 –* Ⓜ *Herrengasse –* ☏ *(01)* Plan: **D3**
5 12 13 20 – www.theguesthouse.at
39 rm – 👤255/316 € 👥👤255/316 € – ⌷ 9 € – 3 suites
• Luxury • Townhouse • Contemporary •

Are you looking for understated, modern comfort and a discreet atmosphere? This boutique hotel behind the Albertina museum and the Opera offers high quality rooms in a Terence Conran interior. Excellent food from the great All Day Breakfast (bread and pastry baked on the premises) to dinner.

Kaiserhof

⅏ 🕭 🔱 ⅍

Frankenberggasse 10 ✉ *1040 –* Ⓜ *Karlsplatz –* ☏ *(01)* Plan I: **B3**
5 05 17 01 – www.hotel-kaiserhof.at
74 rm ⌷ – 👤109/301 € 👥👤143/321 € – 4 suites
• Traditional • Art déco • Contemporary •

Remarkable, friendly service, Viennese charm, and a tasteful juxtaposition of modern and classic features characterise this beautiful 1896 hotel. There is a lovely breakfast room with a buffet service and they serve a snack menu in the bar.

Hollmann Beletage

⅏ 🕭 🔱

Köllnerhofgasse 6 (2nd floor) ✉ *1010* Plan: **E2**
– Ⓜ *Stephansplatz –* ☏ *(01) 9 61 19 60 – www.hollmann-beletage.at*
26 rm – 👤169/229 € 👥👤179/279 € – 1 suite
• Townhouse • Design • Contemporary •

This hotel with its fine 19C architecture boasts a number of attractive features. These include a relaxed, modern atmosphere, a beautifully planted interior courtyard, a small cinema (complete with popcorn machine!), and afternoon delicacies served for hotel guests; not to mention the use of an iPad for the duration of your stay! The highlight is the 95m^2 Spa Suite.

Altstadt Vienna   🅰🅲 ⅖

Kirchengasse 41 ⊠ *1070* – Ⓜ *Volkstheater* – ☎ *(01)*   Plan I: **A3**
5 22 66 66 – *www.altstadt.at*
45 rm ⌓ – ♦109/210 € ♦♦159/250 € – 8 suites
• Historic • Design • Personalised •

From the outside you would never guess the tasteful and original combination of art, design and charm that awaits you behind the attractive old façade of this period hotel. The lovely high-ceilinged rooms are all different and genuinely individual. Central location close to all the major sights.

Hotel Rathaus - Wein & Design   🅰🅲 ⅖

Lange Gasse 13 ⊠ *1080* – Ⓜ *Rathaus* – ☎ *(01)*   Plan I: **A3**
4 00 11 22 – *www.hotel-rathaus-wien.at* – *Closed 23-26 December*
40 rm – ♦130/160 € ♦♦170/220 € – ⌓ 18 € – 1 suite
• Townhouse • Historic • Design •

The atmosphere is relaxing and homely thanks to the wonderful service and the charming building with its historical façade and modern interior. Breakfast is an impressively generous buffet, which can be enjoyed in the pretty interior courtyard. The wine bar offers a selection of some 450 Austrian wines.

Harmonie   🖽 🅰🅲 ⅖

Harmoniegasse 5 ⊠ *1090* – Ⓜ *Schottentor* – ☎ *(01)*   Plan: **C1**
3 17 66 04 – *www.harmonie-vienna.at*
63 rm ⌓ – ♦128/178 € ♦♦138/188 € – 3 suites
• Historic • Cosy • Contemporary •

Set in a fine building dating back to the 19C, Harmonie is close to the Palais Liechtenstein and easily accessible by tram (Line D). A well-run hotel, it offers comfortable, upmarket rooms decorated in tasteful colours. It also has charming service, a good, fresh breakfast and delicious afternoon coffee and cakes. The bistro serves a small selection of regional dishes.

K+K Hotel Maria Theresia   🕸 🅰🅲 ⅖ 🚗

Kirchberggasse 6 ⊠ *1070* – Ⓜ *Volkstheater* – ☎ *(01)*   Plan: **C3**
5 21 23 – *www.kkhotels.com*
132 rm ⌓ – ♦100/450 € ♦♦100/450 €
• Business • Functional •

Located in arty Spittelberg, this hotel offers functional rooms. Ask for one with a view over the city. The spacious lobby has a bar that serves a small menu.

Das Tyrol   🕸 🅰🅲 🚗

Mariahilfer Str. 15 ⊠ *1060* – Ⓜ *Museumsquartier*   Plan: **C3**
– ☎ *(01) 5 87 54 15* – *www.das-tyrol.at*
30 rm ⌓ – ♦109/229 € ♦♦149/358 €
• Townhouse • Personalised •

A beautifully restored corner building offering attractive, timelessly furnished rooms, an excellent breakfast and a small sauna decorated in gold tones. Contemporary art hangs on the walls throughout the hotel. Close to the museum quarter.

Novotel Wien City   🍴 🕸 🅹 🅰🅲 ⅖ 🚗

Aspernbrückengasse 1 ⊠ *1020* – Ⓜ *Nestroyplatz*   Plan: **F1**
– ☎ *(01) 9 03 03* – *www.novotel.com*
124 rm – ♦99/199 € ♦♦99/199 € – ⌓ 16 € – 1 suite
• Chain • Contemporary •

This modern business hotel is located right on the Aspern bridge. It offers seminar facilities and some executive rooms complete with French-style balcony terraces and great views from the top floor. It also makes a great base for tourists – children under 16 can sleep in their parents' room free of charge.

AUSTRIA - VIENNA

Kaiserin Elisabeth

Weihburggasse 3 ⊠ *1010* – **Ⓜ** *Stephansplatz* – ⌀ *(01)*
5 15 26 – *www.kaiserinelisabeth.at*   Plan: **E2**
63 rm � – **†**130/145 € **††**202/225 €
• Traditional • Classic •

The 400-year-old history of the hotel is reflected in the classic decor including paintings by Elisabeth and Kaiser Franz in the stylish lobby. Particularly comfortable superior rooms. Try some of the delicious Kaiserschmarrn for breakfast!

Am Parkring

Parkring 12 ⊠ *1010* – **Ⓜ** *Stubentor* – ⌀ *(01) 51 48 00*
– *www.schick-hotels.com*   Plan: **E2**
55 rm ⊡ – **†**135/236 € **††**175/537 € – 4 suites
• Business • Functional •

Am Parkring is located opposite the Stadtpark, on the upper floors of Vienna's high-rise Gartenbauhochhaus. It offers modern rooms with great views over Vienna, some with balconies. Be sure to ask for a room on the 13th floor.
Das Schick – See restaurant listing

Der Wilhelmshof

Kleine Stadtgutgasse 4 ⊠ *1020* – **Ⓜ** *Praterstern*
– ⌀ *(01) 2 14 55 21* – *www.derwilhelmshof.com*   Plan I: **B2**
105 rm ⊡ – **†**94/396 € **††**104/429 €
• Townhouse • Personalised • Contemporary •

This Hotel is located close to the Prater, the exhibition centre and the city centre. It is a classic 19C townhouse, which has been transformed into an art hotel. The rooms offer an individual feel - the Atelier rooms and junior suites are particularly chic. Fresh buffet breakfast and unexpected garden.

Fleming's Hotel Wien-Westbahnhof

Neubaugürtel 26 ⊠ *1070* – **Ⓜ** *West-Bahnhof* – ⌀ *(01)*
22 73 70 – *www.flemings-hotels.com*   Plan I: **A3**
173 rm ⊡ – **†**99/359 € **††**115/359 € – 2 suites
• Business • Contemporary •

This business hotel close to the west railway station has been maintained in a thoroughly modern style. All the rooms possess glassed-in bathrooms. Restaurant with a brasserie-style atmosphere.

Grand Ferdinand

Schubertring 10 ⊠ *1010* – **Ⓜ** *Karlsplatz* – ⌀ *(01)*
91 88 00 – *www.grandferdinand.com*   Plan: **E3**
188 rm – **†**180/320 € **††**180/320 € – ⊡ 29 € – 1 suite
• Boutique hotel • Elegant •

The chic designer rooms with their fashionable baroque touch are not the only highlight at this stylish, modern hotel. The breakfast room on the first floor affords a great view over the city and the Grand Ferdinand Restaurant serves regional cuisine. Gulasch & Champagne offers a small menu of good plain fare.

Alma

Hafnersteig 7 ⊠ *1010* – **Ⓜ** *Schwedenplatz* – ⌀ *(01)*
5 33 29 61 – *www.hotel-alma.com*   Plan: **E2**
26 rm ⊡ – **†**91/189 € **††**134/220 €
• Business • Townhouse • Contemporary •

A thoroughly modern hotel in a narrow side street, with convenient parking just 3min away. Deluxe rooms with whirlpool baths, a small terrace with a Jacuzzi, and a wonderful view over Vienna from the roof. Water, tea and coffee are free all day.

Kärntnerhof

Grashofgasse 4 ⊠ *1010 –* Ⓜ *Stephansplatz –* ℰ *(01)*   Plan: **E2**
512 19 23 – www.karntnerhof.com
44 rm ⌂ – ♦79/129 € ♦♦139/269 € – 3 suites
• Inn • Traditional • Cosy •

Kärntnerhof boasts a stylish and timeless designer interior that sits perfectly in the period setting of this fine 19C building. A number of attractive features including parquet flooring, antiques and paintings.

XxxX
    ### Steirereck im Stadtpark (Heinz Reitbauer)   🕭 🍴 ₺ 🅰🅺 ⇄

Am Heumarkt 2a ⊠ *1030 –* Ⓜ *Stadtpark –* ℰ *(01)*   Plan: **F2**
7 13 31 68 – www.steirereck.at – Closed Saturday-Sunday and Bank Holidays
Menu 95 € (lunch)/152 € – Carte 70/117 € – *(booking essential)*
• Creative • Design • Chic •

All the ingredients used here are excellent, including produce from the restaurant's long-standing local suppliers and herbs from its own roof garden. The food is creative but never fussy, strong on regional and national influences and full of intense, finely balanced flavours. The service is professional yet relaxed.
→ Mariazeller Saibling im Bienenwachs mit gelber Rübe, Pollen und Rahm. Kalbshirn mit Mispel, Senfgurke und Chupetinho. Java Kaffee mit gelben Datteln, Zwetschken und Zimtblüten.
🕭 **Meierei im Stadtpark** – See restaurant listing

XxxX
£3 £3   ### Silvio Nickol Gourmet Restaurant – Hotel Palais Coburg Residenz

Coburgbastei 4 ⊠ *1010 –* Ⓜ *Stubentor*   🕭 🍴 ₺ 🅰🅺 ⇄ 🚗
– ℰ (01) 51 81 81 30 – www.palais-coburg.com – Closed   Plan: **E2**
1-18 January, 6-30 August and Sunday-Monday
Menu 148/188 € – Carte 108/147 € – *(dinner only) (booking advisable)*
• Modern cuisine • Elegant • Luxury •

The culinary creations served at Silvio Nickol are modern, highly elaborate, considered right down to the smallest detail, and made from nothing but the finest produce and ingredients. Whatever you do, don't forget to take a good look at the wine list as it contains some genuine rarities.
→ Bernstein Makrele, Paprika, Liebstöckl. Luma Schwein, Schwarzkohl, Zwiebel, Madeira. Schokolade, Sanddorn, Rosa Pfeffer, Avocado.

XxxX
Anna Sacher – Hotel Sacher   ₺ 🅰🅺 🚗

Philharmonikerstr. 4 ⊠ *1010 –* Ⓜ *Karlsplatz –* ℰ *(01)*   Plan: **D3**
51 45 68 40 – www.sacher.com – Closed July-August and Monday
Menu 72/97 € – Carte 57/95 € – *(dinner only) (booking advisable)*
• Classic cuisine • Luxury •

Stylish green and fine wood interior adorned with original Anton Faistauer canvases radiates Viennese charm and elegance - a great place to enjoy international haute cuisine including Gut Dornau sheatfish with broccoli and garlic.

XxX
£3   ### Edvard – Hotel Palais Hansen Kempinski   🍴 🅰🅺

Schottenring 24 ⊠ *1010 –* Ⓜ *Schottenring –* ℰ *(01)*   Plan: **D1**
2 36 10 00 80 82 – www.kempinski.com/wien – Closed 1-11 January,
August, Sunday-Monday and Bank Holidays
Menu 89/129 € – Carte 57/77 € – *(dinner only)*
• Modern cuisine • Elegant • Luxury •

This elegant gourmet restaurant offers a successful marriage of the modern and classic, both in its sophisticated aromatic cuisine and the accomplished, pleasantly informal service. The excellent wine suggestions and good wines by the glass are also worth a mention.
→ Fagottini, Parmesan, Salbei. Jakobsmuschel, Karfiol, Ochsenmark. Taube, Bulgur, Feige.

AUSTRIA - VIENNA

AUSTRIA - VIENNA

Le Ciel by Toni Mörwald – Grand Hotel
🛱 ᯣ 🎟 ⇧ 🚗

Kärntner Ring 9 (7th floor) ✉ *1010 –* Ⓜ *Karlsplatz*   Plan: **E3**
– ✆ (01) 5 15 80 91 00 – www.leciel.at – Closed 5-13 February, 16 July-
15 August and Sunday-Monday
Menu 45/120 € (dinner) – Carte 61/90 €
• Classic cuisine • Elegant •

The atmosphere up on the seventh floor is classically elegant and, quite naturally, the best tables are those on the roof terrace. The kitchens serve distinctive and creative food made using the best quality produce. Attentive service.
→ Kaisergranat mit Kürbis, Moujean Tee und Chili. Rehrücken mit jungen Kraut, Radieschen und Lavendel. Eingelegter Cox Orange Apfel mit Dulce, Kräutersalat und Marzipan.

OPUS – Hotel Imperial
ᯣ 🎟

Kärntner Ring 16 ✉ *1015 –* Ⓜ *Karlsplatz – ✆ (01)*   Plan: **E3**
50 11 00 – www.imperialvienna.com – Closed August and Monday
Menu 63/92 € – Carte 58/99 € – *(dinner only) (booking advisable)*
• Country • Elegant • Luxury •

Located in an attractive, classical building, OPUS is decorated in the style of a 1930s Viennese workshop in elegant grey tones with chandeliers and art on the walls. The ambitious cuisine is creative and regionally inspired.
→ Rohnensalat, Molke, Pistazien, Kamille. Forelle, Räucherforellenfond, Belugalinsen, Navetten, Lauch. Bratapfel, Sanddorn, Macadamianuss, Salzkaramell.

Walter Bauer
🍴 🎟

Sonnenfelsgasse 17 ✉ *1010 –* Ⓜ *Stubentor – ✆ (01)*   Plan: **E2**
5 12 98 71 – Closed 24 July-18 August and Saturday-
Monday lunch
Carte 47/74 € – *(booking advisable)*
• Classic cuisine • Cosy • Family •

This listed building in the centre of the old town has oodles of Viennese charm, as well as a wonderful vaulted ceiling in the restaurant. The owners place great importance on providing attentive and personal service, as well as classic cuisine without frills. There is also an excellent wine list.
→ Gänseleberterrine mit Brioche. Lammrücken mit Ratatouille. Marillenpalatschinken.

Konstantin Filippou
🍴 🛋

Dominikanerbastei 17 ✉ *1010 –* Ⓜ *Stubentor – ✆ (01)*   Plan: **E2**
5 12 22 29 – www.konstantinfilippou.com – Closed Saturday-Sunday and
Bank Holidays
Menu 46 € (lunch)/139 € – *(booking advisable)*
• Modern cuisine • Minimalist • Fashionable •

Creative, modern and fashionably informal describe both the interior and the cuisine on offer here. Find attractive wooden tables, a cooking station in the dining room and small windows offering views of the busy chefs at work in the kitchen. Good accompanying wines.
→ Brandade, Black cod, Kaviar. Jakobsmuschel, Haselnuss, Dashi, Trüffel, Mark. Taube, Melanzani, Weinblatt, Miso.
☺ **o boufés** – See restaurant listing

Tian
🍴 ⇧

Himmelpfortgasse 23 ✉ *1010 –* Ⓜ *Stephansplatz*   Plan: **E2**
– ✆ (01) 8 90 46 65 – www.tian-vienna.com – Closed 1-11 January,
18 July-12 August, 24-26 December and Sunday-Monday
Menu 41 € (lunch)/158 € – Carte 66/82 €
• Vegetarian • Elegant • Fashionable •

Distinctive, full of contrast and sophistication, the vegetarian and vegan cuisine served at Tian is of the very highest quality. The fabulously presented, colourful fare – as delightful as the relaxed yet professional service and the modern interior – is served both in the light and airy restaurant with its stucco ceiling and the more intimate basement.
→ Zen Garten, Sellerie, Miso, Yuzu. Artischocke, Fenchel, Parmesan. Sweet Underground, Acaoba Bitterschokolade, Erdbeer-Holunder, Grüntee.

AUSTRIA - VIENNA

XX
(🍴)
Vestibül   ⌘ ☂ ♿

Universitätsring 2 (at Burgtheater) ✉ *1010*   Plan: **C2**
– ⓜ Herrengasse – ℰ (01) 5 32 49 99 – www.vestibuel.at – Closed 22 July-
15 August, Saturday lunch, Sunday and Bank Holidays
Menu 31 € (lunch)/68 € – Carte 33/81 € – *(booking advisable)*
• International • Classic décor • Brasserie •

Though the chef sets great store by high-quality Austrian ingredients, there is
nothing that quite matches the lobster in Vestibül's highly prized Szegediner
lobster with cabbage. The unusual location – in the famous and charming Burg-
theater – is another selling point. Don't miss the excellent wines, some of which
are available as magnums.

XX
Rote Bar – Hotel Sacher   ♿ 🅰🅲 🚗

Philharmonikerstr. 4 ✉ *1010 – ⓜ Karlsplatz – ℰ (01)*   Plan: **D3**
51 45 68 41 – www.sacher.com
Menu 60/67 € – Carte 40/78 €
• Austrian • Elegant • Traditional décor •

A mainstay of the Hotel Sacher, which epitomises the charm of this great Viennese establishment, Rote Bar is also a champion of Austrian cuisine. Treat yourself
to a Wiener Schnitzel or traditional rump of beef and soak up the atmosphere!

XX
Albertina Passage Dinnerclub   🅰🅲

Opernring 4/1/12 (corner Operngasse) ✉ *1010*   Plan: **D3**
– ⓜ Karlsplatz – ℰ (01) 5 12 08 13 – www.albertinapassage.at
– Closed July-August and Sunday - Wednesday
Menu 49/59 € – Carte 48/67 € – *(dinner only) (booking advisable)*
• Modern cuisine • Trendy •

If you are looking for something special, this restaurant – a mix of music venue
and sophisticated restaurant – is both stylish and upmarket. It offers a lounge-
like atmosphere (dimmed lights, bar area, live music), professional and attentive
service and elaborate, ambitious cuisine full of contrasts.

XX
Zum Schwarzen Kameel   ⌘ ☂ 🅰🅲 ⇔

Bognergasse 5 ✉ *1010 – ⓜ Herrengasse – ℰ (01)*   Plan: **D2**
5 33 81 25 11 – www.kameel.at
Menu 68/93 € (dinner) – Carte 44/82 € – *(booking essential)*
• Traditional cuisine • Friendly • Cosy •

One of Vienna's oldest restaurants (1618), fitted out in the much admired Viennese
Art Nouveau style in 1901/02. Guests are offered international and regional cuisine. The restaurant's own delicatessen and patisserie are great for buying gifts.

XX
(🍴)
Eisvogel   ☂ ♿ 🅰🅲 ⇔ 🅿

Riesenradplatz 5 (Prater) ✉ *1022 – ⓜ Praterstern*   Plan I: **B2**
– ℰ (01) 9 08 11 87 – www.stadtgasthaus-eisvogel.at –
Closed 1-15 January
Menu 26/49 € – Carte 27/64 € – *(bookings advisable at dinner)*
• Austrian • Elegant •

Set in the pulsating heart of Vienna next to the giant Riesenrad Ferris wheel at
the entrance to the Prater, Eisvogel is a great place for an aperitif with a view (by
reservation only). The excellent classic Austrian fare on offer includes Beuschel
(veal lung ragout), Wiener Schnitzel and goulash. There is a small, sheltered terrace facing the Prater.

XX
SHIKI   ♿ 🅰🅲 ⇔

Krugerstr. 3 ✉ *1010 – ⓜ Karlsplatz – ℰ (01) 5 12 73 97*   Plan: **E3**
– www.shiki.at – Closed 2-8 January, 7-20 August and Sunday-
Monday, Bank Holidays
Menu 58 € (lunch)/125 € – *(dinner only) (booking advisable)*
• Japanese • Fashionable • Design •

SHIKI offers fine dining Japanese-style in the heart of Vienna, close to the Opera.
The elegant restaurant decorated in dark tones offers a perfect marriage of tradition and modernity. It serves ambitious, seasonal cuisine ('Shiki' means the
four seasons).
SHIKI Brasserie – See restaurant listing

35

XX   **Das Loft** – Hotel Sofitel   ⩽ & AC ⌂
Praterstr. 1 ✉ *1020* – **Ⓜ** *Schwedenplatz* – 𝒞 *(01)*   Plan: **E1**
9 06 16 81 10 – www.sofitel-vienna-stephansdom.com
Menu 89 € (dinner) – Carte 53/97 € – *(bookings advisable at dinner)*
• International • Design • Fashionable •
Das Loft will, quite simply, take your breath away! A light and airy, high-ceilinged room on the 18th floor, entirely glazed and with a wide view. It is the ideal place to eat as you watch the sun go down over the rooftops of Vienna. Well-chosen wine list.

XX   **La Veranda** – Hotel Sans Souci   ⌂ & AC ⌂
Burggasse 2 ✉ *1070* – **Ⓜ** *Volkstheater* – 𝒞 *(01)*   Plan: **C3**
5 22 25 20 19 4 – www.laveranda-wien.com
Menu 55/65 € (dinner) – Carte 40/67 €
• International • Fashionable •
This elegant, modern restaurant sets great store by fresh regional and seasonal produce. The menu options include breast of organic chicken with a duo of pumpkins, almonds and dill, as well as Wiener Schnitzel with multi-coloured salad and parsley potatoes. Pavement terrace in front of the restaurant.

XX   **Fabios**   ⌂ AC
Tuchlauben 6 ✉ *1010* – **Ⓜ** *Stephansplatz* – 𝒞 *(01)*   Plan: **D2**
5 32 22 22 – www.fabios.at – Closed 24-26 December and Sunday
Carte 46/77 € – *(booking essential)*
• Italian • Trendy •
A veritable Who's Who of Vienna! The Italian cuisine served in this fashionable city restaurant is just as modern and minimalist as the interior design – two equally good reasons to give it a try! The bar also serves a range of snacks.

XX   **Do & Co Restaurant am Stephansplatz** – Do & Co Hotel Vienna
Stephansplatz 12 (7th floor) ✉ *1010*   ⩽ 🛏 ⌂ & AC ⌂ ⌂
– **Ⓜ** *Stephansplatz* – 𝒞 *(01) 5 35 39 69*   Plan: **D2**
– www.doco.com
Carte 40/62 € – *(booking essential)*
• Asian • Trendy •
An ultra-modern restaurant on the seventh floor with a great terrace and view of St Stephen's Cathedral. Southeast Asian dishes including chicken kaow soy and sushi alongside Austrian classics such as braised calves' cheeks and goose liver.

XX   **Collio** – Hotel Das Triest   ⌂ & AC
Wiedner Hauptstr. 12 ✉ *1040* – **Ⓜ** *Karlsplatz* – 𝒞 *(01)*   Plan: **B3**
58 91 80 – www.dastriest.at – Closed Saturday lunch, Sunday and Bank Holidays
Carte 33/56 €
• Italian • Friendly •
Collio offers a modern interior and a wonderful terrace in the gloriously green inner courtyard. The food on offer is Italian, focusing particularly on the cuisine of northern Italy. Less expensive lunchtime menu.

XX   **Die Küche Wien** – Hotel Palais Hansen Kempinski   AC
Schottenring 24 ✉ *1010* – **Ⓜ** *Schottenring* – 𝒞 *(01)*   Plan: **D1**
2 36 10 00 80 80 – www.kempinski.com/wien
Carte 32/55 €
• Country • Chic •
The Palais Hansen's second restaurant focuses on new interpretations of Viennese cuisine including dishes such as veal ragout and Wienerwald beef sirloin. The Wohnzimmer, Wintergarten and Küche dining rooms offer their own special atmosphere.

AUSTRIA - VIENNA

XX **Das Schick** – Hotel Am Parkring
Parkring 12 ⊠ 1010 – Ⓜ Stubentor – ℰ (01) Plan: **E2**
51 48 04 17 – www.schick-hotels.com – Closed Saturday lunch, Sunday lunch and Bank Holidays lunch
Carte 43/66 € – *(July-Augsut dinner only)*
• Mediterranean cuisine • Fashionable • Elegant •
Das Schick offers a friendly atmosphere, seasonal cuisine with an upmarket touch and a phenomenal view! That is the recipe that brings diners up here to the 12th floor.

XX **Unkai** – Grand Hotel
Kärntner Ring 9 (7th floor) ⊠ 1010 – Ⓜ Karlsplatz Plan: **E3**
– ℰ (01) 5 15 80 91 10 – www.grandhotelwien.com – Closed Monday lunch
Menu 55 € (lunch)/130 € – Carte 25/66 €
• Japanese • Minimalist •
A pleasantly light and modern restaurant where you can eat either at authentic teppanyaki grill tables or more conventionally. You will also find the Unkai sushi bar on the ground floor serving a sushi brunch on Saturdays, Sundays and public holidays.

XX **Cantinetta Antinori**
Jasomirgottstr. 3 ⊠ 1010 – Ⓜ Stephansplatz – ℰ (01) Plan: **D2**
5 33 77 22 10 – www.cantinettaantinori-vienna.at
Carte 42/76 € – *(booking advisable)*
• Italian • Friendly • Cosy •
The Viennese offshoot of the original Florentine restaurant serves primarily Tuscan cuisine, including succulent braised rabbit. It has a lively but stylish atmosphere. Wide selection of high quality Antinori wines (available by the glass).

XX **at eight** – The Ring
Kärntner Ring 8 ⊠ 1010 – Ⓜ Karlsplatz – ℰ (01) Plan: **E3**
2 21 22 39 30 – www.ateight-restaurant.com
Menu 45/65 € – Carte 44/66 €
• Traditional cuisine • Fashionable •
Simple, modern lines set the tone at this restaurant where the chairs are dressed with covers and the tables with runners in the evenings. The seasonal, classic but contemporary cuisine is accompanied by primarily Viennese wines.

XX **Plachutta**
Wollzeile 38 ⊠ 1010 – Ⓜ Stubentor – ℰ (01) 5 12 15 77 Plan: **E2**
– www.plachutta.at
Carte 31/51 € – *(booking advisable)*
• Austrian • Traditional décor • Inn •
For years, the Plachutta family has been committed to Viennese tradition. They serve beef in many forms in the green panelled dining room or on the large terrace.

XX **Kristian's Monastiri**
Neustiftgasse 16 ⊠ 1070 – Ⓜ Lerchenfelder Str. Plan: **C3**
– ℰ (01) 5 26 94 48 – www.monastiri.at
Carte 32/55 € – *(dinner only)*
• Country • Cosy •
This restaurant is located not far from the Volkstheater. It is a little unprepossessing from the outside but has an attractive interior courtyard terrace. Ask for the little booth in the alcove – it is ideal for couples! The food is largely regional, including pink roast rump steak with wild mushrooms and herb and mustard brioche.

AUSTRIA - VIENNA

XX Gaumenspiel

Zieglergasse 54 ⊠ 1070 – **Ⓜ** *Burgg-Stadthalle*   Plan I: **A3**
– ℰ (0664) 88665021 – www.gaumenspiel.at – Closed Sunday
Menu 40/56 € – Carte 33/58 € – *(dinner only)*
• International • Friendly •

This friendly restaurant has become something of a culinary institution in Vienna's 7th district. In winter the open fire makes it warm and cosy and in summer there is a charming interior courtyard. The ambitious cuisine, prepared using the very best produce, includes fillet of beef with a creamy red wine and onion sauce with pickled turnips.

XX Al Borgo

An der Hülben 1 ⊠ 1010 – **Ⓜ** *Stubentor – ℰ (01)*   Plan: **E2**
5 12 85 59 – www.alborgo.at – Closed Saturday lunch, Sunday and Bank Holidays
Carte 28/47 €
• Italian • Friendly •

Al Borgo enjoys a very central and yet secluded location in the heart of Vienna's 1st district. It serves classic Italian cuisine and a range of excellent seasonal dishes. Regular themed weeks.

XX Julius Meinl am Graben

Graben 19 (1st floor) ⊠ 1010 – **Ⓜ** *Stephansplatz*   Plan: **D2**
– ℰ (01) 5 32 33 34 60 00 – www.meinlamgraben.at – Closed 2 weeks August, Sunday and Bank Holidays
Menu 39/68 € – Carte 46/83 € – *(booking essential)*
• Classic cuisine • Chic • Cosy •

This restaurant and its sister delicatessen (housed in the same building) come to life early in the morning. Ambitious food is served using the finest quality ingredients from breakfast through to dinner (make sure you try the stuffed quail with greengages) complete with a view over Vienna's pedestrian zone.

XX Zum weissen Rauchfangkehrer

Weihburggasse 4 ⊠ 1010 – **Ⓜ** *Stephansplatz – ℰ (01)*   Plan: **E2**
5 12 34 71 – www.weisser-rauchfangkehrer.at
Menu 30/60 € – Carte 31/59 € – *(booking advisable)*
• Austrian • Traditional décor • Chic •

Viennese cuisine including seasonal dishes such as duo of Schneebergland duck and specials like calf's head brawn. These are served throughout the day in comfortable, traditional dining rooms. Wide range of wines and digestifs.

XX The Bank – Hotel Park Hyatt

Am Hof 2 ⊠ 1010 – **Ⓜ** *Herrengasse – ℰ (01)*   Plan: **D2**
2 27 40 12 36 – www.restaurant-thebank.com – Closed. Sunday dinner
Carte 42/86 €
• International • Classic décor •

If you are looking to eat out in an unusual setting, try the period lobby in this former bank with its imposing high ceilings and marble columns. The menu offers French brasserie-style dishes that are prepared in the open show kitchen. The Am Hof café is also popular.

XX Blue mustard

Dorotheergasse 6 ⊠ 1010 – **Ⓜ** *Stephansplatz – ℰ (01)*   Plan: **D2**
934 67 05 – www.bluemustard.at – Closed Sunday
Menu 68/120 € – Carte 62/92 € – *(dinner only)*
• Modern cuisine • Fashionable •

This fashionable address is close to St Stephen's Cathedral. It offers an eclectic mix of dishes – traditional, modern and exotic – all made from good, fresh produce and served in original surroundings. In summer it also operates a food truck serving takeaway meals.

Meierei im Stadtpark – Restaurant Steirereck

Am Heumarkt 2a ✉ *1030 –* Ⓜ *Stadtpark –* ✆ *(01)*   Plan: **F2**
7 13 31 68 – www.steirereck.at – Closed Bank Holidays
Menu 45/54 € (dinner) – Carte 27/51 €
• Country • Friendly •

The Reitbauer family's latest upmarket culinary venture, Meierei serves such seasonal delights as mixed cucumbers braised and marinated with six-row barley, coconut and tartare of Arctic char alongside Austrian classics (including the inevitable Wiener Schnitzel). The interior is light and modern, the service attentive.

Petz im Gußhaus

Gußhausstr. 23 ✉ *1040 –* Ⓜ *Taubstummeng. –* ✆ *(01)*   Plan I: **B3**
5 04 47 50 – www.gusshaus.at – Closed 1 week early February, 3 weeks August and Sunday-Monday
Carte 32/57 € – *(booking advisable)*
• Austrian • Cosy •

Located not far from the Karlsplatz, this restaurant promises excellent, fully-flavoured cuisine with international influences, as well as Austrian dishes. Try the fried chicken with potato and cucumber salad, the lemon and veal ragout with bone marrow dumplings, or the octopus in fennel and curry stock with risotto balls. All served in a smart dining room.

Tempel

Praterstr. 56 ✉ *1020 –* Ⓜ *Nestroyplatz –* ✆ *(01)*   Plan: **F1**
2 14 01 79 – www.restaurant-tempel.at – Closed 23 December-7 January and Saturday lunch, Sunday-Monday
Menu 18 € (lunch)/52 € – Carte 29/51 €
• Country • Bistro •

You may have to search for the slightly concealed entrance to the interior courtyard and lovely terrace that lead to this friendly restaurant. It serves flavoursome, contemporary Mediterranean cuisine and offers a good value lunchtime menu.

Servitenwirt

Servitengasse 7 ✉ *1010 –* Ⓜ *Roßauer Lände –* ✆ *(01)*   Plan I: **A2**
3 15 23 87 – www.servitenwirt.at
Carte 24/47 €
• Austrian • Friendly • Cosy •

If you are looking for flavoursome, authentic Viennese cuisine, that is exactly what you will find alongside the international fare at Servitenwirt. It is set in a quiet square close to the church. The clientele consists mainly of regulars and locals, with the addition of an occasional tourist or two.

Léontine

Reisnerstrasse 39 ✉ *1030 –* Ⓜ *Stadtspark –* ✆ *(01)*   Plan: **F3**
712 54 30 – www.leontine.at – Closed 26 February- 7 March, 16-25 April, 30 July-16 August, 23 December-8 January and Sunday-Monday, Tuesday dinner, Wednesday dinner
Menu 57 € – Carte 45/58 €
• Modern French • Bistro •

If you enjoy a bistro atmosphere, you will love this charming restaurant set in a quiet residential district close to the Stadtpark. It serves modern French cuisine with menu options including turbot with carrots, olives and macadamia nuts.

LABSTELLE

Lugeck 6 ✉ *1010 –* Ⓜ *Stephansplatz –* ✆ *(01)*   Plan: **E2**
2 36 21 22 – www.labstelle.at – Closed Sunday and Bank Holidays
Menu 48/56 € (dinner) – Carte 36/52 € – *(booking advisable)*
• Country • Design • Bistro •

Labstelle offers an attractive, upmarket bistro atmosphere with a relaxed bar area. It serves ambitious seasonal, regional fare including Arctic char, Marschfeld artichoke, parsnips and parsley. There is also a reduced lunchtime menu and a pretty interior courtyard.

AUSTRIA - VIENNA

mochi
🕅   ⛾

Praterstr. 15 ✉ 1020 – Ⓜ Nestroyplatz – ℰ (01)   Plan: **E1**
9 25 13 80 – www.mochi.at – Closed 24 December- 9 January, Sunday and Bank Holidays
Carte 21/46 € – *(booking essential at dinner)*
• Japanese • Trendy • Fashionable •

This is a lively, informal restaurant serving authentic Japanese cuisine with the occasional modern twist at very moderate prices. You can watch the chefs at work as they prepare their rolls, gyoza soup and gyu tataki. At lunchtimes the food is served in simple bowls, in the evenings the presentation is a little more elaborate. Bookings start at 3pm.

o boufés
🕅🕅   🕅

Dominikanerbastei 17 ✉ 1010 – Ⓜ Stubentor – ℰ (01)   Plan: **E2**
5 12 22 29 10 – www.konstantinfilippou.com – Closed Saturday lunch-Sunday and Bank Holidays
Carte 35/49 € – *(booking advisable)*
• Mediterranean cuisine • Bistro •

Located just next door to its gourmet counterpart, this relaxed restaurant with its bare walls, high ceilings and minimalist decor, serves a varied menu. It ranges from a charcuterie plate to keftedes (meatballs) with hilopites (small green pasta squares), as well as black pudding ravioli with cuttlefish, shellfish and peas. The food is accompanied by a choice of natural wines.

Schnattl
🕅

Lange Gasse 40 ✉ 1080 – Ⓜ Rathaus – ℰ (01)   Plan I: **A3**
4 05 34 00 – www.schnattl.com – Closed 2 week Easter, 3 weeks August, Saturday-Sunday and Bank Holidays
Menu 17 € (lunch)/48 € – Carte 30/55 € – *(only lunch, Friday also dinner)*
• Country • Cosy •

This friendly, personally-run restaurant is set a little out of the way but remains popular with regulars and theatregoers, who appreciate the classic cuisine and warm, friendly atmosphere.

Le Salzgries Paris
🕅   🄰🄲

Marc-Aurel-Str. 6 ✉ 1010 – Ⓜ Schwedenplatz – ℰ (01)   Plan: **D1**
5 33 40 30 – www.le-salzgries.at – Closed 3-9 January, 10-18 April, 29 July-15 August, Sunday-Monday and Bank Holidays
Menu 48/67 € (dinner) – Carte 43/67 €
• Classic French • Brasserie • Fashionable •

This exuberant, lively bistro is decorated in warm colours and has a modern bar, which is a real eye-catcher. The tried and tested French cuisine offers classic dishes including entrecote.

SHIKI Brasserie – Restaurant SHIKI
🕅   ♿   🄰🄲

Krugerstr. 3 ✉ 1010 – Ⓜ Karlsplatz – ℰ (01) 5 12 73 97   Plan: **E3**
– www.shiki.at – Closed 2-8 January, 7-20 August, Sunday-Monday and Bank Holidays
Carte 44/68 €
• Japanese • Brasserie • Design •

This minimalist-style brasserie with its large terrace is SHIKI's less formal eatery. It offers a wider range of dishes from miso soup to tempura and sushi – the latter prepared before you as you sit at the sushi bar.

Sakai

Florianigasse 36 ✉ 1080 – Ⓜ Josefstädter Str. – ℰ (01)   Plan I: **A3**
7 29 65 41 – www.sakai.co.at – Closed 24 July-15 August, Monday-Tuesday and Bank Holidays
Menu 29 € (lunch)/75 € – Carte 18/58 €
• Japanese • Minimalist •

Hiroshi Sakai, no stranger in Vienna, has now set up his own restaurant after 10 years at Unkai. He serves seasonally influenced, traditional Japanese cuisine. Take a seat in the authentically simple surroundings and enjoy some sushi and sashimi or better still, one of his sophisticated set Kaiseki menus.

AUSTRIA - VIENNA

𝄆 Motto am Fluss ⇔

Franz Josef Kai 2 ⊠ 1010 – ⓜ Schwedenplatz – ℰ (01)   Plan: **E1**
2 52 55 10 – www.mottoamfluss.at
Carte 39/68 €
• International • Fashionable • Friendly •

As befits its location on the banks of the Danube (by the jetty for the Twin City Liner), this modern building with its glass façade is modelled on a boat. Smart 1950s interior style and international dishes. Less expensive at lunchtimes.

𝄆 Weibel's Wirtshaus

Kumpfgasse 2 ⊠ 1010 – ⓜ Stubentor – ℰ (01)   Plan: **E2**
5 12 39 86 – www.weibel.at
Menu 34 € (dinner) – Carte 26/53 € – *(booking advisable)*
• Austrian • Friendly •

Just a few minutes' walk from St Stephen's Cathedral, Weibel's Wirtshaus is the archetypal Viennese restaurant – warm and friendly, rustic and snug! It also has a charming garden in the small alleyway. The food is traditional and Viennese.

𝄆 La Mia

Lerchenfelder Str. 13 ⊠ 1070 – ⓜ Lerchenfelder Str.   Plan: **C3**
– ℰ (01) 5 22 42 21 – www.lamia.at
Carte 26/38 €
• Italian • Bistro • Rustic •

This informal bistro makes a lively alternative to Kristian's Monastiri next door (under the same management). The fresh Italian cuisine includes antipasti, pasta and grilled meats, such as fillet steak with rosemary potatoes, as well as pizzas baked in the wood-fired oven.

𝄆 loca.

Stubenbastei 10 ⊠ 1010 – ⓜ Stubentor – ℰ (01)   Plan: **E2**
5 12 11 72 – www.bettereatbetter.com
Menu 36/46 € – Carte 35/49 € – *(dinner only) (booking advisable)*
• Country • Cosy •

"Better eat better" is the slogan of this friendly little restaurant close to the Stadtpark. The menu includes dishes such as zander served with two sorts of pumpkin and speck. Don't be afraid to ask for the special theatre menus.

𝄆 Artner auf der Wieden

Floragasse 6 ⊠ 1040 – ⓜ Taubstummengasse   Plan I: **B3**
– ℰ (01) 5 03 50 33 – www.artner.co.at – Closed Saturday lunch, Sunday lunch and Bank Holidays lunch
Menu 13 € (lunch) – Carte 29/52 €
• International • Fashionable • Design •

Alongside classics such as Viennese schnitzel with a salad of chanterelle mushrooms, you will also find creative international fare including spicy short ribs with celery and grilled meats. Add to this the elegant bistro atmosphere and the relaxed service. There is also a good value lunchtime menu that is popular with business guests.

𝄆 Mercado

Stubenring 18 ⊠ 1010 – ⓜ Stubentor – ℰ (01)   Plan: **E2**
5 12 25 05 – www.mercado.at – Closed Saturday lunch
Menu 69 € (dinner) – Carte 36/50 €
• World cuisine • Exotic décor • Cosy •

The ideal restaurant for those who like it hot! Mercado serves "Latin inspired market cuisine" in a relaxed, Latin American atmosphere. Don't miss the pan-fried octopus with potatoes and tamarind barbecue sauce – served à la carte or "family-style".

X **Yohm**

Plan: **D2**

Petersplatz 3 ✉ *1010 –* Ⓜ *Stephansplatz –* ✆ *(01) 5 33 29 00 –* www.yohm.at
Carte 32/87 €

· Asian · Fashionable ·

A pleasant modern restaurant with striking orange decor, occupying two floors. The open kitchen serves up contemporary twists on Southeast Asian cuisine that borrows liberally from around the globe. Good wine selection.

OUTER DISTRICTS

PLAN I

 Park Royal Palace Vienna

Schlossallee 8 (by Mariahilfer Straße **C3**) ✉ *1140 –* ✆ *(01) 8 91 10 –* www.austria-trend.at
233 rm – †79/600 € **††**79/600 € – ☲ 19 € – 21 suites

· Business · Functional ·

The first thing to strike you on entering this conference hotel is the large atrium-style lobby with its modern straight lines and muted colours. The spacious suites offer the best views of Schöllbrunn Castle. Direct access to Vienna's Museum of Technology, which serves as an occasional venue for events.

 Melia

Donau City Str. 7 (by A 22 **B1**) ✉ *1220 –* Ⓜ *Kaisermühlen –* ✆ *(01) 9 01 04 –* www.melia.com
253 rm – †165/390 € **††**165/390 € – ☲ 26 € – 5 suites

· Business · Chain · Design ·

Located in the modern DC Tower, this hotel is just a few metro stations from the city centre. The rooms are just as good as the location; they are all stylish, practical and offer the latest technology and floor-to-ceiling windows. The 57 restaurant (on the 57th floor) serves Mediterranean cuisine with an impressive view.

 Kahlenberg Suite Hotel

Am Kahlenberg 2 (by Heiligenstädter Straße **A1**) ✉ *1190 –* ✆ *(01) 32 81 50 07 00 –* www.kahlenberg.wien
20 rm ☲ – **†**99/209 € **††**119/249 €

· Business · Contemporary ·

Its location is on Vienna's local mountain. The amazing views, as well as the spacious, high quality, very modern rooms with panoramic windows, make this a very unique hotel. This restaurant with a simple, elegant style has a wonderful terrace.

 Falkensteiner Hotel Wien Margareten

Plan: **A3**

Margaretengürtel 142 ✉ *1050 –* Ⓜ *Margaretengürtel –* ✆ *(01) 36 16 39 00 –* www.falkensteiner.com
195 rm – †109 € **††**109 € – ☲ 21 € – 2 suites

· Business · Chain · Contemporary ·

This business hotel is set between Schönbrunn Castle and the city. It offers good conference facilities, easy connections into Vienna and an appealing mix of modern design and Biedermeier style. The seventh floor houses a leisure area complete with terrace for rest and relaxation.

 Courtyard by Marriott Wien Messe

Trabrennstr. 4 (by Handelskai **B2**) ✉ *1020 –* Ⓜ *Praterstern –* ✆ *(01) 7 27 30 –* www.courtyard-wien-messe.at
251 rm – †89/259 € **††**89/259 € – ☲ 20 € – 7 suites

· Contemporary ·

Located in Exhibition Hall D, this hotel is ideal for business travellers but it is also close to the Prater, the race course and the stadium. The rooms are comfortable yet functional. Modern conference facilities and large fitness area. International classics and regional cuisine in a casual setting.

AUSTRIA - VIENNA

 Zeitgeist ✿ ⅃⅗ 🕸 ⅍ 🖼 ⅍ ⇩ 🛏

Sonnwendgasse 15 ⊠ 1100 – **Ⓜ** *Hauptbahnhof*   Plan: **B3**
– 𝒞 (01) 90 26 50 – www.zeitgeist-vienna.com
254 rm – †85 € ††100 € – � 15 €
• Business • Functional • Design •
Located not far from the main railway station, Zeitgeist offers a variety of different room categories. These include Urban, Prestige (with view and terrace) and
Zeitgeist Suite, which are all fashionable, minimalist in style and have the latest
technology. The Pergola bistro serves international fare and there is also a sauna
and a courtyard garden.

 Boutiquehotel Stadthalle ⅊ ⅍ 🛏

Hackengasse 20 ⊠ 1150 – **Ⓜ** *Westbahnhof – 𝒞 (01)*   Plan: **A1**
9 82 42 72 – www.hotelstadthalle.at
79 rm ⊠ – †88/228 € ††108/248 €
• Townhouse • Personalised • Contemporary •
Organic food and sustainability take centre stage in this attractive hotel not
far from the Stadthalle. The rooms offer an individual mix of classic and
modern styling. The garden rooms, which look out onto the beautifully planted interior courtyard (where breakfast is served in summer) are particularly
quiet.

 roomz Vienna ✿ ⅃⅗ ⅊ 🖼

Paragonstr. 1 (by Landstr. Gürtel **B3**) ⊠ *1110 – 𝒞 (01) 7 43 17 77*
– www.roomz-vienna.com
152 rm – †69/124 € ††79/134 € – ⊠ 15 €
• Business • Design •
This well-run and practically equipped hotel has a young, colourful design.
The metro station is a 10min journey from the Dom. Handy, nearby underground car park. The lobby with its open restaurant is also fashionable.

X X X
❀ ❀ **Amador** 🕸 🍸

Grinzingerstr. 86 ⊠ 1190 – **Ⓜ** *Heiligenstadt – 𝒞 (0660)*   Plan: **A1**
9070500 – www.amadors-wirtshaus.com – Closed 1-20 January and
Sunday-Monday
Menu 95/135 € – *(dinner only) (booking essential)*
• Creative • Elegant •
Michelin-starred chef Amador is starting to make a name for himself in this elegant vaulted wine cellar in Vienna. His team combine intensive flavours and
high-quality ingredients to create sophisticated food that is strong on detail. A
glass wall affords diners a fascinating view of the wine barrels stored in another
part of the cellar.
→ Zander, Kaffee, Passionsfrucht, Spinat. Mieral Taube, Mango, Cocos, Purple Curry. Apfelbaum, Salzkaramell, Pink Lady, Vanille.
🍴 **Amadors Wirtshaus & Greißlerei** – See restaurant listing

X X
❀ ❀ **Mraz & Sohn** 🕸 **P**

Wallensteinstr. 59 ⊠ 1200 – **Ⓜ** *Friedensbrücke*   Plan: **A2**
– 𝒞 (01) 3 30 45 94 – www.mraz-sohn.at
– Closed 24 December- 9 January, 12 August-4 September, Saturday-
Sunday and Bank Holidays
Menu 65/112 € – *(dinner only) (booking advisable)*
• Creative • Fashionable •
Distinctive and rich in contrast, the food on offer at Mraz & Sohn is creative,
innovative and truly global in its influences. The interior is modern and minima-
list in style, and the service is friendly, professional and attentive. Excellent wine
suggestions.
→ Wachtel, Kohl, Kren, Moltebeere. Ente, Gurke, Gin, schwarzer Knoblauch.
Nashi Birne.

XX **Eckel**

*Sieveringer Str. 46 (by Billrothstraße **A1**)* ⊠ *1190 –* 𝒞 *(01) 3 20 32 18*
– www.restauranteckel.at – Closed 6-21 August, 23 December-16 January
and Sunday-Monday
Carte 24/62 €
• Country • Family • Traditional décor •

This family run business has a good number of regulars from the 19th district;
one of the most attractive in Vienna. It offers comfortable dining rooms serving
both classic regional fare and lobster specialities. Wonderful garden.

XX **dasTURM**

Wienerbergstr. 7 (22 th floor, at Business Park Vienna, Turm D1) (by
*Wiedner Hauptstraße **B3**)* ⊠ *1100 –* 𝒞 *(01) 6 07 65 00 – www.dasturm.at*
– Closed 1-8 January, 6-12 February, 13-17 April, 24 July-
6 August, Saturday-Sunday and Bank Holidays
Menu 31 € (lunch)/89 € – Carte 42/64 €
• Creative • Fashionable • Friendly •

The ascent in the all-glass external lift here is an experience in itself! On top the
great view is accompanied by two ambitious and creative set menus: 'Kulinarische Ausblicke' and 'Kulinarische Einblicke'. Business lunch at midday. There is
also a bar with a terrace just below on the 21st floor.

XX **Grace**

Danhausergasse 3 ⊠ *1040 –* Ⓜ *Taubstummengasse*   Plan: **B3**
– 𝒞 *(01) 503 10 22 – www.grace-restaurant.at – Closed 7-14 January,*
5-16 September and Sunday-Monday
Menu 29 € – Carte 42/59 € – *(Tuesday-Friday dinner only)*
• Creative • Cosy •

A café in a previous incarnation, Grace has now been converted into a pretty,
modern restaurant with a quiet, secluded terrace. You will still find the original
wood panelling and tiled floor in one of the rooms. Creative cuisine.

X **Hill**

*Sieveringer Str. 137 (by Billrothstr. **A1**)* ⊠ *1190 –* 𝒞 *(01) 3 20 11 11*
– www.hill-restaurant.at – Closed 1-10 January, 2-29 August and Sunday-
Monday
Menu 48/95 € – Carte 41/75 € – *(dinner only)*
• International • Neighbourhood • Friendly •

Fancy fillet of zander with smoked mushroom broth and lovage, or perhaps one
of the chef's suggestions, such as a whole Arctic char? The cuisine at Hill is ambitious and seasonal, the dining rooms are warm and cosy, and the service is
friendly and accomplished with good wine suggestions.

X **Amadors Wirtshaus & Greißlerei** – Restaurant Amador

Grinzingestr. 86 ⊠ *1190 –* Ⓜ *Heiligenstadt –* 𝒞 *(0660)*
90 70 500 – www.amadors-wirtshaus.com –   Plan: **A1**
Closed 1-20 January and Saturday dinner-Monday
Menu 28/55 € – Carte 26/56 €
• Market cuisine • Brasserie •

This brasserie-style alternative to Amador's fine dining restaurant offers more
traditional food in a more traditional setting. The menu includes oyster blade
beef, Viennese-style fried chicken and steaks.

X **Freyenstein**

*Thimiggasse 11 (by Währinger Straße **A2**)* ⊠ *1180 –* 𝒞 *(0664) 4 39 08 37*
– www.freyenstein.at – Closed 6-28 February and Sunday-Monday
Menu 48 € – Carte 33/43 € – *(dinner only) (booking advisable)*
• Traditional cuisine • Family •

This restaurant promises a warm and friendly, family ambience and attentive,
pleasantly informal service. However, attention focuses on the set menu,
which offers two small dishes per course, and all are flavoursome and aromatic.
Demand for tables here is correspondingly high!

AUSTRIA - VIENNA

✗ Kutschker 44

Kutschergasse 44 (by Währinger Straße A2) ☒ *1180 –* ℰ *(01) 4 70 20 47*
– www.kutschker44.at – Closed Sunday-Monday and Bank Holidays
Carte 25/61 € – *(dinner only)*
• Traditional cuisine • Fashionable •

The particularity of this informal, modern restaurant lies in the show kitchen situated in the bar. You can watch your choice from the contemporary, seasonal menu being prepared for you, which adds an extra dimension to your meal.

✗ Woracziczky

Spengergasse 52 ☒ *1050 –* Ⓜ *Pilgramgasse –* ℰ *(0699)*   Plan: **A3**
*11 22 95 30 – www.woracziczky.at – Closed 24 December-13 January,
7-25 August, Saturday-Sunday and Bank Holidays*
Carte 29/45 € – *(during the Advent season open on Saturday evening)*
• Austrian • Neighbourhood • Family •

The chef reserves a warm personal welcome for diners in this friendly, pleasantly informal inn (pronounced 'Vorashitkzy'). It is particularly popular for its casual atmosphere and local Viennese cuisine.

✗ Rudi's Beisl

Wiedner Hauptstr. 88 ☒ *1050 –* Ⓜ *Taubstummengasse*   Plan: **B3**
– ℰ *(01) 5 44 51 02 – www.rudisbeisl.at – Closed Saturday-Sunday and
Bank Holidays*
Carte 16/46 € – *(booking advisable)*
• Country • Bourgeois • Neighbourhood •

Always busy and bustling, Rudi's Beisl is a down-to-earth eatery with lots of decoration on the walls – small, simple and snug! The friendly owner does the cooking himself: traditional fare such as schnitzel, boiled beef and pancakes.

✗ Schübel-Auer

Kahlenberger Str. 22/Zahnradbahnstr. 17 (Döbling)   Plan: **A1**
☒ *1190 –* ℰ *(01) 3 70 22 22 – www.schuebel-auer.at*
*– Closed 23 December-February and Sunday-Monday, March-April and
November-December: Sunday-Tuesday*
Carte 15/28 € – *(open from 4 pm)*
• Country • Wine bar • Cosy •

Today the carefully refurbished former Auerhof (built in 1642 as a wine-grower's house) with its quiet interior courtyard makes a lovely restaurant. Located at the end of tramline D, it is easy to reach from the city centre.

✗ Feuerwehr-Wagner

Grinzingerstr. 53 (Heiligenstadt) ☒ *1190 –* ℰ *(01)*   Plan: **A1**
3 20 24 42 – www.feuerwehrwagner.at
Carte 15/35 € – *(open from 4 pm)*
• Country • Wine bar • Rustic •

This typical, traditional Austrian wine tavern is greatly appreciated by regulars. You'll find a cosy, rustic interior with dark wood and simple tables. The terraced garden is particularly nice.

AT THE AIRPORT

NH Wien Airport

Einfahrtsstr. 1 ☒ *1300 –* ℰ *(01) 70 15 10 – www.nh-hotels.com*
499 rm – †129/195 € ††129/195 € – ☲ 25 €
• Business • Contemporary • Classic •

The lobby, bar and restaurant area are spacious, the rooms well equipped and the hotel enjoys a convenient location close to the airport arrivals hall. All in all an ideal destination for the business traveller. The restaurant serves international cuisine alongside Austrian classics.

Salzburg

SALZBURG

Population: 146 631

Gérald Schléwitz/Fotolia.com

Small but perfectly formed, Salzburg is a chocolate-box treasure, gift-wrapped in stunning Alpine surroundings. It's immortalised as the birthplace and inspiration of one of classical music's greatest stars, and shows itself off as northern Europe's grandest exhibitor of baroque style. Little wonder that in summer its population rockets, as the sound of music wafts from hotel rooms and festival hall windows during rehearsals for the Festspiele. In quieter times of the year, Salzburgers enjoy a leisurely and relaxed pace of life. Their love of music and the arts is renowned; and they enjoy the outdoors, too, making the most of the mountains and lakes, and the paths which run along the river Salzach and zig-zag through the woods and the grounds of Hellbrunn. The dramatic natural setting of Salzburg means you're never likely to get lost. Rising above the left bank (the Old Town) is the Mönchsberg Mountain and its fortress, the Festung Hohensalzburg, while the right bank (the New Town, this being a relative term) is guarded by the even taller Kapuzinerberg. In the New Town stands the Mozart family home, while the graceful gardens of the Schloss Mirabell draw the right bank crowds. The Altstadt (Old Town) is a UNESCO World Heritage Site and its star turn is its Cathedral. To the east is the quiet Nonntal area overlooked by the Nuns' Mountain.

SALZBURG IN...

→ **ONE DAY**
Festung Hohensalzburg, Museum der Moderne, Cathedral, Residenzplatz.

→ **TWO DAYS**
Mozart's birthplace, Nonntal, Kapuzinerberg, Mirabell Gardens, concert at Mozarteum.

→ **THREE DAYS**
Mozart's residence, Hangar 7, Hellbrunn Palace, concert at Landestheater.

PRACTICAL INFORMATION

ARRIVAL-DEPARTURE

✈ Wolfgang Amadeus Mozart Airport is just west of the centre.

🚆 The Hauptbahnhof (railway station) is centrally located on the right bank and is served by trains from all Europe's major locations.

Bus no.2 connects the airport with the Hauptbahnhof.

GETTING AROUND

Salzburg boasts a very efficient bus system. There are two main bus departure points on the left bank (Mozartsteg Bridge and Hanuschplatz) and two on the right (Hauptbahnhof and Mirabellplatz). You can buy tickets in three ways: in blocks of five singles; for a day's duration; or for a week. If you take your sightseeing seriously, then get a Salzburg Card for free travel on public transport and reduced admission to many tourist attractions; choose a card for 24, 48 or 72 hours.

CALENDAR HIGHLIGHTS

January/February
Mozartwoche (Mozart Week).

April
Salzburg Easter Festival.

June
Pfingstfestspiele (Whitsun Festival).

June/July
Sommerszene (Performance Festival).

July/August
Festspiele (Salzburg Festival).

October
Kulturtage (Cultural Days).

December
Weihnachtsmarkt (Christmas market).

EATING OUT

Salzburg's cuisine takes much of its influence from the days of the Austro-Hungarian Empire, with Bavarian elements added to the mix. Over the centuries it was characterised by substantial pastry and egg dishes to fill the stomachs of local salt mine workers; it's still hearty and meaty and is typified by dumplings and broths. In the city's top restaurants, a regional emphasis is still very important but the cooking has a lighter, more modern touch. Beyond the city are picturesque inns and tranquil beer gardens, many idyllically set by lakes. Do try the dumplings: Pinzgauer Nocken are made of potato pastry and filled with minced pork; another favourite is Gröstl, a filling meal of 'leftovers', including potatoes, dumplings, sausages and smoked meat roasted in a pan. If you want a snack, then Jausen is for you – cold meals with bread and sausage, cheese, dumplings, bacon etc, followed by an Obstler, made from distilled fruit. Salzburg's sweet tooth is evident in the Salzburger Nockerl, a rich soufflé omelette made with fruit and soft meringue.

Sheraton Grand

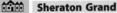

Auerspergstr. 4 ✉ 5020 – ✆ (0662) 88 99 90 Plan: **E1**
– www.sheratongrandsalzburg.com
166 rm – 🚹184/420 € 🚹🚹204/475 € – ☕ 32 € – 14 suites
• Chain • Functional •

This smart hotel with comfortably furnished rooms is situated between the Congress Centre and Mirabell Gardens. A highlight is the elegant, modern Sky Suite on the seventh-floor. Mirabell offers classic cuisine and a garden-facing terrace. Small regional dishes are offered in the bistro.

Schloss Mönchstein

Mönchsberg Park 26 ✉ 5020 – ✆ (0662) 8 48 55 50 Plan: **E1**
– www.monchstein.at – Closed 6 February-15 March, 1-23 November
24 rm ☕ – 🚹316/460 € 🚹🚹350/680 € – 2 suites
• Historic • Personalised •

This hotel is set in a 14C castle at the "top of Salzburg". It offers rooms decorated in the very best of taste, excellent service and great views over the city. There is also an exclusive spa and an outdoor pool set in 3½ acres of grounds.
Schloss Mönchstein – See restaurant listing

Crowne Plaza - The Pitter

Rainerstr. 6 ✉ 5020 – ✆ (0662) 88 97 80 Plan: **F1**
– www.imlauer.com
198 rm – 🚹109/219 € 🚹🚹140/259 € – ☕ 18 € – 5 suites
• Chain • Functional •

Dating back to 1864, the Pitter has undergone something of a makeover. This goes from the ultra-modern lobby and the smart Panorama and Courtyard junior suites to the fitness area with its view over the city. Pitter Keller serves a fine range of beers to accompany the regional fare.
IMLAUER Sky Bar & Restaurant – See restaurant listing

Schloss Leopoldskron

Leopoldskronstr. 56 ✉ 5020 – ✆ (0662) 83 98 30 Plan I: **C1**
– www.schloss-leopoldskron.com
67 rm ☕ – 🚹130/160 € 🚹🚹160/270 € – 12 suites
• Historic • Historic •

With an idyllic setting in 17 acres of grounds, this 18C palace boasts a stunning, almost museum-like hall, the sumptuous Max Reinhardt library and a wonderful stucco-decorated staircase. The main building offers stylish suites, while the adjacent Meierhof annexe is home to attractive, modern guestrooms.

Hotel & Villa Auersperg

Auerspergstr. 61 ✉ 5020 – ✆ (0662) 88 94 40 Plan: **F1**
– www.auersperg.at
55 rm ☕ – 🚹120/190 € 🚹🚹135/295 € – 1 suite
• Townhouse • Contemporary • Elegant •

A veritable oasis in the city! The hotel offers beautifully appointed and generously sized rooms complete with complimentary fruit and water when you arrive. There is a charming garden, pleasant, attentive staff and a friendly bar that serves snacks. Don't miss the great sauna with its roof terrace!

Wolf-Dietrich Altstadthotel

Wolf-Dietrich-Str. 7 ✉ 5020 – ✆ (0662) 87 12 75 Plan: **F1**
– www.wolf-dietrich.at
40 rm ☕ – 🚹73/136 € 🚹🚹127/258 €
• Townhouse • Cosy •

This hotel in the old town is regularly renovated to ensure everything is in perfect working order. The rooms are well appointed and classic in style. There is also a pretty indoor pool complete with sauna in the former wine cellar.

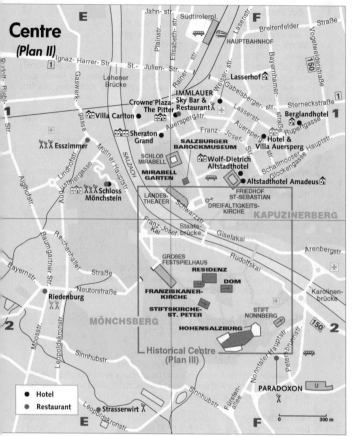

Centre
(Plan II)

🏠 **Villa Carlton** 🅿️

Markus-Sittikus-Str. 3 ⊠ 5020 – ℰ (0662) 88 21 91   Plan: **E1**
– www.villa-carlton.at
39 rm – †87/157 € ††93/195 € – ☑ 16 € – 9 suites
• Townhouse • Contemporary •
This pretty residence has been completely renovated, and this has not been at the expense of its charming high-ceilinged rooms, which come in various styles; these are all modern and include country house, elegant, traditional and pop art.

🏠 **Astoria** 🅿️

Maxglaner Hauptstr. 7 ⊠ 5020 – ℰ (0662) 83 42 77   Plan I: **B2**
– www.salzburgastoria.com
29 rm ☑ – †75/110 € ††95/175 €
• Family • Functional • Contemporary •
Josef Illinger offers a personal welcome, modern rooms come in warm tones, and everything is nicely cared for. Pastries are served to hotel guests throughout the day, as well as snacks and drinks in the evenings. 15min walk to the centre.

AUSTRIA - SALZBURG

 Zur Post ⌂ **P**

Maxglaner Hauptstr. 45 ✉ *5020 – ℰ (0662) 8 32 33 90*   Plan I: **B2**
– www.hotelzurpost.info – Closed 20-27 December
30 rm – ♦60/69 € ♦♦86/96 € – ⌂ 15 €
• Inn • Functional •
You will enjoy the lovely rooms, excellent breakfast and dedicated family management here. The hotel's main building and the Georg and Renate guesthouses offer a classic feel, while the Villa Ceconi, some 200m away, is a little more modern.

 Berglandhotel **P**

Rupertgasse 15 ✉ *5020 – ℰ (0662) 87 23 18*   Plan: **F1**
– www.berglandhotel.at – Closed 3-28 February, 20-26 December
18 rm ⌂ – ♦65/80 € ♦♦85/155 €
• Family • Personalised • Functional •
What distinguishes the Berglandhotel from Vienna's many other city hotels is its warm and friendly welcome. The owners set great store by personal service and the beautifully kept rooms all have an individual touch.

 Haus Arenberg ♨ ⇦ 🏨 **P**

Blumensteinstr. 8 ✉ *5020 – ℰ (0662) 64 00 97*   Plan I: **C2**
– www.arenberg-salzburg.at
16 rm ⌂ – ♦85/112 € ♦♦139/168 €
• Family • Cosy •
Though a little long in the tooth now, the hotel retains a certain charm thanks to its adorable female owner, the slightly elevated location offering a lovely view, and breakfast being served on the terrace overlooking the pretty garden.

 Altstadthotel Amadeus

Linzer Gasse 43 ✉ *5020 – ℰ (0662) 87 14 01*   Plan: **F1**
– www.hotelamadeus.at
20 rm – ♦100/180 € ♦♦140/260 € – ⌂ 20 €
• Historic • Townhouse • Personalised •
This centuries' old hotel is not only very central but also contemporary and tasteful. It boasts a pretty and welcoming breakfast room with a white vaulted ceiling, as well as an Italian restaurant.

 Lasserhof 🅰🅺

Lasserstr. 47 ✉ *5020 – ℰ (0662) 87 33 88*   Plan: **F1**
– www.lasserhof.com
30 rm ⌂ – ♦62/69 € ♦♦79/110 €
• Townhouse • Personalised •
Located not far from the main railway station, Lasserhof reflects the hard work and dedication of its owners. The rooms are smart and equipped with the latest technology, the breakfast is good and fresh and the service is friendly. Parking is available just across the road at reduced rates.

XxX **Esszimmer** (Andreas Kaiblinger) 🍴 🅰🅺
❀
Müllner Hauptstr. 33 ✉ *5020 – ℰ (0662) 87 08 99*   Plan: **E1**
– www.esszimmer.com – Closed 1 week February, 2 weeks September and Sunday–Monday
Menu 87 € (Vegetarian)/129 € – Carte 68/98 € – *(booking advisable)*
• Creative • Fashionable • Elegant •
In his harmonious and elegant restaurant, owner Andreas Kaiblinger and his team continue to produce high quality, creative and classic cuisine using nothing but the best produce. It is served by a highly competent front-of-house team and accompanied by some well-matched wine recommendations. The tables in the rear courtyard are also very attractive.
➜ Jakobsmuschel mit Blutwurst, Krustentiermayonnaise und Gurke. Maiscreme mit Kalbszungerl, Kalbskopf und Pilzen. Zander mit Kraut.

XXX **Schloss Mönchstein** – Hotel Schloss Mönchstein ⇐ ⟨☐⟩ & AC

Mönchsberg Park 26 ✉ *5020* – ☏ *(0662) 8 48 55 50* P
– www.monchstein.at – Closed 6 February-15 March, 1- Plan: **E1**
23 November and Tuesday, except festival period
Menu 55/145 € – Carte 52/101 €
• Classic cuisine • Elegant • Classic décor •

An exceptional place serving ambitious cuisine, in addition to its idyllic location. It offers a classically elegant interior and an elaborate and sophisticated 9-course menu from which to pick and choose. There is also an excellent choice of steaks.

XX **Riedenburg** ⟨☐⟩ P

Neutorstr. 31 ✉ *5020* – ☏ *(0662) 83 08 15* Plan: **E2**
– www.riedenburg.at – Closed 1-11 September and Sunday-Monday,
except festival period
Menu 45/69 € (dinner) – Carte 36/62 € – *(booking advisable)*
• Classic cuisine • Cosy •

Nicole and Helmut Schinwald offer classic Austrian cuisine. Wiener schnitzel, Tauern lamb and sea bass are served in comfortable yet elegant dining rooms with light wood, warm colours and modern pictures. Wonderful garden with chestnut trees.

XX **Gasthof Auerhahn** ⇔ ⟨☐⟩ ↔ P
🙂

Bahnhofstr. 15 ✉ *5020* – ☏ *(0662) 45 10 52* Plan I: **C1**
– www.auerhahn-salzburg.at – Closed 1 week January, 2 weeks June,
1 week September and Sunday dinner-Tuesday
12 rm ☑ – †60/68 € ††90/98 €
Menu 28 € (Vegetarian)/54 € – Carte 27/53 €
• Country • Friendly • Cosy •

Try Topfenknödel (curd cheese dumplings) and classic dishes such as boiled beef with apple and horseradish sauce or medallions of venison with port sauce. If you like the warm and friendly dining rooms, you will love the guestrooms, which although not huge, are pretty and well kept.

X **Strasserwirt** ⟨☐⟩ P
🙂

Leopoldskronstr. 39 ✉ *5020* – ☏ *(0662) 82 63 91* Plan: **E2**
– www.zumstrasserwirt.at – Closed Monday, September-June: Monday-
Tuesday
Menu 39/59 € (dinner) – Carte 36/63 €
• Traditional cuisine • Rural •

Dating back to 1856, Strasserwirt is a traditional restaurant (with lovely cherry wood panelling) complete with a winter garden and an attractive garden outside. The food is regional and includes such delicacies as Kalbsrahmbeuschel (veal ragout) with Serviettenknödel (bread dumplings) and red mullet with saffron risotto.

X **Weiher Wirt** ⟨☐⟩

König Ludwig Str. 2 ✉ *5020* – ☏ *(0662) 82 93 24* Plan I: **B2**
– www.weiherwirt.com – Closed mid January-mid February and Monday
Menu 35 € (dinner) – Carte 25/51 €
• Austrian • Inn •

This restaurant is wonderfully located on the banks of Leopoldskroner Lake. It serves regional dishes such as Szegediner pork goulash with boiled potatoes. Warm colours and modern notes provide a pleasant feel; outside is a lovely garden.

X **IMLAUER Sky Bar & Restaurant** – Hotel Crowne Plaza - The Pitter

Rainerstr. 6 (6th floor) ✉ *5020* – ☏ *(0662) 88 97 80* ⟨☐⟩ AC ↔
– www.imlauer.com Plan: **F1**
Carte 33/67 €
• International • Fashionable •

Enjoying a great location on the sixth floor of one of the city's hotels, this restaurant serves ambitious international and regional cuisine, and all with a great view over Salzburg. Dishes range from black sole meunière with parmesan pasta and a poached organic egg to tafelspitz (boiled topside of veal).

AUSTRIA - SALZBURG

Sacher
Schwarzstr. 5 ✉ *5020* – ☎ *(0662) 88 97 70*
– www.sacher.com
Plan: **G1**
111 rm – ♦385 € ♦♦385 € – ☲ 35 € – 5 suites
• Traditional • Historic • Classic •
The flagship of the Salzburg hotel world, Sacher really is a top international hotel. It offers classically designed, tasteful and luxurious rooms and suites. Alongside the Grill restaurant, don't miss the Café Sacher, the epitome of Viennese coffee house style.
Zirbelzimmer – See restaurant listing

Bristol
Makartplatz 4 ✉ *5020* – ☎ *(0662) 87 35 57*
– www.bristol-salzburg.at – Closed February- March
Plan: **G1**
65 rm ☲ – ♦190/275 € ♦♦270/560 € – 9 suites
• Traditional • Classic •
The stylish decor in the high-ceilinged rooms hints at the history of this hotel, built in 1619 and run as a hotel since 1892. Individually designed rooms with stucco work, crystal chandeliers, antiques, sumptuous fabrics and paintings. The restaurant serves classic cuisine with traditional influences.

Goldener Hirsch
Getreidegasse 37 ✉ *5020* – ☎ *(0662) 8 08 40*
– www.theluxurycollection.com/goldenerhirsch
Plan: **G1**
70 rm – ♦220/380 € ♦♦220/380 € – ☲ 33 € – 5 suites
• Townhouse • Historic • Personalised •
This patrician house built in 1407 stands out not only for its service but also for its thoughtfully retained, traditional style. The attractive rooms boast some lovely wooden furniture including a number of antique pieces. The restaurant offers international cuisine with classic and Austrian influences.

Altstadt Radisson BLU
Rudolfskai 28 (Judengasse 15) ✉ *5020* – ☎ *(0662)*
8 48 57 10 – www.radissonblu.com/hotelsalzburg
Plan: **H1**
62 rm – ♦130 € ♦♦130 € – ☲ 26 € – 13 suites
• Townhouse • Elegant • Classic •
Close to the Mozartplatz, the Altstadt's historical exterior conceals attractive rooms in a classically elegant style, the executive suites and suites being the most spacious. The restaurant with a winter garden overlooking the River Salzach and the terrace in the courtyard both serve international fare. Alternatively, there is the modern Café Altstadt.

arthotel Blaue Gans
Getreidegasse 41 ✉ *5020* – ☎ *(0662) 8 42 49 10*
– www.blauegans.at
Plan: **G1**
35 rm ☲ – ♦135/199 € ♦♦175/245 € – 3 suites
• Townhouse • Contemporary • Personalised •
At 650 years-old, the centrally located arthotel Blaue Gans is the oldest hotel in Salzburg. It offers light, modern rooms including some smart 'Artelier' rooms, as well as contemporary art.
Blaue Gans – See restaurant listing

Goldgasse
Goldgasse 10 ✉ *5020* – ☎ *(0662) 84 56 22*
– www.hotelgoldgasse.at
Plan: **H1**
16 rm – ♦150/180 € ♦♦180/320 € – ☲ 24 €
• Townhouse • Historic • Personalised •
This is a real picture-postcard boutique hotel dating back 700 years. Goldgasse simply oozes history, though the rooms (mostly junior suites) are modern and individually designed. The restaurant serves traditional Austrian cuisine.

	Boutiquehotel am Dom	AC
🏠	*Goldgasse 17 ⊠ 5020 – ℰ (0662) 84 27 65*	Plan: **H2**

– www.hotelamdom.at

15 rm ⌿ – ♦109/229 € ♦♦119/389 €

• Townhouse • Contemporary •

It is hard to imagine that this out of the way little hotel would conceal such generous rooms. They offer smart modern design, beautifully appointed bathrooms and immaculate cleanliness. Use the underground car park in the old town.

	Carpe Diem	AC
XX	*Getreidegasse 50 (1st floor) ⊠ 5020 – ℰ (0662)*	Plan: **G1**
✿		

84 88 00 – www.carpediem.com – Closed 2 weeks February and Sunday

Menu 80/110 € – Carte 49/82 €

• Creative • Fashionable • Design •

Carpe Diem is still one of Salzburg's culinary hotspots. Pop in for a coffee or a delicious snack at Cones on the ground floor. Alternatively, treat yourself to a regionally inspired gourmet meal prepared using the highest quality ingredients and served by the accomplished front-of-house team upstairs.

→ Beef Tatar mit Kartoffelpüree und Kresse im Sancho-Peffer-Cone. Zander, Rote Rübe und Krenschaum. Rosa Grapefruit, Ahornsirup und Erdnuss.

AUSTRIA - SALZBURG

XX **Zirbelzimmer** – Hotel Sacher 🍴 ♿ 🅰🄲 🚗
Schwarzstr. 5 ✉ 5020 – 𝒞 (0662) 88 97 70   Plan: **G1**
– www.sacher.com
Menu 39/59 € – Carte 45/76 €
• International • Elegant •
Sacher's culinary flagship offers a wide and varied menu ranging from poached langoustine to Styrian fried chicken, all served in a warm, friendly and typically Austrian setting. There is also an attractive balcony overlooking the River Salzach.

XX **Pan e Vin**
Gstättengasse 1 (1st floor) ✉ 5020 – 𝒞 (0662) 84 46 66   Plan: **G1**
– www.panevin.at – Closed 1-10 September and Sunday, except festival period
Menu 48/89 € – Carte 33/75 €
• Mediterranean cuisine • Cosy •
Pan e Vin is set in a 600 year-old building with an interior decorated in warm tones. It serves food with a distinctly Mediterranean feel alongside a well-stocked international wine list. Azzuro on the ground floor is also a good option.

X **PARADOXON** 🍴 🚭
Zugallistr. 7 ✉ 5020 – 𝒞 (0664) 1 61 61 91   Plan II : **F2**
– www.restaurant-paradoxon.com – closed Sunday-Monday
Carte 38/62 € – *(dinner only)*
• International • Friendly •
This is probably the only 'permanent' pop-up restaurant in German-speaking Europe! The decor and cuisine change every three months – from Chinese-inspired to workshop-industrial; from dim sum to burgers or spare ribs. One thing that doesn't change however is the excellent level of cooking. Not to be missed!

X **Maier's**
Steingasse 61 ✉ 5020 – 𝒞 (0662) 87 93 79   Plan: **H1**
– www.maiers-salzburg.at – Closed Sunday-Monday
Carte 34/56 € – *(dinner only) (booking advisable)*
• International • Friendly • Cosy •
Many regulars visit this restaurant in an old alleyway to enjoy classic fare including steaks and Szegediner goulash. The feel is welcoming, the service friendly and you can park in the multi-storey car park right opposite the restaurant.

X **Blaue Gans** – arthotel Blaue Gans 🍴 🅰🄲
Getreidegasse 41 ✉ 5020 – 𝒞 (0662) 84 24 91 54   Plan: **G1**
– www.blauegans.at – Closed Sunday, except festival period
Menu 35/54 € (dinner) – Carte 34/48 €
• Country • Friendly •
Blaue Gans is a pleasantly light and airy restaurant complete with a pretty vaulted ceiling and some attractive tables outside on the terrace. The menu offers regional dishes such as stuffed shoulder of lamb with gnocchi, and char with pumpkin, beans and grammeln (scratchings).

ENVIRONS OF SALZBURG AND AIRPORT   **PLAN I**

🏠 **Rosenvilla** 🅿
Höfelgasse 4 ✉ 5020 – 𝒞 (0662) 62 17 65   Plan: **C2**
– www.rosenvilla.com – Closed 5-16 February
14 rm – ♦70/100 € ♦♦120/180 € – ☲ 13 €
• Family • Contemporary • Cosy •
Stefanie Fleischhaker is a born hostess and you are always sure of a warm welcome. Enjoy the great service, tasteful decor and lovely terrace, as well as the excellent breakfasts, which are popular even with non-residents. The single rooms are compact.

Doktorwirt   ⚐ 🕸 ⚐ ⚑ 🕸 ⚒ 🔄 🏊 P

Glaser Str. 9 ✉ 5026 – 𝒞 (0662) 6 22 97 30   Plan: **D3**
– www.doktorwirt.at – Closed 3-28 February, 15 October- 24 November
41 rm � – †80/135 € ††135/185 €
• Inn • Traditional • Cosy •

The Schnöll family run this cosy 12C tavern. There is a spacious spa area and a lovely garden, as well as beautiful tower rooms with small bay windows. Regional cuisine is served in very comfortable rooms or on the terraces in front and behind of the building. There is a wine cellar.

Brandstätter   ⚐ 🕸 🔄 🏊 P

Münchner Bundesstr. 69 ✉ 5020 – 𝒞 (0662) 43 45 35   Plan: **B1**
– www.hotel-brandstaetter.com – Closed 23-27 December
35 rm ⊔ – †95/110 € ††145/165 €
• Family • Cosy •

The hotel's proximity to the main street and the motorway is more than compensated for by the hospitality of the Brandstätter family and their staff. Some of the lovely country house-style rooms face out onto the garden.
🍴 **Brandstätter** – See restaurant listing

Airporthotel   ⚐ ⚑ 🕸 🔄 ⚒ 🏊 🚗

Dr.-Matthias-Laireiter-Str. 9 ✉ 5020 Salzburg-Loig   Plan: **A2**
– 𝒞 (0662) 85 00 20 – www.airporthotel.at
36 rm ⊔ – †105/165 € ††139/199 €
• Inn • Cosy •

This hotel is across from the airport, and consists of two connected hotel buildings, which are typical of the region. Functional rooms, some with air-conditioning.

Bloberger Hof   ⚐ ⚑ P

Hammerauerstr. 4 ✉ 5020 – 𝒞 (0662) 83 02 27   Plan: **B3**
– www.bloblergerhof.at – Closed 8 January-18 February, 23-27 December
20 rm ⊔ – †75/90 € ††90/125 €
• Inn • Cosy •

The Keuschnigg family offer everything you need when you are on the road. Comfortable rooms (book one in the more spacious 'superior' category), a good breakfast with homemade jam, warm, friendly service and parking right outside the door. Some rooms have a view of the Untersberg and others have balconies.

XxxX
Ikarus   🕸 ⚐ 🍴 ⚒ 🔠 ⚙ P
❀❀
Wilhelm-Spazier-Str. 7a ✉ 5020 – 𝒞 (0662) 2 19 70   Plan: **B2**
– www.hangar-7.com – closed 22 December - 27 January
Menu 58 € (lunch)/180 € – *(booking essential)*
• Creative • Fashionable • Elegant •

An unusual concept, the architecturally impressive Hangar-7 is both a Red Bull exhibition space and an ultra-modern luxury restaurant serving top quality creative cuisine. Choose from a menu devised by the international guest chef of the month or the restaurant's own Ikarus selection.
→ Bachforelle, Escabèche, Tomate, Jalapenos. Bayrische Garnele, Bier, Mohn, Sprossen. Ochsenschwanz, Pulpitos, Burrata, Trüffel.

XxX
SENNS.Restaurant   P
❀❀
Söllheimerstr. 16 (at Gusswerk - Object 6c) ✉ 5020   Plan: **C1**
– 𝒞 (0664) 4 54 02 32 – www.senns.restaurant – Closed 24 December-9 January and Sunday-Monday, except festival period
Menu 99/165 € – Carte 58/96 € – *(dinner only) (booking advisable)*
• Creative • Fashionable • Friendly •

The location may take a little getting used to but this is more than made up for by Andreas Senn's splendid, intense cuisine and the unusual and stylish industrial chic decor. Dishes are prepared using the very best ingredients. Excellent parking facilities.
→ Sepia, Passionsfrucht, Saubohnen, Topinambur. Black Cod, Miso, Dashi, Maniok, Lauch. Short Ribs, fermentierte Schalotten, gedörrte Physalis, Artischocken.

AUSTRIA - SALZBURG

55

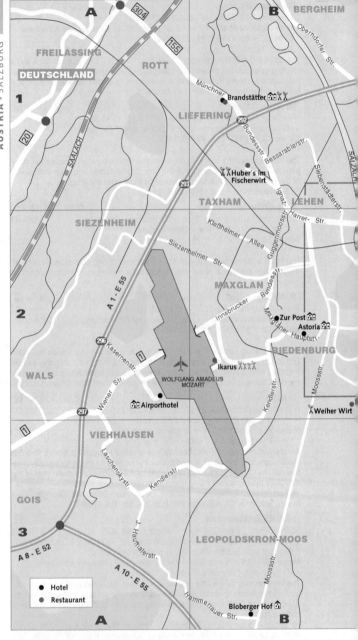

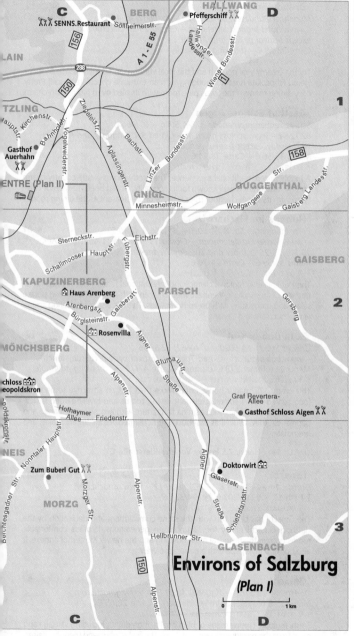

Environs of Salzburg
(Plan I)

XX Brandstätter

Münchner Bundesstr. 69 ⊠ 5020 – ℰ (0662) 43 45 35   Plan: **B1**
– www.hotel-brandstaetter.com – Closed 23-27 December and Sunday,
except festival period and Advent
Carte 28/69 € – *(booking advisable)*
• Country • Cosy •

Try the creamy veal goulash and the local venison, and dont' miss the Mohr im
Hemd (chocolate hazelnut pudding with an exquisite chocolate sauce!) Pretty,
cosy dining rooms – the Swiss pine room with its tiled oven has its own charm.

XX Gasthof Schloss Aigen

Schwarzenbergpromenade 37 ⊠ 5026 – ℰ (0662)   Plan: **D2**
62 12 84 – www.schloss-aigen.at – Closed 9-19 January and Monday-
Wednesday, except festival period
Menu 36/56 € – Carte 28/71 €
• Austrian • Inn • Friendly •

A highly prized, traditional experience! The pretty rooms exude country charm
and the restaurant is well-known for its speciality, boiled beef. The interior courtyard with its sweet chestnut trees is every bit as pleasant as the dining room.

XX Huber's im Fischerwirt

Peter Pfenninger Str. 8 ⊠ 5020 – ℰ (0662) 42 40 59   Plan: **B1**
– www.fischerwirt-liefering.at – Closed 13 February- 1 March, 24 April-
10 May, 9-25 October and Tuesday-Wednesday
Menu 39/59 € – Carte 24/76 €
• Austrian • Cosy • Rural •

The Hubers serve regional classics and international fare in their charming restaurant. Dishes include Viennese fried chicken with lamb's lettuce and potato
salad, and game stew with bread dumplings. There is also a small shop selling
jams, chocolate and caviar.

XX Zum Buberl Gut

Gneiser Str. 31 ⊠ 5020 – ℰ (0662) 82 68 66   Plan: **C3**
– www.buberlgut.at – Closed Tuesday, festival period: Tuesday lunch
Menu 26 € (lunch)/78 € (dinner) – Carte 47/75 € – *(booking advisable)*
• Traditional cuisine • Cosy • Rustic •

This pretty 17C manor house offers more than just an attractive setting. The
food served in the splendid, elegant dining rooms and lovely garden is delicious. It includes dishes such as tuna fish tartare with avocado and mango and
paprika chutney, as well as ossobuco with creamed Jerusalem artichokes and
gremolata.

AT ELIXHAUSEN North: 7,5 km by Vogelweiderstraße C1

⌂ Gmachl

Dorfstr. 14 ⊠ 5161 – ℰ (0662) 48 02 12 – www.gmachl.com
74 rm ⊡ – †118/202 € ††194/324 €
• Country house • Family • Cosy •

The Gmachl has been run with the same commitment and dedication by the
Hirnböck-Gmachl family for 23 unbroken generations. It offers comfortable
rooms both in the historical main building and the newer Klosterhof annexe. It
also boasts a lovely spa with a panoramic view.
Gmachl – See restaurant listing

XX Gmachl – Hotel Gmachl

Dorfstr. 14 ⊠ 5161 – ℰ (0662) 48 02 12 – www.gmachl.com
Menu 55 € (Vegetarian)/85 € (dinner) – Carte 28/65 €
• Country • Inn • Elegant •

Fresh, regional cuisine made of high quality ingredients, including sausage and
meat from the restaurant's own butchery. The feel is warm and friendly - Kaiser-
zimmer and Ahnenstube are elegant yet homely, the Gaststube is more rustic.

XX
ξξ³
Pfefferschiff (Jürgen Vigné)   සි ଲ **P**
Söllheim 3 ⊠ 5300 – ℰ (0662) 66 12 42   Plan: **D1**
*– www.pfefferschiff.at – Closed 2 weeks early March, 2 weeks end June-
early July, 2 weeks early September and Sunday-Monday, except festival
period*
Menu 80 € (Vegetarian)/110 € (dinner)
– Carte 66/97 € – (Tuesday - Friday dinner only) (booking essential)
• Classic cuisine • Elegant • Cosy •

Standing at the gates of Salzburg, this top gourmet restaurant is located in a
lovely 17C former parish house. The owner Jürgen Vigné's flavoursome and distinctive cuisine is matched by the charming front-of-house team managed by
his wife. The dining rooms are delightful and the terrace is wonderful.
➜ Gänseleber mit Marille und Fenchel. Reinanke mit Holunder und Paprika. Reh mit Kirsche und Sellerie.

Schloss Fuschl   ⧈ ◁ ᐸᐸ ₤ⓖ ᠁ 宿 🖺 🖼 ᵫ 🆊 🕏 ᐟ
Schloss Str. 19 ⊠ 5322 – ℰ (06229) 2 25 30
– www.schlossfuschlsalzburg.com
110 rm ☷ – ♦200/750 € ♦♦250/800 € – 13 suites
• Luxury • Classic •

This 'grand' hotel is set on a small peninsular projecting out into the lake. The
rooms are stylishly elegant, and a remarkable collection of paintings pays tribute to the castle's history. Along with a summer restaurant for hotel guests, a
private bathing beach and motorboats, there is even a Rolls Royce at your dis-
posal.
Schloss Restaurant – See restaurant listing

XxX
Schloss Restaurant – Hotel Schloss Fuschl   宿 ᵫ ᐟ
Schloss Str. 19 ⊠ 5322 – ℰ (06229) 2 25 30
– www.schlossfuschlsalzburg.com
Menu 116 € – Carte 44/86 € – *(dinner only)*
• Classic cuisine • Romantic •

Ambitious food is served in this classically elegant setting with its stunning view
of the Fuschlsee Lake. Dishes range from a traditional tafelspitz (boiled topside
of veal) to turbot pan-fried in brown butter. Fantastic terrace!

BELGIUM
BELGIË - BELGIQUE

● Antwerp

BRUSSELS ●

→ **AREA:**
30 528 km² (11 781 sq mi)

→ **POPULATION:**
11 371 928 inhabitants.
Density = 373 per km².

→ **CAPITAL:**
Brussels.

→ **CURRENCY:**
Euro (€).

→ **GOVERNMENT:**
Constitutional parliamentary monarchy (since 1830) and a federal state (since 1994). Member of European Union since 1957 (one of the 6 founding countries).

→ **LANGUAGES:**
Dutch (in Flanders and Brussels), French (in Wallonia and Brussels), German (Eastern cantons); most Belgians also speak English.

→ **PUBLIC HOLIDAYS:**
New Year's Day (1 Jan); Easter Monday (late Mar/Apr); Labor Day (1 May); Ascension Day (May); Whit Monday (late May/June); Independence Day (21 July); Assumption of the Virgin Mary (15 Aug); All Saints' Day (1 Nov); Armistice Day 1918 (11 Nov); Christmas Day (25 Dec); Boxing Day (26 Dec).

→ **LOCAL TIME:**
GMT+1 hour in winter and GMT+2 hours in summer.

→ **CLIMATE:**
Temperate maritime with cool winters and mild summers (Brussels: January 2°C; July 18°C); more continental towards the Ardennes. Rainfall evenly distributed throughout the year.

→ **EMERGENCY:**
Police ☎ **101**; Medical Assistance and Fire Brigade ☎ **100**.
(Dialling **112** within any EU country will redirect your call and contact the emergency services).

→ **ELECTRICITY:**
230 volts AC, 50Hz; 2 round pin sockets.

→ **FORMALITIES:**
Travellers from the European Union (EU), Switzerland, Norway, Iceland and the main countries of North and South America need a national identity card or passport (America: passport required) to visit Belgium for less than three months (tourism or business purpose). For visitors from other countries a visa may be required, in addition to a passport, especially for those wishing to stay for longer than three months. We advise you to check with your embassy before travelling.

BRUSSELS
BRUXELLES/BRUSSEL

Population: 1 175 173

Guitain/Fotolia.com

There aren't many cities where you can use a 16C century map and accurately navigate your way around; or where there are enough restaurants to dine somewhere different every day for five years; or where you'll find a museum dedicated to the comic strip – but then every city isn't Brussels. It was tagged a 'grey' capital because of its EU associations but those who've spent time here know it to be, by contrast, a buzzing town. It's the home of art nouveau, it features a wonderful maze of medieval alleys and places to eat, and it's warm and friendly, with an outgoing, cosmopolitan feel – due in no small part to its turbulent history, which has seen it under frequent occupation. Generally speaking, the Bruxellois believe that you shouldn't take things too seriously: they have a soft spot for puppets and Tintin, street music and majorettes; and they do their laundry in communal places like the Wash Club.

The area where all visitors wend is the Lower Town and the Grand Place but the northwest and southern quarters (Ste-Catherine and The Marolles) are also of particular interest. To the east, higher up an escarpment, lies the Upper Town – this is the traditional home of the aristocracy and encircles the landmark Parc de Bruxelles. Two suburbs of interest are St Gilles, to the southwest, and Ixelles, to the southeast, where trendy bars and art nouveau are the order of the day.

BRUSSELS IN...

→ **ONE DAY**
Grand Place, Musées Royaux des Beaux-Arts, Place Ste-Catherine.

→ **TWO DAYS**
Marolles, Place du Grand Sablon, Musical Instrument Museum, concert at Palais des Beaux-Arts.

→ **THREE DAYS**
Parc du Cinquantenaire, Horta's house, tour St Gilles and Ixelles.

PRACTICAL INFORMATION

ARRIVAL-DEPARTURE

 Brussels Airport is 14km northeast. Trains to and from the airport run every 15min and take 20min.

Eurostar - Brussels Midi Train Station is 2km southwest; high speed Thalys trains also operate from here. Take Metro Line 2, 3, 4 or 6.

GETTING AROUND

Buses, trams and metro all run efficiently. You can buy 1, 5 or 10 trip cards and 1, 2 or 3 day travel cards. These are available from metro stations, travel authority offices (BOOTIK and KIOSK) and newsagents. Remember to stamp your ticket before each journey; red machines are on every metro station concourse and on every tram and bus. Single tickets are valid for an hour and you can hop on and off all forms of public transport. (Roving inspectors impose heavy on-the-spot fines for anyone caught without a valid ticket.)

CALENDAR HIGHLIGHTS

January
Brussels Jazz Festival.

February
Brussels Book Fair.

May
Kunsten Festival des Arts, Queen Elisabeth Music Contest.

June
Brussels Film Festival.

July
Ommegang (Renaissance Procession).

August
Brussels Summer Festival, Fiesta Latina.

July-August
Foire du Midi Funfair.

September
International Comic Strip and Cartoon Festival.

November
Ars Musica.

December
Christmas Market.

EATING OUT

As long as your appetite hasn't been sated at the chocolatiers, or with a cone of frites from a street stall, you'll relish the dining experience in Brussels. As long as you stay off the main tourist drag (i.e. Rue des Bouchers), you're guaranteed somewhere good to eat within a short strolling distance. There are lots of places to enjoy Belgian dishes such as moules frites, Ostend lobster, eels with green herbs, or waterzooi (chicken or fish stew with vegetables). Wherever you're eating, at whatever price range, food is invariably well cooked and often bursting with innovative touches. As a rule of thumb, the Lower Town has the best places, with the Ste-Catherine quarter's fish and seafood establishments the pick of the bunch; you'll also find a mini Chinatown here. Because of the city's cosmopolitan character there are dozens of international restaurants - ranging from French and Italian to more unusual Moroccan, Tunisian and Congolese destinations. Belgium beers are famous the world over and are served in specially designed glasses.

CENTRE (Grand Place, Sainte-Catherine, Sablons)

The Hotel

boulevard de Waterloo 38 ⊠ *1000 –* ℰ *02 504 11 11* Plan: **N3**
– www.thehotel.be
420 rm – ♦130/270 € ♦♦130/270 € – � 27 € – 5 suites
• Townhouse • Grand Luxury • Design •
Enjoy the breathtaking view of Brussels and the hidden charms of the city in this well-preserved district. This establishment is also ideal for exploring the shops along Avenue Louise. Shopaholics take note!
The Restaurant – See restaurant listing

Amigo

rue de l'Amigo 1 ⊠ *1000 –* ℰ *02 547 47 47* Plan: **M2**
– www.roccofortehotels.com
154 rm – ♦197/660 € ♦♦197/660 € – ⊒ 19 € – 19 suites
• Grand Luxury • Townhouse • Personalised •
A real institution, and one of the best hotels in Brussels! Its assets? Its central location (behind the Grand-Place), luxurious rooms, impeccable service and refined charm. You may even run into a celebrity here.
Bocconi – See restaurant listing

Radisson Blu Royal

rue du Fossé aux Loups 47 ⊠ *1000 –* ℰ *02 219 28 28* Plan: **N1**
– www.radissonblu.com/royalhotel-brussels
269 rm – ♦150/400 € ♦♦150/400 € – ⊒ 29 € – 12 suites
• Luxury • Chain • Contemporary •
Impressive modern glass atrium, remains of the city's fortifications, and extremely comfortable suites and guestrooms. Breakfast room adorned with wooden railway sleepers. A contemporary style brasserie illuminated by natural light through the glass roof.

Le Plaza

boulevard Adolphe Max 118 ⊠ *1000 –* ℰ *02 278 01 00* Plan: **F1**
– www.leplaza-brussels.be
184 rm – ♦120/495 € ♦♦140/495 € – ⊒ 20 € – 6 suites
• Palace • Grand Luxury • Elegant •
A 1930s building imitating the George V hotel in Paris. Classic public areas, large cosy guestrooms and a superb Baroque theatre used for receptions and events. An elegant bar and restaurant beneath an attractive dome painted with a trompe l'œil sky.

Métropole

place de Brouckère 31 ⊠ *1000 –* ℰ *02 217 23 00* Plan: **M1**
– www.metropolehotel.com
286 rm ⊒ – ♦102/489 € ♦♦102/519 € – 5 suites
• Grand Luxury • Historic • Personalised •
A 19C luxury hotel overlooking Place de Brouckère. Period lobby and lounges, a retro-style lounge bar with columns, a piano and frescoes, and luxurious bedrooms and suites. Breakfast is served to a backdrop of colonial decor.

Royal Windsor

rue Duquesnoy 5 ⊠ *1000 –* ℰ *02 505 55 55* Plan: **M2**
– www.warwickhotels.com/brussels
260 rm – ♦134/700 € ♦♦134/700 € – ⊒ 24 € – 7 suites
• Luxury • Personalised •
Royal: what better word to describe a stay in this luxury hotel? The historic city centre is a stone's throw from this establishment, which has faultless service. The elegant and comfortable rooms have a nostalgic British flavour. Recommended without hesitation.

The Dominican
rue Léopold 9 ✉ *1000 –* ✆ *02 203 08 08*
Plan: **M1**
– www.thedominican.be
147 rm – ♦130/450 € ♦♦130/450 € – ⌸ 27 € – 3 suites
• Historic building • Grand townhouse • Elegant •
A designer-inspired luxury hotel on the site of a former Dominican convent. Open spaces, elegant furniture and modern comforts which benefit from maximum attention to detail. The Grand Lounge takes full advantage of the natural light from the patio. A modern menu and non-stop service.

Pillows
place Rouppe 17 ✉ *1000 –* ✆ *02 204 00 40*
Plan: **L2**
– www.sandton.eu/pillowsbrussels
45 rm ⌸ – ♦99/499 € ♦♦109/499 €
• Luxury • Contemporary •
Black and white dominate this handsome manor house on Place Rouppe, a few steps from the town centre. The warm, inviting rooms offer all the facilities one has come to expect from a good hotel.

Le Dixseptième
rue de la Madeleine 25 ✉ *1000 –* ✆ *02 517 17 17*
Plan: **M2**
– www.ledixseptieme.be
35 rm ⌸ – ♦100/400 € ♦♦120/430 € – 2 suites
• Luxury • Grand luxury •
This townhouse dating from the 17C was once the official residence of the Spanish ambassador in the city. Elegant lounges, attractive inner courtyard, and guestrooms embellished with furniture of varying styles.

Hôtel des Galeries
rue des Bouchers 38 ✉ *1000 –* ✆ *02 213 74 70*
Plan: **M1**
– www.hoteldesgaleries.be
23 rm – ♦180/300 € ♦♦190/400 € – ⌸ 19 € – 3 suites
• Luxury • Contemporary • Elegant •
This boutique hotel in a classical edifice enjoys a premium location on the corner of Rue des Bouchers and the King's Gallery. The luxury setting combines vintage touches with a contemporary interior, whose attention to detail extends as far as the ceramic tiles in the washrooms. Perfectly located for a stay in Brussels.
Comptoir des Galeries – See restaurant listing

XxxX
❀❀

Sea Grill (Yves Mattagne) – Hôtel Radisson Blu Royal
rue du Fossé aux Loups 47 ✉ *1000 –* ✆ *02 212 08 00*
– www.seagrill.be – closed 9-17 April, 21 July-15 August,
Plan: **N1**
1-6 January, Bank Holidays, Saturday lunch and Sunday
Menu 65 € (lunch), 135/195 € – Carte 135/209 €
• Seafood • Elegant • Luxury •
The menu varies according to the catch of the day. The sea supplies the treasures and the crew steers the ship with flying colours! A challenging, first-rate performance with some prestigious wines in the hold for an unforgettable crossing. It has secluded tables that are ideal for business lunches.
➜ Langoustines cuites et flambées à l'émulsion de châtaigne, truffe et artichaut. Homard bleu breton à la presse. Gaufre de Bruxelles et sorbet mangue.

XxxX
❀

Bruneau (Jean-Pierre Bruneau)
avenue Broustin 75 ✉ *1083 –* ✆ *02 421 70 70*
Plan: **B2**
– www.bruneau.be – closed first 3 weeks July, first 2 weeks January,
Tuesday and Wednesday
Menu 55 € (lunch), 70/125 € – Carte 63/230 €
• Creative French • Elegant •
A renowned restaurant offering a perfect balance between the traditional and the innovative, while at the same time showcasing regional cuisine. Impressive wine list. Outdoor terrace for summer dining.
➜ Fricassée au homard et quinoa. Blanc de coucou de Malines en demi-deuil. Soufflé chaud aux maracujas.

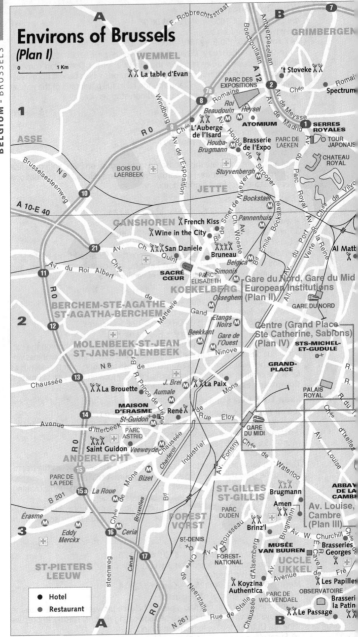

Environs of Brussels
(Plan I)

0   1 Km

A

F. Robbrechtsstraat

WEMMEL

La table d'Evan

PARC DES EXPOSITIONS

Romaine

Roi Beaudouin

Heysel

ATOMIUM

L'Auberge de l'Isard

Houba-Brugmann

Brasserie de l'Expo

PARC DE LAEKEN

ASSE

Windberg

Av. de l'Exposition

R 0

BOIS DU LAERBEEK

Stuyvenbergh

JETTE

Brusselsesteenweg

N 9

A 10-E 40

Bockstael

GANSHOREN French Kiss

Wine in the City

San Daniele

Bruneau

Belgica

Pannenhuis

Simonis

SACRÉ CŒUR

PARC ELISABETH

KOEKELBERG

Osseghem

**BERCHEM-STE-AGATHE
ST-AGATHA-BERCHEM**

Gand

Etangs Noirs

Beekkant

Gare de l'Ouest

Ninove

**MOLENBEEK-ST-JEAN
ST-JANS-MOLENBEEK**

N 8

La Brouette

Aumale

J. Brel

La Paix

Mons

MAISON D'ERASME

St-Guidon

René

Rue Eloy

PARC ASTRID

Saint Guidon

Veeweyde

ANDERLECHT

PARC DE LA PEDE

La Roue

B 201

Érasme

Eddy Merckx

Ceria

Bizet

Bruxelles

Canal

FOREST VORST

ST-DENIS

ST-PIETERS LEEUW

steenweg

N 261

Rue de Stalle

B

GRIMBERGEN

't Stoveke

Romai

Spectrum

SERRES ROYALES

TOUR JAPONAIS

CHATEAU ROYAL

Al Matt

**Gare du Nord, Gare du Midi,
European Institutions
(Plan II)**

GARE DU NORD

**Centre (Grand Place,
Ste Catherine, Sablons)
(Plan IV)**

STS-MICHEL-ET-GUDULE

GRAND-PLACE

PALAIS ROYAL

GARE DU MIDI

Waterloo

Av. d'Ixelles

Louise

**ST-GILLES
ST-GILLIS**

Brugmann

Amen

PARC DUDEN

Brinz'l

MUSÉE VAN BUUREN

FOREST-NATIONAL

Koyzina Authentica

PARC DE WOLVENDAEL

Le Passage

ABBAY DE LA CAMBR

**Av. Louise, Cambre
(Plan III)**

W. Churchill

Brasseries Georges

UCCLE UKKEL

Les Papilles

OBSERVATOIRE

Brasseri la Patin

● Hotel
● Restaurant

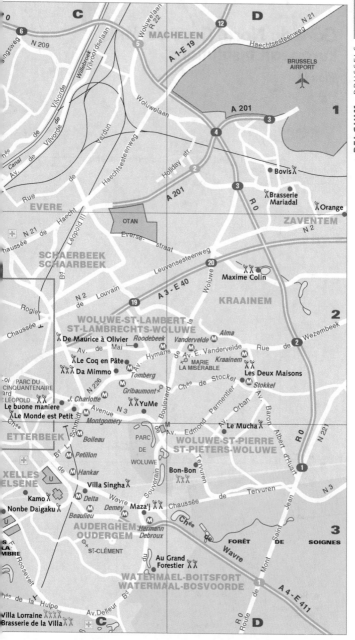

C   D

N 21

6   N 209

MACHELEN   12

Woluwelaan R 22

5

A 1-E 19

Haechtsesteenweg

Willebroek   Vilvoordselaan

née   de   Vilvorde   Verdun   Woluwelaan

BRUSSELS AIRPORT

de   Vilvorde   Av.   de   Haechtsesteenweg

Canal   Rue   de

A 201   3   1

4

Holiday str.

2

EVERE   A 201   3   Bovis ✕

N 21   de   Haecht   Leopold III   ✕ Brasserie Mariadal   ✕ Orange

OTAN   ZAVENTEM   N 2

haussée   Eversg-   straat

SCHAERBEEK   SCHAARBEEK

Leuvensesteenweg   Woluwe

20   Maxime Colin ✕✕

Bd   Louvain   19   A 3 - E 40   KRAAINEM

Rogier   N 2   de   Wezembeek

Chaussée   2   de   2

WOLUWE-ST-LAMBERT   Alma

ST-LAMBRECHTS-WOLUWE   Roodebeek   Vandervelde

✕ De Maurice à Olivier   Av.   de   Mai   Av. E. Vandervelde   Rue

✕ Le Coq en Pâte   Hymans   Kraainem ✕

oi   PARC DU   ✕✕✕ Da Mimmo   Tomberg   ✕ MARIE   LA MISÉRABLE   Les Deux Maisons

CINQUANTENAIRE   N 226   Gribaumont   Chée   de Stockel   Stokkel

ard   LÉOPOLD   ✕✕   J. Charlotte   ✕✕ YuMe   Av.   Orban

Le buone maniere   Avenue   N 3   Parmentier   Baron

✕ Le Monde est Petit   Schmidt   Montgomery   Av. Edmond   ✕ Le Mucha

ETTERBEEK   Boileau   PARC   Av.   R 0   N 221

Petillon   DE   WOLUWE-ST-PIERRE

Hankar   WOLUWE   ST-PIETERS-WOLUWE   1

XELLES   Villa Singha ✕   Souverain   Bon-Bon   Tervuren   N 3

ELSENE   U   Delta   Wavre   ✕✕✕

Kamo ✕   Demey   Maza'j ✕✕   Chaussée   de   Tervuren

Nonbe Daigaku ✕   Beaulieu

S   AUDERGHEM   Hermann   Chée   FORÊT   DE   SOIGNES

LA   OUDERGEM   Debroux

MBRE   ST-CLÉMENT   Mont

Roosevelt   Au Grand   Forestier ✕✕   Saint   Jean   Wavre

Villa Lorraine ✕✕✕✕   WATERMAEL-BOITSFORT   A 4 - E 411

Brasserie de la Villa ✕✕   WATERMAAL-BOSVOORDE   R 0   Route   de   D

hée   de la   Hulpe   Av.Delleur   Bd   C

1   2   3

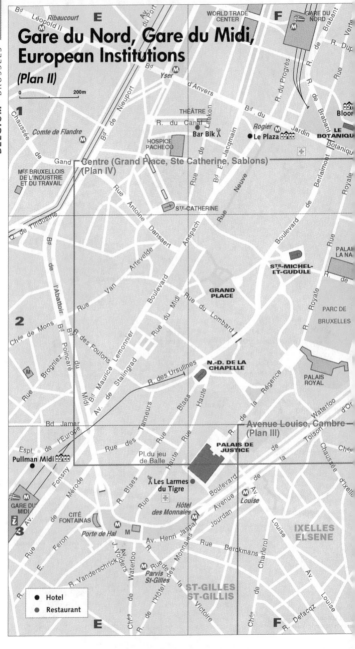

Gare du Nord, Gare du Midi, European Institutions

(Plan II)

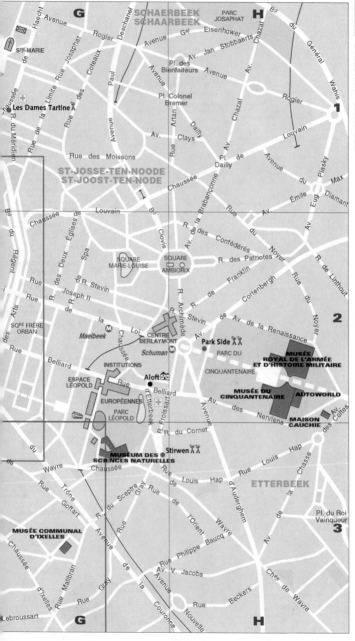

L

Rue de Flandre
Rue du Houblon
Rue N-D. du

⚔ Henri de
● Strofilia ⚔
● Selecto ⚔
Ste-Catherine Ⓜ

⚔ Viva M'Boma
San ⚔
⚔⚔ La Belle Maraîchère
François ⚔⚔
Pl. du Nouveau Marché aux Grains
Antoine ⚔
Pl. Ste-Catherine
⚔ Le Vismet
⚔ Le Fourneau de Bruxelles
STE-CATHERINE Ⓜ

1

⚔ Little Asia

R. des Fabriques
La Manufacture ⚔
Rue des Commines
Chartreux
In 't Spinnekopke ⚔
Dansaert
Arteveide

M

LE BÉGUINAGE
Bd. Jacqmain
Leeken
Bd. Adolphe Max
N.-D. D... FINISTÈ...

Place de Brouckère
Ⓜ ● Métropole 🏨

R. du Fossé aux...
● Samourai ⚔

THÉÂTRE DE LA MONNAIE
R. de l'Écuyer
R. des Fripiers
Anspach
🏨 The Dominic
⚔⚔
Compt... des Gale...
Ho...
De...
Gale...

De l'Ogenblik ⚔
Scheltema ⚔

Pl. de la Bourse
ST-NICOLAS
BOURSE
● Aux Armes de Bruxelles

GALERI... ST-HUBE...

Rue T'Kint
Rue des Van Six Jetons
RICHES CLAIRES
R. des Riches Claires
HALLES ST-GÉRY
Halles St-Géry
Anspach

⚔⚔ Taverne du Passage

GRAND-PLACE
🏨 Amigo
⚔⚔⚔ Bocconi
R. du
● La Maison du Cygne ⚔⚔
L'Ommegang ⚔
M
MADELE...

2

Rue de Vautour
Boulevard
Pl. Fontainas
N.-D. DU BON SECOURS
MANNEKEN PIS
R. de l'Étuve
Rue du Chêne
Lombard
Le Dixseptième 🏨
🏨 Royal Wind...
Place de l'Albertin...

Rue du Midi
R. de la Verdure
Lemonnier
Rue des Foulons
Anneessens Ⓜ
Alexandre ⚔⚔
Comme Chez Sol ⚔⚔⚔
● Pillows 🏨
Rue Maurice
Rue Neuve
Boulevard de l'Empereur
Rue des Alexiens

3

Boulevard Lemonnier Ⓜ
Bd. Poincaré
Stalingrad
Avenue
Rue du Midi
Rue Terre Neuve
Rue des Ursulines
N.-D. DE LA CHAPELLE
Les Brigittines aux Marches de la Chapelle ⚔⚔
Rue Blaes
Rue Haute
Rue des Tanneurs
Rue du Miroir
Rue Blaes
Rue des Capucins
Le Wine Bar des Marolles ⚔
Rue Haute

Peï & Meï ⚔
Genco ⚔
Ⓜ Pl. du G... Sablo...
Lola ⚔
N.-D. D... SABLO...
⚔ Les Petits Oignons
R. E. Allard
CONSERVATOIR...
Pl. Poelaert
PALAIS DE JUSTICE
M
⚔⚔ J...

● Hotel
● Restaurant

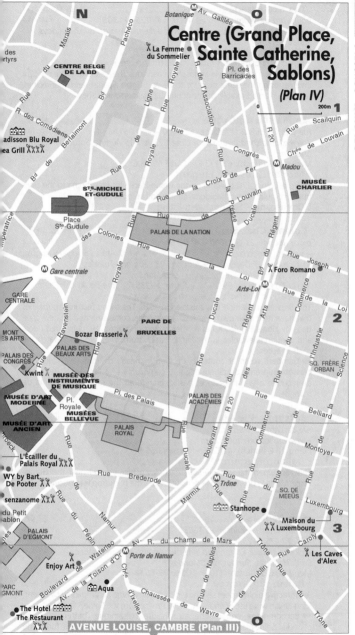

Centre (Grand Place, Sainte Catherine, Sablons)
(Plan IV)

0   200m

BELGIUM - BRUSSELS

XxX The Restaurant – The Hotel ⟨ ⅙ 🄰🄲 ⇔ 🛃 🚗

boulevard de Waterloo 38 ✉ 1000 – ℰ 0 25 04 13 33   Plan: **L3**
– www.therestaurant.be – closed mid July-mid August, Bank Holidays,
Sunday and Monday
Menu 35 € (lunch), 55/110 € – Carte 33/75 €
• Modern cuisine • Chic • Fashionable •

A trendy, sexy lounge-style atmosphere pervades The Restaurant. The concept involves using the same produce to create Belgian, Spanish and Thai recipes, resulting in an admirable choice of unusual, flavoursome dishes.

XxX La Maison du Cygne 🄰🄲 ⇔

rue Charles Buls 2 (1ᵉʳ étage) ✉ 1000 – ℰ 0 2 511 82 44   Plan: **M2**
– www.lamaisonducygne.be – closed 23 July-15 August, Saturday lunch and Sunday
Menu 25 € (lunch), 65/173 € – Carte 69/88 €
• Modern cuisine • Elegant •

This prestigious 17C building on the Grand-Place was once home to the city's butchers' guild. Varied traditional cuisine and an opulent decor.
L'Ommegang – See restaurant listing

XxX Comme Chez Soi (Lionel Rigolet) ⅍ 🄰🄲 ⇔ 🛃
⅍⅍

place Rouppe 23 ✉ 1000 – ℰ 0 2 512 29 21   Plan: **L2**
– www.commechezsoi.be – closed 4, 5, 11 and 12 April, 16 July-15 August, 31 October, 25 December-9 January, 28 February, Tuesday lunch, Wednesday lunch, Sunday and Monday
Menu 60 € (lunch), 99/197 € – Carte 94/235 € – (pre-book)
• Creative French • Elegant •

This Brussels institution was founded in 1926. The menu features specialities that have held their own over four generations, complemented by new creations by Lionel Rigolet. It has all the comfort of a bistro, Horta-inspired decor and comfortable tables in the kitchen itself, from where you can watch the chefs in action.

➜ Gambero rosso et couteaux de mer, marinade de tomate et coulis de cresson. Suprême de pigeonneau au curry fumé et à l'estragon. Petit farci de joconde à la framboise et basilic, granité au thé samba et espuma de mangue.

XxX Bocconi – Hôtel Amigo ⅙ 🄰🄲 ⇔ 🛃

rue de l'Amigo 1 ✉ 1000 – ℰ 0 2 547 47 15   Plan: **M2**
– www.roccofortehotels.com
Menu 18 € (lunch), 42/55 € – Carte 43/65 €
• Italian • Elegant • Elegant •

This renowned Italian restaurant occupies a luxury hotel near the Grand-Place. Modern brasserie-style decor provides the backdrop for enticing Italian cuisine.

XxX San Daniele (Franco Spinelli) ⅍ 🄰🄲 ⇔
⅍

avenue Charles-Quint 6 ✉ 1083   Plan: **A2**
– ℰ 0 2 426 79 23 – www.san-daniele.be
– closed 1 week Easter, mid July-mid August, late December, Bank Holidays, Sunday and Monday
Menu 60 € 🍷 (lunch)/110 € – Carte 72/95 €
• Italian • Intimate •

An attractive dining room serving typical Italian cuisine accompanied by an enticing Italian wine list. Friendly, attentive service from the Spinelli family.

➜ Bar de ligne cru, mariné au vinaigre balsamique, betterave rouge et radis. Saint-pierre rôti aux carottes confites et émulsion de fumet de poisson. Mayonnaise de chocolat noir, polenta à la pistache et sorbet orange-chocolat.

XXX L'Écailler du Palais Royal

rue Bodenbroek 18 ✉ *1000* – ℰ *0 2 512 87 51* Plan: **N3**
– www.lecaillerdupalaisroyal.be – closed 20 July-21 August, 23 December-2 January and Bank Holidays
Carte 76/285 €
• Seafood • Traditional décor •

An elegant and cosy oyster bar frequented by diplomats and top business executives for the past 40 years. Choose from banquette seating and a convivial counter-bar downstairs or round tables upstairs. Refined fish and seafood.

XXX senzanome (Giovanni Bruno)

place du Petit Sablon 1 ✉ *1000* – ℰ *0 2 223 16 17* Plan: **N3**
– www.senzanome.be – closed 1 week at Easter, mid July-mid August, Christmas-New Year, Bank Holidays, Saturday lunch and Sunday
Menu 50 € (lunch), 85/115 € – Carte 77/109 €
• Italian • Design •

All the flavours and aromas of rich Italian, particularly Sicilian, culinary traditions are showcased at senzanome. The talented chef rustles up beautifully prepared and presented dishes of flawless harmony. A prestigious establishment, entirely in keeping with the neighbourhood.
➜ Emulsion de burratina et sorbet de tomate, huile d'olive au basilic et tuile de pain Sarde. Pintade farcie à la mortadelle et pistaches, jus de cuisson au marsala et soja. Baba au limoncello, crème de citron et crumble d'amandes.

XX Aux Armes de Bruxelles

rue des Bouchers 13 ✉ *1000* – ℰ *0 2 511 55 50* Plan: **M1**
– www.auxarmesdebruxelles.com
Menu 23/62 € – Carte 34/109 €
• Belgian • Brasserie • Elegant •

This veritable Brussels institution in the Ilot Sacré district has been honouring Belgian culinary traditions since 1921. Contrasting dining rooms and a lively atmosphere.

XX Lola

place du Grand Sablon 33 ✉ *1000* – ℰ *0 2 514 24 60* Plan: **M3**
– www.restolola.be – closed 2 weeks in August and dinner 24 and 31 December
Carte 40/66 € – *(open until 11pm)*
• Mediterranean cuisine • Brasserie •

Friendly brasserie with a contemporary decor serving Italian dishes based on the freshest ingredients. The pleasant counter is perfect for a meal on the hoof.

XX Les Brigittines Aux Marches de la Chapelle

place de la Chapelle 5 ✉ *1000* – ℰ *0 2 512 68 91* Plan: **M3**
– www.lesbrigittines.com – closed Saturday lunch and Sunday
Menu 35 € (lunch)/55 € – Carte 47/84 €
• Traditional cuisine • Vintage •

This lavish Art Nouveau brasserie will first and foremost delight the eye! Afterwards you will also find it impossible to resist the mouthwatering recipes rustled up by chef Dirk Myny. He is a genuine Brusseler, whose exuberant personality gives character to his traditional market fresh dishes.

XX La Belle Maraîchère

place Sainte-Catherine 11 ✉ *1000* – ℰ *0 2 512 97 59* Plan: **L1**
– www.labellemaraichere.com – closed mid July-early August, 1 week at Carnival, Wednesday and Thursday
Menu 40/64 € – Carte 48/107 € – *(booking advisable)*
• Seafood • Friendly • Elegant •

This welcoming, family-run restaurant is a popular choice for locals with charmingly nostalgic decor in the dining room. Enticing traditional cuisine, including fish, seafood and game depending on the season, as well as high quality sauces. Attractive set menus.

XX WY by Bart De Pooter   🛆 ✿

rue Bodenbroek 22 ⊠ 1000 – ℰ 0 2 400 42 63   Plan: **N3**
– www.wybrussels.be – closed 9-19 April, 23 December-5 January and
Sunday (Change of address planned for July 2017)
Menu 47/93 € – Carte 78/86 €
• Creative • Fashionable •
This haven of fine food nestles in the heart of Brussels' 'Mercedes House'. Once past the car showroom, you will be greeted by a luminous, contemporary restaurant and tasty cuisine. Enjoy fine produce, creative menus and sophisticated service. Flat screens showcase the chefs at work.
➜ Homard fumé au poivron, rouille et herbes aromatiques. Pigeon et dattes à la fleur d'oranger et amandes. Figues au kalamansi, harissa et thé vert.

XX **Comptoir des Galeries** – Hôtel des Galeries   🖾

Galerie du Roi 6 ⊠ 1000 – ℰ 0 2 213 74 74   Plan: **M1**
– www.comptoirdesgaleries.be – closed Sunday and Monday
Menu 26 € (lunch) – Carte 37/62 €
• Classic French • Brasserie • Friendly •
Vintage accents add character to this contemporary brasserie, in the heart of which stands a somewhat incongruous medal press! Pleasant establishment, ideal to savour brasserie classics made with good quality ingredients, or just for a glass of good wine.

XX JB   🛖 🅺 ✿

rue du Grand Cerf 24 ⊠ 1000 – ℰ 0 2 512 04 84   Plan: **M3**
– www.restaurantjb.com – closed August, 24-27 December, Bank Holidays,
Monday lunch, Saturday lunch and Sunday
Menu 37/50 € – Carte 62/73 €
• Modern cuisine • Friendly • Family •
Despite being located close to the Place Louise, this family-run restaurant remains discreet. The regulars all have their favourites, be it Flemish asparagus or grilled veal sweetbreads. Flavours are pronounced and the menu represents good value for money.

XX **Taverne du Passage**

Galerie de la Reine 30 ⊠ 1000 – ℰ 0 2 512 37 31   Plan: **M2**
– www.taverne-du-passage.be – closed Monday
Menu 37 € – Carte 41/61 €
• Belgian • Tavern • Classic décor •
An old-fashioned portrait of Brussels in the delightful Galerie de la Reine with its nostalgic charm and Art Deco features. There are a variety of Belgian delicacies including croquette de crevettes (shrimp) and eels in sorrel sauce.

XX **Alexandre**

rue du Midi 164 ⊠ 1000 – ℰ 0 2 502 40 55   Plan: **L2**
– www.restaurant-alexandre.be – closed last week August-first week
September, first week January, Tuesday lunch, Saturday lunch, Sunday
and Monday
Menu 50 € (lunch), 75/130 €
• Modern cuisine • Intimate •
The restaurant's name gives no hint to the restaurant's feminine character. The charming manageress greets and takes care of patrons, while the female kitchen brigade prepares creative dishes. Their compositions are elegant with a deliciously feminine touch.

X Kwint   ≼ 🛖 🅺

Mont des Arts 1 ⊠ 1000 – ℰ 0 2 505 95 95   Plan: **N2**
– www.kwintbrussels.com
Menu 19 € (lunch), 36/46 € – Carte 30/62 € – *(open until 11pm)*
• Modern French • Brasserie •
An amazing sculpture by artist Arne Quinze adds cachet to this elegant brasserie. It serves a tasty up-to-the-minute menu in which fine quality produce takes pride of place. The view of the city from the Mont des Arts is breathtaking. A great way to see another side of Brussels.

X **La Manufacture**

rue Notre-Dame du Sommeil 12 ⊠ 1000 Plan: **L1**
*– 𝒞 0 2 502 25 25 – www.manufacture.be – closed 21 July-5 August,
24 December-2 January, Bank Holidays, Saturday lunch and Sunday*
Menu 16 € (lunch), 38/70 € ℗ – Carte 40/58 €

• Belgian • Brasserie • Trendy •

Metals, wood, leather and granite provide the decor in this lively, trendy brasserie in the former workshop of a famous Belgian luggage maker. Contemporary cuisine.

X **Bozar Brasserie**

⊛ *rue Baron Horta 3 ⊠ 1000 – 𝒞 0 2 503 00 00* Plan: **N2**
– www.bozarbrasserie.be – closed July-August, Sunday and Monday
Menu 29 € (lunch), 39/59 € – Carte 71/89 €

• Modern French • Fashionable • Brasserie •

Chef Torosyan's pork pie, the house speciality, is emblematic of his cuisine which subtly reinterprets traditional recipes. Do not expect pointlessly complicated dishes – the emphasis is on fine, generously served food.

➔ Noble pâté en croûte au cochon fermier, magret et foie gras de canard, pickles de légumes. Agneau de lait rôti au sautoir, coco de Paimpol, houmous et coriandre. Baba au rhum à l'ananas et gingembre confit.

X **L'Ommegang**

Grand-Place 9 ⊠ 1000 – 𝒞 0 2 511 82 44 Plan: **M2**
– www.brasseriedelommegang.be – closed Bank Holidays, Saturday lunch and Sunday
Carte 32/59 €

• Traditional cuisine • Classic décor • Elegant •

You will enjoy the classic, copious Belgian cuisine served at this brasserie, which is the little sister of the famous Maison du Cygne. It is surrounded by the ambience of "the most beautiful square in the world", as Victor Hugo once said. The affable staff display typical Brussels humour.

X **De l'Ogenblik**

Galerie des Princes 1 ⊠ 1000 – 𝒞 0 2 511 61 51 Plan: **M1**
– www.ogenblik.be – closed 1-15 August, lunch on Bank Holidays and Sunday
Menu 48/60 € – Carte 49/72 € – *(open until midnight)*

• Classic cuisine • Bistro • Simple •

This restaurant, popular with the city's business crowd, has the appearance of an old café. Traditional cuisine including typical bistro dishes.

X **Little Asia**

rue Sainte-Catherine 8 ⊠ 1000 – 𝒞 0 2 502 88 36 Plan: **L1**
– www.littleasia.be – closed 15 July-15 August, Wednesday and Sunday
Menu 25 € (lunch), 45/69 € – Carte 49/75 €

• Vietnamese • Fashionable • Exotic décor •

A restaurant known for its well-prepared Vietnamese specialities, modern decor and smiling waitresses, overseen by a charming female owner.

X **Selecto**

rue de Flandre 95 ⊠ 1000 – 𝒞 0 2 511 40 95 Plan: **L1**
– www.le-selecto.com – closed Sunday and Monday
Menu 20 € (lunch)/42 €

• Modern French • Friendly •

In the heart of the lively Ste-Catherine neighbourhood, the Selecto leads Belgium's vanguard of bistronomic (bistro + gastronomic) culture. Good food, a great atmosphere and reasonable prices!

BELGIUM - BRUSSELS

X **Enjoy Art**   Ⓐ⑃

boulevard de Waterloo 22 ✉ 1000 – ℰ 02 641 57 90   Plan: **N3**
– www.enjoybrussels.be – closed Bank Holidays and Sunday
Menu 23 € (lunch) – Carte 39/61 €
• Creative French • Fashionable •
Diners can choose from the BMW showroom on the left or the trendy restaurant
on the right, which serves brasserie fare amidst modern art. The fresh, flavourful
ingredients are a hit with gourmets.

X **Samourai**   Ⓐ⑃

rue du Fossé aux Loups 28 ✉ 1000 – ℰ 02 217 56 39   Plan: **M1**
*– www.samourai-restaurant.be – closed 10 July-10 August, Sunday and
Monday*
Menu 27 € (lunch), 69/99 € – Carte 59/74 €
• Japanese • Intimate • Minimalist •
A Japanese restaurant which opened in 1975 near the Théâtre de la Monnaie.
Dining rooms on three floors with a Japanese decorative theme. Top-notch cui-
sine based around quality products and adapted to Western tastes.

X **Henri**   ⑧⑧

rue de Flandre 113 ✉ 1000 – ℰ 02 218 00 08   Plan: **L1**
– www.restohenri.be – closed Saturday and Sunday
Carte 43/69 €
• Modern French • Friendly •
Who would not dream of having such a brasserie just down the street? Henri
has been delighting the locals of this Flemish-speaking neighbourhood with
its good food. It is an ideal marriage between flawlessly prepared French dishes
and a laidback ambience. The minute you leave, you will want to return, just like
the many regulars.

X **Les Petits Oignons**   Ⓐ⑃
😊
rue de la Régence 25 ✉ 1000 – ℰ 02 511 76 15   Plan: **M3**
*– www.lespetitsoignons.be – closed 17 April, 24 and 25 December
and 1 January*
Menu 37 € – Carte 38/57 €
• Classic cuisine • Brasserie •
The visitor is of course charmed by the timeless decor and the lively atmosphere in this restaurant, but the delicious brasserie dishes are the real hit!
Good quality produce, carefully prepared and simply presented dishes and an
excellent wine list – you are in for VIP treatment!

X **Scheltema**   ⑯ Ⓐ⑃

rue des Dominicains 7 ✉ 1000 – ℰ 02 512 20 84   Plan: **M1**
– www.scheltema.be – closed 24 and 25 December and Sunday
Menu 20 € (lunch), 33/44 € – Carte 61/88 € – (open until 11.30pm)
• Seafood • Brasserie •
An attractive old brasserie located in the city's Îlot Sacré district. Traditional
dishes and daily specials with fish and seafood specialities. A lively atmosphere
and a pleasant retro-style wooden decor.

X **Peï & Meï**   ⑯

rue Rollebeek 15 ✉ 1000 – ℰ 02 880 53 39   Plan: **M3**
– www.peietmei.be – closed last 2 weeks July and first week January
Menu 21 € (lunch), 49/60 € – Carte 56/70 €
• Classic cuisine • Friendly • Minimalist •
One glimpse of the huge, somewhat battered red brick wall inside is all it takes
to understand that this establishment is far from run of the mill. This first
impression is confirmed when you sample the creative dishes of "Peï" Gauthier,
mingling classicism with originality, served by the smiling "Meï" (Mélissa).

✗ Le Vismet   ⌂

place Sainte-Catherine 23 ✉ *1000*   Plan: **9L1**
– ℰ 0 2 218 85 45 – www.levismet.be
– closed Sunday and Monday
Menu 20 € (lunch)/65 € ⼂ – Carte 43/82 €
• Seafood • Traditional décor •
Le Vismet (Brussels' fish market) is a stone's throw from this traditional restaurant as quickly becomes apparent. The ambience is relaxed, the service typical of Brussels and the food scrumptious. Seafood and fish take pride of place in the dishes with an emphasis on generous, fresh portions.

✗ Genco

rue Joseph Stevens 28 ✉ *1000 – ℰ 0 2 511 34 44*   Plan: **9L3**
– www.gencobrussels.com – closed 15 July-15 August, Sunday dinner and Monday
Carte 38/60 €
• Italian • Traditional décor • Bourgeois •
You are greeted in this Italian restaurant like a long-lost friend. Next you will be regaled by the chef's creations, renowned for their generosity and flawless classicism. It is easy to see why Genco is such a hit and so beloved by its regulars!

✗ Les Larmes du Tigre   ⌂

rue de Wynants 21 ✉ *1000 – ℰ 0 2 512 18 77*   Plan: **F3**
– www.leslarmesdutigre.be – closed Saturday lunch and Monday
Menu 16 € ⼂ (lunch), 34 € ⼂/45 € – Carte 36/47 €
• Thai • Exotic décor •
A real voyage for the taste buds! They have been serving authentic Thai food here for over 30 years, and the enjoyment for money ratio is excellent. Buffet at lunch and Sunday evenings.

✗ Le Fourneau de Bruxelles   ⌂ AC

place Sainte-Catherine 8 ✉ *1000 – ℰ 0 2 513 10 02*   Plan: **L1**
– www.lefourneaudebruxelles.com – closed Sunday and Monday
Menu 19 € (lunch)/47 € – Carte 34/62 €
• Spanish • Design • Fashionable •
We recommend venturing over the threshold of this 'Brussels oven' to feast and make merry on tapas and other Spanish inspired recipes. At the same time admire the kitchen staff wielding knives and spoons in a show worthy of a Broadway stage. A splendid opportunity to hop over to Spain.

✗ Viva M'Boma   ⌂ AC

rue de Flandre 17 ✉ *1000 – ℰ 0 2 512 15 93 – closed*   Plan: **L1**
first week April, 25 July-7 August, first week January and Bank Holidays
Carte 29/53 €
• Belgian • Bistro •
This elegant canteen-style restaurant has closely packed tables and tiled walls reminiscent of a Parisian métro station. It is popular with fans of offal and old Brussels specialities (cow's udder, *choesels* (sweetbreads), marrowbone, ox cheek).

✗ Bar Bik

quai aux Pierres de Taille 3 ✉ *1000 – ℰ 0 2 219 75 00*   Plan: **F1**
– closed Bank Holidays, Saturday and Sunday
Menu 37 € – Carte 38/60 € – *(booking advisable)*
• Traditional cuisine • Friendly • Minimalist •
The Bar Bik (Brussels International Kitchen) features a slate menu with dishes from near and far. Friendly, laidback atmosphere and a minimalist decor.

✗ Le Wine Bar des Marolles   🕸

rue Haute 198 ⊠ 1000 – ℰ 0 2 503 62 50   Plan: **M3**
– www.winebarsablon.be – closed 22 July-18 August, 25 December-
7 January, Sunday dinner, Monday and Tuesday
Menu 15 €
– Carte 32/62 € – (dinner only except Saturday and Sunday and until
11pm)
• Cuisine from South West France • Wine bar •
Are you a fan of dishes that draw on local specialities, redolent of the terroir? If so, don't miss Le Wine Bar! Known only to insiders, this restaurant installed in the heart of the Marolles offers hearty cuisine and a good choice of wines.

✗ La Femme du Sommelier   🕸

rue de l'Association 9 ⊠ 1000 – ℰ 0 476 45 02 10   Plan: **10M1**
– closed 1-15 August, Bank Holidays, Saturday and Sunday
Menu 37 € – *(lunch only) (tasting menu only)*
• Classic cuisine • Wine bar • Neighbourhood •
As the name suggests, this bistro is in the capable hands of a sommelier and his spouse. He advises guests on the choice of wine, while she prepares classic recipes, using only the best ingredients.

✗ San   🆎

rue de Flandre 19 ⊠ 1000 – ℰ 0 2 318 19 19   Plan: **K1**
– www.sanbxl.be – closed 1 week at Easter, 2 weeks in August, late
December-early January, Sunday and Monday
Menu 30 € (lunch), 45/65 € – *(tasting menu only)*
• Creative • Bistro • Vintage •
A spoon, a bowl and dishes that take you to all four corners of the earth. This is the concept dreamt up by star chef Sang Hoon Degeimbre for his bistro, which is decorated in a deliciously vintage 1950s style. Tasty bowls feature rich, balanced flavours. We warrant you will be back for more!

✗ Strofilia   🕸 ✿

rue du Marché aux Porcs 11 ⊠ 1000 – ℰ 0 499 26 00 36   Plan: **L1**
– www.strofilia.be – closed Saturday lunch and Sunday
Menu 45 € ⟁/65 € ⟁ – Carte 23/43 € – *(open until 11pm)*
• Greek • Trendy •
Located close to the trendy Dansaert district, this typical "ouzeri" serves guests in its large loft-style dining rooms and vaulted cellar. A choice of Greek mezze, main courses and wines. The name comes from the attractive grape press on display ("strofilia" in Greek).

✗ In 't Spinnekopke   📶 🆎 ✿

place du Jardin aux Fleurs 1 ⊠ 1000 – ℰ 0 2 511 86 95   Plan: **L1**
– www.spinnekopke.be – closed Saturday lunch and Sunday
Menu 13 € (lunch) – Carte 32/60 € – *(open until 11pm)*
• Belgian • Estaminet •
A charming inn so typical of Brussels, with a bistro-style ambience and a menu that pays homage to the traditions of Belgian brasseries. Terrace on the square.

QUARTIER LOUISE-CAMBRE

🏨 Steigenberger Wiltcher's   🕴 ⛐ 🍸 🐾 🗔 ⅙ 🆎 🛁 🎣 🚗

avenue Louise 71 ⊠ 1050 – ℰ 0 2 542 42 42   Plan: **J1**
– www.wiltchers.com
253 rm – 🛏135/599 € 🛏🛏135/599 € – ☑ 20 € – 14 suites
• Chain • Palace • Classic •
The Steigenberger offers modern luxury within the walls of a historic building dating from 1918. Attractive and stylish guestrooms, excellent leisure and spa options, as well as extensive conference facilities.

Avenue Louise, Cambre
(Plan III)

CENTRE (Plan IV)

Ⓜ Porte de Namur

J   K

Rue

PARC
LÉOPOLD

Ⓜ M

MUSÉUM DES
SCIENCES NATURELLES

Chaussée   M   de   Wavre

✗ Saint
Boniface

R. de la Paix

Chaussée d'Ixelles

Rue

Rue

du

Trône

Goffart

Sq.
Sans Souci

Sans

Souci

Ⓜ Louise

R. du Prince Royal

Keyenveld

Rue

de

l'Arbre

MAISON COMMUNALE
D'IXELLES

Rue

MUSÉE COMMUNAL
D'IXELLES

Colonel
✗

Avenue

Charleroi

R. du Prince Royal

Louise

Steigenberger Wiltcher's
Zoom 🏨
Manos Stephanie 🏨

Berkmans

Bénit

R. de la Croix

Chaussée

Rue

des

Maes

College

Malibran

R. Marie-Henriette

Gray

🏨 Bristol Stephanie

IXELLES
ELSENE

Rue

Rue

Veydt

Notos ✗✗

R. de l'Ermitage

d'Ixelles

Rue

Made in Louise 🏨

Defacqz

✗✗ Rouge Tomate

Pl. E.
Flagey

Kolya ✗✗

Livourne

Bailli

Lesbroussart

Vleurgat

Manos Premier 🏨

Rue

Faider

Avenue

Rue

du

Rue

Dautzenberg

ST-GILLES
ST-GILLIS

STE-TRINITÉ Rue

Rue du Châtelain

Louise

Sq. de
Biarritz

Rue Lanfray

Vallée

Av. de l'Éperon d'Or

Av. de l'Hippodrome

MUSÉE
HORTA

Rue

R. A.
Campenhout

Washington

Chaussée

Rue

Vilain XIV

de

la

Rue du Tabellion

Rue de

Page

de

l'Aqueduc

Tenbosch

Avenue

Vleurgat

Américaine

La Quincaillerie ✗

R. du Mail

Washington

R. Américaine

rtisauce
✗✗

Neuve

La Canne en Ville ✗

Rue

Warwick Barsey 🏨
✗✗ The Avenue

R. de la Réforme
Lepoutre
Toucan

Maru ✗

Sq. H.
Michaux

de

Louise

✗ Toucan
sur Mer

Waterloo

MUSÉE
CONSTANTIN
MEUNIER

l'Abbaye

✗✗ La Villa
Emily

All. du Cloître

ABBAYE
DE LA CAMBRE

Av. Louis

Mignot

Rue

J.-B.

Colyns

Lemonnier

Rue J. Lejeune

Chaussée

Rue

Moliere

✗✗ La Villa in the sky ●

E. de Mot

Avenue

Avenue Louise

Chez ✗
Montaigne

Delstanche

Pl. Guy
d'Arezzo

Avenue

Rue

Rue

de

Legrand

✗✗✗ La Truffe Noire

Av. Lloyd Georges

Rue

Lincoln

Vanderkindere

Waterloo

J   K

● Hotel
● Restaurant

0   100 m

79

Bristol Stephanie

avenue Louise 91 ⊠ *1050 –* ℰ *0 2 543 33 11*   Plan: **J1**
– www.thonhotels.com/bristolstephanie
142 rm – 🛏130/350 € 🛏🛏140/360 € – 🍽 27 € – 1 suite
• Luxury • Business • Personalised •
A luxury hotel with attractive guestrooms spread between two interconnecting buildings. Superb suites. A modern brasserie with the typical decor of a leading hotel.

Warwick Barsey

avenue Louise 381 ⊠ *1050 –* ℰ *0 2 641 51 11*   Plan: **K3**
– www.warwickbarsey.com
94 rm – 🛏100/475 € 🛏🛏120/475 € – 🍽 24 € – 5 suites
• Luxury • Business • Personalised •
This magnificent Second Empire-style hotel is home to characterful guestrooms, making it the darling of artists and cinema crews. Breakfast is served in a neo-Classical, extravagantly glamorous lounge. A real gem.
The Avenue – See restaurant listing

Manos Premier

chaussée de Charleroi 102 ⊠ *1060 –* ℰ *0 2 537 96 82*   Plan: **J2**
– www.manoshotel.com
47 rm – 🛏109/459 € 🛏🛏129/479 € – 🍽 20 € – 3 suites
• Grand townhouse • Business • Elegant •
The Manos Premier has the grace of a late-19C townhouse with its rich Louis XV and Louis XVI furnishings. If possible, book a room overlooking the garden. Authentic oriental hammam in the basement. Stylish restaurant, veranda and lounge bar. Chic and elegant decor, plus a charming patio.
Kolya – See restaurant listing

Manos Stéphanie

chaussée de Charleroi 28 ⊠ *1060 –* ℰ *0 2 539 02 50*   Plan: **J1**
– www.manosstephanie.com
55 rm – 🛏109/359 € 🛏🛏129/379 € – 🍽 20 €
• Manor house • Business • Classic •
A townhouse with warm, classically styled guestrooms with a contemporary feel and light wood furnishings. Cupola above the breakfast room.

Aqua

rue de Stassart 43 ⊠ *1050 –* ℰ *0 2 213 01 01*   Plan: **N3**
– www.aqua-hotel-brussels.com
97 rm 🍽 – 🛏85/300 € 🛏🛏95/300 €
• Business • Design •
Minimalist decor embellished with a blue wood "wave" sculpture, created by contemporary artist Arne Quinze. It offers pared-down rooms with walls painted white and blue and parquet flooring. A calm environment.

Made in Louise

rue Veydt 40 ⊠ *1050 –* ℰ *0 2 537 40 33*   Plan: **11Q1**
– www.madeinlouise.com
48 rm – 🛏70/245 € 🛏🛏70/245 € – 🍽 10 €
• Manor house • Contemporary •
This large mansion has no lack of welcoming, hospitable nooks and crannies for the comfort of guests. The stylish, vintage inspired bedrooms extend an invitation to relax and rest. A charming hotel fully in keeping with its smart neighbourhood.

Zoom

rue de la Concorde 59 ⊠ *1000 –* ℰ *0 2 515 00 60*   Plan: **11Q1**
– www.zoomhotel.be
37 rm – 🛏90/140 € 🛏🛏90/140 € – 🍽 15 €
• Boutique hotel • Vintage •
Photography is the byword of this boutique hotel. All the vintage inspired bedrooms are graced with photos of Brussels, and the same theme is visible in the welcoming lobby. Fine selection of beers at the bar.

XXXX ✿✿ Le Chalet de la Forêt (Pascal Devalkeneer)

drève de Lorraine 43 ✉ 1180 – ✆ 0 2 374 54 16
– www.lechaletdelaforet.be – closed last week December-first
week January, Saturday and Sunday
Menu 54 € (lunch), 145/185 € – Carte 118/170 €
• Creative • Elegant •

This chalet with a lovely terrace on the edge of the Sonian Forest combines elegance and sophistication. The food is particularly stylish with a consummate combination of classicism, creativity, subtlety and generosity. Intense sensations are guaranteed.
➝ Tartare d'huîtres au caviar et parmentier aux fleurs de brocoli. Filet de bœuf au sautoir, risotto de pomme de terre à la truffe noire et lardo di Colonnata. Les 4 "C" : une palette de desserts au chocolat noir, chicorée, café et cacao.

XXXX ✿ La Villa Lorraine

avenue du Vivier d'Oie 75 ✉ 1000 – ✆ 0 2 374 31 63   Plan: **C3**
– www.villalorraine.be – closed 27 March-4 April, 31 July-15 August,
1 January, Sunday and Monday
Menu 49 € (lunch), 125/170 € – Carte 99/219 €
• Creative • Elegant •

Since 1953 this grande dame of the Brussels gastronomic scene has been a popular meeting place for gourmets. The grand, luxurious interior commands respect, as does the cooking. Classical dishes come with modern touches and are packed with flavour. There's also a charming terrace for warmer days.
➝ Langoustines servies nacrées et salées au caviar, mosaïque de céleri et jus à la verveine citronnée. Filet pur de veau de lait aux asperges, girolles, févettes et condiment fenouil-citron. La fraise et la rhubarbe : marmelade de rhubarbe pochée à l'hibiscus, fraises des bois et sorbet aux fraises.
⊛ **La Brasserie de la Villa** – See restaurant listing

XXX ✿ La Truffe Noire

boulevard de la Cambre 12 ✉ 1000 – ✆ 0 2 640 44 22   Plan: **K3**
– www.truffenoire.com – closed 1 week Easter, first 2 weeks August,
Christmas-New Year, Monday lunch, Saturday lunch and Sunday
Menu 50 € (lunch), 135/225 € – Carte 81/154 €
• Italian • Elegant •

As you might expect, The Black Truffle serves the famous *Tuber Melanosporum* in all manner of dishes. An elegant decor with a patio-terrace. Charismatic owner. Splendid choice of wines... some at staggering prices!
➝ Carpaccio aux vieux parmesan et truffe à la façon de Luigi. Saint-pierre farci de truffe cuit à la vapeur et son nectar truffé. Soufflé chaud aux noisettes grillées, sabayon à la vanille et au Frangelico.

XXX Brugmann

avenue Brugmann 52 ✉ 1190 – ✆ 0 2 880 55 54   Plan: **B3**
– www.brugmann.com – closed Monday
Menu 24/39 € – Carte 56/74 € – *(open until 11pm)*
• Modern cuisine • Elegant •

Brugmann is a picture of elegance. The interior is adorned with fine modern art and the rear terrace is superb. What is more the chef's cuisine is equally stylish, combining ingredients and techniques in dishes that are as modern as the decor. A first-class establishment.

XX ⊛ La Brasserie de la Villa

avenue du Vivier d'Oie 75 ✉ 1000 – ✆ 0 2 374 31 63   Plan: **C3**
– www.villalorraine.be – closed 5-8 Mai, 31 July-15 August, 1 January,
Sunday and Monday
Menu 37 € – Carte 42/88 €
• Classic cuisine • Elegant •

The little sister of the Villa Lorraine where you can soak up the atmosphere of that prestigious establishment at more affordable prices. Classic brasserie dishes and appetising light meals.

XX **Rouge Tomate** 🛋 ⟳

avenue Louise 190 ✉ *1050 – ℰ 02 647 70 44*　　　　Plan: **J2**
– www.rougetomate.be – closed Bank Holidays, Saturday lunch and Sunday
Menu 35 € (lunch), 55/60 € – Carte 51/78 €
• Creative • Trendy •
Forgo the bustle of Avenue Louise and venture into this elegant, modern mansion, and perhaps to the lovely terrace at the back. The same harmony is present in the dishes, all of which demonstrate the young chef's desire to experiment with creative, yet balanced recipes.

XX **Brasserie de la Patinoire** 🛋 ⟳

😊 *chemin du Gymnase 1* ✉ *1000 – ℰ 02 649 70 02*　　　Plan: **12R3**
– www.brasseriedelapatinoire.be
Menu 16 € (lunch)/35 € – Carte 34/60 € – *(open until 11.30pm)*
• Classic French • Brasserie •
This establishment cannot be faulted for its stylish, classy allure. Book a table and enjoy this luxury brasserie with a hint of British charm and an ambience that is both friendly yet elegant. Terrace overlooking the Cambre wood. The enthusiastic, generous chef takes a new look at brasserie classics.

XX **Le Passage** 🛋 **P**

avenue Jean et Pierre Carsoel 17 ✉ *1180*　　　　　Plan: **B3**
– ℰ 02 374 66 94 – www.lepassage.be – closed 2 weeks in July, Saturday lunch and Sunday
Menu 35 € (lunch), 55/75 € – Carte 53/98 €
• Classic cuisine • Cosy •
Rocky has found a ring big enough to demonstrate his striking personal interpretation of classic gastronomy. His flavours have a lot of punch! The wine cellar is visible from the dining area.

XX **Kolya** – Hôtel Manos Premier 🛋 Ⓚⓚ ⟳ 🍽 (dinner) 🚗

chaussée de Charleroi 102 ✉ *1060 – ℰ 02 533 18 30*　　Plan: **J2**
– www.kolya.be – closed Saturday lunch and Sunday
Menu 25 € (lunch), 35/65 € – Carte 48/73 €
• Mediterranean cuisine • Cosy •
Enjoy contemporary French cuisine with a Mediterranean accent in the refined setting at Kolya. The veranda and patio are amazing, and the dining room is just as nice.

XX **La Villa in the Sky** (Alexandre Dionisio) 🕸 ⪡ 🛋 🍽

🌼🌼 *avenue Louise 480 (25ᵉᵐᵉ étage)* ✉ *1050*　　　　Plan: **K3**
– ℰ 02 644 69 14 – www.lavillainthesky.be – closed 8-17 April, 29 July-21 August, 24-30 December, Saturday lunch, Sunday and Monday
Menu 125 € ▼ (lunch), 145/195 € – *(booking essential)*
• Creative • Design • Minimalist •
This young chef sparkles! His cuisine, based on fine produce, is both appetising and intelligent. It is poised between modernity and classicism, and has given him a well-earned place in Brussels' limelight.
➜ Crémeux de petits pois au lard confit, girolles et écume noisette. Filet pur de veau au risotto et asperges vertes, morilles et jus de cuisson. Déclinaison autour de la fraise, pain de Gênes, crémeux aux amandes, nougatine et meringue.

XX **Notos** 🛋 ⟳

rue de Livourne 154 ✉ *1000 – ℰ 02 513 29 59*　　　　Plan: **J2**
– www.notos.be – closed first 3 weeks August, 1 week late December, Saturday lunch, Sunday and Monday
Menu 17 € (lunch)/60 € – Carte 48/64 €
• Greek • Minimalist •
A 'new generation' Greek restaurant located in what used to be a garage. Restrained contemporary setting, authentic Greek dishes with a modern touch, and a good selection of Hellenic wines.

XX **The Avenue** – Hôtel Warwick Barsey 🛱 🔣 🛋 🚗

avenue Louise 381 ✉ *1050* – ☎ *02 641 51 11*   Plan: **R2**
– www.warwickbarsey.com – closed Saturday and Sunday
Menu 19 € (lunch), 37/70 € – Carte 34/55 €
• Traditional cuisine • Intimate •

The affluent elegance that prevails along Avenue Louise seems to have ventured over the threshold of this superb establishment. The cuisine displays a blend of brasserie and more modern dishes, all with the inimitable creative stamp of Gaëtan Colin.

XX **Amen** 🛱 🔣 🛋

rue Franz Merjay 165 ✉ *1050* – ☎ *02 217 10 19*   Plan: **11Q2**
– www.amen.restaurant – closed Sunday and Monday
Carte 66/81 €
• Market cuisine • Friendly •

Two-star chef, Pascal Devalkeneer's flair for quality is unerring. His establishment illustrates his undisputed skills: contemporary recipes, intense flavours and a variety of textures. Let's give thanks – Amen!

XX **Artisauce** 🛱

chaussée de Waterloo 421 ✉ *1050* – ☎ *0 483 65 65 16*   Plan: **11Q2**
– www.artisauce.com – closed Saturday lunch, Sunday and Monday
Menu 17 € (lunch)/38 € – Carte 46/66 €
• Classic cuisine • Friendly •

Dad Frédéric greets guests and seats them in the dining room or on the terrace. His son, Christopher, is hard at work in the kitchen creating classic dishes, liberally sprinkled with world influences and flavours.

XX **Brinz'l** 🛋

rue des Carmélites 93 ✉ *1180* – ☎ *02 218 23 32*   Plan: **11P2**
– www.brinzl.be – closed Sunday and Monday
Menu 25 € (lunch), 50/65 € – Carte 56/87 €
• Modern French • Contemporary décor • Bistro •

While Brinzelle (Creole for aubergine) may evoke the chef's Mauritian roots, her cuisine is nonetheless firmly French! After learning her trade in several star restaurants, she now excels in flavoursome, carefully assembled meals that seek above all to enhance the quality of the ingredients.

XX **La Villa Emily** 🕸 🔣 ✿ 🛋
£3

rue de l'Abbaye 4 ✉ *1000* – ☎ *02 318 18 58*   Plan: **K3**
– www.lavillaemily.be – closed first 2 weeks August, Bank Holidays,
Sunday and Monday
Menu 46 € (lunch), 69/109 € – Carte 69/102 €
• Mediterranean cuisine • Elegant • Intimate •

This little jewel combines the elegant atmosphere of a boudoir with subtle designer elements and a huge chandelier. This impressive balance of styles is equally visible in the food. The main course is accompanied by sophisticated sauces and impeccable side dishes. Splendidly classical.

→ Omble chevalier au poireau et girolles. Turbot rôti et fenouil confit au sésame, sauce barbecue. Orange pelée à vif, sorbet butternut et caramel au gingembre.

XX **Toucan** 🛱 ✿ 🛋
😊

avenue Louis Lepoutre 1 ✉ *1050* – ☎ *02 345 30 17*   Plan: **J3**
– www.toucanbrasserie.com – closed dinner 24 and 31 December
Menu 18 € (lunch)/37 €
– Carte 38/65 € – (open until 11pm) (booking advisable)
• Modern cuisine • Bistro • Design •

The plumage of this toucan adds the finishing touch to a lovely classical brasserie, embellished with the occasional modern design twist. The ambience is one of the highlights of the establishment, as is the seamless service. The chef uses only the best quality produce and has no qualms about piling the plates high with tasty fare.

BELGIUM - BRUSSELS

XX Maza'j

boulevard du Souverain 145 ✉ *1160 –* ☎ *0 2 675 55 10* Plan: **C3**
– www.mazaj.be – closed Saturday lunch and Sunday
Menu 20 € (lunch), 37/50 € – Carte 44/63 € – *(bar lunch)*
• Lebanese • Friendly •
If you feel like exploring a new culinary horizon, why not book a table at Maza'j? Don't be misled by the bright contemporary interior, this establishment is the champion of traditional Lebanese cuisine and culture. All the dishes are laid on the table for everyone to sample, in a friendly, relaxed atmosphere.

X Colonel

rue Jean Stas 24 ✉ *1060 –* ☎ *0 2 538 57 36* Plan: **J1**
– www.colonelbrussels.com – closed Sunday and Monday
Menu 24 € (lunch) – Carte 44/70 €
• Meats and grills • Brasserie • Fashionable •
Generous cuts of meat greet you as you enter this brasserie, making the house speciality blatantly clear. The quality of the charcuterie, perfectly cooked red meat, French fries and delicious sauces are quite stunning. Paradise for carnivores!

X La Quincaillerie

rue du Page 45 ✉ *1050 –* ☎ *0 2 533 98 33* Plan: **J2**
– www.quincaillerie.be – closed Sunday lunch
Menu 18 € (lunch)/36 € – Carte 33/69 € – *(open until 11pm)*
• Classic cuisine • Brasserie •
Shiny and majestic brasserie occupying a former Art Deco hardware store. Daily specials and fresh oysters. Very professional service. Doorman.

X Les Papilles

chaussée de Waterloo 782 ✉ *1180 –* ☎ *0 2 374 69 66* Plan: **B3**
– www.lespapilles.be – closed Bank Holidays, Monday dinner and Sunday
Menu 19 € (lunch)/39 €
• Traditional cuisine • Wine bar •
Your taste buds will definitely start tingling when you enter this delightful establishment. It specialises in distinctive and characteristic brasserie fare, and has a sushi bar in the evening. Before sitting down for your meal, pick yourself a bottle of wine directly from the shelves. Friendly and relaxed.

X Kamo (Tomoyasu Kamo)

chaussée de Waterloo 550a ✉ *1050 –* ☎ *0 2 648 78 48* Plan: **C3**
– www.restaurant-kamo.be – closed Bank Holidays, Saturday and Sunday
Menu 23 € (lunch), 50/120 € – Carte 85/108 € – *(booking essential)*
• Japanese • Trendy •
A slice of Tokyo in Ixelles: the classics of Japanese cuisine and remarkable combinations with bold flavours are served in a pared-down setting with a trendy atmosphere. Sit at the counter to admire the skills of the two chefs at work. Good lunch *bento*.
➜ Escabèche de maquereau. Black cod au miso blanc. Sweet potato à la japonaise.

X La Canne en Ville

rue de la Réforme 22 ✉ *1050 –* ☎ *0 2 347 29 26* Plan: **J3**
– www.lacanneenville.be – closed first 2 weeks September, late December-early January, Saturday lunch and Sunday
Menu 18 € (lunch) – Carte 49/61 €
• Classic cuisine • Family • Neighbourhood •
This friendly bistro has taken up abode in a former butchers since 1983, as the tiles and the occasional decorative feature bear witness. The chef treats diners to a succulent repertory of classical dishes, while the lady of the house graciously welcomes diners.

BELGIUM - BRUSSELS

✗ Les Caves d'Alex

rue Caroly 37 ⊠ 1050 – ℰ 0 2 540 89 37   Plan: **N3**
– www.lescavesdalex.be – closed 10-17 April, 21 July-13 August,
26 December-1 January, Saturday and Sunday
Menu 13 € (lunch), 24/38 € – Carte 40/88 €
• Classic French • Bistro • Neighbourhood •
Most of the wines in the cellar of Alex Cardoso, the owner, come from the Côtes
du Rhône and Languedoc regions of France. The food is free of unnecessary
frills offering classical dishes prepared with enthusiasm and know-how – a
genuine treat!

✗ Saint Boniface

rue Saint-Boniface 9 ⊠ 1050 – ℰ 0 2 511 53 66   Plan: **J1**
– www.saintboniface.be – closed Bank Holidays, Saturday lunch, Sunday
and Monday
Carte 37/56 €
• Cuisine from South West France • Bistro •
Tightly packed tables, posters on the walls and a collection of biscuit tins depict
this extremely welcoming bistro. The locals from Brussels flock here to sample
its Basque, Lyons and Southwest France specialities. Generous and delicious!

✗ Maru

chaussée de Waterloo 510 ⊠ 1050 – ℰ 0 2 346 11 11   Plan: **J3**
– closed 17 July-16 August, 24 December-1 January and Monday
Menu 16 € (lunch) – Carte 31/79 €
• Korean • Minimalist •
If your mouth is already watering at the prospect of crunchy deep-fried pancakes or sweet and sour tangsuyuk, head straight for this 'urban-style' Korean restaurant whose fresh ingredients are equalled by the authentic cooking
methods. Even better, the wine list is full of pleasant surprises.

✗ Nonbe Daigaku

avenue Adolphe Buyl 31 ⊠ 1050 – ℰ 0 2 649 21 49   Plan: **C3**
– closed Bank Holidays, Sunday and Monday
Menu 15 € (lunch)/68 € – Carte 43/118 € – *(bookings advisable at dinner)*
• Japanese • Minimalist • Traditional décor •
Japanese restaurant established in 2007 by a veteran of Japanese cuisine in
Brussels. Sushi bar stormed at lunchtimes, specialities cooked in the evening.
Admire the chef's dexterity.

✗ Chez Montaigne

place Georges Brugmann 27 ⊠ 1050 – ℰ 0 2 345 65 23   Plan: **J3**
– www.chezmontaigne.com – closed Bank Holidays except weekends,
Saturday lunch, Sunday dinner and Monday
Menu 22 € (lunch)/45 € – Carte 36/58 €
• Modern cuisine • Bistro •
Artwork by Jean-Luc Moerman sets the scene in the unusual, contemporary
decor of this brasserie, which also doubles as a delicatessen and grocery store.
The chef creates a fine modern repertory that skilfully combines quality ingre-
dients.

✗ Toucan sur Mer

avenue Louis Lepoutre 17 ⊠ 1050 – ℰ 0 2 340 07 40   Plan: **J3**
– www.toucanbrasserie.com – closed dinner 24 and 31 December
Menu 18 € (lunch)
– Carte 43/73 € – (open until 11pm) (booking advisable)
• Seafood • Bistro •
The impeccable quality and freshness of the fish and seafood of the Toucan sur
Mer are more than comparable with seafood restaurants on the coast. We will
take a bet that this pleasant bistro will appeal to seafood lovers.

Villa Singha

rue des Trois Ponts 22 ✉ 1160 Plan: **C3**
– ✆ 02 675 67 34 – www.singha.be
– closed 3-31 July, 25 December-2 January, Bank Holidays, Saturday lunch and Sunday
Menu 12 € (lunch), 19/35 € – Carte 28/37 €
• Thai • Exotic décor •
Singha, the mythological lion, watches over this pleasant Thai restaurant, where fresh produce and authentic flavours enhance the traditional Thai cuisine. One such dish is Kha Nom Jeep, delicious steamed raviolis of chopped pork and Thai spices. The welcome and service are equally charming.

Koyzina Authentica

avenue Brugmann 519 ✉ 1180 – ✆ 02 346 14 38 Plan: **11P3**
– www.koyzinaauthentica.be – closed 3 weeks in August, late December, Sunday and Monday
Menu 15 € (lunch) – Carte 26/48 € – *(open until 11pm)*
• Greek • Mediterranean décor • Neighbourhood •
Greek cuisine has far more to offer than gyros or souvlaki, as this very friendly, if a little cramped, restaurant amply proves. Traditional dishes with an up-to-the-minute twist and almost religious respect for authentic flavours.

EUROPEAN INSTITUTIONS

Stanhope

rue du Commerce 9 ✉ 1000 Plan: **N3**
– ✆ 02 506 91 11 – www.stanhope.be
– closed 22-26 December
125 rm – †95/300 € ††95/300 € – ☕ 30 € – 9 suites
• Grand Luxury • Traditional • Elegant •
The splendours of the Victorian era are brought to life in this British-style townhouse. It offers varying categories of rooms, including superb suites and duplexes. Elegant and classic dining room in line with the menu. Pretty courtyard-terrace.

Aloft

place Jean Rey 3 ✉ 1040 – ✆ 02 800 08 88 Plan: **G2**
– www.aloftbrussels.com
150 rm – †65/260 € ††65/260 € – ☕ 13 €
• Business • Functional •
On the doorstep of Europe's institutions, a loft spirit and design reign throughout this hotel. The spacious, comfortable and practical rooms are equally popular with business travellers and civil servants.

Bon-Bon (Christophe Hardiquest)

avenue de Tervueren 453 ✉ 1150 Plan: **D3**
– ✆ 02 346 66 15 – www.bon-bon.be – closed 1-17 April, 22 July-15 August, 24 December-9 January, Bank Holidays, Monday lunch, Saturday and Sunday
Menu 90/220 € – Carte 108/235 €
• Creative • Elegant •
Bon-Bon deserves its name: this is one of the best restaurants in Belgium! The chef creates refined dishes with top quality ingredients. The popular surprise menu always boasts lots of new finds.
→ Bijoux d'huître , chantilly de livèche et gelée vodka-tonic. Canard au spéculoos cuit en pain de sel. Dessert autour du jardin.

XxX ✿ **Da Mimmo**   🍴 😋 **AC**

avenue du Roi Chevalier 24 ✉ *1200 – ✆ 02 771 58 60*   Plan: **D2**
*– www.da-mimmo.be – closed 20 July-10 August, late December-early
January, Saturday lunch and Sunday*
Menu 42 € (lunch), 125/165 € – Carte 98/130 €
• **Italian** • **Cosy** •
Fine updated classic Italian cuisine with good combined dish and wine sugges-
tions. Friendly atmosphere, careful service, bright fashionable décor and plea-
sant town terrace.
→ Trio d'asperges et cappuccino de parmesan au crabe. Parfait mariage de
ris de veau, langoustines et truffes. Melon au vin santo.

XX 😊 **Park Side**   🍴 ♿ **AC** ⇔

avenue de la Joyeuse Entrée 24 ✉ *1040*   Plan: **H2**
*– ✆ 02 238 08 08 – www.restoparkside.be – closed August, Bank Holidays,
Saturday and Sunday*
Menu 37/55 € – Carte 39/58 €
• **Modern cuisine** • **Fashionable** • **Brasserie** •
English speakers will get the reference right away, since this establishment
abuts the Jubilee Park (parc du Cinquantenaire). A great location for an equally
attractive and chic decor with an ultra-modern design – the main ceiling light in
particular attracts a lot of stares! New-style brasserie specialities on the à la carte
menu.

XX **YuMe**   🍴 ⇔

avenue de Tervueren 292 ✉ *1150 – ✆ 02 773 00 80*   Plan: **D2**
– www.yume.be – closed Bank Holidays, Saturday and Sunday
Menu 35/70 € – Carte 45/70 €
• **Fusion** • **Brasserie** •
YuMe blends East and West. On the Yu side: sushi, gyoza, dim sum and many
Japanese specialities; on the Me side, nice little dishes from the Franco-Belgian
tradition and a nice variety of meats. A fine blend, in a chic contemporary decor.

XX 😊 **Les Deux Maisons**   🍴 **AC**

Val des Seigneurs 81 ✉ *1150 – ✆ 02 771 14 47*   Plan: **D2**
*– www.lesdeuxmaisons.be – closed 1 week Easter, first 3 weeks August,
late December, Bank Holidays, Sunday and Monday*
Menu 21 € (lunch), 37/60 € – Carte 46/72 €
• **Classic French** • **Classic décor** • **Romantic** •
Two houses have merged to create this elegant restaurant, where a classically
trained chef rustles up tempting dishes using excellent ingredients. The 'tradition' menu with its luscious selection of desserts is highly recommended. Fine
wine cellar.

XX **Stirwen**   ⇔

chaussée Saint-Pierre 15 ✉ *1040 – ✆ 02 640 85 41*   Plan: **G3**
*– www.stirwen.be – closed 26 Mai, 21 July-11 August, 24-26 December, 2
and 3 January, Bank Holidays, Saturday and Sunday*
Menu 35 € (lunch), 60/80 € – Carte 63/96 €
• **Modern French** • **Bourgeois** •
This renowned restaurant is today in the capable hands of an ambitious duo.
David is in charge of the service, while François-Xavier takes a new look at
French classics. First-class ingredients are used such as: Noirmoutier sole, Lozère
lamb and Corrèze veal.

XX **Le Buone Maniere**   🍴 ⇔

avenue de Tervueren 59 ✉ *1040 – ✆ 02 762 61 05*   Plan: **D2**
*– www.buonemaniere.be – closed 20 July-20 August, 23 December-
3 January, Saturday lunch and Sunday*
Menu 40 € (lunch)/50 € – Carte 63/92 €
• **Italian** • **Classic décor** •
Le Buone Maniere occupies a mansion along a busy road. Authentic Italian-
Mediterranean cuisine served to a backdrop of contemporary decor or on the
front terrace.

Maison du Luxembourg

rue du Luxembourg 37 ⊠ 1050 – ℰ 02 511 99 95   Plan: **N3**
– www.maisonduluxembourg.be – closed 1-20 August, 24 December-
2 January, Bank Holidays, Friday dinner, Saturday and Sunday
Menu 26 € (lunch)/37 € – Carte 46/73 €
• **Regional cuisine** • **Friendly** •

Country cooking from the Luxembourg region moves to Brussels. This contemporary restaurant offers well-presented classical fare, highlighting produce sourced from the French-speaking province of Luxembourg. The ingredients are superlatively fresh and the vegetable side dishes are delicious. A great advertisement for the region.

Au Grand Forestier

avenue du Grand Forestier 2 ⊠ 1170 – ℰ 02 672 57 79   Plan: **7G6**
– www.augrandforestier.be – closed dinner 24 and 31 December
Carte 37/69 € – *(open until 11pm)*
• **Belgian** • **Contemporary décor** •

Pure luxury is essentially a question of detail, as this delightful brasserie so admirably illustrates! A flawless welcome and personalised service set the scene to make you feel at home. The same attention to detail can be tasted in the immaculately cooked meat, served with delicious sauces – a princely treat for your taste buds!

Le Monde est Petit (Loïc Villers)

rue des Bataves 65 ⊠ 1040 – ℰ 02 732 44 34   Plan: **D2**
– www.lemondeestpetit.be – closed last week July-first 2 weeks
August, late December-early January, Bank Holidays, Saturday and
Sunday
Menu 25 € (lunch) – Carte 53/70 €
• **Creative French** • **Friendly** • **Family** •

The atmosphere at this establishment is really enjoyable, and the regulars are there to prove it. The chef has opted for a rather limited menu in order to focus on contemporary dishes with international touches.

➜ Langoustines rôties à la burrata, coulis d'épinard et tomates marinées au soja fumé. Canette des Dombes : sa cuisse confite et le cou farci aux petits pois à la française et mousseline de fèves et menthe. Espuma de crème brûlée, salade de fraises et rhubarbe, sorbet au yaourt.

Le Coq en Pâte

Tomberg 259 ⊠ 1200 – ℰ 02 762 19 71   Plan: **C2**
– www.lecoqenpate.be – closed Monday
Menu 18 € (lunch), 34/49 € ⓨ – Carte 34/50 €
• **Italian** • **Neighbourhood** •

This family-run restaurant has been regaling diners since 1972. Its secret lies first and foremost in the owner-chef's know-how, born out of his experience, creativity and dedication to Italian cuisine. However, the excellent value for money and comfortable decor are also much appreciated.

De Maurice à Olivier

chaussée de Roodebeek 246 ⊠ 1200 – ℰ 02 771 33 98   Plan: **C2**
– www.demauriceaolivier.be – closed 28 March-11 April, 15 July-
15 August, Monday dinner and Sunday
Menu 22 € (lunch), 33/55 € – Carte 40/52 €
• **Classic cuisine** • **Vintage** •

Maurice, the father, has passed the business onto his son Olivier. He has also bequeathed a rich culinary heritage of French cuisine enriched in Mediterranean influences; the dishes are beautifully presented. Amusingly, the restaurant is also a newsagents.

Le Mucha

🍴

avenue Jules Du Jardin 23 ✉ 1150 – ✆ 0 2 770 24 14 — Plan: **D3**
*– www.lemucha.be – closed last week August-first week September,
Sunday dinner and Monday*
Menu 18 € (lunch)/36 € – Carte 35/60 €
• Classic cuisine • Neighbourhood • Cosy •

The interior of the Mucha is reminiscent of Parisian brasseries in the 1900s, even down to the waiters! Ideal to sample traditional French cuisine from a fine choice of classical dishes, without forgetting a few Italian favourites!

Foro Romano

rue Joseph II 19 ✉ 1000 – ✆ 0 2 280 29 76 – closed Bank — Plan: **N2**
Holidays, Monday dinner, Saturday and Sunday
Menu 35 € (lunch)/50 € – Carte 39/49 €
• Italian • Neighbourhood •

This enoteca offers hearty Italian cuisine, created with its international clientele firmly in mind, and gets very busy at lunchtime.

GARE DU NORD

Bloom!

rue Royale 250 ✉ 1210 – ✆ 0 2 220 66 11 — Plan: **F1**
– www.hotelbloom.com
304 rm – †75/360 € ††75/360 € – 🍽 19 € – 4 suites
• Business • Design • Personalised •

The exclamation mark of Bloom! takes its full meaning when you contemplate the sensational design of its interior. Several European artists were commissioned to adorn the rooms in unique frescoes on a floral theme; some of the rooms' floors even have imitation lawn rugs. Breakfast waffles are sampled in an equally unusual room – but we will let you discover that for yourselves!

Al Matbakh

place Colignon 8 ✉ 1030 – ✆ 0 2 248 23 29 — Plan: **B2**
*– www.almatbakh.be – closed 2nd and 4th Saturday of each month and
Sunday*
Menu 14 € (lunch) – Carte 37/52 €
• North African • Oriental décor • Romantic •

With a name like Al Matbakh ("the kitchen" in Arabic), you would be right to expect an authentic culinary experience of North African origins. This pleasant, colourful restaurant specialises in dishes that combine North African with Lebanese origins. The menu is as varied as it is delicious.

Les Dames Tartine

chaussée de Haecht 58 ✉ 1210 – ✆ 0 2 218 45 49 — Plan: **G1**
– closed first 3 weeks August, Saturday lunch, Sunday and Monday
Menu 20 € (lunch), 36/49 € – Carte 48/56 €
• Classic cuisine • Intimate • Family •

Two women run this restaurant with great panache. Excellent seasonal cuisine, an intimate atmosphere and an impressive wine list.

GARE DU MIDI

Pullman Midi

place Victor Horta 1 ✉ 1060 – ✆ 0 2 528 98 00 — Plan: **E3**
– www.pullmanhotels.com/7431
237 rm – †99/349 € ††99/349 € – 🍽 20 € – 2 suites
• Townhouse • Business • Contemporary •

Just a stone's throw from Brussels-South railway station, this hotel transports you to another world. Trendy decor and modern comforts go hand in hand with elegant, designer inspired guestrooms. Alternatively, you can drop in and enjoy a good meal.

XxX Saint-Guidon 🛗 ♿ 🅿

avenue Théo Verbeeck 2 ✉ *1070 –* 🕿 *0 2 520 55 36*   Plan: **A3**
– www.saint-guidon.be – closed Saturday, Sunday and Club's home match days
Menu 36/75 € – Carte 51/117 € – *(lunch only)*
• Classic French • Elegant •
Anderlecht Football Club does more than play a good game of football because the ground's Tribune 2 is home to Saint Guidon – a fine classical restaurant. Good produce, consummate preparation and refined flavours: the chef is clearly worthy of the Premier League.

XX La Paix *(David Martin)* ♿
🌱

rue Ropsy-Chaudron 49 (opposite abattoirs) ✉ *1070*   Plan: **B2**
– 🕿 *0 2 523 09 58 – www.lapaix.eu – closed July, Christmas – New Year, Bank Holidays, Saturday and Sunday*
Menu 60/110 € – Carte 103/163 € – *(lunch only except Friday)*
• Asian influences • Fashionable • Friendly •
This characterful restaurant is a perfect example of multicultural Brussels! On the food side, chef David Martin deploys the sophistication required for Japanese cuisine. He works with impeccable ingredients such as his own home-grown vegetables or Norwegian king crab, fresh out of the tank. His creative recipes will linger on in your memory.
➜ King crab royal de Norvège, de notre vivier. Volaille de Bresse au shio-koji. Cerises tièdes et glace au romarin.

XX La Brouette 🎱 🍽 🛗
😊

boulevard Prince de Liège 61 ✉ *1070 –* 🕿 *0 2 522 51 69*   Plan: **A2**
– www.labrouette.be – closed 1 week Easter, August, 16 and 17 September, 6-9 January, Carnival holiday, Saturday lunch, Sunday dinner and Monday
Menu 30 € (lunch), 37/56 € – Carte 50/80 €
• Creative French • Friendly •
Herman Dedapper isn't afraid of thinking outside the box. Omnipresent in the dining room, he always wore his chef's hat until passing it onto his right hand man. He is still the owner, and nowadays also the sommelier! Don't miss the 'Brouette' menu, which you can put together yourself.

X René 🍽 🛗

place de la Résistance 14 ✉ *1070 –* 🕿 *0 2 523 28 76*   Plan: **A2**
– closed mid June-late July, Monday and Tuesday
Carte 27/58 €
• Belgian • Family •
This former chippy has been turned into a delightful vintage-style bistro by René who takes us back in time to an era when cooking was simple and unfussy. Mussels, steak and nourishing stews are all served with generous portions of French fries – a treat for lovers of down-to-earth, wholesome food.

ATOMIUM QUARTER

XX L'Auberge de l'Isard 🍽 ♿ 🅿
😊

Romeinsesteenweg 964 ✉ *1780 Wemmel*   Plan: **B1**
– 🕿 *0 2 479 85 64 – www.isard.be – closed dinner on Bank Holidays, Tuesday dinner, Sunday dinner and Monday*
Menu 27 € (lunch), 37/65 € – Carte 50/76 €
• Classic French • Chic •
To escape the bustle of Heysel and Brussels' ring road, head for the elegant villa of Roland Taildeman, who has been at the stove for over 25 years. Guests are particularly taken with the establishment's formula… There is a wide and varied choice with one constant byword – taste.

XX 　　**'t Stoveke** (Daniel Antuna)　　　　　　　　🛖 ⇔
🐕

Jetsestraat 52 ✉ *1853 Strombeek-Bever*　　　　Plan: **B1**
*– ☎ 02 267 67 25 – www.tstoveke.be – closed late July-early August, late
December-early January, Saturday lunch, Sunday dinner, Tuesday and
Wednesday*
Menu 36 € (lunch), 65/75 €
– Carte 55/70 € – (number of covers limited, pre-book)
• Modern cuisine • Cosy • Design •

The chef of 't Stoveke follows in the footsteps of some of the best-known chefs
in the world, but has added his own personal touch. This has ensured that his
cuisine remains resolutely up to date. The dishes reveal an explosion of flavours
that are as much a delight to the eye as to the palate.
➜ Vitello tonato met couscous van bloemkool, coulis van koriander,
miso en gerookte soja. Zonnevis met brandade, grijze garnalen, kreeftenjus
en zeekraal. Pannacotta met witte chocolade, rabarber en vanilleroomijs.

XX 　　**La table d'Evan**　　　　　　　　🛖 ⇔

Brusselsesteenweg 21 ✉ *1780 Wemmel*　　　　Plan: **A1**
*– ☎ 02 460 52 39 – www.evanrestaurants.be – closed Monday in July and
August, Saturday lunch and Sunday*
Menu 55/110 € – Carte 70/90 €
• Mediterranean cuisine • Brasserie • Trendy •

Modern, comfortable and free of unnecessary frills: such is the setting of chef
Evan. On a constant quest for fine produce, he deploys his talent and experience to create delicious dishes. Quality before all else is his motto – to the
delight of our taste buds!

X 　　**Brasserie de l'Expo**　　　　　　　　🛖
😊

avenue Houba de Strooper 188 ✉ *1020*　　　　Plan: **B1**
*– ☎ 02 476 99 70 – www.brasseriedelexpo.be – closed dinner 24 and
31 December*
Menu 15 € (lunch)/35 € – Carte 39/56 €
• Seafood • Brasserie •

The memory of the 1958 Expo continues to linger in this delightful vintage brasserie opposite Heysel stadium. Right from the word go, the seafood bar leaves
you in no doubt that fresh, quality ingredients take pride of place in the chef's
cuisine. Brasserie fare at its best!

X 　　**French Kiss**　　　　　　　　🏛 🛖 AC
😊

rue Léopold I 470 ✉ *1090 – ☎ 02 425 22 93*　　Plan: **B2**
*– www.restaurantfrenchkiss.com – closed 25 July-17 August, 24 and
31 December, 1 January and Monday*
Menu 28/37 € – Carte 38/55 €
• Meats and grills • Friendly •

A pleasant restaurant renowned for its excellent grilled dishes and impressive
wine list. Dining area with a low ceiling and bright paintings adding colour to
the brick walls.

X 　　**Spectrum**　　　　　　　　🛖
😊

Romeinsesteenweg 220 ✉ *1800 Vilvoorde*　　　Plan: **B1**
*– ☎ 02 267 00 45 – www.restospectrum.be – closed Monday dinner,
Saturday lunch and Sunday*
Menu 35 € – Carte 34/55 €
• Classic cuisine • Brasserie •

Good food lovers pay heed! The Spectrum offers one of the best value for
money deals in the region of Brussels. Generous, traditional dishes.

X 　　**La Brasserie de la Gare**　　　　　　🛖 AC
😊

chaussée de Gand 1430 ✉ *1082 – ☎ 02 469 10 09*　Plan: **A2**
– www.brasseriedelagare.be – closed Saturday lunch and Sunday
Menu 13 € (lunch)/37 € – Carte 30/55 €
• Belgian • Brasserie • Neighbourhood •

A whistle-stop from the station, this wood-panelled brasserie bustles. It has a
mural on a railroading theme. Traditional dishes and exciting wine list.

Ϟ **Wine in the City** (Eddy Münster)   88 🏠 AC
place Reine Astrid 34 ⊠ 1090 – 𝒞 0 2 420 09 20   Plan: **B2**
– www.wineinthecity.be – closed last 2 weeks August, Sunday, Monday and Tuesday
Menu 25 € (lunch), 37/70 €
– Carte 60/82 € – (lunch only except Friday and Saturday) (booking essential)
• Creative • Wine bar •
In this restaurant-wine bar, amid rows and rows of bottles, sample the wholesome fare of an enthusiastic and creative chef whose dishes frequently surprise. Excellent produce, faultless combinations and of course a magnificent wine list!
➜ Mosaïque de foie gras et anguille fumée à l'émulsion de poire. Presa iberique et poitrine laqués, poivron et croquette au jambon belotta. Kadaïf aux fruits rouges et sirop au miel.

AIRPORT & NATO

ϞϞ **Maxime Colin**   ⩽ 🛏 🏠 ⇔
Pastoorkesweg 1 ⊠ 1950 Kraainem – 𝒞 0 2 720 63 46   Plan: **D2**
– www.maximecolin.be – closed 1-14 August, first week November, 27 February-7 March, Saturday lunch, Sunday dinner and Monday
Menu 25 € (lunch), 50/85 € – *(tasting menu only)*
• Creative French • Romantic • Friendly •
When you enter chef Colin's establishment you will first want to admire the setting. Established in the gardens of Jourdain castle, the restaurant is depicted by a romantic interior and boasts a handsome terrace by a pond. The modern cuisine uses a wide variety of good quality produce.

Ϟ **Orange**   🏠 P
Leuvensesteenweg 614 ⊠ 1930 Nossegem   Plan: **D1**
– 𝒞 0 2 757 05 59 – www.orangerestaurant.be – closed Saturday lunch, Sunday and Monday
Menu 26 € (lunch)/37 € – Carte 37/74 €
• Modern cuisine • Friendly •
A modern take on good old brasserie cooking, served in an inviting setting: terracotta and chocolate tones, banquettes with fake crocodile-skin upholstery, and designer lighting. Pretty terrace surrounded by greenery.

Ϟ **Brasserie Mariadal**   🛏 🏠 AC ⇔ P
Kouterweg 2 ⊠ 1930 Zaventem – 𝒞 0 2 720 59 30   Plan: **D1**
– www.brasseriemariadal.be
Menu 37 € – Carte 30/64 €
• Classic cuisine • Brasserie •
This modern brasserie occupies an attractive manor house in a public park with a lake. Find an uncluttered, stylish decor, an orangerie, reception rooms and play area. A good value for money menu.

Ϟ **Bovis**   AC
Heldenplein 16 ⊠ 1930 Zaventem – 𝒞 0 2 308 83 43   Plan: **D1**
– www.bovis-zaventem.be – closed Bank Holidays, Saturday and Sunday
Carte 40/71 €
• Meats and grills • Brasserie •
The strapline of this restaurant is 'simply meat', where it uses only the very best quality and ensures that each carcass is aged until it reaches perfect maturity. All is served with handcut chips that are fried in beef fat, along with equally authentic wines.

ANTWERP
ANTWERPEN/ANVERS

Population: 513 570

Brad Pict/Fotolia.com

Antwerp calls itself the pocketsize metropolis, and with good reason. Although it's Europe's second largest port, it still retains a compact intimacy, defined by bustling squares and narrow streets. It's a place with many facets, not least its marked link to Rubens, the diamond trade and, in later years, the fashion collective The Antwerp Six.

The city's centre teems with ornate gabled guildhouses, and in summer, open-air cafés line the area beneath the towering cathedral, giving the place a festive, almost bohemian air. It's a fantastic place to shop: besides clothing boutiques, there are antiques emporiums and diamond stores – to say nothing of the chocolate shops with their appealing window displays. Bold regeneration projects have transformed the skyline and the waterfront's decrepit warehouses have started new lives as ritzy storerooms of 21C commerce. The nightlife here is the best in Belgium, while the beer is savoured the way others might treat a vintage wine. The Old Town is defined by Grote Markt, Groenplaats and The Meir shopping street – these are a kind of dividing line between Antwerp's north and south. North of the centre is Het Eilandje, the hip former warehouse area; to the east is the Diamond District. Antique and bric-a-brac shops are in abundance in the 'designer heart' Het Zuid, south of the centre, which is also home to the best museums and art galleries.

ANTWERP IN...

→ **ONE DAY**
Grote Markt, Our Lady's Cathedral, MoMu, Het Zuid.

→ **TWO DAYS**
Rubens' House, Royal Museum of Fine Arts, a stroll to the Left Bank via the Sint-Anna tunnel.

→ **THREE DAYS**
Het Eilandje and MAS, a river trip, Kloosterstraat, Nationalestraat.

PRACTICAL INFORMATION

ARRIVAL-DEPARTURE

✈ Antwerp Airport is 7km southeast. Buses Number 51, 52 and 53 go to the Central Station.

✈ Brussels Airport is 40km south. The Airport Express train takes 35min. The Antwerp-Brussels Airport Express shuttle bus to Central Station takes 45min.

GETTING AROUND

Antwerp has an efficient network of buses, trams and premetro (trams which run underground at some stage of their journey). Invest in a Dagpas - a day pass - which gives unlimited travel on the whole of the city's public transport system; it's obtainable on board buses and trams and from De Lijn kiosks. On many occasions you'll find it quicker to walk around, as this is a compact city ideal for pedestrians. If you'd rather get about by bike, head to Tourism Antwerp on Grote Markt for more information.

CALENDAR HIGHLIGHTS

May
Sinksenfoor Funfair.

May-September
Free Carillon concerts.

June
Beer Passion Weekend.

Summer
Zomer van Antwerpen (music, theatre, film).

August
Rubens Market, Festival of Flanders, Jazzfestival Middelheim.

September
Laundry Day, Open Monument Day.

EATING OUT

The menus of Flanders are heavily influenced by the lush meadows, the canals swarming with eels and the proximity of the North Sea – but the eating culture in Antwerp offers more than just seafood. With its centuries old connection to more exotic climes, there's no shortage of fragrant spices such as cinnamon in their dishes, especially in the rich stews so beloved by the locals. If you want to eat with the chic, hang around the Het Eilandje dockside or the rejuvenated ancient warehouses south of Grote Markt. For early risers, the grand cafés are a popular port of call, ideal for a slow coffee and a trawl through the papers. Overall the city boasts the same tempting Belgian specialities as Brussels (stewed eel in chervil sauce; mussels; dishes containing rabbit; beef stew and chicory), but also with a focus on more contemporary cuisine. Don't miss out on the local chocolate (shaped like a hand in keeping with the legend which gave Antwerp its name), and be sure to try their De Koninck beer, served in a glass designed like an open bowl.

BELGIUM - ANTWERP

CENTRE (Old Town and Main Station)

Lindner
Lange Kievitstraat 125 ⊠ 2018 – ✆ 03 227 77 00
Plan: **F2**
– www.lindnerhotels.be
173 rm – †99/189 € ††99/189 € – ⌒ 20 € – 4 suites
• Business • Modern •

This modern, almost futuristic hotel was cleverly built near the new station. A good starting point for your trip, whether it is for business or pleasure. Spacious rooms.

De Witte Lelie
Keizerstraat 16 ⊠ 2000 – ✆ 03 226 19 66
Plan: **D1**
– www.dewittelelie.be
10 rm – †225/305 € ††275/355 € – ⌒ 30 € – 1 suite
• Historic • Personalised •

This historic abode fully justifies its reputation for poised sophistication and graceful hospitality. The 17C walls, tasteful decor down to the tiniest detail, and its precious peace and quiet in the city centre explain the appeal of this luxury boutique hotel.

Julien
Korte Nieuwstraat 24 ⊠ 2000 – ✆ 03 229 06 00
Plan: **D2**
– www.hotel-julien.com
21 rm – †179/299 € ††179/299 € – ⌒ 23 €
• Luxury • Design •

Hidden behind its carriage entrance this hotel is a real gem. It boasts a warm welcome, cosy atmosphere and very refined Scandinavian-style rooms. Don't miss the spa built in the 16C cellar. From the roof terrace there is a breathtaking view of the cathedral.

't Sandt
Zand 17 ⊠ 2000 – ✆ 03 232 93 90
Plan: **C2**
– www.hotel-sandt.be
28 rm ⌒ – †160/250 € ††180/270 € – 1 suite
• Luxury • Classic •

This establishment is in an attractive building with a fine Rococo façade near the banks of the Schelde. It offers attentive service, bedrooms full of character, meeting rooms, a patio and a roof terrace.

Les Nuits
Lange Gasthuisstraat 12 ⊠ 2000 – ✆ 03 225 02 04
Plan: **D2**
– www.hotellesnuits.be
25 rm – †129/149 € ††139/159 € – ⌒ 19 €
• Luxury • Cosy • Modern •

Looking for a hip place in town? This boutique hotel offers a nice contrast between the dark colours of the night (la nuit) and lighter shades. Its interior design is really charming.

't Zilte (Viki Geunes)

Hanzestedenplaats 5 ⊠ 2000 – ✆ 03 283 40 40
Plan: **B1**
❀❀
– www.tzilte.be – closed 1 week Easter, 2 weeks July, Autumn break, late December, Saturday and Sunday
Menu 68 € (lunch)/130 € – Carte 153/215 € – *(booking essential)*
• Creative • Design •

This establishment is on the top floor of the MAS, a location at the same level as the food! The urban gastronomy here is indeed top flight, a magnificent blend of craftsmanship and creativity – in one of the loveliest spots in town overlooking the harbour.
→ Bretoense langoustine met champignons, laurier en hijiki. Kalfszwezerik met kreeft, bloemkool en fregola sarda. Creatie met sesam, macha, yuzu en sanchohoning.

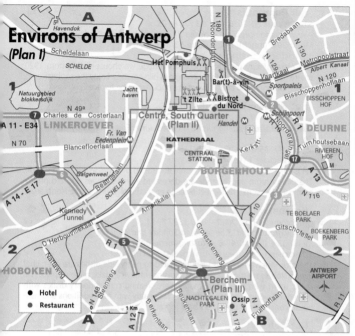

Environs of Antwerp *(Plan I)*

- Hotel
- Restaurant

1 Km

XxX **The Jane** (Nick Bril)   🕸 ċ AK ↔ P
🟊🟊   Plan: **H1**
Paradeplein 1 ⊠ 2018 – 🞰 0 3 808 44 65
*– www.thejaneantwerp.com – closed late March-early April, late June-
early July, late September-early October, 23 December-3 January, Sunday
and Monday*
Menu 100/115 € – *(booking essential) (tasting menu only)*
• Creative • Fashionable • Design •
Jane has managed to transform this imposing chapel into a trendy temple of
food! The former altar has been replaced by an open-plan kitchen, devoted to
the preparation of good food from quality produce. A masterful mixture of
sophistication and simplicity, enhanced by rich flavours. The Upper Room Bar
is ideal for drinks and snacks.
➔ Coquilles met bergamot en knolselderij. Dorade met zeevenkel en dragon. Cannelé met framboos en basilicum.

XxX **'t Fornuis** (Johan Segers)   🕸 ↔
🟊   Plan: **D2**
Reyndersstraat 24 ⊠ 2000 – 🞰 0 3 233 62 70
*– closed 21 July-20 August, late December, Bank Holidays, Saturday and
Sunday*
Carte 70/135 €
• Creative French • Romantic •
Fine classic cuisine and quality wines are served in this rustic restaurant housed
in an old building. The owner/chef has been running the show since 1976 and
was awarded his first Michelin star in 1986. Miniature stoves exhibited downs-
tairs.
➔ Croque-monsieur met kalfshersentjes. Griet met een aardappelmousse-
line, gepocheerd eitje en kaviaar. Frappuccino.

BELGIUM - ANTWERP

XX Het Pomphuis

Siberiastraat ✉ 2030 – ✆ 03 770 86 25 — Plan: **B1**
– www.hetpomphuis.be – closed 24 December and Saturday lunch
Menu 29 € (lunch)/49 € – Carte 53/84 €
• Modern cuisine • Vintage •

This extraordinary restaurant occupies a huge warehouse dating from 1920, where the decor includes three enormous bilge pumps. Enjoy the sophisticated, contemporary menu and views of the docks from the terrace.

XX Het Nieuwe Palinghuis

Sint-Jansvliet 14 ✉ 2000 – ✆ 03 231 74 45 — Plan: **C2**
– www.hetnieuwepalinghuis.be – closed June, Friday, Monday and Tuesday
Menu 44/135 € ♟ – Carte 56/115 €
• Seafood • Friendly •

Eel is king at this fish restaurant, only dethroned by Schelde lobster in season. The dining room and veranda are decorated with seascapes and old photographs of Antwerp. The perfect place to enjoy the pleasures of the North Sea.

XX Graanmarkt 13

Graanmarkt 13 ✉ 2000 – ✆ 03 337 79 91 — Plan: **E2**
– www.graanmarkt13.be – closed Sunday and Monday
Menu 33 € (lunch)/43 € – *(tasting menu only)*
• Modern cuisine • Minimalist • Trendy •

The days when vegetables were relegated to paltry side dishes are over: chef Seppe Nobels masterfully demonstrates how they can take pride of place. He cooks them with talent and imagination, creating contemporary dishes with powerful flavours. The menu changes frequently with new additions and recipes to constantly entice diners back for more.

XX Het Gebaar (Roger van Damme)

❁

Leopoldstraat 24 ✉ 2000 – ✆ 03 232 37 10 — Plan: **D2**
– www.hetgebaar.be – closed Bank Holidays, Sunday and Monday
Carte 66/100 € – *(lunch only) (booking essential)*
• Creative • Cosy •

This restaurant is located in an elegant building on the edge of the botanical park. Luxury tea room cuisine, which the chef enriches with modern twists; mouthwatering desserts! Non-stop service until 6pm.

➜ Carpaccio van wagyurund met een truffelcrème. Op de huid gebakken zeebaars en scheermesje met krabslaatje, structuren van doperwtjes en venkel. Lemon squash: creatie met citroen, limoen, bergamot, basilicum en yoghurt.

XX De Godevaart

Sint-Katelijnevest 23 ✉ 2000 – ✆ 03 231 89 94 — Plan: **D2**
– www.degodevaart.be – closed Sunday and Monday
Menu 70/115 € – Carte approx. 80 € – *(dinner only)*
• Creative • Classic décor •

The chef lets his creativity run riot in the kitchen of this old house that has retained some of its original architectural features (stucco, fireplace, etc.). His cuisine, in which authentic produce takes pride of place, frequently surprises diners with unexpected mixtures and techniques.

XX Lux

Adriaan Brouwerstraat 13 ✉ 2000 – ✆ 03 233 30 30 — Plan: **D1**
– www.luxantwerp.com – closed 9-24 July, 1 January, lunch on Bank Holidays, Saturday lunch, Sunday and Monday
Menu 33 € (lunch), 45/75 € – Carte 66/78 €
• Classic cuisine • Chic •

This restaurant occupies the house of a former ship owner, and has a terrace that overlooks the port. There is a profusion of marble (columns, fireplaces), a wine and cocktail bar, à la carte options, plus an attractive lunch menu.

XX Le Zoute Zoen ⇔

Zirkstraat 23 ✉ 2000 – ℰ 0 3 226 92 20   Plan: **D1**
– www.lezoutezoen.be – closed Saturday lunch and Monday
Menu 30 € (lunch), 57 € 🍷/85 € 🍷 – Carte 50/68 €
• Classic cuisine • Bistro •
This is an intimate and cosy bistro. The culinary emphasis of the chefs is placed as much as possible on Belgian dishes and produce, including the set 'Zoen-menu'.

XX Ardent 🕾

Dageraadplaats 3 ✉ 2018 – ℰ 0 3 336 32 99   Plan: **F3**
– www.resto-ardent.be – closed 28 March-5 April, 4-19 July, 1-5 January, Monday, Tuesday and after 8.30pm
Menu 29 € (lunch), 49/69 € – Carte 54/72 €
• Modern cuisine • Minimalist •
Passion is often said to be the distinctive character trait of great chefs. Wouter Van Steenwinkel is no exception to this rule and his tasteful restaurant will give you an insight into his many talents. You can expect well-thought out and balanced meals with perfectly blended flavours. The French fries are to die for!

XX Renaissance 🕾

Nationalestraat 32 ✉ 2000 – ℰ 0 3 233 93 90   Plan: **D2**
– www.resto-renaissance.be – closed Sunday
Carte 40/74 €
• Italian • Design • Elegant •
What a brilliant idea to locate an Italian restaurant in the same building as the fashion museum! This splendid establishment sports an all-white, minimalist interior. The menu, rich in southern sunshine, is authentic and classical in its origins.

XX Marcel ⇔

Van Schoonbekeplein 13 ✉ 2000 – ℰ 0 3 336 33 02   Plan: **D1**
– www.restaurantmarcel.be – closed Saturday lunch and Sunday
Menu 30 € (lunch), 40/75 € – Carte 51/80 €
• Regional cuisine • Brasserie • Vintage •
Welcome to Marcel's – a vintage bistro with a distinctly French feel. The culinary repertory mingles traditional recipes with touches of modernity, resulting in cuisine steeped in wholesome flavours. Terrace overlooking the MAS.

XX Bistrot du Nord (Michael Rewers)
🕸

Lange Dijkstraat 36 ✉ 2060 – ℰ 0 3 233 45 49   Plan: **B1**
– www.bistrotdunord.be – closed 21 July-15 August, Bank Holidays, Saturday and Sunday
Carte 49/82 €
• Traditional cuisine • Bourgeois • Intimate •
A lesson in tradition! The chef, an authentic craftsman, knows how to get the best out of fine produce. He admits to a weakness for tripe, but diners need have no fears - whatever your choice, your taste buds will be delighted.
➜ Kalfshersentjes met tartaarsaus. Bavette van Black Angus met rodewijns-aus en merg. Dame blanche.

X Brasserie Dock's 🕾 🗚 ⇔ 🐾
😀

Jordaenskaai 7 ✉ 2000 – ℰ 0 3 226 63 30   Plan: **D1**
– www.docks.be – closed Sunday
Menu 18 € (lunch), 30/45 € – Carte 41/68 €
• Seafood • Fashionable • Brasserie •
Set in the post-industrial landscape of the docks, this brasserie encapsulates contemporary taste: Jules Verne decor, trendy clientele and tasty "terre-mer" cuisine (oyster bar). Booking advisable.

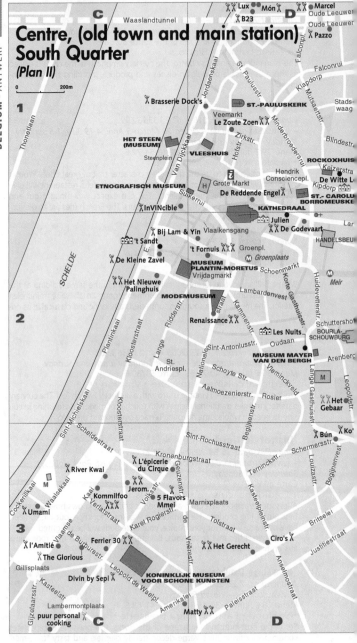

Centre, (old town and main station) South Quarter
(Plan II)

BELGIUM - ANTWERP

Waaslandtunnel

Lux · Món · Marcel
Oude Leeuwer
B23
Oude Leeuwer
Pazzo

Falconpl.
Falconrui
St.-Paulusstr.
Klapdorp
Mutsaertstr.
Stadswaag

Brasserie Dock's
ST.-PAULUSKERK
Jordenskaai
Veemarkt
Le Zoute Zoen
Zirkstr.
Minderbroedersrui
Blindestr.

HET STEEN (MUSEUM)
Van Dijckkaai
Hofstr.
VLEESHUIS
Steenplein
ROCKOXHUIS
Keizerstra
Hendrik Conscienceplein
De Witte L
Kipdorp
ST.-CAROLUS BORROMEUSKE

ETNOGRAFISCH MUSEUM
Suikerrui
Grote Markt
H
De Reddende Engel
KATHEDRAAL
Lar

InVINcible
Vlaaikensgang
Julien
De Godevaart
HANDELSBEU

Bij Lam & Yin
't Sandt
Groenpl.
Groenplaats
De Kleine Zavel
't Fornuis
Schoenmarkt
Meir

SCHELDE
Het Nieuwe Palinghuis
MUSEUM PLANTIN-MORETUS
Vrijdagmarkt
Lambardenvest
Korte Gasthuisstr.
Huidevetterstr.
Schuttershof

MODEMUSEUM
Ridderstr.
Kammenstr.
BOURLA-SCHOUWBURG

Renaissance
Les Nuits
Oudaan
MUSEUM MAYER VAN DEN BERGH
Arenberg

Lange
Kloosterstraat
Nationale str.
Sint-Antoniusstr.
Vlieminckveld
Lange Gasthuisstr.
M
Leopoldstr.

St. Andriespl.
Schoyte Str.
Het Gebaar

Plantinkaai
Aalmoezenierstr.
Rosier

Sint-Michielskaai
Sint-Rochusstraat
Begijnenstr.
Schermersstr.
Bún
Ko'

Scheldestraat
Kronenburgstraat
Geuzenstr.
Terninckstr.
Louizastr.
Begijnenvest

River Kwai
L'épicerie du Cirque
Jerom.
Britselei

Cockerillkaai
M
Waalsekaai
Kaai
Kommilfoo
Verlatstraat
Volkstr.
5 Flavors Mmei
Marnixplaats
Kasteelpleinstr.
Justitiestraat

Umami
Vlaamse de Burburestr.
Karel Rogierstr.
Tolstraat
Ciro's

l'Amitié
Ferrier 30
de Vrièrestr.
Het Gerecht
Anselmostraat

The Glorious
Gillisplaats
Leopold de Waelpl.
KONINKLIJK MUSEUM VOOR SCHONE KUNSTEN
Kasteelstr.

Divin by Sepi
Amerikalei
Paleisstraat

Gijzelaarsstr.
Lambermontplaats
puur personal cooking
Matty

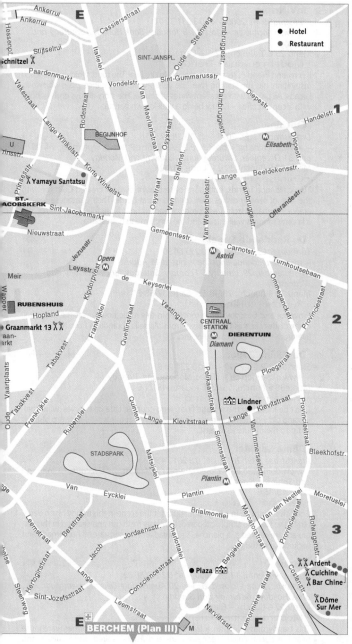

InVINcible
🕸 🛋 AC

Haarstraat 9 ⊠ 2000 – ℰ 03 231 32 07 — Plan: **C1**
– www.invincible.be – closed 1-8 January, Bank Holidays, Saturday and Sunday
Menu 25 € 🍷 (lunch)/37 € – Carte 41/68 €
• **Modern cuisine • Trendy •**

Kenny and Wendy's restaurant really is InVINcible! The food, which is of French inspiration, has the starring role. The vol-au-vent, for instance, plays off sweetbreads! All paired with excellent wines of course. The story always ends happily with a cup of coffee – Kenny being a well-known barista.

Cuichine
🛋

Draakstraat 13 ⊠ 2018 – ℰ 03 289 92 45 — Plan: **F3**
– www.cuichine.be – closed 18-25 April, first 2 weeks September, 24, 25 and 31 December, Saturday lunch, Sunday and Monday
Menu 22 € (lunch)/39 € – Carte 41/62 €
• **Chinese • Friendly •**

Two childhood friends, both sons of restaurant owners, created Cuichine with the idea of serving dishes they used to eat at home. Their Cantonese recipes are well prepared from fresh produce and without fussy frills. Even better, the à la carte menu is well priced and the lunch menu unbeatable.

De Reddende Engel
🛋 ⇆

Torfburg 3 ⊠ 2000 – ℰ 03 233 66 30 — Plan: **D1**
– www.de-reddende-engel.be – closed 16 August-14 September, 29 January-9 February, Saturday lunch, Tuesday and Wednesday
Menu 19 € (lunch), 28/38 € – Carte 37/58 €
• **Regional cuisine • Rustic •**

Provence and Gascony come together in this rustic house near the cathedral. Enjoy dishes such as bouillabaisse from Marseille, brandade from Nîmes, duck liver from the Landes, cassoulet, etc.

De Kleine Zavel
🛋 AC

Stoofstraat 2 ⊠ 2000 – ℰ 03 231 96 91 — Plan: **C1**
– www.dkz-group.be – closed Monday and Tuesday
Menu 38 € (lunch), 55/85 € – Carte 48/71 €
• **Modern cuisine • Bistro •**

Don't be fooled by the vintage floor, retro counter, little bare tables, wine shelves and old wooden beer racks. The food served at this typical Antwerp bistro is as up-to-the-minute as it gets!

Dôme Sur Mer
🛋

Arendstraat 1 ⊠ 2018 – ℰ 03 281 74 33 — Plan: **F3**
– www.domeweb.be – closed 2 weeks in August, 24 December-9 January and Saturday lunch
Carte 40/86 €
• **Seafood • Bistro •**

Goldfish swimming in a huge aquarium set the scene in this trendy bistro devoted to the sea. The simply prepared, flawlessly fresh fish and seafood in this restaurant are cooked à la plancha. The bread and desserts are all homemade and wickedly appetising!

Pazzo
🕸 AC ⇆

Oude Leeuwenrui 12 ⊠ 2000 – ℰ 03 232 86 82 — Plan: **D1**
– www.pazzo.be – closed 20 July-20 August, late December-early January, Bank Holidays, Saturday and Sunday
Menu 22 € (lunch) – Carte 40/73 €
• **Modern cuisine • Friendly •**

This trendy brasserie with a lively atmosphere occupies a former warehouse near the docks. Enjoy Mediterranean- and Asian-inspired bistro cuisine and excellent wines.

BELGIUM - ANTWERP

X B 23

Brouwersvliet 23 ✉ *2000 –* ✆ *0 3 345 15 14*   Plan: **D1**
– www.brouwersvliet23.be – closed 25 July-25 August, 1-16 January,
Wednesday lunch, Saturday lunch and Sunday
Menu 17 € (lunch), 37/60 € – Carte 51/86 €
• Modern cuisine • Brasserie • Wine bar •
Step into this wine bar at N°23 Brouwersvliet and you will find a lively brasserie to the rear. The menu can hold its own with the best, and the fine produce is enhanced by modern techniques and combinations. B 23 brings the promise of an explosion of flavours.

X Món

Sint-Aldegondiskaai 30 ✉ *2000 –* ✆ *0 3 345 67 89*   Plan: **D1**
– www.monantwerp.com
Carte 36/60 €
• Meats and grills • Brasserie • Trendy •
The sculpture of a bull's head immediately gives you a foretaste of the menu, in which red meat takes pride of place. In fact, not just any meat but home raised Limousine beef prepared in a Josper charcoal fire. The cooking and accompaniments are a treat for your taste buds.

X Bar(t)-à-vin

Lange Slachterijstraat 3 ✉ *2060 –* ✆ *0 474 94 17 86*   Plan: **B1**
– www.bartavin.be – closed 2 weeks July, Bank Holidays, Saturday,
Sunday and after 8.30pm
Carte 43/60 €
• Classic cuisine • Bistro •
Bart, the proprietor, converted his wine bar into a bistro in this attractive former butcher shop. Everything has gone smoothly thanks to the food with a focus on ingredients, classic recipes and the limited but varied selections.

X Bij Lam & Yin (Lap Yee Lam)

Reynderstraat 17 ✉ *2000 –* ✆ *0 3 232 88 38 – closed*   Plan: **D2**
Easter holiday, Monday and Tuesday
Carte 46/69 € – (dinner only) (booking essential)
• Chinese • Minimalist • Exotic décor •
This Chinese restaurant goes against the grain, challenging preconceived ideas about Asian cuisine. It has a minimalist decor and a small menu placing the onus on fresh ingredients, originality and flavour. Be sure to book a table!
➔ Stoommandje met dimsum. Gestoomde zeebaars met gember en pijpajuin. Gebakken lam met szechuanpeper.

X Ko'uzi

Leopoldplaats 12 ✉ *2000 –* ✆ *0 3 232 24 88*   Plan: **D3**
– www.kouzi.be – closed 2 weeks in August, Bank Holidays, Sunday,
Monday and after 8pm
Carte 23/59 €
• Japanese • Minimalist • Design •
The minimalist, designer decor is reflected in the cuisine. Classical sushi and sashimi preparations rub shoulders with creative variations. The tea, which can be sampled in the tea room, is equally delicious.

X Schnitzel

Paardenmarkt 53 ✉ *2000 –* ✆ *0 3 256 63 86*   Plan: **K1**
– www.schnitzelantwerpen.be – closed Saturday and Sunday
Carte approx. 40 € – (dinner only)
• Classic cuisine • Neighbourhood • Traditional décor •
Simply but carefully prepared is the motto of this establishment. The chef harnesses his wide experience to prepare delicious cooked meat and beuling, a sort of black pudding. All are incorporated into dishes designed to be shared. Good, wholesome food at its best!

Yamayu Santatsu
Ossenmarkt 19 ⊠ 2000 – ℰ 03 234 09 49 — Plan: **E1**
– www.santatsu.be – closed Sunday lunch and Monday
Menu 16 € (lunch), 23/50 € – Carte 32/59 €
• Japanese • Simple •

A lively and authentic Japanese restaurant that only uses the best hand picked ingredients, and prepares sushi in full view of diners. Assorted à la carte options with four different menus for two people.

Bún

Sint-Jorispoort 22 ⊠ 2000 – ℰ 03 234 04 16 — Plan: **D3**
– www.bunantwerp.be – closed 9-15 January, Sunday and Monday
Carte 27/38 € – (booking essential)
• Vietnamese • Simple •

A fresco on the wall depicts a cockerel fight, transporting you right to the midst of a Vietnamese street! This modest bistro will take you on an amazing gourmet journey from East to West. Vietnamese cooking at its best.

Bar Chine
Draakplaats 3 ⊠ 2018 – ℰ 03 501 28 11 — Plan: **F3**
– www.barchine.be – closed 24, 25 and 31 December, Tuesday and Wednesday
Carte 21/48 € – (dinner only except Friday)
• Chinese • Fashionable •

The paper lanterns are entirely in keeping with the simple, intimate setting. The fuss-free menu includes a mouthwatering array of Asian influenced tapas. Perfect to share with friends or family.

SOUTH QUARTER AND BERCHEM

Firean
Karel Oomsstraat 6 ⊠ 2018 – ℰ 03 237 02 60 — Plan: **G1**
– www.hotelfirean.com
9 rm – ♦160/170 € ♦♦160/170 € – ☐ 18 €
• Luxury • Personalised •

This property full of charm occupies an Art Deco-style building (1929). It features public rooms in the style of the period, a flower-filled patio, and personalised guestrooms with antique furnishings. Impeccable service.
Minerva – See restaurant listing

Kommilfoo (Olivier de Vinck de Winnezeele)
Vlaamse Kaai 17 ⊠ 2000 – ℰ 03 237 30 00 — Plan: **C3**
– www.restaurantkommilfoo.be – closed first 3 weeks July, 25 December, Saturday lunch, Sunday and Monday
Menu 38 € (lunch), 43/80 € – Carte 77/104 €
• Creative • Cosy •

A comfortable, modern dining room is the setting for the culinary creations of this innovative chef who alternates ever-evolving recipes with molecular experimentation. Pyrenean goat is an ever-present dish on the menu here!
→ King krab met burrata en fregola sarda met avocado. Twee bereidingen van melkgeit: het ribstuk met kruidige bulgur en de langzaam gegaarde schouder met houmous. Fantasie van bittere chocolade met yuzu en hazelnoten.

Minerva – Hotel Firean

Karel Oomsstraat 36 ⊠ 2018 – ℰ 03 216 00 55 — Plan: **G1**
– www.restaurantminerva.be – closed 16 July-16 August, 24 December-10 January, Bank Holidays, Saturday and Sunday
Menu 38 € (lunch)/65 € – Carte 65/105 €
• Classic cuisine • Elegant •

Minerva was also the name of the legendary Belgian luxury car, the repair workshops of which were located here. The site is now that of a well-oiled restaurant, serving good quality, traditional fare. You might be interested to know that all the meat is sliced in front of you!

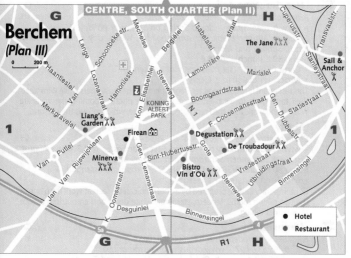

XX **Bistro Vin d'Où**　　　　　　　　　　　🛜 ⇔ **P**

Terlinckstraat 2 ⊠ 2600 Berchem　　　　　　　Plan: **H1**
– ℰ 03 230 55 99 – www.vindou.be
*– closed 6-18 April, 21 July-11 August, 24 December-5 January, Monday
dinner, Tuesday dinner, Wednesday dinner, Saturday lunch and Sunday*
Menu 65/85 € – Carte 69/118 €

• **Modern cuisine • Bistro** •

This smart, contemporary bistro has taken up abode in an attractive bourgeois
home. The chef is a genuine craftsman with a distinct taste for the best produce:
what more can we say? The patio is heaven in summertime and you may even
be forgiven for thinking you are in Italy as you sample a grappa from the house's transalpine distillery!

XX **De Troubadour**　　　　　　　　　　　　🅰️ ⇔ **P**

Driekoningenstraat 72 ⊠ 2600 Berchem　　　　　Plan: **H1**
*– ℰ 03 239 39 16 – www.detroubadour.be – closed first 3 weeks August,
Sunday and Monday*
Menu 26 € (lunch), 37/54 € – Carte 48/81 €

• **Modern cuisine • Trendy** •

A modern, cosy dining room where the gregarious owner fosters a warm and
friendly atmosphere. Classic, creative à la carte options, as well as appetising
menus and daily specials announced at your table. Parking available (prior booking required).

XX **Ferrier 30**　　　　　　　　　　　　　　🛜 🅰️ ⇔

Leopold de Waelplaats 30 ⊠ 2000　　　　　　Plan: **C3**
– ℰ 03 216 50 62 – www.ferrier-30.be
– closed Wednesday
Carte 38/63 €

• **Italian • Design** •

The best Italian restaurant in the area is doubtless Ferrier 30. The meat, fish and
pasta dishes (lasagne al ragu, taglioni con prosciutto) are all steeped in authentic Italian flavours and are are further enhanced by wines brought back by the
owner in person.

BELGIUM - ANTWERP

XX **Het Gerecht** 🛜 ♻

Amerikalei 20 ✉ 2000 – 𝒞 03 248 79 28 Plan: **D3**
*– www.hetgerecht.be – closed Spring break, Easter holiday, 15 July-
5 August, Autumn break, Christmas holiday, Wednesday dinner, Saturday
lunch, Sunday and Monday*
Menu 30 € (lunch), 56/68 €
– Carte 68/92 € – (set menu only at weekends)
• Modern cuisine • Cosy •
This restaurant is full of character. Peggy pampers her customers while Wim treats
their taste buds to his talented creations. The photos adorning the walls are
Wim's handiwork, as is the French inspired cuisine, which follows the seasons.

XX **Matty** 🛜

Brederodestraat 23 ✉ 2018 – 𝒞 03 293 54 41 Plan: **C3**
*– www.restaurantmatty.be – closed 1 week at Easter, first 3 weeks August,
first week November, Saturday lunch, Sunday and Monday*
Menu 30 € (lunch)/58 € – Carte 68/77 € – *(booking essential)*
• Modern cuisine • Design •
Contemporary cuisine prepared by a chef who can be seen at work from one of
the two dining rooms. Modern, startlingly white decor and an outdoor terrace
for summer dining.

XX **Degustation** 🛜 ♻

Frederik de Merodeplein 6 ✉ 2600 Berchem Plan: **H1**
*– 𝒞 0 495 63 04 97 – www.degustation-restaurant.be
– closed Saturday lunch, Sunday lunch, Monday and Tuesday*
Menu 25 € (lunch), 45/55 € – Carte 47/72 €
• Modern French • Fashionable •
The menu boasts many delights, such as turbot with summer truffles and qui-
noa with sage. The chef selects the finest ingredients in preparing his flavourful
dishes, which are offered at reasonable prices.

XX **Liang's Garden** 🄰🄲 ♻

Generaal Lemanstraat 54 ✉ 2000 – 𝒞 03 237 22 22 Plan: **G1**
– closed Sunday
Menu 27 € (lunch), 35/72 € – Carte 35/96 €
• Chinese • Traditional décor •
A stalwart of Chinese cuisine in the city! A spacious restaurant where the
authentic menu covers specialities from Canton (dim sum), Peking (duck) and
Szechuan (fondue).

XX **Jerom.** 🛜

Graaf van Egmontstraat 39a ✉ 2000 – 𝒞 0 487 70 70 70 Plan: **E2**
*– www.restaurantjerom.be – closed 18 July-7 August, 23 December-
4 January, Saturday lunch, Sunday and Monday*
Menu 32 € (lunch), 35/73 € – Carte 60/84 €
• Modern French • Trendy •
Spacious and contemporary, rough yet elegant. This restaurant is both a great
place to eat and eminently welcoming. Masterfully sourced ingredients, distinctive, up-to-the-minute, combinations and flawlessly balanced flavours.

X **The Glorious** 🕮 ⇔ 🛜 🄰🄲

𝄋 *De Burburestraat 4a ✉ 2000 – 𝒞 03 237 06 13* Plan: **C3**
*– www.theglorious.be – closed 1 week at Easter, 2 weeks in July, Sunday
and Monday*
Menu 35 € 🍷 (lunch), 65/95 € – Carte 72/107 €
• Modern French • Wine bar • Chic •
This former warehouse now houses a chic, well-designed restaurant. The owner,
Jurgen, is in charge of the renowned wine selection and the chef, Johan, tempts
you with his cooking, which elevates classic dishes to a whole new level. Enjoy
this glorious adventure surrounded by original baroque and art deco features.
➜ Quenelles van snoek met langoustines en nantuasaus. Jonge duif uit
Anjou met kort gebakken ganzenlever, crème van doperwten en jus met
jeneverbessen. Forêt noire, klassiek met kersen en chocolade.

BELGIUM - ANTWERP

Umami

Luikstraat 6 ⊠ 2000 – ℰ 0 3 237 39 78 Plan: **C3**
– www.umami-antwerp.be – closed Monday and Tuesday
Menu 45/59 € – Carte 30/61 €
– (dinner only except Sunday)
• Asian • Exotic décor •

Asian wood and lounge furniture happily rub shoulders beneath a well of light in this handsome establishment. The menu respects the house's motto - contemporary Asian cuisine. Oriental traditions with an ingenious modern twist.

L'épicerie du Cirque (Dennis Broeckx)

Volkstraat 23 ⊠ 2000 Plan: **C3**
– ℰ 0 3 238 05 71 – www.lepicerieducirque.be
– closed 1 May, 24 and 25 December, 1 week January, Sunday and Monday
Menu 33 € (lunch), 49/95 € – Carte 62/136 €
• Creative • Fashionable • Bistro •

Treat yourself to a simply delicious meal without any unnecessary fuss. The chef focuses on good produce and classical techniques, adding the occasional unusual twist. The dishes sparkle with enticing flavours. The delicatessen shop, which is decked in the same Scandinavian style, is full of tempting delicacies.
➡ Terrine van ganzenlever met beuling en jus van braambessen. Zeebaars met gekonfijte aardappel, salsa verde en king krab. Café glacé : "old school" and "modern".

puur personal cooking

Edward Pecherstraat 51 ⊠ 2000 Plan: **C3**
– ℰ 0 495 83 24 87 – www.puurpersonalcooking.be
– closed last 2 weeks July, late December, Monday lunch, Saturday and Sunday
Menu 38 € (lunch)/58 € – *(booking essential)*
• Modern cuisine • Bistro • Intimate •

One man and his AGA oven occupy the heart of this cosy bistro. The chef develops a personal version of contemporary cuisine, focused on unadulterated flavour. A menu in which quality and passion take pride of place.

Ciro's

Amerikalei 6 ⊠ 2018 Plan: **D3**
– ℰ 0 3 238 11 47 – www.ciros.be
– closed July, Saturday lunch and Monday
Carte 37/63 €
• Belgian • Neighbourhood • Traditional décor •

The nostalgic interior, working class atmosphere and traditional Belgian fare will provide the opportunity to turn a meal at Ciro's into a taste of Antwerp's past. Steak and chips with six sauces is the star of the show. Book ahead – you won't be disappointed!

l'Amitié

Vlaamse Kaai 43 ⊠ 2000 – ℰ 0 3 257 50 05 Plan: **C3**
– www.lamitie.net – closed 2 weeks August, 1 January, Saturday lunch, Sunday and Monday
Carte 38/65 €
• Modern French • Fashionable •

When you arrive in this fully renovated bistro, it won't be friendship, but something more akin to love that you will feel. Fish takes pride of place and the first class ingredients are prepared according to modern techniques and served in small dishes. Scrumptious!

✗ **Divin by Sepi** 🍴 🏠

Verschansingstraat 5 ✉ *2000 –* ☎ *0 3 284 07 40*   Plan: **E2**
– www.divinbysepi.be – closed Saturday lunch, Tuesday and Wednesday
Carte 45/70 € *– (open until 11pm)*
• **Mediterranean cuisine** • **Wine bar** • **Fashionable** •

Sepideh Sedaghatnia first earned a name for herself as a sommelier and this wine bar is the result of her expertise! The excellent wine selection features a number of surprising organic vintages. The menu takes you on a whirlwind world tour of finger food and more classical dishes. Taste without pretentious frills is the watchword here.

✗ **5 Flavors Mmei**
😊

Volkstraat 37 ✉ *2000 –* ☎ *0 3 281 30 37*   Plan: **F2**
– www.5flavors.be – closed Sunday and Monday
Menu 35/45 € – Carte 24/42 €
• **Chinese** • **Simple** •

The most well-known and most obvious can sometimes surprise and this restaurant is a perfect example. The chef pays homage to Chinese tradition with fresh and sometimes surprising preparations, which put paid to many prejudices regarding the cuisine of his place of birth. The dim-sum are to die for!

✗ **River Kwai** 🏠 🆔 ↔

Vlaamse Kaai 14 ✉ *2000 –* ☎ *0 3 237 46 51*   Plan: **C3**
– www.riverkwai.be – closed Monday
Menu 25/49 € ♗
– Carte 34/45 € *– (dinner only except Thursday and Friday)*
• **Thai** • **Exotic décor** •

This reliable restaurant has been serving authentic Thai cuisine for over 20 years. Find an attractive retro façade, dining rooms on separate floors with a typical decor, an elegant lounge and a front terrace.

✗ **Sail & Anchor**

Guldenvliesstraat 60 ✉ *2600 Berchem –* ☎ *0 3 430 40 04*   Plan: **G3**
– www.sailandanchor.be – closed Saturday lunch, Sunday dinner, Tuesday and Wednesday
Menu 25 € (lunch)/65 € *– (tasting menu only)*
• **Modern British** • **Vintage** •

Forget any preconceptions you may have about British cuisine! Chef Yates of this urbane establishment works with classical ingredients (mustard, lemon), combining them into creative masterpieces. Food whose sophisticated blend of tastes and colours will both surprise and delight.

CZECH REPUBLIC
ČESKÁ REPUBLIKA

● PRAGUE

→ **Area:**
78 864 km² (30 449 sq mi).

→ **Population:**
10 627 448 inhabitants.
Density = 135 per km².

→ **Capital:**
Prague.

→ **Currency:**
Czech crown (Kč).

→ **Government:**
Parliamentary republic (since 1993). Member of European Union since 2004.

→ **Language:**
Czech; also German and English.

→ **Public holidays:**
New Year's Day (1 Jan); Easter Monday (late Mar/Apr); Labor Day (1 May); Liberation Day (8 May); St Cyril and St Methodius Day (5 July); Martyrdom of Jan Hus (6 July); Czech Statehood Day (28 Sept); Independence Day (28 Oct); Freedom and Democracy Day (17 Nov); Christmas Eve (24 Dec – Half Day); Christmas Day (25 Dec); 2ⁿᵈ Day of Christmas (26 Dec).

→ **Local Time:**
GMT + 1 hour in winter and GMT + 2 hours in summer.

→ **Climate:**
Temperate continental with cold winters and warm summers (Prague: January 0°C; July 20°C).

→ **Emergency:**
Police ☏ **158**;
Medical Assistance ☏ **155**;
Fire Brigade ☏ **150**.
(Dialling **112** within any EU country will redirect your call and contact the emergency services.)

→ **Electricity:**
230 volts AC, 50Hz; 2 round pin sockets.

→ **Formalities:**
Travellers from the European Union (EU), Switzerland, Iceland and the main countries of North and South America need a national identity card or passport (America: passport required) to visit Czech Republic for less than three months (tourism or business purpose). For visitors from other countries a visa may be required, in addition to a passport, especially for those wishing to stay for longer than three months. We advise you to check with your embassy before travelling.

PRAGUE
PRAHA
Population: 1 272 690

Courtyardpix/Fotolia.com

Prague's history stretches back to the Dark Ages. In the ninth century a princely seat comprising a simple walled-in compound was built where the castle now stands; in the tenth century the first bridge over the Vltava arrived; and by the 13C the enchanting cobbled alleyways below the castle were complete. But Prague has come of age and Europe's most perfectly preserved capital now proffers consumer choice as well as medieval marvels. Its state-of-the-art shopping malls and pulsing nightlife bear testament to its popularity with tourists – the iron glove of communism long since having given way to western consumerism. These days there are practically two versions of Prague: the lively, youthful, 'stag party capital', and the sedate, enchanting 'city of a hundred spires'.

The four main zones of Prague were originally independent towns in their own right. The river Vltava winds its way through their heart and is spanned by the iconic Charles Bridge. On the west side lie Hradčany – the castle quarter, built on a rock spur – and Malá Strana, Prague's most perfectly preserved district, located at the bottom of the castle hill. Over the river are Staré Město, the old town with its vibrant medieval square and outer boulevards, and Nové Město, the new town, which is the city's commercial heart and where you'll find Wenceslas Square and Prague's young partygoers.

PRAGUE IN...

→ **ONE DAY**
Old Town Square, the astronomical clock, Charles Bridge, Prague Castle, Petřín Hill.

→ **TWO DAYS**
Josefov, the National Theatre, Golden Lane.

→ **THREE DAYS**
Wenceslas Square, the National Museum, cross the bridge to look round Malá Strana.

PRACTICAL INFORMATION

ARRIVAL-DEPARTURE

✈ Václav Havel Airport (20km west). The shuttle bus leaves every 30min. International trains stop at Hlavní nádraží.

GETTING AROUND

Trams and buses are frequent and run from early morning to past midnight; there's also a metro covering much of the city. All three are invariably cheap and a short-term (tourist) pass allows unlimited travel on bus, tram, metro and Petrin funicular. Be wary of taxis; although regulations specify rates, it's always best to use a designated rank and avoid flagging down a cab on the street.

CALENDAR HIGHLIGHTS

January
Winter Festival.

May
Spring Music Festival, World Roma Festival.

June
Dance Prague, Many visit Kafka's burial place.

September
Autumn Music Festival.

November
St Martin's Young Wine Celebrations

December
Celebrate Christmas and New Year with various events in the Old Town Square.

EATING OUT

Since the late 1980s, Prague has undergone a bit of a foodie revolution. Global menus have become common currency and the heavy, traditional Czech cuisine is now often served – in the better establishments – with a creative flair and an international touch. Lunch is the main meal of the Czech day and many restaurants close well before midnight. Prague was and still is, to an extent, famous for its infinite variety of dumplings – these were the glutinous staple that saw locals through the long years of stark Communist rule. The favoured local dish is still pork, pickled cabbage and dumplings, and those on a budget can also mix the likes of schnitzel, beer and ginger cake for a ridiculously cheap outlay. Some restaurants include a tip in your final bill, so check closely to make sure you don't tip twice. Czechs consume more beer than anyone else in the world and there are some excellent microbrewery tipples to be had.

CZECH REPUBLIC - PRAGUE

Four Seasons
Veleslavínova 1098/2A ✉ *110 00* – Ⓜ *Staroměstská*   Plan: **G2**
– ℰ *221 427 000* – *www.fourseasons.com/prague*
157 rm – 🛏7850/14100 CZK 🛏🛏7850/14100 CZK – ☕ 1000 CZK – 19 suites
• Grand Luxury • Modern •
This characterful riverside hotel has an understated elegance which sits well with its baroque and Renaissance features. Bedrooms are designed by Pierre-Yves Rochon; the best are duplex suites with river and castle views.

Boscolo Prague
Senovážné Nám. 13 ✉ *110 00* – Ⓜ *Námesti Republiky*   Plan: **H2**
– ℰ *224 593 111* – *www.boscolohotels.com*
152 rm ☕ – 🛏3800/7850 CZK 🛏🛏3950/10000 CZK – 2 suites
• Grand Luxury • Elegant •
This impressive former bank features neo-Renaissance style pillars, a stunning marble lobby and a smart Roman spa and pool. Each of the luxurious bedrooms is unique in shape and style; those in the older building are the most spacious. The elegant restaurant serves a mix of Czech and international dishes.

The Grand Mark
Hybernská 12 ✉ *110 00* – Ⓜ *Námesti Republiky*   Plan: **H2**
– ℰ *226 226 111* – *www.grandmark.cz*
75 rm – 🛏3500/50000 CZK 🛏🛏3500/50000 CZK – ☕ 690 CZK – 61 suites
• Historic • Grand luxury •
A striking 200 year old listed building with a glass-topped atrium, a baroque archway and lovely courtyard gardens. Pass the top-hatted doorman into the sleek, modern interior filled with contemporary art. Many of the bedrooms are suites with kitchenettes. The restaurant has a cool, elegant feel and a modern menu.

Radisson Blu Alcron
Štepánská 40 ✉ *110 00* – Ⓜ *Muzeum* – ℰ *222 820 000*   Plan: **H2**
– *www.radissonblu.com/en/hotel-prague*
204 rm ☕ – 🛏2400/11000 CZK 🛏🛏2400/11000 CZK – 12 suites
• Luxury • Business • Modern •
The art deco features of this imposing 1930s building are superb and its original white and green marble floor has been meticulously maintained. Bedrooms are warmly decorated and well-equipped. La Rotonde has a pleasant summer terrace and serves international and Czech cuisine; Alcron offers modern tasting dishes.
❀ **Alcron** – See restaurant listing

Le Palais
U Zvonarky 1 ✉ *120 00* – Ⓜ *I. P. Pavlova*   Plan: **H3**
– ℰ *234 634 111* – *www.lepalaishotel.eu*
72 rm ☕ – 🛏3180/6750 CZK 🛏🛏3915/8640 CZK – 8 suites
• Townhouse • Luxury • Elegant •
The stylish bedrooms of this 19C mansion come with luxurious pink marble bathrooms and the terrace of the classical dining room has a wonderful outlook. The hotel has one of the largest private collections of Le Corbusier lithographs, along with works by Czech artists Miloš Reindl and Pavel Skalnik.

Art Nouveau Palace
Panská 12 ✉ *111 21* – Ⓜ *Můstek* – ℰ *224 093 111*   Plan: **H2**
– *www.palacehotel.cz*
127 rm ☕ – 🛏2400/10000 CZK 🛏🛏2400/10000 CZK – 2 suites
• Historic • Classic • Elegant •
It's a fitting name: the Viennese art nouveau façade dates from its opening in 1909 and the interior is elegant, with smart wood panelling on display in the lobby and Carrara marble featuring in the bathrooms. Enjoy classic French dishes with a piano accompaniment in the intimate restaurant.

Imperial

Na Poříčí 15 ✉ *110 00 –* Ⓜ *Náměsti Republiky*
Plan: **H1**
– ℰ 246 011 665 – www.hotel-imperial.cz
126 rm ☲ *– ♦4005/10880 CZK ♦♦4005/10880 CZK – 1 suite*
• Business • Vintage • Historic •

The cubist-style façade dates from 1914 and the characterful interior features exquisite art deco mosaics (the building is a listed Czech National Monument). Dark wood furnished bedrooms combine retro styling with modern comforts.
Café Imperial – See restaurant listing

Paris

U Obecního domu 1 ✉ *110 00 –* Ⓜ *Náměsti Republiky*
Plan: **H1**
– ℰ 222 195 195 – www.hotel-paris.cz
86 rm ☲ *– ♦4050/10800 CZK ♦♦4050/10800 CZK – 3 suites*
• Traditional • Classic •

The bright corridors of this charming townhouse are hung with pieces from the owner's art collection and the characterful bedrooms come in soft hues; corner rooms have great city views and the duplex Tower Suite offers a fantastic 360° vista. Dine in the Parisian café or more formal art nouveau restaurant.

Kings Court

U Obecního domu 3 ✉ *110 00 –* Ⓜ *Náměsti Republiky*
Plan: **H1**
– ℰ 224 222 888 – www.hotelkingscourt.cz
137 rm ☲ *– ♦8150/13550 CZK ♦♦8150/13550 CZK – 5 suites*
• Business • Grand luxury • Modern •

This grand building near the Obecni Dum was formerly the Chamber of Commerce. Crystal chandeliers and marble feature in the lobby and the ballroom still has its original stained glass windows. Relax in the spa then head for dinner on the terrace, before retiring to one of the contemporary bedrooms.

Jalta

Václavské Nám. 45 ✉ *110 00 –* Ⓜ *Muzeum*
Plan: **H2**
– ℰ 222 822 111 – www.hoteljalta.com
94 rm ☲ *– ♦2700/9500 CZK ♦♦2700/9500 CZK – 5 suites*
• Business • Traditional • Grand luxury •

There's a real sense of history here, from the opal light fixtures and original doors leading out onto the balcony which overlooks Wenceslas Square, to the UNESCO listed façade and the nuclear bunker in the basement! The chic restaurant unusually blends Czech, Mediterranean and Japanese influences.

Century Old Town

Na Poříčí 7 ✉ *110 00 –* Ⓜ *Náměsti Republiky*
Plan: **H1**
– ℰ 606 548 583 – www.centuryoldtown.com
174 rm *– ♦2200/6580 CZK ♦♦2600/6580 CZK –* ☲ *352 CZK – 2 suites*
• Business • Historic •

Franz Kafka's spirit can be felt throughout this appealing business hotel, which was formerly the Workmen's Accident Insurance Institute HQ – Kafka's place of work from 1908 to 1922. Contemporary bedrooms have compact, shower-only bathrooms. Dine in the courtyard, from an international menu.

Emblem

Platnéřská 19 ✉ *110 00 –* Ⓜ *Staroměstská*
Plan: **G2**
– ℰ 226 202 500 – www.emblemprague.com
59 rm *– ♦4900/9500 CZK ♦♦5500/12200 CZK –* ☲ *500 CZK – 2 suites*
• Townhouse • Design • Contemporary •

It might be housed within a 1907 property but inside you'll find a stylish designer hotel with a private members club in the basement. Head to the lounge to check in, then up to one of the sleek, modern bedrooms with oak flooring and walnut desks. Specially commissioned abstract art hangs in the hallways.
George Prime Steak – See restaurant listing

Environs of Prague
(Plan I)

0 —— 1 km

A
B

1

Podbabská

Horoměřická

DEJVICE

U

BUBENEČ

Korunovacní

Heřákové

Evropská

Milady

nábrěží Edva

VOKOVICE

7

Evropská

STŘEŠOVICE

PRAŽSKÝ HRAD

Karmelit-ská

Křižovnická

KARLŮV MOST

BŘEVNOV

Patočkova

Masarykovo nábřeží

2

BŘEVNOVSKÝ KLÁŠTER

Újzd

Rašínovo nábřeží

Pod stadiony

Prague Centre
(Plan II)

I

Bělohorská

Radlická

Kukulova

MOTOL

SMÍCHOV

KOŠÍŘE

M

Radlická

Smíchovské nádraží

RUZYNĚ ✈

Radlická

M

Na Kopci

Kutvirtova

Jinonice

M

RADLICE

5

Bucharova

JINONICE

STODŮLKY

Nové Butovice

M

Radlická

Hůrka

M

3

Jeremiášova

HLUBOČEPY

4

● Hotel
● Restaurant

A
B

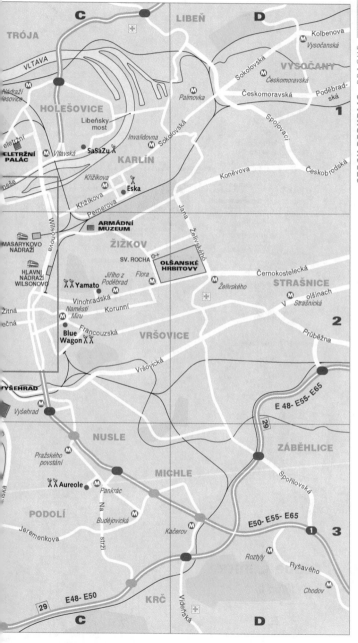

C
LIBEŇ
D

TRÓJA

Kolbenova
Vysočanská

VLTAVA

VYSOČANY

Sokolovská
Českomoravská

Nádraží
lesovice

Poděbrad-
ská

HOLEŠOVICE

Palmovka

Českomoravská

1

Libeňský
most

Spojovací

Českobrodská

eletržní

Invalidovna

Sokolovská

Vltavská

SaSaZu

Koněvova

ELETRŽNÍ
PALÁC

KARLÍN

nešą

Křižíkova

Eska

Křižíkova

Pernerova

Jarva

ARMÁDNÍ
MUZEUM

Wilsonova

ŽIŽKOV

Želivského

Konevova

MASARYKOVO
NÁDRAŽÍ

SV. ROCHA

OLŠANSKÉ
HRBITOVY

Černokostelecká

HLAVNÍ
NÁDRAŽÍ
WILSONOVO

Jiřího z
Poděbrad

Flora

Želivského

STRAŠNICE

olšinach

Žitná

Yamato

Vinohradská

Korunní

Strašnická

ečná

Náměstí
Míru

2

Blue
Wagon

Francouzská

VRŠOVICE

Průběžná

Vršovická

VYŠEHRAD

Vyšehrad

E 48- E55- E65

29

NUSLE

ZÁBĚHLICE

Pražského
povstání

Spořilovská

Aureole

MICHLE

Pankrác

PODOLÍ

Na
Budějovická

E50- E55- E65

1

3

Jeremenkova

strži

Kačerov

Roztyly

Ryšavého

E48- E50

Chodov

29

KRČ

Vídeňská

C

D

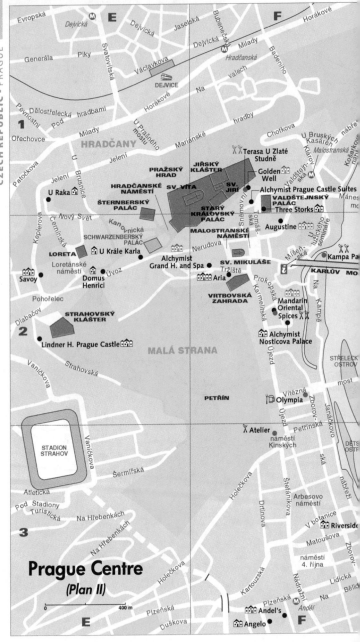

Prague Centre
(Plan II)

0   400 m

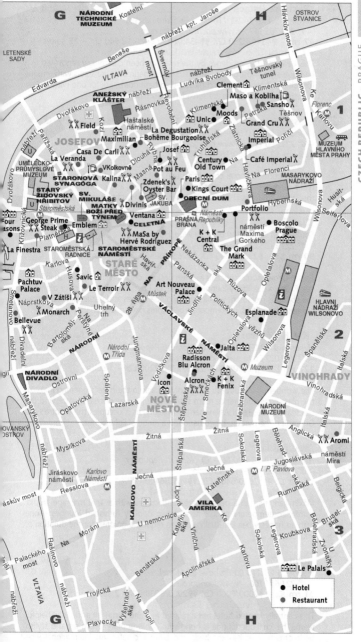

Map labels:

NÁRODNÍ TECHNICKÉ MUZEUM
OSTROV ŠTVANICE
LETENSKÉ SADY
Kostelní
nábřeží kpt. Jaroše
Hlávkův most
Edvarda
Beneše
VLTAVA
Švermův most
Havlodní
nábřeží Ludvíka Svobody
Těšnovský tunel
Wilsonova
Ke Karlovu
Florenc
ANEŽSKÝ KLÁŠTER
nábřeží
Rásnovka
Klimentská
Clement
Maso a Kobliha
Sansho
Klimentská
Petrská
Těšnov
MUZEUM HLAVNÍHO MĚSTA PRAHY
Dvořákovo
Kozí
Haštalské náměstí
Moods
Unic
Zlatnická
Grand Cru
Imperial
Poříčí
JOSEFOV
Field
La Degustation
Bohème Bourgeoise
Truhlářská
Imperial
Café Imperial
MASARYKOVO NÁDRAŽÍ
Maximilian
Josef
Na
Century Old Town
Na Poříčí
Na Florenci
Casa De Carli
Rybná
Dlouhá
Masná
Pot au Feu
Paris
Husitská
La Veranda
VKolkovně
Kalina
Zdenek's Oyster Bar
Kings Court
Na
Seifertova
UMĚLECKO-PRŮMYSLOVÉ MUZEUM
STARONOVÁ SYNAGÓGA
Hybernská
Dvořákovo
STARÝ ŽIDOVSKÝ HŘBITOV
SV. MIKULÁŠE
MATKY BOŽÍ PŘED TÝNEM
Divinis
SV. JAKUBA
OBECNÍ DŮM
Portfolio
Náměstí Republiky
Staroměstská
Ventana
CELETNÁ
Boscolo Prague
Four Seasons
George Prime Steak
Emblem
PRAŠNÁ BRÁNA
náměstí Maxima Gorkého
Křižovnická
Platnéřská
MaSa by Hervé Rodriguez
K + K Central
The Grand Mark
Opletalova
La Finestra
STAROMĚSTSKÁ RADNICE
STAROMĚSTSKÉ NÁMĚSTÍ
Nekázanka
Karlova
Havířská
PŘÍKOPĚ
STARÉ MĚSTO
Panská
Růžova
Husova
NA
Pachtuv Palace
Savic
Le Terroir
Art Nouveau Palace
Politických
HLAVNÍ NÁDRAŽÍ WILSONOVO
Náprstkova
V Zátiší
28. října
Můstek
Jindř.
vězňů
Esplanade
Smetanovo nábřeží
Monarch
Bartoloměj
Uhelný trh
VÁCLAVSKÉ
Bellevue
Divadelní nábřeží
NÁRODNÍ
Národní Třída
Jungmannova
Vodičkova
Štěpánská
NÁMĚSTÍ
Jalta
Opletalova
Wilsonova
Špaňelská
Halská
VINOHRADY
NÁRODNÍ DIVADLO
Ostrovní
Spálená
Lazarská
NOVÉ MĚSTO
Radisson Blu Alcron
Muzeum
Alcron
K + K Fenix
Vinohradská
Masarykovo nábřeží
Icon
Ve Smečkách
Mezibranská
NÁRODNÍ MUZEUM
Haiská
SLOVANSKÝ OSTROV
Myslíkova
Žitná
Žitná
Sokolská
Legerova
Bělehrad
Anglická
Aromi
náměstí Míra
Jiráskovo náměstí
Karlovo Náměstí
Ječná
I. P. Pavlova
Jugoslávská
ská
Resslova
KARLOVO NÁMĚSTÍ
Ječná
Katerinská
Rumunská
Belgická
Jiráskův most
Na Moráni
U nemocnice
VILA AMERIKA
Lipová
Viničná
Ke
Karlovu
Sokolská
Koubkova
Brusel-ská
Palackého most
Na
Rašínovo nábřeží
Benátská
Apolinářská
Bělehradská
Zvonařky
U Zvonařky
Le Palais
VLTAVA
Trojická
Vyšehrad-ská
Na Slupi
Plavecká

Legend:

● Hotel
● Restaurant

Pachtuv Palace

Karolíny Svetlé 34 ✉ *110 00 –* Ⓜ *Staroměstská*
– ☎ *234 705 111 – www.pachtuvpalace.com*
47 rm – 🛏4345/8250 CZK 🛏🛏4345/8250 CZK – 🍽 540 CZK – 28 suites
· Townhouse · Historic building · Elegant ·

This beautiful 18C residence by the river has been charmingly renovated in a baroque style. Most of the spacious, elegant bedrooms are suites with antique furnishings, kitchenettes and mosaic-tiled bathrooms; ask for one with a view. French and Czech dishes are served in the ornate restaurant.

Plan: **G2**

Josef

Rybná 20 ✉ *110 00 –* Ⓜ *Náměsti Republiky*
– ☎ *221 700 111 – www.hoteljosef.com*
109 rm 🍽 – 🛏3300/16500 CZK 🛏🛏3300/16500 CZK
· Townhouse · Design · Minimalist ·

Modern boutique hotel comprising two buildings linked by a delightful courtyard garden. Bedrooms are smart and design-led; ask for one with a view on the 7th or 8th floor. The in-house bakery means that breakfast is a real treat.

Plan: **G1**

Unic

Soukenická 25 ✉ *110 00 –* Ⓜ *Náměsti Republiky*
– ☎ *222 312 521 – www.hotel-unic.cz*
90 rm 🍽 – 🛏2325/6600 CZK 🛏🛏2600/6850 CZK – 8 suites
· Business · Contemporary · Grand luxury ·

This 19C townhouse conceals a stylish design hotel with subtle Spanish influences. Relax in the library-lounge or bright, laid-back bar, then head for dinner in the spacious restaurant with its mix of global dishes and traditional Czech specialities. Clean-lined, contemporary bedrooms have good facilities.

Plan: **H1**

K + K Central

Hybernská 10 ✉ *110 00 –* Ⓜ *Náměsti Republiky*
– ☎ *225 022 000 – www.kkhotels.com*
127 rm 🍽 – 🛏2700/7200 CZK 🛏🛏2700/7200 CZK – 1 suite
· Business · Modern · Historic ·

The wonderful art nouveau façade dates back to the hotel's opening in 1901; the glass cube conference room sits within what was once a theatre; and the spa features bas-relief Asian-themed imagery, as it occupies the theatre's old Orient Bar. The modern bistro-bar offers a range of light dishes.

Plan: **H2**

Maximilian

Haštalská 14 ✉ *110 00 –* Ⓜ *Náměsti Republiky*
– ☎ *225 303 111 – www.maximilianhotel.com*
71 rm 🍽 – 🛏2610/6400 CZK 🛏🛏2610/6400 CZK – 1 suite
· Business · Modern · Minimalist ·

Maximilian is set in a peaceful area and comes with a Thai massage studio, comfy, contemporary bedrooms and two brightly furnished lounges – one with an honesty bar. Unusually, you can request a goldfish for the duration of your stay!

Plan: **G1**

Icon

V Jámě 6 ✉ *110 00 Praha –* Ⓜ *Můstek*
– ☎ *221 634 100 – www.iconhotel.eu*
31 rm 🍽 – 🛏2000/6000 CZK 🛏🛏2000/8000 CZK – 2 suites
· Business · Modern · Design ·

This centrally located hotel has a relaxed feel and is run by a friendly, helpful team. The 'chill-out' lounge is hung with contemporary Czech art and stylish bedrooms feature Hästens beds and biometric safes. An international vibe comes courtesy of a tapas bar and a small Thai massage centre.

Plan: **G2**

CZECH REPUBLIC - PRAGUE

 Ventana AK ⇼

Celetná 7 (Entrance from 2 Stuparska Street) ⊠ *110 00*   Plan: **G2**
– Ⓜ Náměsti Republiky – ☏ 221 776 600 – www.ventana-hotel.net
29 rm ⊊ – 🛉4100/4800 CZK 🛉🛉5400/6000 CZK – 2 suites
• Traditional • Townhouse • Classic •

Once a residential house, Ventana is a hit with tourists, courtesy of its proximity to the Old Town Square and its spacious bedrooms. The loft rooms have separate lounge areas and the top suite has a balcony with Square views.

 K + K Fenix ☆ 🖪 🕅 Ꮽ 🕅 ⇼ 🗚 🚗

Ve Smeckách 30 ⊠ *110 00 – Ⓜ Muzeum*   Plan: **H2**
– ☏ 225 012 000 – www.kkhotels.com
128 rm ⊊ – 🛉2700/7200 CZK 🛉🛉2700/7200 CZK
• Business • Modern •

If you want to be close to the nightlife, this bright, business-focused hotel is the place to be. A classic façade masks a modern interior; be sure ask for one of the more recently refurbished bedrooms to the rear. Light, international dishes are offered in the modern bar-restaurant.

 Esplanade ☆ 🕅 ⇼ 🗚

Washingtonova 1600-19 ⊠ *110 00 – Ⓜ Muzeum*   Plan: **H2**
– ☏ 224 501 111 – www.esplanade.cz
68 rm ⊊ – 🛉2700/6200 CZK 🛉🛉3000/8100 CZK – 6 suites
• Traditional • Classic • Historic •

This charming, atmospheric hotel sits on a peaceful tree-lined street near Wenceslas Square and is something of an architectural gem. Original features abound, from the marble floor of the lobby and the wallpapers in the 'Historical Suites' to the Murano chandelier and stained glass cupola in the restaurant.

 Savic ☆ 🕅 ⇼

Jilská 7 ⊠ *110 00 – Ⓜ Staroměstská – ☏ 224 248 555*   Plan: **G2**
– www.savic.eu
27 rm ⊊ – 🛉2200/7000 CZK 🛉🛉2400/7800 CZK – 1 suite
• Historic • Romantic • Classic •

Just around the corner from the Astronomical Clock is this charming 14C monastery, which is surprisingly peaceful considering its setting. Glittering crystal lights are juxtaposed with exposed stone, beams and 15C frescoes. Start your day with breakfast in the conservatory and end it on the brasserie's terrace.

 Clement Ꮽ 🕅 ⇼ 🗚 🚗

Klimentská 30 ⊠ *110 00 – Ⓜ Náměsti Republiky*   Plan: **H1**
– ☏ 222 314 350 – www.hotelclement.cz
76 rm ⊊ – 🛉1900/5500 CZK 🛉🛉1900/5500 CZK
• Business • Traditional • Functional •

This former office building is close to the river and the city centre. Bedrooms are modern and functional; the Superior rooms with their bold red and black colour schemes are worth paying extra for – some also have panoramic windows.

Moods 🌐 Ꮽ 🕅 ⇼ 🗚

Klimentská 28 ⊠ *110 00 – Ⓜ Náměsti Republiky*   Plan: **H1**
– ☏ 222 330 100 – www.hotelmoods.com
51 rm ⊊ – 🛉2265/12750 CZK 🛉🛉2265/12750 CZK
• Business • Design •

This bright, boutique hotel makes interesting use of natural materials like bamboo and moss. The colourful bedrooms feature Hästens beds and Apple technology, and quotes from Peter Sis's 'The Three Golden Keys' feature throughout.

XxX **Alcron** – Radisson Blu Alcron Hotel   🎨 ⇵ 🅿
☸   *Štepánská 40* ⊠ *110 00* – ⓜ *Muzeum* – ℰ *222 820 000*   Plan: **H2**
      – www.alcron.cz – Closed Saturday lunch and Sunday
      Menu 900/2100 CZK – *(booking essential)*
      • Modern cuisine • Intimate • Vintage •
      An intimate, semi-circular restaurant dominated by an art deco mural of dan-
      cing Manhattan couples by Tamara de Lempicka. Choose 'hot' or 'cold' tasting
      dishes from an international menu; well-presented, creative, contemporary
      cooking uses top ingredients. There's a good choice of wines and staff are
      attentive.
      → Tuna sashimi with tapioca. Breast and leg of pigeon with sour cherries.
      Black sesame seed panna cotta with mandarin sorbet.

XX   **Field** (Radek Kašpárek)
☸   *U Milosrdných 12* ⊠ *110 00* – ⓜ *Staroměstská*   Plan: **G1**
      – ℰ 222 316 999 – www.fieldrestaurant.cz – Closed 24-26 December
      Menu 2600 CZK – Carte 940/1150 CZK
      • Modern cuisine • Intimate • Fashionable •
      Two friends run this chic restaurant, which has a warm, intimate feel. An eye-
      catching mural by artist Jakub Matuška is projected overhead and the Scandi-
      navian style cooking is equally contemporary. Alongside wine pairings they
      offer non-alcoholic drink matches such as tomato, cucumber and chilli juice.
      → Red mullet, Granny Smith apple, avocado and sea buckthorn. Quail with
      black salsify, oyster mushrooms and almonds. Apricot yoghurt, sorrel and
      cocoa beans.

XX   **La Degustation Bohême Bourgeoise** (Oldřich Sahajdák)
☸   *Haštalská 18* ⊠ *110 00* – ⓜ *Náměsti Republiky*   🍴 🎨 ⇵
      – ℰ 222 311 234 – www.ladegustation.cz – Closed   Plan: **G1**
      1 week January and 24 December
      Menu 2450/3350 CZK – *(dinner only)*
      • Modern cuisine • Intimate • Fashionable •
      This intimate L-shaped restaurant is hidden away in a historic building, down
      narrow lanes. Choose between two tasting menus: the 6 course option is inspi-
      red by the refined Czech cuisine of Marie B Svobodová's 19C cookery school.
      Cooking is precise, innovative and flavourful, and the service is charming.
      → Trout, cinnamon, apple and white cabbage. Ox heart, Prague ham and
      cucumber. Potatoes, poppy seeds and berries.

XX   **Bellevue**   ≼ 🌴 🎨 ⇵ ✧
      Smetanovo Nábreží 18 ⊠ *110 00* – ⓜ *Staroměstská*   Plan: **G2**
      – ℰ 222 221 443 – www.zatisigroup.cz – Closed 24 December
      Menu 1490 CZK
      • Modern cuisine • Chic • Classic décor •
      Sit on the pleasant terrace or in the contemporary, pastel-hued dining room of
      this elegant 19C townhouse and take in the view over Charles Bridge and the
      river. Ambitious, original modern dishes consist of many different elements.

XX   **Aureole**   ≼ 🌴 🎨 ⇵
☻   *Tower (27th floor), Hvězdova 1716/2b* ⊠ *140 00*   Plan I: **C3**
      – ⓜ Pankrác – ℰ 222 755 380 – www.aureole.cz – Closed 25-26 December
      Menu 490/1690 CZK – Carte 740/1900 CZK
      • International • Design • Trendy •
      Have a drink in the chic cocktail bar of this hip 27th floor restaurant before
      making for the moody red and black dining room or out onto the fantastic
      panoramic terrace. Refined, original modern cooking cleverly blends East and
      West; the degustation menu best showcases the kitchen's talent.

XX **Grand Cru** 🕸 🛱 & 🄰🄲 ⇧
Lodecká 4 ✉ *110 00* – ⓜ *Florenc* – ℰ *775 044 076*   Plan: **H1**
– *www.grand-cru.cz* – *Closed 24-26 December, 1 January and Sunday*
Menu 450/1300 CZK – Carte 1150/1230 CZK
• Modern cuisine • Fashionable • Elegant •
Choose from homemade pâtés, charcuterie and smokehouse cheeses in the charming wine bar with its Enomatic machine, or cross the cobbled courtyard to the elegant orangery-style room for attractive modern dishes with innovative touches.

XX **V Zátiši** 🄰🄲 ⇜
Liliová 1, Betlémské Nám. ✉ *130 00* – ⓜ *Můstek*   Plan: **G2**
– ℰ *222 221 155* – *www.zatisi.cz*
– *Closed 24 December*
Menu 1190 CZK – Carte 1185/1275 CZK – *(booking essential at dinner)*
• Modern cuisine • Cosy • Elegant •
This modern city centre restaurant is a popular spot. Its name means 'timeless' and with its clever blend of modern Czech and Indian dishes, well-judged spicing and attractive presentation, it looks set to stand up to its name.

XX **MaSa by Hervé Rodriguez** 🛱 🄰🄲
Ovocný trh 12 ✉ *110 00* – ⓜ *Náměsti Republiky*   Plan: **G2**
– ℰ *225 092 900* – *www.masa-prague.cz* – *Closed Sunday*
Menu 395 CZK (weekday lunch)/1200 CZK
• Modern cuisine • Fashionable • Contemporary décor •
A trendy, boldly decorated restaurant on a cobbled street in the Old Town. Simple, good value daily lunches are followed at dinner by 6 and 10 course tasting menus of creative, eye-catching modern dishes. It's run by a friendly team.

XX **Le Terroir** 🕸 🛱 🄰🄲 ⇜
Vejvodova 1 (Entrance from Jilskà Street) ✉ *110 00*   Plan: **G2**
– ⓜ *Můstek* – ℰ *222 220 260* – *www.leterroir.cz* – *Closed Sunday and Monday*
Menu 1390/1890 CZK – *(dinner only)*
• Czech • Rustic • Elegant •
A professionally run, wonderfully atmospheric 12C cellar restaurant with a vaulted ceiling. Create your own 4, 6 or 8 course menu; the classically based Czech cooking has modern touches, while the superb wine list focuses on France.

XX **George Prime Steak** – Emblem Hotel 🕸 & 🄰🄲 ⇧
Platnéřská 19 ✉ *110 00* – ⓜ *Staroměstská*   Plan: **G2**
– ℰ *226 202 599* – *www.georgeprimesteak.com*
Menu 490 CZK (weekday lunch) – Carte 1365/3365 CZK
• Meats and grills • Fashionable •
The dining room of the Emblem hotel is an authentic-feeling American steakhouse decorated in black and grey. The USDA Prime steak comes from the Midwest and is best washed down with something from the impressive Californian wine list.

XX **Casa De Carli** 🛱 🄰🄲 ⇜ ⇧
Vezenskská 5 ✉ *110 00* – ⓜ *Staromestská*   Plan: **G1**
– ℰ *224 816 688* – *www.casadecarli.com* – *Closed Sunday*
Menu 1250 CZK – Carte 485/1145 CZK
• Italian • Friendly • Neighbourhood •
A contemporary, family-run restaurant with bold artwork and tables on the cobbled street. Flavoursome cooking has a subtle Northern Italian bias; the breads, pastas and ice creams are all homemade – go for one of the daily specials.

121

CZECH REPUBLIC - PRAGUE

XX **Pot au Feu** 🔏 ⇔

Rybná 13 ✉ *110 00 –* Ⓜ *Náměsti Republiky* Plan: **G1**
– ℰ 739 654 884 – www.potaufeu.cz – Closed Christmas, Easter, Saturday lunch and Sunday
Menu 495/695 CZK – Carte 615/1235 CZK *– (bookings advisable at dinner)*
• French • Intimate •

The chef-owner's travels inform his cooking – which is inspired largely by the French classics. The intimate interior comes with striking artwork and shelves packed with French wines (sourced directly). Service is relaxed yet clued-up.

XX **Kalina** 🔏 ⇔

Dlouhá 12 ✉ *110 00 –* Ⓜ *Staromestská* Plan: **G1**
– ℰ 222 317 715 – www.kalinarestaurant.cz – Closed 24 December dinner and 25 December
Menu 440/510 CZK – Carte 980/2070 CZK
• Modern cuisine • Intimate •

The eponymous chef-owner's cooking is gutsy yet refined and blends both modern and classic Czech and French influences. The atmospheric interior comprises two 16C rooms; ask for the one to the front, as that's where the action is.

XX **Aromi** 🌿 🍽 🔏 ⇔ 📶

Námestí Míru 6 ✉ *120 00 –* Ⓜ *Náměstí Míru* Plan: **H3**
– ℰ 222 713 222 – www.aromi.cz
Menu 345 CZK (weekday lunch) – Carte 820/1205 CZK
• Italian • Brasserie • Neighbourhood •

A friendly team welcome you to this bright modern restaurant. Simply prepared, classically based Italian dishes are given modern touches; the fresh fish display demonstrates the owners' commitment to sourcing good quality produce.

XX **Portfolio** 🌿 🔏 ⇔ ⇔

Lannŭv Palác, Havlíčkova 1030/1 ✉ *110 00* Plan: **H1**
– Ⓜ *Náměstí Republiky – ℰ 224 267 579 – www.portfolio-restaurant.cz*
– Closed Sunday
Carte 333/1030 CZK
• Modern cuisine • Contemporary décor • Design •

A smart, design-led restaurant set over two floors of an old office building. Unfussy modern dishes have their origins in classical French and Italian cooking and there's an interesting, mainly Old World wine list. Service is smooth.

XX **Blue Wagon** 🍽 🔏 ⇔

Uruguayská 19 ✉ *120 00 –* Ⓜ *Náměstí Míru* Plan I: **C2**
– ℰ 222 561 378 – www.bluewagon.cz – Closed Christmas, Easter, Sunday July-August
Menu 179/970 CZK – Carte 590/970 CZK
• Modern cuisine • Friendly • Elegant •

A very warmly run restaurant with a sleek modern style. The cooking is a blend of classic Czech and Mediterranean influences and comes with a refreshing simplicity. Breads and ice creams are homemade and the wine list is strong in claret.

XX **La Veranda** 🔏 ⇔

Elišky Krásnohorské 2 ✉ *110 00 –* Ⓜ *Staromĕstská* Plan: **G1**
– ℰ 224 814 733 – www.laveranda.cz – Closed 24 December and Sunday
Carte 495/1045 CZK
• Mediterranean cuisine • Cosy • Friendly •

Sit amongst books and bric-a-brac in the colourfully decorated main room or head down to the intimate modern basement. Cooking takes its inspiration from the Med, with Italy playing a big part. Staff are friendly and welcoming.

CZECH REPUBLIC - PRAGUE

XX **Yamato**

U Kanálky 14 ⊠ 120 00 – Ⓜ Jiřiho z Poděbrad   Plan I: **C2**
*– ℰ 222 212 617 – www.yamato.cz – Closed Christmas, Saturday lunch
and Sunday*
Menu 320/1290 CZK – Carte 375/3645 CZK
• Japanese • Elegant • Friendly •

The chef might be a local but he trained in Japan and the room has an authentic Japanese feel. The menus focus on sushi, with beer-marinated tuna a signature dish. A selection of Japanese beers and whiskies complement the cooking.

X **Eska**   🛋 🅰🅲 ⇼ 🎍

😊 *Pernerova 49, Karlín ⊠ 186 00 – Ⓜ Křižíkova*   Plan I: **C1**
– ℰ 731 140 884 – www.eska.ambi.cz – Closed 24 December
Menu 530/550 CZK – Carte 478/741 CZK
• Czech • Design • Fashionable •

A café, bakery and restaurant in a converted fabric factory. The dining room has a stark, industrial feel with exposed bricks, pipework and girders, and the open kitchen adds to the buzz. Old family favourites are given modern makeovers; much use is made of traditional techniques like marinating and fermenting.

X **Divinis**   🅰🅲 ⇼

😊 *Týnská 21 ⊠ 110 00 – Ⓜ Náměsti Republiky*   Plan: **G1**
*– ℰ 222 325 440 – www.divinis.cz – Closed 1-14 August, 24-26 December
and Sunday*
Carte 655/1145 CZK – *(dinner only) (booking essential)*
• Italian • Friendly •

You'll find this intimate, homely restaurant tucked away on a side street; it's run with great passion and has a friendly feel. Rustic, seasonal Italian dishes have original touches and are cooked with flair. The perfect accompaniment comes in the form of a large collection of wines from Italian growers.

X **Sansho**   🛋 🅰🅲

😊 *Petrská 25 ⊠ 110 00 – Ⓜ Florenc – ℰ 222 317 425*   Plan: **H1**
*– www.sansho.cz – Closed Christmas, Saturday lunch, Sunday and
Monday*
Menu 1000 CZK (dinner) – Carte 430/610 CZK – *(booking essential at dinner)*
• Asian • Friendly • Simple •

A homely restaurant set in a small square, with simple styling and a house party type atmosphere. The owner once kept a butcher's shop, so you'll find rare breeds hung for long periods and top class husbandry. Asian cooking has an emphasis on the south-east and dinner offers a set, family-style sharing menu.

X **Zdenek's Oyster Bar**   🛋 🅰🅲

Malá Štupartská 5 ⊠ 110 00 – Ⓜ Náměsti Republiky   Plan: **G1**
– ℰ 725 946 250 – www.oysterbar.cz – Closed 24-25 December
Carte 1185/1985 CZK
• Seafood • Bistro • Wine bar •

Deep in the heart of the city is this romantic, dimly lit restaurant with a pretty pavement terrace. Menus include tapas, caviar, elaborate seafood platters, dishes from the Josper grill and, of course, 8 different types of oyster.

X **La Finestra**   🕸 🅰🅲 ⇔

Platnérská 13 ⊠ 110 00 – Ⓜ Staroměstská   Plan: **G2**
– ℰ 222 325 325 – www.lafinestra.cz
Menu 425 CZK (weekday lunch) – Carte 815/1195 CZK – *(booking essential)*
• Italian • Rustic • Cosy •

You'd never guess but from 1918-1945, this lovely restaurant – with its red-brick vaulted ceiling – was an Alfa Romeo showroom! Expect rustic Italian dishes and fine Italian wines, and be sure to stop-off at their neighbouring shop.

X **Monarch**   🛱 🔣 ✿

Na Perštýně 15 ⊠ 110 00 – ⓜ Můstek – ℰ 224 239 602   Plan: **G2**
– www.monarch.cz – Closed 24-26 December, 1 January and Sunday
Carte 283/603 CZK
• Spanish • Fashionable • Tapas bar •

This sister to Grand Cru brings authentic Spanish tapas to the city. It's boldly
decorated in red and black, with two illuminated bulls' heads and well-stocked
shelves of wine. Gins and cocktails feature, along with live guitar on Weds.

X **Café Imperial** – Hotel Imperial   🔣 4 ⌂

Na Poříčí 15 ⊠ 110 00 – ⓜ Náměstí Republiky   Plan: **H1**
– ℰ 246 011 440 – www.cafeimperial.cz
Menu 750 CZK – Carte 500/850 CZK – (booking essential)
• International • Brasserie • Vintage •

The Imperial hotel's restaurant is an impressive room, with a high ceiling and
colourful mosaic-tiled walls and pillars. Global menus follow the seasons. It was
the place to be seen in the 1920s and, as they say, Kafka's spirit lives on...

🍴 **Maso A Kobliha**   🛱

🍺 *Petrská 23 ⊠ 110 00 – ⓜ Florenc – ℰ 224 815 056*   Plan: **H1**
*– www.masoakobliha.cz – Closed Christmas, Monday, Saturday and
Sunday dinner*
Carte 305/475 CZK
• Traditional cuisine • Neighbourhood • Pub •

Behind the butcher's counter of "Meat and Doughnuts" is a bright, fashionable
bar. Try a local beer from the 'kegerator' alongside a gutsy, classical dish smoked
on-site; the scotch eggs and custard-filled doughnuts are must-tries. Stop off at
the counter on your way out to buy some fresh free range meat.

🍴 **VKolkovně**   🛱 4

V Kolkovně 8 ⊠ 110 00 – ⓜ Staroměstská   Plan: **G1**
– ℰ 224 819 701 – www.vkolkovne.cz
Carte 385/940 CZK
• Traditional cuisine • Traditional décor • Pub •

An authentic pub with a pavement terrace, a copper bar and a lively atmosphere. Traditional Czech cooking comes in generous portions – the goulash
and the smoked sausages are favourites; try them with a Velkopopovický Koze
(dark beer).

ON THE LEFT BANK   **PLAN II**

🏨 **Mandarin Oriental**   🖧 🕼 ⊛ ₺ 🔣 4 � ⌂

Nebovidská 459/1 ⊠ 118 00 – ⓜ Malostranská   Plan: **F2**
– ℰ 233 088 888 – www.mandarinoriental.com/prague
99 rm ⌂ – †6700/20500 CZK ††6700/20500 CZK – 20 suites
• Grand Luxury • Historic • Design •

A former monastery dating from the 14C provides the charming setting for this
luxurious hotel. Chic, tastefully decorated bedrooms have goose down bedding
and an Asian feel courtesy of silk bedspreads and potted orchids. Relax on the
terraces or in the delightful spa which occupies the old chapel.
Spices – See restaurant listing

🏨 **Augustine**   ☆ 🖧 🕼 ⊛ 🍸 ₺ 🔣 4 🔩 **P**

Letenská 12/33 ⊠ 118 00 – ⓜ Malostranská   Plan: **F2**
– ℰ 266 112 233 – www.augustinehotel.com
101 rm ⌂ – †7700/12000 CZK ††8500/13000 CZK – 11 suites
• Historic • Design •

An impressive hotel set over 7 different buildings, including the 13C monastery
after which it is named. Original frescoes and vaulted ceilings remain, yet it has
a contemporary look and feel; the spa is fittingly luxurious. The bar occupies the
old refectory and serves a custom microbrew based on the monks' original
recipe. The chic restaurant serves a modern menu.

CZECH REPUBLIC - PRAGUE

Aria ✿ ⌂ 🅟 ⑂ ⒜ ⇄ ♨ 🛥

Tržiště 9 ⊠ 118 00 – ⓜ Malostranská – ℰ 225 334 111   Plan: F2
– www.ariahotel.net

51 rm ⌁ – ♦6350/10350 CZK ♦♦6350/10350 CZK – 6 suites
• Luxury • Design • Themed •

A musical motif features throughout, from the mosaic music notes in the lobby and the collection of 5,000 CDs and DVDs in the music room, to the bedrooms, which are themed around composers or styles of music. The restaurant boasts a superb rooftop terrace with castle views and the piano is played nightly.

Alchymist Grand H. and Spa ✿ ⌂ ⊕ 🅟 ⬚ ⒜ ⇄ ♨

Tržiště 19 ⊠ 118 00 – ⓜ Malostranská – ℰ 257 286 011   Plan: F2
– www.alchymistgroup.com

45 rm ⌁ – ♦5100/15000 CZK ♦♦5100/15000 CZK – 5 suites
• Luxury • Historic • Personalised •

The Alchymist is a magnificent baroque townhouse characterised by sumptuous gilt furnishings and over-the-top styling. Bedrooms come in rich reds or blues, picked out with gold. Cross the bridge over the koi carp pond to access the atmospheric Indonesian spa with its Turkish bath and mosaic-tiled pool; then enjoy modern international dishes on the restaurant's terrace.

Lindner H. Prague Castle ✿ ⚘ ⌂ 🅟 ⬚ ⒜ ⇄ ♨ 🛥

Strahovská 128 ⊠ 118 00 – ℰ 226 080 000   Plan: E2
– www.lindnerhotels.cz

138 rm – ♦1865/4595 CZK ♦♦1865/4595 CZK – ⌁ 485 CZK – 3 suites
• Business • Historic • Elegant •

This modern hotel is set within the UNESCO protected grounds of the Strahov Monastery and its spacious lobby-lounge was once the stables. Bedrooms feature art deco paintings; those located in the 16C part have characterful timbered ceilings. Summer BBQs use seasonings made from herbs grown in the grounds.

Andel's ✿ ⌂ 🅟 ⬚ ⒜ ⇄ ♨ 🛥

Stroupežnického 21 ⊠ 150 00 – ⓜ Anděl   Plan: F3
– ℰ 296 882 300 – www.viennahouse.com/en/andels-prague – Closed 7 July

290 rm ⌁ – ♦2240/3360 CZK ♦♦2660/3780 CZK – 31 suites
• Business • Modern • Minimalist •

A stylish business hotel close to the Nový Smíchov shopping centre. Its white marble lobby is punctuated by black leather furnishings; the modern, minimalist bedrooms are warmly furnished and the suites with kitchenettes are ideal for longer stays. Dine from an international menu in the small brasserie.

Savoy ✿ ⌂ 🅟 ⬚ ⒜ ⇄ ♨ 🛥

Keplerova 6 ⊠ 118 00 – ℰ 224 302 430   Plan: E2
– www.hotelsavoyprague.com

56 rm ⌁ – ♦4900/5550 CZK ♦♦4900/6250 CZK – 2 suites
• Luxury • Traditional • Elegant •

An imposing period property with professional service and a distinctly British feel, located at the top of the hill. The marble lobby leads to a clubby tartan bar and an elegant restaurant with a retractable roof and an international menu. Bedrooms are warmly decorated; each floor has a different colour scheme.

Golden Well ⚘ ≤ ⒜ ⇄

U Zlaté Studně 166/4 ⊠ 118 00 – ⓜ Malostranská   Plan: F1
– ℰ 257 011 213 – www.goldenwell.cz – Closed 1 week in January

19 rm – ♦5350/8250 CZK ♦♦5350/8250 CZK – ⌁ 550 CZK – 2 suites
• Historic • Townhouse • Elegant •

A charming, intimate hotel, tucked away in a quiet cobbled street close to the Royal Gardens and Charles Bridge. Understated bedrooms have a classical style and come with antique furnishings, modern touches and fresh fruit. The roof terrace offers outstanding views over the castle and city.
Terasa U Zlaté Studně – See restaurant listing

CZECH REPUBLIC - PRAGUE

Alchymist Nosticova Palace

Nosticova 1, Malá Strana ✉ *118 00* – ⓜ *Malostranská*   Plan: **F2**
– ☎ *257 312 513* – *www.nosticova.com*
19 rm ⌧ – ☥3800/7000 CZK ☥☥3800/7000 CZK – 3 suites
• Townhouse • Classic • Personalised •

An intimate 17C residence which is inspired by the period of Emperor Rudolf II. The opulently decorated interior features antiques and Louis XIV style furniture; the Imperial Suite is nestled amongst the beams and even boasts a piano!

Riverside

Janáckovo Nábreži 15 ✉ *150 00* – ⓜ *Anděl*   Plan: **F3**
– ☎ *225 994 611* – *www.mamaison.com*
80 rm ⌧ – ☥2700/3000 CZK ☥☥3750/4000 CZK – 3 suites
• Business • Townhouse • Modern •

A charming riverside townhouse with a cosy bar and a mix of modern and traditional bedrooms – the latter feature mosaic-tiled bathrooms. Those at the front have the view; the most peaceful are to the rear, overlooking the courtyard.

Three Storks

Valdstejnske Nám 8 ✉ *118 00* – ⓜ *Malostranská*   Plan: **F1**
– ☎ *257 210 779* – *www.hotelthreestorks.cz*
21 rm ⌧ – ☥2750/8250 CZK ☥☥3300/11000 CZK
• Townhouse • Modern • Minimalist •

It might have a 19C façade but the Three Storks actually dates from the 17C. Take the glass lift up from the pebble-effect lobby to the contemporary bedrooms; many have original features, including vaulted ceilings and exposed beams. The bright restaurant offers a mix of Czech and international dishes.

Angelo

Radlická 1g ✉ *150 00* – ⓜ *Anděl* – ☎ *234 801 111*   Plan: **F3**
– *www.viennahouse.com*
168 rm ⌧ – ☥1900/5000 CZK ☥☥2300/5400 CZK
• Business • Modern •

Younger sister to Andel's, the Angelo is a chic hotel with a bold red, yellow and black colour scheme running throughout. Bedrooms are spread over 7 floors and have spacious bathrooms with underfloor heating. The lobby-lounge has a jazz motif and the bright restaurant and terrace offer a global menu.

Alchymist Prague Castle Suites

Sněmovní 8 ✉ *118 00* – ⓜ *Malostranká*   Plan: **F1**
– ☎ *257 286 960* – *www.alchymistpraguecastle.com*
8 rm ⌧ – ☥5700/14050 CZK ☥☥5700/14050 CZK
• Townhouse • Personalised • Grand luxury •

A delightfully restored 15C house in a quiet square beneath the castle; its former owners include the painter Brandl and architect Fanta. Its lavish decoration takes in chandeliers, gilt furnishings and hand-painted wallpapers. All 8 bedrooms have butler service and dinner can be taken at the Alchymist Grand.

U Krále Karla

Nerudova-Úvoz 4 ✉ *118 00* – ☎ *257 531 211*   Plan: **E2**
– *www.hotelukralekarla.cz*
19 rm ⌧ – ☥1500/8000 CZK ☥☥1600/9200 CZK
• Historic • Classic • Cosy •

Close to the castle is this Gothic-style townhouse, which was once home to a Benedictine order. Antique-furnished bedrooms are reached via an impressive stone staircase; many feature ornately painted ceilings and stained glass windows.

U Raka ⌂   🐕 𝔸𝕂 ↯ 𝐏

Cernínská 10 ✉ *118 00 –* ☎ *220 511 100*   Plan: **E1**
– www.hoteluraka.cz
6 rm ⌂ *–* ♦2600/3000 CZK ♦♦3650/4450 CZK
• Family • Cosy • Traditional •

You enter through this peaceful hotel's charming cobbled terrace – which is a great spot for summer breakfasts. Rustic bedrooms feature exposed stone, tile and wood, and are decorated with old millstones; one even has its own well!

Domus Henrici ⌂   ↯

Loretánská 11 ✉ *118 00 –* ☎ *220 511 369*   Plan: **E2**
– www.hidden-places.com
8 rm ⌂ *–* ♦1800/3200 CZK ♦♦2700/4000 CZK
• Townhouse • Minimalist •

A privately run townhouse dating back to 1372, perched on a hill in a tranquil location close to the castle. Bedrooms are furnished with art deco pieces and are accessed via the rear terrace, which looks out towards Petřín Hill.

Terasa U Zlaté Studně XX – Golden Well Hotel   ← 🕍 𝔸𝕂 ↯

U Zlaté Studně 166/4 ✉ *118 00 –* Ⓜ *Malostranská*   Plan: **F1**
– ☎ *257 533 322 – www.terasauzlatestudne.cz*
Menu 890 CZK (lunch) – Carte 950/5010 CZK *– (booking essential)*
• Classic cuisine • Cosy • Elegant •

This long-standing restaurant opened in 1901 and, in fact, predates the hotel it sits atop. The intimate room has blue and gold walls and a picture window, while above is a heated terrace with a stunning panoramic view. The classic international menu displays influences ranging from the Med through to Asia.

Kampa Park XX   ← 🕍 𝔸𝕂 ↯

Na Kampe 8b, Malá Strana ✉ *118 00*   Plan: **F2**
– Ⓜ *Malostranská –* ☎ *257 532 685 – www.kampagroup.com – Closed lunch 24-26 December and 1 January*
Menu 785/1950 CZK – Carte 1135/1285 CZK *– (booking essential at dinner)*
• International • Fashionable • Design •

Kampa Park is stunningly located by the water's edge, next to Charles Bridge. Choose from several dining areas: the best spots are the Winter Garden and the riverside terrace. The décor is contemporary, as is the global menu.

Spices XX – Mandarin Oriental Hotel   🕍 𝔸𝕂

Nebovidská 459/1 ✉ *118 00 –* Ⓜ *Malostranská*   Plan: **F2**
– ☎ *233 088 777 – www.mandarinoriental.com/prague*
Carte 795/1465 CZK *– (dinner only)*
• Asian • Intimate • Fashionable •

Softly backlit dark wood panels and decorative Chinoiserie items set the tone in this chic hotel restaurant. The pan-Asian menu is divided into three regions – Northeast, Southeast and Southwest – and there's a separate sushi list too.

SaSaZu X   𝔸𝕂 𝐏

Bubenské nábr. 306 ✉ *170 04 –* Ⓜ *Vltavská*   Plan I: **C1**
– ☎ *284 097 455 – www.sasazu.com – Closed 24-25 December and lunch 1 January*
Menu 600/1250 CZK – Carte 615/960 CZK
• Asian • Exotic décor • Fashionable •

You'll find this chic restaurant and bar within Prague Market. It's a cavernous place with low-level mood lighting and an open kitchen where you can watch the chefs at work. Innovative, flavoursome Southeast Asian dishes are the focus. You can also have a Thai back or hand massage at your table!

CZECH REPUBLIC - PRAGUE

Na Kopci ⌖ 🅰️ ⩋ 🅿️

K Závěrce 2774/20 ✉ *150 00 –* Ⓜ *Smíchovské Nádraží*   Plan I: **B3**
– ℰ 251 553 102 – www.nakopci.com – Closed Christmas
Menu 700 CZK (dinner) – Carte 535/805 CZK – *(booking essential at din-*
ner)
• Traditional cuisine • Bistro • Simple •
Leave the city behind and escape to this busy, buzzy bistro, whose name means
'on the hill'. Expect a warm welcome, an unpretentious atmosphere and great
value, flavoursome Czech classics – along with a few French dishes too. Be sure
to try the local unfiltered beer, which is made just 3km away.

Atelier 🎴 ⌖ 🅰️ ⟷

Rošických 4 ✉ *150 00 –* Ⓜ *Anděl – ℰ 257 218 277*   Plan: **F3**
– www.atelieratelier.cz – Closed Sunday and Monday lunch
Menu 190 CZK (weekday lunch) – Carte 490/770 CZK
• Modern cuisine • Wine bar • Friendly •
This bright, keenly run bistro-cum-wine bar is hidden away off the beaten track.
Wines play a key role – with over 130 on offer – and the unfussy, fiercely seaso-
nal cooking comes with clearly defined flavours and modern twists.

Olympia ⌖ 🅰️ ⩋

Vítezná 7 ✉ *110 00 –* Ⓜ *Národni Třída*   Plan: **F2**
– ℰ 251 511 080 – www.kolkovna.cz
Menu 138 CZK (weekday lunch)/252 CZK – Carte 294/787 CZK
• Traditional cuisine • Vintage • Pub •
This converted bank is now a lively, friendly pub-cum-brasserie. The bar offers a
good range of local beers and the wood-panelled dining room behind is char-
ming. Go for the home-smoked sausages or one of the tasty Czech dishes.

DENMARK
DANMARK

Aarhus

COPENHAGEN

→ **AREA:**
43 069 km² (16 629 sq mi) excluding the Faroe Islands and Greenland.

→ **POPULATION:**
5 745 526 inhabitants. Density = 133 per km².

→ **CAPITAL:**
Copenhagen.

→ **CURRENCY:**
Danish Krone (DKK).

→ **GOVERNMENT:**
Constitutional parliamentary (single chamber) monarchy (since 1849). Member of European Union since 1973.

→ **LANGUAGES:**
Danish; many Danes also understand and speak English.

→ **PUBLIC HOLIDAYS:**
New Year's Day (1 Jan); Maundy Thursday (late Mar/Apr); Good Friday (late Mar/Apr); Easter Monday (late Mar/Apr); Prayer Day (late Apr/May); Ascension Day (May); Whit Monday (late May/June); Constitution Day (5 June); Christmas Eve (24 Dec – Half Day); Christmas Day (25 Dec); 2nd Day of Christmas (26 Dec).

→ **LOCAL TIME:**
GMT + 1 hour in winter and GMT + 2 hours in summer.

→ **CLIMATE:**
Temperate northern maritime with cold winters and mild summers (Copenhagen: January 1°C, July 18°C).

→ **EMERGENCY:**
Police, Medical Assistance and Fire Brigade ☏ 112.

→ **ELECTRICITY:**
230 volts AC, 50Hz; 2 round pin sockets.

→ **FORMALITIES:**
Travellers from the European Union (EU), Switzerland, Norway, Iceland and the main countries of North and South America need a national identity card or passport (America: passport required) to visit Denmark for less than three months (tourism or business purpose). For visitors from other countries a visa may be required, in addition to a passport, especially for those wishing to stay for longer than three months. If you plan to visit Greenland or Faroe Islands while in Denmark, you must purchase a visa in advance in your own country. We advise you to check with your embassy before travelling.

COPENHAGEN
KØBENHAVN

Population: 590 563

HaPu99/Fotolia.com

Some cities overwhelm you, and give the impression that there's too much of them to take in. Not Copenhagen. Most of its key sights are neatly compressed within its central Slotsholmen 'island', an area that enjoyed its first golden age in the early seventeenth century in the reign of Christian IV, when it became a harbour of great consequence. It has canals on three sides and opposite the harbour is the area of Christianshavn, home of the legendary freewheeling 'free-town' community of Christiania. Further up from the centre are Nyhavn, the much-photographed canalside with brightly coloured buildings where the sightseeing cruises leave from, and the elegant Frederiksstaden, whose wide streets contain palaces and museums. West of the centre is where Copenhageners love to hang out: the Tivoli Gardens, a kind of magical fairyland. Slightly more down-to-earth are the western suburbs of Vesterbro and Nørrebro, which were run-down areas given a street credible spit and polish for the 21C, and are now two of the trendiest districts.

Once you've idled away some time in the Danish capital, you'll wonder why anyone might ever want to leave. With its waterfronts, quirky shops and cafés, the city presents a modern, user-friendly ambience – but it also boasts world class art collections, museums, and impressive parks, gardens and lakes, all of which bear the mark of an earlier time.

COPENHAGEN IN...

→ **ONE DAY**
Walk along Strøget, National Museum, Ny Carlsberg Glyptotek, Black Diamond, boat watching at Nyhavn.

→ **TWO DAYS**
Tivoli Gardens, Vesterbro, Opera House, Christiania.

→ **THREE DAYS**
Royal palaces at Frederiksstaden, train ride along the coast.

PRACTICAL INFORMATION

ARRIVAL-DEPARTURE

✈ Copenhagen Airport is located in Kastrup, 9km southeast of the city. The metro will take you to the centre in 15min. A taxi will take 25min.

GETTING AROUND

The metro is a triumph of sleek, smooth efficiency which runs 24 hours a day. If you want to see as much of the city as possible, get a Copenhagen Card, which gives free entry to all museums and galleries, as well as free bus, train and metro travel. They can be purchased from the main tourist office just across the road from the central railway station. Hiring a bicycle is a good way to see the city; it takes about two hours to circumnavigate the major attractions. It's also possible to see the city by kayak. Kajak Ole can get you paddling round the central harbour area for a very different perspective.

CALENDAR HIGHLIGHTS

February
Fashion Festival.

April
Queen Margrethe's birthday.

May
May Day Festival, Copenhagen Beer Festival, Copenhagen Carnival, Copenhagen Marathon.

June
Sankt Hans Eve Festival, Roskilde Music Festival.

July
Jazz Festival.

August
Ballet Festival, Historic Grand Prix, Cooking Festival.

November/December
Tivoli's Special Christmas Market.

EATING OUT

Fresh regional ingredients have revolutionized the menus of Copenhagen's hip restaurants and its reputation for food just keeps getting bigger. The city's dining establishments manage to marry Danish dining traditions such as herring or frikkadeller meatballs with global influences to impressive effect. So impressive that in recent times the city has earned itself more Michelin stars, for its crisp and precise cooking, than any other in Scandinavia. Many good restaurants blend French methods and dishes with regional ingredients and innovative touches and there is a trend towards fixed price, no choice menus involving several courses, which means that dinner can be a pleasingly drawn-out affair, stretching over three or four hours. There's no need to tip, as it should be included in the cost of the meal. Danes, though, have a very good reputation as cheerful, helpful waiting staff, so you might feel like adding a bit extra. But be warned, many restaurants – and even hotels – charge between 2.5% and 5% for using a foreign credit card.

DENMARK - COPENHAGEN

D'Angleterre
Kongens Nytorv 34 ⊠ 1050 K – Ⓜ *Kongens Nytorv* Plan: **C2**
– 𝒞 33 12 00 95 – www.dangleterre.com
90 rm – 🛏2750/3500 DKK 🛏🛏5000/6500 DKK
– ⊊ 285 DKK – 30 suites
• Luxury • Historic • Contemporary •
Smartly refurbished landmark hotel dating back over 250 years. Well-equipped bedrooms come in various shapes and sizes; it's worth paying the extra for a Royal Square view. Unwind in the basement spa or the chic champagne bar.
❀ **Marchal** – See restaurant listing

Copenhagen Marriott
Kalvebod Brygge 5 ⊠ 1560 V – 𝒞 88 33 99 00 Plan: **C3**
– www.copenhagenmarriott.dk
402 rm – 🛏1899/5000 DKK 🛏🛏1899/5000 DKK – ⊊ 230 DKK – 9 suites
• Luxury • Business • Modern •
Striking waterfront hotel; take in the views from the terrace or from the floor to ceiling windows in the large lounge-bar. Bright, spacious bedrooms are handsomely appointed and afford canal or city views. The popular American grill restaurant offers steaks, chops and seafood, and has a lively open kitchen.

Nimb
Bernstorffsgade 5 ⊠ 1577 V Plan: **B3**
– Ⓜ *København Hovedbane Gård*
– 𝒞 88 70 00 00 – www.nimb.dk
17 rm ⊊ *–* 🛏2800/3290 DKK 🛏🛏4200/5900 DKK
• Luxury • Design • Romantic •
An ornate, Moorish-style building dating from 1909, situated in Tivoli Gardens. Smart, stylish bedrooms are sympathetically designed and well-equipped – most overlook the gardens. Eat in the lively bar and grill, the formal French brasserie or the contemporary restaurant. The rustic wine bar offers over 2,000 bottles – and you can enjoy Danish open sandwiches and schnapps in Fru Nimb.

Radisson Blu Royal
Hammerichsgade 1 ⊠ 1611 V Plan: **B3**
– Ⓜ *København Hovedbane Gård – 𝒞 33 42 60 00*
– www.radissonblu.com/royalhotel-copenhagen
260 rm – 🛏995/4895 DKK 🛏🛏1195/5095 DKK – ⊊ 195 DKK – 2 suites
• Business • Design •
Spacious hotel designed by Arne Jacobson, with extensive conference and fitness facilities. Bedrooms have a typical Scandinavian style – the largest are the double-aspect corner rooms; Number 606 still has its original furnishings. Dine informally in all-day Café Royal or enjoy panoramic views from Alberto K.
Alberto K – See restaurant listing

Island
Kalvebod Brygge 53 (via Kalvebod Brygge C3) ⊠ 1560 V – 𝒞 33 38 96 00
– www.copenhagenisland.dk
326 rm – 🛏850/3050 DKK 🛏🛏950/3250 DKK – ⊊ 185 DKK
• Business • Chain • Modern •
Contemporary glass and steel hotel set just outside the city, on a man-made island in the harbour. Bedrooms are well-equipped – some are allergy friendly and some have balconies; choose a water view over a city view. The stylish multi-level lounge-bar and restaurant serves a wide-ranging international menu.

Admiral $\leqslant \widehat{\text{m}}$ 🛴 **P**

Toldbodgade 24-28 ⊠ 1253 K – **Ⓜ** *Kongens Nytorv* Plan: **D2**
– 𝒞 33 74 14 14 – www.admiralhotel.dk
366 rm – **♦**1335/1825 DKK **♦♦**1535/2925 DKK – 🍽 150 DKK
• Business • Historic • Modern •

An impressive 1787 former grain-drying warehouse, with an appealing maritime theme running throughout. Bedrooms feature vintage beams and bespoke wood furniture and have city or harbour views; opt for one of the duplex suites.
Salt – See restaurant listing

 Imperial 𝄞 🕭 🖾 🛴 🚗

Vester Farimagsgade 9 ⊠ 1606 V Plan: **B3**
– **Ⓜ** *København Hovedbane Gård – 𝒞 33 12 80 00*
– www.imperialhotel.dk
304 rm – **♦**1300/2300 DKK **♦♦**1600/2800 DKK – 🍽 170 DKK – 1 suite
• Business • Traditional • Modern •

A well-known hotel, geared up for conferences and centrally located on a wide city thoroughfare. Bedrooms are particularly spacious and have a subtle Danish style. The contemporary restaurant features a brightly coloured Italian theme wall and serves Italian dishes to match.

 Kong Arthur 🕭 🌀 🕭 🛴 **P**

Nørre Søgade 11 ⊠ 1370 K – **Ⓜ** *Nørreport* Plan: **B2**
– 𝒞 33 11 12 12 – www.arthurhotels.dk
155 rm – **♦**1125/1895 DKK **♦♦**1895/2280 DKK – 🍽 175 DKK
• Townhouse • Traditional • Classic •

Four 1882 buildings set around a courtyard, in an elegant residential avenue close to Peblinge Lake. Well-equipped bedrooms have a high level of facilities. Relax in the smart Thai spa and enjoy complimentary drinks from 5-6pm.

 Absalon 🛴

Helgolandsgade 15 ⊠ 1653 V Plan: **B3**
– **Ⓜ** *København Hovedbane Gård – 𝒞 33 24 22 11*
– www.absalon-hotel.dk
162 rm 🍽 – **♦**1150/2100 DKK **♦♦**1300/2850 DKK – 2 suites
• Family • Design • Grand luxury •

A family-run hotel located close to the railway station and furnished with vibrantly coloured fabrics. Elegant, comfortable bedrooms feature an 'artbox' on the wall which celebrates an aspect of Danish design such as Lego or porcelain.

 Andersen

Helgolandsgade 12 ⊠ 1653 V Plan: **B3**
– **Ⓜ** *København Hovedbane Gård – 𝒞 33 31 46 10*
– www.andersen-hotel.dk – Closed 22-26 December
77 rm 🍽 – **♦**1075/2000 DKK **♦♦**1275/3200 DKK
• Family • Design • Contemporary •

Bright and funky boutique styling is the hallmark of this hotel, where the individually furnished bedrooms are classified as 'Cool', 'Brilliant', 'Wonderful' and 'Amazing'. Honesty bar in reception; complimentary glass of wine, 5–6pm.

 Avenue 🛴 **P**

Åboulevard 29 ⊠ 1960 C – **Ⓜ** *Forum – 𝒞 35 37 31 11* Plan: **A2**
– www.brochner-hotels.dk – Closed Christmas
68 rm – **♦**895/6000 DKK **♦♦**1095/6200 DKK – 🍽 160 DKK
• Business • Family • Modern •

Well-maintained, family-run hotel dating back to 1899. Relax around the central bar in the smart modern lounge or out on the courtyard patio. Bedrooms have a bright, crisp style and feature striking Philippe Starck lights.

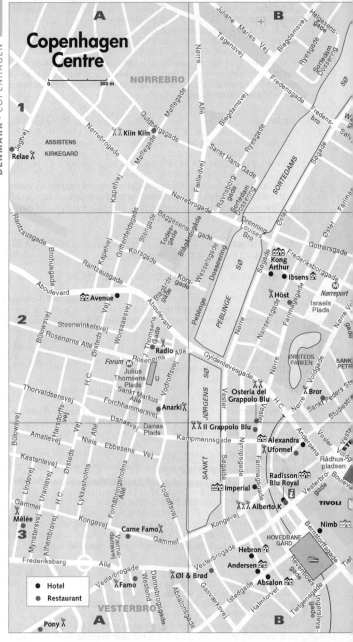

Copenhagen Centre

NØRREBRO

ASSISTENS KIRKEGARD

VESTERBRO

- ● Hotel
- ● Restaurant

Restaurants and places of interest:

Relae, Kiin Kiin, Avenue, Radio, Anarki, Host, Kong Arthur, Ibsens, Osteria del Grappolo Blu, Bror, Il Grappolo Blu, Alexandra, Uformel, Radisson Blu Royal, Imperial, Alberto K, Nimb, Mêlée, Carne Famo, Hebron, Andersen, Absalon, Famo, ØI & Brød, Pony

ØRSTEDS PARKEN

Israels Plads

Nørreport

Rådhus-pladsen

TIVOLI

HOVEDBANE GÅRD

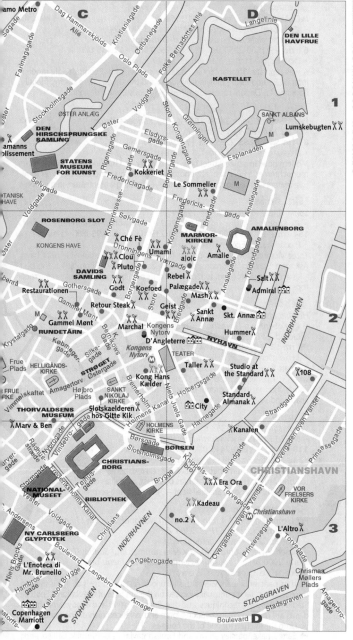

amo Metro
Dag Hammarskjölds Allé
Kristianiagade
Østbanegade
Langelinie

DEN LILLE
HAVFRUE

Sogade
Farimagsgade
Oslo Plads
Folke Bernadottes Allé

KASTELLET

1

Øster
Stockholmsgade
Voldgade
Store Kongensgade
Grønningen

SANKT ALBANS

M
Lumskebugten ✕✕

DEN
HIRSCHSPRUNGSKE
SAMLING
amanns
blissement

ØSTER ANLÆG
Øster
Elsdyrs-
gade
Gemersgade
Borgergade
Esplanaden

M

STATENS
MUSEUM
FOR KUNST
Fredericiagade
Rigensgade
Kokkeriet
Le Sommelier ✕✕

TANISK
HAVE
Sølvgade
Voldgade
Kronprinsesse
Sølvgade
Fredericia-
gade

Amaliegade
Bredgade

ROSENBORG SLOT
Dronningens Tværgade
MARMOR-
KIRKEN
AMALIENBORG

Øster
KONGENS HAVE
✕ Ché Fè
Umami
alolc
Amalie
Toldbodgade

benrå
DAVIDS
SAMLING
✕✕ Clou
✕ Pluto
Borgergade
Store
Rebel ✕
Salt ✕✕

Restaurationen ✕✕
Gothersgade
Godt
Koefoed
Palægade ✕✕
Amaliegade
Admiral 🏛

M
Gammel Mønt
Retour Steak ✕
Store
Geist
Mash ✕✕

Krystalgade
Gammel Mønt
RUNDETÅRN
Møntergade
Købmagergade
Silkegade
Kikkovs gade
Marchal
Kongens Nytorv
Sankt
✕ Annæ
Skt. Annæ 🏛
INDERHAVNEN

2

Frue
Plads
HELLIGANDS-
KIRKE
Niels Juels Gade
D'Angleterre 🏛
NYHAVN
Hummer ✕

FRUE
RKE
Vimmelskaftet
Amagertorv
Højbro
Plads
STRØGET
Østergade
Kongens
Nytorv
TEATER
Taller ✕✕
Studio at
the Standard ✕✕
✕108

THORVALDSENS
MUSEUM
SANKT
NIKOLAJ
KIRKE
Bremerholm
Kong Hans
Kælder
Holbergsgade
Standard-
Almanak ✕
Strandgade

✕ Marv & Ben
Slotskaelderen ✕
hos Gitte Kik
Holmens Kanal
HOLMENS
KIRKE
City 🏛
Havnegade
Overgaden oven Vandet

arver-
gade
Rådhus- Nybrogade
Vindebro-gade
Børsgade
Slotsholmsgade
BØRSEN
✕ Kanalen
Prinsessegade

Stormgade
Frederiksholms Kanal
CHRISTIANS-
BORG
Tøjhus-gade
Brygge
Knippels-bro
Strandgade
CHRISTIANSHAVN

Andersens
Vester Voldgade
BIBLIOTHEK
Christians
✕✕ Era Ora
Torvegade
Overgaden oven Vandet
VOR
FRELSERS
KIRKE

3

NATIONAL
MUSEET
✕ Kadeau
Christianshavn
Prinsessegade

NY CARLSBERG
GLYPTOTEK
Boulevard
INDERHAVNEN
no.2 ✕
L'Altro ✕
Torvegade

Niels Brocks
Gade
✕✕ L'Enoteca di
Mr. Brunello
Langebrogade
Amagerbro-gade

Hambros-gade
Kalvebod Brygge
Langebro
Amager
STADSGRAVEN
Stadsgraven

stortorvs
Copenhagen
Marriott 🏛
SYDHAVNEN
Chrismas
Møllers
Plads

C
Boulevard
D

135

DENMARK - COPENHAGEN

Alexandra

H.C. Andersens Boulevard 8 ✉ *1553 V*   Plan: **B3**
– Ⓜ København Hovedbane Gård – ℰ 33 74 44 94
– www.hotelalexandra.dk – Closed Christmas
61 rm – ♦1500/2250 DKK ♦♦1850/2600 DKK – ➱ 138 DKK
• Boutique hotel • Business • Design •

A well-run, late Victorian hotel in the city centre, with a contrasting modern interior. Bedrooms are individually styled and there's an entire 'allergy friendly' floor; the 12 'Design' rooms are styled by famous Danish designers.

City

Peder Skrams Gade 24 ✉ *1054 K* – Ⓜ *Kongens Nytorv*   Plan: **D2**
– ℰ 33 13 06 66 – www.hotelcity.dk
81 rm ➱ – ♦895/2295 DKK ♦♦1195/2595 DKK
• Business • Traditional • Grand luxury •

Modern hotel in a quiet street between the city and the docks. Bedrooms boast monochrome Jan Persson jazz photos and Jacobsen armchairs. Designer furniture features throughout and there's an eye-catching water feature in the lobby.

Skt. Annæ

Sankt Annæ Plads 18-20 ✉ *1250 K*   Plan: **D2**
– Ⓜ Kongens Nytorv – ℰ 33 96 20 00 – www.hotelsanktannae.dk
154 rm – ♦1090/1990 DKK ♦♦1290/2390 DKK – ➱ 195 DKK – 1 suite
• Business • Townhouse • Cosy •

Three Victorian townhouses not far from the bustling harbourside of Nyhavn. Ask for a 'Superior' bedroom for more space and quiet; Room 601 is the best – it's accessed via the roof terrace and has its own balcony overlooking the rooftops.

Hebron

Helgolandsgade 4 ✉ *1653 V*   Plan: **B3**
– Ⓜ København Hovedbane Gård – ℰ 33 31 69 06 – www.hebron.dk
– Closed 22 December-2 January
99 rm ➱ – ♦700/1900 DKK ♦♦900/2100 DKK – 2 suites
• Traditional • Family • Functional •

A smart hotel behind a Victorian façade – this was one of the city's biggest when it opened in 1899 and some original features still remain. There's a comfy lounge and a grand breakfast room; well-kept bedrooms range in shape and size.

Ibsens

Vendersgade 23 ✉ *1363 K* – Ⓜ *Nørreport*   Plan: **B2**
– ℰ 33 13 19 13 – www.arthurhotels.dk
118 rm ➱ – ♦880/2445 DKK ♦♦1230/2820 DKK
• Historic • Family • Personalised •

A simply, brightly furnished hotel with a relaxed, bohemian feel: the little sister to Kong Arthur. The small bar serves breakfast, as well as complimentary drinks from 5-6pm. Bedrooms are well-kept – 'Tiny' really are compact.

Geranium (Rasmus Kofoed)

Per Henrik Lings Allé 4 (8th Fl), Parken National Stadium (3 km via Dag Hammaraskjölds Allé C1) ✉ *2100 Ø*
– ℰ 69 96 02 20 – www.geranium.dk
– Closed 2 weeks Christmas, 2 weeks summer and Sunday-Tuesday
Menu 2000 DKK – (booking essential) (surprise menu only)
• Creative • Design • Elegant •

With its panoramic park views, this luxurious restaurant feels as if it is inviting the outside in, yet it's unusually located on the 8th floor of the National Football Stadium. Modern techniques and the finest organic and biodynamic ingredients are used to create beautiful, pure and balanced dishes. The chefs invite you into the kitchen for one of the courses.

→ Salted hake, parsley stems and Finnish caviar in buttermilk. Grilled pork, pickled pine and blackcurrant leaves. Wood sorrel and woodruff.

XxX &ঞ্চ
ঞ্চ ঞ্চ

a|o|c

Dronningens Tvaergade 2 ⊠ *1302 K*   Plan: **D2**
– **Ⓜ** *Kongens Nytorv* – *𝒞 33 11 11 45* – *www.restaurantaoc.dk*
– *Closed July, 23-30 December, 1 January, Sunday and Monday*
Menu 1300/1600 DKK – *(dinner only) (tasting menu only)*
• Modern cuisine • Elegant • Romantic •
A spacious, simply decorated restaurant in the vaults of an eye-catching 17C former seafarers building close to Nyhavn harbour and the Royal Palace; owned
and run by an experienced sommelier. Skilful, well-judged and, at times, playful
cooking has a Danish heart and shows great originality as well as a keen eye for
detail, flavour and texture.
→ Baked onion with caviar and elderflower sauce. Roe deer with cherries,
smoked marrow and sorrel. Hazelnut ice cream with burnt Jerusalem artichoke.

XxX &ঞ্চ
ঞ্চ

Kong Hans Kælder

Vingaardsstræde 6 ⊠ *1070 K* – **Ⓜ** *Kongens Nytorv*   Plan: **C2**
– *𝒞 33 11 68 68* – *www.konghans.dk*
– *Closed 24 July-15 August, 24-28 December, 12-27 February, 11-12 April
and Sunday-Tuesday*
Menu 1700 DKK – Carte 1040/2510 DKK – *(dinner only)*
(booking essential)
• Classic French • Elegant • Intimate •
An intimate, historic restaurant in a beautiful vaulted Gothic cellar in the heart of
the city. Classic French cooking uses luxury ingredients and has rich flavours,
with signature dishes like Danish Black lobster. There's a 7 course tasting menu
and Gueridon trolleys add a theatrical element to proceedings.
→ Scallops, smoked butter and caviar. Turbot baked in salt with ramsons
and champagne. Quince, white chocolate and apple.

XxX &ঞ্চ
ঞ্চ

Era Ora

Overgaden Neden Vandet 33B ⊠ *1414 K*   Plan: **D3**
– **Ⓜ** *Christianshavn* – *𝒞 32 54 06 93* – *www.era-ora.dk* – *Closed
Christmas, Easter and Sunday*
Menu 498/950 DKK – *(booking essential) (tasting menu only)*
• Italian • Elegant • Intimate •
A passionately run restaurant on a quaint cobbled street next to the canal;
inside it's grand, with high ceilings, a deep red colour scheme and an air of
formality. The set menu covers all regions of Italy and the well-presented,
modern dishes use top quality Italian produce in vibrant flavour combina-
tions.
→ Crispy turbot with pistachio and bell peppers. Guinea fowl, gooseberries, cime di rapa and chanterelles. Peach with tarragon and liquorice.

XxX &
ঞ্চ

Clou (Jonathan Berntsen)

Borgergade 16 ⊠ *1300 K* – **Ⓜ** *Kongens Nytorv*   Plan: **C2**
– *𝒞 36 16 30 00* – *www.restaurant-clou.dk*
– *Closed first 2 weeks August, 3 weeks late December-early January,
Sunday and Monday*
Menu 1150/1950 DKK – Carte 545/1110 DKK – *(dinner only) (booking
essential)*
• Modern cuisine • Intimate • Neighbourhood •
A comfortable, intimate restaurant set over three converted shops, with
views into the kitchen from the street. Choose between 3, 5 or 7 course
set menus and an à la carte: dishes are modern, attractive and inventive, with
interesting textures and flavours, and accompanying wine matches. Service is
assured.
→ Scallops with Jerusalem artichoke and black truffle. Quail with foie gras
and veal sweetbreads. Oialla chocolate with caramel and berries.

DENMARK - COPENHAGEN

XxX **Mielcke & Hurtigkarl**

Runddel 1 (2 km via Veseterbrogade and Frederiksberg Allé A 3) ⊠ *2000 C*
– ℰ 38 34 84 36 – www.mhcph.com – Closed Christmas-New Year, Sunday and Monday
Menu 800/1100 DKK – *(dinner only) (booking essential)*
• Creative • Elegant • Exotic décor •
Charming 1744 orangery with a fire-lit terrace, set in a delightful spot in Frederiksberg Gardens. The walls are painted with garden scenes and there are backing tracks of birdsong. The ambitious, modern set menus use lots of herbs and vegetables from the gardens. Service is wonderfully attentive.

XxX **Alberto K** – Radisson Blu Royal Hotel ≼ 🅰🅲 🅿

Hammerichsgade 1 ⊠ *1611 V* Plan: **B3**
– ⓜ København Hovedbane Gård – ℰ 33 42 61 61 – www.alberto-k.dk
– Closed 1-8 January, 17 July-8 August, Easter, Christmas, Sunday and bank holidays
Menu 750/950 DKK – *(dinner only) (tasting menu only)*
• Modern cuisine • Chic • Elegant •
Alberto K is located on the 20th floor of the Radisson Blu Royal and is named after its first GM. It has a 1960s inspired, designer interior and offers stunning city views. Monthly set menus offer modern interpretations of classic dishes.

XX **Kadeau** (Nicolai Nørregaard) ⟐
⣿ *Wildersgade 10B* ⊠ *1408 K – ⓜ Christianshavn* Plan: **D3**
– ℰ 33 25 22 23 – www.kadeau.dk – Closed 5 weeks July-August, 1 week Christmas
Menu 1850 DKK – *(dinner only and Saturday lunch) (booking essential) (tasting menu only)*
• Modern cuisine • Design • Elegant •
An intimate, welcoming restaurant with an open kitchen showcasing cuisine and ingredients from Bornholm (an island just to the east of the mainland from where the passionate owners originate). Precise modern dishes feature well-balanced, flavoursome combinations, many texture variations and fermented ingredients.
→ Pickled vegetable terrine with tomato water. Pork with sweet onions and grilled blue cheese. Fermented raspberries with whitecurrant juice.

XX **Kiin Kiin** 🅰🅲 ⟐ 🐾
⣿ *Guldbergsgade 21* ⊠ *2200 N – ℰ 35 35 75 55* Plan: **A1**
– www.kiin.dk – Closed Christmas and Sunday
Menu 495/925 DKK – *(dinner only) (booking essential) (tasting menu only)*
• Thai • Exotic décor • Intimate •
A charming restaurant, whose name means 'come and eat'. Start with refined versions of street food in the moody lounge, then head for the tasteful dining room decorated with golden Buddhas and fresh flowers. Menus offer modern, personal interpretations of Thai dishes with vibrant flavour combinations.
→ Frozen red curry with baby lobster and coriander. Beef with ginger and oyster sauce. Banana cake with salted ice cream and crispy coconut.

XX **Studio at the Standard** (Torsten Vildgaard) 🅰🅲
⣿ *Havnegade 44* ⊠ *1058 K – ⓜ Kongens Nytorv* Plan: **D2**
– ℰ 72 14 88 08 – www.thestandardcph.dk – Closed 12-27 February, 23-26 December, Sunday and Monday
Menu 500/1000 DKK – *(dinner only and lunch Thursday-Saturday) (booking essential) (tasting menu only)*
• Creative • Fashionable • Design •
A showcase restaurant on the top floor of The Standard; sit at the counter to watch the team at work. Dishes are brought to the table by both the charming serving team and the passionate chefs. Classic flavours and modern techniques intertwine in creative, often playful dishes – and ingredients are top-notch.
→ Scallops with blackberries and cream. Neck of Duroc pork with peas and fermented garlic. Roast corn with blackcurrants.

XX **formel B** (Kristian Arpe-Møller) ⟨symbols⟩
⟨symbol⟩

Vesterbrogade 182-184, Frederiksberg (2 km on Vesterbrogade A3)
✉ *1800 C – ☎ 33 25 10 66 – www.formelb.dk – Closed 24-26 December,*
1 January and Sunday
Menu 850 DKK – Carte 410/850 DKK – *(dinner only) (booking essential)*
• Modern cuisine • Fashionable • Design •
Friendly staff create a relaxed environment at this appealing, modern restaurant
with its tree pictures and dark wood branches; ask for a table by the kitchen on
the lower level if you want to get close to the action. Complex and original small
plates are created with an assured and confident touch.
→ Turbot with parsley, garlic and braised veal tail. Pepper-glazed sweetbread with carrots and green rhubarb. Sea buckthorn 'en surprise'.

XX **Kokkeriet** (David Johansen) ⟨symbol⟩
⟨symbol⟩

Kronprinsessegade 64 ✉ *1306 K – ☎ 33 15 27 77*   Plan: **C1**
– www.kokkeriet.dk – Closed 24-26 December, 1 January and Sunday
Menu 900/1200 DKK – *(dinner only) (booking essential) (tasting menu*
only)
• Modern cuisine • Intimate • Design •
A discreet and elegant corner restaurant with two narrow, atmospheric rooms
decorated in grey and black, and a collection of contemporary Danish artwork
on display. Confidently executed, original cooking offers flavoursome, modern
interpretations of classic Danish dishes. Service is smooth and unobtrusive.
→ Apple vinegar marinated celery with split pea purée. Roast poussin with
Danish cheese and spruce. Sorrel sorbet with lemon mousse and caramel.

XX **Marchal** – D'Angleterre Hotel ⟨symbols⟩
⟨symbol⟩

Kongens Nytorv 34 ✉ *1050 K –* Ⓜ *Kongens Nytorv*   Plan: **C2**
– ☎ 33 12 00 95 – www.marchal.dk
Menu 300/500 DKK – Carte 510/2160 DKK
• Modern cuisine • Elegant • Romantic •
A stylish hotel restaurant overlooking the Square and named after the man
who founded the hotel in 1755. Refined, Nordic-style cooking has a classical
French base; menus offer a range of small plates – 3 is about the right amount,
or 4 if you're very hungry. Dinner also includes an extensive caviar collection.
→ Squid with caviar and cucumber. Chateaubriand en croûte with truffle
sauce. Raspberries & peaches with rose hip and champagne sabayon.

XX **Amass** ⟨symbols⟩

Refshalevej 153 (3 km via Torvgade and Prinsessgade D3) ✉ *1432 K*
– ☎ 43 58 43 30 – www.amassrestaurant.com – Closed 24-25 December,
1 January, Sunday and Monday
Menu 395/850 DKK – *(dinner only and lunch Friday-Saturday) (booking*
essential)
• Danish • Minimalist • Friendly •
A large restaurant just outside the city. It has an urban, industrial feel courtesy of
high graffitied concrete walls and huge windows overlooking the old docks. Prices and the authenticity of ingredients are key; cooking is modern Danish.

XX **Taller**

Tordenskjoldsgade 11 ✉ *1055 K –* Ⓜ *Kongens Nytorv*   Plan: **D2**
– ☎ 72 14 08 71 – www.restaurant-taller.dk – Closed 23-27 December, 1-
10 January and Sunday-Tuesday
Menu 375 DKK (lunch)/1175 DKK – *(dinner only and lunch Friday-Satur-*
day) (booking essential)
• World cuisine • Fashionable • Friendly •
Colourful and creative modern interpretations of Venezuelan dishes are served
at this stylish restaurant, whose name translates as 'workshop' in Spanish – take
a seat at the open kitchen counter to see the chef-owner at work close up.

DENMARK - COPENHAGEN

XX
😊
Frederiks Have

Smallegade 41, (entrance on Virginiavej) (1.5 km. via Gammel Kongevej A3) ✉ *2000 F –* Ⓜ *Frederiksberg –* ℰ *38 88 33 35 – www.frederikshave.dk – Closed 24 December-1 January, Easter and Sunday*
Menu 295/395 DKK – Carte 340/530 DKK
• Danish • Neighbourhood • Family •

A sweet neighbourhood restaurant hidden just off the main street in a residential area. Sit inside – surrounded by flowers and vivid local art – or outside, on the terrace. Well-presented, modern Danish dishes have a classical base; tasty sweet and sour combinations feature. The set lunches are great value.

XX
Umami

Store Kongensgade 59 ✉ *1264 K*   Plan: C/D2
– Ⓜ *Kongens Nytorv –* ℰ *33 38 75 00 – www.restaurantumami.dk – Closed 24 December-2 January, Easter Monday and Sunday*
Menu 650 DKK – Carte 350/480 DKK – *(dinner only)*
• Asian • Fashionable • Design •

Attractive building with a large cocktail bar and lounge on the ground floor, and an elegant upper level boasting a stylish, atmospheric dining room, a sushi counter and an open kitchen. Cooking is Japanese, with a European slant.

XX
Geist

Kongens Nytorv 8 ✉ *1050 K –* Ⓜ *Kongens Nytorv*   Plan: C2
– ℰ *33133713 – www.restaurantgeist.dk – Closed 23-26 December and 1 January*
Carte 385/465 DKK – *(dinner only)*
• Modern cuisine • Design • Trendy •

A lively, fashionable restaurant with an open kitchen and a sexy nightclub vibe, set in a striking red-brick property with floor to ceiling windows – in a superb spot overlooking the square. Cleverly crafted dishes display a light touch; 4 should suffice.

XX
Restaurationen

Møntergade 19 ✉ *1116 K –* Ⓜ *Kongens Nytorv*   Plan: C2
– ℰ *33 14 94 95 – www.restaurationen.com – Closed Easter, early July-late August, Christmas-New Year, Sunday and Monday*
Menu 575 DKK – *(dinner only)*
• Classic cuisine • Chic • Romantic •

This restaurant celebrated 25 years in 2016, and is run by a well-known chef who also owns the next door wine bar. Modern Danish dishes are created with quality local produce. The dining room displays some impressive vibrant modern art.

XX
Koefoed

Landegreven 3 ✉ *1301 K –* Ⓜ *Kongens Nytorv*   Plan: C2
– ℰ *56 48 22 24 – www.restaurant-koefoed.dk – Closed 22 December-2 January, Sunday and Monday*
Menu 295/495 DKK – Carte 410/500 DKK – *(booking essential at dinner)*
• Creative • Intimate • Romantic •

An intimate collection of rooms in a former coal cellar, where everything from the produce to the glassware celebrates the island of Bornholm. Modern Danish cooking with deconstructed smørrebrød at lunch and an impressive range of bordeaux.

XX
Palægade

Palægade 8 ✉ *1261 K –* Ⓜ *Kongens Nytorv*   Plan: C2
– ℰ *70 82 82 88 – www.palaegade.dk – Closed Christmas-New Year, Monday dinner and Sunday*
Menu 495 DKK – Carte 350/515 DKK
• Smørrebrød • Friendly • Simple •

More than 40 classic smørrebrød are available at lunch – with plenty of local beers and schnapps to accompany them. Things become more formal in the evenings, when they serve highly seasonal dishes in a traditional Northern European style.

XX **Godt**

Gothersgade 38 ✉ 1123 K – Ⓜ Kongens Nytorv   Plan: **C2**
– ℰ 33 15 21 22 – www.restaurant-godt.dk – Closed mid July to mid
August, Christmas-New Year, Easter, Sunday, Monday and bank holidays
Menu 520/680 DKK – (dinner only) (tasting menu only)
• Classic cuisine • Friendly • Family •
A stylish restaurant seating just 20, where the service is particularly friendly. Tra-
ditional French and European daily menus – of 3, 4 and 5 courses – are formed
around the latest market produce. Old WWII shells act as candle holders.

XX **Salt** – Admiral Hotel   🛜 **P**

Toldbodgade 24-28 ✉ 1253 K – Ⓜ Kongens Nytorv   Plan: **D2**
– ℰ 33 74 14 44 – www.salt.dk
Menu 395 DKK – Carte 500/510 DKK
• Modern cuisine • Design • Fashionable •
A bright and airy hotel restaurant; its vast old timber beams a reminder of the
building's previous life as a granary and its harbourside terrace a great spot in
the summer months. Extensive menus offer interesting modern cooking.

XX **L' Enoteca di Mr. Brunello**   🕸

Rysensteensgade 16 ✉ 1564 K – ℰ 33 11 47 20   Plan: **C3**
– www.lenoteca.dk – Closed 1 July-15 August, Easter, Christmas, Sunday,
Monday and bank holidays
Menu 495 DKK – Carte 495/755 DKK – (dinner only)
• Italian • Elegant • Neighbourhood •
Tucked away near the Tivoli Gardens and run by passionate, experienced
owners. Refined, classic Italian cooking uses good quality produce imported
from Italy. The good value Italian wine list has over 150 different Brunello di
Montalcinos.

XX **Gammel Mønt**

Gammel Mønt 41 ✉ 1117 K – Ⓜ Kongens Nytorv   Plan: **C2**
– ℰ 33 15 10 60 – www.glmoent.dk – Closed July, Christmas,
Easter, Saturday-Monday and bank holidays
Menu 425/565 DKK – Carte 595/920 DKK – (lunch only and dinner Wed-
nesday-Friday)
• Traditional cuisine • Cosy • Friendly •
A part-timbered house in the heart of the city; dating back to 1739, it sports a
striking shade of deep terracotta. The menu celebrates Danish classics and
dishes are hearty, gutsy and reassuringly traditional; try the pickled herrings.

XX **Lumskebugten**   🛜 ⇦

Esplanaden 21 ✉ 1263 K – ℰ 33 15 60 29   Plan: **D1**
– www.lumskebugten.dk – Closed 3 weeks July, Christmas, Easter, Sunday
and bank holidays
Menu 325/475 DKK – Carte 400/735 DKK
• Traditional cuisine • Cosy • Classic décor •
A restored quayside pavilion dating from 1854; the Royal Family occasionally
dine here. A series of small rooms are adorned with maritime memorabilia and
paintings. Local menus offer a wide selection of traditional fish dishes.

XX **Le Sommelier**   🕸 ⇦

Bredgade 63-65 ✉ 1260 K – ℰ 33 11 45 15   Plan: **D1**
– www.lesommelier.dk – Closed 22 December-4 January, Easter and lunch
Saturday and Sunday
Carte 435/585 DKK
• French • Brasserie • Traditional décor •
Attractively refurbished brasserie in the heart of the Old Town, where French
wine posters and a superb wine list hint at the owners' passion. The small à la
carte features classic French dishes and is supplemented by a daily set menu.

DENMARK - COPENHAGEN

XX **Alchemist** 🝔

Århusgade 22 (3.5 km via Dag Hammerskjölds Allé off Østerbrogade C1)
✉ *2100 Ø –* ☏ *51 93 56 23 – www.restaurant-alchemist.dk*
*– Closed 16 December-2 January, 2 July-2 August
and Sunday-Tuesday*
Menu 3000 DKK – *(dinner only) (booking essential) (surprise menu only)*
• Creative • Trendy • Intimate •

The ambitious chef transports diners to another world in this all-encompassing culinary experience. Attentive staff, counter seating and dramatic music provide the setting. The exciting, highly original 45 course menu includes wines.

XX **Mash** 🏦 🝔 ⇔

Bredgade 20 ✉ *1260 K –* Ⓜ *Kongens Nytorv*　　　Plan: **D2**
– ☏ *33 13 93 00 – www.mashsteak.dk – Closed 24 December-2 January,
lunch Saturday and Sunday*
Carte 355/810 DKK – *(booking essential at dinner)*
• Meats and grills • Brasserie • Classic décor •

A smart, lively, American-style steakhouse with a trendy cocktail bar and aged meats on display; sit in the rear room with its red leather booths. Classic steak dishes come with a choice of sides and sauces. French and American wine list.

XX **Il Grappolo Blu**

Vester Farimagsgade 35 ✉ *1606 V –* Ⓜ *Nørreport*　　　Plan: **B3**
– ☏ *33 11 57 20 – www.igb.dk – Closed July, Easter, Christmas, New Year,
Sunday and Monday*
Menu 450/750 DKK – Carte 385/440 DKK – *(dinner only)*
• Italian • Rustic • Cosy •

A cosy restaurant with dark panelling and ornate carvings. 8 and 14 course tasting menus: well-prepared, authentic Italian dishes include appealing antipasti and tasty pastas. The wine list features over 200 different Brunello di Montalcinos.

XX **Osteria del Grappolo Blu**

Vester Farimagsgade 37 ✉ *1606 V –* Ⓜ *Nørreport*　　　Plan: **B2/3**
– ☏ *33 12 57 20 – www.osteria.dk – Closed July, Easter, Christmas, New
Year, Sunday and Monday*
Menu 450/750 DKK – Carte 385/440 DKK – *(dinner only)*
• Italian • Friendly • Traditional décor •

The more informal counterpart to Il Grappolo Blu; a laid-back restaurant with smart 'osteria' styling. Authentic homemade dishes have their roots in southern Italy. Breads, pastas and ice creams are made on the premises daily.

X **Relæ** ❀

Jægersborggade 41 ✉ *2200 N*　　　Plan: **A1**
– ☏ *36 96 66 09 – www.restaurant-relae.dk*
– Closed January and Sunday-Monday
Menu 475/895 DKK – *(dinner only and lunch Friday- Saturday) (booking
essential) (surprise menu only)*
• Modern cuisine • Minimalist • Fashionable •

Book well in advance for a table at this simply styled restaurant, or grab a counter seat to watch the talented team in the open kitchen. Choose the 5 or 10 course surprise menu: unfussy, flavourful dishes come in original combinations and make innovative use of vegetables. Look in the drawers for your cutlery!
→ Green strawberries and marigold. Havervadgård lamb, romaine salad and tarragon. Yoghurt, chervil and lemon.

142

X
£3
108 (Kristian Baumann)
Strandgade 108 ✉ 1401 K – Ⓜ Christianshavn Plan: **D2**
– ℰ 32 96 32 92 – www.108.dk – Closed Christmas and 1 January
Carte 400/460 DKK – *(dinner only) (booking advisable)*
• Modern cuisine • Neighbourhood • Design •
A former whale meat warehouse with floor-to-ceiling windows and water views; bare concrete and a semi-open kitchen give it a cool Nordic style. There's a Noma alumnus in the kitchen and plenty of pickled, cured and fermented ingredients on the 'no rules' menu, from which you pick as many dishes as you like.
→ Rose hip marinated bleak roe with sweet salted plums. Raw lamb with last year's pickles. Rausu kombu ice cream with barley and blackcurrant wood oil.

X
Kanalen
Wilders Plads 1-3 ✉ 1403 K – Ⓜ Christianshavn Plan: **D3**
– ℰ 32 95 13 30 – www.restaurant-kanalen.dk – Closed Sunday and bank holidays
Menu 250/400 DKK – Carte 350/465 DKK – *(booking essential)*
• Danish • Bistro • Cosy •
Former Harbour Police office with a lovely terrace, in a delightful canalside setting. The dining room has a contemporary edge and French windows facing the water. The chefs in the tiny open kitchen prepare a well-balanced Danish menu with light French and Asian touches, which is served by a charming team.

X
Øl & Brød
Viktoriagade 6 ✉ 1620 V Plan: **B3**
– Ⓜ København Hovedbane Gård – ℰ 33 31 44 22 – www.ologbrod.com – Closed Monday
Menu 500 DKK (dinner) – Carte lunch 280/440 DKK – *(lunch only and dinner Thursday-Saturday) (booking essential)*
• Modern cuisine • Neighbourhood • Cosy •
A cosy, hip neighbourhood restaurant where the emphasis is as much on aquavit and craft beers as it is on the refined and flavourful modern food. Lunch sees smørrebrød taken to a new level, while dinner offers a choice of 3 or 6 courses.

X
Rebel
Store Kongensgade 52 ✉ 1264 K Plan: **C/D2**
– Ⓜ Kongens Nytorv – ℰ 33 32 32 09 – www.restaurantrebel.dk – Closed 24 July-6 August, 2 weeks Christmas, Sunday and Monday
Carte 300/600 DKK – *(dinner only)*
• Modern cuisine • Bistro • Fashionable •
Located in a busy part of the city; a simply decorated, split-level restaurant with closely set tables and a buzzy vibe – sit on the more atmospheric ground floor, which looks into the kitchen. Choose 3 or 4 dishes from the list of 11; cooking is modern and refined, and relies on Danish produce.

X
Standard - Almanak
Havnegade 44 ✉ 1058 K – Ⓜ Kongens Nytorv Plan: **D2**
– ℰ 72 14 88 08 – www.thestandardcph.dk – Closed Christmas and New Year
Menu 409/500 DKK – Carte 268/545 DKK – *(bookings advisable at dinner)*
• Modern cuisine • Fashionable •
In a waterfront setting, on the ground floor of an impressive art deco former customs building. At lunch, it's all about tasty smørrebrød, while dinner sees a concise menu of updated Danish classics. An open kitchen adds to the theatre.
£3 **Studio at the Standard** – See restaurant listing

Anarki
ⅲ

Vodroffsvej 47 ✉ 1900 C – **Ⓜ** *Forum*   Plan: **A2**
– ℰ 22 13 11 34 – www.restaurant-anarki.dk
– Closed July-August, Christmas, Sunday and Monday
Menu 385 DKK – Carte 260/425 DKK – *(dinner only)*
• **Traditional cuisine** • **Neighbourhood** • **Bistro** •

An unassuming and proudly run neighbourhood bistro, just over the water into Frederiksberg. The interesting menu of gutsy, flavourful dishes draws inspiration from all over the world, so expect to see words like ceviche, paella and burrata as well as bakskuld – with plenty of offal and some great wines.

Radio

Julius Thomsens Gade 12 ✉ 1632 V – **Ⓜ** *Forum*   Plan: **A2**
– ℰ 25102733 – www.restaurantradio.dk
– Closed 3 weeks summer, 2 weeks Christmas-New Year, Sunday and Monday
Menu 300/400 DKK – *(dinner only and lunch Friday-Saturday) (booking essential) (tasting menu only)*
• **Modern cuisine** • **Minimalist** • **Neighbourhood** •

An informal restaurant with an unfussy urban style, wood-clad walls and cool anglepoise lighting. Oft-changing set menus feature full-flavoured, good value dishes and use organic ingredients grown in the chefs' nearby fields.

56°
⌂ ☼

Krudtløbsvej 8 (2.5 km. via Torvgade, Prinsessgade and Refshalevej D3)
✉ 1439 K – ℰ 31 16 32 05
– www.restaurant56grader.dk
– Closed Christmas, Sunday dinner and Monday
Menu 220/375 DKK
• **Danish** • **Rustic** • **Romantic** •

A sweet, rustic restaurant, unusually set within the 1.5m thick walls of a 17C gunpowder store. Flavoursome Danish cooking mixes modern and traditional elements and keeps Nordic produce to the fore. The large garden is a hit.

L'Altro
Ⓐⓒ

Torvegade 62 ✉ 1400 K – **Ⓜ** *Christianshavn*   Plan: **D3**
– ℰ 32 54 54 06 – www.laltro.dk
– Closed 23-26 December and Sunday
Menu 430 DKK – *(dinner only) (booking essential)*
(tasting menu only)
• **Italian** • **Intimate** • **Traditional décor** •

A cosy, long-standing restaurant with a warm, rustic style; it celebrates 'la cucina de la casa' – the homely Italian spirit of 'mama's kitchen'. Regularly changing set menus feature tasty family recipes from Umbria and Tuscany; dishes are appealing and rely on good quality ingredients imported from Italy.

Marv & Ben

Snaregade 4 ✉ 1205 K – **Ⓜ** *Kongens Nytorv*   Plan: **C2/3**
– ℰ 33 91 01 91 – www.marvogben.dk – Closed Christmas, Sunday and Monday
Menu 350 DKK – Carte 300/500 DKK
– (dinner only) (booking advisable)
• **Modern cuisine** • **Friendly** • **Bistro** •

A simple, two-floored restaurant down a cobbled street off the main tourist track. Styling is stark and modern, with the kitchen on display behind a glass wall. Gutsy, well-crafted dishes focus on produce from the chefs' own fields. Service is friendly, with dishes sometimes brought out by the chefs themselves.

Enomania

Vesterbrogade 187 (2.5 km via Vesterbrogade A3) ⊠ *1800 C
– ℰ 33 23 60 80 – www.enomania.dk – Closed 22 December-8 January,
10-19 February, 29 March-2 April, 13-17 April, 8 July-7 August, 14-
23 October, Saturday-Monday and bank holidays*
Menu 390 DKK – Carte 240/370 DKK – *(dinner only and lunch Thursday-Friday) (booking essential)*
• Italian • Wine bar • Simple •

A simple, bistro-style restaurant near Frederiksberg Park – its name means 'Wine Mania'. The wine cellar comes with a table for tasting and there's an excellent list of over 600 bins, mostly from Piedmont and Burgundy. These are complemented by straightforward, tasty Italian dishes from a daily 4 course menu.

Mêlée

Martensens Allé 16 ⊠ *1828 C –* Ⓜ *Frederiksberg*   Plan: **A3**
*– ℰ 35 13 11 34 – www.melee.dk – Closed Christmas-New Year, Sunday
and Monday*
Menu 385 DKK – Carte 305/445 DKK – *(dinner only) (booking essential)*
• French • Friendly • Bistro •

A bustling neighbourhood bistro with a friendly, laid-back atmosphere; run by an experienced team. Modern, country-style cooking is French-based but has Danish influences; menus might be concise but portions are generous and flavours are bold. An excellent range of wines from the Rhône Valley accompany.

Carne Famo ⇔

Gammel Kongevej 51 ⊠ *1610 V – ℰ 33 22 22 50*   Plan: **A3**
– www.famo.dk – Closed 2 weeks summer, Christmas and Sunday
Menu 450 DKK – Carte 370/445 DKK – *(dinner only) (booking essential)*
• Italian • Minimalist • Friendly •

A laid-back restaurant with the style of a modern osteria. The extensive menu offers authentic, rustic Italian dishes made with fresh seasonal ingredients – and there are plenty of well-priced wines on the all-Italian wine list.

Retour Steak

Ny Østergade 21 ⊠ *1101 K –* Ⓜ *Kongens Nytorv*   Plan: **C2**
– ℰ 33 33 83 30 – www.retoursteak.dk
Menu 450 DKK – Carte 345/530 DKK – *(dinner only) (booking essential)*
• Meats and grills • Bistro • Friendly •

A relaxed, informal restaurant with a stark white interior and contrasting black furnishings. A small menu offers simply prepared grills, good quality American rib-eye steaks and an affordable selection of wines.

Famo

Saxogade 3 ⊠ *1662 V – ℰ 33 23 22 50 – www.famo.dk*   Plan: **A3**
– Closed Christmas and early January
Menu 380 DKK – *(dinner only) (booking essential) (tasting menu only)*
• Italian • Bistro • Neighbourhood •

A modern, simply styled Italian restaurant serving rustic cooking. Extensive daily menus are presented orally: they offer a choice of 8 antipasti, followed by tasty homemade pastas, generous main courses and authentic desserts.

Ché Fè

Borgergade 17a ⊠ *1300 K –* Ⓜ *Kongens Nytorv*   Plan: **C2**
*– ℰ 33 11 17 21 – www.chefe.dk – Closed 21-26 December, 1 January, 9-
31 July and Easter Monday*
Menu 350/490 DKK – Carte 430/485 DKK – *(dinner only) (booking essential)*
• Italian • Simple • Neighbourhood •

An unassuming façade conceals an appealing trattoria with pastel hues and coffee sack curtains. Menus offer authentic Italian classics, including homemade pastas; virtually all ingredients are imported from small, organic producers.

DENMARK - COPENHAGEN

Aamanns Etablissement

X

Plan: **C1**

Øster Farimagsgade 12 ✉ 2100 Ø – ⓜ Nørreport
– ℰ 35 55 33 10 – www.aamanns.dk – Closed July, Christmas and dinner
Sunday-Wednesday
Menu 295 DKK (lunch) – Carte 365/565 DKK – *(booking advisable)*
• Danish • Bistro • Cosy •

A cosy, contemporary restaurant with cheery service and an informal atmosphere. Concise, seasonal menus blend traditional smørrebrød with more modern 'small plates'. The 4 and 6 course dinner menus come with wine pairings.

Kødbyens Fiskebar

X
ⓐ

Den Hvide Kødby, Flæsketorvet 100 (1 km via Halmtorvet B3) ✉ 1711 V
– ℰ 32 15 56 56 – www.fiskebaren.dk – Closed 24-26 December and
1 January and lunch Monday to Friday
Carte 275/485 DKK
• Seafood • Simple • Fashionable •

This buzzy, industrial-style restaurant is set, somewhat incongruously, in a former butcher's shop in a commercial meat market. Concise menus feature fresh, simply prepared seafood dishes which are based around the latest catch; oysters are a speciality. The terrace is a popular spot come summer.

Pluto

X
ⓐ

Plan: **C2**

Borgergade 16 ✉ 1300 K – ⓜ Kongens Nytorv
– ℰ 33 16 00 16 – www.restaurantpluto.dk – Closed Sunday
Menu 450 DKK – Carte 190/470 DKK – *(dinner only)*
• Mediterranean cuisine • Bistro • Rustic •

An appealing restaurant in a residential area, with concrete pillars and an intentionally 'unfinished' feel – sit at wooden tables, at the long metal bar or at communal marble-topped tables. An enticing menu of small plates includes 'cheese' and 'sweets' sections; cooking is rustic, unfussy and flavoursome.

Uformel

X

Plan: **B3**

Studiestraede 69 ✉ 1554 K
– ⓜ København Hovedbane Gård – ℰ 70 99 91 11 – www.uformel.dk
– ⓜ Closed 24-27 December and 1-2 January
Menu 775 DKK – Carte 440/660 DKK – *(dinner only) (booking essential)*
• Modern cuisine • Fashionable • Trendy •

The informal sister of Formel B, with gold table-tops, black cutlery, a smart open kitchen and a cocktail bar (a lively spot at the weekend!) Dishes are tasting plates and all are the same price; 4-6 is about the right amount.

Pony

X

Plan: **A3**

Vesterbrogade 135 ✉ 1620 V – ℰ 33 22 10 00
– www.ponykbh.dk – Closed July-August, 1 week in Christmas and
Monday
Menu 450 DKK – Carte 390/495 DKK – *(dinner only) (booking essential)*
• Danish • Bistro • Neighbourhood •

Neighbourhood restaurant with chatty service and a buzzy vibe: sit at high tables opposite the kitchen or on retro seats in the small dining room. Choose 4 of the tasty, original dishes; refined, modern cooking has a 'nose-to-tail' approach.

no.2

X

Plan: **D3**

Nicolai Eigtveds Gade 32 ✉ 1402 C
– ⓜ Christianshaven – ℰ 33 11 11 68 – www.nummer2.dk – Closed
2 weeks in July, 23-27 December, 1 January, Saturday lunch and Sunday
Menu 250 DKK (weekday lunch)/450 DKK – Carte 300/525 DKK
• Modern cuisine • Design • Fashionable •

Set among smart offices and apartments on the edge of the dock, is this elegant restaurant; the sister to a|o|c. Fresh, flavoursome small plates focus on quality Danish ingredients – be sure to try the cheeses and cured hams.

DENMARK - COPENHAGEN

�✘ **Höst** ✧

Nørre Farimagsgade 41 ✉ *1364 K –* Ⓜ *Nørreport* Plan: **B2**
– ℰ 89 93 84 09 – www.cofoco.dk/en/restaurants/hoest
– Closed 24 December, 1 January and lunch Sunday-Wednesday
Menu 295/495 DKK
• Modern cuisine • Friendly • Rustic •
A busy neighbourhood bistro with fun staff and a lively atmosphere; sit in the Garden Room. The great value monthly set menu comprises 3 courses but comes with lots of extras. Cooking is modern Nordic, seasonal and boldly flavoured.

�✘ **Bror** 𝔸ℂ

Skt Peders Strade 24A ✉ *1453 K –* Ⓜ *Nørreport* Plan: **B2**
– ℰ 32 17 59 99 – www.restaurantbror.dk – Closed 3 weeks January, 24-26 December, Monday and Tuesday
Menu 395 DKK *– (dinner only) (booking essential) (tasting menu only)*
• Regional cuisine • Bistro • Rustic •
Set on a narrow street in an older part of the city, this simple split-level bistro is run by two keen young chefs and a friendly team. Set 4 course menu of rustic bistro dishes; extra courses can be added as desired. Alternatively plump for the no-choice 5 course menu, which comes with additional snacks.

�✘ **Hummer** ⇐ 🏠

Nyhavn 63A ✉ *1051 K –* Ⓜ *Kongens Nytorv* Plan: **D2**
– ℰ 33 33 03 39 – www.restauranthummer.dk
Menu 425 DKK – Carte 220/410 DKK
• Seafood • Friendly • Simple •
Lobster is the mainstay of the menu at this restaurant, situated among the brightly coloured buildings on the famous Nyhavn strip. Enjoy a meal on the sunny terrace or in the modish, nautically styled dining room.

�✘ **Famo Metro** 𝔸ℂ

Øster Søgade 114 ✉ *2100 Ø – ℰ 35 55 66 30* Plan: **C1**
– www.famo.dk – Closed 2 weeks summer and Sunday
Menu 400 DKK *– (dinner only)*
• Italian • Bistro • Simple •
A neighbourhood restaurant with floor to ceiling windows, overlooking Sortedams Lake. Well-priced daily changing menu; classic Italian dishes are authentic and full of flavour. Service is helpful and friendly.

�✘ **Gorilla** 🏠

Flæsketorvet 63 (1 km via Halmtorvet B3) ✉ *1711 V – ℰ 33 33 83 30*
– www.restaurantgorilla.dk – Closed 23-25 December, Sunday and bank holidays
Menu 375/450 DKK – Carte 115/360 DKK *– (dinner only)*
• Modern cuisine • Brasserie • Simple •
A buzzy, canteen-style restaurant in the meatpacking district; the stone floor, zinc ducting and large windows create an industrial feel. The menu offers something for everyone; dishes are well-presented, tasty and designed for sharing.

SMØRREBRØD *The following list of simpler restaurants and cafés/bars specialise in Danish open sandwiches and are generally open from 10.00am to 4.00pm.*

�✘ **Sankt Annæ** 🏠 ✧

Sankt Annæ Plads 12 ✉ *1250 K –* Ⓜ *Kongens Nytorv* Plan: **D2**
– ℰ 33 12 54 97 – www.restaurantsanktannae.dk – Closed Easter, 18 July-7 August, Christmas-New Year, Sunday and bank holidays
Carte 224/368 DKK *– (lunch only) (booking essential)*
• Smørrebrød • Cosy • Classic décor •
An attractive terraced building with a traditional, rather quaint interior. There's a seasonal à la carte and a daily blackboard menu: prices can vary so check before ordering. The lobster and shrimp – fresh from local fjords – are a hit.

X **Amalie**

Amaliegade 11 ⊠ 1256 K – ❶ Kongens Nytorv   Plan: **D2**
– ℰ 33 12 88 10 – www.restaurantamalie.dk – Closed 24 December-
2 January, Easter, Sunday and bank holidays
Menu 269 DKK – Carte 219/322 DKK – *(lunch only) (booking essential)*
• Smørrebrød • Intimate • Rustic •

Charming 18C townhouse by Amalienborg Palace, with two tiny, cosy rooms filled with old paintings and elegant porcelain. The authentic Danish menu offers a large choice of herring, salmon and salads. Service is warm and welcoming.

X **Slotskælderen hos Gitte Kik**

Fortunstræde 4 ⊠ 1065 K – ❶ Kongens Nytorv   Plan: **C2**
– ℰ 33 11 15 37 – www.slotskaelderen.dk – Closed July, Sunday, Monday
and bank holidays
Carte 205/340 DKK – *(lunch only) (booking essential)*
• Smørrebrød • Family • Traditional décor •

Set in a 1797 building and family-run since 1910, this established restaurant sets the benchmark for this type of cuisine. The rustic inner is filled with portraits and city scenes. Go to the counter to see the full selection of smørrebrød.

ENVIRONS OF COPENHAGEN

AT NORDHAVN   North : 3 km by Østbanegade and Road 2

XX **Paustian**

Kalkbrænderiløbskaj 2 ⊠ 2150 Ø – ℰ 39 18 55 01
– www.restaurantpaustian.dk – Closed July, 23 December-14 January and
Sunday
Carte 420/435 DKK – *(lunch only) (booking advisable)*
• Danish • Fashionable • Design •

A friendly, informal restaurant set in an impressive harbourside building designed by renowned architect Jørn Utzon. Traditional Danish cooking with French touches; watch the chefs at work in the open kitchen.

AT KLAMPENBORG   North : 13 km by Østanegade and Road 2

XX **Den Røde Cottage** (Anita Klemensen and Lars Thomsen)

ఔ   *Strandvejen 550 ⊠ 2930 – ℰ 39 90 46 14*
– www.denroedecottage.dk – Closed 22 December-22 February and
Sunday October-May
Menu 525/875 DKK – *(dinner only) (booking essential)*
• Danish • Design •

An attractive former Forestry Officer's house dating back to 1881; built on the site of an old plantation. The small, romantic dining room is set with Royal Copenhagen porcelain and the lovely terrace offers partial sea views. The talented team offer monthly Nordic menus, informed by top seasonal produce.
→ Danish oysters with fennel, almond and horseradish. Poussin, creamy corn, chanterelles and pickled onions. Dark berries, toffee, brioche and sorrel.

X **Den Gule Cottage**

Strandvejen 506 ⊠ 2930 – ℰ 39 64 06 91 – www.dengulecottage.dk
– Closed 22 December-22 February and Monday-Tuesday October-May
Menu 350 DKK – Carte 300/375 DKK – *(booking advisable)*
• Danish • Inn • Minimalist •

A lovely 1844 cottage facing the beach; from the same team as Den Røde. Sit in one of two tiny, simply decorated rooms or on the large terrace with its sea views. Choose from an unfussy menu of five main dishes, salads and cheese plates.

AT **SØLLERØD**   North : 20 km by Tagensvej (take the train to Holte then taxi)
- ⊠ 2840 Holte

XxX   **Søllerød Kro**   🏵 🕝 ⇔ **P**
🏵   *Søllerødvej 35 ⊠ 2840 – 🖰 45 80 25 05 – www.soelleroed-kro.dk – Closed*
3 weeks July, 1 week February, Easter, Sunday dinner, Monday and
Tuesday
Menu 395/1095 DKK – Carte 930/1625 DKK
• Modern cuisine • Inn •
A characterful 17C thatched inn in a truly picturesque setting, with three small
but stylish dining rooms and a delightful courtyard terrace. The superb wine list
features plenty of burgundy and champagne. Choose from an array of menus
which offer classically based dishes with deep, clear flavours.
➜ Organic Oscietra caviar with mussel sauce. Black lobster, vin jaune and
morels à la crème. Gourmandise desserts.

AT **KASTRUP AIRPORT**   Southeast : 10 km by Amager Boulevard

     Hilton Copenhagen Airport   🏖 ≤ ℔ 🌐 ⃞ ᴆ 🎬 🛎 🚗
Ellehammersvej 20 ⊠ 2770 – Ⓜ København Lufthavn – 🖰 32 50 15 01
– www.copenhagen.hilton.com
378 rm – 🛉1395/3095 DKK 🛉🛉1395/3095 DKK – ⌚ 225 DKK – 5 suites
• Business • Luxury • Modern •
A smart, modern business hotel accessed from the airport via a glass walkway.
Spacious, well-maintained bedrooms have excellent sound-proofing and offer
good views from the higher floors. Relax in the Asian-inspired Ni'mat Spa. Horizon offers everything from sandwiches and grills to Nordic specialities.

AARHUS
AARHUS

Population: 324 000

WeEm/Westend61 RM/age fotostock

Known as the world's smallest big city, Denmark's second city is a vibrant, versatile place, yet has the charm of a small town. It was originally founded by the Vikings in the 8th century and has been an important trading centre ever since. It's set on the Eastern edge of Jutland and is the country's main port; lush forests surround it, and there are beautiful beaches to the north and south. It's easy to enjoy the great outdoors, while also benefiting from the advantages of urban life.

There's plenty to see and do, and most of it is within walking distance: the city centre is awash with shops – from big chains to quirky boutiques – as well as museums, bars and restaurants, and the student population contributes to its youthful feel. The most buzzing area is Aboulevarden; a pedestrianized street which runs alongside the river, lined with clubs and cafés. Cultural activities are also high on the agenda of the European Capital of Culture 2017: visit the 12th century Cathedral and the ARoS Art Museum with its colourful rooftop panorama; witness the 2000 year old Grauballe man on display at the Moesgaard prehistoric museum; or step back in time at Den Gamle By. This is not a place that stands still and bold redevelopment projects are reshaping the cityscape, with shiny new apartment and office blocks springing up around the harbour.

AARHUS IN...

➜ **ONE DAY**
ARoS Art Museum, the Viking Museum, Aarhus Cathedral, stroll around the Latin Quarter.

➜ **TWO DAYS**
Den Gamle By (open air 'living' museum), hire a bike and ride into the country.

➜ **THREE DAYS**
Marselisborg Palace (summer residence of the Royal family), Moesgaard Museum.

PRACTICAL INFORMATION

ARRIVAL-DEPARTURE

✈ Aarhus Airport is 45km northeast of the city in Tirstrup. Airport Bus Number 925X to the city centre takes 50min.

GETTING AROUND

Aarhus city centre is fairly small and all the main sights are easily accessible on foot. Another good way to get around is by bike, using the network of bicycle paths which connect the city. City Bikes are available from April-October and are free of charge; a 20 kroner coin is required to unlock them from the rack. If you're catching a yellow city bus, enter by any door and buy a 1-2, 3 or 4 zone ticket from the machine; for the blue regional buses, enter at the front and buy a ticket from the driver. A 24/48hr AarhusCard allows free travel in zones 1 and 2, as well as free or discounted entry to numerous city attractions.

CALENDAR HIGHLIGHTS

May
Classic Car Race, Spot Music Festival.

May-September
Sand Sculpture Festival.

June
Northside Alternative Music Festival.

July
Viking Moot, International Jazz Festival.

September
Aarhus Festival, with concerts, theatre and outdoor shows, Food Festival.

October
International Guitar Festival.

December
Christmas in the Old Town.

EATING OUT

Being a student city, Aarhus hums with café culture all year round; you'll find cosy coffee shops on almost every street, offering breakfasts, cakes, sandwiches and light lunches – some are also popular places to enjoy an evening drink, especially in the lively Aboulevarden area. Eating out is something the Danes excel at and restaurants range from friendly bistros to elegant fine dining establishments; most offer food with a Danish heart but influences come from around the globe. Local produce includes freshly caught fish landed at the harbour and vegetables from the island of Samso; restaurants tend to offer set menus of between 3 and 7 courses and these are great way to sample a varied selection of dishes. They tend to open early – at around 6pm – while the bars and clubs stay open late, and often offer live music. Not to be overlooked are the city's classic Danish smørrebørd restaurants, where satisfying and wonderfully tasty open sandwiches are served, often along with a tempting selection of cakes and pastries. Tipping is not expected, but obviously greatly appreciated.

DENMARK - AARHUS

 Comwell Aarhus　　　　　　☆ ← ｆ& 🅺 🆚 🚗

Værkmestergade 2 ⊠ 8000 – ℰ 86 72 80 00　　Plan: **B2**
– www.comwellaarhus.dk
240 rm ☲ – †998/1698 DKK ††1198/1898 DKK
• Business • Modern • Design •

A stylish, modern hotel set over 12 floors of a tower block. It's aimed at business-people, with 19 meeting rooms; the largest with space for 475. Bedrooms are bright and contemporary with monsoon showers; choose a corner Business Class room for super city views. Guest areas include a bar and buzzy bistro.

 Scandic Aarhus City　　　　　☆ ｆ& 🅺 🆚 🚗

Østergade 10 ⊠ 8000 – ℰ 89 31 81 00　　Plan: **B2**
– www.scandichotels.com
228 rm ☲ – †895/1900 DKK ††995/2700 DKK – 8 suites
• Business • Chain • Modern •

Behind the 19C façade of a Viennese Renaissance café lies a smart, modern hotel with an open-plan lounge, lobby, bar and reception. Bright bedrooms feature photos of city scenes; suites have balconies. Solar panels supply electricity and rooftop hives provide honey. Grill restaurant with an open kitchen.

 Radisson Blu Scandinavia　　　　☆ ｆ& 🅺 🆚 🚗

Margrethepladsen 1 ⊠ 8000 – ℰ 86 12 86 65　　Plan: **A2**
– www.radissonblu.com/hotel-aarhus
234 rm ☲ – †895/1890 DKK ††895/1890 DKK – 5 suites
• Business • Chain • Modern •

A conference-orientated hotel close to the ARoS Museum. Spacious, contemporary bedrooms offer all the facilities a modern traveller would expect. Business Class rooms and suites on the top two floors offer the best views along with extra touches. International dishes are served in the informal restaurant.

 Villa Provence　　　　　　　ｅ 🅿

Fredens Torv 10-12 ⊠ 8000 – ℰ 86 18 24 00　　Plan: **B2**
– www.villaprovence.dk – Closed 22 December-2 January
39 rm ☲ – †1295/1895 DKK ††1395/3000 DKK
• Townhouse • Traditional • Personalised •

Enter through an archway into a lovely cobbled terrace garden: this charming and elegant townhouse is a little piece of Provence in Aarhus. Proudly run by an amiable couple, it's furnished with French antiques and features a traditional lounge full of books, and individual bedrooms; some with four-posters.

 Hotel Royal　　　　　　　　☆ ｆ& 🕸 🅺 🆚

Store Torv 4 ⊠ 8000 – ℰ 86 12 00 11　　Plan: **B2**
– www.hotelroyal.dk
63 rm – †995/1895 DKK ††1195/2045 DKK – ☲ 95 DKK – 5 suites
• Historic • Traditional • Classic •

Beside the cathedral is the city's oldest hotel; open for around 175 years and with a wonderfully classic feel – enhanced by paintings depicting the Kings and Queens of Denmark. Very spacious bedrooms combine antique furniture and modern facilities. The informal restaurant serves international dishes.

Hotel Ritz Aarhus City　　　　　☆ ｆ& 🕸 🅺 🆚

Banegårdspladsen 12 ⊠ 8000 – ℰ 86 13 44 44　　Plan: **A2**
– www.hotelritz.dk – Closed Christmas
67 rm ☲ – †1045/1145 DKK ††1145/1245 DKK
• Historic • Traditional • Art déco •

An iconic 1932 hotel in distinctive yellow brick, situated opposite the railway station. Friendly and welcoming with an appealing art deco style and neatly refurbished, modern bedrooms in warm colours. Showers only in most rooms.

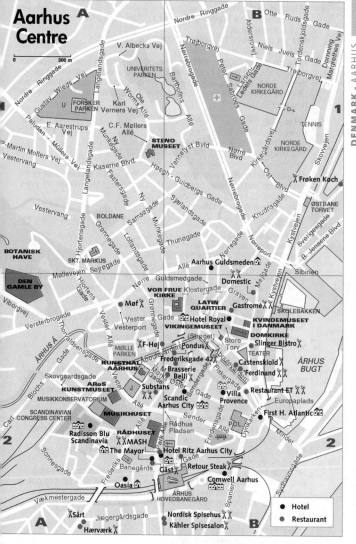

Aarhus
Centre

0 ____ 300 m

Nordre Ringgade
V. Albecks Vej
UNIVERITETS PARKEN
Trøjborgvej
Nørrebrogade
Otte Ruds Gade
Aldersrovej
Niels Juels Gade
Tordenskjoldsgade
Dronning Margrethes Vej
Trøjborgvej
Peter Sabroes Gade
Larssens Gade
NORDRE KIRKEGÅRD

Gustav Wieds Vej
Langelandsgade
Worms Allé
Bartholins Allé
TENNIS
NORDRE KIRKEGÅRD
Skovvejen

U
FORSKER PARKEN
Karl Verners Vej
Ole Allé
Kirkegårdsvej
Øst Blvd

E. Aarestrups Vej
Paludan
Müller - Müllers Vej
C.F. Møllers Allé
STENO MUSEET
Høegh - Guldbergs Gade
Nørrebrogade
Frøken Køch

P-Martin Møllers Vej
Vestervang
Munkegade
Kasern Blvd.
Ny Munkegade
Nørre Blvd
Ost Blvd
ØSTBANE TORVET
Knudrisgade
Sverigesgade
B. Jensens Blvd

Vestervang
Langelandsgade
Fastergade
Samsøgade
Ny Munkegade
Sjællandsgade
Kystvejen
Sibirien

BOLDANE
Grønnegade
Lollandsgade
Thunøgade
Nørregade
Nørreport

BOTANISK HAVE
Hortensgade
Sejrøgade
Allé
Aarhus Guldsmeden

Mølleveien
Hjortens Gade
Nørre Guldsmedgade
Domestic
Melbyg

DEN GAMLE BY
Viborgvej
VOR FRUE KIRKE
Klostergade
Graven
SKOLEBAKKEN

Verstersbrogade
Vester Allé
Vesterport
Møf
Vester Gade
Grønnegade
LATIN QUARTIER
Gastromé
KVINDEMUSEET I DANMARK

ARHUS Å
Thorvaldsensgade
MØLLE PARKEN
Hotel Royal
VIKINGEMUSEET
(Strøget)
Store Torv
DOMKIRKE
Slinger Bistro

Blochs
Skovgaardsgade
KUNSTHAL AARHUS
F-Høj
Pondus
TEATER
ÅRHUS BUGT

ARoS KUNSTMUSEET
Brasserie Belli
Castenskiold
Ferdinand

MUSIKKONSERVATORIUM
Substans
Scandic Aarhus City
Villa Provence
Restaurant ET
Europaplads

SCANDINAVIAN CONGRESS CENTER
MUSIKHUSET
Sønder Allé
Rådhus Pladsen
First H. Atlantic

Radisson Blu Scandinavia
RÅDHUSET
MASH
Park Allé
Fredens
POL.
Mindet

Sonnesgade
The Mayor
Hotel Ritz Aarhus City
Cäst
Retour Steak
Comwell Aarhus

Frederiks Banegårds
Oasia
ÅRHUS HOVEDBANEGÅRD
Skolebakkensgade

Vækmestergade
Jægergårdsgade
Nordisk Spisehus
Kähler Spisesalon

Sårt
Hærværk

● Hotel
● Restaurant

153

DENMARK - AARHUS

 First H. Atlantic ☆ ≤ &

Europaplads 10 ⊠ 8000 – ℰ 86 13 11 11 Plan: **B2**
– www.firsthotels.dk
102 rm ☲ – **♦**995/1895 DKK **♦♦**1095/2195 DKK
• Business • Chain • Modern •

Although its exterior can hardly be deemed charming, its rooms are spacious and modern with good facilities, a balcony and a vista of either the city or the sea. Enjoy breakfast with a view on the top floor. Classic Italian dishes are served in the smart restaurant. Gym membership is available at the adjacent fitness club.

 The Mayor ⚐ 🅿

Banegårdspladsen 14 ⊠ 8000 – ℰ 87 32 01 00 Plan: **A2**
– www.themayor.dk – Closed 23 December-8 January
162 rm ☲ – **♦**795/1995 DKK **♦♦**1045/2095 DKK
• Family • Townhouse • Modern •

Recently refurbished in a contemporary style, this hotel is situated close to the train station and has been owned by the same family for over twenty years. Cosy bedrooms have a modern industrial feel.
Gäst – See restaurant listing

🏠 **Oasia** 🅿

Kriegersvej 27-31 ⊠ 8000 – ℰ 87 32 37 15 Plan: **A2**
– www.hoteloasia.com – Closed 24-25 December
65 rm ☲ – **♦**895/1595 DKK **♦♦**895/1795 DKK
• Townhouse • Traditional • Design •

After a day's sightseeing or shopping, you will be happy to head back to this hotel in a quieter area of the city. Bright, uncluttered bedrooms offer good facilities; go for one of the suites with their modern four posters.

 Aarhus Guldsmeden

Guldsmedgade 40 ⊠ 8000 – ℰ 86 13 45 50 Plan: **B1**
– www.guldsmedenhotels.com – Closed 30 December-2 January
22 rm ☲ – **♦**945/1325 DKK **♦♦**1075/1575 DKK
• Townhouse • Traditional • Personalised •

A relaxed hotel with an eco/organic ethos and a friendly atmosphere. Simply decorated bedrooms vary in shape and size; some feature antique furniture and the larger rooms have four posters. Complimentary tea, coffee and juice.

 Frederikshøj (Wassim Hallal) 🕷 ≤ 🍴 🅰🅺
❀
Oddervej 19 (South: 3.5 km by Spanien and Strandvejen) ⊠ 8000
– ℰ 86 14 22 80 – www.frederikshoj.com – Closed 4 weeks midsummer, 1 week October, Christmas-New Year and Sunday-Tuesday
Menu 895 DKK – *(dinner only) (booking essential) (tasting menu only)*
• Creative • Elegant • Luxury •

Set in the former staff lodge to the Royal Palace, this restaurant is smart, luxurious and contemporary with edgy artwork, iPad menus and floor to ceiling windows affording views over the gardens and out to sea. Dishes are elaborate, creative and visually impressive. Service is professional and knowledgeable.
→ Tuna with caviar. Beef with carrot. Strawberries and cream.

 Gastromé (William Jørgensen) ⇔
❀
Rosensgade 28 ⊠ 8000 – ℰ 28 78 16 17 Plan: **B2**
– www.gastrome.dk – Closed 23 December-3 January, Sunday and Monday
Menu 548/848 DKK – *(dinner only) (tasting menu only)*
• Modern cuisine • Fashionable • Intimate •

This intimate Latin Quarter restaurant features a semi open plan kitchen and stark white walls punctuated with contemporary art. The menu is divided into a 'half throttle' of 4 courses and a 'full throttle' of 8, with wines to match. Complex cooking showcases modern techniques. Informative service.
→ Monkfish, cauliflower, peas and cocoa. Quail with morels and broccoli. Summer berries, elderflower and soured cream.

DENMARK - AARHUS

XX
&3 **Substans** (René Mammen)   [AC]
Frederiksgade 74 ⊠ *8000 –* ☎ *86 23 04 01*   Plan: **A2**
– www.restaurantsubstans.dk – Closed Christmas, 28-30 July, Sunday-
Tuesday
Menu 385/900 DKK *– (dinner only) (tasting menu only)*
• Modern cuisine • Friendly • Simple •
Classically Scandic in style, with a fresh, uncluttered feel, Pondus' older, more
adventurous sister is run by the same experienced husband and wife team.
Creative, contemporary cooking uses top quality, mostly organic, ingre-
dients. Dishes have original touches, distinct flavours and stimulating combi-
nations.
➜ Malt pie, clams and fermented vegetables. Organic pork, carrots and
brown butter. Pickled apples, thyme ice cream, caramel and dried beans.

XX
&3 **Domestic** (Morten Frølich Rastad and Christoffer Norton)   🛱 �&
Mejlgade 35B (through the arch) ⊠ *8000 –* ☎ *61 43 70 10*   ⇔
– www.restaurantdomestic.dk – Closed Easter, 16-   Plan: **B2**
30 December, Sunday and Monday
Menu 500/900 DKK *– (dinner only) (tasting menu only)*
• Danish • Fashionable • Minimalist •
The hottest ticket in town is this rustic yet elegant restaurant where 4 friends
work together to serve skilfully cooked, feel-good food with pure, natural flavours – using only Danish ingredients. Hanging hams, pickling jars and cookbooks feature. Menus offer 4 or 8 set courses; fish dishes are a highlight.
➜ Fjord shrimps, green asparagus and oyster. Beef with ramsons and wild
garlic. Apple and thyme.

XX **Restaurant ET**   🕸 🛱 �& [AC] ⇔
Åboulevarden 7 ⊠ *8000 –* ☎ *86 13 88 00*   Plan: **B2**
– www.restaurant-et.dk – Closed Christmas and Sunday
Menu 358 DKK *–* Carte 374/514 DKK
• French • Design • Fashionable •
You'll find charming service, modern brasserie styling and a central kitchen at
this well-run restaurant. Classic French dishes are full of flavour; some come
with a Danish twist. Superb wine choice, particularly from France.

XX **Nordisk Spisehus**   [AC]
M.P.Bruuns Gade 31 ⊠ *8000 –* ☎ *86 17 70 99*   Plan: **A/B2**
– www.nordiskspisehus.dk – Closed 23-26 December, 1 January and
Sunday except December
Menu 500/800 DKK *–* Carte 240/545 DKK
• Modern cuisine • Neighbourhood • Fashionable •
A smart, intimate restaurant with a unique concept: four themed menus a year
offering their own versions of dishes from Michelin Starred restaurants around
the globe. Décor changes along with the theme: perhaps Japanese, Spanish or
Nordic.

XX **Ferdinand**   🕸 ⇦ 🛱 [AC]
Åboulevarden 28 ⊠ *8000*   Plan: **B2**
– ☎ *87 32 14 44 – www.hotelferdinand.dk*
– Closed 22 December-3 January
19 rm *–* ♦950/1250 DKK ♦♦1150/1450 DKK *–* ⟷ 110 DKK *– 8 suites*
Menu 165/445 DKK *–* Carte 345/435 DKK
• French • Brasserie • Fashionable •
Red-canopied Ferdinand stands out from its neighbours on the liveliest street in
the city. Classic brasserie-style menus offer a mix of French and Danish influenced dishes, with a great value set lunch and small plates in the evening; a bar
also serves tapas in the courtyard. Bedrooms are comfy and spacious.

XX **MASH**   🏦 🍴 AK

Banegaardspladsen 12 ✉ *8000 –* ✆ *33 13 93 00*   Plan: **A2**
– www.mashsteak.dk – Closed 25-27 December and 1 January
Carte 280/1560 DKK
• Meats and grills • Fashionable • Friendly •
This Modern American Steak House (MASH) is bright and smart, with colourful
cow ornaments and red leather banquettes; sit in one of the booths. Top quality
imported USDA steaks are listed alongside Danish and even Japanese Kobe
beef.

X **Hærværk**   ᵴ AK
☺
Frederiks Allé 105 ✉ *8000 –* ✆ *50 51 26 51*   Plan: **A2**
*– www.restaurant-haervaerk.dk – Closed 2 weeks Christmas and 2 weeks
summer*
Menu 450 DKK *– (dinner only) (tasting menu only)*
• Danish • Intimate • Fashionable •
A lively place set in two converted shops; owned and run by four friends. Indust-
rial-chic styling with a concrete floor, stark white décor and a glass-fronted
fridge displaying hanging meats. Well-crafted Danish dishes with a rustic style
and refined touch. Great value daily set menu; enthusiastic service.

X **Frederiksgade 42**

Frederiksgade 42 ✉ *8000 –* ✆ *606 89 606*   Plan: **B2**
– www.frederiksgade42.dk – Closed Sunday and Monday
Menu 198/398 DKK *– (dinner only) (tasting menu only)*
• Danish • Neighbourhood • Bistro •
The experienced owner extends a warm welcome to customers at this delightful restaurant in the heart of the city. The focus is on vegetarian dishes, with
seasonal menus of well-priced small plates designed for sharing.

X **Castenskiold**   🍴 ᵴ AK

Åboulevarden 32 ✉ *8000 –* ✆ *86 18 90 90*   Plan: **B2**
– www.castenskiold.net – Closed Christmas, Easter and Sunday
Menu 350 DKK – Carte 365/450 DKK
• Modern cuisine • Fashionable • Trendy •
Something a little different: set by the river on a busy pedestrianised street, this
trendy restaurant morphs into a bar and club as the day goes on. Creative
modern cooking relies on top quality produce and the flavours shine through.

X **Brasserie Belli**   🍴

Frederiksgade 54 ✉ *8000 –* ✆ *86 12 07 60*   Plan: **B2**
– www.belli.dk – Closed 1 week July, Easter, Christmas and Sunday
Menu 240 DKK – Carte 340/460 DKK
• Classic French • Brasserie • Traditional décor •
An intimate, long-standing, family-owned restaurant on a pedestrianised city
centre street, offering satisfying, good value, French brasserie classics and
polite, friendly service. Check out the owner's costumes from her circus days.

X **Pondus**
☺
Åboulevarden 51 ✉ *8000 –* ✆ *28 77 18 50*   Plan: **B2**
*– www.restaurantpondus.dk – Closed Christmas, 1 week July, Sunday and
Monday*
Menu 295 DKK *– (dinner only) (booking advisable)*
• Danish • Bistro • Rustic •
Set by the narrow city centre canal, this little sister to Substans is a small, rustic
bistro with a friendly vibe and a stripped back style. The blackboard menu offers
great value, flavoursome cooking which uses organic Danish produce. Dishes
are bright and colourful and represent great value.

X
Slinger Bistro

Skolegade 5 ⊠ 8000 – ☏ 30 31 32 45   Plan: **B2**
– www.slingerbistro.dk – Closed Christmas, 2 weeks in summer, Sunday and Wednesday
Menu 300 DKK – Carte 330/550 DKK – *(dinner only)*
• Danish • Neighbourhood • Friendly •

An intimate, personally run neighbourhood restaurant with homely décor and an open kitchen at its heart. Modern, fiercely local cooking on an à la carte and various set menus; 4 courses are sufficient. Good selection of wines by the glass.

X
Møf

Vesterport 10 ⊠ 8000 – ☏ 61 73 33 33   Plan: **A2**
– www.restaurantmoef.com – Closed 23 December - 2 January, Tuesday and Wednesday
Menu 325 DKK – Carte 380/505 DKK – *(dinner only) (booking essential)*
• Danish • Neighbourhood • Trendy •

Owned and run by an experienced young couple, this restaurant features monochrome décor and counter dining. There's a daily 3 course set menu and a concise à la carte; dishes are modern in style but Danish at heart and made with local produce.

X
Frøken Koch   🛋 AK

Kystpromenaden 5 ⊠ 8000 – ☏ 86 18 64 00   Plan: **B1**
– www.kocherier.dk – Closed 22 December-4 January, Sunday and Monday
Menu 295 DKK – Carte 350/400 DKK
• Danish • Bistro • Design •

This bistro overlooks the marina, has a delightful raised terrace and is open all day for hearty, homely Danish classics which are full of flavour. Dishes like potato soup with smoked trout evoke memories of family meals in childhood.

X
Retour Steak   🛋

Banegårdspladsen 4 ⊠ 8000 – ☏ 88 63 02 90   Plan: **B2**
– www.retoursteakaarhus.dk
Carte 265/490 DKK
• Meats and grills • Fashionable • Bistro •

A busy restaurant close to station: the latest outpost of the famed steak group. They serve some simple starters and puddings but the main focus is on meat, with tasty Danish rib-eye in various sizes accompanied by fluffy homemade chips.

X
Gäst – The Mayor Hotel   **P**

Banegårdspladsen 14 ⊠ 8000 – ☏ 87 32 01 67   Plan: **A2**
– www.gaest.dk – Closed 23 December-8 January
Menu 350 DKK – Carte 310/390 DKK
• Italian • Bistro • Fashionable •

This spacious, relaxed Italian restaurant, set on the ground floor of The Mayor Hotel, serves a seasonal, modern menu. Carefully cooked, flavoursome dishes; everything is prepared in-house and pasta is the highlight.

X
Sårt

Jægergårdsgade 6 ⊠ 8000 – ☏ 86 12 00 70   Plan: **A2**
– www.saart.dk – Closed Sunday lunch and Monday
Menu 150/350 DKK – Carte 300/625 DKK
• Danish • Tapas bar • Rustic •

A simple but serious restaurant with its own deli: the first thing you see is a chiller filled with cured meats and preserved legs of ham; they also import whole cheeses, make their own pasta and have fresh bread delivered daily.

SMØRREBRØD *The following simpler restaurants and cafés specialize in Danish open sandwiches*

X **F-Høj**

Plan: **A2**

Grønnegade 2 ✉ 8000 – www.fhoj.dk – Closed 4 weeks midsummer, Christmas-New Year, Sunday and Monday
Menu 120 DKK – Carte 195/205 DKK – *(lunch only) (bookings not accepted)*
• Smørrebrød • Neighbourhood • Friendly •

A bright, busy café with a pavement terrace; fridges and cabinets display a tempting selection of desserts, cakes, biscuits and drinks. Six choices of fresh, flavoursome classics on the smørrebrød menu; two plus a light dessert should suffice.

X **Kähler Spisesalon**

Plan: **A/B2**

M.P. Bruuns Gade 33 ✉ 8000 – ✆ 86 12 20 53 – www.spisesalon.dk – Closed 23-26 December and 1 January
Menu 200/360 DKK – *(bookings not accepted)*
• Smørrebrød • Neighbourhood • Traditional décor •

An informal smørrebrød café, popular with shoppers and open in the evening. They offer soups, salads, smørrebrød and pastries, as well as organic juices and top-notch teas and coffees. Monochrome pictures of Aarhus add to the charm.

FINLAND
SUOMI

→ **AREA:**
338 145 km² (130 558 sq mi).

→ **POPULATION:**
5 523 904 inhabitants.
Density = 16 per km².

→ **CAPITAL:** Helsinki.

→ **CURRENCY:** Euro (€).

→ **GOVERNMENT:**
Parliamentary republic (since 1917).
Member of European Union since 1995.

→ **LANGUAGES:**
Finnish (a Finno-Ugric language
related to Estonian) spoken by
92% of Finns, Swedish (6%) and
Sami (some 7 000 native speakers).
English is widely spoken.

→ **PUBLIC HOLIDAYS:**
New Year's Day (1 Jan); Epiphany
(6 Jan); Good Friday (late Mar/Apr);
Easter Monday (late Mar/Apr);
May Day (1 May); Ascension Day
(May); Epiphany (6 Jan); Midsummer
(mid June); All Saints' Day
(1 Nov); Independence Day (6 Dec);
Christmas Day (25 Dec); Boxing Day
(26 Dec).

→ **LOCAL TIME:**
GMT+2 hours in winter and GMT
+3 hours in summer.

→ **CLIMATE:**
Temperate continental with very
cold winters and mild summers
(Helsinki: January -7°C; July 17°C).
Midnight sun: for several weeks
around Midsummer, the sun never
sets in the north. Snow settles from
early Dec-Apr in the south and
centre of the country.
Northern Lights (Aurora Borealis)
visible in the north on clear, dark
nights; highest frequency in Feb-
Mar and Sep-Oct.

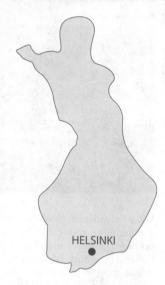

HELSINKI

→ **EMERGENCY:**
Police, Medical Assistance and Fire
Brigade: ✆ **112**

→ **ELECTRICITY:**
230 volts AC, 50Hz; 2 round pin
sockets.

→ **FORMALITIES:**
Travellers from the European Union
(EU), Switzerland, Iceland and the
main countries of North and South
America need a national identity
card or passport (America: passport
required) to visit Finland for less
than three months (tourism or
business purposes). For visitors
from other countries a visa may be
required, in addition to a passport,
especially for those wishing to
stay for longer than three months.
If you plan to visit Russia while in
Finland, you must purchase an
appropriate visa in advance in your
own country. We advise you to
check with your embassy before
travelling.

Helsinki
HELSINGFORS

Population: 620 982

Ph. Robic/MICHELIN

Cool, clean and chic, the 'Daughter of the Baltic' sits prettily on a peninsula, jutting out between the landmasses of its historical overlords, Sweden and Russia. Surrounded on three sides by water, Helsinki is a busy port, but that only tells a small part of the story: forests grow in abundance around here and trees reach down to the lapping shores. This is a striking city to look at: it was rebuilt in the 19C after a fire, and many of the buildings have a handsome neoclassical or art nouveau façade. Shoppers can browse the picturesque outdoor food and tourist markets stretching along the main harbour, where island-hopping ferries ply their trade.

In a country with over 200,000 lakes it would be pretty hard to escape a green sensibility, and the Finnish capital has made sure that concrete and stone have never taken priority over its distinctive features of trees, water and open space. There are bridges at every turn connecting the city's varied array of small islands, and a ten kilometre strip of parkland acts as a spine running vertically up from the centre. Renowned as a city of cool, it's somewhere that also revels in a hot nightlife and even hotter saunas – this is where they were invented. And if your blast of dry heat has left you wanting a refreshing dip, there's always a freezing lake close at hand.

HELSINKI IN...

→ **ONE DAY**
Harbour market place, Uspensky Cathedral, Lutheran Cathedral, Katajanokka, Mannerheimintie.

→ **TWO DAYS**
A ferry to Suomenlinna, Church in the Rock, the nightlife of Fredrikinkatu.

→ **THREE DAYS**
Central Park, the Sibelius monument, Esplanadi.

PRACTICAL INFORMATION

ARRIVAL-DEPARTURE

✈ Helsinki-Vantaa Airport is 19km north of the city.
A taxi will take 20-30min to the centre. Buses to the Central Bus Station take 40min.

GETTING AROUND

Getting across Helsinki is fast and easy: trams and buses whizz you round efficiently. A single ticket is cheap and good for any transfers you make within an hour; buy them from the driver, ticket machines, kiosks, metro stations or the ferry terminal. If you need to make several journeys during one day or several days, a day ticket is a good choice. You can choose a ticket valid for 1 to 7 days. The Helsinki Card is valid for one, two or three days with a sliding scale of prices, and allows you unlimited transport plus free admission to museums and attractions. There are regular ferries from the harbour to Suomenlinna; they sail a little less frequently to the other main islands.

CALENDAR HIGHLIGHTS

June
Helsinki Day (the city's birthday), Juhannus (midsummer).

June-July
Helsinki Cup (international youth football tournament).

August
Helsinki Festival.

October
Baltic Herring Festival.

December
Traditional Christmas Markets, Lucia Parade to the Lutheran Cathedral.

EATING OUT

Local - and we mean local - ingredients are very much to the fore in the kitchens of Helsinki's restaurants. Produce is sourced from the country's abundant lakes, forests and seas, so your menu will assuredly be laden with the likes of smoked reindeer, reindeer's tongue, elk in aspic, lampreys, Arctic char, Baltic herring, snow grouse and cloudberries. Generally speaking, complicated, fussy preparations are overlooked for those that let the natural flavours shine through. In the autumn, markets are piled high with woodland mushrooms, often from Lapland, and chefs make the most of this bounty. Local alcoholic drinks include schnapps, vodka and liqueurs made from local berries: lakka (made from cloudberries) and mesimarja (brambleberries) are definitely worth discovering – you may not find them in any other European city. You'd find coffee anywhere in Europe, but not to the same extent as here: Finns are among the world's biggest coffee drinkers. In the gastronomic restaurants, lunch is a simpler affair, often with limited choice.

FINLAND - HELSINKI

Kämp

Pohjoisesplanadi 29 ✉ 00100 – Ⓜ Kaisaniemi – ✆ (09)   Plan: **C2**
576 111 – www.hotelkamp.fi
179 rm 🖵 – †340/670 € ††370/970 € – 8 suites
• Grand Luxury • Classic •

The grand façade, columned interior and impressive staircase point back to this luxurious hotel's 19C roots and the classically furnished bedrooms follow suit; the superb spa, meanwhile, adds a modern touch. The chic bar offers an excellent selection of champagne and cocktails, while for dining, there's Asian-inspired 'Yume' or a bustling brasserie with a global menu.

Yume – See restaurant listing

Crowne Plaza Helsinki

Mannerheimintie 50 ✉ 00260 – ✆ (09) 2521 0000   Plan: **A1**
– www.crowneplaza-helsinki.fi
349 rm 🖵 – †145/492 € ††145/492 € – 4 suites
• Business • Chain • Contemporary •

Spacious hotel specialising in conferences. Comfy, up-to-date bedrooms have good facilities and city or lake views; the higher the floor, the better the grade. Pay a visit to the huge basement fitness club and spa, then make for the warm, welcoming restaurant which serves Mediterranean cuisine.

Hilton Helsinki Strand

John Stenbergin Ranta 4 ✉ 00530 – Ⓜ Hakaniemi   Plan: **C1**
– ✆ (09) 393 51 – www.hilton.com
190 rm – †129/360 € ††165/395 € – 🖵 22 € – 7 suites
• Business • Luxury • Classic •

This spacious waterfront hotel has a classical 1980s design, an impressive atrium and an 8th floor fitness and relaxation centre; take in the view from the gym or pool. Smartly kept bedrooms boast marble bathrooms – ask for a room overlooking the water. The restaurant offers global classics and local specialities.

Haven

Unioninkatu 17 ✉ 00130 – ✆ (09) 681930   Plan: **C2**
– www.hotelhaven.fi
77 rm 🖵 – †199/270 € ††219/290 €
• Business • Luxury • Modern •

Centrally located office block conversion with an elegant townhouse-style interior and clubby bar offering a great rum selection. Chic bedrooms have top quality furnishings and marble bathrooms with TVs. Have breakfast overlooking the harbour, then at night dine on Russian cuisine in Bystro or in the Nordic fine dining restaurant.

Lilla Roberts

Pieni Roobertinkatu 1-3 ✉ 00130 – ✆ (09) 689 9880   Plan: **C2**
– www.lillaroberts.fi
130 rm 🖵 – †150/330 € ††180/360 € – 1 suite
• Business • Design • Personalised •

The building was designed in 1908 by one of Finland's top architects and was originally head office for the city's energy works. The smart, designer interior uses dark colours and is centred around the concept of 'hygge' (enjoying the simple things in life). The elegant restaurant serves an appealing menu.

Klaus K

Bulevardi 2/4 ✉ 00120 – Ⓜ Rautatientori – ✆ (020)   Plan: **C2**
770 4703 – www.klauskhotel.com
171 rm 🖵 – †120/320 € ††140/640 €
• Luxury • Design •

A landmark building with a funky, laid-back vibe and a striking interior designed to reflect the themes of The Kalevala. Bedroom styles include 'Passion', 'Mystical', 'Desire' and 'Envy'; the top floor 'Sky Lofts' are particularly sumptuous. Modern Tuscan cuisine is served under an embossed metal ceiling.

GLO Hotel Kluuvi

Kluuvikatu 4 ⊠ 00100 – Ⓜ Kaisaniemi – ℰ (010)
3444 400 – www.glohotels.fi   Plan: **C2**
184 rm � – **♦**125/370 € **♦♦**135/380 € – 6 suites
• Luxury • Modern • Design •
Stylish hotel on a fashionable shopping street; a boutique sister to next door Kämp, whose spa it shares. Spacious bedrooms have a contemporary look and come with smart glass shower rooms. There's also a lively bar-lounge and a fashionable restaurant serving cuisine from around the globe.

Radisson Blu Plaza

Mikonkatu 23 ⊠ 00100 – Ⓜ Kaisaniemi – ℰ (020)
1234 703 – www.radissonblu.com/plazahotel-helsinki   Plan: **C2**
302 rm ⊵ – **♦**139/389 € **♦♦**149/399 € – 1 suite
• Business • Chain • Contemporary •
Elegant 20C building set close to the station and completed by a more modern wing. Well-equipped bedrooms come in a choice of modern or classic styles and many have 3D TVs. The bar is a fashionable spot and the large restaurant – unusually set over several rooms – offers five different types of cuisine.

Torni

Yrjönkatu 26 ⊠ 00100 – Ⓜ Rautatientori – ℰ (020)
1234 604 – www.sokoshoteltorni.fi   Plan: **B2**
152 rm ⊵ – **♦**179/269 € **♦♦**179/269 € – 6 suites
• Business • Art déco • Elegant •
Charming early 20C hotel with a palpable sense of history. Bedrooms come in 'Art Deco', 'Art Nouveau' and 'Functionalist' styles – the latter, in the 11 storey tower, have glass-walled bathrooms. The top floor bar has a terrace and superb city views; the restaurant offers traditional Finnish cuisine.

Holiday Inn Helsinki West Ruoholahti

Sulhasenkuja 3 ⊠ 00180 – Ⓜ Ruoholahti – ℰ (09)
4152 1000 – www.holidayinn.com – Closed Saturday,   Plan: **A3**
Sunday and lunch bank holidays
256 rm ⊵ – **♦**65/220 € **♦♦**80/235 €
• Business • Functional •
Set outside the city on a business park but close to a metro station. Modern bedrooms display touches of colour and come with compact shower rooms and excellent soundproofing; the higher, west-facing rooms have pleasant water and city views. The light, bright restaurant serves international cuisine.

Fabian

Fabiankatu 7 ⊠ 00130 – ℰ (09) 6128 2000
– www.hotelfabian.fi   Plan: **C2**
58 rm ⊵ – **♦**139/250 € **♦♦**169/350 €
• Townhouse • Contemporary • Modern •
Charming boutique hotel close to the harbour. Bedrooms have stylish black & white themes and smart bathrooms with heated floors. Have breakfast in the central courtyard in summer – ingredients are organic or from small producers.

Katajanokka

Merikasarminkatu 1 ⊠ 00160 – ℰ (09) 686 450
– www.hotelkatajanokka.fi   Plan: **D2**
106 rm ⊵ – **♦**99/219 € **♦♦**109/229 €
• Historic • Grand luxury •
A pleasantly restored, late 19C prison where they have retained the original staircases and high ceilinged corridors. The old cells are now comfortable, well-equipped bedrooms with modern bathrooms. The traditional cellar restaurant features a preserved prison cell and serves traditional Finnish cuisine.

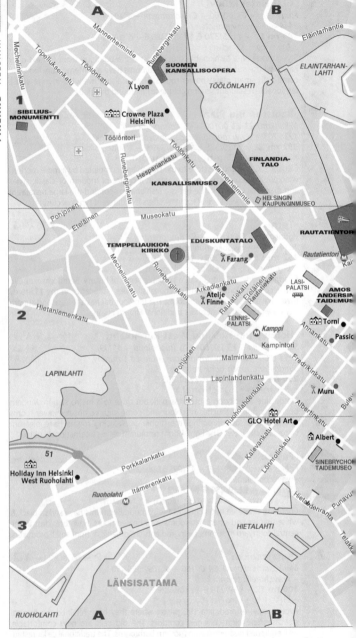

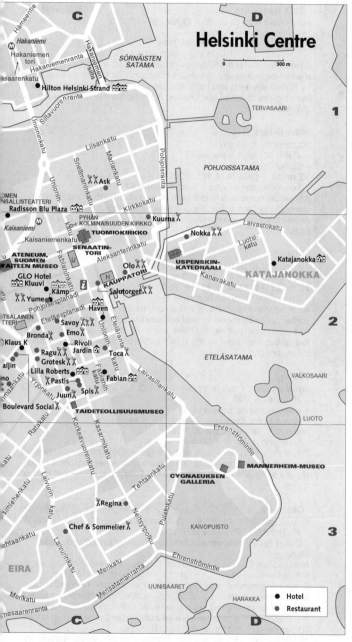

Helsinki Centre

FINLAND - HELSINKI

0 — 300 m

C

Hämeentie
Hakaniemi
M Hakaniemen tori
Hakaniemenranta
isaarenkatu
● Hilton Helsinki Strand

Hakaniemen silta

SÖRNÄISTEN SATAMA

TERVASAARI

Siltavuorenranta
Unioninkatu
Liisankatu

POHJOISSATAMA

Snellmaninkatu
Mariankatu
Pohjoisranta

X X ●Ask

OMEN
NSALLISTEATTERI
● Radisson Blu Plaza

Kaisaniemi

Kirkkokatu
PYHÄN
KOLMINAISUUDEN KIRKKO
● Kuurna X

Laivastokatu

TUOMIOKIRKKO
Kaisaniemenkatu
SENAATIN-TORI
● Nokka X X

Luotsi-katu

ATENEUM,
SUOMEN
TAITEEN MUSEO
Fabianinkatu
Aleksanterinkatu
USPENSKIN-KATEDRAALI
● Katajanokka

GLO Hotel
● Kluuvi
● Kämp
Olo X X

KATAJANOKKA

X X Yume
KAUPPATORI

Kanavakatu

Pohjoisesplanadi
Salutorget X X

TSALAINEN
TTERI
Etelä-esplanadi
Haven

Savoy X X X
Unioninkatu

Bronda X
Emo X

● Klaus K
Rivoli
Jardin
Toca X

ETELÄSATAMA

Ragu X X
Grotesk X X
Etelä-ranta

aljin
Lilla Roberts ●
Fabianinkatu
Katajankatu

VALKOSAARI

no
X Pastis
● Fabian

Laivasillankatu

Juuri X
Spis X

Boulevard Social X
Yrjönkatu

TAIDETEOLLISUUSMUSEO

LUOTO

Ratakatu
Korkeavuorenkatu
Kasarmikatu
Ehrenströmintie

katu

Laivurin-katu
Tehtaankatu

MANNERHEIM-MUSEO

simienkatu

CYGNAEUKSEN
GALLERIA

X Regina ●

htaankatu
Laivurinkatu
Neitsytpolku
Puistokatu

KAIVOPUISTO

3

Chef & Sommelier X

Merikatu
Ehrenströmintie

EIRA

Merikatu
Merisatamanranta

UUNISAARET

HARAKKA

nesaarenranta

C **D**

● Hotel
● Restaurant

165

FINLAND - HELSINKI

GLO Hotel Art
Lönnrotinkatu 29 ✉ *00180* – Ⓜ *Kamppi* – ℰ *(010)*
3444 100 – www.glohotels.fi
Plan: **B3**
171 rm ⌂ – †150/300 € ††165/365 €
• Townhouse • Business • Modern •
Sited in the heart of the lively Design District, a 1903 art nouveau castle with modern extensions and its own art collection. Chic bedrooms were styled by Finnish designers and come in three sizes. You can borrow everything from bicycles to paints and brushes. A Nordic grill menu is served in the old cellars.

Rivoli Jardin
Kasarmikatu 40 ✉ *00130*
Plan: **C2**
– ℰ (09) 681 500 – www.rivoli.fi
– Closed Christmas
55 rm ⌂ – †100/240 € ††120/260 €
• Townhouse • Cosy • Personalised •
A small, city centre oasis hidden away off a courtyard, with an intimate conservatory lounge, and a sauna and meeting room tucked away in the cellar. Bedrooms are cosy and individually decorated; those on the top floor have terraces.

Albert
Albertinkatu 30 ✉ *00180* – ℰ *(020) 1234 638*
Plan: **B3**
– www.sokoshotels.fi – Closed Christmas
95 rm ⌂ – †129/185 € ††144/195 €
• Business • Contemporary •
An unassuming 19C building with a contrastingly cosy interior. Good-sized contemporary bedrooms are well-equipped and come with Nordic furniture and up-to-date bathrooms. Have drinks in the welcoming open-plan lounge-bar, then head to the trattoria-style restaurant for a selection of Italian classics.

XXX Savoy
Eteläesplanadi 14 (8th floor) ✉ *00130* – Ⓜ *Kaisaniemi*
Plan: **C2**
– ℰ (09) 6128 5330
– www.royalravintolat.com/savoy
– Closed Easter, Christmas, Saturday lunch and Sunday
Menu 68 € (lunch) – Carte 83/97 €
• Modern cuisine • Elegant •
The city's most famous restaurant opened in 1937 and offers impressive views from its 8th floor setting. Choose from updated versions of old favourites or a seasonal 4 course menu of refined, attractively presented modern dishes.

XX Olo (Jari Vesivalo)

Pohjoisesplanadi 5 ✉ *00170* – Ⓜ *Kaisaneimi*
Plan: **C2**
– ℰ (010) 3206 250 – www.olo-ravintola.fi
– Closed Easter, midsummer, Christmas, Saturday lunch, Sunday and Monday
Menu 52/139 € – (booking essential) (tasting menu only)
• Modern cuisine • Design • Contemporary décor •
A modern, minimalist restaurant set within an attractive harbourside townhouse. Exciting, innovative cooking features stimulating ingredient combinations with contrasting textures and tastes. At dinner choose 'The Journey' or the 'The Shorter Way'; alternatively book a table in the Creative Kitchen to interact with the chefs and try out their latest creations.
→ Chicken liver with gooseberries. Finnish lamb with onion. Rhubarb and sour milk.

FINLAND - HELSINKI

XX
ॐ **Demo** (Tommi Tuominen)   ⑭⑪

Uudenmaankatu 9-11 ✉ *00120* – ⓜ *Rautatientori*   Plan: **C2**
– ✆ (09) 228 90 840 – www.restaurantdemo.fi – Closed 4 weeks in July-August, Christmas-New Year, Easter, midsummer, Sunday and Monday
Menu 62/102 € – *(dinner only) (booking essential) (tasting menu only)*
• Modern cuisine • Intimate •

An unassuming-looking restaurant decorated in neutral tones and hung with huge cotton pendant lights. Classically based cooking combines French and Finnish influences to produce robust, satisfying dishes with a subtle modern edge. Choose 4-7 courses; the menu is presented verbally and changes almost daily.
➜ Fermented pea soup with pancetta and sour cream. Sautéed pike with cabbage and oat miso. Cloudberry mousse with brown butter ice cream.

XX
ॐ **Ask** (Filip Langhoff)   🅰🅲 ⑭

Vironkatu 8 ✉ *00170* – ⓜ *Kaisaniemi* – ✆ *(040)*   Plan: **C1**
581 8100 – www.restaurantask.com – Closed 3 weeks July, Easter, Christmas, Sunday, Monday and bank holidays
Menu 49/98 € – *(dinner only and lunch Friday-Saturday) (tasting menu only)*
• Modern cuisine • Intimate •

It may be hidden away but this welcoming restaurant is well-known. It's a charming place, run by a delightful, experienced couple, who offer modern Nordic cooking crafted almost entirely from organic ingredients. Dishes are light and original, produce is top quality and flavours are clearly defined.
➜ Reindeer and hazelnut. Pike-perch with parsnip. White chocolate and sorrel.

XX **Yume** – Kämp Hotel   🍴 ⑤ 🅰🅲 ⑭

Kluuvikatu 2 ✉ *00100* – ⓜ *Kaisaniemi* – ✆ *(09) 57611718*   Plan: **C2**
– www.hotelkamp.fi – Closed Christmas, Easter, Sunday and Monday
Menu 54/62 € – Carte 47/62 € – *(dinner only)*
• Asian • Design • Fashionable •

Sit on the large heated terrace or head for the comfy, modern hotel dining room, which is divided up by ornate wooden frames. Alongside Asian-inspired dishes with a Californian twist, you'll find a selection of sushi and sashimi.

XX **Grotesk**   🍴 🅰🅲 ⑭ ⭤

Ludviginkatu 10 ✉ *00130* – ⓜ *Rautatientori* – ✆ *(010)*   Plan: **C2**
470 2100 – www.grotesk.fi – Closed Easter, Christmas, midsummer, Sunday and Monday
Menu 49 € – Carte 39/79 € – *(dinner only)*
• Meats and grills • Fashionable • Brasserie •

A smart, buzzy restaurant behind an impressive 19C façade. It comprises a fashionable cocktail bar, a wine bar serving interesting small plates, and a chic dining room which is decorated in black, white and red and specialises in steaks.

XX **Ragu**   ⑤ 🅰🅲 ⭤

Ludviginkatu 3-5 ✉ *00130* – ⓜ *Rautatientori* – ✆ *(09)*   Plan: **C2**
596 659 – www.ragu.fi – Closed July, Easter, midsummer, Christmas and Sunday
Menu 45 € – Carte 49/56 € – *(dinner only) (booking advisable)*
• Modern cuisine • Design • Chic •

Finland's famed seasonal ingredients are used in unfussy Italian recipes and the welcoming service and lively atmosphere also have something of an Italian feel. Choose the weekly 'House' menu to sample the latest produce to arrive.

XX **Nokka**   🍴 🅰🅲 ⑭ ⭤

Kanavaranta 7F ✉ *00160* – ✆ *(09) 6128 5600*   Plan: **D2**
– www.ravintolanokka.fi – Closed Christmas-New Year, Easter, midsummer, 6 December and Sunday
Menu 50 € (weekday lunch)/66 € – Carte 48/78 €
• Modern cuisine • Elegant •

Converted harbourside warehouse with a nautical feel – look out for the huge anchor and propeller. There's a cookery school, a wine cellar and a smart glass-walled kitchen. Modern Finnish cooking relies on small farm producers.

XX **Salutorget**   ⚇ 🅰🅲 ⇔

Pohjoisesplanadi 15 ✉ 00170 – Ⓜ Kaisaniemi – ℰ (09)   Plan: **C2**
*6128 5950 – www.salutorget.fi – Closed Easter, Christmas, midsummer and
bank holidays*
Menu 39 € (weekday lunch)/49 € – Carte 39/56 €
• International • Brasserie • Elegant •
An old bank, located on the esplanade; now an elegant restaurant with impressive columns and attractive stained glass. The classic, brasserie-style menu has global influences. Enjoy afternoon tea in the plush cocktail bar.

X **Chef & Sommelier** (Sasu Laukkonen)   ⇔
❀
Huvilakatu 28 ✉ 00150 – ℰ (40) 0959 440   Plan: **C3**
*– www.chefetsommelier.fi – Closed late June-early August, 10 days
Christmas-New Year, 1 week February, Easter, Sunday and Monday*
Menu 46/76 € – *(dinner only) (booking essential) (tasting menu only)*
• Modern cuisine • Neighbourhood •
Tiny, simply decorated restaurant with a friendly atmosphere, secreted amongst residential apartment blocks. The open kitchen uses carefully chosen organic and wild ingredients in modern, original Finnish cooking. The passionate chefs deliver dishes to the tables themselves and explain the techniques used.
→ River Teno salmon with summer greens. Lamb with mushrooms and roots. Blueberry and pine.

X **Muru**   🕸 🅰🅲 ⇔

Fredrikinkatu 41 ✉ 00120 – Ⓜ Kamppi – ℰ (30)   Plan: **B2**
*0472 335 – www.murudining.fi – Closed Christmas, New Year, Easter,
1 May, midsummer, Sunday, Monday and bank holidays*
Menu 52 € – Carte 46/52 € – *(dinner only) (booking essential)*
• Modern cuisine • Neighbourhood • Trendy •
Three passionate young owners and a charming, chatty team have created a vibrant, welcoming spot. It's cosy and rustic with a contemporary edge, and displays quirky wine-themed lighting and a bar made from old wine boxes. Cooking is refined yet gutsy; there are two sittings for dinner and booking is a must.

X **Regina**   🅰🅲

Neitsytpolku 10 ✉ 00140 – ℰ (010) 501 4696   Plan: **C3**
– www.restaurantregina.fi – Closed Sunday-Tuesday
Carte 44/64 € – *(dinner only)*
• Modern cuisine • Intimate • Neighbourhood •
This small, cosy bistro sits in a residential area and has a friendly, bustling feel. Unfussy international dishes change every two weeks and showcase produce from all over Europe. The wine list is thoughtfully compiled.

X **Spis**   ⇔

Kasarmikatu 26 ✉ 00130 – ℰ (045) 305 1211   Plan: **C2**
– www.spis.fi – Closed Sunday, Monday and bank holidays
Menu 50/77 € – *(dinner only) (booking essential) (tasting menu only)*
• Modern cuisine • Neighbourhood • Bistro •
Intimate restaurant seating just 18; the décor is 'faux derelict', with exposed brick and plaster walls. Creative, flavoursome cooking features Nordic flavours in attractive, imaginative combinations. Most dishes are vegetable-based.

X **Toca**   ⇔

Unioninkatu 18 ✉ 00130 – ℰ (044) 2379922   Plan: **C2**
– www.toca.fi – Closed July, 22 December-8 January, Sunday and Monday
Menu 65 € – *(dinner only and lunch Tuesday-Thursday-set menu only at
dinner) (booking essential)*
• Modern cuisine • Trendy •
Modest little bistro with an unfinished look. At lunch they serve just two dishes – aimed at local workers – while dinner offers a 3 or 5 set course menu. Cooking is an original mix of Italian simplicity and Finnish modernity.

Ateljé Finne

X   AC ⅙

Arkadiankatu 14 ⊠ 00100 – Ⓜ Kamppi – ℰ (010)   Plan: **B2**
2828242 – www.ateljefinne.fi – Closed Christmas, Easter, midsummer,
weekends in July, Sunday and Monday
Menu 42 € – Carte 42/61 € – *(dinner only) (booking advisable)*
• **Modern cuisine** • **Bistro** •

This is the old studio of sculptor Gunnar Finne, who worked here for over 30 years. Local art decorates the small bistro-style dining rooms set over three levels. Regional dishes are given subtle modern and international twists.

Lyon

X   AC ⅙

Mannerheimintie 56 ⊠ 00260 – ℰ (010) 328 1560   Plan: **A1**
– www.ravintolalyon.fi – Closed July, Easter, Christmas, midsummer,
Sunday and Monday
Menu 58 € – Carte 61/73 € – *(dinner only)*
• **French** • **Bistro** •

Well-established restaurant with a traditional bistro feel; set across from the Opera House. Wide-ranging menus offer seasonal French dishes crafted from Finnish ingredients. These are accompanied by a small selection of French wines.

Emo

X   �& AC ⅙ ⇔

Kasarmikatu 44 ⊠ 00130 – Ⓜ Rautatientori   Plan: **C2**
– ℰ (010) 505 0900 – www.emo-ravintola.fi
– Closed Christmas, Sunday, lunch Saturday and Monday
Menu 27/63 € – Carte 34/56 €
• **Modern cuisine** • **Fashionable** •

Laid-back restaurant with an adjoining bar and a friendly team. The menu is easy-going too, offering around 10 regularly changing dishes that can be taken either as starters or main courses. Quality ingredients feature in flavoursome, unfussy preparations, which are good value and come with a contemporary touch.

Farang

X   ঙ AC ⅙ ⇔

Ainonkatu 3 (inside the Kunsthalle) ⊠ 00100   Plan: **B2**
– Ⓜ Kamppi – ℰ (010) 322 9380 – www.farang.fi – Closed Christmas,
midsummer, Easter, Saturday lunch, Sunday and Monday
Menu 29 € (lunch) – Carte 38/44 €
• **South East Asian** • **Simple** • **Intimate** •

This stylish, modern restaurant is housed in the Kunsthalle art centre. One room is decorated with large photos of Thai scenes and has communal tables; the other is more intimate and furnished in red, black and grey. Zesty, harmonious dishes take their influences from Vietnam, Thailand and Malaysia.

Gaijin

X   🏡 ঙ AC ⅙

Bulevardi 6 ⊠ 00120 – Ⓜ Rautatientori – ℰ (010)   Plan: **C2**
3229381 – www.gaijin.fi – Closed Christmas, midsummer and lunch
Saturday-Monday
Menu 37 € (lunch) – Carte 39/50 € – *(booking essential)*
• **Asian** • **Fashionable** •

Gaijin comes with dark, contemporary décor, a buzzing atmosphere, attentive service and an emphasis on sharing. Its experienced owners offer boldly flavoured, skilfully presented modern takes on Japanese, Korean and Northern Chinese recipes. The tasting menus are a great way to sample the different cuisines.

Boulevard Social

X   🏡 ঙ AC ⅙

Bulevardi 6 ⊠ 00120 – Ⓜ Rautatientori – ℰ (010)   Plan: **C2**
3229382 – www.boulevardsocial.fi – Closed Christmas,
midsummer, Saturday lunch and Sunday
Menu 29 € (lunch) – Carte 26/50 €
• **Mediterranean cuisine** • **Fashionable** •

Owned by the same people as next door Gaijin, this lively, informal restaurant offers an accessible range of authentic North African, Turkish and Eastern Mediterranean dishes; try the set or tasting menus to experience a cross-section of them all. If they're fully booked, ask for a seat at the counter.

Bronda

Eteläesplanadi 20 ✉ 00130 – Ⓜ Rautatientori – ✆ (010) 322 9383 – www.ravintolabronda.fi – Closed Christmas, midsummer and Sunday Plan: **C2**
Menu 29/57 € – Carte 38/70 €
• Modern cuisine • Fashionable • Brasserie •
The floor to ceiling windows of this old furniture showroom flood it with light. Have cocktails and snacks at the bar or comforting, boldly flavoured, Mediterranean sharing plates in the brasserie. Each dish arrives as it's ready.

Pastis

Pieni Roobertinkatu 2 ✉ 00130 – ✆ (030) 04 72 336 – www.pastis.fi – Closed Easter, Christmas and Sunday Plan: **C2**
Menu 30/50 € – Carte 43/56 € – *(booking essential)*
• Classic French • Bistro • Neighbourhood •
The clue is in the name: they serve classic French dishes, alongside several different brands of pastis. It's a popular place, so there's always a lively atmosphere. Come for Saturday brunch or have a private meal in Petit Pastis.

Passio

Kalevankatu 13 ✉ 00100 – Ⓜ Kamppi – ✆ (020) 7352 040 – www.passiodining.fi – Closed Christmas and midsummer Plan: **B2**
Menu 29/50 € – *(dinner only) (booking advisable) (surprise menu only)*
• Modern cuisine • Friendly • Neighbourhood •
With its exposed ducts, dimly lit lamps and leather-topped tables, Passio has a faux industrial look. 3 or 5 course 'Surprise' menus feature regional ingredients. It's run by a local brewer, so be sure to try the artisan beers.

Kuurna

Meritullinkatu 6 ✉ 00170 – Ⓜ Kaisaniemi – ✆ (010) 2818241 – www.kuurna.fi – Closed 10 days Christmas, Good Friday and Sunday Plan: **C2**
Menu 44 € – *(dinner only) (booking essential)*
• Traditional cuisine • Neighbourhood •
Small but very popular restaurant with a lived-in feel and seating for just twenty guests. The set menu offers three choices per course and is supplemented by blackboard specials; cooking is Finnish and follows the seasons.

Juuri

Korkeavuorenkatu 27 ✉ 00130 – ✆ (09) 635 732 – www.juuri.fi – Closed midsummer and 24-26 December Plan: **C2**
Carte 36/53 €
• Traditional cuisine • Bistro •
A small bistro close to the Design Museum, with friendly service and a rustic style. Menus offer a few main dishes along with 'Sapas' – small, tapas-style plates of organic produce. Traditional Finnish recipes are brought up-to-date.

AT HELSINKI-VANTAA AIRPORT

Hilton Helsinki Airport

Lentàjànkuja 1 ✉ 01530 – ✆ (09) 732 20 – www.hilton.com
330 rm – †99/370 € ††109/400 € – ☕ 27 € – 5 suites
• Business • Modern •
3mins from the international terminal (T2); a spacious glass hotel with a relaxed ambience and a large conference capacity. Well-soundproofed bedrooms boast locally designed furniture, good facilities and large bathrooms – some have saunas. The stylish restaurant serves Finnish and international cuisine.

FRANCE
FRANCE

PARIS ●
Strasbourg ●
● Lyons

→ **AREA:**
551 500 km² (212 934 sq mi).

→ **POPULATION:**
66 627 602 inhabitants. Density = 121 per km².

→ **CAPITAL:**
Paris.

→ **CURRENCY:**
Euro (€).

→ **GOVERNMENT:**
Parliamentary republic (since 1946). Member of European Union since 1957 (one of the 6 founding countries).

→ **LANGUAGE:**
French.

→ **PUBLIC HOLIDAYS:**
New Year's Day (1 Jan); Easter Monday (late Mar/Apr); Labor Day (1 May); Victory Day 1945 (8 May); Ascension Day (late Apr/May); Whit Monday (late May/June); Bastille Day (14 July); Assumption of the Virgin Mary (15 Aug); All Saints' Day (1 Nov); Armistice Day 1918 (11 Nov); Christmas Day (25 Dec).

→ **LOCAL TIME:**
GMT+1 hour in winter and GMT +2 hours in summer.

→ **CLIMATE:**
Temperate with cool winters and warm summers (Paris: January 3°C; July 20°C). Mediterranean climate in the south (mild winters, hot and sunny summers, occasional strong wind called the mistral).

→ **EMERGENCY:**
Police ☎ **17**; Medical Assistance ☎ **15**; Fire Brigade ☎ **18**. (Dialling **112** within any EU country will redirect your call and contact the emergency services.)

→ **ELECTRICITY:**
230 volts AC, 50Hz; 2 round pin sockets.

→ **FORMALITIES:**
Travellers from the European Union (EU), Switzerland, Iceland and the main countries of North and South America need a national identity card or passport (America: passport required) to visit France for less than three months (tourism or business purpose). For visitors from other countries a visa may be required, in addition to a passport, especially for those wishing to stay for longer than three months. We advise you to check with your embassy before travelling.

PARIS

PARIS

Population 2 229 621

Cyrille Lips/Fotolia.com

The French capital is one of the truly great cities of the world, a metropolis that eternally satisfies the desires of its beguiled visitors. With its harmonious layout, typified by the grand geometric boulevards radiating from the Arc de Triomphe like the spokes of a wheel, Paris is designed to enrapture. Despite its ever-widening tentacles, most of the things worth seeing are contained within the city's ring road. Paris wouldn't be Paris sans its Left and Right Banks: the Right Bank comprises the north and west; the Left Bank takes in the city south of the Seine. A stroll along the Left Bank conjures images of Doisneau's magical monochrome photographs, while the narrow, cobbled streets of Montmartre vividly call up the colourful cool of Toulouse-Lautrec.

The Ile de la Cité is the nucleus around which the city grew and the oldest quarters around this site are the 1st, 2nd, 3rd, 4th arrondissements on the Right Bank and 5th and 6th on the Left Bank. Landmarks are universally known: the Eiffel Tower and the Arc de Triomphe to the west, the Sacré-Coeur to the north, Montparnasse Tower to the south, and, of course, Notre-Dame Cathedral in the middle. But Paris is not resting on its laurels. New buildings and new cultural sensations are never far away: Les Grands Travaux are forever in the wings, waiting to inspire.

PARIS IN...

→ **ONE DAY**
Eiffel Tower, Notre-Dame Cathedral, a café on Boulevard St Germain, Musée d'Orsay, Montmartre.

→ **TWO DAYS**
The Louvre, Musée du Quai Branly.

→ **THREE DAYS**
Canal Saint-Martin, Centre Pompidou, Picasso Museum and the Marais.

PRACTICAL INFORMATION

ARRIVAL-DEPARTURE

✈ Paris Charles de Gaulle Airport is 23km northeast of Paris. Air France Bus to Montparnasse or Porte Maillot runs every 15min.

✈ Orly Airport is 14km south. Air France Bus runs to Invalides or Montparnasse. Eurostar runs from Gare du Nord, on the Rue de Dunkerque.

GETTING AROUND

A single bus or metro ticket has a flat fare however far you travel; a carnet (book of ten) works out at good value. There are three travel cards: Paris Visite is a 1-day pass for three zones or a 5-day pass for five zones; Mobilis is a 1-day pass giving unlimited travel in either zones 1-2 or zones 1-5; Pass Navigo is a weekly or monthly pass (you'll need a photo). Or try the Velib, the bicycle system; pick up one of the 20,000 bikes at any of the 1,800 points, swipe a travel card to release your bike – then it's just you versus the Parisian traffic...

CALENDAR HIGHLIGHTS

February: Paris Fashion Week.

March: Salon du Livre Paris.

April: Banlieues Bleues.

May: La Nuit des Musées, Foire du Trône funfair.

June: French Open Tennis.

August: Paris Plages.

September: The Autumn Festival, Jazz à la Villette.

October: Nuit Blanche, International Contemporary Art Fair.

November: Great Wines Fair.

EATING OUT

Food plays such an important role in Gallic life that eating well is deemed a citizen's birth-right. Parisians are intensely knowledgeable about their food and wine - simply stroll around any part of the capital and you'll come across lavish looking shops offering perfectly presented treats. Restaurants, bistros and brasseries too can call on the best available bounty around: there are close to a hundred city-wide markets teeming with fresh produce. As Charles De Gaulle said: "How can you govern a country which has 246 varieties of cheese?" Whether you want to linger in a legendary café or dine in a grand salon, you'll find the choice is endless. The city's respect for its proud culinary heritage is palpable but it is not resting on its laurels. Just as other European cities with vibrant restaurant scenes started to play catch-up, so young chefs here took up the cudgels. By breaking away from formulaic regimes and adopting more contemporary styles of cooking, they have ensured that the reputation of the city remains undimmed.

A

L'Abbaye	🏠	226
Atmosphères	🏠	230

B

Baltimore	🏠	186
Banke	🏠	205
Bel Ami		
St-Germain des Prés	🏠	227
Le Bellechasse	🏠	227
La Belle Juliette	🏠	230
Bourg Tibourg	🏠	227
Le Bristol	🏠	180
Le Burgundy	🏠	204

C

Champs-Élysées Plaza	🏠	181
Le Cinq Codet	🏠	217
Concorde Montparnasse	🏠	238
Costes	🏠	204
Le Crayon	🏠	207

D

Les Dames du Panthéon	🏠	230
Delambre	🏠	238
Duc de St-Simon	🏠	226

E

Édouard VII	🏠	205

F

Fabric	🏠	248
Fouquet's Barrière	🏠	181
Four Seasons George V	🏠	180

G

Grand Hôtel		
du Palais Royal	🏠	205

H

Hilton La Défense	🏠	255
Hilton Opéra	🏠	205
Hilton Roissy	🏠	255
Holiday Inn Express		
Canal de la Villette	🏠	248
L'Hôtel	🏠	226
Hôtel de Banville	🏠	247
Hôtel de la Paix	🏠	238
Hôtel de Nell	🏠	205
Hôtel de Noailles	🏠	206
Hôtel de Sers	🏠	187
Hôtel		
des Grands Hommes	🏠	230
Hôtel de Varenne	🏠	218

Hôtel de Vendôme	🏠	204
Hôtel du Continent	🏠	207
Hôtel du Ministère	🏠	206
Hôtel Monsieur	🏠	206

I

Idol	🏠	207
Intercontinental		
Le Grand	🏠	201

J

Jardin de Cluny	🏠	230
Les Jardins de la Villa	🏠	187
Juliana	🏠	217

K

Keppler	🏠	186
Kube	🏠	247

L

Lancaster	🏠	186
La Lanterne	🏠	227
Le Narcisse Blanc	🏠	217
Little Palace	🏠	206

M

La Maison Favart	🏠	206
Mama Shelter	🏠	248
Mandarin Oriental	🏠	201
Marignan		
Champs-Elysées	🏠	186
Le Meurice	🏠	201
Molitor	🏠	247
Montalembert	🏠	227
Muguet	🏠	218

N

Novotel Convention		
et Wellness	🏠	255
Novotel Tour Eiffel	🏠	247

P

Paris Bastille	🏠	243
Park Hyatt		
Paris-Vendôme	🏠	201
Pavillon de la Reine	🏠	241
The Peninsula Paris	🏠	180
Le Petit Moulin	🏠	243
Le Petit Paris	🏠	230
Platine	🏠	218
Plaza Athénée	🏠	180
Prince de Galles	🏠	181
Pulitzer	🏠	206
Pullman Airport	🏠	255

| Pullman Montparnasse | 龠龠龠 | 238 |
| Pullman Paris Centre-Bercy | 龠龠龠 | 247 |

R

Raphael	龠龠龠龠	181
Relais Madeleine	龠	206
Relais Montmartre	龠龠	244
Relais St-Germain	龠龠龠	227
Renaissance Arc de Triomphe	龠龠龠龠	186
La Réserve	龠龠龠龠龠	181
Ritz	龠龠龠龠龠	201
Le Royal Monceau	龠龠龠龠龠	181

S

St-James Paris	龠龠龠龠	246
Scribe	龠龠龠龠	204
Sezz	龠龠龠	217

Shangri-La	龠龠龠龠龠	180
Sofitel le Faubourg	龠龠龠龠	205
Sofitel Paris La Défense	龠龠龠龠	255
Splendid Étoile	龠龠龠	187
Square	龠龠龠	247
Star Champs Élysées	龠	187

T

| Terrass' Hôtel | 龠龠龠 | 244 |

V

Vernet	龠龠龠龠	186
Vice Versa	龠龠	248
Le 20 Prieuré Hôtel	龠	248

W

| The Westin Paris | 龠龠龠龠 | 204 |
| W Paris Opéra | 龠龠龠龠 | 204 |

FRANCE – PARIS

A

L'Abeille	XxxX ✿✿	189
A et M Restaurant	XX	250
L'Affriolé	X	225
Agapé	XX✿	199
Aida	X✿	224
Akrame	XX✿	212
Alain Ducasse au Plaza Athénée	XxXxX ✿✿✿	188
Alcazar	XX	234
Alléno Paris au Pavillon Ledoyen	XxXxX ✿✿✿	188
Alliance	XX✿	233
L'Ambroisie	XxxX ✿✿✿	243
À mère	X	217
Anthocyane	X	241
Antoine	XxX✿	193
L'Antre Amis	X⊕	225
Apicius	XxxX✿	190
L'Archeste	XX✿	250
L'Arôme	XxX✿	194
Arpège	XxX✿✿✿	219
Astrance	XxX✿✿✿	219
AT	X	237
L'Atelier de Joël Robuchon - Étoile	X✿	200
L'Atelier de Joël Robuchon - St-Germain	X✿✿	234
Atelier Maître Albert	XX	233
Atelier Rodier	X	214
Atelier Vivanda - Cherche Midi	X⊕	237
Au Bon Accueil	XX⊕	223
Auguste	XX✿	223
Au Trou Gascon	XX✿	250
Aux Lyonnais	X	214
Aux Prés	X	235
Aux Verres de Contact	X⊕	237

B

Le Baudelaire	XxX✿	210
Benkay	XxX	250
Benoit	XX✿	232
Beurre Noisette	X⊕	252
Bistrot Augustin	X	241
Bistrot Belhara	X	225
Bistrot Paul Bert	X	253
Bistrotters	X⊕	240
Bocca Rossa	X⊕	238
Bofinger	XX	243
Bon Kushikatsu	X	251
Le Bon Saint-Pourçain	X	237
Brasserie Gallopin	XX	213

C

Café Constant	X⊕	226
Le Café de la Paix	XX	211
Camélia	XX	211
Les Canailles	X⊕	216
Carré des Feuillants	XxxX ✿✿	208
Les 110 de Taillevent	XX	196
114, Faubourg	XX✿	195
Le 122	X	225
Chamarré Montmartre	X	245
Chez les Anges	XX⊕	222
Le Chiberta	XxX✿	193
Le Cinq	XxXxX ✿✿✿	187
Le Cinq Codet	XX	222
Circonstances	X⊕	216
Citrus Étoile	XxX	194
Clamato	X⊕	252
Le Clarence	XxXxX ✿✿	189
Les Climats	XX✿	232
Le Clos des Gourmets	X⊕	224
Cobéa	XxX✿	239
Les Cocottes - Tour Eiffel	X⊕	224
Le Comptoir du Relais	X	237
Comptoir Tempero	X⊕	254
Conti	XX	198
Le Cornichon	X	241
La Cour Jardin	XxX	192

D

Le Dali	XX	210
La Dame de Pic	XX✿	232
David Toutain	XX✿	222
D'Chez Eux	XX	223
Divellec	XX✿	219
Le Dôme	XxX	238
Dominique Bouchet	XX✿	198
Drouant	XxX	209

E

Encore	X	215
L'Entredgeu	X⊕	200
L'Envie du Jour	X⊕	252
Épicure	XxXxX ✿✿✿	188
L'Épi Dupin	X	235
ES	XX✿	233
L'Escient	X	200
L'Esquisse	X⊕	245

F

Les Fables de La Fontaine	X✿	224
La Ferrandaise	X	236
Le First	XX	212
Fish La Boissonnerie	X	236
La Fontaine Gaillon	XX	212

La Fourchette du Printemps	✗ ❀	251
Frédéric Simonin	✗✗ ❀	197
Frenchie	✗	216

G

Le Gabriel	✗✗✗ ❀❀	190
Garance	✗✗ ❀	223
La Gauloise	✗✗	224
Gaya Rive Gauche par Pierre Gagnaire	✗ ❀	234
Le George	✗✗✗	191
Graindorge	✗✗ ⊛	199
La Grande Cascade	✗✗✗ ❀	249
Le Grand Restaurant - Jean-François Piège	✗✗✗ ❀❀	208
Le Grand Véfour	✗✗✗ ❀❀	208
Guy Savoy	✗✗✗ ❀❀❀	231

H

Helen	✗✗✗ ❀	194
Hélène Darroze	✗✗✗ ❀	231
Hexagone	✗✗ ❀	195
Hotaru	✗	215

I

Il Carpaccio	✗✗✗ ❀	192
Il Vino d'Enrico Bernardo	✗✗ ❀	219
Impérial Choisy	✗ ⊛	254
L'Inattendu	✗✗	250
Itinéraires	✗✗ ❀	233

J

Les Jardins de l'Espadon	✗✗✗ ❀	209
Jin	✗ ❀	213
Jouvence	✗ ⊛	253
Le Jules Verne	✗✗✗ ❀	218

K

Kei	✗✗✗ ❀❀	210
Ken Kawasaki	✗	246
Kiku	✗	215
Kunitoraya	✗	215

L

Lasserre	✗✗✗✗ ❀	189
Laurent	✗✗✗✗ ❀	189
Lili	✗✗✗	191
Liza	✗	214
Lucas Carton	✗✗✗ ❀	209
Le Lulli	✗✗	211
Le Lumière	✗✗	212

M

Macéo	✗✗✗	210
Maison Blanche	✗✗✗	192
La Maison du Jardin	✗ ⊛	236
Maison Rostang	✗✗✗✗ ❀❀	190
Manko	✗	200
Mansouria	✗	254

Le Marché du Lucas	✗✗	213
La Marée Passy	✗	252
Marius et Janette	✗✗	197
La Marlotte	✗ ⊛	235
Mathieu Pacaud - Histoires	✗✗✗✗ ❀❀	190
Matsuhisa	✗✗	197
Maxan	✗✗	198
Le Meurice Alain Ducasse	✗✗✗✗✗ ❀❀	207
1728	✗✗✗	209
Mini Palais	✗✗	197
Le Moderne	✗	214
Moissonnier	✗	235
Monsieur K	✗	216
Mon Vieil Ami	✗	235
Le Moulin de la Galette	✗	246

N

Nakatani	✗✗ ❀	223
Neige d'Été	✗✗ ❀	222
Nina	✗ ⊛	239
Noglu	✗	216
Nolita	✗✗	198
Nubé	✗✗	197
N° 41	✗ ⊛	252

O

L'Office	✗ ⊛	216
Officina Schenatti	✗	237
L'Oiseau Blanc	✗✗	196
L'Orangerie	✗✗ ❀	196
L'Oriental	✗	246
L'Os à Moelle	✗ ⊛	253
L'Ourcine	✗	253

P

Pages	✗✗ ❀	199
Le Pantruche	✗ ⊛	214
Passage 53	✗✗ ❀❀	211
Passerini	✗	244
Penati al Baretto	✗✗✗ ❀	195
Le Pergolèse	✗✗✗ ❀	194
La Petite Sirène de Copenhague	✗	214
Petrossian - Le 144	✗✗✗	219
Pho Tai	✗ ⊛	254
Pierre Gagnaire	✗✗✗ ❀❀❀	189
Pomze	✗✗ ⊛	198
Pramil	✗	253
Le Pré Carré	✗✗	199
Le Pré Catelan	✗✗✗✗ ❀❀❀	248
Prémices	✗✗	212
Prunier	✗✗✗	191
Pur' - Jean-François Rouquette	✗✗✗ ❀	209

Q		
Le Quinzième - Cyril Lignac	XxX ✿	249
Qui plume la Lune	X ✿	243
R		
Le Radis Beurre	X ⊛	225
Le Réciproque	X ⊛	246
La Régalade	X	251
La Régalade Conservatoire	X	213
Relais d'Auteuil	XxX ✿	249
Relais Louis XIII	XxX ✿	231
Le Relais Plaza	XX	196
Le Restaurant	XX ✿	232
Restaurant du Palais Royal	XX ✿	211
Restaurant H	X ✿	244
La Rotonde	XX	239
S		
St-James Paris	XxX ✿	249
Saturne	XX ✿	212
La Scène	XxX ✿	191
La Scène Thélème	XX ✿	196
Septime	X ✿	251
Shang Palace	XxX ✿	191
Shu	X	236
Silk & Spice	X	215
6 New York	XX	199
Sola	X ✿	234
Sormani	XxX	193
Stéphane Martin	X	224
Sushi B	X ✿	213
Sur Mesure par Thierry Marx	XxX ✿✿	208
Sylvestre	XxX ✿✿	218
T		
Table - Bruno Verjus	X	251
La Table de l'Espadon	XxXxX ✿✿	207
La Table d'Eugène	XX ✿	244
La Table du Baltimore	XxX	193
La Table du Lancaster	XxX ✿	192
Les Tablettes de Jean-Louis Nomicos	XxX ✿	193
Le Taillevent	XxXxX ✿✿	188
Taokan - St-Germain	X	236
Tempero	X ⊛	254
Le Timbre	X ⊛	239
Timgad	XX	197
Tintilou	X	254
Tomy & Co	X	225
Tour d'Argent	XxXxX ✿	231
Toyo	X	241
Le 39V	XX ✿	195
Le Troquet	X ⊛	226
Tsé Yang	XxX	194
U		
Un Dimanche à Paris	XX	234
V		
Le V	XxX	192
Vaudeville	XX	213
Le Versance	XxX	210
Villaret	X ⊛	253
Le Vinci	XX	200
20 Eiffel	X ⊛	226
Le Violon d'Ingres	XX ✿	222
Le Vitis	X ⊛	239
Y		
Yam'Tcha	XX ✿	233
Yard	X ⊛	252
Yen	X	236
Z		
Ze Kitchen Galerie	X ✿	235
Zen	X ⊛	215

A

L'Affriolé	✗	225
Aida	✗❄	224
Alcazar	✗✗	234
L'Ambroisie	✗✗✗❄❄❄	243
L'Antre Amis	✗⊛	225
L'Atelier de Joël Robuchon - Étoile	✗❄	200
L'Atelier de Joël Robuchon - St-Germain	✗❄❄	234
Atelier Maître Albert	✗✗	233
Au Bon Accueil	✗✗⊛	223
Aux Prés	✗	235

B

Benkay	✗✗✗	250
Benoit	✗✗❄	232
Bistrot Belhara	✗	225
Bistrot Paul Bert	✗	253
Bofinger	✗✗	243
Brasserie Gallopin	✗✗	213

C-D

Le Café de la Paix	✗✗	211
Camélia	✗✗	211
Les 110 de Taillevent	✗✗	196
114, Faubourg	✗✗❄	195
Chamarré Montmartre	✗✗	245
Le Cinq	✗✗✗✗❄❄❄	187
Le Cinq Codet	✗✗	222
Circonstances	✗⊛	216
Clamato	✗⊛	252
Le Comptoir du Relais	✗	237
Comptoir Tempero	✗⊛	254
La Cour Jardin	✗✗✗	192
Le Dali	✗✗	210
La Dame de Pic	✗✗❄	232
D'Chez Eux	✗✗	223
Divellec	✗✗❄	219
Le Dôme	✗✗✗	238
Drouant	✗✗✗	209

E-F-G

Épicure	✗✗✗✗❄❄❄	188
Les Fables de La Fontaine	✗❄	224
Le First	✗✗	212
Fish La Boissonnerie	✗	236
Le Gabriel	✗✗✗❄❄	190
La Gauloise	✗✗	224
Le George	✗✗✗❄	191
La Grande Cascade	✗✗✗❄	249
Guy Savoy	✗✗✗✗❄❄❄	231

I-J-K-L

Impérial Choisy	✗⊛	254
Le Jules Verne	✗✗✗❄	218
Kunitoraya	✗	215
Lili	✗✗✗	191
Le Lumière	✗✗	212

M-N-O

Macéo	✗✗✗	210
Maison Blanche	✗✗✗	192
La Marée Passy	✗	252
Marius et Janette	✗✗	197
Mini Palais	✗✗	197
Le Moderne	✗	214
Mon Vieil Ami	✗	235
Le Moulin de la Galette	✗	246
Nolita	✗✗	198
N° 41	✗⊛	252
L'Oiseau Blanc	✗✗	196
L'Orangerie	✗✗❄	196
L'Oriental	✗	246

P-R

Le Pantruche	✗⊛	214
Pomze	✗✗⊛	198
Pramil	✗	253
Pur' - Jean-François Rouquette	✗✗✗❄	209
La Régalade Conservatoire	✗	213
Le Relais Plaza	✗✗	196
La Rotonde	✗✗	239

S-T

St-James Paris	✗✗✗❄	249
Shang Palace	✗✗✗❄	191
Sushi B	✗❄	213
La Table de l'Espadon	✗✗✗✗❄❄	207
Les Tablettes de Jean-Louis Nomicos	✗✗✗❄	193
Taokan - St-Germain	✗	236
Tempero	✗⊛	254
Timgad	✗✗	197
Tintilou	✗	254
Tsé Yang	✗✗✗	194

U-V-Z

Un Dimanche à Paris	✗✗	234
Vaudeville	✗✗	213
Le Violon d'Ingres	✗✗❄	222
Yard	✗⊛	252
Zen	✗⊛	215

FRANCE - PARIS

Plaza Athénée

25 av. Montaigne (8th) – Ⓜ *Alma Marceau*
Plan: **G3**
– ℰ 01 53 67 66 65
– *www.dorchestercollection.com/paris/hotel-plaza-athenee*
154 rm – ♦990/2150 € ♦♦990/2150 € – � 60 € – 54 suites
• Palace • Grand Luxury • Classic •
The Parisian luxury hotel par excellence: inaugurated in 1911, the Plaza Athénée is wearing the passing years wonderfully well. Nothing alters the establishment's primacy, which is at the zenith of French-style luxury and elegance. Brilliant classicism, exceptional amenities, including the fabulous Christian Dior Spa. The legend lives on.
❀❀❀ **Alain Ducasse au Plaza Athénée** • **La Cour Jardin** • **Le Relais Plaza** – See restaurant listing

Four Seasons George V

31 av. George-V (8th) – Ⓜ *George V* – ℰ 01 49 52 70 00
Plan: **G3**
– *www.fourseasons.com/paris*
185 rm – ♦1090/1890 € ♦♦1090/1890 € – ⊒ 70 € – 59 suites
• Palace • Historic • Elegant •
This mythical luxury hotel, founded in 1928, has an interior design that reflects the splendours and refinement of the 18C. Its sumptuous and spacious guestrooms, art collections, superb spa and lovely interior courtyard – not to mention its gastronomic history – make this a truly exceptional place!
❀❀❀ **Le Cinq** • ❀ **Le George** • ❀ **L'Orangerie** – See restaurant listing

Le Bristol

112 r. du Faubourg-St-Honoré (8th) – Ⓜ *Miromesnil*
Plan: **H2**
– ℰ 01 53 43 43 00 – *www.lebristolparis.com*
148 rm – ♦1300/2100 € ♦♦1300/2100 € – ⊒ 60 € – 42 suites
• Palace • Grand luxury •
This luxury hotel, built in 1925 and boasting a new wing added in 2009, is arranged around a magnificent garden. Sumptuous guestrooms decorated in Louis XV or Louis XVI style, as well as a stunning swimming pool, reminiscent of a 19C yacht, on the top floor.
❀❀❀ **Épicure** • ❀ **114, Faubourg** – See restaurant listing

Shangri-La

10 av. d'Iéna (16th) ✉ *75116* – Ⓜ *Iéna*
Plan: **F3**
– ℰ 01 53 67 19 98 – *www.shangri-la.com*
75 rm – ♦695/1675 € ♦♦695/1675 € – ⊒ 58 € – 25 suites
• Palace • Historic • Grand luxury •
The hallmark of this palatial hotel, opened in 2011, is its fusion of French Empire and Asian styles. Occupying the former home of Prince Roland Bonaparte (1896), its classic architecture encompasses grandiose lounges, opulent luxury and dining options for every taste. A true sense of exclusivity!
❀❀ **L'Abeille** • ❀ **Shang Palace** – See restaurant listing

The Peninsula Paris

19 av. Kléber (16th) ✉ *75116* – Ⓜ *Kléber*
Plan: **F2**
– ℰ 01 58 12 28 88 – *http://paris.peninsula.com/fr/*
166 rm – ♦750/1350 € ♦♦750/1350 € – ⊒ 55 € – 34 suites
• Palace • Historic • Elegant •
So it is with this hotel that the Hong Kong Peninsula group arrived in Paris in 2014. A master stroke! Just minutes from the Arc de Triomphe, in a beautiful Belle Epoque building, the hotel has the greatest of everything. Find luxurious interiors, hi-tech equipment and top of the range amenities. 'Tis a rock, a peak, a cape... no, a peninsula!
L'Oiseau Blanc • **Lili** – See restaurant listing

FRANCE - PARIS

Le Royal Monceau

37 av. Hoche (8th) – Ⓜ Charles de Gaulle-Etoile
– ☏ 01 42 99 88 00 – www.leroyalmonceau.com   Plan: **G2**
108 rm – ♦1200/1600 € ♦♦1200/1600 € – ☲ 58 € – 41 suites
• Palace • Grand Luxury • Design •

This 21C luxury hotel, decorated by Philippe Starck, plays with current expectations. There is an art gallery, a bookshop, a hi-tech cinema and a superb spa. Since 2016, it has had a new restaurant: Matsuhisa, the brainchild of emblematic chef Nobu Matsuhisa.
❀ **Il Carpaccio • Matsuhisa** – See restaurant listing

La Réserve

42 av. Gabriel (8th) – Ⓜ Champs Elysées Clemenceau   Plan: **H3**
– ☏ 01 58 36 60 60 – www.lareserve-paris.com
14 rm – ♦1100/9000 € ♦♦1100/9000 € – ☲ 41 € – 26 suites
• Palace • Grand Luxury • Elegant •

Handsome wooden floors, inviting sofas and gold-plated cornices are a few of the exclusive details that set the Belle Epoque scene in this handsome 19C Parisian mansion, revamped by Jacques Garcia. The suites enjoy views over the Elysée palace gardens, the Grand Palais or the Eiffel Tower. The quintessence of luxury.
❀❀ **Le Gabriel** – See restaurant listing

Raphael

17 av. Kléber (16th) ✉ 75116 – Ⓜ Kléber
– ☏ 01 53 64 32 00 – www.raphael-hotel.com   Plan: **F2**
83 rm – ♦330/455 € ♦♦405/665 € – ☲ 40 € – 37 suites
• Luxury • Classic •

A magnificent entrance gallery with woodwork, very elegant rooms (some with views over Paris) and an undeniably elegant English bar: such are the treasures of the Raphael. Founded in 1925, and a stone's throw from the Arc de Triomphe, it is a legend among Parisian hotels.

Prince de Galles

33 av. George-V (8th) – Ⓜ George V – ☏ 01 53 23 77 77   Plan: **G3**
– www.hotelprincedegalles.fr
115 rm – ♦659/1290 € ♦♦659/1290 € – ☲ 38 € – 44 suites
• Grand Luxury • Art déco • Historic •

This legendary jewel of Parisian Art Deco is a beacon of elegance on Avenue George V. Built in 1928 and exuding a new freshness, the charm of the place remains intact; from the luxurious and refined guestrooms to the "Les Heures" bar, where time stands still, opposite the listed patio.
❀ **La Scène** – See restaurant listing

Fouquet's Barrière

46 av. George-V (8th) – Ⓜ George V – ☏ 01 40 69 60 00   Plan: **G2**
– www.fouquets-barriere.com
48 rm – ♦630/1700 € ♦♦630/1700 € – ☲ 49 € – 33 suites
• Luxury • Townhouse • Personalised •

This luxury hotel follows in the tradition of mythical Parisian brasseries. Founded in 2006, its interior was designed by Jacques Garcia and blends French Empire-style with Art Deco. There is plenty of mahogany, silk, and velvet combined with hi-tech facilities and a superb spa.

Champs-Élysées Plaza

35 r. de Berri (8th) – Ⓜ George V – ☏ 01 53 53 20 20   Plan: **G2**
– www.champselyseesplaza.com
35 rm ☲ – ♦299/1500 € ♦♦299/1500 € – 10 suites
• Townhouse • Personalised • Elegant •

With its elegance and space, its harmony of colours, its fusion of styles and its attentive service, this hotel is the epitome of luxury. Fitness centre.

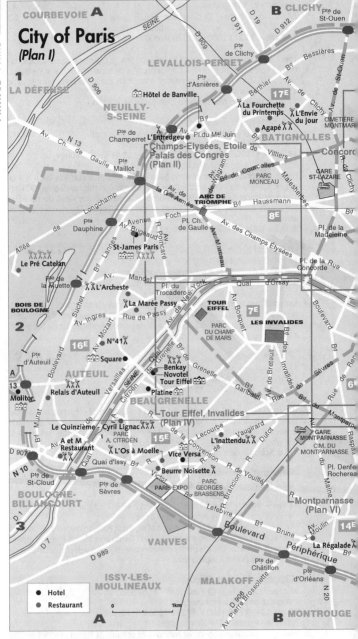

City of Paris
(Plan I)

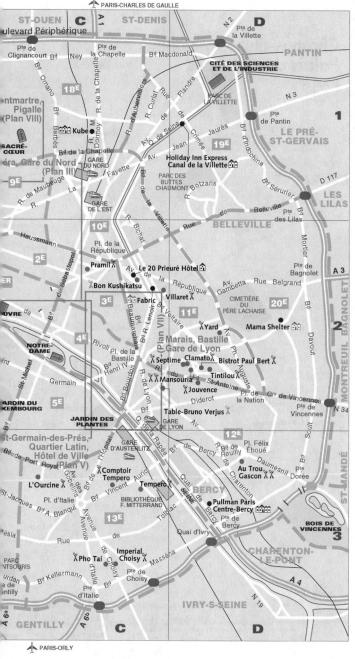

Champs-Élysées, Étoile, Palais des Congrès
(Plan II)

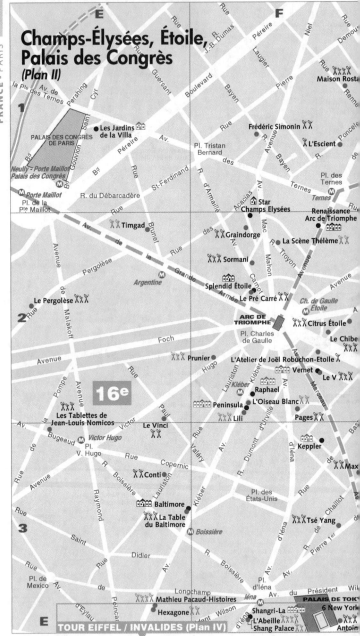

Av. de Pershing

Av. de la Pte des Ternes

PALAIS DES CONGRÈS DE PARIS

Neuilly - Porte Maillot Palais des Congrès

M Porte Maillot
Pl. de la Pte Maillot

R. du Débarcadère

Boulevard Bayen

Rue Guersant

Rue Laugier

Rue Pereire

R. J.-B. Dumas

Rue Niel

Rue Demou

Maison Rosta ✗✗✗✗

Les Jardins de la Villa 🏨

Pl. Tristan Bernard

Frédéric Simonin ✗✗

L'Escient ✗

Rue Poncele

Pl. des Ternes

M Ternes

Renaissance Arc de Triomphe 🏨

Star Champs Elysées 🏨

La Scène Thélème ✗✗

Timgad ✗✗

Graindorge ✗✗

Sormani ✗✗✗

Splendid Étoile 🏨

Le Pré Carré ✗✗

Le Pergolèse ✗✗✗

ARC DE TRIOMPHE

Pl. Charles de Gaulle

Ch. de Gaulle **M** Étoile

Citrus Étoile ✗✗✗

Le Chibe ✗✗✗

Prunier ✗✗✗

L'Atelier de Joël Robuchon-Etoile ✗

Vernet 🏨

Le V ✗✗✗

Raphael 🏨

Peninsula 🏨

L'Oiseau Blanc ✗✗

Les Tablettes de Jean-Louis Nomicos ✗✗✗

Lili ✗✗✗

Pages ✗✗

Le Vinci ✗✗

Keppler 🏨

Max ✗✗

Victor Hugo **M**
Pl. V. Hugo

Conti ✗✗

Baltimore 🏨

La Table du Baltimore ✗✗✗

M Boissière

Pl. des États-Unis

Tsé Yang ✗✗✗

Pl. d'Iéna

16e

Mathieu Pacaud-Histoires ✗✗✗✗

Hexagone ✗✗

Shangri-La 🏨

L'Abeille ✗✗✗

Shang Palace ✗✗

PALAIS DE TOKY

6 New York

Antoin ✗✗

TOUR EIFFEL / INVALIDES (Plan IV)

184

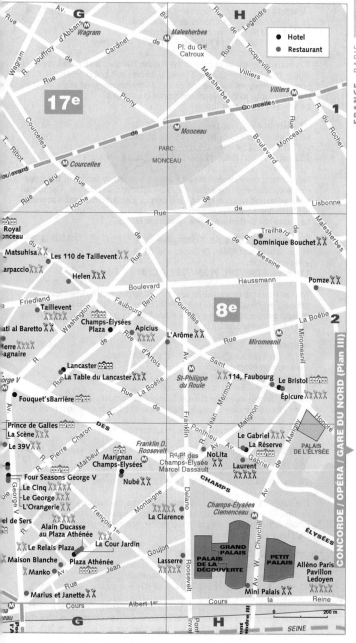

Av. G

Wagram

Rue d'Abbans

Malesherbes

Pl. du Gal Catroux

Rue de Legendre

H

Rue de Tocqueville

● Hotel
● Restaurant

Wagram

R. Jouffroy de

Rue Cardinet

de

Villiers

Prony

Villiers

17e

Courcelles

1

Courcelles

de

Monceau

R. du Rocher

T. Ribot

Boulevard

Courcelles

Monceau

Boulevard

Monceau

Courcelles

PARC MONCEAU

oulevard

Rue Daru

Rue Hoche

de

Lisbonne

Rue

de

Av.

Treilhard

de

Malesherbes

Royal Monceau

Dominique Bouchet ✕✕

Matsuhisa

Les 110 de Taillevent ✕✕

Messine

arpaccio✕✕✕

Helen ✕✕✕

Boulevard

Haussmann

Pomze ✕✕

Friedland

Taillevent ✕✕✕✕✕

Faubourg

Berri

Courcelles

8e

La Boétie

ati al Baretto ✕✕

Washington

Champs-Élysées Plaza ●

Apicius ✕✕✕✕

L'Arôme ✕✕

Miromesnil

ierre agnaire ✕✕✕✕

de

Rue

d'Artois

Saint

Rue

Miromesnil

Lancaster ⌂⌂⌂⌂

St-Philippe du Roule

✕✕ 114, Faubourg

Le Bristol ⌂⌂⌂⌂⌂

orge V

La Table du Lancaster ✕✕✕

Rue La Boétie

Épicure ✕✕✕✕✕

Fouquet'sBarrière ⌂⌂⌂⌂

Rue La Boétie

Honoré

Prince de Galles ⌂⌂⌂⌂

DES

Jean Mermoz

Malignon

Le Gabriel ✕✕✕

La Scène ✕✕✕

R. Pierre Charon

Franklin D. Roosevelt

Franklin

Ponthieu

Av.

La Réserve ⌂⌂⌂⌂⌂

PALAIS DE L'ÉLYSÉE

Le 39V✕✕

Marbeuf

Marignan Champs-Élysées ⌂⌂⌂

R^d-Pt des Champs-Élysée Marcel Dassault

NoLita ✕✕

Gabriel

Four Seasons George V ⌂⌂⌂⌂⌂

Nubé ✕✕

CHAMPS

Laurent ✕✕✕✕

George V

Le Cinq ✕✕✕✕✕

Montaigne

Delano

Champs-Élysées Clemenceau

Le George ✕✕✕

François 1er

L'Orangerie ✕✕

La Clarence ✕✕✕✕

ÉLYSÉES

el de Sers ⌂⌂

Alain Ducasse au Plaza Athénée ✕✕

La Cour Jardin

Churchill

✕✕ Le Relais Plaza

Maison Blanche ✕

Plaza Athénée ⌂⌂⌂⌂⌂

Lasserre ✕✕✕✕

GRAND PALAIS

PETIT PALAIS

Alléno Paris Pavillon Ledoyen ✕✕✕✕✕

✕ Manko ●

Goujon

Jean

Roosevelt

PALAIS DE LA DÉCOUVERTE

● Marius et Janette ✕✕

Rue

Mini Palais ✕✕

la

Reine

na eau

Cours

Albert 1er

Cours

Av. W.

G

H

Pont Inval

Pont andre III

SEINE

0   200 m

FRANCE - PARIS

Vernet   🔥 🅰 🛁

25 r. Vernet (8th) – Ⓜ *Charles de Gaulle-Etoile*
– ☎ *01 44 31 98 00 – www.hotelvernet.com*
41 rm – ♦250/890 € ♦♦250/890 € – ☑ 25 € – 9 suites

Plan: **F2**

• Historic • Townhouse • Elegant •

This building, which dates back to the Roaring Twenties, is in a small street set slightly back from the Champs-Élysees and home to a brand new hotel. It has been completely refurbished and exudes a very Parisian 'je ne sais quoi', from the bright lobby to the elegant and refined guestrooms.
Le V – See restaurant listing

Baltimore   🔥 🔥 🅰 🛁 🚗

88 bis av. Kléber (16th) ✉ *75116 –* Ⓜ *Boissière*
– ☎ *01 44 34 54 54 – www.sofitel.com*
103 rm – ♦230/1150 € ♦♦236/1185 € – ☑ 33 € – 1 suite

Plan: **E3**

• Historic • Elegant • Cosy •

The contemporary decor, elegant furniture and trendy fabrics in the guestrooms contrast with the building's 19C Haussmann architecture. The overall feel is warm and welcoming. The bar is worth a special mention and is appreciated by business travellers in particular.
La Table du Baltimore – See restaurant listing

Renaissance Arc de Triomphe   🏊 🔥 🔥 🅰 🛁 🚗

39 av. Wagram (17th) – Ⓜ *Ternes –* ☎ *01 55 37 55 37*
– www.marriott.fr
118 rm – ♦234/729 € ♦♦234/729 € – ☑ 30 € – 5 suites

Plan: **F2**

• Luxury • Chain • Design •

You can't miss the impressive façade of this hotel designed by Christian de Portzamparc, which stands close to Place de l'Étoile. Originality and contemporary style are also the name of the game inside, from the elegant guestrooms to the vast lobby. Try the Sunday brunch.

Lancaster   🔥 🅰 🛁

7 r. de Berri (8th) – Ⓜ *George V –* ☎ *01 40 76 40 76*
– www.hotel-lancaster.com
45 rm – ♦350/2000 € ♦♦350/2000 € – ☑ 42 € – 11 suites

Plan: **B2**

• Historic • Townhouse • Classic •

Marlene Dietrich loved the discreet luxury of this property, built in 1889 just a stone's throw from the Champs-Élysées. Pleasant lobby and lounges filled with antique furniture.
❀ **La Table du Lancaster** – See restaurant listing

Keppler   🔥 🛁 🔥 🅰 🛁

10 r. Keppler (16th) ✉ *75116 –* Ⓜ *George V*
– ☎ *01 47 20 65 05 – www.keppler.fr*
34 rm – ♦300/500 € ♦♦300/500 € – ☑ 22 € – 5 suites

Plan: **F3**

• Luxury • Personalised • Cosy •

The Keppler's luxurious and refined decor bears the hallmark of Pierre-Yves Rochon. There is a sense of magic pervading the lounges, library and guestrooms. A hammam, sauna and fitness room complete the picture at one of the city's most elegant addresses.

Marignan Champs-Elysées   🔥 🅰 🛁

12 r. de Marignan (8th) – Ⓜ *Franklin D. Roosevelt*
– ☎ *01 40 76 34 56 – www.hotelmarignanelyseesparis.com*
45 rm – ♦270/880 € ♦♦270/880 € – ☑ 40 € – 5 suites

Plan: **G3**

• Luxury • Townhouse • Contemporary •

This hotel in a former townhouse, just off the Champs-Élysées, offers a discreet take on luxury. All of the guestrooms are done out in an elegant and sleek style with oak floorboards, chic 1950s and 1960s furniture and large beds. Style and subtlety.
Nubé – See restaurant listing

Hôtel de Sers

41 av. Pierre-1er-de-Serbie (8th) — Plan: **G3**
– Ⓜ *George V* – ℰ 01 53 23 75 75
– *www.hoteldesers.com*
45 rm – †350/690 € ††500/800 € – ⊏ 30 € – 7 suites
• Grand townhouse • Historic • Elegant •

The Marquis de Sers would fail to recognise his late-19C property! The mix of styles is, however, a success. While the entrance hall has preserved its original character, the guestrooms are resolutely contemporary. An elegant address.

Splendid Étoile

1bis av. Carnot (17th) — Plan: **F2**
– Ⓜ *Charles de Gaulle-Étoile* – ℰ 01 45 72 72 00
– *www.hsplendid.com*
55 rm – †220/430 € ††220/430 € – ⊏ 25 € – 2 suites
• Traditional • Business • Personalised •

The Splendid Étoile is recognisable by its attractive stone façade and wrought-iron balconies. It offers large guestrooms (some with views of the Arc de Triomphe), which owe their character to the Louis XV inspired furniture and heavy drapes. Overall, a very pleasant, elegant style.
Le Pré Carré – See restaurant listing

Les Jardins de la Villa

5 r. Bélidor (17th) – Ⓜ *Porte Maillot* — Plan: **E1**
– ℰ 01 53 81 01 10
– *www.jardinsdelavilla.com*
33 rm – †155/400 € ††155/400 € – ⊏ 22 €
• Boutique hotel • Luxury • Design •

Fashionistas will be thrilled by this small boutique hotel with numerous references to the fashion world, along with black, shocking pink and grey tones. It also boasts a spa with fitness facilities, a sauna and a hammam. Original, chic and comfortable!

Star Champs Élysées

18 r. de l'Arc-de-Triomphe (17th) — Plan: **F2**
– Ⓜ *Charles de Gaulle-Étoile* – ℰ 01 43 80 27 69
– *www.hotelstarchampselysees.com*
62 rm – †100/290 € ††120/390 € – ⊏ 13 €
• Business • Traditional • Functional •

This hotel is in a quiet street near the Place de l'Étoile and the Arc de Triomphe. It offers guestrooms which, although small, are functional and well maintained. The reception area with its medieval decoration makes for an original detail! A good place that caters to both business travellers and tourists.

Le Cinq – Hôtel Four Seasons George V

31 av. George V (8th) – Ⓜ *George V* — Plan: **G3**
– ℰ 01 49 52 71 54
– *www.fourseasons.com/paris*
Menu 145 € (lunch), 210/310 € – Carte 195/395 €
• Modern cuisine • Luxury • Elegant •

After the fabulous years at Ledoyen, Christian Le Squer is now at the helm of this renowned establishment. The majesty of the Grand Trianon inspired decor remains intact, waiters in uniform still perform their dizzying ballet, and the expertise of the chef does the rest, keeping the finest tradition alive!
→ Gratinée d'oignons à la parisienne. Bar de ligne au caviar et lait ribot. Givré laitier au goût de levure.

XxXxX **Alain Ducasse au Plaza Athénée** – Hôtel Plaza Athénée

✿✿✿ *25 av. Montaigne (8th) –* Ⓜ *Alma Marceau*
– ✆ 01 53 67 65 00 – www.alain-ducasse.com – Closed Plan: **G3**
22 July-30 August, 22 to 31 December, Monday lunch, Tuesday lunch,
Wednesday lunch, Saturday and Sunday
Menu 210 € ♟ (lunch)/390 € – Carte 245/350 €
– (booking advisable)
• Creative • Luxury • Design •

Alain Ducasse has rethought his entire restaurant along the lines of 'naturality'
– his culinary Holy Grail is to uncover the truth of each ingredient. Based on the
trilogy fish-vegetables-cereals (here too, a respect for nature prevails), some of
the dishes are really outstanding, and the setting is magnificent!
→ Lentilles vertes du Puy et caviar, délicate gelée d'anguille. Turbot du
golfe de Gascogne, maïs grand roux et huître de l'étang de Thau. Chocolat
et café de notre manufacture, badiane et praliné.

XxXxX **Épicure** – Hôtel Bristol

✿✿✿ *112 r. du Faubourg-St-Honoré (8th) –* Ⓜ *Miromesnil*
– ✆ 01 53 43 43 40 – www.lebristolparis.com Plan: **H2**
Menu 145 € (lunch)/320 € – Carte 171/365 €
• Modern cuisine • Luxury • Classic décor •

The bright dining room overlooking the garden boasts a restrained, distinguished elegance in which the glamour of the 18C shines forth. The virtuosity of Éric
Fréchon's classic cuisine bears witness to his freedom of expression with regard
to great tradition. He creates dishes that are fresh and endowed with the finest
flavours!
→ Macaronis farcis de truffe noire, artichaut et foie gras de canard gratinés au vieux parmesan. Sole farcie aux girolles et persil plat, sucs des
arêtes au vin jaune. Chocolat nyangbo, cacao liquide et sorbet doré à
l'or fin.

XxXxX **Alléno Paris au Pavillon Ledoyen** (Yannick Alléno)

✿✿✿ *8 av. Dutuit (carré Champs-Élysées) (8th)*
– Ⓜ *Champs-Elysées Clemenceau – ✆ 01 53 05 10 01* Plan: **H3**
– www.yannick-alleno.com – Closed 2 weeks in August, Saturday lunch
and Sunday
Menu 135 € (lunch), 295/380 € – Carte 170/290 €
• Modern cuisine • Luxury •

Taken over by Yannick Alléno, this Parisian institution – in an elegant Second
Empire pavilion in the Jardins des Champs Elysées – has embarked on a new
chapter in its history. The chef produces a tour de force, immediately stamping
his hallmark on dishes. He manages with all his mastery to put a new spin on
haute cuisine, magnifying for example jus and sauces through clever extra-
ctions. Prepare to be impressed!
→ Avocat en millefeuille de céleri, extraction coco aux éclats de chia. Bœuf
Wagyu en aiguillettes, onigiri iodé, langues d'oursin et anguille fumée.
Charlotte norvégienne moderne aux pommes.

XxXxX **Le Taillevent**

✿✿ *15 r. Lamennais (8th) –* Ⓜ *Charles de Gaulle-Etoile* Plan: **G2**
– ✆ 01 44 95 15 01 – www.taillevent.com – Closed 29 July-28 August,
Saturday, Sunday and Bank Holidays
Menu 88 € (lunch), 178/218 € – Carte 155/250 € – *(booking advisable)*
• Classic cuisine • Luxury • Elegant •

Wainscoting and works of art adorn this former private residence dating from
the 19C. It was once home to the Duke of Morny, and is now a guardian of
French haute cuisine. Exquisite dishes and a magnificent wine list.
→ Rémoulade de tourteau à l'aneth, sauce fleurette citronnée. Bar de ligne
étuvé, caviar osciètre, poireau et champagne. Soufflé chaud au chocolat.

FRANCE - PARIS

XxXxX Lasserre

17 av. F.-D.-Roosevelt (8th) – Ⓜ Franklin D. Roosevelt   Plan: **H3**
– ℰ 01 43 59 02 13 – www.restaurant-lasserre.com – Closed August,
Sunday and Monday
Menu 90 € (weekday lunch), 195/375 € ₸ – Carte 190/435 €
• Classic cuisine • Luxury • Chic •

One of the temples of Parisian gastronomy. The elegance of the interior
(columns, draperies, tassels etc), the tableware, the quality of the service – it all
comes together to magnify the haute cuisine of accomplished chef, Michel
Roth.
→ Macaroni, truffe noire et foie gras de canard. Bœuf Rossini, pommes
soufflées. Crêpes Suzette.

XxXxX Le Clarence

31 av. F.-D.-Roosevelt (8th) – Ⓜ Franklin D. Roosevelt   Plan: **H3**
– ℰ 01 82 82 10 10 – www.le-clarence.paris – Closed Sunday and Monday
Menu 65 € (lunch), 130/320 € – Carte 120/175 € – (booking advisable)
• Modern cuisine • Luxury • Historic •

This superb 1884 mansion located close to the Champs-Elysées hosts the remarkable talent of Christophe Pelé (former chef of La Bigarrade, in Paris). He is an
artist when it comes to marrying produce from land and sea. As for the sumptuous wine list, it is enough to make you dizzy even before you have had a glass!
→ Saint-Jacques, épinards et anchois. Saint-pierre, ris de veau et cocos de
Paimpol. Soufflé à la fève de cacao, crème glacée au cognac.

XxXxX Laurent

41 av. Gabriel (8th) – Ⓜ Champs Elysées Clemenceau   Plan: **H3**
– ℰ 01 42 25 00 39 – www.le-laurent.com – Closed Christmas Holidays,
Saturday lunch, Sunday and Bank Holidays
Menu 95/180 € – Carte 165/250 €
• Classic cuisine • Elegant • Luxury •

A stone's throw from the Champs Élysées, this former hunting lodge belonging
to Louis XIV with its elegant shaded terraces has a loyal following. Traditional
cuisine and a good wine list.
→ Araignée de mer dans ses sucs en gelée, crème de fenouil. Tronçon de
turbot nacré à l'huile d'olive, bardes et légumes verts dans une fleurette
iodée. Glace vanille minute.

XxxX Pierre Gagnaire

6 r. Balzac (8th) – Ⓜ George V – ℰ 01 58 36 12 50   Plan: **G2**
– www.pierregagnaire.com – Closed 3 weeks in August, 1 week Christmas
Holidays, Saturday and Sunday
Menu 85 € (lunch)/310 € – Carte 325/405 €
• Creative • Elegant • Chic •

The restaurant's chic and restrained contemporary decor is in complete contrast
to the renowned inventiveness of this famous chef. Pierre Gagnaire's cooking,
which draws on his passion for jazz and art, is a festival for the senses.
→ Gambas de Palamos coraillées, raidies au four, pistes, casserons et poul-
pitos à l'omiza. Saint-pierre pimenté saisi à la poêle, compote de concombre, tomate et txistorra. Le grand dessert de Pierre Gagnaire.

XxxX L'Abeille – Hôtel Shangri-La

10 av. d'Iéna (16th) ✉ 75116 – Ⓜ Iéna   Plan: **F3**
– ℰ 01 53 67 19 90 – www.shangri-la.com – Closed 30 July-29 August, 17
to 30 December, Sunday, Monday and lunch
Menu 210 € – Carte 155/215 €
• Modern cuisine • Luxury • Elegant •

The Shangri-La Hotel's 'French restaurant' has a name that gives a nod to the
Napoleonic emblem of the bee. As you might expect, France's grand culinary
tradition is honoured here under the auspices of a team led by Christophe
Moret. The menu promotes fine classicism and noble ingredients.
→ Oursin et caviar en délicate royale. Homard des îles Chausey en cocotte
lutée, sucs savoureux. Miel du maquis corse givré aux parfums de citron et
d'eucalyptus.

FRANCE - PARIS

XxxX
❀❀ **Mathieu Pacaud - Histoires**   Plan: **E3**
85 av. Kléber (16th) ✉ 75016 – ⓜ Trocadéro
– ☎ 01 70 98 16 35
– www.histoires-paris.fr
– Closed August, Tuesday lunch, Saturday lunch, Sunday
and Monday
Menu 95 € (lunch), 230/350 € – Carte 230/355 € – *(booking advisable)*
• Creative • Elegant • Cosy •

Mathieu Pacaud and his team took many months to explore countless combinations and hatch an original and well-crafted menu. The chef draws on numerous techniques – infusion, maceration, deglazing, marinades – and produces
innovative dishes: each one an experience in itself!
➜ Marquise d'œuf, émulsion d'artichaut breton et truffe noire. Turbot sauvage, fleur de courgette, fumée de romarin et crémeux de chorizo. Grande
valse brillante.

XxxX
❀ **Apicius** (Jean-Pierre Vigato)   Plan: **G2**
20 r. d'Artois (8th) – ⓜ St-Philippe du Roule
– ☎ 01 43 80 19 66
– www.restaurant-apicius.com
– Closed August, Saturday, Sunday and Bank Holidays
Menu 140 € (lunch), 180/220 € – Carte 125/215 €
• Classic cuisine • Elegant • Luxury •

Restaurant on the ground floor of a listed town house with a garden. There is a
succession of fine rooms in a chic mix of classic, rococo and modern styles. Up-
to-date cuisine; superb wine list.
➜ Foie gras de canard poêlé et grillé en aigre-doux. Ris de veau rôti, feuilles et jeunes pousses. Soufflé au chocolat guanaja, chantilly sans sucre.

XxxX
❀❀ **Maison Rostang**   Plan: **F1**
20 r. Rennequin (17th) – ⓜ Ternes
– ☎ 01 47 63 40 77 – www.maisonrostang.com
– Closed 2 weeks in August, Monday lunch, Saturday lunch
and Sunday
Menu 90 € (lunch), 185/225 € – Carte 150/215 €
• Classic cuisine • Elegant • Luxury •

Wood panelling, Robj figurines, works by Lalique and an Art Deco stained-glass
window make up the interior that is at once luxurious and unusual. The fine and
superbly classical food is by Nicolas Beaumann, formerly Yannick Alleno's sous-
chef at Le Meurice. His remarkable compositions are enhanced by a magnificent
wine list.
➜ Homard bleu confit, risotto d'artichaut et jus de presse au Condrieu. Ris
de veau croustillant, pâtes farcies de champignons et écrevisses au vin
jaune. Cigare croustillant au tabac Havane et mousseline Cognac.

XxX
❀❀ **Le Gabriel** – Hôtel La Réserve   Plan: **H3**
42 av. Gabriel (8th) – ⓜ Champs Elysées Clemenceau
– ☎ 01 58 36 60 50 – www.lareserve-paris.com
– Closed Saturday lunch
Menu 105 € (weekday lunch)/220 € – Carte 145/255 €
• Modern cuisine • Elegant • Luxury •

The restaurant is nestled in the elegant setting of La Réserve and features Versailles wooden flooring and *cuir de Cordoue* with a gold patina. Chef Jérôme
Banctel, no stranger to Paris' *grandes maisons*, cooks his own superb take on
the classics, with a smattering of Asian touches and executed in the proper
way. A success!
➜ Saumon de Norvège, raviole de daïkon et aubergine fumée. Cabillaud
de ligne, curry et riz japonais, avocat bio. Grains de café meringués, crème
glacée au sirop de merisier.

ξξξ   **La Scène** – Hôtel Prince de Galles   🏢 ❧ 🅰🅲 ⇔ 🍴
⌘   *33 av. George V (8th) –* 🄼 *George V*   Plan: **G3**
      – ℰ 01 53 23 78 50 – www.restaurant-la-scene.fr
      – Closed August, Saturday lunch and Sunday
      Menu 65 € (lunch), 110/195 € – Carte lunch 125/165 €
      • Modern cuisine • Elegant • Luxury •

Within the elegant Prince de Galles Hotel, La Scène shines the spotlight on the kitchens, which are separated from the dining area by just a white marble counter. They are the realm of Stéphanie Le Quellec, no stranger to the limelight since winning France's 'Top Chef' TV show in 2011. Imaginative, harmonious and precise dishes.

→ Caviar impérial, pain mi-perdu et mi-soufflé, pomme Pompadour. Ris de veau, pomme dorée, morilles et café. Vanille en crème glacée, esprit d'une omelette norvégienne.

ξξξ   **Shang Palace** – Hôtel Shangri-La   ❧ 🅰🅲 ⇔ 🍴
⌘   *10 av. d'Iéna (16th)* ✉ *75116 –* 🄼 *Iéna*   Plan: **F3**
      – ℰ 01 53 67 19 92 – www.shangri-la.com – Closed 6 to 21 February,
      11 July-2 August, Tuesday and Wednesday
      Menu 52 € 🍷 (lunch), 78/128 € – Carte 60/230 €
      • Chinese • Exotic décor •

The Shang Palace occupies one of the lower floors of the Shangri-La hotel. It gracefully recreates the decor of a luxury Chinese restaurant with its jade columns, sculpted screens and crystal chandeliers. The menu pays homage to the full flavours and authenticity of Cantonese gastronomy.

→ Saumon Lo Hei. Canard laqué façon pékinoise en deux services. Crème de mangue, poméla et perles de sagou.

ξξξ   **Lili** – Hôtel Peninsula   ❧ 🅰🅲 ⇔
      19 av. Kléber (16th) ✉ *75116 –* 🄼 *Kléber*   Plan: **F2**
      – ℰ 01 58 12 67 50 – http://paris.peninsula.com/fr/ – Closed 22 to
      28 February and 13 to 30 August
      Menu 58 € (lunch), 68/150 € – Carte 80/120 €
      • Chinese • Elegant • Exotic décor •

Opened by the Hong Kong luxury hotel group of the same name, the already famous Peninsula Hotel is the rightful home of an Asian restaurant, Lili. It is named after a famous Chinese singer of the 1920s. In a very theatrical setting, the long menu unveils a wide range of Chinese specialties. A real embassy!

ξξξ   **Prunier**   🍽 🅰🅲 ⇔ 🍴
      16 av. Victor-Hugo (16th) ✉ *75116*   Plan: **F2**
      – 🄼 *Charles de Gaulle-Etoile*
      – ℰ 01 44 17 35 85 – www.prunier.com
      – Closed August, Saturday lunch, Sunday and Bank Holidays
      Menu 47 € (lunch), 85/175 € – Carte 62/215 €
      • Seafood • Classic décor • Cosy •

A culinary institution created in 1925 by the architect Boileau. It has a superb, listed Art Deco interior of black marble, mosaics and stained-glass windows. In addition to enjoying excellent fish and seafood, mark the occasion by tasting the house caviar from southwest France.

ξξξ   **Le George** – Hôtel Four Seasons George V   🏢 ❧ 🅰🅲 🍴
⌘   *31 av. George-V (8th) –* 🄼 *George V – ℰ 01 49 52 72 09*   Plan: **G3**
      – www.legeorge.com
      Menu 110/140 € – Carte 70/100 €
      • Italian • Elegant • Cosy •

In the kitchens of the George since September 2016, Simone Zanoni has made an impression with his light, Italian-inspired cooking, often served in tasting-size portions. Superb dining room or conservatory in the courtyard.

→ Consommé de bœuf, tortellini au parmesan. Côte de veau à la milanaise. Dessert caramel au beurre salé.

FRANCE - PARIS

XxX
۞

Il Carpaccio – Hôtel Le Royal Monceau   🐕 🍽 ᶑ 🅐 ⇔ ⛱

37 av. Hoche (8th) – Ⓜ *Charles de Gaulle-Etoile*   Plan: **G2**
– ℰ 01 42 99 88 12 – www.leroyalmonceau.com – Closed 1 to 21 August,
Sunday and Monday
Menu 120/145 € – Carte 100/185 €
• Italian • Elegant •

You reach the restaurant via a remarkable corridor decorated with thousands of shells. The restaurant decor, reminiscent of a winter garden, is also delightful. The menu is unapologetically simple and in the great tradition of Italian home cooking.

→ Tartelette d'artichaut, épinard, céleri et vinaigrette de truffe. Noix de veau cuite en calzone, millefeuille de légumes d'automne et fromage. Biscuit cuillère imbibé au café et à l'amaretto, crème de mascarpone.

XxX

La Cour Jardin – Hôtel Plaza Athénée   🍽 🅐 ⛱

25 av. Montaigne (8th) – Ⓜ *Alma Marceau*   Plan: **G3**
– ℰ 01 53 67 66 20
– www.dorchestercollection.com/paris/hotel-plaza-athenee – Open mid-May to mid-September
Menu 64 € – Carte 85/130 € – *(booking advisable)*
• Mediterranean cuisine • Elegant • Romantic •

First comes delight at finding such a ravishing, flower-filled courtyard, planted with trees and with ivy, Virginia creeper and geraniums scaling its walls... And then the food: created by Alain Ducasse, it is summery, light and aromatic. The ingredients are exceedingly fresh and the flavours speak for themselves. Impeccable service.

XxX

Maison Blanche   🐕 ⪦ 🍽 🅐 ⛱

15 av. Montaigne (8th) – Ⓜ *Alma Marceau*   Plan: **G3**
– ℰ 01 47 23 55 99 – www.maison-blanche.fr – Closed 2 weeks in August,
Saturday lunch and Sunday lunch
Menu 58 € (lunch), 69/125 € – Carte 78/209 €
• Modern cuisine • Design • Friendly •

Majestically located on the rooftop of the Champs Elysées Theatre, this immense two-floor loft overlooks the Eiffel Tower and a big chunk of Paris! The contemporary cuisine with Mediterranean accents bears witness to the chef's international background.

XxX
۞

La Table du Lancaster – Hôtel Lancaster   🐕 🍽 🅐 ⇔ ⛱

7 r. de Berri (8th) – Ⓜ *George V – ℰ 01 40 76 40 18*   Plan: **G2**
– www.hotel-lancaster.fr – Closed 3 weeks in August, Saturday, Sunday
and Bank Holidays
Menu 75 € (lunch), 175/205 € – Carte 155/185 €
• Modern cuisine • Elegant •

In this Haussman building on a street off the Champs-Élysées, you will appreciate the exclusive and confidential atmosphere of a grand hotel restaurant. The food is nicely presented and in summer, the pleasant inner terrace offers an original experience.

→ Foie gras de canard poêlé, verveine et amertume d'abricot. Grillon de ris de veau français aux cèpes et sureau maison. Cylindre de chocolat et mélilot glacé.

XxX

Le V – Hôtel Vernet   🅐 ⇔

25 r. Vernet (8th) – Ⓜ *Charles de Gaulle-Etoile*   Plan: **F2**
– ℰ 01 44 31 98 00 – www.hotelvernet.com – Closed August, Saturday
lunch and Sunday
Carte 58/106 €
• Modern cuisine • Elegant •

The stunning dining room of the Hôtel Vernet is crowned by a large Eiffel-designed glass canopy and embellished with pilasters and drapes. The perfect setting for a special occasion, where the refined cuisine encompasses a classic repertoire with new combinations of flavours.

XXX

La Table du Baltimore – Hôtel Baltimore

1 r. Léo-Delibes (16th) ✉ 75016 – Ⓜ Boissière Plan: **E3**
– ✆ 01 44 34 54 34 – www.latabledubaltimore.fr – Closed August, Saturday, Sunday and Bank Holidays
Carte 80/100 €

• Modern cuisine • Cosy •

The Hotel Baltimore is also home to this chic restaurant boasting old wood panelling, contemporary furniture and artwork. An elegant setting for cuisine in keeping with the times.

XXX
✿

Le Chiberta

3 r. Arsène-Houssaye (8th) – Ⓜ Charles de Gaulle-Etoile Plan: **F2**
– ✆ 01 53 53 42 00 – www.lechiberta.com – Closed 2 weeks in August, Saturday lunch and Sunday
Menu 49 € (lunch), 110/165 € 🍷 – Carte 90/140 €

• Creative • Minimalist •

Find a serene atmosphere, soft lighting and simple decor designed by J M Wilmotte (dark colours and unusual wine bottle walls). This provides the setting for inventive cuisine supervised by Guy Savoy.

➜ Salade de homard, vinaigrette de corail. Filet de bœuf charolais à la truffe, girolles et pommes noisette, jus truffé. Terrine d'orange et de pamplemousse, tuile au thé earl grey.

XXX

Sormani

4 r. Gén.-Lanrezac (17th) – Ⓜ Charles de Gaulle-Étoile Plan: **F2**
– ✆ 01 43 80 13 91 – www.restaurantsormani.fr – Closed 3 weeks in August, Saturday, Sunday and Bank Holidays
Carte 70/140 €

• Italian • Romantic • Elegant •

Fabric wallpaper, Murano glass chandeliers, mouldings and mirrors: all the elegance of Italy comes to the fore in this chic and sophisticated restaurant. The cooking of Pascal Fayet (grandson of a Florentine cabinet maker) pays a subtle homage to Italian cuisine. From the lobster ravioli and veal with ceps to the remarkable dessert, the "gigantesco".

XXX
✿

Les Tablettes de Jean-Louis Nomicos

16 av. Bugeaud (16th) ✉ 75116 – Ⓜ Victor Hugo Plan: **E3**
– ✆ 01 56 28 16 16 – www.lestablettesjeanlouisnomicos.com
Menu 42 € (lunch), 80 € 🍷/145 € – Carte 100/150 €

• Modern cuisine • Elegant •

Having manned the kitchens at Lasserre, Jean-Louis Nomicos is now pursuing his solo career on the premises formerly occupied by Joël Robuchon's La Table. Savour his fine, Mediterranean-inspired cuisine to a backdrop of original and contemporary decor.

➜ Macaroni, truffe noire, foie gras de canard, céleri et jus de veau. Filet de bœuf de Salers, aubergine brûlée, pommes soufflées et sauce provençale. Granité à la Chartreuse verte, framboises et glace à l'eau de rose.

XXX
✿

Antoine

10 av. de New-York (16th) ✉ 75116 – Ⓜ Alma Marceau Plan: **F3**
– ✆ 01 40 70 19 28 – www.antoine-paris.fr – Closed 3 weeks in August, 1 week Christmas Holidays, Sunday and Monday
Menu 48 € (weekday lunch), 86/155 € – Carte 125/155 €

• Seafood • Elegant •

With chef Thibault Sombardier at the helm, this is a sure bet for fish and seafood in Paris. Delivered directly from the ports of Brittany, the Basque Country or the Mediterranean, the quality ingredients are handled with expertise and inspiration. Elegant contemporary decor.

➜ Gamberoni et fins coquillages au naturel, citron noir d'Iran et bouillon de roquette. Aiguillette de saint-pierre de petit bateau, épinards, pomme de mer et sabayon à l'estragon. Galet noisette, compotée de mirabelle.

FRANCE - PARIS

XxX ☆
Le Pergolèse (Stéphane Gaborieau)   🗨 AC ⇄ 🥛
40 r. Pergolèse (16th) ✉ *75116* – Ⓜ *Porte Maillot*   Plan: **E2**
– ☏ 01 45 00 21 40 – www.lepergolese.com – Closed 3 weeks in August,
Saturday lunch and Sunday
Menu 54 € (lunch), 75/125 € – Carte 80/120 €
• Modern cuisine • Elegant •
A successful reinterpretation of southern cuisine with a smattering of Japanese touches by a chef awarded the 'Meilleur Ouvrier de France'. It is served in a decor that is at once pared down and elegant.
→ Moelleux de filets de sardines marinés aux épices, sorbet à la tomate. Sole façon "Meilleur Ouvrier de France 2004". Soufflé chaud de saison.

XxX
Tsé Yang   AC ⇄
25 av. Pierre-1er-de-Serbie (16th) ✉ *75016* – Ⓜ *Iéna*   Plan: **F3**
– ☏ 01 47 20 70 22
Menu 34 € ⚹ (lunch), 45/53 € – Carte 45/100 €
• Chinese • Exotic décor •
Elegant dining rooms (gilded ceilings and dominant black colour scheme) provide the setting for traditional Chinese cuisine from Peking, Shanghai and Sichuan. An exotic location in which guests will also appreciate the attentive and stylish service.

XxX
Citrus Étoile   ↴ AC 🥛
6 r. Arsène-Houssaye (8th) – Ⓜ *Charles de Gaulle-Étoile*   Plan: **F2**
– ☏ 01 42 89 15 51 – www.citrusetoile.com – Closed Christmas Holidays,
Saturday, Sunday and Bank Holidays
Menu 49/120 € ⚹ – Carte 83/133 €
• Modern cuisine • Fashionable • Friendly •
In a restaurant decorated with flair by his wife Élisabeth, Gilles Épié creates original and skilfully prepared cuisine. It is testament as much to his solid classical training as it is to the experience he clocked up in the USA (the couple lived in California for 10 years) and Asia. Friendly and professional service.

XxX ☆
Helen   AC ⇄
3 r. Berryer (8th) – Ⓜ *George V* – ☏ *01 40 76 01 40*   Plan: **G2**
– www.helenrestaurant.com – Closed 3 weeks in August, 24 December-
2 January, Saturday lunch, Sunday and Monday
Menu 48 € (lunch)/130 € – Carte 76/162 €
• Seafood • Elegant • Design •
Founded in 2012, Helen has made its mark among the fish restaurants of Paris' chic neighbourhoods. If you love fish, you will be bowled over: from the quality of the ingredients (only wild fish sourced from day boats) to the care taken over the recipes. Sober and elegant decor.
→ Carpaccio de daurade royale au citron caviar. Bar de ligne aux olives taggiasche. Paris-brest.

XxX ☆
L'Arôme   🗨 AC ⇿ ⇄ 🥛
3 r. St-Philippe-du-Roule (8th)   Plan: **G-H2**
– Ⓜ St-Philippe-du-Roule – ☏ 01 42 25 55 98 – www.larome.fr – Closed
1 week in February, 3 weeks in August, Saturday and Sunday
Menu 59 € (lunch), 99/155 € – Carte 85/110 €
• Modern cuisine • Chic • Romantic •
Attractive restaurant run by Eric Martins (front of house) and Thomas Boullault (in the kitchen). Comfortable dining room with a warm atmosphere and an open kitchen. Modern cuisine.
→ Pressé de tourteau, avocat, riz koshihikari et eau de tomate au piment fumé. Filet de biche rôti aux baies de genièvre, coing poché au romarin et sauce Périgueux. Fruits rouges aux parfums d'agrumes et de citronnelle, croustillant aux amandes.

XxX ❋❋ ❗

Penati al Baretto (Alberico Penati)

9 r. Balzac (8th) – **Ⓜ** *George V*   Plan: **G2**
– ℰ *01 42 99 80 00*
– *www.penatialbaretto.eu*
– *Closed Saturday lunch and Sunday*
Menu 45 € (lunch) – Carte 75/120 €
• Italian • Classic décor • Elegant •

Alberico Penati's restaurant, opened mid-2014, has imposed itself as one of the best in the city! In accordance with the finest Italian tradition, generosity and refinement distinguish each recipe. The dishes are brimming with flavour as they explore all the regions of the peninsula. A succulent voyage.

→ Pressé de lapin de Carmagnola en escabèche aux gambas rouges sautées. Spaghettis di Verrigni aux sardines à la sicilienne. Tiramisu.

XX ❋❋

Hexagone

85 av. Kléber (16th) ✉ *75116* – **Ⓜ** *Trocadéro*   Plan: **E3**
– ℰ *01 42 25 98 85*
– *www.hexagone-paris.fr*
– *Closed Sunday and Monday*
Menu 59 € (weekday lunch), 135/185 €
– Carte 100/140 €
• Modern cuisine • Trendy • Design •

After many years working with his father Bernard at L'Ambroisie, Mathieu Pacaud has embarked on his own gourmet adventure. Here he brilliantly concocts his own version of French culinary classics, whilst preserving a unity of technique, flavour and sauce. Inspiring!

→ Œuf de poule mollet, fine ratatouille et crème glacée de céleri. Limande-sole à la viennoise, poêlée de girolles, amandes fraîches et sauce au vin jaune. Ganache bayano, glace au miel, croquant à la noisette, sarrasin glacé et soufflé.

XX ❋❋

Le 39V (Frédéric Vardon)

39 av. George V (6th floor - entrance at 17 r. Quentin-   Plan: **G3**
Bauchart) (8th) – **Ⓜ** *George V*
– ℰ *01 56 62 39 05* – *www.le39v.com*
– *Closed August, Saturday and Sunday*
Menu 50 € (lunch), 95/195 € 🍷 – Carte 75/145 €
• Modern cuisine • Design • Friendly •

The temperature is rising at 39, avenue George V! On the 6th floor of this impressive Haussmann-style building overlooking the rooftops of Paris, diners can enjoy the chef's refined cuisine in a stylish setting. Dishes are based around a classic repertoire, top quality ingredients and fine flavours.

→ Macaronis gratinés, fin ragoût de truffe noire. Saint-pierre de Bretagne aux artichauts cuits et crus en tempura, sucs persillés. Paris-brest.

XX ❋❋

114, Faubourg – Hôtel Bristol

114 r. du Faubourg-St-Honoré (8th)   Plan: **H2**
– **Ⓜ** *Miromesnil*
– ℰ *01 53 43 44 44*
– *www.lebristolparis.com*
– *Closed 3 weeks in August, Saturday lunch and Sunday lunch*
Menu 114 € – Carte 85/170 €
• Modern cuisine • Elegant •

This chic brasserie within the premises of Le Bristol has a lavish interior with gilded columns, floral motifs and a grand staircase. Savour dishes from the menu of fine brasserie classics cooked with care and lots of taste.

→ Soupe d'artichaut, escalope de foie gras poêlée, émulsion truffe noire. Merlan frit, sauce tartare, tétragones à l'huile d'olive et citron. Millefeuille à la vanille Bourbon, caramel au beurre demi-sel.

FRANCE - PARIS

FRANCE - PARIS

La Scène Thélème
     🔄 📶 🍴

18 rue Troyon (17th) – Ⓜ *Charles de Gaulle-Étoile*   Plan: **F2**
– ☎ *01 77 37 60 99* – *www.lascenetheleme.fr* – *Closed Saturday lunch,*
Sunday and Monday
Menu 49 € (weekday lunch), 115/145 € – Carte 110/150 €
• Modern cuisine • Contemporary décor • Cosy •

An unusual restaurant, where theatre and gastronomy come together. Some evenings, you can attend a theatrical show before being seated at your table. A wonderful idea! The generous and tasty ingredient-focused cuisine, created by a young chef who is perfectly at ease in his role, also works a treat. The scene is set for a memorable culinary intermission.
➜ Ravioles de foie gras de canard, artichaut, aubergine et jus de volaille acidulé. Saint-Jacques de plongée, arancini, mouron des oiseaux et marmelade de citron. Crème légère à la vanille tahitensis et poivre de sarawak.

Les 110 de Taillevent
     🍷 🔄 📶 🍴

195 r. du Faubourg-St-Honoré (8th)   Plan: **G2**
– Ⓜ *Charles de Gaulle-Etoile* – ☎ *01 40 74 20 20*
– *www.taillevent.com/les-110-de-taillevent-brasserie.com* – *Closed 3 to 24 August*
Menu 44 € – Carte 45/95 €
• Traditional cuisine • Cosy •

Under the aegis of the prestigious Taillevent name, this ultra-chic brasserie puts the onus on food and wine pairings. The concept is a success, with its remarkable choice of 110 wines by the glass, and nicely done traditional food (pâté en croûte, bavette steak with a peppercorn sauce etc). Elegant and inviting decor.

L'Oiseau Blanc – Hôtel Peninsula
     🍷 🔄 📶

19 av. Kléber (16th) ✉ *75116* – Ⓜ *Kléber*   Plan: **F2**
– ☎ *01 58 12 67 30* – *http://paris.peninsula.com/fr/*
Menu 69 € (lunch), 109/129 €
• Modern cuisine • Design • Elegant •

This is the Peninsula's rooftop restaurant for 'contemporary French gastronomy'. Part of the luxury hotel that opened in 2014 near the Arc de Triomphe, the restaurant is presided over by a replica of the White Bird (in homage to the plane in which Nungesser and Coli attempted to cross the Atlantic in 1927) and offers stunning views.

L'Orangerie – Hôtel Four Seasons George V
     🍷 🍷 📶

31 av. George-V (8th) – Ⓜ *George V* – ☎ *01 49 52 72 24*   Plan: **G3**
– *www.fourseasons.com/paris*
Menu 95/125 € – Carte 90/150 € – *(booking advisable)*
• Modern cuisine • Elegant •

This tiny restaurant (18 seats only) is between La Galerie restaurant and the handsome courtyard of the Four Seasons George V hotel. It features a concise, seasonal menu in which tradition is updated thanks to elegant, perfumed notes and a delicate blend of flavours.
➜ Œuf de poule fumé, caviar impérial et cresson. Poulette du Perche, girolles, citronnelle et Chartreuse. Fines feuilles et soufflé, chocolat noir et cardamome.

Le Relais Plaza – Hôtel Plaza Athénée
     📶

21 av. Montaigne (8th) – Ⓜ *Alma Marceau*   Plan: **G3**
– ☎ *01 53 67 64 00*
– *www.dorchestercollection.com/paris/hotel-plaza-athenee* – *Closed late July-late August*
Menu 64 € – Carte 80/135 €
• Classic cuisine • Elegant • Brasserie •

Within the Plaza Athénée is this chic and exclusive brasserie, popular with regulars from the fashion houses nearby. It is impossible to resist the charm of the lovely 1930s decor inspired by the liner SS Normandie. A unique atmosphere for food that has a pronounced sense of tradition. As Parisian as it gets.

FRANCE - PARIS

XX **Matsuhisa** – Hôtel Le Royal Monceau   🎿 🛋 ఈ 🗚 🍽
37 av. Hoche (8th) – Ⓜ *Charles de Gaulle-Etoile*   Plan: **G2**
– ℰ *01 42 99 98 80 – www.leroyalmonceau.com – Closed Saturday lunch
and Sunday lunch*
Menu 130/170 € – Carte 80/200 €
• Japanese • Design • Chic •

The chef Nobu Matsuhisa is known as being the inventor of the Peruvian-Japanese style. He entrusts sushi master Hideki Endo with the task of sublimating Japanese – but also French – ingredients, such as crunchy oysters with caviar, wasabi and aioli sauce. All in the sumptuous setting of the Royal Monceau.

XX **Timgad**   🗚 🍽
21 r. Brunel (17th) – Ⓜ *Argentine –* ℰ *01 45 74 23 70*   Plan: **E2**
– www.timgad.fr
Carte 45/90 €
• North African • Oriental décor • Exotic décor •

Experience the historic splendour of the city of Timgad in this elegant Moroccan restaurant adorned with fine stuccowork. Fragrant North African cuisine, including couscous and tagines.

XX **Frédéric Simonin**   🗚
🕸 *25 r. Bayen (17th) –* Ⓜ *Ternes –* ℰ *01 45 74 74 74*   Plan: **F1**
*– www.fredericsimonin.com – Closed 30 July-21 August, Sunday and
Monday*
Menu 49 € (lunch), 86/139 € – Carte 95/155 €
• Modern cuisine • Cosy • Elegant •

Black-and-white decor forms the backdrop to this chic restaurant close to Place des Ternes. Fine, delicate cuisine from a chef with quite a career behind him already.
➜ Langoustines croustillantes, petits pois et fraises des bois, bavarois d'amande. Veau de Normandie cuit en cocotte, condiment truffe noire et jus au macis. Dacquoise croustillante au praliné feuilleté, ganache chocolat-noisette.

XX **Marius et Janette**   🍴 🗚 🍽
4 av. George-V (8th) – Ⓜ *Alma Marceau*   Plan: **G3**
– ℰ 01 47 23 41 88 – www.mariusjanette.com
Menu 48 € (weekday lunch) – Carte 91/180 €
• Seafood • Mediterranean décor • Friendly •

This seafood restaurant's name recalls Marseille's Estaque district. It has an elegant nautical decor and a pleasant street terrace in summertime.

XX **Nubé** – Hôtel Marignan Champs-Elysées   ఈ 🗚
12 r. de Marignan (8th) – Ⓜ *Franklin D. Roosevelt*   Plan: **G3**
*– ℰ 01 40 76 34 56 – www.hotelmarignanelyseesparis.com – Closed
Sunday dinner*
Menu 60/80 € – Carte 50/66 €
• Modern cuisine • Design • Elegant •

The chef describes his cooking as "salsa cancan": his fusion recipes borrow as much from his South American roots (he is Colombian) as the French culinary tradition, which he also adores. The result is this cuisine without borders, full of colour and downright inventive. Sample in a modern and rather original interior.

XX **Mini Palais**   🍴 ఈ ♿ 🍽
Au Grand Palais - 3 av. Winston-Churchill (8th)   Plan: **H3**
– Ⓜ *Champs-Elysées Clemenceau – ℰ 01 42 56 42 42*
– www.minipalais.com
Carte 35/77 €
• Modern cuisine • Fashionable • Brasserie •

Concealed within the Grand Palais, the Mini Palace is dedicated to the full pleasures of the palate, with a focus on generosity, abundance and the finest ingredients. The snack menu is available from midday to midnight. Tea room and an exquisite terrace.

FRANCE - PARIS

XX Conti 🔳 🍴

72 r. Lauriston (16th) ✉ *75116 –* Ⓜ *Boissière*   Plan: **E3**
– ℰ 01 47 27 74 67 – www.leconti.fr – Closed 31 July-20 August,
24 December-1 January, Saturday, Sunday and Bank Holidays
Menu 39 € (weekday lunch)/47 € – Carte 57/87 €
• Italian • Intimate • Cosy •

The intimate decor of this restaurant brings to mind a private club or an Italian theatre with its red velvet, crystal mirrors and chandeliers. The many regulars are drawn here by the excellent, classic Italian cuisine.

XX Maxan 🔳 ⇔

3 r. Quentin-Bauchart (8th) – Ⓜ *George V*   Plan: **F3**
– ℰ 01 40 70 04 78 – www.rest-maxan.com – Closed 14 to 19 August,
Saturday lunch and Sunday
Menu 40 € – Carte 48/82 €
• Modern cuisine • Elegant •

It is here, a stone's throw from Avenue George V, that Maxan is to be found, since moving from its previous spot near Miromesnil. In an elegant and discreet interior, decorated in a palette of greys, it is a pleasure to rediscover the flavour-some market-based cuisine. The set lunch menu is great value.

XX Nolita 🦪 🔳

1 av. Matignon (Motor Village - 2nd floor) (8th)   Plan: **H3**
– Ⓜ *Franklin D. Roosevelt – ℰ 01 53 75 78 78 – www.nolitaparis.fr*
– Closed 2 weeks in August, Saturday lunch and Sunday dinner
Menu 39 € (weekday lunch) – Carte 58/85 €
• Italian • Design •

A chic restaurant within MotorVillage (the showroom of a major Italian car manufacturer). The chef draws on the great Italian tradition, composing a menu to make your mouth water. Try linguine with sardines, risotto with Italian ham and mushrooms, Venetian-style calf's liver and onions, and an excellent tiramisu!

XX Dominique Bouchet ⇔
🍀

11 r. Treilhard (8th) – Ⓜ *Miromesnil – ℰ 01 45 61 09 46*   Plan: **H2**
– www.dominique-bouchet.com – Closed 3 weeks in August, 1 week in
December, Saturday and Sunday
Menu 55 € (weekday lunch), 105/140 €
– Carte 80/115 € – (booking advisable)
• Classic cuisine • Elegant •

This is the sort of place that you want to recommend to your friends: a nicely refurbished contemporary interior with an intimate atmosphere, tasty and well put-together market cuisine, and alert service.

→ Carpaccio de Saint-Jacques, mangue et pomme verte. Gigot d'agneau mitonné au vin rouge, sauce aux fèves de cacao et pomme purée. Pêche pochée sur un granité de champagne, gelée de groseille.

XX Pomze 🔳 ⇔
😊

109 bd Haussmann (1st floor) (8th) – Ⓜ *St-Augustin*   Plan: **H2**
– ℰ 01 42 65 65 83 – www.pomze.com – Closed 22 December-2 January,
Saturday except dinner from September to June and Sunday
Menu 36 € – Carte 48/70 €
• Modern cuisine • Minimalist •

The unusual concept behind Pomze is to take the humble apple as a starting point for a culinary voyage! From the food shop (where you will find cider and calvados) to the restaurant, this 'forbidden fruit' provides the central theme. Creative and intrepid dishes offer excellent value for money.

XX **Le Pré Carré** – Hôtel Splendid Étoile   AC

1 bis av. Carnot (17th) – ⓜ *Charles de Gaulle-Étoile*   Plan: **F2**
– ☎ 01 46 22 57 35 – www.restaurant-le-pre-carre.com – Closed 3 weeks in
August, 1 week Christmas Holidays, Saturday lunch and Sunday
Menu 39 € (dinner) – Carte 44/75 €
• Traditional cuisine • Fashionable • Elegant •

In the dining room, two mirrors facing each other reflect Le Pré Carré's infinite elegance and welcoming decor. Aromatic herbs and spices add a gentle touch to the gourmet cuisine, which is very much in keeping with the times.

XX **Agapé**   ಟಿ AC ♨
ಟ೦
51 r. Jouffroy-D'Abbans (17th) – ⓜ *Wagram*   Plan I: **B1**
– ☎ 01 42 27 20 18 – www.agape-paris.fr – Closed Saturday and Sunday
Menu 44 € (lunch), 99/205 € ♉ – Carte 105/160 €
• Modern cuisine • Elegant • Friendly •

Agápe meant unconditional love of another in Ancient Greece. Here, you do indeed feel the love, as you taste this good quality food, which cultivates classicism and sometimes takes liberties – such as the Caesar salad made with calf sweetbreads and crayfish! The finesse of the flavours and the precision of the cooking makes it a sure-fire winner.
→ Noix de veau fumée au bois de hêtre. Homard des côtes bretonnes, girolles, courgette et sauce homardine. Crêpe dentelle au sarrasin, crémeux au chocolat, chantilly vanille et glace sarrasin.

XX **Graindorge**
☺
15 r. Arc-de-Triomphe (17th)   Plan: **F2**
– ⓜ Charles de Gaulle-Étoile – ☎ 01 47 54 00 28 – www.le-graindorge.fr
– Closed 2 weeks in August, Monday lunch, Saturday lunch and Sunday
Menu 32 € (lunch), 36/50 € – Carte 45/65 €
• Flemish • Vintage • Friendly •

Potjevlesch (potted meat), bintje farcie (stuffed potatoes), waterzoï (a stew with Ostend grey prawns) and kippers from Boulogne are just some of the hearty Northern dishes on offer in the Graindorge's attractive Art Deco setting, washed down with some delicious traditional beers.

XX **Pages** (Ryuji Teshima)
ಟ೦
4 r. Auguste-Vacquerie (16th) ✉ *75016*   Plan: **F2**
– ⓜ Charles de Gaulle-Etoile – ☎ 01 47 20 74 94 – www.restaurantpages.fr
– Closed 3 weeks in August, Sunday and Monday
Menu 50 € (lunch), 75/90 € – (booking advisable)
• Creative • Minimalist • Trendy •

Explosive marriages of flavours are cooked in this restaurant. For example, veal tartare meets lemon zest, botarga and anchovy cream, and celeriac comes together with lobster and Saint Nectaire cheese. It was opened in 2014 by a young Japanese chef with a passion for French cuisine and its sleek decor is just as up to the minute.
→ Cuisine du marché.

XX **6 New York**   AC ♨
6 av. de New-York (16th) ✉ *75016* – ⓜ *Alma Marceau*   Plan: **F3**
– ☎ 01 40 70 03 30 – www.6newyork.fr – Closed August, Saturday lunch
and Sunday
Menu 45 € (lunch), 70/90 € ♉ – Carte 46/76 €
• Modern cuisine • Design •

Although the name gives away the address – on Avenue de New York – the restaurant is not a typical North American restaurant. Well-defined, honest flavours and a respect for the seasons are behind cuisine in perfect harmony with the elegant and contemporary setting.

FRANCE - PARIS

FRANCE - PARIS

Le Vinci ⚏ 🕭

23 r. Paul-Valéry (16th) ✉ *75116 –* ⓜ *Victor Hugo* Plan: **E2-3**
– ☎ 01 45 01 68 18 – www.restaurantlevinci.fr – Closed 1 to 22 August,
Saturday and Sunday
Menu 38 € – Carte 48/84 €
• Italian • Elegant • Friendly •
The pleasing interior design and friendly service make Le Vinci a very popular choice a stone's throw from avenue Victor-Hugo. The impressive selection of pastas and risottos, as well as the à la carte meat and fish dishes vary according to the seasons.

Manko ⚏ ⇦

15 av. Montaigne (8th) – ⓜ *Alma Marceau* Plan: **G3**
– ☎ 01 82 28 00 15 – www.manko-paris.com – Closed Saturday lunch and
Sunday
Menu 65 € – Carte 40/80 €
• Peruvian • Elegant • Exotic décor •
Star chef, Peruvian Gaston Acurio, and Canadian singer Garou are the driving force behind Manko. This restaurant, lounge and cabaret bar in the Théâtre des Champs-Elysées basement proposes Peruvian recipes peppered with Asian and African touches. The food is nicely done and ideal for sharing.

L'Atelier de Joël Robuchon - Étoile ⚏ ⇦ 🕭

133 av. des Champs-Élysées (Publicis Drugstore Plan: **F2**
basement) (8th) – ⓜ *Charles de Gaulle-Étoile – ☎ 01 47 23 75 75*
– www.joel-robuchon.com
Menu 49 € (lunch), 99/199 € – Carte 95/205 €
• Creative • Design • Minimalist •
Paris, London, Las Vegas, Tokyo, Taipei, Hong Kong, Singapore and back to Paris: the destiny of these Ateliers, in tune with the times, has been an international one. The chef has come up with a great concept: serving dishes drawing on France, Spain and Asia cooked with precision, on a long counter with bar stools and a red and black colour scheme.
➜ Langoustine en ravioli truffé à l'étuvée de chou vert. Caille caramélisée au foie gras, pomme purée. Chocolat tendance, crémeux onctueux au chocolat araguani, sorbet cacao et biscuit Oréo.

L'Escient ⚏

28 r. Poncelet (17th) – ⓜ *Ternes – ☎ 01 47 64 49 13* Plan: **F1**
– www.restaurantescient.fr – Closed 6 to 17 August, Sunday and Bank
Holidays
Menu 37/55 € – Carte approx. 47 €
• Modern cuisine • Fashionable • Family •
King prawns, taramasalata, daikon, lime and ginger; fresh cod, dried fig crust, chorizo and lemon preserves etc. L'Escient offers a menu with plenty of original associations and remains true to its name, always choosing these judiciously! A very tasty fusion, in an understated decor.

L'Entredgeu

83 r. Laugier (17th) – ⓜ *Porte de Champerret* Plan I: **AB1**
– ☎ 01 40 54 97 24 – Closed Sunday
Menu 36 € – *(booking advisable)*
• Traditional cuisine • Bistro • Friendly •
You are greeted with a smile on entering L'Entredgeu, with its unpronounceable name and lively atmosphere! The chef, who hails from the Béarn, cooks up a storm of classics. This includes smoked mackerel, homemade Béarnais black pudding macaire, roast cod in a pepper crust, and orzo risotto. One of the best deals in the capital.

FRANCE - PARIS

Ritz
15 pl. Vendôme (1st) – Ⓜ *Opéra* – ✆ *01 43 16 30 30*   Plan: K3
– *www.ritzparis.com*
71 rm – †1200/2300 € ††1200/2300 € – ☲ 120 € – 71 suites
• Grand Luxury • Historic • Personalised •
The mythical hotel has reopened after four years of refurbishment and is as luxurious as ever. On legendary Place Vendôme, César Ritz opened the "perfect hotel" in 1898. Proust, Hemingway and Coco Chanel were a few of its illustrious patrons, enticed by the incomparable sophistication of a 28 000m²/92 000ft² luxury hotel. Everything is lavish, from the Hemingway Bar and the 1 500m²/5 000ft² spa to the Mansard suite, whose huge terrace overlooks Place Vendôme and reveals a 360° panorama over Paris. The legend continues.
⸙⸙ **La Table de l'Espadon** • ⸙ **Les Jardins de l'Espadon** – See restaurant listing

Le Meurice
228 r. de Rivoli (1st) – Ⓜ *Tuileries* – ✆ *01 44 58 10 10*   Plan: J-K3
– *www.dorchestercollection.com/fr/paris/le-meurice/*
136 rm – †695/4000 € ††695/4000 € – ☲ 58 € – 24 suites
• Palace • Grand Luxury • Historic •
This luxury hotel opposite the Tuileries was founded at the start of the 19C, making it one of the first to be built in Paris. It has opulent guestrooms and a superb suite on the top floor that has breathtaking panoramic views. The hotel now also bears the contemporary touch of Philippe Starck. A truly fabulous place to stay.
⸙⸙ **Le Meurice Alain Ducasse** • **Le Dali** – See restaurant listing

Mandarin Oriental
251 r. St-Honoré (1st) – Ⓜ *Concorde* – ✆ *01 70 98 78 88*   Plan: J3
– *www.mandarinoriental.fr/paris/*
98 rm – †875/1500 € ††875/1500 € – ☲ 47 € – 40 suites
• Palace • Elegant • Personalised •
Among all the major new hotels in Paris, the opening of the Mandarin Oriental in mid-2011 made quite an impact. Faithful to the principles of this Hong Kong group, the property is the height of refinement. It combines French elegance with the delicate touches of Asia and features sleek lines, lots of space and peace and quiet. A capital address in the heart of the French capital!
⸙⸙ **Sur Mesure par Thierry Marx** • **Camélia** – See restaurant listing

Park Hyatt Paris-Vendôme
5 r. de la Paix (2nd) – Ⓜ *Opéra* – ✆ *01 58 71 12 34*   Plan: K3
– *www.parisvendome.park.hyatt.com*
110 rm – †980 € ††1400 € – ☲ 38 € – 43 suites
• Luxury • Elegant •
Ed Tuttle designed his dream hotel, which stands on the famous rue de la Paix. It has a collection of contemporary art and French-style classicism with a subtle blend of Louis XVI-style and 1930s furnishings. There is a spa and hi-tech equipment, as well as restaurants for all tastes. An authentic palace.
⸙ **Pur' - Jean-François Rouquette** – See restaurant listing

Intercontinental Le Grand
2 r. Scribe (9th) – Ⓜ *Opéra* – ✆ *01 40 07 32 32*   Plan: K2
– *www.paris.intercontinental.com*
442 rm – †335/950 € ††335/950 € – ☲ 45 € – 28 suites
• Historic • Grand luxury • Historic •
Opened in 1862, the Intercontinental stands on the Place de l'Opéra in the heart of Haussmann's Paris. With its superbly decorated Café de la Paix, interior courtyard with a Proustian ambience and its Second Empire-style guestrooms, this is a real Parisian landmark.
Le Café de la Paix – See restaurant listing

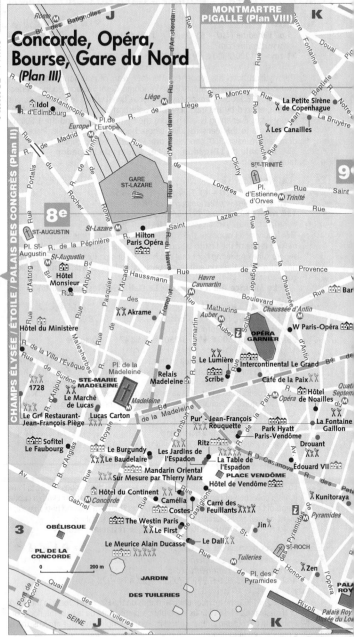

FRANCE - PARIS

Concorde, Opéra, Bourse, Gare du Nord
(Plan III)

MONTMARTRE
PIGALLE (Plan VIII)

CHAMPS ÉLYSÉE / ÉTOILE / PALAIS DES CONGRÈS (Plan II)

Bd des Batignolles

Rome

Rue de Constantinople
R. d'Edimbourg
Idol

Pl. de l'Europe
Europe

R. de Madrid
R. de Vienne

Liège

Rue d'Amsterdam

Rue de Londres

GARE ST-LAZARE

La Petite Sirène de Copenhague
Les Canailles

R. Moncey
Rue Blanche
Rue de Clichy

STE-TRINITÉ
Pl. d'Estienne d'Orves
Trinité

9e

Portalis
Rue du Rocher
Rue de Rome

St-Lazare

Hilton Paris Opéra

Saint Lazare

8e

ST-AUGUSTIN
Pl. St-Augustin
St-Augustin

R. de la Pépinière

Hôtel Monsieur

Rue d'Anjou
Rue Pasquier
Rue de l'Arcade
Rue Tronchet

Rue Haussmann

des

Havre Caumartin

Akrame

Boulevard Haussmann

Rue de Mogador
Chaussée d'Antin

Rue de Provence

Bar

Hôtel du Ministère

R. de la Ville l'Évêque
Rue de Surène

Pl. de la Madeleine
STE-MARIE MADELEINE

Rue des Mathurins
Auber
Rue Scribe

Boulevard
Auber

OPÉRA GARNIER

W Paris-Opéra

Rue de Caumartin

Le Lumière
Intercontinental Le Grand

Malesherbes

1728
Le Marché de Lucas
Le Grd Restaurant-Jean-François Piège

Lucas Carton

Relais Madeleine

Scribe

Café de la Paix

Hôtel de Noailles
Opéra

Quati
Septem
du

Sofitel Le Faubourg

Rue Boissy d'Anglas

Madeleine
Bd de la Madeleine

Rue Royale

Pur' - Jean-François Rouquette

Park Hyatt Paris-Vendôme

La Fontaine Gaillon

Drouant

Le Burgundy
Le Baudelaire
Sur Mesure par Thierry Marx

Les Jardins de l'Espadon
Mandarin Oriental
La Table de l'Espadon

Ritz

PLACE VENDÔME

Rue de Casanova
Édouard VII

Av. Gabriel

Hôtel du Continent
Camélia
Costes

Rue de Rivoli

Rue Cambon

Hôtel de Vendôme

Jin

Kunitoraya

Rue des Pyramides

OBÉLISQUE

PL. DE LA CONCORDE

The Westin Paris
Le First

Carré des Feuillants

Rue de Castiglione

Le Dali

Rue St-Honoré

ST-ROCH

Zen

3

0   200 m

Le Meurice Alain Ducasse

JARDIN DES TUILERIES

Tuileries

Pl. des Pyramides

l'Opéra

PALAI
ROY

Pont de la Concorde
SEINE

Quai des Tuileries

Palais Roy
Musée du Lou

202

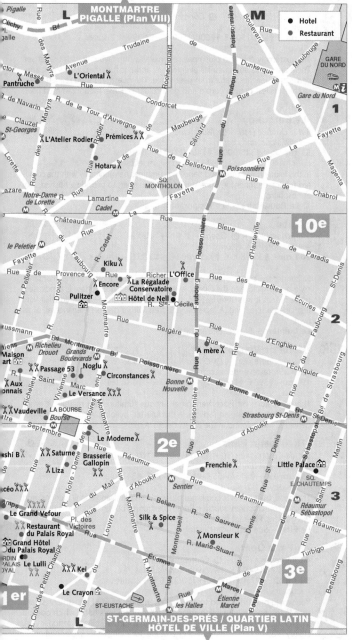

MONTMARTRE
PIGALLE (Plan VIII)

● Hotel
● Restaurant

GARE
DU NORD

Gare du Nord

1

L'Oriental ✗

Pantruche ●

L'Atelier Rodier ✗ ✗ Prémices ✗ ✗

Hotaru ✗

Notre-Dame
de Lorette

SQ.
MONTHOLON

10e

Kiku ✗

Encore ✗

Pulitzer

Richer L'Office ✗
La Régalade
Conservatoire
Hôtel de Nell

2

A mère ✗

Richelieu
Drouot Grands
Maison
art Montmartre
Boulevards

✗ ✗ Passage 53   Noglu ✗

✗ Aux   Circonstances ✗
onnais   Le Versance ✗ ✗ ✗

✗ ✗ Vaudeville LA BOURSE
Bourse

Le Moderne ✗

2e

ushi B ✗   ✗ ✗ Saturne   Frenchie ✗   Little Palace
Brasserie
✗ Liza   Gallopin
✗ ✗   SQ.
E. CHAUTEMPS

céo ✗✗✗   3

mps ✗✗✗✗   Réaumur
Le Grand Vefour   Sébastopol
✗ ✗ Restaurant   Silk & Spice
● du Palais Royal   ✗   Monsieur K ✗

Grand Hôtel
du Palais Royal
Le Lulli   Kei ✗✗✗

Le Crayon   3e

les Halles

L   ST-EUSTACHE

ST-GERMAIN-DES-PRÉS / QUARTIER LATIN
HÔTEL DE VILLE (Plan V)

Costes
⚒ 🛎 ⬜ 🚿 🅐🅒

239 r. St-Honoré (1st) – Ⓜ *Concorde* – ℰ *01 42 44 50 00*   Plan: **K3**
– www.hotelcostes.com
84 rm – ❖500/1500 € ❖❖600/1500 € – ⬡ 35 € – 2 suites
• Luxury • Personalised • Cosy •
This extremely chic and plush palace remains a firm favourite with the jet set. There are nooks and crannies everywhere, and it is furnished with squat armchairs and benches made from pear wood. The guestrooms are refined down to the smallest details: purple and gold colour scheme, monogrammed linen etc.

Le Burgundy
🛎 🌐 🎶 ⬜ 🚿 🅐🅒

6-8 r. Duphot (1st) – Ⓜ *Madeleine* – ℰ *01 42 60 34 12*   Plan: **J3**
– www.leburgundy.com
51 rm ⬡ – ❖345/900 € ❖❖400/1100 € – 8 suites
• Grand Luxury • Design • Personalised •
In this luxury hotel, the wood panelling combines harmoniously with the coloured fabrics, designer furniture and contemporary art to provide a hushed, arty atmosphere.
❀ **Le Baudelaire** – See restaurant listing

Scribe
🛎 🌐 🚿 🅐🅒 🧖

1 r. Scribe (9th) – Ⓜ *Opéra* – ℰ *01 44 71 24 24*   Plan: **K2**
– www.hotel-scribe.com
204 rm – ❖350/800 € ❖❖350/800 € – ⬡ 35 € – 9 suites
• Luxury • Personalised • Classic •
Fall under the charm of this chic, very Parisian hotel occupying a Haussmann-style building close to the Opéra, where the hushed atmosphere is almost secretive in feel. It was here, in 1895, that the Lumière brothers hosted their very first cinema screening. A legendary address with a discreet elegance all of its own.
Le Lumière – See restaurant listing

Hôtel de Vendôme
⚒ 🚿 🅐🅒 🧖

1 pl. Vendôme (1st) – Ⓜ *Opéra* – ℰ *01 55 04 55 00*   Plan: **K3**
– www.hoteldevendome.com
19 rm – ❖390 € ❖❖650/920 € – ⬡ 39 € – 10 suites
• Luxury • Palace • Grand luxury •
The other hotel on Place Vendôme! Antique furniture and marble sit easily alongside state-of-the-art facilities in this fine 18C building. A sense of elegance pervades, and is found in the tiniest details. A real gem.

The Westin Paris
🛎 🌐 🚿 🅐🅒 🧖

3 r. de Castiglione (1st) – Ⓜ *Tuileries* – ℰ *01 44 77 11 11*   Plan: **J3**
– www.thewestinparis.fr
394 rm ⬡ – ❖315/4465 € ❖❖315/4465 € – 34 suites
• Luxury • Personalised •
This hotel, built in 1878, combines old-world charm (Napoleon III lounges) and elegant contemporary touches. Some guestrooms boast views across the Tuileries gardens. Pleasant spa.
Le First – See restaurant listing

W Paris Opéra
⚒ 🛎 🚿 🅐🅒 🧖 🏊

4 r. Meyerbeer (9th) – Ⓜ *Chaussée d'Antin*   Plan: **K2**
– ℰ 01 77 48 94 94 – www.wparisopera.fr
89 rm ⬡ – ❖750/3200 € ❖❖750/3200 € – 2 suites
• Luxury • Contemporary • Design •
You would be hard-pushed to get any closer to the heart of Haussmann's Paris than in this fine 1870 building adjacent to the Opéra. This hotel, which opened in 2012, may plump for a "Paris-chic" decor, but it is in a resolutely designer vein. Luxury is combined with a laid-back attitude (for example, a circular bed and a view over the Palais Garnier). Very trendy and very enticing.

FRANCE - PARIS

Hilton Opéra ⛱ 🛁 ♿ 🅰 🛋

108 r. St-Lazare (8th) – Ⓜ *Saint-Lazare* — Plan: **J2**
– ℰ 01 40 08 44 44 – www.parisopera.hilton.com
257 rm ⌷ – **♦**239/1200 € **♦♦**239/1200 € – 11 suites
• Chain • Contemporary •
Completely refurbished in 2015, this hotel is in touch with its Belle Époque past: a lobby with marble columns and ceiling crafted with gold leaf, a large majestic lounge, with a glass roof and frescoes... the bright and contemporary guestrooms are very comfortable.

Sofitel le Faubourg ⛱ 🛁 ♿ 🅰 🛋

15 r. Boissy-d'Anglas (8th) – Ⓜ *Concorde* — Plan: **J3**
– ℰ 01 44 94 14 14 – www.sofitel-paris-lefaubourg.com
118 rm – **♦**370/810 € **♦♦**370/910 € – ⌷ 36 € – 29 suites
• Luxury • Contemporary • Personalised •
This elegant hotel occupies two 18C and 19C residences. It offers attractive suites in a contemporary style, as well as elegant guestrooms. There is also a lounge crowned with a glass roof, a fitness centre and a hammam.

Hôtel de Nell ♿ 🅰 🛋

7-9 r. du Conservatoire (9th) – Ⓜ *Bonne Nouvelle* — Plan: **M2**
– ℰ 01 44 83 83 60 – www.charmandmore.com
33 rm – **♦**180/1200 € **♦♦**180/1200 € – ⌷ 21 €
• Luxury • Townhouse • Design •
A very fine hotel, housed in a Haussmann building next to the Conservatoire National Supérieur d'Art Dramatique. You can't find fault with its fittings, in a confident style designed by Jean-Michel Wilmotte. Untreated wood, pale tones, clean lines... in keeping with the spirit of contemporary luxury.
La Régalade Conservatoire – See restaurant listing

Banke ⛱ ♿ 🅰 🛋

20 r. Lafayette (9th) – Ⓜ *Chaussée d'Antin* — Plan: **K2**
– ℰ 01 55 33 22 22 – www.derbyhotels.com
104 rm – **♦**250/530 € **♦♦**300/705 € – ⌷ 24 €
• Luxury • Design •
Situated in the heart of the Belle Epoque business district between the Bourse and the Opera, this former bank building was converted into a unique luxury hotel in 2009. The opulent lobby, crowned by a glass ceiling, is highly striking, while the guestrooms have a warm, welcoming feel.

Édouard VII ⛱ 🛁 ♿ 🅰 🛋

39 av. de l'Opéra (2nd) – Ⓜ *Opéra* – ℰ 01 42 61 86 11 — Plan: **K3**
– www.edouard7hotel.com
59 rm – **♦**280/490 € **♦♦**280/490 € – ⌷ 30 € – 10 suites
• Luxury • Personalised • Cosy •
Shimmering fabrics and refined decor in the Couture rooms, while the mood in the Edouard VII rooms is more understated. The hotel exudes elegance and the suites are superb. Cosy bar and light meals in a very pleasant contemporary setting.

Grand Hôtel du Palais Royal 🛁 ♿ 🅰

4 r. de Valois (1st) – Ⓜ *Palais Royal* – ℰ 01 42 96 15 35 — Plan: **L3**
– www.grandhoteldupalaisroyal.com
64 rm – **♦**390/790 € **♦♦**390/1090 € – ⌷ 34 € – 4 suites
• Luxury • Contemporary • Elegant •
Set next to the Palais Royal, the Ministry of Culture and the Conseil d'État, this 18C building boasts an impeccable location! Inside, the place is elegant but without pomp. The guestrooms are sober and decorated with contemporary furnishings and white walls. Although very central, the neighbourhood is quiet.
Le Lulli – See restaurant listing

FRANCE - PARIS

Hôtel du Ministère 🖼 🖼 🖼 🖼

31 r. de Surène (8th) – Ⓜ *Madeleine* – ℰ *01 42 66 21 43*
– *www.ministerehotel.com*

41 rm – ♦150/576 € ♦♦170/576 € – ☲ 19 € – 2 suites

Plan: **J2**

• Boutique hotel • Luxury • Personalised •

This hotel is a stone's throw from the French Home Office, the Palais de l'Élysée, and Faubourg St Honoré. The comfortable and very functional guestrooms pay tribute to the 1970s, which won't fail to please fans of the era, nor those who are feeling nostalgic. Charming service.

La Maison Favart 🖼 🖼 🖼

5 r. Marivaux (2nd) – Ⓜ *Richelieu Drouot*
– ℰ *01 42 97 59 83* – *www.lamaisonfavart.com*

36 rm – ♦230/390 € ♦♦230/690 € – ☲ 24 € – 3 suites

Plan: **L2**

• Luxury • Townhouse • Elegant •

A timeless atmosphere reigns in this hotel (1824), where painter Francisco de Goya once stayed. The guestrooms – some facing the Opéra Comique – are very pleasant. This is a charming hotel, full of romanticism and poetry.

Hôtel de Noailles 🖼 🖼

9 r. de la Michodière (2nd) – Ⓜ *Quatre Septembre*
– ℰ *01 47 42 92 90* – *www.hotelnoailles.com*

51 rm – ♦200/425 € ♦♦200/455 € – ☲ 18 € – 5 suites

Plan: **K2**

• Townhouse • Contemporary • Cosy •

Hip, contemporary elegance behind a pretty 1900 façade. Sleek, minimalist rooms, most of which open on to the patio (with a balcony on the 5th and 6th floors).

Little Palace 🖼 🖼

4 r. Salomon-de-Caus (3rd) – Ⓜ *Réaumur-Sébastopol*
– ℰ *01 42 72 08 15* – *www.littlepalacehotel.com*

49 rm – ♦172/265 € ♦♦182/265 € – ☲ 15 € – 4 suites

Plan: **M3**

• Townhouse • Functional • Elegant •

The charming Little Palace is a successful fusion of Belle Époque and contemporary styles. Welcoming guestrooms with those on the 6th and 7th floors (with a balcony and views of Paris) preferable.

Pulitzer 🖼 🖼

23 r. du Faubourg-Montmartre (9th)
– Ⓜ *Grands Boulevards* – ℰ *01 53 34 98 10* – *www.hotelpulitzer.com*

44 rm – ♦110/385 € ♦♦115/385 € – ☲ 18 €

Plan: **L2**

• Business • Personalised •

The charm of a British library (comfy Chesterfield armchairs) and the contemporary elegance of industrial-style come together at this hotel. It is located in the heart of the city's theatres and department stores. This Pulitzer would be a worthy winner of a prize for originality.

Hôtel Monsieur 🖼 🖼 🖼

62 r. des Mathurins (8th) – Ⓜ *Havre-Caumartin*
– ℰ *01 43 87 17 11* – *www.hotelmonsieur.com*

29 rm ☲ – ♦180/370 € ♦♦180/370 € – 2 suites

Plan: **J2**

• Townhouse • Personalised •

A stone's throw from the Théâtre des Mathurins, this recent hotel pays a discreet homage to the world of the theatre and one of its prominent figures, Sacha Guitry. The guestrooms are comfortable and truly inviting; some even have a terrace. Small fitness space.

Relais Madeleine 🖼 🖼

11 bis r. Godot-de-Mauroy (9th) – Ⓜ *Havre Caumartin*
– ℰ *01 47 42 22 40* – *www.relaismadeleine.fr*

23 rm – ♦209/549 € ♦♦209/549 € – ☲ 15 €

Plan: **J2**

• Traditional • Personalised • Classic •

Staying at this small hotel is a bit like spending time in a family home, but right in the centre of Paris! It has undeniable charm with carefully chosen furniture, sparkling colours and delightful fabrics - not to mention the attentive service.

Hôtel du Continent ℻

30 r. Mont-Thabor (1st) – Ⓜ *Tuileries –* ℰ *01 42 60 75 32*   Plan: **J3**
– www.hotelcontinent.com
25 rm – ✝129/400 € ✝✝142/400 € – ⌷ 12 €
• Traditional • Townhouse • Elegant •

Set near the Tuileries, this hotel is run with a personal touch and was completely redesigned in 2013 by Christian Lacroix. The six continents are the theme for the decor. Elegance, interplay of colours and overall character – it is a pleasure to venture into this new territory.

Le Crayon ℻ ⊬

25 r. du Bouloi (1st) – Ⓜ *Palais Royal*   Plan: **L3**
– ℰ *01 42 36 54 19 – www.hotelcrayon.com*
26 rm – ✝129/311 € ✝✝149/347 € – ⌷ 7 €
• Townhouse • Personalised •

This far from banal hotel is halfway between an artist's residence and a family home, featuring an explosive mix of colours, contrasts and vintage decor. Each bedroom is its own original creation, adorned with furniture tracked down personally by the hotel's designer.

Idol ♿ ℻

16 r. d'Édimbourg (8th) – Ⓜ *Europe –* ℰ *01 45 22 14 31*   Plan: **J1**
– www.idolhotel-paris.com
32 rm – ✝130/300 € ✝✝150/500 € – ⌷ 17 €
• Townhouse • Personalised • Design •

Vintage 1970s furniture and a "jazzy" theme adorn this hotel, refurbished in 2014, near the station Gare Saint-Lazare. The style is in keeping with this music-orientated area with more than its fair share of stringed instrument shops. The guestrooms have names like Lady Soul and Light My Fire. A real music box.

⚜⚜⚜⚜⚜ **Le Meurice Alain Ducasse** – Hôtel Le Meurice   ❀ ℻ ⇄ ⊠
❀❀

228 r. de Rivoli (1st) – Ⓜ *Tuileries –* ℰ *01 44 58 10 55*   Plan: **J-K3**
– www.alainducasse-meurice.com/fr – Closed 6 to 20 February, 31 July-28 August, Saturday and Sunday
Menu 110 € (lunch), 130/380 € – Carte 230/340 €
• Modern cuisine • Luxury • Romantic •

In the heart of the famous luxury hotel, this stylish place is the archetype of the great French restaurant. Its eminently luxurious decor is inspired by the royal apartments of Versailles and revisited with talent by designer Philippe Starck. Under the aegis of Alain Ducasse, the dishes fete the finest ingredients.
➔ Pâté chaud de pintade. Bar, fenouil et citron. Chocolat de notre manufacture.

⚜⚜⚜⚜⚜ **La Table de l'Espadon** – Hôtel Ritz   ❀ ♿ ℻ ⇄ ⊠
❀❀

15 pl. Vendôme (1st) – Ⓜ *Opéra*   Plan: **K3**
– ℰ *01 43 16 33 74 – www.ritzparis.com*
– Closed lunch
Menu 195/330 € – Carte 186/456 €
• Modern cuisine • Elegant • Luxury •

The dining room, submerged in gold and sumptuous fabrics, is dazzling. In this magical setting, the precise cooking of the young Nicolas Sale sparkles. Choose the bait, then the line, then reel in : the descriptions of dishes conjure images of game fishing. Taste, personality, intensity : a fresh wind blows on the Ritz. Superb!
➔ Air de foie gras, melon semi-confit, lait d'amande et graines de courge. Saint-pierre rôti au beurre de safran, mousseline et barigoule d'artichaut, émulsion de coquillages. Tablettes crémeuse et sorbet chocolat sambirano.

FRANCE - PARIS

XXXX Le Grand Véfour (Guy Martin)   ❀ 🅰🅲 ⇦ 🍴

😋😋 *17 r. de Beaujolais (1st) –* ⓜ *Palais Royal*   Plan: **L3**
– 𝒞 01 42 96 56 27 – www.grand-vefour.com – Closed 3 weeks in August,
Saturday and Sunday
Menu 115 € (lunch)/315 € – Carte 230/295 €
• Creative • Classic décor •

Bonaparte and Joséphine, Lamartine, Hugo, Sartre… For more than two centuries, the former Café de Chartres has been cultivating the legend. Nowadays it is Guy Martin who maintains the aura. Influenced by travel and painting – colours, shapes, textures – the chef 'sketches' his dishes like an artist… between invention and history.
→ Ravioles de foie gras, crème foisonnée truffée. Parmentier de queue de bœuf aux truffes. Palet noisette et chocolat au lait, glace au caramel brun et sel de Guérande.

XXXX Carré des Feuillants (Alain Dutournier)   ❀ 🅰🅲 ⇦ 🍴

😋😋 *14 r. de Castiglione (1st) –* ⓜ *Tuileries*   Plan: **K3**
– 𝒞 01 42 86 82 82
– www.carredesfeuillants.fr
– Closed August, Saturday and Sunday
Menu 60 € (lunch)/178 € – Carte 125/160 €
• Modern cuisine • Elegant •

Elegant and minimalist contemporary restaurant on the site of the old Feuillants convent. Modern menu with strong Gascony influences. Superb wines and Armagnacs.
→ Fines aiguillettes de bar sauvage, copeaux de poutargue, bonbon de tomate et jus de griotte. Caneton croisé au foie gras, cuisse poudrée d'olive et sauce bigarade. Tarte à la rhubarbe caramélisée, gariguette pistachée et crème glacée vanille.

XXX Le Grand Restaurant - Jean-François Piège   ❀ ♿ 🅰🅲

😋😋 *7 r. d'Aguesseau (8th) –* ⓜ *Madeleine*   Plan: **J2**
– 𝒞 01 53 05 00 00 – www.jeanfrancoispiege.com
– Closed 31 July-22 August, 24 december-4 January, Saturday
and Sunday
Menu 85 € (lunch), 195/255 € – Carte 165/220 € – *(booking advisable)*
• Modern cuisine • Elegant • Design •

Jean-François Piège has found the perfect setting to showcase the great laboratory kitchen he had been dreaming of for so long. The lucky few to get a seat (25 maximum) can sample delicate, light dishes whose emotion can both be tasted and experienced. The quintessence of talent!
→ Pomme de terre agria soufflée craquante en chaud-froid, pulpe foisonnée d'extraits de crustacés, nage concentrée et caviar. Mijoté moderne de ris de veau de lait cuit sur des coques de noix, mousseline de noix. Blanc à manger.

XXX Sur Mesure par Thierry Marx – Hôtel Mandarin Oriental

😋😋 *251 r. St-Honoré (1st) –* ⓜ *Concorde*   ❀ ♿ 🅰🅲
– 𝒞 01 70 98 71 25 – www.mandarinoriental.fr/paris/   Plan: **J3**
– Closed late July-late August, Sunday and Monday
Menu 85 € (weekday lunch), 180/210 €
• Creative • Design • Elegant •

Precise 'tailor-made' (sur mesure) cuisine is the hallmark of Thierry Marx, who confirms his talent as a master culinary craftsman at the Mandarin Oriental's showcase restaurant. Every dish reveals his tireless scientific approach, which is sometimes teasing but always exacting. An experience in itself, aided by the stunning, immaculate and ethereal decor.
→ Soupe à l'oignon en trompe-l'œil. Bœuf charbon, aubergine grillée, sirop d'érable et vinaigre de feuille de cerisier. Ylang-ylang.

XXX ✿

Lucas Carton

9 pl. de la Madeleine (8th) – Ⓜ Madeleine Plan: **J2**
– ✆ 01 42 65 22 90 – www.lucascarton.com – Closed 3 weeks in August, Sunday and Monday
Menu 89 € (weekdays), 132/182 € 🍷 – Carte 125/190 €
• Modern cuisine • Historic • Chic •

Another page in the history of Lucas Carton, the famous address on the Place de la Madeleine. The young chef, Julien Dumas, knows how to bring out the best in fine produce (special mention for the spring lamb), and his balanced dishes are infused with Mediterranean touches.

➜ Chou-fleur croustillant. Noix de ris de veau, jeunes carottes. Île flottante aux pistaches.

XXX

1728

8 r. d'Anjou (8th) – Ⓜ Madeleine – ✆ 01 40 17 04 77 Plan: **J2**
– www.1728-paris.com – Closed Saturday lunch and Sunday
Menu 45 € (lunch), 70/130 € – Carte 61/95 €
• Creative • Romantic • Elegant •

A place replete with history! Built in 1728, this town house was the residence of La Fayette from 1827 until his death. At the stove, Gaëtan Joly (ex-Ze Kitchen Galerie) demonstrates clear inventiveness and scatters his dishes with pleasing Asian touches. Great wine list.

XXX ✿

Pur' - Jean-François Rouquette - Hôtel Park Hyatt Paris-Vendôme

5 r. de la Paix (2nd) – Ⓜ Opéra – ✆ 01 58 71 10 60
– www.paris-restaurant-pur.fr – Closed August and lunch Plan: **K3**
Menu 145/185 € – Carte 100/230 €
• Creative • Elegant •

Experience a sense of pure enjoyment as you dine in this restaurant. The highly elegant contemporary decor and creative dishes are carefully conjured by the chef using the finest ingredients. Attractive, delicious and refined.

➜ Homard, betterave, groseilles et vinaigrette acidulée au shiso. Turbot cuisiné dans un beurre de colombo, crevettes grises, couteaux et salicornes. Calisson glacé de poire et kalamensi, millefeuille caramélisé et crème anglaise.

XXX ✿

Les Jardins de l'Espadon - Hôtel Ritz

15 pl. Vendôme (1st) – Ⓜ Opéra – ✆ 01 43 16 33 74 Plan: **K3**
– www.ritzparis.com – Closed Saturday, Sunday and dinner
Menu 120/145 €
• Modern cuisine • Romantic •

This retractable conservatory, surrounded by greenery and entered by a flower-filled, gilded gallery, is one of the main new features of the revamped Ritz. It serves as a setting for Nicolas Sale's inspired cuisine: langoustine cannelloni, spring cabbage and Meursault sauce or roast breast of pigeon. A concise menu, inventive dishes, flawless service – Bravo!

➜ Cannelloni de langoustine, chou pointu et sauce au vin de Meursault. Merlan de ligne et crème de charlotte grenobloise. Chocolat de Madagascar, textures de meringue et sauce chocolat frappé.

XXX

Drouant

16 pl. Gaillon (2nd) – Ⓜ Quatre Septembre Plan: **K3**
– ✆ 01 42 65 15 16 – www.drouant.com
Menu 45 € (weekday lunch)/65 € – Carte 70/100 €
• Traditional cuisine • Elegant •

A legendary restaurant where the Prix Goncourt has been awarded since 1914. With Antoine Westermann at the helm, it serves traditional cuisine with a modern touch. Elegant, richly decorated interior.

XxX **Le Baudelaire** – Hôtel Le Burgundy   🖼 ♨

6-8 r. Duphot (1st) – Ⓜ Madeleine – ☎ 01 71 19 49 11   Plan: **J3**
– www.leburgundy.com – Closed lunch in August, Saturday lunch and
Sunday
Menu 58 € (lunch), 105/210 € 🍷 – Carte 100/170 €
• Modern cuisine • Elegant •
This restaurant is within the luxurious Hotel Burgundy. It is a quality, gourmet
establishment, where the food reveals finesse and lightness. There is a lovely
atmosphere around the inner patio.
➜ Foie gras de canard en fines ravioles, bouillon clair, bigorneaux et ama-
rante. Lieu jaune de ligne étuvé aux algues, gnocchis de céleri et jus d'arêtes. Fraises mara des bois, sorbet yaourt et estragon, sablé noisette et
meringue craquante.

XxX **Macéo**   🐟 🖼 ⇔

15 r. Petits-Champs (1st) – Ⓜ Bourse – ☎ 01 42 97 53 85   Plan: **L3**
– www.maceorestaurant.com – Closed Saturday lunch, Sunday and Bank
Holidays
Menu 30 € (weekday lunch)/40 € – Carte 50/58 €
• Modern cuisine • Classic décor •
Macéo is first a tribute by the owner to Maceo Parker, a great American saxo-
phonist who played with James Brown. It also has a Second Empire interior
and serves seasonal recipes that invariably delight; roast duckling and miniature
vegetables with a Spanish twist or slow-cooked beef ravioli, for example. Vegetarian menu and international wine list.

XxX **Le Versance**   🍽 🖼

16 r. Feydeau (2nd) – Ⓜ Bourse – ☎ 01 45 08 00 08   Plan: **L2**
– www.leversance.fr – Closed 1 to 22 August, 22 december-4 January,
Saturday lunch, Sunday and Monday
Menu 38 € (lunch) – Carte 74/90 €
• Modern cuisine • Elegant •
A minimalist stage enhanced by beams, stained glass and designer furnishings.
The globetrotting chef's cuisine is ambitious: ceviche of tuna, chicken broth,
lemon verbena and combawa. Opposite, a delicatessen proposes homemade
sandwiches and carefully selected produce.

XxX **Kei** (Kei Kobayashi)   🖼

5 r. du Coq-Héron (1st) – Ⓜ Louvre Rivoli   Plan: **L3**
– ☎ 01 42 33 14 74 – www.restaurant-kei.fr – Closed Easter Holidays,
3 weeks in August, Christmas Holidays, Thursday lunch, Sunday and
Monday
Menu 56 € (lunch), 99/195 €
• Modern cuisine • Elegant • Minimalist •
Japanese-born Kei Kobayashi's discovery of French gastronomy on TV was a
revelation to him. So much so that as soon as he was old enough, he headed
to France to train in some of the country's best restaurants. His fine cuisine
reflects this passion and his twin influences.
➜ Jardin de légumes croquants, saumon fumé d'Écosse, mousse de
roquette, émulsion de citron et crumble d'olives. Bar de ligne rôti sur ses
écailles, marmelade d'algue nori. Vacherin aux fraises et au miso.

XX **Le Dali** – Hôtel Le Meurice   🖼

228 r. de Rivoli (1st) – Ⓜ Tuileries – ☎ 01 44 58 10 44   Plan: **J-K3**
– www.dorchestercollection.com/fr/paris/le-meurice/
Menu 64/78 € – Carte 65/125 €
• Mediterranean cuisine • Chic • Romantic •
In the heart of the Meurice, Le Dali is both a meeting place and an elegant restaurant. It serves tasty, seasonal cuisine with lovely Mediterranean accents. The
handsome classical interior, columns and mirrors pay tribute to the artist, who
was a loyal patron of the establishment.

FRANCE - PARIS

XX **Camélia** – Hôtel Mandarin Oriental 🍽 � AC

251 r. St-Honoré (1st) – Ⓜ *Concorde*   Plan: **J3**
– 𝒞 01 70 98 74 00
– www.mandarinoriental.fr/paris/
Menu 60 € (weekday lunch)/88 € – Carte 75/130 €
• Modern cuisine • Elegant • Design •

Keep it simple, concentrate on the flavour of the top-notch ingredients, draw inspiration from France's gastronomical classics and enhance them with Asian touches. This is the approach of Thierry Marx at Camélia; an elegant, soothing, zen place. An unequivocal success.

XX **Le Lulli** – Grand Hôtel du Palais Royal   AC

4 r. de Valois (1st) – Ⓜ *Palais Royal*   Plan: **L3**
– 𝒞 01 42 96 15 35
– www.grandhoteldupalaisroyal.com – Closed 31 July-27 August,
Saturday, Sunday and Bank Holidays
Menu 38 € – Carte 58/72 €
• Modern cuisine • Elegant • Romantic •

A profusion of plants and contemporary art set the scene of this welcoming interior. Clément Le Norcy, a chef with a fine track record, can be found in the kitchen rustling up wholesome, distinctive dishes in tune with the seasons. The friendly yet professional service is yet another bonus.

XX **Le Café de la Paix** – Hôtel Intercontinental Le Grand   ⅗ AC ⇔

2 r. Scribe (9th) – Ⓜ *Opéra* – 𝒞 01 40 07 32 32   Plan: **K2**
– www.paris.intercontinental.com
Menu 55 € (weekday lunch)/82 € – Carte 90/110 €
• Modern cuisine • Elegant • Chic •

Frescoes, gilded panelling and Napoleon III-inspired furniture provide the backdrop for this luxurious and legendary brasserie. Open from 7am to midnight, it is still the place to meet in Paris.

XX **Restaurant du Palais Royal**   🍽 ⅗ AC ⇔ 🥢
❀

110 galerie de Valois (1st) – Ⓜ *Palais Royal*   Plan: **L3**
– 𝒞 01 40 20 00 27 – www.restaurantdupalaisroyal.com – Closed Sunday
and Monday
Menu 48 € (lunch)/142 € – Carte 90/115 €
• Creative • Elegant •

Magnificently located beneath the arcades of the Palais Royal, this elegant restaurant is the playground of young chef Philip Chronopoulos, formerly of the Atelier de Joël Robuchon. Philip concocts creative, striking meals, such as flash-fried scampi with girolle mushrooms and fresh almonds.
→ Poulpe au piment fumé, pommes grenaille caramélisées. Grosses langoustines saisies, lait d'amande aux herbes et chou-fleur rôti. Citron meringué, crémeux à la noix de coco.

XX **Passage 53** (Shinichi Sato)   ❀❀ AC
❀❀

53 passage des Panoramas (2nd)   Plan: **L2**
– Ⓜ Grands Boulevards
– 𝒞 01 42 33 04 35 – www.passage53.com
– Closed 2 weeks in August, Sunday and Monday
Menu 120 € (lunch)/180 € – *(booking advisable)*
• Creative • Intimate • Design •

In an authentic covered passage, this restaurant has a minimalist decor and offers a fine panorama of contemporary cuisine. Using market-fresh produce, the young Japanese chef – trained at L'Astrance – turns out irrefutably precise compositions that are cooked to perfection.
→ Langoustines, crème et gelée de kombu, lamelles de radis. Turbot et déclinaison de cèpes. Dessert autour du citron.

FRANCE - PARIS

XX **Akrame** (Akrame Benallal)

7 r. Tronchet (8th) – **Ⓜ** Madeleine – 𝒞 01 40 67 11 16   Plan: **J2**
– www.akrame.com – Closed 2 weeks in August, 1 week Christmas
Holidays, Saturday and Sunday
Menu 60 € (lunch), 115/145 € – (booking advisable)
• Creative • Design •

Akrame Benallal now dons his chef's hat in this restaurant tucked away behind a
heavy porte cochère (coach gateway). With a single, well put-together set menu,
he unleashes great inventiveness to capitalise on excellent quality ingredients.
The dishes are meticulously prepared. Needless to say, it's a hit!
→ Cuisine du marché.

XX **Le Lumière** – Hôtel Scribe

1 r. Scribe (9th) – **Ⓜ** Opéra – 𝒞 01 44 71 24 24   Plan: **K2**
– www.hotel-scribe.com
Menu 45 € (weekday lunch)/95 € – Carte 55/92 €
• Modern cuisine • Elegant •

The Lumière brothers presented their first film to the public in this very setting.
The dining room, crowned by a superb glass roof, evokes the elegance of the
Belle Epoque period. This image is continued in the kitchen, directed to perfection by a chef who embraces both vivacity and sparkle in his cooking. Simpler à
la carte choices at weekends.

XX **La Fontaine Gaillon**

pl. Gaillon (2nd) – **Ⓜ** Quatre Septembre – 𝒞 01 47 42 63 22   Plan: **K2-3**
– www.restaurant-la-fontaine-gaillon.com – Closed 3 weeks in August and Sunday
Menu 55 € (weekday lunch)/110 € ♟ – Carte 67/86 €
• Seafood • Elegant •

Beautiful 17C townhouse owned by Gérard Depardieu with an elegant setting
and terrace around a fountain. Spotlight on seafood, accompanied by a pleasant selection of wines.

XX **Le First** – Hôtel The Westin Paris

234 r. de Rivoli (1st) – **Ⓜ** Tuileries – 𝒞 01 44 77 10 40   Plan: **J3**
– www.lefirstrestaurant.com/fr/
Menu 51 € ♟ – Carte 56/77 €
• Modern cuisine • Elegant • Vintage •

Inside the Westin, this veritable boudoir with its soft lighting (in Jacques Garcia trademark style) is a stone's throw from the Tuileries. The cuisine puts a
new spin on traditional dishes (like young rabbit with sage). In summer, head
for the peaceful terrace in the courtyard.

XX **Prémices**

24 r. Rodier (9th) – **Ⓜ** Cadet – 𝒞 01 45 26 86 26   Plan: **L1**
– Closed 1 week in May, 3 weeks in August, 1 week Christmas Holidays,
Monday lunch, Saturday and Sunday
Menu 36 € (lunch), 65/90 € – Carte 55/95 € – (booking advisable)
• Modern cuisine • Fashionable •

Financier in a merchant bank, Alexandre Weill left that behind, started from
scratch to indulge his passion for food, and learnt how to cook – so much the
better! In his tastefully decorated restaurant he serves flavoursome dishes,
which are lucid, unfussy and made with choice ingredients.

XX **Saturne** (Sven Chartier)

17 r. N.-D.-des-Victoires (2nd) – **Ⓜ** Bourse   Plan: **L3**
– 𝒞 01 42 60 31 90 – www.saturne-paris.fr – Closed August, Christmas
Holidays, Saturday and Sunday
Menu 45 € (lunch)/90 € – Carte approx. 60 €
• Creative • Trendy •

The young chef at this restaurant named after Saturn (the god of agriculture)
offers a single menu with an emphasis on excellent ingredients and naturally
produced wines. A typically Scandinavian loft-style atmosphere (with pale
wood and polished concrete).
→ Cuisine du marché.

FRANCE - PARIS

XX **Le Marché du Lucas** – Restaurant Lucas Carton   🔲

9 pl. de la Madeleine (8th) – Ⓜ Madeleine   Plan: **J2**
– ☎ 01 42 65 56 66 – www.lucascarton.com – Closed 3 weeks in August,
Sunday and Monday
Menu 49 €
• Traditional cuisine • Classic décor • Cosy •
Above Lucas Carton, in a pleasant Art Nouveau setting, chef Julien Dumas
plumps for simplicity and generosity with a daily-changing spoken menu.
Free-range pork chop with black olives, black pudding….hearty cooking!

XX **Brasserie Gallopin**   ⏃ 🔲 ⇦

40 r. N.-D.-des-Victoires (2nd) – Ⓜ Bourse   Plan: **L3**
– ☎ 01 42 36 45 38 – www.brasseriegallopin.com
Menu 29 € – Carte 40/85 €
• Traditional cuisine • Brasserie •
This brasserie, set opposite Palais Brongniart, is a genuine institution founded in
1876 by a Mr Gallopin. Parisians and tourists are attracted by its handsome Victorian interior of mahogany, its turn of the 20C conservatory and its bourgeois
bistro classics: calf's head, Noirmoutier turbot, baked Alaska with raspberry
liqueur.

XX **Vaudeville**   🏠

29 r. Vivienne (2nd) – Ⓜ Bourse – ☎ 01 40 20 04 62   Plan: **L2**
– www.vaudevilleparis.com
Menu 32/50 € – Carte 35/65 €
• Traditional cuisine • Brasserie • Vintage •
A grand Art Deco brasserie in the pure Parisian tradition. Seafood, fresh taglia-
telle with morels and Beaufort, calf's head with ravigote sauce, andouillette and
choucroute are on the menu. By day, a regular lunchtime spot for journalists
and in the evening, a haunt for theatre-goers after the show.

X **Jin**   🔲 ⇦
🕸

6 r. de la Sourdière (1st) – Ⓜ Tuileries   Plan: **K3**
– ☎ 01 42 61 60 71 – Closed 2 weeks in August,
Christmas Holidays, Sunday and Monday
Menu 95 € (lunch)/145 € – (booking advisable)
• Japanese • Elegant • Design •
A showcase for Japanese cuisine, right in the heart of Paris! Jin is first and fore-
most about the know-how of chef Takuya Watanabe, who comes from Sapporo.
Before your eyes, he creates delicious sushi and sashimi, using fish sourced from
Brittany, Oléron and Spain. The whole menu is a treat.
➜ Cuisine du marché.

X **Sushi B**   🔲
🕸

5 r. Rameau (2nd) – Ⓜ Bourse – ☎ 01 40 26 52 87   Plan: **L3**
– www.sushi-b-fr.com – Closed 2 weeks in August and Tuesday
Menu 58 € (weekday lunch), 95/160 € – (booking advisable)
• Japanese • Minimalist •
It is enjoyable to linger in this tiny restaurant (with just seven places) on the
edge of the pleasant Square Louvois for its sleek, soothing interior, of course...
but paticularly to witness for oneself the chef's great talent. Like an excellent
artisan, he uses only the freshest top-notch ingredients, which he handles with
surgical precision.
➜ Cuisine du marché.

X **La Régalade Conservatoire** – Hôtel de Nell   ⏃ 🔲 ⇦ 🍴

7-9 r. du Conservatoire (9th) – Ⓜ Bonne Nouvelle   Plan: **M2**
– ☎ 01 44 83 83 60 – www.charmandmore.com
Menu 37 € – (booking advisable)
• Modern cuisine • Fashionable • Friendly •
With Régalades in the 14th and 1st arrondissements, this is Bruno Doucet's third
Parisian address, this time close to Grands Boulevards inside the luxurious Hôtel
de Nell. Here bistro-style goes chic, and the chef's cooking is as well-executed,
generous and tasty as ever.

FRANCE - PARIS

X Atelier Rodier

17 r. Rodier (9th) – Ⓜ *Notre-Dame de Lorette*   Plan: **L1**
*– ℰ 09 67 19 94 90 – www.latelier-rodier.com – Closed August, 1 week
Christmas Holidays, Sunday, Monday and lunch*
Menu 42/95 € Ⓨ – Carte 53/77 €
• Modern cuisine • Fashionable • Trendy •

Visible from the dining area, the kitchens are proudly on display and reveal a certain flair for the art of cooking. Santiago Torrijos is a young chef who has done stints in some stellar establishments and is quite at ease in his role here as head 'bistronome'. His recipes are creative, inspired and full of surprises.

X La Petite Sirène de Copenhague

47 r. Notre-Dame-de-Lorette (9th) – Ⓜ *St-Georges*   Plan: **K1**
*– ℰ 01 45 26 66 66 – www.lapetitesireneparis.com – Closed August,
23 December-2 January, Saturday lunch, Sunday and Monday*
Menu 35 € (lunch)/41 € – Carte 50/82 € – *(booking advisable)*
• Danish • Bistro •

The Danish flag flying above the entrance provides a strong clue to the gourmet offerings inside. There is a daily menu chalked up on a slate board, as well as a more expensive à la carte, from which guests can feast on Danish specialities such as pickled herrings.

X Le Moderne   🌿 🅰🅲

40 r. N.-D.-des-Victoires (2nd) – Ⓜ *Bourse*   Plan: **L3**
*– ℰ 01 53 40 84 10 – www.le-moderne.fr – Closed 3 weeks in August,
Saturday and Sunday*
Menu 38/49 €
• Modern cuisine • Friendly •

Close to the Palais Brongniart, now stripped of its vocation as the Bourse de Paris, the Café Moderne plunges you into the still bustling atmosphere of the neighbourhood. At lunchtime, the place is packed to the rafters, while in the evening it has an intimate feel. On the menu are good, fresh ingredients, cooked with taste.

X Liza   🅰🅲

14 r. de la Banque (2nd) – Ⓜ *Bourse – ℰ 01 55 35 00 66*   Plan: **L3**
– www.restaurant-liza.com – Closed Saturday lunch and Sunday dinner
Menu 38 € (dinner)/48 € – Carte 35/65 €
• Lebanese • Oriental décor •

Originally from Beirut, Liza Asseily gives pride of place to her country's cuisine. In a contemporary interior dotted with Middle Eastern touches, opt for the shish taouk or mechoui kafta (lamb, hummus and tomato preserves). Dishes are meticulously prepared using fresh ingredients. A real treat!

X Aux Lyonnais   🅰🅲 ⇔

32 r. St-Marc (2nd) – Ⓜ *Richelieu Drouot*   Plan: **L2**
*– ℰ 01 42 96 65 04 – www.auxlyonnais.com – Closed August, Saturday
lunch, Sunday and Monday*
Menu 34 € (weekday lunch)/35 € – Carte 46/64 € – *(booking advisable)*
• Lyonnaise • Bistro • Vintage •

This bistro, founded in 1890, serves delicious cuisine which explores the gastronomic history of the city. Deliciously retro decor, featuring a zinc counter, banquettes, bevelled mirrors and moulded fixtures and fittings.

X Le Pantruche

3 r. Victor-Massé (9th) – Ⓜ *Pigalle – ℰ 01 48 78 55 60*   Plan: **L1**
*– Closed 1 week Easter Holidays, 3 weeks in August, 1 week Christmas
Holidays, Saturday and Sunday*
Menu 36 € – Carte 41/50 € – *(booking advisable)*
• Modern cuisine • Bistro •

'Pantruche' is slang for Paris... An apt name for this bistro with a chic retro decor, which happily cultivates a 1940s-1950s atmosphere. As for the food, the chef and his small team put together lovely seasonal dishes in keeping with current culinary trends.

X **Hotaru**

18 r. Rodier (9th) – Ⓜ *Notre-Dame de Lorette*   Plan: **L1**
*– ℰ 01 48 78 33 74 – Closed 3 weeks in August, 2 weeks
in Winter, Sunday and Monday*
Menu 24 € (lunch) – Carte 26/53 €
• Japanese • Rustic • Simple •

A welcoming Japanese restaurant with a young chef who produces traditional,
family cuisine with an emphasis on fish. Enjoy sushi, maki and sashimi, as well as
a selection of cooked and fried dishes.

X **Encore**   &

43 r. Richer (9th) – Ⓜ *Le Peletier – ℰ 01 72 60 97 72*   Plan: **L2**
*– www.encore-restaurant.fr – Closed 2 weeks in August, Christmas
Holidays, Saturday and Sunday*
Menu 30 € (lunch)/42 € – Carte 40/60 €
• Modern cuisine • Trendy • Friendly •

Don't be too quick to dismiss this place as just another trendy bistro: having a
real chef/owner toiling in the kitchens, it is by no means a mere copy! He creates pure cuisine that respects the ingredients, sometimes with Japanese touches, such as *lomo* of tuna in a dashi stock. "Encore!" exclaim our delighted
taste buds.

X **Kunitoraya**   🅰🅲 ⇄

5 r. Villedo (1st) – Ⓜ *Pyramides – ℰ 01 47 03 07 74*   Plan: **K3**
*– www.kunitoraya.com – Closed 2 weeks in August, Christmas Holidays,
Sunday dinner and Monday*
Menu 32 € (weekday lunch), 70/100 € – Carte approx. 40 €
• Japanese • Vintage • Minimalist •

With its old zinc counter, mirrors and Métro-style tiling, Kunitoraya has the feel
of a late-night Parisian restaurant from the early 1900s. Refined Japanese cuisine
is based around "udon", a thick homemade noodle prepared with wholemeal
flour imported from Japan.

X **Zen**   🍴 🅰🅲
☺

8 r. de L'Échelle (1st) – Ⓜ *Palais Royal*   Plan: **K3**
*– ℰ 01 42 61 93 99 – www.restaurantzenparis.fr – Closed 2 weeks in
August and 31 December-5 January*
Menu 20 € (weekday lunch), 30/60 € – Carte 20/40 €
• Japanese • Minimalist •

This enticing restaurant combines a refreshing contemporary interior design
and authentic Japanese cooking. The menu is well-rounded and faithful to the
classic sushi, grilled dishes and tempura, with house specialities of gyoza and
chirashi. Ideal for a quick lunch or a relaxing 'zen' dinner.

X **Silk & Spice**   & 🅰🅲 ⇄

6 r. Mandar (2nd) – Ⓜ *Sentier – ℰ 01 44 88 21 91*   Plan: **L3**
– www.silkandspice.fr – Closed Saturday lunch and Sunday
Menu 25 € (lunch), 36/45 € – Carte 28/50 €
• Thai • Exotic décor •

A hushed atmosphere and delicious Thai-inspired cuisine. The signature dishes
here are king prawns and shrimps in a lemon grass reduction, and green beef
curry.

X **Kiku**   🅰🅲 ⇔

56 r. Richer (9th) – Ⓜ *Cadet – ℰ 01 44 83 02 30 – Closed*   Plan: **L2**
1 week in August and in December, Saturday, Sunday and dinner
Menu 17/21 € – Carte 17/33 €
• Japanese • Intimate •

In Japan, they are called 'izakaya': sake bars serving small tasting dishes. The
concept is original but totally convincing. Very flavoursome and distinct, this
delicious Japanese food is a treat – and just a stone's throw from Les Folies Bergère.

FRANCE - PARIS

Les Canailles

25 r. La Bruyère (9th) – Ⓜ St-Georges — Plan: **K1**
– ℰ 01 48 74 10 48 – www.restaurantlescanailles.fr – Closed 3 weeks in August, Saturday and Sunday
Menu 35 € – Carte 52/69 € – *(booking advisable)*
• Modern cuisine • Bistro • Friendly •

This pleasant restaurant was created in 2012 by two Bretons with impressive culinary backgrounds. They slip into the *bistronomy* (gastro bistro), serving bistro and seasonal dishes. Specialities: ox tongue carpaccio and sauce ravigote, and rum baba with vanilla whipped cream... Tuck in!

L'Office

3 r. Richer (9th) – Ⓜ Poissonnière – ℰ 01 47 70 67 31 — Plan: **M2**
– www.office-resto.com – Closed 3 weeks in August, 1 week Christmas Holidays, Saturday and Sunday
Menu 27 € – *(booking advisable)*
• Modern cuisine • Bistro • Friendly •

A tiny bistro a stone's throw from Les Folies Bergère. Seated at tightly packed tables, diners dig into food that changes with the seasons. Precise, flavoursome dishes are accompanied by a well-selected wine list - all at reasonable prices.

Frenchie

5 r. du Nil (2nd) – Ⓜ Sentier – ℰ 01 40 39 96 19 — Plan: **M3**
– www.frenchie-restaurant.com – Closed 31 July-22 August, 22 December-2 January, Monday lunch, Tuesday lunch, Wednesday lunch, Saturday and Sunday
Menu 45 € (lunch)/74 € – *(booking advisable)*
• Modern cuisine • Friendly • Fashionable •

Near the Sentier metro station, this small, loft-style restaurant has exposed brickwork, stones and beams. It specialises in contemporary-style cuisine created by a young chef with an international CV.

Circonstances

174 r. Montmartre (2nd) – Ⓜ Grands Boulevards — Plan: **L2**
– ℰ 01 42 36 17 05 – www.circonstances.fr – Closed 3 weeks in August, Monday dinner, Tuesday dinner, Saturday and Sunday
Menu 36/45 €
• Traditional cuisine • Friendly •

On the doorstep of the Grands Boulevards metro station, this bistro was founded by two old hands determined to uphold the tradition of good market-fresh cuisine and fine produce. Shrimp ravioli with "coriander mint", salt cod and potato mash with coconut milk and olive oil, or dark chocolate mousse.

Noglu

16 passage des Panoramas (2nd) — Plan: **L2**
– Ⓜ Grands Boulevards – ℰ 01 40 26 41 24 – www.noglu.fr – Closed Monday dinner and Sunday
Menu 37 € (dinner) – Carte 35/50 €
• Modern cuisine • Simple • Trendy •

As its name suggests, Noglu offers food that is certified gluten-free. Try the white asparagus and smoked trout, sautéed veal with mushrooms or chocolate parfait with candied orange. There is an array of beautifully made dishes that diners can savour in a convivial atmosphere. For those in a hurry, you can even take it away!

Monsieur K

10 r. Marie-Stuart (2nd) – Ⓜ Sentier – ℰ 01 42 36 01 09 — Plan: **M3**
– www.kapunkaparis.com – Closed 1 week in August and Sunday
Menu 27/42 € – Carte 30/55 €
• Thai • Friendly •

The chef is a true Asia enthusiast. He has travelled the length and breadth of Thailand 16 times to sample its many cuisines and to reproduce a replica of the best dishes. He is a perfectionist fighting for the good cause, and makes a mean Pad Thai.

FOR ALL WHO MAKE IT TASTE AS GOOD AS IT LOOKS.

From pork to Wagyu beef:
METRO lets you discover an exciting
variety of meats.

Follow us on:

METRO

À mère

49 r. de l'Échiquier (10th) – **Ⓜ** *Bonne Nouvelle*   Plan: **M2**
– ☎ 01 48 00 08 28 – www.amere.fr – *Closed 2 weeks in August, Saturday and Sunday*
Menu 39/65 € – **Carte approx. 50 €**
• Creative • Fashionable • Trendy •

Maurizio Zillo, an Italian-Brazilian chef who has had a dazzling career (Bocuse, Alléno, Atala in São Paulo...), has put together a dream team (including a sommelier from the George V) to create this trendy bistro. His dishes are packed with flavour, and his inventiveness hits the nail on the head every time. What a lovely surprise!

TOUR EIFFEL – INVALIDES   PLAN IV

Le Cinq Codet   🛗 📶 ♿ 🅰️

5 r. Louis-Codet (7th) – **Ⓜ** *École-Militaire*   Plan: **P2**
– ☎ 01 53 85 15 60 – www.le5codet.com
59 rm ☲ – **♦**239/2000 € **♦♦**239/2000 € – 8 suites
• Luxury • Design • Elegant •

A stone's throw from the Invalides, this striking, exclusive hotel is full of attractions. It has an unbeatable location, and rooms with smart, comfortable furnishings and hi-tech fixtures and fittings. There are over 400 contemporary artworks, a stylish restaurant, a well-being centre and a lovely patio terrace. Concierge and valet parking.
Le Cinq Codet – See restaurant listing

Juliana   🛗 📶 ♿ 🅰️

10-12 r. Cognacq-Jay (7th) – **Ⓜ** *Alma-Marceau*   Plan: **P1**
– ☎ 01 44 05 70 00 – www.hoteljuliana.paris
35 rm – **♦**450/900 € **♦♦**450/900 € – ☲ 29 € – 5 suites
• Luxury • Elegant • Contemporary •

The superlative elegance of this brand new hotel is undeniable. Find chandeliers, extravagant mirrors, ethnic sculptures and mother-of-pearl furnishings. The rooms satisfy the two-fold demand for good taste and optimum comfort (Japanese toilets). Attractive, flower-decked façade come summertime.

Le Narcisse Blanc   🍴 🛜 📶 🖥 ♿ 🅰️ 🧖

19 bd de la Tour-Maubourg (7th)   Plan: **P1**
– **Ⓜ** *La Tour Maubourg* – ☎ 01 40 60 44 32 – www.lenarcisseblanc.com
34 rm – **♦**280/800 € **♦♦**280/800 € – ☲ 39 € – 3 suites
• Luxury • Grand townhouse • Contemporary •

An attractive conversion for this former army administrative building, now a refined hotel. The Art Nouveau decoration pays homage to Cléo de Mérode, Belle Epoque dancer and icon, nicknamed "pretty little narcissus". She inspired Nadar, Lautrec, Proust... and now this charming establishment. Pleasant spa.

Sezz   ♿ 🅰️ 🧖 🚗

6 av. Frémiet (16th) ✉ 75016 – **Ⓜ** *Passy*
– ☎ 01 56 75 26 26 – www.paris.hotelsezz.com
19 rm – **♦**239/587 € **♦♦**239/587 € – ☲ 30 € – 7 suites
• Luxury • Design •

Behind the beautiful and elaborately sculpted façade of this building, dating from 1913, the interior has adopted an ultra-design style. It features grey stone, original furniture, hi-tech gadgetry and a sauna. Every guest is also assigned an individual assistant for the duration of his or her stay.

FRANCE - PARIS

Platine
⅋ ⏃ 🛗 ⚐

20 r. de l'Ingénieur-Robert-Keller (15th)
Plan I: **A2**
– **Ⓜ** Charles Michels
– 𝒞 01 45 71 15 15 – www.platinehotel.fr
46 rm – ♦139/315 € ♦♦149/345 € – 🍽 15 €
• Townhouse • Personalised •

Platine or platinum blonde – like Marilyn Monroe – to whom this hotel pays homage. The guestrooms are comfortable and well kept. Go for one of those with a round bed for optimum glamour and to channel your inner star! There is a pleasant relaxation suite in the basement.

Muguet
🅰🅲

11 r. Chevert (7th) – **Ⓜ** École Militaire
Plan: **P2**
– 𝒞 01 47 05 05 93 – www.hotelparismuguet.com
40 rm – ♦100/190 € ♦♦120/290 € – 🍽 14 €
• Family • Classic •

In a quiet street a stone's throw from Les Invalides, this hotel has been refurbished in a classic style. Attractively maintained guestrooms; those overlooking the small flower-decked garden are generally quieter.

Hôtel de Varenne
⅋ 🅰🅲

44 r. de Bourgogne (7th) – **Ⓜ** Varenne
Plan: **Q2**
– 𝒞 01 45 51 45 55 – www.hoteldevarenne.com
24 rm – ♦163/280 € ♦♦222/380 € – 🍽 15 € – 2 suites
• Family • Cosy •

Located between the Rodin Museum and the National Assembly, this hotel is nestled in an attractive and tranquil small courtyard. The overall feel is very classical (Louis XVI and Empire-style) – a look appreciated by the many tourists in search of a true Parisian bolt hole.

Le Jules Verne
❀ ⋜ 🅰🅲 🗗

😋

2ᵉᵐᵉ floor Tour Eiffel (private lift, South pillar) (7th)
Plan: **O1**
– **Ⓜ** Bir-Hakeim – 𝒞 01 45 55 61 44
– www.lejulesverne-paris.com
Menu 105 € (weekday lunch), 190/230 €
• Modern cuisine • Design • Chic •

The designer decor on the second floor of the Eiffel Tower lives up to expectations, with a magical view as a bonus! French culinary heritage is the focus here, where classic dishes are accompanied by some excellent wines.
➜ Foie gras de canard confit, melon et poivre. Volaille jaune aux champignons des bois, sauce Albufera. Écrou croustillant au chocolat de notre manufacture à Paris.

Sylvestre
❀ 🅰🅲 ⇔

😋😋

79 r. St-Dominique (1st floor) (7th)
Plan: **P1**
– **Ⓜ** La Tour Maubourg
– 𝒞 01 47 05 79 00 – www.thoumieux.fr
– Closed 1 to 28 August, Tuesday lunch, Wednesday lunch, Saturday lunch, Sunday and Monday
Menu 85 € (lunch), 175/250 € – Carte 155/195 € – (booking advisable)
• Modern cuisine • Elegant • Intimate •

It took aplomb, and even courage, to step into the shoes of media star Jean-François Piège at the Thoumieux Hotel. Yet Sylvestre Wahid has done it! This multicultural chef concocts magical, and above all seasonal recipes like cucumber water and vegetable cannelloni or three preparations of cèpes in tribute to autumn.
➜ Œuf de poule, céleri et truffe noire en chaud-froid. Pigeon des Costières à la feuille de sauge, navet glaçon fumé-brûlé. Fine tarte au citron soufflée au chocolat grand cru, sorbet aux agrumes.

FRANCE - PARIS

XxX · **Arpège** (Alain Passard) · 🅰🅒 ↭
🕸🕸🕸 *84 r. de Varenne (7th)* – Ⓜ *Varenne* – 𝒞 *01 47 05 09 06* · Plan: **Q2**
– www.alain-passard.com – Closed Saturday and Sunday
Menu 145 € (lunch), 320/380 € – Carte 225/305 €
• Creative • Elegant •
Precious woods and a Lalique crystal decor provide the backdrop for the dazzling, vegetable-inspired cuisine of this culinary genius. He creates his astonishing dishes from organic produce grown in his three vegetable gardens!
➔ Fines ravioles potagères multicolores, consommé aux légumes. Corps-à-corps de volaille haute couture. Tarte aux pommes bouquet de roses.

XxX · **Astrance** (Pascal Barbot) · 🕸🕸 🅰🅒
🕸🕸🕸 *4 r. Beethoven (16th)* ✉ *75016* – Ⓜ *Passy* · Plan: **N1**
– 𝒞 01 40 50 84 40 – www.astrancerestaurant.com – Closed August,
1 week in November, Christmas Holidays, Saturday, Sunday, Monday and
Bank Holidays
Menu 70 € (lunch), 150/230 € – *(booking advisable)*
• Creative • Minimalist • Elegant •
No à la carte choices in this restaurant, where chef Pascal Barbot produces a different 'surprise menu' at each sitting. Sample the inventive cuisine of a chef at the height of his art, who focuses on excellent ingredients and creative flair. An unforgettable culinary experience.
➔ Millefeuille de champignons de Paris, foie gras mariné au verjus et pâte de citron rôti. Légine à la vapeur, coulis raisin et tamarin, poudre de gingembre. Tartelette aux agrumes.

XxX · **Petrossian - Le 144** · 🅰🅒 ↭ 🍽
144 r. de l'Université (7th) – Ⓜ *Invalides* · Plan: **P1**
– 𝒞 01 44 11 32 32 – www.petrossian.fr – Closed August, Sunday and
Monday
Menu 39 € (lunch), 95/150 € – Carte 56/96 €
• Seafood • Chic • Elegant •
The Petrossians have been serving Parisians with caviar from the Caspian Sea since 1920. Enjoy fish and seafood in the elegant dining room above the boutique.

XX · **Il Vino d'Enrico Bernardo** · 🕸🕸 🅰🅒 🍽
🕸 *13 bd La Tour-Maubourg (7th)* – Ⓜ *Invalides* · Plan: **P1**
– 𝒞 01 44 11 72 00 – www.enricobernardo.com – Closed Saturday lunch,
Sunday and Monday
Menu 38 € (weekday lunch)/95 € 🍷 – Carte approx. 75 €
• Modern cuisine • Elegant • Cosy •
The themed menus 'On the roads of the world' and 'On the roads of France and Italy' enable Enrico Bernardo, a leading sommelier, to introduce diners to his favourite wines of the moment, as an accompaniment to the delicious dishes. The decor, with its vine shoots and wine cabinet, is in tune with the rest!
➔ Menu surprise.

XX · **Divellec** · 🕸🕸 ᴺ 🅰🅒 ↭ 🍽
🕸 *18 r. Fabert (7th)* – Ⓜ *Invalides* – 𝒞 *01 45 51 91 96* · Plan: **P-Q1**
– www.divellec-paris.fr
Menu 55 € (weekday lunch), 90/190 € – Carte 60/110 €
• Seafood • Chic • Elegant •
The famous restaurant of Jacques Le Divellec has treated itself to a makeover. At the helm is the starred chef Mathieu Pacaud (Hexagone and Histoires in Paris), who channels his considerable talent into impeccable fish and seafood cuisine. The delicacies come thick and fast. Le Divellec is back with a vengeance!
➔ Minestrone d'écrevisses, nage montée au beurre de basilic. Saint-pierre à l'oseille et cocos de Paimpol à la moutarde de Cremone. Soufflé au chocolat et glace à la vanille Bourbon.

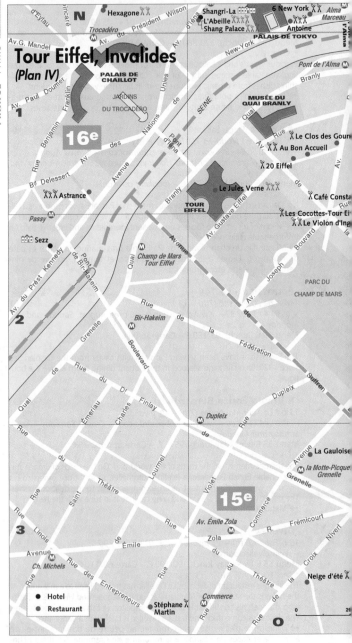

Tour Eiffel, Invalides
(Plan IV)

16e

15e

- ● Hotel
- ● Restaurant

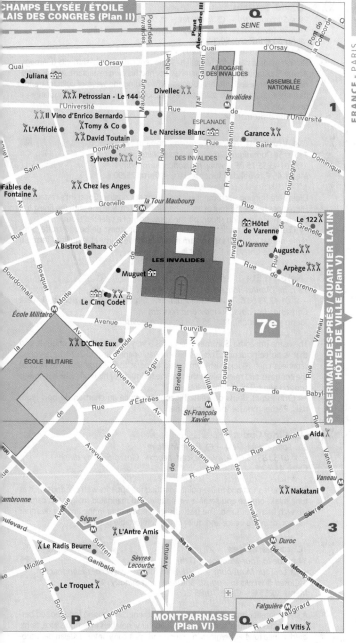

CHAMPS ÉLYSÉE / ÉTOILE
PALAIS DES CONGRÈS (Plan II)

SEINE

Quai d'Orsay

Quai d'Orsay

AÉROGARE
DES INVALIDES

ASSEMBLÉE
NATIONALE

Juliana

Petrossian - Le 144

l'Université

Il Vino d'Enrico Bernardo

L'Affriolé

Tomy & Co

David Toutain

Dominique

Sylvestre

Divellec

Invalides

Rue de

l'Université

ESPLANADE

Le Narcisse Blanc

Rue du

DES INVALIDES

Garance

Saint

Dominique

1

Fables de
Fontaine

Chez les Anges

Grenelle

la Tour Maubourg

Rue de

Bourgogne

Rue de Grenelle

Le 122

Hôtel
de Varenne

Varenne

Auguste

Arpège

Bistrot Belhara

LES INVALIDES

Muguet

Le Cinq Codet

École Militaire

Avenue de

Tourville

7e

Rue de

Varenne

Varenne

Vaneau

St-François
Xavier

D'Chez Eux

ÉCOLE MILITAIRE

Duquesne

Ségur

d'Estrées

Rue de

Breteuil

Boulevard de Villars

Rue de

Babyl

Duquesne

Rue Oudinot

Rue Éblé

Aida

Vaneau

Nakatani

Duroc

Bd de Montparnasse

Cambronne

Ségur

Suffren

L'Antre Amis

Le Radis Beurre

Sèvres
Lecourbe

Garibaldi

Avenue de Saxe

Rue de

3

Miollis

Le Troquet

Borvin

Rue Lecourbe

MONTPARNASSE
(Plan VI)

Falguière

R. de Vaugirard

Le Vitis

XX

David Toutain

29 r. Surcouf (7th) – Ⓜ *Invalides – ℰ 01 45 50 11 10*
Plan: **P1**
– www.davidtoutain.com – Closed Saturday and Sunday
Menu 55 € (lunch), 80/110 €
• Modern cuisine • Design • Fashionable •

Having made a name for himself at some renowned establishments (L'Arpège, Agapé Substance), David Toutain has opened his own restaurant. All this experience is channelled into his cooking. While riding the wave of culinary trends, its finesse, creativity and palette of expressions reveal insight and singularity – a great balance!

→ Cuisine du marché.

XX

Le Violon d'Ingres (Christian Constant)

135 r. St-Dominique (7th) – Ⓜ *École Militaire*
Plan: **O1**
– ℰ 01 45 55 15 05 – www.maisonconstant.com
Menu 45 € (weekday lunch)/110 € – Carte 75/90 €
• Traditional cuisine • Elegant •

Diners are fighting each other off for a spot at Christian Constant's restaurant! His recipes reveal the soul of an authentic cook, firmly in line with the finest tradition. Their execution shows off the know-how of a talented team.

→ Œuf de poule mollet roulé à la mie de pain, toast de beurre truffé. Suprême de bar croustillant aux amandes, huile de curry et piquillos. Tarte au chocolat de Christian Constant.

XX

Neige d'Été (Hideki Nishi)

12 r. de l'Amiral-Roussin (15th) – Ⓜ *Avenue Émile Zola*
Plan: **O3**
– ℰ 01 42 73 66 66 – www.neigedete.fr – Closed 2 weeks in August, 1 week Christmas Holidays, Sunday and Monday
Menu 45 € (lunch), 80/135 € – *(booking advisable)*
• Modern cuisine • Minimalist •

The name (meaning 'Summer Snow') has a very Japanese poetry about it, and that is no coincidence. This restaurant was opened in mid-2014 by a young Japanese chef, Hideki Nishi, who used to be at the George V. It also hints at the contrasts and minimalism that are the hallmarks of his work, which is always spot-on and full of counterpoints.

→ Cromesquis de ris de veau. Pigeonneau grillé au charbon de bois japonais. Pêche, mousse au champagne.

XX

Le Cinq Codet - Hôtel Le Cinq Codet

5 r. Louis-Codet (7th) – Ⓜ *École-Militaire*
Plan: **P2**
– ℰ 01 53 85 15 60 – www.le5codet.com – Closed Sunday dinner
Carte 44/62 €
• Modern cuisine • Elegant • Friendly •

The menu is short and to the point, whetting the appetite with offerings such as tuna tataki, orange and sesame vinaigrette, and marinated maigre fish carpaccio with baby leaf salad. The tasty dishes are savoured in the inviting designer interior, or in the peace and quiet of the comfortable patio.

XX

Chez les Anges

54 bd de la Tour-Maubourg (7th)
Plan: **P1**
– Ⓜ *La Tour Maubourg – ℰ 01 47 05 89 86 – www.chezlesanges.com*
– Closed 3 weeks in August, Saturday and Sunday
Menu 36/55 € – Carte 70/85 €
• Classic cuisine • Elegant •

A stylish interior provides the setting for authentic, appetising food, poised between tradition and modernity. Joël Thiébault vegetables in lemon sauce, farmbred guinea fowl, aubergines in orange and spelt curry or Venezuelan dark chocolate tart. Splendid wine and whisky list.

FRANCE - PARIS

XX ❀ **Auguste** (Gaël Orieux)   AC

54 r. de Bourgogne (7th) – Ⓜ *Varenne*   Plan: **Q2**
– ℰ 01 45 51 61 09 – www.restaurantauguste.fr – Closed 1 to 15 August,
Saturday and Sunday
Menu 37 € (lunch), 88/154 € ♆ – Carte 85/113 € – *(booking advisable)*
• Modern cuisine • Elegant •
Intimate atmosphere, mirrors, white walls and pretty armchairs... Auguste is perfectly tailored to the cuisine of Gaël Orieux, a chef who is passionate about food
and ingredients. His dishes? A quest for harmony and inventiveness, finely wea-
ving together ingredients from land and sea. Affordable prices at lunch; they
pull out all the stops at dinner.
→ Croustillant de langoustine à la verveine, bavarois de céleri branche et
réduction de kumquat. Ris de veau, pralin de cacahouètes caramélisées,
girolles aux abricots secs et vin du Jura. Soufflé au chocolat pur Caraïbe,
glace au miel.

XX ❀ **Nakatani** (Shinsuke Nakatani)   AC

27 r. Pierre-Leroux (7th) – Ⓜ *Vaneau – ℰ 01 47 34 94 14*   Plan: **Q3**
– www.restaurant-nakatani.com – Closed 3 weeks in August, Sunday and
Monday
Menu 40 € (lunch)/135 € – *(tasting menu only)*
• Modern cuisine • Intimate • Romantic •
Japanese chef Shinsuke Nakatani (formerly at Hélène Darroze) is now standing
on his own two feet. With a keen sense of seasoning, technique and the aesthe-
tics of the dishes, he cooks fabulous French cuisine using seasonal ingredients.
All this is served by discreet and efficient staff. Impeccable!
→ Caviar et anguille fumée, mousseline de chou-rave et purée de navet.
Ris de veau, fèves, aubergine grillée et huile de pépins de courge. Panna-
cotta au laurier, fraises, rhubarbe, thym citron et huile d'olive.

XX ❀ **Garance** (Guillaume Iskandar)   ⅍ AC ⇔

34 r. St-Dominique (7th) – Ⓜ *Invalides*   Plan: **Q1**
– ℰ 01 45 55 27 56 – www.garance-saintdominique.fr – Closed Saturday
and Sunday
Menu 39 € (lunch), 68/88 € – Carte 77/90 € – *(booking advisable)*
• Creative • Design • Elegant •
Guillaume Muller and Guillaume Iskandar (both formerly of L'Arpège) have tea-
med up to open this contemporary bistro in an old building near Invalides. The
recipes are very contemporary and always highlight the ingredients (celery coo-
ked in hay and Italian bacon, lamb two ways). Success guaranteed!
→ Cuisine du marché.

XX **D'Chez Eux**   ⅍ AC

2 av. Lowendal (7th) – Ⓜ *École Militaire*   Plan: **P2**
– ℰ 01 47 05 52 55 – www.chezeux.com
Menu 34 € (weekday lunch) – Carte 46/111 €
• Cuisine from South West France • Rustic • Friendly •
This restaurant has had a winning formula for over 40 years – and the place
shows no sign of ageing! Sample the generous portions of dishes inspired by
the southwest of France. These are made with quality ingredients and served
by waiters in old-fashioned aprons in a provincial inn ambience.

XX ☺ **Au Bon Accueil**   AC

14 r. Monttessuy (7th) – Ⓜ *Pont de l'Alma*   Plan: **O1**
– ℰ 01 47 05 46 11 – www.aubonaccueilparis.com – Closed 3 weeks in
August, Saturday and Sunday
Menu 36/55 € – Carte 69/96 €
• Modern cuisine • Bistro • Cosy •
In the shadow of the Eiffel Tower, this chic and discreet restaurant serves appe-
tising cuisine based around seasonal produce. Excellent value.

XX **La Gauloise** 🛱 ⇔

59 av. La Motte-Picquet (15th) Plan: **O3**
– Ⓜ La Motte Picquet Grenelle – 𝒞 01 47 34 11 64 – Closed August,
Saturday and Sunday
Menu 31 € – Carte 35/68 €
• Traditional cuisine • Elegant • Vintage •

This Belle Epoque brasserie boasts the delightful air of Parisian life from yesteryear. It has a menu that features dishes such as poached eggs and vegetable
pot-au-feu, pork crepinettes, turbot with a Béarnaise sauce, and onion soup. La
Gauloise's attractive terrace is also much appreciated by diners.

X **Aida** (Koji Aida) 🍴 🆔 ⇔
𝓔𝓑
1 r. Pierre-Leroux (7th) – Ⓜ Vaneau – 𝒞 01 43 06 14 18 Plan: **Q3**
– www.aida-paris.net – Closed 1 week in March, 3 weeks in August,
Monday and lunch
Menu 160/280 € – *(booking advisable)*
• Japanese • Elegant • Minimalist •

Be transported to the Land of the Rising Sun in this restaurant. It breathes
authenticity and purity through its delicious Japanese cuisine full of finesse.
The fish, presented alive and then prepared in front of you, couldn't be fresher.
The art of simplicity and transparency at its best!
→ Sashimi. Teppanyaki. Wagashi.

X **Les Fables de La Fontaine** 🛱 🆔
𝓔𝓑
131 r. St-Dominique (7th) – Ⓜ École Militaire Plan: **P1**
– 𝒞 01 44 18 37 55 – www.lesfablesdelafontaine.net
Menu 70 € – Carte 45/65 € – *(booking advisable)*
• Modern cuisine • Bistro • Friendly •

The former sous-chef of Les Fables has slipped effortlessly into the role of chef.
She composes modern cuisine that is fragrant and bursting with colours,
demonstrating an impressive maturity and undeniable talent. Relish your meal
in a sleek, light and elegant bistro decor.
→ Jaune d'œuf croustillant, poireau croquant en vinaigrette d'algues, haddock cru et cuit. Aïoli de lieu, petits légumes de saison glacés et huile
d'olive. Sablé breton, crème et sorbet citron, meringue au poivre.

X **Stéphane Martin** 🆔 ⇔

67 r. des Entrepreneurs (15th) – Ⓜ Charles Michels Plan: **N3**
– 𝒞 01 45 79 03 31 – www.stephanemartin.com – Closed 9 to 17 April,
30 July-21 August, 23 December-2 January, Sunday and Monday
Menu 30 € (weekday lunch)/38 € – Carte 47/71 €
• Modern cuisine • Friendly •

This Left Bank address is well known to gourmets. The cosy setting and tasteful
decor provide the backdrop for appetising traditional fare with a modern twist.
Enjoy the pleasure of dishes such as calf's liver meunière or knuckle of pork braised in spiced honey.

X **Le Clos des Gourmets** 🍴 ⇔
🙂
16 av. Rapp (7th) – Ⓜ Alma Marceau – 𝒞 01 45 51 75 61 Plan: **O1**
– www.closdesgourmets.com – Closed 1 to 25 August, Sunday and Monday
Menu 30 € (lunch), 35/39 € – Carte lunch 44/60 €
• Modern cuisine • Fashionable •

Sleek and welcoming modern bistro where the chef loves good food and cares
enough to do it well. Asparagus crème brûlée, fennel slow cooked with mellow
spices: the cuisine is honest and full of delicious flavours.

X **Les Cocottes - Tour Eiffel**
🙂
135 r. St-Dominique (7th) – Ⓜ École Militaire Plan: **O1**
– 𝒞 01 45 50 10 28 – www.maisonconstant.com
Menu 28 € (weekday lunch) – Carte 35/67 €
• Traditional cuisine • Fashionable •

The concept in this friendly eatery is based around bistro cuisine with a modern
touch cooked in cast-iron casserole pots (cocottes), and includes popular dishes
such as country paté, roast veal etc. No advance booking.

FRANCE - PARIS

Le Radis Beurre

51 bd Garibaldi (15th) – Ⓜ *Sèvres Lecourbe*   Plan: **P3**
– ℰ 01 40 33 99 26 – www.restaurantleradisbeurre.com – Closed 3 weeks in August, Saturday and Sunday
Menu 34 € – Carte approx. 41 €
• Traditional cuisine • Bistro •

It was in 2015 on Boulevard Garibaldi in Paris that chef Jérôme Bonnet found the perfect site for his restaurant. He prepares tasty, carefully created food that bears the hallmark of his southern upbringing. An example? Pig's trotters with duck foie gras and meat juices. You may even get to nibble on a few radishes with butter while you wait.

L'Antre Amis

9 r. Bouchut (15th) – Ⓜ *Ségur – ℰ 01 45 67 15 65*   Plan: **P3**
– www.lantreamis.com – Closed August, Saturday and Sunday
Menu 35/75 € 🍷
• Modern cuisine • Contemporary décor •

Enter this haven of friendship (a play on words in French) and sample the enthusiastic cuisine of the owner-chef. Excellent market fresh ingredients (meat, fish, shellfish) go into well-presented, flawlessly prepared dishes. Very concise menu and extensive wine list – some 170 references.

Le 122

122 r. de Grenelle (7th) – Ⓜ *Solférino*   Plan: **Q2**
– ℰ 01 45 56 07 42 – www.le122.fr – Closed August, Saturday and Sunday
Menu 29 € (lunch)/72 € – Carte 50/62 €
• Modern cuisine • Design •

A stone's throw from the town hall of the 7th arrondissement, this pleasant restaurant draws in numerous politicians at every mealtime. The chef produces flavoursome and skilfully done cuisine such as pan-fried scallops, black rice risotto, bottarga, as well as fillet of John Dory, quince and grape condiments, celeriac mash...

Tomy & Co

22 r. Surcouf (7th) – Ⓜ *Invalides – ℰ 01 45 51 46 93*   Plan: **P1**
– Closed August, 23 to 30 December, 1 week in February, Saturday and Sunday
Menu 45/65 €
• Modern cuisine • Friendly • Bistro •

This restaurant, a stone's throw from rue Saint-Dominique, bears the mark of Tomy Gousset (Meurice, Taillevent), who flashes his tattoos and his talent with equal ostentation. His style is gastro-bistro cooking that is in touch with its time, as he juggles simplicity and sophistication with dishes such as Apicius duck.

Bistrot Belhara

23 r. Duvivier (7th) – Ⓜ *École Militaire*   Plan: **P2**
– ℰ 01 45 51 41 77 – www.bistrotbelhara.com – Closed 31 July-25 August, 24 to 29 December, Sunday and Monday
Menu 34 € (lunch)/52 € – Carte 43/54 €
• Traditional cuisine • Bistro •

Belhara is a site that is famous for its superb waves on the Basque coast - and this is the chef's nod to his origins. It is a tough call to summarise his impressive career path (Guérard, Loiseau, Ducasse etc). A convert to the bistro mode, Thierry Dufroux works wonders as he revisits the classics – the chef is definitely on the crest of the wave!

L'Affriolé

17 r. Malar (7th) – Ⓜ *Invalides – ℰ 01 44 18 31 33*   Plan: **P1**
– www.laffriole.fr – Closed 3 weeks in August, Sunday and Monday
Menu 39 € – Carte approx. 47 €
• Modern cuisine • Fashionable •

With his daily specials board and monthly menu, the chef closely follows seasonal market availability. The contemporary designer decor adds a certain charm to the overall feel. A 'bento' menu is also available for those in a hurry.

X

Le Troquet

21 r. François-Bonvin (15th) – Ⓜ *Cambronne*   Plan: **P3**
– ☎ 01 45 66 89 00 – Closed 1 week in May, 3 weeks in
August, 1 week in December, Sunday and Monday
Menu 31 € (lunch), 33/41 € – Carte lunch approx. 35 €
• Traditional cuisine • Vintage • Bistro •
A typical Parisian 'troquet' (café-bar) in all its splendour! Although Christian
Etchebest is no longer at the helm, a young promising chef is working with
the same team. He has the same reliance on ultra-fresh ingredients and the
same culinary focus on southwest France.

X

Café Constant   AC

139 r. St-Dominique (7th) – Ⓜ *École Militaire*   Plan: **O1**
– ☎ 01 47 53 73 34 – www.maisonconstant.com
Menu 24 € (weekday lunch) – Carte 36/60 € – *(bookings not accepted)*
• Traditional cuisine • Bistro • Friendly •
This unpretentious and friendly brasserie run by Christian Constant occupies an
old café. The gourmet bistro cuisine includes classics such as eggs mimosa, oyster tartare, roast lamb, rice pudding etc. No advance bookings.

X

20 Eiffel   AC

20 r. de Monttessuy (7th) – Ⓜ *Alma Marceau*   Plan: **O1**
– ☎ 01 47 05 14 20 – www.restaurant20eiffel.fr – Closed 14 to 31 August
and Sunday
Menu 31 € – Carte 47/55 €
• Traditional cuisine • Classic décor •
In a quiet street a stone's throw from the Eiffel Tower, this restaurant offers a
understated interior full of light. On the menu, you can choose from a range of
updated dishes, prepared by two chefs, all of which place the focus on flavour
and taste. For example, a delicious fillet of pollock with squash.

SAINT-GERMAIN DES PRES – QUARTIER LATIN – HOTEL DE VILLE   PLAN V

Duc de St-Simon   AC

14 r. St-Simon (7th) – Ⓜ *Rue du Bac – ☎ 01 44 39 20 20*   Plan: **R1**
– www.hotelducdesaintsimon.com
29 rm – †250/295 € ††250/295 € – ⭢ 19 € – 5 suites
• Luxury • Personalised •
The small paved courtyard comes into view as you pass through the entrance,
revealing the full beauty of this fine 18C townhouse. The fabrics, woodwork, old
prints and antique furniture enhance the sense of an aristocratic property from
bygone days. The charm here is on an equal par with the peace and quiet.

L'Hôtel   AC

13 r. des Beaux-Arts (6th) – Ⓜ *St-Germain des Prés*   Plan: **S1**
– ☎ 01 44 41 99 00 – www.l-hotel.com
20 rm ⭢ – †305/1150 € ††305/1150 €
• Luxury • Historic • Personalised •
It was at L'Hôtel that the great Oscar Wilde died in 1900. The atypical, aesthetic
decor, updated by Jacques Garcia, still manages to pay homage to artistic pomp
and splendour. There is a nod to Baroque, Empire and Oriental styles.
❀ **Le Restaurant** – See restaurant listing

L'Abbaye   AC

10 r. Cassette (6th) – Ⓜ *St-Sulpice – ☎ 01 45 44 38 11*   Plan: **S2**
– www.hotel-abbaye.com
40 rm ⭢ – †250/712 € ††250/712 € – 4 suites
• Luxury • Historic • Personalised •
A hotel with a rare charm occupying a former 17C abbey. It features highly refined guestrooms, which are both bright and classically styled, as well as a peaceful and leafy courtyard where the only noise is from the bubbling fountain.
Thoughtful and attentive staff.

FRANCE - PARIS

Relais St-Germain　　　　　　　　　　　　　　　AC

9 carr. de l'Odéon (6th) – Ⓜ *Odéon* – ✆ *01 44 27 07 97*　　　Plan: **S2**
– *www.hotelrsg.com*
22 rm ☲ – ♦295/460 € ♦♦295/460 €
• Traditional • Townhouse • Personalised •

Life never seems to stand still at the Carrefour de l'Odéon – a good reason for
taking refuge in this refined hotel. The painted wood beams, shimmering fabrics and antique furniture bestow a unique character on the guestrooms, which
are perfect for literary inspiration!
Le Comptoir du Relais – See restaurant listing

La Lanterne　　　　　　　　　　　　　　🛏 🕉 🖥 ♿ AC

12 r. de la Montagne-Sainte-Geneviève (5th)　　　　　　Plan: **T2**
– Ⓜ *Maubert Mutualité* – ✆ *01 53 19 88 39* – *www.hotel-la-lanterne.com*
27 rm – ♦210/670 € ♦♦210/670 € – ☲ 19 € – 1 suite
• Boutique hotel • Cosy • Trendy •

In the heart of the Latin Quarter, between Notre-Dame and the Pantheon, this
oh-so-chic boutique hotel has comfortable guestrooms (including four in a little
interior garden). The bonus? The relaxation suite with a pool, hammam and sen-
sory shower, which is a rarity in the area.

Bel Ami St-Germain des Prés　　　　　🛗 🕉 ♿ AC ♨

7 r. St-Benoit (6th) – Ⓜ *St-Germain des Prés*　　　　Plan: **S2**
– ✆ *01 42 61 53 53* – *www.hotel-bel-ami.com*
108 rm ☲ – ♦229/700 € ♦♦229/700 € – 7 suites
• Townhouse • Contemporary •

The name of this hotel has nothing to do with the famous novel by Maupassant,
even if it is located in the literary district of St Germain. The hotel will suit guests
looking for a chic, urban ambience. It has a trendy bar and simple, contemporary-style guestrooms, some of which have been renovated. Attractive well-
being area.

Montalembert　　　　　　　　　　　　　　🍴 AC ♨

3 r. Montalembert (7th) – Ⓜ *Rue du Bac*　　　　　　Plan: **R1**
– ✆ *01 45 49 68 68* – *www.hotelmontalembert-paris.fr*
44 rm – ♦280/500 € ♦♦280/500 € – ☲ 30 € – 6 suites
• Historic • Personalised • Design •

Located between St-Germain-des-Prés and the Orsay Museum, this particularly
attractive building dates back to 1926. It has very pleasant guestrooms; some
are decorated in Louis-Philippe style, and the majority, in a chic and contemporary style bearing the hallmark of Christian Liaigre. A few even boast an attractive view of the city's rooftops.

Bourg Tibourg　　　　　　　　　　　　　　　　　AC

19 r. du Bourg-Tibourg (4th) – Ⓜ *Hôtel de Ville*　　　Plan: **U1**
– ✆ *01 42 78 47 39* – *www.bourgtibourg.com*
30 rm – ♦220/290 € ♦♦290/400 € – ☲ 20 € – 1 suite
• Luxury • Townhouse • Cosy •

Hotel entirely styled by Jacques Garcia. Each room has its own individual decor
(neo-Gothic, Baroque, Eastern etc) and exudes luxury and refinement. A little
gem in the heart of the Marais district.

Le Bellechasse　　　　　　　　　　　　　　　♿ AC

8 r. de Bellechasse (7th) – Ⓜ *Musée d'Orsay*　　　　Plan: **R1**
– ✆ *01 45 50 22 31* – *www.lebellechasse.com*
33 rm – ♦159/470 € ♦♦159/470 € – ☲ 21 €
• Luxury • Personalised • Design •

A lovely hotel that has been entirely decorated by Christian Lacroix. The fashion
house has created designer guestrooms with splashes of colour. They have old
or contemporary details that often have a dreamlike quality. It makes for a 'journey within a journey' – fashionable and full of character!

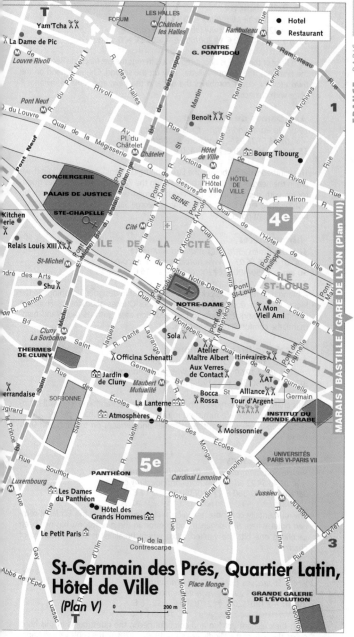

St-Germain des Prés, Quartier Latin,
Hôtel de Ville

(Plan V)   0   200 m

FRANCE - PARIS

La Belle Juliette
92 r. du Cherche-Midi (6th) – **Ⓜ** *Vaneau*
– ℰ 01 42 22 97 40 – www.labellejuliette.com
39 rm – ♦190/520 € ♦♦200/600 € – ⌂ 22 € – 6 suites
• Townhouse • Elegant • Personalised •

Plan: **R3**

Each floor of the hotel is decorated on a different theme: Madame Récamier on the first floor (the famous Juliette), Italy on the second, Chateaubriand on the third etc. The decor combines the old and the new, and remains inviting. A place with character.

Les Dames du Panthéon
19 pl. du Panthéon (5th) – **Ⓜ** *Luxembourg*
– ℰ 01 43 54 32 95 – www.hoteldupantheon.com
35 rm – ♦200/450 € ♦♦200/450 € – ⌂ 18 €
• Luxury • Traditional • Cosy •

Plan: **T3**

The Panthéon, the Sorbonne, the Luxembourg Gardens... no doubt about it, we are in the heart of the Latin Quarter! Facing the Panthéon, this hotel has guestrooms with decor inspired by French women who have left their mark on history: Marguerite Duras, Juliette Gréco, George Sand and Édith Piaf. A romantic and elegant hotel.

Atmosphères
31 r. des Écoles (5th) – **Ⓜ** *Maubert Mutualité*
– ℰ 01 43 26 56 02 – www.hotelatmospheres.com
56 rm – ♦150/400 € ♦♦200/600 € – ⌂ 16 €
• Business • Luxury • Design •

Plan: **T2-3**

A brand new hotel with sleek lines and the latest in designer furnishings. In the lobby, there is a fine exhibition of Thierry des Ouches photographs. From the lounge and the guestrooms to the relaxation area (with its sauna and hammam), the comfort is total. A success.

Hôtel des Grands Hommes
17 pl. du Panthéon (5th) – **Ⓜ** *Luxembourg*
– ℰ 01 46 34 19 60 – www.hoteldesgrandshommes.com
30 rm – ♦180/340 € ♦♦190/450 € – ⌂ 14 €
• Traditional • Townhouse • Historic •

Plan: **T3**

This charming hotel enjoys a fine location near the Panthéon. The well-maintained guestrooms are furnished in Directoire-style and have plenty of character. Superb views from the balconies and terraces on the fifth and sixth floors.

Jardin de Cluny
9 r. du Sommerard (5th) – **Ⓜ** *Maubert Mutualité*
– ℰ 01 43 54 22 66 – www.hoteljardindecluny.com
39 rm – ♦130/360 € ♦♦130/360 € – ⌂ 17 €
• Business • Townhouse • Personalised •

Plan: **T2**

Environmentally conscious travellers will enjoy staying at this Écolabel-certified hotel, where the elegance and comfort in the guestrooms has not been sacrificed one bit. The vaulted room where breakfast is served has lots of charm.

Le Petit Paris
214 r. St-Jacques (5th) – **Ⓜ** *Luxembourg*
– ℰ 01 53 10 29 29 – www.hotelpetitparis.com
20 rm – ♦180/420 € ♦♦240/500 € – ⌂ 18 €
• Townhouse • Design • Contemporary •

Plan: **T3**

With their elegant yet fun and colourful decor, the guestrooms in this hotel evoke the style of the Middle Ages, the 1920s, 1970s, or the Louis VX and Napoleon III periods.

Tour d'Argent

15 quai de la Tournelle (5th) – **M** *Maubert Mutualité*   Plan: **U2**
– ☎ 01 43 54 23 31
– www.tourdargent.com
– Closed 2 weeks in August, Sunday and Monday
Menu 105 € (lunch), 220/350 € – Carte 175/330 €
• Modern cuisine • Luxury • Elegant •

This establishment, dating from 1582, has undergone a velvet revolution. Chef Philippe Labbé prepares modern, lively cuisine with a new take on the classics, such as five dishes of duck (with the tongue as dessert!). Elegant service and a fantastic wine cellar of 400 000 bottles. A traditional hand in a modern glove.
➙ Foie gras de canard grillé, tomatillos, tomates anciennes et pourpier. Homard bleu de casier en deux services. Crêpes "mademoiselle" préparées au guéridon, sorbet au caillé de lait cru.

Guy Savoy

11 quai de Conti (6th) – **M** *St-Michel*   Plan: **S1**
– ☎ 01 43 80 40 61 – www.guysavoy.com
– Closed August, Christmas Holidays, Saturday lunch, Sunday and Monday
Menu 385/490 € – Carte 205/335 €
• Creative • Luxury • Romantic •

Guy Savoy: the second act! In 2015, the chef set up shop in the Hôtel de la Monnaie, on the banks of the Seine. The setting is sumptuous with six dining rooms decorated with contemporary artworks, on loan from François Pinault. The host is true to form, injecting the place with sincerity and enthusiasm, inventiveness without excess, and unfailing generosity. Irresistible!
➙ Soupe d'artichaut à la truffe noire, brioche feuilletée aux champignons et aux truffes. Autour du veau, jus classique sous la croûte. Millefeuille à la gousse de vanille.

Relais Louis XIII (Manuel Martinez)

8 r. des Grands-Augustins (6th) – **M** *Odéon*   Plan: **T2**
– ☎ 01 43 26 75 96 – www.relaislouis13.com – Closed August, 1 week in January, Sunday and Monday
Menu 60 € (lunch), 90/140 € – Carte approx. 130 €
• Classic cuisine • Elegant • Elegant •

Very close to the Seine, this old house located in historical Paris takes us back to Louis XIII's day. The decor is full of character with exposed beams, stonework and stained-glass windows. This forms an elegant backdrop for Manuel Martinez's cooking, which is in line with French culinary classicism. Good value lunch menu.
➙ Quenelle de bar, mousseline de champignons et glaçage au champagne. Canard challandais rôti aux épices, garniture de saison. Millefeuille.

Hélène Darroze

4 r. d'Assas (6th) – **M** *Sèvres Babylone*   Plan: **R2**
– ☎ 01 42 22 00 11 – www.helenedarroze.com – Closed Sunday and Monday
Menu 58 € (lunch), 98/185 €
• Modern cuisine • Cosy • Fashionable •

Hélène Darroze, the descendent of a family of cooks from southwest France (Aquitaine, Landes, Basque country), finds the raw ingredients for her cuisine in her homeland. To this heritage, she has added her experience, insatiable curiosity and own distinctive blend of talent and intuition.
➙ Huître, caviar d'Aquitaine et haricots maïs du Béarn. Homard tandoori, carotte, agrumes et coriandre fraîche. Chocolat et framboises.

FRANCE - PARIS

FRANCE - PARIS

XX
&3
Le Restaurant – Hôtel L'Hôtel   AC

13 r. des Beaux-Arts (6th) – Ⓜ *St-Germain des Prés*   Plan: **S1**
– ☎ 01 44 41 99 01
– www.l-hotel.com
– Closed August, 19 to 26 December, Sunday and Monday
Menu 55 € (lunch), 110/190 € ⦿ – Carte 100/130 €
• Modern cuisine • Elegant • Luxury •

Le Restaurant is part of L'Hôtel, with a decor also created by Jacques Garcia. The chef revisits classic French gastronomy with creative dishes based around evocative flavours and superb ingredients.
→ Tourteau de Loctudy, mousse avocat et yuzu. Ris de veau "crousti-moelleux" et petits pois à la française. Meringue italienne, biscuit craquant, crémeux et zeste de citron.

XX
&3
La Dame de Pic   � & AC ⇔

20 r. du Louvre (1st) – Ⓜ *Louvre Rivoli*   Plan: **T1**
– ☎ 01 42 60 40 40 – www.anne-sophie-pic.com
– Closed 7 to 20 August
Menu 59 € (weekday lunch), 105/135 €
• Creative • Design • Elegant •

Anne-Sophie Pic's Parisian restaurant, depicted by a soft feminine interior, is 2min from the Louvre. A fine blend of flavours, precise creations and the ability to mix unexpected ingredients are the hallmark of this talented chef, embodied by her frog's legs in Lapsang Souchong tea or roast lamb chartreuse with spring vegetables.
→ Œuf de poule et champignons bruns de Paris, consommé infusé au gingembre et au géranium rosat. Paleron de bœuf Black Angus légèrement fumé au café, girolles au jus. Poire pochée, crème légère et glace à la vanille de Madagascar.

XX
&3
Les Climats   ⸱ ⸱ AC ⇔ ⸰ (dinner)

41 r. de Lille (7th) – Ⓜ *Rue du Bac*   Plan: **R1**
– ☎ 01 58 62 10 08 – www.lesclimats.fr
– Closed 12 to 20 February, 3 weeks in August, 25 December-2 January, Sunday and Monday
Menu 45 € (lunch), 110/180 € ⦿ – Carte 95/130 €
• Modern cuisine • Vintage • Elegant •

A restaurant in the unusual setting of the former Maison des Dames des Postes, which housed postal and telecommunications service operators from 1905. The French cuisine is spiced up with modern touches. The mosaic floors, antique brass light fittings and vert d'Estours marble gives character to the decor.
→ Tourteau, daurade royale, couteaux et légumes de saison assaisonnés d'une sauce tosazu. Poitrine de pigeonneau rôtie, caillette de cuisse au chou et sauce salmis. Biscuit soufflé chaud parfumé à l'amaretto et sucs de cerises noires.

XX
&3
Benoit   ⸱ AC ⇔

20 r. St-Martin (4th) – Ⓜ *Châtelet-Les Halles*   Plan: **U1**
– ☎ 01 42 72 25 76 – www.benoit-paris.com
Menu 39 € (lunch) – Carte 70/100 €
• Classic cuisine • Bistro • Classic décor •

Alain Ducasse supervises this chic and lively bistro, one of the oldest in Paris: Benoit celebrated its 100th anniversary in 2012! The classic food is prepared in time-honoured tradition, and respects the soul of this authentic and fine establishment.
→ Foie gras de canard confit, brioche parisienne toastée. Sauté gourmand de ris de veau, crêtes et rognons de coq, foie gras et jus truffé. Profiteroles Benoit, sauce au chocolat chaud.

FRANCE - PARIS

XX **Itinéraires** (Sylvain Sendra)   ⚬ ♿ Ⓐ

✿ *5 r. de Pontoise (5th) –* Ⓜ *Maubert Mutualité*   Plan: **U2**
*– ✆ 01 46 33 60 11 – www.restaurant-itineraires.com – Closed 7 to
13 February, 6 to 27 August, Saturday lunch, Sunday and Monday*
Menu 49 € (lunch), 65/105 € – Carte 60/95 € – *(booking advisable)*
• Modern cuisine • Fashionable • Friendly •

Talented young chef Sylvain Sendra set up his attractive restaurant – very light
and bright – among the capital's quality restaurants. Finesse, flavours, originality
and quality ingredients: you won't regret including a meal here on your itine-
rary.
➔ Tarte à l'oignon doux des Cévennes, foie gras et corolle de champignons de Paris. Lieu jaune, purée de navet kabu, salicornes croquantes.
Ganache au chocolat noir, condiment cassis, pousses de betteraves et
glace à la vanille de Madagascar.

XX **Alliance** (Toshitaka Omiya)   Ⓐ

✿ *5 r. de Poissy (5th) –* Ⓜ *Maubert Mutualité*   Plan: **U2**
*– ✆ 01 75 51 57 54 – www.restaurant-alliance.fr – Closed 5 to 28 August,
Saturday and Sunday*
Menu 39 € (lunch), 75/95 € – Carte 65/110 € – *(booking advisable)*
• Modern cuisine • Contemporary décor • Minimalist •

Alliance brings together two alumni of the restaurant Agapé Substance as partners in this new adventure. A starter of oyster, onion and lemon; foie gras, vegetable pot-au-feu and Corsican broth... The chef's dishes are flashes of simplicity,
at once subtle and well executed. We will be going back for more.
➔ Pommes de terre "Allians", échalote et champignons. Homard bleu de
l'Île Chausey, maïs et sauge. Abricot et romarin.

XX **ES** (Takayuki Honjo)   Ⓐ

✿ *91 r. de Grenelle (7th) –* Ⓜ *Solférino – ✆ 01 45 51 25 74*   Plan: **R1**
*– http://www.es-restaurant.fr – Closed 3 weeks in August, Tuesday lunch,
Sunday and Monday*
Menu 42 € (weekday lunch)/105 € – *(booking advisable)*
• Modern cuisine • Minimalist •

A restaurant founded in 2013 by Takayuki Honjo, a young Japanese chef who is
an adept of French cuisine. From the first mouthful, his talent strikes a chord
with your taste buds. Foie gras and sea urchin, pigeon and cocoa... all the associations work a treat. He masters flavours and never forgets the harmony of the
whole.
➔ Cuisine du marché.

XX **Yam'Tcha** (Adeline Grattard)

✿ *121 r. St-Honoré (1st) –* Ⓜ *Louvre Rivoli*   Plan: **T1**
*– ✆ 01 40 26 08 07 – www.yamtcha.com – Closed August, Christmas
Holidays, Tuesday lunch, Sunday and Monday*
Menu 65 € (weekday lunch)/135 € – *(booking advisable)*
• Creative • Elegant •

Adeline Grattard has a remarkable feel for ingredients with simple and striking
associations – influences of France and Asia – devised to be paired with a selection of excellent teas. This young chef, trained at L'Astrance and in Hong Kong,
cultivates clarity with style.
➔ Cuisine du marché.

XX **Atelier Maître Albert**   Ⓐ ⇄ 🔥

1 r. Maître-Albert (5th) – Ⓜ *Maubert Mutualité*   Plan: **U2**
*– ✆ 01 56 81 30 01 – www.ateliermaitrealbert.com – Closed 2 weeks in
August, Christmas Holidays, Saturday lunch and Sunday lunch*
Menu 35/70 € – Carte 40/58 €
• Traditional cuisine • Cosy • Friendly •

An attractive medieval fireplace and roasting spits take pride of place in this
handsome interior designed by Jean-Michel Wilmotte. Guy Savoy is responsible
for the mouthwatering menu.

XX **Un Dimanche à Paris**   ⅏ 🄰🄲 ↻

4 cours du Commerce-St-André (6th) – 🚇 *Odéon*   Plan: **S2**
– 𝒞 01 56 81 18 18 – www.un-dimanche-a-paris.com – Closed 1 to
22 August, Sunday dinner and Monday
Menu 29 € (weekday lunch), 37/62 € – Carte 40/64 €
• Modern cuisine • Fashionable • Friendly •

Chocolate is king in this concept store! In the restaurant, the spicy hint of the cocoa bean can even be detected in the meat and fish dishes. The delicious desserts are a particular highlight - and the elegant setting is equally perfect for a mid-afternoon hot chocolate.

XX **Alcazar**   ⅏ 🄰🄲 ↻

62 r. Mazarine (6th) – 🚇 *Odéon – 𝒞 01 53 10 19 99*   Plan: **S2**
– www.alcazar.fr
Menu 34 € (lunch) – Carte 55/65 €
• Modern cuisine • Trendy • Brasserie •

This former cabaret was given a makeover in autumn 2015, under the direction of architect and decorator Lola Gonzalez. With its plant-filled decor, the whole place exudes the timeless elegance of a large winter garden. As for the food, you can still enjoy an appetising contemporary brasserie menu.

X
❀ **Gaya Rive Gauche par Pierre Gagnaire**   🄰🄲

44 r. du Bac (7th) – 🚇 *Rue du Bac – 𝒞 01 45 44 73 73*   Plan: **R1**
– www.pierre-gagnaire.com – Closed 2 weeks in August, Christmas
Holidays, Sunday and Monday
Menu 65 € (lunch) – Carte 55/100 €
• Seafood • Cosy • Elegant •

Under the impulsion of designer Violaine Jeantet, this restaurant (Pierre Gagnaire's second in Paris) has become cosier and more refined, thanks in particular to the sapele wall panelling. As for the food, it still celebrates fish and seafood in original ways but without excess. Delicious!
➜ Carpaccio de daurade royale, avocat, céléri branche et groseille. Fine tranche de maigre pimentée et saisie à l'huile d'olive, mousseline de maïs et mousse de concombre. Parfait à la Chartreuse verte, poire et raisins pochés au vin doux.

X
❀❀ **L'Atelier de Joël Robuchon - St-Germain**   🕸 🄰🄲 ↻ 🍷

5 r. de Montalembert (7th) – 🚇 *Rue du Bac*   Plan: **R1**
– 𝒞 01 42 22 56 56 – www.joel-robuchon.net – Open from 11.30am to
3.30pm and 6.30pm to midnight. Reservations possible for certain times
only: please enquire
Menu 179 € – Carte 80/170 €
• Creative • Design • Minimalist •

This contemporary Atelier by Joël Robuchon – the first in a long line – is a must! Find the long counter flanked by high stools, a small, intimate dining area, and a red and black colour scheme. The studied half-light is directed onto the stunning food, prepared with a watchmaker's precision.
➜ Langoustine en ravioli truffé à l'étuvée de chou vert. Agneau de lait en côtelettes à la fleur de thym. Ganache onctueuse au chocolat araguani, glace au grué de cacao et biscuit Oréo.

X
❀ **Sola**   🄰🄲 ↻

12 r. de l'Hôtel-Colbert (5th) – 🚇 *Maubert Mutualité*   Plan: **T-U2**
– 𝒞 01 43 29 59 04 – www.restaurant-sola.com – Closed 2 weeks in
August, 30 December-7 January and Sunday
Menu 65 € (lunch)/98 €
• Modern cuisine • Exotic décor • Elegant •

This restaurant is just a few yards from the banks of the Seine overlooking Notre Dame and yet you'd be forgiven for thinking you were already in Japan! The young Japanese chef is living proof that the cuisine of his home and adopted countries can combine to create harmonious and gracefully presented culinary creations. Ingredients sourced from France are transformed with traditional Far Eastern flavours.
➜ Cuisine du marché.

FRANCE - PARIS

Ze Kitchen Galerie (William Ledeuil)

4 r. des Grands-Augustins (6th) – Ⓜ *St-Michel*　　　　　　Plan: **T2**
– ☏ *01 44 32 00 32* – *www.zekitchengalerie.fr* – *Closed 2 weeks in August, 1 week in December, Saturday lunch and Sunday*
Menu 48 € (lunch), 85/98 € – Carte approx. 85 €
• Creative • Friendly •
William Ledeuil has breathed his love of Southeast Asian flavours (Thailand, Vietnam and Japan) that inspire his creations into this establishment. Galanga, ka-chaï, curcuma, wasabi and ginger – herbs, roots, spices and condiments from all over the world at the service of French classics.
➔ Thon rouge de ligne, condiment kalamensi. Bœuf Wagyu confit et grillé, condiment tamarin, jus teriyaki. Glace chocolat blanc et wasabi, jus à la fraise et condiment pistache.

Mon Vieil Ami

69 r. St-Louis-en-l'Île (4th) – Ⓜ *Pont Marie*　　　　　　Plan: **U2**
– ☏ *01 40 46 01 35* – *www.mon-vieil-ami.com* – *Closed Monday and Tuesday*
Carte 35/55 €
• Traditional cuisine • Inn • Contemporary décor •
Savour tasty, traditional dishes with a modern twist in this trendy inn with old beams and contemporary decor. Test out the house specialities, the pâté en croûte and the rum baba… along with rigorously sourced vegetables.

Moissonnier

28 r. des Fossés-St-Bernard (5th) – Ⓜ *Jussieu*　　　　　　Plan: **U3**
– ☏ *01 43 29 87 65* – *Closed August, Sunday and Monday*
Carte 35/64 €
• Lyonnaise • Bistro • Minimalist •
The decor in this bistro has resisted every passing trend with its gleaming zinc counter, walls showing the patina of age, and comfy banquettes. Veal sweetbread turnovers and oxtail terrine are just two examples of the specialities of the skilful chef.

Aux Prés

27 r. du Dragon (6th) – Ⓜ *St-Germain des Prés*　　　　　　Plan: **S2**
– ☏ *01 45 48 29 68* – *www.restaurantauxpres.com*
Menu 48 €
• Modern cuisine • Vintage • Friendly •
Cyril Lignac is clearly not short of a project or two! After changing the name and concept of his St Germain establishment, he now serves international, decidedly creative and spontaneous cuisine, without losing sight of French country roots. The Sunday brunch is a great success.

La Marlotte

55 r. du Cherche-Midi (6th) – Ⓜ *St-Placide*　　　　　　Plan: **R2**
– ☏ *01 45 48 86 79* – *www.lamarlotte.com*
Menu 29 € (weekday lunch)/34 € – Carte 34/60 €
• Traditional cuisine • Rustic •
This modern take on a provincial-style inn is not far from the Bon Marché department store and is a popular haunt for publishers and politicians. The copious and seasonal cuisine honours tradition with dishes such as herring and potatoes in oil, chicken liver terrine, and Grenoble-style skate.

L'Épi Dupin

11 r. Dupin (6th) – Ⓜ *Sèvres Babylone*　　　　　　Plan: **R2**
– ☏ *01 42 22 64 56* – *www.epidupin.com* – *Closed 1 to 24 August, Monday lunch, Saturday and Sunday*
Menu 39/52 € – *(booking advisable)*
• Modern cuisine • Friendly • Fashionable •
True to his beliefs, chef François Pasteau runs an eco-friendly establishment. He buys his fruit and vegetables locally, recycles organic waste, filters the drinking water on site, etc. This respect for the health of our planet and bodies can be tasted in his recipes, which provide an appetising tribute to French country traditions.

FRANCE - PARIS

La Maison du Jardin

27 r. Vaugirard (6th) – Ⓜ Rennes – ℰ 01 45 48 22 31 — Plan: **S3**
– Closed 3 weeks in August, Saturday lunch and Sunday
Menu 35 € – (booking advisable)
• Traditional cuisine • Bistro •

This bistro, a stone's throw from the Palais du Luxembourg, explores the flavours and simplicity of traditional cuisine. Try dishes such as homemade terrines, seasonal soups, lamb pastilla, cod with courgette polenta, and the chocolate dessert selection... all accompanied by sensibly priced wines.

Yen

22 r. St-Benoît (6th) – Ⓜ St-Germain-des-Prés — Plan: **S2**
– ℰ 01 45 44 11 18 – www.yen-paris.fr – Closed 2 weeks in August and Sunday
Menu 71 € (dinner) – Carte 24/84 €
• Japanese • Fashionable • Friendly •

The highly refined Japanese decor in this restaurant will appeal to fans of the minimalist look. The menu showcases the chef's speciality, soba – buckwheat noodles served hot or cold and prepared in front of you.

La Ferrandaise

8 r. de Vaugirard (6th) – Ⓜ Odéon – ℰ 01 43 26 36 36 — Plan: **T2**
– www.laferrandaise.com – Closed dinner in August, Monday lunch, Saturday lunch and Sunday
Menu 37/55 €
• Traditional cuisine • Bistro • Friendly •

This pretty restaurant close to the Luxembourg gardens pays homage to the cuisine of the Auvergne and the Puy-de-Dôme. The owner has even developed a partnership with breeders of the traditional 'Ferrandaise' cattle from his homeland, while the Breton chef creates cuisine that is both honest and tasty. A winning combination.

Taokan - St-Germain

8 r. du Sabot (6th) – Ⓜ St-Germain des Prés — Plan: **S2**
– ℰ 01 42 84 18 36 – www.taokan.fr – Closed 1 to 16 August and Sunday lunch
Menu 24 € (lunch), 29/37 € – Carte 43/66 €
• Chinese • Fashionable • Friendly •

Come inside this pretty restaurant, in the heart of St-Germain des Prés, to enjoy Chinese cuisine. Cantonese specialities feature; for example dim sum, steamed fish, duck breast with honey, and caramelised sliced chicken. Beautiful presentation and good ingredients: this is a real ambassador for Chinese food!

Shu

8 r. Suger (6th) – Ⓜ St-Michel – ℰ 01 46 34 25 88 — Plan: **T2**
– www.restaurant-shu.com – Closed Easter Holidays, 3 weeks in August, Sunday and lunch
Menu 38/63 € – (booking advisable)
• Japanese • Minimalist • Friendly •

You will need to duck to get through the door that leads to this 17C cellar. To a backdrop of minimalist decor, discover authentic and impressively crafted Japanese cuisine. The freshness of the ingredients is showcased to the full in dishes such as kushiage, sushi and sashimi.

Fish La Boissonnerie

69 r. de Seine (6th) – Ⓜ Odéon – ℰ 01 43 54 34 69 — Plan: **S2**
– www.laboissonnerie.com – Closed 1 week in August and 23 December-2 January
Carte 37/57 €
• Traditional cuisine • Bistro • Friendly •

It is worth coming here just to admire the mosaic façade! For more than 15 years, this convivial restaurant has been paying homage to Bacchus, fish and seafood. The menu features dishes such as oyster vichyssoise, scallops with Paimpol beans, and sea bream with barigoule-style artichokes.

FRANCE - PARIS

X

Atelier Vivanda - Cherche Midi   AK

20 r. du Cherche-Midi (6th) – **M** *Sèvres Babylone*   Plan: **R2**
*– 𝒞 01 45 44 50 44 – www.ateliervivanda.com – Closed Sunday and
Monday*
Menu 36/71 €
• Meats and grills • Bistro • Friendly •
Welcome to this bistrot à viande run by Akrame Benallal. Superb pieces of meat
are of course on the menu: Black Angus beef (flank and marbled cuts), chicken
supreme and Iberian pork chop, all lovingly prepared and accompanied by gra-
tin dauphinois or homemade fries. Wildly good.

X

Le Bon Saint-Pourçain   🏠

10 bis r. Servandoni (6th) – **M** *Mabillon*   Plan: **S2**
– 𝒞 01 42 01 78 24 – Closed Sunday and Monday
Carte 38/67 € – *(booking advisable)*
• Traditional cuisine • Bistro • Neighbourhood •
Tucked away behind St Sulpice church in the heart of the high-brow Saint Ger-
main des Prés district, this former 'bougnat' restaurant reopened in the spring of
2015. Bistro traditions with a modern twist depict the delicious food – doubtless
due to the high quality fresh produce. Booking advisable!

X

Le Comptoir du Relais – Hôtel Relais St-Germain   🏠 AK

5 carr. de l'Odéon (6th) – **M** *Odéon* – 𝒞 01 44 27 07 50   Plan: **S2**
– www.hotelrsg.com
Menu 60 € (weekday dinner) – Carte 26/72 € – *(booking advisable)*
• Traditional cuisine • Bistro • Friendly •
In this pocket-sized 1930s bistro, chef Yves Camdeborde delights customers
with his copious traditional cuisine. Brasserie dishes are to the fore at lunchtime,
with a more refined single menu available in the evening.

X

Officina Schenatti   ⇔

15 r. Frédéric-Sauton (5th) – **M** *Maubert Mutualité*   Plan: **U2**
*– 𝒞 01 46 34 08 91 – www.officinaschenatti.com – Closed 3 weeks in
August, 24 to 28 December, Monday lunch and Sunday*
Menu 35 € – Carte 56/77 €
• Italian • Trendy • Fashionable •
Ivan Schenatti, who comes from Lombardy, chose this street near the Seine to
set up his 'officina' (studio) with a decor blending stone and designer furniture.
He creates tasty cuisine from Italy's regions, such as homemade ravioli stuffed
with chanterelles, and pairs them with good Italian wines.

X

AT   AK ⇔

4 r. Cardinal-Lemoine (5th) – **M** *Cardinal Lemoine*   Plan: **U2**
*– 𝒞 01 56 81 94 08 – www.atushitanaka.com – Closed Monday lunch and
Sunday*
Menu 55 € (lunch)/95 €
• Creative • Design • Minimalist •
A stone's throw from the banks of the Seine and the Tour d'Argent, the minima-
list interior of this small restaurant embodies the quintessence of Japan. Chef
Tanaka, formerly with Pierre Gagnaire, loves fresh ingredients and precise coo-
king and is forever surprising us with his creative recipes. Vaulted basement.

X

Aux Verres de Contact   ఓ ⇔

33 r. de Bièvre (corner of bd St-Germain) (5th)   Plan: **U2**
*– **M** Maubert Mutualité – 𝒞 01 46 34 58 02*
– www.auxverresdecontact.com – Closed Saturday lunch and Sunday
Menu 35 €
• Traditional cuisine • Bistro • Friendly •
The team from Le Jadis in the 15th arrondissement runs this pleasant and
colourful contemporary bistro. The name is inspired by the writer and journalist
Antoine Blondin (it refers to a euphemism he coined on his expense claim
forms). The food is generous market based cooking, accompanied by good
wine. Cheers!

FRANCE - PARIS

✗ Bocca Rossa

8 r. de Poissy (5th) – ⓜ Maubert Mutualité — Plan: **U2**
– ℰ 09 51 88 52 44 – Closed Sunday
Carte 30/40 € – *(booking advisable)*
· Italian · Trattoria · Contemporary décor ·

This place is the outpost of Itinéraires, the nearby restaurant of starred chef Sylvain Sendra. Fine Italian ingredients go into the purest trattoria-spirit dishes – antipasti, carpaccio, Sicilian salad, pasta... Quality Italian cucina and attractive prices.

MONTPARNASSE – DENFERT   PLAN VI

🏨 Pullman Montparnasse   ✗ ≤ ⅃ゟ & ⅋ ﹩

19 r. du Cdt-Mouchotte (14th) — Plan: **V1**
– ⓜ Montparnasse Bienvenüe – ℰ 01 44 36 44 36
– www.pullmanhotels.com
926 rm – ♥159/517 € ♥♥159/517 € – ☐ 26 € – 31 suites
· Business · Contemporary ·

This is one of the largest business hotels in the capital with its 900 guestrooms and some 50 meeting rooms. Almost half of the rooms boast panoramic views of Paris and all are very comfortable.

🏨 Concorde Montparnasse   ✗ & ⅋ ﹩ 🚗

40 r. du Cdt-Mouchotte (14th) – ⓜ Gaîté — Plan: **V1**
– ℰ 01 56 54 84 00 – www.montparnasse.concorde-hotels.fr
354 rm – ♥125/500 € ♥♥129/500 € – ☐ 19 €
· Business · Contemporary ·

Situated on Place de Catalogne, this hotel offers functional guestrooms that are ideal for business travellers. Guests can relax in the trendy bar or enjoy a meal in the 'salad bar' or on the outdoor patio.

🏨 Delambre   & ⅋

35 r. Delambre (14th) – ⓜ Edgar Quinet — Plan: **W1**
– ℰ 01 43 20 66 31 – www.hoteldelambreparis.com
30 rm – ♥95/160 € ♥♥95/160 € – ☐ 13 €
· Traditional · Functional ·

The memory of André Breton and Paul Gauguin is still alive in this hotel situated near Montparnasse railway station. Relax in one of the simple, functional guestrooms before taking a stroll through this lively district.

🏠 Hôtel de la Paix   ⅋

225 bd Raspail (14th) – ⓜ Raspail – ℰ 01 43 20 35 82 — Plan: **W1**
– www.paris-montparnasse-hotel.com
40 rm – ♥95/170 € ♥♥95/290 € – ☐ 10 €
· Traditional · Personalised ·

Don't be fooled by the façade: this hotel has real charm. The owners have decorated the building with enthusiasm, using carefully chosen objects and old furniture. The guestrooms are bright, pretty and simple in style.

✗✗✗ Le Dôme   ⅋ ⇔

108 bd Montparnasse (14th) – ⓜ Vavin — Plan: **W1**
– ℰ 01 43 35 25 81
Carte 70/140 €
· Seafood · Brasserie ·

One of the temples of literary and artistic bohemia from the Roaring Twenties with a legendary Art Deco setting. Le Dôme continues to serve the freshest fish and seafood in the best time-honoured fashion.

XxX 　 **Cobéa** (Philippe Bélissent)   ✿
❀ *11 r. Raymond-Losserand (14th)* – Ⓜ *Gaîté*   Plan: **V2**
 – ☎ 01 43 20 21 39 – www.cobea.fr
 – Closed 1 week Easter Holidays, August, 1 week Christmas Holidays,
 Sunday and Monday
 Menu 50 € (lunch), 85/120 € *– (booking advisable)*
 • Modern cuisine • Elegant •
 Co, as in Jérôme Cobou, front-of-house, Bé, as in Philippe Bélissent, in the kitchens, and A for Associates. Cobéa is the venture of two passionate young pro-
 fessionals, who have created a place in their image, that is, guided by the taste
 for good things! A feel for ingredients, harmony and strength of flavours and
 finesse. A delicious restaurant.
 → Tourteau sauvage de Bretagne. Quasi de veau à la plancha. Framboise
 et litchi.

XX **La Rotonde**   🏠 🅰🅲
 105 bd Montparnasse (6th) – Ⓜ *Vavin*   Plan: **W1**
 – ☎ 01 43 26 68 84 – www.rotondemontparnasse.com
 Menu 44 € *– Carte 30/80 €*
 • Traditional cuisine • Brasserie • Friendly •
 A stone's throw from the theatres of the Rue de la Gaîté, La Rotonde has been
 the incarnation of the very essence of the Parisian brasserie for over a century.
 The decor is typical – very 1930s – all brass fittings and red banquettes, and the
 dishes are brasserie classics, such as Salers beef and oyster platters. Plus, it is
 open until 2am!

X **Le Vitis**   🅰🅲 ✧
☺ *8 r. Falguière (15th)* – Ⓜ *Falguière*   Plan: **V1**
 – ☎ 01 42 73 07 02 – www.levitis.fr – Closed 2 weeks in August,
 24 December-3 January, Sunday and Monday
 Menu 36 € *– Carte 40/48 € – (booking advisable)*
 • Traditional cuisine • Bistro •
 The Delacourcelle brothers, whom we last saw at the Pré Verre in the 5th arrondissement, are back with this pocket-handkerchief bistro. Their tempting selection of skilfully prepared, distinctive dishes include pig's head with date purée
 and melting suckling pig with sweet spices. Superb wine list.

X **Le Timbre**
☺ *3 r. Ste-Beuve (6th)* – Ⓜ *Notre-Dame des Champs*   Plan: **W1**
 – ☎ 01 45 49 10 40 – www.restaurantletimbre.com – Closed August, 1 to
 6 January, Sunday and Monday
 Menu 28 € (lunch), 36/45 € *– (booking advisable)*
 • Traditional cuisine • Bistro • Friendly •
 The young chef of this bistro, which is no bigger than a postage stamp, has preserved all the charm of the establishment. Find wooden tables, benches and a
 simple, unpretentious ambience. The chef serves unusual, appetising, market-
 fresh cuisine and Agnès, his partner, will happily guide your choice of wine.

X **Nina**
☺ *139 r. du Château (14th)* – Ⓜ *Mouton Duvernet*   Plan: **V2**
 – ☎ 09 83 01 88 40 – Closed Sunday and Monday
 Menu 19 € (weekday lunch), 22/39 € *– Carte 25/49 €*
 • Creative • Bistro • Trendy •
 The impressive choice of flawlessly cooked, fine produce (stone bass, scorpion
 fish, Galician beef) will already have set your taste buds tingling but Nina's real
 speciality is vegetables, in all forms, shapes, sizes, colours and textures. A
 genuine culinary exploit – well done Nina!

FRANCE - PARIS

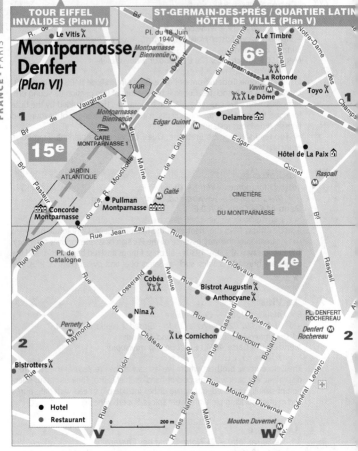

Montparnasse, Denfert
(Plan VI)

TOUR EIFFEL INVALIDES (Plan IV)

ST-GERMAIN-DES-PRÉS / QUARTIER LATIN
HÔTEL DE VILLE (Plan V)

Le Vitis

Pl. du 18 Juin 1940

Montparnasse Bienvenüe

Le Timbre

6e

La Rotonde

Vavin

Le Dôme

Toyo

1

Montparnasse Bienvenüe

GARE MONTPARNASSE 1

15e

Edgar Quinet

Delambre

Edgar

Hôtel de La Paix

Raspail

JARDIN ATLANTIQUE

Gaîté

Pullman Montparnasse

CIMETIÈRE DU MONTPARNASSE

Concorde Montparnasse

Rue Jean Zay

Pl. de Catalogne

Froidevaux

14e

Cobéa

Bistrot Augustin
Anthocyane

Nina

PL. DENFERT ROCHEREAU

Denfert Rochereau

2

Pernety

Le Cornichon

Daguerre

Liancourt

Bistrotters

Mouton Duvernet

● Hotel
● Restaurant

0   200 m

V   W

Bistrotters   AC

9 r. Decrès (14th) – Ⓜ Plaisance   Plan: **V2**
– ☎ 01 45 45 58 59 – www.bistrotters.com – Closed 24 December-
2 January, Sunday and Monday
Menu 23 € (weekday lunch)/36 €
• Modern cuisine • Bistro • Simple •
A very lovely find in the southern reaches of the 14th arrondissement, close
to métro Plaisance. The values of bistronomie and Epicureanism are at the
fore with hearty, elaborate fare made from fine ingredients (small producers
from the Île-de-France area are preferred). Bistro interior and laid-back service.

FRANCE - PARIS

✗ **Anthocyane** 🕸 AC
63 r. Daguerre (14th) – Ⓜ *Denfert-Rochereau*   Plan: **W2**
– 🕾 01 43 27 86 02 – Closed 3 weeks in August, 1 week
Christmas Holidays, Sunday and Monday
Menu 39 € 🍷 (weekday lunch), 62/97 € 🍷 – Carte 62/70 €
• Modern cuisine • Contemporary décor •

An experienced Italian chef prepares heart-warming modern food (crispy squid with basil and caper mash, cod fillets and emerald vegetables, melted chocolate soufflé), served in a restaurant with contemporary decor. A fine wine list and modest prices, particularly at lunchtime, add the final touch to this engaging portrait.

✗ **Bistrot Augustin** 🕽 ᕘ AC
79 r. Daguerre (14th) – Ⓜ *Gaîté*   Plan: **W2**
– 🕾 01 43 21 92 29 – www.augustin-bistrot.fr
– Closed Sunday
Menu 39 € – Carte 46/67 €
• Traditional cuisine • Bistro • Friendly •

This chic bistro with an intimate interior proposes market (and seasonal) cuisine with southern influences to whet the appetite. An example: the superb Périgord pork chop... Ingredients take pride of place here, and our taste buds aren't complaining!

✗ **Toyo** AC ⇔
17 r. Jules-Chaplain (6th) – Ⓜ *Vavin – 🕾 01 43 54 28 03*   Plan: **W1**
– www.restaurant-toyo.com – Closed 2 weeks in August, Monday lunch
and Sunday
Menu 39 € (lunch), 49/130 €
• Creative • Design • Minimalist •

In a former life, Toyomitsu Nakayama was the private chef for the couturier Kenzo. Nowadays, he excels in the art of fusing flavours and textures from France and Asia to create dishes that are both fresh and delicate.

✗ **Le Cornichon**
34 r. Gassendi (14th) – Ⓜ *Denfert Rochereau*   Plan: **W2**
– 🕾 01 43 20 40 19 – www.lecornichon.fr – Closed August, 1 week
Christmas Holidays, Saturday and Sunday
Menu 35 € (lunch)/37 € – Carte approx. 59 €
• Modern cuisine • Bistro • Friendly •

This business is run by two real food lovers: the first is a computer engineer who has always wanted to get into the restaurant business and the second is a well-trained young chef. They came together to create this bistro with a very modern feel. With its fine ingredients, appealing dishes and full flavours, Le Cornichon is sure to win you over!

MARAIS – BASTILLE – GARE DE LYON   **PLAN VII**

🏨 **Pavillon de la Reine** 🕸 ᕘ AC ᘚ 🚗
28 pl. des Vosges (3rd) – Ⓜ *Bastille – 🕾 01 40 29 19 19*   Plan: **Y2**
– www.pavillon-de-la-reine.com
51 rm – ♦330/890 € ♦♦330/890 € – � 35 € – 5 suites
• Luxury • Historic • Personalised •

The elegance and noble discretion of historical Paris. Beyond the arches of the Place des Vosges, the first flash of inspiration comes at the sight of the beautiful leafy courtyard, and the refined guestrooms are cause for further delight. Luxury without ostentation!

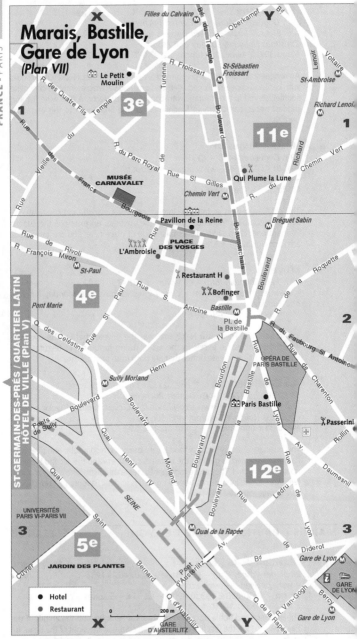

Marais, Bastille, Gare de Lyon
(Plan VII)

Le Petit Moulin

MUSÉE CARNAVALET

Pavillon de la Reine

L'Ambroisie

PLACE DES VOSGES

St-Paul

Restaurant H

Bofinger

Bastille

Pl. de la Bastille

Qui Plume la Lune

Bréguet Sabin

OPÉRA DE PARIS BASTILLE

Paris Bastille

Passerini

Sully Morland

ST-GERMAIN-DES-PRÉS / QUARTIER LATIN HÔTEL DE VILLE (Plan V)

Pont Marie

UNIVERSITÉS PARIS VI-PARIS VII

JARDIN DES PLANTES

SEINE

Quai de la Rapée

Pont d'Austerlitz

GARE D'AUSTERLITZ

GARE DE LYON

Gare de Lyon

3e

11e

4e

12e

5e

● Hotel
● Restaurant

0   200 m

FRANCE - PARIS

Le Petit Moulin ⚐

29 r. du Poitou (3rd) – Ⓜ *St-Sébastien Froissart*   Plan: **X1**
– ℰ 01 42 74 10 10 – www.hoteldupetitmoulin.com
17 rm – ♦185/495 € ♦♦185/495 € – ⌷ 16 €
• Luxury • Personalised •

Christian Lacroix is behind the unique and refined decor in this hotel in the Marais, which plays on the contrasts between the traditional and the modern. Every bedroom is a delight, with vibrant tones and free-standing bathtubs.

Paris Bastille ♿ ⚐ 🛁

67 r. de Lyon (12th) – Ⓜ *Bastille* – ℰ *01 40 01 07 17*   Plan: **Y2**
– www.hotelparisbastille.com
37 rm – ♦82/332 € ♦♦85/332 € – ⌷ 15 €
• Business • Functional • Contemporary •

Fine fabrics, exotic woods and selected hues characterise the bedrooms and the breakfast room in this comfortable modern hotel opposite Opera Bastille.

L'Ambroisie (Bernard Pacaud) ⚐ 🍽

9 pl. des Vosges (4th) – Ⓜ *St-Paul*   Plan: **X2**
– ℰ 01 42 78 51 45 – www.ambroisie-paris.com
– Closed 5 to 20 February, 1 to 8 May, 6 to 28 August, Sunday and Monday
Carte 205/330 € – *(booking advisable)*
• Classic cuisine • Luxury • Elegant •

Ambrosia was the food of the gods on Mount Olympus. Without question, the cuisine of Bernard Pacaud reaches similar heights, with its explosion of flavours, its scientific approach and its perfect execution. Incomparable classicism and an immortal feast for the senses in the regal setting of a townhouse on Place des Vosges.
➝ Feuillantine de langoustines aux graines de sésame, sauce au curry. Escalopine de bar à l'émincé d'artichaut, caviar golden. Tarte fine sablée au chocolat, glace à la vanille Bourbon.

Bofinger ⚐ ⇔ 🍽 (dinner)

5 r. de la Bastille (4th) – Ⓜ *Bastille* – ℰ *01 42 72 87 82*   Plan: **Y2**
– www.bofingerparis.com
Menu 38 € – Carte 40/80 €
• Traditional cuisine • Brasserie • Historic •

This is a real Paris institution with striking, Alsace-style decor, including a dome, inlaid wood, mirrors, and paintings by Hansi. Opened in 1864, this brasserie is as charming as ever.

Qui plume la Lune (Jacky Ribault) ⇗

50 r. Amelot (11th) – Ⓜ *Chemin Vert*   Plan: **Y1**
– ℰ 01 48 07 45 48 – www.quiplumelalune.fr
– Closed 23 July-15 August, 1 to 9 January, Sunday, Monday and Tuesday
Menu 60 € *(weekday lunch)*/130 € – *(booking advisable)*
• Modern cuisine • Cosy •

First, there is the place itself, which is very pretty, inviting and romantic and then there is the food, which is created by a passionate cook. It is fresh, full of vitality and made with carefully selected ingredients (organic produce, great vegetables etc). An enjoyable culinary moment.
➝ Raviole d'huîtres, citron confit, fromage blanc, herbes et plantes sauvages. Filet de rouget à l'anis vert et au yuzu, sésame noir et mangue fraîche. Sorbet au citron jaune, lait émulsionné, macaron à l'azuki et coriandre fraîche.

X
දි **Restaurant H** (Hubert Duchenne) &. AC
13 r. Jean-Beausire (4th) – Ⓜ Bastille – ℰ 01 43 48 80 96 Plan: **Y2**
– www.restauranth.com – Closed 3 weeks in August, 1 week Christmas
Holidays, Sunday and Monday
Menu 30 € (lunch), 50/70 € – *(booking advisable)*
• Creative • Cosy • Intimate •

A good restaurant near Bastille may sound like a contradiction in terms, but at this eatery with barely 20 places, diners tuck into a single set menu (for example: mussels, cream of parsley and samphire greens). "H" stands for Hubert Duchenne, a young chef who learned the ropes from Akrame Benallal and Jean-François Piège. Inventive and skilful cooking.
➔ Cuisine du marché.

X **Passerini** &. AC
65 r. Traversière (12th) – Ⓜ Ledru Rollin Plan: **Y3**
– ℰ 01 43 42 27 56 – www.passerini.paris – Closed 3 weeks in August,
Tuesday lunch, Sunday and Monday
Menu 30 € (lunch)/48 € (lunch) – Carte dinner 44/92 €
• Italian • Contemporary décor • Friendly •

An Italian feel reigns in this nicely renovated former café. Tuck into aptly named "grosses pièces" (generous platters of fish and poultry) for sharing, or other dishes bursting with freshness and good ideas, such as roast guinea fowl, leeks, spinach and hazelnut, or tagliolini, marinated John Dory with sage and lemon.

MONTMARTRE – PIGALLE PLAN VIII

 Terrass' Hôtel ⌂ &. AC ⚐
12 r. J.-de-Maistre (18th) – Ⓜ Place de Clichy Plan: **Z1**
– ℰ 01 46 06 72 85 – www.terrass-hotel.com
92 rm ⌐ – †150/400 € ††160/450 € – 6 suites
• Traditional • Business • Personalised •

A few minutes from Montmartre cemetery, this hotel was entirely revamped in 2015. The interior now sports an eclectic mixture of Scandinavian and industrial influences, while the rooms echo the neighbourhood's bohemian artistic spirit.

 Relais Montmartre ⚐ AC
6 r. Constance (18th) – Ⓜ Abbesses – ℰ 01 70 64 25 25 Plan: **Z2**
– www.relaismontmartre.fr
26 rm – †119/249 € ††119/249 € – ⌐ 15 €
• Business • Traditional • Cosy •

Not far from the shops on rue Lepic, this small hotel is a somewhat unexpected find in such a lively district. It is full of character and has all the charm of a bourgeois house. It offers charming guestrooms embellished with period furniture, not to mention the welcome peace and quiet.

XX **La Table d'Eugène** (Geoffroy Maillard)
දි *18 r. Eugène-Sue (18th) – Ⓜ Jules Joffrin* Plan: **AA 1**
– ℰ 01 42 55 61 64 – www.latabledeugene.com – Closed August, 1 week
Christmas Holidays, Sunday and Monday
Menu 42 € (lunch), 89/120 € – *(booking advisable)*
• Modern cuisine • Design • Fashionable •

Without any difficulty, Geoffroy Maillard – who already had a stint at Frechon behind him – has propelled his charming Table d'Eugène to rank among the best. Good news for the 18th arrondissement, and all foodies! He creates very fresh food, bursting with flavours and colour, which is hearty even in its subtlety. Power and finesse.
➔ Calamar, chou-fleur et yuzu. Agneau en deux cuissons, jeunes carottes aux épices. Sphère chocolat et fève tonka.

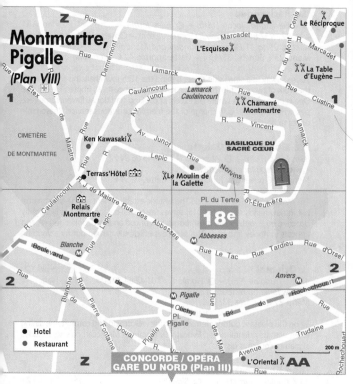

Montmartre, Pigalle
(Plan VIII)

XX

Chamarré Montmartre

📇 🍴 AC ♿

52 r. Lamarck (18th) – Ⓜ Lamarck Caulaincourt   Plan: **AA1**
– ℰ 01 42 55 05 42 – www.chamarre-montmartre.com
Menu 32 € (lunch), 45/70 € – Carte 60/80 €
• Creative • Fashionable •

This contemporary restaurant on Montmartre hill serves creative cuisine with a blend of culinary influences. Dishes include Seychelles-style sea bass, lobster in a calamansi sauce and rum baba, all of which can be enjoyed on the attractive terrace.

X

L'Esquisse

151 bis r. Marcadet (18th) – Ⓜ Lamarck-Caulaincourt   Plan: **AA1**
– ℰ 01 53 41 63 04 – Closed 3 weeks in August,
Sunday and Monday
Menu 22 € (weekday lunch) – Carte 34/46 €
• Modern cuisine • Bistro • Fashionable •

Two young enthusiastic food lovers have pooled their talents to create this inviting vintage bistro with solid wooden floors and benches. The eye-catching, no-frills dishes pay tribute to the high quality produce. Flawlessly cooked with contrasting seasonings. Delicious!

245

X

😋

Le Réciproque

14 r. Ferdinand-Flocon (18th) – Ⓜ Jules Joffrin   Plan: **AA1**
– ℰ 09 86 37 80 77 – www.lereciproque.com – Closed mid-July to early
August, 25 to 31 December, Sunday and Monday
Menu 23 € (lunch), 35/49 € – Carte approx. 42 € – *(booking advisable)*
• Traditional cuisine • Bistro • Contemporary décor •

Tucked away in a small side street behind the 18th town hall, this restaurant is
the work of two youthful partners, each of whom boasts an impressive résumé.
One is in the kitchen where he excels at cooking traditional, flavoursome recipes, while the other is in charge of the friendly, courteous service. Reasonable
prices to boot!

X

Le Moulin de la Galette

83 r. Lepic (18th) – Ⓜ Abbesses – ℰ 01 46 06 84 77   Plan: **AA1**
– www.lemoulindelagalette.fr
Menu 29 € (weekday lunch)/38 € – Carte 41/59 €
• Traditional cuisine • Bistro • Elegant •

The Moulin de la Galette is back! The historic establishment on the Montmartre
hill, in new hands since late 2015, serves fresh, well-balanced dishes like lightly
poached eggs with girolle mushrooms, loin of cod and raw-cooked fennel, and
apricots in honey and basil. The service is efficiently carried out by a youthful
team.

X

L'Oriental

47 av. Trudaine (9th) – Ⓜ Pigalle – ℰ 01 42 64 39 80   Plan: **AA2**
– www.loriental-restaurant.com
Menu 37 € – Carte 33/52 €
• North African • Exotic décor •

Sit on the pleasant outdoor terrace or in the welcoming and comfortable dining
room with its oriental decor. Evocatively flavoured Moroccan cuisine, includes
signature couscous dishes.

X

Ken Kawasaki

15 r. Caulaincourt (18th) – Ⓜ Blanche   Plan: **Z1**
– ℰ 09 70 95 98 32 – www.kenkawasaki.fr – Closed 3 weeks in July,
2 weeks in December, Wednesday lunch, Thursday lunch, Saturday lunch
and Sunday
Menu 30 € (lunch), 45/70 € – *(booking advisable)*
• Creative • Minimalist •

This establishment invites you to celebrate a splendid marriage between Japanese and French cuisine. Japanese chef Ken Kawasaki has put together a fine
team, who together prepare exquisitely graphic dishes, full of unusual flavours
using market-fresh ingredients. Simply excellent.

OUTSIDE CENTRAL AREA   PLAN I

St-James Paris

43 av. Bugeaud (16th) ✉ 75116 – Ⓜ Porte Dauphine   Plan: **A2**
– ℰ 01 44 05 81 81 – www.saint-james-paris.com
15 rm – †385/1690 € ††385/1690 € – 🍴 36 € – 34 suites
• Historic • Luxury • Personalised •

This superb late-19C mansion has been given a new look by designer Bambi
Sloan. Napoleon-III style flirts with a very British brand of originality and includes
lovely materials and shimmering prints. There is a delightful library, a majestic
staircase and some fabulous collections of books. The blueprint for a unique
place.
 St-James Paris – See restaurant listing

FRANCE - PARIS

Pullman Paris Centre-Bercy ✿ 𝐿𝑎 & 🅰𝒸 𝔰𝔞

1 r. de Libourne (12th) – Ⓜ *Cour St-Émilion* Plan: **D3**
– ☎ 01 44 67 34 00 – www.pullmanhotels.com
396 rm ⌷ – **♦**110/600 € **♦♦**120/705 € – 20 suites
• Business • Chain • Contemporary •

Between Bercy village (home to shops, cinemas and restaurants) and the Seine, this huge glass edifice can be seen from all around! The rooms are very comfortable and those on the upper floors command a fine view of Paris.

Square ✿ ⓦ & 🅰𝒸 𝔰𝔞 ☎

3 r. Boulainvilliers (16th) ✉ *75016 –* Ⓜ *Mirabeau* Plan: **A2**
– ☎ 01 44 14 91 90 – www.hotelsquare.com
22 rm – **♦**180/660 € **♦♦**180/660 € – ⌷ 20 €
• Luxury • Design •

This contemporary hotel is located just opposite the Maison de la Radio. It has guestrooms that are spacious and quiet, thanks to the excellent soundproofing. The hi-tech facilities and modern art collection underline the Square's boutique hotel image.

Molitor ✿ ⓦ ⌁ 🖽 & 🅰𝒸 𝔰𝔞 🐾

2 av. de la Porte-Molitor (16th) ✉ *75016* Plan: **A2**
– Ⓜ *Michel Ange Molitor – ☎ 01 56 07 08 69 – www.mltr.fr*
117 rm ⌷ – **♦**250/700 € **♦♦**480/1400 € – 7 suites
• Luxury • Townhouse • Design •

A true emblem of western Paris since the 1920s, the Piscine Molitor was resurrected in 2014 and has been converted into a gorgeous luxury hotel. There are nods to its history with the blue and yellow façade around the pool and the restaurant's decoration, along with ultra-modern minimalism in the guestrooms.

Kube ✿ 𝐿𝑎 & 🅰𝒸 𝔰𝔞 🐾 ☎

1-5 passage Ruelle (18th) – Ⓜ *La Chapelle* Plan: **C1**
– ☎ 01 42 05 20 00 – www.kubehotel-paris.com – Closed August
39 rm – **♦**159/449 € **♦♦**159/449 € – ⌷ 18 €
• Luxury • Design • Minimalist •

Although not located in one of the city's most attractive districts, this resolutely 21C hotel with its designer look and hi-tech gadgetry, will appeal to a more contemporary clientele. Transparent glass, clean white lines and loft-style guestrooms provide the decor in this cutting-edge property. It has a restaurant, as well as two bars, including the Ice Kube (-10°C, warm clothing provided!).

Novotel Tour Eiffel ✿ ≤ 𝐿𝑎 🕊 🖽 & 🅰𝒸 𝔰𝔞 ☎

61 quai de Grenelle (15th) – Ⓜ *Bir-Hakeim* Plan: **A2**
– ☎ 01 40 58 20 00 – www.novotel-paris-toureiffel.com
758 rm – **♦**140/375 € **♦♦**140/375 € – ⌷ 20 € – 6 suites
• Chain • Business • Contemporary •

This contemporary-style Novotel overlooking the Seine and surrounded by 1970s high-rise buildings boasts a hi-tech conference centre. The main bonus is that nearly all the guestrooms enjoy views of the river.
Benkay – See restaurant listing

Hôtel de Banville 🅰𝒸

166 bd Berthier (17th) – Ⓜ *Porte de Champerret* Plan: **B1**
– ☎ 01 42 67 70 16 – www.hotelbanville.fr
38 rm ⌷ – **♦**125/350 € **♦♦**125/350 €
• Luxury • Boutique hotel • Personalised •

This charming boutique hotel is decorated with great taste, and guestrooms are embellished with shiny wood and opulent detail. Jazz evenings in the piano-bar every Tuesday.

FRANCE - PARIS

Vice Versa

213 r. de la Croix-Nivert (15th) – Ⓜ *Porte de Versailles* Plan: **A3**
– ℰ *01 55 76 55 55* – *www.viceversahotel.com*
37 rm – ✝100/315 € ✝✝120/365 € – ⌶ 15 €
• Townhouse • Personalised • Design •

Greed, gluttony, pride, lust, wrath, sloth and envy: the guestrooms of this hotel decorated by Chantal Thomass illustrate the seven deadly sins! To get here, cross the hall with its heavenly feel. However, if you go down to the basement to visit the hammam, you will find yourself in hell... Diabolically inspired!

Fabric

31 r. de la Folie-Méricourt (11th) – Ⓜ *Saint-Ambroise* Plan: **C2**
– ℰ *01 43 57 27 00* – *www.hotelfabric.com*
33 rm – ✝200/380 € ✝✝200/380 € – ⌶ 18 €
• Townhouse • Design • Contemporary •

In a former textile factory, lying halfway between République and Bastille, this beautiful hotel has retained some of its industrial heritage. Find elegant, designer guestrooms, as well as iron girders and light fixtures, antique furniture and a palette of grey tones.

Mama Shelter

109 r. de Bagnolet (20th) – Ⓜ *Gambetta* Plan: **D2**
– ℰ *01 43 48 48 48* – *www.mamashelter.com*
172 rm – ✝79/399 € ✝✝89/399 € – ⌶ 16 € – 1 suite
• Townhouse • Design •

Philippe Starck is behind the refined, fantasy decor in this huge hotel, which is at the cutting edge of contemporary design. It is characterised by a young and slightly bohemian atmosphere in keeping with this district, which is enjoying an urban revival.

Holiday Inn Express Canal de la Villette

68 quai de Seine (19th) – Ⓜ *Crimée* – ℰ *01 44 65 01 01*
– *www.holidayinnexpress.com/paris-canal* Plan: **D1**
144 rm ⌶ – ✝89/299 € ✝✝89/299 €
• Business • Chain • Contemporary •

Those who enjoy a stroll around the Bassin de la Villette know this building well: its twin (a warehouse dating from 1853) still stands on the opposite bank. The hotel, rebuilt in 2008, is striking for its unusual metal cladding and has a warm, friendly atmosphere. Some of the spacious guestrooms overlook the water.

Le 20 Prieuré Hôtel

20 r. Grand-Prieuré (11th) – Ⓜ *Oberkampf* Plan: **C2**
– ℰ *01 47 00 74 14* – *www.hotel20prieure.com*
32 rm – ✝99/189 € ✝✝99/199 € – ⌶ 13 €
• Traditional • Contemporary •

This hotel subscribes to the urban contemporary look and offers small yet agreeable rooms which feature shades of white, designer furniture, and huge photos of Paris.

XxXxX Le Pré Catelan

✿✿✿ *in Bois de Boulogne - rte de Suresnes (16th)* ✉ *75016* Plan: **A2**
– ℰ *01 44 14 41 14* – *www.precatelanparis.com* – *Closed 5 to 20 February, 6 to 28 August, 29 October-6 November, Sunday and Monday*
Menu 130 € (lunch), 220/280 € – Carte 250/315 €
• Creative • Luxury • Elegant •

Based on classic recipes that pay homage to the local produce, Frédéric Anton's inventive cuisine is perfectly accomplished. Each dish is a masterpiece, to be enjoyed to the full amid a magnificent decor of white and silver in the heart of the Bois de Boulogne.

→ Crabe, crème légère à l'aneth, caviar de France, soupe au parfum de fenouil. Cabillaud aux algues, beurre aux zestes de citron vert. Pomme soufflée croustillante, crème glacée au caramel, cidre et sucre pétillant.

FRANCE - PARIS

La Grande Cascade 🍴🍴🍴 ⛄ 😋🏠⬧🏠 🅿

in Bois de Boulogne - allée de Longchamp (16th) ✉ *75016*
– ☎ 01 45 27 33 51 – www.restaurantsparisiens.com – Closed
19 December-14 January
Menu 89/192 € – Carte 169/216 €
• Modern cuisine • Classic décor • Elegant •

A charming pavilion (1850) just a stone's throw from the large waterfall (Grande Cascade) in the Bois de Boulogne. To savour the refined cuisine here beneath the majestic rotunda or on the delightful terrace is a rare and elegant treat.
→ Tourteau de Bretagne au naturel, avocat et caviar osciètre royal. Carré d'agneau du pays d'Oc, tomates, olives de Kalamata et prune noire. Baba au rhum ambré et chantilly.

St-James Paris – Hôtel St-James Paris 🍴🍴🍴 🍺🏠🔳⬧🅿

43 av. Bugeaud (16th) ✉ *75116 –* Ⓜ *Porte Dauphine* Plan: A2
– ☎ 01 44 05 81 88 – www.saint-james-paris.com – Closed lunch and
Sunday dinner
Menu 130 € – Carte 95/155 €
• Modern cuisine • Classic décor • Elegant •

An exclusive hotel with the atmosphere of an English member's-only club. The setting is superb, as chic as it is elegant with its wood panelling, golden brown fabrics, trompe-l'oeil ceiling and very secret garden. The food is in keeping with the rest: delicate, precise and finely composed. A place with plenty of good taste!
→ Velouté glacé aux huîtres, pomme de terre et caviar. Homard mijoté, émulsion de jus des carcasses façon cappuccino à l'estragon. Fraîcheur de fruits de saison au parfum de verveine.

Relais d'Auteuil (Patrick Pignol) 🍴🍴 ⛄🔳🍺

31 bd Murat (16th) ✉ *75016 –* Ⓜ *Michel Ange Molitor* Plan: A2
– ☎ 01 46 51 09 54 – www.relaisdauteuil-pignol.fr
– Closed August, Christmas Holidays, Saturday lunch, Sunday
and Monday
Menu 100 € 🍷 (lunch)/135 € – Carte 90/155 €
• Modern cuisine • Intimate • Classic décor •

This restaurant's intimate setting highlights the numerous modern paintings and sculptures on display. The fine contemporary cuisine is inspired by top quality produce, including game in season. Superb wine list, as well as an impressive choice of champagnes.
→ Encornets farcis aux oignons doux des Cévennes, senteurs de speck. Côte et filet d'agneau des Pyrénées rôtis, jus aux brins de sarriette. Feuillantine croustillante aux fruits de saison parfumés aux épices.

Le Quinzième - Cyril Lignac 🍴🍴 🏠🔳⬧🍺

14 r. Cauchy (15th) – Ⓜ *Javel* Plan: A2-3
– ☎ 01 45 54 43 43
– www.restaurantlequinzieme.com
– Closed 3 weeks in August, Saturday and Sunday
Menu 65 € (lunch), 130/160 €
• Modern cuisine • Elegant •

Cyril Lignac has definitely perfected the art of creating distinctive cuisine. Not only are his dishes visually striking, the combination of unusual, complimentary flavours is heavenly. An example: three super-fresh, juicy scallops served with a purée of carrot and Corsican clementines.
→ Foie gras poêlé, condiment citron vert et vinaigrette aigre-douce. Ris de veau rôti au beurre demi-sel, crème au vin jaune et fine raviole de betterave blanche. Poire comice, chantilly légère au citron yuzu, marmelade et sorbet poire.

XxX　**Benkay** – Novotel Tour Eiffel　　　　　　　　⪬ & 🄰🄲 ⇆ 🕭
61 quai de Grenelle (15th) – **Ⓜ** *Bir-Hakeim*　　　Plan: **A2**
– ☏ 01 40 58 21 26 – www.restaurant-benkay.com – Closed 2 weeks in
August
Menu 100/160 € – Carte 44/77 €
• Japanese • Elegant • Elegant •
On the banks of the Seine, with a view over the river, the elegant Benkay artfully honours Japanese gastronomy. You can opt for the teppanyaki (the hot plate where the dishes are cooked in front of you) or the 'washoku' (table service) - not to mention the sushi counter, which is simply divine.

XX　**Au Trou Gascon**　　　　　　　　　　　　🕸 🄰🄲
✿　*40 r. Taine (12th)* – **Ⓜ** *Daumesnil*　　　　　Plan: **D3**
– ☏ 01 43 44 34 26 – www.autrougascon.fr
– Closed August, 1 to 7 January, Saturday and Sunday
Menu 42 € (lunch)/68 € – Carte 65/80 €
• Cuisine from South West France • Elegant •
This institution, dedicated to the cuisine of Southwest France, transports diners to the area between the River Adour and the ocean. It has earned the loyalty of many long-standing regulars with its pâté en croûte with duck foie gras, lièvre à la royale (hare), and warm and crusty tourtière - not to mention the ever-popular cassoulet.
→ Gambas vapeur en crème de tête, chutney de billes de melon et gaspacho safrané au pistou. Agneau de lait rôti, petits farcis en surprise. Pêche blanche de vigne pochée, mini baba et granité Bellini.

XX　**L'Archeste** (Yoshiaki Ito)　　　　　　　　& 🄰🄲
✿　*79 r. de la Tour (16th)* – **Ⓜ** *Rue de la Pompe*　Plan: **A2**
– ☏ 01 40 71 69 68 – www.archeste.com – Closed Saturday lunch, Sunday
and Monday
Menu 38 € (weekday lunch), 56/96 € – (booking advisable)
• Modern cuisine • Minimalist • Contemporary décor •
This restaurant has a refined interior and food to match. It is the brainchild of the chef formerly at Hiramatsu. Bonito fish, vegetables and celeriac; pigeon, ceps, mixed green salad: there is no à la carte here, only the set menus, evolving daily with the seasons and the chef's moods. Precise and modern. A delight.
→ Cuisine du marché.

XX　**A et M Restaurant**　　　　　　　　　　🕸 🕭
136 bd. Murat (16th) ✉ *75016* – **Ⓜ** *Porte de St-Cloud*　Plan: **A3**
– ☏ 01 45 27 39 60 – www.am-restaurant.paris – Closed August, Saturday
lunch and Sunday
Menu 38 € – Carte 46/69 €
• Modern cuisine • Elegant • Friendly •
A true chef's bistro in a chic and welcoming setting. The menu includes dishes such as calf's head with a ravigote sauce, and velouté of Paimpol beans with haddock. The menu offers excellent value for money for a Parisian restaurant.

XX　**L'Inattendu**　　　　　　　　　　　　　🄰🄲
99 r. Blomet (15th) – **Ⓜ** *Vaugirard* – ☏ *01 55 76 93 12*　Plan: **B3**
– www.restaurant-inattendu.fr – Closed Sunday and Monday
Menu 25 € (weekdays)/37 €
• Traditional cuisine • Cosy •
This small, elegantly decorated restaurant is run by two experienced partners who have opened a fishmonger's next door – a real guarantee of fresh produce! Reliable, well-presented cuisine with the occasional unexpected surprise.

FRANCE - PARIS

Bon Kushikatsu   ♿ 🄰🄲

24 r. Jean-Pierre-Timbaud (11th) – Ⓜ *Oberkampf*   Plan: **C2**
– ✆ 01 43 38 82 27 – Closed Sunday
Menu 30 € (weekday lunch)/60 € *– (booking advisable)*
• Japanese • Intimate • Elegant •

This restaurant is an express trip to Osaka to discover the city's culinary speciality of *kushikatsu* (meat, vegetables or seafood skewers coated with breadcrumbs and deep-fried). Dish after dish reveals fine flavours, such as: beef sancho, peppered foie gras, and shiitake mushrooms. The courteous service transports you to Japan.

Table - Bruno Verjus   🕸 ✿

3 r. de Prague (12th) – Ⓜ *Ledru Rollin*   Plan: **C2**
– ✆ 01 43 43 12 26 – www.tablerestaurant.fr – Closed 3 weeks in August, Saturday lunch and Sunday
Carte 62/82 € *– (booking advisable)*
• Modern cuisine • Design • Trendy •

Choosing the finest ingredients and cooking them humbly is the way of Bruno Verjus – a remarkable character, entrepreneur, blogger and food critic... turned chef! His dishes are full of energy and flavour, and reveal a rich interplay of textures, hinting at the chef's sincere and contagious passion.

Septime (Bertrand Grébaut)   ✿

80 r. de Charonne (11th) – Ⓜ *Charonne*   Plan: **D2**
– ✆ 01 43 67 38 29 – www.septime-charonne.fr – Closed 3 weeks in August, Monday lunch, Saturday and Sunday
Menu 32 € (lunch)/70 € *– (booking advisable)*
• Modern cuisine • Contemporary décor •

Since 2011, when this restaurant opened, word of mouth has spread throughout the city and beyond. The key to its success? The neo-industrial decor, resolutely seasonal cuisine and high quality ingredients. Professionalism and simplicity all in one!
➜ Cuisine du marché.

La Fourchette du Printemps (Nicolas Mouton)   🄰🄲

30 r. du Printemps (17th) – Ⓜ *Wagram*   Plan: **B1**
– ✆ 01 42 27 26 97 – www.lafourchetteduprintemps.com – Closed August, Sunday and Monday
Menu 30 € (weekday lunch), 55/75 € – Carte approx. 62 € *– (booking advisable)*
• Modern cuisine • Bistro • Friendly •

Whatever the season, this contemporary bistro stands out from the crowd. The young chef, an alumnus of some top restaurants, hones ingredients to reveal lovely flavours - surrounded by unpretentious decor that matches the laid-back service. Here, taste goes hand in hand with simplicity.
➜ Raviole ouverte de tourteau, mangue, pomme verte, avocat et crumble de fruits secs. Saint-pierre poêlé aux olives taggiasche, risotto crémeux et jus de coques monté au beurre. Sphère citron et verveine.

La Régalade   🕸 🄰🄲

49 av. Jean-Moulin (14th) – Ⓜ *Porte d'Orléans*   Plan: **B3**
– ✆ 01 45 45 68 58 – www.laregalade.paris – Closed 31 July-20 August, Monday lunch, Saturday and Sunday
Menu 37 € *– (booking advisable)*
• Traditional cuisine • Friendly •

A friendly and relaxed bistro serving well-presented and copious seasonal cuisine accompanied by an astutely compiled choice of wines. La Régalade is always full and it is easy to see why. Make sure you book ahead!

FRANCE - PARIS

La Marée Passy

71 av. Paul-Doumer (16th) ✉ *75016 –* Ⓜ *La Muette*   Plan: **A2**
– ☎ 01 45 04 12 81 – www.lamareepassy.com
Carte 45/60 €
• Seafood • Friendly •

With its wood panelling, red tones and maritime-inspired backdrop, the decor is in perfect harmony with the cuisine, which focuses on fish and seafood. The daily specials board changes according to deliveries from the Atlantic coast.

L'Envie du Jour

106 r. Nollet (17th) – Ⓜ *Brochant – ☎ 01 42 26 01 02*   Plan: **B1**
– www.lenviedujour.com – Closed Sunday and Monday
Menu 32/44 €
• Modern cuisine • Friendly • Fashionable •

This restaurant is the brainchild of enthusiastic young chef Sergio Dias Lino. All eyes are on the kitchens, which open out onto the small dining room. The cook's movements are the focus, as he carefully prepares his lovely ingredients to bring out their best in the form of colourful and fragrant dishes.

N° 41

41 av. Mozart (16th) ✉ *75016 –* Ⓜ *Ranelagh*   Plan: **A2**
– ☎ 01 45 03 65 16 – Closed 2 weeks in August
Carte 30/50 €
• Traditional cuisine • Bistro •

This pleasant industrial-style bistro serves tasty, quality cuisine, such as eggs baked in ramekins and cream of foie gras. This restaurant has a modern feel and is run by a couple of restaurateurs who are passionate about what they do.

Beurre Noisette

68 r. Vasco-de-Gama (15th) – Ⓜ *Lourmel*   Plan: **A3**
– ☎ 01 48 56 82 49 – Closed 6 to 21 August, Sunday and Monday
Menu 32 € (lunch), 36/55 € – *(booking advisable)*
• Traditional cuisine • Friendly •

A cosy bistro serving delicious food. Thierry Blanqui draws inspiration from the local markets with dishes such as duck and foie gras pâté en croûte, and slow-cooked shoulder of suckling lamb with seasonal vegetables. Even the humblest ingredients are transformed into beautiful dishes. There is plenty to enjoy in this happy marriage of tradition and innovation.

Yard

6 r. Mont-Louis (11th) – Ⓜ *Philippe Auguste*   Plan: **D2**
– ☎ 01 40 09 70 30 – Closed August, 24 to 31 December, Saturday and Sunday
Menu 19 € (lunch) – Carte dinner 33/49 € – *(booking advisable)*
• Modern cuisine • Bistro •

The restaurant is very much of its time with a pretty little façade, an inviting bistro interior and laid-back service. The young British chef produces uninhibited cuisine according to the inspiration of the moment, with dishes such as homemade rabbit ravioli. There's also a friendly tapas bar and a lively pavement terrace.

Clamato

80 r. de Charonne (11th) – Ⓜ *Charonne*   Plan: **D2**
– ☎ 01 43 72 74 53 – www.clamato-charonne.fr – Closed 3 weeks in August, Wednesday lunch, Thursday lunch, Friday lunch, Monday and Tuesday
Carte 34/50 € – *(bookings not accepted)*
• Seafood • Fashionable •

The Septime's little sister is becoming something of a bistronomic hit, thanks to its fashionable interior and concise menu focused on seafood and vegetables. Each ingredient is selected carefully and meals are served in a genuinely friendly atmosphere. No bookings are taken – it's first in, first served!

FRANCE - PARIS

X
☺ ### Jouvence   AC

172 bis r. du Faubourg-St-Antoine (12th)   Plan: **D2**
– ⓜ Faidherbe-Chaligny – ✆ 01 56 58 04 73 – www.jouvence.paris
– Closed 3 weeks in August, Sunday and Monday
Menu 24 € (lunch)/55 € – Carte 35/54 € – *(booking advisable)*
• Modern cuisine • Vintage • Fashionable •
Situated on the corner of rue de Cîteaux, this former apothecary-style shop from
the 1900s does not merely rest on its decorative laurels. They serve contempo-
rary cuisine, replete with quality ingredients, such as prawn tempura, cucumber
kimchi and celery juice. The young chef, formerly with Dutournier (Pinxo restaurant) certainly has talent.

X
Bistrot Paul Bert   ⭐ 🍴

18 r. Paul-Bert (11th) – ⓜ Faidherbe Chaligny   Plan: **D2**
– ✆ 01 43 72 24 01 – Closed Sunday and Monday
Menu 19 € (weekday lunch)/41 € – Carte approx. 50 € – *(booking advisable)*
• Traditional cuisine • Vintage • Bistro •
The façade of this pleasant bistro promises "cuisine familiale". Translate this as:
feuilleté of calf sweetbreads with mushrooms, and roast venison with cranberries and celeriac purée. Generous, tasty dishes are prepared without frills. You
will be asking for more but be sure to save some room for the rum baba!

X
☺ ### Villaret   ⭐ AC 🍴 (dinner)

13 r. Ternaux (11th) – ⓜ Parmentier – ✆ 01 43 57 75 56   Plan: **C2**
– Closed 2 weeks in August, Saturday lunch and Sunday
Menu 27 € (lunch), 35/55 € – Carte 45/59 €
• Traditional cuisine • Friendly • Bistro •
From the moment you arrive, cooking aromas will entice you! This convivial
bistro serves appealing seasonal fare: baked eggs with foie gras, salted monk-
fish, and chocolate biscuits. Good choice of wines.

X
Pramil   AC

9 r. Vertbois (3rd) – ⓜ Temple – ✆ 01 42 72 03 60   Plan: **C2**
*– www.pramil.fr – Closed 2 to 8 May, 14 to 28 August, Sunday lunch and
Monday*
Menu 33 € – Carte 35/45 €
• Modern cuisine • Bistro •
The elegant yet restrained decor helps focus the senses on the attractive and
honest seasonal cuisine conjured up by Alain Pramil. He is a self-taught chef
passionate about food who, in another life, was a physics teacher!

X
L'Ourcine   Plan: **C3**

92 r. Broca (13th) – ⓜ Les Gobelins – ✆ 01 47 07 13 65
*– www.restaurant-lourcine.fr – Closed 3 weeks in August, Sunday and
Monday*
Menu 38 €
• Traditional cuisine • Bistro • Friendly •
Quality and modesty summarise nicely the spirit of L'Ourcine, a pleasant little
bistro which offers inspired, seasonal cuisine. The menu du jour and the 'coups
de cœur' set menu on the blackboard offer an array of great suggestions.

X
☺ ### L'Os à Moelle

3 r. Vasco-de-Gama (15th) – ⓜ Lourmel   Plan: **A3**
*– ✆ 01 45 57 27 27 – Closed 3 weeks in August, Sunday
and Monday*
Menu 35 €
• Traditional cuisine • Friendly • Bistro •
After relinquishing the reins for a few years (so as to focus on his Barbezingue
restaurant in Châtillon), Thierry Faucher is back at L'Os à Moelle, where he was
one of bistronomy's forerunners. This restaurant provides the perfect opportunity to get to grips with his philosophy, which involves restoring bistro cuisine
to its rightful place!

FRANCE - PARIS

X
(a) **Tempero**

5 r. Clisson (13th) – Ⓜ *Chevaleret* – ℰ *09 54 17 48 88*   Plan: **C3**
– *www.tempero.fr* – *Closed August, 1 week Christmas Holidays, Monday dinner, Tuesday dinner, Wednesday dinner, Saturday and Sunday*
Menu 21 € (lunch) – Carte dinner 32/47 € – *(booking advisable)*
• Creative • Bistro • Friendly •

A friendly little bistro, which is rather like its chef, Alessandra Montagne. Originally from Brazil, she worked at some fine Parisian establishments before opening her own place. Here she cooks with market-fresh ingredients, creating invigorating and reasonably priced dishes that draw on French, Brazilian and Asian cooking. A lovely fusion!

X
(a) **Comptoir Tempero**

124 bd Vincent-Auriol (13th) – Ⓜ *Nationale*   Plan: **C3**
– ℰ *01 45 84 15 35* – *www.tempero.fr* – *Closed August, 1 week Christmas Holidays, Monday dinner, Tuesday dinner, Wednesday dinner, Saturday and Sunday*
Menu 21 € (lunch) – Carte 34/46 € – *(booking advisable)*
• Creative • Bistro • Friendly •

Take a seat at one of the tightly packed tables in this friendly restaurant and get ready to sample the brilliant cuisine of Olivier, responsible for the success of parent establishment, the Tempero. Fresh ingredients and a focus on dishes inspired by French and Brazilian classics, with a few nods to Asia. Simply irresistible!

X
(a) **Impérial Choisy**   🅰🅲

32 av. de Choisy (13th) – Ⓜ *Porte de Choisy*   Plan: **C3**
– ℰ *01 45 86 42 40*
Carte 19/40 €
• Chinese • Simple •

A genuine Chinese restaurant frequented by many local Chinese people who use it as their lunchtime canteen. Hardly surprising given the delicious Cantonese specials on offer!

X
(a) **Pho Tai**   🅰🅲 ᛩ

13 r. Philibert-Lucot (13th) – Ⓜ *Maison Blanche*   Plan: **C3**
– ℰ *01 45 85 97 36* – *Closed August and Monday*
Carte 25/35 €
• Vietnamese • Simple •

In a quiet street in the Asian quarter, this small Vietnamese restaurant stands out from the crowd. All credit to the chef, Mr Te, who arrived in France in 1968 and is a magnificent ambassador for Vietnamese cuisine. Dumplings, crispy chicken with fresh ginger, bo bun and phô soups: everything is full of flavour.

X
Mansouria   🅰🅲

11 r. Faidherbe (11th) – Ⓜ *Faidherbe-Chaligny*   Plan: **D2**
– ℰ *01 43 71 00 16* – *www.mansouria.fr* – *Closed Monday lunch and Sunday*
Menu 28/36 € – Carte 35/60 € – *(booking advisable)*
• North African • Oriental décor •

Tajines, couscous, and crème à la fleur d'oranger are among the aromatic dishes prepared by the talented female chefs here under the baton of Fatema Hal, an ethnologist, writer and leading figure in North African gastronomy.

X
Tintilou   ⇔

37 bis r. de Montreuil (11th) – Ⓜ *Faidherbe-Chaligny*   Plan: **D2**
– ℰ *01 43 72 42 32* – *www.letintilou.fr* – *Closed 3 weeks in August, 1 week in January, Monday lunch, Saturday lunch and Sunday*
Menu 25 € (weekday lunch), 36/49 € – Carte 48/60 €
• Modern cuisine • Cosy •

This 16C former *relais de mousquetaires* – frequented by Louis XIII's guards – is elegant and original. The flavoursome cuisine served here evokes travel. The menu is short and changes every month, presenting dishes with enigmatic marriages of flavour: salmon, pumpkin, fennel, botargo; wild duck and cocoa. Tasty simplicity!

Hilton La Défense 🛍 ♨ ⅙ ⅙ 🅰🅲 ♨
2 pl. de la Défense ✉ 92053 – Ⓜ La Défense – ℰ 01 46 92 10 10
– www.hiltonparisladefense.com
153 rm – ⅊155/450 € ⅊⅊170/465 € – ☲ 26 € – 4 suites
• Business • Chain • Contemporary •

Hotel situated within the CNIT complex. Some of the rooms have been particularly designed with the business traveller in mind: work, rest, relaxation and jacuzzi tubs in the bathrooms.

Sofitel Paris La Défense 🛍 ⅙ 🅰🅲 ♨ 🚗
34 cours Michelet (on the ring road, exit La Défense 4) ✉ 92060 Puteaux
– Ⓜ Esplanade de la Défense – ℰ 01 47 76 44 43
– www.sofitel-paris-ladefense.com
151 rm – ⅊180/435 € ⅊⅊180/435 € – ☲ 27 €
• Luxury • Chain • Personalised •

This business hotel not far from the CNIT and Grande Arche blends in perfectly with the high-rise buildings of the Défense district. Spacious, well-equipped guestrooms, as well as a restaurant (Mediterranean cuisine) and a small fitness suite.

PARIS AIRPORT ROISSY

At Roissypole

Hilton Roissy 🛍 ⅙ 🔲 ⅙ 🅰🅲 ♨ 🚗
Roissypôle – ℰ 01 49 19 77 77 – www.hiltonhotels.com/fr_fr
392 rm – ⅊179/809 € ⅊⅊179/809 € – ☲ 25 €
• Chain • Business • Personalised •

There reigns a certain excess in this top-class hotel, which is a veritable modern town within the airport perimeter. It has a huge lobby with a vertiginous glass roof, particularly spacious guestrooms, and many amenities including restaurants, a swimming pool, meeting rooms etc.

Pullman Airport 🛍 ⅙ 🏨 🔲 ⅙ 🅰🅲 ♨ 🚗
3 bis r. de la Haye – ℰ 01 70 03 11 63 – www.pullmanhotels.com
294 rm – ⅊169/450 € ⅊⅊169/450 € – ☲ 26 € – 11 suites
• Business • Contemporary • Design •

A modern and contemporary complex, which is the perfect addition to the hotels on offer around the airport. The guestrooms are elegant and well appointed with wifi, safe, iron, flat screen TV etc. On the lower floors, there is a sauna, a hammam and a large fitness centre.

At Roissy-Ville

Novotel Convention et Wellness 🛍 ⅙ 🌐 🔲 ⅙ 🅰🅲 ♨
10 allée du Verger – ℰ 01 30 18 20 00   🚗
– www.novotel.com/5418
288 rm – ⅊90/215 € ⅊⅊90/215 € – ☲ 20 € – 7 suites
• Chain • Business • Contemporary •

This hotel, which is used to receiving travellers and business clients, has perfectly oiled wheels. Its amenities are at the forefront when it comes to seminar organisation (there's a large space dedicated to fully-equipped meeting rooms) and relaxation (there's a spa and a Novotel Café etc).

Lyons
Lyon

Population: 491 268

Calzada/Fotolia.com

Lyons is a city that needs a second look, because the first one may be to its disadvantage: from the outlying autoroute, drivers get a vision of the petrochemical industry. But strip away that industrial façade and look what lies within: the gastronomic epicentre of France; a wonderfully characterful old town of medieval and Renaissance buildings with a World Heritage Site stamp of approval; and the peaceful flow of two mighty rivers. Lyons largely came of age in the 16C thanks to its silk industry; many of the city's finest buildings were erected by Italian merchants who flocked here at the time. What they left behind was the largest Renaissance quarter in France, with glorious architecture and an imposing cathedral.

Nowadays it's an energised city whose modern industries give it a 21C feel but that hasn't pervaded the three-hour lunch ethos of the older quarters. The rivers Saône and Rhône provide the liquid heart of the city. Modern Lyons in the shape of the new Villeurbanne and La Part Dieu districts are to the east of the Rhône. The medieval sector, the old town, is west of the Saône. Between the two rivers is a peninsula, the Presqu'île, which is indeed almost an island. This area is renowned for its red-roofed 16C and 17C houses. Just north of here on a hill is the old silk-weavers' district, La Croix-Rousse.

LYONS IN...

➜ **ONE DAY**
Old town including funicular up Fourvière hill, Musée des Beaux-Arts.

➜ **TWO DAYS**
Musée des Tissus, La Croix-Rousse, evening river trip, Opera House.

➜ **THREE DAYS**
Traboule hunting (map in hand), antique shops in rue Auguste Comte.

ARRIVAL-DEPARTURE

✈ Lyon Saint Exupéry Airport is 27km east of the city centre.
The Express Bus takes around 45min and runs every 20min.

GETTING AROUND

The transport system in the city includes the funicular, as well as the bus, tram and metro. The 'Liberty' ticket is valid for one day's travel on the network; you can also buy single tickets and a carnet of ten tickets. The Lyons City Card is available for 1, 2 or 3 days, and grants unlimited access to the transport network, plus many museums (including the Roman ruins in St-Romain-en-Gal), short river trips and guided city tours. The card is available from the tourist office and major public transport offices. Lyons boasts one of Europe's biggest 'swipe a bike' schemes: using a smart card, you can help yourself to a bicycle at one of 350 places around town.

CALENDAR HIGHLIGHTS

March
International Fair.

May
Nuits Sonores (Electronic music).

June
Fête de la Musique, Fourvière Festival .

July
Bastille Day celebrations.

September
Lyons Dance Biennial.

October
Red Carpet Antiques Festival.

November
Baroque Music Festival.

December
Festival of Lights.

EATING OUT

Lyons is a great place for food. In the old town virtually every square metre is occupied by a restaurant but if you want a real encounter with the city, step inside a Lyonnais bouchon. These provide the true gastronomic heartbeat of the city - authentic little establishments where the cuisine revolves around the sort of thing the silk workers ate all those years ago: tripe, pigs' trotters, calf's head; fish lovers go for quenelles. For the most atmospheric example of the bouchon, try one in a tunnel-like recess inside a medieval building in the old town. Lyons also has plenty of restaurants serving dishes from every region of France and is a city that loves its wine: it's said that Lyons is kept afloat on three rivers: the Saône, the Rhône and the Beaujolais. Furthermore, the locals still enthusiastically embrace the true concept of lunch and so, unlike in many cities, you can enjoy a midday meal that continues for quite a few hours. With the reputation the city has for its restaurants, it's usually advisable to book ahead.

FRANCE - LYONS

Villa Florentine ✆ ⟨ 🛏 ♨ ℉ ♨ 🛗 ♨ 🚗

25 montée St-Barthélémy ⊠ 69005 – Ⓜ Fourvière Plan: **E2**
– ℰ 04 72 56 56 56 – www.villaflorentine.com
24 rm – ♦195/1200 € ♦♦195/1200 € – ⊊ 27 € – 5 suites
• Historic • Luxury • Romantic •

On the Fourvière hill, this 18C Renaissance-inspired residence enjoys an incomparable view of the town. In the rooms, refinement and classic styling are the watchwords.

❀ **Les Terrasses de Lyon** – See restaurant listing

Cour des Loges ✆ ♨ 🌐 🅰🅲 🛗 🅿

6 r. du Bœuf ⊠ 69005 – Ⓜ Vieux Lyon Plan: **E2**
– ℰ 04 72 77 44 44 – www.courdesloges.com
56 rm ⊊ – ♦222/422 € ♦♦244/704 € – 4 suites
• Luxury • Historic • Personalised •

Vaults, galleries, passages... this magical place has all the character of the Renaissance in the middle of Vieux-Lyon with design and contemporary elegance as a bonus. Trendy bistro ambience and daily changing dishes at the Café-Épicerie. At the Loges, the atmosphere is romantic and the cuisine, creative.

❀ **Les Loges • Café-Épicerie** – See restaurant listing

Collège ♿ 🅰🅲 🛗 🚗

5 pl. St-Paul ⊠ 69005 – Ⓜ Vieux Lyon Plan: **E-F1**
– ℰ 04 72 10 05 05 – www.college-hotel.com
40 rm – ♦130/175 € ♦♦130/175 € – ⊊ 17 €
• Business • Townhouse • Personalised •

Desks, a pommel horse, geography maps: everything here evokes the schools of yesteryear, and all in a designer style. Immaculately white rooms with balcony or terrace and pleasant bar serving 'gôneries' – Lyonnais tapas!

✗✗✗ Têtedoie (Christian Têtedoie) ❀ ⟨ ♿ 🅰🅲 ⇄ 🍴 🅿

❀ *montée du Chemin-Neuf ⊠ 69005 – Ⓜ Minimes* Plan: **E2**
– ℰ 04 78 29 40 10 – www.tetedoie.com
Menu 45 € (weekday lunch), 65/130 € – Carte 90/130 €
• Modern cuisine • Design • Chic •

Perched on Fourvière hill, this restaurant, with its ultra-contemporary design, is a vantage point over the city. Christian Têtedoie applies his talent to exploring French tradition. His signature dish, casseroled lobster and calf's head cromesquis, is quite simply exquisite. At La Terrasse de l'Antiquaille, the Mediterranean has the place of honour.

➜ Foie gras de canard en textures, asperges vertes et marmelade de citron. Cannelloni de tête de veau confite, médaillon, pince et émulsion de homard. Soufflé au Grand Marnier et sorbet à l'orange safrané.

✗✗✗ Les Terrasses de Lyon – Hôtel Villa Florentine ❀ ⟨ 🛏 ♿ 🅰🅲

❀ *25 montée St-Barthélémy ⊠ 69005 – Ⓜ Fourvière* 🅿
– ℰ 04 72 56 56 02 – www.villaflorentine.com Plan: **E2**
– Closed Sunday and Monday
Menu 49 € (lunch), 89/115 € – Carte 105/125 €
• Classic cuisine • Elegant • Luxury •

In the heights of Fourvière; an elegant restaurant with a splendid view of the city. Classical cooking which places the emphasis on quality regional produce.

➜ Quenelle de langoustines, courgette beurre et morilles au vin jaune. Pigeon fumé aux sarments de vigne, courgettes grises et tomates de pleine terre. Soufflé au chocolat kalapaia, glace à la fève tonka.

Old Town, Bellecour, Hôtel de Ville
(Plan II)

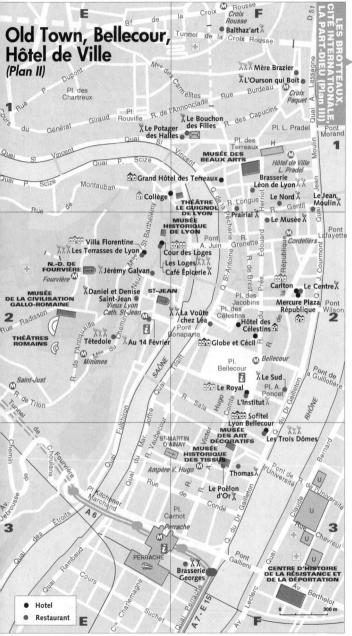

Balthaz'art
Mère Brazier
L'Ourson qui Boit
Croix Paquet
Le Bouchon des Filles
Le Potager des Halles
Pl. des Terreaux
MUSÉE DES BEAUX ARTS
Hôtel de Ville L. Pradel
Brasserie Léon de Lyon
Grand Hôtel des Terreaux
Collège
Le Nord
Le Jean Moulin
THÉÂTRE LE GUIGNOL DE LYON
MUSÉE HISTORIQUE DE LYON
Prairial
Le Musée
Villa Florentine
Les Terrasses de Lyon
N.-D. DE FOURVIÈRE
Jérémy Galvan
Cour des Loges
Les Loges
Café Épicerie
Cordeliers
MUSÉE DE LA CIVILISATION GALLO-ROMAINE
Daniel et Denise Saint-Jean
Vieux Lyon
Cath. St-Jean
ST-JEAN
La Voûte chez Léa
Carlton
Le Centre
Mercure Plaza République
Hôtel des Célestins
THÉÂTRES ROMAINS
Têtedoie
Au 14 Février
Pont Bonaparte
Globe et Cécil
Le Royal
L'Institut
Le Sud
Sofitel Lyon Bellecour
MUSÉE DES ART DÉCORATIFS
Les Trois Dômes
MUSÉE HISTORIQUE DES TISSUS
Thomas
Le Poêlon d'Or
ST-MARTIN D'AINAY
PERRACHE
Brasserie Georges
CENTRE D'HISTOIRE DE LA RÉSISTANCE ET DE LA DÉPORTATION

• Hotel
• Restaurant

0   300 m

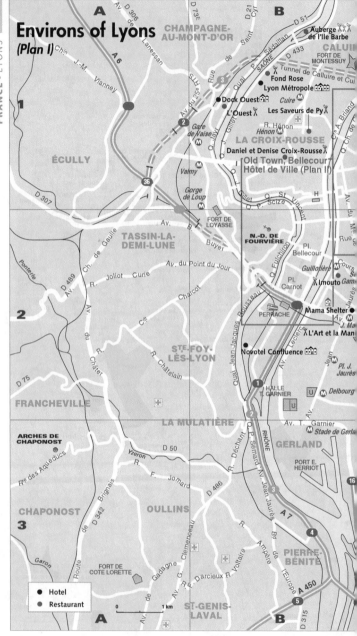

Environs of Lyons
(Plan I)

CHAMPAGNE-AU-MONT-D'OR

Auberge de l'Île Barbe

CALUI

FORT DE MONTESSUY

Tunnel de Calluire et Cui

Fond Rose

Lyon Métropole

Cuire

Dock Ouest

L'Ouest

Les Saveurs de Py

R. Hénon

Hénon

LA CROIX-ROUSSE

Gare de Vaise

Daniel et Denise Croix-Rousse

Old Town, Bellecour
Hôtel de Ville (Plan II)

ÉCULLY

Valmy

Gorge de Loup

FORT DE LOYASSE

N.-D. DE FOURVIÈRE

Pl. Bellecour

TASSIN-LA-DEMI-LUNE

Av. Buyer

Av. du Point du Jour

Guillotière

Pl. Carnot

Imouto

Charcot

PERRACHE

Mama Shelter

STE.-FOY-LÈS-LYON

R. Châtelain

L'Art et la Man

Novotel Confluence

Pl. J. Jaurès

FRANCHEVILLE

HALLE T. GARNIER

Delbourg

LA MULATIÈRE

Av. T. Garnier

Stade de Gerla

ARCHES DE CHAPONOST

D 50

GERLAND

PORT E. HERRIOT

CHAPONOST

OULLINS

PIERRE-BÉNITE

FORT DE COTE LORETTE

● Hotel
● Restaurant

0   1 km

ST-GENIS-LAVAL

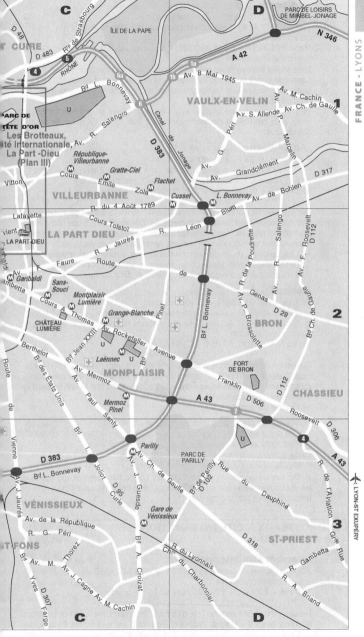

FRANCE - LYONS

XXX **Les Loges** – Hôtel Cour des Loges [AC]

*6 r. du Bœuf ⊠ 69005 – **Ⓜ** Vieux Lyon*   Plan: **E2**
– 𝒞 04 72 77 44 44 – www.courdesloges.com – Closed August and lunch except Sunday
Menu 105/125 € – Carte 90/120 € – *(booking advisable)*
• Modern cuisine • Romantic • Elegant •

Time seems to have stood still in this enchanting and romantic setting. Find a Florentine courtyard ringed by three floors of galleries and crowned by a contemporary glass ceiling. Savour the refined and inventive cuisine with flickering candlelight adding a final touch.
→ Truffe noire, crème soubise et ris de veau braisé en pithiviers. Pigeonneau, pain croustillant de champignons et fruit épicé. Variation de cacaos grands crus.

X **Au 14 Février** (Tsuyoshi Arai) [AC]

*6 r. Mourguet ⊠ 69005 – **Ⓜ** Vieux Lyon*   Plan: **E2**
– 𝒞 04 78 92 91 39 – www.au14fevrier.com – Closed 2 weeks in August and in January, Sunday, Monday and lunch except Saturday
Menu 87 € – *(booking advisable) (tasting menu only)*
• Creative • Intimate • Cosy •

The gastronomic worlds of France and Japan continue to enjoy a great romance... and this pocket-sized restaurant, named after Valentine's Day, is one of the finest examples of the trend. Under the direction of a talented Japanese chef, the meal is a revelation with its variety of textures, sweet-and-sour contrasts etc.
→ Langoustines, coulis de nectarine et fenouil, vinaigre balsamique blanc. Turbot sauvage poêlé, sauce citron au safran, artichaut et petits pois. Raviolis d'ananas, crème d'avocat, sorbet ananas et fleur de sureau.

X **Jérémy Galvan** [AC]

*29 r. du Bœuf ⊠ 69005 – **Ⓜ** Vieux-Lyon*   Plan: **E2**
– 𝒞 04 72 40 91 47 – www.jeremygalvanrestaurant.com – Closed 1 week in April, 3 weeks in August, 1 week Christmas Holidays, Saturday lunch, Sunday and Monday
Menu 26 € (lunch), 49/85 € – Carte 60/75 €
• Creative • Cosy • Contemporary décor •

Cuisine based on instinct is what is promised here, with menus labelled "Interlude", "Let go" and "Perfume" setting the tone for the dishes. These are original, creative and playful; deviating from well-trodden paths but always respecting the seasons and nature.
→ Cuisine du marché.

X **Café-Épicerie** – Hôtel Cour des Loges [AC]

*2 r. du Bœuf ⊠ 69005 – **Ⓜ** Vieux Lyon*   Plan: **E2**
– 𝒞 04 72 77 44 44 – www.courdesloges.com
Carte 40/60 €
• Modern cuisine • Trendy • Friendly •

In the marvellous setting of the Cour des Loges, this Café-Épicerie boasts a trendy bistro-style ambience. The locals come to enjoy unpretentious yet well-prepared dishes that change daily.

LES BROTTEAUX – CITÉ INTERNATIONALE – LA PART-DIEU   **PLAN III**

🏨 **Marriott Cité Internationale**

70 quai Charles-de-Gaulle ⊠ 69006 – 𝒞 04 78 17 50 50   Plan: **H1**
– www.marriottlyon.com
199 rm – †90/450 € ††90/450 € – ⊡ 24 € – 5 suites
• Chain • Business • Contemporary •

Between the Rhône and the Tête d'Or park, this impressive red-brick and glass structure bears the Marriott hallmark. The rooms are well equipped, spacious and contemporary in style. Guests also appreciate the large meeting rooms and fitness facilities.

Crowne Plaza Cité Internationale ⚐ ⅃ᵔ ₺ ₳ ₰ ⌂

22 quai Charles-de-Gaulle ✉ *69006 –* ✆ *04 78 17 86 86* Plan: **H1**
– www.crownplaza.com/lyonciteintl
156 rm – ♦85/440 € ♦♦85/440 € – ⌇ 22 € – 7 suites
• Chain • Business • Contemporary •
Modern building designed by Renzo Piano. It has bright rooms overlooking the
Tête-d'Or park or the Rhône. Traditional French cuisine and regional ingredients
in the restaurant, as well as a pleasant terrace.

 Mercure Lyon Centre Saxe Lafayette ⚐ ⅃ᵔ ₺ ₳ ₰

29 r. Bonnel ✉ *69003 –* Ⓜ *Place Guichard* ⌂
– ✆ *04 72 61 90 90* Plan: **G3**
– www.mercure-lyon-saxe-lafayette.com
156 rm – ♦95/270 € ♦♦95/270 € – ⌇ 19 €
• Chain • Business • Contemporary •
This former garage, built in 1932, is conveniently located between the Gare de
la Part-Dieu (railway station) neighbourhood and the quays of the Rhône. The
guestrooms are spacious and elegant. There is a small indoor pool and fitness
facilities in the basement.

XxxX **Pierre Orsi** ⅋⅋ ⌂ ₺ ₳ ⇄ ⅏
✿
3 pl. Kléber ✉ *69006 –* Ⓜ *Masséna* Plan: **G2**
– ✆ *04 78 89 57 68 – www.pierreorsi.com*
– Closed Sunday and Monday except Bank Holidays
Menu 65 € (weekday lunch), 115/135 € – Carte 85/190 €
• Classic cuisine • Bourgeois • Romantic •
First, you come face to face with the lovely ochre Florentine façade, then, on
entering, you discover the elegance and luxurious comfort of an opulent bourgeois house. As for the food: the cuisine is fine and precise, of the moment,
based on top-notch ingredients and accompanied by superb wines.
➔ Ravioles de foie gras de canard au jus de porto et truffes. Filet de bœuf
au poivre vert de Madagascar. Crêpes Suzette au beurre d'orange.

XxX **Le Neuvième Art** (Christophe Roure) ⅋⅋ ₺ ₳
✿✿
173 r. Cuvier ✉ *69006 –* Ⓜ *Brotteaux* Plan: **H2**
– ✆ *04 72 74 12 74 – www.leneuviemeart.com – Closed 19 February-*
6 March, 6 to 29 August, Sunday and Monday
Menu 88/148 € – Carte approx. 105 €
• Creative • Design • Contemporary décor •
Christophe Roure's cooking - a subtle sense of invention, precise marriages of
flavours and an understanding of textures - marks him out as an artist. Nor
does he put a foot wrong in the very fine wine list, with close to 400 bottles to
choose from!
➔ Royale de tourteau, râpée de poutargue et pois gourmands. Bœuf
Wagyu cuit au feu de bois, céleri en croûte de sel et poudre de menthe.
Soufflé chaud à la pistache, crème glacée pistache et guimauve vaporeuse.

XxX **Le Gourmet de Sèze** (Bernard Mariller) ₺ ₳ ⇄
✿
125 r. de Sèze ✉ *69006 –* Ⓜ *Masséna* Plan: **H2**
– ✆ *04 78 24 23 42 – www.le-gourmet-de-seze.com – Closed 15 to*
18 February, 29 July-24 August, Sunday, Monday and Bank Holidays
Menu 56/120 € – (booking advisable)
• Classic cuisine • Elegant • Cosy •
In a spacious yet cosy interior, diners can enjoy dishes that show off chef Bernard Mariller's inventiveness and attention to detail. He continues to pay a fitting tribute to his mentors, who include Joël Robuchon and Philippe Chavent.
➔ Coquilles Saint-Jacques d'Erquy. Poitrine de poulet fermier farci de ris
de veau, racines de légumes et sauce poulette au fois gras. Fraîcheur de
menthe dans une tarte aux fruits rouges.

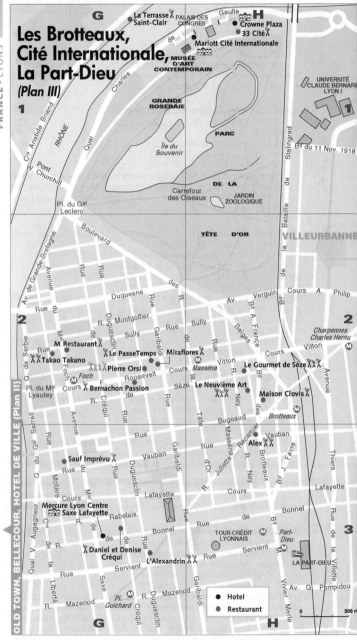

Les Brotteaux,
Cité Internationale,
La Part-Dieu
(Plan III)

G La Terrasse ✗ **PALAIS DES** Gaulle 🏨🏨 **H**
Saint-Clair CONGRÈS ● Crowne Plaza
de ● 33 Cité ✗
Mariott Cité Internationale
MUSÉE 🏨🏨
D'ART
Charles **CONTEMPORAIN**

UNIVERSITÉ
CLAUDE BERNARD
LYON I

1

GRANDE
ROSERAIE

1

RHÔNE

Quai

Île du
Souvenir

PARC

Bd du 11 Nov. 1918

Crs Aristide Briand

Pont
W. Churchill

Carrefour
des Oiseaux

DE LA

JARDIN
ZOOLOGIQUE

Pl. du Gal
Leclerc

Boulevard

TÊTE D'OR

VILLEURBANNE

de la Bataille
de Stalingrad

Av. de Grande-Bretagne

Avenue

Rue

Rue
des

Av. Verguin

Cours A. Philip

2

Duquesne

Rue
R. Duguesclin

Montgolfier

Rue

Sully

Bd A. France

Bd des Belges

2

Charpennes
Charles Hernu

Rue du

Sully

Garibaldi

de

Rue

Vitton

Vitton

Q. de Serbie
Rue

M̂ Restaurant

Le PasseTemps ✗

Miraflores ✗

Cours Masséna

Le Gourmet de Sèze ✗✗✗

Avenue

✗ Takao Takano

✗✗✗✗ Pierre Orsi

Roosevelt

Sèze

Le Neuvième Art

Foch

Foch
Cours ✗ Bernachon Passion

de

✗✗✗

Maison Clovis ✗

Pl. du Mal
Lyautey

R. Créqui

de

Rue

Rue

Tête

Ney

Bugeaud

Masséna

Récamier

des

Brotteaux

Q. du Gal Sarrail

Avenue

Rue

Rue

Vauban

Garibaldi

R. d'Or

Juliette

Brotteaux

Vauban

Alex ✗✗

Thiers

✗ Sauf Imprévu

Ney

Bd J. Favre

Molière

Cours Mal

Duguesclin

Lafayette

Rue

de

Lafayette

Q. Augagneur
Crs V. Augagneur

Mercure Lyon Centre 🏨🏨
Saxe Lafayette

Rabelais

Bonnel

Rue

de

Bd

Rue de la Villette

3

de

Rue

✗ Daniel et Denise
Créqui

Bonnel

Cours

TOUR CRÉDIT
LYONNAIS

Servient

Part-
Dieu

3

Rue
Mazenod

L'Alexandrin ✗✗

Servient

Rue

Av. G. Pompidou

LA PART-DIEU

Rue
R. de la Liberté

Saxe

Pl.
Guichard

Mazenod

Garibaldi

Duguesclin

Créqui

Vivier-Merle

● **Hotel**
● **Restaurant**

0   300 m

XX   **Takao Takano**   &. 🅰🅺
£3   *33 r. Malesherbes* ✉ *69006 –* Ⓜ *Foch*   Plan: **G2**
      – ℰ 04 82 31 43 39
      – www.takaotakano.com
      – Closed 3 weeks in August, Sunday and Monday
      Menu 35 € (weekday lunch), 60/90 €
      – (booking advisable)
      • Creative • Design • Elegant •
      It would be hard not to be won over by Japanese chef Takao Takano's sense of
      precision, his humility before his ingredients, his absolute respect of flavours
      and his subtle compositions. Exquisite. Book to avoid disappointment.
      → Langoustine, concombre et raifort. Rouget barbet, persil et encornet.
      Mirabelle, fromage blanc et tilleul.

XX   **L'Alexandrin** (Laurent Rigal)   🅰🅺
£3   *83 r. Moncey* ✉ *69003 –* Ⓜ *Place Guichard*   Plan: **G3**
      – ℰ 04 72 61 15 69 – www.lalexandrin.fr – Closed 30 July-23 August,
      Sunday and Monday
      Menu 38 € (weekday lunch), 60/115 €
      • Modern cuisine • Traditional décor • Neighbourhood •
      L'Alexandrin combines originality with generosity, serving dishes made using
      fine, locally sourced produce. Each menu (vegetarian, revisited Lyon classics or
      pure creation) proposes a different take on the art of fine dining in an exclusive
      atmosphere. One novelty is the table d'hôte with four guests seated in the kit-
      chen at the heart of the action!
      → Salade de tête de veau panée, escargots en persillade et petits poi-
      reaux en vinaigrette. Volaille de Bresse au vinaigre, girolles sautées et
      petits légumes glacés. Madeleines au chocolat guanaja, marmelade
      d'orange confite.

X   **Maison Clovis** (Clovis Khoury)   🅰🅺
£3   *19 bd Brotteaux* ✉ *69006 –* Ⓜ *Brotteaux*   Plan: **H2**
      – ℰ 04 72 74 44 61
      – www.maisonclovis.com
      – Closed 30 April-8 May, 6 to 28 August, 1 to 8 January, Sunday and
      Monday
      Menu 59/95 € – Carte 60/110 €
      • Modern cuisine • Contemporary décor • Trendy •
      This designer restaurant is elegant without being uptight. Clovis Khoury prepa-
      res delicious seasonal cuisine using fine ingredients. The menu is short, but the
      choice is nevertheless impossible.
      → Oursin d'Islande servi dans sa coque, cuisses de grenouilles et raviole de
      champignons. Lotte confite et marinée servie dans l'esprit d'un tajine.
      Soufflé chocolat grand cru et menthe poivrée.

X   **Le Passe Temps** (Younghoon Lee)   🅰🅺
£3   *52 r. Tronchet* ✉ *69006 –* Ⓜ *Masséna*   Plan: **G2**
      – ℰ 04 72 82 90 14 – www.lepassetemps-restaurant.com – Closed August,
      Sunday, Monday and Bank Holidays
      Menu 30 € (weekday lunch), 50/70 €
      – (booking advisable)
      • Creative • Minimalist • Design •
      Mr Lee, originally from Seoul, has brought a little of his native country to the
      Brotteaux neighbourhood. With a sharp sense of aestheticism and flavours,
      he reinterprets French cuisine by adding Korean touches. His speciality, foie
      gras with root and other vegetables in a soya broth, is quite simply deli-
      cious!
      → Foie gras, bouillon de soja et oignon cébette. Agneau de lait, ail des
      ours et courgette. Fraises au thé vert, mascarpone.

FRANCE - LYONS

X
£3
Miraflores (Carlos Camino)

60 r. Garibaldi ⊠ 69006 – Ⓜ Massena   Plan: **G2**
– ℰ 04 37 43 61 26 – www.restaurant-miraflores.com – Closed 3 weeks in
August, Sunday, Monday and lunch
Menu 47/90 € – Carte 60/80 € – *(booking advisable)*
• Peruvian • Intimate • Elegant •
The young chef, originally from Peru, takes you on a joyful, French-Peruvian culi-
nary journey. All of the Peruvian ingredients are organic, such as *aji* (chilli), *camu*
camu (fruit) and *huacatay* (black mint). If you are not familiar with these names, you
can simply turn to the glossary at the end of the menu.
➜ Ceviche de maigre mariné au citron vert, coriandre, aji limo, maïs chulpe
et camu camu. Pigeonneau rôti, sauce à la bière malta, huacatay, risotto de
quinoa noir et blanc. Velours et contrastes de cacao péruvien.

X
(☺)
M Restaurant   ⛱ AK

47 av. Foch ⊠ 69006 – Ⓜ Foch – ℰ 04 78 89 55 19   Plan: **G2**
– www.mrestaurant.fr – Closed 18 to 26 February, 31 July-20 August,
Saturday and Sunday
Menu 26/36 € – Carte approx. 43 €
• Market cuisine • Trendy • Friendly •
The charming and fashionable M serves delicious gourmet cuisine which is full
of flavour. The decor is slightly psychedelic.

X
(☺)
33 Cité   ఔ ⛱ ⅗ AK ⇔

33 quai Charles-de-Gaulle ⊠ 69006 – ℰ 04 37 45 45 45   Plan: **H1**
– www.33cite.com – Closed 3 weeks in August
Menu 27 € – Carte 33/59 €
• Traditional cuisine • Brasserie • Contemporary décor •
Three talented chefs – Mathieu Viannay (Meilleur Ouvrier de France), Christophe
Marguin and Frédéric Berthod (alumnus of Bocuse) – joined forces to create this
chic, tasty brasserie. It opens onto the Tête-d'Or Park. On the menu find great
brasserie specialities.

X
(☺)
Sauf Imprévu   ⇔

40 r. Pierre-Corneille ⊠ 69006 – Ⓜ Foch   Plan: **G3**
– ℰ 04 78 52 16 35 – Closed 2 weeks in August,
Saturday, Sunday and dinner except Thursday
Menu 25 € – Carte approx. 34 €
• Traditional cuisine • Simple • Family •
"Marguerite" terrine in homage to his great-grandmother, coco de Paimpol
beans with shellfish, grilled prime rib of beef with homemade chips... With his
focus firmly on tradition, Félix Gagnaire proposes delicious and copious dishes.
Everything is fresh, homemade and spot on, and the prices are also fair!

X
Bernachon Passion   AK

42 cours Franklin-Roosevelt ⊠ 69006 – Ⓜ Foch   Plan: **G2**
– ℰ 04 78 52 23 65 – www.bernachon.com – Closed 23 July-22 August,
Sunday, Monday, Bank Holidays and dinner
Menu 30 € – Carte 36/54 € – *(booking advisable)*
• Traditional cuisine • Simple • Intimate •
The famous Lyon-based chocolatier of Bernachon needs no introduction. The
son of the founder married the eldest daughter of Paul Bocuse and it is the
grandchildren of the great chef who are at the reins here! On the menu find
good traditional recipes (such as pike quenelles and pâté en croûte) and pastries... made by Bernachon, of course.

X
La Terrasse St-Clair   ⛱

2 Grande-Rue-St-Clair ⊠ 69300 Caluire-et-Cuire   Plan: **G1**
– ℰ 04 72 27 37 37 – www.terrasse-saint-clair.com – Closed 5 to
22 August, 23 December-7 January, Sunday and Monday
Menu 29 €
• Traditional cuisine • Bistro • Friendly •
A restaurant with the air of an old-fashioned French café, serving good, traditio-
nal cuisine. There's a terrace shaded by plane trees and a petanque ground!

Sofitel Lyon Bellecour

20 quai Gailleton ✉ *69002 –* Ⓜ *Bellecour* — Plan: **F3**
– ☎ 04 72 41 20 20 – www.sofitel.com
135 rm – ♦205/1200 € ♦♦205/1200 € – ☲ 26 € – 29 suites
• Business • Luxury • Contemporary •
A luxurious and elegant Sofitel in a contemporary building with futuristic facilities. Bill Clinton stayed in the presidential suite here. There are two options for dinner: the beautiful Trois Dômes restaurant (see restaurants) or Le Silk restaurant (an international menu in a sleek setting).
⛛ **Les Trois Dômes** – See restaurant listing

Le Royal

20 pl. Bellecour ✉ *69002 –* Ⓜ *Bellecour* — Plan: **F2**
– ☎ 04 78 37 57 31 – www.sofitel.com
72 rm – ♦140/500 € ♦♦160/500 € – ☲ 25 € – 5 suites
• Luxury • Traditional • Elegant •
Established in 1912, Le Royal wins over hotel guests with its blend of comfort and refinement. A century on, the institution has lost none of its charm and style. Mouldings, Toiles de Jouy fabrics, traditional old furniture… it is quite simply elegant.
L'Institut – See restaurant listing

Carlton

4 r. Jussieu ✉ *69002 –* Ⓜ *Cordeliers –* ☎ *04 78 42 56 51* — Plan: **F2**
– www.mgallery.com
80 rm – ♦155/530 € ♦♦155/530 € – ☲ 25 €
• Business • Traditional • Art déco •
This illustrious establishment was completely refurbished in 2013. It transports guests back in time to a 1930s ambience with an interior in predominantly red tones. The guestrooms are spacious and well appointed, and the period lift is magnificent. A marriage of comfort and charm.

Globe et Cécil

21 r. Gasparin ✉ *69002 –* Ⓜ *Bellecour* — Plan: **F2**
– ☎ 04 78 42 58 95 – www.globeetcecilhotel.com
60 rm – ♦116/220 € ♦♦126/270 € – ☲ 18 €
• Traditional • Classic • Personalised •
This hotel, dating back to the end of the 19C, is located a stone's throw from Place Bellecour. It has pretty and immaculately kept guestrooms (some have floorboards and fireplaces). The foyer and lounge offer first-rate amenities.

Grand Hôtel des Terreaux

16 r. Lanterne ✉ *69001 –* Ⓜ *Hôtel de Ville* — Plan: **F1**
– ☎ 04 78 27 04 10 – www.hotel-lyon-grandhoteldesterreaux.fr
53 rm – ♦95/175 € ♦♦115/275 € – ☲ 16 €
• Traditional • Classic •
This 19C post house is conducive to relaxing in the centre of town. Find tastefully decorated rooms, a small indoor pool and attentive service.

Mercure Plaza République

5 r. Stella ✉ *69002 –* Ⓜ *Cordeliers –* ☎ *04 78 37 50 50* — Plan: **F2**
– www.mercure.com
82 rm – ♦109/219 € ♦♦109/219 € – ☲ 20 €
• Business • Chain • Functional •
This pleasant chain hotel is well located and very popular with business travellers.

FRANCE - LYONS

🏠 **Hôtel des Célestins**   AC

4 r. des Archers ✉ *69002 –* Ⓜ *Bellecour*   Plan: **F2**
– ☏ *04 72 56 08 98 – www.hotelcelestins.com*
29 rm – †81/169 € ††81/169 € – ☲ 11 €
• Traditional • Family • Functional •

A hotel in a residential building is rather unusual. Pleasant rooms including a very attractive junior suite on the fifth floor (with a large Italian-style shower, a flat screen TV, etc).

XxX **Mère Brazier** (Mathieu Viannay)   ⌘ AC ⇕ 🥢
£3£3   *12 r. Royale* ✉ *69001 –* Ⓜ *Hôtel de Ville*   Plan: **F1**
– ☏ *04 78 23 17 20 – www.lamerebrazier.fr –* Closed 1 week in February, 3 weeks in August, Saturday and Sunday
Menu 100/160 € – Carte 130/170 €
• Modern cuisine • Elegant • Chic •

The guardian of Lyon cuisine, Eugénie Brazier (1895-1977) is without doubt looking down on Mathieu Viannay – winner of the Meilleur Ouvrier de France award – with pride. An emblematic restaurant where high-powered classics and creativity continue to be served.
➔ Artichaut et foie gras. Poularde de Bresse demi-deuil. Paris-brest.

XxX **Les Trois Dômes** – Hôtel Sofitel Lyon Bellecour   ⌘ ≤ AC 🥢
£3   *20 quai Gailleton (8th floor)* ✉ *69002 –* Ⓜ *Bellecour* Plan: **F3**
– ☏ *04 72 41 20 97 – www.les-3-domes.com –* Closed August, Sunday and Monday
Menu 47 € (lunch), 81/125 € – Carte 100/180 €
• Modern cuisine • Fashionable • Luxury •

On the top floor of the hotel; high-level cooking with the accent on delicious food and wine pairings. From a terrine of pot au feu with foie gras to leg of Limousin lamb, the classics are skillfully reworked. Magical views of the city from the elegant and contemporary dining room.
➔ Quenelles de brochet, sauce écrevisse et pousses d'épinard. Filet de bœuf Salers, foie gras chaud, artichauts violets et sauce vin rouge. Macaron au chocolat nyangbo, glace safran.

XX **Brasserie Léon de Lyon**   ⌘ 🏠 AC ⇕
1 r. Pleney (corner of r. du Plâtre) ✉ *69001*   Plan: **F1**
– Ⓜ *Hôtel de Ville –* ☏ *04 72 10 11 12 – www.leondelyon.com*
Menu 26 € – Carte 43/52 €
• Traditional cuisine • Brasserie • Chic •

This Lyon institution, founded in 1904, has kept its affluent setting and its convivial atmosphere. Excellent ingredients combine to produce hearty gourmet dishes.

XX **La Voûte - Chez Léa**   AC

11 pl. A.-Gourju ✉ *69002 –* Ⓜ *Bellecour*   Plan: **F2**
– ☏ *04 78 42 01 33 – www.lavoutechezlea.com*
Menu 30 € – Carte 36/46 €
• Traditional cuisine • Friendly • Traditional décor •

One of the oldest restaurants in Lyon: in a welcoming atmosphere, tradition carries on with verve. A fine menu with tasty regional dishes and game in autumn.

XX **Brasserie Georges**   🏠 ♿ ⇕
30 cours de Verdun ✉ *69002 –* Ⓜ *Perrache*   Plan: **F3**
– ☏ *04 72 56 54 54 – www.brasseriegeorges.com*
Menu 23/28 € – Carte 28/50 €
• Traditional cuisine • Brasserie • Vintage •

'Good beer and good cheer since 1836' in the jealously guarded Art Deco setting of this brasserie that is a veritable institution. Lively atmosphere.

✗
☺

Balthaz'art   ⇦

7 r. des Pierres-Plantées ✉ *69001 –* Ⓜ *Croix-Rousse*   Plan: **F1**
– ℰ 04 72 07 08 88 – www.restaurantbalthazart.com – Closed 6 to 21 August,
24 December-1 January, Tuesday lunch, Wednesday lunch, Sunday and Monday
Menu 17 € (weekday lunch), 29/34 € – Carte 33/46 €
• Modern cuisine • Bistro • Friendly •

You have to earn your meal at this restaurant located near the top of La Croix-Rousse! Housed in the former French Communist Party HQ, red dominates the interior, and Picasso and Modigliani prints hang on the walls. The imagination and beauty found in the decoration are also present in the dishes, which are paired with well-chosen wines.

✗

L'Institut – Hôtel Le Royal   ♿ ⒶⒸ ⇦

20 pl. Bellecour ✉ *69002 –* Ⓜ *Bellecour*   Plan: **F2**
– ℰ 04 78 37 23 02 – www.institutpaulbocuse.com – Closed 6 to
28 August, 24 December-8 January, Sunday and Monday
Carte 48/65 € – (booking advisable)
• Traditional cuisine • Elegant • Design •

On Place Bellecour, the training restaurant of the Paul Bocuse Institute feels nothing like a school! In a contemporary decor designed by Pierre-Yves Rochon, with open kitchens giving onto the restaurant, the students deliver a high standard of service. The dishes are extremely well prepared and deserve a high mark.

✗
✿

Prairial (Gaëtan Gentil)   ⒶⒸ

11 r. Chavanne ✉ *69001 –* Ⓜ *Cordeliers*   Plan: **F1**
– ℰ 04 78 27 86 93 – www.prairial-restaurant.com – Closed 19 February-
6 March, 27 August-18 September, Sunday and Monday
Menu 33 € (weekday lunch), 53/79 €
• Modern cuisine • Design • Trendy •

In spring 2015 Gaëtan Gentil took over this restaurant on the Presqu'île that boasts a designer decor (white tables, hanging lamps) and a vertical garden. He offers diners what he terms "uninhibited gastronomy": creative and contemporary dishes in which vegetables take pride of place.
→ Cuisine du marché.

✗
☺

L'Ourson qui Boit

23 r. Royale ✉ *69001 –* Ⓜ *Croix-Paquet*   Plan: **F1**
– ℰ 04 78 27 23 37 – Closed 4 weeks in July-August,
2 weeks in December, Wednesday, Sunday and Bank Holidays
Menu 18 € (lunch)/32 €
• Modern cuisine • Friendly • Bistro •

The Japanese chef at this contemporary bistro has worked in some of the finest restaurants. His cuisine blends the subtle flavours of yuzu and ginger with traditional French ingredients – all at reasonable prices. Not to be missed!

✗
☺

Le Jean Moulin   ⒶⒸ

22 r. Gentil ✉ *69002 –* Ⓜ *Cordeliers – ℰ 04 78 37 37 97*   Plan: **F1**
– www.lejeanmoulin-lyon.com – Closed 3 weeks in August, Sunday and Monday
Menu 26 € (weekday lunch)/29 €
• Modern cuisine • Friendly • Elegant •

Find great value at this elegant, welcoming bistro, opened in late 2011 by a chef who trained at some of the top establishments (Bocuse, Viannay, Pic). The cooking is not so different from the man himself: lively, serious, tasteful, colourful and generous. Good enough to whet any appetite!

✗

Le Sud   🍽 ♿ ⒶⒸ ⇦

11 pl. Antonin-Poncet ✉ *69002 –* Ⓜ *Bellecour*   Plan: **F2**
– ℰ 04 72 77 80 00 – www.nordsudbrasseries.com
Menu 27 € (weekdays)/33 € – Carte 39/65 €
• Mediterranean cuisine • Brasserie • Mediterranean décor •

There is a kind of Greek elegance about this Bocuse brasserie located a stone's throw from the Place Bellecour. And it is not by chance as it is all about the Mediterranean here with the Italian-style penne rigate, the soupe marseillaise and the tajine à l'orientale... all the more so in summer, on the terrace.

✗ **Le Centre**　　　　　　　　　　　　　　　　　&. 风 ⇔
14 r. Grolée ⊠ 69002 – ⓜ Cordeliers – ℰ 04 72 04 44 44　　Plan: **F2**
– www.lespritblanc.com
Menu 24 € 🍷 (weekday lunch), 26/32 € – Carte 45/76 €
• Meats and grills • Fashionable • Friendly •
Georges Blanc, the famous chef from the restaurant in Vonnas, is the mastermind
behind this contemporary brasserie. It is dedicated to meat – and fine meats at
that. Find Charolais, Wagyu beef, Aveyron lamb and Bresse chicken served with
a large choice of accompaniments and sauces. Calling all carnivores!

✗ **Le Nord**　　　　　　　　　　　　　　　　　　&. 风 ⇔
18 r. Neuve ⊠ 69002 – ⓜ Hôtel de Ville　　　　　Plan: **F1**
– ℰ 04 72 10 69 69 – www.nordsudbrasseries.com
Menu 27 € (weekdays)/33 € – Carte 36/62 €
• Traditional cuisine • Vintage • Brasserie •
The smallest (or least large!) brasserie in Bocuse's collection is organised into
several areas. This includes a veranda onto the street and private lounges ups-
tairs. The team working in the kitchens has clearly been schooled by the best.
The freshness of ingredients is the mantra here, and tradition goes hand-in-
hand with generosity and flavour. A sure-fire dining option.

✗ **Le Potager des Halles**　　　　　　　　　　　　风 ⇔
3 r. de la Martinière ⊠ 69001 – ⓜ Hôtel de Ville　　Plan: **F1**
– ℰ 04 72 00 24 84 – www.lepotagerdeshalles.com – Closed 3 weeks in
August, Sunday and Monday
Menu 39 € – Carte approx. 46 €
• Traditional cuisine • Bistro • Friendly •
This pleasant restaurant is between the Quais de la Saône and the Halles de la Marti-
nière. It serves dishes like veal rump with different coloured carrots, and skate wing
with samphire. Organic ingredients and fresh market produce take pride of place.

✗ **Thomas**　　　　　　　　　　　　　　　　　　　风
6 r. Laurencin ⊠ 69002 – ⓜ Bellecour　　　　　Plan: **F3**
– ℰ 04 72 56 04 76 – www.restaurant-thomas.com – Closed 24 December-
2 January, Saturday and Sunday
Menu 21 € (lunch), 33/45 €
• Modern cuisine • Bistro • Friendly •
This cosy, modern bistro is under the auspices of a young chef who communica-
tes his passion for delicious, refined cuisine (on a monthly changing menu). Game
is a feature, as is one of the house classic desserts, pain perdu (French toast).

BOUCHONS *Regional wine tasting and local cuisine in a typical
Lyonnaise atmosphere*

✗ **Daniel et Denise Saint-Jean**　　　　　　　　风 ⇔
🐵
32 r. Tramassac ⊠ 69005 – ⓜ Vieux Lyon – ℰ 04 78 42 24 62　　Plan: **E2**
– www.daniel-et-denise.fr – Closed 31 December-3 January, Sunday and Monday
Menu 31/50 € 🍷 – Carte 35/54 €
• Lyonnaise • Lyonnaise bistro • Friendly •
A stone's throw from Cathédrale St-Jean, this bouchon in the picturesque Old
Town is run by chef Joseph Viola (Meilleur Ouvrier de France). Like the two
other branches (Créqui and the Croix-Rousse), the menu offers Lyonnaise cuisine that is hearty and tasty.

✗ **Daniel et Denise Créqui**　　　　　　　　　　🍴 风
🐵
156 r. de Créqui ⊠ 69003 – ⓜ Place Guichard　　Plan: **G3**
– ℰ 04 78 60 66 53 – www.daniel-et-denise.fr – Closed Saturday, Sunday
and Bank Holidays
Menu 31/50 € 🍷 – Carte 27/52 € – (booking advisable)
• Lyonnaise • Lyonnaise bistro • Friendly •
A dyed-in-the-wool 'bouchon', smooth with the patina of age, serving tasty,
generous cuisine with excellent ingredients. Unsurprisingly, typical dishes take
pride of place.

X

Daniel et Denise Croix-Rousse 🏠 🖾

8 r. de Cuire – ⓜ Croix-Rousse – ℰ 04 78 28 27 44   Plan: **F1**
– www.daniel-et-denise.fr – Closed Sunday and Monday
Menu 21 € (weekday lunch)/31 € – Carte 37/52 €
• Lyonnaise • Lyonnaise bistro • Friendly •

There is no doubt that this Daniel and Denise (the third in the saga, after Rue de Créqui and the St Jean district) is certain to enjoy the same success as its elder sisters. It must be said that Joseph Viola is unparalleled in the art of fresh, tasty Lyonnaise classics. There is also a delightful vintage decor.

X

Le Bouchon des Filles

20 r. Sergent-Blandan ✉ 69001 – ⓜ Hôtel de Ville   Plan: **F1**
– ℰ 04 78 30 40 44 – Closed Christmas Holidays and
lunch except Saturday and Sunday
Menu 26/29 €
• Lyonnaise • Bistro • Cosy •

Next to the charming Place Sathonay, in a little cobbled street, is this picture-postcard bouchon, which is as sweet-looking as it is inviting. Run by a pair of filles, the food consists of lighter versions of Lyon's traditional dishes. It is simple, fresh, tasty and generous.

X

Le Musée

2 r. des Forces ✉ 69002 – ⓜ Cordeliers – ℰ 04 78 37 71 54   Plan: **F2**
– Closed August, 24 December-2 January, Saturday dinner, Sunday and Monday
Menu 24 € (lunch)/29 € – Carte approx. 31 € – *(booking advisable)*
• Lyonnaise • Bistro • Rustic •

A sincere and authentic bouchon with a decor of checked tablecloths, closely packed tables and a buzzing atmosphere. In the kitchen, the young chef creates the classics with real know-how, such as Lyonnaise pork, foie de veau persillé (calf's liver), trotters and brawn salad.

X

Le Poêlon d'or 🖾 ⇔

29 r. des Remparts-d'Ainay ✉ 69002 – ⓜ Ampère   Plan: **F3**
– ℰ 04 78 37 65 60 – www.lepoelondor-restaurant.fr – Closed 5 to
20 August, Saturday and Sunday
Menu 20/32 € – Carte 26/50 € – *(booking advisable)*
• Lyonnaise • Bistro • Vintage •

It's hard to say whether or not the chef does actually use a golden saucepan (poêlon d'or), but he must have a secret weapon – he revisits Lyon's terroir so well and creates food that is as tasty as it is perfectly put together - from the gâteau de foie de volaille (chicken liver) with tomato coulis, to the pike quenelle gratin with béchamel sauce. A must!

AROUND THE CENTRE

🏨

Lyon Métropole 🏊 🖪 📶 ⚒ 🖵 ✗ ⇔ ᕻ 🖾 🛄 🚗

85 quai J.-Gillet ✉ 69004 – ℰ 04 72 10 44 44   Plan: **B1**
– www.lyonmetropole.com
174 rm – ✝99/360 € ✝✝99/360 € – ☲ 20 €
• Business • Spa and wellness • Functional •

A hotel popular for its Olympic size swimming pool and its sports facilities: a superb spa, a gym, tennis and squash courts, etc. In the restaurant, seafood and fish are to the fore.

🏨

Novotel Confluence 🏊 🖪 ᕻ 🖾 🛄 🚗

3 r. Paul-Montrochet ✉ 69002 – ⓜ Perrache   Plan: **B2**
– ℰ 04 37 23 64 00 – www.accorhotel.com/7325
150 rm – ✝95/250 € ✝✝95/250 € – ☲ 17 € – 3 suites
• Chain • Contemporary •

In this new neighbourhood on the banks of the Saône, you cannot miss this hotel with its resolutely contemporary architecture. It has a large and inviting lobby, a restaurant with a designer look and a terrace on the river. The pleasant guestrooms boast all the latest mod cons.

Dock Ouest
🕭 🕭 🕭

39 r. des Docks ✉ *69009* – Ⓜ *Gare de Vaise*
Plan: **B1**
– ☏ 04 78 22 34 34 – www.dockouest.com
43 rm – †75/242 € ††75/242 € – ☲ 13 €
• Townhouse • Business • Contemporary •

Dock Ouest is located in an up-and-coming district of Lyon, just opposite Paul Bocuse's fast food outlet. The guestrooms are comfortable and decorated in a restrained style, with the added bonus of a kitchenette. Gourmet breakfasts.

Mama Shelter
🕭 🕭 🕭 🕭 🕭

13 r. Domer ✉ *69007* – Ⓜ *Jean Macé*
Plan: **B2**
– ☏ 04 78 02 58 58 – www.mamashelter.com
156 rm – †69/129 € ††89/269 € – ☲ 16 €
• Business • Townhouse • Design •

Like the branches in Paris and Marseille, Mama Shelter is a delight! The decor is as trendy as ever (raw concrete, designer flourishes, offbeat touches), guestrooms are modern and public transport is close by. Splendid.

Auberge de l'Île Barbe (Jean-Christophe Ansanay-Alex)
🕭

pl. Notre-Dame (on Barbe Island) ✉ *69009*
🖘 🕭 (dinner) 🅿
– ☏ 04 78 83 99 49 – www.aubergedelile.com – Closed
Plan: **B1**
Sunday dinner and Monday
Menu 50 € (weekday lunch), 128/158 €
• Classic cuisine • Romantic • Elegant •

A country feel in the heart of the leafy île Barbe, an island in the Saône. The walls date from 1601 and there is a softly intimate atmosphere. The very refined cuisine has remarkable flavour associations and creative flights of fancy.
→ Velouté de cèpe comme un cappuccino, vapeur de foie gras. Selle d'agneau de lait servie comme au dîner de gala du patrimoine de l'Unesco. Soufflé chaud de pêche blanche.

Les Saveurs de Py
🕭 🕭 🕭

8 r. Pailleron ✉ *69004* – Ⓜ *Hénon* – ☏ 04 78 28 80 86
Plan: **B1**
– www.saveursdepy.fr – Closed August, Sunday and Monday
Menu 18 € (lunch), 31/39 €
• Modern cuisine • Friendly • Bistro •

Right in the heart of the lively Croix-Rousse neighbourhood, this is one of those lovely, contemporary, convivial and colourful little bistros. In the kitchens is a chef who demonstrates talent in his use of market ingredients, daring to throw in wonderful Japanese touches. Bold flavours and excellent value.

L'Art et la Manière
🕭 🖘

102 Gde-Rue de la Guillotière ✉ *69007*
Plan: **B-C2**
– Ⓜ Saxe-Gambetta
– ☏ 04 37 27 05 83 – www.art-et-la-maniere.fr
– Closed 3 weeks in August, Saturday and Sunday
Menu 21 € (lunch), 30/45 € – (booking advisable)
• Traditional cuisine • Bistro • Friendly •

A contemporary bistro that champions conviviality, seasonal cuisine and enticing, reasonably priced wines. It is also a great excuse for discovering the La Guillotière district. As it has a loyal local following, you are best advised to book ahead.

Imouto
🕭

21 r. Pasteur ✉ *69007* – Ⓜ *Guillotière*
Plan: **B2**
– ☏ 04 72 76 99 53 – Closed Sunday and Monday
Menu 21 € (lunch), 32/64 € – (booking advisable)
• Fusion • Design • Simple •

Originally from Vietnam, Gaby Didonna has opened Imouto ("little sister" in Japanese) in a working class district of Lyon. He is part of a team of two, along with Guy Kendell, his Australian second-in-command. The result is delicious fusion cuisine combining French tradition and Japanese influences. Tasty and always very impressive!

L'Ouest ✗

*1 quai du Commerce (North via the banks of the Saône, Plan: B1
D51)* ✉ *69009 –* Ⓜ *Gare de Vaise
–* ☎ *04 37 64 64 64 – www.nordsudbrasseries.com*
Menu 27 € (weekdays)/33 € – Carte 31/69 €
• Traditional cuisine • Brasserie • Contemporary décor •

Another of Paul Bocuse's brasseries, but this one is quite simply huge! The menu pays homage to the tradition that made a name for this great chef. Dishes include calf's liver with onions (*foie de veau à la lyonnaise*), spit-roast Bresse chicken, and sole meunière. It has a designer interior and a pretty terrace by the Saône.

Fond Rose ✗

23 chemin de Fond-Rose ✉ *69300 Caluire-et-Cuire* Plan: B1
– ☎ *04 78 29 34 61 – www.nordsudbrasseries.com*
Menu 31 € (weekdays)/35 € – Carte 38/55 €
• Classic cuisine • Brasserie • Elegant •

A 1920s mansion transformed into a chic brasserie by the Bocuse group. With its terrace surrounded by 100 year-old trees, it is the epitome of peace and quiet. The food is tasty and generous and squarely in the tradition of the areas around the River Saône, with frogs' legs and quenelles etc.

COLLONGES-AU-MONT-D'OR

Paul Bocuse ✗✗✗✗

40 quai de la Plage – ☎ *04 72 42 90 90 – www.bocuse.fr*
Menu 165/260 € – Carte 145/240 €
• Classic cuisine • Elegant • Luxury •

A high temple of tradition and old-style service, which is oblivious to passing culinary trends. Paul Bocuse is still offering the same "presidential" truffle soup first served in 1975, and has had three Michelin stars since 1965!
→ Soupe aux truffes noires V.G.E. Rouget en écailles de pommes de terre. Crème brûlée à la cassonade.

CHARBONNIÈRES-LES-BAINS

Le Pavillon de la Rotonde

3 av. Georges-Bassinet – ☎ *04 78 87 79 79 – www.pavillon-rotonde.com
– Closed 30 July-23 August and 2 to 9 January*
16 rm – ♦150/570 € ♦♦150/570 € – ☑ 22 €
• Luxury • Spa and wellness • Contemporary •

A stone's throw from the casino and set in wooded parkland, this luxury hotel blends the modern with discreet touches of Art Deco. Some of the guestrooms have a hammam and a terrace. A very fine establishment on the outskirts of Lyons.
❀ **La Rotonde** – See restaurant listing

La Rotonde ✗✗✗

20 av. du Casino (Domaine du Lyon Vert) ✉ *69260 La Tour de Salvagny
–* ☎ *04 78 87 00 97 – www.restaurant-rotonde.com – Closed 30 July-23 August,
2 to 9 January, Tuesday lunch, Saturday lunch, Sunday and Monday*
Menu 45 € (lunch), 78/135 € – Carte 105/125 €
• Modern cuisine • Elegant • Luxury •

In this pleasantly leafy area on the outskirts of town: a fine legacy of the Art Deco period which also houses the casino Le Lyon Vert. The menu is in a classic French vein and combines timeless dishes with new influences - not forgetting the great repertoire of Lyon cuisine.
→ Pâté en croûte "Champion du Monde 2013". Turbot confit et escargots, pomme charlotte, céleri et sauce cresson. Finger praliné au citron, noisettes et crème glacée au chocolat gianduja.

STRASBOURG
STRASBOURG

Population: 274 394

DX/Fotolia.com

Would it be stretching things to call Strasbourg the ultimate European city? It can make an impressive claim. Although in France, it sits just across the Rhine from Germany; it's home to the Court of Human Rights and the Council of Europe; its stunning cathedral is the highest medieval building on the continent; and it's a major communications hub as it connects the Mediterranean with the Rhineland, Central Europe, the North Sea and the Baltic. Oh, and the Old Town is a UNESCO World Heritage Site. What's more, there's a real cosmopolitan buzz here. A large student population, courtesy of the city's ancient university, helps generate a year-round feeling of liveliness.

The name 'Strasbourg' translates as 'crossroads', and the city bounced back and forth between France and Germany for over three hundred years. Its unique geographical position also lends the city a great gastronomic tradition, with two cuisine cultures colliding head on and hungry visitors reaping the benefits. Meanwhile, street signs in both French and Alsatian add to a gently teasing schizophrenia, enhanced by distinct areas of medieval French and German architecture. The final brushwork of this striking picture is the handsome waterway that completely encircles the Old Town; the ideal setting for a lingering boat journey on a summer's afternoon.

STRASBOURG IN...

→ **ONE DAY**
Old Town, Notre-Dame Cathedral, Petite France.

→ **TWO DAYS**
Boat trip on the Ill, Museum of Modern and Contemporary Art, meal in a winstub.

→ **THREE DAYS**
Alsatian Museum (or Rohan Palace museum), European Parliament, Orangerie.

PRACTICAL INFORMATION

ARRIVAL-DEPARTURE

 Strasbourg Entzheim International Airport is 12km southwest of the city. The train to Central Station runs from Entzheim Station (a 5min walk from the terminal) and takes 15min.

GETTING AROUND

Strasbourg is covered by a bus and tram service. You can buy a single ticket or carnets (multipasses). There's also a Tour Pass which gives unlimited travel for 24hr. The city has impressive green credentials: buses run on natural gas, trams are slick and efficient, and there are 130,000 cyclists and 270 miles of cycle paths – hiring a bike is a great way of getting about here. If you're staying longer, invest in a Strasbourg Pass. This is a three-day pass which offers free travel, plus free admission or discounts to many city-wide monuments and visitor attractions.

CALENDAR HIGHLIGHTS

May
Les Nuits de Musées.

June
Festival de Musique.

July
Les Nuits de Strasbourg, L'Ill aux Lumieres.

August
Route Romane Festival.

September
European Days of Heritage.

November
St-Art Contemporary Art Fair, Jazz d'Or.

December
Christmas Markets.

EATING OUT

Strasbourg is generally considered one of the best cities in France for great food. There's the attention to quality and detail that's the epitome of the French gourmet philosophy, allied to bold and hearty Alsatian fare with its roots firmly set across the Rhine. A favourite of the region is choucroute (or sauerkraut if you're leaning towards Germany), which is a rumbustious mixture of cabbage, potatoes, pork, sausage and ham; then there's baeckoffe, a tasty Alsace stew, which translates as 'ovenbake'

and blends pieces of stewing lamb, beef and pork with liberal splashes of Riesling. Talking of which, the fragrant wines of the area have a distinct character of their own: they're white, spicy and floral. The local fruit liquor, eau de vie, has a definite Alsatian kick, too – it's sweetened entirely by fruit without a hint of sugar. A good place to try the local specialities is a typical Strasbourg winstub. Most of the city's smarter restaurants are around the cathedral, in the Petite France quarter, and along the canal and river banks.

FRANCE - STRASBOURG

Régent Petite France & Spa

5 r. des Moulins – ℰ 03 88 76 43 43
– www.regent-petite-france.com
83 rm – ♥165/690 € ♥♥165/690 € – ☲ 25 € – 9 suites
Plan: **F2**
• Luxury • Personalised • Elegant •

A beautiful, large hotel occupying a former ice-making factory on the banks of the river Ill in the historic Petite France district. Comfortable, modern, stylish and unostentatious interior with pleasant rooms. Restaurant with a modern menu, lounge bar and terrace over the river.
Le Pont Tournant – See restaurant listing

Sofitel

4 pl. St-Pierre-le-Jeune – ℰ 03 88 15 49 00
– www.sofitel-strasbourg.com
146 rm – ♥140/396 € ♥♥140/396 € – ☲ 26 € – 4 suites
Plan: **F1**
• Chain • Business • Contemporary •

This, the very first Sofitel opened to the world in 1964, is right in the heart of the old town. The perfectly-maintained guestrooms are elegant and tailored to a business clientele (there are also numerous seminar rooms).

Cour du Corbeau

6 r. des Couples – ℰ 03 90 00 26 26 – www.cour-corbeau.com
63 rm – ♥155/680 € ♥♥155/680 € – ☲ 24 €
Plan: **G2**
• Historic • Luxury • Elegant •

A stone's throw from the Pont du Corbeau and the cathedral, this attractive hotel occupies several 16C buildings. Contemporary decor and top of the range facilities. Friendly service.

Les Haras

23 r. des Glacières – ℰ 03 90 20 50 00
– www.les-haras-hotel.com
55 rm – ♥150/595 € ♥♥150/595 € – ☲ 24 €
Plan: **F2**
• Historic • Luxury • Design •

This hotel in the centre of Strasbourg is located in the former national stud farm: an exceptional setting for an exceptional hotel! The guestrooms, done out in a minimalist design, range in size from large to very large (17-35 m^2).

Régent Contades

8 av. de la Liberté – ℰ 03 88 15 05 05
– www.regent-contades.com
46 rm – ♥104/590 € ♥♥194/760 € – ☲ 21 € – 2 suites
Plan: **H1**
• Luxury • Historic • Classic •

Behind the beautiful façade of this 19C townhouse is a refined, classical interior (with wood panelling and paintings) - as well as services to match.

Villa Novarina

11 r. Westercamp – ℰ 03 90 41 18 28
– www.villanovarina.com
24 rm – ♥150/450 € ♥♥175/850 € – ☲ 24 €
Plan: **D2**
• Boutique hotel • Contemporary • Personalised •

Near the Parc de l'Orangerie in the well-heeled embassy district, this large 1950s building was designed by architect Maurice Novarina (1907-2002). The lobby pays homage to Modernism (with furnishings by Eames, Knoll and Le Corbusier). Sleek guestrooms, a lovely pool and a tranquil garden.

Beaucour

5 r. des Bouchers – ℰ 03 88 76 72 00
– www.hotel-beaucour.com
49 rm – ♥96/132 € ♥♥164/209 € – ☲ 14 €
Plan: **G2**
• Traditional • Personalised • Cosy •

Two 18C Alsatian houses built around a charming flower-filled patio. Very comfortable Alsatian-style or classic rooms, some with wooden beams and a spa bathtub etc.

FRANCE - STRASBOURG

Maison Rouge   ♿
4 r. des Francs-Bourgeois – ☏ *03 88 32 08 60*   Plan: **F2**
– www.maison-rouge.com
139 rm ♻ – ⚟113/227 € ⚟⚟123/237 € – 3 suites
• Traditional • Classic •
A traditional hotel offering top-quality comfort and service. Spacious, immaculate rooms with designer fabrics and top-quality furnishings are accessed via landings decorated with objets d'art.

Hannong   ♿
15 r. du 22-Novembre – ☏ *03 88 32 16 22*   Plan: **F2**
– www.hotel-hannong.com – Closed 1 to 8 January
72 rm – ⚟79/289 € ⚟⚟89/369 € – ♻ 16 €
• Traditional • Functional • Personalised •
This hotel, which is full of character, was built on the site of the Hannong earthenware factory (18C). Expect objets d'art, contemporary facilities, quality materials and meticulous upkeep. Pleasant terrace area.

Hotel.D   ♿
15 r. du Fossé-des-Treize – ☏ *03 88 15 13 67 – www.hoteld.fr*   Plan: **F1**
37 rm – ⚟109/485 € ⚟⚟109/485 € – ♻ 16 €
• Business • Townhouse • Contemporary •
This contemporary hotel is close to the waterfront and the city centre. It has a unique, eye-catching and colourful interior. The comfortable guestrooms (large bed, Italian shower) and good breakfast (locally-sourced yogurts, apple and plum juice) make this a pleasant place to stay.

XxxX   Au Crocodile
☘   *10 r. de l'Outre –* ☏ *03 88 32 13 02 – www.au-crocodile.com*   Plan: **F1**
– Closed Sunday and Monday except in December
Menu 39 € (lunch), 82/120 € – Carte 90/105 €
• Classic cuisine • Elegant • Luxury •
Taken over in 2015 by Cédric Moulot (also the owner of the 1741), the Crocodile is in the process of regaining its former colours. The professional service showcases recipes that are quite simply delicious. First-class ingredients, subtle flavours and skilful preparation are combined in well-balanced dishes.
→ Carpaccio de langoustines au citron vert, salade de tourteau et huître végétale. Côte de veau de lait dorée au sautoir, échalote confite, gnocchis aux herbes et fricassée de girolles. Vacherin à la framboise et fromage blanc.

XxX   1741
☘   *22 quai des Bateliers –* ☏ *03 88 35 50 50 – www.1741.fr*   Plan: **G2**
– Closed 2 weeks in January, Tuesday and Wednesday except in December
Menu 39 € (weekday lunch), 95/135 € – Carte 90/105 €
• Modern cuisine • Cosy • Elegant •
This town house, built under the First Empire, faces the Château des Rohan. In an elegant boudoir-style decor, tuck into tasty, flavoursome and expertly done cuisine that promises fine moments. Interesting selection of Alsace wines.
→ Œuf cuit à 64°. Noisette de chevreuil des chasses d'Alsace, betterave et sauce grand veneur. Chocolat, caramel et fève tonka.

XxX   Buerehiesel (Eric Westermann)
☘   *in the parc de l'Orangerie –* ☏ *03 88 45 56 65*   Plan I: **D1**
– www.buerehiesel.fr – Closed 19 February-1 March, 30 July-21 August, 31 December-15 January, Sunday and Monday
Menu 39 € (weekday lunch), 68/98 € – Carte 65/100 €
• Modern cuisine • Elegant •
An exquisite restaurant housed in a beautiful half-timbered 17C farmhouse that was dismantled from its original location and rebuilt in the Parc de l'Orangerie (with bucolic views from the conservatory dining room and terrace). Refined and reliable regional cuisine, accompanied by a wonderful choice of Alsace wines. Pleasant service.
→ Cuisses de grenouilles poêlées au cerfeuil et schniederspaetzle. Pillette de Bresse cuite entière comme un baeckeofe. Brioche caramélisée à la bière, glace à la bière et poire rôtie.

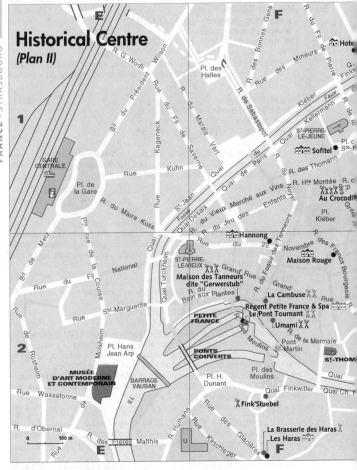

Historical Centre
(Plan II)

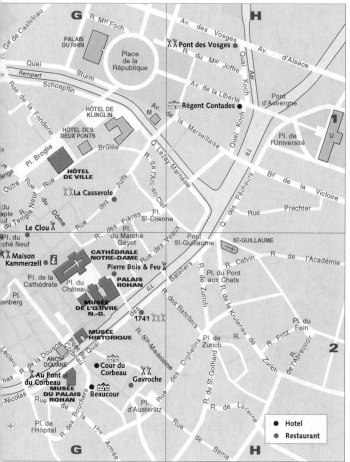

La Cambuse

XX   � AC

*1 r. des Dentelles – ℰ 03 88 22 10 22 – Closed 2 to   Plan: **F2***
15 May, 1 to 22 August, 23 December-8 January, Sunday and Monday
Carte 46/63 € – (booking advisable)
• Seafood • Cosy • Intimate •

La Cambuse's intimate dining room is decorated in the style of a boat cabin.
Simple yet refined fish and seafood are the specialities here, prepared in a
fusion of French and Asian styles based around spices and a minimum of cooking time.

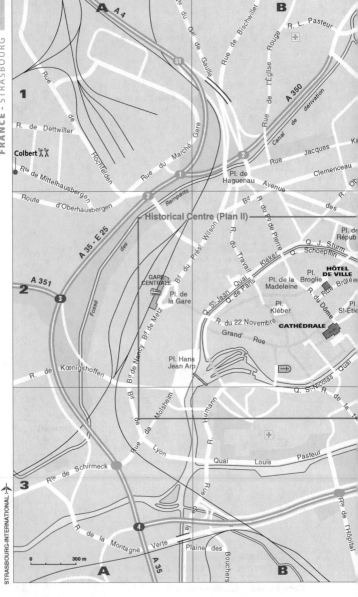

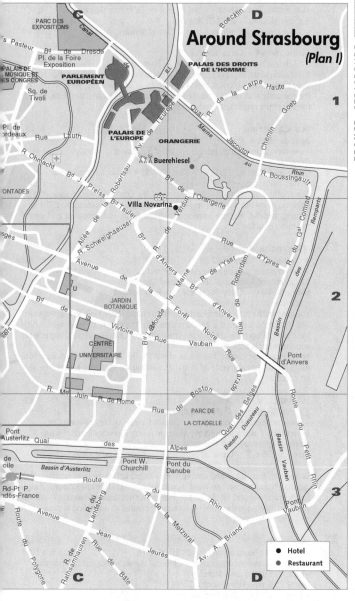

PARC DES
EXPOSITIONS

C

Canal

's Pasteur

B^d de Dresde
Pl. de la Foire
Exposition

PALAIS DE
MUSIQUE ET
ES CONGRÈS

PARLEMENT
EUROPÉEN

D

Boeckflin

Around Strasbourg
(Plan I)

PALAIS DES DROITS
DE L'HOMME

Haute

de la Carpe

Goeb

Sq. de
Tivoli

Pl. de
ordeaux

Rue

Lauth

PALAIS DE
L'EUROPE

Av. de l'Europe

ORANGERIE

Quai P. de la Marne

Jacquotot

au Rhin

Chemin

1

R. Ohmacht

R. J. Preiss

B^d

Buerehiesel

R. Boussingault

ONTADES

Allée de la

R. Schweighaeuser

B^d Tauler

Robertsau

Villa Novarina

B^d de l'Orangerie

de Verdun

Rue

d'Ypres

R. du Gal Conrad

Remparts

eges

Avenue

de

la

B^d d'Anvers

Marne

R. de l'Yser

B^d d'Anvers

Rotterdam

Rue

des

Bassin

2

B^d

de

JARDIN
BOTANIQUE

Vivtoire

B^d Lamboisle

Rue

Forêt

Noire

Vauban

d'Anvers

Rue de

Pont
d'Anvers

CENTRE
UNIVERSITAIRE

R. Mal

Juin

R. de Rome

Rue

de

Boston

Rue

Tarade

Route

du

Petit

Pont
Austerlitz

Quai

des

Alpes

PARC DE
LA CITADELLE

Quai des Belges

Bassin Dusuzeau

Bassin

Rhin

de
oile

Bassin d'Austerlitz

Pont W.
Churchill

Pont du
Danube

du

Bassin Vauban

3

Rd-Pt P.
ndès-France

Route

Avenue

R. du Landsberg

R. de la Metzeral

Rhin

Av. A. Briand

Pont
Vauban

Route du Polygone

Jean

Rue de Bâle

Jaurès

R. de Ratisanhausen

● Hotel

● Restaurant

C

D

FRANCE - STRASBOURG

XX **Le Pont Tournant** – Hôtel Régent Petite France & Spa ⇐ 🏠

5 r. des Moulins – ☏ 03 88 76 43 43   ⅙ 🅰🅒 🚗
– www.regent-petite-france.com – Closed Sunday,   Plan: **F2**
Monday and lunch
Menu 55/75 € – Carte 40/54 €
• Modern cuisine • Elegant • Chic •

Its location in the heart of La Petite France quarter is delightful and the cooking shows talent, allying good, fresh ingredients. In fine weather, you can dine on the romantic teak terrace installed on the edge of the canal and lock. Bear in mind that the restaurant is only open for dinner.

XX **La Casserole** 🅰🅒

24 r. des Juifs – ☏ 03 88 36 49 68   Plan: **G1**
– www.restaurantlacasserole.fr – Closed Sunday and Monday except in December
Menu 39 € (lunch), 79/115 € – Carte 77/99 € – (booking advisable)
• Modern cuisine • Cosy • Elegant •

The youthful owner, former head waiter of the Crocodile, would appear to be enjoying every second in his very own restaurant, as do his customers! The welcoming, tasteful, modern interior showcases fresh, well-prepared and up-to-the-minute cuisine.

XX **Gavroche** (Benoit Fuchs) 🅰🅒
❀
4 r. Klein – ☏ 03 88 36 82 89   Plan: **G2**
– www.restaurant-gavroche.com – Closed 22 July-16 August,
22 December-3 January, Saturday and Sunday
Menu 50/80 € – Carte 85/95 € – (booking advisable)
• Modern cuisine • Intimate •

You can feel the desire to make the customer happy here, both in the restaurant and the kitchens. Spend a pleasant time over the course of your meal, which has plenty of finesse and character. The dishes concentrate on good ingredients and the result is a treat!
→ Foie gras de canard fumé aux sarments de vigne. Dos de maigre rôti, rougaille de tomate verte et piquillos. Gâteau au chocolat sans farine cuit en cocotte.

XX **Umami** (René Fieger) 🅰🅒
❀
8 r. des Dentelles – ☏ 03 88 32 80 53   Plan: **F2**
– www.restaurant-umami.com – Closed 1 week in May, 3 weeks in September, 1 week in January, Monday lunch, Tuesday lunch, Friday lunch, Wednesday and Thursday
Menu 50/95 € 🍷 – Carte approx. 70 € – (booking advisable)
• Creative • Cosy • Intimate •

Sweet, salt, sour, bitter and umami, the so-called fifth taste long recognised in Japanese gastronomy. The word wonderfully heralds this tasty cuisine, fusing foods from near and far. As for the interior, with its intimate atmosphere and subdued lighting in the evening, it certainly creates an appealing setting.
→ Cuisine du marché.

XX **Colbert** 🏠 ♻ 🅿
🚲
127 rte Mittelhausbergen – ☏ 03 88 22 52 16   Plan I: **A1**
– www.restaurant-colbert.com – Closed 2 weeks in August, Christmas Holidays, Sunday and Monday
Menu 25 € (weekday lunch), 32/48 €
– Carte 41/53 € – (booking advisable)
• Modern cuisine • Cosy • Bistro •

The young owner-chef concocts recipes that are in tune with modern tastes, combining flavour and precision in original, elegant dishes; pan-fried frogs' legs, macaroni and cooking juices to name only one. Given the quality of the cuisine, it is hardly surprising that the restaurant is frequently fully booked.

XX **Le Violon d'Ingres** 🏠

1 r. du Chevalier-Robert (at La Robertsau) – ✆ *03 88 31 39 50 – Closed
2 weeks in August, 1 week in October and in January, Saturday lunch,
Sunday dinner and Monday*
Menu 36 € (weekday lunch), 58/64 €
– Carte 60/70 € – (booking advisable)
· Classic cuisine · Intimate · Classic décor ·
This historic Alsace house in the Robertsau district near the European Parliament serves impeccably prepared modern cuisine in an elegant dining room
or on the shady terrace.

XX **Maison Kammerzell** 🆎 ⇔

16 pl. de la Cathédrale – ✆ *03 88 32 42 14*   Plan: **G2**
– www.maison-kammerzell.com
Menu 30/47 € – Carte 36/55 €
· Alsatian · Historic · Friendly ·
A typical 16C Strasbourg house near the cathedral with an authentic medieval
feel, featuring stained-glass windows, paintings, wood carvings and Gothic vaulting. Local cuisine (choucroute is a speciality) and brasserie-style dishes.

XX **Pont des Vosges** 🏠 🆎

15 quai Koch – ✆ *03 88 36 47 75*   Plan: **H1**
– www.lepontdesvosges.fr – Closed Sunday
Carte 37/70 €
· Traditional cuisine · Brasserie ·
Located on the corner of an old building, this brasserie is renowned for its
copious, traditional cuisine. Vintage advertising posters and mirrors decorate
the dining room.

X **La Brasserie des Haras** 🏠 ⟋ 🆎 ⇔ 🔥

23 r. des Glacières – ✆ *03 88 24 00 00*   Plan: **F2**
– www.les-haras-brasserie.com
Menu 34/71 € – Carte 34/59 €
· Modern cuisine · Design · Chic ·
An elegant and refined restaurant with lovely traditional dishes and a handful of
local specialities. In addition, the kitchen opens onto the contemporary dining
room, so you can see the chef at work!

X **Pierre Bois & Feu** 🆎

6 r. du Bain-aux-Roses – ✆ *03 88 36 25 59*   Plan: **G2**
*– www.pierreboisetfeu.fr – Closed 1 week in February, 2 weeks in August,
Monday lunch, Wednesday lunch and Sunday*
Menu 44 € – Carte 59/79 €
· Traditional cuisine · Bistro · Friendly ·
In a side street close to the quays, this contemporary little bistro is housed in a
building dating from the 17C. It is a charming spot with its bare wood tables
and open kitchen. On the menu find seasonal dishes and fine local produce, as
well as a speciality that begs to be tried: Salers beef "cuit au fer à repasser" (cooked with an iron!).

WINSTUBS *Regional specialities and wine tasting in a typical
Alsatian atmosphere*

X **Au Pont du Corbeau** ⅋ 🏠 🆎

😊 *21 quai St-Nicolas –* ✆ *03 88 35 60 68 – Closed 1 week*   Plan: **G2**
*February Holidays, 25 July-22 August, Sunday lunch and Saturday except
in December*
Menu 31 € (dinner) – Carte 29/52 €
· Alsatian · Winstub · Friendly ·
Experience local gastronomic specialities and traditional decor (Renaissance
features, posters) in this restaurant next door to the Musée Alsacien, with its displays of popular art.

Le Clou

AC

3 r. du Chaudron – ✆ *03 88 32 11 67*   Plan: **G1-2**
– www.le-clou.com
Menu 18 € (weekday lunch) – Carte 30/55 €
• Alsatian • Winstub • Rustic •

Located a short distance from the cathedral, this authentic winstub (typical Alsace bistro) is packed with olde worlde objects and scenes from yesteryear (beautiful marquetry). Typical cuisine which pays homage to the region.

Fink'Stuebel

26 r. Finkwiller – ✆ *03 88 25 07 57*   Plan: **F2**
– www.restaurant-finkstuebel.com – Closed 3 weeks in August, Sunday and Monday except in December
Carte 36/66 €
• Alsatian • Winstub • Inn •

Half-timbering, wooden floorboards, painted woodwork, regional furniture and floral tablecloths provide the decor in the Fink'Stuebel, the epitome of a traditional winstub. Local cuisine predominates here, of course, with foie gras to the fore.

GERMANY
DEUTSCHLAND

→ **Area:**
357 111 km² (137 735 sq mi).

→ **Population:**
82 200 000 inhabitants.
Density = 230 per km².

→ **Capital:**
Berlin.

→ **Currency:**
Euro (€).

→ **Government:**
Parliamentary federal republic, comprising 16 states (Länder) since 1990. Member of European Union since 1957 (one of the 6 founding countries).

→ **Language:**
German.

→ **Public holidays:**
New Year's Day (1 Jan); Epiphany (6 Jan - certain regions only); Good Friday (late Mar/Apr); Easter Monday (late Mar/Apr); Labor Day (1 May); Ascension Day (May); Whit Monday (late May/June); Corpus Christi (late May/June – certain regions only); Assumption of the Virgin Mary (15 Aug); Day of German Unity (3 Oct); Reformation Day (31 Oct - new Federal States only); All Saints' Day (1 Nov); Day of Prayer & Repentance (21 Nov, certain regions only); Christmas Day (25 Dec); Boxing Day (26 Dec).

→ **Local Time:**
GMT+1 hour in winter and GMT +2 hours in summer.

→ **Climate:**
Temperate continental, with cold winters and warm summers (Berlin: January 0°C; July 20°C).

● Hamburg

BERLIN ●

Cologne
●

● Frankfurt

Munich
●

→ **Emergency:**
Police ℰ **110**; Medical Assistance and Fire Brigade ℰ **112**.
(Dialling **112** within any EU country will redirect your call and contact the emergency services.)

→ **Electricity:**
230 volts AC, 50Hz; 2 round pin sockets.

→ **Formalities**
Travellers from the European Union (EU), Switzerland, Iceland and the main countries of North and South America need a national identity card or passport (America: passport required) to visit Germany for less than three months (tourism or business purpose). For visitors from other countries a visa may be required, in addition to a passport, especially for those wishing to stay for longer than three months. We advise you to check with your embassy before travelling.

BERLIN
BERLIN

Population: 3 501 880

S. Guillot/MICHELIN

Berlin's parliament faces an intriguing dilemma when it comes to where to call its heart, as, although they are homogeneous in many other ways, the east and the west of the city still lay claim to separate centres after 40 years of partition. Following the tempestuous 1990s, Berlin sought to resolve its new identity, and it now stands proud as one of the most dynamic and forward thinking cities in the world. Alongside its idea of tomorrow, it's never lost sight of its bohemian past, and many parts of the city retain the arty sense of adventure that characterised downtown Berlin during the 1920s: turn any corner and you might find a modernist art gallery, a tiny cinema or a cutting-edge club.

The eastern side of the River Spree, around Nikolaiviertel, is the historic heart of the city, dating back to the 13C. Meanwhile, way over to the west of the centre lie Kurfürstendamm and Charlottenburg; smart districts which came to the fore after World War II as the heart of West Berlin. Between the two lie imposing areas which swarm with visitors: Tiergarten is the green lung of the city, and just to its east is the great boulevard of Unter den Linden. Continuing eastward, the self-explanatory Museum Island sits snugly and securely in the tributaries of the Spree. The most southerly of Berlin's sprawling districts is Kreuzberg, renowned for its bohemian, alternative character.

BERLIN IN...

→ **ONE DAY**
Unter den Linden, Museum Island, Nikolaiviertel, coffee at TV Tower.

→ **TWO DAYS**
Potsdamer Platz, Reichstag, Regierungsviertel including the Gemäldegalerie, concert at Philharmonie.

→ **THREE DAYS**
KaDeWe, Kurfürstendamm, Charlottenburg Palace.

PRACTICAL INFORMATION

ARRIVAL-DEPARTURE

✈ Berlin Tegel Airport lies 12km northwest.

✈ Berlin Schönefeld is 21km southeast.
U-Bahn and S-Bahn trains operate from both.

GETTING AROUND

The U- and S-Bahn trains are quick and efficient but the bus is another good alternative; routes 100 and 200 incorporate most of the top attractions. Trams operate mainly within East Berlin. There are various ticketing options - check with a tourist information office or simply invest in a Berlin Welcome Card, which provides unlimited travel on the S-Bahn, and discounts for selected theatres, museums, attractions and city tours; buy one from a public transport ticket desk, a tourist information office or one of many hotels. Cyclists are well looked after here; there are many cycling routes and most of the main roads have separate cycle lanes and special traffic lights at intersections.

CALENDAR HIGHLIGHTS

January
International Green Week.

February
Berlin Film Festival (Berlinale).

June
Karneval der Kulturen.

July
Classic Open Air Festival.

September
Berlin Music Week, International Literary Festival.

October
Berlin Festival of Lights.

EATING OUT

Many of Berlin's best restaurants are found within the grand hotels and you only have to go to Savignyplatz near Ku'damm to realise how smart dining has taken off. Dinner is the most popular meal and you can invariably eat late, as lots of places stay open until 2 or 3am. Berlin also has a reputation for simple, hearty dishes, inspired by the long, hard winter and, when temperatures drop, the city's comfort food has an irresistible allure – there's pork knuckle, Schnitzel, Bratwurst in mustard, chunky dumplings... and the real Berlin favourite, Currywurst. Bread and potatoes are ubiquitous but since reunification, many dishes have also incorporated a more global influence, so produce from the local forests, rivers and lakes may well be given an Asian or Mediterranean twist (Berlin now claims a wider range of restaurants than any other German city). Service is included in the price of your meal but it's customary to round up the bill. Be sure to try the local 'Berliner Weisse mit Schuss' – a light beer with a dash of raspberry or woodruff.

Adlon Kempinski

Unter den Linden 77 ✉ *10117* – Ⓜ *Brandenburger Tor* – ✆ *(030) 2 26 10* – *www.hotel-adlon.de* Plan: **G1**

307 rm – †265/720 € ††265/720 € – ☕ 42 € – 78 suites

• Grand Luxury • Historic • Classic •

Situated in the capital, this imposing grand hotel, which has hosted a list of crowned heads far too long to cite here, is synonymous with glitz and glamour. Magical, luxurious ambience, plus presidential suites with limousine and butler service.

✿✿ **Lorenz Adlon Esszimmer • Quarré** – See restaurant listing

The Ritz-Carlton

Potsdamer Platz 3 ✉ *10785* – Ⓜ *Potsdamer Platz* – ✆ *(030) 33 77 77* – *www.ritzcarlton.com* Plan: **F2**

263 rm – †195/450 € ††195/450 € – ☕ 38 € – 40 suites

• Grand Luxury • Chain • Classic •

One of the most exclusive hotel addresses in Germany. The elegant lobby with its cantilevered marble staircase is home to a stylish lounge where guests gather for classic 'teatime' treats.

Brasserie Desbrosses – See restaurant listing

Regent

Charlottenstr. 49 ✉ *10117* – Ⓜ *Französische Str.* – ✆ *(030) 2 03 38* – *www.regenthotels.com/berlin* Plan: **G1**

156 rm – †260/850 € ††260/850 € – ☕ 35 € – 39 suites

• Grand Luxury • Classic •

The guests here expect first class service and they are not disappointed. A pleasant custom is the taking of tea – English, Russian or Saxony-style (the hotel's own blend) – on nothing but the finest Meissen porcelain in the elegant lounge.

✿✿ **Fischers Fritz** – See restaurant listing

Grand Hyatt Berlin

Marlene-Dietrich-Platz 2 (Entrance on Eichhornstraße) ✉ *10785* – Ⓜ *Potsdamer Platz* – ✆ *(030) 25 53 12 34* – *www.berlin.grand.hyatt.com* Plan: **F2**

326 rm – †179/439 € ††179/469 € – ☕ 36 € – 16 suites

• Grand Luxury • Chain • Design •

This trapezoid hotel on the Potsdamer Platz impresses with modern, hi-tech rooms decorated in a minimalist style. The Club Olympus Spa with its impressive swimming pool and views over the roofs of Berlin is also worth a look. Restaurant options include Vox and Mesa, which serves a range of dishes from curry wurst to beef roulade.

Vox – See restaurant listing

Hotel de Rome

Behrenstr. 37 ✉ *10117* – Ⓜ *Französische Str.* – ✆ *(030) 4 60 60 90* – *www.hotelderome.de* Plan: **G1**

136 rm – †270/555 € ††270/555 € – ☕ 37 € – 9 suites

• Grand Luxury • Classic •

A luxury hotel on the Bebelplatz in the impressive framework of a building dating from 1889, formerly used by the Dresdner Bank. Today, the old strongroom is a pool.

La Banca – See restaurant listing

The Mandala

Potsdamer Str. 3 ✉ *10785* – Ⓜ *Potsdamer Platz* – ✆ *(030) 5 90 05 00 00* – *www.themandala.de* Plan: **F2**

131 rm – †160/500 € ††160/500 € – ☕ 30 € – 26 suites

• Business • Luxury • Design •

This hotel, set opposite the Sony Center in the Potsdamer Platz, has a range of spacious and simple yet luxurious rooms and suites and also boasts an unusual spa. The trendy Bar Qiu serves business lunches.

✿✿ **FACIL** – See restaurant listing

Titanic Gendarmenmarkt

Französische Str. 30 ☒ *10117* – ⓜ *Hausvogteiplatz* — Plan: **G1**
– ℰ *(030) 20 14 37 00* – *www.titanic-hotels.de*
200 rm – ♦160/290 € ♦♦160/290 € – ☲ 28 € – 8 suites
• Townhouse • Business • Contemporary •

Despite its city centre location, the Titanic Deluxe – set in the former costume department of the Berlin State Opera – really is a little world of its own. The design is chic, from the bright, marble lobby to the stylishly modern rooms and the large hammam. Café Parisienne.
Beef Grill Club by Hasir – See restaurant listing

Steigenberger Hotel am Kanzleramt

Ella-Trebe-Str. 5 ☒ *10557* – ⓜ *Hauptbahnhof* – ℰ *(030)*
7 40 74 30 – *www.steigenberger.de* — Plan: **F1**
328 rm – ♦119/299 € ♦♦119/299 € – ☲ 25 € – 11 suites
• Business • Contemporary •

A modern, minimalist style hotel with a spacious lobby and an attractive leisure area with a view of Berlin's Government Quarter. Breakfast is served in a light and airy room on the first floor and meals are served at No. 5 (restaurant and bar). Convenient location next to the main railway station.

Boutique Hotel i-31

Invalidenstr. 31 ☒ *10115* – ⓜ *Naturkundemuseum* — Plan I: **C1**
– ℰ *(030) 3 38 40 00* – *www.hotel-i31.de*
117 rm – ♦104/159 € ♦♦104/159 € – ☲ 18 €
• Business • Personalised • Contemporary •

This boutique hotel with its designer interior stands in the heart of Berlin-Mitte, still one of the trendiest parts of Berlin. The fresh, comfortable rooms – categorised as 'Pure', 'White' and 'Brown' – all come with a free mini-bar and the latest in modern technology.

nhow

Stralauer Allee 3 ☒ *10245* – ⓜ *Warschauer Str.* — Plan I: **D2**
– ℰ *(030) 2 90 29 90* – *www.nhow-berlin.com*
303 rm – ♦110/180 € ♦♦110/180 € – ☲ 25 € – 1 suite
• Business • Design • Minimalist •

No other hotel in Berlin combines music and lifestyle in such an unconventional and cosmopolitan manner. Clean lines and functional architecture outside; upbeat design, curved forms and young, fresh colours inside. And with its recording studio looking out over the city, it really is one of a kind!
fabrics – See restaurant listing

Titanic Chaussee

Chausseestr. 30 ☒ *10115* – ⓜ *Naturkundemuseum* — Plan I: **C1**
– ℰ *(030) 3 11 68 58 00* – *www.titanic-hotels.de*
376 rm – ♦90/190 € ♦♦90/190 € – ☲ 19 € – 13 suites
• Business • Spa and wellness • Elegant •

The Titanic Chaussee offers tasteful, modern design with a retro touch. This is evident from its spacious lobby to its comfortable guestrooms, as well as in the 3000m^2 wellness suite (this costs extra) and the Pascarella (Italian) and Hasir Burger restaurants. All just a short walk from the fashionable Oranienburger Straße.

The Dude

Köpenicker Str. 92 ☒ *10179* – ⓜ *Heinrich-Heine-Str.* — Plan I: **D2**
– ℰ *(030) 411 988 177* – *www.thedudeberlin.com*
27 rm – ♦109/219 € ♦♦139/249 € – ☲ 24 €
• Townhouse • Historic • Personalised •

This is design in its purest form. The mix of historical detail (the building dates back to 1822) and modern style is reminiscent of a mansion house. If you are in search of a snack, the Deli serves sandwiches at lunchtime. Breakfast is also available.
The Brooklyn – See restaurant listing

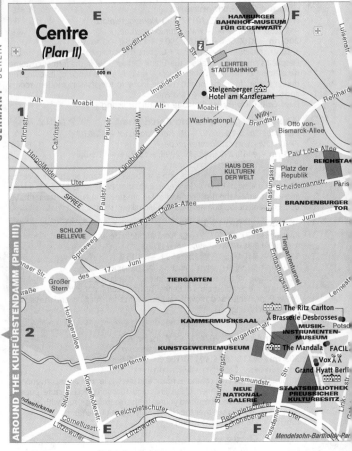

Centre
(Plan II)

0   500 m

HAMBURGER BAHNHOF-MUSEUM FÜR GEGENWART

LEHRTER STADTBAHNHOF

Steigenberger Hotel am Kanzleramt

Moabit

Washingtonpl.

HAUS DER KULTUREN DER WELT

Otto von-Bismarck-Allee

Paul Löbe Allee

REICHSTAG

Platz der Republik

Scheidemannstr.

Paris

BRANDENBURGER TOR

SCHLOß BELLEVUE

17. Juni

Straße des

TIERGARTEN

The Ritz Carlton

Brasserie Desbrosses

KAMMERMUSIKSAAL

MUSIK-INSTRUMENTEN-MUSEUM

Potsd

KUNSTGEWERBEMUSEUM

The Mandala

FACIL

Vox

Grand Hyatt Berli

NEUE NATIONAL-GALERIE

STAATSBIBLIOTHEK PREUSSICHER KULTURBESITZ

Mendelsohn-Bartholdy-Par

Großer Stern

Garden Living

P

Invalidenstr.101 ⊠ 10115 – Ⓜ Zinnowitzer Straße – ℰ (030) 2 84 45 59 00 – www.gardenliving.de

Plan I: **C2**

27 rm – ♦99/159 € ♦♦114/174 € – ⌂ 8 €

• Townhouse • Personalised •

Part of the ethos at the Garden Living is to make you feel as if you are 'staying at home'. This is indeed the impression you get in this pretty group of three old townhouses with their generously sized and tastefully appointed apartments, each with their own small kitchen. The attractive interior courtyard or 'Green Oasis' makes the ideal place for breakfast on a lovely summer's morning.

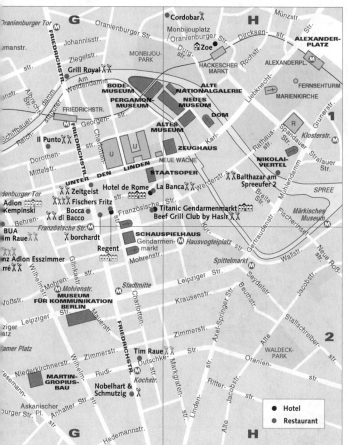

Catalonia

Köpenicker Str. 80 ✉ *10178*
– Ⓜ *Märk. Museum*
– 𝒞 *(030) 24 08 47 70*
– *www.hoteles-catalonia.com*
131 rm – †79/299 € ††89/299 € – ⌑ 16 €

☆ ⅙ ㏅ ⅏
Plan I: **D2**

• Chain • Contemporary • Grand luxury •

Catalonia is the so-called 'pilot project' of a Catalan hotel group in Germany. The unusual lobby design reflects the variety and changing landscape of Berlin and the landings feature some impressive graffiti. The restaurant serves a mix of Berlin and Spanish cuisine including tapas.

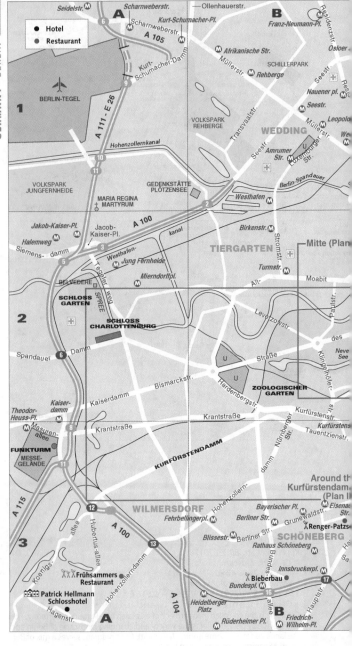

Legend:
- ● Hotel
- ● Restaurant

Seidelstr.

Scharnweberstr. — Ollenhauerstr.

A

B

Scharnweberstr.

Kurt-Schumacher-Pl.

A 105

Franz-Neumann-Pl.

Residenzstr.

Osloer

Afrikanische Str.

SCHILLERPARK

Müllerstr.

Rehberge

Seestr.

Nauener pl.

Seestr.

Leopold

BERLIN-TEGEL

VOLKSPARK REHBERGE

Müllerstr.

WEDDING

Transvaalstr.

Seestr.

Amrumer Str.

Seestr.

Wee

Luxemburger Str.

Hohenzollernkanal

Berlin-Spandauer

VOLKSPARK JUNGFERNHEIDE

GEDENKSTÄTTE PLÖTZENSEE

Westhafen

MARIA REGINA MARTYRUM

Jakob-Kaiser-Pl.

Jacob-Kaiser-Pl.

A 100

kanal

Birkenstr.

Mitte (Plan

Halemweg

Westhafen-

TIERGARTEN

Stromstr.

Siemens-damm

Jung Fernheide

Turmstr.

Moabit

BELVEDERE

Mierndorffpl.

All-

SCHLOSS GARTEN

Levetzowstr.

Paulstr.

SPREE

SCHLOSS CHARLOTTENBURG

Straße

des

Neve See

Klingelhöfer-

Spandauer

Damm

U

Kaiser-damm

Kaiserdamm

Bismarckstr.

Hardenbergstr.

U

ZOOLOGISCHER GARTEN

Theodor-Heuss-Pl.

Krantstraße

Kurfürstenstr.

Masuren-allee

Krantstraße

Nürnberger Str.

Kurfürstens

FUNKTURM

Tauentzienstr.

MESSE-GELÄNDE

KURFÜRSTENDAMM

Around th
Kurfürstendam
(Plan I

A 115

WILMERSDORF

Hohenzollern-

Bayerischer Pl.

Eisenau
Str.

Fehrbellinerpl.

Berliner Str.

Grunewaldstr.

Renger-Patzs

damm

SCHÖNEBERG

Blissestr.

Berliner Str.

Rathaus Schöneberg

Bundes-

Koenigs-

allee

Hubertus-allee

Hohenzollerndamm

Frühsammers Restaurant

Innsbruckerpl.

Bieberbau ●

Patrick Hellmann Schlosshotel

A 104

Bundespl.

Heidelberger Platz

Hauptstr.

A

Hagenstr.

Rüderheimer Pl.

Friedrich-Wilhelm-Pl.

B

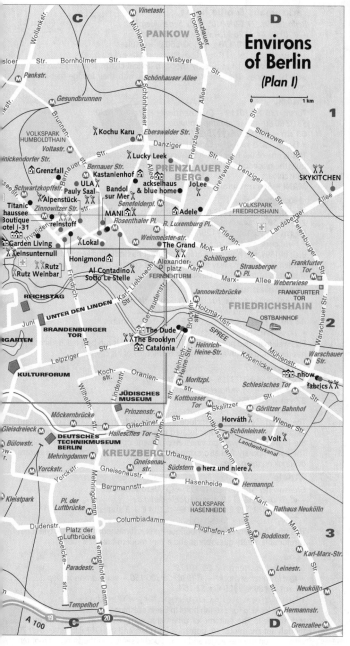

Environs of Berlin
(Plan I)

0   1 km

C   **D**

Wollankstr.

Vinetastr.

sloer   Str.   Bornholmer   Str.   Wisbyer   Str.

Mühlenstr.

Prenzlauer Promenade

PANKOW

Pankstr.

kstr.

Pankstr.

Schönhauser Allee

Gesundbrunnen

Schönhauser Allee

Brunnen

Storkower   Str.

VOLKSPARK
HUMBOLDTHAIN

Kochu Karu   Eberswalder Str.

Voltastr.

inickendorfer Str.

Grenzfall

Bernauer   Str.

Danziger

Lucky Leek

Prenzlauer   Allee

Danziger   Str.

SKYKITCHEN

PRENZLAUER
BERG

Schwartzkopffstr.

Bernauer Str.

Kastanienhof

ackselhaus
& blue home

JoLee

Greifswalder   Str.

seestr.

Pauly Saal

Bandol
sur Mer

VOLKSPARK
FRIEDRICHSHAIN

Titanic
haussee
Boutique
otel I-31

Alpenstück

ULA

Zinnowitzer str.

MANI

reinstoff

Senefelderpl.

Rosenthaler Pl.

Adele

Invalidenstr.

Landsberger

Petersburger   Str.

Garden Living

R. Luxemburg Pl.

Weinmeister-str.

Meinsunternull

Friedrichstr.

Lokal

The Grand

Moll-   str.

Rutz
Rutz Weinbar

Honigmond

Alexander-
platz

Karl-

Schillingstr.

Strausberger
Pl.

Frankfurter
Tor

Al Contadino
Sotto Le Stelle

FERNSEHTURM

Marx-

Allee

Weberwiese

FRANKFURTER
TOR

REICHSTAG

Karl-   Str.

Jannowitzbrücke

OSTBAHNHOF

Juni

UNTER DEN LINDEN

Grenzdienststr.

Holzmarktstr.

FRIEDRICHSHAIN

Warschauer Str.

BRANDENBURGER
TOR

str.

SPREE

Mühlenstr.

IGARTEN

Leipziger

Str.

The Dude
The Brooklyn
Catalonia

Heinrich-
Heine-Str.

Köpenicker

Warschauer
Str.

KULTURFORUM

Koch-
str.

Oranien-

Lindenstr.

Heinrich-Heine-Str.

Moritzpl.

Schlesisches Tor

nhow

fabrics

Wilhelm-

JÜDISCHES
MUSEUM

Prinzenstr.

Kottbusser
Tor

Skalitzer

Görlitzer Bahnhof

Str.

Möckernbrücke

Gitschiner

Str.

Horváth

Kottbusser Damm

Wiener   Str.

Gleisdreieck

Halleschen Tor

Prinzenstr.

Schönleinstr.

Bülowstr.

DEUTSCHES
TECHNIKMUSEUM
BERLIN

Landwehrkanal

Volt

wr.

Mehringdamm

KREUZBERG

Urbanstr.

Gneisenau-
str.

herz und niere

Yorckstr.

Gneisenaustr.

Südstern

Hermannpl.

Kleistpark

Bergmannstr.

Hasenheide

Karl-

Rathaus Neukölln

Pl. der
Luftbrücke

Dudenstr.

Platz der
Luftbrücke

Boelcke-

Columbiadamm

VOLKSPARK
HASENHEIDE

Flughafen-str.

Hermann-

Boddinstr.

Marx-

Str.

Paradestr.

Leinestr.

Neukölln

Tempelhof

A 100

19

20

Tempelhofer Damm

Hermannstr.

Grenzallee

C   **D**

ackselhaus & blue home

Belforter Str. 21 ✉ *10405 –* Ⓜ *Senefelderplatz*   Plan I: **D1**
– ℰ (030) 44 33 76 33 – www.ackselhaus.de
31 rm ⌷ *–* ♦110/170 € ♦♦150/360 € *– 4 suites*
• Townhouse • Historic • Personalised •
This establishment has a really special historical charm. It is Venetian in style with blue tones. The green inner courtyards with their lounge feel are very pretty.

MANI   ♿ 🅰🅲

Torstr. 136 ✉ *10119 –* Ⓜ *Rosenthaler Platz – ℰ (030)*   Plan I: **C2**
53 02 80 80 – www.amanogroup.de
63 rm *–* ♦75/250 € ♦♦75/250 € *–* ⌷ *15 €*
• Boutique hotel • Contemporary •
This is one of the new stylish boutique hotels in Berlin – chic, fashionable and truly the place to be. The guestrooms are decorated in a minimalist-style with dark colours.
MANI – See restaurant listing

Honigmond   ⚒ 🈳

Tieckstr. 11 ✉ *10115 –* Ⓜ *Zinnowitzer Str. – ℰ (030)*   Plan I: **C2**
2 84 45 50 – www.honigmond.de
60 rm *–* ♦95/130 € ♦♦129/199 € *–* ⌷ *10 €*
• Historic • Classic • Personalised •
Built in 1895, this house in a quiet side street has individually-styled rooms. The Garden Hotel 350m away has a lovely inner courtyard garden. Pleasant coffee shop-cum-restaurant in a classic setting.

Kastanienhof   🈳 🅿

Kastanienallee 65 ✉ *10119 –* Ⓜ *Senefelderpl.*   Plan I: **C1**
– ℰ (030) 44 30 50 – www.kastanienhof.biz
44 rm *–* ♦79/154 € ♦♦98/216 € *–* ⌷ *9 € – 2 suites*
• Townhouse • Functional •
This well-managed hotel offering functional rooms is run by a real Berliner who has decorated it with a vast array of mementos of his city.

Grenzfall   ⚒ 🛏 ♿ 🈳 🚗

Ackerstr. 136 ✉ *13355 –* Ⓜ *Bernauer Str. – ℰ (030)*   Plan I: **C1**
34 33 33 00 – www.hotel-grenzfall.de
37 rm *–* ♦63/159 € ♦♦83/179 € *–* ⌷ *11 €*
• Townhouse • Functional •
The Grenzfall's attractions include a friendly welcome, a 3000m² garden and reasonable prices. The hotel, located in a quiet side street close to the site of the former Berlin wall, provides employment opportunities for the disabled. The contemporary feel also extends to the restaurant, which boasts a terrace overlooking the garden.

Adele

Greifswalder Str. 227 ✉ *10405 –* Ⓜ *Alexanderplatz*   Plan I: **D1**
– ℰ (030) 44 32 43 10 – www.adele-berlin.de
13 rm *–* ♦79/129 € ♦♦89/139 € *–* ⌷ *14 € – 3 suites*
• Townhouse • Design •
This small and very exclusive boutique hotel is furnished in Art Deco-style. It has comfortable, pretty guestrooms and a very modern breakfast room.

Zoe   ♿ 🅰🅲 🚗

Große Präsidentenstr. 7 ✉ *10178*   Plan: **H1**
– Ⓜ *Hackescher Markt – ℰ (030) 21 300 150 – www.amanogroup.de*
88 rm *–* ♦89 € ♦♦89 € *–* ⌷ *15 €*
• Boutique hotel • Contemporary • Trendy •
If you are looking for a stylish hotel in Berlin's fashionable Hackescher Markt district, this is it. The epitome of urban chic with calm, dark tones, the rooms, though not enormous, are upmarket and chic, and the G&T Bar serves over 70 variations on the classic gin and tonic. Food is served on the stunning roof terrace.

XxXxX **Lorenz Adlon Esszimmer** – Hotel Adlon Kempinski 🕸 ⅙ 🔟
🕸 🕸 *Unter den Linden 77* ✉ *10117* – Ⓜ *Brandenburger Tor* ⇧ 🚗
– ☏ (030) 22 61 19 60 – www.lorenzadlon-esszimmer.de Plan: **G1**
*– Closed 1-17 January, 16-25 April, 30 July-22 August, 29 October-
7 November and Sunday-November*
Menu 145/205 € – Carte 126/156 € – *(dinner only)*
• Creative • Luxury • Elegant •
Eminently elegant and luxurious, this restaurant pays tribute to the hotel's founder Lorenz Adlon. You can eat in the dining room with its fine wood panelling
and open fire, or in the library. Sample either of Hendrik Otto's two menus to
find out just how skilfully he combines classic dishes and contemporary elements.
➜ Rottstocker Saibling, Fischextrakt, Grapefruit, Limette, Kopfsalat, Erbsen,
Szechuan Pfeffer, Dill. Rehrücken, Wildpfeffersauce, Bohne, gedörrte Bee-
ren, fermentierter Pfeffer, Majoran. Opalis Schokolade Kerbel-Koriandereis,
karamellisierter Blätterteig, Kokosnuss, Gurke, Molke.

XxxX **Fischers Fritz** – Hotel Regent 🕸 ⅙ 🔟 ⇧ 🚗
🕸 🕸 *Charlottenstr. 49* ✉ *10117* – Ⓜ *Französische Str.* Plan: **G1**
*– ☏ (030) 20 33 63 63 – www.fischersfritz-berlin.com – Closed 2-8 January,
31 July - 20 August*
Menu 105/170 € – Carte 105/168 € – *(dinner only) (booking advisable)*
• Classic cuisine • Elegant •
The elegant wood panelling, open fire and fine chandeliers at Fischers Fritz are
somewhat reminiscent of a classic English style, while Christian Lohse's fish-
inspired cuisine, unforgettable for its use of high quality produce and painstaking preparation, clearly shares equally classic roots. It is not for nothing that the
restaurant has held two Michelin stars since 2008!
➜ Geröstete Atlantik Jakobsmuschel, Püree von glatter Petersilie und Schalotten, Verjus gebunden mit gesalzener Butter. Bretonischer Hummer
geröstet mit Salz, Chili und Koriander. Kiwi Gold Label in Marsala-Passions-
fruchtkaramell geschmort und geschäumte Pistazienbutter.

XxX **reinstoff** (Daniel Achilles) 🕸 ⅙ 🔟
🕸 🕸 *Schlegelstr. 26c (Edison Höfe)* ✉ *10115* Plan I: **C2**
*– Ⓜ Zinnowitzerstr. – ☏ (030) 30 88 12 14 – www.reinstoff.eu – Closed
Sunday-Monday*
Menu 110/198 € – *(dinner only) (booking advisable)*
• Creative • Fashionable • Intimate •
The delightfully creative set menus ('Close to home' and 'Further afield') are
more than matched by the friendly, professional wine waiters. They are always
ready with a sometimes unorthodox but always well-matched recommenda-
tion – including a beer with your starter or vermouth to accompany dessert.
The room-within-a-room concept in this old industrial setting is particularly
appealing.
➜ Kalmar Cocktail, Kiwi und grüner Wacholder, Zitronenblattöl, Salicorn-
Vinaigrette. Salzwiesenlamm, Pastrami vom Tafelspitz, Akazienblüten,
geschmorte feine Rippchen. Litschi, kleine Eiswaffel, Mangostane, Sesam
und Wasabi.

XxX **FACIL** – Hotel The Mandala 🕸 🍴 ⅙ 🔟 🚗
🕸 🕸 *Potsdamer Str. 3 (5th floor)* ✉ *10785* Plan: **F2**
*– Ⓜ Potsdamer Platz – ☏ (030) 5 90 05 12 34 – www.facil.de – Closed
2 weeks early January, 3 weeks July - August and Saturday-Sunday*
Menu 48 € (weekday lunch)/185 €
– Carte 100/123 € – *(booking advisable)*
• Creative • Chic •
FACIL is an oasis of calm amid the hustle and bustle of the Potsdamer Platz. It is
pleasantly light and airy, especially in the summer with plenty of greenery out-
side even though it is on the fifth floor! The modern, creative food is beautifully
presented.
➜ Gillardeau Auster mit Wacholderholz geräuchert, Knollensellerie. Perl-
huhnbrust mit Artischocke, Kopfsalat und Earl-Grey-Tee. Shabu Shabu vom
Wagyu Rind mit Erdnuss, Salzpflaume und Strandkrabben Dashi.

XX   Tim Raue   ♿ ⓚ
▷▷ *Rudi-Dutschke-Str. 26* ✉ *10969* – Ⓜ *Kochstr.*   Plan: **G2**
– ℰ *(030) 25 93 79 30 – www.tim-raue.com – Closed 24-26 December and*
Sunday-Tuesday lunch
Menu 48 € (lunch)/198 € – Carte 125/156 €
• Asian • Fashionable •

Tim Raue's pared down Southeast Asian cuisine uses a small number of high
quality ingredients to great advantage. Sweet and savoury, mild and sharp,
soft and crispy – his dishes are a riot of contrasting textures and flavours, always
combined to perfection. The lunchtime menu is particularly popular.
→ Kaisergranat, Wasabi, Kanton Style. Zander, Kamebishi Soja und Lauch.
Spanferkel, Dashi und japanischer Senf.

XX   Rutz   🛏 🏠 ⓚ
▷▷ *Chausseestr. 8 (1st floor)* ✉ *10115*   Plan: **C2**
– Ⓜ *Oranienburger Tor – ℰ (030) 24 62 87 60 – www.rutz-restaurant.de*
– *Closed 1 week early January and Sunday-Monday*
Menu 98/165 € – Carte 103/123 € – *(dinner only)*
• Modern cuisine • Trendy •

Nowadays it would be hard to imagine Berlin's gourmet dining scene without
the deeply flavoured, contrast-rich cuisine of Rutz. You can sample its perfect
marriages of exquisite ingredients from the four to 10 course 'Inspirations'
menu or the à la carte. The interior is modern but welcoming, the service
expertly done, and the wine list excellent.
→ Douglasie Meerforelle, saures Wachtelei, Senfsaat. Dry Aged Schwarzfe-
derhuhn, Petersilienbutter, fermentierte Zitronenblätter. Grüner Apfel, Back-
kartoffelschaum, Hefeeis, Sauerampfer.
🍷 **Rutz Weinbar** – See restaurant listing

XX   Richard
▷ *Köpenicker Str. 174 (by Köpenicker Straße D2)* ✉ *10997*
– Ⓜ *Schlesisches Tor – ℰ (030) 49 20 72 42 – www.restaurant-richard.de*
– *Closed Sunday - Monday*
Menu 48/98 € – *(dinner only)*
• Modern French • Fashionable • Trendy •

Yes, this really is it, but don't be put off by the somewhat lacklustre exterior.
Inside the former Köpenicker Hof, built in 1900, the fine interior has an ornate
ceiling, designer lighting and artworks (the owner Hans Richard is also a painter). It provides the perfect setting for an excellent, artful and reasonably priced
set menu.
→ Kaisergranat mit Panna Cotta vom Blumenkohl, Mandelmilch und Sauerklee. Vichysoisse mit Sylter Royal Auster, verkohltem Lauch und Lardo di
Colonnata. Konfierte Quitte mit Hagebutte und weißer Schokoladen-
mousse.

XX   einsunternull
▷ *Hannoversche Str. 1* ✉ *10115* – Ⓜ *Oranienburger Tor*   Plan I: **C2**
– ℰ *(030) 27 57 78 10 – www.einsunternull.com – Closed Sunday-Monday*
lunch
Menu 77/117 € – Carte 39/57 € – *(booking advisable)*
• Creative • Design •

Take the lift down to the basement in the evenings at einsunternull and you
will find a minimalist-style former brewery cellar serving simple and seasonal, flavoursome cuisine. The suggested wine accompaniments come in
two versions: 'Spaß am Leben' and 'Besondere Momente' or by the glass.
Reduced lunchtime menu available upstairs on the ground floor with a
view of the kitchens.
→ Spannrippe vom Rind und Knollensellerie. Broiler, gebeiztes Eigelb und
Bärlauchtabak. Schwarzwurzel, Joghurt und Waldmeister.

XX
🕸 **Pauly Saal** 🏮

Auguststr. 11 ✉ *10117 –* Ⓜ *Rosenthaler Pl. –* 𝒞 *(030)* Plan I: **C2**
33 00 60 70 – www.paulysaal.com – Closed Sunday-Monday
Menu 46 € (weekday lunch)/97 € – *(booking advisable)*
• Modern cuisine • Fashionable •
If you are looking for somewhere elegant yet relaxed to eat, this is the place for
you. The high-ceilinged hall in this former Jewish girls' school boasts a striking
decorative rocket above the window into the kitchen, as well as some stylish
Murano glass chandeliers. The classic cuisine, based on high quality produce,
comes without frills. Smaller lunchtime menu.
➔ Taschenkrebs, Avocado, Sesam, Algen. Austern, Fenchel, Kohlrabi, Safran. Ochsenbacke, Lauch, Petersilienwurzel, Blutwurst.

XX **SRA BUA by Tim Raue** – Hotel Adlon Kempinski 🕸 🛓 🅰🅲

Behrenstr. 72 ✉ *10117 –* Ⓜ *Brandenburger Tor –* 𝒞 *(030)* 🚗
22 61 15 90 – www.srabua.berlin Plan: **G1**
Menu 58/105 € – Carte 50/82 € – *(dinner only)*
• Asian • Elegant • Exotic décor •
SRA BUA, the latest hotspot at the Hotel Adlon, is well worth a visit. It offers
ambitious, pan-Asian cuisine which combines Thai and Japanese influences
and uses top quality ingredients. The truly unusual, elegant decor provides the
perfect foil to the slightly exotic food. The charming front-of-house team completes the picture with its professional and attentive service.

XX **Bocca di Bacco** 🕸 🅰🅲 ⇔

Friedrichstr. 167 ✉ *10117 –* Ⓜ *Französische Str.* Plan: **G1**
*– 𝒞 (030) 20 67 28 28 – www.boccadibacco.de – Closed Sunday lunch and
Bank Holidays lunch*
Menu 22 € (weekday lunch) – Carte 36/66 €
• Italian • Fashionable •
This restaurant with a modern design has a bar and lounge area where good
Italian cuisine is served. Very friendly atmosphere. Beautiful function room on
the first-floor.

XX **Grill Royal** 🕸 🏮

Friedrichstr. 105b ✉ *10117 –* Ⓜ *Oranienburger Tor* Plan: **G1**
– 𝒞 (030) 28 87 92 88 – www.grillroyal.com
Carte 46/122 € – *(dinner only) (booking advisable)*
• Grills • Trendy • Fashionable •
The place to eat on the River Spree, known for its grilled meats. Diners select the
cuts themselves from a glass chiller cabinet! Great selection of Bordeaux and
Italian wines.

XX **Il Punto** 🏮 🛓 🅰🅲 ⇔

Neustädtische Kirchstr. 6 ✉ *10117 –* Ⓜ *Friedrichstr.* Plan: **G1**
*– 𝒞 (030) 20 60 55 40 – www.ilpunto.net – Closed Saturday lunch and
Sunday*
Menu 30 € (weekday lunch) – Carte 35/71 €
• Italian • Elegant •
Popular with fans of Italian cuisine, Il Punto boasts a loyal clientele. The *paccheri
alla Ciampi* owe their name to a visit to Germany of Italian President Carlo
Ciampi. Attractive glass-roofed interior courtyard.

XX **Zeitgeist** 🅰🅲

Friedrichstr. 84 / Ecke Unter den Linden (1st floor) Plan: **G1**
✉ *10177 –* Ⓜ *Französische Str. –* 𝒞 *(030) 20 92 13 13*
*– www.drive-volkswagen-group.com – Closed 1-16 January, 24 July-
22 August and Monday dinner, Saturday lunch, Sunday*
Menu 29 € (weekday lunch)/56 € – Carte 48/55 €
• Country • Design • Trendy •
With a view out over the pulsating Unter den Linden, Zeitgeist is a quiet and relaxing restaurant on the first floor of the Drive Volkswagen Group Forum. The interior is modern and elegant and the cuisine is ambitious, regional and seasonal.
Menu offerings include wild boar with celeriac, potato mash and orange.

XX **Quarré** – Hotel Adlon Kempinski ⟨ 🛜 ⅋ 🄼 🚘

Unter den Linden 77 ✉ *10117 –* Ⓜ *Brandenburger Tor* Plan: **G1**
– ☏ (030) 22 61 15 55 – www.hotel-adlon.de
Carte 43/89 €
• Classic cuisine • Brasserie •

A hotel like the Adlon naturally takes great pains to provide its guests with a suitably stylish setting for their stay. Here at Quarré, for example, they have succeeded in creating an elegant dining environment and a cosmopolitan meeting place for a business lunch, dinner or Sunday brunch.

XX **Vox** – Hotel Grand Hyatt 🛜 ⅋ 🄼 ⇔

Marlene-Dietrich-Platz 2 (Entrance on Eichhornstraße) Plan: **F2**
✉ *10785 –* Ⓜ *Potsdamer Platz – ☏ (030) 25 53 17 72*
– www.vox-restaurant.de
Carte 54/73 € – *(dinner only)*
• Modern cuisine • Brasserie • Design •

The decor at Vox is bright and modern. The large show kitchen offers guests the chance to watch the team, including the sushi chefs, at work.

XX **The Brooklyn** – Hotel The Dude

Köpenicker Str. 92 ✉ *10179 –* Ⓜ *Heinrich-Heine-Str.* Plan I: **D2**
– ☏ (030) 20 21 58 20 – www.thebrooklyn.de – Closed Sunday
Carte 46/160 € – *(dinner only)*
• Grills • Cosy • Vintage •

The Brooklyn Beef Club provides the necessary New York-style to make sure you really enjoy your American steak from the grill. It is worth taking a look at the bar, where some 160 different whiskies are available by the glass.

XX **fabrics** – Hotel nhow ⅋ 🄼 🚘

Stralauer Allee 3 ✉ *10245 –* Ⓜ *Warschauer Str.* Plan I: **D2**
– ☏ (030) 2 90 29 90 – www.nhow-berlin.com – Closed Sunday
Menu 38/48 € (dinner) – Carte 28/54 €
• Modern cuisine • Minimalist •

Cool design throughout in white, pink and a trendy green, giving a light and airy feel. The top quality produce in the kitchen is used to create house specials including classics such as steak Chateaubriand. Small lunchtime menu.

XX **La Banca** – Hotel de Rome 🛜 ⅋ 🄼 ⇔ 🚘

Behrenstr. 37 ✉ *10117 –* Ⓜ *Französische Str. – ☏ (030)* Plan: **G1**
46 06 09 12 01 – www.hotelderome.de
Menu 21 € (lunch) – Carte 31/72 €
• Mediterranean cuisine • Cosy • Design •

A casual yet classy restaurant which offers Mediterrenean cuisine made using fresh produce There is a terrace in the beautiful interior courtyard. The lunch menu is good value for money.

XX **Beef Grill Club by Hasir** – Hotel Titanic Gendarmenmarkt

Französische Str. 30 ✉ *10117 –* Ⓜ *Hausvogteiplatz* 🛜 🄼
– ☏ (030) 20 14 37 08 60 – www.titanic-hotels.de Plan: **G1**
Menu 34/90 € (dinner) – Carte 35/78 €
• Grills • Friendly •

This stylish grill/restaurant with its open kitchen is a great place to sample some really excellent steak. Take a look in the meat maturing cabinet – this is where the excellent dry aged beef comes from.

XX **Balthazar am Spreeufer 2** 🛜 ⇔

Spreeufer 2 ✉ *10178 –* Ⓜ *Märkisches Museum* Plan: **H1**
– ☏ (030) 30 88 21 56 – www.balthazar-spreeufer.de
Menu 44/95 € – Carte 34/53 €
• Classic cuisine • Friendly • Cosy •

This cosy, friendly restaurant offers classic cuisine. This ranges from Wiener Schnitzel with roast potatoes to redfish with pearl barley, and black salsify stew with chorizo. Its location on the River Spree makes the terrace particularly popular.

XX   **The Grand**   🍴 ⇔

Hirtenstr. 4 ✉ 10178 – Ⓜ Alexanderplatz – ℰ (030)   Plan I: **C2**
*27 89 09 95 55 – www.the-grand-berlin.com – Closed Saturday lunch and
Sunday lunch*
Menu 17 € *(weekday lunch)*
– Carte 41/79 € – *(August: dinner only) (bookings advisable at dinner)*
• Grills • Trendy • Design •
The interior is chic with a shabby touch and the gallery tables overlooking the
restaurant are particularly attractive. The main focus of the ambitious cuisine is
steaks from the 800°C Southbent grill, which are on view in the glazed meat
maturing cabinet. Reduced lunchtime menu with good value specials. Bar and
club.

X   **Horváth** (Sebastian Frank)   🍴 ఉ

❀❀   *Paul-Lincke-Ufer 44a ✉ 10999 – Ⓜ Schönleinstr.*   Plan I: **D2**
*– ℰ (030) 61 28 99 92 – www.restaurant-horvath.de – Closed 30 January-
5 February, 21 August-3 September and Monday-Tuesday*
Menu 99/129 € – *(dinner only) (booking advisable)*
• Creative • Minimalist •
Try Horváth if you fancy some really imaginative cuisine full of interesting combinations, full-bodied flavours and intensity. The food has its own particular
style, which is elaborate yet harmonious. The service is friendly and accomplished, and in good weather you can sit outside in the garden overlooking the
lively street.
→ Spargel, Kürbiskernöl, Riesling. Stör, Milchbruch, Kochschinken. Kalbsba-
cke, Erbse, Eierschwammerl.

X   **Nobelhart & Schmutzig**   ❀ 𝗔𝗖

❀   *Friedrichstr. 218 ✉ 10969 – Ⓜ Kochstr. – ℰ (030)*   Plan: **G2**
*25 94 06 10 – www.nobelhartundschmutzig.com – Closed 2 weeks early
January, mid July - mid August and Sunday-Monday*
Menu 95 € – *(dinner only) (booking essential)*
• Creative • Trendy • Friendly •
This 'food bar' offers its own special mix of trendy, urban chic and relaxed but
professional service. The cuisine also has its own particular style, consciously
eschewing any hint of luxury or chichi. The powerful and creative food is
made using predominantly regional Brandenburg produce.
→ Ike Jime Saibling, Zwiebel, Dill. Kartoffel, Blutwurst, Senf. Rharbarber,
Weizengras, Kirschpflaumenblüten.

X   **Bandol sur Mer**

❀   *Torstr. 167 ✉ 10115 – Ⓜ Rosenthaler Platz – ℰ (030)*   Plan I: **C2**
67 30 20 51 – www.bandolsurmer.de – Closed Tuesday-Wednesday
Menu 79/125 € – Carte 61/71 € – *(dinner only) (booking essential)*
• Modern French • Neighbourhood •
This friendly, low-key little restaurant is proof that down-to-earth food can also
be ambitious. The open kitchen produces creative, flavoursome cuisine which is
full of contrast and rich in intensity, as well as being a feast for the eyes.
→ Gebeizte Wildgarnele, Seegras, Bitterzitrone, Tomate. Gegrillter Lamm-
bauch, fermentierter Spitzkohl, Auster, Alge. Mirabelle, weißes Schokola-
deneis, Ysop, Lakritze.

X   **Rutz Weinbar** – Restaurant Rutz   ❀ 🍴 𝗔𝗖

☺   *Chausseestr. 8 (1st floor) ✉ 10115*   Plan I: **C2**
*– Ⓜ Oranienburger Tor – ℰ (030) 24 62 87 60 – www.rutz-restaurant.de
– Closed 1 week early January and Sunday-Monday*
Carte 35/63 € – *(dinner only open from 4pm)*
• Country • Wine bar •
This genuinely German restaurant has a regionally inspired menu. It offers tradi-
tional specialities such as smoked Neuköllner Rauchknacker sausage and Man-
galitza ham hock; in contrast to the more sophisticated Rutz.

GERMANY - BERLIN

GERMANY - BERLIN

✗ Lucky Leek
⊛

Kollwitzstr. 54 ✉ 10178 – Ⓜ Senefelderplatz – ☏ (030)   Plan: **D1**
66 40 87 10 – www.lucky-leek.com – Closed Monday-Tuesday
Menu 33/55 € – Carte 34/43 € – *(dinner only)*
• Vegan • Neighbourhood • Trendy •
Lucky Leek is a genuinely modern restaurant with a friendly, personal note.
Josita Hartanto cooks vegan cuisine including vegetable consommé with
potato and cress ravioli, pear and chilli risotto with tandoori cabbage and nori
tempeh rolls.

✗ Kochu Karu
⊛

Eberswalder Str. 35 ✉ 10437 – Ⓜ Eberswalder Str.   Plan I: **C1**
– ☏ (030) 80 93 81 91 – www.kochukaru.de – Closed 3-11 August
Carte 23/40 € – *(dinner only) (booking advisable)*
• Korean • Minimalist • Neighbourhood •
Korea meets Spain in this small, minimalist-style restaurant. Bin-Lee Zauner (a
famous Korean opera singer) and José Miranda Morillo (a Düsseldorfer of Spanish origin) combine the culinary traditions of the two countries. The menu includes gogi dumplings and octopus with chorizo. Don't miss their 'Musical Meal'.

✗ Lokal
⊛

Linienstr. 160 ✉ 10115 – Ⓜ Rosenthaler Platz   Plan I: **C2**
– ☏ (030) 28 44 95 00 – www.lokal-berlinmitte.de
Menu 40 € – Carte 29/52 € – *(dinner only) (booking advisable)*
• Country • Friendly •
Relaxed, friendly and pleasantly unpretentious, it is no surprise that Lokal is
popular with Berliners and visitors alike. The food is fresh, flavoursome and seasonal and includes dishes such as ox cheek with swede, chicory and broccoli.

✗ Cordobar
⊛

Große Hamburger Str. 32 ✉ 10115   Plan: **H1**
– Ⓜ Hackescher Markt – ☏ (030) 27 58 12 15 – www.cordobar.net
– Closed Sunday-Monday
Carte 20/52 € – *(dinner only)*
• International • Minimalist •
This minimalist, urban-style restaurant has forged itself a reputation as one of
the gourmet hotspots of Berlin, not just as an Austrian/German wine bar but
also for its great food. The menu includes creative hot and cold snacks ranging
from zander, sauerkraut and grapefruit to veal sweetbreads with miso and
spring onions.

✗ borchardt

Französische Str. 47 ✉ 10117 – Ⓜ Französische Str.   Plan: **G1**
– ☏ (030) 81 88 62 62 – www.borchardt-restaurant.de
Carte 34/80 €
• International • Brasserie •
A traditional townhouse in the Gendarmenmarkt is home to this trendy restaurant which serves international cuisine. It also has a charming interior courtyard
terrace.

✗ Al Contadino Sotto Le Stelle

Auguststr. 36 ✉ 10119 – Ⓜ Rosenthaler Platz   Plan I: **C2**
– ☏ (030) 2 81 90 23 – www.alcontadino.eu – Closed 23 December-
5 January and Sunday
Carte 44/54 € – *(dinner only)*
• Italian • Cosy •
It's located in the centre of Berlin-Mitte, close to the Marienkirche, and Lucio
Massaro has been running this friendly trattoria successfully for a number of
years. It is popular for both its lively atmosphere and its flavoursome Italian
fare. Try the ravioli with sea bass or the ossobuco. Two doors down you will
find a delicatessen and snacks in the Mozzarella-Bar.

X **ULA**   AC

Anklamer Str. 8 ✉ *10178 –* Ⓜ *Bernauer Str. –* 𝒸 *(030)*   Plan I: **C1**
89 37 95 70 – www.ula-berlin.de – Closed Sunday dinner-Monday
Menu 35/58 € – Carte 16/41 € – *(Monday to Saturday dinner only)*
• Japanese • Minimalist •

If you fancy some authentic Japanese cuisine, try the white miso soup with
grilled salmon, monkfish tempura or sushi here at ULA. In the same building as
the gallery of the same name, the restaurant offers a minimalist-style eatery
away from the hustle and bustle of the city.

X **Alpenstück**   🍴 ♿ ⇄

Gartenstr. 9 ✉ *10115 –* Ⓜ *Rosenthaler Platz –* 𝒸 *(030)*   Plan I: **C1**
21 75 16 46 – www.alpenstueck.de
Menu 39/49 € – Carte 41/45 € – *(dinner only) (booking advisable)*
• Country • Fashionable •

This relaxed and friendly restaurant uses regional produce in dishes such as
pan-fried fillet of trout with beetroot, yellow turnip and fondant potatoes. At
lunchtimes the restaurant's own bakery over the road sells fine pastries and
small snacks. In the delicatessen you can buy Maultaschen (Swabian pasta squares) and fond (caramelised meat dripping for making gravy) to take home.

X **MANI** – Hotel MANI   🍴 ♿ AC

Torstr. 136 ✉ *10119 –* ⓂRosenthaler Platz –* 𝒸 *(030)*   Plan I: **C2**
53 02 80 80 – www.hotel-mani.com
Carte 29/68 € – *(August: Monday-Saturday dinner only)*
• Modern cuisine • Trendy •

MANI is one of Berlin's 'places to be' at the moment. Its open kitchen, minimalist
styling and rich dark tones lend the place a slightly oriental feel, which chimes
perfectly with the spirit of the times. Try the interesting evening menu or, if you
prefer, sample the simpler lunchtime offerings.

X **Brasserie Desbrosses** – Hotel The Ritz-Carlton   🍴 ♿ AC 🛋

Potsdamer Platz 3 ✉ *10785 –* ⓂPotsdamer Platz*   Plan: **F2**
– 𝒸 *(030) 3 37 77 54 02 – www.ritzcarlton.de/berlin*
Carte 54/74 €
• French • Brasserie •

An eclectic group of diners come here to savour the typically French bistro
dishes on offer. The original 1875 interior comes from a brasserie in southern
Burgundy.

X **herz und niere**   🍴 ⊘

Fichtestr. 31 ✉ *10967 –* ⓂSüdstern –* 𝒸 *(030)*   Plan I: **D3**
69 00 15 22 – www.herzundniere.berlin – Closed Monday
Menu 38/88 € – Carte 30/48 € – *(dinner only)*
• Country • Friendly • Cosy •

The flavoursome food at this restaurant is made from locally sourced produce
and served in warm and welcoming surroundings with friendly service and
good wine recommendations. Try the ox muzzle salad or perhaps one of the
vegetarian dishes.

X **VOLT**   🍴 ♿ ⇄

Paul-Lincke-Ufer 21 ✉ *10999 –* ⓂSchönleinstr.*   Plan I: **D3**
– 𝒸 *(030) 3 38 40 23 20 – www.restaurant-volt.de – Closed 1 week end*
December-early January, 3 weeks July-August and Sunday-Monday
Menu 58/87 € – *(dinner only)*
• Country • Fashionable •

Matthias Gleiß's restaurant is very popular and you can see why. With its well-
chosen industrial design features and good food – including vegetables sourced from local farmers – this former electricity substation built in 1928 fits perfectly into Kreuzberg's lively gastro scene.

Waldorf Astoria

Plan: **K2**

*Hardenbergstr. 28 ✉ 10623 – Ⓜ Zoologischer Garten
– ☎ (030) 8 14 00 00 – www.waldorfastoria.com/berlin*
202 rm – †220/380 € ††220/380 € – 立 38 € – 30 suites
• Grand Luxury • Elegant • Classic •

The modern, elegant interior here is designed in classic 1920s-style with perfectly judged colours and lines throughout. As befits its legendary name, it also has its own Peacock Alley restaurant serving international cuisine – a genuine piece of New York hotel tradition in Berlin! ROCA serves sandwiches and cakes.

Sofitel Berlin Kurfürstendamm

Plan: **K2**

*Augsburger Str. 41 ✉ 10789 – Ⓜ Kurfürstendamm
– ☎ (030) 8 00 99 90 – www.sofitel-berlin-kurfuerstendamm.com*
291 rm – †159/490 € ††189/520 € – 立 30 € – 20 suites
• Business • Grand Luxury • Contemporary •

This hotel is set in the midst of lively central Berlin with a striking façade of shell-bearing limestone. It offers a huge lobby and attractive, modern and spacious rooms with lots of art.
Le Faubourg – See restaurant listing

InterContinental

Plan: **L2**

*Budapester Str. 2 ✉ 10787 – Ⓜ Zoologischer Garten
– ☎ (030) 2 60 20 – www.berlin.intercontinental.com*
545 rm – †109/399 € ††129/428 € – 立 32 € – 13 suites
• Business • Luxury • Classic •

The Intercontinental is smart and upmarket throughout. Elegant, contemporary guestrooms are equipped with the latest technology; there is a tasteful Vitality Club, plus conference and events facilities.
❀ **Hugos** – See restaurant listing

Swissôtel

Plan: **K2**

*Augsburger Str. 44 ✉ 10789 – Ⓜ Kurfürstendamm
– ☎ (030) 220100 – www.swissotel.com/berlin*
316 rm – †119/399 € ††119/399 € – 立 23 €
• Business • Contemporary •

This modern town hotel with its glass façade welcomes its guests with a spacious atrium hall. It has comfortable guestrooms, including business and executive rooms.
❀ **44** – See restaurant listing

Zoo Berlin

Plan: **K2**

*Kurfürstendamm 25 ✉ 10179 – Ⓜ Uhlandstr. – ☎ (030)
88 43 70 – www.hotelzoo.de*
131 rm – †180/1200 € ††180/1200 € – 立 32 €
• Luxury • Design • Elegant •

Well-known designer Dayna Lee has brought a bit of Berlin hotel history back to life at Zoo Berlin. She has successfully combined the elegance and class of the old hotel with a new, modern feel. The rooms are tasteful and upmarket, opulent yet functional, with all the atmosphere of a real 'grand hotel'.
Grace – See restaurant listing

Das Stue

Plan: **L2**

*Drakestr. 1 ✉ 10787 – Ⓜ Wittenbergplatz – ☎ (030)
3 11 72 20 – www.das-stue.com*
78 rm – †230 € ††550 € – 立 35 €
• Luxury • Design • Elegant •

'Stylish' is the only word that fits! In this listed 1930's building that once housed the Danish embassy, the interior is a great mixture of neo-Classical and modern design. The lobby with its impressive staircases is a highlight, while rooms are individually designed; some offering a view over Berlin Zoo. Casual is both relaxed and sophisticated and offers tapas-style international dishes.
❀ **5 - cinco by Paco Pérez** – See restaurant listing

Am Steinplatz

$\hat{\mathbf{A}}$ 𝄞 ⓘ ⅏ ⵙ 𝄢

Steinplatz 4 ✉ 10623 – Ⓜ Ernst-Reuter-Platz – ℰ (030)
5 54 44 40 – www.hotelsteinplatz.com   Plan: **K2**
84 rm – ♦165/255 € ♦♦165/255 € – ⌧ 35 € – 3 suites
• Luxury • Townhouse • Elegant •

Formerly Berlin's artists' hotel, Am Steinplatz is now a small, exclusive boutique hotel in the heart of Charlottenburg. The rooms are upmarket, chic and comfortable, the service attentive and personal, and the decor is characterised by period charm and high, stuccoed ceilings. Regionally inspired restaurant concept.

25hours Hotel Bikini

𝄞 ⓘ ⅏ ⵙ

Budapester Str. 40 ✉ 10787 – Ⓜ Zoologischer Garten   Plan: **K2**
– ℰ (030) 1 20 22 10 – www.25hours-hotels.com
149 rm – ♦150 € ♦♦150 € – ⌧ 21 €
• Business • Personalised • Grand luxury •

One of Berlin's most interesting hotel hotspots, built onto the Bikini Mall in a trendy, 'urban jungle' style, the 25hours offers uninterrupted views of the zoo (the sauna on the ninth floor looks onto the monkey house!). Don't miss the Woodfire Bakery and the lounge-style Monkey Bar with its great city views. Free bicycle hire.
NENI – See restaurant listing

Louisa's Place

𝄞 ⅏

Kurfürstendamm 160 ✉ 10709 – Ⓜ Adenauerplatz   Plan: **J3**
– ℰ (030) 631030 – www.louisas-place.de
47 suites – ♦145/625 € ♦♦145/625 € – ⌧ 26 €
• Business • Personalised • Cosy •

This hotel has friendly service and offers tasteful, spacious suites with kitchens. There is also a stylish breakfast room and library.
Balthazar – See restaurant listing

Ellington

𝄞 ⅏ ⵙ 𝄢

Nürnberger Str. 50 ✉ 10789 – Ⓜ Wittenbergplatz   Plan: **L2**
– ℰ (030) 68 31 50 – www.ellington-hotel.com
280 rm – ♦118/208 € ♦♦128/228 € – ⌧ 20 € – 5 suites
• Business • Contemporary • Minimalist •

Numerous photographs of Duke Ellington, after whom the hotel is named, adorn this simply furnished hotel. It has a beautiful lobby area and a lounge-style interior courtyard. Many details preserve its historic charm.
Duke – See restaurant listing

Hecker's Hotel Kurfürstendamm

⅏ ⵙ 𝄢

Grolmanstr. 35 ✉ 10623 – Ⓜ Uhlandstr. – ℰ (030)   Plan: **K2**
8 89 00 – www.heckers-hotel.de
69 rm – ♦85/290 € ♦♦95/310 € – ⌧ 17 €
• Business • Design •

This establishment offers contemporary living just a few steps from the Kurfürstendamm. The Bauhaus, Toskana and Colonial themed rooms are tastefully done out. There is a quiet sun terrace on the fourth-floor, and a modern breakfast room. The Cassambalis offers Mediterranean cuisine in a warm and charming atmosphere.
Cassambalis – See restaurant listing

XxX
£3

Hugos – Hotel InterContinental

Budapester Str. 2 (14th floor) ✉ 10787   Plan: **L2**
– Ⓜ Zoologischer Garten – ℰ (030) 26 02 12 63
– www.hugos-restaurant.de – Closed Sunday-Monday
Menu 70 € (Vegetarian)/150 € – (dinner only) (booking advisable)
• Modern cuisine • Chic • Elegant •

It is true that the view from the 14th floor is fantastic but this elegant, minimalist-style restaurant is known first and foremost for its classic, modern cuisine, which is both beautifully crafted and delicious.
→ Jakobsmuschel, Pekannuss, Bärlauch, Pfifferlinge, Rollgerste. Gegrilltes Linumer Kalbsfilet, Zunge, Bries, Schulter und Kohlrabi. Gin Tonic und Grapefruit, eingelegte Gurke.

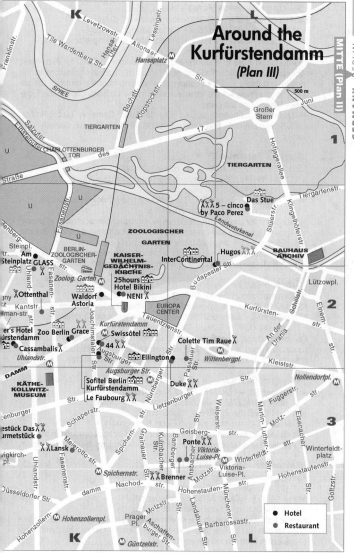

Around the Kurfürstendamm
(Plan III)

0   500 m

TIERGARTEN

CHARLOTTENBURGER TOR

Großer Stern

TIERGARTEN

5 – cinco by Paco Perez

Das Stue

ZOOLOGISCHER GARTEN

KAISER-WILHELM-GEDÄCHTNIS-KIRCHE

Hugos

InterContinental

BAUHAUS ARCHIV

Am Steinplatz

GLASS

BERLIN-ZOOLOGISCHER-GARTEN

25hours Hotel Bikini

NENI

Ottenthal

Waldorf Astoria

EUROPA CENTER

Kurfürsten-

Zoo Berlin Grace

Kurfürstendamm

Swissôtel

44

Ellington

Colette Tim Raue

Cassambalis

Sofitel Berlin Kurfürstendamm

Le Faubourg

Duke

KÄTHE-KOLLWITZ-MUSEUM

Nollendorfpl.

estück Das urmetstück

Lansk

Ponte

Viktoria-Luise-Pl.

Brenner

Hohenzollernpl.

Güntzelstr.

Spichernstr.

| | Hotel |
| | Restaurant |

305

GERMANY - BERLIN

XxX **5 - cinco by Paco Pérez** – Hotel Das Stue ⸙ &. 🅰🅺
🆂
Drakestr. 1 ✉ *10787 –* Ⓜ *Wittenbergplatz – ℰ (030)* Plan: **L2**
3 11 72 20 – www.5-cinco.com – Closed Sunday-Monday
Menu 165 € – Carte 96/150 € – *(dinner only) (booking advisable)*
• Creative • Design • Trendy •
You no longer have to make the journey to Miramar in Spain for Paco Pérez'
Michelin-starred cuisine. You can now sample his upmarket creations in this
modern restaurant – with 86 copper pans hanging from the centre of the cei-
ling – as you marvel at the intense activity in the kitchens. Choose the 'Expe-
rience Menu' or go à la carte.
→ Saubohne, Saubohnenjus und "Cap de Creus" Garnelen. Taube, Profite-
roles, Schwarzwurzeln und Kaffee. Schokolade 2014, Mousse, Ganache und
Sorbet.

XX **Markus Semmler** 🛖
🆂
Sächsische Str. 7 ✉ *10707 –* Ⓜ *Hohenzollernpl.* Plan: **J3**
– ℰ (030) 89 06 82 90 – www.semmler-restaurant.de – Closed July-August
and Sunday-Tuesday
Menu 85/145 € – Carte 91/110 € – *(dinner only) (booking essential)*
• Classic cuisine • Fashionable •
Markus Semmler cooks fresh classic cuisine including delicacies such as peppe-
red tuna with tomato and bread salad, and turbot with oxtail praline. The star-
ters and desserts are prepared in the open kitchen before your eyes.
→ Herzkalbsbries, Pfifferlinge, Schnittlauch. Wildwassergarnele, Spargel,
Römersalatherzen, Amalfi Zitrone. Maibock, Wacholder-Schalotten, Spargel.

XX **Grace** – Hotel Zoo Berlin 🛖 &. 🅰🅺
Kurfürstendamm 25 ✉ *10719 –* Ⓜ *Uhlandstr. – ℰ (030)* Plan: **K2**
88 43 77 50 70 – www.grace-berlin.de – Closed Sunday-Monday
Menu 50/90 € – Carte 56/101 € – *(dinner only) (booking advisable)*
• International • Chic • Design •
Combining stylish, modern design and vintage flair, Grace is a really smart place
to eat. The food is modern and international and includes such delights as
creamy rock shrimps with cucumber, coriander, peanuts and chilli.

XX **44** – Hotel Swissôtel 🛖 &. 🅰🅺 🚗
Augsburger Str. 44 ✉ *10789 –* Ⓜ *Kurfürstendamm* Plan: **K2**
– ℰ (030) 220102288 – www.restaurant44.de – Closed Sunday
Menu 44 € – Carte 35/68 € – *(dinner only)*
• Swiss • Contemporary décor • Friendly •
This simple, modern and elegant restaurant serves imaginative food in the form
of a tasting menu. Glass frontage and a terrace overlooking the Kurfürstendamm.

XX **Balthazar** – Hotel Louisa's Place 🛖 &. 🅰🅺 ⇔
Kurfürstendamm 160 ✉ *10709 –* Ⓜ *Adenauerplatz* Plan: **J3**
– ℰ (030) 89408477 – www.balthazar-restaurant.de
Menu 44/95 € – Carte 38/53 € – *(dinner only)*
• International • Fashionable • Trendy •
A great little place to eat on the Ku'damm! The restaurant in the Louisa's Place
Hotel serves what it refers to as 'metropolitan cuisine' – German food with a mix
of influences from around the world.

XX **Duke** – Hotel Ellington 🛖 &. 🅰🅺 🚗
Nürnberger Str. 50 ✉ *10789 –* Ⓜ *Wittenbergplatz* Plan: **L2**
– ℰ (030) 6 83 15 40 00 – www.duke-restaurant.com – Closed Sunday
Menu 22 € (weekday lunch)/68 € (dinner) – Carte 56/94 €
• Modern French • Fashionable • Trendy •
Fancy scallops with sourdough, quince and swede or perhaps some Icelandic
redfish in beurre blanc with oyster mushrooms? The menu at this friendly,
modern restaurant is divided into two parts: the classic 'Legère' menu and its
creative 'Logique' counterpart (evenings only). Attractive interior courtyard.

GERMANY - BERLIN

XX **Alt Luxemburg**

Windscheidstr. 31 ⊠ 10627 – Ⓜ *Wilmersdorfer Str.*   Plan: **I2**
– 𝒞 (030) 3 23 87 30 – www.altluxemburg.de – Closed Sunday
Menu 58/78 € – Carte 53/62 € – *(dinner only) (booking advisable)*
• Classic French • Family •

Attractive, friendly colours contribute to the atmosphere of this restaurant. It offers classic cuisine, and has been traditionally run by the Wannemacher family since 1982.

XX **Brenner**

Regensburger Str. 7 ⊠ 10777 – Ⓜ *Viktoria-Luise-Platz*   Plan: **L3**
– 𝒞 (030) 23 62 44 70 – www.restaurant-brenner.de – closed Sunday
Menu 44/67 € – Carte 35/59 € – *(dinner only)*
• Modern cuisine • Cosy •

The food served in the cosy, rustic yet elegant dining rooms is ambitious, creative and modern. It includes delights such as European perch fillet with sweetheart cabbage, gherkins and mustard, and a tapas menu. Over 350 different wines.

XX **Ponte**

Regensburger Str. 5 ⊠ 10777 – Ⓜ *Viktoria-Luise-Platz*   Plan: **L3**
– 𝒞 (030) 21 91 24 10 – www.ponte-ristorante.de – Closed Monday-Tuesday
Carte 35/54 € – *(dinner only and Sunday lunch)*
• Italian • Neighbourhood • Friendly •

The food on offer at Ponte is fresh and classically Italian with dishes including a salad of spinach, pancetta and parmesan and veal shank slow-cooked with vegetables, as well as fish and seafood. Good Italian wines. There is an attractive terrace outside the restaurant.

XX **Lansk**

Meierottostr. 1 ⊠ 10719 – Ⓜ *Spichernstraße – 𝒞 (030)*   Plan: **K3**
88 70 88 60 – www.lansk-restaurant.de
Menu 39/80 € – Carte 50/64 €
• Country • Cosy • Friendly •

The food served in this lovely listed building is seasonal and regional. The evening brings two set menus – try the venison with black salsify, Brussels sprouts and brioche dumplings. The lunchtime menu is a little simpler and offers great value for money.

XX **Filetstück Das Gourmetstück**

Uhlandstr. 156 ⊠ 10719 – Ⓜ *Uhlandstr. – 𝒞 (030)*   Plan: **K3**
54 46 96 40 – www.filetstueck.de – Closed Sunday
Menu 59/109 € – Carte 53/75 €
• Modern cuisine • Brasserie •

In the evenings this relaxed and friendly restaurant with its brasserie feel serves an ambitious, creative 'Gourmetstückset' menu. This has four to seven courses including sturgeon, beluga lentils, Chinese spinach and tandoori relish. Alternatively, a variety of steaks are also available.

XX **Le Faubourg** – Hotel Sofitel Berlin Kurfürstendamm   🍴 ♿ Ⓐ🅚

Augsburger Str. 41 ⊠ 10789 – Ⓜ *Kurfürstendamm – 𝒞 (030)*   🚗
8009997700 – www.lefaubourg.berlin – Closed Saturday   Plan: **K2**
lunch, Sunday lunch
Menu 21 € (weekday lunch) – Carte 51/67 €
• French • Design • Elegant •

This elegant restaurant – the black latex flooring, lights and large temperature-controlled wine cabinet are particularly striking – serves ambitious French cuisine. The starters are great to share, and the main courses are either traditional or more modern. Simpler and very reasonably priced lunchtime menu.

Bieberbau (Stephan Garkisch)

Durlacher Str. 15 ✉ *10715 –* Ⓜ *Bundesplatz –* ✆ *(030)*   Plan I: **B3**
8 53 23 90 – www.bieberbau-berlin.de – Closed Sunday-Monday
Menu 44/66 € – *(dinner only) (booking advisable)*
• Modern cuisine • Cosy •

This wonderful example of the stucco plasterer's art was created by Richard Bieber in the 19C. The food prepared at the Molteni ranges is based on regional products and fine herbs. So try not to fill up too much on the homemade bread and flavoured butters!
→ Stettiner Haff-Zander mit Roter Bete, Ayran, Gewürzgurke. Münsterländer Wildtaube, Cima di Rapa, Schwarzwurzel, Pickels und Blutwurst. Topfenknödel, Zitrus süß-bitter, Oliven und Kürbiskerne.

Ottenthal

Kantstr. 153 ✉ *10623 –* Ⓜ *Uhlandstr. –* ✆ *(030)*   Plan: **K2**
3 13 31 62 – www.ottenthal.com – Closed 1 week mid August
Menu 34 € – Carte 34/52 € – *(dinner only) (booking advisable)*
• Austrian • Classic décor •

The typically Austrian tavern fare is a great success. In his friendly restaurant (named after his home town in Lower Austria) chef Arthur Schneller produces unfussy dishes including Wiener Tafelspitz (boiled rump of beef Viennese style) and apple strudel. Good wine selection.

Renger-Patzsch

Wartburgstr. 54 ✉ *10823 –* Ⓜ *Eisenacher Str.*   Plan I: **B3**
– ✆ (030) 7 84 20 59 – www.renger-patzsch.com – Closed Sunday
Menu 34/36 € – Carte 29/43 € – *(dinner only) (booking advisable)*
• Traditional cuisine • Inn • Cosy •

Traditional, tasty and well-executed dishes such as Alsatian sauerkraut with shoulder of pork or flammekueche. The restaurant owes its name to one of the pioneers of landscape photography - a number of his black and white photos adorn the walls. A great place to eat and a very popular one. Wonderful terrace.

Jungbluth

Lepsius Str. 63 (by Hauptstraße B3) ✉ *12163 –* Ⓜ *Steglitzer Rathaus*
– ✆ (030) 79 78 96 05 – www.jungbluth-restaurant.de – Closed Monday
Menu 34/58 € – Carte 37/50 €
• Modern cuisine • Neighbourhood • Friendly •

The young team that runs Jungbluth have created a pleasant little restaurant serving tasty food at reasonable prices. Try the delicious roast shoulder of beef with cima di rapa and creamed garlic and celery.

Die Nussbaumerin

Leibnizstr. 55 ✉ *10629 –* Ⓜ *Adenauerpl. –* ✆ *(030)*   Plan: **J3**
50 17 80 33 – www.nussbaumerin.de – Closed Sunday
Carte 30/43 € – *(dinner only) (booking advisable)*
• Austrian • Cosy •

Here in her cosy restaurant Johanna Nußbaumer recreates a little bit of Austria in the heart of Berlin. Specialities include breaded fried chicken, Wiener Schnitzel, sirloin steak, and a range of Austrian stews and sweet dishes. The excellent wines also hail from her home country.

Colette Tim Raue

Passauer Str. 5 ✉ *10789 –* Ⓜ *Wittenbergplatz*   Plan: **L2**
– ✆ (030) 2 199 21 74 – www.brasseriecolette.de – Closed Sunday-Monday
Carte 36/62 €
• Classic French • Brasserie •

A well-known name on the Berlin gastro scene, Colette Tim Raue has created a friendly, modern and uncomplicated brasserie, which could easily be in Paris. Try the paysanne pie, duck confit or lemon tart.

Brasserie Lamazère

Stuttgarter Platz 18 ✉ 10178 – Ⓜ Wilmersdorfer Str. Plan: **I3**
– ✆ (030) 31 80 07 12 – www.lamazere.de
– Closed 1-4 January and Monday
Menu 38 € – Carte 42/56 € – *(dinner only) (booking advisable)*
• French • Brasserie • Neighbourhood •

You might almost be in France here in the heart of Charlottenburg at Brasserie Lamazère thanks to its charming, straightforward bistro feel and authentic, constantly changing menu of fresh and tasty seasonal fare. Try the *oeufs en cocotte* with Bayonne ham or Atlantic cod with tomato and paprika mussels.

GLASS

Uhlandstr. 195 ✉ 10623 – Ⓜ Zoologischer Garten Plan: **K2**
– ✆ (030) 54 71 08 61 – www.glassberlin.de
– Closed 2 weeks early January, 2 weeks early August and Sunday-Monday
Menu 75/95 € – *(dinner only) (booking advisable)*
• Creative • Minimalist •

The decor is as minimalist and modern in style as the food is creative and full of contrast. The real eye catcher is the reflective, metal curtain from behind which emerges a five to seven course menu including such delights as lamb with dates, cabbage and capers. Vegetarian options are also available. Wine comes by the bottle or the glass.

Cassambalis – Hecker's Hotel Kurfürstendamm

Grolmanstr. 35 ✉ 10623 – Ⓜ Uhlandstr. – ✆ (030) 8 85 47 47 – www.cassambalis.de – Closed Sunday dinner Plan: **K2**
Menu 35/68 € – Carte 41/66 €
• Mediterranean cuisine • Friendly •

You can't get any closer to the action than this. Close to the Ku'Damm, this restaurant is reminiscent of a bright, friendly brasserie with lots of art on the walls, open wine shelves and bright colours. Mediterranean cuisine.

NENI – 25hours Hotel Bikini

Budapester Str. 40 (10th floor) ✉ 10787 Plan: **K2**
– Ⓜ Zoologischer Garten – ✆ (030) 1 20 22 10
– www.25hours-hotels.com
Menu 35 € – Carte 25/58 € – *(booking advisable)*
• Mediterranean cuisine • Trendy •

With its glasshouse decor and stunning view, Neni is a restaurant with a difference. The food coming out of the open kitchens is an eclectic mix of Mediterranean, Oriental and local cuisines, including houmous with chicken liver, baba ghanoush and Eifel lamb. The ideas come courtesy of Haya Molcho. Spectacular terrace!

ENVIRONS OF BERLIN — PLAN I

AT BERLIN-GRUNEWALD

Patrick Hellmann Schlosshotel

Brahmsstr. 10 ✉ 14193 – ✆ (030) 89 58 40 Plan: **A3**
– www.schlosshotelberlin.com
43 rm – †249/490 € ††249/490 € – ☕ 29 € – 10 suites
• Luxury • Design • Classic •

This unique building, formerly part of a large chain, has reverted to a private hotel. It has of course retained its tasteful 1914 palace interior full of pretty period details, its lovely grounds and its attractive leisure area. All this in a quiet location just a short 10min walk from the Kurfürstendamm.

XXX **Frühsammers Restaurant** 🕸 🍴

Flinsberger Platz 8 ⊠ 14193 – 𝒞 (030) 89 73 86 28 Plan: **A3**
– www.fruehsammers-restaurant.de – Closed 1-11 January and Sunday-Monday
Menu 94/109 € – *(dinner only) (booking advisable)*
• Classic cuisine • Friendly •

This red villa is set in the grounds of a tennis club. It provides a suitably classic setting for Sonja Frühsammer's elegant and sophisticated cuisine centred on high-quality produce. Her husband Peter heads the charming front-of-house team and provides excellent wine suggestions. Simple bistro menu at lunchtimes.
→ Kobe Beef, Champignon, Rettich, Soja-Saibling, Spargel, Morcheln. Bauch vom Iberico, Knackerbsen, Salzzitrone, Traubenmost, Hamachi-Makrele, Topinambur. Variation von der Schokolade, Rhabarber, Erdbeere, Mandelkuchen.

AT BERLIN-LICHTENBERG

XX **SKYKITCHEN** ⇦ ⟨ 🛋 🏮 ⌚ 🆔 🧳 🚗

Landsberger Allee 106 ⊠ 10369 – Ⓜ Landsberger Allee Plan: **D1**
– 𝒞 (030) 4530532620 – www.skykitchen.berlin – Closed Sunday-Monday
534 rm ⌷ – ♦94/120 € ♦♦219/245 € – 23 suites
Menu 45 € (Vegetarian)/142 € – *(dinner only) (booking advisable)*
• Modern cuisine • Fashionable •

It is worth making your way out to Lichtenberg to sample the *'voyage culinaire'* on offer on the 12th floor of andel's Hotel. The 3- to 11-course set menu showcases a creative, modern cuisine full of contrasts, with local and international influences. The setting is relaxed yet stylishly chic, and the view is wonderful. The SKYBAR is two floors further up.
→ Müritz Aal und Linumer Kalb, Senfgurke, Meerrettich, Escabeche. Blaue Garnele und Husumer Krabben, Sanddorn, Röstsalat, Radieschen. Iberico Schwein, Knollensellerie, Schmorzwiebel, Spitzpaprika.

COLOGNE
KÖLN

Population: 1 060 582

Jürgen Feldhaus/Fotolia.com

Cologne is one of Germany's oldest cities and its name was instigated by the Romans, who set up a 'colony' to fend off the Barbarians. It became a Free City, and later fell under the rule of Napoleon and then the Prussians; all of which has given the locals a cosmopolitan, laid-back and sociable outlook. Although it may never be described as Europe's prettiest city, it has an eye-catching old town (largely rebuilt after World War II) and some world-class museums. It also boasts one of the finest collections of medieval churches in Europe, and ploughs its own furrow by celebrating Carnival like it's Rio. Most famously, it has its Cathedral, a massive structure that took over half a millennium to build, stood tall during the War and remains one of the biggest tourist attractions in Germany to this day.

The River Rhine cuts a swathe right through the heart of Cologne, with four central bridges allowing plentiful passage from east to west. The main hub of the city is on the west bank, with the Altstadt (old town) practically on the river bank itself. Out to the west, the old medieval walls are now a ring road which neatly encircles the city centre and just northwest of the ring road is Mediapark, a brash modern development. To the east of the Rhine is the massive Trade Fair Centre, with its 80m-high tower, while to its north is Cologne's biggest and most popular park, Rheinpark.

COLOGNE IN...

→ **ONE DAY**
Altstadt, Dom, Romanesque churches.

→ **TWO DAYS**
Museum Ludwig, Wallraf-Richartz Museum (or Chocolate Museum), Stadtgarten (or Opera House).

→ **THREE DAYS**
Romano-Germanic Museum, Rheinpark.

PRACTICAL INFORMATION

ARRIVAL-DEPARTURE

✈ Cologne / Bonn Airport lies 17km southeast of the city centre. The S13 train takes about 15min.

GETTING AROUND

You can get around Cologne by bus, tram or metro. Validate your ticket by stamping it each time you board. Single and day tickets for Cologne not only take you from one side of the city to the other but are also valid for a journey to nearby Bonn. If you're in the city for a while, invest in a Köln Welcome Card, available from tourist information offices and many hotels. As well as providing free travel on the public transport network, it offers almost ninety deals and discounts at venues ranging from galleries and museums to shops, leisure facilities and eateries.

CALENDAR HIGHLIGHTS

February
Crazy Days (carnival).

March
lit.cologne (international literature festival).

July
Cologne Lights, Christopher Street Day (gay pride celebration), Summerjam.

August
Street Festival.

October
Long Night of Cologne Museums, Cologne International Comedy Festival.

November
Carnival begins.

EATING OUT

Cologne is known throughout Germany for its Kölsch. It's the name of the local people and it's the name of their brew, a light beer with the yeast risen to the top rather than sunk to the bottom of the glass. 20 local breweries produce their own versions and you can try them out in an old town brauhaus – atmospheric, dark wood-panelled places where buzzy waiters continuously refill your empty stangen (0.2 litre glass). After that, make the most of the city's ethnic diversity by selecting a restaurant from an impressive global range; pick of the bunch are the fine Italian, Japanese and Turkish establishments. If your preference is for something local, favoured dishes include Himmel un Äad (bloodsausage and mash), Sauerbraten vom Pferd (braised horse) or Töttchen (ragout of brains and calf's head, cooked with herbs). Bars, cafés and restaurants all stay open late, many until 11pm or midnight. Service charge is generally included but most people round up the bill. In summer, seek out an ice-cream parlour, sit under a parasol and tuck into a full-on sundae.

GERMANY - COLOGNE

Excelsior Hotel Ernst   🛗 🦢 🅰🅲 🛅 🚗

Domplatz/Trankgasse 1 ✉ *50667*   Plan: I1
– **Ⓜ** *Dom-Hauptbahnhof* – ℰ *(0221) 27 01* – *www.excelsiorhotelernst.com*
140 rm – ♦220/495 € ♦♦270/690 € – ☲ 32 € – 28 suites
• Grand Luxury • Traditional • Classic •

Traditional and modern elements have been combined with style and taste in this grand hotel by the cathedral. Exclusive reception area, elegant rooms. Particularly luxurious are the rooms in the Hanseflügel wing.

❀ **taku** • **Hanse Stube** – See restaurant listing

Eden Hotel Früh am Dom   ✿ 🛅

Sporergasse 1 ✉ *50667* – **Ⓜ** *Dom-Hauptbahnhof*   Plan: J1
– ℰ *(0221) 2 61 32 95* – *www.hotel-eden.de*
78 rm ☲ – ♦90/230 € ♦♦115/255 €
• Townhouse • Contemporary •

An established hotel close to the cathedral square. The rooms are up to date in terms of style and technology. Some also have a view of the cathedral – which can also be enjoyed while having breakfast. On the first floor the modern Hof 18 restaurant serves international cuisine.

🕱🕱🕱 Hanse Stube – Excelsior Hotel Ernst   🕸 🌅 🅰🅲 ⟷

Domplatz/Trankgasse 1 ✉ *50667*   Plan: I1
– **Ⓜ** *Dom-Hauptbahnhof* – ℰ *(0221) 2701* – *www.excelsiorhotelernst.com*
Menu 39 € (lunch)/117 € – Carte 64/82 €
• Classic cuisine • Classic décor •

The Hanse Stube is one of the most elegant restaurants in the city and serves good classic cuisine. Many business people come for the fairly priced, daily changing business lunch.

🕱🕱 taku – Excelsior Hotel Ernst   🕸 🅰🅲 🦢
❀
Domplatz/Trankgasse 1 ✉ *50667*   Plan: I1
– **Ⓜ** *Dom-Hauptbahnhof* – ℰ *(0221) 2 70 1* – *www.taku.de* – *Closed 1 week during Carnival, 1 week during Easter, 4 weeks July-August, Sunday-Monday and Bank Holidays lunch*
Menu 41 € (lunch)/130 € – Carte 83/95 € – *(booking advisable)*
• Asian • Minimalist • Fashionable •

If you have a taste for high quality Southeast Asian cuisine, you should try the dishes served in this bright, minimalist-style restaurant by a largely Asian kitchen team headed up by chef Mirko Gaul. Interestingly, his European roots are also evident in the chef's authentic Asian fare. Make sure you book 24hr in advance if you want to sample the 6-course Peking Duck menu.
➜ "Japanischer Garten" - Wurzelgemüse, Yuzu, Quinoa. "Siu Mai" - Schwein & Garnele, Krabben, Shoaxing. Banane, Kokos, Himbeere.

🕱🕱 Alfredo (Roberto Carturan)   🅰🅲
❀
Tunisstr. 3 ✉ *50667* – ℰ *(0221) 2 57 73 80*   Plan: I2
– *www.ristorante-alfredo.com* – *Closed 3 weeks July-August, Saturday-Sunday and Bank Holidays*
Menu 69/95 € – Carte 60/84 € – *(booking advisable)*
• Italian • Friendly •

Roberto Carturan is following unashamedly in the footsteps of this father, Alfredo, and his authentic Italian cuisine. His food is fresh and unfussy, each dish a tribute to high quality ingredients simply combined. Wait for the waiter's suggestions as you take your seat. The service is professional and accomplished with just the right amount of informality.
➜ Jakobsmuscheln, gefüllte Totanelli. Steinbutt, Spargel. Nocciola delle Langhe, Tonkabohne.

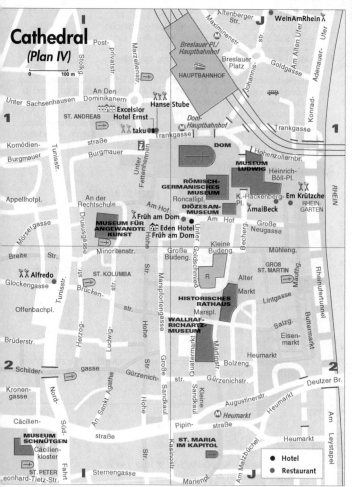

Cathedral
(Plan IV)

0   100 m

Post-privatstr.

Unter Sachsenhausen

An Den Dominikanern

Marzellenstr.

Stolkg.

Excelsior Hotel Ernst
ST. ANDREAS

Hanse Stube

Komödien-Burgmauer

Tunisstr.

straße

taku

Burgmauer

Trankgasse

Altenberger Str.

Maximinenstr.

str.

WeinAmRhein

Am Alten Ufer

Adenauer- Uter

Breslauer Pl./ Hauptbahnhof

Breslauer Platz

HAUPTBAHNHOF

Johannis-

Goldgasse

Konrad-

Dom-Hauptbahnhof

Trankgasse

DOM

Appellhofpl.

An der Rechtschule

Unter Fettenhennen

Hohenzollernbr.

MUSEUM LUDWIG

Heinrich-Böll-Pl.

RHEIN

RÖMISCH-GERMANISCHES MUSEUM

Roncallipl.

DIÖZESAN-MUSEUM

Am Hof

K.-Hackenberg-Pl.

Em Krützche

RHEIN-GARTEN

Früh am Dom

Am Hof

maiBeck

MUSEUM FÜR ANGEWANDTE KUNST

Eden Hotel
Früh am Dom

Unter

Hohe

Becherg.

Große Neugasse

Mörsergasse

Drususgasse

Minoritenstr.

Große Budeng.

Goldschmied

Kleine Budeng.

Mühleng.

Breite   Str.

Alfredo
Glockengasse

ST. KOLUMBA

str.

Brücken-

Marspfortengasse

str.

Hohe   Str.

GROß ST. MARTIN

Alter

Rheinufertunnel

Mäuthg.

Offenbachpl.

Tunisstr.

Herzog-

Markt

Lintgasse

Brüderstr.

HISTORISCHES RATHAUS

Marspl.

Salzg.

Buttermarkt

WALLRAF-RICHARTZ-MUSEUM

Eisen-markt

Martinstr.

Heumarkt

2

Schilder-

gasse

Gürzenich-

str.

Große Sandkaul

Quatermarkt

Kleine Sandkaul

Bolzeng.

Gürzenichstr.

Deutzer Br.

2

Kronen-gasse

Nord-

Süd-

An Sankt Agatha

Hohe   Str.

Augustinerstr.

Heumarkt

Am Leystapel

Cäcilien-

straße

Heumarkt

Pipin-

straße

MUSEUM SCHNÜTGEN
Cäcilien-kloster

Fahrt

ST. MARIA IM KAPITOL

Kasinostr.

Heumarkt

ST. PETER
Leonhard-Tietz-Str.

Sternengasse

Marienpl.

Am Malzbüchel

●	Hotel
●	Restaurant

XX **Em Krützche**

Am Frankenturm 1 ⊠ 50667 – Ⓜ Dom-Hauptbahnhof   Plan: **J1**
– ☎ (0221) 2 58 08 39 – www.em-kruetzche.de – Closed durimg Christmas,
10-18 April and Monday
Menu 25/39 € – Carte 37/57 € – *(bookings advisable at dinner)*
• Classic cuisine • Traditional décor • Family •

Run for around 40 years by the Fehn family, this historic guesthouse has pretty rooms set over two floors, which range from charmingly rustic to elegant. Goose is the speciality in winter.

315

maiBeck (Jan C. Maier and Tobias Becker)

Am Frankenturm 5 ✉ 50667 – Ⓜ Dom-Hauptbahnhof Plan: **J1**
– ✆ (0221) 96 26 73 00 – www.maibeck.de
– Closed Monday
Menu 42 € – Carte 41/61 € – *(booking advisable)*
• Modern cuisine • Fashionable • Design •

This restaurant is the brainchild of Jan Maier and Tobias Becker, two ambitious young men with a passion for cooking and a feel for combining tastes and flavours. Their speciality is homemade pasta. The best place to eat in summer is the terrace with its view of the Rhine.
→ Offener Raviolo vom Euskirchener Eigelb, Spinat, Sonnenblumenkerne. Räucheraal von Herr Ihnken, Rhabarber, Rübchen, Estragon. Gebackenes Kalbsbries von Kremer, Rübstiel, Monschauer Senf.

WeinAmRhein

Johannisstr. 64 ✉ 50668 Plan: **J1**
– Ⓜ Breslauer Pl./Hauptbahnhof – ✆ (0221) 91 24 88 85
– www.weinamrhein.eu – Closed 2 weeks July-August, Saturday lunch, Sunday-Monday and Bank Holidays
Menu 22 € (weekday lunch)/59 € – Carte 37/60 €
• International • Chic •

This restaurant has a chic, stylish interior, charming, attentive service and modern but classically based cuisine full of flavour and finesse. WeinAmRhein uses high-quality, fresh ingredients to produce food that offers great value for money. Wine lovers will appreciate the excellent wine list.

Früh am Dom

Am Hof 12 ✉ 50667 – Ⓜ Dom-Hauptbahnhof Plan: **J1**
– ✆ (0221) 2 61 32 15 – www.frueh-gastronomie.de
Carte 18/37 €
• Country • Traditional décor • Rustic •

Brewery tradition since 1904. In the many rooms, each with its own atmosphere, Kölsch beer and typical dishes are served by the waiters at ancient bare tables.

CENTRE PLAN II

Marriott

Johannisstr. 76 ✉ 50668 Plan: **F1-2**
– Ⓜ Breslauer Pl. / Hauptbahnhof – ✆ (0221) 94 22 20
– www.koelnmarriott.de
355 rm – 🛉129/499 € 🛉🛉149/499 € – ☕ 27 € – 10 suites
• Business • Contemporary •

This comfortable and modern hotel has a touch of luxury. The Dom Suite is very pleasant with its large roof terrace and fantastic view. Various conference rooms. 'Plüsch-Bar' in the lobby. 'Fou' is the casual French brasserie-stye restaurant.

Savoy

Turiner Str. 9 ✉ 50668 Plan: **F1**
– Ⓜ Breslauer Pl. / Hauptbahnhof – ✆ (0221) 1 62 30 – www.savoy.de
145 rm – 🛉147/179 € 🛉🛉194/285 € – ☕ 22 € – 5 suites
• Business • Personalised •

For guests looking for something special, Gisela and Daniela Ragge have created very high quality and individual rooms with an eye to detail: New York, Venice, Geisha... In the evening dine in the Mythos restaurant and at lunchtime in the bar. Superb roof terrace.

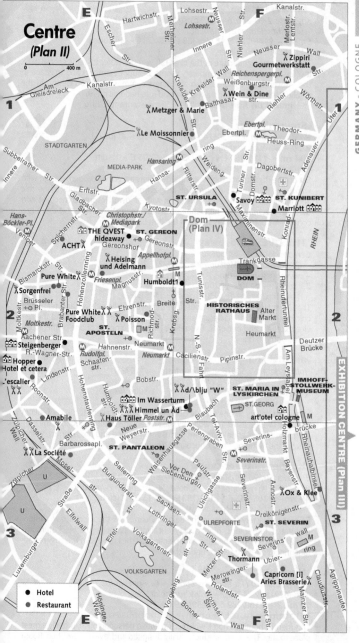

Centre
(Plan II)

0   400 m

Hartwichstr.

Lohsestr.

Kanalstr.

Am-Gleisdreieck

Kanalstr.

Escher Str.

Merheimer Str.

Innere

Neusser Str.

Merlostr.
Lentzstr.

Wall

× Zippiri
Gourmetwerkstatt

Reichenspergerpl.

Weißenburgstr.

Neusser Str.

Wörthstr.

Uferstr.

× Metzger & Marie

Krefelder Wall

Balthasar-str.

× Wein & Dine

STADTGARTEN

× Le Moissonnier

Ebertstr.

Ebertpl.

Theodor-Heuss-Ring

Subbelrather Str.

Innere

Hansaring

Ritterstr.

Weidengasse

Turiner Str.

Dagobertstr.

Maximinenstr.

Adenauer-

MEDIA-PARK

Erftstr.

Hansa-

Kyotostr.

ST. URSULA

Domstr.

× Savoy 🏨🏨

ST. KUNIBERT

● Marriott 🏨🏨

Hans-Böckler-Pl.

Christophstr./
Mediapark

Gladbacher Str.

Stickernstr.

Hohenzollernring

🏨 THE QVEST
hideaway

ST. GEREON

Gereonstr.

Dom
(Plan IV)

Konrad-

RHEIN

× ACHT

Gereonshof

Venloer Str.

Bismarckstr.

× Heising
und Adelmann

Appellhofpl.

Friesenpl.

Magnusstr.

Trankgasse

Rheinufertunnel

× Pure White

Brabanter Str.

Humboldt1 ●

Tunisstr.

DOM

× Sorgenfrei

Brüsseler
Pl.

Ehrenstr.

Breite

Krebsg.

HISTORISCHES
RATHAUS

Molkerei

Moltkestr.

× Pure White
Foodclub

× × Poisson

Richmod-str.

N.-S.-Fahrt

Alter
Markt

Deutzer
Brücke

Aachener Str.

ST.
APOSTELN

Hahnenstr.

Neumarkt

Heumarkt

🏨 Steigenberger

R.-Wagner-Str.

Rudolfpl.

Neumarkt

Cäcilienstr.

Pipinstr.

Am Leystapel

🏨 Hopper
Hotel et cetera

Lindenstr.

Schaafen-str.

Bobstr.

× ×d/\blju "W"

ST. MARIA IN
LYSKIRCHEN

IMHOFF-
STOLLWERK-
MUSEUM

l'escalier × ×

Roonstr.

Hohenstaufenring

🏨 Im Wasserturm

Blaubach

ST.GEORG

Hohenzollernring

● Amabile

× × Himmel un Äd

Poststr.

art'otel cologne

brücke

Holzmarkt

Rheinauhalbinsel

Zülpicher
Wall

Dasselstr.

× Haus Töller

Neue
Weyerstr.

Tel-Aviv-Str.

Perlengraben

Severins-

Bayenstr.

× × La Société

Barbarossapl.

ST. PANTALEON

Waisenhausgasse

Vor Den
Siebenburgen

Paulstr.

Severinstr.

Annostr.

× Ox & Klee

Mosel-str.

Zülpicher
Str.

Sachsen-

Lothringer
Str.

Ulrichgasse

Severinstr.

Dreikönigenstr.

ST. SEVERIN

U

Sälzerring

Burgunder-str.

ring

Eifel-str.

ULREPFORTE

SEVERINSTOR

Severins-
ring

wall

ring

U

Volksgartenstr.

Metzer Str.

× Thormann

Ubier-ring

Luxemburger

Eifelwall

VOLKSGARTEN

Merowinger-str.

Rolandstr.

Bonner Str.

× Capricorn [i]
Aries Brasserie ×

Claudiusstr.

Aggripinaufer

Honinger Weg

Vorgebirg-str.

Bonner Str.

Wörmser Str.

Mainzer Str.

Wall

● **Hotel**
● **Restaurant**

E   F

GERMANY - COLOGNE

Im Wasserturm

Kaygasse 2 ⊠ 50676 – Ⓜ Poststr. – ℰ (0221) 2 00 80
– www.hotel-im-wasserturm.de
54 rm – †148/280 € ††166/380 € – ⊡ 28 € – 34 suites
• Historic • Business • Design •

Plan: **F2**

The imposing architecture of the over 130 year-old water tower is special here. It offers tasteful and contemporary rooms, beauty treatments and massage in the 'Atelier Beaut'. There is also a business centre. Clean-lined design in the d∧blju "W" restaurant with a regional and international menu.
❀ **Himmel un Äd • d∧blju "W"** – See restaurant listing

Steigenberger

Habsburgerring 9 ⊠ 50674 – Ⓜ Rudolfplatz – ℰ (0221) 2280 – www.koeln.steigenberger.com
304 rm – †115/350 € ††115/350 € – ⊡ 25 € – 1 suite
• Business • Trendy •

Plan: **E2**

Set on the Rudolfplatz, the Steigenberger offers attractive, modern design with warm colours and simple forms. This ranges from the spacious lobby to the chic and intelligently designed rooms (each with its own Nespresso machine and the latest technology). The restaurant serves international fare and there is a convenient public car park beneath the hotel.

THE QVEST hideaway
Gereonskloster 12 ⊠ 50670
– Ⓜ Christophstr./Mediapark – ℰ (0221) 2 78 57 80
– www.qvest-hotel.com
33 rm ⊡ – †140 € ††200 € – 1 suite
• Boutique hotel • Business • Design •

Plan: **E2**

The Qvest is a unique hotel housed in the former city archives and features a chic mix of neo-Gothic, design and art. The atmosphere is relaxed and the service excellent and personal. If you like a piece of furniture or one of the accessories, you can buy it!

art'otel cologne
Holzmarkt 4 ⊠ 50676 – Ⓜ Severinstr. – ℰ (0221) 80 10 30 – www.artotels.com/cologne
208 rm ⊡ – †79/179 € ††89/189 € – 1 suite
• Business • Design •

Plan: **F3**

Hotel and gallery in one: trendy designer interior, excellent technical facilities with free W-LAN, as well as works by the Korean artist SEO throughout the building. The Chino Latino restaurant serves Asian cuisine and has a terrace with a view of the Rhine port and Chocolate Museum.

Hopper Hotel et cetera

Brüsseler Str. 26 ⊠ 50674 – Ⓜ Moltkestr. – ℰ (0221) 92 44 00 – www.hopper.de – Closed 24 December-1 January
49 rm – †105/155 € ††150/180 € – ⊡ 13 € – 1 suite
• Townhouse • Personalised •

Plan: **E2**

Former monastery located in the Belgian Quarter. All the rooms have design-orientated furnishings, high quality eucalyptus parquet, marble bathrooms and free W-LAN. The imposing altar painting catches the eye in the cosy restaurant. Inner courtyard terrace under the trees.

Humboldt1
Kupfergasse 10 (1st floor) ⊠ 50667 – Ⓜ Appellhofpl.
– ℰ (0221) 27 24 33 87 – www.humboldt1.de
7 rm ⊡ – †160/289 € ††259/319 €
• Boutique hotel • Family • Personalised •

Plan: **F2**

This friendly boutique hotel, which is run with a personal touch, is really a great place to stay. The rooms are individually designed and lavishly furnished. Room 6 – a duplex with bath under the eaves – is particularly attractive.

XxX 🕸️ **Himmel un Äd** – Hotel Im Wasserturm   🆎 ⟷

Kaygasse 2 (11th floor) ✉ *50676* – 🚇 *Poststr.*   Plan: F2
*– 𝒞 (0221) 2 00 80 – www.hotel-im-wasserturm.de – Closed 2 weeks early
January, during Carnival, mid July-early August and Sunday-Monday*
Menu 99/139 € – Carte 74/95 € – *(dinner only) (booking advisable)*
• Modern cuisine • Fashionable • Elegant •
This impressive building is once again the site of a gourmet restaurant. High up
on the 11th floor the chefs serve modern cuisine with regional accents in an
elegant setting with a wonderful view.
➜ Haff-Zander, Weinbergschnecke, Taubnessel, Birne. U.S. Short Rib, Lieb-
stöckel, Steinpilz, Weiße Johannisbeere. Campari Orange, Rote Paprika,
Manjari, Pistazie.

XX 🕸️ **La Société**   🏵️

Kyffhäuser Str. 53 ✉ *50674* – 🚇 *Poststr.* – 𝒞 *(0221)*   Plan: E3
23 24 64 – www.lasociete.info – Closed 2 weeks July
Menu 55/109 € – Carte 69/89 € – *(dinner only) (booking advisable)*
• Classic cuisine • Neighbourhood • Intimate •
La Société has it all: food, service and setting. Enjoy excellent classic cuisine with
modern, regional influences (try starting with the 'Kölsche Tapas') served by a
charming front-of-house team who give good wine suggestions. It has a cosy,
almost intimate interior with an impressive decor.
➜ Angebratenes Tatar "Stroganoff Style" mit Wachtel-Senfei. Brust und
Keule von der Bresse Poularde mit Erbsen, Morcheln und grünem Spargel.
Dies und Das vom Rhabarber mit weißer Schokolade und karamellisiertem
Blätterteig.

XX 🕸️ **L'escalier** (Maximilian Lorenz)   🏵️ 🍽️ 🆎

Brüsseler Str. 11 ✉ *50674* – 🚇 *Moltkestr.* – 𝒞 *(0221)*   Plan: E2
*2 05 39 98 – www.lescalier-restaurant.de – Closed 20 February-5 March
and Saturday lunch, Sunday-Monday*
Menu 59 € (lunch)/109 €
• Modern cuisine • Bistro •
Small, intimate and friendly, L'escalier is everything a really good bistro should
be. The classic modern fare comes in the form of two set menus, one traditional
and the other more innovative.
➜ Bretonische Steinpilze, Blutwurst, Schalotte, Schnittlauch. Bayerischer
Rehrücken, Sellerieknolle, Kirsche, Holunder, Zitrusfrüchte. Guanaja Schoko-
lade, Sanddorn, Erdnuss, Passepierre.

XX **d/\blju "W"** – Hotel Im Wasserturm   🍽️ 🆎 ⟷ 🛋️

Kaygasse 2 ✉ *50676* – 🚇 *Poststr.* – 𝒞 *(0221) 2 00 80*   Plan: F2
– www.hotel-im-wasserturm.de – Closed Saturday lunch, Sunday lunch
Menu 54 € – Carte 33/78 €
• International • Fashionable • Elegant •
The interior of this restaurant is light and modern, with the elegant light fittings
providing much of the atmosphere. The glass frontage offers a view of the terrace, which boasts an open-air kitchen in fine weather.

XX **Pure White Foodclub**

Brabanter Str. 48 ✉ *50672* – 🚇 *Friesenplatz* – 𝒞 *(0221)*   Plan: E2
96 02 65 56 – www.pure-white-food.de – Closed Sunday
Carte 41/129 € – *(dinner only)*
• Grills • Fashionable •
The sister restaurant to the trendy Pure White bistro just around the corner is a
little more comfortable, but the principle is the same. Top quality, flavoursome
produce, simply prepared on the Josper charcoal grill. If you chose the right
table you can even see into the kitchen.

Le Moissonnier

AC

Krefelder Str. 25 ⊠ 50670 – ℰ (0221) 72 94 79 — Plan: **F1**
– www.lemoissonnier.de – Closed 1 week Christmas-early January, 2 weeks during Easter, 3 weeks July-August and Sunday-Monday except Bank Holidays
Menu 92 € (weekday lunch)/140 € – Carte 80/122 € – *(booking essential)*
· Creative French · Bistro · Friendly ·

Liliane and Vincent Moissonnier are French and know all there is to know about French brasserie style. Not surprising then that this lively and uncomplicated restaurant has carved out quite a reputation for itself in Cologne. It serves the creative cuisine of fellow countryman Eric Menchon. The 4-course menu with wine suggestions offers unbeatable value for money.
→ Foie Gras Maison. Ris de Veau caramélisé. Short Rib de Boeuf.

Ox & Klee

AC

Im Zollhafen 18 ⊠ 50678 – Ⓜ Severinstr. – ℰ (0221) — Plan: **F3**
16956603 – www.oxundklee.de – Closed during Carnival, 2 weeks Easter, 2 weeks July, Sunday-Monday and Bank Holidays
Menu 69/144 € – *(dinner only) (booking advisable)*
· Modern cuisine · Chic · Friendly ·

Daniel Gottschlich and his team have moved to the middle of the three Crane Buildings. The interior is chic and ultramodern and the cuisine is sophisticated and rich in contrasts. The Bayleaf bar now offers a new cocktail + food format.
→ Jakobsmuschel, Beef, Fenchel, Dill. Schweinebauch, Auster, Alge, Bottarga. "Blüten, Blätter, Knospen".

Metzger & Marie

Kasparstr. 19 ⊠ 50670 – Ⓜ Ebertpl. – ℰ (0221) — Plan: **F1**
99 87 93 53 – www.metzgermarie.de – Closed Tuesday-Wednesday
Carte 34/60 € – *(dinner only) (booking advisable)*
· Traditional cuisine · Rustic · Neighbourhood ·

A trained butcher and a former waitress from the Rhenish family serve traditional fare at this restaurant. Wiener schnitzel, marinated pot roast and a vegetarian option are on the menu, all accompanied by good German and Austrian wines. These are served in an equally traditional setting that offers a pleasant mix of the rustic and the modern. There's a young, relaxed atmosphere.

Capricorn [i] Aries Brasserie

Alteburgerstr. 31 ⊠ 50678 – Ⓜ Severinstr. – ℰ (0221) — Plan: **F3**
3 97 57 10 – www.capricorniaries.com – Closed Saturday lunch, Sunday and Wednesday
Menu 25 € (weekday lunch)/59 € – Carte 29/50 €
· Classic French · Bistro · Cosy ·

This street corner brasserie is everything it should be – warm, friendly and down-to-earth. All the food on offer is based on good quality ingredients; try the fish soup with pan-fried scallops or the 'steak frites'. The delicious desserts include crème brûlée with tonka bean ice cream.

Poisson

AC

Wolfsstr. 6 ⊠ 50667 – Ⓜ Neumarkt – ℰ (0221) — Plan: **E2**
27 73 68 83 – www.poisson-restaurant.de – Closed during Carnival, Sunday-Monday and Bank Holidays
Menu 32 € (lunch)/78 € – Carte 54/99 € – *(booking advisable)*
· Seafood · Bistro · Trendy ·

Top quality products are deliciously prepared at this modern bistro with a fish orientated menu. The chef allows Asian, as well as Mediterranean and classic components to influence his food.

X **Amabile**

Görrestr. 2 ⊠ 50674 – Ⓜ Moltkestr. – ℰ (0221) 21 91 01   Plan: **E2**
– www.restaurant-amabile.de – Closed 2 weeks during Carnival, 2 weeks
September and Sunday-Monday
Menu 38/70 € – Carte 46/52 € – *(dinner only)*
• International • Friendly • Intimate •

You will find this lovingly decorated restaurant with a rustic touch between the Millowitsch Theatre and the University. The best way to discover the seasonal cuisine is to order the surprise menu.

X **Heising und Adelmann**

Friesenstr. 58 ⊠ 50670 – Ⓜ Friesenplatz – ℰ (0221)   Plan: **E2**
1 30 94 24 – www.heising-und-adelmann.de – Closed Sunday-Monday and
Bank Holidays
Menu 35/69 € – Carte 31/60 € – *(dinner only)*
• International • Bistro • Trendy •

Guests are served modern international cuisine in the relaxed atmosphere of this lively bistro restaurant with its delightful terrace. It has a pleasant lounge and a large bar area.

X **Sorgenfrei**

Antwerpener Str. 15 ⊠ 50672 – Ⓜ Moltkestr.   Plan: **E2**
– ℰ (0221) 3 55 73 27 – www.sorgenfrei-koeln.com – Closed during
Carnival, during Christmas and Saturday lunch, Sunday
Menu 37/42 € (dinner) – Carte 38/52 €
• International • Friendly • Rustic •

A really appealing and lively address in the Belgian Quarter, next door to which is a wine dealer with a good European range. No-frills international dishes. The classic is Argentinean 'Black Ranch' entrecote steak. Simpler lunchtime menu.

X **Pure White**

Antwerpener Str. 5 ⊠ 50672 – Ⓜ Rudolfpl. – ℰ (0221)   Plan: **E2**
29 43 65 07 – www.pure-white-food.de – Closed Sunday
Carte 37/117 € – *(dinner only) (booking advisable)*
• Seafood • Neighbourhood • Trendy •

Located close to the Friesenplatz, Pure White serves fresh food based on top quality ingredients in a casual, informal setting. Try the Norwegian king crab, the oysters or the wild halibut. If you prefer meat, you will enjoy the US, Scottish and Japanese dry-aged beef from the Josper grill.

X **ACHT**

Spichernstr. 10 ⊠ 50672 – Ⓜ Hans-Böckler-Pl.   Plan: **E2**
– ℰ (0221) 16 81 84 08 – www.restaurant-acht.de – Closed Christmas-New
Year, Sunday and Bank Holidays
Menu 39/59 € – Carte 41/52 € – *(dinner only)*
• International • Fashionable • Minimalist •

A fashionable city address in the Spichernhöfen warehouse district on the edge of the Belgian Quarter. Take your seat at a bare wooden table with a view of the kitchens, and enjoy the seasonal international fare including US beef tartare and the ACHT fish soup. Lovely interior courtyard.

X **Thormann**

Elsaßstr. 4 ⊠ 50677 – Ⓜ Severinstr. – ℰ (0221)   Plan: **F3**
3 10 44 91 – www.restaurant-thormann.de – Closed 1 week early January,
1 week during Carnival. 2 weeks end July and Monday
Menu 35/75 € – Carte 43/55 € – *(dinner only)*
• Classic cuisine • Intimate • Cosy •

This little restaurant with its charmingly intimate atmosphere serves largely classic cuisine, such as entrecôte of Spanish suckling calf in sherry and chocolate jus. Friendly service.

GERMANY - COLOGNE

X **Zippiri Gourmetwerkstatt**
Riehler Str. 73 ⊠ *50668 –* Ⓜ *Reichenspergerpl.*   Plan: **F1**
– ℰ (0221) 92 29 95 84 – www.zippiri.de – Closed 1-5 January,
23 February-8 March, 6-13 June, 28 August-29 September and Tuesday
Menu 55/85 € – Carte 44/83 € – *(dinner only and Sunday lunch)*
• Sardinian • Friendly •
The family owners here – restaurateurs to their very core – boast Sardinian roots that come through clearly in their cuisine. Top quality produce is used to create flavoursome dishes including tagliata of horse fillet served with rocket and parmesan.

X **The New Yorker Long Island Grill & Bar**
Agrippinawerft 30 ⊠ *50678 –* Ⓜ *Clodwigplatz*   Plan: **F3**
– ℰ (0221) 920710 – www.long-island.eu – Closed Saturday lunch,
Sunday-Monday
Carte 34/68 €
• International • Fashionable •
The USP here is undoubtedly the great location on the Agrippinawerft wharf with the museums and the Rhine close at hand, not to mention the wonderful terrace. The international menu focuses on grilled dishes, such as half a grilled lobster with tagliarini and aioli.

X **Wein & Dine**
Weißenburgerstr. 32 ⊠ *50670 –* Ⓜ *Reichenspergerpl.*   Plan: **F1**
– ℰ (0221) 91 39 18 75 – www.wein-dine.de – Closed Saturday lunch,
Sunday-Monday
Menu 15 € (weekday lunch) – Carte 37/52 €
• Modern cuisine • Fashionable •
With its fashionable yet welcoming atmosphere, open kitchen and friendly service, this smart little restaurant has much to offer. The modern international menu includes wild sea bass with pea puree, mountain lentils and beetroot.

X **Haus Töller**
Weyerstr. 96 ⊠ *50676 –* Ⓜ *Poststr. – ℰ (0221)*   Plan: **E3**
2 58 93 16 – www.haus-toeller.de – Closed Christmas-mid January, June-August, Sunday and Bank Holidays
Carte 22/28 € – *(dinner only) (booking advisable)*
• Country • Traditional décor • Cosy •
The former 'Steynen Huys' 1343 is really something for connoisseurs with its original wooden tables and floors, coffer ceiling and confession chair. Specialities include pork knuckles, Rhenish marinated roast (horsemeat) and on Friday evenings potato pancakes – all washed down with Päffgen Kölsch draught beer.

AT THE EXHIBITION CENTRE   **PLAN III**

🏨 **Hyatt Regency**
Kennedy-Ufer 2a ⊠ *50679 –* Ⓜ *Deutzer Freiheit*   Plan: **G2**
– ℰ (0221) 8 28 12 34 – www.cologne.regency.hyatt.de
288 rm – ♦140/800 € ♦♦140/800 € – ☒ 30 € – 18 suites
• Luxury • Luxury • Classic •
Classic business hotel directly by the Rhine at the Hohenzollern bridge. The lobby is large and refined, the rooms sleek, modern, elegant and technically up to date. Even the standard rooms are 36m² in size. International cuisine in the bright Glashaus restaurant on the first floor.

🏨 **Stadtpalais**
Deutz-Kalker-Str. 52 ⊠ *50679 –* Ⓜ *Deutz-Kalker Bad*   Plan: **G2**
– ℰ (0221) 88 04 20 – www.hotelstadtpalais.de
115 rm ☒ – ♦135/289 € ♦♦154/307 €
• Business • Contemporary •
This attractive group of buildings directly opposite the LANXESS Arena combines historical and modern architecture. Technically well equipped rooms come in a purist style. The restaurant offers a small range of dishes from a set menu.

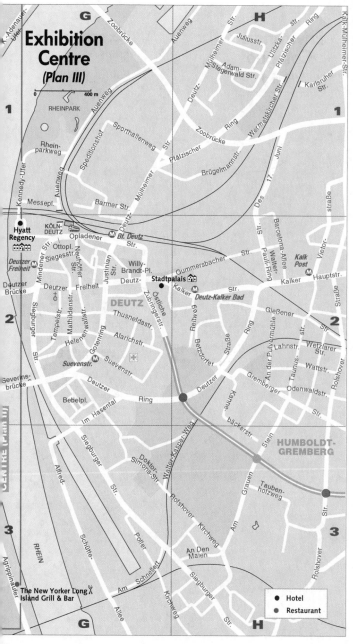

Exhibition Centre
(Plan III)

0 400 m

RHEINPARK

Zoobrücke

Auenweg

Juliusstr.

Mülheimer Str.

Adam-Stegerwald Str.

Ulitzka-Str.

Pfälzischer Ring

Kalk-Mülheimer-Str.

Karlsruher Str.

Rhein-parkweg

Speditionshof

Sporthallenweg

Mülheimer Str.

Zoobrücke Ring

Pfälzischer Str.

Des 17 Juni

straße

Auenweg

Barmer Str.

Deutz-

Brügelmannstr.

Kennedy-Ufer

Messepl.

Hyatt Regency

KÖLN-DEUTZ

Opladener

Bf. Deutz Str.

Barcelona-Allee

Str.

Walter-Pauli-Ring

Vietor-

Kalk Post

Deutzer Freiheit

Mindener Str.

Ottopl.

Siegesstr.

Neuhöfer Str.

Justinian Str.

Willy-Brandt-Pl.

Deutz-

Stadtpalais

Gummersbacher

Kalker Str.

Str.

Hauptstr.

Kalker

Straße

Deutzer Brücke

Deutzer Freiheit

DEUTZ

Östliche Zubringerstr.

Deutz-Kalker Bad

Siegburger

Tempelstr.

Helenenwallstr.

Mathildenstr.

Gotenring

Thusneldastr.

Alarichstr.

Rehweg

Betzdorfer Straße

Ring

Gießener

Str.

An der Pulvermühle

Lahnstr.

Wetzlarer Str.

Str.

Wattstr.

Rolshover

Severins-brücke

Str.

Suevenstr.

Suevenstr.

Deutzer

Ring

Deutzer

Taunus-

Gremberger

Odenwaldstr.

Str.

Bebelpl.

Im Hasental

Kamme-bäckerstr.

Stein

HUMBOLDT-GREMBERG

CENTRE (Plan III)

Siegburger

Str.

Doktor-Simons-Str.

Walter-Kasper-Weg

Rolshover

Grauen

Tauben-holzweg

Str.

Alfred-

Schütte-

Poller

Kirchweg

Am

Rolshover

RHEIN

Agrippinaufer

An Den Maien

Schnellert

Siegburger

Kirchweg

Str.

The New Yorker Long Island Grill & Bar

Am

Aallee

●	Hotel
●	Restaurant

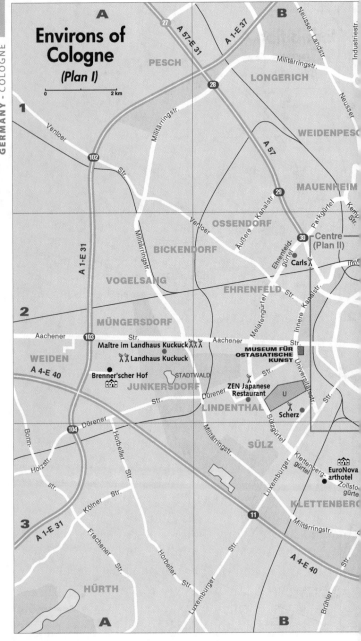

Environs of Cologne
(Plan I)

0   2 km

A 57-E 31

A 1-E 37

Neusser Landstr.

Industriestr.

PESCH

Militärringstr.

LONGERICH

WEIDENPES

Neusser

Venloer

Militärringstr.

A 57

MAUENHEIM

A 1-E 31

Militärringstr.

Venloer

Äußere Kanalstr.

Parkgürtel

Kem... Str.

OSSENDORF

Centre (Plan II)

Ehrenfeld gürtel

BICKENDORF

Carls ✗

Inne...

VOGELSANG

EHRENFELD Str.

Innere Kanalstr.

Melatengürtel Str.

MÜNGERSDORF

Str.

Aachener

A 103

Aachener

Str.

MUSEUM FÜR OSTASIATISCHE KUNST

Maître im Landhaus Kuckuck ✗✗✗

Universitätsstr.

WEIDEN

✗ ✗ Landhaus Kuckuck

A 4-E 40

Brenner'scher Hof

STADTWALD

ZEN Japanese Restaurant

Str.

JUNKERSDORF

Str.

Dürener

U

LINDENTHAL

Scherz

Str.

A 104

Dürener

Militärringstr.

SÜLZ

Bonn-

Holzstr.

Horbeller

Str.

Luxemburger

Klettenberg gürtel

EuroNova arthotel

Südgürtel

Zollsto...

gürte...

KLETTENBER

Kölner

Str.

Str.

A 11

Militärringstr.

A 1-E 31

Frechener

Str.

HÜRTH

Horbeller

Str.

Luxemburger

Str.

A 4-E 40

Brühler

Str...

A

B

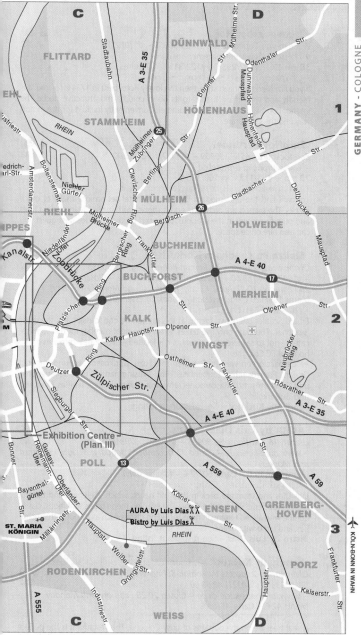

Brenner'scher Hof
Wilhelm-von-Capitaine-Str. 15 ⊠ *50858* – *ℰ (0221)* Plan: **A2**
9 48 60 00 – *www.brennerscher-hof.de*
38 rm ⊆ – ∳102/295 € ∳∳122/315 € – 2 suites
• Country house • Historic • Cosy •
If you like Mediterranean style, then this lovely hotel built in 1754 is for you. It is friendly and welcoming thanks to its warm colours and attractive decor. The interior courtyard is lovely in the summer. Conveniently located for the motorway and the city centre.

EuroNova arthotel
Zollstockgürtel 65 ⊠ *50969* – *ℰ (0221) 9 33 33 00* Plan: **B3**
– *www.euronova-arthotel.de*
73 rm – ∳85/115 € ∳∳100/130 € – ⊆ 15 €
• Business • Design • Contemporary •
You will find the ultra-modern EuroNova arthotel set amid a maze of office blocks. The owners are architects and it shows: both in the clean straight lines and pure forms and in the spacious, upmarket rooms. As a business guest you can also hire office space.

Maître im Landhaus Kuckuck (Erhard Schäfer)
Olympiaweg 2 (access by Roman-Kühnel-Weg) ⊠ *50933* Plan: **A2**
– *ℰ (0221) 48 53 60* – *www.landhaus-kuckuck.de* – *Closed 20-28 April, 10-23 February, 17 July-13 August and Monday-Tuesday*
Menu 109/129 € – *(dinner only) (booking essential)*
• Classic French • Elegant •
Erhard Schäfer offers two menus at this restaurant, one 'classic', and the other 'seasonal'. There are only five tables, exactly the right number for this sophisticated – not to say exclusive – venue. It is located just a stone's throw from the home of FC Cologne.
→ Carpaccio von weißen Garnelen mit Yuzu, Aprikosenessig und Imperial Caviar. Französische Taubenbrust im Wirsingmantel mit Selleriepüree und Gerstenrisotto. Mascarponecrème mit Carameltoffee, weißes Moccaeis und Butterkeks.
Landhaus Kuckuck – See restaurant listing

AURA by Luis Dias
Uferstr. 16 (1st floor) ⊠ *50996* – *ℰ (0221) 37984606* Plan: **C3**
– *www.aura-koeln.de* – *Closed 27 December-5 January, 31 July-13 August and Monday*
Menu 59/119 € – Carte 60/77 € – *(dinner only)*
• Classic cuisine • Chic • Elegant •
Luis Dias and team are back in their old haunt, which is elegant and tasteful with a wonderful view of the Rhine. The evening menu offers ambitious, classic cuisine with a Mediterranean note, including dishes such as turbot with artichokes, and lamb with beans.
Bistro by Luis Dias – See restaurant listing

Landhaus Kuckuck – Restaurant Maître im Landhaus Kuckuck
Olympiaweg 2 (access by Roman-Kühnel-Weg) Plan: **A2**
⊠ *50933* – *ℰ (0221) 48 53 60*
– *www.landhaus-kuckuck.de* – *Closed 20-28 February and Monday*
Menu 42 € – Carte 45/63 €
• Country • Elegant • Luxury •
A real treasure on the outskirts of busy Cologne. This restaurant is the perfect place to relax and unwind with its magnificent countryside location and elegant English country house-style interior.

X

ZEN Japanese Restaurant

Bachemer Str. 236 ✉ *50935 –* ✆ *(0221) 28 28 57 55*　　　Plan: **B2**
– www.restaurant-zen.de – Closed Monday
Carte 20/57 € – *(dinner only) (booking advisable)*
• Japanese • Minimalist •

Set in the middle of a residential district, ZEN promises what is probably the most authentic Japanese cuisine in Cologne… and at very reasonable prices to boot! The chefs use the very best ingredients to prepare dishes such as *kinpira gobou* (braised burdock root) and *harami yakiniku* (grilled beef skirt), as well as sushi and sashimi. Informal, minimalist-style decor.

X

Scherz

Berrenrather Str. 242 ✉ *50667 –* ✆ *(0221) 16 92 94 40*　　　Plan: **B2**
– www.scherzrestaurant.de – Closed 18 June-18 July and Monday, Saturday lunch
Menu 45/55 € (dinner) – Carte 32/56 €
• Austrian • Neighbourhood •

Austrian-born Michael Scherz has his pleasantly informal restaurant in the heart of the lively Sülz district. Find Austro-Hungarian classics like fried breaded chicken, Wiener Schnitzel and offal, alongside a more modern evening menu. Whatever you do, leave room for a glorious dessert of Kaiserschmarrn! Austrian wines.

X

Bistro by Luis Dias – Restaurant AURA by Luis Dias

Uferstr. 16 ✉ *50996 –* ✆ *(0221) 37984606*　　　Plan: **C3**
– www.aura-koeln.de – Closed 27 December-5 January, 31 July-13 August and Monday, Saturday lunch
Carte 38/60 €
• Mediterranean cuisine • Fashionable •

Bistro is simpler but also chic and the cuisine is still prepared to the same high standards. It provides a pleasantly relaxed setting for Mediterranean fare, which includes pan-fried octopus with watermelon, risotto with porcini mushrooms or lamb chops.

X

Carls

Eichendorffstr. 25 (at Neu-Ehrenfeld) ✉ *50823*　　　Plan: **B2**
– ✆ *(0221) 58 98 66 56 – www.carlsrestaurant.de – Closed during Carnival, 23 October-4 November and Monday*
Carte 23/46 € – *(dinner only)*
• International • Neighbourhood • Bourgeois •

If you want something friendly and local, you will love the charm of this rustic, down-to-earth eatery. It serves international and regional fare from tuna steak with chicory and lemon risotto to himmel un äd', a local speciality of black pudding, fried onions, mash and apple sauce.

FRANKFURT
FRANKFURT AM MAIN

Population: 732 000

Tom Bayer/Fotolia.com

European travellers might feel there's no need to go all the way to New York when they've got Frankfurt. After all, it's earned itself the nickname 'Mainhattan', what with all those slinky, shiny skyscrapers reaching up from the banks of the River Main. This may be a city of big corporations, but you'll also find half-timbered medieval houses (admittedly rebuilt), and an array of museums along the south bank of the river. Located at the crossing point of Germany's north-south and east-west roads, Frankfurt is a city that takes its cultural scene very seriously. It's said that it spends more money on the arts per year than any other European city, and has also become something of a gourmet hotspot with a cuisine range that gets more eclectic by the month.

The centre of Frankfurt is Cathedral Hill, where the cathedral has stood for eight hundred years; it towers over Römerberg, the medieval square, rebuilt following the war. To the west, amongst the mighty skyscrapers of international banks and corporations, lie the main railway station and the Exhibition Centre, while south of the River Main is the famous 'museum embankment' and Frankfurt's oldest area, Sachsenhausen, full of bars, cafés and restaurants. Germany's great poet, novelist and dramatist, Johann Wolfgang von Goethe, was born and bred here; no doubt he wouldn't believe his eyes if he saw Frankfurt today.

FRANKFURT IN...

→ **ONE DAY**
Old Town, Römerberg, the view from Main Tower.

→ **TWO DAYS**
Goethe House, Museum Embankment, an apfelwein lokal restaurant in Sachsenhausen.

→ **THREE DAYS**
Boat trip on the Main, window shopping (Zeil), a concert at the Opera House.

PRACTICAL INFORMATION

ARRIVAL-DEPARTURE

✈ Frankfurt Airport is 9km southeast of the city centre. S-Bahn trains S8 and S9 leave every 15min for Frankfurt station and take just over 10min.

GETTING AROUND

Frankfurt runs an efficient bus, metro and tram system. You can buy a day ticket for one person or for a group (max. 5), which is valid until the last ride of the day. Tickets are available at vending machines and from bus drivers, but cannot be bought on trams, the U-Bahn or S-Bahn. A Frankfurt Card entitles you to free public transport, discounts at a variety of museums and attractions, and reductions of up to thirty per cent on selected boat trips. You can buy the Card at many travel agencies, at tourist information offices and in both terminals at the airport; it's valid for 24 or 48 hours.

EATING OUT

Not so long ago, Frankfurt's gastronomic fame came courtesy of its Apfelwein (a sweet or dry variant of cider), its Handkäs mit Musik (small yellow cheese with vinegar, oil and onions) and its Grüne Sauce (various herbs and sour cream served with boiled eggs). That's not the case now. Head along to the Fressgass (near Opernplatz) – which translates as 'Eatery Alley' or 'Glutton's Lane' – and you've got a pedestrian mile of eateries; choose from a whole range of food to take away or to graze over, all at good prices. Nearly thirty per cent of Frankfurt's citizens have come to the city from overseas,

CALENDAR HIGHLIGHTS

February
Carnival.

May
Forest Folk Festival, Rose and Light Festival (music and illuminations in the Palm Garden).

August
Museum Quay Festival, River Main Festival.

September
Autumn Dippe Fair (funfair and fireworks), IAA (International Motor Show - odd-numbered years).

October
Book Fair.

so a wealth of eating possibilities has been opened up. It's now easy to 'eat globally' all round the city and foreign communities have added a real touch of spice to the culinary landscape, with the likes of Turkish, Italian and Chinese establishments. Nevertheless, a visit to this city wouldn't be complete without a trip to the äppelwoilokale in Sachsenhausen, the casual but lively cafés where tradition is the key, and Apfelwein is served up in ceramic mugs.

329

GERMANY - FRANKFURT ON MAIN

Steigenberger Frankfurter Hof   🕅 🖪 🌐 🕥 🕹 🖾 🕸 🚘

Am Kaiserplatz ✉ *60311 –* Ⓜ *Willy-Brandt-Platz*   Plan: **E1**
– ℰ (069) 2 15 02
– www.frankfurter-hof.steigenberger.de
261 rm ☲ – **♦**249/699 € **♦♦**249/699 € – 42 suites
• Grand Luxury • Traditional • Classic •

This classic grand hotel has a tradition that stretches back to 1876. With an impressive, historical façade outside and pure luxury within, it boasts an imposing lobby with plenty of space to sit and relax. There are tasteful, spacious guestrooms and an attractive 1 000m2 spa area.
❀ **Français** – See restaurant listing

Jumeirah   🕅 🕥 🕹 🖾 🕸 🚘

Thurn-und-Taxis-Platz 2 (access via Große Eschenheimer   Plan: **E1**
Str. 8) ✉ *60313 –* Ⓜ *Hauptwache – ℰ (069) 2 97 23 70*
– www.jumeirah.com/frankfurt
217 rm – **♦**239/349 € **♦♦**239/349 € – ☲ 32 € – 49 suites
• Grand Luxury • Contemporary • Elegant •

At the Jumeirah the very best in comfort, technology and interior decor speak for themselves. No praise is too high for the 220m^2 Presidential Suite which boasts its own massage and beauty facility, a Talise spa and direct access to the adjacent leisure centre. Breakfast and snacks are served in Le Petit Palais adjoining the MyZeil shopping mall.
Max on One – See restaurant listing

Villa Kennedy   🖫 🖪 🕥 🗔 🕹 🖾 🕸 🚘

Kennedyallee 70 ✉ *60596 –* Ⓜ *Schweizer Platz*   Plan I: **B3**
– ℰ (069) 71 71 20 – www.roccofortehotels.com
137 rm – **♦**245/945 € **♦♦**245/945 € – ☲ 35 € – 26 suites
• Grand Luxury • Classic • Contemporary •

The Villa Speyer, built in 1904, has been converted into an impressive luxury hotel with great architectural flair. The interior successfully combines the classic and the modern. The exquisite spa offers Éminence beauty treatments (the only one in Germany).
Gusto – See restaurant listing

The Westin Grand   🖪 🌐 🕥 🗔 🕹 🖾 🚘

Konrad-Adenauer-Str. 7 ✉ *60313 –* Ⓜ *Konstablerwache*   Plan: **F1**
– ℰ (069) 2 98 10 – www.westingrandfrankfurt.com
353 rm – **♦**199/699 € **♦♦**199/699 € – ☲ 33 € – 18 suites
• Luxury • Chain • Contemporary •

Enjoying a central location, this large international business hotel boasts comfortable, modern guestrooms and numerous conference areas. Executive club on the first floor. Swimming pool with great views of the city.
san san • Sushimoto – See restaurant listing

Fleming's Deluxe   🕅 ❮ 🖪 🕥 🕹 🖾 🕸 🚘

Eschenheimer Tor 2 ✉ *60318 –* Ⓜ *Eschenheimer Tor*   Plan: **E1**
– ℰ (069) 4 27 23 20
– www.flemings-hotels.com
202 rm ☲ – **♦**198/258 € **♦♦**218/278 € – 4 suites
• Business • Contemporary •

In the Eschenheimer centre you'll find this listed former office building from the 1950s with its original Peternoster still operational. It has modern furnishings with a bar and lounge on the seventh-floor. The rooftop restaurant with its show kitchen offers a view of the Skyline.

25hours Hotel The Goldman

Hanauer Landstr. 127 ✉ *60314 –* Ⓜ *Ostbahnhof* — Plan I: **D2**
– ℰ (069) 40 58 68 90 – www.25hours-hotels.com/goldman
97 rm – �120/405 € ♥♥120/405 € – ☞ 18 €
• Business • Design • Personalised •
This hotel has all manner of endearing and stylish decor in the form of lamps, fabrics, paintings etc. The very pleasant, modern rooms couldn't be more individual.
Goldman – See restaurant listing

Villa Orange

Hebelstr. 1 ✉ *60318 –* Ⓜ *Merianplatz – ℰ (069)* — Plan: **F1**
40 58 40 – www.villa-orange.de
38 rm ☞ – ♥95/265 € ♥♥135/375 €
• Family • Contemporary • Cosy •
This beautifully appointed villa-style townhouse is one of the Bio Hotels. Modern-style and warm tones from the foyer via the library to the rooms. Organic, quality breakfast.

XxXx
❀

Français – Hotel Steigenberger Frankfurter Hof

Am Kaiserplatz ✉ *60311 –* Ⓜ *Willy-Brandt-Platz* — Plan: **E1**
– ℰ (069) 2 15 118 – www.restaurant-francais.de – Closed 1 week January, 2 weeks Easter, 4 weeks July-August, Saturday lunch, Sunday-Monday and Bank Holidays
Menu 59 € (weekday lunch)/135 € (dinner)
– Carte 90/110 € – *(booking advisable)*
• Modern French • Elegant • Classic décor •
The best quality produce is used here to create subtle, beautifully balanced, unusual combinations that you can enjoy in the stylish, high-ceilinged dining rooms served by the attentive front-of-house team. In summer, enjoy alfresco dining outside in the courtyard. The lunchtime menu offers great value for money.
→ Elsässer Gänseleber, grüne Tomate, Nori Alge, Cashewkerne. Bretonischer Wolfsbarsch, grüner Spargel, Karotte, Miso. Reh aus der Eifel, Erbse, Feige, Cassis-Ingwer.

XxX
❀❀

Tiger-Gourmetrestaurant

Heiligkreuzgasse 20 ✉ *60313 –* Ⓜ *Konstablerwache* — Plan: **F1**
– ℰ (069) 9 20 02 20 – www.tigerpalast.de – Closed 1-10 January, mid May-mid August and Sunday-Monday
Menu 98 € (Vegetarian)/135 €
– Carte 88/124 € – *(dinner only) (booking essential)*
• Modern French • Elegant • Fashionable •
Modern techniques and textures, subtle contrasts and intense aromas: that's the classically based cuisine on offer here at Tiger. And should the elaborately and meticulously prepared food make you forget you're sitting in the Variety Theatre, there are always the historical posters which adorn the walls of this small, almost intimate restaurant to remind you!
→ Bretonische Felsenrotbarbe in Arbequina Olivenöl sautiert. Kalb aus der Corréze in 2 Gängen serviert. Fruchtiger Thaigarten, süß-sauer.
Palastbar-Restaurant – See restaurant listing

XxX

Max on One – Hotel Jumeirah

Thurn-und-Taxis-Platz 2 (access via Große Eschenheimer — Plan: **E1**
Str. 8, 1st. floor) ✉ *60313 –* Ⓜ *Hauptwache – ℰ (069) 2 97 23 71 98*
– www.jumeirah.com/frankfurt – Closed Saturday lunch, Sunday
Carte 33/89 € – *(August: Monday-Friday dinner only) (booking advisable)*
• International • Elegant •
Max on One is located on the first floor of an upmarket hotel in the city centre. It boasts an open show kitchen where you can watch the staff at work surrounded by Japanese interior designer Takashi Sugimoto's smart decor. The cleverly integrated glass wine cabinet is particularly eye-catching.

GERMANY - FRANKFURT ON MAIN

GERMANY - FRANKFURT ON MAIN

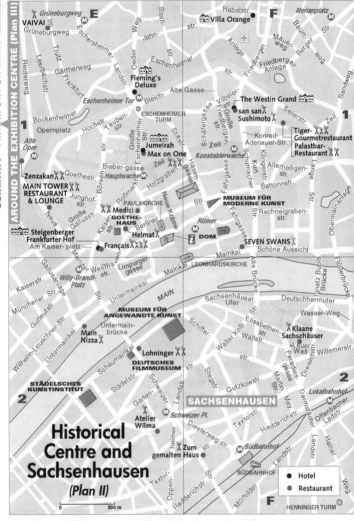

XX Carmelo Greco

🕸️

Ziegelhüttenweg 1 ⊠ 60598 – Ⓜ Südbahnhof – 𝒞 (069)   Plan I: **C3**
60 60 89 67 – www.carmelo-greco.de – Closed Saturday lunch, Sunday
Menu 46 € (weekday lunch)/125 € – Carte 62/97 €
• Italian • Fashionable • Chic •

Carmelo Greco offers Italian-cum-Mediterranean cuisine based on the use of
good, fresh ingredients. This can be enjoyed in the attractively elegant and
modern interior or outside on the pretty terrace. Popular lunch menu.
➜ Jakobsmuschel, Martini Bianco, Yuzu-Sakejus. Risotto, Artischocke, Hummer. Blak Cod, Bagna Cauda, Kartoffel.

XX **Lohninger** 🛜 📶 ⇔
Schweizer Str. 1 ✉ *60594 –* Ⓜ *Schweizer Pl. –* ☏ *(069)*   Plan: **E2**
2 47 55 78 60 – www.lohninger.de
Menu 39 € (lunch)/88 € (dinner) – Carte 44/76 € – *(booking advisable)*
• Austrian • Friendly • Fashionable •
This modern restaurant can be found in the beautiful high-ceilinged rooms of a
classic townhouse. It offers Austrian cuisine with international influences.

XX **MAIN TOWER RESTAURANT & LOUNGE** ⇐ 📶
Neue Mainzer Str. 52 (53rd floor, fee) ✉ *60311*   Plan: **E1**
– Ⓜ *Alte Oper –* ☏ *(069) 36 50 47 77 – www.maintower-restaurant.de*
– Closed Saturday lunch, Sunday-Monday and Bank Holidays lunch
Menu 35 € (weekday lunch)/105 € (dinner)
– Carte 57/69 € – (booking essential)
• Modern cuisine • Fashionable •
In addition to its unique view of the city, Main Tower offers some excellent food
including dishes such as king prawns with cauliflower and fennel salad or beef
fillet with romanesco and macadamia nuts. In the evenings you can make up
your own set menu from the à la carte offerings for an all-in price. Separate
lunchtime menu.

XX **Medici** 🛜 📶
Weißadlergasse 2 ✉ *60311 –* Ⓜ *Hauptwache –* ☏ *(069)*   Plan: **E1**
21 99 07 94 – www.restaurantmedici.de – Closed Sunday and Bank
Holidays
Menu 21 € (lunch)/64 € – Carte 44/64 €
• International • Friendly •
Two brothers are your hosts in this city centre restaurant. International dishes
with a Mediterranean influence are served in a modern atmosphere.

XX **Zenzakan** 🛜 ♿ 📶 ⇔ 🚗
Taunusanlage 15 ✉ *60325 –* Ⓜ *Alte Oper –* ☏ *(069)*   Plan: **E1**
970 86 908 – www.mook-group.de – Closed 24 December-7 January and
Sunday
Menu 99 € – Carte 44/107 € – *(dinner only)*
• Asian • Trendy • Exotic décor •
This "Pan-Asian Supper Club" has striking, black Far Eastern decor, great lighting
and its own "cherry garden". It has a very particular atmosphere that is matched
by the primarily Southeast Asian food including modern takes on Japanese
dishes. Try the "freestyle sushi".

XX **Gusto** – Hotel Villa Kennedy 🛜 ♿ 📶 🚗
Kennedyallee 70 ✉ *60596 –* Ⓜ *Schweizer Platz*   Plan I: **B3**
– ☏ *(069) 717 121 205 – www.villakennedy.com*
Menu 76/89 € – Carte 57/112 €
• Italian • Elegant • Cosy •
Take a seat in this friendly restaurant with its tastefully modern, minimalist-style
interior and sample some of its upmarket Italian food, such as the homemade
ravioli with salsa verde. The imposing interior courtyard is also very impressive.

XX **Palastbar-Restaurant** – Tiger-Gourmetrestaurant 📶 ⇔
Heiligkreuzgasse 20 ✉ *60313 –* Ⓜ *Konstablerwache*   Plan: **F1**
– ☏ *(069) 92 00 220 – www.tigerpalast.de – Closed mid May-mid August*
and Monday
Menu 54 € – Carte 47/70 € – *(dinner only)*
• International • Cosy • Intimate •
With its comfortable bench seats upholstered in black leather, impressive brick
arches and clever lighting, this restaurant is definitely the place to see and be
seen.

GERMANY - FRANKFURT ON MAIN

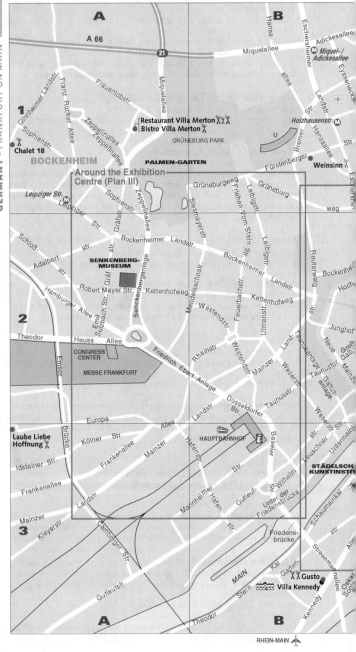

FRANKFURT ON MAIN - EXCHIBITION CENTRE - SENKENBERG MUSEUM - PLAN...

A

A 66

21

Miquelallee

B

Hansa...

Escherisheimer

Adickesallee

Miquel- / Adickesallee

allee

Str. Landstr.

Eyssenecke...

1

Ginnheimer Landstr.

Franz Rücker Allee

Frauenlobstr.

Miquelallee

Brener

Hansaallee

Str.

Holzhausenstr.

Ⓜ

Sophienstr.

Zeppelinallee

Zeppelinallee

Restaurant Villa Merton 🍴🍴🍴
Bistro Villa Merton 🍴

GRÜNEBURG PARK

Fürstenberger

Weinsinn 🍴

Chalet 18

BOCKENHEIM

PALMEN-GARTEN

U

Escherisheime...

– Around the Exhibition –
Centre (Plan III)

Leipziger Str.

Ⓜ

Leipziger

Str.

Sophienstr.

Zeppelinallee

Grüneburgweg

Grüneburg-

weg

Gräfst.

Bockenheimer Landstr.

Friehen-Vom-Stein-Str.

Leibigstr.

Grüneburg-

Leibigstr.

Reuterweg

Bockenheit

Hoch

Schloß

Adalbert-

str.

Emil Sulzbach Str.

Senkenberganlage

Gräf. str.

SENKENBERG-MUSEUM

Robert Mayer Str.

Kettenhofweg

Mendelsschnstr.

Westendstr.

Bockenheimer Landstr.

Kettenhofweg

Feuerbachstr.

Ulmenstr.

str.

Land-

Taunusanlage

Junghor

2

Hamburger Allee

Theodor

Heuss Allee

CONGRESS CENTER

MESSE FRANKFURT

Emser

Friedrich Ebert Anlage

Rheinstr.

Westendstr.

Mainzer

Weserstr.

Taunusstr.

Taunusstr.

Taunusanlage

Gallus-anlage

Neue

Große Galli...

Taunusto...

Mainz

Düsseldorfer

Europa

Allee

Landstr.

HAUPTBAHNHOF

ℹ️

Baseler

Weser st. Str.

Leuschner

Untermain

Laube Liebe Hoffnung 🍴

Kölner

Str.

Brücke

Frankenallee

Mainzer

Hafenstr.

Str.

STÄDELSCH KUNSTINSTI

Idstainer Str.

Frankenallee

Mahnhelmer

Hafen-

Gutleut-

Wilhelm

Str.

Unter der

str.

Schaumainkai

Mainzer

Landstr.

Friedensbrücke

str.

3

Kleyerstr.

Cramberger Str.

Friedens-brücke

Stresemannallee

Gutleutstr.

MAIN

Stern

Kai

Garten-

Gusto 🍴🍴

Villa Kennedy

Kennedy

Oeskar

Sol...

Theodor

A

B

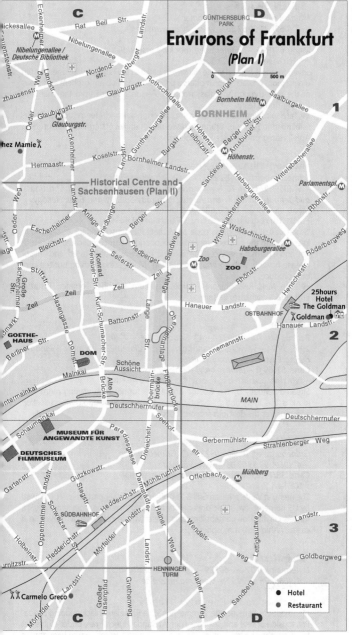

Environs of Frankfurt
(Plan I)

0   500 m

C   **D**

GÜNTHERSBURG
PARK

ickesallee

Eckenheimer

Rat Beil Str.

Nibelungenallee /
Deutsche Bibliothek

Nibelungenallee

Nordendstr.

Friedberger Landstr.

Rothschildallee

Burgstr.

Saalburgallee

Bornheim Mitte Ⓜ

BORNHEIM

Glauburgstr.

Höhenstr.

Berger Str.

Arnsburger Str.

Leibnizstr.

Ⓜ Höhenstr.

Wittelsbacherallee

Chez Mamie ✕

Koselstr.

Günthersburgallee

Bornheimer Landstr.

Burgstr.

Sandweg

Habsburgerallee

Parlamentspl. Ⓜ

Hermannstr.

Eckenheimer Landstr.

Rhönstr.

**Historical Centre and
Sachsenhausen (Plan II)**

Eschenheimer

Bleichstr.

Stiftstr.

Friedberger Anlage

Berger Str.

Seilerstr.

Zeil

Wittelsbacherallee

Waldschmidtstr.

Ⓜ

Habsburgerallee Ⓜ

Röderbergweg

Zoo

ZOO

Ⓜ

Rhönstr.

Henschelstr.

Große
Eschenheimer
Str.

Zeil

Hasengasse

Konrad-Adenauer-Str.

Kurt-Schumacher-Str.

Lange Str.

Hanauer Landstr.

25hours
Hotel
The Goldman
Ⓜ Goldman

OSTBAHNHOF

Hanauer Landstr.

2

**GOETHE-
HAUS**

Berliner Str.

Domstr.

DOM

Battonstr.

Schöne
Aussicht

Obermainanlage

Sonnemannstr.

Mainkai

Alte
Brücke

Obermainbrücke

Flößerbrücke

Untermainkai

Deutschherrnufer

MAIN

Deutschherrnufer

Schaumainkai

**MUSEUM FÜR
ANGEWANDTE KUNST**

Paradiesgasse

Seehof

Dreieichstr.

Gerbermühlstr.

Strahlenberger Weg

**DEUTSCHES
FILMMUSEUM**

Gartenstr.

Landstr.

Gutzkowstr.

Mühlbruchstr.

Offenbacher

Ⓜ Mühlberg

Landstr.

Oppenheimer

Schweizer

SÜDBAHNHOF

Hedderichstr.

Darmstädter Landstr.

Wendels-

weg

Lettigkautweg

Landstr.

Holbeinstr.

Hedderichstr.

Mörfelder Landstr.

Hainer Weg

Goldbergweg

urnitzstr.

✕✕ Carmelo Greco ●

Mörfelder Landstr.

Gröfer
Hasenpfad

Grethenweg

**HENNINGER
TURM**

Hainer Weg

Am Sandberg

C   **D**

● Hotel
● Restaurant

335

SEVEN SWANS [AC]

Mainkai 4 ⊠ *60311 –* Ⓜ *Römer*   Plan: **F1**
– 𝒞 (069) 21 99 62 26 – www.sevenswans.de
– Closed Sunday-Monday
Menu 65/89 € – *(dinner only) (booking essential)*
· Modern cuisine · Design ·

Seven Swans is housed in the narrowest building in Frankfurt with one 4 x 10m dining room on each floor. It offers a private dining club atmosphere and views of the river through the glass frontage. Personal service from the charming front-of-house team.

→ Tafelspitz vom Kalb mit Karotte, Brennnessel und Meerrettich. Eismeer-saibling mit Senfsaat, Brunnenkresse und Kamille. Hafermilch mit grünem Apfel, Honig und weißer Schokolade.

Atelier Wilma (Michael Riemenschneider) [AC] ⟷

Schneckenhofstr. 11 ⊠ *60311 –* Ⓜ *Schweizer Platz*   Plan: **E2**
– 𝒞 (069) 97 69 16 76 – www.atelierwilma.restaurant – Closed Christmas-mid January, mid July-end August, Saturday-Sunday and Bank Holidays
Menu 45/149 € – Carte 58/101 €
· Modern cuisine · Chic · Fashionable ·

'Smart casual' is the dress code at Michael Riemenschneider's restaurant, in keeping with the relaxed, upmarket decor and the uncomplicated, professional and charming service. The food is modern, sophisticated and full of intense flavours with a 'certain something'. Made using nothing but the very best produce.

→ Ente, Mais, Reis, Chicorée. Pulpo, Basilikum, Kartoffel, Tomaten. Pistazie, Erdbeere, Frischkäse, Balsamico.

Heimat [🍴] 🍴

Berliner Str. 70 ⊠ *60311 –* Ⓜ *Hauptwache – 𝒞 (069)*   Plan: **E1**
29 72 59 94 – www.restaurant-heimat.de – Closed 23 December-8 January, during Easter and during Whitsun
Carte 51/69 € – *(dinner only) (booking essential)*
· Market cuisine · Trendy · Fashionable ·

Situated centrally by the Goethe house in a former tram waiting room with kiosk is this lively and pleasantly relaxed restaurant. A good wine selection accompanies the delicious seasonal food.

VAIVAI

Grüneburgweg 16 ⊠ *60322 –* Ⓜ *Grüneburgweg*   Plan: **E1**
– 𝒞 (069) 90 55 93 05 – www.vaivai.de
Carte 38/71 € – *(dinner only) (booking essential)*
· Italian · Trendy ·

The menu at VaiVai's 'Italian Grill & Bar' offers antipasti or pasta to start, followed by US prime rib-eye steak, dry aged *bistecca alla Fiorentina*, *gamberoni grigliati* (grilled crayfish) or perhaps *branzino intero* (whole sea bass), all served in a casual, fashionable atmosphere.

MainNizza 🍴 ⟷

Untermainkai 17 ⊠ *60329 –* Ⓜ *Willy-Brandt-Platz*   Plan: **E2**
– 𝒞 (069) 26 95 29 22 – www.mainnizza.de
Carte 27/51 €
· International · Friendly · Trendy ·

Menu options here include 'Himmel & Ääd', a Rhineland black pudding speciality, topside of veal and sea bass fillet. At Sunday lunchtimes, under-eights eat free from the children's menu. Attractive veranda and self-service beer garden overlooking the Main.

X **Goldman** – 25hours Hotel The Goldman
Hanauer Landstr. 127 ⊠ 60314 – Ⓜ *Ostbahnhof* Plan I: **D2**
– 𝒞 (069) 40 58 68 98 06 – www.goldman-restaurant.com – Closed Sunday and Bank Holidays
Menu 62 € – Carte 44/70 € – *(Monday to Saturday dinner only)*
• Mediterranean cuisine • Design •
Comfortable dining in a smart, modern restaurant with an open kitchen and large glass frontage. Mediterranean dishes with a contemporary interpretation are served.

X **Chez Mamie**
Sömmeringstr. 4 ⊠ 60322 – Ⓜ *Glauburgstr. – 𝒞 (069)* Plan I: **C1**
95 20 93 60 – www.chezmamie.de – Closed Saturday lunch, Sunday-Monday
Menu 15 € *(weekday lunch)* – Carte 21/43 €
• Classic French • Bistro •
If you have been to Chez Mamie in Wiesbaden, you will recognise the same system here. This friendly bistro and wine bar serves traditional fare from a menu in the form of an Asterix comic, which includes steak tartare and boeuf bourguignon. Simple menu at lunchtimes.

X **san san** – Hotel The Westin Grand
Konrad-Adenauer-Str. 7 ⊠ 60313 – Ⓜ *Konstablerwache* Plan: **F1**
– 𝒞 (069) 91399050 – www.sansan-restaurant.de – Closed Sunday
Carte 29/58 €
• Chinese • Traditional décor •
A restaurant offering typical Chinese fare in a Chinese setting, with a choice of three dining options: the Bamboo Lounge, the Shanghai Suite or an intimate private dining room.

X **Sushimoto** – Hotel The Westin Grand
Konrad-Adenauer-Str. 7 ⊠ 60313 – Ⓜ *Konstablerwache* Plan: **F1**
– 𝒞 (069) 1310057 – www.sushimoto.eu – Closed Monday, Sunday lunch except during fairs
Menu 45/95 € – Carte 37/126 € – *(booking advisable)*
• Japanese • Elegant •
The atmosphere is authentic and austere, just as you might expect from a Japanese restaurant. Explore the many facets of Japanese cuisine including sushi and teppanyaki.

X **Klaane Sachsehäuser**
Neuer Wall 11 (Sachsenhausen) ⊠ 60594 Plan: **F2**
– Ⓜ *Lokalbahnhof – 𝒞 (069) 61 59 83 – www.klaanesachsehaeuser.de*
– Closed Sunday
Carte 17/28 € – *(dinner only open from 4pm)*
• Country • Rustic •
This popular pub-style restaurant, reached through an interior courtyard, has been serving traditional "Stöffche" brewed on the premises and good Frankfurt fare since 1876. And you'll always find someone to share your evening with!

X **Zum gemalten Haus**
Schweizer Str. 67 (Sachsenhausen) ⊠ 60594 Plan: **F2**
– Ⓜ *Schweizer Platz – 𝒞 (069) 61 45 59 – www.zumgemaltenhaus.de*
– Closed 3 weeks July and Monday
Carte 12/21 €
• Country • Rustic •
Huddle up, talk shop and chat in the midst of these wall murals and mementoes from bygone days. The main thing is the "Bembel" is always full!

GERMANY - FRANKFURT ON MAIN

Hessischer Hof

Friedrich-Ebert-Anlage 40 ✉ 60325 – Ⓜ Hauptbahnhof – ✆ (069) 7 54 00 – www.hessischer-hof.de Plan: **G2**

114 rm – 🚹159 € 🚹🚹209 € – ☕ 35 € – 7 suites

• Luxury • Classic • Personalised •

Thanks to the excellent service, from the welcome drink, via the free minibar to the good quality breakfast, guests feel very well looked after here. New executive rooms in a classic-elegant style. The exhibition of fine Sèvre porcelain gives the restaurant an exclusive feel.

Sèvres – See restaurant listing

Roomers

Gutleutstr. 85 ✉ 60329 – Ⓜ Hauptbahnhof – ✆ (069) 2 71 34 20 – www.roomers-frankfurt.com Plan: **H2**

116 rm – 🚹230/550 € 🚹🚹230/550 € – ☕ 32 € – 3 suites

• Business • Design • Contemporary •

This trendy address impresses with its harmonious, high quality and tasteful interior in dark tones. Muted lights and music give the bar a lounge atmosphere. Guests are made to feel very welcome. Superb design in the sauna and fitness area.

Roomers – See restaurant listing

25hours Hotel by Levi's

Niddastr. 58 ✉ 60329 – Ⓜ Hauptbahnhof – ✆ (069) 2 56 67 70 – www.25hours-hotels.com Plan: **H2**

76 rm – 🚹120/160 € 🚹🚹120/160 € – ☕ 18 €

• Townhouse • Design • Contemporary •

This designer hotel is by the main railway station. The floors have been individually decorated in the style of the denim in fashion from the 1930s to 1980s. There is a 'Gibson Music Room' in the basement. The cosy restaurant is colourful, trendy and lively.

Liebig

Liebigstr. 45 ✉ 60323 – Ⓜ Westend – ✆ (069) 24 18 29 90 – www.hotelliebig.de Plan: **H1**

19 rm – 🚹135/175 € 🚹🚹165/215 € – ☕ 16 €

• Family • Contemporary • Personalised •

This pretty Art Nouveau-style villa in Frankfurt's West End offers individually designed guestrooms that range from the modern to the classic. Some have a particular charm thanks to their period furniture and antique-style bath fittings. The restored old wooden staircase is also worth a closer look.

Lafleur

Palmengartenstr. 11 ✉ 60325 – Ⓜ Westend – ✆ (069) 90 02 91 00 – www.restaurant-lafleur.de – Closed 22 December-15 January and Saturday lunch, Sunday-Tuesday lunch Plan: **G1**

Menu 102 € (weekday lunch)/148 € – Carte 88/135 €

• Modern French • Elegant •

Lafleur serves beautifully presented, classic yet modern cuisine full of masterful aromatic combinations. Set in a glazed, Bauhaus-style annex to the prestigious Palmengarten hospitality complex, it also offers an upmarket, minimalist-style interior and attractive walk-in temperature-controlled wine store.

➜ Pilzcannelloni in getrüffelter Artischockenvelouté. Gebratener Kaisergranat mit Schinkencrunch in eigener Bisque. Variation von Coppeneur Bio Grand Cru Schokoladen mit Cru de Cacao Eis.

WESTEND – EXHIBITION-CENTRE – STATION - PLAN III

XxX
&

Restaurant Villa Merton

Am Leonhardsbrunn 12 (Corner of Ditmarstraße, at   Plan I: **A1**
Union International Club) ✉ 60487 – ✆ (069) 70 30 33
– www.restaurant-villa-merton.de – Closed 23 December-10 January,
Saturday-Sunday and Bank Holidays
Menu 85/135 € – *(dinner only) (booking advisable)*
• Classic cuisine • Fashionable • Elegant •

This listed villa in the diplomatic quarter makes a great place to eat. The decor is elegant and the sophisticated classic cuisine with modern notes comes in the form of three set menus: 'Vegetarian', 'Villa Merton' and 'For Body and Soul'.
→ Aal und Eisbein vom Duroc Schwein mit Kopfsalat, Radieschen und Apfel. Lauwarmes Linsengemüse mit geräuchertem Sellerie und Belper Knolle. Zunge, Bries und Karree vom Schottischen Lamm mit Senf, grünem Spargel und Ricotta-Praline.
Bistro Villa Merton – See restaurant listing

XxX

Sèvres – Hotel Hessischer Hof

Friedrich-Ebert-Anlage 40 ✉ 60325 – Ⓜ *Hauptbahnhof*   Plan: **G2**
– ✆ (069) 7 54 00 – www.restaurant-sevres.de
Menu 55/96 € – Carte 55/85 € – *(bookings advisable at dinner)*
• Modern French • Elegant •

This elegant restaurant is named after the famous French porcelain of which it offers a stunning display. The food coming out of the kitchen is classic, seasonal fare including braised leg of rabbit with tomatoes, pearl onions and gnocchi. At lunchtimes you will find a popular business lunch including wine, water and coffee. Good parking.

XX

Roomers – Hotel Roomers

Gutleutstr. 85 ✉ 60329 – Ⓜ *Hauptbahnhof* – ✆ (069)   Plan: **H2**
2 71 34 20 – www.roomers.eu – Closed Saturday lunch, Sunday lunch
Menu 29 € (weekday lunch) – Carte 34/83 €
• International • Fashionable •

This fashionable address in central 'Mainhattan' has a decor that is simply stunning. It features sand coloured upholstered sofas, indirect lighting and fine materials combined with black accessories.

XX

Stanley Diamond La Buvette

Ottostr. 16 ✉ 60329 – Ⓜ *Hauptbahnhof* – ✆ (069)   Plan: **H2**
26 94 28 92 – www.stanleydiamond.com – Closed Saturday lunch, Sunday-Monday
Menu 52/72 € – Carte 49/72 €
• Modern cuisine • Trendy • Cosy •

A trendy mix of restaurant and bar, the interior at Stanley Diamond is stylish and upmarket and the service is simple and professional. The ambitious cuisine features reinventions of classic dishes such as jellied oxtail with potato foam and imperial caviar.

X
&

Ernos Bistro

Liebigstr. 15 ✉ 60323 – Ⓜ *Westend* – ✆ (069) 72 19 97   Plan: **H1**
– www.ernosbistro.de – Closed 2 weeks end December-early
January, 1 week during Easter, 3 weeks August, Saturday-Sunday and
Bank Holidays
Menu 39 € (lunch)/125 € – Carte 73/128 € – *(booking advisable)*
• Classic French • Bistro • Cosy •

The very epitome of *savoir vivre*, this charming little bistro could hardly be more authentic with its panelling and traditional decor of lamps and wine bottles. A lively atmosphere and simple, fully flavoured, French food made from the finest ingredients complete the picture.
→ Marinierte Jakobsmuscheln mit Trüffel und Selleriecrème, Trüffelvinaigrette. Seezungenfilets mit Tatar von der Gillardeau Auster, Lauchgemüse und Noilly Pratsauce. Wildentenbrust mit Blutwurst und Apfel, Wirsing und Preiselbeersauce.

GERMANY · FRANKFURT ON MAIN

339

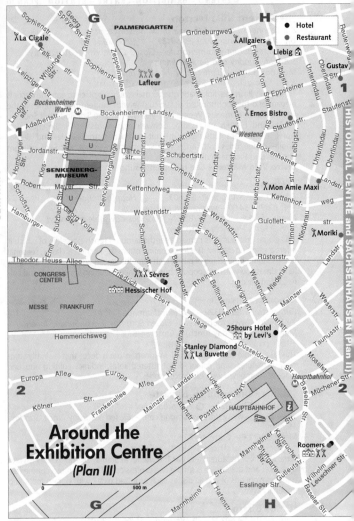

Around the Exhibition Centre (Plan III)

0 _____ 500 m

X ❀ **Weinsinn**

Fürstenbergerstr. 179 ☒ 60322 – Ⓜ Holzhausenstr.   Plan I: **B1**
– 𝄐 (069) 56 99 80 80 – www.weinsinn.de – Closed 4-15 April, 11-28 July,
Sunday-Monday and Bank Holidays
Menu 63/93 € – *(dinner only) (booking essential)*
• International • Minimalist • Vintage •

It is hardly surprising that this restaurant is in such demand. The atmosphere is
lively, the decor modern and attractive, and the intensely flavoured and pleasantly
simple food is really special! The wine list boasts over 200 different names.
➔ Fjordforelle, Avocado, Gurke. Steinbutt, Spinat, Safran, Paellasud. Reh,
Sellerie, Spitzkohl.

GERMANY - FRANKFURT ON MAIN

Gustav

Reuterweg 57 ⊠ 60323 – Ⓜ Westend – 𝒞 (069)   Plan: **H1**
74 74 52 52 – www.restaurant-gustav.de – Closed 3-14 January, 4-15 April,
11-28 July, Saturday lunch, Sunday-Monday and Bank Holidays
Menu 65/93 € (dinner) – (bookings advisable at dinner)
• Creative • Minimalist • Trendy •
The interior at this restaurant is classy and minimalist and the front-of-house
team is young, charming and relaxed. The food is creative, sophisticated and
fully flavoured and some of the tables afford a view of the kitchen. Reduced
lunchtime menu for diners in a hurry.
→ Geräucherte Spanferkelbäckchen, Rettich, Alblinsen, Senfsaat. Gerösteter
Spargel, gebeiztes Eigelb, Leinsamen, braune Butter. Lammschulter, Gurke,
Bärlauch, Kümmel.

La Cigale

Falkstr. 38 ⊠ 60487 – Ⓜ Bockenheimer Warte   Plan: **G1**
– 𝒞 (069) 70 41 11 – www.lacigale-restaurant.de – Closed Sunday-Tuesday
lunch, Wednesday lunch, Thursday lunch, Saturday lunch
Menu 54 € – Carte 31/60 € – (booking advisable)
• International • Cosy •
La Cigale's many regulars are attracted here by the restaurant's friendly, welco-
ming atmosphere, as well as the fresh cuisine. This is prepared by chef Martin
Kofler, and his braised ox cheeks are a particular favourite.

Mon Amie Maxi

Bockenheimer Landstr. 31 ⊠ 60311 – Ⓜ Westend   Plan: **H1**
– 𝒞 (069) 7140 2121 – www.mook-group.de – Closed 24 December-
6 January and Saturday lunch
Carte 19/118 € – (Bank Holidays dinner only)
• French • Brasserie •
Take a table in the comfortable, casual interior at Mon Amie Maxi and enjoy
fresh, authentic brasserie-style fare from the open kitchen. The menu ranges
from oysters to calves' kidneys and a cheese board, but whatever you do,
don't miss the delicious seafood buffet.

Chalet 18

Grempstr. 18 ⊠ 60487 – Ⓜ Leipziger Str. – 𝒞 (069)   Plan I: **A1**
70 28 14 – www.chalet-18.de – Closed 1 week early January, July and
Monday-Tuesday
Menu 79/99 € – (dinner only) (booking essential)
• Asian influences • Friendly • Bistro •
This French bistro-style restaurant serves a fusion of European and Southeast Asian
cuisine full of sophisticated contrasts. Try the whole set menu or, alternatively, just
the excellent dim sum: Peking duck, Irish lobster or wagyu beef – you choose!

Moriki

Taunusanlage 12 ⊠ 60325 – Ⓜ Hauptbahnhof   Plan: **H1**
– 𝒞 (069) 71 91 30 70 – www.moriki.de
Menu 59 € (dinner) – Carte 26/63 € – (booking advisable)
• Japanese • Trendy • Fashionable •
You will find this stylish, uncomplicated restaurant and sushi bar on the ground
floor of Deutsche Bank's headquarters building. The appealing menu – Japanese
with Pan-Asian influences – includes crunchy spicy tuna rolls, miso duck and
chilli ginger prawn.

Laube Liebe Hoffnung

Pariser Str. 11 ⊠ 60486 – 𝒞 (069) 75 84 77 22   Plan I: **A3**
– www.laubeliebehoffnung.de
Menu 28/47 € (dinner) – Carte 38/53 €
• International • Bistro •
Located in the new European Quarter, this modern wooden building has a charming, relaxed interior. It serves an interesting mix of freshly made food ranging
from Laube bratwurst to sea bream served on a bed of olive risotto. There is also
a pretty terrace complete with grill.

X **Allgaiers** 🅑 🍴

Liebigstr. 47 ⊠ 60323 – ⓜ Westend – ℰ (069) Plan: **H1**
98 95 66 11 – www.allgaiers.eu – Closed 23 December-6 January, Saturday lunch and Sunday
Menu 23 € (weekday lunch)/69 € – Carte 37/58 €
• French • Cosy • Friendly •

A great place for good brasserie cuisine. Try the tasty calf's sweetbread ravioli with spring vegetables and light and creamy morel mushrooms. On weekdays the lunch menu served in this friendly restaurant with its striking wine racks is also popular.

X **Bistro Villa Merton** – Restaurant Villa Merton 🍴

Am Leonhardsbrunn 12 (Corner of Ditmarstraße, at Plan I: **A1**
Union International Club) ⊠ 60487 – ℰ (069) 70 30 33
– www.restaurant-villa-merton.de
Menu 36 € (weekday lunch)/48 € – Carte 40/66 €
• Country • Elegant •

The Villa Merton now has an attractive dining alternative in Bistro, in terms of both cuisine and price. It serves fresh and flavoursome food with regional and international influences. Try the Hessen fish and chips or the pan-fried beefsteak with fried onions and potato and chive puree.

ENVIRONS OF FRANKFURT

AT THE RHEIN-MAIN AIRPORT **by Kennedy Allee** B3

🏨 **Kempinski Hotel Gravenbruch** 🛏 Ⅰ🅢 📶 ⏳ 🔲 🍽 ⅄

Graf zu Ysenburg und Büdingen-Platz 1 ⊠ 63263 🆎 🅢 🅿
– ℰ (069) 38 98 80 – www.kempinski.com/gravenbruch
187 rm – †149/409 € **††**149/409 € – 🍽 31 € – 38 suites
• Luxury • Classic •

Following a programme of investment, the Gravenbruch now offers a choice of bright, modern and more classical guestrooms. You can also relax with a massage or beauty treatment or try a training session in the gym which enjoys a view over the adjacent park. Indeed, the hotel even boasts its own lake. The Torschänke and beer garden serves traditional Hessen food.
❀ **Sra Bua by Juan Amador** • **Torschänke** • **EssTisch** – See restaurant listing

🏨 **Hilton** 🛏 Ⅰ🅢 📶 ⅄ 🆎 🅢 🚗

Am Flughafen (The Squaire) ⊠ 60549 – ℰ (069) 26 01 20 00
– www.frankfurtairport.hilton.com
232 rm – †159/599 € **††**159/599 € – 🍽 32 € – 17 suites
• Business • Contemporary • Contemporary •

This 625m-long futuristic construction of glass and steel (designed as a recumbent tower block!) hides an interior that is urban chic in the best sense of the word. Close to the A3 motorway, the Intercity Express station and Terminal 1.

🏨 **Steigenberger Airport** 🛏 Ⅰ🅢 📶 ⅄ 🆎 🅢 🚗

Unterschweinstiege 16 ⊠ 60549 – ℰ (069) 69750
– www.airporthotel-frankfurt.steigenberger.com
560 rm – †149/189 € **††**169/209 € – 🍽 28 € – 10 suites
• Chain • Business • Contemporary •

This hotel is characterised by its elegant hall, comfortable rooms (in particular the modern Tower room) and the 'Open Sky' leisure area with fantastic views. A cosy atmosphere in the Unterschweinstiege.
Faces – See restaurant listing

XX
£3 **Sra Bua by Juan Amador** – Kempinski Hotel Gravenbruch

Graf zu Ysenburg und Büdingen-Platz 1 ✉ 63263 – ☎ (069)
38 98 80 – www.kempinski.com/gravenbruch – Closed Sunday-Monday
Menu 79/129 € – Carte 80/90 € – *(dinner only) (booking advisable)*
• Fusion • Elegant • Design •

It is not just the elegant, minimalist Sra Bua-style design on a classic Buddha theme that draws the crowds here. The real focal point is the pan-Asian cuisine prepared with precision and a real feel for fusion. The ambitious young kitchen team uses top quality produce.

➜ Saibling, Shiitake, Limette. Kalbskopf, Wasabi, Grüner Apfel. Valrhona Dulcey, Zitronenverbene, Rhabarber.

XX **Faces** – Hotel Steigenberger Airport

Unterschweinstiege 16 ✉ 60549 Frankfurt – ☎ (069) 69 75 0
– www.airporthotel-frankfurt.steigenberger.de – Closed Saturday-Sunday and Bank Holidays
Carte 45/71 € – *(dinner only)*
• International • Design •

Behind the glass frontage lies a smart, modern restaurant with original lighting. It serves contemporary international cuisine focusing on high quality ingredients. Separate bar.

XX **EssTisch** – Kempinski Hotel Gravenbruch

Graf zu Ysenburg und Büdingen-Platz 1 ✉ 63263 – ☎ (069) 38 98 80
– www.kempinski.com/gravenbruch
Menu 46 € – Carte 41/80 €
• International • Elegant •

The main restaurant in the hotel's new wing is bright and welcoming. You can choose from an international menu, which also includes a couple of classic regional dishes, or from the specialities available from the buffet. This feast is known as the 'Perfume of the Sea' on Fridays when it offers a wide range of fish and seafood.

X **Torschänke** – Kempinski Hotel Gravenbruch

Graf zu Ysenburg und Büdingen-Platz 1 ✉ 63263 – ☎ (069) 38 98 96 70
– www.kempinski.com/gravenbruch – Closed Monday-Tuesday
Carte 30/51 € – *(dinner only)*
• Country • Rustic •

Once the starting point for wild boar hunts, Torschänke continues to include wild boar on its menu, alongside other regional specialities. Pleasant, informal setting.

HAMBURG

HAMBURG

Population: 1 814 600

Matthias Krüttgen/Fotolia.com

With a maritime role stretching back centuries, Germany's second largest city has a lively and liberal ambience. Hamburg is often described as 'The Gateway to the World', and there's certainly a visceral feel here, particularly around the big, buzzy and bustling port area. Locals enjoy a long-held reputation for their tolerance and outward looking stance, cosmopolitan to the core. Space to breathe is seen as very important in Hamburg: the city authorities have paid much attention to green spaces, and the city can proudly claim an enviable amount of parks, lakes and tree-lined canals.

There's no cathedral here (at least not a standing one, as war-destroyed St Nikolai remains a ruin), so the Town Hall acts as the central landmark. Just north of here are the Binnenalster (inner) and Aussenalster (outer) lakes. The old walls of the city, dating back over eight hundred years, are delineated by a distinct semicircle of boulevards that curve attractively in a wide arc south of the lakes. Further south from here is the port and harbour area, defined by Landungsbrücken to the west and Speicherstadt to the east. The district to the west of the centre is St Pauli, famed for its clubs and bars, particularly along the notorious Reeperbahn, which pierces the district from east to west. The contrastingly smart Altona suburb and delightful Blankenese village are west of St Pauli.

HAMBURG IN...

→ ONE DAY
Boat trip from Landungsbrücken, Speicherstadt, Kunsthalle, Fishmarket (Sunday morning). Elbphilharmonie

→ TWO DAYS
Steamboat on the Alster, Hamburg History Museum, St Pauli by night.

→ THREE DAYS
Arts and Crafts Museum, canal trip, concert at Musikhalle.

ARRIVAL-DEPARTURE

✈ Hamburg Airport is 15km north of the city centre. Airport buses leave for Hamburg Hauptbahnhof every 15-20min and Altona Station every 30min; both take 20min.

GETTING AROUND

Hamburg Transport Authority controls all of the bus routes, the overground S-Bahn trains, the U-Bahn underground lines, and several river and ferry services. Tickets are available for single journeys, or for one-day or three-day duration; you can buy them from vending machines or bus drivers. The Hamburg Card is valid for the transport network, and offers discounts in museums, theatres and some restaurants, as well as for tours on land and water. Buy it from Tourist Information offices, vending machines, hotels or travel agents.

CALENDAR HIGHLIGHTS

April, August and November
Dom Festivals (huge funfairs)

April
Long Night of Hamburg Museums.

May
Hafengeburtstag (harbour's birthday celebration), Japanese Cherry Blossom Festival.

July
Duckstein Festival.

August-September
Alster Fair.

September
Hamburg Cruise Days.

October
Film Festival.

October-November
International Boat Show.

EATING OUT

Being a city immersed in water, it's no surprise to find Hamburg is a good place for fish. Though its fishing industry isn't the powerhouse of old, the city still boasts a giant trawler's worth of seafood places to eat. Eel dishes are mainstays of the traditional restaurant's menu, as is the herring stew with vegetables called Labskaus. Also unsurprisingly, considering it's the country's gateway to the world, this is somewhere that offers a vast range of international dishes. Wherever you eat, the portions are likely to be generous. There's no problem with finding somewhere early: cafés are often open at seven, with the belief that it's never too early for coffee and cake. Bakeries also believe in an early start, and the calorie content here, too, can be pretty high. Bistros and restaurants, usually open by midday, are proud of their local ingredients, so keep your eyes open for Hamburgisch on the menu. Service charges are always included in the bill, so tipping is not compulsory, although most people will round it up and possibly add five to ten per cent.

Fairmont Hotel Vier Jahreszeiten

*Neuer Jungfernstieg 9 ✉ 20354 – **Ⓜ** Jungfernstieg*
– ✆ (040) 3 49 40 – www.fairmont-hvj.de   Plan: **F2**
139 rm – ♦295/405 € ♦♦315/495 € – ☲ 39 € – 17 suites
• Grand Luxury • Traditional • Classic •

This hotel is the very epitome of Hamburg tradition and was first established in 1897. Cleverly combining smart, fresh design and classical elegance, the rooms are both lavish and sumptuous. You can relax on the great roof terrace with a bar, take afternoon tea in the stylish Wohnhalle or enjoy a snack or cake in the trendy Condi Lounge.

❀❀ **Haerlin** • **Jahreszeiten Grill** – See restaurant listing

Atlantic Kempinski

*An der Alster 72 ✉ 20099 – **Ⓜ** Jungfernstieg – ✆ (040)*   Plan: **H1**
2 88 80 – www.kempinski.com/hamburg
221 rm – ♦199 € ♦♦229 € – ☲ 36 € – 33 suites
• Grand Luxury • Classic • Contemporary •

Following extensive renovation work, the Atlantic Kempinski is now even more magnificent than before. It has an elegant, classic lobby, timeless, sumptuously decorated rooms (complete with fine ebony and state-of-the-art technology) and stylish reception and conference facilities.
Atlantic Restaurant – See restaurant listing

Park Hyatt

Bugenhagenstr. 8 (at Levantehaus) ✉ 20095   Plan: **H2**
*– **Ⓜ** Mönckebergstr. – ✆ (040) 33 32 12 34 – www.hamburg.park.hyatt.de*
262 rm – ♦185/550 € ♦♦239/590 € – ☲ 34 € – 21 suites
• Grand Luxury • Chain • Contemporary •

This former Hanseatic League trading post welcomes guests on the first floor where they can make themselves comfortable in the tasteful lounge. Combining high quality and modern elegance this is a luxury hotel without equal. The Apples restaurant invites diners to watch the chef working in the show kitchen.

Le Méridien

*An der Alster 52 ✉ 20099 – **Ⓜ** Hauptbf. Nord*   Plan: **H1**
– ✆ (040) 21000 – www.lemeridienhamburg.com
275 rm – ♦139/429 € ♦♦159/449 € – ☲ 30 € – 7 suites
• Chain • Luxury • Contemporary •

This modern hotel has an attractive, clear style extending from the brightly furnished rooms (with specially designed therapeutic beds) to the wellness area. The restaurant on the ninth floor offers a fantastic view over the Außenalster lake.

Grand Elysée

*Rothenbaumchaussee 10 ✉ 20148 – **Ⓜ** Stephanspl.*   Plan: **F1**
– ✆ (040) 41 41 20 – www.grand-elysee.com
494 rm – ♦190 € ♦♦210 € – ☲ 25 € – 17 suites
• Luxury • Classic •

The Grand Elysée is Hamburg's largest privately operated hotel. It promises elegant rooms, a spacious lobby with shop and café, a brasserie and THEO'S restaurant serving prime beef. Around the hotel you will find some 800 artworks from the family owners' personal collection. The rooms facing the garden courtyard are quiet, and those giving onto the Moorweidenpark are south facing.
Piazza Romana – See restaurant listing

SIDE

Drehbahn 49 ✉ *20354* – Ⓜ *Stephanspl.* – ℰ *(040)* Plan: **F2**
30 99 90 – *www.side-hamburg.de*
168 rm – ♦165/450 € ♦♦165/450 € – ☐ 28 € – 10 suites
• Luxury • Design •

Behind the natural stone and glass façade lies an impressive 30m high lobby, with lighting design by Robert Wilson. The hotel has tasteful rooms designed in white and brown by Matteo Thun.
[m]eatery – See restaurant listing

 Sofitel Alter Wall

Alter Wall 40 ✉ *20457* – Ⓜ *Rödingsmarkt* – ℰ *(040)* Plan: **F3**
36 95 00 – *www.sofitel.com*
223 rm – ♦150 € ♦♦180 € – ☐ 32 € – 18 suites
• Chain • Luxury • Design •

Simultaneously luxurious and minimalist, the Alter Wall boasts a clean, modern design and a great location on the Alsterfleet, which is best appreciated from the terrace right on the water. The hotel even has its own jetty! The Ticino restaurant serves Italian cuisine.

 Steigenberger

Heiligengeistbrücke 4 ✉ *20459* – Ⓜ *Rödingsmarkt* Plan: **F3**
– ℰ *(040) 36 80 60* – *www.hamburg.steigenberger.de*
227 rm – ♦159/399 € ♦♦179/419 € – ☐ 29 € – 6 suites
• Luxury • Classic •

Right beside the Alster canal stands this well-run and elegant hotel in the shape of a ship. From the fitness area roof terrace there is a wonderful view over the city.
Bistro am Fleet – See restaurant listing

 AMERON Hotel Speicherstadt

Am Sandtorkai 4 ✉ *20457* – Ⓜ *Überseequartier* Plan: **G3**
– ℰ *(040) 6 38 58 90* – *www.hotel-speicherstadt.de*
192 rm – ♦139 € ♦♦139 € – ☐ 19 €
• Historic • Vintage •

This charming hotel is located in the middle of Hamburg's Speicherstadt district. It boasts a trendy retro decor from the 1950s with warm colours that creates a friendly and welcoming feel. The restaurant in the modern glass annexe serves Italian food.

 The George

Barcastr. 3 ✉ *22087* – Ⓜ *Lohmühlenstr.* – ℰ *(040)* Plan: **D2**
2 80 03 00 – *www.thegeorge-hotel.de*
123 rm – ♦147/177 € ♦♦157/187 € – ☐ 20 € – 2 suites
• Townhouse • Design • Elegant •

Elegant, British-style meets young, modern design throughout this hotel. The library, bar and rooms are decorated in muted tones with feature pictures, furnishing fabrics and wallpapers. Highlights include the roof terrace with its view over Hamburg and the garden behind the hotel. The restaurant serves Mediterranean/Italian cuisine.

 HENRI

Bugenhagenstr. 21 ✉ *20095* – Ⓜ *Mönckebergstr.* Plan: **H2**
– ℰ *(040) 5 54 35 70* – *www.henri-hotel.com*
60 rm – ♦98/118 € ♦♦118/138 € – ☐ 15 € – 5 suites
• Business • Vintage • Personalised •

This former office building has been redeveloped with taste, quality and all the modern facilities you would expect… and with a strong 1950/60s retro feel. There are charming details such as the homely lounge, a kitchen that serves snacks and drinks, as well as a daily 'Abendbrot' and German tea and cakes at the weekend.

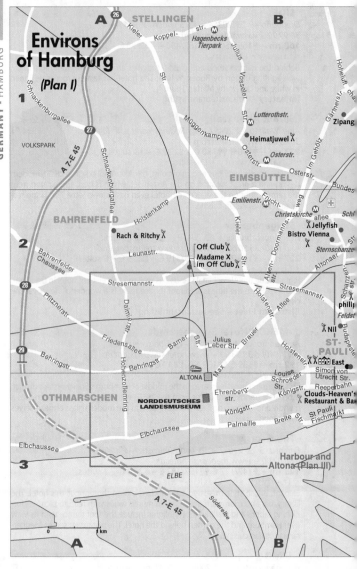

Environs of Hamburg
(Plan I)

STELLINGEN

Kieler

Koppel-

str.

Hagenbecks
Tierpark

Julius

Vosseler

Str.

Hoheluft- cha

Gärtnerstr.

Zipang

Schnackenburgallee

Lutterothstr.

Müggenkampstr.

Osterstr.

Heimatjuwel X

VOLKSPARK

A 7-E 45

Schnackenburgallee

Osterstr.

Im Gehölz

EIMSBÜTTEL

Osterstr.

Bundes

Frucht-

weg

Holstenkamp

Emilienstr.

BAHRENFELD

Christskirche

allee

Schl

Aiken- Doormanns-

Rach & Ritchy X

Bistro Vienna

X **Jellyfish**

Leunastr.

Kieler

Str.

X

Str

Off Club X

Madame X

Sternschanze

im Off Club X

Bahrenfelder

Chaussee

Stresemannstr.

Altonaer

Stresemannstr.

X

philip

Pfitznerstr.

Daimlerstr.

Holstenstr.

Allee

Feldst

Budapester

Friedensallee

Barner

Julius

Brauer

X **Nil**

Leber Str.

ST-

PAULI

Hohenzollernring

Str.

Holstenstr.

X X □□□ **East**

Behringstr.

Behringstr.

Max

ALTONA

Louise

Simon von

Schroeder

Utrecht Str.

Str.

Reeperbahn

Ehrenberg-

Königstr

Clouds-Heaven's

OTHMARSCHEN

str.

X **Restaurant & Bar**

NORDDEUTSCHES

LANDESMUSEUM

Königstr.

St Pauli

Breite str.

Fischmarkt

Elbchaussee

Palmaille

Elbchaussee

Harbour and

Altona (Plan III)

ELBE

ELBE

A 7-E 45

Süderelbe

0   1 km

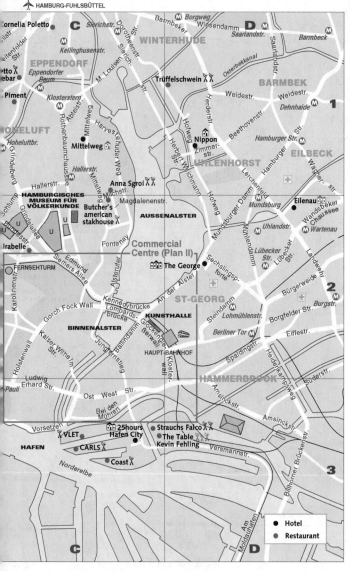

HAMBURG-FUHLSBÜTTEL

GERMANY - HAMBURG

Hotel
Restaurant

349

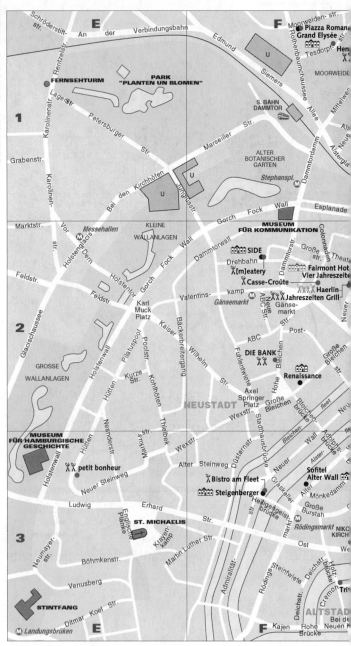

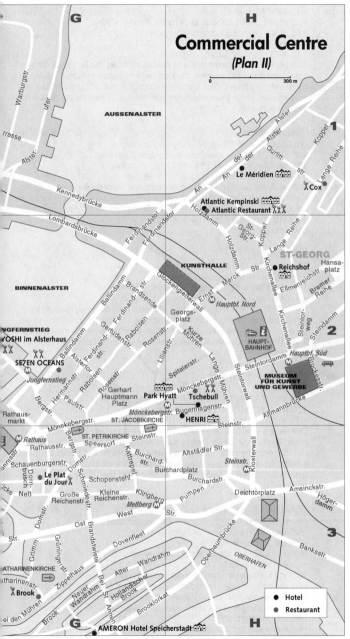

Commercial Centre
(Plan II)

0   300 m

G

H

AUSSENALSTER

Alster

An der Alster

An der Alster

Gurlitt str.

Koppel

Lange Reihe

1

● Le Méridien

✗ Cox

Kennedybrücke

Holzdamm

● Atlantic Kempinski
● Atlantic Restaurant ✗✗✗

Lombardsbrücke

Ferdinandstor

Ferdinandstor

St. Georg Str.

Koppel

Lange Reihe

ST-GEORG

BINNENALSTER

Ballindamm

Brandsende

Glockengießerwall

KUNSTHALLE

Ernst Merck Str.

● Reichshof

Hansa-platz

Ellmenreichstr.

Bremer Reihe

Ferdinand-str.

Gertudenstr.

Raboisen

Rosenstr.

Georgs-platz

Kurze Mühren

Hauptbf. Nord

Kirchenallee

Steintor-weg

Steindamm

2

NGFERNSTIEG

OSHI im Alsterhaus ✗✗

Ballindamm

Alstertor

Rosenstr.

Lilienstr.

Spitalerstr.

Lange Mühren

HAUPT-BAHNHOF

ℹ

Hauptbf. Süd

SE7EN OCEANS ✗✗

Hermannstr.

Jungfernstieg

Rabolsen

Paulstr.

Rosenstr.

Gerhart Hauptmann Platz

Mönckebergstr.

Park Hyatt

Tschebull ✗✗

Steintordamm

Steintorwall

MUSEUM FÜR KUNST UND GEWERBE

Brockesstr.

Bergstr.

Mönckebergstr.

Bugenhagenstr.

● HENRI

Almannbrücke

Rathaus-markt

● Rathaus

ST. JACOBIKIRCHE

Mönckebergstr.

ST. PETRIKIRCHE

Steinstr.

Steinstr.

Rathausstr.

Speersort

Schmiedestr.

Altstädter Str.

Steinstr.

Klosterwall

Schauenburgstr.

Domstr.

Burchard-str.

3

● Le Plat du Jour ✗

Schopenstehl

Burchardplatz

Burchardstr.

Pumpen

Amsinckstr.

Domstr.

Bergstr.

Kattrepel

Deichtorplatz

Höger-damm

Neß

Große Reichenstr.

Kleine Reichenstr.

Klingberg

Meßberg

Str.

Dohrn

Ost

Brandstwiete

West

Str.

Grimm

Gröningerstr.

Dovenfleet

Oberbaumbrücke

OBERHAFEN

Banksstr.

ATHARINENKIRCHE

tharinenstr.

✗ Brook

Zippelhaus

Neuer Wandrahm

Brook

Alter Wandrahm

Bei St. Annen

Hollandischer Brook

Brooklorkat

ei den Mühren

G

● AMERON Hotel Speicherstadt

H

●	Hotel
●	Restaurant

GERMANY - HAMBURG

 Reichshof   ⚐ ᵘ⁴ 🍴 ⅄ 🔲 🛁

Kirchenallee 34 ✉ 20099 – Ⓜ Hauptbf. Nord – ☏ (040)   Plan: **H2**
3 70 25 90 – www.reichshof-hamburg.com
278 rm – †149/359 € ††149/359 € – ☕ 21 €
• Business • Elegant • Historic •
Built in 1910 as a "grand hotel" and now partly listed, the Reichshof contains many reminders of its heyday – the lobby with its imposing marble columns is particularly impressive. This creates a successful mix of historical flair and modern style, which also extends to the restaurant. The rooms are contemporary and upmarket.

 Renaissance   ⚐ 🍴 🔲 🛁 🚗

Große Bleichen 36 ✉ 20354 – Ⓜ Jungfernstieg   Plan: **F2**
– ☏ (040) 34 91 80 – www.renaissance-hamburg.com
205 rm ☕ – †149/200 € ††169/249 € – 1 suite
• Business • Contemporary • Elegant •
With a central location in the Hanseviertel, the Renaissance offers a classic, minimalist-style lobby and very tasteful rooms equipped with the latest technology, all decorated in chic, grey tones. The restaurant's name and interior are both inspired by the Broschek family's print works, which were once based here.

 Eilenau   🍴

Eilenau 36 ✉ 22089 – Ⓜ Mundsburg – ☏ (040)   Plan I: **D2**
2 36 01 30 – www.eilenau.de
17 rm – †109 € ††139/159 € – ☕ 15 € – 5 suites
• Townhouse • Personalised • Elegant •
Anything but a typical city hotel, the Eilenau is housed in two carefully renovated buildings dating back to 1890. Antiques, stucco, chandeliers and old parquet flooring mix with stylish modern furniture beneath the high ceilings. There is also a small, quiet garden where breakfast is served in the summer.

 25hours Hafen City   ⚐ 🍴 ⅄ 🔲 🛁 🚗

Überseeallee 5 ✉ 20457 – Ⓜ Überseequartier   Plan I: **C3**
– ☏ (040) 2 57 77 70 – www.25hours-hotels.com
170 rm – †125/350 € ††135/360 € – ☕ 19 €
• Townhouse • Personalised • Design •
One thing is sure, for individuality and originality you can't beat this Hamburg hotel. Bright, new design meets warm wood and stories of the sea. Old records cover the walls in the lounge-style Vinyl Room and guests are given a sailors' kit bag for their personal belongings in the rooftop sauna. It's no surprise in a hotel full of seafaring references to find that all the rooms have a cabin feel.

XᵡXᵡX **Haerlin** – Fairmont Hotel Vier Jahreszeiten   🎩 ⪡ ⅄ 🔲 🔄 🚗

❀❀   *Neuer Jungfernstieg 9 ✉ 20354 – Ⓜ Jungfernstieg*   Plan: **F2**
– ☏ (040) 34 94 33 10 – www.fairmont-hvj.de
– Closed Sunday-Monday
Menu 145/185 € – *(dinner only) (booking advisable)*
• Creative French • Luxury • Elegant •
The food at Haerlin is powerful and intensely flavoured. The dishes brought to your table are creative and technically perfect, and use nothing but the very best ingredients. The culinary quality is matched by the exquisite interior where everything is of the finest quality. The view over the Inner Alster Lake adds the finishing touch.
→ Kaisergranat mit indonesischem Salat und Kaffir-Zwiebelcrème. Taubenbrust mit Waldorfvinaigrette, Morcheln, Chicorée und Apfel. Rhabarber mit Heumilch, gerösteter Gerste und Petersilie.

GERMANY - HAMBURG

The Table Kevin Fehling

Shanghaiallee 15 ⊠ 20457 – ℰ (040) 22 86 74 22 — Plan I: **C2**
– www.the-table-hamburg.de – Closed 24 December-2 January, 13-19 March, 31 July-20 August and Sunday-Monday
Menu 195 € – *(dinner only) (booking essential)*
• Creative • Design •

This relaxed restaurant really is one of a kind! Diners sit at a long, curved table as the chefs – a study of concentration – combine fine international ingredients to perfection before their eyes with the precision, subtlety and stunning presentation for which Kevin Fehling is famed. Excellent wine recommendations.
→ Lachs von den Faröer Inseln mit Passionsfrucht, Yuzu, Miso und Champonzusud. Lammrücken mit Orangen-Hollandaise, Focaccia, Olive und Rosmarinjus. Baby Banane „Indisch", Kurkuma, Tandoori, Jasminreis und Sanddorn.

Atlantic Restaurant – Hotel Atlantic Kempinski

An der Alster 72 ⊠ 20099 – ⓜ Jungfernstieg – ℰ (040) — Plan: **H1**
2 88 88 60 – www.kempinski.com/hamburg – Closed Sunday
Menu 80/115 € – Carte 54/115 €
• Classic cuisine • Elegant •

The elegant restaurant of this traditional Hamburg hotel serves as a lounge for significant numbers of the city's rich and famous. Its classic cakes are particularly popular.

Jahreszeiten Grill – Fairmont Hotel Vier Jahreszeiten

Neuer Jungfernstieg 9 ⊠ 20354 – ⓜ Jungfernstieg – ℰ (040)
34 94 33 12 – www.fairmont-hvj.de — Plan: **F2**
Menu 32 € (weekday lunch)/105 € – Carte 68/94 €
• Classic French • Elegant •

This restaurant is a stylish Hamburg institution with an impressive Art Deco interior. It serves classics including smoked eel and scrambled eggs with herbs on wholewheat bread, as well as more sophisticated fare, including codfish in a thyme crust with chanterelle mushrooms and grilled meats. The very best ingredients are always used.

SE7EN OCEANS

Ballindamm 40 (2nd floor) (Europa-Passage) ⊠ 20095 — Plan: **G2**
– ⓜ Jungfernstieg – ℰ (040) 32 50 79 44 – www.se7en-oceans.de
– Closed 6-12 February, 7-27 August and Sunday, Tuesday
Menu 43 € (lunch)/129 € – Carte 78/85 €
• Classic French • Chic • Design •

Ideal for escaping the crowds, this modern eatery has a great view of the Inner Alster Lake and the Jungfernstieg promenade. It offers peace and quiet in the midst of the Europa Passage shopping centre and serves classic international cuisine. The glass front opens up in the summer.
→ Norwegische Jakobsmuscheln, Bergamotte, Blumenkohl, Lengua Iberico. Bretonischer Steinbutt, Erbsen, Kopfsalat, Algenbutter. Kumquat, Eierlikör, Rauchmandel.

Tschebull

Mönckebergstr. 7 ⊠ 20095 – ⓜ Mönchebergstr. — Plan: **H2**
– ℰ (040) 32 96 47 96 – www.tschebull.de – Closed Sunday and Bank Holidays
Menu 30 € (lunch)/69 € (dinner) – Carte 32/73 € – *(booking advisable)*
• Austrian • Cosy •

In the centre of this exclusive shopping arcade sits a little piece of Austria, courtesy of Carinthian chef Alexander Tschebull. As you would expect, the Austrian classics, such as Tafelspitz (Viennese-style boiled beef) and Fiaker (beef) goulash are excellent, as are the more modern dishes. These include skrei cod with potato and caper champ, radish and pearl onions.

GERMANY - HAMBURG

XX DIE BANK

Hohe Bleichen 17 ✉ *20354 –* Ⓜ *Gänsemarkt – ℰ (040)* Plan: **F2**
2380030 – www.diebank-brasserie.de – Closed Sunday and Bank Holidays
Menu 23 € (lunch)/69 € – Carte 53/69 € – *(bookings advisable at dinner)*
• International • Brasserie • Trendy •
This brasserie and bar are one of the city's hotspots. The banking hall on the first-floor of this former bank, built in 1897, is an impressive feature of this fashionable venue.

XX Henriks

Tesdorpfstr. 8 ✉ *20148 –* Ⓜ *Stephanspl. – ℰ (040)* Plan: **F1**
2 88 08 42 80 – www.henriks.cc
Carte 27/110 € – *(booking essential)*
• International • Design • Elegant •
This chic designer restaurant offers ambitious cuisine that mixes Southeast Asian, Mediterranean and regional influences. Dishes include gravlax with curly kale and beetroot mayonnaise or tuna tataki steak with wasabi puree and miso soy sauce. The large terrace and lounge are always popular. Good value lunch menu.

XX YOSHI im Alsterhaus

Jungfernstieg 16 (Alsterhaus 4th. floor direct elevator Plan: **G2**
entrance Poststr. 8) ✉ *20354 –* Ⓜ *Jungfernstieg – ℰ (040) 35 71 44 93*
– www.yoshi-hamburg.de – Closed Sunday and Bank Holidays
Menu 20 € (weekday lunch)/98 € – Carte 34/117 €
• Japanese • Fashionable •
Christened 'Gourmet Boulevard', the fourth floor of Hamburg's upmarket Alsterhaus shopping plaza is the meeting place for enthusiasts of Japanese food and culture. The teriyaki and sushi dishes prepared by the Japanese chefs achieve a perfect marriage of the traditional and the modern. Popular roof terrace.

XX Piazza Romana – Hotel Grand Elysée

Rothenbaumchaussee 10 ✉ *20148 –* Ⓜ *Stephanspl.* Plan: **F1**
– ℰ (040) 41 41 20 – www.grand-elysee.com
Carte 33/50 €
• Italian • Classic décor •
If you fancy carpaccio di vitello, a plate of linguine or tiramisu, then the Italian cuisine on offer at this restaurant is for you.

XX Strauchs Falco

Koreastr. 2 ✉ *20354 – ℰ (040) 2 26 16 15 11* Plan I: **C3**
– www.falco-hamburg.de
Carte 38/84 €
• International • Fashionable •
Strauchs Falco serves a wide range of good Mediterranean dishes, steaks and classic fare. The restaurant itself is modern in style with an open kitchen and a large terrace in summer. The tapas bar on the first floor doubles up as a café during the day.

X Brook

Bei den Mühren 91 ✉ *20457 –* Ⓜ *Meßberg – ℰ (040)* Plan: **G3**
37 50 31 28 – www.restaurant-brook.de – Closed Sunday
Menu 35/39 € – Carte 38/51 €
• International • Fashionable •
The most popular dishes at this relaxed modern restaurant include classics such as braised calves' cheeks, but fish fresh from the famous fish market just round the corner are also firm favourites, as is the very reasonable set lunchtime menu. It is worth coming here in the evenings too, when you can enjoy views of the illuminated warehouse district.

Le Plat du Jour 🏠 🎿

Dornbusch 4 ⊠ *20095 –* Ⓜ *Rathaus – 𝒞 (040) 32 14 14*   Plan: **G3**
– www.leplatdujour.de – Closed during Christmas
Menu 35 € (dinner) – Carte 31/49 € – *(booking advisable)*
• Classic French • Bistro •

With a reputation forged largely by word of mouth, you will find the lively Le Plat du Jour busy from lunchtime onwards. Both the interior, with its black and white photos and closely packed tables, and the food it serves, are authentic brasserie in style. As an alternative to the dish of the day, try the Mediterranean French fish soup with croutons or the classic 'steak frites'.

Casse-Croûte 🕸 🎿

Büschstr. 2 ⊠ *20354 –* Ⓜ *Gänsemarkt – 𝒞 (040)*   Plan: **F2**
34 33 73 – www.casse-croute.de – Closed during Christmas, Sunday lunch and Bank Holidays lunch
Menu 28/36 € – Carte 36/94 € – *(booking advisable)*
• Classic French • Bistro •

French *art de vivre* combined with a local Hamburg feel draws a good number of regulars into this lively and pleasantly relaxed bistro close to the Gänsemarkt. Classic dishes on offer include a northern bouillabaisse, as well as Königsberg meatballs with potato mash and caper sauce.

Cox

Lange Reihe 68 ⊠ *20099 –* Ⓜ *Hauptbf. Nord – 𝒞 (040)*   Plan: **H1**
24 94 22 – www.restaurant-cox.de – Closed Saturday lunch, Sunday lunch and Bank Holidays lunch
Carte 34/48 € – *(mid July-mid August dinner only)*
• International • Bistro • Cosy •

More casual and urban than chic and elegant, Cox is a bistro in the best sense of the word. A colourful mix of diners enjoys a varied selection of dishes including braised lamb shanks, grass-fed beef rissoles and cod. Good value lunchtime menu.

Trific

Holzbrücke 7 ⊠ *20459 –* Ⓜ *Rödingsmarkt – 𝒞 (040)*   Plan: **F3**
41 91 90 46 – www.trific.de – Closed Saturday lunch, Sunday
Menu 18 € (lunch)/35 € (dinner) – Carte 35/47 € – *(booking advisable)*
• International • Fashionable • Neighbourhood •

The location is new but the culinary concept remains the same: guests create their own menu from a range of delicious dishes including spiny loach, asparagus and potatoes. The restaurant extends over two floors with the floor-to-ceiling windows on the ground floor giving views over the dyke.

VLET

Sandtorkai 23 (entrance by Kibbelstegbrücke 1, 1st   Plan I: **C3**
floor, Block N) ⊠ *20457 –* Ⓜ *Baumwall – 𝒞 (040) 3 34 75 37 50*
– www.vlet.de – Closed Sunday
Menu 62/78 € – Carte 45/64 € – *(dinner only)*
• Modern cuisine • Trendy •

The deliberate warehouse feel, typical of Hamburg's Speicherstadt area, makes an ideal venue for fashionable cuisine. It is best to park in the Contipark and cross the Kibbelstegbrücke bridge to reach the restaurant.

Coast 🕸 🏠 &

Großer Grasbrook 14 ⊠ *20457 –* Ⓜ *Überseequartier*   Plan I: **C3**
– 𝒞 (040) 30 99 32 30 – www.coast-hamburg.de
Menu 63/72 € – Carte 45/85 €
• Fusion • Friendly • Fashionable •

With a great location close to the water on the Marco Polo Terrace at the edge of the Hafencity, Coast serves an interesting mix of European and Southeast Asian food and creative sushi delicacies. Downstairs in the basement you will find the Enoteca, which serves Italian cuisine. From 6pm you can park in the Unilever garage next door.

X **CARLS** ⟨ 🛱 & 🎇 ⟺

Am Kaiserkai 69 ⊠ 20457 – Ⓜ Baumwall – ℰ (040) Plan I: **C3**
3 00 32 24 00 – www.carls-brasserie.de
Menu 42 € – Carte 32/76 €
• Country • Brasserie •

This elegant brasserie is at the New Elbe Philharmonic Hall. It serves up French cuisine with a North German slant alongside great views of the port. Savoury tarts and nibbles in the bistro; spices and other gourmet treats in the delicatessen.

X **La Mirabelle**

Bundesstr. 15 ⊠ 20146 – Ⓜ Hallerstr. – ℰ (040) Plan I: **C2**
4 10 75 85 – www.la-mirabelle-hamburg.de – Closed 1-6 January, Sunday-Monday and Bank Holidays
Menu 33 € (weekdays)/62 € – Carte 44/67 € – *(dinner only)*
• Classic French • Cosy • Family •

As the name suggests, the cuisine is French, flavoursome and without frills. Try the delicious sounding Atlantic cod with mustard sauce. Cheese lovers beware: the restaurant boasts some 50 different French cheeses!

X **[m]eatery** – Hotel SIDE & 🎇 ⟺ 🚗

Drehbahn 49 ⊠ 20354 – Ⓜ Stephanspl. – ℰ (040) Plan: **F2**
30 99 95 95 – www.meatery.de
Carte 39/124 €
• Meats and grills • Design •

The strong colours may shock some as the furniture and walls in this fashionable restaurant come in various shades of bright green. Steakhouse with glass-fronted meat maturing cabinet.

X **Bistro am Fleet** – Hotel Steigenberger 🛱 & 🎇 🚗

Heiligengeistbrücke 4 ⊠ 20459 – Ⓜ Rödingsmarkt Plan: **F3**
– ℰ (040) 36 80 61 22 – www.hamburg.steigenberger.de
Menu 35 € – Carte 26/64 €
• International • Cosy •

The cool feel of this restaurant is due to the conservatory, which makes the transition from inside to outside almost seamless. A range of international dishes are on offer.

NORTH OF THE CENTRE **PLAN I**

🏠 **Mittelweg** 🕁 🅿

Mittelweg 59 ⊠ 20149 – Ⓜ Klosterstern – ℰ (040) Plan: **C1**
4 14 10 10 – www.hotel-mittelweg-hamburg.de
30 rm ⊑ – ♦105/135 € ♦♦145/189 €
• Grand townhouse • Cosy •

This 1890 villa is full of turn of the century charm. Find it at the staircase, through to the stucco ceilings in the stylish breakfast room, and in the carefully selected combinations of colours, motifs and classic furniture in the bedrooms. Quiet, secluded garden.

XX **Piment** (Wahabi Nouri) 🛱

😳 *Lehmweg 29 ⊠ 20251 – Ⓜ Eppendorfer Baum* Plan: **C1**
– ℰ (040) 42 93 77 88 – www.restaurant-piment.de – closed Wednesday and Sunday
Menu 78/108 € – Carte 68/92 € – *(dinner only) (booking advisable)*
• Creative • Friendly •

Wahabi Nouri's two set menus – 'Piment' and 'Nouri's' – are the perfect expression of his creative, sophisticated style and ambitious minimalist presentation. These are both informed by his Moroccan roots, which he uses in a pleasingly underplayed manner in the form of exotic spices and perfumes – more in one menu, less in the other.
→ Gänseleber mit Salzzitrone, Datteln und Berberitzen. Couscous, Gemüsevielfalt und Safranglace. Etouffée Taube mit Himbeer-Essigjus und B'stilla.

GERMANY - HAMBURG

XX
✿✿ **Trüffelschwein** (Kirill Kinfelt) 〻

Mühlenkamp 54 ✉ 22303 – Ⓜ Sierichstr. – ℰ (040) Plan: **D1**
69 65 64 50 – www.trueffelschwein-restaurant.de – Closed 6-13 March, 22-
29 May, 7-21 August and Sunday-Monday
Menu 79/119 € – *(dinner only) (booking advisable)*
• Modern cuisine • Friendly •

The cuisine is modern, elaborate and sophisticated right down to the last detail. The attractive interior, which is warm and minimalist in style, makes a great setting for this fine food.
➔ Rindertatar, Gurke, Gin, Dill. Auster, Schweinebauch 48h, Couscous, Safran. Iberico Schwein, Trüffel, Sellerie, Mandel.

XX **Anna Sgroi** 〻

Milchstr. 7 ✉ 20148 – Ⓜ Hallerstr. – ℰ (040) Plan: **C1**
28 00 39 30 – www.annasgroi.de – Closed Saturday lunch, Sunday-
Monday and Bank Holidays lunch
Menu 39 € (lunch)/95 € – Carte 71/82 €
• Italian • Elegant • Cosy •

This charming and attractively renovated townhouse with its simple yet stylishly comfortable interior offers an informal setting in which to enjoy unfussy, classic Italian cuisine. Additional good value lunchtime menu.

X
㊉ **Zipang**

Eppendorfer Weg 171 ✉ 20253 – Ⓜ Eppendorfer Baum Plan: **B1**
– ℰ (040) 43 28 00 32 – www.zipang.de – Closed Sunday-Tuesday lunch,
Wednesday lunch
Menu 62 € (dinner) – Carte 32/78 €
• Japanese • Minimalist •

The minimalist interior at Zipang has clean lines, muted colours and a smart silver sheen. This makes a perfect match for chef Toshiharu Minami's mix of traditional and modern Japanese cooking styles. The restaurant is popular with Japanese diners – always a good sign.

X
㊉ **Heimatjuwel** 〻🝙

Stellinger Weg 47 ✉ 20255 – Ⓜ Lutterothstr. – ℰ (040) Plan: **B1**
42106989 – www.heimatjuwel.de – Closed 1-15 January and Sunday-
Monday
Menu 37/67 € – Carte 40/56 € – *(dinner only) (booking advisable)*
• Creative • Minimalist • Rustic •

Marcel Görke, no stranger to the Hamburg culinary scene, runs this rustic, minimalist-style little restaurant with its friendly, informal atmosphere. It serves creative, fully-flavoured regional cuisine that represents great value for money. There is a very short and simple lunchtime menu. Small pavement terrace.

X **Cornelia Poletto**

Eppendorfer Landstr. 80 ✉ 20249 – Ⓜ Kellenhusenstr. Plan: **C1**
– ℰ (040) 4 80 21 59 – www.cornelia-poletto.de – Closed Sunday-Monday
and Bank Holidays
Menu 59/98 € – Carte 41/84 € – *(booking advisable)*
• Italian • Friendly • Cosy •

Cornelia Poletto (who Germans will know from the television if not from her previous restaurant) serves Italian specialities in the restaurant and sells them (spices, wine, pasta, cheese) in the shop. Booked out almost daily.

X **Poletto Winebar** ⌘〻

Eppendorfer Weg 287 ✉ 20251 – Ⓜ Eppendorfer Baum Plan: **C1**
– ℰ (040) 38 64 47 00 – www.poletto-winebar.de
Menu 19 € (lunch)/89 € (dinner)
– Carte 26/57 € – (bookings advisable at dinner)
• Italian • Cosy •

This lively wine bar is definitely one of the places to be in Eppendorf. The food is flavoursome and Italian in style, including classics such as vitello tonnato and tiramisu served alongside excellent cold meats straight from the Berkel meat slicer. Great wine selection also in the adjacent wine shop.

GERMANY - HAMBURG

✗ Jellyfish

Weidenallee 12 ✉ 20357 – Ⓜ Christkirche – ℰ (040)   Plan: **B2**
*4 10 54 14 – www.jellyfish-restaurant.de – Closed 24 December-5 January
and Monday-Tuesday*
Menu 69/99 € – *(dinner only)*
• Seafood • Bistro •

If you are looking for an alternative to Hamburg's established fish restaurants, try Jellyfish. Uncomplicated, urban and minimalist, it serves ambitious food made using excellent produce in the form of a set menu or from the 'Seafood Etagère' – a speciality you will have to order in advance.

✗ Bistrot Vienna

Fettstrasse 2 ✉ 20357 – Ⓜ Christkirche – ℰ (040)   Plan: **B2**
4 39 91 82 – www.vienna-hamburg.de – Closed Monday
Menu 25 € – Carte 21/53 € – *(dinner only)*
• Market cuisine • Bistro •

A small restaurant in a slightly out-of-the-way location, Bistrot Vienna is charming, lively and well frequented. The popular combination of vibrant yet relaxed atmosphere and Sven Bunge's seasonal, international, homemade cuisine means that the tightly packed tables are always in demand. No reservations though.

✗ Butcher's american steakhouse

Milchstr. 19 ✉ 20148 – ℰ (040) 44 60 82   Plan: **C2**
*– www.butchers-steakhouse.de – Closed Saturday lunch, Sunday lunch
and Bank Holidays lunch*
Carte 81/163 €
• Meats and grills • Family • Cosy •

Here you can taste fine Nebraska beef that the chef presents to the table. A cosy restaurant with a decor dominated by dark wood and warm colours.

Empire Riverside Hotel

Bernhard-Nocht-Str. 97 (via Davidstraße) ✉ 20359   Plan: **J1**
– Ⓜ Reeperbahn – ℰ (040) 31 11 90 – www.empire-riverside.de
327 rm – †129/379 € ††129/379 € – ☲ 22 €
• Business • Design • Contemporary •

Famous architect David Chipperfield designed this contemporary hotel close to the St Pauli pontoon bridges. Rooms have a view of either the river or the city as does "20", the panoramic bar on the 20th floor. This wharf-side restaurant offers international cuisine in a simple, contemporary setting.

East

Simon-von-Utrecht-Str. 31 ✉ 20359 – Ⓜ St. Pauli   Plan I: **B2**
– ℰ (040) 30 99 30 – www.east-hamburg.de
120 rm – †169/329 € ††169/329 € – ☲ 26 € – 8 suites
• Business • Design •

The design in this former iron foundry is resolutely modern and trendy. It runs from the guestrooms through to the bar-lounge and the leisure and beauty area with its professionally staffed fitness club.
East – See restaurant listing

MY PLACE

Lippmannstr. 5 ✉ 22769 – Ⓜ Feldstr. – ℰ (040)   Plan: **J1**
28 57 18 74 – www.myplace-hamburg.de
17 rm – †75/112 € ††99/112 € – ☲ 5 € – 1 suite
• Townhouse • Personalised • Contemporary •

Close to the trendy Schanze district, a dedicated hostess runs a small hotel with individually styled, charming modern rooms named after districts of Hamburg.

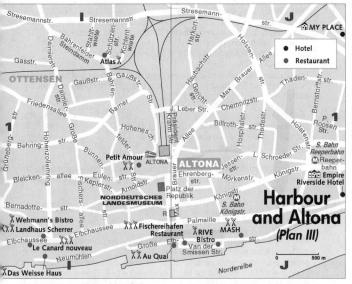

XxX Landhaus Scherrer (Heinz O. Wehmann)   🕸 🄰🄲 ⇔ 🅿

£3
Elbchaussee 130 ⊠ 22763 – 𝒞 (040) 8 83 07 00 30   Plan: I1
– www.landhausscherrer.de – Closed Sunday
Menu 98/128 € – Carte 73/98 €

• Classic French • Elegant •

Heinz O. Wehmann has been at the helm at Landhaus Scherrer since 1980. He is still serving classic cuisine in this elegant restaurant where Otto Bachmann's large erotic painting remains the decorative focus. Adding a modern note, the 600 plus wines on the wine list are presented to you on an iPad.

→ Geräucherter Saibling mit Schmorgurken und Senfaromen. Krosse Vierländer Ente. Holsteiner Rehrücken mit Pfifferlingen und Kirschen.

Wehmann's Bistro – See restaurant listing

XxX Fischereihafen Restaurant   ⇐ 🕸 ⇔ 🅿

Große Elbstr. 143 ⊠ 22767 – 𝒞 (040) 38 18 16   Plan: J1
– www.fischereihafenrestaurant.de
Menu 25 € (lunch)/75 € – Carte 35/83 € – *(booking advisable)*

• Seafood • Classic décor •

This fish restaurant overlooking the port is a veritable Hamburg institution. The service is excellent, as is the great value lunchtime menu.

XX Petit Amour (Boris Kasprik)   🛖

£3
Spritzenplatz 11 ⊠ 22765 – Ⓜ Altona – 𝒞 (040)   Plan: I1
30 74 65 56 – www.petitamour-hh.com – Closed 1 week end January,
2 weeks end July and Sunday-Monday
Menu 65/112 € – *(dinner only and Thursday lunch) (booking advisable)*

• Classic cuisine • Chic • Cosy •

This is a very popular restaurant for a number of reasons… The upmarket design (modern and minimalist yet warm and friendly), the professional service and wine suggestions, and the unfussy, ambitious cuisine with international influences.

→ Königskrabbe mit Ossietra Kaviar, Avocado und Staudenselleriesud. Ente aus der Dombes, Shiitake Tarte und Kopfsalatherzen. Frühlingskräuterflan, Süßholz, Johannisbeeren und Limettensorbet.

GERMANY - HAMBURG

XX Au Quai
 ≤ 斎 **P**

Große Elbstr. 145 b ☒ *22767 –* ℰ *(040) 38 03 77 30*   Plan: **J1**
– www.au-quai.com – Closed during Christmas, 1-15 January and
Saturday lunch, Sunday
Menu 19 € (weekday lunch)/47 € – Carte 42/79 €
• Seafood • Trendy •

This popular establishment is situated close to the harbour and has a terrace
facing the water. The modern interior is complemented by designer items and
holographs.

XX East – Hotel East
 斎 & 🚗

Simon-von-Utrecht-Str. 31 ☒ *20359 –* Ⓜ *St. Pauli*   Plan I: **B2**
– ℰ *(040) 30 99 33 – www.east-hamburg.de*
Carte 27/97 € – *(dinner only)*
• Fusion • Design • Fashionable •

The atmosphere in this former factory building draws on many styles and influences. Far Eastern charm combines skilfully with Western industrial heritage. A
restaurant not to be missed.

XX MASH
 ⅋⅋ ✿

Große Elbstr. 148 ☒ *22767 –* Ⓜ *Königstr. –* ℰ *(040)*   Plan: **J1**
8 09 00 81 11 – www.mashsteak.de
Menu 30 € (weekday lunch) – Carte 54/113 € – *(pre-book at weekends)*
• Steakhouse • Elegant • Friendly •

An upmarket steak restaurant, MASH offers any number of high-quality cuts
from rib-eye to NY strip and the very exclusive kobe beef. The temperature con-
trolled wine cabinets contain over 1 500 different wines – including some excellent vintages by the glass!

X philipps
 斎
🍸

Turnerstr. 9 ☒ *20038 –* Ⓜ *Feldstr. –* ℰ *(040)*   Plan I: **B2**
63 73 51 08 – www.philipps-restaurant.de – Closed Sunday-Monday
Menu 36 € – Carte 34/52 €
• International • Trendy • Friendly •

Hidden away in a side street, phillips is a great place to eat. Walk down the few
stairs to this friendly little restaurant with low ceilings, a relaxed atmosphere
and international menu. It promises flavoursome and skilfully prepared dishes
such as ox cheeks with leek champ.

X Nil
 斎
🍸

Neuer Pferdemarkt 5 ☒ *20359 –* Ⓜ *Feldstr. –* ℰ *(040)*   Plan I: **B2**
4 39 78 23 – www.restaurant-nil.de – Closed Tuesday except in December
Menu 26/42 € – Carte 34/61 € – *(dinner only)*
• International • Neighbourhood • Friendly •

The casual, trendy atmosphere here is perfectly in keeping with the times. Set
over three floors, the tables are a little tightly packed but the feel is friendly and
comfortable for all that. The food itself is another reason for Nil's popularity. Try
the Mangalitza bratwurst with pumpkin and potato mash and pointed cabbage
– the delicious sausages are homemade. In summer the best tables are outside
in the garden behind the restaurant. Cookery courses available next door.

X Clouds - Heaven's Restaurant & Bar
 ≤ 斎 **K**

Reeperbahn 1 (at 23. floor der Tanzenden Türme)   Plan I: **B3**
☒ *20359 –* Ⓜ *St. Pauli –* ℰ *(040) 30 99 32 80 – www.clouds-hamburg.de*
– Closed Saturday lunch, Sunday lunch
Carte 49/102 € – *(booking essential)*
• French • Design •

The view from Hamburg's highest restaurant is simply amazing! High above the
River Elbe and St Michael's church you can choose between the ambitious
French/Mediterranean cuisine (try the salt-baked turbot for two) or something
from the rotisserie. One floor higher up and you will find yourself on the rooftop
terrace.

Das Weisse Haus

Neumühlen 50 ✉ *22763 – ℰ (040) 3 90 90 16*   Plan: I1
– www.das-weisse-haus.de – Closed Saturday lunch, Sunday lunch and Monday
Menu 39/59 € – Carte 41/58 € – *(booking advisable)*
• International • Friendly •
In the little white building on the Elbpromenade your host Patrick Voelz proposes a range of international dishes alongside a now established seasonal surprise menu. The atmosphere is casual and friendly and you can sit outside too.

Wehmann's Bistro – Restaurant Landhaus Scherrer

Elbchaussee 130 ✉ *22763 – ℰ (040) 8 83 07 00 50*   Plan: I1
– www.wehmanns-bistro.de – Closed Sunday
Menu 38 € – Carte 36/50 €
• Country • Bistro •
The decor in this lovely bistro gives the impression of classic comfort. Culinary delights are prepared by the owner, Heinz O Wehmann.

RIVE Bistro

Van-der-Smissen Str. 1 (at Kreuzfahrt-Center) ✉ *22767*   Plan: J1
– Ⓜ Königstr. – ℰ (040) 3 80 59 19 – www.rive.de
Menu 20 € (weekday lunch)/48 € – Carte 34/60 € – *(booking advisable)*
• Seafood • Bistro •
Find excellent fish and friendly service at this restaurant in Hamburg's famous docks, along with a view of passing ships. The menu boasts local classics such as Hamburger Pannfisch, international fare including yellowfin tuna with pak choi and mango and chilli couscous, along with some meat dishes.

Louis C. Jacob

Elbchaussee 401 (by Elbchaussee A3) ✉ *22609 – ℰ (040) 82 25 50*
– www.hotel-jacob.de
66 rm – ♦185/225 € ♦♦225/425 € – ⯑ 32 € – 19 suites
• Luxury • Traditional • Classic •
The successful management and services in this elegant hotel on the Elbe are exemplary. Equally pleasant is the classical furnishing of the rooms, some of which are as spacious as junior suites.
❀❀ **Jacobs Restaurant** • ❀ **Weinwirtschaft Kleines Jacob** – See restaurant listing

Strandhotel

Strandweg 13 (by Elbchaussee A3) ✉ *22587 – ℰ (040) 86 13 44*
– www.strandhotel-blankenese.de – Closed 25 December-18 January
13 rm – ♦100/120 € ♦♦160/205 € – ⯑ 15 € – 2 suites
• Family • Classic •
The Elbstrand is the epitome of the lifestyle hotel. Despite its many modern features, the charm of this listed white Art Nouveau villa is omnipresent. Its high-ceilinged, stuccoed rooms match the designer furnishings to perfection. The excellent buffet breakfast comes with a lovely view of the Elbe.

Landhaus Flottbek

Baron-Voght-Str. 179 (by Stresemannstraße A2) ✉ *22607 – ℰ (040) 82 27 41 60 – www.landhaus-flottbek.de*
25 rm – ♦110 € ♦♦120/150 € – ⯑ 16 €
• Family • Cosy •
A well-run hotel consisting of several 18C farmhouses converted to create tasteful, comfortable guestrooms. Try and book one of the rooms that look out onto the lovely garden.
❀ **Landhaus Flottbek** – See restaurant listing

GERMANY - HAMBURG

XxxX ✿✿ Süllberg - Seven Seas (Karlheinz Hauser)

Süllbergsterrasse 12 (by Elbchaussee A3) ✉ *22587 –* ✆ *(040)*
*8 66 25 20 – www.suellberg-hamburg.de – Closed January-mid February
and Monday-Tuesday*
10 rm – †170/190 € – ††190/230 € – ☲ 17 € – 1 suite
Menu 79 € (Vegetarian)/180 € – *(dinner only and Sunday lunch)*
• Modern French • Luxury •

The Süllberg is a Blankenese institution and along with the Seven Seas has become one of Hamburg's top gourmet addresses. It offers a genuinely upmarket dining experience, from the classy interior to Karlheinz Hauser's fragrant, classic cuisine, as well as the accomplished and attentive service and expert wine recommendations. The rooms are as attractive and stylish as the restaurant.
→ Gänseleber roh mariniert, Dörraprikose, Salzkaramell, Kokos. Hummer "Dreierlei", Mais, Ingwer, fermentierter Knoblauch. Limousinlamm, Rücken und Brust, Aubergine, Bärlauch, Orange.
Deck 7 – See restaurant listing

XxX ✿✿ Jacobs Restaurant – Hotel Louis C. Jacob

Elbchaussee 401 (by Elbchaussee A3) ✉ *22609 –* ✆ *(040) 82 25 54 07
– www.hotel-jacob.de – Closed Monday-Tuesday*
Menu 98/135 €
– Carte 70/116 € – *(Wednesday to Friday dinner only) (booking advisable)*
• Classic French • Chic •

Thomas Martin's food – classic, simple and free of fancy flourishes, placing great emphasis on top-quality ingredients – is now available from a new à la carte menu. The dining experience is rounded off by the accomplished service, the stylish decor and the magnificent lime tree shaded terrace overlooking the Elbe.
→ Saint Pierre mit Mangold, Zitrone und Pinienkernen. Sardinen aus der Bretagne in provençalischer Vinaigrette mariniert. Karamellisierte Altländer Apfeltarte, Crème chantilly.

XX ☺ Landhaus Flottbek – Hotel Landhaus Flottbek

Baron-Voght-Str. 179 (by Stresemannstraße A2) ✉ *22607 –* ✆ *(040)
82 27 41 60 – www.landhaus-flottbek.de – Closed Saturday lunch, Sunday lunch*
Menu 25 € (lunch)/36 € (dinner) – Carte 37/61 €
• Country • Rustic • Elegant •

Both the pretty half-timbered building with its country house style and the comfortable garden terrace here are charming. The seasonal, regional food on offer includes venison daube with braised vegetables. The small lounge area in the bar is also attractive.

XX Witthüs

Elbchaussee 499a (access via Mühlenberg) (by Elbchaussee A3) ✉ *22587
–* ✆ *(040) 86 01 73 – www.witthues.com – Closed Monday*
Menu 30/39 € – Carte 38/55 € – *(dinner only)*
• International • Friendly •

This historic farmhouse is idyllically located near the Elbe. Enjoy international cuisine and professional service in a classic, elegant setting with Nordic flair. Outdoor terrace.

XX Deck 7 – Restaurant Süllberg - Seven Seas

Süllbergsterrasse 12 (by Elbchaussee A3) ✉ *22587 –* ✆ *(040) 86 62 52 77
– www.suellberg-hamburg.de*
Menu 44 € – Carte 39/65 €
• Country • Cosy • Elegant •

In defiance of many a passing trend, this restaurant with its smart, brown leather upholstered chairs and parquet flooring has opted for the versatility of a classic yet modern interior. In summer, eat outside with stunning views of the Elbe.

Weinwirtschaft Kleines Jacob – Hotel Louis C. Jacob

Elbchaussee 404 (by Elbchaussee A3) ✉ *22609 –* ℰ *(040)*
82 25 55 10 – www.kleines-jacob.de
Menu 36 € – Carte 31/49 € – *(dinner only) (booking advisable)*
• Classic cuisine • Wine bar • Cosy •

No wonder so many people describe Kleines Jacob as their favourite restaurant with its wine bar charm, candlelit tables and attentive service. The dishes coming out of the open kitchens include chicken fricassee vol-au-vents and rice. All the wines come from vineyards in German-speaking countries.

Madame X im Off Club – Restaurant Off Club

Leverkusenstr. 54 ✉ *22761 –* ℰ *(040) 89 01 93 33*
– www.offclub.de – Closed Sunday-Monday
Plan I: **AB2**
Menu 77 € – *(dinner only) (booking essential)*
• Creative • Fashionable •

Madame X offers a very particular kind of gourmet experience combining a cool vibe, its creative 'Carte Blanche' set menu and a relaxed front-of-house team that explain the dishes to you at your table. Simple fare using few ingredients, sourced largely from the restaurant's own farm or farmer and hunter friends.

Off Club

Leverkusenstr. 54 ✉ *22761 –* ℰ *(040) 89 01 93 33*
– www.offclub.de – Closed Sunday-Monday
Plan I: **AB2**
Carte 31/55 €
• International • Fashionable •

The Off Club is set in a renovated factory building. As part of a trendy dual concept, it serves flavoursome dishes such as braised ox cheeks with fennel alongside "Japanese bar food in Hamburg", which includes octopus with sweet miso. Good value daily menu at lunchtimes.

Madame X im Off Club – See restaurant listing

Rach & Ritchy

Holstenkamp 71 ✉ *22525 –* ℰ *(040) 89 72 61 70*
– www.rach-ritchy.de – Closed Saturday lunch, Sunday and Bank Holidays lunch
Plan I: **A2**
Carte 34/78 € – *(booking advisable)*
• Meats and grills • Friendly • Fashionable •

TV chef Christian Rach is now a household name. It is the second member of the duo, Richard 'Ritchy' Mayer, who does the cooking in his fashionable, modern grill restaurant. Specialities include succulent steaks from the glass-fronted maturing cabinet.

Atlas

Schützenstr. 9a (entrance Phoenixhof) ✉ *22761*
– ℰ *(040) 8 51 78 10 – www.atlas.at – Closed Saturday lunch and Sunday dinner*
Plan: **I1**
Menu 21 € (weekday lunch)/33 € – Carte 21/52 €
• International • Bistro •

This former fish smokery is now a restaurant in the modern bistro style. Shorter menu available at lunchtimes. Pleasant ivy-covered terrace.

MUNICH
MÜNCHEN

Population: 1 534 935

Situated in a stunning position not far north of the Alps, Munich is a cultural titan. Famously described as the 'village with a million inhabitants', its mix of German organisation and Italian lifestyle makes for a magical mix, with an enviable amount of Italian restaurants to seek out and enjoy. This cultural capital of Southern Germany boasts over forty theatres and dozens of museums; temples of culture that blend charmingly with the Bavarian love of folklore and lederhosen. Perhaps in no other world location – certainly not in Western Europe – is there such an enjoyable abundance of folk festivals and groups dedicated to playing the local music. And there's an abundance of places to see them, too: Munich is awash with Bierhallen, Bierkeller, and Biergarten.

The heart of Munich is the Old Town, with its epicentre the Marienplatz in the south, and Residenz to the north: there are many fine historic buildings around here. Running to the east is the River Isar, flanked by fine urban thoroughfares and green areas for walks. Head north for the area dissected by the Ludwig-strasse and Leopoldstrasse – Schwabing – which is full of students as it's the University district. To the east is the English Garden, a denizen of peace. West of here, the Museums district, dominated by the Pinakothek, is characterised by bookshops, antique stores and galleries.

MUNICH IN...

→ **ONE DAY**
The old town, Frauenkirche, English Garden, Wagner (if possible!) at the National Theatre.

→ **TWO DAYS**
Schwabing, Pinakothek, Hofbräuhaus.

→ **THREE DAYS**
Olympic Park, Schloss Nymphenburg, Deutsches Museum, an evening in a traditional Bavarian inn.

PRACTICAL INFORMATION

ARRIVAL-DEPARTURE

 Airport Frank Josef Strauss is 28km northeast of the city. Munich S-Bahn Lines S1 or S8 take 45min to the centre.

GETTING AROUND

The underground network (U-Bahn) operates the same fare system as on Munich's buses and trams: it's divided into 4 ring-shaped price zones; zone 1 (the white zone) is the most important for visitors, as it covers the city centre. Prices rise in accordance with the amount of zones you intend to travel. If you plan to make several journeys, invest in a strip-card (Streifenkarte). You can also buy a 1 or 3-day Tageskarte: good value for tourists and available from tourist information offices, hotel receptions, travel agents and newsagents. The München Welcome Card is available for 1 or 3 days and gives free use of public transport as well as reduced entry to many museums, palaces and sights.

EATING OUT

Munich is a city in which you can eat well - especially if you're a meat-eater – and in large quantities. The local specialities are meat and potatoes,

CALENDAR HIGHLIGHTS

March
Starkbierfest (Strong Beer Festival).

June/July
Münchner Opernfestspiele (opera and ballet), Summer Tollwood Festival.

July
Sommernachtstraum (concert and fireworks).

August
Theatron Music Summer.

September-October
Oktoberfest.

October
Long Night of Museums, Munich Marathon.

November-December
Winter Tollwood Festival, Christkindlmarkt

with large dollops of cabbage on the side; you won't have trouble finding roast pork and dumplings or meatloaf and don't forget the local white veal sausage, weisswurst. The meat is invariably succulent, and cabbage is often adorned with the likes of juniper berries. Potatoes, meanwhile, have a tendency to evolve into soft and buttery dumplings. And sausage? Take your pick from over 1,500 recognised species. Other specialities include Schweinshaxe (knuckle of pork) and Leberkäs (meat and offal pâté). Eating out in Munich, or anywhere in Bavaria, is an experience in itself, with the distinctive background din of laughter, singing and the clinking of mugs of Bavarian Weissbier. It's famous for the Brauereigaststätten or brewery inn; be prepared for much noise, and don't be afraid to fall into conversation with fellow diners and drinkers. The many Italian restaurants in the city provide an excellent alternative.

GERMANY - MUNICH

Mandarin Oriental   🏝 🕭 🛋 🏊 🛗 🛁 🚗

Neuturmstr. 1 ✉ *80331 –* Ⓜ *Isartor*   Plan: **H2**
– ☎ (089) 29 09 80
– www.mandarinoriental.com/munich
67 rm – †575/895 € ††575/895 € – 🍽 44 € – 6 suites
· Grand Luxury · Historic · Classic ·

This neo-Renaissance style palace is now a luxury hotel with an international reputation and one of Germany's most select addresses. A byword for exclusive accommodation and premier service, it guarantees the very highest standards – not least when it come to breakfast! The roof-top pool with its view of the Alps is the icing on the cake.
Matsuhisa Munich – See restaurant listing

Bayerischer Hof   🏝 🕭 🖤 🛋 🛗 🛁 🚗

Promenadeplatz 2 ✉ *80333 –* Ⓜ *Marienplatz – ☎ (089)*   Plan: **G2**
2 12 00 – www.bayerischerhof.de
319 rm – †310/395 € ††390/580 € – 🍽 40 € – 21 suites
· Grand Luxury · Traditional · Classic ·

This grand hotel set in a magnificent palace was first opened in 1841. The rooms are exclusively designed in six different styles. The Blue Spa restaurant with its small menu looks out over Munich to the Alps beyond. Other restaurants include Trader Vic's, which serves Polynesian food.
⊛⊛ **Atelier · Garden-Restaurant** – See restaurant listing

The Charles   🏝 🕭 🖤 🛋 🛗 🛁 🚗

Sophienstr. 28 ✉ *80333 –* Ⓜ *Hauptbahnhof*   Plan: **E1**
– ☎ (089) 5445550
– www.sophiasmuenchen.de
136 rm – †270/740 € ††270/740 € – 🍽 38 € – 24 suites
· Grand Luxury · Elegant · Contemporary ·

This attractive hotel in the Old Botanical Gardens is the epitome of luxury with its chic and elegant, minimalist-style interior, high-class spa and every conceivable service. Sophia's restaurant promises 'Botanical Bistronomy', as well as a chic but friendly bar and pleasant terrace.

Königshof   🕭 🛋 🛗 🛁 🚗

Karlsplatz 25 ✉ *80335 –* Ⓜ *Karlsplatz – ☎ (089)*   Plan: **F2**
55 13 60 – www.koenigshof-hotel.de
79 rm – †280/320 € ††310/350 € – 🍽 35 € – 8 suites
· Luxury · Traditional · Elegant ·

The Geisel family have a long history in the hotel trade stretching back to 1900. It has reached its pinnacle in this classic, luxury hotel in a choice location on the Karlsplatz. The professional front of house team are always on hand to guide and advise.
⊛ **Gourmet Restaurant Königshof** – See restaurant listing

Vier Jahreszeiten Kempinski   🏝 🕭 🛋 🛗 🛁 🚗

Maximilianstr. 17 ✉ *80539 –* Ⓜ *Lehel – ☎ (089) 2 12 50*   Plan: **H2**
– www.kempinski.com/vierjahreszeiten
230 rm – †240/665 € ††320/725 € – 🍽 42 € – 67 suites
· Luxury · Traditional · Classic ·

This classic Munich grand hotel dates back to 1858. It has the sort of historic charm you don't often find, though it is not without the modern conveniences required to make it comfortable and homely. Tagesbar, facing onto Maximilianstraße, serves international fare.
Schwarzreiter – See restaurant listing

Sofitel Munich Bayerpost

Bayerstr. 12 ✉ *80335 –* Ⓜ *Hauptbahnhof –* ☎ *(089) 59 94 80 – www.sofitel-munich.com*
388 rm – ♦210/360 € ♦♦210/360 € – ☲ 38 € – 8 suites
• Chain • Luxury • Design •

Modern architecture and contemporary design have been incorporated into this imposing listed building dating from the latter part of the 19C with great success as you can see for yourself both in the upmarket spa and the numerous events facilities.
Délice La Brasserie – See restaurant listing

Plan: **E2**

Hilton Munich Park

Am Tucherpark 7 ✉ *80538 –* ☎ *(089) 3 84 50 – www.hilton.de/muenchenpark*
481 rm – ♦139/479 € ♦♦139/479 € – ☲ 29 € – 3 suites
• Chain • Business • Contemporary •

The Hilton Park's location (in the English Garden) and the comfortable accommodation, which includes business and executive rooms, are both excellent. The restaurant offers an international menu and there is beer garden on the River Eisbach.

Plan I: **C2**

Derag Livinghotel

Frauenstr. 4 ✉ *80469 –* Ⓜ *Fraunhoferstr. –* ☎ *(089) 8 85 65 60 – www.deraghotels.de*
83 rm – ♦190/240 € ♦♦220/280 € – ☲ 21 €
• Business • Design • Functional •

With a great central location on the lively Viktualienmarkt and beautiful designer rooms with all the latest technology, Derag Livinghotel offers a number of apartments with kitchenettes perfect for long-stay guests. There is lots of attention to detail, such as a free mini-bar, Nespresso machine and Wi-Fi. The hotel also boasts the Tian restaurant, which serves vegetarian and vegan cuisine.

Plan: **G3**

Louis

Viktualienmarkt 6 ✉ *80331 –* Ⓜ *Marienplatz –* ☎ *(089) 41 11 90 80 – www.louis-hotel.com*
72 rm – ♦139/399 € ♦♦189/449 € – ☲ 29 €
• Townhouse • Elegant • Design •

With an excellent location in the Viktualienmarkt – where the excellent ingredients for breakfast come from – the Louis offers both modern design and comfort, alongside additional services such as shoe cleaning and daily newspapers. In summer, the Japanese cuisine on offer at Emiko can be enjoyed on the roof terrace facing the courtyard.

Plan: **G2**

Cortiina

Ledererstr. 8 ✉ *80331 –* Ⓜ *Isartor –* ☎ *(089) 2 42 24 90 – www.cortiina.com*
70 rm – ♦149/409 € ♦♦189/429 € – ☲ 25 € – 5 suites
• Townhouse • Business • Elegant •

The interior of this hotel in its improbable but nonetheless central location comes as something of a surprise. It has beautiful materials including wood, slate and Jura marble, which are combined perfectly with natural colours. Some of the guestrooms are spacious and include their own kitchenette.

Plan: **H2**

anna hotel

Schützenstr. 1 ✉ *80335 –* Ⓜ *Karlsplatz (Stachus) –* ☎ *(089) 5 99 94 0 – www.annahotel.de*
73 rm – ♦185/370 € ♦♦185/370 € – ☲ 22 € – 2 suites
• Business • Contemporary •

The clientele in this modern hotel right on the Karlsplatz – the 'Stachus' as it's known locally – is young or at least young at heart! For a panoramic view take a room on the top floor, and if you feel like some sushi, you need go no further than the hotel's bistro, which also boasts a popular bar.

Plan: **F2**

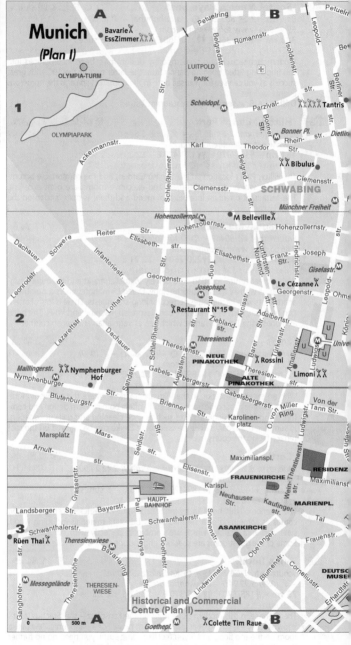

Munich
(Plan I)

A

B

Bavarie ✗
EssZimmer ✗✗✗

✗✗✗ Tantris

OLYMPIA-TURM

1

OLYMPIAPARK

Petuelring

Leopold-

Petuel

Be

Belgradstr.

Rümannstr.

Isoldenstr.

Berliner Str.

LUITPOLD PARK

✚

Str.

Ackermannstr.

Scheidpl. Ⓜ

Parzival-

Bonner Str.

Bonner Pl.

Rhein-

Str.

Dietlin

SCHWABING

Karl

Theodor

✗✗ Bibulus

Clemensstr.

Schleißheimer

Belgrad-

str.

Clemensstr.

Clemensstr.

Münchner Freiheit

2

Hohenzollernpl. Ⓜ

M Belleville ✗

Dachauer

Schwere

Reiter

Str.

Hohenzollernstr.

Hohenzollernstr.

Leonrodstr.

Str.

Infanteriestr.

Elisabeth-

str.

Elisabethstr.

Kurfürsten-Nordend

Franz-Str.

Joseph

Friedrichstr.

Giselastr. Ⓜ

Leopold-

Ohms

Lazarettstr.

Lothstr.

Georgenstr.

Str.

Teng-

str.

Aicisstr.

Le Cézanne ✗

Georgenstr.

Josephspl. Ⓜ

✗ Restaurant N°15

Ziebland-str.

Adalbertstr.

str.

Turkenstr.

Ⓤ

Univer

Dachauer

Schleißheimer

str.

Theresienstr.

Theresienstr. Ⓜ

Bayer

str.

Amalienstr.

Ⓤ Ⓜ Ludwigstr.

Ⓤ

Kön

Maillingerstr. ✗✗ Nymphenburger Hof

Sandstr.

Augusten-

Gabels-

NEUE PINAKOTHEK

✗ Rossini

Theresien-str.

Limoni ✗✗

Nymphenburger

Str.

bergerstr.

ALTE PINAKOTHEK

Blutenburgstr.

Brienner

Str.

Gabelsbergerstr.

von Miller

Von der Tann Str.

Marsplatz

Mars-

Karolinen-platz

Ring

Arnulf-

str.

Grasserstr.

Seidlstr.

str.

Elisenstr.

Maximianspl.

Ludwigstr.

gden Str

RESIDENZ

Maximilianst

3

HAUPT-BAHNHOF

Paul

FRAUENKIRCHE

Wein-Theatinerstr.

str.

MARIENPL.

Landsberger

Str.

Bayerstr.

Karlspl.

Neuhauser Str.

Kaufinger-

str.

Tal

Rüen Thai ✗

Schwanthalerstr.

Theresienwiese

Schwanthalerstr.

Heyse

Goethestr.

Sonnenstr.

ASAMKIRCHE

Oberanger

Frauenstr.

Ⓜ Messegelände

Theresienhöhe

Bavariaring

THERESIEN-WIESE

Str.

Lindwurmstr.

Blumenst.

Cornelliusstr.

DEUTSC MUSE

Ganghofer-

Historical and Commercial Centre (Plan II)

Goethepl.

✗ Colette Tim Raue

Erhardst

0 ____ 500 m

A

B

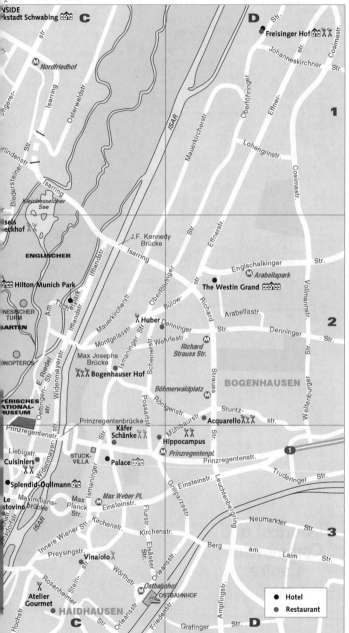

NSIDE
rkstadt Schwabing **C**

Freisinger Hof ✗ ✗

D

Str.

Johanneskirchner Str.

Cosimastr.

Nordfriedhof

Osterwaldstr.

Isarring

ISAR

Mauerkircherstr.

Oberföhringer

Effner

Str.

Lohengrinstr.

Cosimastr.

1

Biedersteiner Str.

Isarring

Kleinhesseloher See

sels eckhof ✗ ✗

J.F. Kennedy Brücke

Isarring

Str.

Effnerstr.

ENGLISCHER

Englschalkinger Str.

Arabellapark

The Westin Grand

Hilton Munich Park

Tucherpark

Ifflandstr.

Oberföhringer

Str.

Richard

Bülow

Arabellastr.

Vollmannstr.

NESISCHER TURM

ARTEN

Am

Mauerkircherstr.

✗ Huber

Denninger

Str.

Denninger

Str.

2

ONOPTEROS

Montgesastr.

Ismaninger str.

Scheinerstr.

Wehrlestr.

Richard Strauss Str.

Max Josephs Brücke

E. Riedel

Widenmayerstr.

✗✗✗ Bogenhauser Hof

Welfenburger

ERISCHES ATIONAL-USEUM

Oetingen- str.

Possartstr.

Böhmerwaldplatz

Röntgenstr.

Strauss

BOGENHAUSEN

Stuntz- str.

Prinzregentenbrücke

Prinzregentenstr.

Käfer Schänke ✗ ✗

Mühlbaurstr.

Acquarello ✗✗✗

Liebigstr.

Cuisiniers ✗ ✗

STUCK-VILLA

Widenmayerstr.

Str.

Palace

Hippocampus ✗ ✗

Prinzregentenpl.

Prinzregentenstr.

1

Truderinger Str.

●**Splendid-Dollmann**

Ismaninger Str.

Max Weber Pl.

Einsteinstr.

Grillparzerstr.

Einsteinstr.

Leuchtenbergring

Le stovino

Maximilians-Brücke

Max Planck Str.

Einsteinstr.

Flurstr.

Neumarkter Str.

3

ISAR

Innere Wiener Str.

Kirchenstr.

Kirchenstr.

Elsässer Str.

Berg

am

Laim

Str.

Preysingstr.

Vinaiolo ✗

Stein- str.

Wörthstr.

Orleansstr.

Rosenheimer

Ostbahnhof

OSTBAHNHOF

Ampfingstr.

✗ **Atelier Gourmet**

HAIDHAUSEN

C

Hochstr.

Orleansstr.

Friedenstr.

Grafinger Str.

D

| ● | Hotel |
| ● | Restaurant |

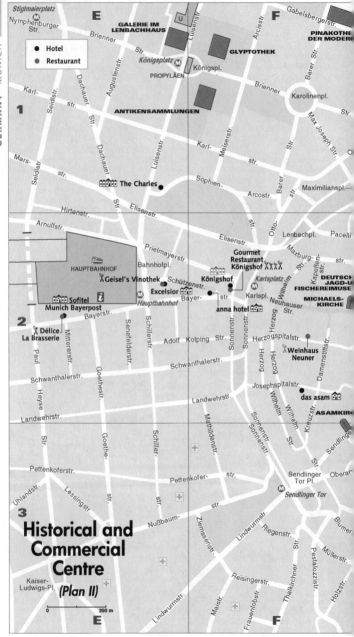

Stiglmaierplatz
Nymphenburger Str.

E

Brienner Str.

GALERIE IM LENBACHHAUS

Luisenstr.

F

Gabelsbergerstr.

PINAKOTHE DER MODER

Königsplatz

GLYPTOTHEK

Königspl.

PROPYLÄEN

Arcisstr.

Barer Str.

Brienner Str.

Karolinenpl.

● Hotel
● Restaurant

Augustenstr.

Dachauer str.

ANTIKENSAMMLUNGEN

Karl-

Seidlstr.

Karl- str.

Meiserstr.

Luisenstr.

1

Mars- str.

Seidlstr.

Dachauer str.

Sophien-

Karl-

str.

Arcostr.

Max-Joseph Str.

Maximilianspl.

🏨🏨🏨 The Charles ●

Hirtenstr.

Elisenstr.

Arnulfstr.

Prielmayerstr.

Elisenstr.

Otto-

Lenbachpl.

Pacelli

🚉 **HAUPTBAHNHOF**

Bahnhofpl.

X Geisel's Vinothek

Bahnhofstr.

Schützenstr.

Gourmet Restaurant Königshof XXXX

Marburg- str.

Kapellen str.

DEUTSCH JAGD-U FISCHEREIMUSE

🏨🏨 **Königshof**

🏨🏨 Sofitel
Munich Bayerpost

Excelsior 🏨🏨

Bayer-

str.

Karlspl. 🅼

Karlspl.

Neuhauser Str.

MICHAELS-KIRCHE

2

X Délice
La Brasserie

Bayerstr.

🅼 Hauptbahnhof

Bayer-

anna hotel 🏨🏨

Herzogspitalstr.

Sonnenstr.

Sonnenstr.

Herzog

Herzog

Neuhauser

Paul Heyse str.

Mitterstr.

Schillerstr.

Adolf Kolping Str.

Schwanthalerstr.

X **Weinhaus Neuner**

Damenstiftstr.

Schwanthalerstr.

Senefelderstr.

Goethestr.

Landwehrstr.

Josephspitalstr.

Herzog Wilhelm

Herzog Wilhelm

das asam 🏨🏨

ASAMKIR

Landwehrstr.

Str.

Goethe-

Schiller-

Mathildenstr.

Sonnenstr.

Sonnenstr.

Kreuzstr.

Sendlinger

Str.

Oberan

Pettenkoferstr.

Pettenkofer-

str.

Sendlinger
Tor Pl.

Uhlandstr.

Lessingstr.

str.

🅼 Sendlinger Tor

Blumer

3

Historical and Commercial Centre *(Plan II)*

Kaiser-Ludwigs-Pl.

Nußbaum-

Ziemssenstr.

Lindwurmstr.

Fliegenstr.

Str.

Müllerstr.

Pestalozzistr.

0 ——— 200 m

E

Reisingerstr.

Maistr.

Frauenlobstr.

Thalkirchner

Lindwurmstr.

Holzstr.

F

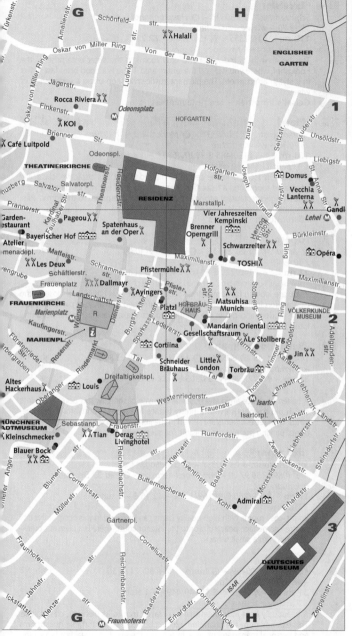

G

H

Schönfeld- str.

✗✗ Halali

Von der Tann Str.

ENGLISHER
GARTEN

Oskar von Miller Ring

Ludwigstr.

Jägerstr.

Oskar von Miller Ring

Finkenstr.

Rocca Riviera ✗✗

Odeonsplatz

Ⓜ

1

Franz

Seitzstr.

Bruderstr.

Unsöldstr.

✗ KOI

Brienner

Str.

Odeonspl.

HOFGARTEN

Joseph

Liebigstr.

✗ Café Luitpold

THEATINERKIRCHE

Salvatorpl.

Salvator- str.

Hofgarten- str.

St. Anna Str.

🏠 Domus

Vecchia
Lanterna
✗✗

Ⓜ Lehel

Gandl

husberg

Theatinerstr.

Residenzstr.

RESIDENZ

Marstallpl.

Straub

Herzog

Ring

Seitzstr.

Prannerstr.

Garden-
restaurant

✗✗ Pageou

Kardinal-
Faulhaber Str.

Spatenhaus
an der Oper ✗

Vier Jahreszeiten
Kempinski
🏠

Brenner
Operngrill

Schwarzreiter ✗✗

Bürkleinstr.

🏠 Opéra

Atelier

Bayerischer Hof 🏠

Maffeistr.

Maximilianstr.

● TOSHI ✗

Maximilianstr.

menadepl.

✗✗ Les Deux

Schäftlerstr.

Schrammer-
str.

Pfistermühle ✗✗

Pfister-
str.

rengrube

Frauenplatz

✗✗✗ Dallmayr

Neuturm-
str.

Stollberg str.

Matsuhisa
Munich
✗✗

VÖLKERKUNDE
MUSEUM

FRAUENKIRCHE

Landschaftstr.

✗ Ayingers

Alter Hof

Sparkassenstr.

Platzl HOFBRÄU-
🏠 HAUS

Mandarin Oriental 🏠

Adelgunden-
str.

2

Marienplatz

Dienerstr.

Gesellschaftsraum ✗ Le Stollberg

Herrnstr.

Knöbelstr.

Kaufingerstr.

R

Burgstr.

Ledererstr.

Kanalstr.

Jin ✗✗

MARIENPL.

ℹ

🏠 Cortiina

Liebherrstr.

Fürstenfelder-

Rosenstr.

Tal

Schneider
Bräuhaus

Little ✗
London

Torbräu 🏠

Wimmer

Landstr.

rbergraben

Dreifaltigkeitspl.

Tal

Thomas Ⓜ Isartor

Kanalstr.

Altes
Hackerhaus ✗

🏠 Louis

Westenriederstr.

Frauenstr.

Isartorpl.

Thierschstr.

Steinsdorfstr.

MÜNCHNER
STADTMUSEUM

Sebastianpl.

✗✗ Tian

Derag 🏠
Livinghotel

Rumfordstr.

Zweibrückenstr.

✗ Kleinschmecker

Frauenstr.

Blauer Bock
✗✗ 🏠

Blumen-
str.

Reichenbachstr.

Klenzestr.

Aventinstr.

Baaderstr.

Morassistr.

Erhardstr.

Anger

Corneliusstr.

Buttermelcherstr.

Kohl-
str.

Admiral 🏠

Müllerstr.

Gärtnerpl.

Corneliusstr.

3

Fraunhofer-

Reichenbachstr.

Baaderstr.

Erhardtstr.

DEUTSCHES
MUSEUM

ckstattstr.

Jahnstr.

Klenze-

str.

ISAR

Corneliusbrücke

Zeppelinstr.

G

Ⓜ *Fraunhoferstr*

H

Excelsior

Schützenstr. 11 ⊠ 80335 – Ⓜ *Hauptbahnhof – 𝒞 (089)*   Plan: **E2**
55 13 70 – www.excelsior-hotel.de
118 rm – ∤145/355 € ∤∤150/370 € – ⌑ 22 €
• Business • Classic •

This hotel, with its individual and cosy rooms, is the sister enterprise of the Königshof, where you will find the leisure area. There is a good breakfast buffet in a stylish atmosphere. The pleasant, rustic-style shop offers a wide range of wines.

Geisel's Vinothek – See restaurant listing

Platzl

Sparkassenstr. 10 ⊠ 80331 – Ⓜ *Marienplatz – 𝒞 (089)*   Plan: **G2**
23 70 30 – www.platzl.de
166 rm ⌑ – ∤130/485 € ∤∤200/685 € – 1 suite
• Traditional • Cosy •

This hotel is located in the centre of the old city. It has attractive, classically decorated rooms and a relaxation area in the style of Ludwig II's Moorish pavilion. Ayingers restaurant provides a more relaxed alternative to the formal Pfistermühle.

Pfistermühle • Ayingers – See restaurant listing

Opéra

St.-Anna-Str. 10 ⊠ 80538 – Ⓜ *Lehel – 𝒞 (089)*   Plan: **H2**
2 10 49 40 – www.hotel-opera.de
22 rm ⌑ – ∤140/220 € ∤∤160/240 € – 3 suites
• Grand townhouse • Personalised • Classic •

If you are looking for something special, this little jewel of a hotel close to the Opera offers individually designed rooms furnished with antique pieces but also some modern accents. In the summer you can take breakfast in the delightful interior courtyard.

Splendid-Dollmann

Thierschstr. 49 ⊠ 80538 – Ⓜ *Lehel – 𝒞 (089) 23 80 80*   Plan I: **C3**
– www.hotel-splendid-dollmann.de
36 rm – ∤95/275 € ∤∤135/305 € – ⌑ 15 € – 1 suite
• Historic • Personalised •

A haven of peace amid the hustle and bustle of the city, this hotel is set in a stylish old townhouse with a pretty terrace in the rear courtyard. In the evenings, light refreshments are served in the library. Two parking spaces and residents' parking permits are available for guests with cars.

das asam

Josephspitalstr. 3 ⊠ 80331 – Ⓜ *Sendlinger Tor*   Plan: **F2**
– 𝒞 (089) 2 30 97 00 – www.hotel-asam.de – Closed 22 December-
6 January
17 rm – ∤149/260 € ∤∤169/430 € – ⌑ 16 € – 8 suites
• Business • Classic •

Bright, cosy rooms with high quality baths can be found in this hotel in the city centre - some face peacefully onto the interior court. There is a pleasant breakfast area with a small terrace.

Admiral

Kohlstr. 9 ⊠ 80469 – Ⓜ *Isartor – 𝒞 (089) 21 63 50*   Plan: **H3**
– www.hotel-admiral.de
31 rm ⌑ – ∤119/399 € ∤∤149/449 € – 1 suite
• Family • Classic • Cosy •

A beautifully kept little hotel that has stayed true to its pleasant, classic style. This extends from the charming, plush lobby to the comfortable guestrooms and personal management style. In summer the excellent breakfast is also served in the little garden.

Torbräu
Tal 41 ⊠ 80331 – ⓂIsartor – ℰ (089) 24 23 40
– www.torbraeu.de
Plan: **H2**
88 rm ⊑ – †165/245 € ††225/285 € – 2 suites
• Traditional • Classic •
The oldest hotel in Munich, Torbräu has been in business since 1490. Now a smart, family-run property it is constantly being upgraded and modernised. Attractive and bright breakfast room on the first floor. Bavarian and Mediterranean food served in the Schapeau.

Domus
St.-Anna-Str. 31 ⊠ 80538 – ⓂLehel
– ℰ (089) 2 17 77 30 – www.domus-hotel.de
Plan: **H1**
45 rm ⊑ – †120/190 € ††165/280 €
• Business • Functional •
Aldo Diaco's beautifully kept Domus hotel offers contemporary guestrooms in warm colours with modern bathrooms. In summer you can breakfast outside on the pretty little terrace.
Vecchia Lanterna – See restaurant listing

Blauer Bock
Sebastiansplatz 9 ⊠ 80331 – ⓂMarienplatz – ℰ (089)
45 22 23 33 – www.restaurant-blauerbock.de
Plan: **G3**
68 rm ⊑ – †99/235 € ††155/310 € – 4 suites
• Family • Business • Contemporary •
Just a stone's throw from the Viktualienmarkt, this smart, well-appointed hotel offers rooms decorated in a variety of different styles. Note that those giving onto the interior courtyard are a little quieter.
Blauer Bock – See restaurant listing

✕✕✕✕ Gourmet Restaurant Königshof – Hotel Königshof
ℰ
Karlsplatz 25 (1st floor) ⊠ 80335
– ⓂKarlsplatz – ℰ (089) 551360
Plan: **F2**
– www.koenigshof-hotel.de
– Closed Sunday-Monday
Menu 162 € – Carte 97/127 € – *(booking advisable)*
• Classic French • Elegant • Classic décor •
Stalwarts of the restaurant trade since 1900, the Geisels' choice of chef amply demonstrates their experience and flair. Martin Fauster, who matches their dedication and commitment, has been at the helm in the kitchen for many years. His sophisticated, classic cuisine is accompanied by interesting wines recommended by an expert team of sommeliers.
➜ Flusskrebse, Mispeln, Artischocken, Fichtensprossen und Pistazien. Kalbsschulter, Briesraviolo und Mairübchen. Mascarpone knusprig, Soufflé, Rhabarber, Grapefruit, Limette und Rosenwasser.

✕✕✕ Dallmayr
Dienerstr. 14 (1st floor) ⊠ 80331 – ⓂMarienplatz
Plan: **G2**
– ℰ (089) 21 35 100 – www.restaurant-dallmayr.de – Closed 2 weeks
24 December-early January, 2 weeks during Easter, 3 weeks August,
Sunday-Monday and Bank Holidays
Menu 95/175 € – *(dinner only and Sunday lunch) (booking advisable)*
• Modern French • Elegant •
In the same building as the famed delicatessen, it is no surprise that the first floor restaurant prides itself on the quantity of its raw ingredients. The classically modern cuisine shuns any hint of gimmickry, centring instead on skilful craftsmanship and intense flavours. The excellent service is equally convincing.
➜ Langoustine, Rose, Avocado, Haselnuss. Taube, Liebstöckel, Rote Bete. Lammrücken, Curry, Kichererbse, Brin d'Amour.

XXX **Atelier** – Hotel Bayerischer Hof 88 AC 🚗

£3 £3 *Promenadeplatz 2* ✉ *80333* – Ⓜ *Marienplatz* – ℰ *(089)* Plan: **G2**
2 12 07 43 – *www.bayerischerhof.de* – *Closed 24 December-10 January
and Sunday-Monday*
Menu 135/180 € – *(dinner only)*
• Creative French • Elegant • Design •
Atelier offers the perfect marriage of Axel Vervoordt's classy, minimalist yet
warm interior, pleasant service and excellent, multi-faceted food. This is carefully planned down to the smallest detail and skilfully executed. Modern elements from Japanese and other cuisines successfully complement the classic
basis.
→ Schottischer Loch Duart Lachs mit Miso gebeizt, Shiso rot und grün,
Essigkarotten, Mango und Dashi. Wagyu Short Rib, Sellerie, Zwiebeln,
Lauch und geflämmtes Rindermark. Exotische Früchte mit Vanille, Kokos
und Amaranth-Ganache.

XX **Les Deux** 88 🛋 AC

£3 *Maffeistr. 3a (1st floor)* ✉ *80333* – Ⓜ *Marienplatz* Plan: **G2**
– ℰ *(089) 7 10 40 73 73* – *www.lesdeux-muc.de* – *Closed Sunday and Bank
Holidays*
Menu 48 € (weekday lunch)/95 € – Carte 71/135 € – *(booking advisable)*
• Modern French • Friendly • Fashionable •
Les Deux in question are Fabrice Kieffer and Johann Rappenglück, now running
their own brasserie-style restaurant in what used to be the Dukatz. The food on
offer downstairs is simple but excellent, while on the first floor you can enjoy
fine, modern French cuisine and over 400 different wines. There is also an
exemplary front-of-house team. What more could you want?
→ Gebratene Entenleber, Sellerie, Ziegenkäse, Balsamico 25 Jahre, Haselnuss. Black Cod, Erdnüsse, Rettich, Alge, Englischer Curry. Brust und Keule
von der Barbarie Ente, Blaukraut, Purple Curry, Walnuss.

XX **Le Barestovino** 88 🛋 AC ↔

🅐 *Thierschstr. 35* ✉ *80538* – Ⓜ *Lehel* – ℰ *(089)* Plan I: **C3**
23 70 83 55 – *www.barestovino.de* – *Closed Sunday-Monday*
Menu 37/64 € – Carte 37/52 € – *(dinner only)*
• Classic French • Bistro •
Owner Joel Bousquet runs a friendly operation here, in both the modern restaurant and the Le Bouchon wine bar. The cuisine is similarly unpretentious – it includes delicious dishes such as mi-cuit salmon with fennel and potato mash, all
accompanied by French wines, making this a delightful dining experience.

XX **Pfistermühle** – Hotel Platzl 🛋 🚗

Pfisterstr. 4 ✉ *80331* – Ⓜ *Marienplatz* – ℰ *(089)* Plan: **G2**
23 70 38 65 – *www.pfistermuehle.de* – *Closed Sunday*
Menu 59 € – Carte 40/65 €
• Country • Rustic • Cosy •
A separate entrance leads into this historic hostelry that started life as a ducal
mill in 1573. Stylish Bavarian bar crowned by a vaulted ceiling.

XX **Garden-Restaurant** – Hotel Bayerischer Hof 🛋 AC 🚗

Promenadeplatz 2 ✉ *80333* – Ⓜ *Marienplatz* – ℰ *(089)* Plan: **G2**
2 12 09 93 – *www.bayerischerhof.de*
Menu 39 € (lunch)/74 € – Carte 49/96 € – *(booking advisable)*
• International • Friendly • Design •
Belgian designer Axel Vervoordt has given this restaurant a very particular look.
The industrial-style conservatory design creates a setting reminiscent of an
artist's studio.

XX **Limoni**

Amalienstr. 38 ✉ 80799 – Ⓜ Universität Plan I: **B2**
– ℰ (089) 28 80 60 29 – www.limoni-ristorante.com
– Closed Sunday
Menu 50/64 € – Carte 40/53 € – *(dinner only)*
• Italian • Elegant • Friendly •
At this restaurant, the decor is minimalist yet welcoming, the service attentive
and responsive, and the Italian cuisine fresh and ambitious. Go for a classic such
as vitello tonnato or try one of the dishes from the frequently changing menu.

XX **Blauer Bock** – Hotel Blauer Bock

Sebastiansplatz 9 ✉ 80331 – Ⓜ Marienplatz – ℰ (089) Plan: **G3**
45 22 23 33 – www.restaurant-blauerbock.de – Closed Sunday-Monday
and Bank Holidays
Menu 19 € (lunch)/83 € (dinner) – Carte 42/90 €
• International • Chic • Fashionable •
A chic, modern restaurant with clean lines. It offers an appealing French and
regional menu including pan-fried ducks' liver and braised calves' cheeks.

XX **Halali**

Schönfeldstr. 22 ✉ 80539 – Ⓜ Odeonsplatz – ℰ (089) Plan: **H1**
28 59 09 – www.restaurant-halali.de – Closed Saturday lunch, Sunday and
Bank Holidays; October-Christmas: Saturday lunch, Sunday lunch
Menu 25 € (weekday lunch)/66 € – Carte 37/70 € – *(booking advisable)*
• Classic cuisine • Cosy •
The sophisticated restaurant in this 19C guesthouse has almost become an
institution already. The dark wood panelling and lovely decoration has created
a cosy atmosphere.

XX **Tian**

Frauenstr. 4 ✉ 80469 – Ⓜ Isartor – ℰ (089) Plan: **G3**
8 85 65 67 12 – www.taste-tian.com – Closed Sunday-Monday lunch and
Bank Holidays
Menu 19 € (lunch)/49 € (dinner) – Carte 40/50 €
• Vegetarian • Fashionable •
Right on the Viktualienmarkt you will find the first Tian spin-off restaurant in
Germany serving a range of refined and skilfully executed vegetarian dishes.
There is also a trendy bar with a pretty interior courtyard. Reduced lunchtime
menu.

XX **Nymphenburger Hof**

Nymphenburger Str. 24 ✉ 80335 – Ⓜ Maillingerstr. Plan I: **A2**
– ℰ (089) 1 23 38 30 – www.nymphenburgerhof.de – Closed Sunday-
Monday and Bank Holidays
Menu 29 € (weekday lunch)/75 € – Carte 43/74 € – *(booking advisable)*
• International • Friendly •
The Austrian inspired cuisine tastes just as good on the lovely terrace as it does
in the friendly restaurant. Live piano music is also played on some evenings.

XX **Pageou**

Kardinal-Faulhaber-Str. 10 (1st floor) ✉ 80333 Plan: **G2**
– Ⓜ Marienplatz – ℰ (089) 24 23 13 10 – www.pageou.de – Closed
Sunday-Monday and Bank Holidays
Menu 47 € (lunch)/108 € (dinner) – Carte 69/81 € – *(booking advisable)*
• Mediterranean cuisine • Cosy •
Behind Pageou's magnificent historical façade, the clean lines, beautiful mate-
rials and colours of the interior provide the perfect setting for the modern cui-
sine. The quiet courtyard terrace is also very appealing.

GERMANY - MUNICH

XX **Les Cuisiniers**
Plan I: **C3**
Reitmorstr. 21 ⊠ *80538 –* ⓜ *Lehel – ℰ (089)*
*23 70 98 90 – www.lescuisiniers.de – Closed Saturday lunch, Sunday and
Bank Holidays*
Menu 25 € (lunch)/98 € (dinner) – Carte 36/69 € – *(booking advisable)*
• Classic French • Bistro •
The atmosphere, service and food here are pleasantly uncomplicated – just as
you would imagine a French bistro should be. French and half-French respecti-
vely, the chef and owner serve authentic French food that is chalked up on a
blackboard menu.

XX **Vecchia Lanterna** – Hotel Domus
Plan: **H1**
St.-Anna-Str. 31 ⊠ *80538 –* ⓜ *Lehel – ℰ (089)*
81892096 – www.vecchia-lanterna.de – Closed Sunday-Monday
Menu 49/80 € – Carte 46/67 €
• Italian • Elegant • Fashionable •
After years working in Germering, Mirka Otta and Antonio Denami have now
moved to the heart of Munich. In this elegantly modern restaurant with its
quiet rear courtyard terrace they offer classic Mediterranean cuisine including
an interesting lunch menu accompanied by wines mainly from Italy.

XX **Jin**
Plan: **H2**
Kanalstr. 14 ⊠ *80538 –* ⓜ *Isartor – ℰ (089) 21 94 99 70*
– www.restaurant-jin.de – Closed Monday
Menu 66/96 €
– Carte 43/69 € – *(July-September: Tuesday-Friday dinner only)*
• Asian • Minimalist • Elegant •
Hao Jin combines influences from various South-East Asian countries including
China and Japan in his creative cuisine. Guests can choose from two menus, but
the chef is always pleased to respond to individual wishes. The contents of the
fish tank (including prawns and blue fin tuna) are particularly appetising.

XX **Matsuhisa Munich** – Hotel Mandarin Oriental
Plan: **H2**
Neuturmstr. 1 ⊠ *80331 –* ⓜ *Isartor – ℰ (089)*
290 98 1875 – www.mandarinoriental.com
Menu 95/138 € – Carte 77/113 €
• Asian • Fashionable •
This elegant, minimalist-style restaurant on the first floor offers Asian cuisine
from Nobu Matsuhisa. His dishes are simple yet sophisticated, the produce
good and fresh, and you can rely on the presence of classics such as black cod.

XX **Schwarzreiter** – Hotel Vier Jahrszeiten Kempinski
Plan: **H2**
Maximilianstr. 17 ⊠ *80539 –* ⓜ *Lehel – ℰ (089)*
*21 25 21 25 – www.schwarzreiter-muenchen.de – Closed August and
Sunday-Monday*
Menu 92/121 € – *(dinner only)*
• Modern cuisine • Elegant •
Schwarzreiter offers modern Bavarian cuisine in an elegant, minimalist-style
interior. The food served by the friendly front-of-house team includes sheatfish
and cabbage, as well as breaded fried chicken with morel mushrooms, carrots,
farrotto and chicken ragout.

XX **Rocca Riviera**
Plan: **G1**
Wittelsbacherplatz 2 ⊠ *80331 –* ⓜ *Odeonsplatz*
*– ℰ (089) 28724421 – www.roccariviera.com – Closed Saturday lunch,
Sunday*
Menu 30 € (lunch)/100 € – Carte 44/80 €
• Mediterranean cuisine • Fashionable • Chic •
Rocca Riviera is a relaxed and stylish restaurant with a pleasant atmosphere not
far from the Odeonsplatz. It serves Mediterranean-French fusion cuisine on a
sharing plate basis, as well as meat and fish from the charcoal grill.

GERMANY - MUNICH

Colette Tim Raue

Klenzestr. 72 ✉ *80469* – **⓪** *Frauenhoferstraße* — Plan I: **B3**
*– 𝒞 (089) 23 00 25 55 – www.brasseriecolette.de – Closed Monday-
Tuesday*
Carte 36/62 €
• French • Brasserie •

Tim Raue really has his finger on the pulse with his new culinary concept at
Colette. It is as relaxed as a French brasserie, friendly with pleasantly informal
service, and offers good food at great prices. The first class ingredients speak
for themselves in dishes such as *boeuf bourguignon* with speck, mushrooms
and shallots.

Weinhaus Neuner

Herzogspitalstr. 8 ✉ *80331* – **⓪** *Karlsplatz* – 𝒞 *(089)* — Plan: **F2**
2603954 – www.weinhaus-neuner.de
Carte 36/73 € – *(booking advisable)*
• Traditional cuisine • Traditional décor •

With its cross-vaulted ceiling, herringbone parquet and wood panelling this old
restaurant has lost nothing of its traditional charm. The food is just what you
would expect from an upmarket Munich restaurant – try the flaky pastry crust
chicken fricassee pie.

Geisel's Vinothek – Hotel Excelsior

Schützenstr. 11 ✉ *80335* – **⓪** *Hauptbahnhof* – 𝒞 *(089)* — Plan: **E2**
5 51 37 71 40 – www.excelsior-hotel.de – Closed Sunday lunch
Menu 20 € (lunch)/42 € – Carte 28/60 €
• Country • Rustic •

The Geisel family offer a great alternative in their Königshof restaurant with the
focus on gourmet cuisine. Perfect for those who prefer a lighter regional or
Mediterranean fare accompanied by a glass of good wine.

Délice La Brasserie – Hotel Sofitel Munich Bayerpost

Bayerstr. 12 ✉ *80335* – **⓪** *Hauptbahnhof* – 𝒞 *(089)*
5 99 48 29 62 – www.delice-la-brasserie.com — Plan: **E2**
Carte 51/70 €
• French • Brasserie • Minimalist •

With its smart decor and incredibly high ceilings, Délice La Brasserie strikes a
perfect balance between casual urban eatery and historic setting. The international cuisine has a distinct French flavour.

Le Stollberg

Stollbergstr. 2 ✉ *80539* – **⓪** *Isartor* – 𝒞 *(089)* — Plan: **H2**
24 24 34 50 – www.lestollberg.de – Closed Sunday
Menu 45 € – Carte 40/61 €
• Classic cuisine • Bistro • Elegant •

After spells at several good restaurants, the charming Anette Huber has started
her own venture with this modern restaurant. The classic, French and seasonal
cuisine includes offerings such as calves' kidneys in red wine sauce with mashed
potato. Good value lunch. Open throughout the day on Saturdays.

Gesellschaftsraum

Bräuhausstr. 8 ✉ *80331* – **⓪** *Isartor* – 𝒞 *(089)* — Plan: **H2**
*55 07 77 93 – www.der-gesellschaftsraum.de – Closed Saturday lunch and
Sunday*
Menu 56/85 € – Carte 49/63 €
• Creative • Trendy • Fashionable •

If you like things casual, urban and trendy, you will find the atmosphere in this
restaurant in the centre of the old town to your taste. The food is creative,
modern and ambitious, and the service is pleasantly relaxed.

GERMANY - MUNICH

X   Brenner Operngrill   ⌂

Maximilianstr. 15 ✉ 80539 – Ⓜ Lehel – 𝒞 (089)   Plan: **H2**
4 52 28 80 – www.brennergrill.de
Carte 24/108 €
• Grills • Trendy •

A place to see and be seen... The bar, café and restaurant housed in this impressive hall with its high-vaulted ceiling (once the stables of this great residence) are a hot item on the Munich culinary scene. Homemade pasta, as well as meat and fish served hot from the open grill in the centre of the room.

X   TOSHI   🅰🅒

Wurzerstr. 18 ✉ 80539 – Ⓜ Lehel – 𝒞 (089)   Plan: **H2**
25 54 69 42 – www.restaurant-toshi.de – Closed Saturday lunch, Sunday and Bank Holidays lunch
Menu 80/140 € – Carte 30/101 €
• Japanese • Minimalist •

It is just a short hop from the ritzy Maximilianstraße to this authentic Japanese restaurant. The menu – as characteristic as the minimalist design – offers fresh Far Eastern dishes. These include sushi, teppanyaki and 'pan-Pacific' cuisine.

X   KOI   ⌂ � 🅰🅒

Wittelsbacherplatz 1 ✉ 80333 – Ⓜ Odeonsplatz   Plan: **G1**
– 𝒞 (089) 89 08 19 26 – www.koi-restaurant.de – Closed Christmas, Sunday and Bank Holidays lunch
Carte 28/153 €
• Japanese • Friendly • Bistro •

You can look forward to an interesting mix of visual and culinary styles on the two floors at Koi. The kitchens produce a combination of Japanese and European cuisine, including sushi and Robata-grilled meats, all based on fresh produce.

X   Gandl   ⌂

St.-Anna-Platz 1 ✉ 80538 – Ⓜ Lehel – 𝒞 (089)   Plan: **H1**
29 16 25 25 – www.gandl.de – Closed Sunday and Monday dinner
Menu 59 € (dinner) – Carte 35/54 €
• Classic cuisine • Cosy • Bistro •

Gandl is located in a former colonial goods store, which has retained some of its old shelving and still sells one or two items. The food ranges from classic French to international. If you are here in summer don't miss the terrace overlooking the square.

X   Little London   ⌂

Tal 31 ✉ 80331 – Ⓜ Marienplatz – 𝒞 (089) 22 23 94 70   Plan: **H2**
– www.little-london.de – Closed 2 weeks early August
Carte 36/95 € – *(dinner only)*
• Grills • Friendly •

This lively steakhouse at the Isartor is fronted by a large, classic bar with a great selection of gins and whiskeys and makes a great place to enjoy some top-quality meat. The Nebraska steaks, but also the roast topside of veal and shoulder of lamb, are in particular demand.

X   Kleinschmecker   ⌂

Sebastiansplatz 3 ✉ 80331 – Ⓜ Marienplatz – 𝒞 (089)   Plan: **G3**
26 94 91 20 – www.restaurant-kleinschmecker.de – Closed 1-15 January, Sunday and Bank Holidays
Menu 57/85 € – Carte 45/63 €
• Creative • Fashionable •

This friendly, fashionable restaurant close to the Viktualienmarkt is pleasantly informal. The food is creative and sensitively combines good, fresh produce and pleasing tastes. Additional midday menu at lunchtimes.

Cafe Luitpold

Brienner Str. 11 ✉ 80333 – Ⓜ Odeonsplatz – ✆ (089) 2 42 87 50 – www.cafe-luitpold.de – Closed Sunday dinner and Monday dinner except Bank Holidays Plan: **G1**

Menu 39/69 € (dinner) – Carte 27/58 €

• Traditional cuisine • Friendly • Traditional décor •

Guests can sit in the lively coffee house atmosphere of Cafe Leopold and enjoy its good, fresh homemade cakes. There is also a museum on the first floor from which you can see right into the bakery – make sure you try the tarts, pralines and other delicacies!

Ayingers – Hotel Platzl

Sparkassenstr. 10 ✉ 80331 – ✆ (089) 23 70 36 66 – www.ayingers.de Plan: **G2**

Carte 21/46 €

• Country • Cosy •

In keeping with its tavern style, classic Bavarian fare is the staple on the menu here, although you will also find locally hunted game and there is always a pretzel to start with! Don't miss the barrel tapping ritual at 5pm every day.

Schneider Bräuhaus

Tal 7 ✉ 80331 – Ⓜ Isartor – ✆ (089) 2 90 13 80 – www.schneider-brauhaus.de Plan: **G2**

Carte 18/47 €

• Country • Cosy •

This Bavarian hostelry is like something out of a picture book. People from Munich come here for the 'Kronfleisch' or skirt of beef – just one of the many specialities from the restaurant's own butchery. Squeezing together in the rustic dining areas is also traditional!

Spatenhaus an der Oper

Residenzstr. 12 ✉ 80333 – Ⓜ Marienplatz – ✆ (089) 2 90 70 60 – www.kuffler.de Plan: **G2**

Carte 29/69 €

• Country • Traditional décor •

The attractive rooms in this townhouse, opposite the Bavarian State Opera, exude rural charm. On the ground floor the food is local; on the first-floor the menu is international.

Altes Hackerhaus

Sendlinger Str. 14 ✉ 80331 – Ⓜ Marienplatz – ✆ (089) 2 60 50 26 – www.hackerhaus.de Plan: **G2**

Carte 22/52 €

• Country • Cosy • Romantic •

A very cared-for and well-run rustic restaurant where Bavarian delicacies are served in warm and homely rooms. There is a beautiful covered interior courtyard.

ENVIRONS PLAN I

The Westin Grand

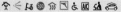

Arabellastr. 6 ✉ 81925 – Ⓜ Arabellapark – ✆ (089) 92640 – www.westingrandmunich.com Plan: **D2**

599 rm – †139/650 € ††139/650 € – ☕ 29 € – 28 suites

• Business • Luxury • Contemporary •

This business and conference address is the largest hotel is Munich and also has the largest day spa in the city. There is a great roof lounge for the Westin Club rooms and suites, as well as pretty alternatives in the form of comfortable, modern Bavarian rooms. Paulaner's offers traditional, tavern-style charm.

GERMANY - MUNICH

Palace 🔧 🛏 🛎 AC ⚙ 🚗

Trogerstr. 21 ✉ *81675 –* 🚇 *Prinzregentenplatz*   Plan: **C3**
– ☎ *(089) 41 97 10 – www.hotel-muenchen-palace.de*
70 rm ⌷ – 🛏155/407 € 🛏🛏185/478 € – 4 suites
• Traditional • Classic • Elegant •

This tasteful, impeccably run hotel includes many musicians amongst its regulars. The natural tones and parquet floors combine to create a warm and friendly atmosphere. Pleasant garden and roof terrace. This restaurant serves classic international cuisine.

INNSIDE Parkstadt Schwabing 🔧 🛎 AC ⚙ 🚗

Mies-van-der-Rohe-Str. 10 ✉ *80807 –* 🚇 *Nordfriedhof*   Plan: **C1**
– ☎ *(089) 35 40 80 – www.innside.com*
160 rm – 🛏109/199 € 🛏🛏119/209 € – ⌷ 22 €
• Business • Functional •

Designed by famous architect Helmut Jahn, this hotel enjoys a convenient location close to the striking HighLight Towers. The whole building is beautifully light, with clean modern lines. This bistro-style restaurant decorated with its modern white interior serves international cuisine.

🏠 Freisinger Hof 🛎 ⚙ 🚗

Oberföhringer Str. 191 ✉ *81925 –* ☎ *(089) 95 23 02*   Plan: **D1**
– www.freisinger-hof.de – Closed 28 December - early January
51 rm ⌷ – 🛏125/145 € 🛏🛏156/170 €
• Country house • Cosy •

The hotel annexe which has been added to this historical inn offers comfortable country-style rooms. The small lobby is bright and welcoming. Enjoy tasty regional food in this cosy inn dating from 1875. Boiled beef and other classic Austrian dishes served.
🍴 **Freisinger Hof** – See restaurant listing

✕✕✕ Tantris 🕸 🌡 AC ⇔ P

 Johann-Fichte-Str. 7 ✉ *80805 –* 🚇 *Dietlindenstr.*   Plan: **B1**
– ☎ *(089) 3 61 95 90 – www.tantris.de – Closed 2 weeks early January,*
Sunday-Monday and Bank Holidays
Menu 95 € (weekday lunch)/210 € – Carte 81/175 € – *(booking advisable)*
• Classic French • Vintage •

Tantris is quite simply THE place to eat with its near legendary 1970s-style and Hans Haas' sublime, product-based classic cuisine. The cult setting and fine dining are accompanied by a well-practised, friendly and professional front-of-house team, as well as good wine recommendations.
→ Konfierte Crevetten mit cremiger Zitronenpolenta und Röstsud. Taubenbrust und Gänseleber mit Radicchiorisotto und Portwein Verjus. Mango-Kokos Panna Cotta mit Schokolade und Haselnuss.

✕✕ EssZimmer 🕸 🛗 AC 🚗

Am Olympiapark 1 (3th floor) (at BMW Welt) ✉ *80809*   Plan: **A1**
– ☎ *(089) 3 58 99 18 14 – www.esszimmer-muenchen.de – Closed 3 weeks*
January, August, Sunday-Monday and Bank Holidays
Menu 100/190 € – *(dinner only) (booking advisable)*
• Modern French • Chic • Cosy •

There is a double pleasure on offer at EssZimmer: a view of the impressive shipping hall at BMW Welt with its smart exhibition pieces, as well as the chance to enjoy Bobby Bräuer's delicate cuisine. Dine in the elegant, modern setting with a choice of two set menus. Free parking.
→ Bretonische Langoustine, Buttermilch, Bergamotte, grüner Spargel. Atlantik Steinbutt, Ochsenbacke, gelbe Pflaume, Pfifferlinge. Salzwiesenlamm, Kichererbse, Paprika, Garam Masala.
Bavarie – See restaurant listing

GERMANY - MUNICH

Acquarello (Mario Gamba)

Mühlbaurstr. 36 ✉ *81677 –* ⓜ *Böhmerwaldplatz*   Plan: **D2**
– 𝒞 (089) 4 70 48 48 – www.acquarello.com – Closed 1-3 January and
Saturday lunch, Sunday lunch and Bank Holidays lunch
Menu 49 € (weekday lunch)/119 € – Carte 71/101 €
• Mediterranean cuisine • Friendly • Mediterranean décor •
Whether Mario Gamba's cuisine is Italian with a French influence or French with Italian roots is largely irrelevant when it comes to tasting his delicious dishes made from only the finest quality ingredients. Mario has now been joined by his son, Massimiliano, who assists his father as part of the excellent front-of-house team.
→ Vitello Tonnato. Feigentortelli. Weißweinschaum, gebratene Gänseleber und Reduktion von Cassis. Rinderschmorbraten, Barolosauce, Selleriepüree.

Bogenhauser Hof

Ismaninger Str. 85 ✉ *81675 –* ⓜ *Böhmerwaldplatz*   Plan: **C2**
– 𝒞 (089) 98 55 86 – www.bogenhauser-hof.de – Closed 24 December-
8 January, Sunday and Bank Holidays
Menu 45/119 € – Carte 48/78 € – *(booking advisable)*
• Classic cuisine • Traditional décor • Cosy •
This elegant yet comfortable restaurant, housed in a building dating back to 1825, serves classic cuisine prepared using the finest ingredients, which explains why it has so many regulars. It also has a leafy garden complete with mature chestnut trees.

Geisels Werneckhof

Werneckstr. 11 ✉ *80802 –* ⓜ *Münchner Freiheit*   Plan: **C2**
– 𝒞 (089) 38 87 95 68 – www.geisels-werneckhof.de – Closed
24 December-4 January, end July-mid August and Sunday-Monday
Menu 130/160 €
– Carte 95/130 € – (dinner only and Sunday lunch) (booking essential)
• Creative • Cosy • Traditional décor •
The cuisine prepared by Tohru Nakamura is anything but "off the peg". The finesse and fluency with which he combines top-quality produce, classic principles and Japanese influences to create elegant, creative dishes are genuinely impressive and clearly bear his inimitable signature.
→ Seeforelle, Frühlingskräuter und junge Zwiebeln. Lozère Kalb, Morcheln, Räucheraal und Kalbsschwanzkrokette. Kirschblüte, Salzmandel und 20-jähriger Mirin.

Käfer Schänke

Prinzregentenstr. 73 (1st floor) ✉ *81675*   Plan: **C3**
– ⓜ *Prinzregentenplatz – 𝒞 (089) 4168247 – www.feinkost-kaefer.de*
– Closed Sunday and Bank Holidays
Menu 40 € (lunch)/119 € (dinner)
– Carte 59/93 € – (booking essential at dinner)
• International • Cosy •
In this popular restaurant with its 12 highly individual dining rooms the international menu is determined by the availability of the best quality produce. The delicatessen sells a range of fine foods.

Freisinger Hof – Hotel Freisinger Hof

Oberföhringer Str. 189 ✉ *81925 – 𝒞 (089) 95 23 02*   Plan: **D1**
– www.freisinger-hof.de – Closed 28 December-9 January
Carte 35/58 €
• Country • Inn •
This is just what you imagine a traditional Bavarian restaurant to be like. Dating back to 1875, it stands just outside the city gates and serves typical Bavarian and Austrian cuisine. Dishes include Krosser saddle of suckling pig, and Vienna-style beef boiled in broth.

XX **Hippocampus**

Mühlbaurstr. 5 ⌧ 81677 – ⓜ Prinzregentenplatz   Plan: **C3**
*– 𝒞 (089) 47 58 55 – www.hippocampus-restaurant.de – Closed Monday
and Saturday lunch*
Menu 30 € (weekday lunch)/59 € – Carte 48/62 €
• Italian • Elegant •

Hippocampus offers friendly service, an informal atmosphere and ambitious
Italian cuisine. Beautiful fixtures and fittings help create the elegant yet warm
and welcoming interior.

XX **Bibulus**

Siegfriedstr. 11 ⌧ 80803 – ⓜ Münchner Freiheit   Plan: **B1**
*– 𝒞 (089) 39 64 47 – www.bibulus-ristorante.de – Closed Saturday lunch
and Sunday*
Menu 20 € (weekday lunch)/72 € – Carte 38/63 €
• Italian • Elegant •

It says something when a restaurant is popular with the locals, and the people
of Schwabing clearly appreciate the uncomplicated and flavoursome Italian
food. It is especially nice outside in the little square under the plane trees. Charming service.

X **Acetaia**

*Nymphenburger Str. 215 (by A2) ⌧ 80639 – 𝒞 (089) 13 92 90 77
– www.restaurant-acetaia.de – Closed Saturday lunch*
Menu 29 € (lunch)/95 € – Carte 47/69 €
• Italian • Cosy •

This friendly restaurant with its Art Nouveau decor offers Italian cuisine and the
best espresso in the city. The olive oil and balsamic vinegar which gave the
place its name are also very good. Attractive terrace.

X **Vinaiolo**

Steinstr. 42 ⌧ 81667 – ⓜ Ostbahnhof – 𝒞 (089)   Plan: **C3**
48 95 03 56 – www.vinaiolo.de – Closed Saturday lunch
Menu 27 € (lunch)/52 € – Carte 40/62 € – (bookings advisable at dinner)
• Italian • Cosy • Friendly •

Sample a taste of the 'dolce vita' in this restaurant. The service exudes southern
charm, the food could not be better, even in Italy, and the lunchtime menu is
very reasonably priced. The image of authentic Italy is completed by fixtures
and fittings from an old grocer's shop in Trieste.

X **M Belleville**
☺

Fallmerayerstr. 16 ⌧ 80796 – ⓜ Hohenzollernpl.   Plan: **B2**
*– 𝒞 (089) 30 74 76 11 – www.m-belleville.com – Closed Saturday lunch,
Sunday-Monday*
Menu 37 €
• Classic French • Bistro • Brasserie •

A little bit of Paris in Munich, this charming, lively bistro offers some excellent
food. The young, relaxed front-of-house team serves such delights as *rôti de
porc* with mash and calves' cheeks in braised in red wine, followed perhaps by
a classic *riz au lait caramel* for dessert. You will also find some rare natural wines
and regular live music.

X **Le Cézanne**
☺

Konradstr. 1 ⌧ 80801 – ⓜ Giselastr. – 𝒞 (089) 39 18 05   Plan: **B2**
*– www.le-cezanne.de – Closed during Easter, 3 weeks early August and
Monday*
Menu 45 € – Carte 32/59 € – (dinner only) (booking advisable)
• French • Family • Friendly •

In this friendly corner restaurant the chef cooks dishes from his French homeland. You can choose from the blackboard or the small menu of classic dishes. In
summer, enjoy your meal outdoors or by the open, glass façade.

✗ Restaurant N° 15   😵 🍽

Neureutherstr. 15 ✉ 80331 – Ⓜ Josephspl. – ☏ (089)   Plan: **B2**
39 99 36 – www.restaurant-n15.com – Closed Sunday-Monday and bank
Holidays
Menu 76/120 € – Carte 65/85 € – *(dinner only)*
• Classic cuisine • Elegant • Family •
Diners at N° 15 enjoy French cuisine with a modern touch and a fine selection of
Bordeaux and Burgundies that will delight wine lovers. If you can, take a table
on the pretty terrace under the mature trees.

✗ Atelier Gourmet   🍽

Rablstr. 37 ✉ 81669 – Ⓜ Ostbahnhof – ☏ (089)   Plan: **C3**
48 72 20 – www.ateliergourmet.de – Closed Sunday
Menu 39/75 € – Carte 49/55 € – *(dinner only) (booking advisable)*
• Classic French • Bistro •
Small, intimate, lively and popular, Atelier Gourmet is quite simply a great little
restaurant. The food is fresh, delicious and good value for money thanks to
chefs Duchardt and Bousquet. It is served in a casual, friendly atmosphere with
efficient service and good wine recommendations from the female owner. Try
the capon and duck crépinette.

✗ Bavarie – Restaurant Esszimmer   🍽 ⅍ 🅰🅒 🚗

Am Olympiapark 1 (2nd floor) (at BMW Welt) ✉ 80809   Plan: **A1**
– ☏ (089) 3 58 99 18 18 – www.feinkost-kaefer.de – Closed 2 weeks August,
Sunday dinner and Bank Holidays dinner
Menu 33 € – Carte 41/51 €
• International • Bistro • Fashionable •
Grounded in the principles of regionality and sustainability, the Bavarie concept
on offer here creates a combination of Bavarian and French cuisine based on
local produce. Dishes include goose liver crème brûlée and Gutshof Polting
lamb. The terrace offers views of the Olympia Park and Tower.

✗ Rüen Thai   😵 🅰🅒

Kazmairstr. 58 ✉ 80339 – Ⓜ Messegelände – ☏ (089)   Plan: **A3**
50 32 39 – www.rueen-thai.de – Closed 31 July-20 August
Menu 49/99 €
– Carte 29/55 € – *(Thursday-Sunday and Bank Holidays dinner only)*
• Thai • Family • Bourgeois •
True to his roots, Anuchit Chetha has dedicated himself to the cuisine of southern Thailand, preparing a range of dishes including gung pla and nüe san
kua, as well as a finger food menu. In addition to specialising in interesting
spice combinations, he is also passionate about wine – the restaurant boasts a
cellar containing a number of real rarities.

✗ Huber   🍽 ♻

Newtonstr. 13 ✉ 81679 – Ⓜ Richard Strauss Str.   Plan: **C2**
– ☏ (089) 985152 – www.huber-restaurant.de – Closed Saturday lunch,
Sunday-Monday
Menu 29 € (lunch)/95 € (dinner) – Carte 49/65 €
• International • Fashionable •
This appealing, modern restaurant offers friendly service and quality contempo-
rary cuisine created by a young chef. The selection of Austrian wines is particu-
larly good. The interior is by a Munich designer.

GREECE
ELLÁDA

ATHENS

→ **AREA:**
131 944 km²
(50 944 sq mi).

→ **POPULATION:**
10 919 459 inhabitants.
Density = 83 per km².

→ **CAPITAL:** Athens.

→ **CURRENCY:** Euro (€).

→ **GOVERNMENT:**
Parliamentary republic
(since 1974). Member of European
Union since 1981.

→ **LANGUAGE:** Greek.

→ **PUBLIC HOLIDAYS:**
New Year's Day (1 Jan); Epiphany
(6 Jan); Orthodox Shrove Monday
(late Feb-Mar); Independence Day
(25 Mar); Orthodox Good Friday
(late Mar/Apr); Orthodox Easter
Monday (late Mar/Apr); Labor Day
(1 May); Pentecost Sunday (late
May/June); Orthodox Whit Monday
(late May/June); Assumption of
the Virgin Mary (15 Aug); Ochi Day
(28 Oct); Christmas Day (25 Dec);
Boxing Day (26 Dec).

→ **LOCAL TIME:**
GMT+2 hours in winter and GMT
+3 hours in summer.

→ **CLIMATE:**
Temperate Mediterranean, with
mild winters and hot, sunny
summers (Athens: January 10°C;
July 27°C).

→ **EMERGENCY:**
Police ✆ **100**; Medical Assistance
✆ **166**; Fire Brigade ✆ **199**;
Tourist Police ✆ **171**.
(Dialing **112** within any EU country
will redirect your call and contact
the emergency services.)

→ **ELECTRICITY:**
230 volts AC, 50Hz; 2 round pin
sockets.

→ **FORMALITIES:**
Travellers from the European Union
(EU), Switzerland, Iceland and
the main countries of North and
South America need a national
identity card or passport (America:
passport required) to visit Greece
for less than three months (tourism
or business purpose). For visitors
from other countries a visa may be
required, in addition to a passport,
especially for those wishing to
stay for longer than three months.
We advise you to check with your
embassy before travelling.

ATHENS
ATHÍNA
Population: 664 046

Stefanos Kyriazis/Fotolia.com

Inventing democracy, the theatre and the Olympic Games... and planting the seeds of philosophy and Western Civilisation – Athens was central to all of these, a city that became a byword for glory and learning, a place whose golden reputation could inspire such awe that centuries later just the mention of its name was enough to turn people misty-eyed. It's a magical place, built upon eight hills and plains, with a history stretching back at least 3,000 years. Its short but highly productive golden age resulted in the architectural glory of The Acropolis, while the likes of Plato, Aristotle and Socrates were in the business of changing the mindset of society.

The Acropolis still dominates Athens and can be seen peeking through alleyways and turnings all over the city. Beneath it lies a teeming metropolis, part urban melting pot, part über-buzzy neighbourhood. Plaka, below the Acropolis, is the old quarter, and the most visited, a mixture of great charm and cheap gift shops. North and west, Monastiraki and Psiri have become trendy zones; to the east, Syntagma and Kolonaki are notably modern and smart, home to the Greek parliament and the famous. The most northerly districts of central Athens are Omonia and Exarcheia, distinguished by their rugged appearance and steeped in history; much of the life in these parts is centred round the polytechnic and the central marketplace.

ATHENS IN...

→ **ONE DAY**
Acropolis (Parthenon), Agora and Temple of Hephaestus, Plaka.

→ **TWO DAYS**
Kolonaki, National Archaeological Museum, Filopappou Hill.

→ **THREE DAYS**
Monastiraki flea-market (Sunday), Benaki Museum, Technopolis, National Gardens, Lykavittos Hill.

PRACTICAL INFORMATION

ARRIVAL-DEPARTURE

 Athens International Airport is 33km east of the city. Metro Line 3 takes you to Monastiraki.

 Piraeus Port is the third largest port in the Mediterranean and is 10km southwest of Athens. Metro Line 1 takes you to Monastiraki.

GETTING AROUND

The most sensible way of getting around town is by the metro; buses and trolley-buses run an excellent service but are hampered by traffic. Carnets of 10 tickets are available from newsstands, OASA booths and kiosks, and at metro or subway stations.

Be sure to have some Euros in your wallet when you arrive, as tickets for all forms of public transport can only be paid for in cash; cards are not accepted by either ticket agents or ticket machines.

CALENDAR HIGHLIGHTS

March-April
Candlelit procession up Lykavittos Hill to the chapel of Agios Georgios.

May-September
Greek folk dances at Dora Stratou Theatre.

June
European Music Day, Rockwave Festival (rock music).

June-August
Hellenic Festival.

August
Nights Under The Full Moon (moonlit classical performances at monuments and archaeological sites).

EATING OUT

In recent times, a smart wave of restaurants has hit the city and, with many chefs training abroad before returning home, this is a good time to eat out in the shadow of The Acropolis. If you want the full experience, dine with the locals rather than the tourists and make your reservation for late evening, as Greeks rarely go out for dinner before 10pm. The trend towards a more eclectic restaurant scene now means that you can find everything from classical French and Italian cuisine to Asian and Moroccan dishes, and even sushi. Modern tavernas offer good attention to detail, but this doesn't mean they're replacing the wonderfully traditional favourites. These older tavernas, along with mezedopoleia, are the backbone of Greek dining, and most visitors wouldn't think their trip was complete without eating in one; often the waiter will just tell you what's cooking that day - and you're usually very welcome to go into the kitchen and make your selection. Greece is a country where it is customary to tip good service; ten per cent is the normal rate.

Grande Bretagne

≤ ₤ₒ ⑩ 份 ⊐ ◌ ₤ 瓜 ⁴ⁿ ₤ₐ

1 Vas Georgiou A, Constitution Sq ⊠ 105 64 — ⓜ *Syntagma* – ℰ *(210) 3330 000 – www.grandebretagne.gr*
320 rm – ✝240/360 € ✝✝250/370 € – ☲ 25 € – 46 suites

Plan: **C2**

• Grand Luxury • Palace • Elegant •

Take in fantastic views of Syntagma Square and the surrounding area from this impressive 19C hotel. The grand interior is filled with luxurious hand-made furnishings. Opulent bedrooms display excellent attention to detail and come with extremely spacious marble bathrooms; the suites are particularly striking.

GB Roof Garden – See restaurant listing

Hilton

⇧ ≤ ₤ₒ ⑩ 份 ⊐ ◌ ₤ 瓜 ⁴ⁿ ₤ₐ 龠

46 Vasilissis Sofias Ave ⊠ 115 28 – ⓜ *Evangelismos* – ℰ *(210) 7281 000 – www.hiltonathens.gr*
506 rm – ✝199/349 € ✝✝199/349 € – ☲ 38 €

Plan: **D2**

• Chain • Business • Modern •

One of the biggest hotels in Athens comes with a great fitness centre and spa, along with a huge lobby boasting a bookshop and a hairdresser. Modern bedrooms have balconies and sea or mountain outlooks. The restaurants serve Greek and international dishes – rooftop 'Galaxy' offers sea and Acropolis views.

Athenaeum Inter-Continental

⇧ ≤ ₤ₒ ⑩ 份 ⊐ ₤ 瓜 ⁴ⁿ ₤ₐ 龠

89-93 Syngrou Ave (Southwest: 2.5 km) ⊠ 117 45 – ℰ *(210) 9206 000 – www.intercontinental.com/athens*
543 rm – ✝235/320 € ✝✝235/320 € – ☲ 32 € – 60 suites

• Grand Luxury • Business • Modern •

Corporate hotel with impressive meeting spaces, a business centre and jewellery and gift shops. The owner is one of the world's top 5 modern art collectors. Bedrooms are spacious and well-equipped; the Club floors offer dedicated services. Eat in the lounge-bar, the casual restaurant or more formal Première.

Première – See restaurant listing

King George

⇧ ≤ ₤ₒ 份 ₤ 瓜 ⁴ⁿ ₤ₐ

3 Vas Georgiou A, Syntagma Sq ⊠ 105 64 – ⓜ *Syntagma* – ℰ *(210) 3222 210 – www.kinggeorgeathens.com*
102 rm ☲ – ✝230/390 € ✝✝230/750 € – 13 suites

Plan: **C2**

• Palace • Grand Luxury • Classic •

A luxuriously converted 1930s mansion located in Syntagma Square. Bedrooms have an elegant, classical style and come with smart marble bathrooms. The rooftop Penthouse Suite boasts a veranda and a stunning private pool with panoramic city and Acropolis views. Dine informally in the fashionable lounge-bar or head to the 7th floor Tudor Hall for a greater sense of occasion.

Divani Caravel

⇧ ≤ ₤ₒ 份 ⊐ ₤ 瓜 ⁴ⁿ ₤ₐ 龠

2 Vas Alexandrou Ave ⊠ 161 21 – ⓜ *Evelangismos* – ℰ *(210) 7207 000 – www.divanis.com*
471 rm – ✝390/500 € ✝✝410/530 € – ☲ 29 € – 44 suites

Plan: **D2**

• Business • Luxury • Classic •

Pass through the marble lobby with its impressive chandelier and up to the elegant bedrooms, which combine classic charm with mod cons. Take in breathtaking views of The Acropolis and Lykavittos Hill from the rooftop pool, then head to the all-day café-restaurant or chic Brown's for modern Mediterranean fare.

Electra Palace 🏔️ ≤ ⬚ 🛗 📶 ⛱ 🔲 ⬚ 🆑 🅦 🧖 🚗
18-20 Nikodimou St ⊠ 105 57 – ⓜ Syntagma – ℰ (210)   Plan: **C3**
3370 000 – www.electrahotels.gr
155 rm ⌑ – 🛉120/175 € 🛉🛉130/225 € – 11 suites
• Luxury • Classic •

An attractive hotel on a peaceful city street in the Plaka district. Its classical façade conceals an elegantly furnished interior; head up to the rooftop pool for fantastic panoramic views over downtown Athens and towards The Acropolis. The two restaurants serve traditional Greek and international fare.
Electra Roof Garden – See restaurant listing

Electra Metropolis 🏔️ 🆑 🅿️ 📶 ⛱ 🔲 ⬚ 🅦 🧖
15 Mitropoleos ⊠ 105 57 – ⓜ Syntagma – ℰ (214)   Plan: **C2**
1006200 – www.electrahotels.gr
216 rm ⌑ – 🛉175/190 € 🛉🛉200/395 €
• Business • Luxury • Modern •

The interior of the Electra Metropolis is surprisingly spacious considering its central location and the light-filled atrium is 9 floors high! Modern bedrooms come in warm tones and the Suites have balconies with stunning Acropolis views. Look out over the city from the top floor bar or Roof Garden restaurant.

Radisson Blu Park H. Athens 🏔️ ≤ 🆑 📶 ⛱ ⬚ 🅦 🧖
10 Alexandras Ave ⊠ 106 82 – ⓜ Victoria – ℰ (210)   🚗
8894 500 – www.radissonblu.com   Plan: **B1**
153 rm ⌑ – 🛉110/170 € 🛉🛉120/250 €
• Business • Chain • Contemporary •

It's been in the family since 1976 and its elegant tree trunk pillars and colour-changing leaves are inspired by the park opposite. Contemporary bedrooms come in browns and greens and most have park views. The Asian restaurant overlooks The Acropolis and moves up to the rooftop to serve BBQ and pasta dishes in summer. Casual Gallo Nero offers Tuscan-inspired fare.

New Hotel 🏔️ 🆑 ⬚ 🅦 🧖
16 Filellinon St ⊠ 105 57 – ⓜ Syntagma – ℰ (210)   Plan: **C3**
327 3000 – www.yeshotels.gr
79 rm ⌑ – 🛉175/245 € 🛉🛉195/265 €
• Business • Traditional • Design •

A quirky, contemporary hotel designed by the Campana brothers. The lobby walls feature wood reclaimed from old furniture and bedsteads, and the minimalist bedrooms showcase furnishings made from recycled materials. Organic ingredients feature in Mediterranean dishes in the all-day restaurant.

AthensWas 🏔️ ≤ 🆑 📶 🅦 🧖
5 Dionysiou Areopagitou St ⊠ 117 42 – ⓜ Acropolis   Plan: **C3**
– ℰ (210) 924 9954 – www.athenswas.gr
21 rm ⌑ – 🛉175/240 € 🛉🛉190/1550 €
• Townhouse • Grand luxury • Design •

This stylishly understated hotel sits on a pedestrianised street in a historic part of the city and its ethos is one of relaxation. Dine on modern Mediterranean dishes on the roof terrace. The best bedrooms have large balconies with great views of The Acropolis – no other hotel is this close to the citadel!

Athenian Callirhoe 🏔️ 🆑 📶 🅦 🧖
32 Kallirois Ave and Petmeza ⊠ 117 43 – ⓜ Syngrou-Fix   Plan: **C3**
– ℰ (210) 9215 353 – www.tac.gr
84 rm ⌑ – 🛉85/140 € 🛉🛉90/150 €
• Business • Modern •

This contemporary hotel sits between two main Avenues and has an elegant lobby filled with smart design furniture. Its comfortable bedrooms come with wooden furnishings and some have balconies and jacuzzis. The 8th floor roof garden restaurant offers international dishes and a panoramic view.

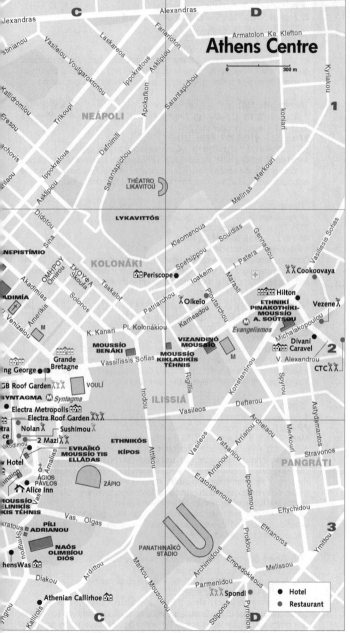

Athens Centre

0   300 m

C Alexandras

Armatolon Ke Klefton

D

Alexandras

Fanarioton

Laskareos

Vasileiou Voulgaroktonou

stinianou

Ippokratous

Asklipiou

Apokafkon

Kallidromiou

Sarantapichou

Trikoupi

Kyriakou

Eresou

NEÁPOLI

achovis

Dafnimili

Ippokratous

Sarantapichou

koniari

Melinas Merkouri

riliou

Asklipiou

THÉATRO LIKAVITOÚ

Didorou

LYKAVITTÓS

Sina

LYKAVITTÓS

NEPISTÍMIO

Kleomenous

Souidias

Gennadiou

Vasilissis Sofias

KOLONÁKI

Spefsippou

I. Patera

OMÍROU
Omirou

ΣΚΟΥΦΑ
Skoufa

Periscope ●

Ioakeim

Marasli

X X Cookoovaya

Akadimias

Tsakalof

Patriarchou

Ploutarchou

Hilton

ADIMÍA

Solonos

X Oikeío

Karneadou

Vezene X

Venizelou

K. Kanari

Pl. Kolonákiou

ETHNIKÍ PINAKOTHÍKI-MOUSSÍO A. SOÚTSOU

M

Michalakopoulou

M

Evangelismos

Divani Caravel

Grande Bretagne

MOUSSÍO BENÁKI

VIZANDINÓ MOUSSÍO

V. Alexandrou

ng George ●

Vasillissis Sofias

MOUSSÍO KIKLADIKÍS TÉHNIS

Konstantinou

CTC X X

GB Roof Garden X X X

VOULÍ

Rigillis

M

Spyrou

SYNTAGMA M Syntagma

ILISSIÁ

Defterou

Astydamantos

Electra Metropolis

Irodou

Vasileos

Archelaou

tra
ce

Electra Roof Garden X X X

Nolan X — Sushimou X

Vasileos

Pafsaniou

Arrianou

Merkouri

Stravonos

Vikodimou

2 Mazi X X

ETHNIKÓS KÍPOS

Attikou

Arrianou

Ippodamou

PANGRÁTI

v Hotel

EVRAÏKÓ MOUSSÍO TIS ELLÁDAS

Eratosthenous

ÁGIOS PÁVLOS

Alice Inn

ZÁPIO

Eftychidou

MOUSSÍO ELINIKÍS KIS TÉHNIS

Vas. Olgas

PÍLI ADRIANOU

Proklou

Effranoros

kratous

Symgrou

NAÓS OLIMBÍOU DIÓS

Archimidous

Empedokleous

Ymitou

hensWas

Ardittou

Markou Mousourou

Melissou

Diakou

PANATHINAÏKÓ STADIO

Parmenidou

X X X Spondi ●

ngrou

Kallirois

Athenian Callirhoe

Archimidous

Stilponos

Pyrronos

C

D

● Hotel
● Restaurant

391

Periscope

22 Haritos St ⊠ 106 75 – Ⓜ Evangelismos – ℰ (210)   Plan: **D2**
7297 200 – www.yeshotels.gr
21 rm ⊡ – †135/190 € ††150/440 €

• Business • Modern • Minimalist •

An elegant residential district is home to this small hotel decorated in shades of grey. Minimalist bedrooms come with balconies and large aerial photos of Athens – some on the ceiling. The stylish bar features Mini Cooper seating.

Acropolis Hill

7 Mousson St ⊠ 117 42 – Ⓜ Singrou-Fix – ℰ (210)   Plan: **B3**
9235 151 – www.acropolishill.gr
37 rm ⊡ – †60/130 € ††65/160 €

• Traditional • Business • Contemporary •

A traditional-looking hotel set close to the Philopappos Monument. It has a nice outdoor pool and a contemporary, boutique style interior. Bedrooms are simple and practical; those at the front have balconies and Acropolis views.

Hermes

19 Apollonos St ⊠ 105 57 – Ⓜ Syntagma – ℰ (210)   Plan: **B3**
3235 514 – www.hermeshotel.gr
45 rm ⊡ – †55/95 € ††60/105 €

• Family • Functional •

Compact, modern hotel located between Monastiraki and Syntagma Square. Bedrooms are bright and simply furnished; the family rooms have two bedrooms and two bathrooms. Buffet breakfasts are served in the first floor restaurant.

Alice Inn

9 Tsatsou St ⊠ 105 58 – Ⓜ Syntagma – ℰ (210)   Plan: **C3**
3237139 – www.aliceinnathens.com
4 rm ⊡ – †60/195 € ††60/195 €

• Boutique hotel • Townhouse • Personalised •

This private house on a quiet street in the heart of Plaka has been transformed into a boutique guesthouse with four uniquely designed, apartment-style bedrooms. You can prepare your own meals in the communal kitchen and dining room.

Spondi   ✿✿

5 Pyronos, off Varnava Sq, Pangrati ⊠ 116 36 – ℰ (210)   Plan: **D3**
7564 021 – www.spondi.gr – Closed Easter
Menu 73/136 € – Carte 100/132 € – *(dinner only)*

• French • Romantic • Elegant •

A discreet, intimate restaurant with two delightful courtyards and two equally charming dining rooms – one an elegant room built from reclaimed bricks in the style of a vaulted cellar. Top quality seasonal ingredients are used in imaginative, deftly executed and stunningly presented modern French dishes. Greek, French and Italian wines feature on an impressive list.

→ Langoustines with lemon, caviar, celery and grapefruit. Duck with almonds, peach and sweet potato. Alpaco chocolate with cinnamon, caramel, peanuts and pistachio ice cream.

GB Roof Garden – Grande Bretagne Hotel

1 Vas Georgiou A, Constitution Sq ⊠ 105 64   Plan: **C2**
– Ⓜ Syntagma – ℰ (210) 3330 766 – www.gbroofgarden.gr
Carte 38/134 € – *(booking essential)*

• Mediterranean cuisine • Fashionable • Elegant •

Set on the 8th floor of the Grande Bretagne hotel, this elegant rooftop restaurant offers spectacular views across Syntagma Square towards The Acropolis. Sunny, modern Mediterranean cooking uses fresh ingredients and is accompanied by an extensive wine list. Service is smooth and efficient.

Première – Athenaeum Inter-Continental Hotel

89-93 Syngrou Ave (9th floor) (Southwest: 2.5 km) ✉ *117 45* – ✆ *(210)*
9206 981 – www.intercontinental.com/athens – Closed Sunday and Monday
Menu 65/90 € – Carte 61/94 € – *(dinner only)*
• Mediterranean cuisine • Friendly • Minimalist •
Start with a drink in the cocktail bar then head through to the elegant restaurant or out onto the terrace to take in views of The Acropolis. Top quality produce features in carefully crafted, delicate Mediterranean dishes.

Electra Roof Garden – Electra Palace Hotel

18-20 Nikodimou St ✉ *105 57* – Ⓜ *Syntagma* – ✆ *(210)*   Plan: **C3**
3370 000 – www.electrahotels.gr
Menu 35 € – Carte 30/54 € – *(dinner only)*
• Mediterranean cuisine • Romantic • Elegant •
Set on the top floor of the Electra Palace hotel, this superbly located restaurant offers unrivalled views of The Acropolis and downtown Athens. Well-made dishes are a mix of traditional Greek and more international flavours.

Funky Gourmet (Georgianna Chiliadaki and Nikos Roussos)   AC

13 Paramythias St and Salaminos, Keramikos ✉ *104 35*   ✿
– Ⓜ *Keramikós* – ✆ *(210) 5242 727*   Plan: **A2**
– *www.funkygourmet.com – Closed August, Sunday and Monday*
Menu 90/150 € – *(dinner only) (booking essential)*
• Innovative • Minimalist • Intimate •
A charming neoclassical house in downtown Athens, off the main tourist track. The minimalist black, white and grey first floor dining room looks out over the city. Wonderfully well-crafted, innovative dishes feature unusual but well-thought-through combinations, and many display playful, theatrical elements.
➔ Funky Gourmet dolmas. Greek salad. Bacon, chocolate and caramel.

Hytra

Onassis Cultural Centre (6th Floor), 107-109 Syngrou Ave C3 (Southwest: 2.5 km) ✉ *11745* – ✆ *(210) 3316 767 – www.hytra.gr*
Menu 58/75 € – Carte 64/71 € – *(dinner only)*
• Modern • Design • Fashionable •
Take the express lift up to the 6th floor of the striking Onassis Cultural Centre; here you'll find a sultry restaurant looking out over Syngrou. Classic Greek recipes are executed in a refined modern manner – for something a little different try the cocktail pairings. They also offer a bistro menu at the bar.
➔ Quail with spelt, chestnut and fresh truffle. Sea bass with artichoke, lemon potatoes and foraged greens. Yoghurt with camomile-infused honey, walnuts and bee pollen.

CTC   AC ✿

27 Diocharous ✉ *11528* – Ⓜ *Evangelismos* – ✆ *(210)*   Plan: **D2**
722 8812 – www.ctc-restaurant.com – Closed July-August, Sunday and Monday
Menu 60/80 € – Carte 57/69 € – *(dinner only) (booking essential)*
• Modern • Intimate • Fashionable •
Its name is short for "the art of feeding" and the sleek, intimate room seats just 28, with a private table on the mezzanine. The chef has worked in both Greece and France, so his dishes are a modern blend of Greek and Gallic elements.

2 Mazi

48 Nikis St ✉ *105 58* – Ⓜ *Syntagma* – ✆ *(210) 3222 839*   Plan: **C3**
– *www.2mazi.gr – Closed Easter*
Carte 36/55 €
• Greek • Trendy • Historic •
Within this neoclassical building you'll find a modern dining room offering a menu inspired by fresh Greek ingredients and Cretan herbs and vegetables. They also have a good selection of local wines by the glass. Mazi means 'together'.

GREECE - ATHENS

✗✗ Cookoovaya
⌂ & AK

2A Chatzigianni Mexi St ✉ 115 28 – Ⓜ Evangelismos — Plan: **D2**
– 𝒞 (210) 723 5005 – www.cookoovaya.gr – Closed 1 January, Easter and 1 week August
Carte 34/91 € – *(booking advisable)*
• Greek • Friendly • Fashionable •
Five of the city's leading chefs have come together to open this bustling restaurant, where rustic, homely cooking is the order of the day and generous dishes are designed for sharing. The homemade pies from the wood-oven are a hit.

✗ Sushimou
AK

6 Skoufou ✉ 105 57 – Ⓜ Syntagma – 𝒞 (211) 4078457 — Plan: **C3**
– www.sushimou.gr – Closed Christmas-New Year, Easter, Saturday-Sunday
Carte 30/50 € – *(dinner only)*
• Asian • Bistro • Trendy •
Set within a large complex near Syntagma Square is this narrow sushi bar with minimalist Japanese styling and 12 seats arranged around the counter. The Greek chef spent several months at the Tokyo Sushi Academy learning the art; simply tell him your preferences and let him know when you have had enough.

✗ Athiri
⌂

15 Plateon ✉ 104 35 – Ⓜ Keramikós – 𝒞 (210) — Plan: **A2**
3462 983 – www.athirirestaurant.gr – Closed 2 weeks August, 1 week Easter, 1-5 January, Sunday dinner in winter and Monday
Menu 35 € – Carte 24/37 € – *(dinner only and Sunday lunch)*
• Greek • Neighbourhood •
In winter, sit inside, surrounded by blue, white and grey hues; in summer, head out to the courtyard and well-spaced tables surrounded by lush green plants. Local, seasonal ingredients are simply prepared in order to reveal their natural flavours. Dishes are generous, good value and have creative touches.

✗ Oikeio
⌂ AK

15 Ploutarhou St ✉ 106 75 – Ⓜ Evangelismos — Plan: **D2**
– 𝒞 (210) 7259 216 – Closed Easter, Christmas and Sunday
Carte 15/28 €
• Greek • Rustic • Traditional décor •
Sweet little restaurant in a chic neighbourhood, with tables on two different levels, as well as outside. The décor is traditional and the place has a warm, cosy feel. Menus offer great value family-style cooking made with fresh ingredients and feature the likes of sardines, moussaka and octopus in vinegar.

✗ Nolan
⌂ AK

31 Voulis St ✉ 105 57 – Ⓜ Syntagma – 𝒞 (210) — Plan: **C3**
3243545 – www.nolanrestaurant.gr – Closed Christmas, Easter, 15 August and Sunday
Carte 27/37 €
• Fusion • Fashionable • Minimalist •
This small, contemporary bistro stands out from the other restaurants in this busy neighbourhood. The young chef has Greek, German and Asian roots and his cooking fuses influences from all three countries along with many other international flavours. Dishes provide plenty of appeal and are great for sharing.

✗ Kuzina
⌂ AK

9 Adrianou St ✉ 105 55 – Ⓜ Thissio – 𝒞 (210) 3240 133 — Plan: **B3**
– www.kuzina.gr – Closed Easter Sunday, 25 December and 1 January
Menu 19 € – Carte 26/50 €
• Mediterranean cuisine • Friendly • Bistro •
A lively split-level restaurant in a busy pedestrianised street; its shelves crammed with alcohol and homemade preserves. Cooking makes good use of local produce. Sit on the terrace for a panoramic view which takes in Hephaestus Temple.

Ⓧ **Vezene**

Vrasida 11 ✉ 115 28 – ℰ (210) 723 2002 — Plan: **D2**
– www.vezene.gr – Closed Christmas-New Year and Sunday
Carte 25/64 € – *(dinner only)*
• Meats and grills • Friendly • Minimalist •

An easy-going eatery specialising in wood-fired steaks and seafood. The dark wood interior opens into a glass-enclosed veranda. The friendly team guide guests as the menu evolves. Try the mini Wagyu burger and the sliced-to-order salumi.

Ⓧ **Mama Tierra**

84 Akadimias ✉ 106 78 – Ⓜ Omonia – ℰ (211) — Plan: **B2**
411 4420 – www.mamatierra.gr – Closed Christmas, Easter and Sunday
Carte 12/18 €
• Vegetarian • Simple • Neighbourhood •

'Mother Earth' is a small, simple neighbourhood restaurant befitting of her name. The chef comes from India and brings many flavours from his homeland to the international vegan dishes. They also offer a takeaway service.

ENVIRONS OF ATHENS

AT HALANDRI Northeast : 11 km by Vas. Sofias

ⓇⓇⓇ **Botrini's** (Ettore Botrini)

☆

24b Vasileos Georgiou ✉ 152 33 – Ⓜ Halandri – ℰ (210) 6857323
– www.botrinis.com – Closed 14-17 April, Sunday and Monday
Menu 55/90 € – Carte 67/87 € – *(dinner only)*
• Mediterranean cuisine • Design • Contemporary décor •

A converted school in a quiet suburb – now a passionately run restaurant with an ultra-modern interior, a sleek glass-fronted kitchen and verdant terraces. Appealing modern menus feature local produce in creative, attractively presented dishes. Many of the oils, salamis and wines are produced by the family.
→ Swordfish carpaccio. Organic veal cheek with potato croquettes and praline. Sweet tzatziki.

AT MAROUSSI Northeast : 12.5 km by Vas. Sofias

Ⓧ **Aneton**

Stratigou Lekka 19 ✉ 151 22 – Ⓜ Maroussi – ℰ (210) 8066 700
– www.aneton.gr – Closed August, 25 December, 1 January and Easter
Carte 24/53 € – *(dinner only and Sunday lunch) (booking essential)*
• Greek • Friendly • Intimate •

It's worth travelling into the smart city suburbs to seek out this appealing neighbourhood restaurant. Menus follow the seasons; in summer they have a Mediterranean base and some Middle Eastern spicing, while in winter, hearty stews and casseroles feature. The hands-on owner really brings the place to life.

AT KIFISSIA Northeast : 15 km by Vas. Sofias

 Kefalari Suites

1 Pentelis and Kolokotroni St, Kefalari ✉ 145 62 – Ⓜ Kifissia – ℰ (210)
6233 333 – www.yeshotels.gr
13 rm ☑ – †145/180 € ††160/285 € – 1 suite
• Townhouse • Elegant • Cosy •

A cosy 19C villa in a smart residential area. Elegantly furnished bedrooms come with kitchenettes and are themed around everything from Jaipur to the sea. Have breakfast on the veranda, then take in the view from the rooftop jacuzzi.

 Semiramis

48 Charilaou Trikoupi St, Kefalari ✉ 145 62 – Ⓜ Kifissia – ℰ (210)
6284 400 – www.yeshotels.gr
51 rm ☑ – †165/200 € ††185/220 € – 1 suite
• Business • Design • Minimalist •

A bold design hotel set on the main plaza of a leafy suburb. Luminous pinks and greens feature inside and out and are complemented by curvaceous modern furnishings. Minimalist bedrooms boast hi-tech facilities and balconies and there's a quirky pool and sun terrace. A new restaurant is set to open as we go to print.

AT VOULIAGMENI South : 18 km by Singrou

Divani Apollon Palace & Thalasso

10 Ag Nikolaou and Iliou St (Kavouri) off Athinas ✉ *166 71 –* ℰ *(210) 8911 100 – www.divaniapollonhotel.com*
280 rm 🛏 **– ♦420/560 € ♦♦460/600 € – 7 suites**
• Palace • Luxury • Classic •
Chic resort with a particularly impressive spa and thalassotherapy centre, two out-door swimming pools and an underground walkway to a private beach. Luxu-rious bedrooms boast balconies and gulf views. Dine on fresh seafood in beach-side Mythos, global cuisine in Anemos or all-day snacks in the coffee lounge.

Apollon Suites

11 Nikolaou St ✉ *166 71 –* ℰ *(210) 8911 100 – www.divanis.com – Closed November-April*
56 rm 🛏 **– ♦135/220 € ♦♦155/450 €**
• Luxury • Contemporary • Elegant •
The peaceful annexe of the Divani Apollon Palace shares its facilities but has a more intimate atmosphere. Spacious bedrooms feature hand-chosen fabrics and terraces (some with sea views). Room service and concierges are available 24/7.

Margi

11 Litous St ✉ *166 71 –* ℰ *(210) 8929 000 – www.themargi.gr*
89 rm 🛏 **– ♦130/350 € ♦♦150/375 € – 8 suites**
• Traditional • Personalised • Mediterranean •
Stylish hotel on the peninsula, close to the beach. The lobby has a Mediterra-nean feel, bedrooms are furnished in a modern colonial style and offer sea or forest views from their balconies. The sun loungers are beautifully arranged in and around the pool. Cooking uses produce from their nearby farm.

AT PIRAEUS Southwest: 8 km by Singrou

Piraeus Theoxenia

23 Karaoli and Dimitriou St ✉ *185 31 –* Ⓜ *Piraeus –* ℰ *(210) 4112 550 – www.theoxeniapalace.com*
77 rm 🛏 **– ♦105/114 € ♦♦105/114 € – 1 suite**
• Business • Luxury • Contemporary •
The Theoxenia is set in the heart of town, close to the bustling local markets and the harbour. The large marble lobby opens onto a classical restaurant which ser-ves global dishes with Mediterranean influences. Spacious bedrooms combine traditional and modern styles and the business centre is well-equipped.

Varoulko (Lefteris Lazarou)

Akti Koumoundourou 52, Mikrolimano Marina (Southeast: 1.5 km by coastal road) ✉ *185 33 –* Ⓜ *Piraeus –* ℰ *(210) 522 8400 – www.varoulko.gr – Closed Easter, Christmas and New Year*
Menu 60 € – Carte 42/60 € – *(booking essential)*
• Seafood • Classic décor • Friendly •
Varoulko sits in a great spot in Mikrolimano Marina – the chef's old neighbour-hood. Watch the yachts glide by from the maritime-themed dining room which opens onto the water. Greek and Mediterranean dishes feature organic vegeta-bles, Cretan olive oil and the freshest seafood; squid and octopus feature highly.
→ Grilled squid with caramelised lentil and orange sauce. Grouper risotto with mushrooms and Amaretto. Valrhona chocolate pie.

Papaioannou

Akti Koumoundourou 42, Mikrolimano Marina (Southeast: 1.5 km by coastal road) ✉ *185 33 –* Ⓜ *Piraeus –* ℰ *(210) 4225 059 – www.papaioannoufish.com – Closed Christmas, Easter and Sunday lunch*
Carte 23/56 €
• Seafood • Traditional décor • Family •
A traditional seafood restaurant where diners select the type, weight and coo-king style of their fish. Shrimp, mussels and crayfish come 'saganaki' style – in tomato sauce with feta cheese. Menus evolve as more fresh produce arrives.

HUNGARY
MAGYARORSZÁG

→ **AREA:**
93 032 km²
(35 920 sq mi).

→ **POPULATION:**
9 821 318 inhabitants.
Density = 106 per km².

→ **CAPITAL:**
Budapest.

→ **CURRENCY:**
Hungarian Forint (Ft or HUF).

→ **GOVERNMENT:**
Parliamentary republic (since 1989).
Member of European Union since
2004.

→ **LANGUAGE:**
Hungarian; many Hungarians also
speak English and German.

→ **PUBLIC HOLIDAYS:**
New Year's Day (1 Jan); 1848
Revolution Day (15 Mar); Easter
Monday (late Mar/Apr); Labor Day
(1 May); Whit Monday (late May/
June); St Stephen's Day (20 Aug);
1956 Uprising Remembrance Day
(23 Oct); All Saints' Day (1 Nov);
Christmas Eve (24 Dec); Christmas
Day (25 Dec); Boxing Day (26 Dec).

→ **LOCAL TIME:**
GMT+1 hour in winter and GMT+2
hours in summer.

→ **CLIMATE:**
Temperate continental with
cold winters and warm summers
(Budapest: January -1°C; July 22°C).

→ **EMERGENCY:**
Police ☎ **107**; Medical Assistance
☎ **104**; Fire Brigade ☎ **105**;
Roadside breakdown service
☎ **188**.
(Dialling **112** within any EU country
will redirect your call and contact
the emergency services.)

→ **ELECTRICITY:**
230 volts AC, 50Hz; 2 round pin
sockets.

→ **FORMALITIES:**
Travellers from the European Union
(EU), Switzerland, Iceland and
the main countries of North and
South America need a national
identity card or passport (America:
passport required) to visit Hungary
for less than three months (tourism
or business purpose).
For visitors from other countries a
visa may be required, in addition
to a passport, especially for those
wishing to stay for longer than
three months. We advise you to
check with your embassy before
travelling.

BUDAPEST
BUDAPEST

Population: 1 740 041

Jonathan/Fotolia.com

No one knows quite where the Hungarian language came from: it's not quite Slavic, not quite Turkic, and its closest relatives appear to be in Finland and Siberia. In much the same way, Hungary's capital is a bit of an enigma. A lot of what you see is not as old as it appears. Classical and Gothic buildings are mostly neoclassical and neo-Gothic, and the fabled baroque of the city is of a more recent vintage than in other European capitals. That's because Budapest's frequent invaders and conquerors, from all compass points of the map, left little but rubble behind them when they left; the grand look of today took shape for the most part no earlier than the mid-19C.

It's still a beautiful place to look at, with hilly Buda keeping watch – via eight great bridges – over sprawling Pest on the other side of the lilting, bending Danube. These were formerly two separate towns, united in 1873 to form a capital city. It enjoyed its heyday around that time, a magnificent city that was the hub of the Austro-Hungarian Empire. Defeats in two world wars and fifty years behind the Iron Curtain put paid to the glory, but battered Budapest is used to rising from the ashes and now it's Europe's most earthily beautiful capital, particularly when winter mists rise from the river to shroud it in a thick white cloak. In summer the days can swelter, and the spas are definitely worth a visit.

BUDAPEST IN...

➜ **ONE DAY**
Royal Palace, the Parliament Building, a trip on the Danube.

➜ **TWO DAYS**
Gellert Baths, a stroll down Váci utca, a concert at the State Opera House.

➜ **THREE DAYS**
Museum of Applied Arts, Margaret Island, coffee and cake at Gerbeaud.

ARRIVAL-DEPARTURE

🛬 Liszt Ferenc National Airport is 24km southeast of the city. A taxi will take about 45min. Shuttle Minibuses do the rounds of the hotels. A train will take you from Terminal 1 to the Western Railway Station.

GETTING AROUND

Budapest has an extensive public transport system, with a three-line metro, buses, trolley buses and trams. Tickets must be bought in advance and validated in the ticket stampers at the start of the journey. Buy your tickets at metro stations, ticket machines, newsagents or tobacconists.

The Budapest Card includes unlimited travel on public transport; free or reduced price admission to many museums and sights, cultural and folklore programmes; and discounts in some shops, restaurants and thermal baths. Valid for two or three days, it can be bought at the airport, main metro stations, tourist offices and some hotels.

CALENDAR HIGHLIGHTS

April
Spring Festival (classical, opera and folk music).

June-August
Summer Festival (open-air theatre).

August
Sziget Festival (rock music).

October
Contemporary Arts Festival (cutting edge theatre, dance, music and film).

November-December
Winter Festival and Christmas Fair at Vörösmarty tér.

EATING OUT

The city is most famous for its coffee houses so, before you start investigating restaurants, find time to tuck into a cream cake with a double espresso in, say, the Ruszwurm on Castle Hill, the city's oldest, and possibly cosiest, café. In tourist areas, it's not difficult to locate goulash on your menu, and you never have to travel far to find beans, dumplings and cabbage in profusion. Having said that, Budapest's culinary scene has moved on apace since the fall of communism, and Hungarian chefs have become much more inventive with their use of local, seasonal produce. Pest is where you'll find most choice but even in Buda there are plenty of worthy restaurants. Lots of locals like to eat sausage on the run and if you fancy the idea, buy a pocket knife. Sunday brunch is popular in Budapest, especially at the best hotels. Your restaurant bill might well include a service charge; don't feel obliged to pay it, as tipping is entirely at your own discretion – though you may find the persistence of the little folk groups that pop up in many restaurants hard to resist.

HUNGARY - BUDAPEST

Four Seasons Gresham Palace

Szechenyi István tér 5-6 ⊠ *1051* – Ⓜ *Vörösmarty tér*
– ℰ *(1) 268 6000 – www.fourseasons.com/budapest*   Plan: **E2**
179 rm ☲ – ╪137800/188700 HUF ╪╪137800/188700 HUF – 18 suites
• Grand Luxury • Palace • Art déco •
Beautifully renovated art nouveau building constructed in 1906 for the Gresham Life Assurance Company. It boasts a stunning lobby with a mosaic floor and a stained glass cupola, along with an impressive rooftop spa and superb river views. Elegant bedrooms are the ultimate in luxury. The chic brasserie offers a mix of international, Hungarian and rotisserie dishes.

Kempinski H. Corvinus

Erzsébet tér 7-8 ⊠ *1051* – Ⓜ *Deák Ferenc tér* – ℰ *(1)*   Plan: **E2**
429 3777 – www.kempinski.com/budapest
349 rm – ╪54900/103700 HUF ╪╪54900/164700 HUF – ☲ 12000 HUF
– 18 suites
• Business • Luxury • Elegant •
Stylish, well-equipped hotel with a striking lobby, lounge and bar; overlooking a central square and named after the charismatic 15C king, Matthias Corvinus. Spacious bedrooms feature Empire-style furniture and boast excellent facilities. The bistro serves modern Hungarian and Viennese cuisine.
Nobu Budapest – See restaurant listing

Corinthia Budapest

Erzsébet krt 43-49 ⊠ *1073* – Ⓜ *Oktogon* – ℰ *(1)*   Plan: **F1**
479 4000 – www.corinthia.com/budapest
413 rm – ╪70000/148000 HUF ╪╪70000/150000 HUF – ☲ 8700 HUF
– 28 suites
• Grand Luxury • Historic • Classic •
Superbly restored and comprehensively equipped hotel with a splendid 19C façade and a spectacular atrium, where a marble staircase leads to a rococo-style ballroom. There's a stunning swimming pool and spa, several shops and a patisserie. The Brasserie offers international cuisine; intimate Rickshaw serves wide-ranging Chinese, Thai, Indian and Indonesian dishes.

Ritz-Carlton

Erzsébet tér 9-10 ⊠ *1051* – Ⓜ *Deák Ferenc tér* – ℰ *(1)*   Plan: **E2**
429 5500 – www.ritzcarlton.com
200 rm – ╪109700/181500 HUF ╪╪109700/181500 HUF – ☲ 9600 HUF
– 30 suites
• Luxury • Elegant • Contemporary •
Opened in 1918, this grand former insurance office and police HQ is now a luxurious hotel with plenty of original features and an understated feel. Have afternoon tea beneath a beautiful stained glass cupola and drinks amongst doric columns. The stylish brasserie serves Hungarian dishes with a modern twist.

Aria

Hercegprímás utca 5 ⊠ *1051* – Ⓜ *Bajcsy-Zsilinszky út*
– ℰ *(1) 445 4055 – www.ariahotelbudapest.com*   Plan: **E2**
49 rm ☲ – ╪94000/180000 HUF ╪╪94000/180000 HUF – 4 suites
• Luxury • Spa and wellness • Personalised •
An 1870s building houses this luxurious hotel, which boasts a stunning glass-enclosed courtyard with views of the sky above. Chic, spacious bedrooms are set in 4 wings and each is themed around a style of music – classical, jazz, opera and contemporary. Modern Hungarian dishes feature in the restaurant. In summer, have a drink in the rooftop bar and take in the view.

Prestige 㿇 🕭 & 🔳 ⇄ 🚿 🚗

Vigyázó Ferenc utca 5 ⊠ 1051 – Ⓜ Vörösmarty tér   Plan: **E1**
– ℰ (1) 920 1000 – www.prestigehotelbudapest.com
85 rm – 📍63900/113000 HUF 📍📍71400/120500 HUF – ⚌ 8450 HUF – 13 suites
• Luxury • Elegant • Personalised •

In the heart of the city centre you'll find this 19C townhouse designed by neo-classical architect Jozsef Hild. Most of the refined, elegant bedrooms are set around a central atrium; they differ in size and colour but all are equally well-equipped with the likes of coffee machines, bathrobes and spa bags.
🌼 **Costes Downtown** – See restaurant listing

Boscolo Budapest 🏔 㿇 🕭 ⊞ 🔳 & 🔳 🚿 🚗

Erzsébet krt 9-11 ⊠ 1073 – Ⓜ Blaha Lujza tér – ℰ (1)   Plan I: **B2**
886 6111 – www.boscolohotels.com
185 rm – 📍41600/132500 HUF 📍📍50000/213000 HUF – ⚌ 8000 HUF – 7 suites
• Grand Luxury • Historic • Modern •

Stunning New York Insurance Company building constructed in 1891; set around an impressive five-floor, Italian Renaissance style atrium. A feeling of luxury pervades: vast bedrooms feature silk wallpapers, chandeliers and marble bathrooms, and there's an unusual ice-house style spa. The all-day café offers international dishes, while the stunning salon serves modern fare.
Salon – See restaurant listing

Buddha-Bar Klotild Palace 🏔 㿇 🕭 & 🔳 ⇄ 🚿

Váci utca 34 ⊠ 1052 – Ⓜ Ferenciek ter – ℰ (1)   Plan: **E2**
799 7300 – www.buddhabarhotel.hu
102 rm – 📍43000/156000 HUF 📍📍43000/200000 HUF – ⚌ 7800 HUF
• Luxury • Modern • Themed •

Chic hotel in a palace built for Princess Klotild of the Habsburg family. It has an oriental theme, with a Zen garden and bedrooms featuring crimson fabrics, intimate lighting and state-of-the-art facilities. The opulent restaurant with its huge gold Buddha serves Chinese, Thai and Japanese dishes.

Iberostar Grand H. Budapest 🏔 㿇 🕭 & 🔳 ⇄ 🚿

Október 6 utka 26 ⊠ 1051 – Ⓜ Arány Janos utca   Plan: **E1**
– ℰ (1) 354 3050 – www.iberostar.com
50 rm – 📍32550/82550 HUF 📍📍32550/82550 HUF – ⚌ 6100 HUF
• Chain • Modern • Personalised •

A classic-looking hotel with a contrastingly modern interior. The lobby-lounge features padded silver chairs on a black marble floor, while bright bedrooms come with good facilities, boldly patterned furnishings and a Spanish edge. The comfy restaurant serves globally influenced lunches and Hungarian dinners.

Moments 🏔 㿇 🕭 & 🔳 ⇄ 🚿

Andrássy utca 8 ⊠ 1061 – Ⓜ Opera – ℰ (1) 611 7000   Plan: **F1**
– www.hotelmomentsbudapest.hu
99 rm ⚌ – 📍34000/68000 HUF 📍📍34000/68000 HUF – 2 suites
• Townhouse • Modern • Centrally located •

Not far from the State Opera and the bustle of Andrássy Avenue, is this 19C townhouse. Original inlaid floors and an impressive decorative ceiling remain. Bedrooms are sleek and modern with a subtle art deco style; the suite has a balcony and Basilica views. Dine in the brasserie or on the pavement terrace.

K + K Opera 㿇 🕭 & 🔳 ⇄ 🚿 🚗

Révay utca 24 ⊠ 1064 – Ⓜ Opera – ℰ (1) 269 0222   Plan: **F1**
– www.kkhotels.com
200 rm ⚌ – 📍24000/61000 HUF 📍📍24000/61000 HUF – 2 suites
• Business • Modern • Functional •

Friendly hotel on a quiet side street behind the Opera House, close to the smart shops of Andrássy Avenue. Uniform bedrooms are comfortable and up-to-date. The cool bar-lounge serves a range of snacks; breakfasts are comprehensive.

HUNGARY - BUDAPEST

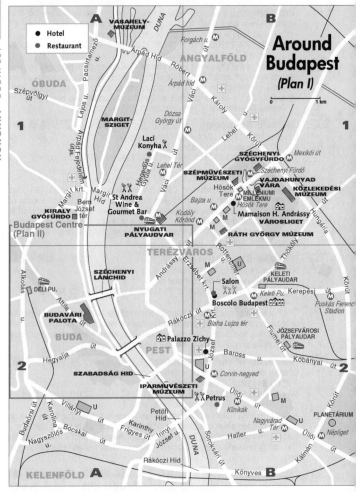

Around Budapest
(Plan I)

Legend:
- ● Hotel
- ● Restaurant

0 — 1 km

A B

ÓBUDA
Szépvölgyi út

ANGYALFÖLD
Forgách u.

MARGIT-SZIGET

Laci Konyha

Lehel Tér

St Andrea Wine & Gourmet Bar

KIRÁLY GYÓFÜRDÖ

Budapest Centre (Plan II)

NYUGATI PÁLYAUDVAR

SZÉCHENYI GYÓGYFÜRDÖ
Mexikói út
Széchenyi Fürdö

SZÉPMÜVÉSZETI MÚZEUM

Hösök Tere
MILLENIUMI EMLÉKMÜ
Hösök Tere

VAJDAHUNYAD VÁRA
KÖZLEKEDÉSI MÚZEUM
VÁROSLIGET

Mamaison H. Andrássy

RÁTH GYÖRGY MÚZEUM

TERÉZVÁROS

SZÉCHENYI LÁNCHÍD

DÉLI PU.

BUDAVÁRI PALOTA

BUDA

Salon

Boscolo Budapest

KELETI PÁLYAUDVAR
Keleti Pu. Kerepesi út
Puskás Ferenc Stadion

Blaha Lujza tér

Palazzo Zichy

PEST

JÓZSEFVÁROSI PÁLYAUDVAR

Baross u.
Köbányai út

SZABADSÁG HÍD

IPARMÜVÉSZETI MÚZEUM

Corvin-negyed

Petrus

Klinikák

PLANETÁRIUM
Népliget

KELENFÖLD

Rákóczi Híd

Könyves

🏨 **Palazzo Zichy**   Plan I: **B2**

Lörinc pap tér 2 ✉ 1088 – **M** *Kálvin tér – ✆ (1)*
235 4000 – www.hotel-palazzo-zichy.hu

80 rm ☲ – ♦27550/67750 HUF ♦♦30650/71000 HUF

• **Business • Historic building • Modern •**

Beautiful rococo building with an impressive 1899 façade; once home to writer Count Zichy. The glass-roofed atrium has a striking modern design. Bedrooms are generously sized and well-equipped, with a cool, minimalist style.

HUNGARY - BUDAPEST

Mamaison H. Andrássy
🏕 🎬 ↳ 🛁 🅿

Munkáczy Mihály utca 5-7 ✉ 1063 – Ⓜ Bajza utca   Plan I: **B1**
– 𝒞 (1) 462 2100 – www.mamaison.com
68 rm – 🛏27500/78700 HUF 🛏🛏27500/78700 HUF – 🍽 4800 HUF
– 5 suites
• Business • Townhouse • Design •

Classical 1937 Bauhaus building in a superb location on the elegant main street. The modern lobby-lounge features pillars of stainless steel filigree. Light, spacious bedrooms have good facilities and most come with balconies. The stylish monochrome restaurant offers modern international dishes.

La Prima Fashion
🛁 ↳ 🎬 ↳ 🛁

Piarista utca 6 ✉ 1052 – Ⓜ Ferenciek ter – 𝒞 (1)   Plan: **E2**
799 0088 – www.laprimahotelbudapest.com
80 rm 🍽 – 🛏28000/82000 HUF 🛏🛏31500/175500 HUF
• Business • Modern • Design •

Simple, modern hotel located near Elizabeth Bridge. A beige and turquoise colour scheme runs throughout. The small lobby lounge has deep padded armchairs; bedrooms have velour bedheads, bold feature walls and TVs set into large mirrors.

Parlament
🏨 ↳ 🎬 ↳ 🛁

Kálmán Imre utca 19 ✉ 1054 – Ⓜ Arany János utca   Plan: **E1**
– 𝒞 (1) 374 6000 – www.parlament-hotel.hu
65 rm 🍽 – 🛏24500 HUF 🛏🛏27500 HUF
• Townhouse • Business • Modern •

A well-run boutique hotel; its stylish, modern interior a contrast to its classical 19C façade. The splendid open-plan atrium has an unusual display depicting famous Hungarians. Compact, modern bedrooms have an art deco style.

Casati
🛁 🏨 🎬

Paulay Ede utca 31 ✉ 1078 – Ⓜ Opera – 𝒞 (1)   Plan: **F1**
343 1198 – www.casatibudapesthotel.com
25 rm 🍽 – 🛏24700/43250 HUF 🛏🛏27800/74100 HUF
• Townhouse • Personalised • Contemporary •

18C townhouse with an Italian Renaissance style façade. The glass-roofed breakfast room features an old well and leads to a '70s lounge-bar. The gym is in the stone-walled basement. Bedrooms range from bohemian to elegant to minimalist.

Bohem Art
🎬 ↳ 🛁

Molnár utca 35 ✉ 1056 – Ⓜ Kálvin tér – 𝒞 (1)   Plan: **F3**
327 9020 – www.bohemarthotel.hu
60 rm 🍽 – 🛏18500/49500 HUF 🛏🛏21500/59000 HUF
• Townhouse • Modern • Design •

A trendy hotel in a bohemian area of the city, run by a hip, friendly team. Modern Hungarian art features throughout. Stylish bedrooms have large screen prints and are furnished in white; the standard rooms are fairly compact.

12 Revay
↳ 🎬 ↳

Révay utca 12 ✉ 1065 – Ⓜ Opera – 𝒞 (1) 909 1212   Plan: **F1**
– www.12revayhotel.com
53 rm 🍽 – 🛏20000/32000 HUF 🛏🛏20000/38000 HUF – 3 suites
• Business • Modern • Functional •

12 Revay is a bright, modern hotel ideally situated between the Basilica and the Opera House. Uniform bedrooms feature large black and white prints of the city's monuments; the 3 apartments have small kitchenettes and wonderful views.

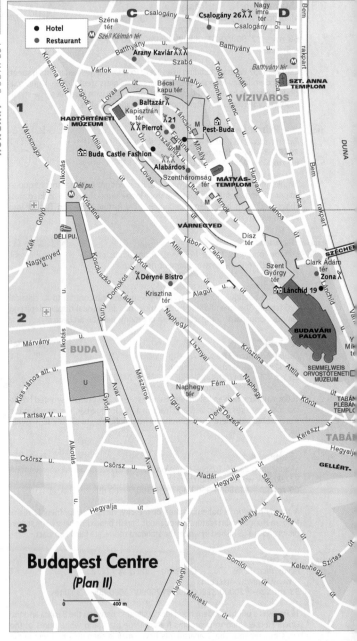

Budapest Centre
(Plan II)

0 — 400 m

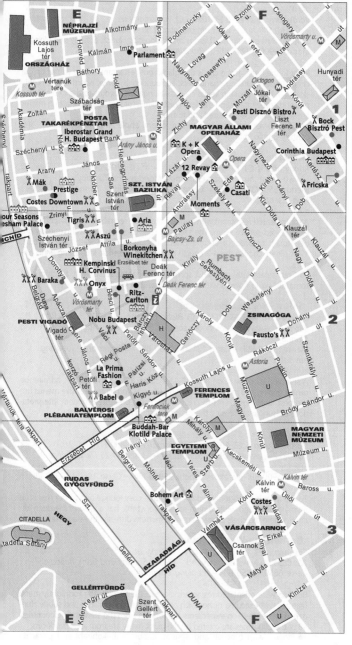

NÉPRAJZI MÚZEUM

Kossuth Lajos tér

ORSZÁGHÁZ

Kossuth tér

Parlament

POSTA TAKARÉKPÉNZTAR

Iberostar Grand H. Budapest Bank

Mák

Prestige

Costes Downtown

Four Seasons Gresham Palace

Tigris

Ászú

Baraka

Onyx

PESTI VIGADÓ

Kempinski H. Corvinus

Borkonyha Winekitchen

Ritz-Carlton

Vörösmarty tér

Nobu Budapest

La Prima Fashion

Babel

BALVÉROSI PLÉBANIATEMPLOM

FERENCES TEMPLOM

Buddah-Bar Klotild Palace

EGYETEMI TEMPLOM

RUDAS GYÓGYFÜRDŐ

Bohem Art

CITADELLA

Citadella Sétány

GELLÉRTFÜRDŐ

Szent Gellért tér

SZT. ISTVÁN BAZILIKA

Aria

12 Revay

Moments

Casati

MAGYAR ÁLLAMI OPERAHÁZ

K + K Opera

Pesti Disznó Bistro

Bock Bisztró Pest

Corinthia Budapest

Fricska

PEST

ZSINAGÓGA

Fausto's

Hunyadi tér

Astoria

MAGYAR NEMZETI MÚZEUM

Kálvin tér

Costes

VÁSÁRCSARNOK

Csarnok tér

Szent Gellért tér

DUNA

405

HUNGARY - BUDAPEST

XxX ✿ **Onyx** 🕸 AC

Vörösmarty Square 7-8 ⊠ 1051 – ⓜ *Vörösmarty tér*   Plan: **E2**
– ✆ (030) 508 0622 – www.onyxrestaurant.hu – Closed 3 weeks
January, 3 weeks August, Tuesday and Wednesday lunch, Sunday and Monday
Menu 19900/29900 HUF *– (booking essential)*
• Modern cuisine • Elegant • Intimate •

Right in the heart of the city is this glamorous restaurant, where you sit on gilt chairs under sparkling chandeliers, surrounded by onyx adornments. Highly skilled, detailed cooking keeps classical Hungarian flavours to the fore but also presents some interesting modern twists. On Saturdays, only the tasting menus are served. Service is assured and formal.
➜ Goose liver and grapes. Venison, celery, apple and black pudding. 21st century Somló sponge cake.

XxX ✿ **Costes** 🕸 AC

Ráday utca 4 ⊠ 1092 – ⓜ *Kálvin tér – ✆ (1) 219 0696*   Plan: **F3**
– www.costes.hu – Closed Christmas, Monday and Tuesday
Menu 26500/37500 HUF *– Carte 21000/24600 HUF – (dinner only) (booking essential)*
• Modern • Design • Elegant •

A sophisticated restaurant with immaculately dressed tables, run by a confident, experienced service team. The talented chef uses modern techniques and a deft touch to produce accomplished, innovative dishes with clear flavours. Most diners choose the 4-7 course set menus and their interesting wine pairings.
➜ Crab salad with corn and sprouts. Mangalitsa lecsó with zucchini and tomatoes. Wild flowers with violet, lemon and vanilla.

XxX **Salon** – Boscolo Budapest Hotel   AC

Erzsébet krt. 9-11 ⊠ 1073 – ⓜ *Blaha Lujza tér – ✆ (1)*   Plan I: **B2**
886 6191 – www.boscolohotels.com – Closed 2 weeks August, Sunday and Monday
Menu 18300 HUF *– Carte 13100/20500 HUF – (dinner only) (booking advisable)*
• Hungarian • Classic décor • Luxury •

A stunning baroque salon behind glass doors, in a luxurious hotel; admire the ornate gilding and impressive painted ceiling as you dine. Extensive menus use the best local ingredients to create attractively presented modern interpretations of Hungarian classics; the 7 course tasting menu is a highlight.

XxX **Baraka** AC

Dorottya utca 6 ⊠ 1051 – ⓜ *Vörösmarty tér – ✆ (1)*   Plan: **E2**
200 0817 – www.barakarestaurant.hu – Closed 24-25 December and Sunday
Menu 6900 HUF (weekday lunch)/25900 HUF *– Carte 14500/29300 HUF*
• Modern • Elegant • Intimate •

To the front is a beautiful cocktail bar with a cosy lounge and to the rear is an intimate black and white dining room. Every table has a view of the open kitchen, where the chefs prepare creative modern dishes with Asian touches.

XX ✿ **Borkonyha Winekitchen** 🕸 AC

Sas utca 3 ⊠ 1051 – ⓜ *Bajcsy-Zsilinszky út – ✆ (1)*   Plan: **E2**
266 0835 – www.borkonyha.hu – Closed Sunday and bank holidays
Carte 6850/13850 HUF *– (booking essential)*
• Modern • Fashionable • Friendly •

Bustling wine-orientated restaurant close to the Basilica. The fortnightly menu features well-executed dishes with an elaborate modern style and subtle Hungarian influences. Top ingredients are sourced from the surrounding countries. 48 of the 200 wines are offered by the glass; many are from local producers.
➜ Pigeon with broccoli and apricot. Rabbit with kohlrabi and pistachio crisps. Bitter chocolate, passion fruit and coffee.

XX   **Costes Downtown** – Prestige Hotel   & AC

☆   *Vigyázó Ferenc utca 5* ✉ *1051 –* Ⓜ *Vörösmarty tér*   Plan: **E1**
– 𝒞 (1) 920 1015 – www.costesdowntown.hu
Menu 6900 HUF (weekday lunch)/22000 HUF
– Carte 15200/20200 HUF
• Modern • Fashionable • Contemporary décor •
The more informal sister to Costes sits within the Prestige hotel and has chic
bistro styling and a friendly atmosphere; ask to be seated in one of the booths.
Refined modern dishes follow the seasons and feature excellent texture and fla-
vour combinations. They offer a good value business lunch.
→ Quail with corn and radicchio. John Dory with poached crayfish and bis-
que sauce. Chocolate, chocolate and chocolate.

XX   **Babel**   ॐ AC

Piarista Köz 2 ✉ *1052 –* Ⓜ *Ferenciek ter – 𝒞 (70)*   Plan: **E2**
*6000 800 – www.babel-budapest.hu – Closed 2 weeks Christmas, 2 weeks
late summer, Sunday and Monday*
Menu 18500 HUF – Carte 10500/18600 HUF
– (dinner only) (booking essential)
• Modern cuisine • Elegant • Design •
It's all about tradition at this intimate restaurant, where brick walls, parquet
floors and a striking concrete ceiling contrast with stylish modern furnishings. Creative, complex cooking is inspired by the Austrian-Hungarian
Empire; texture and temperature play their part and dishes are beautifully
presented.

XX   **St. Andrea Wine & Gourmet Bar**   ॐ 🏠 & AC ⇔

Bajcsy-Zsilinszky utca 78 ✉ *1055*   Plan I: **A1**
– Ⓜ *Nyugati pályaudvar – 𝒞 (1) 269 0130 – www.standreaborbar.hu
– Closed Saturday lunch, Sunday and bank holidays*
Menu 3200 HUF (weekday lunch) – Carte 6400/14700 HUF
• Modern cuisine • Elegant • Wine bar •
A stylish bar-cum-restaurant with wine-themed décor; owned by a small bou-
tique winery. Well-presented, creative dishes are designed to match their
wines – some of which aren't sold anywhere else in the world!

XX   **Fausto's**   AC ⇔

Dohány utca 5 ✉ *1072 –* Ⓜ *Astoria*   Plan: **F2**
– 𝒞 (30) 589 1813 – www.fausto.hu
*– Closed 2 weeks August, 24-26 December, 1 May, Saturday lunch and
Sunday*
Menu 6200 HUF (weekday lunch)/21700 HUF – Carte 11500/19600 HUF –
(booking essential)
• Italian • Cosy • Intimate •
Expect a friendly welcome at this personally run eatery. Dine on sophisticated
modern Italian dishes at linen-laid tables in the restaurant or on simpler, more
classically based fare in the laid-back, wood-furnished osteria; the daily home-
made pasta is a hit. Good quality Hungarian and Italian wines feature.

XX   **Tigris**   ॐ AC ⇔

Mérleg utca 10 ✉ *1051 –* Ⓜ *Bajcsy-Zsilinszky út – 𝒞 (1)*   Plan: **E2**
*317 3715 – www.tigrisrestaurant.hu – Closed 1 week August, Christmas
and Sunday*
Carte 7600/13700 HUF *– (booking essential at dinner)*
• Hungarian • Traditional décor • Neighbourhood •
Traditional bistro in a historic building designed by a Hungarian architect; it
exudes a luxurious feel. Classic dishes have an appealing, earthy quality and
feature foie gras specialities. The wine list champions up-and-coming producers.

HUNGARY - BUDAPEST

XX Petrus

Ferent tér 2-3 ⊠ 1094 – ❻ Klinikák – ℰ (1) 951 2597 Plan I: **B2**
*– www.petrusrestaurant.hu – Closed 2 weeks August, 24-26 December,
Sunday and Monday*
Menu 8200 HUF – Carte 7580/10900 HUF
• Classic/traditional • Bistro • Neighbourhood •
Friendly neighbourhood bistro where Budapest meets Paris – both in the décor
and the food. The chef-owner's passion is obvious and the cooking is rustic and
authentic, with bold flavours and a homely touch. If you're after something a
little different, ask to dine in the old Citroën 2CV!

XX Nobu Budapest – Kempinski H. Corvinus

Erzsébet tér 7-8 ⊠ 1051 – ❻ Deák Ferenc tér – ℰ (1) Plan: **E2**
429 4242 – www.noburestaurants.com
Menu 5000 HUF – Carte 5800/14500 HUF
• Japanese • Minimalist • Fashionable •
Minimalist restaurant in a stylish hotel, with well-spaced wooden tables, Japanese lanterns, fretwork screens and an open kitchen. Numerous menus offer a
huge array of Japanese-inspired dishes; some come with matching wine flights.

XX Aszú

Sas utca 4 ⊠ 1051 – ❻ Bajcsy-Zsilinszky út – ℰ (1) Plan: **E2**
328 0360 – www.aszuetterem.hu
Carte 7300/13700 HUF
• Hungarian • Elegant • Design •
As its name suggests, this restaurant celebrates Tokaj and its wines. The cooking showcases updated Hungarian classics, and the striking room features an
ornate mirrored wall, a golden-hued vaulted ceiling and handcrafted wooden
carvings.

X Fricska

Dob utca 56-58 ⊠ 1073 – ❻ Oktogon – ℰ (1) 951 8821 Plan: **F1**
*– www.fricska.eu – Closed 2 weeks July, 1 week March, 1 week August,
Sunday, Monday and bank holidays*
Menu 2400 HUF (weekday lunch) – Carte 6550/9300 HUF – *(bookings
advisable at dinner)*
• Modern cuisine • Bistro • Contemporary décor •
The subtitle 'gastropub' is misleading, as this is a contemporary cellar bistro with
crisp white décor and a laid-back vibe. The blackboard menu offers appealingly
unadorned dishes with Hungarian, French and Italian influences. The homemade pastas are a highlight and the weekday lunch menu is a steal.

X Mák

Vigyázó Ferenc utca 4 ⊠ 1051 – ❻ Vörösmarty tér Plan: **E1**
*– ℰ (30) 723 9383 – www.mak.hu – Closed 1 week in summer, Sunday
and Monday*
Menu 4275 HUF (weekday lunch)/18000 HUF – Carte 10000/13950 HUF –
(bookings advisable at dinner)
• Modern cuisine • Bistro • Rustic •
Rustic restaurant with whitewashed brick walls, semi-vaulted ceilings and a
relaxed feel: its name means 'poppy seed'. The talented young chef prepares
creative dishes which play with different texture and flavour combinations.

X Laci Konyha

Hegedűs Gyula utca 56 ⊠ 1134 – ❻ Lehel Tér Plan I: **A1**
*– ℰ (70) 370 7475 – www.lacikonyha.com – Closed 24 December-
5 January, Saturday, Sunday and bank holidays*
Menu 2500/9000 HUF – Carte dinner 6500/9800 HUF
• Modern cuisine • Neighbourhood • Simple •
Original menus and an edgy vibe make this restaurant a hit with one and all;
gather your friends and make for one of the larger tables. Ingredients are well-
sourced and accurately cooked, and while combinations are traditionally based,
the techniques used provide the cooking with modern overtones.

X **Pesti Disznó Bistro**

Nagymező utca 19 ⊠ *1065 –* Ⓜ *Oktogon –* 𝒞 *(1)*   Plan: **F1**
951 4061 – www.pestidiszno.hu – Closed 24-25 December
Menu 1190 HUF (weekday lunch) – Carte 5170/10170 HUF
• Meats and grills • Bistro • Wine bar •
A lively, easy-going Hungarian bistro; as you cross the threshold, wonderful aromas hint at what is to come. Carefully sourced ingredients feature in authentic recipes and prices are fair; their native Mangalitsa pork is a speciality.

X **Bock Bisztró Pest**

Erzsébet krt. 43-49 ⊠ *1073 –* Ⓜ *Oktogon –* 𝒞 *(1)*   Plan: **F1**
321 0340 – www.bockbisztro.hu – Closed Sunday and bank holidays
Carte 6200/10500 HUF – *(booking essential)*
• Hungarian • Bistro • Rustic •
A busy, buzzy bistro; its shelves packed with wine. Choose something from the à la carte or try one of the blackboard specials – the friendly, knowledgeable staff will guide you. Cooking is gutsy and traditional with a modern twist.

BUDA   **PLAN II**

🏨 **Lánchíd 19**

Lánchíd utca 19 ⊠ *1013 –* 𝒞 *(1) 419 1900*   Plan: **D2**
– www.lanchid19hotel.hu
48 rm – †22850/45650 HUF ††22850/114100 HUF – ⊑ 4000 HUF
• Business • Design • Modern •
Stylish hotel overlooking the river and castle, and featuring a glass-floored lounge looking down to the ruins of a 14C water tower. Bedrooms boast designer chairs, feature walls and modern facilities; those to the front have impressive views. The mezzanine restaurant offers an international menu.

🏨 **Buda Castle Fashion**

Úri utca 39 ⊠ *1014 –* Ⓜ *Széll Kálmán tér –* 𝒞 *(1)*   Plan: **C1**
224 7900 – www.budacastlehotel.eu
20 rm ⊑ – †20000/38000 HUF ††24500/45000 HUF – 5 suites
• Townhouse • Functional • Modern •
Lovely 15C merchant's house on a quiet street in the heart of Old Buda; a former HQ of the Hungarian Hunting Association. Bedrooms are spacious, comfy and pleasantly modern. There's also a delightfully peaceful courtyard terrace.

🏨 **Pest-Buda**

Fortuna utca 3 ⊠ *1014 –* Ⓜ *Széll Kálmán tér –* 𝒞 *(1)*   Plan: **C1**
800 9213 – www.pest-buda.com
11 rm – †31200/104000 HUF ††31200/104000 HUF – ⊑ 3000 HUF
• Inn • Historic • Contemporary •
The oldest hotel in Hungary dates from 1696 and sits in a charming cobbled street in the Old Town. Bedrooms are furnished in a contemporary country style and have smart travertine-tiled bathrooms. Sit on red leather banquettes in the vaulted bistro, where gingham-covered tables spill out onto the terrace.

XxX **Alabárdos**

Orszaghaz Utca 2 ⊠ *1014 –* Ⓜ *Széll Kármán tér*   Plan: **D1**
– 𝒞 *(1) 356 0851 – www.alabardos.hu – Closed 25-26 December and Sunday*
Menu 13500/21500 HUF – Carte 11600/12600 HUF – *(dinner only and Saturday lunch) (booking essential)*
• Hungarian • Chic • Elegant •
Set in a series of 15C buildings opposite the castle and named after its guards, this professionally run restaurant has stood here for over 50 years. It's formal yet atmospheric, with subtle modern touches and a delightful terrace. Cooking is rich and flavourful and features classic dishes with a modern edge.

⭐⭐⭐ Arany Kaviár

Ostrom utca 19 ✉ *1015* – Ⓜ *Széll Kálmán tér* – ☎ *(1)*   Plan: **C1**
201 6737 – *www.aranykaviar.hu* – *Closed 24-26 December, 20 August,*
Monday and bank holidays
Menu 3900 HUF (weekday lunch) – Carte 11300/40300 HUF
• Russian • Intimate • Elegant •

Choose between an opulent, richly appointed room and a larger, more modern extension which opens onto the garden. French and Russian influences guide the creative, ambitious cooking; Hungarian and Siberian caviar is a speciality.

⭐⭐ Pierrot

Fortuna utca 14 ✉ *1014* – Ⓜ *Széll Kálmán tér* – ☎ *(1)*   Plan: **C1**
375 6971 – *www.pierrot.hu*
Carte 6800/14600 HUF
• Hungarian • Elegant • Intimate •

Characterful two-roomed restaurant in a vaulted 13C property within the castle walls. European and Hungarian classics are prepared with a contemporary touch; service is efficient. Pierrot themed artwork and live piano music feature.

⭐⭐ Csalogány 26

Csalogány utca 26 ✉ *1015* – Ⓜ *Batthyány tér* – ☎ *(1)*   Plan: **D1**
201 7892 – *www.csalogany26.hu* – *Closed 2 weeks summer, 2 weeks*
winter, Sunday, Monday and bank holidays
Menu 2500/13000 HUF – Carte 6700/11700 HUF – *(booking advisable)*
• Modern • Bistro • Friendly •

Homely neighbourhood restaurant with a simple bistro style. A passionate father and son team offer two daily menus; go for 4 or 8 courses or choose from the à la carte. Cooking is full of flavour and presented in a modern style.

⭐ Baltazár

Országház utca 31 ✉ *1014* – Ⓜ *Széll Kálmán tér*   Plan: **C1**
– ☎ *(1) 300 7050* – *www.baltazarbudapest.com*
11 rm – ♦45034/77480 HUF ♦♦67600/136700 HUF – ⌑ 4650 HUF
Carte 6120/14020 HUF
• Meats and grills • Design • Bistro •

A hidden gem, tucked away to the north of the Old Town, away from the crowds. Sit on the pretty terrace or head into the striking bistro, where stage spotlights illuminate boldly painted concrete walls. Cooking focuses on Hungarian classics and meats from the Josper grill. Its bedrooms are also ultra-modern.

⭐ Vendéglő a KisBíróhoz

Szarvas Gábor utca 8/d (Northwest: 3.5 km by Attila utca, Kristina Körut
and Szilágyi Erzsébet off Kutvölgyi utca) ✉ *1125* – ☎ *(1) 376 6044*
– *www.vendegloakisbirohoz.hu* – *Closed Monday and bank holidays*
Menu 11700 HUF – Carte 6800/10400 HUF
• Hungarian • Bistro • Neighbourhood •

Contemporary glass and wood building with a large terrace, in a peaceful suburban location. Wine takes centre stage: staff will recommend a match for your dish from the extensive list. Cooking is hearty and classical with a modern edge.

⭐ Zona

Lánchíd utca 7-9 ✉ *1013* – ☎ *(30) 422 5981*   Plan: **D2**
– *www.zonabudapest.com*
Menu 3590 HUF (weekday lunch) – Carte 7100/11800 HUF
• Modern cuisine • Design • Trendy •

Contemporary restaurant with floor to ceiling windows overlooking the river and a huge shelving unit packed with wines. Gold glass balls illuminate sleek wooden tables. Modern dishes follow the seasons and arrive smartly presented.

21

Fortuna utca 21 ⊠ 1014 – Ⓜ Széll Kálmán tér – 𝒸 (1)
202 2113 – www.21restaurant.hu
Menu 8960 HUF – Carte 6100/10440 HUF

Plan: **C1**

• Hungarian • Bistro • Friendly •

Situated within the castle walls is this contemporary take on a traditional bistro.
Classic Hungarian dishes are subtly reinvented with an appealing contemporary
touch. Sit on the terrace for great views down the cobbled street.

Déryné Bistro

Krisztina tér 3 ⊠ 1013 – Ⓜ Déli pu. – 𝒸 (1) 225 1407
– www.bistroderyne.com – Closed 24 December
Carte 4110/8610 HUF

Plan: **C2**

• Classic French • Bistro • Traditional décor •

Wonderfully old bistro-cum-brasserie with a horseshoe bar and lots of old-fashioned charm. French classics sit alongside a few Hungarian dishes. It's open for
breakfast, they have their own bakery, and a pianist plays from 3-8pm.

Tanti

Apor Vilmos tér 11-12 (West: 4.25 km by Hegyalja and Jagelló utca)
⊠ 1124 – 𝒸 (20) 243 1565 – www.tanti.hu – Closed 15-23 August and
Sunday
Menu 4700 HUF (weekday lunch)/20000 HUF

• Modern cuisine • Minimalist • Neighbourhood •

'Auntie' is located in the corner of a pleasant little shopping mall and comes
with an appealing terrace. It's light, bright and simply kitted out and offers a
concise menu of attractive dishes. Well-chosen native wines accompany.

Republic of IRELAND
ÉIRE

→ **AREA:**
70 284 km² (27 137 sq mi).

→ **POPULATION:**
4 713 993 inhabitants.
Density = 67 per km².

→ **CAPITAL:** Dublin.

→ **CURRENCY:** Euro (€).

→ **GOVERNMENT:**
Parliamentary republic
(since 1921). Member of
European Union since 1973.

→ **LANGUAGES:**
Irish and English.

→ **PUBLIC HOLIDAYS:**
New Year's Day (1 Jan);
St Patrick's Day (17 Mar); Easter
Monday (late Mar/Apr); May Bank
Holiday (first Mon in May); June
Bank Holiday (first Mon in June);
August Bank Holiday (first Mon
in Aug); October Bank Holiday (last
Mon in Oct); Christmas Day
(25 Dec); St Stephen's Day (26 Dec).

→ **LOCAL TIME:**
GMT in winter and GMT+1 hour in
summer.

→ **CLIMATE:**
Temperate maritime with cool
winters and mild summers (Dublin:
January 5°C; July 15°C), fairly high
rainfall.

→ **EMERGENCY:**
Police, Medical Assistance, Fire
Brigade ☏ 999 – also used for
Mountain, Cave, Coastguard and
Sea Rescue.
(Dialling 112 within any EU country
will redirect your call and contact
the emergency services.)

DUBLIN ●

→ **ELECTRICITY:**
230 volts AC, 50 H; 3 flat pin
sockets.

→ **FORMALITIES:**
Travellers from the European Union
(EU), Switzerland, Iceland and the
main countries of North and South
America need a national identity
card or passport (except for British
nationals travelling from the UK;
America: passport required) to visit
Ireland for less than three months
(tourism or business purpose).
For visitors from other countries a
visa may be required, in addition
to a passport, especially for those
wishing to stay for longer than
three months. We advise you to
check with your embassy before
travelling.

DUBLIN
BAILE ÁTHA CLIATH

Population: 565 000

Marek Slusarczyk/Fotolia.com

For somewhere touted as the finest Georgian city in the British Isles, Dublin enjoys a very young image. When the 'Celtic Tiger' roared to prominence in the 1990s, Ireland's old capital took on a youthful expression, and for the first time revelled in the epithets 'chic' and 'trendy'. Nowadays it's not just the bastion of Guinness drinkers and those here for the 'craic', but a twenty-first century city with smart restaurants, grand new hotels, modern architecture and impressive galleries. Its handsome squares and façades took shape 250 years ago, designed by the finest architects of the time. Since then, it's gone through uprising, civil war and independence from Britain, and now holds a strong fascination for foreign visitors.

The city can be pretty well divided into three. Southeast of the river is the classiest, defined by the glorious Trinity College, St Stephen's Green, and Grafton Street's smart shops. Just west of here is the second area, dominated by Dublin Castle and Christ Church Cathedral – ancient buildings abound, but it doesn't quite match the sleek aura of the city's Georgian quarter. Across the Liffey, the northern section was the last part to be developed and, although it lacks the glamour of its southern neighbours, it does boast the city's grandest avenue, O'Connell Street, and its most celebrated theatres.

DUBLIN IN...

→ **ONE DAY**
Trinity College, Grafton Street, St Stephen's Green, Merrion Square, Temple Bar.

→ **TWO DAYS**
Christ Church Cathedral, Dublin Castle, Chester Beatty Library, the quayside.

→ **THREE DAYS**
O'Connell Street, Parnell Square, Dublin Writers' Museum, DART train to the coast.

PRACTICAL INFORMATION

ARRIVAL-DEPARTURE

 Dublin Airport is 7 miles north. There are a number of coaches and buses (including Airlink and Aircoach), which take you to the centre of the city in approximately 30mins.

GETTING AROUND

The bus network covers the whole city from the Central Bus Station in Store Street and is cheap and efficient, while the exciting LUAS (meaning 'speed') light rail network will get you to places a little quicker; ticket prices for both relate to the number of stages travelled. If you want to visit the coast, then jump on a DART (Dublin Area Rapid Transport) train. They operate at regular intervals, are amazingly efficient, and leave central Dublin from Connolly, Tara Street and Pearse stations. If you'd rather spend your time in the city, the Dublin Pass provides access to over thirty attractions, and ranges from one to six days.

EATING OUT

It's still possible to indulge in Irish stew but nowadays you can also dine on everything from tacos and Thai to Malaysian and Middle Eastern cuisine, particularly in the Temple Bar area. The city makes the most of its bay proximity, so seafood features highly, with smoked salmon and oysters the favourites; the latter washed down with a pint of Guinness. Meat is particularly tasty in Ireland, due to the healthy livestock and a wet climate, and Irish beef is world famous for its fulsome flavour. However, there's never been a better time to be a vegetarian

CALENDAR HIGHLIGHTS

March
St Patrick's Day, Celtic Flame, Temple Bar Fleadh (traditional music).

April
Colours Boat Race, Feis Ceoil (classical music).

June
Bloomsday.

July-August
Diversions (free concerts and open-air theatre).

August
Horse Show.

September
Fringe Theatre Festival.

October
Dublin Theatre Festival.

November
Opera Ireland.

in Dublin, as every type of veg from spinach to seaweed now features, and chefs insist on the best seasonal produce, cooked for just the right amount of time to savour all the taste and goodness. Dinner here is usually served until about 10pm, though many global and city centre restaurants stay open later. If you make your main meal at lunchtime, you'll pay considerably less than in the evening: the menus are often similar, but the bill in the middle of the day will probably be about half the price.

Shelbourne

27 St Stephen's Grn. ✉ *D2 –* ℰ *(01) 6634500*
– www.theshelbourne.ie Plan: **E3**
265 rm – 🛏229/750 € 🛏🛏229/750 € – ⌷29 € – 12 suites
• Grand Luxury • Classic • Elegant •

Famed hotel dating from 1824, overlooking an attractive green; this is where
the 1922 Irish Constitution was signed. Elegant guest areas and classical architecture; it even has a tiny museum. The bar and lounge are THE places to go for
drinks and afternoon tea. Chic spa and characterful, luxurious bedrooms.
Saddle Room – See restaurant listing

Merrion

Upper Merrion St ✉ *D2 –* ℰ *(01) 6030600*
– www.merrionhotel.com Plan: **F3**
142 rm – 🛏495/635 € 🛏🛏515/656 € – ⌷29 € – 10 suites
• Townhouse • Luxury • Classic •

A Georgian façade conceals a luxury hotel and a compact spa with an impressive pool. Opulent drawing rooms are filled with antique furniture and fine artwork – enjoy 'art afternoon tea' with a view of the formal parterre garden. Stylish bedrooms have a classic, understated feel and smart marble bathrooms.
Dine from an accessible menu in the barrel-ceilinged bar.

Fitzwilliam

St Stephen's Grn ✉ *D2 –* ℰ *(01) 478 70 00*
– www.fitzwilliamhotel.com Plan: **E3**
139 rm – 🛏219/500 € 🛏🛏219/500 € – ⌷22 € – 2 suites
• Business • Modern •

Stylish, modern hotel set around an impressive roof garden. Contemporary
bedrooms display striking bold colours and good facilities; most overlook the
roof garden and the best have views over St Stephen's Green. The bright first
floor brasserie offers original Mediterranean-influenced menus.

The Dean

33 Harcourt St ✉ *D2 –* ℰ *(01) 607 8110 – www.deandublin.ie* Plan: **E3**
51 rm – 🛏109/450 € 🛏🛏109/450 € – ⌷15 € – 3 suites
• Townhouse • Design • Modern •

A cool, informal, urban boutique. Stylish bedrooms include compact rooms
named 'Mod Pods'; suites with record players, amps and guitars; and a penthouse
with table football, a poker table and a bar! The moody lobby serves an all-day
menu and loft-style Sophie's offers Mediterranean dishes and rooftop views.

Number 31

31 Leeson Cl. ✉ *D2 –* ℰ *(01) 6765011 – www.number31.ie* Plan: **H1**
21 rm ⌷ – 🛏150/240 € 🛏🛏190/280 €
• Townhouse • Design •

Unusual and very individual property – once home to architect Sam Stephenson.
It's classically styled around the 1960s, with a striking sunken lounge; the most
modern bedrooms are found in the Georgian house across the terraced garden.

XXXX ✿✿ Patrick Guilbaud (Guillaume Lebrun)

21 Upper Merrion St ✉ *D2 –* ℰ *(01) 6764192* Plan: **F3**
– www.restaurantpatrickguilbaud.ie – Closed 25-31 December, 17 March,
14 April, Sunday, Monday and bank holidays
Menu 45/105 € – *(booking essential)*
• Modern French • Elegant •

A truly sumptuous restaurant in an elegant Georgian house; the eponymous owner
has run it for over 35 years. Accomplished, original cooking uses luxurious ingredients and mixes classical French cooking with modern techniques. Dishes are
well-crafted and visually stunning with a superb balance of textures and flavours.
→ Blue lobster ravioli with coconut-scented lobster cream, toasted
almonds and curry dressing. Spiced Wicklow lamb with Basque pepper
stew, bergamot and olive jus. Chocolate and peanut parfait with salted
caramel and popcorn ice cream.

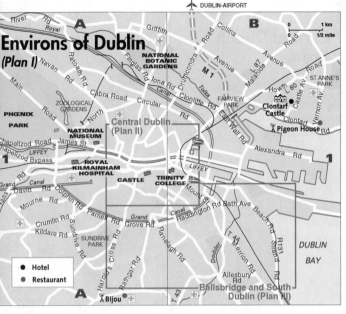

XXX   **Chapter One** (Ross Lewis)   AC ⇔ 🚗

❁   *The Dublin Writers Museum, 18-19 Parnell Sq ⊠ D1*   Plan: **E1**
– 𝒞 (01) 8732266 – www.chapteronerestaurant.com – Closed 2 weeks
August, 2 weeks Christmas, Sunday, Monday and bank holidays
Menu 40/70 € – *(booking essential)*
• Modern cuisine • Intimate • Design •

Good old-fashioned Irish hospitality meets with modern Irish cooking in this sty-lish basement restaurant beneath the Writers Museum. The series of intercon-necting rooms have an understated elegance and striking bespoke art hangs on the walls. Boldly flavoured dishes showcase produce from local artisan pro-ducers.

→ Pig's tail stuffed with Fingal Ferguson's bacon and Dublin Bay prawn. Turbot with fermented horseradish, cauliflower and pickled red dulse. Sal-ted butter ice cream with caramelised soda bread and soda bread mousse.

XXX   **L'Ecrivain** (Derry Clarke)   🍴 AC ⇔ 🕅

❁   *109a Lower Baggot St ⊠ D2 – 𝒞 (01) 6611919*   Plan: **F3**
– www.lecrivain.com – Closed Sunday and bank holidays
Menu 45/75 € – *(dinner only and lunch Thursday-Friday) (booking essen-tial)*
• Modern cuisine • Fashionable • Design •

A well-regarded restaurant with an attractive terrace, a glitzy bar and a private dining room which screens live kitchen action. The refined, balanced menu has a classical foundation whilst also displaying touches of modernity; the ingre-dients used are superlative. Service is structured yet has personality.

→ Lambay scallop with cabbage, onion, apple and oyster cream. Aged beef with chanterelles, foie gras, crisp potato and oxtail jus. 'Irish Coffee' mousse with vanilla ice cream and whiskey foam.

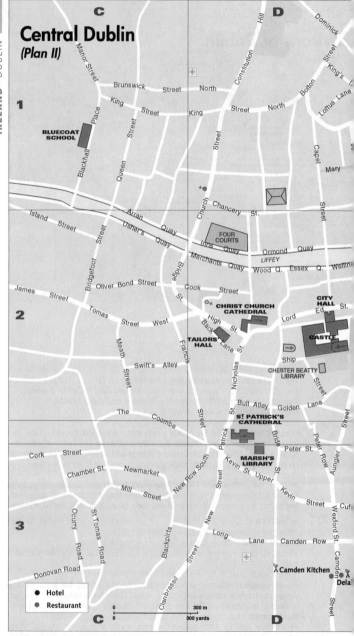

Central Dublin
(Plan II)

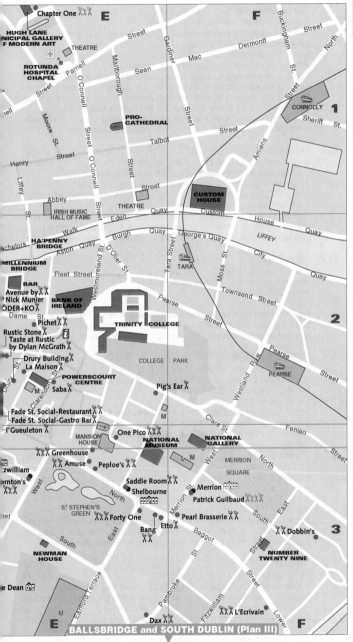

E

Chapter One ✕✕✕

HUGH LANE
MUNICIPAL GALLERY
OF MODERN ART

THEATRE

Street

ROTUNDA
HOSPITAL
CHAPEL

F

Buckingham Street

Dermott

Mac

Sean

Gardiner Street

Marlborough

Parnell Street

O'Connell

Moore St.

Street

North

St.

Street

Sheriff

CONNOLLY **1**

St.

Henry Street

Liffey

St.

Abbey

IRISH MUSIC
HALL OF FAME

PRO-
CATHEDRAL

O'Connell Street

Marlborough Street

Talbot

Street

Amiens Street

Street

THEATRE

Eden Quay

Custom

CUSTOM
HOUSE

House

LIFFEY

Quay

HA'PENNY
BRIDGE

MILLENNIUM
BRIDGE

Batchelors

Walk

Burgh Quay

George's Quay

City

Quay

Aston Quay

Fleet Street

Westmoreland St.

D'Olier St.

Tara Street

Moss St.

Townsend Street

TARA

BAR

Avenue by ✕✕
Nick Munier
ODER+KO ✕

Dame St.

Pichet ✕✕

BANK OF
IRELAND

Pearse

Street

Townsend Street

2

Rustic Stone ✕
Taste at Rustic
by Dylan McGrath ✕

Drury Building ✕
La Maison ✕

POWERSCOURT
CENTRE

Saba ✕

Drury

Clarendon

M

TRINITY COLLEGE

COLLEGE PARK

Pig's Ear ✕

Westland Row

Clare St.

Pearse

PEARSE

Street

Fenian

Fade St. Social-Restaurant ✕ ✕
Fade St. Social-Gastro Bar ✕
l'Gueuleton ✕

One Pico ✕✕✕

M

MANSION
HOUSE

NATIONAL
MUSEUM

NATIONAL
GALLERY

M

MERRION
SQUARE

North

Street

✕✕✕ Greenhouse

Fitzwilliam

Thornton's
✕✕✕

✕✕ Amuse ●

West

North

Peploe's ✕✕

Saddle Room ✕✕
Shelbourne

ST STEPHEN'S
GREEN

✕✕✕ Forty One

East

Bang
✕✕

Merrion St.

Merrion

Merrion

West

Merrion ▦▦▦

Patrick Guilbaud ✕✕✕✕

Pearl Brasserie ✕✕

South

East

✕✕ Dobbin's

3

Etto ✕

Baggot

St.

NUMBER
TWENTY NINE

NEWMAN
HOUSE

South

East

Street

Pembroke

Fitzwilliam Street Lower

The Dean ▦▦

Earlsfort Terrace

U

Dax ✕✕

Papbroke

Fitzwilliam

✕✕✕ L'Ecrivain ●

E

BALLSBRIDGE and SOUTH DUBLIN (Plan III)

F

XxX · 🌼 **Greenhouse** (Mickael Viljanen) · AC

Dawson St ⊠ *D2 – ℰ (01) 676 7015* · Plan: **E3**
*– www.thegreenhouserestaurant.ie – Closed 2 weeks July, 2 weeks
Christmas, Sunday and Monday*
Menu 36 € (weekday lunch)/89 €
• Modern cuisine • Elegant • Fashionable •
Stylish restaurant with turquoise banquettes and smooth service. Menus include a good value set lunch, midweek set and tasting menus and a 5 course 'Surprise' on Friday and Saturday evenings. Accomplished, classically based cooking has stimulating flavour combinations and creative modern overtones.
→ Foie gras, apple, walnut and smoked eel. Kerry lamb with wild garlic, artichoke and turnip. Milk chocolate and yuzu bar, banana and lime.

XxX **Forty One** · ⇔

41 St. Stephen's Grn. ⊠ *D2 – ℰ (01) 6620000* · Plan: **E3**
*– www.restaurantfortyone.ie – Closed first 2 weeks August, 25-
26 December, 17 March, Good Friday, Sunday and Monday*
Menu 35 € (weekday lunch)/75 € – Carte 63/79 € – (booking advisable)
• Modern cuisine • Elegant • Intimate •
Intimate, richly furnished restaurant on the first floor of an attractive, creeper-clad townhouse, in a corner of St Stephen's Green. Accomplished, classical cooking features luxurious Irish ingredients and personal, modern touches.

XxX **One Pico** · AC ⇔ 🕰

5-6 Molesworth Pl ⊠ *D2 – ℰ (01) 6760300* · Plan: **E3**
– www.onepico.com – Closed bank holidays
Menu 27/49 €
• Classic French • Elegant •
Stylish modern restaurant tucked away on a side street; a well-regarded place that's a regular haunt for MPs. Sit on comfy banquettes or velour chairs, surrounded by muted colours. Classic French cooking offers plenty of flavour.

XX **Pearl Brasserie** · AC 🕰

20 Merrion St Upper ⊠ *D2 – ℰ (01) 6613572* · Plan: **F3**
– www.pearl-brasserie.com – Closed 25 December and Sunday
Menu 25 € (lunch) – Carte 39/66 €
• Classic French • Brasserie •
Formal basement restaurant with a small bar-lounge and two surprisingly airy dining rooms; sit in a stylish booth in one of the old coal bunkers. Intriguing modern dishes have a classical base and Mediterranean and Asian influences.

XX **Amuse** · AC

22 Dawson St ⊠ *D2 – ℰ (01) 639 4889 – www.amuse.ie* · Plan: **E3**
*– Closed 2 weeks Christmas-New Year, last week July, first week August,
Sunday and Monday*
Menu 29 € (weekday lunch)/65 € – (booking advisable)
• Modern cuisine • Friendly •
Modern, understated décor provides the perfect backdrop for the intricate, innovative cooking. Dishes showcase Asian ingredients – including kombu and yuzu; which are artfully arranged according to their flavours and textures.

XX · 🐸 **Pichet** · AC 🕰

14-15 Trinity St ⊠ *D2 – ℰ (01) 6771060* · Plan: **E2**
– www.pichetrestaurant.ie – Closed 25 December and 1 January
Menu 25 € (lunch and early dinner) – Carte 34/50 € – (booking essential)
• Classic French • Fashionable • Brasserie •
You can't miss the bright red signs and blue and white striped canopies of this buzzy brasserie – and its checkerboard flooring makes it equally striking inside. Have breakfast or snacks at the bar or classic French dishes in the main room. A good selection of wines are available by the glass or pichet.

XX **Avenue by Nick Munier** 🔳 ⇔ 🏵
1 Crow St ⊠ *D2* – ℰ *(01) 645 5102* – *www.avenue.ie*   Plan: **E2**
– *Closed 1 week January*
Menu 25 € *(early dinner)*
– *Carte 39/42 €* – *(dinner only and lunch Friday-Saturday)*
• French • Brasserie • Design •
A surprisingly large establishment set over 4 levels – the basement houses a
private dining room, the top floor a jazz venue and the other two floors a
smart brasserie with blue leather chairs. Menus offer unfussy bistro favourites.

XX **Saddle Room** – Shelbourne Hotel   ⅃ 🔳 ⇔
27 St Stephen's Grn. ⊠ *D2* – ℰ *(01) 6634500*   Plan: **E3**
– *www.shelbournedining.ie*
Menu 23/45 € – Carte 39/109 €
• Meats and grills • Elegant • Fashionable •
Renowned restaurant with a history as long as that of the hotel in which it
stands. The warm, inviting room features intimate gold booths and a crustacea
counter. The menu offers classic dishes and grills; West Cork beef is a speciality.

XX **Bang**   🔳 ⇔ 🐸
11 Merrion Row ⊠ *D2* – ℰ *(01) 4004229*   Plan: **E3**
– *www.bangrestaurant.com*
Menu 25 € *(early dinner)*/50 € – Carte 41/74 € – *(dinner only)*
• Modern cuisine • Bistro • Fashionable •
Stylish restaurant with an intimate powder blue basement, a bright mezzanine
level and a small, elegant room above. There are good value pre-theatre menus,
a more elaborate à la carte and tasting menus showcasing top Irish produce.

XX **Fade St. Social - Restaurant**   ⅃ ⇔ 🐸 🏵
4-6 Fade St ⊠ *D2* – ℰ *(01) 604 0066*   Plan: **E2**
– *www.fadestsocial.com* – *Closed 25-26 December*
Menu 35 € *(lunch and early dinner)*
– *Carte 31/83 €* – *(dinner only and lunch Thursday-Saturday)*
• Modern cuisine • Brasserie • Fashionable •
Have cocktails on the terrace then head for the big, modern brasserie with its
raised open kitchen. Dishes use Irish ingredients but have a Mediterranean
feel; they specialise in sharing dishes and large cuts of meat such as chateaubriand.

XX **Suesey Street**   ⌂ 🔳 ⇔
26 Fitzwilliam Pl ⊠ *D2* – ℰ *(01) 669 4600*   Plan: **H1**
– *www.sueseystreet.ie* – *Closed 25-30 December, Saturday lunch, Sunday
and Monday*
Menu 25/48 € – Carte 34/60 €
• Modern cuisine • Intimate • Cosy •
An intimate restaurant with sumptuous, eye-catching décor in the basement of
a Georgian townhouse; sit on the superb courtyard terrace with its retractable
awning. Refined, modern cooking brings out the best in home-grown Irish
ingredients.

XX **Dax**   🔳
23 Pembroke St Upper ⊠ *D2* – ℰ *(01) 6761494*   Plan: **E3**
– *www.dax.ie* – *Closed 10 days Christmas, Saturday lunch, Sunday and
Monday*
Menu 30 € *(weekday lunch)* – Carte 44/66 € – *(booking essential)*
• French • Bistro • Classic décor •
Smart, masculine restaurant in the cellar of a Georgian townhouse near Fitzwilliam Square. Tried-and-tested French dishes use top Irish produce and flavours
are clearly defined. The Surprise Menu best showcases the kitchen's talent.

XX **Peploe's**   𝖆 🅰🄲 ▨

16 St Stephen's Grn. ✉ *D2 –* ☏ *(01) 6763144*   Plan: **E3**
*– www.peploes.com – Closed 25-26 December, Good Friday and lunch
bank holidays*
Menu 29 € (lunch and early dinner) – Carte 39/59 € – *(booking essential)*
• Mediterranean cuisine • Cosy • Brasserie •
Atmospheric cellar restaurant – formerly a bank vault – named after the artist.
Comfy room with a warm, clubby feel and a large mural depicting the owner.
The well-drilled team present Mediterranean dishes and an Old World wine list.

X **Delahunt**   𝖆 ⇔

39 Camden Street Lower ✉ *D2 –* ☏ *(01) 5984880*   Plan: **D3**
– www.delahunt.ie – Closed 15 August-1 September, Sunday and Monday
Menu 27 € (lunch) – Carte 34/44 €
– (dinner only and lunch Thursday-Saturday) (booking essential)
• Modern cuisine • Bistro • Fashionable •
An old Victorian grocer's shop mentioned in James Joyce's 'Ulysses'; the clerk's
snug is now a glass-enclosed private dining room. Precisely executed, flavoursome dishes are modern takes on time-honoured recipes. Lunch offers two
choices per course and dinner, four; they also serve snacks in the upstairs bar.

X **Locks**   ⇔

1 Windsor Terr ✉ *D8 –* ☏ *(01) 416 3655*   Plan III : **G1**
*– www.locksrestaurant.ie – Closed Sunday dinner, Monday, Tuesday Lunch
and Wednesday*
Menu 22/45 € – Carte 35/56 € – *(booking essential)*
• Modern cuisine • Bistro • Neighbourhood •
Locals love this corner restaurant overlooking the canal – the downstairs is
buzzy, while upstairs it's more intimate, and the personable team only add to
the feel. Natural flavours are to the fore and dishes are given subtle modern touches; come at the start of the week or before 7pm for the best value menus.

X **Pig's Ear**   ⇔

4 Nassau St ✉ *D2 –* ☏ *(01) 6703865*   Plan: **E2**
*– www.thepigsear.ie – Closed first week January, Sunday and bank
holidays*
Menu 22 € (lunch and early dinner) – Carte 33/49 € – *(booking essential)*
• Modern cuisine • Bistro • Friendly •
Well-established restaurant in a Georgian townhouse overlooking Trinity College. Floors one and two are bustling bistro-style areas filled with mirrors and
porcine-themed memorabilia; floor three is a private room with a Scandinavian
feel. Good value menus list hearty dishes with a modern edge.

X **Etto**

18 Merrion Row ✉ *D2 –* ☏ *(01) 6788872 – www.etto.ie*   Plan: **E3**
– Closed Sunday and bank holidays
Menu 25/28 € (weekdays) – Carte 29/44 € – *(booking essential)*
• Mediterranean cuisine • Rustic • Neighbourhood •
The name of this rustic restaurant means 'little' and it is totally apt! Blackboards
announce the daily wines and the lunchtime 'soup and sandwich' special. Fla-
voursome dishes rely on good ingredients and have Italian influences; the chef
understands natural flavours and follows the 'less is more' approach.

X **Taste at Rustic by Dylan McGrath**

17 South Great George's St (2nd Floor) ✉ *D2 –* ☏ *(01)*
707 9596 – www.tasteatrustic.com – Closed Sunday and Monday   Plan: **E2**
Menu 45 € – Carte 33/100 € – *(dinner only) (booking advisable)*
• Asian • Rustic •
Dylan McGrath's love of Japanese cuisine inspires dishes which explore the five
tastes; sweet, salt, bitter, umami and sour. Ingredients are top-notch and flavours, bold and masculine. Personable staff are happy to recommend dishes.

X **Bastible**

111 South Circular Rd ⊠ *D8 – 𝒞 (01) 473 7409*   Plan III : **G1**
– www.bastible.com – Closed Sunday dinner, Monday and Tuesday
Menu 36/38 € *– (dinner only and lunch Saturday-Sunday) (booking essential)*
• Modern cuisine • Simple • Neighbourhood •

The name refers to the cast iron pot which once sat on the hearth of every family home; they still use it here to make the bread. Modern cooking showcases one main ingredient with minimal accompaniments; menus offer 3 choices per course.

X **Osteria Lucio**   🍴 ᗕ 🅰🅲

The Malting Tower, Clanwilliam Terr ⊠ *D2 – 𝒞 (01)*   Plan: **H1**
662 4198 – www.osterialucio.com – Closed 25-29 December and bank holiday Mondays
Menu 23 € *(early dinner) – Carte 24/44 €*
• Italian • Intimate • Romantic •

Smart restaurant under the railway arches, run by two experienced chefs. Robust, rustic dishes showcase local produce, alongside ingredients imported from Italy; sit by the bar to watch pizzas being cooked in the oak-burning stove.

X **Drury Buildings**   🍴 ♻ 🆐

52-55 Drury St ⊠ *D2 – 𝒞 (01) 960 2095*   Plan: **E2**
– www.drurybuildings.com – Closed 25-26 December, dinner 24 December and Good Friday
Carte 32/54 €
• Italian • Trendy • Brasserie •

A high, laid-back 'New York loft': its impressive terrace has a retractable roof and reclaimed furniture features in the stylish cocktail bar, which offers cicchetti and sharing boards. The airy restaurant serves rustic Italian dishes.

X **Fade St. Social - Gastro Bar**   🍴 ᗕ

4-6 Fade St ⊠ *D2 – 𝒞 (01) 604 0066*   Plan: **E2**
– www.fadestreetsocial.com – Closed 25-26 December and lunch Monday-Tuesday
Menu 35 € *(early dinner) – Carte 23/39 € – (booking essential)*
• International • Fashionable • Tapas bar •

Buzzy restaurant with an almost frenzied feel. It's all about a diverse range of original, interesting small plates, from a bacon and cabbage burger to a lobster hot dog. Eat at the kitchen counter or on leather-cushioned 'saddle' benches.

X **La Maison**   🍴 🅰🅲

15 Castlemarket ⊠ *D2 – 𝒞 (01) 672 7258*   Plan: **E2**
– www.lamaisonrestaurant.ie – Closed 25-27 December and 1-2 January
Menu 22 € *(weekday dinner) – Carte 24/56 €*
• Classic French • Bistro • Cosy •

Sweet little French bistro with tables on the pavement and original posters advertising French products. The experienced, Breton-born chef-owner offers carefully prepared, seasonal Gallic classics, brought to the table by a personable team.

X **SÖDER+KO**   🅰🅲

64 South Great George's St ⊠ *D2 – 𝒞 (01) 478 1590*   Plan: **E2**
– www.soderandko.ie – Closed bank holidays
Carte 22/42 € *– (booking essential)*
• Asian • Fashionable • Trendy •

A vast, vibrant bar-cum-bistro in a former nightclub, with numerous rooms and even a chill-out lounge. Skilfully prepared Asian small plates are a mix of the modern and the classic; they are appealing, satisfying and good value.

X **Rustic Stone**   🍴 ᗕ 🅰🅲

17 South Great George's St ⊠ *D2 – 𝒞 (01) 707 9596*   Plan: **E2**
– www.rusticstone.ie – Closed 25-26 December and 1 January
Menu 30/55 € *– Carte 28/59 €*
• Modern cuisine • Fashionable •

Split-level restaurant offering something a little different. Good quality ingredients are cooked simply to retain their natural flavours and menus focus on healthy and special dietary options; some meats and fish arrive on a sizzling stone.

IRELAND - DUBLIN

X **l'Gueuleton**   🛏 ❤

1 Fade St ⊠ D2 – 𝒞 (01) 6753708   Plan: **E2**
– www.lgueuleton.com – Closed 25-26 December
Menu 25/37 € – Carte 37/50 €
• Classic French • Bistro •

Rustic restaurant with beamed ceilings, Gallic furnishings, a shabby-chic bistro feel and a large pavement terrace. Flavoursome cooking features good value, French country classics which rely on local, seasonal produce. Service is friendly.

X **Camden Kitchen**

3a Camden Mkt, Grantham St ⊠ D8 – 𝒞 (01) 4760125   Plan: **D3**
– www.camdenkitchen.ie – Closed 24-26 December, Sunday and Monday
Menu 19/25 € – Carte 30/50 €
• Classic cuisine • Bistro • Neighbourhood •

Simple, modern, neighbourhood bistro set over two floors; watch the owner cooking in the open kitchen. Tasty dishes use good quality Irish ingredients prepared in classic combinations. Relaxed, friendly service from a young team.

X **Saba**   ❤

26-28 Clarendon St ⊠ D2 – 𝒞 (01) 679 2000   Plan: **E2**
– www.sabadublin.com – Closed Good Friday and 25-26 December
Menu 14 € (weekday lunch)/35 € – Carte 23/46 €
• Thai • Fashionable • Simple •

Trendy, buzzy Thai restaurant and cocktail bar. Simple, stylish rooms with refectory tables, banquettes and amusing photos. Fresh, visual, authentic cooking from an all-Thai team, with a few Vietnamese dishes and some fusion cooking too.

BALLSBRIDGE   **PLAN III**

🏨 **InterContinental Dublin**   🏊 ⌗ ⅃ᴬ 🌐 🐾 ⊡ ❤ 🛎 🚗

Simmonscourt Rd. ⊠ D4 – 𝒞 (003531) 665 4000   Plan: **J2**
– www.intercontinental.com/dublin
197 rm – ⭡245/390 € ⭡⭡245/390 € – ⊊ 28 € – 58 suites
• Luxury • Business • Classic •

Imposing hotel bordering the RDS Arena. Elegant guest areas, state-of-the-art meeting rooms and impressive ballrooms boast ornate décor, antique furnishings and Irish artwork. Spacious, classical bedrooms have marble bathrooms and plenty of extras. A wide-ranging menu is served in the bright, airy restaurant.

🏨 **Dylan**   🏊 ❤ 🛎

Eastmoreland Pl ⊠ D4 – 𝒞 (01) 6603000   Plan: **H1**
– www.dylan.ie – Closed 24-26 December
44 rm – ⭡304/455 € ⭡⭡304/455 € – ⊊ 25 €
• Townhouse • Design • Contemporary •

Red-brick Victorian nurses' home with a sympathetically styled extension and a funky, boutique interior. Tasteful, individually decorated bedrooms offer a host of extras; those in the original building are the most spacious. The stylish restaurant offers a menu of modern Mediterranean dishes and comes complete with a zinc-topped bar and a smartly furnished terrace.

🏨 **Ariel House**   ⌗ 🅿

50-54 Lansdowne Rd ⊠ D4 – 𝒞 (01) 668 5512   Plan: **J1**
– www.ariel-house.net – Closed 22 December-4 January
37 rm ⊊ – ⭡130/290 € ⭡⭡130/290 €
• Townhouse • Luxury • Classic •

Close to the Aviva Stadium and a DART station; a personally run Victorian townhouse with comfy, traditional guest areas and antique furnishings. Warmly decorated bedrooms have modern facilities and smart bathrooms; some feature four-posters.

Pembroke Townhouse   🅿

88 Pembroke Rd ⊠ D4 – ☎ (01) 66 00 277   Plan: **H1**
– www.pembroketownhouse.ie – Closed 2 weeks Christmas-New Year
48 rm – ♦70/350 € ♦♦70/350 € – ⌒ 15 €
• Townhouse • Traditional • Classic •

Friendly, traditionally styled hotel set in 3 Georgian houses. Small lounge with honesty bar and pantry. Sunny breakfast room offering homemade bread, cakes and biscuits. Variously sized, neutrally hued bedrooms; go for a duplex room.

Old Spot   ⅏ AC ⇔

14 Bath Ave ⊠ D4 – ☎ (01) 660 5599   Plan: **J1**
– www.theoldspot.ie – Closed 25-26 December and 1 January
Carte 31/51 €
• Traditional cuisine • Pub • Friendly •

The appealing bar has a stencilled maple-wood floor and a great selection of snacks and bottled craft beers. There's also a relaxed, characterful restaurant filled with vintage posters, which serves pub classics with a modern edge.

Chop House   🍴

2 Shelbourne Rd ⊠ D4 – ☎ (01) 6602390   Plan: **J1**
– www.thechophouse.ie – Closed Saturday lunch
Menu 32 € – Carte 30/55 €
• Meats and grills • Pub • Neighbourhood •

Imposing pub close to the stadium, with a small side terrace, a dark bar and a bright, airy conservatory. The relaxed lunchtime menu is followed by more ambitious dishes in the evening, when the kitchen really comes into its own.

ENVIRONS OF DUBLIN

AT DONNYBROOK

XX   Mulberry Garden   🕽

Mulberry Ln (off Donnybrook Rd) ⊠ D4 – ☎ (01)   Plan: **H2**
269 3300 – www.mulberrygarden.ie – Closed Sunday-Wednesday
Menu 49/70 € – *(dinner only) (booking essential)*
• Modern cuisine • Cosy • Intimate •

Delightful restaurant hidden away in the city suburbs; its interesting L-shaped dining room set around a small courtyard terrace. Choice of two dishes per course on the weekly menu; original modern cooking relies on tasty local produce.

AT RANELAGH

XX   Kinara Kitchen   ⅏ AC 🕽

17 Ranelagh Village ⊠ D6 – ☎ (01) 406 0066   Plan: **H2**
– www.kinarakitchen.ie – Closed 25-26 December and Good Friday
Menu 22 € (lunch and early dinner) – Carte 29/50 €
• Pakistani • Exotic décor • Neighbourhood •

This smart restaurant has become a destination not just for its cooking but for its cocktails too. The friendly, professional team serve a menu of homely, well-spiced Pakistani classics, including a selection from the tandoor oven.

X   Brioche   ⅏ 🕽

51 Elmwood Ave Lower ⊠ D6 – ☎ (01) 4979163   Plan: **H1**
– www.brioche.ie – Closed 25-27 December, 1 January, Sunday, Monday and lunch Tuesday-Wednesday
Menu 25/35 €
• Modern cuisine • Chic • Neighbourhood •

It's all about France at this lovely bistro in the buzzy village-like Ranelagh district. Attractive, modern French-inspired plates use top Irish ingredients and many have playful touches. Brioche is served at the start of every meal.

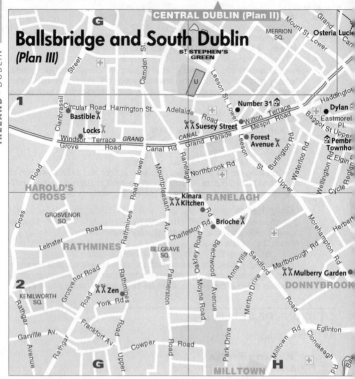

X **Forest Avenue**   ☝

8 Sussex Terr. ✉ *D4 –* ☎ *(01) 667 8337*   Plan: **H1**
– www.forestavenuerestaurant.ie – Closed last 2 weeks August,
25 December-10 January, 11-16 April, Sunday-Tuesday and lunch
Wednesday
Menu 30 € (weekday lunch)/52 € – *(booking essential)*
• Modern cuisine • Neighbourhood • Rustic •
This rustic neighbourhood restaurant is named after a street in Queens and has
a fitting 'NY' vibe, with its jam jar and antler light fittings and stags' heads lining
the walls. Top ingredients feature in well-crafted modern dishes.

AT RATHMINES

XX **Zen**   ☝ 🅰

89 Upper Rathmines Rd ✉ *D6 –* ☎ *(01) 4979428*   Plan: **G2**
– www.zenrestaurant.ie – Closed 25-27 December
Menu 31 € – Carte 23/35 € – *(dinner only and Friday lunch)*
• Chinese • Elegant • Friendly •
Long-standing family-run restaurant, unusually set in an old church hall. At the
centre of the elegant interior is a huge sun embellished with gold leaf. Imaginative Chinese cooking centres around Cantonese and spicy Sichuan cuisine.

426

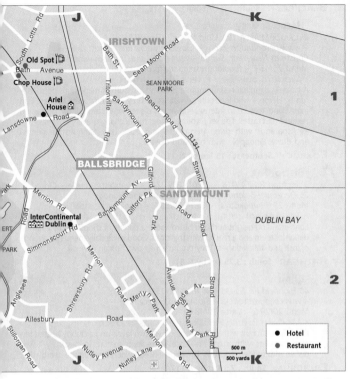

AT CLONTARF Northeast : 5.5 km by R105

Clontarf Castle ⌂ ᵫ ⅙ 🎬 🛗 🅿
Plan: **B1**

Castle Ave. ✉ D3 – ℰ (01) 833 2321
– www.clontarfcastle.ie
111 rm ⌂ – ♥199/469 € ♥♥219/489 €

• Business • Historic building • Historic •

A historic castle dating back to 1172, with sympathetic Victorian extensions; well-located in a quiet residential area close to the city. Contemporary bedrooms are decorated with bold, warm colours and many have four-poster beds. The restaurant offers local meats and seafood in a medieval ambience.

✗ Pigeon House 🛋
🖼

11b Vernon Ave (East : 1km by Clontart rd on Vernon   Plan: **B1**
Ave (R808)) ✉ D3 – ℰ (01) 8057567 – www.pigeonhouse.ie – Closed 25-26 December
Menu 27 € (dinner) – Carte 30/48 €

• Modern cuisine • Neighbourhood • Bistro •

Slickly run neighbourhood bistro that's open for breakfast, lunch and dinner. It's just off the coast road in an up-and-coming area and has a lovely front terrace and a lively feel. Cooking is modern and assured. The bar counter is laden with freshly baked goodies and dishes are full of flavour.

427

AT BLACKROCK Southeast : 7.5 km by R 118

X
 E3 **Heron & Grey** (Damien Grey)

Blackrock Market, 19a Main St – 𝒞 (01) 212 3676
– www.heronandgrey.com – Closed 2 weeks late August, 2 weeks
Christmas-New Year, Sunday-Wednesday and Thursday lunch
Menu 26/48 € – *(booking essential) (tasting menu only)*
• Modern cuisine • Friendly • Intimate •

A homely, candlelit restaurant in a bohemian suburban market; it's personally run by Heron – who leads the service – and Grey, who heads the kitchen. Irish ingredients feature in intensely flavoured dishes which are full of contrasting textures and tastes. The set 5 course dinner menu changes every 2 weeks.
➔ Asparagus with dried trompettes and duck egg. Langoustine, fennel and dulse. Pineapple with rum and clove.

AT FOXROCK Southeast : 13 km by N 11

XX **Bistro One**

3 Brighton Rd ⊠ D18 – 𝒞 (01) 289 7711 – www.bistro-one.ie – Closed
25 December-3 January, 18 April, Sunday and Monday
Menu 29 € (weekdays) – Carte 29/55 € – *(booking essential)*
• Traditional cuisine • Neighbourhood •

Long-standing neighbourhood bistro above a parade of shops; run by a father-daughter team and a real hit with the locals. Good value daily menus list a range of Irish and Italian dishes. They produce their own Tuscan olive oil.

AT RATHGAR South : 3.75 km by N 81

X **Bijou**   🛋 & 🅰🅲 ⇔

46 Highfield Rd ⊠ D6 – 𝒞 (01) 496 1518   Plan: **A1**
– www.bijourathgar.ie – Closed 25-26 December
Menu 20/29 € – Carte 30/48 €
• Modern British • Brasserie • Classic décor •

Friendly restaurant with dining spread over two levels and a clubby heated terrace complete with a gas fire. Local ingredients feature in classically based dishes with modern touches. The experienced owners also run the nearby deli.

AT DUNDRUM South : 7.5 km by R 117

XX **Ananda**   & 🅰🅲 🏵

Sandyford Rd, Dundrum Town Centre ⊠ D14 – 𝒞 (01) 296 0099
– www.anandarestaurant.ie – Closed 25-26 December
Menu 20/50 € – Carte 31/60 € – *(dinner only and lunch Friday-Sunday)*
• Indian • Exotic décor • Fashionable •

Its name means 'bliss' and it's a welcome escape from the bustle of the shopping centre. The stylish interior encompasses a smart cocktail bar, attractive fretwork and vibrant art. Accomplished Indian cooking is modern and original.

AT SANDYFORD South : 10 km by R 117 off R 825

XX **China Sichuan**   🛋 & 🅰🅲

The Forum, Ballymoss Rd. ⊠ D18 – 𝒞 (01) 293 5100
– www.china-sichuan.ie – Closed 25-31 December, Good Friday, lunch
Saturday and bank holidays
Menu 15 € (weekday lunch)/35 € – Carte 27/57 €
• Chinese • Fashionable • Classic décor •

A smart interior is well-matched by creative menus, where Irish produce features in tasty Cantonese classics and some Sichuan specialities. It was established in 1979 and is now run by the third generation of the family.

ITALY
ITALIA

→ **AREA:**
301 262 km² (116 317 sq mi).

→ **POPULATION:**
60 665 551 inhabitants.
Density = 201 per km².

→ **CAPITAL:**
Rome.

→ **CURRENCY:**
Euro (€).

→ **GOVERNMENT:**
Parliamentary republic with two chambers (since 1946). Member of European Union since 1957 (one of the 6 founding countries).

→ **LANGUAGE:**
Italian.

→ **PUBLIC HOLIDAYS:**
New Year's Day (1 Jan); Epiphany (6 Jan); Easter Monday (late Mar/Apr); Liberation Day (25 Apr); Labor Day (1 May); Republic Day (2 June); Assumption of the Virgin Mary (15 Aug); All Saints' Day (1 Nov); Immaculate Conception (8 Dec); Christmas Day (25 Dec); St Stephen's Day (26 Dec).

→ **LOCAL TIME:**
GMT+1 hour in winter and GMT +2 hours in summer.

→ **CLIMATE:**
Temperate Mediterranean with mild winters and hot, sunny summers (Rome: January 8°C; July 30°C).

→ **EMERGENCY:**
Police ☎ **112**; Medical Assistance ☎ **118**; Fire Brigade ☎ **115**. (Dialling **112** within any EU country will redirect your call and contact the emergency services.)

→ **ELECTRICITY:**
230 volts AC, 50Hz; 2 round pin sockets.

→ **FORMALITIES:**
Travellers from the European Union (EU), Switzerland, Iceland and the main countries of North and South America need a national identity card or passport (America: passport required) to visit Italy for less than three months (tourism or business purpose). For visitors from other countries a visa may be required, in addition to a passport, especially for those wishing to stay for longer than three months. We advise you to check with your embassy before travelling.

ROME
ROMA

Population: 2 864 731

Scaliger/iStock

Rome wasn't built in a day, and, when visiting, it's pretty hard to do it justice in less than three. The Italian capital is richly layered in Imperial, Renaissance, baroque and modern architecture, and its broad piazzas, hooting traffic and cobbled thoroughfares all lend their part to the heady fare: a theatrical stage cradled within seven famous hills. Being Eternal, Rome never ceases to feel like a lively, living city, while at the same time a scintillating monument to Renaissance power and an epic centre of antiquity. Nowhere else offers such a wealth of classical remains; set alongside palaces and churches, and bathed in the soft, golden light for which it is famous. When Augustus became the first Emperor of Rome, he could hardly have imagined the impact his city's language, laws and calendar would have upon the world.

The River Tiber snakes its way north to south through the heart of Rome. On its west bank lies the characterful and 'independent' neighbourhood of Trastevere, while north of here is Vatican City. Over the river the Piazza di Spagna area to the north has Rome's smartest shopping streets, while the southern boundary is marked by the Aventine and Celian hills, the latter overlooking the Colosseum. Esquiline's teeming quarter is just to the east of the city's heart; that honour goes to The Capitol, which gave its name to the concept of a 'capital' city.

ROME IN...

→ **ONE DAY**
Capitol, Forum, Colosseum, Pantheon, Trevi Fountain, Spanish Steps.

→ **TWO DAYS**
Via Condotti, Piazza Navona and surrounding churches, Capitoline museums.

→ **THREE DAYS**
A day on the west bank of the Tiber at Trastevere, Vatican City.

PRACTICAL INFORMATION

ARRIVAL-DEPARTURE

Leonardo da Vinci Airport at Fiumicino is 32km southwest of Rome. The Fiumicino Leonardo Express train to Stazione Termini runs every 30min and takes 35min. Every 30min the Cotral bus travels to Cornelia Station (Metro Line A).

GETTING AROUND

Rome is served by a metro, bus and tram system. Tickets are available from metro stations, bus terminals, ticket machines, tobacconists, newsagents, cafés and tourist information centres. Choose your ticket type: a single ticket, which must be time stamped on board, or travelcards for one, three or seven days. Rome is best seen on foot, so make sure you have a good pair of walking shoes. Avoid the likes of sleeveless tops, shorts and miniskirts if you want to visit religious sites.

CALENDAR HIGHLIGHTS

February
Carnival.

March
Spring Festival, Independent Film Festival, Cultural Heritage Week, Rome Marathon.

April
Rome's Birthday, Parklife Festival.

June-August
Cinema Isle.

June-September
The Roman Summer.

July
Festa de Noantri, Tevere Expo.

July-August
Secret Passages.

July-September
New Operafestival.

September
White Night.

October
Rome Film Festival.

November
Romaeuropa Festival.

EATING OUT

Despite being Italy's capital, Rome largely favours a local, traditional cuisine, typically found in an unpretentious trattoria or osteria. Although not far from the sea, the city doesn't go in much for fish, and food is often connected to the rural, pastoral life with products coming from the surrounding Lazio hills, which also produce

good wines. Pasta, of course, is not to be missed, and lamb is favoured among meats for the main course. So too, the 'quinto quarto': a long-established way of indicating those parts of the beef (tail, tripe, liver, spleen, lungs, heart, kidney) left over after the best bits had gone to the richest families. For international cuisine combined with a more refined setting, head for the elegant hotels: very few other areas of Italy have such an increasing number of good quality restaurants within a hotel setting. Locals like to dine later in Rome than say, Milan, with 1pm, or 8pm the very earliest you'd dream of appearing for lunch or dinner. In the tourist hotspots, owners are, of course, only too pleased to open that bit earlier.

Hassler

piazza Trinità dei Monti 6 ✉ *00187 –* Ⓜ *Spagna* Plan: **F1**
– ☎ 06 699340 – www.hotelhasslerroma.com
93 rm – ♦380/505 € ♦♦465/920 € – ☱ 38 € – 13 suites
• Grand Luxury • Historic • Elegant •
Superbly located at the top of the Spanish Steps, this hotel combines tradition, prestige and elegance. The height of splendour is reached in the magnificent suite that occupies the whole of the eighth floor. It has a private lift, additional accommodation for security staff, two panoramic terraces, modern furnishings and all the latest technology.
❀ **Imàgo** – See restaurant listing

De Russie

via del Babuino 9 ✉ *00187 –* Ⓜ *Flaminio* Plan: **F1**
– ☎ 06 328881 – www.roccofortehotels.com/hotel-de-russie
121 rm – ♦363/687 € ♦♦506/958 € – ☱ 38 € – 25 suites
• Grand Luxury • Historic • Personalised •
One of the best in Rome, this hotel occupying a building designed by Valadier in the early 19C boasts a light, harmonious decor. Elegant guestrooms, as well as the Popolo and Picasso suites, which were completely refurbished in spring 2016: these two private apartments are decorated with original art works and antiques. The hotel's 'secret garden' is planted with rose bushes and jasmine.
Le Jardin de Russie – See restaurant listing

Grand Hotel Plaza

via del Corso 126 ✉ *00186 –* Ⓜ *Spagna – ☎ 06 67495* Plan: **F2**
– www.grandhotelplaza.com
196 rm – ♦200/430 € ♦♦250/460 € – ☱ 25 € – 8 suites
• Grand Luxury • Palace • Personalised •
This hotel boasts huge, stunning, late-19C lounges decorated in Art Nouveau-style with coffered ceilings and a profusion of marble, frescoes and glass. The guestrooms are also furnished in period style, as is the atmospheric dining room. Panoramic terrace with a Champagne bar.

Indigo Rome St. George

via Giulia 62 ✉ *00186 – ☎ 06 686611* Plan: **E2**
– www.hotelindigo.com/romestgeorge
64 rm – ♦260/440 € ♦♦260/440 € – ☱ 29 €
• Boutique hotel • Traditional • Design •
This boutique, designer-style hotel is in one of the most beautiful streets in Rome. It offers an elegant ambience and luxurious furnishings in its public areas and spacious guestrooms.
I Sofà di Via Giulia – See restaurant listing

Grand Hotel de la Minerve

piazza della Minerva 69 ✉ *00186 – ☎ 06 695201* Plan: **F2**
– www.grandhoteldelaminerve.com
135 rm – ♦220/700 € ♦♦270/750 € – ☱ 35 € – 4 suites
• Luxury • Historic • Elegant •
An historic building surrounded by ancient monuments. Elegant atmosphere and an imaginative menu of traditional cuisine. Attractive views from the terrace.

D'Inghilterra

via Bocca di Leone 14 ✉ *00187 – ☎ 06 699811* Plan: **F2**
– www.hoteldinghilterra.com
88 rm – ☱ 230/480 € ♦♦290/633 € – 7 suites
• Historic building • Grand Luxury • Romantic •
A haven for tourists from around the world since as early as the 17C, this hotel has the charming ambience of an elegant private house with delightful, indivi-dual-style guestrooms. Find elegant lounges, an atmospheric bar, and a restau-rant serving simple, classic cuisine at lunchtime and more elaborate, ambitious fare in the evening.

ITALY - ROME

Raphaël

largo Febo 2 ✉ *00186* – ☎ *06 682831*
– *www.raphaelhotel.com*
49 rm – ♦200/480 € ♦♦250/530 € – ⊡ 28 € – 1 suite
• Boutique hotel • Luxury • Romantic •
With its collection of porcelain, antiquarian artefacts and sculptures by famous artists, the entrance to this hotel resembles a museum. The recently renovated guestrooms are modern in style. The menu in this attractive restaurant with a panoramic terrace focuses mainly on Italian cuisine, along with some French dishes.

Plan: **E2**

Dei Borgognoni

via del Bufalo 126 ✉ *00187* – Ⓜ *Spagna*
– ☎ *06 69941505* – *www.hotelborgognoni.it*
51 rm ⊡ – ♦180/260 € ♦♦215/295 €
• Traditional • Luxury • Contemporary •
Occupying a 19C palazzo, this elegant hotel's spacious, modern public rooms and comfortable guestrooms combine both traditional and modern features.

Plan: **F2**

Nazionale

piazza Montecitorio 131 ✉ *00186* – ☎ *06 695001*
– *www.hotelnazionale.it*
100 rm ⊡ – ♦220/290 € ♦♦270/390 € – 1 suite
• Traditional • Luxury • Elegant •
Overlooking Piazza di Montecitorio, this hotel occupies an 18C building with elegant public areas and guestrooms furnished in different styles. In this city so often crowded with visitors, the fact that the restaurant is open non-stop from noon until 7pm will appeal, as will the delicious Mediterranean cuisine.

Plan: **F2**

D.O.M.

via Giulia 131 ✉ *00186 Roma* – ☎ *06 6832144*
– *www.domhotelroma.com*
14 rm – ♦240/1250 € ♦♦240/1250 € – 4 suites
• Luxury • Traditional • Modern •
The initials of this hotel stand for Deo Optimo Maximo. The 17C palazzo combines decor from the adjacent church with contemporary furnishings, subtle colours and three works by Andy Warhol. Terrace bar on the top floor.

Plan: **E3**

Grand Hotel del Gianicolo

viale delle Mura Gianicolensi 107 ✉ *00152*
– Ⓜ *Cipro Musei Vaticani* – ☎ *06 58333405* – *www.grandhotelgianicolo.it*
48 rm ⊡ – ♦110/495 € ♦♦130/495 €
• Traditional • Business • Classic •
A stylish hotel on the Gianicolo offering comfortable guestrooms and elegant public areas. You also have the illusion of being a guest in a smart country house, thanks to the beautiful outdoor pool – an unusual sight in Rome. Contemporary cuisine is served in the Corte degli Angeli.

Plan: **B3**

Piranesi-Palazzo Nainer

via del Babuino 196 ✉ *00187* – Ⓜ *Flaminio*
– ☎ *06 328041* – *www.hotelpiranesi.com*
32 rm ⊡ – ♦108/160 € ♦♦125/290 €
• Traditional • Luxury • Classic •
The lobby, guestrooms and corridors of this hotel are decorated with marble, elegant furnishings and an unusual exhibition of old fabrics. The hotel also boasts a roof garden and sun terrace.

Plan: **F1**

Manfredi Suite in Rome

via Margutta 61 ✉ *00187* – Ⓜ *Spagna* – ☎ *06 3207676*
– *www.hotelmanfredi.it*
21 rm ⊡ – ♦119/240 € ♦♦120/299 € – 1 suite
• Inn • Traditional • Elegant •
Housed on the third floor of a palazzo on the famous Via Margutta. Elegant, individually furnished guestrooms, all of which boast the latest in modern facilities. Excellent international breakfast of natural products, including yoghurt and homemade pastries.

Plan: **F1**

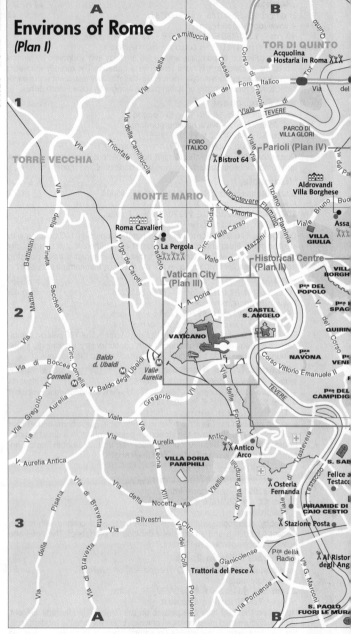

Environs of Rome
(Plan I)

Camilluccia

TOR DI QUINTO
Acquolina
● Hostaria in Roma ✗✗✗

Via della Camilluccia

Cassia

Via del Foro Italico

Viale TEVERE

Via del

TORRE VECCHIA

Triontale

FORO
ITALICO

✗ Bistrot 64

PARCO DI
VILLA GLORI

Parioli (Plan IV)

MONTE MARIO

Lungotevere

Tiziano Flaminia

Flaminio

Aldrovandi
Villa Borghese

Bruno   Buo

Roma Cavalieri

V. Cadlolo

● La Pergola
✗✗✗✗✗

Clodia

L. di Vittoria

Circ. Viale Carso

Viale

G.   Mazzini

Viale

Assa
✗✗✗

VILLA
GIULIA

Historical Centre
(Plan II)

V. Ugo de Carolis

Vatican City
(Plan III)

V. A. Doria

CASTEL
S. ANGELO

VILL
BORGH

Pza DEL
POPOLO

Pza I
SPAG

Battistini   Pineta   Sacchetti

Via   Mattia

Circ Cornelia

Via di Boccea

Cornelia

V. Baldo degli Ubaldi

Baldo
d. Ubaldi

Ⓜ Valle
Aurelia

VATICANO

Gregorio

VII

Via delle Fornaci

del   Corso

NAVONA

Corso Vittorio Emanuele II

QUIRIN

Pza
VENE

F

Pza DEL
CAMPIDIG

Via di Gregorio XI

Aurelia

Viale

Via

Aurelia

Antica

✗✗ Antico
Arco

✗

TEVERE

Testaccio

S. SAB

V. Aurelia Antica

Via della

Leona

VILLA DORIA
PAMPHILI

Vitellia

Ostería
Fernanda

Felice a
Testacc

PIRAMIDE DI
CAIO CESTIO

✗

Nocetta

Via

XIII   Circ.

✗ Stazione Posta ●

Via   di   Bravetta

Silvestri

V. dei   Colli

N. di Villa Pamph

Pza della
Radio

✗ Al Ristor
degli Ang

Via   della

Via di Bravetta

● Gianicolense
Trattoria del Pesce ✗

Via G. Marconi

Via Portuense

Portuensi

Pisana

S. PAOLO
FUORI LE MURA

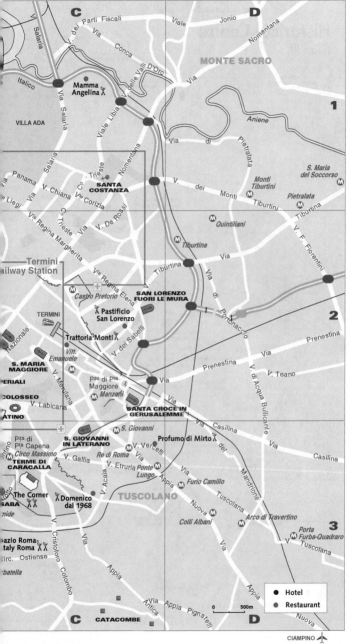

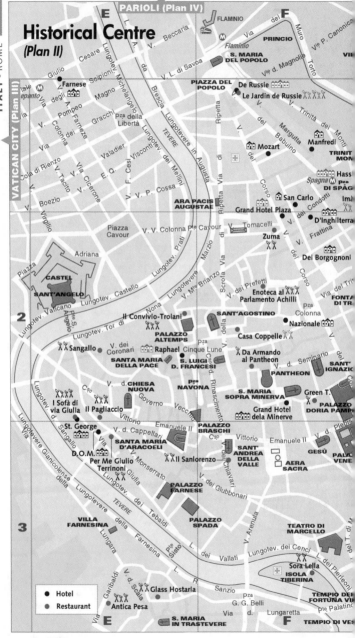

Historical Centre
(Plan II)

FLAMINIO

del

PRINCIO

Via

Flaminio

Lungotev. Beccaria

Lungotev. L. A. da

Cesare

Giulio

Via

Farnese

Lungotev. Scipioni, Michelangelo

V. degli A.

Magno

Pompeo

V. Colonna dei

Gracchi

Pza della Libertà

Valadier

Via

Cola di Rienzo

V. Tacito

V. Cicerone

E. Q.

F. Cesi Viscontev. del Mellini

Boezio

V. P. Cossa

Virgilio

Piazza Cavour

Adriana

Piazza

CASTEL SANT'ANGELO

Lungotev. Vaticano

Lungotev. Castello

Pte S. Angelo

Lungotev. Tor di Nona

V. dei Coronari

Sangallo

Lungotevere Gianicolense della

Lungotev. d. Sangallo

Via

St. George

D.O.M.

Per Me Giulio Terrinoni

Lungotev. dei Tebaldi

VILLA FARNESINA

Lungara

V. d. Cappellari

Lungotev. della Farnesina

TEVERE

Pte Sisto

L. dei Vallati

V. di Monserrato

Via Giulia

Garibaldi

V. d. Scala

Antica Pesa

Glass Hostaria

S. MARIA IN TRASTEVERE

S. MARIA DEL POPOLO

PIAZZA DEL POPOLO

De Russie
Le Jardin de Russie

Via di Ripetta

Brescia

Lungotevere in Augusta

TEVERE

Via V. V. Colonna

Pte Cavour

Lungotevere Prati

Lungotevere

V. M.te Brianzo

V. della Scrofa

Mozart

Manfredi

Vle d. Magnolie

V. L. di Savoia

Trinità dei Monti

Margutta

Via del Babuino

TRINITÀ MON

Hass

Spagna

DI SPAG

San Carlo

Imà

Via del Corso

V. dei Condotti

D'Inghilterra

Frattina

ARA PACIS AUGUSTAE

Grand Hotel Plaza

Tomacelli

Zuma

Dei Borgognoni

V. dei Prefetti

Enoteca al Parlamento Achilli

SANT'AGOSTINO

Il Convivio-Troiani

PALAZZO ALTEMPS

Raphael

Cinque Lune

SANTA MARIA DELLA PACE

S. LUIGI D. FRANCESI

V. d. CHIESA NUOVA

Casa Coppelle

Pza NAVONA

Da Armando al Pantheon

V. d. Seminario

PANTHEON

SANT' IGNAZIO

Pza Colonna

Nazionale

Via del Tri

FONTA DI TR.

Corso

S. MARIA SOPRA MINERVA

Grand Hotel dela Minerve

PALAZZO DORIA PAMP

Green T.

I Sofà di via Giulia

Il Pagliaccio

Governo

Vittorio

Emanuele II

Vecchia

Rinascimento

PALAZZO BRASCHI

SANTA MARIA D'ARACOELI

Il Sanlorenzo

Vittorio Emanuele II

SANT'ANDREA DELLA VALLE

AERA SACRA

V. d. Plebis

GESÙ

PALA VENE

PALAZZO FARNESE

C.so

V. dei Giubbonari

V. Arenula

PALAZZO SPADA

TEATRO DI MARCELLO

Lungotev. dei Cenci

L. dei Pierleon

Sora Lella

ISOLA TIBERINA

Pza G. G. Belli

Sanzio

Lungaretta

Via d.

TEMPIO DEL FORTUNA VIR

Pte Palatino

TEMPIO DI VES

● Hotel
● Restaurant

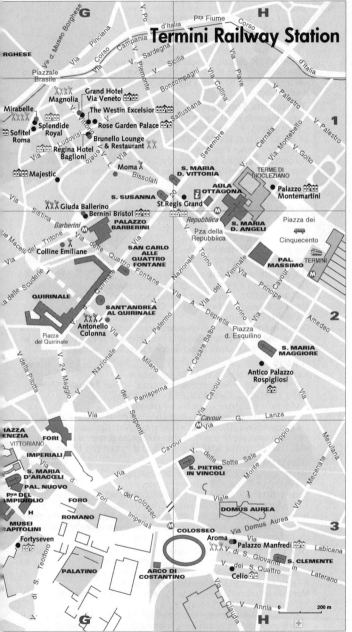

Termini Railway Station

RGHESE

Piazzale
Brasile

Mirabelle

Sofitel
Roma

Splendide
Royal

Magnolia

Grand Hotel
Via Veneto

The Westin Excelsior

Rose Garden Palace

Brunello Lounge
& Restaurant

Regina Hotel
Baglioni

Majestic

Moma

Giuda Ballerino

Bernini Bristol

S. SUSANNA

St.Regis Grand

S. MARIA
D. VITTORIA

AULA
OTTAGONA

TERME DI
DIOCLEZIANO

Palazzo
Montemartini

Bissolati

PALAZZO
BARBERINI

Barberini

Repubblica

Pza della
Repubblica

S. MARIA
D. ANGELI

Piazza dei

Cinquecento

Colline Emiliane

SAN CARLO
ALLE
QUATTRO
FONTANE

PAL.
MASSIMO

TERMINI

QUIRINALE

SANT'ANDREA
AL QUIRINALE

Antonello
Colonna

Piazza
del Quirinale

Piazza
d. Esquilino

S. MARIA
MAGGIORE

Antico Palazzo
Rospigliosi

Cavour

Lanza

IAZZA
ENEZIA

FORI
VITTORIANO

IMPERIALI

S. MARIA
D'ARACŒLI

PAL. NUOVO

Pza DEL
AMPIDIGLIO

FORO
ROMANO

S. PIETRO
IN VINCOLI

DOMUS AUREA

MUSEI
CAPITOLINI

Fortyseven

PALATINO

COLOSSEO

ARCO DI
COSTANTINO

Aroma

Palazzo Manfredi

Cello

S. CLEMENTE

0   200 m

437

🏨 Mozart 〔AC〕

via dei Greci 23/b ✉ *00187 –* Ⓜ *Spagna* Plan: **F1**
– ℰ 06 36001915 – www.hotelmozart.com
78 rm ⌧ – ♦69/300 € ♦♦99/350 €
• Traditional • Family • Cosy •

Housed in a 19C palazzo, this hotel boasts elegant public areas and guestrooms in the same refined style. The Vivaldi Luxury Rooms annexe situated just a stone's throw from the hotel offers slightly larger, modern rooms, as well as its own breakfast room.

🏨 Fontanella Borghese 〔AC〕

largo Fontanella Borghese 84 ✉ *00186 –* Ⓜ *Spagna* Plan: **F2**
– ℰ 06 68809504 – www.fontanellaborghese.com
24 rm ⌧ – ♦90/130 € ♦♦130/205 €
• Family • Inn • Personalised •

In a central yet peaceful location, on the 2nd and 3rd floors of a historical building looking out over Palazzo Borghese, is this distinguished and refined hotel with classy finishings.

🏨 San Carlo 〔AC〕

via Delle Carrozze 92/93 ✉ *00187 –* Ⓜ *Spagna* Plan: **F1**
– ℰ 06 6784548 – www.hotelsancarloroma.com
50 rm ⌧ – ♦80/130 € ♦♦100/230 €
• Traditional • Cosy • Centrally located •

This inviting hotel is parallel to Via Condotti. It offers pleasant guestrooms and a charming breakfast terrace, which is particularly delightful in the summer months.

🏨🏨🏨🏨 Le Jardin de Russie – Hotel De Russie 🛏🍴♿〔AC〕

via del Babuino 9 ✉ *00187 –* Ⓜ *Piazzale Flaminio* Plan: **F1**
– ℰ 06 32888870 – www.roccofortehotels.com/hotel-de-russie
Menu 40 € (weekday lunch)/58 € – Carte 68/124 €
• Mediterranean cuisine • Luxury • Chic •

Despite its French name, this restaurant serves decidedly Italian cuisine with a creative and contemporary flavour. At lunchtime, an extensive buffet offers an alternative to the à la carte. Brunch is available on Saturdays and Sundays.

🏨🏨🏨 Imàgo – Hotel Hassler 〔AC〕
❀

piazza Trinità dei Monti 6 ✉ *00187 –* Ⓜ *Spagna* Plan: **F1**
– ℰ 06 69934726 – www.imagorestaurant.com – Closed 2 January-9 February
Menu 120/150 € – Carte 100/166 € – *(dinner only)*
• Modern cuisine • Luxury • Friendly •

This restaurant continues to be a perennial favourite, thanks to its large windows and unforgettable views of Rome. Modern cuisine made with high quality ingredients.
➔ Risotto cacio, pepi e sesami. Merluzzo carbonaro glassato al sake, verdurine viola. Dolce mozzarella di bufala, grattachecca di frutta rossa e balsamico.

🏨🏨🏨 Hostaria dell'Orso ❀🍴〔AC〕↻

via dei Soldati 25/c ✉ *00186 – ℰ 06 68301192* Plan: **E-F2**
– www.hdo.it – Closed August and Sunday
Carte 116/155 € – *(dinner only) (booking advisable)*
• Modern cuisine • Luxury • Traditional décor •

Housed in an historic building, this restaurant has intimate, romantic dining rooms decorated in a simple, elegant style. The elegant cuisine is based around the highest quality ingredients.

🏨🏨🏨 Il Pagliaccio (Anthony Genovese) ❀〔AC〕
❀❀

via dei Banchi Vecchi 129/a ✉ *00186 – ℰ 06 68809595* Plan: **E2**
– www.ristoranteilpagliaccio.it – Closed 3 weeks in August, 25 January-8 February, Sunday, Monday and Tuesday lunch
Menu 75 € (lunch)/155 € – Carte 95/140 € – *(booking advisable)*
• Creative • Chic • Luxury •

This restaurant strikes a modern note in the heart of Renaissance Rome. The cuisine is modern and innovative, reinterpreting traditional dishes with a contemporary twist.
➔ Spaghetti di grano arso, granita di ricci e lumachine di mare. Agnello, aglio nero, carciofi e gel di acqua di mare. Praline di caffè e nocciole, ananas allo zenzero.

Enoteca al Parlamento Achilli

via dei Prefetti 15 ⊠ 00186 – Ⓜ *Spagna*　Plan: **F2**
– ℰ 06 86761422 – www.enotecalparlamento.com – Closed August and Sunday
Menu 70/130 € – Carte 80/112 €
• Creative • Elegant •
Although there is little to suggest a restaurant from the exterior, this elegant wine bar in the city centre leads to two wood-vaulted and interconnecting dining rooms. The striking individual cuisine is based on bold combinations and contrasts, perfect for anyone looking for a change from more traditional fare. A truly delightful and imaginative exploration of culinary flavours!
→ Cioccolato bianco, olive in tapenade, pesce marinato. Spugnole in salsa di albicocche. Cremoso di rognone, gamberi scottati, patate al gin.

Il Convivio-Troiani (Angelo Troiani)

vicolo dei Soldati 31 ⊠ 00186 – ℰ 06 6869432　Plan: **E2**
– www.ilconviviotroiani.com – Closed 1 week in August, 24-26 December and Sunday
Menu 110/125 € – Carte 81/136 € – *(dinner only)*
• Modern cuisine • Luxury • Chic •
This elegant restaurant is in the heart of the historic centre. Amid a decor of frescoes, paintings and modern minimalism, enjoy quintessential Italian cuisine. Choose from risottos and pasta, as well as a selection of specialities from the Lazio region.
→ Spaghettoni all'amatriciana. Dall'agnello... tutto carré: quattro differenti preparazioni con le diverse parti. Ciliegie, rosa e cioccolato.

Antica Pesa

via Garibaldi 18 ⊠ 00153 – ℰ 06 5809236　Plan: **E3**
– www.anticapesa.it – Closed Sunday
Carte 49/98 € – *(dinner only)*
• Cuisine from Lazio • Elegant • Cosy •
Typical Roman dishes made from carefully selected ingredients grace the menu of this restaurant, which is housed in a grain storehouse that once belonged to the neighbouring Papal State. Large paintings by contemporary artists hang on the walls and there is a small lounge with a fireplace near the entrance.

Il Sanlorenzo

via dei Chiavari 4/5 ⊠ 00186 – ℰ 06 6865097　Plan: **F3**
– www.ilsanlorenzo.it – Closed 6-30 August, Sunday, lunch Monday and Saturday
Menu 65 € (weekdays)/85 € – Carte 86/130 €
• Seafood • Elegant • Trendy •
A historic palazzo built over the foundations of the Teatro Pompeo is home to this atmospheric restaurant, which brings together history and contemporary art. However, the real star is the fish on the menu, most of which comes from the island of Ponza, and is served either raw or cooked very simply in a modern style.

I Sofà di Via Giulia – Hotel Indigo Rome St. George

via Giulia 62 ⊠ 00186 – ℰ 06 68661245　Plan: **E2**
– www.isofadiviagiulia.com
Carte 44/75 €
• Modern cuisine • Elegant • Luxury •
Regional cuisine with a modern twist, and an impressive wine list that more than meets the high standards of this restaurant. Lively, designer-style decor, as well as a delightful roof garden for summer dining with panoramic views of the city centre as a backdrop.

Per Me Giulio Terrinoni 🛖 ♿ 𝔸𝕂

ⓒ *vicolo del Malpasso 9* ✉ *00186 Roma –* ☎ *06 6877365*   Plan: **E3**
– www.giulioterrinoni.it – Closed 3 weeks in August
Menu 75/120 € – Carte 74/146 € – *(number of covers limited, pre-book)*
• Creative • Contemporary décor • Intimate •
This intimate and minimalist-style restaurant situated in a narrow street crossing Via Giulia was opened in late 2015 by chef Terrinoni. He has created an imaginative menu that is balanced and full of flavour. Renowned for his excellent fish specialities, the chef is just as skilful in his preparation of meat. The new lunchtime formula offers either a classic menu or a selection of reasonably priced tapas-style options.
➜ Carpaccio di scampi, fegato grasso e gel di cipolla rossa. Ricciola di profondità arrosto, raviolo di melanzane affumicate, harissa (salsa nordafricana), salsa di zuppa di pesce. Cacio e pepe (dessert!): millefoglie di pasta, mousse di ricotta, gelato al pepe affumicato, arancio.

Glass Hostaria (Cristina Bowerman) 𝟴𝟴 𝔸𝕂

ⓒ *vicolo del Cinque 58* ✉ *00153 –* ☎ *06 58335903*   Plan: **E3**
– www.glasshostaria.it – Closed 3-26 July, 9-31 January and Monday
Menu 75/110 € – Carte 66/106 € – *(dinner only)*
• Creative • Design • Fashionable •
Situated in the heart of Trastevere, this restaurant boasts an ultra-modern design with an interesting play of light and a slightly unsettling atmosphere. The excellent cuisine also features highly modern touches.
➜ Raviolo liquido di parmigiano 60 mesi, burro d'Isigny e asparagi. Astice, avocado, tapioca, semi di senape fritti. Zuppetta di caffè, mandorle sabbiate, gelato al liquore a base di whiskey.

Casa Coppelle 𝟴𝟴 ♿ 𝔸𝕂 ⇔

piazza delle Coppelle 49 ✉ *00186 –* ☎ *06 68 89 17 07*   Plan: **F2**
– www.casacoppelle.com
Menu 35 € – Carte 41/155 € – *(booking advisable)*
• Mediterranean cuisine • Chic • Elegant •
Situated in the heart of the city, this delightfully intimate restaurant offers a number of different dining rooms, from a 'gallery of portraits' to the British-style library rooms and the 'herbier' with prints on the walls. There is something for everyone here, although every guest will enjoy the same modern reinterpretations of Mediterranean cuisine.

Sangallo ai Coronari 🛖 𝔸𝕂 ⇔

via dei Coronari 180 ✉ *00186 –* ☎ *06 68134055*   Plan: **E2**
– www.ristorantesangallo.com – Closed 9-23 August
Menu 45/75 €
– Carte 53/87 € – (dinner only 2 August-6 September) (booking advisable)
• Modern cuisine • Elegant • Traditional décor •
A pleasing blend of old and new in a 16C palazzo near San Salvatore in Lauro church. Various elegant dining rooms act as a stylish setting for the contemporary cuisine.

Sora Lella 𝔸𝕂

via di Ponte Quattro Capi 16 (Tiber Island) ✉ *00186*   Plan: **F3**
– ☎ *06 6861601 – www.trattoriasoralella.it – Closed 15-20 August and Tuesday*
Menu 40/50 € – Carte 32/63 €
• Roman • Traditional décor • Friendly •
Son and grandchildren of the famous late ""Sora Lella"", perpetuate in a dignified way the tradition both in the warmth of the welcome and in the typical Roman elements of the offer.

XX **Zuma** 🏵 🕭 🎧

via della Fontanella di Borghese 48 ✉ *00186 –* Ⓜ *Spagna*   Plan: **F2**
– ℰ 06 99266622 – www.zumarestaurant.com – Closed 8-22 August and Monday
Menu 85/145 € – Carte 31/180 € – *(booking advisable)*
• **Fusion** • **Fashionable** • **Trendy** •

An international chain dedicated to contemporary Japanese food, Zuma has
chosen the fourth and fifth floors (with a terrace) of Palazzo Fendi for its first
Italian restaurant. The striking and decidedly fashionable cuisine consists of a
delicious sushi corner, the robata grill and a selection of modern and creative
dishes. A huge success ever since it opened.

X **Felice a Testaccio** 🎧

😊 *via Mastrogiorgio 29* ✉ *00153 – ℰ 06 5746800*   Plan: **B3**
– www.feliceatestaccio.com – Closed 1 week in August
Carte 34/45 € – *(booking advisable)*
• **Traditional cuisine** • **Friendly** • **Traditional décor** •

The simple, family, trattoria-style atmosphere of Felice a Testaccio is so popular that
it is now almost essential to book ahead for a table. Make sure you try the legendary roast lamb with potatoes, as well as the *cacio e pepe* tonnarelli pasta and the
tiramisù. Without a doubt, one of the standard-bearers of Latium cuisine.

X **Da Armando al Pantheon** 🎧

salita dè Crescenzi 31 – Ⓜ *Spagna – ℰ 06 68803034*   Plan: **F2**
– www.armandoalpantheon.it – Closed August, Saturday dinner and Sunday
Carte 36/67 € – *(number of covers limited, pre-book)*
• **Roman** • **Family** • **Friendly** •

Just a few metres from the Pantheon, this small family-run restaurant has been
delighting locals and visitors for years with its traditional cuisine. Booking ahead
is essential if you want to be sure of a table.

X **Green T.** 🎧 ⇔

Via del Piè di Marmo 28 ✉ *00186 – ℰ 06 679 8628*   Plan: **F2**
– www.green-tea.it – Closed 2 weeks in August and Sunday
Menu 14 € (weekday lunch)/18 € – Carte 28/66 €
• **Chinese** • **Minimalist** • **Friendly** •

Owner Yan introduces tea lovers to the 'Tao of Tea' (an introduction and tasting of
this ancient beverage) in this original restaurant situated on four floors of a building
not far from the Pantheon. Asian cuisine takes pride of place on the menu.

ST-PETER'S BASILICA (Vatican City and Monte Mario)   **PLAN III**

 Rome Cavalieri

via Cadlolo 101 ✉ *00136 – ℰ 06 35091*   Plan: **A2**
– www.romecavalieri.it
345 rm – 🕇265/915 € 🕇🕇299/950 € – ♻ 38 € – 25 suites
• **Grand Luxury** • **Chain** • **Elegant** •

This imposing building overlooks the entire city of Rome. The hotel has excellent facilities, including extensive gardens, an outdoor swimming pool, plus a
fine art collection. Restaurant with an informal atmosphere by the edge of the
swimming pool for dining with live music.
❀❀❀ **La Pergola** – See restaurant listing

🏛 **Gran Melià Roma**   🏵 🌳 🕭 🎧 🏟 🏊 ⚓ 🎧 🛄 🏝

via del Gianicolo 3 ✉ *00165 – ℰ 06925901*   Plan: **K2**
– www.granmeliarome.com
116 rm – 🕇295/800 € 🕇🕇295/800 € – ♻ 36 € – 22 suites
• **Luxury** • **Chain** • **Modern** •

This hotel boasts a truly historic setting in an old monastery on the site of the
villa that once belonged to Nero's mother, Agrippina. There is an elegant,
modern feel to the public areas and guestrooms, some of which feature designer bathtubs that can be seen from the bed. A superb address with a charming
atmosphere and an excellent choice of facilities.
Vivavoce – See restaurant listing

ST. PETER'S BASILICA: PLAN III

Villa Laetitia
☖ ₤ð AK
lungotevere delle Armi 22/23 ✉ 00195
Plan: L2
– Ⓜ *Lepanto* – ℰ 06 3226776
– *www.villalaetitia.com*
21 rm ☷ – †100/250 € ††130/600 €
· Historic building · Luxury · Romantic ·
Enjoying a charming location on the banks of the Tiber, this delightful Art Nouveau villa welcomes its guests as if they were visiting a private home - and what
a home! The elegant and individual guestrooms all bear the stamp of the
famous designer, Anna Fendi.
❀ **Enoteca la Torre** – See restaurant listing

Farnese
AK P
via Alessandro Farnese 30 ✉ 00192
Plan: E1
– Ⓜ *Lepanto* – ℰ 06 3212553
– *www.hotelfarnese.com*
23 rm ☷ – †90/350 € ††120/450 €
· Traditional · Elegant ·
Decorated in period style, this hotel has elegant rooms and an attractive lobby
housing a 17C polychrome marble frontal. Fine views of St Peter's from the terrace.

ITALY - ROME

 Alimandi Vaticano

viale Vaticano 99 ✉ *00165* – Ⓜ *Ottaviano-San Pietro*   Plan: **J1**
– ✆ *06 39745562 – www.alimandi.com*
24 rm ⌑ – †90/200 € ††100/240 €
• Traditional • Elegant •

This pleasant hotel enjoys an excellent location directly opposite the Vatican Museums. The marble and wood decor in the well-appointed guestrooms adds to their elegant atmosphere.

 Sant'Anna 🅰🅺

borgo Pio 133 ✉ *00193* – Ⓜ *Ottaviano-San Pietro*   Plan: **K1-2**
– ✆ *06 68 80 16 02 – www.hotelsantanna.com*
20 rm ⌑ – †120/250 € ††150/350 €
• Traditional • Historic •

An original coffered ceiling and pleasant interior courtyard add a decorative touch to this small, welcoming hotel occupying a 16C building a short distance from St Peter's.

 Bramante 🅰🅺

vicolo delle Palline 24 ✉ *00193*   Plan: **K2**
– Ⓜ *Ottaviano-San Pietro –* ✆ *06 68806426 – www.hotelbramante.com*
16 rm ⌑ – †90/180 € ††140/320 €
• Historic • Elegant •

This historic hotel is situated in the heart of the typical, pedestrianised Borgo district. The oldest sections date back to the 15C.

XxXxX **La Pergola** – Hotel Rome Cavalieri   ✿ ≼ 🏠 ⅏ 🅰🅺 ⇔ 🅿
❁❁❁   *via Cadlolo 101* ✉ *00136* – ✆ *06 35092152*   Plan: **A2**
– www.romecavalieri.it – Closed 2 weeks in August, January, Sunday and Monday
Menu 125/230 € – Carte 120/238 € – *(dinner only) (booking essential)*
• Modern cuisine • Luxury • Romantic •

This superb restaurant is suspended above the Eternal City in the magnificent setting of a panoramic roof garden. Mediterranean cuisine (chef Heinz Beck's constant passion), a systematic search for the best quality ingredients, and an added dose of creativity all come together in La Pergola. The restaurant's success speaks for itself.
→ Crudo di gamberi rossi e San Pietro su crema di grana padano e infuso di peperoni. Fiore di zucca in pastella su fondo di crostacei e zafferano con caviale. Lombo di agnello al finocchietto in crosta di cereali con perle di caprino.

XxxX **Vivavoce** – Hotel Gran Melià Roma   ⇔ ⅏ 🅰🅺

via del Gianicolo 3 ✉ *00165* – ✆ *06925901*   Plan: **K2**
– www.ristorantevivavoce.com – Closed January and Sunday
Menu 75/95 € – Carte 67/107 € – *(dinner only)*
• Mediterranean cuisine • Elegant • Classic décor •

This restaurant in the Eternal City serves beautifully prepared gourmet dishes inspired by the flavours of the Amalfi Coast.

XxX **Enoteca la Torre** – Hotel Villa Laetitia   ✿ 🏠 🅰🅺
❁   *lungotevere delle Armi 22/23* ✉ *00195* – Ⓜ *Lepanto*   Plan: **L2**
– ✆ *0645668304 – www.enotecalatorreroma.com – Closed 10 days in August, Monday lunch and Sunday*
Menu 60 € (weekday lunch)/120 € – Carte 80/125 €
• Modern cuisine • Liberty • Romantic •

This restaurant has a distinctly refined and elegant look. The antique furniture, flowers, columns and stucco all contribute to an Art Nouveau feel that would not be out of place in Paris. Although a new chef has been at the helm since early 2016, the cuisine continues to celebrate creativity with excellent results.
→ Ravioli di grano saraceno, ricotta di bufala, scampi al lime, consommé di crostacei. Piccione marinato alla soya, sedano rapa e chutney di pomodoro del piennolo. Crema bruciata di pastiera, pompelmo, sorbetto agli agrumi e achillea.

XX **Antico Arco**   ⚜ 🅰 ⇔

piazzale Aurelio 7 ☒ 00152 – 𝒞 06 5815274   Plan: **B3**
– www.anticoarco.it
Menu 38 € (dinner)/78 € – Carte 56/87 €
• Creative • Chic • Cosy •

The chef at this modern, bright and fashionable restaurant selects the best
Italian ingredients to create innovative dishes based on traditional specialities.

XX **Tordomatto**   ᵹ 🅰 ⇔

via Pietro Giannone 24 ☒ 00195 – 𝒞 06 69352895   Plan: **J1**
*– www.tordomattoroma.com – Closed 2 weeks in August, 2 weeks in
January, lunch Tuesday and Monday*
Menu 25/80 € – Carte 53/71 € – *(booking advisable)*
• Modern cuisine • Fashionable • Minimalist •

A minimalist-style restaurant with contemporary decor and the option of eating
at a bar in the kitchen. The dishes are full of character, demonstrating the skilful
expertise of the chef. Herbs in pots behind the windows add an attractive
touch.

X **Trattoria del Pesce**   🅰

via Folco Portinari 27 ☒ 00186 – 𝒞 349 3352560   Plan: **B3**
– www.trattoriadelpesce.it – Closed 15-22 August
Carte 34/79 €
• Seafood • Bistro • Family •

A good selection of fresh and raw fish dishes served in a welcoming, vaguely
bistro-style restaurant with young and competent staff. Parking can be difficult,
but your patience is definitely rewarded!

X **Settembrini**   ⚜ 🍴 🅰 ⇔

via Settembrini 25 ☒ 00195 – Ⓜ Lepanto   Plan: **B2**
*– 𝒞 06 97610325 – www.viasettembrini.com – Closed 11-24 August
and Sunday*
Carte 23/68 € – *(bookings advisable at dinner)*
• Modern cuisine • Bistro • Minimalist •

In just over 10 years, this fashionable bistro has become one of the leading restaurants in Rome. Recent changes have moved the dining room to the living
area, which was previously occupied by the café. The cuisine served is simple,
fresh and contemporary in feel. If you like unusual settings, ask for the table surrounded by bottles in the wine cellar.

PARIOLI   **PLAN IV**

🏨 **Parco dei Principi Grand Hotel & Spa**   ⚘ ≤ � Lⱼ 📶

via Gerolamo Frescobaldi 5 ☒ 00198   ⓌⒹ🅰 ᵹ 🅰 ♨ ⇔ 🍴
– 𝒞 06 854421 – www.parcodeiprincipi.com   Plan: **M2**
179 rm ⌂ – †225/380 € ††305/645 € – 14 suites
• Palace • Grand luxury •

This hotel is situated in a quiet, residential district not far from the Villa Borghese
gardens. The dome of St Peter's is visible from the top floor rooms. Wood panelling, carpets and reproductions of famous paintings contribute to the luxurious
ambience, while the 2 000m² spa offers all the latest treatments and technology.

🏨 **Lord Byron**   🐾 🅰

via G. De Notaris 5 ☒ 00197 – 𝒞 06 3220404   Plan: **L-M1**
– www.lordbyronhotel.com
22 rm ⌂ – †150/700 € ††200/1000 € – 6 suites
• Luxury • Boutique hotel • Art déco •

Situated just a few metres from the greenery of the Villa Borghese gardens, this
elegant aristocratic hotel is adorned with Art Deco features. The guestrooms
and public areas have been carefully decorated with fabrics and furniture that
bring out the original character of the building.
Sapori del Lord Byron – See restaurant listing

ITALY - ROME

Aldrovandi Villa Borghese 🛇 🕼 🗉 😘 🗏 🕹 🚾 🖾 🖸

via Ulisse Aldrovandi 15 ✉ *00197* – Ⓜ *Policlinico*
Plan: **B2**
– ℰ *06 3223993 – www.aldrovandi.com*
103 rm – †300/600 € ††400/800 € – � 28 € – 12 suites
• Luxury • Palace • Classic •
Off the beaten track, yet exclusive, this hotel situated in a smart district a stone's throw from the Villa Borghese boasts classic rooms, the best of which have been recently renovated.
❀ **Assaje** – See restaurant listing

Assaje – Hotel Aldrovandi Villa Borghese 🖨 🕹 🚾 🖸

❀ *via Ulisse Aldrovandi 15* – Ⓜ *Policlinico* – ℰ *06 3223993*
Plan: **B2**
– www.aldrovandi.com
Menu 120/140 € – Carte 73/106 €
• Modern cuisine • Mediterranean décor • Luxury •
The new owner of this hotel has completely renovated its restaurant, now named Assaje, which means "abundance" in the Neapolitan dialect. The focus is on Mediterranean cuisine. The menu offers imaginative, modern dishes alongside more traditional, classic fare with a range of fish and meat options available. Professional, friendly service.
➜ Spaghettoni ai ricci di mare. Baccalà con crema ai peperoncini verdi, pomodoro e maionese all'aglio. Cioccolato!

Sapori del Lord Byron – Hotel Lord Byron 🚾 ⬌

via G. De Notaris 5 ✉ *00197* – ℰ *06 3220404*
Plan: **L-M1**
– www.lordbyronhotel.com – Closed Sunday
Carte 44/70 € – *(dinner only)*
• Italian • Luxury • Classic décor •
Be prepared to be stunned by the opulence of this luxury restaurant, which is adorned with mirrors, paintings and white marble. The skills of the chef combine with a respect for tradition to bring out the very best of Italian cuisine. The menu includes original dishes such as carpaccio of beetroot with crayfish and wasabi.

Metamorfosi (Roy Caceres) 🚾 ⬌

❀ *via Giovanni Antonelli 30/32* ✉ *00197* – ℰ *06 8076839*
Plan: **M1**
– www.metamorfosiroma.it
Menu 45 € (weekday lunch)/130 €
– Carte 81/115 € – (dinner only in August)
• Creative • Elegant • Cosy •
Enjoy excellent fusion cuisine with an eclectic and international feel. These are prepared by a young Colombian chef and his colleagues who hail from all four corners of the globe. Whether the dishes come from Lazio or South America, they are all colourful, exciting and full of flavour.
➜ "Foglia di grano": tonno rosso ed erbe (piatto da degustare con le mani). Anguilla di Comacchio, farro franto e carpione di gelato. Mela, pinoli e gelsomino.

Acquolina Hostaria in Roma 🕸 🖨 🚾

❀ *via Antonio Serra 60* ✉ *00191* – ℰ *06 3337192*
Plan: **B1**
– www.acquolinahostaria.it – Closed 10-20 August and Sunday
Menu 85/130 € – Carte 67/133 € – *(dinner only) (booking advisable)*
• Seafood • Cosy • Classic décor •
Situated in the greenery of the Fleming district, this is an excellent restaurant for anyone in search of classic cuisine with an emphasis on fish dishes. The good wine list and attentive service are two additional reasons for making your way out to this district.
➜ Spaghettone "ajo e ojo", gamberi rossi, pecorino, limone e menta romana. Tataki di ricciola e panzanella come a Roma. Birra e noccioline.

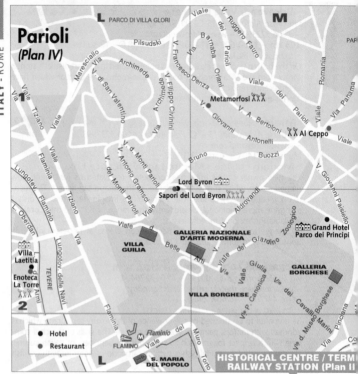

Parioli
(Plan IV)

L PARCO DI VILLA GLORI

M

Metamorfosi XXX

XX Al Ceppo

Lord Byron

Sapori del Lord Byron XXXX

GALLERIA NAZIONALE
D'ARTE MODERNA

VILLA
GUILIA

Grand Hotel
Parco dei Principi

GALLERIA
BORGHESE

VILLA BORGHESE

Villa
Laetitia

Enoteca
La Torre
XXX

● Hotel
● Restaurant

FLAMINO

L

S. MARIA
DEL POPOLO

HISTORICAL CENTRE / TERM
RAILWAY STATION (Plan II

XX **Al Ceppo**

via Panama 2 ✉ *00198 –* ☎ *06 8551379*   Plan: **M1**
*– www.ristorantealceppo.it – Closed 10-25 August, lunch Saturday June-
September, Monday lunch rest of the year*
Menu 25 € (weekday lunch) – Carte 42/73 €
• Mediterranean cuisine • Elegant • Traditional décor •
Elegant bistro-style wood panelling welcomes guests to this rustic yet elegant
restaurant which serves Mediterranean cuisine reinterpreted with a contemporary twist. Specialities include grilled fish and meat dishes prepared in front of
guests in the dining room.

XX **Marzapane**

via Velletri 39 ✉ *00198 –* ☎ *06 6478 1692*   Plan: **N2**
*– www.marzapaneroma.com – Closed 11-21 August, 2-10 January,
Wednesday*
Menu 39/69 € – Carte 47/79 € – (booking advisable)
• Creative • Classic décor • Cosy •
A young and informal atmosphere with skill and expertise to the fore in the kitchen. Originally from Spain, the chef has fully adopted the flavours of Roman
cuisine. He serves classic dishes with the occasional Iberian twist and a few
more creative options of excellent quality. Weekday lunchtime dishes are simpler and the service is quicker.

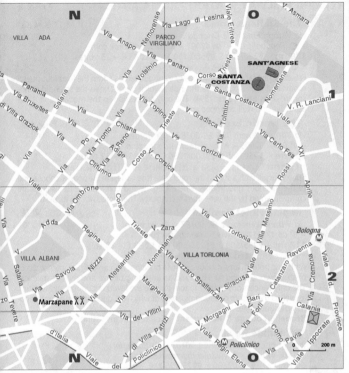

🍴 ⭐

Bistrot 64 [AK]

via Guglielmo Calderini 64 ✉ *00196* – ☎ *06 3235531*　　　Plan: **B1**
– *www.bistrot64.it* – *Closed 15 days in August, 1 week in January and Tuesday*
Menu 40/70 €
– Carte 45/74 € – *(dinner only except Friday, Saturday and Sunday) (booking advisable)*
· Mediterranean cuisine · Bistro · Fashionable ·
This restaurant boasts the attractive, informal decor of a bistro combined with surprisingly creative and imaginative cuisine. Courteous and attentive service.
➙ Spaghetto di patate, burro e alici. Risotto, vaniglia, spinaci e limone. Rombo e astice, bisque e taccole.

🍴

Mamma Angelina [AK]

viale Arrigo Boito 65 ✉ *00199* – ☎ *06 8608928* – *Closed*　　Plan: **C1**
August and Wednesday
Carte 25/44 €
· Seafood · Trattoria · Neighbourhood ·
After the antipasto buffet, the cuisine in this restaurant follows two distinct styles – fish and seafood, or Roman specialities. The paccheri pasta with seafood and fresh tomatoes sits in both camps!

ITALY - ROME

The St. Regis Rome   ✤ ⅃ẞ 🛎 & ᴀⅽ 🕸

via Vittorio Emanuele Orlando 3 ✉ *00185*   Plan: **H1**
– Ⓜ *Repubblica* – ✆ *06 47091* – www.stregisrome.com
138 rm – 🛇280/350 € 🛇🛇560/1500 € – ⌑ 43 € – 23 suites
• Grand Luxury • Palace • Elegant •
Frescoes, fine fabrics and Empire-style antique pieces adorn the luxurious guest-rooms and lavish lounges of this hotel, which has retained the splendid atmo-sphere of its early years (1894). The only concession to the modern age is the attractive and well-equipped spa.

The Westin Excelsior   ⅃ẞ 🄯 🛎 🖻 & ᴀⅽ 🕸 🚗

via Vittorio Veneto 125 ✉ *00187* – Ⓜ *Barberini*   Plan: **G1**
– ✆ *0647082805* – www.restaurantdoney.com
284 rm – 🛇250/365 € 🛇🛇500/1050 € – ⌑ 35 € – 32 suites
• Grand Luxury • Spa and wellness • Traditional •
Spoil yourself with a stay in the royal suite (the largest in Europe) or choose one of the luxurious guestrooms, where elegant and comfortable furnishings are complemented by the very latest technology. The "dolce vita" at its best!

Regina Hotel Baglioni   ⅃ẞ 🄯 & ᴀⅽ 🕸

via Vittorio Veneto 72 ✉ *00187* – Ⓜ *Barberini*   Plan: **G1**
– ✆ *06 421111* – www.baglionihotels.com
117 rm – 🛇285/500 € 🛇🛇285/500 € – ⌑ 33 € – 10 suites
• Historic • Luxury • Elegant •
A historic hotel in an Art Nouveau-style building, with an elegant interior decor of stuccowork, period furniture and an imposing bronze and marble staircase. The only concessions to the modern day are the levels of comfort and facilities, as well as the superb guestrooms, some of which are decorated in a contempo-rary designer style.
Brunello Lounge & Restaurant – See restaurant listing

Splendide Royal   ⅃ẞ & ᴀⅽ 🕸

via di porta Pinciana 14 ✉ *00187* – Ⓜ *Barberini*   Plan: **G1**
– ✆ *06 421689* – www.splendideroyal.com
60 rm ⌑ – 🛇250/2500 € 🛇🛇250/2500 € – 9 suites
• Luxury • Historic • Elegant •
Gilded stucco, damask fabrics and sumptuous antique furnishings combine to make this Baroque hotel perfect for those looking for a change from the ubiqui-tous minimalist style. This ambience of classic luxury continues in the guest-rooms, which are decorated in shades of periwinkle blue, golden yellow and cardinal red.
Mirabelle – See restaurant listing

Majestic   ✤ ⅃ẞ & ᴀⅽ 🕸 ⇔

via Vittorio Veneto 50 ✉ *00187* – Ⓜ *Barberini*   Plan: **G1**
– ✆ *06 421441* – www.hotelmajestic.com
94 rm – 🛇190/465 € 🛇🛇315/720 € – ⌑ 30 € – 4 suites
• Historic • Luxury • Elegant •
Film-buffs may recognise the backdrop to the famous Italian movie 'La Dolce Vita' at this hotel, which was opened in the late 19C. The Majestic remains one of the bastions of luxury accommodation on the Via Veneto, with its antique furniture, tapestries and frescoes, nowadays accompanied by modern comforts and facilities.

Sofitel Rome Villa Borghese   ᴀⅽ 🕸

via Lombardia 47 ✉ *00187* – Ⓜ *Barberini*   Plan: **G1**
– ✆ *06 478021* – www.sofitel.com
78 rm ⌑ – 🛇660 € 🛇🛇680 € – 3 suites
• Boutique hotel • Palace • Elegant •
The neo-Classical style dominates in this hotel just a stone's throw from the cos-mopolitan Via Veneto. Superb guestrooms and elegant public areas. Situated on the top floor, the panoramic restaurant with its Lounge Bar boasts romantic views of the Villa Medici.
La Terrasse – See restaurant listing

Bernini Bristol

piazza Barberini 23 ✉ *00187* – Ⓜ *Barberini*
– ☎ *06 488931* – *www.berninibristol.com*
Plan: **J3**

117 rm – ♦380/470 € ♦♦600/660 € – ☲ 33 € – 10 suites
• Luxury • Elegant • Personalised •

This elegant hotel is an integral part of the famous Piazza Barberini. It has guest-rooms decorated either in classic or contemporary style (those with panoramic views on the upper floors are recommended). Enjoy a light à la carte menu in the 'Giuda Ballerino A pranzo' restaurant.
Giuda Ballerino! – See restaurant listing

Palazzo Montemartini

largo Giovanni Montemartini 20 ✉ *00186 Roma*
– Ⓜ *Termini* – ☎ *06 45661* – *www.palazzomontemartini.com*
Plan: **H1**

82 rm ☲ – ♦180/600 € ♦♦200/650 € – 4 suites
• Luxury • Spa and wellness • Elegant •

The theme of water links this hotel in an aristocratic 19C palazzo with the Roman Baths of Diocletian next door. The hotel's modern interior decor is bright, functional and minimalist.

Grand Hotel Via Veneto

via Vittorio Veneto 155 ✉ *00187* – Ⓜ *Barberini*
– ☎ *06 487881* – *www.ghvv.it*
Plan: **J3**

105 rm – ♦275/620 € ♦♦275/850 € – ☲ 33 € – 11 suites
• Grand Luxury • Spa and wellness • Modern •

Situated on one of Rome's most famous streets, this hotel offers luxury in the true sense of the word, with superb, retro-style guestrooms and a collection of more than 500 original paintings on display. A love of Italian flavours and traditions is clearly evident in the cuisine served in this restaurant. This restaurant serves Italian and international cuisine, as well as a good choice of cocktails.
❀ **Magnolia** – See restaurant listing

Rose Garden Palace

via Boncompagni 19 ✉ *00187* – Ⓜ *Barberini*
– ☎ *06 421741* – *www.rosegardenpalace.com*
Plan: **G1**

62 rm – ♦180/385 € ♦♦200/400 € – ☲ 15 € – 3 suites
• Traditional • Traditional • Elegant •

A modern, minimalist design is the inspiration behind the furnishing of this hotel housed in an early-20C palazzo. The building has nonetheless retained some of its original architectural features, such as its high ceilings and marble decor.

Palazzo Manfredi

via Labicana 125 ✉ *00184* – Ⓜ *Colosseo*
– ☎ *06 77591380* – *www.palazzomanfredi.com*
Plan: **H3**

14 rm ☲ – ♦350/700 € ♦♦350/850 € – 2 suites
• Luxury • Historic • Modern •

The elegant rooms and superb suites of this hotel overlook the Colosseum and the Domus Aurea. Without a doubt the hotel's most striking feature is its delightful roof-garden terrace, which is perfect for a relaxing breakfast or romantic dinner.
❀ **Aroma** – See restaurant listing

Fortyseven

via Luigi Petroselli 47 ✉ *00186* – ☎ *06 6787816*
– *www.fortysevenhotel.com*
Plan: **G3**

59 rm ☲ – ♦170/315 € ♦♦170/315 € – 2 suites
• Traditional • Luxury • Personalised •

The name of this hotel housed in an austere 1930s palazzo refers to the number of the street which leads down to the Teatro di Marcello. Each of the five floors here is dedicated to a 20C Italian artist (Greco, Quagliata, Mastroianni, Modigliani and Guccione) and the hotel is adorned with a collection of paintings, sculptures and lithographs.

ITALY - ROME

Celio
via dei Santi Quattro 35/c ✉ *00184* – Ⓜ *Colosseo*
– ℰ *06 70495333* – *www.hotelcelio.com*
Plan: **H3**
19 rm ⌿ – †120/190 € ††140/270 € – 1 suite
• Family • Traditional • Personalised •

This hotel opposite the Colosseum has floors decorated with artistic mosaics in its public spaces and elegant guestrooms alike. Careful attention to detail is evident in the latter, where the carpets add a touch of warmth to the decor. A hammam and relaxation area are also available.

Antico Palazzo Rospigliosi
via Liberiana 21 ✉ *00185* – Ⓜ *Cavour*
– ℰ *06 48930495* – *www.hotelrospigliosi.com*
Plan: **G2**
39 rm ⌿ – †115/165 € ††149/220 €
• Historic • Traditional • Classic •

This 16C mansion has retained much of its period elegance in its large lounges, as well as in the fine detail of its beautiful bedrooms. The cloister-garden, with its bubbling fountain and splendid 17C chapel, is particularly delightful.

Magnolia – Grand Hotel Via Veneto
via Sicilia 24 ✉ *00187* – Ⓜ *Barberini*
– ℰ *06 487881* – *www.magnoliarestaurant.it*
Plan: **OU**
– *Closed Sunday and Monday*
Menu 65/90 € – Carte 55/102 €
– *(dinner only) (booking advisable)*
• Creative • Luxury • Elegant •

Having made your way through a tunnel of black marble, water and changing lights, you come to a superb cloister-style courtyard, which offers the perfect setting for alfresco dining in fine weather. The new chef here creates modern and inventive cuisine. Dishes are presented in the form of paintings and strike a truly innovative note – culinary works of art available either à la carte or on a tasting menu.
➔ "Nel blu": crudità di pescato e crostacei. Capesante alla vaniglia bourbon, prosciutto, crema di patate, carciofi ed erbette. "Sinfonia".

Mirabelle – Hotel Splendide Royal
via di porta Pinciana 14 ✉ *00187* – Ⓜ *Barberini*
– ℰ *06 42168838* – *www.mirabelle.it*
Plan: **G1**
Menu 80 € (lunch)/160 € – Carte 83/155 €
• Classic cuisine • Elegant • Luxury •

Mirabelle means 'beautiful sight' and the view doesn't disappoint - you can even pick out Villa Borghese in the magical skyline of the historic city centre. Enjoy classical Italian fare in the luxurious dining room; cooking ranges from regional specialities right through to dishes with a more international touch.

Aroma – Hotel Palazzo Manfredi
via Labicana 125 ✉ *00184* – Ⓜ *Colosseo*
– ℰ *06 97615109* – *www.aromarestaurant.it*
Plan: **H3**
Menu 115/150 € – Carte 108/194 €
– *(bookings advisable at dinner)*
• Creative • Luxury • Romantic •

The terrace offers breathtaking views of Ancient Rome, from the Colosseum to the dome of St Peter's, while the name of this restaurant pays tribute to both the city and to the aromas provided by the creative and imaginative Mediterranean cuisine served here.
➔ Spaghetti con ricotta stagionata, pomodorini confit, melanzane e basilico. Tagliata di manzo di Kobe, con patate e verdurine di stagione. Soufflé al cioccolato con coulis ai lamponi.

XxX ✿ **Antonello Colonna** 🕸 🅰🅒

scalinata di via Milano 9/a ✉ *00184 –* Ⓜ *Termini*   Plan: **G2**
– ℰ 06 47822641 – www.antonellocolonna.it – Closed August, Sunday and Monday
Menu 95 € – Carte 80/116 € – *(dinner only) (booking advisable)*
• Creative • Contemporary décor • Elegant •
This open-plan, glass-walled restaurant is within the imposing Palazzo delle Esposizioni. It serves inventive cuisine inspired by traditional dishes, which will please the most discerning guests.
→ "Negativo" di carbonara. Maialino croccante con patate affumicate e mostarda. Diplomatico con crema, cioccolato e caramello al sale.

XxX **La Terrasse** – Hotel Sofitel Rome Villa Borghese   🕸 🍴 🅰🅒 ⇔

via Lombardia 47 ✉ *00187 –* Ⓜ *Barberini – ℰ 06 478022944*
– www.laterrasseroma.com
Menu 60 € (weekday lunch)/60 €
– Carte 70/120 € – *(bookings advisable at dinner)*
• Modern cuisine • Chic • Fashionable •
As its name suggests, the jewel in the crown of this restaurant is the splendid terrace that offers panoramic views of the city. The cuisine, however, is equal to the view with imaginative Mediterranean dishes featured on the menu, as well as a simpler choice of fare available at lunchtime.

XxX **Giuda Ballerino!** – Hotel Bernini Bristol   🕸 🍴 🅰🅒

piazza Barberini 23 ✉ *00187 – ℰ 06 42010469*   Plan: **G2**
– www.giudaballerino.com – Closed 2 weeks in January and Sunday
Menu 90/130 € – Carte 90/142 € – *(dinner only)*
• Modern cuisine • Elegant • Contemporary décor •
The roof garden on the eighth floor of the historic Hotel Bernini provides an elegant, panoramic setting for Giuda Ballerino's modern dishes. It is decorated with some of the chef's favourite iconic cartoon-strip characters (such as Dylan Dog). Creative cuisine and an excellent wine list.

XX ✿ **The Corner** (Marco Martini)   ⇔ 🍴 🅰🅒

viale Aventino 121 ✉ *00186 – ℰ 06 45597350*   Plan: **C3**
– www.thecornerrome.com – Closed 12-17 Agosto, 1°-10 January
11 rm ⊡ – ♦89/119 € ♦♦129/159 €
Menu 22/95 € – Carte 56/80 € – *(booking advisable) (bar lunch)*
• Creative • Trendy • Bistro •
Chef Martini and his team create modern and imaginative cuisine in this restaurant which boasts a winter garden-style dining room with a contemporary feel as well as a terrace-cum-lounge for aperitifs and snacks, dominated by a life-size marble Superman. The gourmet menu is also available at lunchtime if you book ahead.
→ Gambero, zucchine e provolone. Ricciola in porchetta. Cioccolato affumicato, scorzonera (pianta) e vermouth.

XX **Spazio Roma-Eataly Roma**   ♿ 🅰🅒

piazzale XII Ottobre 1492 ✉ *00186 –* Ⓜ *Piramide*   Plan: **C3**
– ℰ 0690279240 – www.nikoromitoformazione.it – Closed 3 weeks in August, 10 days in January and Wednesday
Carte 37/55 € – *(number of covers limited, pre-book)*
• Modern cuisine • Fashionable • Vintage •
This 'laboratory-cum-restaurant' has grown out of the training school run by Michelin-starred chef Niko Romito in Castel di Sangro. This stylish restaurant on the top floor of the famous Eataly supermarket provides new culinary talents with real experience as they create a whole host of delicious dishes.

ITALY - ROME

XX **Brunello Lounge & Restaurant** – Regina Hotel Baglioni   ♿ 🅰🅲 ⇔
via Vittorio Veneto 72 ✉ *00187* – Ⓜ *Barberini*
– 📞 *06 421111* – *www.brunellorestaurant.com*   Plan: **G1**
Menu 90 € – Carte 56/118 €
• Modern cuisine • Intimate • Elegant •
This warm, elegant restaurant has a faintly Oriental feel. It provides the perfect
setting to enjoy superb Mediterranean cuisine, as well as international dishes
that will appeal to foreign visitors to the capital.

X **Stazione di Posta**   ⇐ 🅰🅲 🅿
🕄 *largo Dino Frisullo snc* ✉ *00153* – Ⓜ *Piramide*   Plan: **B3**
– 📞 *06 5743548* – *www.stazionediposta.eu* – *Closed Tuesday*
Menu 45/90 € – Carte 50/80 €
• Creative • Trendy • Friendly •
Part of the 'Città dell' Altra Economia' housed in an old abattoir, this restaurant
has an exciting and lively ambience thanks to its open-plan layout and post-
industrial feel. The imaginative cuisine is created by a new chef and his young
dynamic team. There is also a cocktail bar and simpler options available at
lunchtime.
➜ Risotto, brodo di insalata, anguilla affumicata, crème fraiche (panna
acida). Triglia, zuppa di provola affumicata, pomodoro e basilico. Dolce
bianco.

X **Domenico dal 1968**   🌐 🅰🅲
🕄 *via Satrico 21* ✉ *00183* – 📞 *06 70494602*   Plan: **C3**
– *www.domenicodal1968.it* – *Closed 20 days in August, Sunday dinner
and Monday*
Carte 30/49 €
• Roman • Simple • Family •
It is worth heading off the tourist track to experience this authentic Roman trattoria. The fritto (fried seafood and vegetables) and linguine with mullet roe and
clams are the house specialities.

X **Profumo di Mirto**   🅰🅲
🕄 *viale Amelia 8/a* ✉ *00181* – 📞 *06 786206*   Plan: **C3**
– *www.profumodimirto.it* – *Closed August and Monday*
Menu 25 € (weekdays)/55 € – Carte 23/79 €
• Seafood • Family • Friendly •
The name of this restaurant pays tribute to Sardinia, the owner's native region.
Fish from the Mediterranean takes pride of place on the menu. It is prepared in
delicious, home-style dishes such as the excellent octopus ravioli served with a
crayfish sauce.

X **Colline Emiliane**   🅰🅲 ⇔
via degli Avignonesi 22 ✉ *00187* – Ⓜ *Barberini*   Plan: **G2**
– 📞 *06 4817538* – *Closed August, Sunday dinner and
Monday*
Carte 37/60 € – *(booking advisable)*
• Emilian • Trattoria •
Just a stone's throw from Piazza Barberini, this simple, friendly, family-run restaurant has just a few tables arranged close together. It serves typical dishes
from the Emilia region, including fresh pasta stretched by hand in the traditional
way.

X **Al Ristoro degli Angeli**   🌐 🅰🅲
🕄 *via Luigi Orlando 2* ✉ *00154* – 📞 *06 51436020*   Plan: **B3**
– *www.ristorodegliangeli.it* – *Closed Sunday*
Carte 29/55 € – *(dinner only)*
• Roman • Vintage • Simple •
Situated in the Garbatella district, this restaurant with a bistro feel is decorated
with vintage tables, chairs and lighting. The menu focuses on dishes from Lazio,
such as *spaghetti cacio e pepe* (with a cheese and black pepper sauce) in a crunchy parmesan wafer, although vegetable and fish options are also available.

X Moma

AC

via San Basilio 42/43 ✉ *00186 –* Ⓜ *Barberini*   Plan: **G1**
– ☏ 0642011798 – www.ristorantemoma.it – Closed Sunday
Menu 50 € (weekday dinner) – Carte 46/84 €
• **Modern cuisine** • **Trendy** • **Minimalist** •

The versatile nature of this bar-cum-bistro and restaurant makes it well worth a visit. At lunchtime, the ambience is busy and lively, while in the evening the restaurant becomes more intimate and atmospheric. Attractive modern cuisine with some imaginative dishes on the menu.

X Trattoria Monti

AC

via di San Vito 13/a ✉ *00185 –* Ⓜ *Cavour*   Plan: **C2**
– ☏ 06 4466573 – Closed Christmas Holidays, 1 week-
Easter, August, Sunday dinner and Monday
Carte 31/51 € – *(booking advisable)*
• **Cuisine from the Marches** • **Traditional décor** • **Family** •

As a result of renovation work completed a few years ago, this trattoria is resolutely contemporary in style with wooden chairs, copper piping and low-hanging lamps. Specialities include dishes from Lazio and The Marches, the owner's birthplace.

X Pastificio San Lorenzo

AC

via Tiburtina 196 ✉ *00186 – ☏ 06 97273519*   Plan: **C2**
– www.pastificiosanlorenzo.com
Menu 40 € (weekdays)/60 €
– Carte 34/57 € – (bookings advisable at dinner) (bar lunch)
• **Modern cuisine** • **Colourful** • **Friendly** •

The name of this modern restaurant with an international feel hints at its origins. An old industrial building once home to a pasta factory, the site subsequently became a centre for artists – right in the middle of the San Lorenzo university area – and it has retained this lively ambience despite being away from the city's main tourist sites. The food doesn't disappoint with its intriguing blend of regional flavours and modern influences.

X Osteria Fernanda

AC

via Crescenzo Del Monte 18/24 ✉ *00186*   Plan: **B3**
– ☏ 06 5894333 – www.osteriafernanda.com – Closed 14-24 August,
1 week in February, Saturday lunch and Sunday
Menu 38/59 € – Carte 38/62 €
• **Creative** • **Minimalist** • **Neighbourhood** •

In the district famous for its Porta Portese market, this restaurant run by two talented business partners is definitely worth a visit. One of the partners manages the front of house, while the other shows real passion in his creative cuisine made from locally sourced ingredients, as well as produce from further afield.

FLORENCE
FIRENZE

Population: 382 808

Giovanni Simeone/Sime/Photononstop

Florence has always stood for beauty, and represents Italy's greatest contribution to the world of arts: the Renaissance. It is said that Cupid lives in Florence and it's hard to imagine a city more romantic than this; lovers visit from around the world, while those not yet in love are thought to find their match here. Florence is surrounded by a ring of hills, and winding streets flanked with cypress and olive trees lead you to the heart of Dante's beloved hometown. The city centre and many of its monuments lie on the northern side of the Arno, a river closely connected with Florence's history and celebrated by poets throughout the years. The river is crossed by many delightful bridges, Ponte Vecchio being the most famous, but, despite its charm, the Arno has in the past wreaked havoc in the form of regular flooding, which has caused huge amounts of damage.

In each area of Florence, civic and religious powers occupy their own distinct site. Piazza della Signoria is home to the town hall, while the Duomo sits in the piazza of the same name at the end of Via dei Calzaiuoli, the city's most famous shopping street. Cross one of the bridges to the south side of the city for a more relaxed, village-like atmosphere; here you will find the Palazzo Pitti and the Giardino di Boboli. Walking eastwards will bring you to the Piazzale Michelangelo, which boasts probably the best views in Florence.

FLORENCE IN...

→ **ONE DAY**
Piazza della Signoria, Via dei Calzaiuoli, the Duomo, Santa Croce, Ponte Vecchio.

→ **TWO DAYS**
The Uffizi, Santa Maria Novella, San Lorenzo.

→ **THREE DAYS**
Palazzo Pitti/Galleria Palatina, Giardino di Boboli, Santa Maria del Carmine, Piazzale Michelangelo.

PRACTICAL INFORMATION

ARRIVAL-DEPARTURE

🛫 Amerigo Vespucci, Florence's airport, lies 5km outside of the city. A bus will take you to the Santa Maria Novella Railway Station.

GETTING AROUND

If you are staying in the city centre, the best and most interesting way to see Florence is by foot, as most of the sights are within easy walking distance. Alternatively, one of the municipal orange buses will take you everywhere you need. There are two main tourist offices in Florence; one is in Piazza Stazione (Santa Maria Novella), 4; the other is in Via Cavour 1/R.

CALENDAR HIGHLIGHTS

January
Pitti Immagine Fashion Fair.

February
Carnival.

April
Easter Sunday Celebration in the Piazza del Duomo, Arts and Crafts exhibition.

May
Trofeo Marzocco (flag-waving competition).

June
Festa di San Giovanni (Feast of St John the Baptist – fireworks and a football match).

August
Festa di San Lorenzo (Feast of St Lawrence).

September
Festa della Rificolona (paper lantern festival).

November
Florence Marathon.

EATING OUT

Tuscan food is one of the most famous and highly regarded of Italy's regional cuisines, and it will come as no surprise to learn that some of the best examples are to be found here in Florence. Soups are particularly renowned; don't miss pappa col pomodoro – made with bread and tomatoes – or ribollita – made from cannellini, a local variety of beans, black cabbage, bread and other vegetables. Pasta can certainly not be ignored; pappardelle con la lepre (with hare) and pici (a sort of spaghetti) are two of the most popular.

Meat is a favourite for second courses: the fiorentina, a grilled T-bone steak which takes its name from the city, has now become a favourite nationwide. Restaurants in tourist areas can be very pricey – for a quick, inexpensive meal you're better off opting for a pizza. Wines are equally important in Florence as the cooking: a Chianti, a Morellino di Scansano or a Nobile di Montepulciano will give you good value for money but, if price is not an issue, opt for the Super Tuscans – Ornellaia, Sassicaia, Solaia or Tignanello.

455

ITALY - FLORENCE

Four Seasons Hotel Firenze

borgo Pinti 99 ⊠ *50121 –* ☏ *055 26261* Plan: **F2**
– www.fourseasons.com/florence
116 rm – ♦395/925 € ♦♦695/1150 € – ⊈45 € – 20 suites
• Historic building • Grand luxury •
The austere walls of a 15C palazzo surround this hotel, which boasts the largest private garden in Florence. Sumptuous guestrooms, classic-style decor and bright, secluded courtyards all contribute to the hotel's exclusive charm. The Conventino annexe is popular with guests looking for privacy and tranquility. Delicious choice of Tuscan and Italian cuisine in the Atrium restaurant, as well as pizza and summer barbecues in the garden.
❀ **Il Palagio** – See restaurant listing

The St. Regis Florence

piazza Ognissanti 1 ⊠ *50123 –* ☏ *055 27163* Plan: **D2**
– www.stregisflorence.com
83 rm ⊈ – ♦300/600 € ♦♦500/1000 € – 17 suites
• Historic building • Grand luxury •
This hotel is even more luxurious and exclusive after its recent renovation. It offers spacious guestrooms, where modern accessories provide a contrast with the classic decor of frescoes, Murano glass chandeliers and antique furniture.
❀ **Winter Garden by Caino** – See restaurant listing

The Westin Excelsior

piazza Ognissanti 3 ⊠ *50123 –* ☏ *055 27151* Plan: **C2**
– www.westinflorence.com
167 rm – ♦730/1210 € ♦♦985/1890 € – ⊈43 € – 4 suites
• Grand Luxury • Classic •
Sumptuous interiors of an old nobleman's dwelling on the Arno, where history and tradition combine with more modern accessories for an exclusive aristocratic stay. The dining hall of this restaurant is princely. Among its features are the boxed ceilings and decor in Carrara marble.
SE.STO On Arno – See restaurant listing

Portrait Firenze

lungarno Acciaiuoli 4 ⊠ *50123 –* ☏ *055 27268000* Plan: **D3**
– www.lungarnocollection.com
7 rm – ♦480/1900 € ♦♦500/1950 € – ⊈35 € – 30 suites
• Grand Luxury • Vintage • Modern •
Luxurious, elegant and original – this stylish hotel offers suite-only accommodation of varying sizes, all equipped with the latest accessories. One of Florence's stand-out luxury hotels.
Caffè dell'Oro – See restaurant listing

Relais Santa Croce

via Ghibellina 87 ⊠ *50122 –* ☏ *055 2342230* Plan: **E3**
– www.baglionihotels.com
18 rm ⊈ – ♦256/700 € ♦♦300/800 € – 6 suites
• Historic building • Luxury • Personalised •
Luxury and elegance in the heart of Florence, where period furnishings blend with designer-style decor and rich fabrics to create a unique blend of the traditional and the modern. Time, experience and passion are the essential ingredients here, combining to create simple, delicious dishes from old Tuscan recipes.

Regency

piazza Massimo D'Azeglio 3 ⊠ *50121 –* ☏ *055 245247* Plan: **F2**
– www.regency-hotel.com – Closed 3 January-5 April
29 rm ⊈ – ♦157/467 € ♦♦172/482 € – 3 suites
• Luxury • Historic •
This elegant hotel was built to offer accommodation for local political figures. It boasts a tranquil, comfortable atmosphere and has retained much of its traditional charm.

Brunelleschi

piazza Santa Elisabetta 3 ✉ *50122 – ℰ 055 27370*
Plan: **E2**
– www.hotelbrunelleschi.it
82 rm ⌓ – †224/864 € ††239/919 € – 14 suites
• Luxury • Centrally located •
Housed in the Byzantine Torre della Pagliazza, this hotel with welcoming guest-rooms boasts a small museum with Roman remains. A dining room partly enc-losed by old walls is home to the gourmet Santa Elisabetta restaurant, while the hotel also offers bistro dining in the elegant Osteria della Pagliazza.

Savoy

Piazza della Repubblica 7 ✉ *50123 – ℰ 055 27351*
Plan: **D2**
– www.hotelsavoy.it
102 rm – †260/560 € ††330/950 € – ⌓ 30 € – 14 suites
• Luxury • Classic •
This elegant, historic hotel is situated near the Duomo, the city's museums and luxury fashion boutiques. It offers spacious, comfortable guestrooms with mosaic adorned bathrooms.

Helvetia e Bristol

via dei Pescioni 2 ✉ *50123 – ℰ 055 26651*
Plan: **D2**
– www.royaldemeure.com
52 rm ⌓ – †200/650 € ††200/870 € – 15 suites
• Palace • Personalised •
Situated near the Duomo and Palazzo Strozzi, this elegant 19C hotel evokes the charm of bygone days. It has personalised guestrooms decorated with period paintings and antique furniture.

Bernini Palace

piazza San Firenze 29 ✉ *50122 – ℰ 055 288621*
Plan: **E3**
– www.hotelbernini.duetorrihotels.com
63 rm ⌓ – †180/600 € ††200/750 € – 11 suites
• Luxury • Elegant •
When Florence was the capital of Italy, members of parliament and senators would meet in the Sala Parlamento of this hotel. With its spacious corridors, magnificent guestrooms (those on the Tuscan Floor are particularly impressive), and an excellent restaurant, this hotel now attracts visitors looking for the hig-hest quality.

Lungarno

borgo San Jacopo 14 ✉ *50125 – ℰ 055 27261*
Plan: **D3**
– www.lungarnocollection.com
63 rm – †240/950 € ††250/990 € – ⌓ 40 € – 10 suites
• Luxury • Personalised •
The name of this hotel situated between Ponte Vecchio and Santa Trinità refers to its excellent location overlooking the River Arno. Every corner of the hotel is stylish and elegant. It has numerous terraces and balconies and many of the guestrooms offer views of the river.
✿ **Borgo San Jacopo** – See restaurant listing

Continentale

vicolo dell'Oro 6 r ✉ *50123 – ℰ 055 27262*
Plan: **D3**
– www.lungarnocollection.com
43 rm – †190/460 € ††190/460 € – ⌓ 28 €
• Business • Centrally located •
A modern, elegant hotel built around a medieval tower with a lounge bar over-looking the Arno and the Ponte Vecchio, plus a new White Iris Beauty Spa. The designer-style interior is decorated in bright, warm colours.

ITALY - FLORENCE

457

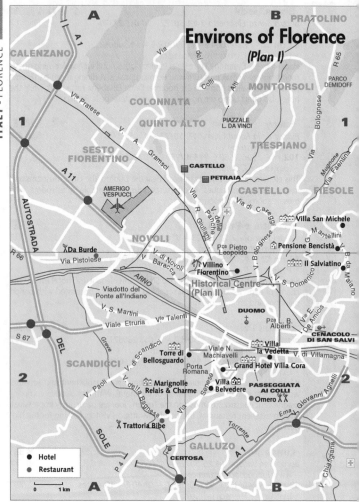

Environs of Florence
(Plan I)

● Hotel
● Restaurant

0   1 km

Santa Maria Novella ← ʅᴚ 🛏 ♿ 𝔸𝐂

piazza Santa Maria Novella 1 ⊠ 50123 – ℰ 055 271840 Plan: **D2**
– www.hotelsantamarianovella.it
69 rm ⌤ – ♦150/350 € ♦♦185/520 € – 2 suites
• Business • Elegant •
Overlooking Piazza Santa Maria Novella, this welcoming hotel offers small lounge areas and elegant guestrooms, all of which have different decor and furnishings. Enjoy superb views of this magical city from the hotel's delightful panoramic terrace.

Gallery Hotel Art

vicolo dell'Oro 5 ✉ *50123* – ☎ *055 27263*
– *www.lungarnocollection.com*   Plan: **D3**
71 rm – 🛏200/720 € 🛏🛏200/720 € – ☷ 28 € – 3 suites
• Business • Minimalist •
African wood in the guestrooms, bathrooms furnished with stone from the Middle East and views of Florence on the walls – the cosmopolitan art in this museum-like hotel creates a strikingly modern ambience.
The Fusion Bar & Restaurant – See restaurant listing

Adler Cavalieri

via della Scala 40 ✉ *50123* – ☎ *055 277810*
– *www.hoteladlercavalieri.com*   Plan: **D2**
60 rm ☷ – 🛏115/335 € 🛏🛏115/420 €
• Traditional • Cosy •
This pleasant hotel is located in the immediate vicinity of the station. The soundproofing is excellent and wood has been used to very good effect. The management is youthful and competent.

Grand Hotel Adriatico

via Maso Finiguerra 9 ✉ *50123* – ☎ *055 27931*
– *www.hoteladriatico.it*   Plan: **C2**
126 rm ☷ – 🛏90/270 € 🛏🛏100/410 € – 3 suites
• Business • Cosy •
Conveniently situated in the city centre, this hotel has a large lobby and modern guestrooms decorated in a simple, yet elegant style. Tuscan and Italian cuisine is served in the quiet, recently renovated dining room, as well as in the attractive garden.

Palazzo Magnani Feroni

borgo San Frediano 5 ✉ *50124* – ☎ *055 2399544*
– *www.palazzomagnaniferoni.it*   Plan: **C3**
13 suites ☷ – 🛏200/960 € 🛏🛏200/960 €
• Historic building • Romantic •
An extraordinary 17th century palace which houses a beautiful collection of artwork, princely corridors, enormous bedrooms and an enchanting terrace with a view on the Duomo and the Palazzo Vecchio.

Cellai

via 27 Aprile 14 ✉ *50129* – ☎ *055 489291*
– *www.hotelcellai.it*   Plan: **E1**
68 rm ☷ – 🛏120/169 € 🛏🛏150/298 €
• Historic building • Cosy •
This luxurious hotel in Florence offers a welcoming atmosphere, period furnishings and antique prints of plants and animals. The top floor is home to an attractive terrace decked with jasmine, which acts as an open-air lounge in which to relax and enjoy views of the city.

Pierre

via Dè Lamberti 5 ✉ *50123* – ☎ *055 216218*
– *www.remarhotels.com*   Plan: **D3**
49 rm ☷ – 🛏120/265 € 🛏🛏160/370 € – 1 suite
• Traditional • Centrally located •
This elegant hotel in the city centre has comfortable, stylishly furnished rooms and modern amenities. You can see the Duomo from some of the tables in the breakfast room.

Firenze Number Nine

via dei Conti 9/31r ✉ *50123* – ☎ *055293777*
– *www.firenzenumbernine.com*   Plan: **D2**
45 rm ☷ – 🛏90/300 € 🛏🛏160/1000 €
• Boutique hotel • Design •
Soft, subtle colours add a hint of contemporary style to the traditional Florentine decor in this smart hotel (room 107 is particularly stylish). Friendly service, as well as an excellent gym for fitness enthusiasts.

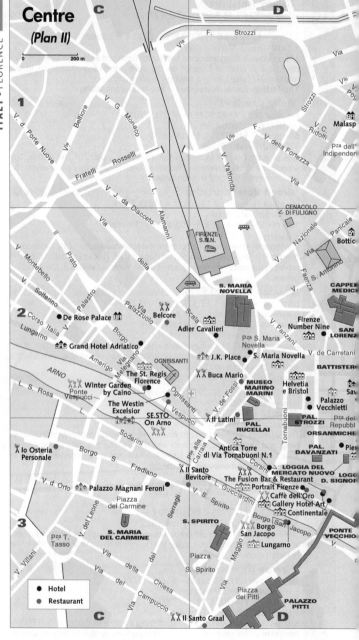

Centre
(Plan II)

0 ___ 200 m

C   **D**

F. Strozzi

V. d. Porte Nuove

Belfiore

V. G. Monaco

Via

Vle

V. C. Ridolfi

Malasp

Pza dell'Indipenden

Rosselli

Fratelli

V. L.

V. J. da Diacceto

Alamanni

V. della Fortezza

V. Vallonda

Nazionale

CENACOLO DI FULIGNO

Botti

Il Prato

V. Montebello

V. Sollenino

Via

della

Palestro

Via Palazzuolo

FIRENZE S.M.N.

Faenza

V. S. Antonino

CAPPE MEDIC

2 Corso Italia

Lungarno

●De Rose Palace

Belcore

S. MARIA NOVELLA

Adler Cavalieri

Firenze Number Nine

SAN LORENZ

Borgo

Via Melagrino

Via

Scala

Pza S. Maria Novella

V. Panzani

●Grand Hotel Adriatico

ARNO

L. S. Rosa

Amerigo

J.K. Place ● S. Maria Novella

V. de Carretani

BATTISTER

The St. Regis Florence

OGNISSANTI

Buca Mario

MUSEO MARINO MARINI

Helvetia e Bristol

Sav

Winter Garden by Caino

Ponte Vespucci

The Westin Excelsior

Ognissanti

V. de Fossi

Palazzo Vecchietti

SE.STO On Arno

Vespucci

Il Latini

PAL. RUCELLAI

Tornabuoni

PAL. STROZZI

Pza del Repubbl

Io Osteria Personale

Soderini

Pie. alla Carraia

Antica Torre di Via Tornabuoni N.1

ORSANMICHE

PAL. DAVANZATI

Pie

Borgo

S.

Frediano

Corsini

LOGGIA DEL MERCATO NUOVO

LOG D. SIGNOR

V. d. Orto

Palazzo Magnani Feroni

Il Santo Bevitore

L. Guicciardini

The Fusion Bar & Restaurant

Portrait Firenze

Caffè dell'Oro

Gallery Hotel Art

Piazza del Carmine

V. S. Spirito

Continentale

3

Pza T. Tasso

V. del Leone

S. MARIA DEL CARMINE

S. SPIRITO

Serragli

Borgo San Jacopo

San Jacopo

Lungarno

PONTE VECCHIO

V. Villani

Via

della

Piazza S. Spirito

Maggio

Via

Piazza dei Pitti

Campuccio

PALAZZO PITTI

● Hotel
● Restaurant

Il Santo Graal

C   **D**

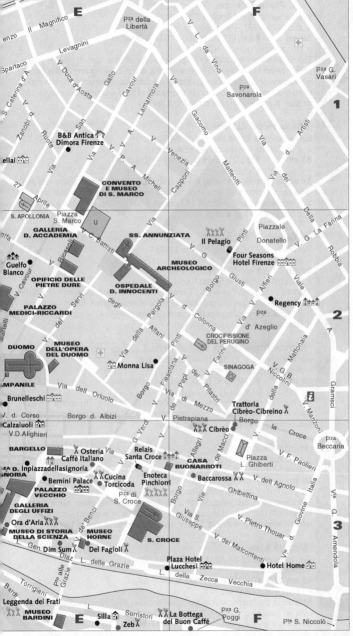

E

F

Pza della Libertà

enzo Il Magnifico

Levagnini

V. L. da Vinci

Pza G. Vasari

Spartaco

V. Duca d'Aosta

Gallo

Cavour

Lamarmora

Vie

Pza Savonarola

S. Caterina d'A.

Zanobi

Ruote

San

V. P. A. Micheli

V. A.

V. A.

Giacomo

Venezia

Matteotti

Via d. Artisti

Via d.

1

ellai 🏠

B&B Antica Dimora Firenze 🏠

CONVENTO E MUSEO DI S. MARCO

Capponi

27 Aprile

S. APOLLONIA

Piazza S. Marco

U

Della Robbia

GALLERIA D. ACCADEMIA

SS. ANNUNZIATA

Pinti

Piazzale Donatello

Il Pelagio 𝕏𝕏𝕏

elfa

Guelfo Bianco ●

C. Battisti

Ricasoli

Four Seasons Hotel Firenze 🏨

V. G.

V. Cavour

OPIFICIO DELLE PIETRE DURE

MUSEO ARCHEOLOGICO

Borgo

Giusti

V. Alfieri

Viale

Regency 🏨

PALAZZO MEDICI-RICCARDI

Servi

OSPEDALE D. INNOCENTI

Pergola

V. della

degli

V. dei

Alfani

Colonna

pza

d' Azeglio

DUOMO

MUSEO DELL'OPERA DEL DUOMO

🏠 **Monna Lisa**

V. della Alfani

Fiesolana

V. dei Pinti

CROCIFISSIONE DEL PERUGINO

V. Farini

Mattonaia

V. G. B. Niccolini

2

A.

Gramsci

MPANILE

Via dell' Oriuolo

Borgo

Pepi

V. dei Pilastri

SINAGOGA 🕍

della

Brunelleschi 🏠

V. d. Corso

Borgo d. Albizi

V. Pietrapiana

V. di Mezzo

ℹ️

Calzaiuoli 🏠

Trattoria Cibrèo-Cibreino 𝕏

V.D.Alighieri

Borgo

la

Croce

Pza Beccaria

BARGELLO

𝕏 **Osteria** Via G. Verdi

𝕏𝕏𝕏 **Cibrèo**

V. de' Macci

ZA D. Inpiazzadellasignoria

Caffè Italiano 🏠

Relais Santa Croce 🏨

V. F. Paolieri

-NORIA

𝕏𝕏 **Cucina**

CASA BUONARROTI

Piazza L. Ghiberti

Via G.

Bernini Palace 🏠

Torcicoda ●

Enoteca Pinchiorri

Baccarossa 𝕏𝕏

V. dell'Agnolo

Italia

PALAZZO VECCHIO 🏠

Pza di S. Croce

𝕏𝕏𝕏𝕏

Borgo

Ghibellina

V. Pietro Thouar

Giovine

GALLERIA DEGLI UFFIZI

Via S. Giuseppe

d.

3

Amendola

Ora d'Aria 𝕏𝕏𝕏

de' Benci

MUSEO DI STORIA DELLA SCIENZA

MUSEO HORNE

S. CROCE

V. dei Malcontenti

Via G.

L. Gen. Diaz 𝕏 **Dim Sum**

Del Fagioli 𝕏

Plaza Hotel Lucchesi 🏠

Hotel Home 🏠

Diaz

L. delle Grazie

L. della Zecca Vecchia

Pte alle Grazie

Torrigiani

Bardi

L.

Serristori

Pza G. Poggi

F

Leggenda dei Frati 𝕏𝕏𝕏

MUSEO BARDINI

E **Silla** 🏠

Zeb 𝕏

𝕏𝕏 **La Bottega del Buon Caffè**

Pte S. Niccolò

J.K. Place Firenze
piazza Santa Maria Novella 7 ✉ *50123*
– ☎ *055 2645181* – *www.jkplace.com*
18 rm ☲ – **♦**500/1100 € **♦♦**500/1100 € – 2 suites

☆ ≤ AC
Plan: **G1**

• Boutique hotel • Quirky •
This smart hotel with the feel of a private house offers a romantic refuge with a stylish blend of history and modernity. It is worth booking one of the rooms with a view of the magnificent piazza or the rooftops of Florence. There is a spacious outdoor area opening on to the square at the J.K. Lounge, where you can be sure of excellent cuisine throughout the day.

Plaza Hotel Lucchesi
lungarno della Zecca Vecchia 38 ✉ *50122*
– ☎ *05526236* – *www.hotelplazalucchesi.it*
83 rm ☲ – **♦**130/250 € **♦♦**180/700 € – 10 suites

☆ ≤ ⌇ & AC 🚗
Plan: **E3**

• Palace • Elegant •
An elegant hotel overlooking the Arno with generously sized public areas and guestrooms decorated with Imperial-style furnishings. There is a 360° view of the monuments and rooftops of Florence from the top floor terrace, which also boasts a bar and a small pool.

Il Guelfo Bianco
via Cavour 29 ✉ *50129* – ☎ *055 288330*
– *www.ilguelfobianco.it*
40 rm ☲ – **♦**90/160 € **♦♦**99/257 €

& AC
Plan: **E2**

• Traditional • Personalised • Cosy •
Situated in the heart of Medici Florence, this hotel offers contemporary-style public areas and spacious guestrooms, some of which have frescoes on the ceilings. Small bistro selling hot food from 12-3pm.
Il Desco – See restaurant listing

Antica Torre di via Tornabuoni 1 – Residenza d'epoca
via Tornabuoni 1 ✉ *50123* – ☎ *055 2658161*
– *www.tornabuoni1.com*
19 rm ☲ – **♦**200/495 € **♦♦**200/495 € – 6 suites

AC
Plan: **D3**

• Historic building • Elegant •
The hotel premises include the upper floors of the building. The rooms are spacious and bright and an outstanding feature is the breathtaking view from the two terraces overlooking the entire town.

Home Florence
piazza Piave 3 ✉ *50122* – ☎ *055 243668*
– *www.hhflorence.it*
39 rm ☲ – **♦**100/300 € **♦♦**120/450 €

🛗 & AC 🛁
Plan: **F3**

• Boutique hotel • Minimalist •
This charming small palazzo with a predominantly white decor has a young, fashionable feel while at the same time – as the name suggests – manages to retain a homely atmosphere. Breakfast is served on three shared tables.

Monna Lisa
via Borgo Pinti 27 ✉ *50121* – ☎ *055 2479751*
– *www.monnalisa.it*
45 rm ☲ – **♦**89/209 € **♦♦**139/279 € – 4 suites

🐾 🛗 🛗 AC 🛁
Plan: **E2**

• Historic • Classic •
Situated in the historic centre, this hotel occupies an original medieval palazzo with an imposing staircase, brick flooring and coffered ceilings. Rooms and communal areas have Renaissance-style furnishings. The newer rooms, which are just as elegant as the rest of the hotel, can be found in the two annexes in the splendid garden.

Palazzo Vecchietti
via degli Strozzi 4 – 𝒞 055 2302802
– www.palazzovecchietti.com
Plan: **D2**
7 rm ☲ – **†**299/599 € **††**299/599 € – 5 suites
• Luxury • Personalised •
Remains of Florence's 13C walls are still visible in this palazzo, which offers a delightful inner courtyard now transformed into a small lounge. Romantic galleries overlook the courtyard and lead to the luxurious rooms. All of these are decorated in an elegant contemporary style and equipped with a small kitchen.

Inpiazzadellasignoria – Residenza d'epoca
via de' Magazzini 2 ✉ *50122 – 𝒞 055 2399546*
– www.inpiazzadellasignoria.com
Plan: **E3**
10 rm ☲ – **†**200/250 € **††**250/300 € – 2 suites
• Family • Personalised •
As the name implies, this establishment faces the Piazza della Signoria, the political centre of old Florence. It is welcoming and pleasantly elegant.

De Rose Palace
via Solferino 5 ✉ *50123 – 𝒞 055 2396818*
– www.florencehotelderose.com
Plan: **C2**
18 rm ☲ – **†**60/180 € **††**80/350 €
• Traditional • Personalised •
In a renovated 19th Century building a hotel with a simple, elegant interior, with period style furnishings and beautiful Venetian lamps; pleasant family atmosphere.

Malaspina
piazza dell'Indipendenza 24 ✉ *50129 – 𝒞 055 489869*
– www.malaspinahotel.it
Plan: **D1**
31 rm ☲ – **†**53/185 € **††**68/275 €
• Business • Functional •
In the 13C the Malaspina family received Dante as their guest at the Castello di Fosdinovo. This tradition of hospitality is upheld by the descendants of the Malaspina, who run this 20C hotel decorated in period style. Spacious, well-equipped guestrooms.

Calzaiuoli
via Calzaiuoli 6 ✉ *50122 – 𝒞 055 212456*
– www.calzaiuoli.it
Plan: **E3**
52 rm ☲ – **†**120/550 € **††**120/700 € – 1 suite
• Traditional • Cosy •
In the pedestrian street between Piazza del Duomo and Piazza della Signoria lies a hotel which has a restricted number of public areas but comfortable and welcoming bedrooms, and recently renovated bathrooms.

Botticelli
via Taddea 8 ✉ *50123 – 𝒞 055 290905*
– www.hotelbotticelli.it
Plan: **D2**
34 rm ☲ – **†**70/150 € **††**100/240 € – 1 suite
• Family • Cosy •
Near to the S.Lorenzo market, in a 16th Century building, is a charming hotel with frescoes in the public areas and a small covered balcony; bedrooms recently refurbished.

Silla
via dei Renai 5 ✉ *50125 – 𝒞 055 2342889*
– www.hotelsilla.it
Plan: **E3**
36 rm ☲ – **†**120/280 € **††**120/360 €
• Inn • Vintage •
It is pleasant in summer to eat your breakfast or just relax on the wide balcony of this hotel with its family atmosphere, situated as it is on the left bank of the Arno.

B&B Antica Dimora Firenze

via Sangallo 72 ✉ *50129 –* ✆ *055 4627296*
– www.antichedimorefiorentine.it
Plan: **E1**
6 rm ⌿ *–* ♥70/130 € ♥♥80/150 €
• Manor house • Elegant •

This hotel is in the area of the San Marco convent. Its rooms are distinctive thanks to their interesting colours, and are set off by the quite exceptional elegance of the period furniture and canopied beds.

Villino Fiorentino

via delle Cinque Giornate 12 ✉ *50122 –* ✆ *389 9992606*
– www.villinofiorentino.com
Plan: **B2**
6 rm ⌿ *–* ♥118/136 € ♥♥136/146 €
• Inn • Elegant •

This property is the pride and joy of its owner Sara, who has transformed what was a typical 1930s Florentine villa into an elegant boutique B&B. It is an excellent base for visiting Florence if you are travelling by car (there is a convenient car park). Well worth a visit.

Enoteca Pinchiorri (Annie Féolde)

via Ghibellina 87 ✉ *50122 –* ✆ *055 242777*
Plan: **E3**
– www.enotecapinchiorri.com – Closed 3 weeks in August, 1 week Christmas Holidays, Sunday and Monday
Menu 175/225 € – Carte 165/295 € – *(dinner only) (booking advisable)*
• Modern cuisine • Luxury • Romantic •

For decades Pinchiorri has represented luxury and haute cuisine at the highest level in Italy. The restaurant has a number of dining rooms, including a historic room, which has an almost museum-like feel. Highly attentive service from the legendary owners, Annie and Giorgio, and an excellent menu featuring the best of Tuscan, Italian and international cuisine. The wine list is renowned across the globe.

➜ Cappelletti di mela e spezie, crema di ricotta e salsiccia di agnello del casentino. Petto d'anatra arrosto con indivia brasata, latte di mandorla e salsa al vin santo. Pesca, stracciatella, frolla al grano tostato e fiammiferi di meringa.

Winter Garden by Caino – Hotel The St. Regis Florence

piazza Ognissanti 1 – ✆ *055 2716*
Plan: **D2**
– www.stregisflorence.com
Menu 95 € – Carte 83/125 € – *(dinner only) (booking advisable)*
• Creative • Luxury •

Horse-drawn carriages once entered the old courtyard of the St Regis hotel, now converted into a winter garden. Enjoy delicious dishes from the Maremma created by Valeria Piccini in the luxurious surroundings of one of Florence's most elegant hotels.

➜ Tagliolini al nero di seppia con scampi e crema di zafferano. Il gioco del galletto. Diversamente tiramisù.

Il Palagio – Four Seasons Hotel Firenze

borgo Pinti 99 ✉ *50121 –* ✆ *055 2626450*
Plan: **F2**
– www.ilpalagioristorante.it – Closed 15 January-15 February and Sunday dinner October-May
Menu 125/254 € – Carte 98/173 € – *(dinner only)*
• Modern cuisine • Historic • Luxury •

The magnificent decor of one of the most impressive palazzi in Florence has been given a more contemporary feel in this restaurant. It offers delicious and carefully prepared reinterpretations of traditional Italian cuisine.

➜ Insalata di astice con crema di "soffritto" e cavolfiore. Tonno arrostito su crema di fagioli di Rotonda e ciambotta lucana. Barretta croccante al caramello con gelato alle nocciole.

XxX ❀ **La Leggenda dei Frati** (Filippo Saporito e Alessandro Rossi)
Costa San Giorgio 6/a ✉ 50122 – ℰ 055 0680545 🏠 **P**
– www.laleggendadeifrati.it – Closed 1 week in August Plan: **E3**
and Monday
Menu 35 € (weekday lunch)/90 € – Carte 60/95 € – *(booking advisable)*
• Creative • Historic • Design •
Things start well and only get better… Once you have entered the beautiful Villa Bardini not far from Palazzo Vecchio, you are plunged into an elegant and welcoming ambience. This serves as the perfect setting for delicious creative and modern cuisine. There is an additional treat: anyone who dines at the restaurant can also choose to visit the museum accompanied by the restaurant owner who has a set of keys. A truly multi-sensory experience!
→ Gamberi di Mazara del Vallo crudi con patate e crema all'whisky. Pancia di maialino croccante, spinaci, carciofo e senape. Mandorla, vaniglia e pera.

XxX ❀ **Borgo San Jacopo** – Hotel Lungarno 🕸 **AC**
borgo San Jacopo 14 ✉ 50125 – ℰ 055 281661 Plan: **D3**
– www.borgosanjacopo.com
Menu 105/115 € – Carte 81/153 € – *(dinner only)*
• Modern cuisine • Romantic • Intimate •
The flavours of the region have been given a lighter touch in this restaurant, which also offers an excellent wine list of over 600 labels. In summer, treat yourself to dinner on the delightful small terrace overlooking the Arno, where the candlelight is reflected on the surface of the water.
→ Senza farina: spaghetto di patata gialla, crema all'uovo, guanciale, erba cipollina. Agnello infuso al fieno e camomilla, cavolfiore, scalogno, asparagi, fondo ristretto. La dama fiorentina: praline dolci e salate di cioccolato bianco e fondente.

XxX ❀ **Ora D'Aria** (Marco Stabile) **AC**
via dei Georgofili 11r ✉ 50122 – ℰ 055 2001699 Plan: **F3**
– www.oradariaristorante.com – Closed 5-27 August, 29 January-
12 February, Monday lunch and Sunday
Menu 80/90 € – Carte 75/123 € – *(booking advisable)*
• Modern cuisine • Elegant • Cosy •
The dining room at this restaurant faces the open-view kitchen, allowing a continuous exchange of dialogue between chefs and diners. The cuisine focuses on mainly Tuscan produce served in dishes that blend traditional skill with contemporary style.
→ Tortellini farciti di faraona, Champagne solido e polvere di frutti rossi. Manzo croccante alla fiorentina, sedano rapa e vin santo. Latte, caramello e sale.

XxX **SE.STO On Arno** – Hotel The Westin Excelsior 🏠 **AC** ⟷
piazza Ognissanti 3 ✉ 50123 – ℰ 055 2715 2783 Plan: **C2**
– www.sestoonarno.com
Menu 85/115 € – Carte 81/135 € – *(booking advisable)*
• Creative • Chic • Luxury •
This restaurant boasts the highest terrace in Florence, offering stunning views of the Duomo, Giotto's bell tower, the Palazzo della Signoria and Ponte Vecchio. The Mediterranean cuisine, which is reinterpreted with a contemporary twist, provides a real treat for the taste buds.

XxX **The Fusion Bar & Restaurant** – Gallery Hotel Art ♿ **AC**
vicolo dell'Oro 5 ✉ 50123 – ℰ 055 27266987 Plan: **D3**
– www.lungarnocollection.com
Carte 23/77 € – *(dinner only)*
• Fusion • Fashionable • Cosy •
This bar-cum-restaurant is young and stylish. It offers an interesting choice of cocktails, a simple menu at lunchtime and a good mix of Western and Asian cuisine in the evening, including sushi.

XxX   Cibrèo   ⌗ ﹠ AC ⇦

via A. Del Verrocchio 8/r ✉ *50122* – ✆ *055 2341100*   Plan: **F3**
– *www.cibreo.com* – *Closed August, 1 week in February and Monday*
Menu 77/120 €
• Tuscan • Elegant • Neighbourhood •
This restaurant has an informal, fashionable atmosphere, with young, confident
staff and fine, inventive cuisine inspired by traditional dishes.

XX   La Bottega del Buon Caffè   ⌗ AC
☸

lungarno Benvenuto Cellini, 63/r ✉ *50122*   Plan: **F3**
– ✆ *055 5535677* – *www.borgointhecity.com* – *Closed Monday lunch and
Sunday*
Menu 95 €, 115/115 € – Carte 83/126 €
• Creative • Contemporary décor • Elegant •
This elegant restaurant on the Lungarno combines urban chic with Florentine
style. There is a terrace for alfresco dining in fine weather. In the open-view kitchen top-quality ingredients are skilfully transformed into imaginative and carefully prepared dishes with a host of culinary influences.
➜ Taglierini alle triglie, sedano e pane croccante al prezzemolo. Spalla
d'agnello, topinambur, yogurt ed agretti. Il cheesecake de La Bottega.

XX   Caffè dell'Oro – Hotel Portrait Firenze   AC

lungarno Acciaiuoli 4 – ✆ *055 27268912*   Plan: **D3**
– *www.lungarnocollection.com* – *Closed Sunday in winter*
Carte 46/73 € – *(booking advisable)*
• Mediterranean cuisine • Romantic • Elegant •
Tuscan and Mediterranean dishes take pride of place in this restaurant with
superb views of Ponte Vecchio. The elegant atmosphere is in the same style as
the hotel next door.

XX   Baccarossa   AC

via Ghibellina 46/r ✉ *50122* – ✆ *055240620*   Plan: **F3**
– *www.baccarossa.it* – *Closed Sunday*
Menu 30/70 € – Carte 38/84 € – *(dinner only) (booking advisable)*
• Mediterranean cuisine • Trendy • Cosy •
This elegant, bistro-style wine bar is decorated in bright colours and furnished
with wooden tables. It serves delicious Mediterranean cuisine including fish
specialities, homemade pasta and some meat dishes. All the wines available
can be ordered by the glass.

XX   Belcore   AC

via dell'Albero 30r ✉ *50123* – ✆ *055 211198*   Plan: **C2**
– *www.ristorantebelcore.it* – *Closed 16-25 August, 25-31 January,
Wednesday*
Menu 35/50 € – Carte 38/59 € – *(dinner only)*
• Classic cuisine • Contemporary décor •
An excellent selection of wines complement the different types of cuisine ser-
ved in this restaurant. Taste the fish specialities, traditional favourites from Italy
and Tuscany, and more modern dishes.

XX   Buca Mario   AC ⇦

piazza Degli Ottaviani 16 r ✉ *50123* – ✆ *055 214179*   Plan: **D2**
– *www.bucamario.it* – *Closed 9-20 December*
Carte 40/109 € – *(dinner only)*
• Regional cuisine • Traditional décor • Neighbourhood •
This typical Florentine restaurant opened in 1886. Housed in the cellars of the
Palazzo Niccolini in the heart of Florence, it is popular for its excellent, traditional
Tuscan cuisine.

XX **Il Santo Graal**   🖿 AK ⇔

via Romana 70r ✉ *50122 Firenze* – ☏ *055 2286533*   Plan: **D3**
– *www.ristorantesantograal.it* – *Closed 7-21 August and Monday*
Menu 35/50 € – Carte 42/69 € – *(booking advisable)*
• Modern cuisine • Minimalist • Design •
An elegant and minimalist ambience pervades the Santo Graal. This gourmet restaurant, run by a young chef, brings new life to Tuscan traditions with intense flavours and reinterpretations of local culinary favourites.

XX **Cucina Torcicoda**   🛖 AK

via Torta 5/r – ☏ *055 2654329*   Plan: **E3**
– *www.cucinatorcicoda.com* – *Closed Monday in November-March*
Carte 37/81 €
• Tuscan • Cosy •
An osteria, pizzeria and restaurant (in the evenings) all-in-one. This property has three different options under the same roof, offering informal or more elegant dining depending on your mood. Enjoy traditional Tuscan cuisine at the osteria, Neapolitan-style pizzas at the pizzeria and more refined cuisine at the restaurant. All three serve the house speciality: Florentine steak made from different types of beef.

XX **Io Osteria Personale**   🖿 AK

Borgo San Frediano 167r ✉ *50124 Firenze*   Plan: **D2**
– ☏ *055 9331341* – *www.io-osteriapersonale.it* – *Closed 3 weeks in August, 3 weeks in January and Sunday*
Menu 40/55 € – Carte 39/62 € – *(dinner only) (booking advisable)*
• Creative • Bistro • Cosy •
The young owner of this restaurant has an interesting background – a former vet with a passion for food. He has opened one of the most fascinating restaurants in Florence, serving original dishes to diners looking for a change from more traditional fare.

X **Il Santo Bevitore**   ⇔

via Santo Spirito 64/66 r ✉ *50125* – ☏ *055 211264*   Plan: **C3**
– *www.ilsantobevitore.com* – *Closed 10-20 August and Monday lunch*
Carte 27/60 €
• Tuscan • Rustic • Friendly •
This restaurant offers home-style cooking, such as spelt pappardella pasta with wild boar and bilberries, and duck leg with chicory and foie gras, as well as a touch of creativity in the evening. Good value for money.

X **Osteria Caffè Italiano**   AK ⇔

via Isola delle Stinche 11 ✉ *50122* – ☏ *055 289368*   Plan: **E3**
– *www.caffeitaliano.it*
Menu 38 € – Carte 31/59 €
• Traditional cuisine • Rustic • Bistro •
These fine premises are part of a historic building. Wood furnishings predominate in the three small dining halls where the cuisine is largely based on Tuscan recipes. There is a fine wine list.

X **Trattoria Cibrèo-Cibreino**   AK

🙂 *via dei Macci 122/r* ✉ *50122* – ☏ *0552 341100*   Plan: **F3**
– *www.edizioniteatrodelsalecibreofirenze.it* – *Closed August, 10 days in February and Monday*
Carte 30/37 €
• Country • Bistro • Simple •
This trattoria is named after the famous cibreo, a typical stew from Florence that Catherine de Medici was said to enjoy so much that she even attempted, unsuccessfully, to export it to France. It is often crowded, but there is no point in trying to book a table as they don't take reservations. Roast rack of beef (gran pezzo) is one of the specialities.

ITALY - FLORENCE

Il Latini
AC

via dei Palchetti 6 r ⊠ 50123 – 𝒞 055 210916   Plan: **D2**
– www.illatini.com – Closed 1-15 August, 20 December-2 January
and Monday
Carte 27/80 €
• Tuscan • Neighbourhood • Osteria •
Flasks of wine on the walls, hams hanging from the ceiling, friendly informal service and a tradition dating back a hundred years. This famous Florentine trattoria celebrates Tuscan cuisine in all its glory, from ribollita soups to roast meat dishes.

Zeb
�&. AC

via San Miniato 2r ⊠ 50122 – 𝒞 055 2342864   Plan: **E3**
– www.zebgastronomia.com – Closed 16-31 August, Wednesday and
dinner Sunday, Monday and Tuesday except in April-October
Carte 20/48 €
• Tuscan • Simple • Family •
A new take on traditional cuisine in this unique restaurant in the delightful San Niccolò district. Diners sit side-by-side around a central table, as in a sushi bar, enjoying a selection of delicious homemade dishes.

Da Burde
AC

via Pistoiese 154 ⊠ 50122 – 𝒞 055 317206   Plan: **A2**
– www.burde.it – Closed 12-20 August and Bank Holidays
Carte 23/42 € – (lunch only except Friday)
• Regional cuisine • Friendly • Simple •
Opened at the beginning of the 20C as a grocer's shop and trattoria, this historic restaurant is a long way off the usual tourist trail. The two brothers who now run Da Burde have kept everything as it was with cured hams on sale and a bar selling tobacco. To the rear, there is a small dining room in which authentic Tuscan cuisine, such as the famous Florentine steak and pappa al pomodoro soup, is served.

Il Desco – Hotel Il Guelfo Bianco
🛖

via Cavour 29 – 𝒞 055 288330 – www.ildescofirenze.it   Plan: **E2**
– Closed Sunday except in April-October
Carte 31/43 € – (booking advisable)
• Regional cuisine • Osteria • Fashionable •
The tables laid with tablecloths and the informal ambience gives this charming restaurant a genuine bistro feel, as does the range of authentic Tuscan specialities served here. The internal courtyard is popular in summer, but the indoor dining room is also appealing. There is also a small terrace on the pavement of the main road outside.

Del Fagioli
AC 🍴

corso Tintori 47 r ⊠ 50122 – 𝒞 055 244285 – Closed   Plan: **E3**
August, Saturday and Sunday
Carte 26/73 €
• Tuscan • Trattoria • Osteria •
A traditional trattoria that is typical of its genre with an open-view kitchen, lively informal ambience and Tuscan cuisine, including a wide selection of meat dishes and grills. A convivial atmosphere that attracts locals and tourists alike.

Dim Sum
AC

Via de' Neri 37/r ⊠ 50122 – 𝒞 055 284331   Plan: **E3**
– www.dimsumrestaurant.it – Closed Sunday
Carte 9/30 € – (booking advisable)
• Cantonese • Oriental décor • Bistro •
This Chinese restaurant is very popular with locals and for good reason. The menu focuses on small portions of fish and meat (dim sum, hence the restaurant's name) accompanied by an excellent selection of teas.

ITALY - FLORENCE

Villa Cora   ⛲ 🕭 ⟨ 🛏 🖪 ⊕ 🏠 🛌 ⎙ Ⅲ 🏊 🅿
viale Machiavelli 18 ⊠ 50125 – ℰ 055 228790   Plan: **B2**
– www.villacora.it
44 rm – ♥275/781 € ♥♥308/825 € – ⊒ 30 € – 8 suites
• Historic building • Elegant •
An elegant late-19C villa offering a maze of rooms decorated with frescoes, marble and stucco. It is surrounded by mature grounds, which include a swimming pool. There is a small terrace-lounge with exquisite views, as well as a restaurant serving fine cuisine and a veranda for alfresco dining in summer.

Torre di Bellosguardo   🕭 ⟨ 🛏 ⎙ Ⅲ 🚗
via Roti Michelozzi 2 ⊠ 50124 – ℰ 055 2298145   Plan: **A2**
– www.torrebellosguardo.com
9 rm – ♥110/160 € ♥♥260/350 € – ⊒ 20 € – 7 suites
• Historic building • Elegant •
There's a hint of the past in the lounge areas and guestrooms of this simple yet elegant hotel, which has breathtaking views of Florence. It has a magical, fairy tale atmosphere. There is a park with a botanical garden, an aviary and a swimming pool.

Villa La Vedetta   ⛲ 🕭 ⟨ 🛏 🏠 ⎙ 🛌 Ⅲ 🏊 🅿
viale Michelangiolo 78 ⊠ 50125 – ℰ 055 681631   Plan: **B2**
– www.villalavedettahotel.com – Closed 16 January-16 February
11 rm ⊒ – ♥150/980 € ♥♥150/1100 € – 7 suites
• Historic building • Luxury • Elegant •
Surrounded by mature parkland, this neo-Renaissance-style villa has been transformed into an elegant hotel decorated with a mix of designer-style furnishings and antique pieces. Every guestroom has its own personality, with each boasting charming details, such as bedside tables made from onyx or crocodile, crystal writing desks and precious silk furnishings.

Marignolle Relais & Charme   🕭 ⟨ 🛏 ⎙ Ⅲ 🅿
via di San Quirichino 16, località Marignolle   Plan: **A2**
– ℰ 055 2286910 – www.marignolle.com
8 rm ⊒ – ♥130/215 € ♥♥145/285 € – 1 suite
• Luxury • Personalised •
The pleasant rooms in this rustic dwelling in a holding in the hills are all different from one another and are characterized by refined blends of lively materials; panoramic swimming pool in the greenery.

Villa Belvedere   🕭 ⟨ 🛏 ⎙ 🍴 Ⅲ 🅿
via Benedetto Castelli 3 ⊠ 50124 – ℰ 055 222501   Plan: **B2**
– www.villabelvederefirenze.it – Open 1° March-15 November
26 rm ⊒ – ♥80/150 € ♥♥120/207 €
• Traditional • Cosy •
Villa dating from the 1950s, with a swimming pool in the gardens and a splendid view over the town and the hills, for a quiet stay in a luxury but family orientated environment.

XX   Omero   🕭 ⟨ 🏠
via Pian de' Giullari 49 – ℰ 055 220053   Plan: **B2**
– www.ristoranteomero.it
Menu 35/45 € – Carte 57/70 €
• Tuscan • Rustic • Family •
Offering views of the hills, this beautifully kept restaurant has been run by the same family for 30 years. Traditional trattoria ambience and typical regional cuisine. Evening dining on the terrace in summer.

Trattoria Bibe ⇔ 🏠 **P**

via delle Bagnese 15 – ☏ 055 2049085 Plan: **A2**
– www.trattoriabibe.com – Closed 1 week in November, 2 weeks in February and Wednesday
3 rm ☕ – �100 € ♦♦140 € Carte 35/49 € – *(dinner only)*
• Tuscan • Regional décor • Friendly •
Immortalised by the Italian writer Montale in his poetry, this trattoria has been run by the same family for almost two centuries. The menu features traditional Tuscan dishes, such as pici pasta with wild boar sauce. Alfresco dining in summer. There are also apartments with kitchens for guests that wish to extend their stay.

AT BAGNO A RIPOLI

 Villa La Massa 🌿 ≤ 🏠 🛁 ᗉ ᶜ AC ᐟ **P**

via della Massa 24 – ☏ 055 62611 – www.villalamassa.com – Open April-November
23 rm ☕ – ♦460/740 € ♦♦460/740 € – 14 suites
• Grand Luxury • Historic •
More than just a hotel, this building is an architectural jewel from the Medici period and a bucolic oasis overlooking the River Arno situated just 15min from Florence (easily accessible thanks to the hotel's free shuttle service). Four-poster beds, wood panelling, frescoed ceilings, tapestries and marble bathrooms all combine to provide a warm yet elegant ambience, offering guests a taste of aristocratic Florentine life – with all the comforts of our modern age.
Il Verrocchio – See restaurant listing

XxX **Il Verrocchio** – Hotel Villa La Massa 🏠 🏠 ᗉ AC ✿ **P**

via della Massa 24 – ☏ 055 62611533 – www.villalamassa.com – Open April-November
Menu 70/100 € – Carte 73/118 € – *(dinner only)*
• Modern cuisine • Romantic • Luxury •
This restaurant is named after the Florentine artist in whose studio the great Leonardo da Vinci trained. It boasts an elegant dining room with a vaulted ceiling, as well as a delightful terrace overlooking the Arno for alfresco dining. Regional specialities and traditional Italian favourites are on the menu.

AT FIESOLE PLAN I

Villa San Michele ✿ 🌿 ≤ 🏠 ᗉ ᶜ AC ᐟ ✿ **P**

via Doccia 4 – ☏ 055 5678200 – www.belmond.com – Open 1° April-30 October Plan: **B1**
39 rm ☕ – ♦600 € ♦♦970/1280 € – 6 suites
• Historic building • Grand luxury •
A free shuttle bus takes guests from this hotel to the heart of Florence (10min). Or you may prefer simply to relax in the tranquil grounds of this elegant 15C building and enjoy the superb views of the city below.

 Il Salviatino ✿ 🌿 ≤ 🏠 ᗉ ♒ ᶜ AC **P**

via del Salviatino 21 – ☏ 055 9041111 – www.salviatino.com Plan: **B2**
45 rm ☕ – ♦350/2500 € ♦♦380/2600 € – 8 suites
• Grand Luxury • Historic •
Luxury is evident not only in the rooms of this 16C villa – which is surrounded by gardens and boasts fine views of the city – but also in its "service ambassadors", who are on hand to deal with guests' requests 24 hours a day. A truly idyllic place to stay!

 Pensione Bencistà

via Benedetto da Maiano 4 – ℰ 055 59163
– www.bencista.com – Open 15 March-15 November
41 rm ⬮ – †80/130 € – ††158/250 € – 2 suites

Plan: **B1**

• Historic building • Vintage •

Situated on the slopes of the hills surrounding Fiesole, this 14C villa offers picture-postcard views of Florence. The interior decor is attractively retro, if occasionally a little dated in style, but full of charm and old-world romance.

✗ **Tullio a Montebeni**

via Ontignano 48 – ℰ 055 697354 – www.ristorantetullio.it – Closed
August, 22-28 February, Monday, Tuesday lunch
Carte 25/60 € – *(dinner only except Saturday, Sunday) (booking advisable)*

• Tuscan • Family • Friendly •

This restaurant started as a simple grocery shop and in 1958 it began serving simple meals to locals and hunters in the region. Today the restaurant is enthusiastically run by Tullio's children, who continue to offer regional cuisine accompanied by their own home produced wine.

 Villa il Poggiale

via Empolese 69 (North-West: 1 km) – ℰ 055 828311
– www.villailpoggiale.it
24 rm ⬮ – †80/150 € ††90/250 € – 2 suites

• Luxury • Historic • Personalised •

Situated in the heart of Chianti just a few kilometres from Florence, this Renaissance-style villa is an oasis of peace surrounded by delightful gardens. Guests here are spoilt with a whole host of attentive details which combine to make their stay a truly unforgettable experience, as well as a new spa which offers a range of treatments created exclusively for the hotel. The restaurant serves typical Tuscan cuisine accompanied by a good selection of local wines.

✗✗✗ **La Tenda Rossa**

piazza del Monumento 9/14 – ℰ 055 826132 – www.latendarossa.it
– Closed 2 weeks in August, Monday lunch and Sunday
Menu 45 € (lunch)/120 € – Carte 58/126 €

• Creative • Elegant • Family •

Italian restaurants are traditionally family-run, and three families run this one! Its quality of service and the food is three times as good.

ITALY - FLORENCE

MILAN
MILANO

Population: 1 345 851

Bruno Bernier/Fotolia.com

If it's the romantic charm of places like Venice, Florence or Rome you're looking for, then best avoid Milan. If you're hankering for a permanent panorama of Renaissance chapels, palazzi, shimmering canals and bastions of fine art, then you're in the wrong place. What Milan does is relentless fashion, churned out with oodles of attitude and style. Italy's second largest city is constantly reinventing itself, and when Milan does a makeover, it invariably does it with flair and panache. That's not to say that Italy's capital of fast money and fast fashion doesn't have an eye for its past. The centrepiece of the whole city is the magnificent gleaming white Duomo, which took five hundred years to complete, while up la via a little way, La Scala is quite simply the world's most famous opera house. But this is a city known primarily for its sleek and modern towers, many housing the very latest threads from the very latest fashion gurus.

MILAN IN...

→ **ONE DAY**
Duomo, Leonardo da Vinci's 'The Last Supper' (remember to book first), Brera, Navigli.

→ **TWO DAYS**
Pinacoteca Brera, Castello Sforzesco, Parco Sempione, Museo del Novecento, a night at La Scala.

→ **THREE DAYS**
Giardini Pubblici and its museums, trendy Savona district.

Just north of Milan's centre lies Brera, with its much prized old-world charm, and Quadrilatero d'Oro, with no little new-world glitz; the popular Giardini Pubblici are a little further north east from here. South of the centre is the Navigli quarter, home to rejuvenated Middle Age canals, while to the west are the green lungs of the Parco Sempione. For those into art or fashion, the trendy Savona district is also a must.

PRACTICAL INFORMATION

ARRIVAL-DEPARTURE

 Malpensa Airport is 48km north-west of the city and Linate Airport, 7km east. A train connects Malpensa with Stazione Cadorna, Garibaldi and Centrale train stations every 30min and takes 40min. From Linate take the Airport Bus No. 73 to Piazza San Babila metro station (every 10min, it takes 25min).

GETTING AROUND

The best way to get about Milan is by bus, tram or metro. Tickets are valid for one metro ride, or ninety minutes of travel on buses or trams. You can also purchase books of ten tickets, or

unlimited one-day or two-day passes. Buy them at metro stations, kiosks, bars or tobacconists. The metro provides a fast and efficient service, with frequent trains running on three different lines. Walking is a good alternative: most of Milan's attractions are based in the small and compact centre.

CALENDAR HIGHLIGHTS

February
Milan Fashion Week.

March
MiArt (international modern art fair).

April
Naviglio Grande Flower Market.
International Furniture Fair.

June
Gods of Metal Festival, Festival Latino Americano, Festa del Naviglio, Notte Bianca.

September
September Music, Panoramica (film festival), Milan Fashion Week.
Formula 1 Grand Prix in Monza.

October
Wellness World Exhibition, Celtic New Year celebrations.

December
Opera season at La Scala gets underway.

EATING OUT

For a taste of Italy's regional cuisines, Milan is a great place to be. The city is often the goal of those leaving their home regions in the south or centre of the country; many open trattoria or restaurants, with the result that Milan offers a wide range of provincial menus. Excellent fish restaurants, inspired by recipes from the south, are a big draw despite the fact that the city is a long way from the sea. Going beyond the local borders, the emphasis on really good food continues and the quality of internationally diverse places

to eat is better in Milan than just about anywhere else in Italy, including Rome. You'd expect avant-garde eating destinations to be the thing in this city of fashion and style, and you'd be right: there are some top-notch cutting-edge restaurants, thanks to Milan's famous tendency to reshape and experiment as it goes. For those who want to try out the local gastronomic traditions, risotto allo zafferano is not to be missed, nor is the cotoletta alla Milanese (veal cutlet) or the casoeula (a winter special made with pork and cabbage).

Four Seasons Hotel Milano

via Gesù 6/8 ✉ *20121 –* Ⓜ *Montenapoleone* Plan: **G1**
– ✆ 02 77088 – www.fourseasons.com/milan
68 rm – †590/950 € ††590/950 € – ☕ 35 € – 50 suites
• Grand Luxury • Luxury • Classic •
This evocative hotel has achieved a perfect balance between the original architectural features of the 15C monastery in which it is housed and its elegant contemporary design. Don't be surprised by the highly modern technology available in the superb guestrooms that occupy the former monks' cells.
La Veranda – See restaurant listing

Mandarin Oriental Milano

via Andegari 9 ✉ *20121 Milano –* Ⓜ *Montenapoleone* Plan: **G1**
– ✆ 02 87318888 – www.mandarinoriental.com
72 rm – †560/1200 € ††560/1200 € – ☕ 35 € – 32 suites
• Grand Luxury • Historic building • Design •
This prestigious chain has now opened a hotel in four sober 18C buildings situated in Milan's fashion quarter. Choose between standard rooms (in name only!) and various suites decorated in warm colours, with an elegant Italian designer style. The attractive spa also has original features, such as the wooden beams that are deliberately arranged asymmetrically, evoking the image of an Asian cane thicket. The ambience is distinctly 1950s in the Mandarin Bar, where guests can choose from a selection of sandwiches, large salads and typical Italian dishes.
✿✿ **Seta** – See restaurant listing

Park Hyatt Milano

via Tommaso Grossi 1 ✉ *20121 –* Ⓜ *Duomo* Plan: **G2**
– ✆ 02 88211234 – www.milan.park.hyatt.com
90 rm – †520/1575 € ††520/1575 € – ☕ 38 € – 16 suites
• Luxury • Grand Luxury • Modern •
Housed in a palazzo dating from 1870, this contemporary-style hotel boasts the best of modern comforts, including spacious guestrooms and equally large bathrooms. Travertine marble covers the building and a splendid work of art by Anish Kapoor "Untitled 2013" can be admired in the lobby.
✿ **Vun • Mio Bar** – See restaurant listing

Grand Hotel et de Milan

via Manzoni 29 ✉ *20121 –* Ⓜ *Montenapoleone* Plan: **G1**
– ✆ 02 723141 – www.grandhoteletdemilan.it
77 rm – †396/813 € ††421/838 € – ☕ 35 € – 18 suites
• Grand Luxury • Historic building • Historic •
This hotel opened over 150 years ago. Big names in the field of music, theatre and politics have stayed in its elegant rooms that are full of charm. Bright restaurant dedicated to the great tenor, who recorded his first record in this hotel.
Don Carlos – See restaurant listing

Carlton Hotel Baglioni

via Senato 5 ✉ *20121 –* Ⓜ *San Babila – ✆ 02 77077* Plan: **H1**
– www.baglionihotels.com
87 rm – †395/600 € ††682/968 € – ☕ 36 €
• Luxury • Traditional • Elegant •
Celebrities and well-known personalities are among the guests who have stayed in this splendid hotel, which describes itself as 'home from home'. It provides luxury in a warm, family atmosphere. Antique pieces and original works of art grace the public areas, while the guestrooms offer stucco decor and modern technology.

Bulgari
🛎 ⓘ ⚙ 🖥 👤 🔖 AC ♨ 🚗

via privata Fratelli Gabba 7/b ✉ 20121   Plan: **G1**
– Ⓜ *Montenapoleone* – ✆ *02 8058051* – *www.bulgarihotels.com*
47 rm – ▮550/820 € ▮▮550/820 € – ☕ 40 € – 11 suites
• Boutique hotel • Grand Luxury • Design •
Owned by the famous jewellery company, this luxury hotel is decorated in warm colours with fine materials gracing the guestrooms. The hotel boasts one of the best spas in the city with a hammam whose green glass decor evokes an emerald. Exclusive terrace overlooking an unexpected garden.
Bulgari-Il Ristorante – See restaurant listing

Armani Hotel Milano
🍴 🖥 ⓘ 🏠 👤 AC ♨

via Manzoni 31 ✉ 20123 – Ⓜ *Montenapoleone*   Plan: **G1**
– ✆ *02 8883 8888* – *www.armanihotels.com*
95 rm – ▮500/1500 € ▮▮500/1500 € – ☕ 40 € – 32 suites
• Grand Luxury • Boutique hotel • Minimalist •
This innovative hotel is housed in an austere building dating from 1937, typical of the Armani style. It is run by a 'lifestyle manager' who offers a warm welcome to guests. Luxurious 1 000m² spa and very spacious guestrooms.
❀ **Armani** – See restaurant listing

Starhotels Rosa Grand
🍴 🖥 🏠 👤 AC ♨

piazza Fontana 3 ✉ 20122 – Ⓜ *Duomo* – ✆ *02 88311*   Plan: **G2**
– *www.starhotels.com*
324 rm ☕ – ▮300/1300 € ▮▮300/1300 € – 6 suites
• Palace • Modern • Design •
Situated in the heart of Milan, this hotel has recently undergone a major refurbishment. The interior is arranged around a courtyard, with simple, square shapes creating a naturally elegant look. The guestrooms here are comfortable and stylish, although only a few offer views of the Duomo.

Château Monfort
🍴 🖥 ⓘ 🖥 👤 AC ♨

corso Concordia 1 ✉ 20129 – ✆ *02 776761*   Plan: **H1**
– *www.hotelchateaumonfort.com*
77 rm – ▮250/990 € ▮▮250/990 € – ☕ 26 €
• Grand Luxury • Boutique hotel • Romantic •
Discreet elegance in a superb Art Nouveau-style palazzo designed by Paolo Mezzanotte. The guestrooms have a chic, glamorous feel – the opera inspired rooms are delightful – and there is also a small spa to relax in.

The Gray
🍴 👤 AC

via San Raffaele 6 ✉ 20121 – Ⓜ *Duomo*   Plan: **G2**
– ✆ *02 7208951* – *www.sinahotels.com* – *Closed August*
19 rm – ▮500/650 € ▮▮550/900 € – ☕ 33 € – 2 suites
• Boutique hotel • Traditional • Personalised •
All different in style, the rooms in this hotel feature a host of interesting details, as well as up-to-date technology such as Wi-Fi internet connection and LCD televisions. 'Gray' in name only (perhaps an ironic reference to Milan's occasional dull weather?), this hotel is one of the most stylish and elegant in the city.

Milano Scala
🍴 🖥 👤 AC ♨

via dell'Orso 7 ✉ 20121 – Ⓜ *Cairoli* – ✆ *02 870961*   Plan: **F1**
– *www.hotelmilanoscala.it* – *Closed 12-27 August*
58 rm ☕ – ▮170/630 € ▮▮260/820 € – 4 suites
• Boutique hotel • Traditional • Personalised •
A charming hotel built in 2010 with an emphasis on sustainability. The public areas are fairly small but stylish, while the breakfast room is a real delight, decorated with musical notes on the walls. There is a good choice of dishes in the restaurant for dinner. At lunchtime the menu is lighter with a focus on snacks.

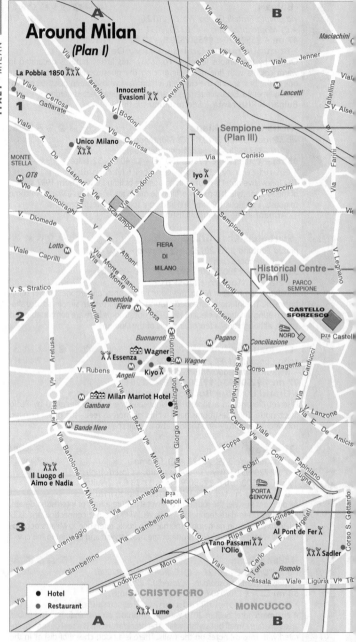

Around Milan
(Plan I)

La Pobbia 1850 ✗✗✗

Innocenti
Evasioni ✗✗

Unico Milano
✗✗✗

MONTE
STELLA
Ⓜ QT8

Sempione
(Plan III)

Iyo ✗

FIERA
DI
MILANO

Historical Centre
(Plan II)
PARCO
SEMPIONE

Lotto Ⓜ

Amendola
Fiera Ⓜ

CASTELLO
SFORZESCO
NORD
Pza Castell

Buonarroti
✗✗ Essenza 🏨🏨 Wagner
Ⓜ Wagner

Conciliazione

Angeli Kiyo ✗

Ⓜ 🏨🏨 Milan Marriot Hotel

Gambara

Ⓜ Bande Nere

Il Luogo di
Aimo e Nadia
✗✗✗

Pza
Napoli

PORTA
GENOVA

Al Pont de Fer ✗

Tano Passami
l'Olio ✗✗

✗✗✗ Sadler

Romolo

S. CRISTOFORO

MONCUCCO

✗✗✗ Lume ●

● Hotel
● Restaurant

476

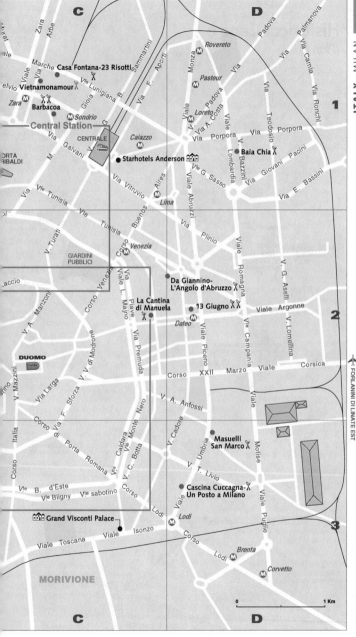

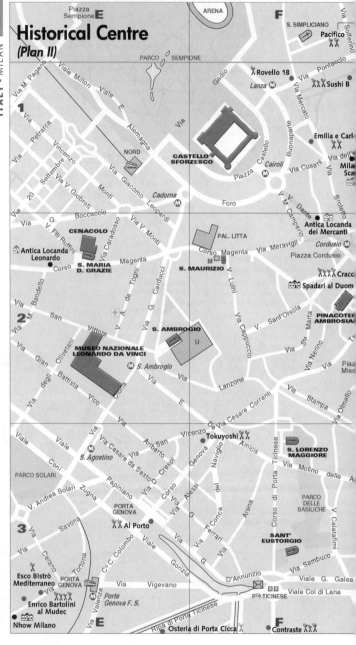

Historical Centre
(Plan II)

Piazza Sempione **E**

ARENA

F

PARCO SEMPIONE

S. SIMPLICIANO

Pacifico ✗✗

Rovello 18 ✗

Lanza Ⓜ

Sushi B ✗✗✗

NORD

CASTELLO SFORZESCO

Emilia e Carl ✗✗

Cadorna Ⓜ

Piazza Cairoli Ⓜ

Foro

Mila Sca

Antica Locanda dei Mercanti

CENACOLO

PAL. LITTA

Cordusio Ⓜ

Antica Locanda Leonardo

S. MARIA D. GRAZIE

Corso Magenta

S. MAURIZIO

Piazza Cordusio

Crac

Spadari al Duom

2

S. AMBROGIO

PINACOTEC AMBROSIA

MUSEO NAZIONALE LEONARDO DA VINCI

Ⓜ S. Ambrogio

Piaz Miss

Lanzone

Via Cesare Correnti

Tokuyoshi ✗✗

S. LORENZO MAGGIORE

Ⓜ S. Agostino

PARCO SOLARI

Via Molino delle

PARCO DELLE BASILICHE

3

XX Al Porto

SANT' EUSTORGIO

PORTA GENOVA

Esco Bistrò Mediterraneo

PORTA GENOVA

Porta Genova F. S.

Via Vigevano

D'Annunzio

PTA TICINESE

Viale G. Galea

Enrico Bartolini al Mudec

Viale Col di Lana

Nhow Milano

E

Ripa di Porta Ticinese

Osteria di Porta Cicca ✗

F

Contraste ✗✗✗

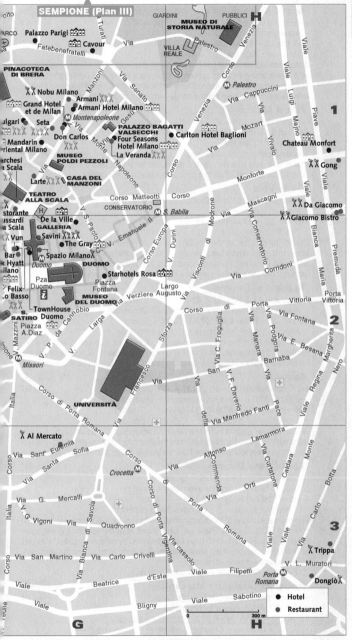

SEMPIONE (Plan III)

GIARDINI PUBBLICI

MUSEO DI STORIA NATURALE

Palazzo Parigi
Fatebenefratelli
Cavour
Via Turati

VILLA REALE
Palestro

PINACOTECA DI BRERA

Nobu Milano
Armani
Armani Hotel Milano
Grand Hotel et de Milan
Bulgari
Seta
Mandarin Oriental Milano
Don Carlos
Montenapoleone

PALAZZO BAGATTI VALSECCHI
Four Seasons Hotel Milano
La Veranda

Carlton Hotel Baglioni

Chateau Monfort

Gong

Marchesi a Scala
MUSEO POLDI PEZZOLI
Larte
CASA DEL MANZONI

TEATRO ALLA SCALA
Ristorante Bussardi a Scala
De la Ville
GALLERIA
Savini
Vun
Bar
Park Hyatt Milano
The Gray
Spazio Milano
Felix Lo Basso
S. SATIRO
TownHouse Duomo
Piazza A.Diaz

Corso Matteotti
CONSERVATORIO
S. Babila

Da Giacomo
Giacomo Bistro

Monforte
Mascagni

DUOMO
Starhotels Rosa
Piazza Fontana
MUSEO DEL DUOMO
Largo Augusto
Verziere

Porta Vittoria
Via Fontana

Missori
UNIVERSITÀ

Al Mercato
Sant' Eufemia
Crocetta

Lamarmora

G. Mercalli
Vigoni
Quadronno

Trippa

San Martino
Carlo Crivelli
d'Este

Porta Romana
Dongiò

Sabotino

Bligny

0   300 m

● Hotel
● Restaurant

G   H

479

ITALY - MILAN

Grand Visconti Palace

viale Isonzo 14 ✉ *20135 –* Ⓜ *Lodi TIBB – ☎ 02 540341* Plan: **C3**
– www.grandviscontipalace.com
166 rm ⌧ – ♦100/1000 € ♦♦100/1100 € – 6 suites
• Palace • Business • Industrial •
A large old industrial mill has been converted to house this elegant grand hotel with a welcoming well-being centre, conference rooms and a delightful garden. Make sure you try the Quinto Piano restaurant, which delights guests with its refined and imaginative cuisine made with real care and attention.

Nhow Milano

via Tortona 35 ✉ *20144 – ☎ 02 4898861 – www.nhow-hotels.com* Plan: **E3**
245 rm ⌧ – ♦80/800 € ♦♦100/1000 € – 1 suite
• Luxury • Design •
This designer-style hotel located in a former industrial district has plenty of charm, and acts as a permanent showcase for artistic and stylistic excellence. Eclectic guestrooms offering impeccable standards of comfort.

De la Ville

via Hoepli 6 ✉ *20121 –* Ⓜ *Duomo – ☎ 02 8791311* Plan: **G2**
– www.sinahotels.com
107 rm ⌧ – ♦250/480 € ♦♦300/500 € – 1 suite
• Traditional • Elegant • Personalised •
Despite its location in the bustling centre of Milan, there's nothing Milanese about this hotel, which has a French name and a distinctly British decor. It features wood panelling, fireplaces and attractive prints depicting horses and fox hunting. The same stylish elegance is evident in the guestrooms.

Spadari al Duomo

via Spadari 11 ✉ *20123 –* Ⓜ *Duomo – ☎ 02 72002371* Plan: **F2**
– www.spadarihotel.com – Closed 22-27 December
39 rm ⌧ – ♦185/450 € ♦♦200/600 € – 1 suite
• Traditional • Modern • Contemporary •
This modern hotel has the twin advantage of a central location, as well as a fine display of contemporary art collected by its art enthusiast owners. Note the Giò Pomodoro fireplace in the lobby and the careful play of light throughout the hotel.

Cavour

via Fatebenefratelli 21 ✉ *20121 –* Ⓜ *Turati* Plan: **G1**
– ☎ 02 620001 – www.hotelcavour.it – Closed 7-25 August
120 rm ⌧ – ♦115/700 € ♦♦126/900 € – 7 suites
• Traditional • Elegant • Contemporary •
This simple yet elegant hotel not far from the city's main cultural sights is decorated with high quality materials, from the floors to the wood panelling. The restaurant serves reasonably priced brasserie-style dishes from 11am-7pm.

Townhouse Duomo

via Silvio Pellico 2 ✉ *20121 –* Ⓜ *Duomo* Plan: **G2**
– ☎ 02 45397600 – www.townhousehotels.com
6 rm – ♦♦400/1500 € – ⌧ 25 € – 8 suites
• Luxury • Historic • Centrally located •
The main attractions of this luxury hotel are its views of Milan cathedral and the splendid Piazza Duomo. These can be enjoyed from the luxurious guestrooms (all on the third floor), which have been designed by different architects, as well as from the small breakfast terrace on the first floor, from where the centuries-old spires appear close at hand.
❀ **Felix Lo Basso** – See restaurant listing

Antica Locanda dei Mercanti

via San Tomaso 6 ✉ *20121 –* Ⓜ *Cordusio* Plan: **F2**
– ☎ 02 8054080 – www.locanda.it
12 rm ⌧ – ♦195/245 € ♦♦225/325 € – 3 suites
• Manor house • Boutique hotel • Romantic •
A small, cosy hotel, simple and elegant in style, and furnished with antique furniture. Many of the light and spacious guestrooms have a small terrace.

XxxX **Seta** – Hotel Mandarin Oriental Milano   器 斎 & 岡
❀❀ *via Monte di Pietà 18 ⊠ 20121 –* Ⓜ *Montenapoleone*   Plan: **G1**
– 𝒞 02 87318897 – www.mandarinoriental.com – Closed 7-28 August,
Saturday lunch and Sunday
Menu 130 € – Carte 89/147 € – *(booking advisable)*
• Creative • Design • Luxury •

The characteristic structure of this restaurant includes large windows that allow
a real connection between indoors and out, while the top-quality cuisine prepared by Antonio Guida is as light as the restaurant's name suggests (*seta* is the
Italian for silk). The menu features meat and fish dishes with influences from
northern and southern Italy, as well as a choice of exotic desserts.
→ Riso in cagnone con crema di riso alle erbe, maccagno (formaggio) e
polvere di lamponi. Pollo ficatum con crema di cannellini alle alghe, fregola
e garusoli (lumache di mare). Parfait alla liquirizia, cristalli di foglie di
tabacco del Kentucky e crema al caffè.

XxxX **Cracco**   器 & 岡
❀❀ *via Victor Hugo 4 ⊠ 20123 –* Ⓜ *Duomo – 𝒞 02 876774*   Plan: **F2**
– www.ristorantecracco.it – Closed August, 23 December-9 January,
Saturday lunch, Monday lunch and Sunday
Menu 190 € – Carte 118/209 € – *(booking advisable)*
• Creative • Luxury • Chic •

This restaurant offers traditional dishes from Milan and elsewhere in Italy reinterpreted with a modern twist and playing on contrasts of textures, flavours and
colours. The elegantly discreet ambience is made even more hushed by the cher-
rywood panelling on the walls. There is also a "table d'hôte" – a small table for a
maximum of four diners, which offers views of the team at work in the kitchen.
→ Risotto allo zafferano e midollo alla piastra. Vitello impanato alla milanese. Nuvola di mascarpone.

XxxX **Vun** – Hotel Park Hyatt Milano   器 & 岡 ⇔
❀ *via Silvio Pellico 3 ⊠ 20121 –* Ⓜ *Duomo*   Plan: **G2**
– 𝒞 02 88211234 – www.ristorante-vun.it – Closed August, Christmas
Holidays, Sunday and Monday
Menu 150 € – Carte 90/118 € – *(dinner only) (booking advisable)*
• Modern cuisine • Elegant • Fashionable •

A young Neapolitan chef is at the helm in this restaurant. Enjoy dishes and
ingredients from his native region as well as top quality produce from the heel
of Italy. Elegant and cosmopolitan ambience.
→ Seppia alla diavola, patata, rafano, cavolo acidulo. Riso carnaroli riserva,
limone, capperi, rosmarino, scampi. Zuppa di latte, pane, caffè, mandorle.

XxxX **Il Ristorante Trussardi alla Scala**   器 & 岡
piazza della Scala 5 (palazzo Trussardi) ⊠ 20121   Plan: **G1**
– Ⓜ *Duomo – 𝒞 02 80688201 – www.trussardiallascala.com – Closed 2 weeks*
in August, 2 weeks December-January, Saturday lunch and Sunday
Menu 100/160 € – Carte 90/120 € – *(booking advisable)*
• Modern cuisine • Luxury •

There has been a change in the style of cuisine served at this modern restaurant, which overlooks one of the most famous squares in Milan. A careful selection of produce and imaginative creativity are the hallmarks of the young, talented chef, Luigi Taglienti.
Café Trussardi – See restaurant listing

XxxX **Savini**   器 & 岡 ⇔
galleria Vittorio Emanuele II ⊠ 20121 – Ⓜ *Duomo*   Plan: **G2**
– 𝒞 02 72003433 – www.savinimilano.it – Closed 3 weeks in August, 1-
7 January, Saturday lunch and Sunday
Menu 110/160 € – Carte 86/135 €
• Classic cuisine • Luxury • Chic •

The entrance to this restaurant is through the Caffè Savini, which offers a selection of Italy's most famous dishes. A lift takes diners to the first floor, where the
gourmet restaurant has been delighting guests with its mix of Milanese favourites and more creative fare since 1867.

ITALY - MILAN

XxX ✿ **Felix Lo Basso** – Hotel Townhouse Duomo ≼ 🏠 � ⅋ AC

piazza Duomo 21 (5° piano) ✉ *20122 –* Ⓜ *Duomo*   Plan: **G2**
– ✆ 02 49528914 – Closed 13-27 August, 1-8 January,
Saturday lunch and Sunday
Menu 95/130 € – Carte 79/120 €
• Creative • Fashionable • Elegant •
Puglian chef Felice Lo Basso is now at new premises offering breathtaking views of the Duomo. He continues to prove his talent with his recognised trademark of light, creative and colourful cuisine, which is often playful and always focuses on the use of top-quality Italian ingredients.
→ Canederlo di gamberi in consommè di porcini, limone e speck. Il mio risotto alla parmigiana. La cotoletta alla milanese con ortaggi e verdure.

XxX ✿ **Armani** – Armani Hotel Milano ≼ ⅋ AC ⇔

via Manzoni 31 ✉ *20121 –* Ⓜ *Montenapoleone*   Plan: **G1**
– ✆ 02 8883 8888 – www.armanihotels.com – Closed 7-31 August, Sunday
dinner
Menu 150 € (dinner) – Carte 78/132 € – *(booking advisable) (bar lunch)*
• Modern cuisine • Luxury • Design •
This exclusive, designer-style restaurant has checkerboard-style flooring and floor-to-ceiling glass windows offering superb views of Milan. The menu features excellent Italian cuisine alongside international dishes inspired by the Umami philosophy, which focuses on the fifth sense.
→ Pisarei (gnocchi di pane), ragù di culatello, finocchio confit, pecorino toscano. Astice, burrata, pera, 'nduja, patanegra, coriandolo. Cassis: cremoso al cassis, biscotto al cioccolato e sale, sorbetto al lemongrass.

XxX **Larte** AC ⇔

via Manzoni 5 ✉ *20123 –* Ⓜ *Montenapoleone*   Plan: **G1**
– ✆ 0289096950 – www.lartemilano.com – Closed August, 24 December-
3 January, Saturday lunch and Sunday
Menu 25 € (lunch)/80 € – Carte 55/98 € – *(booking advisable)*
• Mediterranean cuisine • Fashionable • Trendy •
This new Milanese 'salon' showcases the best of Italian culture with a menu featuring a fine selection of meat and fish classics from around the country, as well as a boutique selling Italian products. Larte is not just a restaurant, but also a chocolate shop, osteria, café and, last but not least, an art gallery!

XxX **Don Carlos** – Grand Hotel et de Milan AC

via Manzoni 29 ✉ *20121 –* Ⓜ *Montenapoleone*   Plan: **G1**
– ✆ 02 72314640 – www.ristorantedoncarlos.it – Closed August
Menu 75/90 €
– Carte 79/117 € – (dinner only) (number of covers limited, pre-book)
• Modern cuisine • Romantic • Vintage •
Named after one of Verdi's operas, this charming restaurant has a quiet atmosphere and elegant decor, including wood panelling, red appliqué and old photos. The menu focuses on traditional cuisine from Lombardy and Piedmont with a creative touch.

XxX **Marchesi alla Scala** ⅋ AC

via Filodrammatici 2 ✉ *20121 –* Ⓜ *Duomo*   Plan: **G1**
– ✆ 02 72094338 – www.ilmarchesino.it – Closed 7-26 August, 2-
7 January, Saturday lunch and Sunday
Menu 46 € (weekday lunch)/150 € – Carte 66/146 € – *(booking advisable)*
• Modern cuisine • Classic décor •
Housed within the La Scala opera house, this restaurant with a café and tearoom offers a careful mix of classic columns, modern paintings and designer-style furniture. Fine cuisine presented in the simple yet elegant style that is typical of Gualtiero Marchesi.

XxX **Bulgari-Il Ristorante** – Hotel Bulgari   🛏 🗐 ♿ 🆑 🚗
via privata Fratelli Gabba 7/b ✉ *20121*   Plan: **G1**
– Ⓜ *Montenapoleone –* 📞 *02 8058051 – www.bulgarihotels.com*
Menu 90 € (dinner), 65/110 € – Carte 73/122 € – *(booking advisable)*
• **Modern cuisine • Design • Minimalist •**
Overlooking an unexpected yet beautiful garden, this attractive restaurant boasts
the same exclusive style as the rest of the hotel. The cuisine showcases top quality
Italian produce in dishes that are modern and contemporary in flavour.

XxX **La Veranda** – Four Seasons Hotel Milano   🛏 🗐 🆑 ⇕ 🚗
via Gesù 6/8 ✉ *20121 –* Ⓜ *Montenapoleone*   Plan: **G1**
– 📞 *02 77081478 – www.fourseasons.com/milan*
Menu 39 € (weekday lunch)/80 € – Carte 79/135 €
• **Classic cuisine • Luxury • Traditional décor •**
Younger guests will have no problem choosing a dish at this restaurant, thanks to
its special children's menu. While other diners can enjoy Mediterranean cuisine
and a wide selection of vegetarian specialities as they admire views of the clois-
ters, which are visible through the large windows of the modern dining room.

XxX **Mio Bar** – Hotel Park Hyatt Milano   🗐 ♿ 🆑
via Tommaso Grossi 1 – 📞 *02 88211234*   Plan: **G2**
– www.milan.park.hyatt.com
Menu 43 € (weekday lunch) – Carte 64/84 €
• **Modern cuisine • Trendy • Luxury •**
This welcoming and lively bar in the prestigious Park Hyatt Milan hotel is open
from six in the morning until 1am, serving a small selection of à la carte dishes,
as well as an "Assaggi" menu just before dinner.

XxX **Sushi B**   🗐 🆑
via Fiori Chiari 1/A ✉ *20121 –* 📞 *02 89092640*   Plan: **F1**
– www.sushi-b.it – Closed 6-21 August, 23 December-9 January,
Sunday and Monday
Menu 95 € – Carte 79/85 €
• **Japanese • Minimalist • Elegant •**
This new, glamorous and extremely elegant restaurant has a minimalist decor
that is decidedly Japanese in feel. There is an attractive bar at the entrance for
pre-dinner drinks, while the actual restaurant is on the first floor. This offers well-
spaced tables and the option of eating at the teppanyaki bar, where a glass
window separates the guests from the kitchen. Delightful vertical garden that
brightens up the outdoor summer dining area.

XX **Tokuyoshi**   ♿ 🆑
❀ *via San Calogero 3* ✉ *20123 –* Ⓜ *Sant'Ambrogio*   Plan: **F3**
– 📞 *02 84254626 – www.ristorantetokuyoshi.com – Closed 3 weeks in*
August, 2 weeks in January and Monday
Menu 90/135 € – Carte 74/144 € – *(dinner only except Sunday)*
• **Creative • Minimalist • Trendy •**
After gaining experience in a number of major restaurants, Yoji Tokuyoshi is
now the owner and manager of his own establishment. He creates delicious
fusion cuisine, which he describes as "cucina italiana contaminata". With typical
Japanese humility and real attention to detail, Yoji conjures up dishes that are
unique, full of flavour and definitely unforgettable.
→ Gyotaku (sgombro). Noto (spaghetti). Cemento e terra (dolce).

XX **Nobu Milano**   🆑 ⇕
via Pisoni 1 ✉ *20121 –* Ⓜ *Montenapoleone*   Plan: **G1**
– 📞 *02 62312645 – www.armanirestaurants.com – Closed 14-21 August*
and Sunday lunch
Menu 85/140 € – Carte 57/103 €
• **Fusion • Minimalist • Design •**
The pure minimalist lines of this restaurant with numerous branches dotted
around the world are not only typical of the Armani style but also distinctly
Japanese in feel. Fusion cuisine takes pride of place with a hint of South American influence.

XX **Emilia e Carlo** 🕸 🔼

via Sacchi 8 ⊠ 20121 – Ⓜ *Cairoli –* ℰ *02 875948*   Plan: **F1**
*– www.emiliaecarlo.it – Closed August, Christmas Holidays, Saturday lunch
and Sunday*
Carte 53/80 €
• **Modern cuisine • Rustic •**
Housed in an early 19C palazzo, this trattoria has a rustic feel with arches and
wooden beams. Creative contemporary cuisine, and a fine choice of wines.

XX **Al Porto** 🔼

piazzale Generale Cantore ⊠ 20123   Plan: **E3**
– Ⓜ *Porta Genova FS –* ℰ *02 89407425 – www.alportomilano.it*
– Closed August, 24 December-3 January, Monday lunch and Sunday
Carte 48/100 €
• **Seafood • Classic décor • Cosy •**
There is a definite maritime flavour to this restaurant, which occupies the old
19C Porta Genova toll house. Always busy, Al Porto specialises exclusively in
fresh fish dishes, including raw fish.

XX **Da Giacomo** 🔼

via P. Sottocorno 6 ⊠ 20129 – ℰ *02 76023313*   Plan: **H1**
– www.giacomoristorante.com
Menu 35 € (lunch) – Carte 56/85 €
• **Seafood • Friendly • Neighbourhood •**
This old Milanese trattoria dates from the early 20C. Seafood enthusiasts will be
delighted by the numerous fish specialities on offer. The menu also includes a
few meat dishes, as well as Alba truffles, Caesars' mushrooms and cep mushrooms in season.

XX **Giacomo Bistrot** 🔼

via P. Sottocorno 6 ⊠ 20129 – ℰ *0276022653*   Plan: **H1**
– www.giacomobistrot.com
Carte 57/98 €
• **Classic cuisine • Bistro •**
This restaurant, which stays open until late at night, boasts tables set close together in French-bistro style, while its shelves of leather-bound volumes evoke the
distinctly British ambience of a traditional bookshop. The menu features meat
dishes, game, oysters and truffles (in season).

X **Café Trussardi** – Il Ristorante Trussardi alla Scala   ⅗ 🔼

piazza della Scala 5 ⊠ 20121 – Ⓜ *Duomo*   Plan: **G1**
– ℰ *02 80688295 – www.cafetrussardi.com – Closed 2 weeks in
August, 2 weeks in December-January and Sunday*
Carte 40/78 €
• **Mediterranean cuisine • Fashionable • Trendy •**
If you are looking for a quick, simple meal with a minimum of fuss, then this is
the place for you. There is a lively, cosmopolitan ambience and a menu focusing
on delicious Mediterranean flavours.

X **Masuelli San Marco** 🔼

viale Umbria 80 ⊠ 20135 – Ⓜ *Lodi TIBB*   Plan: **D3**
– ℰ *02 55184138 – www.masuellitrattoria.it – Closed 24 July-7 August, 1-
6 January and Sunday*
Menu 22 € (weekday lunch) – Carte 35/65 €
• **Lombardian • Vintage • Inn •**
A rustic atmosphere with a luxurious feel in a typical trattoria, with the same
management since 1921; cuisine strongly linked to traditional Lombardy and
Piedmont recipes.

ITALY - MILAN

X **Rovello 18**   🐝 AC

via Tivoli 2 ang. Corso Garibaldi ⊠ 20123 – ⓂLanza   Plan: **F1**
*– ☏ 02 72093709 – www.rovello18.com – Closed 3 weeks in August
and Sunday lunch*
Carte 38/76 €
• Italian • Vintage • Traditional décor •
This restaurant has kept its original name and is situated just 300m from its old premises. Nothing else has changed and the ambience is still attractively retro, managing to be both informal and elegant at the same time. The cuisine is Italian in style, with fish and excellent meat dishes on the menu, as well as a carefully selected wine list.

X **Al Mercato**   ♿ AC

via Sant'Eufemia 16 ⊠ 20121 – ⓂMissori   Plan: **G3**
*– ☏ 02 87237167 – www.al-mercato.it – Closed July-August, 24 December-
4 January, Sunday dinner*
Menu 50/100 € – Carte 63/79 € – *(number of covers limited, pre-book)*
• Modern cuisine • Bistro • Intimate •
An original and modern concept created by two young chefs. The tiny, intimate and well-furnished dining room serves as a backdrop for gourmet cuisine in the evening and a more restricted menu at lunchtime. In another part of the restaurant, the lively Burger Bar (no reservations; the queue can be long) offers various tasty snacks, including the inevitable hamburger.

X **Spazio Milano**   AC

*galleria Vittorio Emanuele II (3° piano del Mercato del
Duomo) ⊠ 20123 – ⓂDuomo – ☏ 02 878400*   Plan: **G2**
– www.nikoromitoformazione.it – Closed 15-31 August
Carte 39/61 € – *(booking advisable)*
• Creative • Design •
This restaurant on the top floor of the Mercato del Duomo acts as a training ground for youngsters from the cookery school run by Romito (a 3 Star restaurant in Abruzzo); although you would never guess from the food that these chefs are beginners. Three rooms offer views of the kitchen, Galleria and cathedral respectively and the food, made from top quality produce, is full of flavour.

CENTRAL STATION - VITTORIA   **PLAN III**

🏨 **Principe di Savoia**   ⓕⓢ 🛜 🔲 AC 👙

piazza della Repubblica 17 ⊠ 20124 – ⓂRepubblica   Plan: **M2**
– ☏ 02 62301 – www.dorchestercollection.com
257 rm – ✝255/1040 € ✝✝285/1070 € – ☲ 45 € – 44 suites
• Grand Luxury • Palace • Elegant •
Overlooking Piazza della Repubblica, this majestic white building dating from the 19C is an imposing sight. With a truly international atmosphere, this luxury hotel boasts superb guestrooms, a well-equipped fitness area and a wellbeing centre. Perfect for a relaxing stay.
Acanto – See restaurant listing

🏨 **Excelsior Hotel Gallia**   ⓕⓢ 🛜 🔲 AC 👙

piazza Duca d'Aosta 9 ⊠ 20124 – ⓂCentrale FS   Plan: **M1**
– ☏ 02 67851 – www.excelsiorgallia.com
182 rm – ✝300/900 € ✝✝300/900 € – ☲ 40 € – 53 suites
• Grand Luxury • Modern •
Now boasting a fully restored exterior, the Excelsior Gallia successfully combines the elegance of an early 20C historic building with a contemporary design that is typical of Milan. It has a mix of chrome and marble that comes together to striking effect. Top class leisure options, including a splendid spa where modern facilities and a luxury brand of cosmetics set the scene for moments of sheer indulgence and relaxation.
Terrazza Gallia – See restaurant listing

The Westin Palace

piazza della Repubblica 20 ✉ 20124 – Ⓜ Repubblica Plan: **M2**
– ✆ 02 63361 – www.westinpalacemilan.it
227 rm – †220/1150 € ††220/1150 € – ☕ 40 € – 5 suites
• Palace • Luxury • Grand luxury •

The Milanese apotheosis of the Imperial style – a luxury hotel with sober, austere decor. Some of the rooms have views of the Duomo, while all guests can enjoy the roof terrace in summer. Recently refurbished and just as elegant as ever, the restaurant now also offers a private dining area. Mediterranean dishes dominate the menu.

Palazzo Parigi

corso di Porta Nuova 1 ✉ 20121 – ✆ 02625625 Plan: **G1**
– www.palazzoparigi.com
65 rm – †400/990 € ††400/990 € – ☕ 40 € – 33 suites
• Grand Luxury • Elegant •

This extraordinary palazzo has been renovated to provide the highest level of luxury accommodation. It features carefully chosen elegant furnishings, precious marble, plenty of natural light and stunning views of the city from the top floor guestrooms.

Starhotels Anderson

piazza Luigi di Savoia 20 ✉ 20124 – Ⓜ Centrale FS Plan: **C1**
– ✆ 02 6690141 – www.starhotels.com
106 rm ☕ – †900 € ††900 €
• Palace • Business • Design •

This hotel has a warm, designer-style atmosphere, with fashionable and intimate public rooms and welcoming guestrooms offering all the usual comforts of a hotel of this standard. The elegant lounge is home to a small restaurant (open only in the evenings) which serves contemporary-style cuisine.

Acanto – Hotel Principe di Savoia

piazza della Repubblica 17 ✉ 20124 – Ⓜ Repubblica Plan: **M2**
– ✆ 02 62302026 – www.dorchestercollection.com – Closed 8-23 August
Menu 35 € (weekday lunch)/90 € – Carte 72/157 €
• Modern cuisine • Luxury • Chic •

A modern restaurant with spacious and elegant dining rooms where guests can enjoy attentive service and classic contemporary-style cuisine. The lunchtime buffet and business menu also add to the modern feel, as does the option of enjoying the same dishes at a table in the bar.

Terrazza Gallia – Excelsior Hotel Gallia

piazza Duca d'Aosta 9 – ✆ 02 67851 Plan: **M1**
– www.excelsiorgallia.com
Menu 35 € (weekday lunch) – Carte 70/90 €
• Creative • Luxury • Contemporary décor •

Run by two experienced brothers from Naples, this splendid terrace restaurant is reserved for the Milanese tradition of the aperitif in the evening and for lunches of creative, colourful cuisine at midday. The dining room is decorated in contemporary-style, as is the rest of this splendid hotel.

Berton

via Mike Bongiorno 13 ✉ 20123 – Ⓜ Gioia Plan: **L1**
– ✆ 02 67075801 – www.ristoranteberton.com – Closed 2 weeks in August, Christmas Holidays, Saturday and Monday lunch, Sunday
Menu 45 € (weekday lunch), 110/135 € – Carte 77/180 €
• Creative • Design • Minimalist •

Light, modern and minimalist in style, the restaurant decor echoes the cuisine served here, which uses just a few ingredients to create original and beautifully presented dishes.

→ Risotto con gambero crudo e corallo di crostacei. Brodo di prosciutto crudo con merluzzo, pane al prezzemolo e rapanelli. Uovo di yogurt e mango.

XxX
⭐

Alice-Eataly Smeraldo (Viviana Varese)   ⴲ 🅰️

piazza XXV Aprile 10 ⊠ 20123 – Ⓜ Porta Garibaldi FS   Plan: **L2**
– ℰ 02 49497340 – www.aliceristorante.it – Closed 24-26 December
Menu 43 € (weekday lunch)/130 € – Carte 72/132 € – *(booking advisable)*
• Creative • Design • Fashionable •
In 2014, the famous Teatro Smeraldo in Milan became the setting for a large
Eataly complex, in which the Alice restaurant is certainly one of the highlights.
The attractive designer-style decor makes the perfect backdrop for the imaginative
cuisine that includes a number of fish dishes.
➔ "Superspaghettino" con brodo affumicato, julienne di calamaro, vongole,
polvere di tarallo e limone. Ali di razza con scaloppa di foie gras,
crema e julienne di finocchi. Rivisitazione della pastiera napoletana.

XxX
⭐

Joia (Pietro Leemann)   ⅋ 🅰️ ⇦

via Panfilo Castaldi 18 ⊠ 20124 – Ⓜ Repubblica   Plan: **M2**
– ℰ 02 29522124 – www.joia.it – Closed 6-29 August, 25 December-
7 January, Sunday
Menu 35 € (weekday lunch)/120 € – Carte 73/110 €
• Vegetarian • Minimalist • Chic •
The dishes always let you sense their essence, in their colour, taste, texture and
presentation. To quote the chef, they are a "summary of research, where the
ingredients of Mediterranean cuisine meet with the cultures of the world; a
natural choice, without meat – a philosophy where nature is welcomed and respected".
You'll be lulled by sweet, melodious background music, in this pure,
minimalist setting.
➔ Di non solo pane vive l'uomo (panzanella con verdure croccanti, cannellini
e ciliegia profumati al wasabi). Una porta per il Paradiso (verdure estive
servite tiepide con crema di crescenza e tartufo, fumante sorbetto
di sedano verde). Pomo d'oro.

XxX

Daniel   ⴲ 🅰️

via Castelfidardo 7, angolo via San Marco ⊠ 20121   Plan: **L2**
– ℰ 02 63793837 – www.ristorantedanielmilano.com – Closed 3 weeks in
August, 25 December-6 Jamuary, Saturday lunch and Sunday
Menu 50 € (dinner)/70 € – Carte 46/102 €
• Italian • Contemporary décor • Elegant •
One of the first things to strike you in this restaurant is the open-view kitchen,
where the young friendly chef happily interacts with diners. His menu focuses on
traditional Italian classics, as well as a few more inventive offerings, all of which are
prepared using the very best ingredients. Simpler fare available at lunchtime.

XX

I Malavoglia   🅰️

via Lecco 4 ⊠ 20124 – Ⓜ Porta Venezia   Plan: **M2**
– ℰ 02 29531387 – www.ristorante-imalavoglia.com – Closed August,
25 December-7 January, Sunday, Monday lunch
Menu 48 € – Carte 52/72 €
• Sicilian • Traditional décor • Cosy •
The name of this restaurant near the Porta Venezia ramparts hints at its Sicilian
origins. The fish and seafood dishes served here are modern yet inspired by traditional
recipes and include delicious specialities such as the beautifully presented
swordfish involtini.

XX

13 Giugno   🅰️ ⇦

via Goldoni 44 ang.via Uberti 5 ⊠ 20129   Plan: **D2**
– ℰ 02 719654 – www.ristorante13giugno.it
Carte 55/119 €
• Sicilian • Colourful • Mediterranean décor •
This lively restaurant boasts a charming winter garden. Pasta with sea urchins,
aubergine caponata, stuffed sardines and couscous are just some of the Sicilian
specialities on the menu.

ITALY - MILAN

XX **Il Liberty** 〔AC〕

viale Monte Grappa 6 ✉ 20124 – ℰ 02 29011439 Plan: **L2**
*– www.il-liberty.it – Closed 12-18 August, 1°-7 January, Saturday lunch and
Sunday*
Menu 55/60 € – Carte 46/75 €
• Creative • Simple • Cosy •

Occupying an Art Nouveau-style palazzo, this small restaurant with two rooms
and a loft area has a friendly, welcoming atmosphere. The menu includes a
selection of fish and meat dishes, with a choice of simpler and more reasonably
priced options at lunchtime.

XX **Barbacoa** 〔AC〕

via delle Abbadesse 30 ✉ 20123 – Ⓜ Zara Plan: **C1**
– ℰ 02 6883883 – www.barbacoa.it
Menu 47 € – Carte 40/75 € – *(dinner only except Sunday)*
• International • Minimalist • Cosy •

The first European restaurant of a Brazilian chain, Barbacoa is a true celebration
of meat. Beef takes pride of place, although chicken, pork and lamb also feature
on the menu. The traditional caipirinha, a cocktail based on cane sugar and
lime, continues the Brazilian theme, while mixed salads and exotic fruit desserts
complete the picture.

XX **Pacifico** 〔AC〕

via Moscova 29 ✉ 20123 Milano – ℰ 02 8724 4737 Plan: **F1**
– www.wearepacifico.com – Closed 7-21 August
Menu 70 € – Carte 48/64 € – *(booking advisable)*
• Peruvian • Bistro • Elegant •

Cosmopolitan Milan has warmly embraced this lively restaurant, which acts as
an ambassador for Peruvian cuisine with the occasional Asian influence. There is
an excellent choice of ceviche – raw fish or seafood dishes marinated in lemon
and flavoured with spices such as chilli pepper and coriander – which are a typical speciality of Latin American countries along the Pacific coast.

XX **Gong** 〔AC〕

corso Concordia 8 ✉ 20123 – ℰ 02 76023873 Plan: **H1**
– www.gongmilano.it – Closed 14-19 August and Monday
Menu 80 € – Carte 45/62 €
• Chinese • Minimalist • Elegant •

A modern take on Chinese cuisine, the occasional international influence and
carefully chosen ingredients all contribute to the success of this restaurant,
one of the most fashionable ethnic eateries in the city.

X **Pisacco** 〔AC〕

via Solferino 48 ✉ 20121 – Ⓜ Moscova Plan: **L2**
– ℰ 02 91765472 – www.pisacco.it – Closed 12-19 August and Monday
Menu 12 € (weekday lunch) – Carte 34/48 €
• Modern cuisine • Trendy • Colourful •

A modern and informal restaurant with attentive service and reasonable prices.
Excellent selection of creative dishes, as well as some reinterpretations of classic
favourites, such as polenta and baccalà (salted cod) and Caesar salad.

X **Serendib** 〔AC〕

via Pontida 2 ✉ 20121 – Ⓜ Moscova – ℰ 02 6592139 Plan: **K2**
– www.serendib.it
Menu 15/23 € – Carte 21/40 €
• Indian • Simple • Oriental décor •

Serendib, the old name for Sri Lanka, means "to make happy" – an ambitious
promise, but one which this restaurant manages to keep! True to its origins,
the tempting menu focuses on Indian and Sri Lankan cuisine.

Casa Fontana-23 Risotti

✗

piazza Carbonari 5 ✉ *20125 –* Ⓜ *Sondrio – ℰ 02 6704710*   Plan: **C1**
– www.23risotti.it – Closed 2 weeks in August, 1°-12 January, Monday and Saturday lunch in summer
Menu 33 € – Carte 41/68 €
• Lombardian • Traditional décor • Cosy •
Despite the obligatory 25min wait for your food, this restaurant is well worth a visit for its excellent risottos. Attractive pictures of rice fields on the walls.

Trippa

✗
🍴

Via Giorgio Vasari, 3 ✉ *20135 –* Ⓜ *Porta Romana*   Plan: **H3**
– ℰ 327 668 7908 – www.trippamilano.it – Closed 2 weeks in August and Sunday
Menu 42 € – Carte 29/49 € – *(dinner only) (booking advisable)*
• Italian • Trattoria • Vintage •
Simple, informal and just a little old-fashioned, this restaurant is named after the tripe that can often be found on the menu, alongside other dishes from all over Italy. This is plain, unfussy cuisine emphasising the quality of the ingredients used and the expert skills of the young chef. This makes it one of the best *trattorie* in the city.

Da Giannino-L'Angolo d'Abruzzo

✗
🍴

via Pilo 20 ✉ *20129 –* Ⓜ *Porta Venezia – ℰ 02 29406526*   Plan: **D2**
Carte 29/40 €
• Cuisine from Abruzzo • Traditional décor •
A warm welcome combined with a simple but lively atmosphere and typical dishes from the Abruzzo region make this a popular place to eat. Generous portions and excellent roast dishes.

Vietnamonamour

✗

via Taramelli 67 ✉ *20124 Milano –* Ⓜ *Zara*   Plan: **C1**
– ℰ 02 70634614 – www.vietnamonamour.com – Closed August and Monday
4 rm – ♦65/160 € ♦♦85/250 €   Menu 13/25 € – Carte 29/59 €
• Vietnamese • Intimate • Oriental décor •
This Vietnamese restaurant in the Isola district has a twin of the same name in the Città Studi area of the city. Both restaurants offer the same exotic charm and attention to individual detail, as well as delicious cuisine and delightful guestrooms that are perfect for a relaxing stay.

Dongiò

✗
🍴

via Corio 3 ✉ *20135 –* Ⓜ *Porta Romana – ℰ 02 5511372*   Plan: **H3**
– Closed 3 weeks in August, Saturday lunch and Sunday
Carte 30/39 € – *(booking advisable)*
• Calabrian • Family • Rustic •
This family-run restaurant introduces a flavour of traditional Calabria to Milan with a simple, lively atmosphere that is quite rare nowadays. Home cooking based on fresh pasta, 'nduja (spicy sausage) and the ubiquitous peperoncino (chilli pepper).

La Cantina di Manuela

✗

via Carlo Poerio 3 ✉ *20129 – ℰ 02 76318892*   Plan: **C2**
– www.lacantinadimanuela.it
Carte 34/50 € – *(booking advisable)*
• Modern cuisine • Bistro • Colourful •
The dining room in this young, dynamic restaurant is surrounded by bottles of wine. Elaborate dishes feature on the menu, with antipasti available in the evening. At lunchtime these are replaced by various salads aimed at a business clientele in a hurry. Milanese-style cutlets are the house speciality.

Baia Chia

✗

via Bazzini 37 ✉ *20131 –* Ⓜ *Piola – ℰ 02 2361131*   Plan: **D1**
– www.ristorantesardobaiachia.it – Closed 7-24 August, Christmas Holidays
Carte 31/53 €
• Sardinian • Family •
This pleasant restaurant with a family atmosphere is divided into two small dining rooms, plus a veranda which can also be used in winter. Excellent fish dishes and Sardinian specialities on the menu. Many of the wines also come from Sardinia.

Un Posto a Milano-Cascina Cuccagna

via Cuccagna 2 ⊠ 20121 Milano – ℰ 02 5457785
– www.unpostoamilano.it – Closed 1-6 January and Monday
Plan: **D3**
Menu 15 € (weekday lunch)/38 € – Carte 37/60 €
• Classic cuisine • Country house • Traditional décor •
Occupying an old restored farmhouse in urban Milan, the Cascina Cuccagna is both a restaurant and a cultural centre. It is surrounded by greenery, providing a delightful oasis in the city. At lunchtime, choose from a copious and reasonably priced buffet. The evening menu is more elaborate but still offers good value for money.

FIERAMILANOCITY - SEMPIONE - NAVIGLI (viale Fulvio Testi, Niguarda, viale Fermi, viale Certosa, corso Sempione, piazza Carlo Magno, via Monte Rosa, San Siro, via Novara, via Washington, Ripa di porta Ticinese, Corso S. Gottardo) **PLAN I**

Milan Marriott Hotel

via Washington 66 ⊠ 20146 – ⓜ Wagner
Plan: **A2**
– ℰ 02 48521 – www.milanmarriotthotel.com
321 rm – †120/590 € ††120/590 € – ⌒ 20 €
• Chain • Contemporary •
Not far from the bustling Corso Vercelli, this hotel combines a modern exterior with a more traditional interior decor. Functional guestrooms. Enjoy regional dishes and Mediterranean cuisine in the La Brasserie de Milan restaurant.

Leonardo Hotels Milan City Centre

via Messina 10 ⊠ 20154 – ⓜ Cenisio – ℰ 02 318170
Plan: **K1**
– www.leonardo-hotels.com
122 rm ⌒ – †109/509 € ††129/509 € – 8 suites
• Luxury • Business • Elegant •
In a district buzzing with shops and businesses, this hotel remains a solid choice amid the accommodation options in Milan. This is partly thanks to its new management team who continue to offer elegant, comfortable rooms and modern facilities.
Il Giorno Bistrot – See restaurant listing

Wagner

via Buonarroti 13 ⊠ 20149 – ⓜ Wagner
Plan: **A2**
– ℰ 02 463151 – www.hotelwagnermilano.it – Closed 12-19 August
49 rm ⌒ – †80/399 € ††80/399 €
• Business • Traditional •
This hotel, next to the eponymous metro station, has attractive rooms with marble and modern furnishings.

Antica Locanda Leonardo

corso Magenta 78 ⊠ 20123 – ⓜ Conciliazione
Plan: **E2**
– ℰ 02 48014197 – www.anticalocandaleonardo.com – Closed 6-25 August, 2-7 January
16 rm ⌒ – †95/170 € ††158/395 €
• Family • Cosy •
The luxury atmosphere combines with the family-style welcome in a hotel which overlooks a small inner courtyard, in an ideal location near the place where Leonardo da Vinci's painting of the "Last Supper" is housed.

Enrico Bartolini al Mudec

via Tortona 56 ⊠ 20123 – ⓜ Porta Genova
Plan: **E3**
– ℰ 02 84293701 – www.enricobartolini.net – Closed 2 weeks in August, Monday lunch and Sunday
Menu 45 € (weekday lunch)/160 € – Carte 115/195 €
• Creative • Contemporary décor • Trendy •
Many different adjectives could be used to describe Enrico Bartolini's cuisine, which is among the best in Milan. The food is balanced, innovative and carefully prepared, with a real "contemporary-classic" feel, to use one of the chef's favourite expressions.
→ Gamberi mezzi fritti in due passaggi. Ravioli di arachidi con ricci di mare e ristretto di pollo. Ventresca di tonno e dintorni.

ITALY - MILAN

XxX ✿✿ **Il Luogo di Aimo e Nadia** (Alessandro Negrini e Fabio Pisani)

via Montecuccoli 6 ✉ *20147 –* Ⓜ *Primaticcio* 🕸 🅰🅲 ⇄
– ☏ 02 416886 – www.aimoenadia.com – Closed Plan: **A3**
3 weeks in August, 1-8 January, Saturday lunch and Sunday
Menu 45 € (weekday lunch)/145 € – Carte 87/181 €
• Creative • Design •

Although Aimo and Nadia are no longer at the helm of this restaurant, their style of cuisine is echoed by two excellent chefs. They have maintained the restaurant's tradition of creating Italian regional dishes with a modern twist. The focus has always been on top-quality ingredients (even before it was fashionable), making this restaurant in Via Montecuccoli one of the cradles of this culinary ethos. This is now kept alive through exciting, memorable cuisine created by two fine chefs.
→ Tagliolini di semola e crescione con tartufi di mare, crema di ceci, erba lippia, melaleuca. Piccione: petto ai porcini e nocciole, coscia confit con fegatino, agnoli nel suo ristretto. Dedicato ad Aimo e Nadia: dolce zuppa etrusca!

XxX ✿✿ **Sadler** 🕸 🅰🅲 ⇄

via Ascanio Sforza 77 ✉ *20141 –* Ⓜ *Romolo* Plan: **B3**
– ☏ 02 58104451 – www.sadler.it – Closed 2 weeks in August, 1 week in January and Sunday
Menu 75 € (weekdays)/170 € – Carte 72/156 € – *(dinner only)*
• Creative • Elegant •

Overlooking the Naviglio canal on the outskirts of the city, this restaurant focuses all its attention on its cuisine, which features traditional recipes reinterpreted with a contemporary flavour. Fish is the speciality here, although there is also a vegetarian menu. The children's options are designed to introduce the younger generation to gourmet dining.
→ Risotto all'acqua di funghi porcini con polvere di funghi trombetta. San Pietro in casseruola con scarola farcita alla napoletana e acqua di provola affumicata. THEramisù: ricordo di Tokyo a tè matcha (tè verde giapponese).

XxX **La Pobbia 1850** 🍽 ⴲ 🅰🅲 ⇄

via Gallarate 92 ✉ *20151 – ☏ 02 38006641* Plan: **A1**
– www.lapobbia.com – Closed 3 weeks in August, 26 December-6 January and Sunday
Menu 22 € – Carte 44/76 €
• Lombardian • Elegant • Family •

Housed in an old but elegant farmhouse, this restaurant is named after the poplar trees growing alongside the road, which ran through open countryside until as recently as the late 19C. Milanese cuisine and specialities from Lombardy take pride of place, with just a few options (almost all meat dishes) on the menu. A new attractive outdoor dining area has recently been opened in the garden.

XxX **Ceresio 7** ⬰ 🍽 🅰🅲

via Ceresio 7 ✉ *20123 –* Ⓜ *Monumentale* Plan: **K1**
– ☏ 0231039221 – www.ceresio7.com – Closed 14-17 August, 1-3 January
Menu 85 € (dinner) – Carte 64/115 € – *(bookings advisable at dinner)*
• Modern cuisine • Design • Trendy •

This designer-style restaurant is housed on the fourth floor of the historic ENEL palazzo, remodelled and converted into the Dsquared2 building. It combines the use of brass, marble and wood to create a successful blend of attractive colours and vintage decor. The view of Milan (even better from the long outdoor terrace with its two swimming pools) completes the picture, while the cuisine reinterprets Italian classics with a contemporary twist.

XxX **Unico Milano** ⬰ ⴲ 🅰🅲

via Achille Papa 30, palazzo World Join Center Plan: **A1**
✉ *20149 –* Ⓜ *Portello – ☏ 02 39214847 – www.unicorestaurant.it*
Menu 25 € (weekday lunch)/140 € – Carte 67/113 € – *(dinner only)*
• Creative • Elegant • Design •

From the 20th floor of the WJC Tower – home to the only restaurant offering views of the city's entire skyline – Milan resembles a plastic model. The cuisine served by the new chef here is creative in style.

XxX   Contraste   🏠 AC

via Meda 2 ✉ 20123 – 𝒞 02 49536597   Plan: **F3**
– www.contrastemilano.it – Closed 2 weeks in August, 2 weeks in December-January, Sunday dinner and Tuesday
Menu 80/130 € – Carte 74/124 € *– (dinner only except Sunday)*
• **Modern cuisine** • **Elegant** • **Historic** •

Glittering red silicon chandeliers hover above diners at this restaurant, which is decorated here and there with Art Nouveau touches. The cuisine is traditional yet reinterpreted in presentation and appearance, offering contrasting flavours that leave guests impressed and delighted.

XxX   Lume   ⴵ AC P
☸

via Watt 37 ✉ 20123 – 𝒞 02 80888624 – www.lumemilano.com   Plan: **B3**
– Closed 14-23 August, 10 days in January, Sunday dinner and Monday
Menu 40 € (weekday lunch), 120/150 € – Carte 90/155 €
• **Modern cuisine** • **Design** • **Minimalist** •

The name of this restaurant situated in an industrial setting evokes the importance of light in the premises, which boasts large windows overlooking an internal garden. The cuisine revolves around the personality of the chef, Luigi Taglienti. He creates elegant, modern and inventive dishes with influences from Lombardy and his native Liguria.

→ Musetto di vitello allo spumante, insalata di mostarda dolce e cetriolo. Animella di vitello in dolceforte. Ibisco, barbabietola e insalata di pompelmo rosa.

XX   Iyo   🏠 AC
☸

via Piero della Francesca 74 ✉ 20154   Plan: **B1**
– Ⓜ Gerusalemme – 𝒞 02 45476898 – www.iyo.it – Closed 2 weeks in August, Christmas Holidays, Monday and Tuesday lunch
Menu 95 € – Carte 46/126 € *– (booking advisable)*
• **Japanese** • **Minimalist** • **Design** •

This restaurant features simple Japanese elegance and tatami dining rooms, which will appeal to traditionalists. It offers creative, Western-influenced fusion cuisine alongside classic Japanese specialities, followed by a grand finale of European desserts and Asian fruit. Thoughtful, attentive service completes the picture.

→ Crudo di calamaro sfrangiato, verdure croccanti, uovo di quaglia e salsa "soba dashi". Wagyu tataki: tagliata di manzo nobile giapponese. Bittersweet simphony: dessert con miele, tè matcha (tè verde giapponese) e pompelmo.

XX   Innocenti Evasioni *(Arrigoni e Picco)*   🐝 ⴴ 🏠 AC ⟷
☸

via privata della Bindellina ✉ 20155 – Ⓜ Portello   Plan: **A1**
– 𝒞 02 33001882 – www.innocentievasioni.com – Closed 6-31 August, 1°-10 January and Sunday
Menu 49/68 € – Carte 47/84 € *– (dinner only) (booking advisable)*
• **Creative** • **Fashionable** •

This pleasant establishment, with large windows facing the garden, offers classic cuisine reinterpreted with imagination. Enjoyable outdoor summer dining.

→ Ravioli di baccalà mantecato in salsa di piselli, soft di grana padano e patate alla paprica. Filetto di rombo, senape speziata, asparagi e birra di riso nero. Dulce de leche, banana alla liquirizia, rhum e sbrisolona demi-sel.

XX   Tano Passami l'Olio *(Gaetano Simonato)*   AC
☸

via Villoresi, 16 ✉ 20143 – 𝒞 02 8394139   Plan: **B3**
– www.tanopassamilolio.it – Closed August, 24 December-6 January and Sunday
Carte 90/135 € *– (dinner only) (booking advisable)*
• **Creative** • **Elegant** • **Classic décor** •

Situated near the Naviglio Grande canal, where it has been in business for 20 years. This classic, elegant restaurant provides the setting for decidedly original cuisine featuring unusual combinations and elegant presentation. Excellent olive oils are also available to add a touch of seasoning to your meal. Smoking room.

→ Tiramisù di seppia, mascarpone e patate. Piccione laccato nel suo fondo e crema di amarena, tarassaco in gel e rabarbaro. Parfait di cioccolato bianco, meringa, mezza sfera di cioccolato, spuma di lamponi e sorbetto.

XX **Il Giorno Bistrot** – Leonardo Hotels Milan City Centre   🛜 🅰️
via Messina 10 ✉ *20154 –* Ⓜ *Cenisio – ℰ 02 318170*   🚘
– www.fedegroup.it – Closed Sunday lunch and Saturday   Plan: **K1**
Carte 33/65 €
• Classic cuisine • Bistro • Elegant •
The historic restaurant of the Hotel Hermitage demonstrates a real passion for local cuisine, with dishes such as risotto and *cotoletta alla milanese* on the menu. There is also a good choice of gluten-free options.

XX **Arrow's**   🛜 ♿ 🅰️
via A. Mantegna 17/19 ✉ *20154 –* Ⓜ *Gerusalemme*   Plan: **J1**
– ℰ 02 341533 – www.ristorantearrows.it – Closed 3 weeks in August, Monday lunch and Sunday
Carte 37/77 €
• Seafood • Family • Cosy •
Packed, even at midday, the atmosphere becomes cosier in the evening but the seafood cuisine, prepared according to tradition, remains the same.

XX **La Cantina di Manuela**   🕸 ♿ 🅰️
🉐 *via Procaccini 41* ✉ *20154 –* Ⓜ *Gerusalemme*   Plan: **J1**
– ℰ 02 3452034 – www.lacantinadimanuela.it
Carte 31/57 €
• Modern cuisine • Neighbourhood • Friendly •
Although the chef has changed, the dishes that made the reputation of this restaurant, such as *risotto alla Milanese*, Fassone beef cheek in a Barolo sauce, and tiramisu, are still very much on the menu. Updated traditional cuisine.

XX **Essenza**   🛜 🅰️
via Marghera 34 ✉ *20149 – ℰ 02 498 6865*   Plan: **A2**
– www.essenzaristorante.it – Closed 3 weeks in August, Christmas Holidays, Monday lunch and Sunday
Menu 50/90 € – Carte 61/99 €
• Modern cuisine • Classic décor • Elegant •
Born out of the passion of an excellent chef with plenty of experience to his name, this restaurant was opened in 2015 and is the place to go if you are looking for modern, imaginative cuisine. Truly memorable fish and meat dishes are served in a quiet and elegant dining room with a classic decor. The charming outdoor area has just a few tables, so booking ahead is essential.

X **Osteria di Porta Cicca**   🛜 ♿ 🅰️
ripa di Porta Ticinese 51 ✉ *20143 –* Ⓜ *Porta Genova*   Plan: **E3**
– ℰ 02 8372763 – www.osteriadiportacicca.com – Closed 14-21 August and Monday
Menu 35/55 €
– Carte 41/86 € – (dinner only except Sunday) (booking advisable)
• Modern cuisine • Romantic • Cosy •
A welcoming, intimate ambience with a hint of Provence in an attractive canal side setting. The only sign of a traditional osteria is in the name – the cuisine is modern and innovative in style.

X **Kiyo**   🛜 🅰️
via Carlo Ravizza 4 ✉ *20121 –* Ⓜ *Wagner*   Plan: **A2**
– ℰ 02 4814295 – www.kiyo.it
Menu 20 € (weekday lunch) – Carte 37/80 €
• Japanese • Chic • Minimalist •
The manager of this restaurant is Italian and the chef Japanese (the name kiyo means limpid and pure). Enjoy typical Japanese dishes followed by a choice of delicious European desserts in the wood-furnished dining rooms.

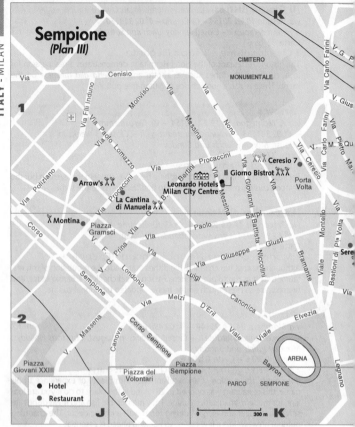

Sempione
(Plan III)

Ceresio 7

Il Giorno Bistrot

Leonardo Hotels
Milan City Centre

Arrow's

La Cantina
di Manuela

Montina

Piazza
Gramsci

Porta
Volta

Sere

CIMITERO
MONUMENTALE

Piazza
Giovani XXIII

Piazza del
Volontari

Piazza
Sempione

ARENA

PARCO   SEMPIONE

● Hotel
● Restaurant

0   300 m

X **Trattoria Montina**   📶 🅰🅒

via Procaccini 54 ✉ 20154 – Ⓜ *Gerusalemme*   Plan: **J2**
*– 𝒞 02 3490498 – www.trattoriamontina.it – Closed Easter, 5-
27 August, 25 December-3 January, Monday lunch and Sunday*
Carte 28/51 €
• **Traditional cuisine • Friendly • Cosy •**
Nice bistro atmosphere, tables close together, defused lighting in the evening in an
establishment managed by twin brothers; seasonal national and Milanese dishes.

X **Al Pont de Ferr**   🅰🅒

Ripa di Porta Ticinese 55 ✉ 20143   Plan: **B3**
– Ⓜ *Porta Genova FS – 𝒞 02 89406277 – www.pontdeferr.it – Closed
24 December-6 January*
Menu 20 € (weekday lunch)/130 € – Carte 39/86 €
• **Creative • Osteria • Trendy •**
This rustic osteria is situated near an old wrought-iron bridge alongside an arti-
ficial canal designed and built in 1179. This was initially used to irrigate the surrounding fields and is now frequented by boats. The cuisine is seasonal with an
equal emphasis on fish and meat dishes.

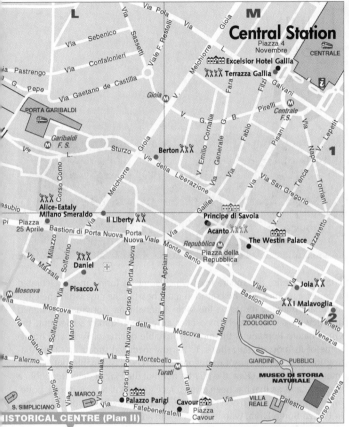

X **Esco Bistrò Mediterraneo** &. AC

via Tortona 26 ⊠ *20123 – 𝒞 028358144* Plan: **E3**
– www.escobistromediterraneo.it – Closed Saturday lunch and Sunday
Menu 15 € (weekday lunch)/55 € – Carte 35/49 €
• Mediterranean cuisine • Trendy • Friendly •
This modern restaurant is informal and welcoming. Your first impression is that of finding yourself in an architect's studio, as a guest of the owner. However, this is just a preamble to the main event – that of savouring the delicious cuisine made by the talented chef. He manages to combine the use of top-quality ingredients with expert and innovative techniques.

TURIN
TORINO

Population: 890 529

fbxx/iStock

Piazza Castello, the square from which some of Turin's most celebrated avenues start, may well be considered the heart of the city; while the city's landmark building has to be the Mole Antonelliana – originally designed as a Jewish synagogue. Named after an ancient Roman settlement, the Quadrilatero Romano is the most fashionable quarter of Turin and boasts some of its most elegant shops; its narrow medieval streets are a fascinating interlude to the city's orthogonal plan. Less fashionable but equally interesting is Borgo Dora, the quarter north of the Piazza della Repubblica – a popular area that has been given a facelift but still retains its old, bohemian atmosphere – and don't miss the Cortile del Maglio, inside the arsenal in Piazza Borgo Dora, with its markets and art.

At the other end of the scale, la Collina provides some of the city's smartest addresses, while crossing the River Po – the longest in Italy – at Piazza Vittorio Veneto will lead you to Turin's luxurious period houses. Those interested in residential architecture can also find some of the city's most beautiful houses – dating back to the 19C – in the Via Galileo Ferraris area of the Crocetta quarter. For a more vibrant atmosphere, head for the embankment between Piazza Vittorio Veneto and Corso Vittorio Emanuele and you will find the 'murazzi', where you will get the best of Turin's nightlife with its bars and clubs.

TURIN IN...

→ ONE DAY
Piazza Castello, Via Roma, Piazza San Carlo, Mole Antonelliana, Piazza Vittorio Veneto, Duomo, Sacra Sindone.

→ TWO DAYS
Egyptian Museum, Sabaudia Gallery, Palazzo Carignano & Madama.

→ THREE DAYS
Valentino Park, Reggia di Venaria, Museum of Cinema.

PRACTICAL INFORMATION

ARRIVAL-DEPARTURE

✈ Better known as Caselle – after the nearby town – Turin's airport, Sandro Pertini, is 16km north of the city.
Trains run every 30min and bring you into Torino Dora Railway Station in 20min. A shuttle bus takes 50min to the centre. A taxi will take about 40min.

GETTING AROUND

Turin has a very efficient public transport network, with buses and trams crossing the city from 5am until midnight. Tickets for buses, trams and the underground can be bought at tobacconists, newsagents and other places exhibiting a special GTT sign, and must be stamped on board. Options range from 90min travel to unlimited daily use, as well as blocks of 5 or 25 tickets.

CALENDAR HIGHLIGHTS

February
CioccolaTò Chocolate Festival.

May
Fiera Internazionale del Libro (International Book Fair).

June
Feast of Patron Saint John the Baptist.

September
Mito (over 200 music events).

October
Salone del Gusto (biennial food fair, organised by the Slow Food Movement).

November
Torino Film Festival.

EATING OUT

Turin can rightly boast of being one of Italy's gastronomic centres. Not to be missed are the fresh egg pastas, and the local braised beef, lamb and pigeons. White truffles deserve a mention, although they've become so rare that prices are often incredibly high; they are usually served with pasta or fonduta (melted cheese, milk and egg yolks). With some of the best Italian chocolate produced in Turin, desserts are a real treat. You might find bonèt (chocolate pudding with almond biscuits), torta di nocciole (hazelnut cake) or panna cotta (cooked cream). Alongside Tuscany, Piedmont's red wines are indisputably the best in Italy; try a local Barbera, a reliable Nebbiolo or a world famous Barbaresco or Barolo. Cafés have a long tradition in Turin; try a bicerin (a drink made from coffee, cream and chocolate) with a gianduiotto (a chocolate made with 'tonda gentile', a famous variety of hazelnut). Look out for the world's biggest food market, 'Eataly': 2,500m² of delicacies brought to you by local producers, who pride themselves on their excellent, often rare, ingredients.

Golden Palace 🕭 ⚐ 🕲 ⚇ 🗝 ⚐ 🞈 🕭 ⛟

via dell'Arcivescovado 18 ✉ 10121 – Ⓜ Re Umberto   Plan: **D2**
– ℰ 011 5512111 – www.allegroitalia.it
182 rm ⚐ – ♦139/519 € ♦♦159/519 € – 13 suites
• Grand Luxury • Palace • Art déco •
When Palazzo Toro (now home to this hotel) was built during the Second World
War, the building was cited in some of the most authoritative books on architecture as a fine example of design and structure. Over half a century later, the
decor and minimalist design continue to impress. The G Ristorante Italiano serves modern cuisine with, as its name suggests, an emphasis on Italian dishes.

NH Piazza Carlina 🕭 🞈 ⚐ 🕲 🕭 ⛟

piazza Carlo Emanuele II 15 – ℰ 011 8601611   Plan: **E2**
– www.nh-collection.com
160 rm ⚐ – ♦149/669 € ♦♦169/699 € – 7 suites
• Luxury • Historic • Personalised •
A splendid hotel housed in a 17C palazzo originally designed as an orphanage.
The home of intellectual Antonio Gramsci in the early 20C, the building has
been one of the best hotels in Turin for years. It offers an elegant and stylish
ambience embellished by a discreet display of works of art. The Carlina restaurant completes the picture, serving a selection of Piedmontese specialities
alongside other modern Italian options.

Grand Hotel Sitea 🞈 🞈 ⚐ 🕭

via Carlo Alberto 35 ✉ 10123 – ℰ 011 5170171   Plan: **E2**
– www.grandhotelsitea.it
119 rm ⚐ – ♦105/400 € ♦♦168/1000 € – 1 suite
• Luxury • Palace • Elegant •
Opened in 1925, this refined, traditional hotel boasts elegant, classic and period
furnishings that contribute to its stylish atmosphere. The American Bar offers an
easy alternative for lunch when the Carignano restaurant is closed.
Carignano – See restaurant listing

Principi di Piemonte 🕭 ≤ 🞈 🕲 ⚐ 🕭

via Gobetti 15 ✉ 10123 – Ⓜ Porta Nuova   Plan: **E2**
– ℰ 011 5515.1 – www.atahotels.it/principi-di-piemonte
81 rm ⚐ – ♦170/650 € ♦♦200/750 € – 18 suites
• Luxury • Business • Elegant •
This historic 1930s building is situated just a stone's throw from the centre. It
offers spacious guestrooms decorated in marble, an elegant atmosphere and
resolutely modern comfort.

Victoria 🞈 🕲 🗝 ⚐ 🕭

via Nino Costa 4 ✉ 10123 – ℰ 011 5611909   Plan: **E2**
– www.hotelvictoria-torino.com
106 rm ⚐ – ♦180/220 € ♦♦300/350 € – 4 suites
• Luxury • Traditional • Classic •
Attentive service, antique furniture, Oriental features and a colour scheme that
is distinctly British, all combine to create a warm ambience in this elegant residence run by a family of keen travellers. The Egyptian-style spa is particularly
striking and inviting.

Art Hotel Boston ⚐ 🕭

via Massena 70 ✉ 10128 – ℰ 011 500359   Plan: **D3**
– www.hotelbostontorino.it
71 rm ⚐ – ♦80/150 € ♦♦90/180 € – 5 suites
• Business • Luxury • Design •
Comfortable guestrooms decorated with striking works of contemporary art are
the main feature of this designer-style hotel situated not far from the city's main
art collections. The modern Pain Perdu restaurant next door specialises in Mediterranean cuisine.

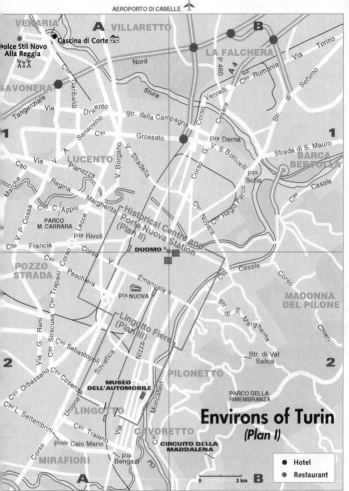

AEROPORTO DI CASELLE

Environs of Turin
(Plan I)

● Hotel
● Restaurant

0   2 km

Genova   ♬ ⋒ ♿ 🅐🅒 🏖

via Sacchi 14/b ✉ 10128 – Ⓜ *Porta Nuova*   Plan: **E2**
– ☏ 011 5629400 – www.albergogenova.it
88 rm ☲ *–* ♦70/200 € ♦♦99/280 € – 4 suites
• Traditional • Historic • Personalised •
A 19C building is home to this elegant, beautifully kept hotel. Classic features
combine harmoniously with modern standards of comfort and individual
details, especially in the guestrooms – ten of which boast frescoes on the ceiling. Highly recommended for business travellers and holidaymakers alike.

Via San Giovanni Bosco   **C**   Via Maria Ausiliatrice   **D**

Piazza della Repubblica

Corso   Regina   Margherita

Via Pierdionigi Pinelli   V. Carlo Ignazio Giulio   Consolata   ✕✕ Tre Galline

SAN DOMENICO

Via San   **Capriccioli**   Magazzini San Domenico   ✕✕   San   Domenico   L'Aci

Le Chiuse   Donato   Via   del   Carmine   Corso   Via Corte d'Appello

Via Amedeo Peyron   Luigi   Cibrario   Francia   Piazza Statuto   PZA SAVOIA   Via   Giuseppe   **H**   Garibal

Principi d'Acaja Ⓜ   V. C. Boucheron   Palestro   Via   G.   Botero   Barbarou

Inghilterra   Cso S. Martino   V. F. Juvarra   Corso   Via A. Fabro   Via G. Siccardi   V. S. Maria   G.   Via Mo

XVIII Dicembre Ⓜ   Via   A.   **Galante** ✕✕   Corso   Giuseppe   **Consorzio**

Via   Cernaia   V.

Corso   d'Acaja   Avogadro   Ferraris   ✕✕ **Solferino**   S. F. d'Assisi

Via   Duchessa   Jolanda   Bolzano   V. Beato S. Valfrè   ✕✕✕ **Vintage 1997**   Piazza Solferino

Vinzaglio   V. D. Bertolotti

Via   Principi   Avigliana   V. Ettore de Sonnaz   Galileo   V. Confienza   Umberto   **Go Pa**

Via   G.   Cavalli   Ⓜ Porta Susa   Corso   Giacomo   Amedeo   Matteotti

Via San Quintino   Corso   Via San Quin

✕✕✕ **Piano 35**   Vittorio   **NH Ambasciatori** 🏨   Emanuele II   Corso V.   Emanue

Corso   Vinzaglio Ⓜ   Via   Magenta   Via   Re Um   Magenta

Borsellino   Abruzzi   Via   Vincenzo   Vela   Via   Assie

Castelfidardo   Corso   Stati   Uniti   Ferraris

Francesco   Paolo   Corso   Rodolfo   Re   ✕ **Tave delle**

V. Vigone   degli   Triestre   Via   Legnano

V. Monginevro   Paolo   Ferrucci   Coo   Piazzale Duca d'Aosta   Cso   Galileo   Via   Pastre

3   Corso   Peschiera   **U**   Duca   Trento   Via   Valeggio   Corso

San   Via   Via Governolo

Corso   Luigi   Einaudi   Corso

Via   Marco   Polo   🏨 **Art Hotel Boston**

V.   Paolo   Braccini   Via   Cristoforo   Colombo

C   **D**

● Hotel
● Restaurant

0 ——— 300 m

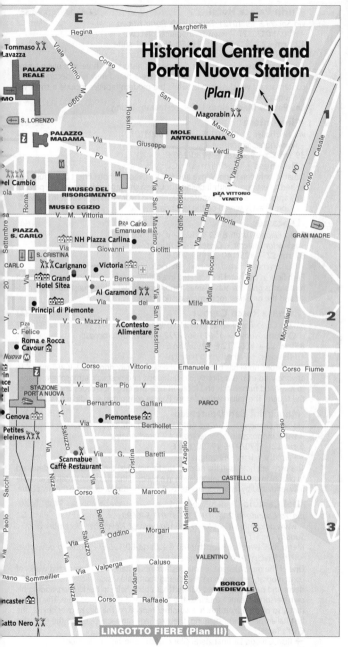

Historical Centre and Porta Nuova Station

(Plan II)

N

ITALY - TURIN

Turin Palace Hotel
I_6 ⊕ 🏠 ⧠ & 🗚 🔧
Plan: **E2**

via Sacchi 8 ✉ *10121 Torino –* **Ⓜ** *Porta Nuova*
– ℰ 011 0825321 – www.turinpalacehotel.com
123 rm ⌇ – †120/400 € ††150/450 € – 1 suite
• Traditional • Boutique hotel • Classic •

After being closed for almost a decade, this historic city hotel was given a new lease of life in 2015. Inside, the rooms have a brand new feel, decorated in a contemporary yet classic style, while the modern facilities include a small yet well-equipped spa.

Les Petites Madeleines – See restaurant listing

Piemontese
& 🗚
Plan: **E2**

via Berthollet 21 ✉ *10125 – ℰ 011 6698101*
– www.hotelpiemontese.it
39 rm ⌇ – †60/180 € ††80/260 €
• Business • Traditional • Cosy •

Situated between Porta Nuova and the Po river, this hotel offers colourfully furnished guestrooms with individual touches; the attic-style rooms are particularly attractive with their exposed beams and hydro-massage baths. In fine weather, breakfast is served on the veranda.

Lancaster
🗚 🔧
Plan: **E3**

corso Filippo Turati 8 ✉ *10128 – ℰ 011 5681982*
– www.lancaster.it – Closed 3-23 August
82 rm ⌇ – †75/140 € ††99/200 €
• Business • Traditional • Modern •

Each floor in this hotel is decorated in a different colour. Attractive, personalised furnishings give the public areas a modern look, while the guestrooms are classic and the breakfast room more rustic in feel.

Roma e Rocca Cavour
🔧
Plan: **E2**

piazza Carlo Felice 60 ✉ *10121 Torino*
– **Ⓜ** *Porta Nuova – ℰ 011 5612772 – www.romarocca.it*
85 rm ⌇ – †65/112 € ††95/156 €
• Historic • Family • Vintage •

This historic hotel has been run by the same family since 1854. It will appeal to anyone who enjoys a slightly old-fashioned and nostalgic atmosphere, thanks to its period furnishings and location near the elegant arcades and gardens of the square. The Italian writer Cesare Pavese committed suicide in room 346.

Magazzini San Domenico
& 🗚
Plan: **D1**

via San Domenico 21 a ✉ *10122 – ℰ 011 4368341*
– www.magazzinisandomenico.it – Closed August
6 rm ⌇ – †70/90 € ††100/120 €
• Family • Inn • Design •

This excellent hotel is in the heart of the former royal capital. It has been designed to offer high-quality accommodation in a building that has been tastefully and skilfully renovated by its owner-architects. A superb base for exploring the city centre.

XxxX
⣿

Del Cambio (Matteo Baronetto)
🥂 🎐 & 🗚
Plan: **G2**

piazza Carignano 2 ✉ *10123 – ℰ 011 546690*
– www.delcambio.it – Closed Monday except November-December and Sunday dinner
Menu 35 € (weekday lunch)/140 € – Carte 80/125 € – *(booking advisable)*
• Piedmontese • Historic • Luxury •

One of the most elegant historic restaurants in Italy, with unexpected works of contemporary art adorning the dining room, alongside more traditional 19C decor and furniture. Matteo Baronetto is at the helm in the kitchen, adding his own personal creative touch to the traditional dishes served there. The restaurant also offers a light lunch, a summer terrace on the piazza overlooking the first Italian parliament building, the excellent Farmacia cafe and the exclusive Chef's Table.

→ Riso Cavour. La finanziera. Giandujotto e sorbetto alle more.
Bar Cavour – See restaurant listing

ITALY - TURIN

XxX **Vintage 1997** (Pierluigi Consonni)   &&& 🅰️🅲️
❊   Plan: **D2**

piazza Solferino 16/h ✉ *10121*

– 🅜 *Re Umberto* – ☏ *011 535948* – *www.vintage1997.com*

– *Closed 3 weeks in August, 1-6 January, Saturday lunch and Sunday*

Menu 20 € (weekday lunch)/75 € – Carte 50/106 €

• Classic cuisine • Elegant • Traditional décor •

Scarlet fabrics, lampshades and elegant wood panelling all add to the muted ambience of this elegant restaurant. It serves imaginative cuisine inspired by traditional favourites using carefully selected ingredients. Champagne imported from France.

→ Tajarin con burro di montagna e parmigiano da vacche bianche. Scampi e filetto di coniglio su crema di scalogno. Tiramisù del Vintage 1997.

XxX **Piano 35**   ≤ 🅰️🅲️

corso Inghilterra 3 (grattacielo Intesa Sanpaolo)   Plan: **C2**
✉ *10121* – ☏ *011 4387800* – *www.piano35.com* – *Closed 15 days in August, Sunday, Monday lunch*

Menu 35/100 € – Carte 75/115 € – *(booking essential)*

• Modern cuisine • Design • Elegant •

A variety of herbs and wild ingredients feature in the creative dishes served in this restaurant, which nonetheless have their roots in traditional recipes. As the name suggests, the restaurant occupies the 35th floor of one of the city's brand-new tower blocks – it's no surprise, then, that the views are breathtaking!

XxX **Les Petites Madeleines** – Hotel Turin Palace Hotel   &. 🅰️🅲️

via Sacchi 8 – ☏ *011 0825321*   Plan: **E2**
– *www.turinpalacehotel.com* – *Closed Monday*

Carte 40/81 € – *(dinner only)*

• Modern cuisine • Classic décor • Elegant •

This restaurant on the ground floor of the hotel boasts an attractive and elegant decor in keeping with the rest of the building. The contemporary-style menu includes fish and meat dishes alike, while options are restricted to a lighter menu for lunch, which is served on the terrace in fine weather.

XX   **Magorabin** (Marcello Trentini)   &&& &. 🅰️🅲️
❊

corso San Maurizio 61/b ✉ *10124* – ☏ *011 8126808*   Plan: **F1**
– *www.magorabin.com* – *Closed Monday lunch, Sunday*

Menu 50/90 € – Carte 67/90 € – *(booking advisable)*

• Creative • Contemporary décor • Design •

Forget the noisy, traffic-filled avenue and soak up the atmosphere of this enchanting restaurant. It serves imaginative, creative cuisine with the occasional hint of the Piedmont. A real contrast to conservative, traditional Turin.

→ Spaghetti pane, burro e acciughe. Anatra all'orientale. Sweet fossil.

XX   **Al Garamond**   &&& 🅰️🅲️ ⇔

via Pomba 14 ✉ *10123* – ☏ *011 8122781*   Plan: **E2**
– *www.algaramond.it* – *Closed August, Saturday lunch, Sunday*

Menu 48/80 € – Carte 42/75 €

• Modern cuisine • Fashionable • Intimate •

Bearing the name of a lieutenant in Napoleon's Dragoons, this restaurant offers creative modern cuisine run by young, skilled and enthusiastic management.

XX   **Al Gatto Nero**   &&& 🅰️🅲️

corso Filippo Turati 14 ✉ *10128* – ☏ *011 590414*   Plan: **E3**
– *www.gattonero.it* – *Closed August and Sunday*

Menu 25 € (weekday lunch)/65 € – Carte 42/75 € – *(pre-book)*

• Classic cuisine • Vintage • Traditional décor •

This restaurant is renowned for its excellent cuisine with a menu featuring traditional specialities from Piedmont alongside Mediterranean dishes and a few fish options. The wine cellar boasts around 1 000 different wines and is one of the best in the city.

ITALY - TURIN

XX **Galante** 🗛

corso Palestro 15 ✉ 10122 – Ⓜ XVIII Dicembre Plan: **E1**
– ℰ 011532163 – www.ristorantegalante.it
– Closed 4-28 August, 26 December-6 January, Saturday lunch, Sunday
Menu 42 € – Carte 34/66 € – *(bookings advisable at dinner)*
• Seafood • Classic décor • Intimate •
Soft shades and padded seating in the small, well-cared for elegant restaurant
with neo classical setting; on the menu with its wide selection there are both
meat and fish dishes.

XX **Tre Galline** 🞔 🗛 ⇔

via Bellezia 37 ✉ 10122 – ℰ 011 4366553 Plan: **D1**
*– www.3galline.it – Closed Sunday dinner in October-May, also Sunday
lunch in other months*
Menu 50 € – Carte 38/84 € – *(dinner only except Saturday)*
• Country • Vintage • Classic décor •
Well cared-for rustic environment in the dining rooms, with wooden ceiling
beams characterising this historic city restaurant, where you can sample typical
and tasty Piedmontese cuisine.

XX **Solferino** 🞔 🗛

piazza Solferino 3 ✉ 10121 – ℰ 011 535851 Plan: **D2**
– www.ristorantesolferino.com
Carte 30/64 €
• Regional cuisine • Classic décor • Friendly •
Renowned and always very busy, despite the changes in staff over the years,
Solferino overlooks a picturesque city square. Classic regional and Italian cuisine
served in classically decorated dining rooms.

XX **Capriccioli** 🗛

via San Domenico 40 ✉ 10122 Plan: **C1**
*– ℰ 011 4368233 – Closed 3 weeks in August, 1 week in January, Monday,
Tuesday lunch*
Carte 42/90 €
• Seafood • Chic • Family •
A tiny corner of Sardinia in northern Italy. The menu at this elegant restaurant
features specialities such as mullet roe and Carloforte tuna, as well as a good
selection of fish and seafood from other parts of the country. The ecru tones
evoke the sandy beach of Capriccioli.

XX **San Tommaso 10 Lavazza** 🗛

via San Tommaso 10 ✉ 10122 – ℰ 011 534201 Plan: **E1**
– www.lavazza.it – closed August and Sunday
Carte 26/80 €
• Classic cuisine • Cosy • Contemporary décor •
The Lavazza grocery store opened here in 1895 and now you will find a bar with
a restaurant to the rear. Enthusiasts of the brand can admire old adverts and
calendars while enjoying the classic Italian cuisine served here.

XX **Carignano** – Grand Hotel Sitea 🞔 🗛 ⇔

via Carlo Alberto 35 ✉ 10123 – ℰ 011 5170171 Plan: **CY**
*– www.grandhotelsitea.it – Closed August and Sunday, also Saturday in
July*
Menu 44/180 € – Carte 46/70 € – *(dinner only)*
• Mediterranean cuisine • Elegant • Intimate •
Part of the Grand Hotel Sitea, this elegant restaurant boasts large picture wind-
ows overlooking the hotel garden. The menu focuses on Mediterranean cuisine
and specialities from Piedmont.

ITALY - TURIN

XX **Bar Cavour** – Ristorante Del Cambio
piazza Carignano 2 ✉ 10123   Plan: **G2**
– *☎ 011 19211270*
– *www.barcavour.com*
– *Closed Monday except November-December*
Carte 35/70 € – *(dinner only)*
• Classic cuisine • Fashionable • Elegant •
Situated above the famous Del Cambio restaurant on the attractive Piazza
Carignano, this establishment with dark furniture and subtle lighting serves
mouthwatering classic cuisine with the occasional contemporary twist. There is
also an attractive bar serving wine, cocktails and spirits, which can be enjoyed
either as an aperitif or as an after-dinner drink.

X **Consorzio**
via Monte di Pietà 23 ✉ 10122 – ☎ 011 2767661   Plan: **D1**
– *www.ristoranteconsorzio.it – Closed 3 weeks in August, Saturday lunch
and Sunday*
Menu 34 € – Carte 31/56 € – *(booking advisable)*
• Piedmontese • Friendly • Trendy •
Run by two young partners, this simple and informal restaurant focuses on
regional and traditional cuisine. It offers delicious Piedmontese specialities
such as local cheese and wine, *agnolotti gobbi* (a type of pasta), braised Fassone beef and panna cotta with various sauces (hazelnut, vincotto, and bitter orange). The nearby Banco Vini e Alimenti bistro is run by the same
owners.

X **Taverna delle Rose**
via Massena 24 ✉ 10128 – Ⓜ Re Umberto – ☎ 011 538345   Plan: **D3**
– *Closed August, Saturday lunch and Sunday*
Carte 27/64 €
• Italian • Family • Traditional décor •
Eclectic cuisine that includes regional specialities, Italian dishes and a few fish
options, all served in an attractive and informal ambience. The romantic dining
room with exposed brick walls and soft lighting is perfect for dinner.

X **L'Acino**
via San Domenico 2/a ✉ 10121   Plan: **D1**
– *☎ 011 5217077 – Closed 3 weeks in August, 1 week in January
and Sunday*
Carte 29/40 € – *(dinner only) (number of covers limited, pre-book)*
• Regional cuisine • Rustic • Family •
This small trattoria with friendly staff has delicious Piedmontese cuisine, which
goes well with the excellent choice of wines. House specialities include onion
stuffed with Bra sausage and served with melted cheese, regional cheeses, Fas-
sona beef, and pears cooked in wine and spices. Be warned: if you haven't made
a booking you are unlikely to get a table.

X **Scannabue Caffè Restaurant**
largo Saluzzo 25/h ✉ 10125 – Ⓜ Marconi   Plan: **E3**
– *☎ 011 6696693 – www.scannabue.it*
– *Closed 1 week in August*
Menu 30/45 €
– *Carte 32/60 € – (dinner only in August) (booking advisable)*
• Country • Vintage • Neighbourhood •
This lively local trattoria has an old-fashioned feel. All the focus is on excellent
Piedmontese dishes, including specialities such as tajarin pasta, Fassone beef
and hazelnuts. A few fish options are also available.

✗
🕸
Contesto Alimentare ⏣

via Accademia Albertina 21/e ✉ *10123* — Plan: **E2**
— Ⓜ *Porta Nuova* – ✆ *011 8178698* – *www.contestoalimentare.it*
– *Closed Monday*
Menu 25/35 € – Carte 28/48 € – *(number of covers limited, pre-book)*
• Piedmontese • Simple • Family •

A tiny modern trattoria with simple tables set close together, where the fine cuisine on offer is the real attraction. Using regional produce, the female chef prepares delicious specialities from Piedmont. Classic dishes such as *tajarin* pasta and *plin* ravioli always feature among the first courses, followed by beef with savoy cabbage and hazelnut cake and ice cream.

LINGOTTO FIERE   PLAN III

🏨
NH Lingotto Tech ⏣ 🛗 ⛴ ⏣ ⏣ 🚗

via Nizza 230 ✉ *10126* – Ⓜ *Lingotto* – ✆ *011 6642000* — Plan: **C2**
– *www.nh-hotels.it/lingotto* – *Closed August*
141 rm ⌷ – 🛏109/199 € 🛏🛏109/199 € – 1 suite
• Business • Palace • Modern •

The panoramic lift at this hotel leads up to the balconies overlooked by its guestrooms, which are all decorated with design-style furnishings. The twin of the Hotel Lingotto, this hotel boasts more modern facilities, as well as the Tech restaurant, which serves classic cuisine in an open-plan dining room.

🏨
AC Hotel Torino by Marriott ⏣ 🛗 🦚 ⛴ ⏣ ⏣ 🚗

via Bisalta 11 ✉ *10126* – Ⓜ *Spezia* – ✆ *011 6395091* — Plan: **H2**
– *www.hotelactorino.com*
86 rm – 🛏100/450 € 🛏🛏110/460 € – ⌷ 14 € – 3 suites
• Chain • Business • Minimalist •

Once a pasta factory, this early 20th century building in the Lingotto area is now an up-to-date hotel that offers ideal comfort and completely modern facilities.

✗✗✗
🌸
Casa Vicina-Eataly Lingotto *(Claudio Vicina)* 🕸 ⛴ ⏣

via Nizza 224 ✉ *10126* – Ⓜ *Lingotto* — Plan: **H2**
– ✆ *011 19506840* – *www.casavicina.com* – *Closed 4 August-7 September,*
Christmas Holidays, Sunday dinner and Monday
Menu 43 € (lunch)/120 € – Carte 62/124 €
• Piedmontese • Minimalist • Elegant •

Housed in the first Eataly store opened in Italy (from which its excellent wine list is supplied), this restaurant is expertly run by the experienced and enthusiastic Vicina family. The decor is elegant and minimalist in style, while the Piedmontese cuisine has just a touch of contemporary flavour.
➜ Agnolotti pizzicati a mano al sugo d'arrosto. Rognone à la coque con vellutata di senape ed aglio in camicia. Torrone al cucchiaio.

AT RIVOLI

✗✗✗✗
🌸
Combal.zero *(Davide Scabin)* 🕸 ⩽ ⏣

piazza Mafalda di Savoia – ✆ *011 9565225* – *www.combal.org*
– *Closed August, Christmas Holidays, Sunday and Monday*
Menu 130/200 € – Carte 100/185 € – *(dinner only)*
• Creative • Design • Luxury •

This modern, minimalist-style restaurant is next to the Museo d'Arte Contemporanea in Rivoli's castle. It serves beautifully presented classic Piedmontese dishes alongside a selection of Italian favourites. The owner-chef also creates more inventive and imaginative dishes that feature mainly on the restaurant's tasting menu, where he demonstrates his full culinary expertise.
➜ Maccherone soufflé, ragù alla bolognese e fonduta di grana padano riserva Combal.zero. Piccione all'ortolana. Zuppa di cannoli, mandorle e caffè.

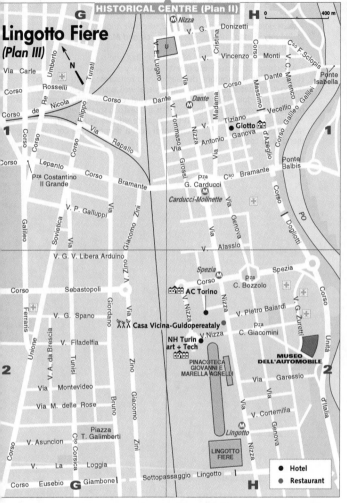

Lingotto Fiere
(Plan III)

● Hotel

● Restaurant

AT VENARIA REALE

PLAN I

Cascina di Corte

Plan: A1

*via Amedeo di Castellamonte 2 – ℰ 011 4593278
– www.cascinadicorte.it*
12 rm ⌂ – ♦120/180 € ♦♦140/280 €
• Family • Country house • Elegant •
Not far from the famous palace, this 19C farmhouse with adjoining ice-cream
parlour has a simple architectural style that is typical of the region. A rustic interior with exposed brickwork in the bedrooms goes hand-in-hand with modern,
comfortable furnishings and facilities.

XxX
€3

Dolce Stil Novo alla Reggia (Alfredo Russo)   🏠 ᴼᴸ AC ⟷

piazza della Repubblica 4 – 𝒞 3462690588   Plan: **A1**
– www.dolcestilnovo.com – Closed 2 weeks in August, 2 weeks
in January, Sunday dinner, Tuesday lunch and Monday
Menu 38 € (weekday lunch)/90 €
– Carte 70/121 € – (number of covers limited, pre-book)
• Modern cuisine • Elegant • Luxury •

Housed inside the Torrione del Garove, this restaurant boasts light and airy dining rooms decorated in minimalist-style, as well as an attractive terrace over-looking the Reggia di Venaria gardens. The chef serves regional cuisine with the occasional modern touch, alongside fish and seafood specialities.

→ Zuppetta di legumi con frutti del mare ed olio crudo. "Gran bollito" misto del Dolce Stil Novo. Cremoso di ricotta di montagna con gli ingredienti della cassata.

LUXEMBOURG
LËTZEBUERG

LUXEMBOURG

→ **Area:**
2 586 km² (998 sq mi).

→ **Population:**
576 243 inhabitants (nearly 62% nationals, 38% resident foreigners). Density = 223 per km².

→ **Capital:** Luxembourg.

→ **Currency:** Euro (€).

→ **Government:**
Constitutional parliamentary monarchy (since 1868). Member of European Union since 1957 (one of the 6 founding countries).

→ **Languages:**
The national language is Lëtzebuergesch, a variant of German, similar to the Frankish dialect of the Moselle valley; German is used for general purposes and is the first language for teaching; French is the legislative language. Both French and German are used as administrative languages.

→ **Public holidays:**
New Year's Day (1 Jan); Easter Monday (late Mar/21 Apr); Labor Day (1 May); Ascension Day (May); Whit Monday (late May/June); National Day (23 June); Assumption of the Virgin Mary (15 Aug); All Saints' Day (1 Nov); Christmas Day (25 Dec); St Stephen's Day (26 Dec).

→ **Local Time:**
GMT+1 hour in winter and GMT +2 hours in summer.

→ **Climate:**
Temperate continental with cold winters and mild summers (Luxembourg: January 1°C; July 17°C).

→ **Emergency:**
Police ☎ 113; Medical Assistance ☎ 112; Fire Brigade ☎ 118. (Dialling 112 within any EU country will redirect your call and contact the emergency services.)

→ **Electricity:**
230 volts AC, 50Hz; 2 round pin sockets.

→ **Formalities:**
Travellers from the European Union (EU), Switzerland, Norway, Iceland and the main countries of North and South America need a national identity card or passport (America: passport required) to visit the Grand Duchy of Luxembourg for less than three months (tourism or business purpose). For visitors from other countries a visa may be required, in addition to a passport, especially for those wishing to stay for longer than three months. We advise you to check with your embassy before travelling.

LUXEMBOURG

LËTZEBUERG

Population: 111 287

Luxembourg may be small but it's perfectly formed. Standing high above two rivers on a sandstone bluff, its commanding position over sheer gorges may be a boon to modern visitors, but down the centuries that very setting has rendered it the subject of conquest on many occasions. Its eye-catching geography makes it a city of distinctive districts, linked by spectacular bridges spanning lush green valleys.

The absolute heart of the city is the old town, its most prominent landmarks the cathedral spires and the city squares with their elegant pastel façades – an ideal backdrop to the 'café culture' and a worthy recipient of UNESCO World Heritage Status. Winding its way deep below to the south west is the river Pétrusse, which has its confluence with the river Alzette in the south east. Follow the Chemin de la Corniche, past the old city walls and along the Alzette's narrow valley to discover the ruins of The Bock, the city's first castle, and the Casemates, a labyrinth of rocky 17C and 18C underground defences. Directly to the south of the old town is the railway station quarter, while down at river level to the east is the altogether more attractive Grund district, whose northerly neighbours are Clausen and Pfaffenthal. Up in the north east, connected by the grand sounding Pont Grand-Duchesse Charlotte, is Kirchberg Plateau, a modern hub of activity for the EU.

LUXEMBOURG CITY IN...

→ **ONE DAY**
Place d'Armes, Ducal Grand Palace, National Museum of History and Art, Chemin de la Corniche.

→ **TWO DAYS**
Luxembourg City History Museum, Bock Casemates, the Grund.

→ **THREE DAYS**
Kirchberg Plateau, Museum of Modern Art, concert at Luxembourg Philharmonic Hall.

PRACTICAL INFORMATION

ARRIVAL-DEPARTURE

✈ Luxembourg Findel Airport is 6km northeast of the city centre. City bus Number 16 runs every 10min and takes 25min.

GETTING AROUND

Buses run from 5am to 10pm and there's an additional late night service on Fridays and Saturdays (there's no metro). The most convenient bus stations are at the exit of the Gare Centrale and on Place Hamilius in the old town. The fare system (valid for trains too) is simple enough: for trips of 10km or less you buy a 'short' ticket; for an unlimited day ticket (valid until 8am the next day) you buy a Billet Reseau. Available from Easter-October, the Luxembourg Card offers unlimited travel and free admission to many attractions countrywide. In winter, the Stater Muséeskaart offers three days of free admission to important sights in the city.

CALENDAR HIGHLIGHTS

March-May
Printemps Musical.

May
Foire du Printemps (Spring festival).

June
National Day Eve - Fireworks over the Pétrusse Valley and partying on Place d'Armes and Place Guillaume II.

June-September
Summer in the City.

August-September
Schueberfouer (One of Europe's biggest funfairs).

November-January
Winterlights Festival.

EATING OUT

The taste buds of Luxembourg have been very much influenced by French classical cuisine, particularly around and about the Old Town, an area that becomes a smart open-air terrace in summer. Look out for the local speciality Judd mat Gaardebounen, smoked neck of pork with broad beans. The centre of town is an eclectic place to eat as it runs the gauntlet from fast-style pizzeria to expense account restaurants favoured by businessmen. A good bet for atmosphere is the Grund, which offers a wide variety of restaurants and price ranges, and is certainly the area that boasts the most popular cafés and pubs. A few trendy places have sprouted over recent times near the Casemates, and these too are proving to be pretty hot with the younger crowd. A service charge is included in your bill but if you want to tip, ten per cent is reasonable. The Grand Duchy produces its own white and sparkling wines on the borders of the Moselle. Over the last decade it has produced some interesting varieties but you'll rarely find these abroad, as they're eagerly snapped up by the locals.

Le Royal

12 boulevard Royal ⊠ *2449* – ℰ *241 61 61*   Plan: **C1**
– *www.leroyalluxembourg.com*
190 rm – †190/480 € ††190/480 € – ☲ 31 € – 20 suites
• Grand Luxury • Business • Classic •

Nothing in this hotel is left to chance, to such an extent that a king would feel perfectly at home! Guests are waited on hand and foot by an army of staff that are available day and night. It is ideally located in the city's 'Wall Street' neighbourhood.
La Pomme Cannelle – See restaurant listing

Le Place d'Armes

18 place d'Armes ⊠ *1136* – ℰ *27 47 37*   Plan: **C1**
– *www.hotel-leplacedarmes.com*
21 rm – †250/570 € ††250/570 € – ☲ 26 € – 7 suites
• Grand Luxury • Historic • Elegant •

Although on the liveliest square in the town centre, this establishment is a real haven of peace. This former townhouse has been given a complete makeover. It exudes charm and an old Luxembourg atmosphere without feeling stuffy. A must.
❀ **La Cristallerie • Plëss • Café de Paris** – See restaurant listing

Sofitel Le Grand Ducal

40 boulevard d'Avranches ⊠ *1160* – ℰ *24 87 71*   Plan: **B3**
– *www.sofitel.com*
126 rm – †350/550 € ††350/550 € – ☲ 30 € – 2 suites
• Business • Luxury •

This Sofitel has everything you would expect from a top class, international hotel. The plush, understated ambience is offset by an interior that combines designer details with luxurious comfort. It also has a view over the town and the lush gardens of the Pétrusse Valley (from the bathtub of some rooms).

Parc Beaux-Arts

1 rue Sigefroi ⊠ *2536* – ℰ *26 86 76*   Plan: **D1**
– *www.goeres-group.com*
11 rm – †170/455 € ††170/455 € – ☲ 20 € – 11 suites
• Historic • Luxury • Elegant •

This delightful hotel stands right next door to the Museum of Art and History and the Grand Ducal Palace, with whom it shares a taste for beauty and refinement. Each individually appointed spacious room has its own distinctive character. For lovers of sophisticated art de vivre!

Simoncini

6 rue Notre-Dame ⊠ *2240* – ℰ *22 28 44*   Plan: **C1**
– *www.hotelsimoncini.lu*
35 rm ☲ – †125/200 € ††145/220 €
• Business • Townhouse • Design •

This fashionable establishment, which is half hotel, half art gallery, is something of a wild card in Luxembourg's traditional hotel landscape. Well located right in the centre, it is ideal for a city trip and has a public car park nearby.

XxxX Clairefontaine (Arnaud Magnier)
❀

9 place de Clairefontaine ⊠ *1341* – ℰ *46 22 11*   Plan: **D1**
– *www.restaurantclairefontaine.lu – closed 1 week Easter, last
2 weeks August-first week September, Christmas-New Year, first week
January, Bank Holidays, Saturday and Sunday*
Menu 57 € (lunch)/99 € – Carte 88/115 €
• Creative French • Elegant •

This attractive restaurant with a terrace stands on an elegant square. It has traditional decor with old wooden panelling and contemporary furnishings. Creative, modern cuisine and astute wine pairings.
➔ Foie gras de canard confit et différentes textures de maïs, voile de caramel. Lotte lardée et gaufre de pommes de terre, fricassée de petits pois et girolles. Éclair farci aux fruits rouges, marmelade et crème à la vanille Bourbon.

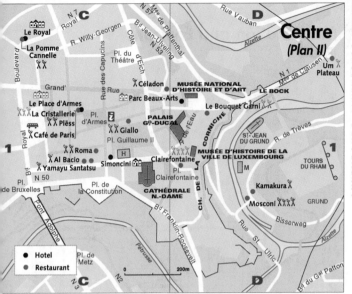

Centre
(Plan II)

XXXX Mosconi (Ilario Mosconi)

13 rue Münster ⊠ *2160 –* ℰ *54 69 94 – www.mosconi.lu*   Plan: **D1**
*– closed 1 week Easter, last 3 weeks August, 24 December-early January,
Bank Holidays, Saturday lunch, Sunday and Monday*
Menu 44 € (lunch)/130 € – Carte 99/129 €
• Italian • Elegant • Luxury •

Ilario and Simonetta Mosconi are an enthusiastic couple that proudly pay
homage to the gastronomic traditions of Italy. Their Italian cuisine is as full of
flair as it is steeped in flavours. The secret of their success no doubt lies in the
infinite care and attention they devote to choosing their suppliers.
→ Linguini de Gragnano, tartare de sardines marinées, huile et citron confit. Truffes blanches d'Alba en saison. Caramel à la sicilienne, sauce à
l'orange et pistaches de Bronte.

XXX La Cristallerie – Hôtel Le Place d'Armes

18 place d'Armes (1ᵉʳ étage) ⊠ *1136*   Plan: **C1**
– ℰ 274 73 74 21 – www.hotel-leplacedarmes.com
*– closed 30 July-28 August, 26-30 December, 19-27 February, Saturday
lunch, Sunday and Monday*
Menu 78 € (lunch)/228 € – (tasting menu only)
• Modern French • Classic décor • Elegant •

In terms of decor, this crystal glassworks is the epitome of stylish, classical elegance. The chef amply demonstrates how subtle touches of creativity can enhance fine ingredients. His well-balanced creations feature the occasional Asian
influence.
→ King crabe juste tiédi au caviar et cœur de cocotier. Hampe de bœuf
grillée au feu de bois, anguille fumée et échalote noire. Cheese cake aux
fruits rouges.

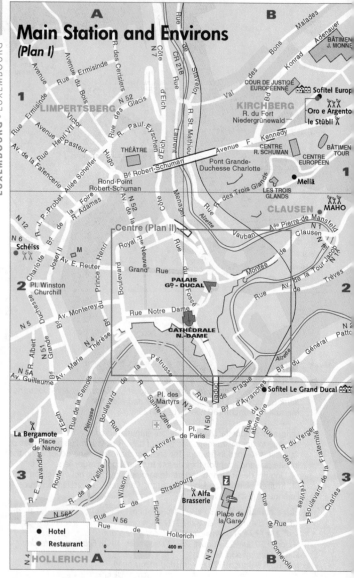

Main Station and Environs
(Plan I)

XX **La Pomme Cannelle** – Hôtel Le Royal

12 boulevard Royal ✉ *2449* – ✆ *241 61 67 36*
Plan: **C1**
– www.leroyalluxembourg.com – closed August, first week January, Bank Holidays, Saturday and Sunday
Menu 68 € (lunch) – Carte 61/78 €
• Creative French • Romantic •
La Pomme Cannelle represents a culinary marriage between French traditions and Oriental flavours. The Indian Empire style interior echoes that of the hotel to which it belongs.

XX **Schéiss**

142 Val Sainte-Croix ✉ *1370*
Plan: **A2**
– ✆ 24 61 82 – www.scheiss.lu
– closed Bank Holidays, Sunday and Monday
Menu 28 € (lunch)/49 € – Carte 52/68 €
• Modern cuisine • Design •
Despite the elegant minimalist interior, you need have no fear of the usual hefty bill associated with such decor. Enjoy delicious, contemporary cuisine that is steeped in simplicity.

XX **Le Bouquet Garni** (dinner)

32 rue de l'Eau ✉ *1449* – ✆ *26 20 06 20*
Plan: **D1**
– www.lebouquetgarni.lu – closed Bank Holidays, Sunday and Monday
Menu 30 € (lunch)/45 €
• Classic French • Romantic • Rustic •
As the establishment's name suggests, the dishes are steeped in the aroma of French cuisine. Chef Thierry Duhr demonstrates his talent by the quality, sophistication and generosity of his recipes. The dining room, both elegant and rustic, provides the perfect backdrop to the menu.

XX **Roma**

5 rue Louvigny ✉ *1946* – ✆ *22 36 92* – *www.roma.lu*
Plan: **C1**
– closed Sunday dinner and Monday
Carte 51/65 €
• Italian • Friendly •
The Roma, Luxembourg's first Italian restaurant, specialises in homemade pasta, ultra fresh ingredients and, more unusually, themed festivals; all of which have enabled it to become a firm favourite with the locals. There is a popular range of daily specials.

XX **Plëss** – Hôtel Le Place d'Armes

18 place d'Armes ✉ *1136* – ✆ *274 73 74 11*
Plan: **C1**
– www.hotel-leplacedarmes.com
Menu 39 € (lunch) – Carte 50/80 €
• Classic cuisine • Brasserie •
Plëss means 'square' in Luxembourgish – an obvious reference to the Place d'Armes. This is where this lovely contemporary brasserie is located, in the heart of town. Glamorous, urban atmosphere.

XX **Giallo**

24 rue du Curé ✉ *1368* – ✆ *26 20 00 27*
Plan: **3E1**
– www.giallo.lu – closed Sunday and Monday
Menu 19 € (lunch) – Carte 50/68 €
• Italian • Design • Design •
The two-storey water feature is one of the most striking elements of this handsome modern interior, setting the scene for the oh so stylish Giallo. The establishment is also rich in culinary ambition, backed up by first-class produce, which is perhaps unsurprising when the aim is to serve authentic Italian cuisine.

LUXEMBOURG - LUXEMBOURG

X

(⊛)

La Bergamote

2 place de Nancy ✉ *2212 –* ☎ *26 44 03 79*   Plan: A3
– www.labergamote.lu – closed 1 week Easter, last 2 weeks August, late
December, Bank Holidays, Saturday lunch, Sunday and Monday
Menu 26 € (lunch)/35 € – Carte 52/69 €
• Modern cuisine • Trendy • Friendly •

Have you ever actually tasted bergamot? The subtle, fresh taste of this small
citrus fruit is a recurring ingredient in Philippe Bridard's sun-drenched cuisine.
Vitello tonnato, roast sea bream and shrimp polenta, without forgetting a few
modern, French touches...

X

Alfa Brasserie   &. AC

16 place de la Gare ✉ *1616 –* ☎ *49 00 11 30 00*   Plan: B3
– www.alfabrasserie.lu
Menu 22 € (lunch), 25/80 € – Carte 35/53 €
• Classic cuisine • Brasserie • Elegant •

Alfa Brasserie will take you back in time. Copper pots, high ceilings and Art Deco
features recreate the authentic setting of a 1930s Parisian brasserie. The menu is
deliciously classical, with the occasional Luxembourg specialty.

X

Céladon   ⇔

1 rue du Nord ✉ *2229 –* ☎ *47 49 34 – www.thai.lu*   Plan: C1
– closed Saturday lunch and Sunday
Menu 47/57 € – Carte 42/50 €
• Thai • Intimate •

Lovers of Thai cuisine won't be disappointed by the fresh produce and authentic Asian flavours of the Céladon. Vegetarians will no doubt be in seventh heaven with the range that is on offer.

X

(⊛)

Kamakura   ⇔

4 rue Münster ✉ *2160 –* ☎ *47 06 04 – www.kamakura.lu*   Plan: D1
– closed 2 weeks Easter, last 2 weeks August-early September, late
December-early January, Bank Holidays, Saturday lunch and Sunday
Menu 15 € 🍷 (lunch), 36/68 € – Carte 41/69 €
• Japanese • Minimalist •

The minimalist design of this Japanese restaurant has made no concessions to
the West. It is named after the former capital of the Land of the Rising Sun and
embodies the essence of Japanese cooking: understated, low-key presentation
and virtuoso preparation. Kamakura will celebrate its 30th anniversary in 2018!

X

Yamayu Santatsu   ⇔

26 rue Notre-Dame ✉ *2240 –* ☎ *46 12 49 – closed last*   Plan: C1
week July-first 2 weeks August, late December-early January, Bank
Holidays, Sunday and Monday
Menu 16 € (lunch), 34/61 € – Carte 26/61 €
• Japanese • Minimalist •

Yamayu Santatsu's sushi is fully equal to that of Tokyo, explaining the establishment's popularity by gourmets who know how to appreciate the subtlety of
Japanese cuisine. It has understated decor and private rooms for business mee-
tings.

X

Al Bacio   AC

24 rue Notre-Dame ✉ *2240 –* ☎ *27 99 48 81 – closed*   Plan: C1
last 2 weeks August, late December-early January, Bank Holidays, Monday
dinner, Tuesday dinner and Sunday
Carte 32/45 €
• Italian • Trendy • Simple •

Presto, presto! The characteristic liveliness associated with Italian towns forms
the backdrop to this popular restaurant. The regulars return for the authentic,
super fresh cuisine. Who could resist such a delicious Italian kiss (bacio)?

X **Café de Paris** – Hôtel Le Place d'Armes
16 place d'Armes ✉ *1136* – ☎ *26 20 37 70*   Plan: **C1**
– www.hotel-leplacedarmes.com – closed Sunday dinner
Menu 35 € (lunch) – Carte 32/56 €
· Regional cuisine · Bistro · Intimate ·
The lively ambience and cosy décor set the scene in this inviting bistro. The chefs work with the best of Luxembourg's fine country produce to create fine, flavoursome dishes.

ENVIRONS OF LUXEMBOURG

 Sofitel Europe
4 rue du Fort Niedergrünewald (European Centre)   Plan: **B1**
✉ *2015 Kirchberg* – ☎ *43 77 61 – www.sofitel.com*
105 rm – ♦140/460 € ♦♦160/480 € – ☷ 28 € – 4 suites
· Business · Grand Luxury · Contemporary ·
A bold, oval shaped hotel at the heart of the European Institutions district, with a central atrium and spacious, extremely comfortable guestrooms. The service is attentive and friendly, as you would expect from this upmarket chain. The typical restaurant serves regional cuisine; a warm atmosphere is enhanced by staff in traditional costumes.
Oro e Argento – See restaurant listing

 Meliã
1 Park Dräi Eechelen ✉ *1499 Kirchberg* – ☎ *27 33 31*   Plan: **B1**
– www.melia-luxembourg.com
160 rm ☷ – ♦95/550 € ♦♦100/570 € – 1 suite
· Business · Functional ·
The first hotel of this Spanish chain in Benelux, located next to the conference centre. Rooms are stylish, comfortable and functional. Lovely view of the city.

XxX **Oro e Argento** – Hôtel Sofitel Europe
6 rue du Fort Niedergrünewald (European Centre)   Plan: **B1**
✉ *2015 Kirchberg* – ☎ *43 77 68 70 – www.sofitel.com – closed 31 July-1 September and Saturday lunch*
Menu 41 € (lunch), 49/80 € – Carte 71/123 €
· Italian · Intimate ·
An attractive Italian restaurant in a luxury hotel. Contemporary cuisine served to a backdrop of plush decor with a Venetian touch. Intimate atmosphere and stylish service.

XxX **MAHO**
2 place Sainte-Cunégonde ✉ *1367 Clausen*   Plan: **2D2**
– ☎ 28 99 80 00 – www.maho.lu – closed Saturday lunch and Sunday
7 rm ☷ – ♦105/180 € ♦♦200/280 €
Menu 32 € (lunch), 48/150 € – Carte 58/75 €
· Classic French · Contemporary décor ·
Silence and elegance are the bywords of MAHO. The classical, refined cuisine demonstrates the chef's skill and know-how and the guestrooms are delightful. It is located close to the city centre.

XX **Mamma Bianca**
33 avenue J.F. Kennedy (Ellipse Kirchberg 2) ✉ *1855 Kirchberg*
– ☎ 27 04 54 – www.mammabianca.lu – closed late December-early January, Bank Holidays, Saturday and Sunday
Menu 22 € (lunch)/37 € – Carte 42/70 €
· Italian · Trendy ·
Mamma mia – what a restaurant! A spacious interior done up in a trendy, designer style, bordering on a lounge ambience. The menu features Italian classics. The chef rustles up dishes full of generous flavours and devoid of unnecessary frills. A delicious Bib Gourmand!

X

Bick Stuff

95 rue de Clausen ✉ *1342 Clausen –* ✆ *26 09 47 31 – www.bickstuff.lu*
– closed week after Pentecost, 2 weeks in August, late December, Thursday
dinner, Saturday lunch, Sunday dinner and Monday
Menu 23 € (lunch), 36/46 € – Carte 53/67 €
• Home cooking • Classic décor •

Bick is a local word which literally means beak in English but loosely translates
as "food". A family-run establishment where you will instantly feel at home. Vir-
ginie and Denis Laissy have the same goal: good food in a relaxed atmosphere.
Chef Denis rustles up reassuringly classical recipes, adding his own distinctive
touch. We recommend the set menu.

X

Um Plateau

6 Plateau Altmünster ✉ *1123 Clausen –* ✆ *26 47 84 26*   Plan: **D1**
– www.umplateau.lu – closed Saturday lunch and Sunday
Menu 27 € (lunch) – Carte 39/65 € – (open until 11pm)
• Modern cuisine • Chic •

Diners appreciate the smart lounge ambience and cosy interior of this restaurant. After a glass of wine in the lively bar, treat yourself to a meal in which
fine produce takes pride of place. Authentic flavours and painstaking preparations are the hallmarks of this establishment.

X

Le Stübli – Hôtel Sofitel Europe

4 rue du Fort Niedergrünewald ✉ *2015 Kirchberg*   Plan: **D1**
– ✆ *43 77 68 83 – www.sofitel.com – closed weekends and July-August*
Menu 25 € (lunch)/35 € – Carte 47/58 €
• Traditional cuisine • Romantic •

You may find the all-wood interior more reminiscent of an Alpine chalet, but
you are well and truly in the heart of Luxembourg! Traditional dishes prepared
with the best of local produce await the discerning diner.

NETHERLANDS
NEDERLAND

→ **AREA:**
41 543 km² (16 163 sq mi).

→ **POPULATION:**
16 979 729 inhabitants.
Density = 409 per km².

→ **CAPITAL:**
Amsterdam; The Hague
is the seat of government
and Parliament.

→ **CURRENCY:**
Euro (€).

→ **GOVERNMENT:**
Constitutional parliamentary
monarchy (since 1815). Member
of European Union since 1957
(one of the 6 founding countries).

→ **LANGUAGE:**
Dutch; many Dutch people also
speak English.

→ **PUBLIC HOLIDAYS:**
New Year's Day (1 Jan); Easter
Monday (late Mar/Apr); King's Day
(26/27 Apr); Liberation Day (5 May);
Ascension Day (May); Whit Monday
(late May/June); Christmas Day
(25 Dec); St Stephen's Day (26 Dec).

→ **LOCAL TIME:**
GMT+1 hour in winter and GMT
+2 hours in summer.

→ **CLIMATE:**
Temperate maritime with cool
winters and mild summers
(Amsterdam: January 2°C; July
17°C), rainfall evenly distributed
throughout the year.

AMSTERDAM

● The Hague
● Rotterdam

→ **EMERGENCY:**
Police, Medical Assistance and Fire
Brigade ✆ **112**.

→ **ELECTRICITY:**
230 volts AC, 50Hz; 2 round pin
sockets.

→ **FORMALITIES:**
Travellers from the European
Union (EU), Switzerland, Norway,
Iceland and the main countries of
North and South America need a
national identity card or passport
(America: passport required) to
visit the Netherlands for less than
three months (tourism or business
purpose). For visitors from other
countries a visa may be required, in
addition to a passport, especially
for those wishing to stay for longer
than three months. We advise you
to check with your embassy before
travelling.

AMSTERDAM
AMSTERDAM

Population: 812 895

Packshot/Fotolia.com

Once visited, never forgotten; that's Amsterdam's great claim to fame. Its endearing horseshoe shape – defined by 17C canals cut to drain land for a growing population – allied to finely detailed gabled houses, has produced a compact city centre of aesthetically splendid symmetry and matchless consistency. Exploring the city on foot or by bike is the real joy here and visitors rarely need to jump on a tram or bus.

'The world's biggest small city' displays a host of distinctive characteristics, ranging from the world-famous red light district to the cosy and convivial brown cafés, from the wonderful art galleries and museums to the quirky shops, and the medieval churches to the tree-lined waterways with their pretty bridges. There's the feel of a northern Venice, but without the hallowed and revered atmosphere. It exists on a human scale, small enough to walk from one end to the other. Those who might moan that it's just too small should stroll along to the former derelict docklands on the east side and contemplate the shiny new apartments giving the waterfront a sleek, 21C feel. Most people who come here, though, are just happy to cosy up to old Amsterdam's sleepy, relaxed vibe. No European city does snug bars better: this is the place to go for cats kipping on beat-up chairs and candles flickering on wax-encrusted tables…

AMSTERDAM IN...

→ ONE DAY
A trip on a canal boat, Rijksmuseum, Anne Frank Museum, Van Gogh Museum.

→ TWO DAYS
Begijnhof, shopping in the '9 Straatjes', Vondelpark, evening in a brown café.

→ THREE DAYS
The Jordaan, Plantage and Entrepotdok, red light district.

PRACTICAL INFORMATION

ARRIVAL-DEPARTURE

✈ Schiphol International Airport is 18km southwest of the city. Trains run regularly to Amsterdam Central Station, and take 15min.

GETTING AROUND

With its narrow streets and canals, this is a city geared to walking. It's also one of the most bike-friendly capitals in the world, so rent one if you want to experience life as a local. Trams and buses run mostly from the central station; the metro has four short lines, mostly used by commuters. The Amsterdam Card entitles the holder to free public transport, admission to major museums, a canal cruise and discounts in some restaurants. Valid for 24hr, 48hr, or 72hr, it is available from the Tourist Information Office opposite the central station.

EATING OUT

Amsterdam is a vibrant and multi-cultural city and, as such, has a wide proliferation of restaurants offering a varied choice of cuisines, where you can eat well without paying too much. Head for an eetcafe and you'll get a satisfying three course meal at a reasonable price. The Dutch consider the evening to be the time to eat your main meal, so some restaurants shut at lunchtime. Aside from the eetcafe, you can top up your middle-of-day fuel levels with simple, home-cooked meals and local beers at a bruin (brown) café, or for something

CALENDAR HIGHLIGHTS

June
Kunst RAI (modern art exhibition). Holland Festival (theatre, concerts and ballets), Open Garden Days.

July
Roots Festival (music and dance).

August
Uitmarkt (theatre/music shows), Gay Pride's Canal Parade, Grachtenfestival (classical concerts).

September
Jordaan Festival (music shows and fairs).

November
Museumnacht (many museums stay open during the night).

lighter, a café specialising in coffee and cake. If you wish to try local specialities, number one on the hit list could be rijsttafel or 'rice table', as the Dutch have imported much from their former colonies of Indonesia. Fresh raw herring from local waters is another nutritious local favourite, as are apple pies and pancakes of the sweet persuasion; often enjoyed with a hot chocolate. Restaurants are never too big but are certainly atmospheric and busy, so it's worth making reservations.

NETHERLANDS - AMSTERDAM

Amstel
Prof. Tulpplein 1 ✉ *1018 GX* – ☎ *(0 20) 622 60 60*   Plan: **H3**
– *www.amsterdam.intercontinental.com*
63 rm – ♦200/500 € ♦♦350/600 € – ☲ 33 € – 16 suites
• Grand Luxury •
A veritable haven of luxury and good taste in this grand hotel on the banks of the Amstel. The vast rooms are decorated with attention to detail and stylish furnishings. Complete, efficient service.
La Rive – See restaurant listing

Sofitel Legend The Grand
O.Z. Voorburgwal 197 ✉ *1012 EX* – ☎ *(0 20) 555 31 11*   Plan: **G2**
– *www.sofitel-legend-thegrand.com*
177 rm – ♦295/610 € ♦♦410/695 € – ☲ 38 € – 29 suites
• Grand Luxury •
This magnificent building, where William of Orange once stayed, oozes historic grandeur. The guestrooms and public spaces breathe luxury and French elegance – and there is even a butler service. Le Petit Bistro will delight fans of bistro cuisine with its many classic favourites.
❀ **Bridges** – See restaurant listing

Hotel de l'Europe
Nieuwe Doelenstraat 2 ✉ *1012 CP* – ☎ *(0 20) 531 17 77*   Plan: **G2**
– *www.deleurope.com*
88 rm – ♦399/699 € ♦♦399/799 € – ☲ 38 € – 23 suites
• Luxury •
This luxury hotel, which dates back to the end of the 19C, offers a chic combination of charm and tradition. The rooms are elegant and the junior suites were inspired by the Dutch School. Views of the canals.
❀❀ **Bord'Eau** • ❀ **Hoofdstad** – See restaurant listing

Grand Hotel Amrâth
Prins Hendrikkade 108 ✉ *1011 AK* – ☎ *(0 20) 552 00 00*   Plan: **G1**
– *www.amrathamsterdam.com*
165 rm – ♦209/369 € ♦♦239/429 € – ☲ 25 € – 9 suites
• Chain •
The monumental staircase in this imposing Art Nouveau hotel will be your stairway to heaven as you won't want for anything here. The location is nice and central, the rooms are comfortable and the service is very personal and attentive. In the restaurant, you will find a hint of retro in the decor and an international flavour on your plate.

Andaz
Prinsengracht 587 ✉ *1016 HT* – ☎ *(0 20) 523 12 34*   Plan: **F2**
– *www.amsterdam.prinsengracht.andaz.com*
117 rm – ♦335/495 € ♦♦335/495 € – ☲ 30 € – 5 suites
• Luxury •
Design hotel on the Prinsengracht with interior decor by Marcel Wanders. This former library lends itself to an experience encapsulating both luxury and style, accompanied by a personal welcome and service. In the restaurant, the charcoal oven is used for freshly cooked dishes served in large or small portions.

Waldorf Astoria
Herengracht 542 ✉ *1017 CG* – ☎ *(0 20) 718 46 00*   Plan: **G3**
– *www.waldorfastoria.com/amsterdam*
83 rm – ♦385/995 € ♦♦385/995 € – ☲ 38 € – 10 suites
• Palace •
Six canal houses from the 17C have been transformed into a luxury hotel with stylish decor, marble bathrooms and staff who are ever attentive to guests' needs. The views add to the appeal, with the front rooms overlooking the Herengracht and those to the rear overlooking the beautiful courtyard. Wonderful!
❀❀ **Librije's Zusje Amsterdam** – See restaurant listing

Pulitzer ☆ 🛎 ℔ & 🅰🅲 🕍 🚗
Plan: **F1**
Prinsengracht 315 ⊠ 1016 GZ – ℰ (020) 523 52 35
– www.pulitzeramsterdam.com
225 rm ⌑ – ♦200/500 € ♦♦200/500 € – 9 suites
• Chain • Historic •

Characterful complex of no less than 25 houses (17C and 18C), set around a beautifully kept garden. The rooms have been tastefully redecorated and the artwork in the communal areas creates a pleasant ambience. Luxury brasserie Jansz is a trendy spot for tasty contemporary dishes at any time of day.

 NH Grand Hotel Krasnapolsky ℔ 🕭 & 🅰🅲 🕍 🚗
Plan: **G1**
Dam 9 ⊠ 1012 JS – ℰ (0 20) 554 91 11
– www.nh-collection.com
451 rm – ♦179/559 € ♦♦179/559 € – ⌑ 30 € – 2 suites
• Luxury • Classic •

Monuments should be cherished, that is why this historic grand hotel dating back to 1855 has been fully renovated. Business people and holidaymakers alike will appreciate the modern luxury and the more classic features. Breakfast in the winter garden and dinner in the stylish Grand Café complete the experience.
The White Room – See restaurant listing

 Conservatorium ☆ ℔ 🌐 🕭 🔲 🅰🅲 🕍
Plan: **E3**
Van Baerlestraat 27 ⊠ 1071 AN – ℰ (0 20) 570 00 00
– www.conservatoriumhotel.com
129 rm – ♦415/900 € ♦♦415/900 € – ⌑ 37 € – 7 suites
• Historic •

The Conservatorium is one of Amsterdam's finest hotels. Neither expense nor effort was spared in the renovation of this neo-Classical jewel that dates back to the end of the 19C. Excellent service, with staff at hand to meet your every need. Pure, unadulterated luxury.
Taiko – See restaurant listing

 art'otel ☆ ℔ 🕭 🔲 🅰🅲 🕍 ✥
Plan: **G1**
Prins Hendrikkade 33 ⊠ 1012 TM – ℰ (0 20) 719 72 00
– www.artotelamsterdam.com
107 rm ⌑ – ♦249/749 € ♦♦249/749 €
• Chain •

From the exhibition in the cellar to the creations in the corridors and bedrooms, art is the theme of this modern hotel. It also exhibits a good grasp of the art of indulgence, from the luxury and comfort of the bedrooms to the exquisite care in the wellness suite. All this with the backdrop of beautiful works of art.

 NH Barbizon Palace ☆ ℔ 🕭 & 🅰🅲 🕍 🚗
Plan: **G1**
Prins Hendrikkade 59 ⊠ 1012 AD – ℰ (0 20) 556 45 64
– www.nh-hotels.com
271 rm ⌑ – ♦320/440 € ♦♦350/480 € – 3 suites
• Chain •

This elegant property directly opposite the station has a hint of 17C charm. Renovations are taking place to upgrade the traditional comfort. The famous Amsterdam canals await discovery from the private jetty. At Bar Mar-Dique discover dishes prepared in a modern bistro style, with a penchant for vegetables.
❀ **Vermeer** – See restaurant listing

 Ambassade ☆ ≤ 🅰🅲
Plan: **F2**
Herengracht 341 ⊠ 1016 AZ – ℰ (0 20) 555 02 22
– www.ambassade-hotel.nl
54 rm – ♦185/315 € ♦♦185/325 € – ⌑ 20 € – 3 suites
• Luxury •

The CoBrA collection and the books in the library signed by authors who have stayed here all testify to the artistic style of this hotel. It is just perfect for art loving Amsterdam!

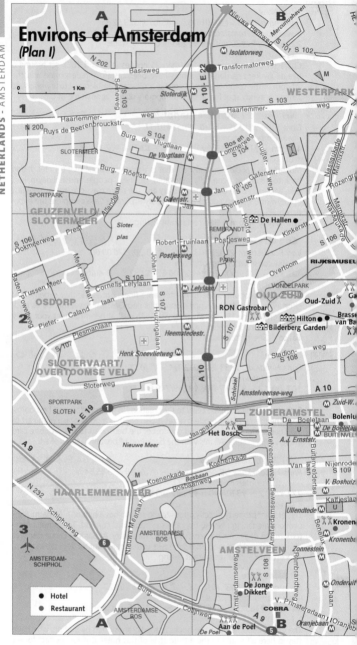

Environs of Amsterdam
(Plan I)

0   1 Km

A

B

N 202

Nieuwe Hemweg

Mercuriushaven

Nieuwe Hemweg

S 101   S 102

Isolatorweg

Transformatorweg

M

Basisweg

A 10 - E 22

WESTERPARK

Sloterdijk

S 103

Haarlemmer-

weg

Haarlemmer-

S 103

weg

1

Haarlemmer-

Ruys de Beerenbrouckstr.

N 200

S 104

Burg. de Vlugtlaan

Bos en

Lommerweg

S 104

SLOTERMEER

De Vlugtlaan

Galenstr.

Burg. Röellstr.

Jan van

S 105

weg

Hoofd

Ruijter

weg

Nassaukade

Marnixstr.

Rozengr

SPORTPARK

J.V. Galenstr.

Evertsenstr.

De Hallen

Kinkerstr.

Nassaukade

Marnixstr.

GEUZENVELD/
SLOTERMEER

Jan

REMBRANDT

S 106

Allendelaan

Pres

Sloter

plas

Robert Fruinlaan

Postjesweg

Postjesweg

PARK

S 106

Meer

en Vaart

RIJKSMUSEI

S 106

Ookmeerweg

Baden Powellweg

Tussen Meer

OSDORP

Cornelis Lelylaan

S 106

Johan-

Huizingalaan

S 107

Lelylaan

Overtoom

VONDELPARK

OUD-ZUID

Oud-Zuid

Gal

Pieter-

Caland

laan

RON Gastrobar

Hilton

Brasse
van Ba

2

Plesmanlaan

Heemstedestr.

S 107

Bilderberg Garden

S 107

Henk Sneevlietweg

A 10

Stadion-
S 108

weg

SLOTERVAART/
OVERTOOMSE VELD

Sloterweg

A 10

Schinkel

Amstelveense-weg

A 10

SPORTPARK
SLOTEN

Zuid-W.

A4 - E 19

ZUIDERAMSTEL

Boleniu

A 9

Jaagpad

Het Bosch

De Boelelaan

De Boelela

A.J. Ernststr.

BUITENVEL

N 232

Nieuwe Meer

Koenenkade

Amstelveenseweg

Buitenveldertse

laan

Van

Nijenrode
S 109

Schipholweg

Koenenkade

Bosbaan

V. Boshuiz

HAARLEMMERMEER

Bosbaanweg

Ullendtede

Kalfjeslaan

U

3

AMSTERDAM-
SCHIPHOL

Nieuwe Meerlaan

AMSTERDAMSE
BOS

Benelux

Kronen

Kronenbu

Zonnestein

AMSTELVEEN

Rembrandtweg

Onderuit

Burg.

De Jonge
Dikkert

Amsteldamseweg

V. Prinstererlaan

Oranje

baan

COBRA

A 9

Oranjebaan

AMSTERDAMSE
BOS

Colijnweg

Aan de Poel

De Poel

A

B

● Hotel

● Restaurant

524

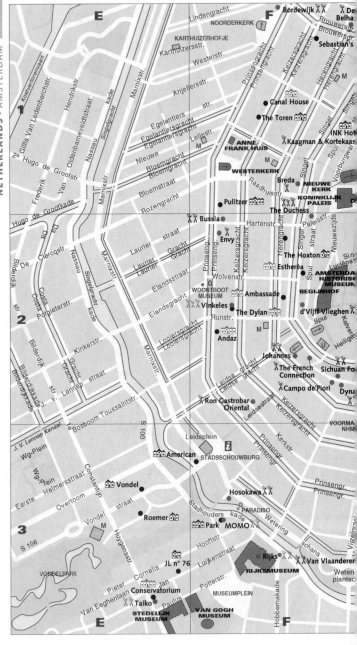

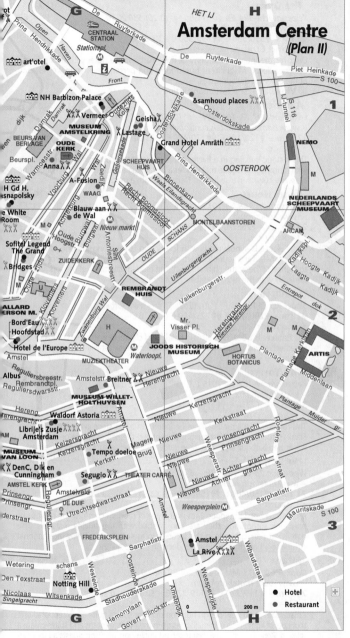

Amsterdam Centre

(Plan II)

HET IJ

H

NETHERLANDS - AMSTERDAM

Prins Hendrikkade
De Ruyterkade
CENTRAAL STATION
Stationspl.
Front
art'otel
G

Piet Heinkade — S 100
S 116
IJ-tunnel

NH Barbizon Palace
Vermeer
Oosterdokskade
&samhoud places

Damrak
Open
Haven
Damrak

dijk

MUSEUM AMSTELKRING
Geisha
Lastage
Grand Hotel Amrâth
NEMO

BEURS VAN BERLAGE
OUDE KERK
Anna
Beurspl.
Prins Hendrikkade

OOSTERDOK

H Gd H. snapolsky
A-Fusion
WAAG

Warmoesstr.
Voorburgw.
Oudezijde
Kolk
Oosterdokskade

Binnenkant
SCHEEPVAART HUIS

e White Room
Blauw aan de Wal
SCHANS
Recht Boomssloot
Recht Boomssloot
Waals Eilandsgracht

NEDERLANDS SCHEEPVAART MUSEUM

Sofitel Legend The Grand
Bridges

Nieuw markt!
MONTELBAANSTOREN
ARCAM

ZUIDERKERK
OUDE

Kadijkspl.
Hoogte Kadijk
Laagte Kadijk

ALLARD PIERSON M.
Bord'Eau
Hoofdstad
Hotel de l'Europe

Uilenburgergracht

Entrepot dok

2

REMBRANDT HUIS

Valkenburgerstr.

M

ARTIS

Amstel
Albus
Regulier sbreestr.
Rembrandtpl.
Reguliersdwarsstr.

Breitner

Mr. Visser Pl.
JOODS HISTORISCH MUSEUM
MUZIEKTHEATER
Waterloopl.
Nieuwe Herengracht
HORTUS BOTANICUS

Plantage Kerklaan
Plantage Middenlaan
Plantage Muider gr.

Hereng.
Herengracht
Waldorf Astoria
MUSEUM WILLET-HOLTHUYSEN

Keizersgracht
Kerkstraat
Roeiersstraat

Librije's Zusje Amsterdam
Keizersgracht
Kerkstr.
Tempo doeloe
Magere Brug

Nieuwe Keizersgracht
Nieuwe Prinsengracht
Prinsengracht
Weesperstr.

MUSEUM VAN LOON
DenC, Dik en Cunningham
Segugio
THEATER CARRÉ

Nieuwe Achter gracht
Nieuwe Achter gracht

AMSTEL KERK
Prinsengr.
Prinsengr.
derstraat

Amstelveld
DE DUIF
Utrechtsedwarsstraat

Amstel
Sarphatistr.

Weesperplein
Mauritskade — S 100

3

FREDERIKSPLEIN

Sarphatistr.
Oosteinde

Amstel
La Rive

Amsteldijk
Wibaudstraat

Wetering
Den Texstraat
Nicolaas
Singelgracht

schans
Notting Hill
Witsenkade
Weteringschans
Stadhouderskade
Hemonylaan
Govert Flinckstr.

0 ___ 200 m

| ● | Hotel |
| ● | Restaurant |

G

H

527

The Dylan

Keizersgracht 384 ✉ *1016 GB* – ℰ *(0 20) 530 20 10*
Plan: **F2**
– *www.dylanamsterdam.com*
40 rm – **†**350/550 € **††**495/550 € – ⥮ 28 € – 2 suites
• Grand Luxury •

Discover the intimate harmony of this 17C boutique hotel with its surprising designer decor. Magnificent guestrooms and personal service make this one of the city's special addresses.

❀ **Vinkeles** – See restaurant listing

American

Leidsekade 97 ✉ *1017 PN* – ℰ *(0 20) 556 30 00*
Plan: **F3**
– *www.hampshire-hotels.com/american*
175 rm – **†**120/180 € **††**120/480 € – ⥮ 20 €
• Palace •

This historic building in a lively square immediately commands your attention with its imposing façade that exudes a certain dignity. Café Americain offers fine brasserie cuisine in a stylish Art Deco pub with a magnificent ceiling.

Canal House

Keizersgracht 148 ✉ *1015 CX* – ℰ *(0 20) 622 51 82*
Plan: **F1**
– *www.canalhouse.nl*
23 rm ⥮ – **†**285/700 € **††**285/700 € – 1 suite
• Luxury •

Canal House is synonymous with luxury and is set alongside one of Amsterdam's canals. Take your pick from guestrooms ranging in category from 'good' to 'better' to 'best', the ultimate treat! The modern character of the rooms fits in perfectly with the historic ambience of this hotel.

Estheréa

Singel 305 ✉ *1012 WJ* – ℰ *(0 20) 624 51 46* – *www.estherea.nl*
Plan: **F2**
91 rm – **†**200/450 € **††**225/480 € – ⥮ 18 € – 2 suites
• Traditional •

The Estheréa is a beautiful, elegant hotel full of charm. Its warm, classic interior clad in red velvet will tempt you in, and its excellent breakfast will win you over completely.

The Toren

Keizersgracht 164 ✉ *1015 CZ* – ℰ *(0 20) 622 63 52*
Plan: **F1**
– *www.thetoren.nl*
38 rm – **†**80/330 € **††**150/600 € – ⥮ 14 € – 2 suites
• Traditional •

This romantic boutique hotel can be found just a few steps away from the Anne Frank House. The breakfast room is elegant and the bedrooms are decorated in a warm, neo-Baroque style. The three garden suites will ensure a memorable stay.

Notting Hill

Westeinde 26 ✉ *1017 ZP* – ℰ *(0 20) 523 10 30*
Plan: **G3**
– *www.hotelnottinghill.nl*
71 rm – **†**150/400 € **††**150/400 € – ⥮ 24 €
• Luxury •

A boutique hotel equipped with every type of modern comfort. The rooms not only look sumptuous, they are also finished with top quality materials. The hotel's car park is handy in this location in the city centre. Enjoy international cuisine to a backdrop of designer decor in the restaurant.

Aitana

IJdok 6 ✉ *1013 MM* – ℰ *(0 20) 891 48 00*
Plan: **C1**
– *www.room-matehotels.com*
285 rm – **†**119/279 € **††**119/279 € – ⥮ 19 € – 6 suites
• Chain •

Amsterdam has a new design hotel on the river IJ, and quite an exceptional one too! Lots of light and a minimalist design in the themed rooms and suites create a relaxed 'Zen-like' feel. Breakfast is served until noon, allowing guests a lazy morning in the comfortable beds. A nice extra touch: the hotel has its own marina.

Park

Stadhouderskade 25 ✉ *1071 ZD* – ℰ *(0 20) 671 12 22*
Plan: **F3**
– www.parkhotel.nl
189 rm – ♦179/409 € ♦♦179/409 € – ⌷ 19 €
• Palace •
Fully renovated, hi-tech hotel set between the Vondelpark and the busy centre.
Five types of spacious and pleasant, trendy rooms. Meeting and fitness facilities.
Stylish service.
MOMO – See restaurant listing

INK Hotel

Nieuwezijds Voorburgwal 67 ✉ *1012 RE* – ℰ *(0 20)*
Plan: **K1**
627 59 00 – www.ink-hotel-amsterdam.com
149 rm – ♦169/369 € ♦♦169/389 € – ⌷ 25 € – 1 suite
• Townhouse • Contemporary •
Full of charm and character, this modern hotel owes its name to the rich history
of the building. Housed in the former home of the newspaper *De Tijd*, the hotel
boasts a decor that is reminiscent of that past, with maps of Amsterdam promi-
nently featured on the walls. Another good story is in the making here.

The Albus

Vijzelstraat 49 ✉ *1017 HE* – ℰ *(0 20) 530 62 00*
Plan: **G2**
– www.albushotel.com
74 rm – ♦99/369 € ♦♦99/369 € – ⌷ 19 €
• Business •
A bright, modern design hotel in the city centre, where the guestrooms have been
named 'smart', 'superb' and 'stunning' depending on their size. A useful tip: the
rooms at the back are particularly quiet. The Senses restaurant also has a relaxed
atmosphere with slow food prepared from top quality produce in a traditional way.

Roemer

Roemer Visscherstraat 10 ✉ *1054 EX* – ℰ *(0 20)*
Plan: **E3**
589 08 00 – www.hotelroemer.com
37 rm – ♦150/300 € ♦♦150/300 € – ⌷ 20 €
• Business •
An attractive hotel with an elegant, designer-style interior, in an early 20C townhouse situated close to the Vondelpark. Modern interior, immaculate rooms and
breakfast served in the garden in summer.

Vondel

Vondelstraat 26 ✉ *1054 GD* – ℰ *(0 20) 612 01 20*
Plan: **E3**
– www.hotelvondel.com
86 rm – ♦150/300 € ♦♦150/300 € – ⌷ 20 €
• Business •
This boutique hotel was created out of seven 1900s houses. Communal areas,
bedrooms and conference room in a decidedly contemporary style. Breakfasts
on the stylish patio when the weather is good. Hip, stylish bistro serving local
and international cuisine.

JL n° 76

Jan Luijkenstraat 76 ✉ *1071 CT* – ℰ *(0 20) 348 55 55*
Plan: **F3**
– www.hoteljlno76.com
39 rm – ♦150/300 € ♦♦150/300 € – ⌷ 20 €
• Luxury •
On Jan Luijkenstraat two 18C townhouses have been converted to form this
pleasant boutique hotel. The rooms are modern, stylish and peaceful, despite
the hotel's location in the bustling, fashionable museum quarter. The restaurant
offers a choice from a concise contemporary menu.

De Hallen

⚒ ♿ 📻 🛁 🚘

Bellamyplein 47 ✉ *1053 AT*   Plan: **B2**
– ☏ *(0 20) 820 86 70*
– *www.hoteldehallen.com*
55 rm – 🧍150/300 € – 🧍🧍150/300 € – 🍴 20 €
• Historic •

The tram depot near Amsterdam's Foodhallen has been converted into a contemporary hotel. You will discover a combination of retro, industrial, trendy and Scandinavian design elements, all of which result in a warm and charming hotel.

The Hoxton

⚒ 🛁

Herengracht 255 ✉ *1016 BJ*   Plan: **K2**
– ☏ *(0 20) 888 55 55*
– *www.thehoxton.com*
111 rm 🍴 – 🧍89/299 € 🧍🧍99/529 €
• Townhouse • Cosy •

The sign outside is tiny, so you might be surprised to step inside The Hoxton and discover a bustling, homely living room. The cosy feel reaches as far as the bedrooms, where vintage and modern elements intertwine. In the restaurant guests can enjoy an à la carte breakfast in the morning and contemporary cuisine later in the day.

Sebastian's

Keizersgracht 15 ✉ *1055 CC* – ☏ *(0 20) 423 23 42*   Plan: **F1**
– *www.hotelsebastians.nl*
34 rm – 🧍70/170 € 🧍🧍100/260 € – 🍴 10 €
• Traditional •

A boutique hotel with an adventurous, yet warm colour scheme. Its convenient location on the Keizersgracht canal, close to the Jordaan area, will suit business travellers and night-owls alike. Trendy bar.

XXXX ✺✺ Bord'Eau – Hotel de l'Europe

🛁 < 🍽 📻 ⇕ 🛋 🅿

Nieuwe Doelenstraat 2 ✉ *1012 CP*   Plan: **G2**
– ☏ *(0 20) 531 16 19* – *www.bordeau.nl*
– *closed 16 July-8 August, first 2 weeks January, Saturday lunch, Sunday and Monday*
Menu 48 € (lunch), 128/176 € – Carte 114/194 € – *(open until 11pm)*
• Creative • Elegant •

Delicious and sophisticated, or deliciously sophisticated, is the best way of summing up this beautiful restaurant. The chef makes every effort to please his clientele with his distinguished, original style of cooking and his use of well-sourced produce. The way he really brings out the flavours is fantastic!
→ Kalfstartaar met kaviaar en aardappel met merg. Rode mul met jus 'à la becasse', artisjok barigoule en toast. Groene appel met walnoot en karamel.

XXXX ✺✺ Librije's Zusje Amsterdam – Hotel Waldorf Astoria

📻 ⇕
🛋

Herengracht 542 ✉ *1017 CG* – ☏ *(0 20) 718 46 43*
– *www.librijeszusje.com* – *closed 23-27 April, 30 July-*   Plan: **G3**
21 August, 1-16 January, Sunday and Monday
Menu 80/150 €
– Carte 98/210 € – *(dinner only except Friday and Saturday)*
• Creative • Luxury •

Extraordinarily beautiful and classy! This refined, classic restaurant offers a true fine dining experience. The food is elegant, with a unique interplay of textures and tastes that is spot on, creating a wonderful harmony where every bite surprises. Definitely worth a visit!
→ Kabeljauwrug met fenergiek, morieljes, konijnniertjes en pecannoot. Ganzenlever en yuzu met buikspek van tonijn, chocolade en krokante garnaaltjes. Taco met suikermais, popcorn, jalapeño en limoen.

NETHERLANDS - AMSTERDAM

XxXX **La Rive** – Hotel Amstel ⇐ 🈯 🄰🄲 ⇔ 🕭 🅿

Prof. Tulpplein 1 ⊠ *1018 GX* – ☎ *(0 20) 520 32 64* Plan: **H3**
– *www.restaurantlarive.com* – *closed 2-21 January*
Menu 105/125 € – Carte approx. 150 € – *(dinner only)*
• Modern French • Chic •

An intimate ambience, refined decor, sublime comfort and exquisite wines characterise this gastronomic restaurant in the Amstel Hotel. The kitchen is modern, producing dishes that show touches of Asian inspiration. The canalside tables are particularly sought after.

XxX **The Duchess** 🄰🄲

Spuistraat 172 ⊠ *1012 VT* – ☎ *(0 20) 811 33 22* Plan: **F2**
– *www.the-duchess.com*
Carte 60/85 € – *(open until 11pm)*
• Mediterranean cuisine • Elegant •

The Duchess has flair. Once the vault of a bank, this is now a stylish restaurant dominated by dark marble with a Belle Epoque atmosphere. The beautiful Molteni kitchen produces Mediterranean dishes with a modern twist.

XxX **Vinkeles** – Hotel The Dylan Plan: **F2**
✿
Keizersgracht 384 ⊠ *1016 GB* – ☎ *(0 20) 530 20 10*
– *www.vinkeles.com* – *closed 1-17 August, 1-20 January, Bank Holidays and Sunday*
Menu 85/140 € – Carte approx. 100 € – *(dinner only)*
• Creative • Friendly • Elegant •

Smart restaurant set in a characterful hotel. Creative, tasty cuisine, served stylishly in the former bakery (view of the old ovens) or facing the courtyard.
➜ Geglaceerde kalfszwezerik met ossenstaartbouillon, fregola en groene tomaat. Wilde zeebaars met serranoham, radijs en pijlinktvis. Rabarber met macadamianoten, havermout en vlierbesbloesem.

XxX **&samhoud places** (Moshik Roth) 🄰🄲 ⇔
✿✿
Oosterdokskade 5 ⊠ *1011 AD* – ☎ *(0 20) 260 20 94* Plan: **H1**
– *www.samhoudplaces.com* – *closed first 2 weeks August, first 2 weeks January, Monday and Tuesday*
Menu 130/170 €
– Carte 123/295 € – *(dinner only except Friday and Sunday)*
• Creative • Design •

Moshik Roth invites you on an adventure. This fashionable establishment will take you from one pleasant surprise to the next. The chef knows how to combine inventiveness with refinement for a fantastic flavour experience, extracting the best from top-quality ingredients with absolute precision.
➜ Mona Lisa aardappel met een zwartetruffelemulsie. Kalfszwezerik in hooi gegaard met kumquat en een kumbava-infusie. Guanaja chocoladessoufflé met citrusfruit en angelica.

XxX **The White Room** – NH Grand Hotel Krasnapolsky 🅖 🄰🄲 🕭 🚗

Dam 9 ⊠ *1012 JS* – ☎ *(020) 554 94 54* Plan: **L1**
– *www.nh-collection.com* – *closed 26 July-9 August, 3-18 January, Tuesday lunch, Wednesday lunch, Sunday and Monday*
Menu 38 € (lunch), 65/105 € – Carte approx. 95 € – *(booking essential at dinner)* *(set menu only at weekends)*
• Modern cuisine • Classic décor • Elegant •

The white and gold dining room (1885) has the feel of an ancient Austrian palace, magnificently combining classic elegance with modern furnishings. The influence of top chef Jacob Jan Boerma is clear here from the interplay of acidity and citrus in modern combinations. Beautifully seasoned and a delight for the eyes.

Bridges – Hotel Sofitel The Grand

O.Z. Voorburgwal 197 ⊠ 1012 EX – ✆ (0 20) 555 35 60   Plan: **G2**
– www.bridgesrestaurant.nl – closed Monday
Menu 30 € (lunch), 69/89 € – Carte 68/96 €
• Seafood • Elegant •

The dishes on offer in this beautiful fish restaurant combine refinement, surprise, originality and quality, and are worthy of the utmost praise. Overall, good quality, reasonably priced cuisine.

→ Langoustines met gekonfijte aardappel, zilverui, wortel en dennennaaldenbouillon. Gelakte rogvleugel op crème van rijst met garnalenjus, zeegroenten en amandel. Haagse passie met bittere chocolade, Haagsche hopjes en passievrucht.

Vermeer – Hotel NH Barbizon Palace

Prins Hendrikkade 59 ⊠ 1012 AD – ✆ (0 20) 556 48 85   Plan: **G1**
– www.restaurantvermeer.nl – closed 24 July-13 August, 25 December-8 January, Bank Holidays and Sunday
Menu 65/85 € – (dinner only)
• Organic • Design • Elegant •

The simple design makes this beautiful restaurant a relaxed spot. Chef Naylor offers food with a personal touch, with generous use of produce from his own vegetable garden, located on the hotel roof. His dishes are well thought through and inventive, creating delicious contrasts and harmonies for an intense flavour experience.

→ Met appel en zurkel gemarineerde makreel, komkommer, yoghurt en avocado. Gebraden lamsrug met knoflook en munt, gebakken artisjok en walnootjus. Slaatje van aardbeien met agavelikeur en chiboustcreme met limoen.

RIJKS®

Museumstraat 2 ⊠ 1077 XX – ✆ (0 20) 674 75 55   Plan: **F3**
– www.rijksrestaurant.nl – closed 27 April, 31 December dinner and 1 January
Menu 40 € (lunch)/68 € – Carte 38/63 €
• Modern French • Brasserie •

This lively, luxurious brasserie belonging to the Rijksmuseum is a surefire winner. The flavours are recognizable but the inventive style of cooking is a surprise and, despite the huge range of flavours and textures, everything is well-balanced. The descriptions are intriguing and exciting and dishes certainly live up to expectations.

→ Gestoomde heek met gekonfijte Opperdoezer Ronde en aïoli van geroosterde mosselen. Zacht gegaarde schol met fregola, tomaat en basilicumvinaigrette. Perzik met Texelse geitenkaas, verse amandelen en waterkers.

Hoofdstad – Hotel de l'Europe

Nieuwe Doelenstraat 2 ⊠ 1012 CP – ✆ (0 20) 531 16 19   Plan: **G2**
– www.hoofdstadbrasserie.nl
Menu 37 € – Carte 60/102 € – (open until 11 pm)
• Classic cuisine • Cosy •

On the terrace of this luxurious canal-side brasserie, with its views of bridges and passing boats, Amsterdam really comes into its own. The delicious dishes, which are uncomplicated yet always full of flavour, can also be enjoyed indoors. Sole Meunière and charcoal-grilled entrecote are just two of the kitchen's culinary delights.

Dynasty

Reguliersdwarsstraat 30 ⊠ 1017 BM – ✆ (0 20)   Plan: **F2**
626 84 00 – www.fer.nl – closed 27 December-31 January and Tuesday
Menu 45/68 € – Carte 38/69 € – (dinner only ; open until 11pm)
• Chinese • Exotic décor •

A pleasant, long-standing restaurant featuring cuisine from around Asia. The trendy, exotic décor is warm and colourful. There's a lovely terrace at the back and service is attentive.

XX **d'Vijff Vlieghen** 🏧 ⇔

Spuistraat 294 (via Vlieghendesteeg 1) ⊠ 1012 VX Plan: **F2**
*– ℰ (0 20) 530 40 60 – www.vijffvlieghen.nl – closed 27 April, 24 July-
6 August, 24 December-3 January*
Menu 40/116 € 🍷 – Carte 51/61 € – *(dinner only)*
• Traditional cuisine • Rustic •

The classic dishes on offer at these charming 17C premises are all prepared with
typical Dutch products. A set menu is served in various attractive, country-style
dining rooms where original Rembrandt sketches decorate the walls.

XX **Taiko** – Hotel Conservatorium ⅄ 🏧

Van Baerlestraat 27 ⊠ 1071 AN – ℰ (0 20) 570 00 00 Plan: **E3**
– www.conservatoriumhotel.com – closed Sunday
Menu 78/115 € – Carte 43/128 € – *(dinner only)*
• Asian influences • Intimate •

Taiko is an atmospheric, cosmopolitan restaurant and deliciously trendy. The
establishment serves a contemporary take on Asian cuisine. It is beautifully presented, diverse and pure in flavour.

XX **Breitner** ⇐

Amstel 212 ⊠ 1017 AH – ℰ (0 20) 627 78 79 Plan: **G2**
*– www.restaurant-breitner.nl – closed 24 July-7 August, 25 December-
8 January and Sunday*
Menu 40/45 € – Carte 53/68 € – *(dinner only)*
• Creative French • Chic •

Creative and elaborate meals are served in a classical modern setting. There are
views over the Amstel with sightseeing boats and landmarks (drawbridges, the
Hermitage museum) in the background.

XX **Anna** 🏧

Warmoesstraat 111 ⊠ 1012 JA – ℰ (0 20) 428 11 11 Plan: **G1**
*– www.restaurantanna.nl – closed Easter Monday, Whit Monday, 24, 25
and 26 December and Sunday*
Menu 48/65 € – Carte 49/58 € – *(dinner only)*
• Modern cuisine • Fashionable •

There is no lack of vitality at Anna given its location in the middle of the vibrant
red-light district. This cosmopolitan restaurant has a relaxed and informal atmosphere – a choice setting for balanced, modern cooking.

XX **Hosokawa** 🏧 ⇔

Max Euweplein 22 ⊠ 1017 MB – ℰ (0 20) 638 80 86 Plan: **F3**
– www.hosokawa.nl – closed 31 December, 1 January and Tuesday
Menu 50/95 € – Carte 37/98 €
• Teppanyaki • Minimalist •

A sober, modern Japanese restaurant with a sushi bar; it's worth a detour to
watch the entertaining show of food rotating past your eyes!

XX **Segugio** 🏧 ⇔

Utrechtsestraat 96 ⊠ 1017 VS – ℰ (0 20) 330 15 03 Plan: **G3**
*– www.segugio.nl – closed 27 April, 24, 25 and 31 December-1 January
and Sunday*
Menu 45/58 € – Carte 53/63 € – *(dinner only)*
• Italian • Friendly •

This establishment with three modern dining rooms on several levels features
sunny Italian cuisine made right before your eyes. Good selection of Italian
wines.

XX **Sichuan Food** 🏧 ⇔

Reguliersdwarsstraat 35 ⊠ 1017 BK – ℰ (0 20) 626 93 27 Plan: **F2**
– www.sichuanfood.nl – closed 31 December
Menu 32/76 € – Carte 36/88 € – *(dinner only)*
• Chinese • Exotic décor •

Small Chinese restaurant with a good local reputation, situated in a lively area.
The Beijing duck is prepared and served in the dining room.

XX **Van Vlaanderen** 🏠 AC ⇔

Weteringschans 175 ⊠ *1017 XD* – ☎ *(0 20) 622 82 92* Plan: **F3**
– *www.restaurant-vanvlaanderen.nl* – *closed 27 December-3 January,*
Saturday lunch, Sunday and Monday
Menu 30 € (lunch), 37/60 € – Carte 54/67 €
• Modern cuisine • Classic décor •
Van Vlaanderen has long been recognised as the place to go for the good
things in life. It has a pleasant location in the centre of Amsterdam with its
own jetty on the patio. The restaurant's success lies in attentive service and a
young, spirited team whose enthusiasm is evident in the modern, original versions of the classic dishes served here.

XX **DenC, Dik en Cunningham** AC ⇔

Kerkstraat 377 ⊠ *1017 HW* – ☎ *(0 20) 422 27 66* Plan: **G3**
– *www.restaurantdenc.nl* – *closed Saturday lunch and Sunday*
Menu 28 € (lunch), 36/65 €
• Creative French • Classic décor •
The deer heads on the walls of this contemporary restaurant hint at chef Dik's
hunter-family upbringing and, unsurprisingly, his cooking puts the spotlight
firmly on game. Sommelier Cunningham's choice of wines make a good match.

XX **Bussia** ⇔

Reestraat 28 ⊠ *1016 DN* – ☎ *(0 20) 627 87 94* Plan: **F2**
– *www.bussia.nl* – *closed Tuesday lunch, Wednesday lunch and Monday*
Menu 36 € (lunch), 46/79 € – Carte 53/62 €
• Italian • Trendy •
A restrained yet stylish modern restaurant that conjures up Italian cuisine with a
French influence. This is accompanied by an impressive choice of fine Italian
wines presented by the female owner. As a bonus, the open kitchen enables
you to look behind the scenes.

XX **Bordewijk** 🏠 AC

Noordermarkt 7 ⊠ *1015 MV* – ☎ *(0 20) 624 38 99* Plan: **F1**
– *www.bordewijk.nl* – *closed mid July-mid August, 24 December-*
2 January, Sunday and Monday
Menu 39 € – Carte 52/71 € – *(dinner only until 11pm)*
• Modern cuisine • Friendly •
Popular restaurant due to its modern menu with inventive touches and minimalist décor: bare floorboards, Formica tables and designer chairs. Noisy atmosphere when busy.

XX **Johannes** 🏠

Herengracht 413 ⊠ *1017 BP* – ☎ *(0 20) 626 95 03* Plan: **F2**
– *www.restaurantjohannes.nl* – *closed 27 April, 31 December and 1 January*
Menu 49 € – *(dinner only) (tasting menu only)*
• International • Trendy •
Take your place in the pleasant dining room or on the terrace, and let Johannes surprise you. All you have to do is choose the number of courses, then sit back and
enjoy balanced dishes. These often feature bold and unusual combinations and
techniques, as well as distinctive flavours blended together in delicious harmony.

XX **MOS** 🏠 ⇔

IJdok 185 ⊠ *1013 MM* – ☎ *(0 20) 638 08 66* Plan: **G1**
– *www.mosamsterdam.nl* – *closed Sunday and Monday*
Menu 36 € (lunch), 50/65 € – Carte 62/76 € – *(bookings advisable at dinner)*
• Creative French • Trendy •
The interior is relaxed and chic, the large windows offer a fantastic view of the IJ
river, and the food is delicious. MOS is sublime. The chef shows how a little creativity
conjures up a variety of prominent flavours, producing balanced combinations that
are both rich and refined. Guests are advised to ask about parking when reserving.
➔ Gebrande dorade met ganzenlever, manzanilla, krokante kippenhuid en
blauwe bessen. Geroosterde Iberico procureurstuk met tortilla, paarse spits-
kool, cashewnoten en een chorizovinaigrette. Dessert van ananas met
kokos en kaffirlimoen.

XX **MOMO** – Hotel Park   ᚠ 🅰🅲

Hobbemastraat 1 ⊠ 1071 XZ – 𝒞 (0 20) 671 74 74   Plan: **F3**
– www.momo-amsterdam.com
Menu 23 € (lunch), 62/72 €
– Carte 40/90 € – (open until 11pm) (bar lunch)
• Asian • Brasserie •

MOMO is still one of the city's hot spots, with fusion cuisine in a fashionable setting. Bento (Japanese lunch box) at lunchtime and a menu designed for sharing in the evening.

XX **Blauw aan de Wal**   🕸 🛋 🅰🅲 ⇔

O.Z. Achterburgwal 99 ⊠ 1012 DD – 𝒞 (0 20) 330 22 57   Plan: **G2**
– www.blauwaandewal.com – closed Sunday
Menu 55/68 € – *(dinner only until 11pm) (booking advisable) (tasting menu only)*
• Market cuisine • Friendly •

A popular restaurant at the end of a cul-de-sac in the lively red light district. Discreet décor, simple and tasty modern cuisine, good wine selection and a shady terrace.

X **Envy**   🅰🅲
🙂
Prinsengracht 381 ⊠ 1016 HL – 𝒞 (0 20) 344 64 07   Plan: **F2**
– www.envy.nl
Carte 30/55 € – *(dinner only except Friday, Saturday and Sunday)*
• Mediterranean cuisine • Brasserie •

A new-style brasserie with dining on either side of a long refectory table under low, spherical lights or standing at one of the smaller tables. All the food is on display in glass showcases.

X **Lastage** (Rogier van Dam)   🅰🅲
❀
Geldersekade 29 ⊠ 1011 EJ – 𝒞 (0 20) 737 08 11   Plan: **G1**
– www.restaurantlastage.nl – closed 27 and 28 April, 24 July-14 August, 26 December-2 January and Monday
Menu 43/89 € – *(dinner only)*
• Creative • Bistro •

At Lastage you'll find a concise selection of tempting dishes full of character and depth, like vichyssoise of potato with mackerel tartare or veal cheek confit with lobster. The relatively small bill at the end will make the experience even more enjoyable.
→ Rode mul en garnaal met garam masalacrème, augurk en saus van rode paprika en saffraan. Beemsterlam met artisjok, tomaat en lamsjus. Aarbeien en witte chocolade met speculaas en rabarbersorbet.

X **De Belhamel**   ≼ 🛋 🅰🅲 ⇔

Brouwersgracht 60 ⊠ 1013 GX – 𝒞 (0 20) 622 10 95   Plan: **F1**
– www.belhamel.nl
Menu 35/45 € – Carte 45/53 €
• Classic cuisine • Bistro •

This art nouveau style restaurant is located at the confluence of two canals and has a delightful terrace overlooking the water. Influences from France and Italy combine to deliver tasty dishes with clearly defined flavours.

X **Tempo doeloe**   🅰🅲
🙂
Utrechtsestraat 75 ⊠ 1017 VJ – 𝒞 (0 20) 625 67 18   Plan: **G3**
– www.tempodoeloerestaurant.nl – closed 27 April, 25, 26 and 31 December-1 January and Sunday
Menu 37/50 € – Carte 37/62 € – *(dinner only)*
• Indonesian •

Regular diners at Tempo doeloe or 'Times Gone By' find it difficult to hide their enthusiasm when they visit this restaurant. They know that an Indonesian feast like no other in Amsterdam awaits them. The food here is authentically Indonesian, with no concessions to Western tastes. Selamat makan!

A-Fusion
Zeedijk 130 ⊠ *1012 BC – ℰ (0 20) 330 40 68*   Plan: **G1**
– www.a-fusion.nl
Menu 18 € (lunch), 34/45 € – Carte 23/41 € – *(open until 11pm)*
• Asian • Bistro •
A fusion of Chinese and Japanese cuisine in the heart of Amsterdam's Chinatown. This restaurant boasts a grill, sushi bar, dim sum and wok kitchen. Be sure to try the prawn dim sum, the beef with a black pepper sauce and the oysters with ginger. Alternatively, give the cooks carte blanche to come up with some surprising choices.

Bistrot Neuf
Haarlemmerstraat 9 ⊠ *1013 EH – ℰ (0 20) 400 32 10*   Plan: **G1**
– www.bistrotneuf.nl
Menu 20/34 € – Carte 42/72 €
• Classic cuisine • Bistro •
With its clean, modern design, this relaxed bistro is ideally located in a lively area of Amsterdam. Traditional French dishes exhibit original Amsterdam flair and are impeccably cooked to bring out the true flavours of the ingredients. Efficient service.

Geisha
Prins Hendrikkade 106a ⊠ *1011 AJ – ℰ (0 20) 626 24 10*   Plan: **G1**
– www.restaurantgeisha.nl – closed 27 April, 25 and 31 December,
1 January and Sunday
Menu 33/55 € – Carte 27/74 € – *(dinner only)*
• Asian • Fashionable •
Run by the Wang sisters, this restaurant decorated in a trendy style specialises in innovative Asian cuisine. The small portions allow diners to sample a variety of dishes.

Ron Gastrobar Oriental
Kerkstraat 23 ⊠ *1017 GA – ℰ (0 20) 223 53 52*   Plan: **F2**
– www.rongastrobaroriental.nl – closed 27 April, 31 December and
1 January
Carte 32/62 € – *(dinner only until 11 pm) (booking advisable)*
• Chinese • Trendy •
Subtle lighting, Asian decor and natural materials set the mood at this stylish restaurant, while a renowned bartender shakes cocktails at the extensive bar. Full of flavour, the delicious dishes offer a contemporary take on traditional Chinese cuisine.

Campo de' Fiori
Regulierdwarsstraat 32 ⊠ *1017 BM – ℰ (0 20) 303 95 00*   Plan: **F2**
– www.campodefiori.nl – closed Monday lunch, Tuesday lunch and
Wednesday lunch
Menu 33 € (lunch)/39 € – Carte 41/62 €
• Italian • Trendy •
Close your eyes, savour the cuisine and imagine you are on the Campo de' Fiori in Rome. The chef may include modern features in his dishes but the flavours remain deliciously authentic. This welcoming establishment is well worth a visit, as is its enclosed garden.

The French Connection
Singel 460 ⊠ *1017 AW – ℰ (0 20) 737 30 51*   Plan: **K2**
– www.tfcrestaurant.nl
Menu 38/70 € – Carte 39/54 € – *(dinner only)*
• Creative French • Friendly •
France is clearly the theme here, from the rustic interior to the menu. The experienced chefs serve up tasty dishes delivering a creative take on classic French recipes, achieving refined precision and great value for money.

✗ Breda

Singel 210 ✉ 1016 AB – ℰ (0 20) 622 52 33   Plan: **J1**
– www.breda-amsterdam.com
Menu 30 € (lunch), 50/80 € – *(bookings advisable at dinner) (surprise menu only)*
• Modern cuisine • Brasserie •

Welcome to Breda: dazzling, a touch retro, and luxurious too, but above all a place for delicious food. Choose from surprise menus featuring a range of inventive dishes created by the chef. International, varied and tasty.

✗ Kaagman & Kortekaas

Sint Nicolaasstraat 43 ✉ 1012 NJ – ℰ (0 20) 233 65 44   Plan: **J1**
– www.kaagmanenkortekaas.nl – closed Sunday and Monday
Menu 37/57 € – *(dinner only) (booking essential)*
• Market cuisine • Traditional décor •

Giel Kaagman and Bram Kortekaas focus on quality in their informal bistro. The chef likes to work with game and poultry, making his own charcuterie and terrines. These are cleverly worked into dishes that present an up-to-date take on traditional flavours.

✗ BAK restaurant

Van Diemenstraat 408 ✉ 1013 CR – ℰ (0 20) 737 25 53   Plan: **C1**
– www.bakrestaurant.nl – closed 25 December-2 January, Monday, Tuesday and after 8.30pm
Menu 50/60 € – *(dinner only except Saturday and Sunday) (tasting menu only)*
• Vegetarian • Vintage •

Responsibly produced, respectfully cultivated ingredients are like gold dust, and that is what it takes to create dazzling dishes. The chef here produces particularly convincing vegetarian combinations, while also using a little meat and fish from time to time. Make sure you ask for a table at the window, where you will have a lovely view of the IJ river.

SOUTH and WEST QUARTERS

🏨 Okura

Ferdinand Bolstraat 333 ✉ 1072 LH – ℰ (0 20)   Plan: **C2**
678 71 11 – www.okura.nl
291 rm – ♦220/470 € ♦♦220/470 € – ☲ 30 € – 9 suites
• Palace •

A luxurious Japanese-style hotel set in a modern tower building. Various types of rooms and suites, superb wellness centre, extensive conference facilities and a full range of services.
❀❀ **Ciel Bleu** • ❀ **Yamazato** • ❀ **Sazanka** • 🍴 **Serre** – See restaurant listing

🏨 Hilton

Apollolaan 138 ✉ 1077 BG – ℰ (0 20) 710 60 00   Plan: **B2**
– www.amsterdam.hilton.com
271 rm – ♦199/499 € ♦♦229/529 € – ☲ 27 € – 4 suites
• Chain • Elegant •

A modern apartment-style building with a waterside garden and several terraces. Contemporary rooms and suites with panoramic views, one of which was the scene of John and Yoko's 'bed-in' in 1969.

🏨 Bilderberg Garden

Dijsselhofplantsoen 7 ✉ 1077 BJ – ℰ (0 20) 570 56 00   Plan: **B2**
– www.bilderberg.nl/hotels/garden-hotel
122 rm – ♦129/329 € ♦♦129/329 € – ☲ 19 € – 2 suites
• Business • Elegant •

A chain hotel catering mainly to corporate customers and set in the business district. It has an inviting interior, spacious, comfortable guestrooms, good meeting facilities and valet parking.

The College
Roelof Hartstraat 1 ✉ *1071 VE –* ☎ *(0 20) 571 15 11* Plan: **C2**
– www.thecollegehotel.com
40 rm – ♦119/390 € ♦♦119/470 € – ☲ 20 €
• **Grand Luxury** •

In this 19C school building, The College gives promising students the chance to gain experience, and they do so with conviction - their enthusiasm ensuring that guests lack nothing. Stay in stylish rooms where authentic elements provide a touch of distinction. The bar-lounge is open for a bite to eat at any time of the day.

Arena
's-Gravesandestraat 51 ✉ *1092 AA –* ☎ *(0 20) 850 24 00* Plan: **C2**
– www.hotelarena.nl
116 rm – ♦89/229 € ♦♦89/229 € – ☲ 19 €
• **Historic** • **Townhouse** •

This historic building dating back to 1890 was once an orphanage; today it is an ultra-trendy hotel. Three beautiful staircases and other authentic features remain as reminders of the past, but Arena combines these with modern comfort and smart design. The restaurant is also thoroughly contemporary.

The Manor
Linnaeusstraat 89 ✉ *1093 EK –* ☎ *(0 20) 700 84 00* Plan: **C2**
– www.hampshirehotelmanoramsterdam.com
125 rm ☲ **–** ♦140/500 € ♦♦155/500 €
• **Chain** •

A former civic hospital that has been transformed into a delightful place to stay. This is thanks to its carefully maintained historic character and the harmonious use of modern, trendy materials. Every comfort is provided for your stay, and you can easily explore the city from the tram that stops nearby.

Albert
Albert Cuypstraat 6 ✉ *1072 CT –* ☎ *(0 20) 305 30 20* Plan: **C2**
– www.siralberthotel.com
87 rm – ♦160/425 € ♦♦160/425 € – ☲ 24 € – 3 suites
• **Townhouse** • **Design** •

Sir Albert receives you with open arms in his boutique hotel. The spirit of the hotel's namesake is kept alive through subtle touches, such as notes on the mirrors and works of art. Design and luxury rule supreme in all the rooms, which are decorated mainly in black and white. This top quality address is situated in De Pijp, a residential district of Amsterdam.

Ciel Bleu – Hotel Okura, 23ste etage
Ferdinand Bolstraat 333 ✉ *1072 LH –* ☎ *(0 20)* Plan: **C2**
678 74 50 – www.cielbleu.nl – closed 6-20 August, 31 December-
8 January and Sunday
Menu 110/185 € – Carte 110/175 € – *(dinner only)*
• **Creative** • **Elegant** •

A chic restaurant at the top of the Okura Hotel with superb contemporary décor and a fascinating urban panorama. Experience stylish service, delicious creative cuisine with exotic touches, a fine wine list and sunset views from the lounge.
→ Koningskrab met kaviaar, roomijs van 'beurre blanc' en gezouten citroen. Dorset lamsrug op twee manieren bereid. Virunga cacao met bramen, yuzu en oude rum.

Yamazato – Hotel Okura
Ferdinand Bolstraat 333 ✉ *1072 LH –* ☎ *(0 20)* Plan: **C2**
678 74 50 – www.yamazato.nl – closed 19-28 July and Monday
Menu 40 € (lunch), 75/115 € – Carte 29/173 €
• **Japanese** • **Minimalist** •

Excellent Japanese restaurant featuring authentic Kaiseki cuisine, Sukiya-style décor and a sushi bar. Meticulous and friendly service. Simplified lunch menu possible (bento box).
→ Omakase en nigiri sushi. Tempura van kreeft. Shabu shabu, dunne plakjes entrecote en groenten in een bouillon.

XX **The Roast Room** 🛋 ⇔

Europaplein 2 ✉ 1078 GZ – ℰ (0 20) 723 96 14   Plan: **C2**
– www.theroastroom.nl – closed 27 April
Menu 35 € (lunch), 65/85 € – Carte 57/80 € – *(open until 11.30pm)*
• Meats and grills • Trendy •

An impressive steakhouse. Glass, steel and meat are the dominant features of the Roast Bar (brasserie on the ground floor) and the Rotisserie (restaurant upstairs). See the meat hanging ready to cook, smell it on the grill and taste the results when it has been cooked to perfection. Excellent side dishes complete the picture.

XX **Het Bosch** ⩽ 🛋 🅿

Jollenpad 10 ✉ 1081 KC – ℰ (0 20) 644 58 00   Plan: **B3**
– www.hetbosch.com – closed 26 December-8 January and Sunday
Menu 40 € (lunch), 45/75 € – Carte 46/83 €
• Modern French • Trendy •

The restaurant and patio of this cube-shaped, up-to-the-minute restaurant offer views of the marina at Nieuwe Meer. Classic dishes with an adventurous twist feature on the menu. In summer, Het Bosch Waterfront serves cocktails and barbecued choices on – as its name suggests – the waterfront.

XX **Visaandeschelde** 🛋 🅰🅲 🥘 (dinner)

Scheldeplein 4 ✉ 1078 GR – ℰ (0 20) 675 15 83   Plan: **C2**
– www.visaandeschelde.nl – closed 27 April, 31 December-1 January,
Saturday lunch and Sunday lunch
Menu 35 € (lunch)/45 € – Carte 51/93 € – *(open until 11pm)*
• Seafood • Traditional décor •

Set opposite the RAI congress centre, this restaurant is popular with Amsterdammers for its dishes full of the flavours of the sea, its contemporary brasserie décor and its lively atmosphere.

XX **Le Garage** 🅰🅲 ⇔ 🥘
🍂
Ruysdaelstraat 54 ✉ 1071 XE – ℰ (0 20) 679 71 76   Plan: **B2**
– www.restaurantlegarage.nl – closed Saturday lunch and Sunday lunch
Menu 30 € (lunch), 37/48 € – Carte 55/65 €
• French • Fashionable •

Smart restaurant with a luxury brasserie interior where guests can choose from an appealing set menu and an extensive à la carte. Both are founded on quality ingredients and prepared in a French style, with a touch of creativity. At En Pluche, the lively neighbouring establishment, the dishes are slightly simpler but no less sublime.

XX **Serre** – Hotel Okura 🅰🅲 🥘 🅿
🍂
Ferdinand Bolstraat 333 ✉ 1072 LH – ℰ (0 20)   Plan: **C2**
678 74 50 – www.okura.nl – closed 16-27 January
Menu 37/40 € – Carte 37/65 €
• Modern cuisine • Brasserie •

Luxurious, French brasserie ambience, select menus, sensible prices and a young enthusiastic team in the kitchen. A favourite hotel restaurant for locals.

XX **Sazanka** – Hotel Okura 🅰🅲 🥘 🅿
❀
Ferdinand Bolstraat 333 ✉ 1072 LH – ℰ (0 20)   Plan: **C2**
678 74 50 – www.okura.nl
Menu 83/115 € – Carte 52/131 € – *(dinner only)*
• Teppanyaki • Friendly •

Sazanka takes you on an adventure to Japan. The sober interior and waitresses dressed in kimonos set the tone; then enters the chef, who proudly takes his place behind the teppan-yaki grill. He confidently demonstrates his skills and uses excellent ingredients to create flavours which provide contrast but are always well balanced. What a show!
→ Gegrilde oesters met yuzuboter. Teppanyaki van zeebaars in zeezoutkorst met prei. Sukiyakirol van wagyurund en tamago saus.

XX
🍽️ **Brasserie van Baerle**   🏵️ 🏠 ⇔

Van Baerlestraat 158 ✉ 1071 BG – ☏ (0 20) 679 15 32   Plan: **B2**
– www.brasserievanbaerle.nl – closed 27 April, 25, 26 and 31 December-
1 January, Monday lunch and Saturday lunch
Menu 37 € – Carte 48/63 €
• Classic cuisine • Vintage •

This retro brasserie attracts regular customers, mainly from the local area because of its appealing menu, tasty steak tartare and well-matched wines. Courtyard terrace.

XX
Jaspers   ⇔

Ceintuurbaan 196 ✉ 1072 GC – ☏ (0 20) 471 52 33   Plan: **C2**
– www.restaurantjaspers.nl – closed 28 July-28 August, 30 December-
4 January, Sunday and Monday
Menu 38/78 € – (dinner only) (tasting menu only)
• Creative French • Trendy •

Although there is no choice on offer in this restaurant (only a set menu), this is more than compensated for by the fresh ingredients used. Jaspers' cooking style demonstrates French roots with a modern twist.

XX
Restaurant C   🏠 ⇔

Wibautstraat 125 ✉ 1091 GL – ☏ (0 20) 210 30 11   Plan: **G3**
– www.c.amsterdam – closed 1 January
Menu 25 € (lunch), 45/65 € – Carte 32/44 €
• Creative French • Trendy • Chic •

The contemporary, chic Restaurant Celsius is a dazzling spot, especially the kitchen bar. The reference to degrees emphasises the precision the chefs strive for, because that is what makes the difference between good food and delicious cuisine. Creativity in the combination of strong flavours and textures makes C a top choice.

XX
🕸️ **Bolenius**   🏵️ 🏠 ⇔

George Gershwinlaan 30 ✉ 1082 MT – ☏ (0 20)   Plan: **B2**
404 44 11 – www.bolenius-restaurant.nl – closed Easter, 27 April,
Pentecost, 29 July-14 August, 27 December-3 January and Sunday
Menu 35 € (lunch), 69/99 € – Carte 67/86 €
• Creative • Design •

At Bolenius you will discover how sleek Scandinavian design can be – and this is reflected in the meticulous presentation of the dishes. The chef is a creative soul who likes to experiment and provoke reactions. Vegetables play an important role in this exciting culinary experience, which really explores the power of natural flavours.
→ Langoustines met komkommer, zeewier en witte ui. Lam en gepofte aubergine, sjalot en tuinkruiden. Aardbeien en tomaat met sorbetijs van pittig gekruide olie.

XX
🕸️ **RON Gastrobar** (Ron Blaauw)   🏠 🎦 ⇔ 🎋

Sophialaan 55 ✉ 1075 BP – ☏ (0 20) 496 19 43   Plan: **B2**
– www.rongastrobar.nl – closed 27 April, 31 December-1 January
Carte approx. 60 €
• Creative French • Fashionable •

Ron Blaauw returns to basics here, creating cuisine that is pure and prepared with quality ingredients. This urban gastro-bar combines a hip, lively ambience with top class cuisine without the frills. It also means little formality but original, delicious food and sensational flavours. Phenomenal value for money, which is also reflected in the wine list.
→ Gebakken ganzenlever met gemarineerde bietjes, krenten in madeira en parmezaanschuim. Barbecue spare ribs met huisgemaakte sambal. Surprise ei.

Sinne (Alexander Ioannou)

Ceintuurbaan 342 ✉ *1072 GP –* ✆ *(0 20) 682 72 90*   Plan: **C2**
– www.restaurantsinne.nl – closed Monday and Tuesday
Menu 38/85 € – *(dinner only except Sunday) (booking essential)*
• Modern cuisine • Trendy •

The open kitchen at the back of this warm and friendly restaurant is reminiscent of a theatre scene. While chef Ioannou plays the lead role, the top quality produce steals the show in the form of modern, meticulously prepared dishes. Attentive service from hostess Suzanne, as well as reasonable prices.
➜ Zachtgegaarde kabeljauw met rettich en bouillon van appel, venkel en bleekselderij. Black angusrund op de barbecue geroosterd met seizoensgarnituur en rodewijnsaus. Aardbeien met verveine, olijfoliepoeder, yoghurt en basilicum.

Le Hollandais

Amsteldijk 41 ✉ *1074 HV –* ✆ *(0 20) 679 12 48*   Plan: **C2**
– www.lehollandais.nl – closed 26 April, 3 weeks in August, Sunday and Monday
Menu 37/53 € – Carte 52/60 € – *(dinner only)*
• Classic cuisine • Vintage •

Feeling a little nostalgic? Then this is the place for you, as Le Hollandais really turns the clock back. The dining hall is reminiscent of the 1970s and the chef still serves up generous dishes with rich flavours, just like the old days. You will experience classic French cuisine the way it is meant to taste.

Elkaar

Alexanderplein 6 ✉ *1018 CG –* ✆ *(0 20) 330 75 59*   Plan: **C2**
– www.etenbijelkaar.nl – closed 27 April, 25 and 31 December-1 January, Saturday lunch and Sunday dinner
Menu 30 € (lunch), 37/55 € – Carte approx. 46 €
• Modern French • Family •

If you are looking for a relaxed meal out together, this friendly establishment with a pleasant summer terrace is a great option. The set menu is a good choice, offering a selection from the à la carte menu. The chef combines quality ingredients in a contemporary manner, creating beautiful flavours without overcomplicating things.

Oud-Zuid

Johannes Verhulststraat 64 ✉ *1071 NH –* ✆ *(0 20)*   Plan: **B2**
676 60 58 – www.restaurantoudzuid.nl – closed 27 April, 25, 26 and 31 December-1 January
Menu 28 € (lunch)/35 € – Carte 47/59 €
• Classic cuisine • Brasserie •

This characterful restaurant with a brasserie-style dining room presents traditional dishes with a modern touch. For music lovers, Oud-Zuid is less than a 10 min walk from the Concertgebouw.

Volt

Ferdinand Bolstraat 178 ✉ *1072 LT –* ✆ *(0 20) 471 55 44*   Plan: **F3**
– www.restaurantvolt.nl – closed 27 April and 1 January
Carte 30/40 € – *(dinner only except Saturday and Sunday)*
• Modern French • Bistro • Simple •

Certain elements of the austere decor at Volt are reminiscent of the lamp shop previously housed here. This is still a vibrant location, but now the excitement comes in the form of flavours. The chef produces classic cuisine as it should be, as well as a very good wine and beer list.

Rijsel

Marcusstraat 52b ✉ *1091 TK –* ✆ *(0 20) 463 21 42*   Plan: **G3**
– www.rijsel.com – closed 1-14 August, Saturday and Sunday
Menu 34/75 € – Carte 35/105 € – *(dinner only) (booking essential)*
• Classic French • Simple •

Rijsel's simple interior resembles a classroom, and the restaurant happens to share its entrance with a school. In the open kitchen you can see the master at work preparing his delicious French cuisine. He has an excellent knowledge of ingredients and his traditional dishes also include a nod to Flemish food.

NETHERLANDS - AMSTERDAM

XXXX **Aan de Poel** (Stefan van Sprang)   🕸 ≼ 🛋 AK ⇔ 🦞

❀❀ *Handweg 1 ⊠ 1185 TS Amstelveen – ℰ (0 20) 345 17 63*   Plan: **B3**
– www.aandepoel.nl – closed 27 April, 24 July-7 August, 27 December-
10 January, Saturday lunch, Sunday and Monday
Menu 50 € (lunch), 89/99 € – Carte 72/100 €
• Creative • Trendy •

A successful marriage of technical skill and brilliant produce ensures that every dish is a feast for the senses. Here, contemporary cuisine can be savoured in one of its most beautiful and tasteful forms. What's more, this restaurant benefits from a superb lakeside setting, a chic and sophisticated designer interior and a skilled sommelier.

➜ Grietfilet met dragon, meiknol en foie gras. Gebakken kalfszwezerik en -sukade met morieljes. Soufflé van karamel met moka en banaan.

XX **De Jonge Dikkert**   🛋 ⇔ 🅿

🙂 *Amsterdamseweg 104a ⊠ 1182 HG Amstelveen*   Plan: **B3**
– ℰ (0 20) 643 33 33 – www.jongedikkert.nl – closed 3 weeks in August, 24
and 31 December-6 January, Saturday lunch and Sunday lunch
Menu 35 € (lunch), 36/70 € – Carte 44/59 €
• Regional cuisine • Trendy • Inn •

This timber windmill dating back to the 17C feels nice and cosy thanks to the new contemporary interior. Indulge yourself in this fantastic setting, which is equalled by the superb cuisine featuring local ingredients, beautifully crafted dishes, and modern techniques and combinations. A strong Bib Gourmand.

XX **Kronenburg**   🛋 ⅋ AK ⇔ 🅿

Prof. E.M. Meijerslaan 6 ⊠ 1183 AV Amstelveen   Plan: **B3**
– ℰ (0 20) 345 54 89 – www.restaurant-kronenburg.nl – closed 27 April,
24 July-6 August, Saturday lunch and Sunday
Menu 29 € (lunch)/35 € – Carte 42/51 €
• Mediterranean cuisine • Trendy •

An oasis in the Kronenburg business quarter on the edge of a lake in a verdant setting. Dine on the terrace or behind the glass façade in an elegant, bright interior that is positively sparkling. The dishes have a Mediterranean flair and are inspired by French cuisine.

THE HAGUE
DEN HAAG –'S GRAVENHAGE

Population: 510 909

H. Conodul/Iconotec/Photononstop

The Hague appears to be a city of anomalies. Although the seat of Dutch government, it's not the capital of the Netherlands (which is Amsterdam); although a city of Europe-wide importance, it's just as famous for its modern seaside resort of Scheveningen; and although populated for hundreds of years by the well-to-do, its canal-side houses share little of Amsterdam's flamboyance. The Hague earned its nickname 'the biggest village in Europe' because of its relatively small population sprawled about a large area: that 'village' is marked by an aristocratic charm, which is why it's rightly obtained another title – Holland's most elegant town.

The Hague is also doffing its neatly tailored cap to the 21C: parts of the centre now shoot skywards courtesy of shiny government high-rises, while a rash of reasonably priced, buzzy restaurants and bars has brightened the streets. An outward-thinking city council has helped loosen the staid image with a lively programme of concerts and events, and there's an enticing range of museums clustered in the centre. A village, however large, wouldn't be a village without its sections of green and pleasant land, and The Hague doesn't disappoint, with a kaleidoscope of leafy lanes and large parks. The air of gentle manners is all-pervasive, and bureaucrats and bankers know that in a few minutes they can be sitting in a deckchair on a sandy beach.

THE HAGUE IN...

→ **ONE DAY**
Binnenhof, Mauritshuis, Panorama Mesdag.

→ **TWO DAYS**
Gemeentemuseum, 'The Fred', a stroll around Noordeinde, a show at Lucent Dans Theater.

→ **THREE DAYS**
A day out by the sea at Scheveningen, Madurodam.

PRACTICAL INFORMATION

ARRIVAL-DEPARTURE

 Rotterdam The Hague Airport is 16km southeast of The Hague. Bus Number 33 to Central Station takes 45min. The train to Schiphol Airport takes 30min.

GETTING AROUND

Single tickets can be purchased from the bus driver but saver tickets must be bought in advance from the tourist information office, post offices, tobacconists, newsagents and hotels. You can buy good value stripcards in two varieties – as a 15-stripcard or a 45-stripcard – and these are valid throughout the country on buses, trams and metro. A one-day pass is also available; with the price dependent on the amount of zones to be covered. The only rail travel within the city is the line linking the two stations, Den Haag Centraal Station and Den Haag Hollands Spoor, which is a kilometre to the south of the centre.

EATING OUT

Locals like to think that their 'biggest village in Europe' is the result of a lot made from a little; they call it the Hague Bluff. But what's that got to do with food? Well, the Hague Bluff is also a local pudding, a gooseberry fool made with eggs and sugar, representing the idea that something grand can be made from humble ingredients. There's no bluff, though, about the city's restaurant scene. It's first rate in every respect, and although some establishments are targeted full-on at the embassy army, many more are very affordable. With the cuisine

CALENDAR HIGHLIGHTS

April
King's Night Festival.

April-June
International Sand Sculpture Festival.

May
North Sea Regatta.

May-June
Tong Tong Fair (the world's biggest Eurasian fair).

July
De Parade (fairground rides, music, theatre).

August
International Fireworks Festival.

September
Todaysart Festival.

November
Crossing Border Festival (literature, music and visual arts).

of more than 20 nationalities on offer, the choice is broad and pleasingly sophisticated, and the number of exotic restaurants reflects the many cultures found here. Asian influences are everywhere, but in particular, the Indonesian connection is clear. There's a host of top-notch restaurants in the area just beyond Lange Voorhout, around Denneweg and Frederikstraat. If you can't find what you want there, then head to Molenstraat, near the Noordeinde Palace, for another exciting cluster.

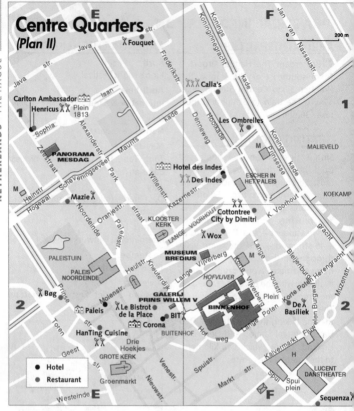

Centre Quarters
(Plan II)

CENTRE

 Hotel Des Indes   ⓕ ⓢ ⓘ ☒ ⓖ ⓢ ⓟ

Lange Voorhout 54 ☒ 2514 EG – ℰ (0 70) 361 23 45   Plan: **F1**
– www.luxurycollection.com/desindes

90 rm – †155/549 € – ††175/559 € – ☲ 29 € – 2 suites

• Grand Luxury •

Hotel Des Indes describes itself as *the* hotel in The Hague and it is difficult to argue with this description. Already renowned for its beauty when it opened at the end of the 19C, this fairytale palace has become simply more stunning over the years. It boasts opulent decor that is characteristic of its colonial past.
Des Indes – See restaurant listing

Carlton Ambassador   ⓢ ⓐ ⓢ ⓟ

Sophialaan 2 ☒ 2514 JP – ℰ (0 70) 363 03 63   Plan: **E1**
– www.carlton.nl/ambassador

88 rm ☲ – †99/299 € – ††99/299 € – 3 suites

• Palace •

A pearl in the heart of the embassy quarter. This charming little hotel breathes warmth and character, from the distinguished lobby to the elegant guestrooms. The personnel are excellent ambassadors for this splendid establishment and will ensure that you lack nothing during your stay.
Henricus – See restaurant listing

546

Corona 🏧 🛗

Buitenhof 42 ⊠ 2513 AH – ℰ (0 70) 363 79 30 – www.corona.nl   Plan: **E2**
36 rm – ♦80/160 € ♦♦85/180 € – ☲ 17 € – 1 suite
• Palace •

Corona's rich history gives it an international allure, a reputation upheld by guestrooms that live up to the expectations of today's guests and business people. The location in the heart of the city, opposite the government buildings of the Binnenhof, is a trump card.
BIT – See restaurant listing

Paleis ⬡ 🏧

Molenstraat 26 ⊠ 2513 BL – ℰ (0 70) 362 46 21   Plan: **E2**
– www.paleishotel.nl
20 rm – ♦119/169 € ♦♦119/169 € – ☲ 17 €
• Luxury •

A luxury hotel inspired by the Louis XVI-style. Details that make all the difference include fabrics used for the curtains, chairs and bedspreads sourced from Pierre Frey, a renowned French furnishings company, and even a luxurious hassock at the foot of the bed. The royal welcome you will receive is enhanced by the king-size beds.

Mozaic 🏧 🅿

Laan Copes van Cattenburch 38 ⊠ 2585 GB   Plan: **B1**
– ℰ (0 70) 352 23 35 – www.mozaic.nl
25 rm – ♦70/110 € ♦♦70/160 € – ☲ 15 €
• Family •

The team at Mozaic offer their guests that little bit extra. Find a warm personal welcome, a townhouse with a hint of history and a touch of modern design in the bedrooms. An inspired alternative to the usual chain hotels.

Calla's (Marcel van der Kleijn) 🕸 🏧

Laan van Roos en Doorn 51a ⊠ 2514 BC – ℰ (0 70)   Plan: **F1**
345 58 66 – www.restaurantcallas.nl – closed 23 July-16 August,
25 December-4 January, Saturday lunch, Sunday and Monday
Menu 40/99 € – Carte 86/105 €
• Creative French • Elegant •

'Calla' refers to a Mexican lily, which derives its name from the Greek word for beauty. To continue with the international theme, the cuisine is French and the wine list a combination of the Old World and the New. The delicious, simple yet refined cuisine served here provides a truly memorable dining experience.
→ Schelpdieren met gekoelde 'nage' en verjus. Gebraden lam met een piperade en saus van bonenkruid en knoflook. Handgerolde couscous met appel, amandel en honingroomijs.

Cottontree City by Dimitri 🍽 🏧

Lange Voorhout 98 ⊠ 2514 EJ – ℰ (0 70) 360 11 70   Plan: **F2**
– www.cottontree.nl – closed 24-31 December, Saturday lunch and Sunday
Menu 28 € (lunch), 35/45 € – Carte 34/53 €
• Market cuisine • Cosy •

Red booths and designer chairs light up the austere interior of this lively establishment. The traditional dishes will certainly cheer you. These form the foundation of the menu with beautifully combined flavours. A top venue since 1968!

HanTing Cuisine (Xiaohan Ji) 🏧 ⇔

Prinsestraat 33 ⊠ 2513 CA – ℰ (0 70) 362 08 28   Plan: **E2**
– www.hantingcuisine.nl – closed Monday
Menu 37/68 € – Carte approx. 55 € – *(dinner only)*
• Fusion • Exotic décor •

HanTing Cuisine is certainly the place to discover fusion cooking at its best. Han, the chef, brings all his expertise to bear in balancing the flavours of China with those of the West. He creates cuisine that is delicate and pleasingly harmonious. Not surprisingly, the place is also very popular.
→ Coquille en langoustine met kumquat, soja en bieslook. Geroosterde eend met eendentong, -maag en -lever, zeekwal en ananas. Black Forest: chocolade, kersen, peer en 5 specerijen.

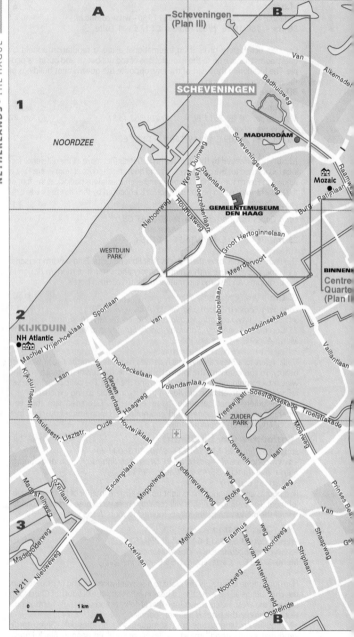

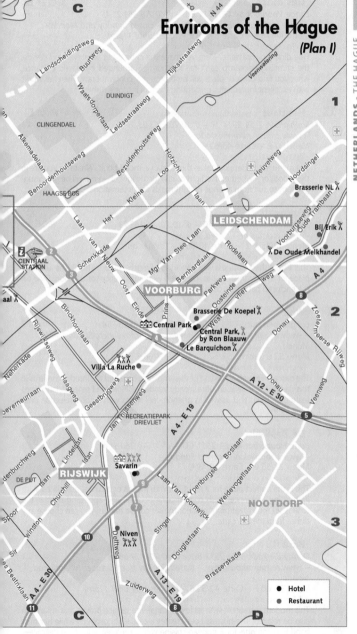

XX **Des Indes** – Hotel Des Indes   👌 🔄 🐾 🅿

Lange Voorhout 54 ⊠ 2514 EG – ℰ (0 70) 361 23 45   Plan: **F1**
– www.luxurycollection.com/desindes – closed Sunday and Monday
Menu 44/78 € – Carte 51/68 € – *(open until 11pm)*
• Modern cuisine • Elegant •

Fine dining or brasserie? Here you have the choice, but whatever you decide, the stunning backdrop can't fail to charm. Surrounded by classic elegance, what you find on your plate will be thoroughly contemporary. The chef works with excellent ingredients, presenting them in intricate dishes.

XX **Henricus** – Hotel Carlton Ambassador   🆎 🔄 🅿

Sophialaan 2 ⊠ 2514 JP – ℰ (0 70) 363 03 63   Plan: **E1**
– www.carlton.nl/ambassador
Menu 37 € – Carte 43/62 €
• International • Cosy •

The menu at the Henricus takes the form of a 'mood book'. Whatever you are in the mood for – whether it is 'light & easy' or 'delightful' – you will be given suggestions to suit from a range of light meals and international dishes.

X **Fouquet**   🛜 🔄

Javastraat 31a ⊠ 2585 AC – ℰ (0 70) 360 62 73   Plan: **E1**
– www.fouquet.nl – closed Sunday
Menu 30/85 € ♈ – Carte 40/86 € – *(dinner only)*
• Market cuisine • Brasserie •

This established business still swears by French cuisine. This is the ultimate place for market fresh dishes, prepared with a reverence for tradition. Dine on the enclosed patio terrace in summer.

X **Wox**   🦀 🆎 🔄

Lange Voorhout 51 ⊠ 2514 EC – ℰ (0 70) 365 37 54   Plan: **F2**
– www.wox.nl – closed Bank Holidays, Saturday lunch, Sunday and Monday
Menu 32 € (lunch), 52/62 € – Carte 47/66 €
• Fusion • Tapas bar •

The name gives you an inkling of the ambience here and the interior confirms it: this flashy brasserie is an ultra trendy venue. Fashionable Franco-Asian dishes feature on the menu, as well as phenomenal wines with a good selection available by the glass.

X **De Basiliek**   🛜 🔄

Korte Houtstraat 4a ⊠ 2511 CD – ℰ (0 70) 360 61 44   Plan: **F2**
– www.debasiliek.nl – closed Sunday
Menu 28/55 € – Carte 38/49 €
• Modern cuisine • Design •

This is the perfect place for a night out with friends or business associates. With its bustling ambience, fresh contemporary cuisine and appealing menus, the tone is set for a great night out. For the set course menus, you can choose any dishes from the à la carte.

X **Basaal**   🛜 🔄
🈁
Dunne Bierkade 3 ⊠ 2512 BC – ℰ (0 70) 427 68 88   Plan: **C2**
– www.restaurantbasaal.nl – closed Sunday from October till April and Monday
Menu 37/60 € – Carte 42/52 € – *(dinner only until 11pm)*
• Modern cuisine • Intimate •

This modern restaurant with its lovely canal-side terrace proves that smart can also be relaxed. The hostess Loes creates a casual atmosphere, while her husband Bastiaan opts for European cuisine with a preference for local delicacies. Whatever you pick, the ingredients will be fresh and the flavours distinctive.

X ☺ | **Les Ombrelles** 🛜 ⇔ 🍽 (dinner) 🅿

Hooistraat 4a ⊠ 2514 BM – 𝒞 (0 70) 365 87 89 — Plan: **F1**
– www.lesombrelles.nl – closed 25 December-3 January and Sunday
Menu 27 € (lunch), 37/61 € – Carte 47/95 €
• Seafood • Trendy •
You don't need to be an expert in Molière's language to know the meaning of Ombrelles – just glance at the ceiling full of umbrellas to find the clue. The chef focuses on fish and shellfish dishes, adding his own original touches to traditional French recipes.

X | **Le Bistrot de la Place** 🛜

Plaats 27 ⊠ 2513 AD – 𝒞 (0 70) 364 33 27 — Plan: **E2**
– www.bistrotdelaplace.nl – closed Saturday lunch and Sunday
Menu 38 € – Carte 38/61 €
• Classic French • Bistro •
The record sleeves on the walls, the French music in the background and the flavours of archetypal French cuisine: the spirit of France has penetrated every fibre of this exceptional bistro. On Fridays and Saturdays, the owner performs French songs.

X | **Sequenza** 🛜

Spui 224 ⊠ 2511 BX – 𝒞 (0 70) 345 28 53 – closed — Plan: **F2**
Sunday and Monday
Menu 43 € – (dinner only until 11pm) (tasting menu only)
• Market cuisine • Trendy •
The cosy atmosphere of Sequenza has won the hearts of its many regular customers. They return time and time again for the French inspired cuisine made from fresh, market-sourced produce. The restricted menu may offer only a small selection of dishes, but the food is full of flavour.

X | **Mazie** 🛜

Maziestraat 10 ⊠ 2514 GT – 𝒞 (0 70) 302 02 86 — Plan: **E1**
– www.restaurantmazie.nl – closed late December-early January, Tuesday lunch, Saturday lunch, Sunday and Monday
Menu 43 € (lunch), 48/78 €
• Creative • Neighbourhood •
The atmosphere is cosy in this little neighbourhood restaurant; situated in a side street of het Noordeinde. Dishes arrive in tasty, modern combinations and are nicely presented. This all comes at a satisfyingly honest price.

X | **Bøg** 🛜

Prinsestraat 130 ⊠ 2513 CH – 𝒞 (0 70) 406 90 44 — Plan: **E2**
– www.bøg.com – closed 27-31 March, 23 July-20 August, 20 December-5 January, Sunday and Monday
Menu 56 € – (dinner only)
• Scandinavian • Design •
Slick Scandinavian design is beautifully executed at Bøg. You have the choice between a vegetarian menu and a meat/fish menu, both as creative as they are appealing. The pure flavours drawn from local ingredients are truly delicious.

X | **BIT** – Hotel Corona 🛜 🆎

Buitenhof 42 ⊠ 2513 AH – 𝒞 (0 70) 790 00 32 — Plan: **E2**
– www.bitgrill.nl
Carte 26/60 €
• Meats and grills • Brasserie •
This urban establishment focuses on quality. BIT stands for Best In Town and they aim to prove that their name is justified with first-rate meat prepared on the Josper grill. Grilling is an art and they clearly understand that here. The restaurant also serves breakfast.

Kurhaus ☆ ≤ ♨ ᷓ 🅰 🖧 🅿

Gevers Deynootplein 30 ✉ *2586 CK – ℰ (0 70) 416 26 36* Plan: **G1**
– www.amrathkurhaus.nl
253 rm – †119/269 € ††119/269 € – ☲ 25 € – 8 suites
• Palace •

This grand residence is much more than a hotel; it's an institution. With its superb seaside location, a refined ambience and a restaurant with an impressive terrace, it more than justifies its reputation.

XxX Cottontree Mer ஃ ≤ 🅰

Zeekant 60 ✉ *2586 AD – ℰ (0 70) 355 52 50* Plan: **G1**
– www.cottontree.nl/mer – closed Bank Holidays, Saturday lunch, Sunday and Monday
Menu 30 € (lunch), 43/63 € – Carte 43/63 €
• Seafood • Elegant •

Tasty seafood and a fantastic view of the sea make for a mouthwatering combination. In order to fully explore the delicious fish and shellfish on offer you will need to pick at least four dishes, as this establishment works with small portions.

XX Waterproef ஃ 🍴 🅰 ⇕

Dr. Lelykade 25 ✉ *2583 CL – ℰ (0 70) 358 87 70* Plan: **G2**
– www.restaurantwaterproef.nl – closed 26 December-1 January, Saturday lunch, Sunday lunch, Monday lunch and Wednesday
Menu 30 € (lunch), 40/63 € – Carte 48/65 €
• Modern French • Fashionable •

A very large restaurant beside the quay, where up to 100 guests can be served in a beautiful room combining the old and the new. The cuisine is modern (the fixed menus offer the best value) and the service informal. The wine list is a real eye-catcher, offering a spectacular choice for diners.

X Catch by Simonis 🍴 🅰 ⇕

Dr. Lelykade 43 ✉ *2583 CL – ℰ (0 70) 338 76 09* Plan: **G2**
– www.catchbysimonis.nl
Menu 20 € (lunch), 25/40 € – Carte 34/58 €
• Seafood • Fashionable •

No, you are not in New York, although this impressive restaurant wouldn't be out of place there with its fashionable interior, trendy ambience, prestigious bottles adorning the wine wall and delicious food. Fish and shellfish steal the show in dishes that are as fresh as they are modern. A great catch!

X De Dis

Badhuisstraat 6 ✉ *2584 HK – ℰ (0 70) 350 00 45* Plan: **G1**
– www.restaurantdedis.nl – closed Monday and Tuesday
Menu 45/59 € – *(dinner only) (surprise menu only)*
• Creative • Bistro •

This restaurant has very modest decor and is located in a working class area of Scheveningen. There are plenty of surprises on the plate, ensuring that guests will want to spend time appreciating the cuisine on offer. Top quality seasonal produce is beautifully flavoured and presented.

ENVIRONS OF THE HAGUE (Rijswijk, Voorburg, Leidschendam)

Savarin ♨ 🕸 ⑂ 🍴 🖹 ᷓ 🅰 🖧 🅿

Laan van Hoornwijck 29 ✉ *2289 DG Rijswijk – ℰ (0 70)* Plan: **C3**
307 20 50 – www.savarin.nl
35 rm – †139/219 € ††139/219 € – ☲ 22 € – 2 suites
• Business •

An oasis between motorways and huge office buildings, where you'll find a winning mix of leisure and wellness facilities and personal service. Guestrooms are intimate and extremely comfortable. It's a real delight!
Savarin – See restaurant listing

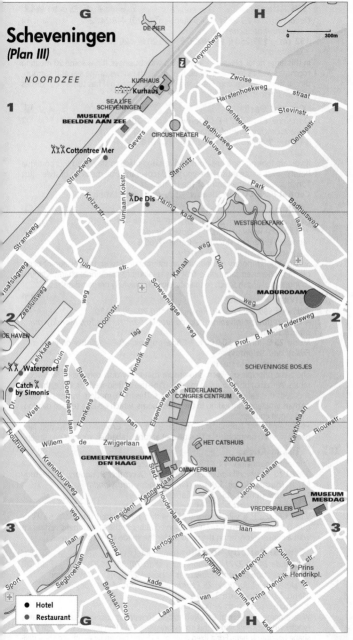

Scheveningen
(Plan III)

NOORDZEE

DE PIER

0   300m

Deynootweg

Zwolse straat

Harstenhoekweg

Stevinstr.

KURHAUS
Kurhaus
SEA LIFE SCHEVENINGEN
MUSEUM BEELDEN AAN ZEE

CIRCUSTHEATER

Gentsestr.

Gentsestr.

Gevers

Badhuisweg

Nieuwe

Stevinstr.

Cottontree Mer

Strandweg

Keizerstr.

Juniaan Kokstr.

De Dis

Haring kade

Park

WESTBROEKPARK

Badhuisweg laan

Strandweg

Duin str.

weg

Kanaal weg

Duin

weg

safslagweg

Zeesluisweg

Duin weg

Doornstr.

Scheveningse lag

MADURODAM

Weg

DE HAVEN

Lelykade

van Boetzelaer laan

Duin

Staten laan

Frankens

Fred. Hendrik laan

Scheveningse weg

Prof. B. M. Teldersweg

SCHEVENINGSE BOSJES

Waterproef

Catch by Simonis

West

Dr.

Eisenhowerlaan

NEDERLANDS CONGRES CENTRUM

Scheveningse weg

Kerkhoflaan

Riouwstr.

Hortrust

Willem   de   Zwijgerlaan

Kranenburgweg

weg

laan

Sport

Segbroeklaan

GEMEENTEMUSEUM DEN HAAG

President   Kennedylaan

Stadhouderslaan

HET CATSHUIS

ZORGVLIET

OMNIVERSUM

Jacob Catslaan

MUSEUM MESDAG

VREDESPALEIS

Conrad

Hertoginne

laan

Koningin

kade

Meerdervoort

Zoutman str.

Prins Hendrikpl.

Prins Hendrik str.

Beeklaan

Groot

Laan   van

Emma

kade

- ● Hotel
- ● Restaurant

553

NH Atlantic
Deltaplein 200 ⊠ 2554 EJ Kijkduin – ℰ (0 70) 448 24 82 — Plan: **A2**
– www.nh-hotels.com
132 rm – ♦99/250 € ♦♦99/250 € – 🖵 20 € – 20 suites
• Classic •

In this large hotel, pleasure is combined with business. It has some 20 meeting rooms, as well as leisure facilities. Best of all, the views of the sea and surrounding nature are stunning. For many years the same chef has turned out dishes with an international flavour.

Central Park
Oosteinde 14 ⊠ 2271 EH Voorburg – ℰ (0 70) 387 20 81 — Plan: **D2**
– www.centralparkronblaauw.com
14 rm – ♦99/175 € ♦♦175/295 € – 🖵 18 €
• Luxury •

If you are looking for a luxurious and relaxing place to stay, then this boutique hotel is an absolute must. Here you will discover the true meaning of style – just 10min drive from the centre of The Hague.
Central Park by Ron Blaauw – See restaurant listing

Savarin – Hotel Savarin
Laan van Hoornwijck 29 ⊠ 2289 DG Rijswijk – ℰ (0 70) — Plan: **C3**
307 20 50 – www.savarin.nl – closed Sunday
Menu 35 € (lunch), 40/75 € – Carte 47/66 €
• Modern cuisine • Trendy •

Serving contemporary cuisine with an international twist, this restaurant occupies a modernised farmhouse that has retained its traditional charm. Original flavours add a fresh touch to the occasionally playfully prepared dishes.

Niven (Niven Kunz)
Delftweg 58a ⊠ 2289 AL Rijswijk – ℰ (0 70) 307 79 70 — Plan: **C3**
– www.restaurantniven.nl – closed late December, Sunday, Monday and after 8.30pm
Menu 25 € (lunch), 50/100 € – Carte approx. 80 € – *(dinner only except Friday and Saturday)*
• Creative • Elegant •

The basic principle of Niven is to ensure that every dish consists of 80% vegetables. With that philosophy in mind and the use of field-fresh produce, the chef succeeds in creating imaginative delicacies. This fresh, modern business exudes a smart ambience, including in the guestrooms, which boast a terrace overlooking a golf course.
➜ Asperges met langoustines, framboos en roos. Groene groenten met lam, paddestoel en gestoofde sla. Creatie met aardbei, rabarber, yoghurt en citroen.

Villa la Ruche
Prinses Mariannelaan 71 ⊠ 2275 BB Voorburg – ℰ (0 70) — Plan: **C2**
386 01 10 – www.villalaruche.nl – closed 27 December-9 January, Wednesday lunch, Thursday lunch, Saturday lunch, Sunday and Monday
Menu 35 € (lunch), 45/75 € – Carte 68/80 €
• Modern French • Elegant •

Villa la Ruche is a villa from the 19C with a modernised interior. It treats its guests to up-to-the-minute cuisine, served either in the atmospheric restaurant with a conservatory or on the patio under the shade of the plane trees.

Central Park by Ron Blaauw – Hotel Central Park
Oosteinde 14 ⊠ 2271 EH Voorburg – ℰ (0 70) 387 20 81 — Plan: **D2**
– www.centralparkronblaauw.com – closed 27 April, 4 May dinner, 31 December-1 January, 25 February-5 March and Saturday lunch
Menu 39/49 € – Carte 39/60 €
• Modern French • Trendy •

With a name like Central Park you expect something cosmopolitan, and that is exactly what you will find at this luxury brasserie. Chef Ron Blaauw's concept takes shape beautifully here. For a fixed price of €15 you can enjoy exciting dishes, deliciously combining different preparation methods with quality ingredients.

Brasserie De Koepel

Oosteinde 1 ⊠ 2271 EA Voorburg – 𝒞 (0 70) 369 35 72   Plan: **D2**
– www.brasseriedekoepel.nl – closed 17-30 July, 27-31 December and
Sunday
Menu 32/52 € – Carte 39/51 € – *(dinner only until 11pm)*
• Market cuisine • Brasserie •

A former orangery located in a park where you can sit and enjoy nature on the terrace. Beneath the dome, with its paintings of scantily clad women, enjoy the house specialities of Caesar salad, lobster and cream soup, hare fillet with a spicy sauce and tarte Tatin.

Brasserie NL

Neherpark 5 ⊠ 2264 ZD Leidschendam – 𝒞 (0 70)   Plan: **D1**
320 85 50 – www.brasserienl.com – closed 25-31 December, Sunday and
Monday
Menu 25 € (lunch), 37/80 € ♈
– Carte 40/53 € – (dinner only except Thursday and Friday)
• Modern cuisine • Brasserie •

The large, concrete radio tower with its telephone paraphernalia inside is a reminder of its history as the headquarters of the postal service in the Netherlands. What stands out most about this restaurant is its vintage appeal and the designer chairs from the sixties. The menu is straightforward: modern, generous and based on excellent produce.

De Oude Melkhandel

Sluiskant 22 ⊠ 2265 AB Leidschendam – 𝒞 (0 70)   Plan: **D2**
317 82 70 – www.deoudemelkhandel.nl – closed late December-early
January and Monday
Menu 20 € (lunch), 33/48 € – Carte approx. 45 €
• Market cuisine • Brasserie •

A picturesque waterside location with views over the lock. This former dairy is now home to a contemporary brasserie, where the kitchen follows the rhythms of the seasons. The up-to-date dishes are based around fresh and authentic ingredients.

Le Barquichon

Kerkstraat 6 ⊠ 2271 CS Voorburg – 𝒞 (0 70) 387 11 81   Plan: **D2**
– www.lebarquichon.nl – closed 31 July-21 August, Saturday lunch,
Sunday lunch, Tuesday and Wednesday
Menu 28 € (lunch), 33/47 € – Carte 46/56 € – *(bar lunch)*
• Classic cuisine • Bistro •

A young couple breathed new life into this little neighbourhood restaurant. Given its location along a pedestrian walkway, the pavement terrace is opened up whenever the weather allows. The menu is short and traditional; the dining room small but cosy.

Bij Erik

Sluisplein 9 ⊠ 2266 AV Leidschendam – 𝒞 (0 70)   Plan: **D2**
301 04 51 – www.bijerik.nl – closed 27 December-10 January, Monday and
Tuesday
Menu 25 € (lunch)/35 € – *(tasting menu only)*
• Modern French • Trendy •

The highly motivated and enthusiastic chef of this cosy establishment, Erik Tas, works with a single set menu that is sure to impress. The power of his cuisine lies in the strong, well-balanced flavours that bring out the best in the ingredients. Bij Erik is also excellent value for money.

ROTTERDAM
ROTTERDAM

Population: 619 879

Jérôme Dancette/Fotolia.com

Rotterdam trades on its earthy appeal, on a rough and ready grittiness that ties in with its status as the largest seaport in the world; it handles 350 million tonnes of goods a year, with over half of all the freight that is heading into Europe passing through it. Flattened during the Second World War, Rotterdam was rebuilt on a grand scale, jettisoning the idea of streets full of terraced houses in favour of a modern cityscape of concrete and glass, and there are few places in the world that have such an eclectic range of buildings to keep you entertained (or bewildered): try the Euromast Space Tower, the Groothandelsgebouw (which translates as 'wholesale building'), the 'Cube Houses' or the fabulous sounding Boompjestorens for size. The city is located on the Nieuwe Maas but is centred around a maze of other rivers – most importantly the Rhine and the Maas – and is only a few dozen kilometres inland from the North Sea. It spills over both banks, and is linked by tunnels, bridges and the metro; the most stunning connection across the water is the modern Erasmusbridge, whose graceful, angular lines of silver tubing have earned it the nickname 'The Swan', and whose sleek design has come to embody the Rotterdam of the new millennium. It's mirrored on the southern banks by the development of the previously rundown Kop Van Zuid area into a sleek, modern zone.

ROTTERDAM IN...

→ **ONE DAY**
Blaak area including Kijk-Kubus and Boompjestorens, Oude Haven, Museum Boijmans Van Beuningen.

→ **TWO DAYS**
More Museumpark, Delfshaven, take in the view from Euromast, cruise along the Nieuwe Maas.

→ **THREE DAYS**
Kop Van Zuid, a show at the Luxor Theatre.

PRACTICAL INFORMATION

ARRIVAL-DEPARTURE

The Airport is 8km northwest of the city. Shuttle bus No. 33 runs every 10min and takes 20min to Centraal Railway Station.

GETTING AROUND

There are a variety of stripcards to ease your way around on the metro, bus, tram and train: from two-strip right up to forty-five strip tickets. That could entail a lot of fiddling about and franking. A better bet could be to invest in a one-day, two-day, or three-day card, which gives you unlimited travel on any form of transport. A Rotterdam Card provides unlimited use of the transport network as well as free admission to most attractions and is available for either 24 or 72 hours. You can hire bicycles from the Centraal Station cycle shop. These work out at good value, and can be hired for either a day or a week.

CALENDAR HIGHLIGHTS

January-February
International Film Festival.

March
Museum Night.

June
Poetry International Festival.

July
North Sea Jazz Festival,
Summer Carnival (street parade),
Rotterdam Unlimited (music, dance, art, street theatre).

September
World Port Days (ship tours, demos and cruises).

EATING OUT

Rotterdam is a hot place for dining, in the literal and metaphorical sense. There are lots of places to tuck into the flavours of Holland's colonial past, in particular the spicy delicacies of Indonesia and Surinam. The long east/west stretch of Oude and Nieuwe Binnenweg is not only handy for many of the sights, it's also chock-full of good cafés, café-bars and restaurants, and the canal district of Oudehaven has introduced to the city a good selection of places to eat while taking in the relaxed vibe. Along the waterfront, various warehouses have been transformed into mega-restaurants, particularly around the Noordereiland isle in the middle of the river, while in Kop Van Zuid, the Wilhelminapier Quay offers quality restaurants and tasty views too. Many establishments are closed at lunchtime, except business restaurants and those that set a high gastronomic standard and like to show it off in the middle of the day as well as in the evening. The bill includes a service charge, so tipping is optional: round up the total if you're pleased with the service.

Hilton 🏃 🛴 ♿ 🆔 🏋 🏊 🚗

Weena 10 ✉ 3012 CM – ☎ (0 10) 710 80 00   Plan: **E1**
– www.rotterdam.hilton.com
246 rm – ♦99/269 € ♦♦99/269 € – 🛏 25 € – 8 suites
• Chain •

This established business hotel has been fully renovated, with bedrooms and meeting rooms decorated in warm hues, lots of timber and earthy colours, and modern comfort guaranteed. The smart lobby is the biggest in the city. Dine on creative cuisine in eclectically decorated Joelia or choose from simpler dishes in Roots.
🌸 **Joelia** – See restaurant listing

Parkhotel ≼ 🛴 🍴 🆔 🏋 🅿

Westersingel 70 ✉ 3015 LB – ☎ (0 10) 436 36 11   Plan: **E2**
– www.bilderberg.nl
187 rm – ♦79/209 € ♦♦99/209 € – 🛏 25 € – 2 suites
• Business •

A contemporary hotel with a history dating back to 1922, situated in the heart of modern Rotterdam. The two tower blocks built in the 1980s offer panoramic views of the 'Architectural Capital of the Netherlands'.
The Park - Inspired by Erik van Loo – See restaurant listing

Pincoffs 🆔 🏋 🅿

Stieltjesstraat 34 ✉ 3071 JX – ☎ (0 10) 297 45 00   Plan: **C2**
– www.hotelpincoffs.nl – closed 1-16 August
16 rm 🛏 – ♦139 € ♦♦169/199 € – 1 suite
• Historic •

This trendy renovated customs office is the place to be for visitors wanting to explore the city and indulge in a little pampering. Bulgari accessories in the bathroom, your favourite music on the iPod docking station and impeccable, friendly service all add to the appeal.

New York 🏃 ≼ ♿ 🆔 🏋 ⊕

Koninginnenhoofd 1 (Wilhelminapier) ✉ 3072 AD   Plan: **F3**
– ☎ (0 10) 439 05 00 – www.hotelnewyork.nl
72 rm – ♦99/315 € ♦♦99/315 € – 🛏 18 €
• Traditional •

Stay at the New York hotel and experience the excitement of the fortune-seekers who came to buy their tickets here for the ocean crossing to New York. The whole place radiates character and dynamic energy, from the elegant rooms to the large restaurant, which has a pleasant lively ambience.

Quartier du Port 🏃 🆔 🏋

Van Vollenhovenstraat 48 ✉ 3016 BJ – ☎ (010)   Plan: **E3**
240 04 25 – www.quartierduport.nl
20 rm 🛏 – ♦99/199 € ♦♦99/199 €
• Townhouse •

A boutique hotel with a warm, welcoming atmosphere, a feeling of space and openness in the guestrooms, and just a hint of nostalgia in the reception area. The bread at breakfast is a real treat. The restaurant menu is traditional and changes regularly.

Stroom 🏃 🛴 🆔 🏋

Lloydstraat 1 ✉ 3024 EA – ☎ (0 10) 221 40 60   Plan: **B2**
– www.stroomrotterdam.nl
18 rm – ♦99/125 € ♦♦125/165 € – 🛏 15 € – 3 suites
• Townhouse •

Once energy was generated in this former power station, today it houses a boutique hotel. The interior has a rather austere design, but the personal approach of the managers brings warmth to the place. The effect is truly electric.

XxxX · ✿✿ · **Parkheuvel** (Erik van Loo) 🕸 ⩻ ⌂ ⇔ **P**

Heuvellaan 21 ✉ *3016 GL* — Plan: **E3**
– ✆ *(0 10) 436 07 66*
– *www.parkheuvel.nl*
– *closed 27 April, 31 July-20 August, 27 December-8 January,*
27 February-2 March, Bank Holidays except Christmas, Saturday lunch
and Sunday
Menu 55/140 € – Carte 89/128 €
· Creative · Elegant ·

Parkheuvel has an almost legendary reputation in Dutch gastronomy. Its tradition of culinary excellence, combined with the very best ingredients (wagyu beef, caviar and more), results in creations that have been carefully considered but never overthought. Beautifully situated by the River Maas.

➔ Briocheboterham met gel, parel en medaillons van oosterscheldekreeft. Gebraad van wagyurund met radijsjes, brunoise van merg, gebrande zilveruitjes en een longpepperjus. Chocolade en pindareep.

XxxX · ✿✿ · **Fred** (Fred Mustert) AC 🍴 (dinner)

Honingerdijk 263 ✉ *3063 AM* — Plan: **C2**
– ✆ *(0 10) 212 01 10* – *www.restaurantfred.nl*
– *closed 24 July-6 August, 25 December-1 January, Saturday lunch and*
Sunday
Menu 48 € (lunch), 117/137 € – Carte 85/113 €
· Creative French · Elegant ·

'Less is more' is Fred's philosophy. The decor is contemporary and elegant; stunning because of its class and simplicity. And the dishes? They are refined, well considered creations, where every ingredient has a function. Fred Mustert delivers a personalised experience, where everything matches.

➔ Gebakken langoustines met meloen, komkommer en langoustinecrème. Tarbot met palingtartaar en vinaigrette van zuring en aceto balsamico. Bombe van nougatparfait, pistachecrème en kaneelkletskop.

XxX · **Old Dutch** 🍴 ⇔ 🐾 **P**

Rochussenstraat 20 ✉ *3015 EK* — Plan: **E2**
– ✆ *(0 10) 436 03 44* – *www.olddutch.net*
– *closed Bank Holidays, Saturday and Sunday*
Menu 38 € (lunch), 43/60 € – Carte 55/108 €
· Modern French · Classic décor ·

With its serving staff decked out in suits and bow ties, this traditional restaurant with an incredibly spacious terrace has the atmosphere of a gentlemen's club. Familiar produce is given a fresh twist, such as marinated Scottish salmon served with chicory, walnuts, apple and crème fraîche. Meat is even sliced at your table.

XxX · ✿ · **Wereldmuseum** ⅙ AC

Willemskade 25 ✉ *3016 DM* — Plan: **F3**
– ✆ *(0 10) 270 71 85* – *www.wereldmuseum.nl*
– *closed 27 April, 1-20 August, 24 December-3 January, Saturday lunch*
and Monday
Menu 30 € (lunch), 40/95 € – Carte 50/71 €
· Modern cuisine · Trendy ·

Just like the neighbouring museum, this fashionable restaurant has plenty of draws; starting with beautiful views over the historic port. The ambitious cooking style of the chef has evolved and is now an attraction in its own right. Dishes are modern, without unnecessary frippery, and are full of flavour.

➔ Geroosterde langoustines met rode biet, hibiscus en haringkuit. Gebraden duif met tuinbonen, gekonfijte pootjes en dauphine-aardappel. Gerookte chocolade met banaan, gierst, pinda, yoghurt en koffie.

559

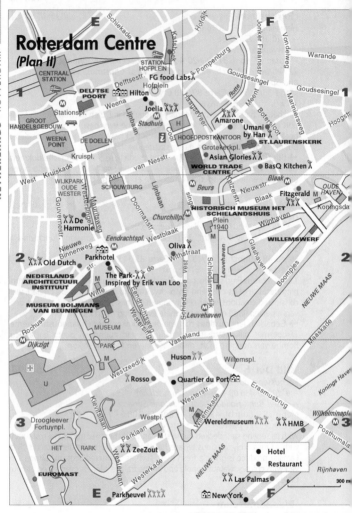

XXX **Joelia** (Mario Ridder) – Hotel Hilton   🏨 ✿

✿ *Coolsingel 5 ⊠ 3012 AA – 𝒞 (0 10) 710 80 34*   Plan: **E1**
– www.joelia.eu – closed 31 December-1 January
Menu 39 € (lunch), 55/113 € – Carte 80/157 €
• Creative French • Trendy •

Joelia proves that refinement does not need to be complex. Her eclectic decor
beautifully combines vintage and design to unique effect. Her cuisine is creative
without being fussy, and serves one aim: to achieve a harmony of subtle perfumes and intense flavours.

➜ Gouden gebak van brioche met ganzenlever en truffel. Tarbot met eek-
hoorntjesbrood en kruidengnocchi. Vijg met gekaramelliseerde druivensi-
roop en vanilleroomijs.

NETHERLANDS - ROTTERDAM

XxX Amarone (Gert Blom)   ⁜ AC
ॐ

Meent 72a ⊠ 3011 JN – ℰ (0 10) 414 84 87   Plan: **F1**
– www.restaurantamarone.nl – closed 31 July-20 August, 31 December-
4 January, Bank Holidays, Saturday lunch and Sunday
Menu 35 € (lunch), 50/80 € – Carte 71/93 €
• Creative • Chic •

This fashionable city restaurant emanates the same elegance and superior quality as the fine wine from which it takes its name. Inventive cuisine made from the best ingredients.
→ Kreeft met groene asperges, chips en vinaigrette van morieljes. Gebraden duif en gyoza van de pootjes met bereidingen van wortel. Gekaramelliseerde sinaasappel, crème van tonkabonen en limoncellosorbet.

XxX In den Rustwat   ⅏ AC ⇔
☺

Honingerdijk 96 ⊠ 3062 NX – ℰ (0 10) 413 41 10   Plan: **C2**
– www.idrw.nl – closed 23 July-14 August, 27 December-
3 January, Sunday and Monday
Menu 35 € (lunch), 37/57 € – Carte 53/70 €
• Modern cuisine •

In den Rustwat adds an exotic touch to metropolitan Rotterdam with its thatched roof, history dating back to the 16C and an idyllic setting close to an arboretum. The food here is anything but traditional, offering contemporary-style dishes with an abundance of ingredients and cooking methods.

XxX FG - François Geurds   AC ⇔ ⌷
ॐॐ

Katshoek 37B ⊠ 3032 AE – ℰ (0 10) 425 05 20   Plan: **B2**
– www.fgrestaurant.nl – closed 11-18 April, 23 July-18 August, 1-
18 January, Sunday and Monday
Menu 45 € (lunch), 91/151 € – Carte 98/168 €
• Creative • Design • Chic •

François Geurds has a clear vision and he brings it to life in this restaurant, which is urban, trendy and original. The chef adopts a style that is very detailed, sometimes even playful, but always keeps his focus on the flavours of his high quality ingredients and sauces. FG could easily stand for Fantastically Good!
→ Oester met rabarber en ganzenlever. Piepkuiken en langoustines in drie bereidingen. Miljonairsbiscuit.

XxX Fitzgerald   ⅏ ⇔

Gelderseplein 49 ⊠ 3011 WZ – ℰ (0 10) 268 70 10   Plan: **F2**
– www.restaurantfitzgerald.nl – closed 27 April, 24 July-7 August,
27 December-5 January, Tuesday lunch, Wednesday lunch, Saturday
lunch, Sunday and Monday
Menu 27 € (lunch), 43/80 € – Carte 55/72 €
• Modern French • Elegant •

Fitzgerald has real allure with its Italian marble, large glass windows, and design and vintage elements. The same goes for the experienced staff who will introduce you to cuisine that is thoroughly modern, varied and delicious.

XX Huson   ⅏ AC ⇔
☺

Scheepstimmermanslaan 14 ⊠ 3011 BS – ℰ (0 10)   Plan: **E3**
413 03 71 – www.huson.nl – closed Saturday lunch and Sunday dinner
after 7.30pm
Menu 34/62 € – Carte 42/55 €
• Creative • Brasserie •

Huson is a trendy restaurant with class, and like the nearby harbour, there is always a lively buzz here. Feast on the wondrous marriage of French and creative cuisine in attractive combinations that capture both subtlety and exuberance. Fantastic prices too.

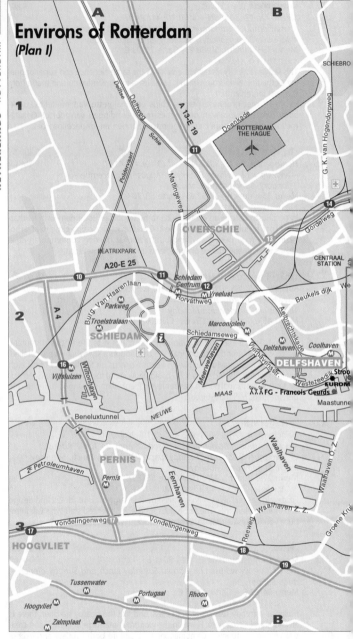

Environs of Rotterdam
(Plan I)

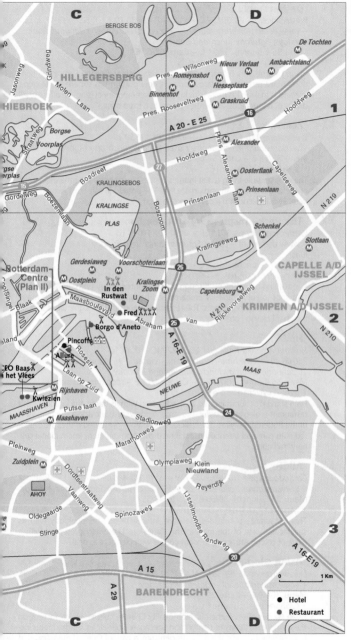

Legend:
- ● Hotel
- ● Restaurant

XX **De Harmonie**

Westersingel 95 ⊠ 3015 LC – ℰ (0 10) 436 36 10 Plan: **E2**
– www.deharmonierotterdam.nl – closed 25 December-1 January, Bank Holidays, Saturday lunch and Sunday
Menu 35 € (lunch), 55/71 € – Carte 45/60 €
• Modern cuisine • Trendy •

Having learned his culinary craft from chefs such as Gordon Ramsay (in London's Maze restaurant), Marco Somer is now putting this experience to good use and is making his mark with his own contemporary cuisine. He offers small dishes of harmonious, authentic flavours at a fixed price.

XX **Zeezout**

Westerkade 11b ⊠ 3016 CL – ℰ (0 10) 436 50 49 Plan: **E3**
– www.restaurantzeezout.nl – closed Sunday lunch and Monday
Menu 35/68 € – Carte 58/65 €
• Seafood • Design •

The only sensible thing to eat in the skippers' quarter of one of the main ports of the world is fish, fish and... more fish! The dorado in salt crust is a real treat here. Stylish decor with a cosy atmosphere.

XX **The Park - Inspired by Erik van Loo** – Parkhotel

Westersingel 70 ⊠ 3015 LB – ℰ (0 10) 440 81 65 Plan: **E2**
– www.thepark.nl – closed Saturday lunch and Sunday lunch
Menu 29 € (lunch), 36/53 € – Carte 43/64 €
• Modern cuisine • Trendy •

A refreshing breeze blows through this blue-tinted luxury brasserie. It is a pleasant spot to enjoy carefully prepared and beautifully presented cuisine made from top quality ingredients. The restaurant stands out for signature dishes by top chef Erik van Loo.

XX **HMB**

Holland Amerika Kade 104 ⊠ 3072 MC – ℰ (0 10) Plan: **F3**
760 06 20 – www.hmb-restaurant.nl – closed 1-15 August, 28 December-10 January, Saturday lunch, Sunday and Monday
Menu 35 € (lunch), 57/77 € – Carte 54/71 € – (booking advisable)
• International • Fashionable •

HMB stands for hummingbird, and in keeping with its name, the interior of this restaurant is elegantly playful. The large windows also provide a stunning view of the Rotterdam skyline. The delicious, beautifully presented dishes are prepared with care and attention using ingredients from different international culinary traditions.

XX **Allure**

Cargadoorskade 107 ⊠ 3071 AW – ℰ (0 10) 486 65 29 Plan: **C2**
– www.restaurant-allure.nl – closed 26 December-4 January and Monday
Menu 25 € (lunch), 38/60 € – Carte 48/55 €
• Market cuisine • Design •

This restaurant's purple designer-style interior blends harmoniously with its spectacular view of the marina. The dishes are beautifully presented with a blaze of colour. Attractive, modern cuisine with plenty of appeal.

XX **Asian Glories**

Leeuwenstraat 15 ⊠ 3011 AL – ℰ (0 10) 411 71 07 Plan: **F1**
– www.asianglories.nl – closed Wednesday
Menu 30/49 € – Carte 29/54 €
• Chinese • Family •

Asian Glories offers authentic, high quality Chinese cuisine, which focuses on the culinary traditions of Canton and Szechuan. Specialities on the menu include Peking duck and the delicious dim sum, a type of Oriental dumpling that is served either boiled or fried.

XX **Las Palmas**

Wilhelminakade 330 ⊠ 3072 AR – ℰ (0 10) 234 51 22
– www.restaurantlaspalmas.nl – closed Saturday lunch
Menu 23 € (lunch) – Carte 35/130 €
• Classic cuisine • Brasserie •

Plan: **F3**

There's always plenty going on at Herman den Blijker's brasserie, which is styled as a loft. You get a sneak preview before your meal arrives: meats age in special cabinets, the shellfish is on display and the open kitchen is on a raised platform. Dishes are recognisable and produce is fresh. The lunch menu is great.

X **C.E.O baas van het vlees**

Sumatraweg 1 ⊠ 3072 ZP – ℰ (0 10) 290 94 54
– www.ceobaasvanhetvlees.nl – closed 25, 26 and 31 December and Monday
Carte 35/77 € – (dinner only until 11pm)
• Meats and grills • Bistro •

Plan: **C2**

A lively bistro where prime quality American meat takes pride of place on the menu. All you have to decide is how you would like your meat cooked and whether you would like French fries and homemade mayonnaise as part of your meal.

X **Oliva**

Witte de Withstraat 15a ⊠ 3012 BK – ℰ (0 10) 412 14 13
– www.restaurantoliva.nl – closed 25 December-1 January
Menu 34/44 € – Carte approx. 40 € – (dinner only)
• Italian • Bistro •

Plan: **E2**

Enjoy down-to-earth Italian cuisine in this delightful trattoria. The menu changes daily and the dishes are made from ingredients imported straight from Italy. Authentic and delicious.

X **FG Food Labs**
🕸

Katshoek 41 ⊠ 3032 AE – ℰ (0 10) 425 05 20
– www.fgfoodlabs.nl – closed 24-31 May, 9-23 August and 1-17 January
Menu 45 € (lunch), 70/120 € – Carte 42/88 €
• Creative • Fashionable •

Plan: **E1**

This 'taste laboratory' housed in a trendy version of a train tunnel is definitely part of the Rotterdam scene. The emphasis is on new flavours and textures and on pushing culinary boundaries. This results in inventive cuisine that is bold and full of character.
→ Tuna ceviche. Porkbelly 48 uur. Dropdessert met banaan.

X **Umami by Han**
🐦

Binnenrotte 140 ⊠ 3011 HC – ℰ (0 10) 433 31 39
– www.umami-restaurant.com
Menu 25/38 € – Carte approx. 30 € – (dinner only) (booking advisable)
• Asian • Fashionable •

Plan: **F1**

The trendy, modern interior with bright colours immediately catches the eye, but the trump card of this restaurant is its rock solid concept... a range of Asian dishes with a French twist from which you can choose your heart's desire. A wonderful journey of discovery at amazing prices!

X **Rosso**

Van Vollenhovenstraat 15 (access via Westerlijk Handelsterrein) ⊠ 3016 BE – ℰ (0 10) 225 07 05 – www.rossorotterdam.nl – closed 1-10 August and Sunday
Menu 46/57 € – Carte 38/66 € – (dinner only)
• Creative French • Trendy •

Plan: **E3**

Shades of red lend colour to the relaxed and intimate interior of this trendy restaurant. It offers fine wines and a menu that you can put together as you please, choosing from a variety of small dishes prepared with top quality produce. Excellent food and an enjoyable ambience.

Kwiezien 🛱 🗚

Delistraat 20 ✉ 3072 ZK – ℰ (0 10) 215 14 40 Plan: **C2**
– www.kwiezien.nl – closed 25 and 26 December, 1 January and Monday
Menu 29/48 € – *(dinner only)*
• Market cuisine • Family •

The concept of cosy Kwiezien is simple: you put together your own meal with little dishes costing 9.50 euros each. Karin and Remco work in their open kitchen, using exclusively fresh ingredients in a continual quest for exciting combinations. A modest price for a rich palette of flavours.

Borgo d'Aneto ⇐ 🛱 🗚

Nijverheidstraat 2 ✉ 3071 GC – ℰ (0 10) 290 77 32 Plan: **C2**
– www.borgodaneto.nl – closed Sunday, Monday and Tuesday
Menu 35 € – *(dinner only)*
• Italian • Bistro •

In a bustling but cosy atmosphere, Faouzi Chihabi dishes up pure Italian cuisine with an emphasis on beautiful and tasty produce. The chef's passion is evidenced by the food, which can be savoured while admiring the fantastic view of the Rotterdam skyline.

BasQ Kitchen

Grote Markt 188 ✉ 3011 PA – ℰ (0 10) 414 00 99 Plan: **F1**
– www.basqkitchen.nl
Menu 35 € – Carte 27/41 €
• Basque • Brasserie •

Rotterdam's Markthal is a place of delicacies and BasQ fits in perfectly here. In this lively bistro you will discover different aspects of Basque cuisine from traditional to modern. The pintxos and tapas offer an authentic flavour of the Basque Country.

NORWAY
NORGE

→ AREA:
323 878 km² (125 049 sq mi).

→ POPULATION:
5 302 697 inhabitants. Density = 16 per km².

→ CAPITAL:
Oslo.

→ CURRENCY:
Norwegian Krone (kr or NOK) divided into 100 øre.

→ GOVERNMENT:
Constitutional parliamentary monarchy with single-chamber Parliament (since 1945).

→ LANGUAGES:
Norwegian has two written variants: Bokmål - influenced by Danish and spoken by 80% of the population - and Nynorsk (New Norwegian). Sami is the language of the Sami people in the far north. English is widely spoken.

→ PUBLIC HOLIDAYS:
New Year's Day (1 Jan); Maundy Thursday and Good Friday (late Mar/Apr); Easter Monday (late Mar/Apr); Labor Day (1 May); Constitution Day (17 May); Ascension Day (May); Whit Monday (late May/June); Christmas Day (25 Dec); St Stephen's Day (26 Dec).

→ LOCAL TIME:
GMT+1 hour in winter and GMT +2 hours in summer.

→ CLIMATE:
Temperate northern maritime with cold winters and mild summers (Oslo: January -4°C; July 16°C). Colder interior, fairly high precipitation in the coastal regions.

→ EMERGENCY:
Police ℰ 112; Medical Assistance ℰ 113; Fire Brigade ℰ 110. (Dialling 112 within any EU country will redirect your call and contact the emergency services.)

→ ELECTRICITY:
230 volts AC, 50Hz; 2 round pin sockets.

→ FORMALITIES:
Travellers from the European Union (EU), Switzerland, Iceland and the main countries of North and South America need a national identity card or passport (America: passport required) to visit Norway for less than three months (tourism or business purpose). For visitors from other countries a visa may be required, in addition to a passport, especially for those wishing to stay for longer than three months. We advise you to check with your embassy before travelling.

567

Oslo

OSLO

Population: 648 300

Gräfenhain/Sime/Photononstop

Oslo has a lot going for it – and one slight downside: it's one of the world's most expensive cities. It also ranks high when it comes to its standard of living, however, and its position at the head of Oslofjord, surrounded by steep forested hills, is hard to match for drama and beauty. It's a charmingly compact place to stroll round, particularly in the summer, when the daylight hours practically abolish the night and, although it may lack the urban cool of some other Scandinavian cities, it boasts its fair share of trendy clubs and a raft of Michelin Stars. There's a real raft, too: Thor Hyerdahl's famous Kon-Tiki – one of the star turns in a city that loves its museums.

Oslo's uncluttered feel is enhanced by parks and wide streets and, in the winter, there are times when you feel you have the whole place to yourself. Drift into the city by boat and land at the smart harbour of Aker Brygge; to the west lies the charming Bygdøy peninsula, home to museums permeated with the smell of the sea. Northwest is Frogner, with its famous sculpture park, the place where locals hang out on long summer days. The centre of town, the commercial hub, is Karl Johans Gate, bounded at one end by the Royal Palace and at the other by the Cathedral, while further east lie two trendy multi-cultural areas, Grunerlokka and Grønland, the former also home to the Edvard Munch Museum.

OSLO IN...

→ ONE DAY
Aker Brygge, Karl Johans Gate, Oslo Opera House.

→ TWO DAYS
Akershus, Astrup Fearnley Museum, ferry trip to Bygdøy.

→ THREE DAYS
Vigeland Park, Holmenkollen Ski Jump, Grunerlokka, Munch Museum.

PRACTICAL INFORMATION

ARRIVAL-DEPARTURE

✈ Oslo International Airport, Gardermoen, is 47km north of the city. The train station is located beneath the terminal and the Flytoget train takes 19min to Oslo's central station. The Express Bus to Oslo city centre leaves every 20min and takes 45min.

GETTING AROUND

The integrated transport system comprises bus, tram or metro and you can obtain single or day tickets; alternatively, hire one of the many free Citybike scheme bicycles parked at different points around the city. You pay a toll if you arrive by car. The Oslo Pass, which covers the transport system and entry to all museums, is valid for one to three days and is available from the Information Centre next to Oslo Central Station.

CALENDAR HIGHLIGHTS

March
By:Larm (music festival), Oslo International Church Music Festival.

May
St Hallvard's Day (concerts and theatre productions).

June
Norwegian Wood Rock Festival.

August
International Jazz Festival.

November
Oslo World Music Festival.

December
Nobel Peace Prize awarded (parades and festivities).

EATING OUT

Oslo has a very vibrant dining scene, albeit one that is somewhat expensive, particularly if you drink wine. The cooking can be quite classical and refined but there are plenty of restaurants offering more innovative menus too. What is in no doubt is the quality of the produce used, whether that's the ever-popular game or the superlative shellfish, which comes from very cold water, giving it a clean, fresh flavour. Classic Norwegian dishes often include fruit, such as lingonberries with venison. Lunch is not a major affair; most prefer just a snack or sandwich at midday while making dinner the main event of the day. You'll find most diners are seated by 7pm and are offered a 6, 7 or 8 course menu which they can reduce at their will, with a paired wine menu alongside. It doesn't have to be expensive, though. Look out for konditoris (bakeries) where you can pick up sandwiches and pastries, and kafeterias which serve substantial meals at reasonable prices. Service is a strength; staff are generally very polite, speak English and are fully versed in the menu.

NORWAY - OSLO

Continental

Stortingsgaten 24-26 ⊠ 0117 – ⓜ National Theatret Plan: **C2**
– ℰ 22 82 40 91 – www.hotelcontinental.no – Closed Christmas
155 rm � – †1695/3660 NOK ††2295/4060 NOK – 3 suites
• Grand Luxury • Traditional • Classic •
A classic hotel situated by the National Theatre and run by the 4th generation of
the family, who ensure the service remains very personal. Bedrooms are stylish
and contemporary – Deluxe are spacious and come with bathrobes and sofas.
Dine in the grand café or from an inventive daily menu in Annen Etage.
Theatercaféen – See restaurant listing

Grand

Karl Johans Gate 31 ⊠ 0159 – ⓜ Stortinget Plan: **C2**
– ℰ 23 21 20 00 – www.grand.no
292 rm ⊠ – †1550/3100 NOK ††1550/3100 NOK – 7 suites
• Grand Luxury • Traditional • Classic •
An imposing, centrally located hotel built in 1874; the guest areas and grand
ballrooms reflect this. Bedrooms are charming: some are modern, some are
feminine and others are in a belle époque style. The winners of the Nobel
Prize are interviewed here! International fare in elegant Palmen. Nordic-inspired
cooking in the Grand Café.

Radisson Blu Plaza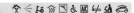

Sonja Henies Plass 3 ⊠ 0134 – ⓜ Jernbanetorget Plan: **D2**
– ℰ 22 05 80 00 – www.radissonblu.com/plazahotel-oslo
676 rm ⊠ – †1195/5745 NOK ††1395/5945 NOK – 19 suites
• Business • Modern • Functional •
This is Norway's tallest hotel and it boasts more bedrooms than any other in
Oslo; the modern 'Business' rooms are the most comfortable. It has a large
marble lobby with a lounge and bar, extensive conference facilities, an Irish
pub, and a top floor restaurant offering a Norwegian menu and city views.

Thief

Landgangen 1 ⊠ 0252 – ℰ 24 00 40 00 Plan: **B3**
– www.thethief.com
116 rm ⊠ – †2290/4290 NOK ††2590/4590 NOK – 9 suites
• Luxury • Contemporary •
A smart hotel with a superb spa, located on a huge development on Thief
Island. Works from global artists – including Andy Warhol – feature throughout;
facilities are state-of-the-art and a tablet controls all of the technology in the
bedrooms.
Fru K – See restaurant listing

Rosenkrantz

Rosenkrantz gate 1 ⊠ 0159 – ⓜ National Theatret Plan: **C2**
– ℰ 23 31 55 00 – www.thonhotels.no
151 rm ⊠ – †1145/2895 NOK ††1445/4095 NOK
• Business • Chain • Functional •
Located in the city centre and perfect for the business traveller. The brightly sty-
led 8th floor guest lounge has complimentary coffee, mineral water, fruit and
cakes. Functional bedrooms come with Smart TVs and modern bathrooms.
Brasserie Paleo – See restaurant listing

Comfort H. Grand Central

Jernbanetorget 1 ⊠ 0154 – ⓜ Jernbanetorget Plan: **D2**
– ℰ 22 98 28 00 – www.comfortgrandcentral.no
170 rm ⊠ – †1420/1949 NOK ††1610/2249 NOK
• Chain • Business • Functional •
A great choice for businesspeople, this delightful hotel has a superb location
above the main train station. Many of the soundproofed bedrooms have been
individually styled and boast coordinating fabrics and colour schemes, as well
as feature bathrooms. The restaurant offers a menu of simple Italian dishes.

Opera

🏛️🏛️🏛️ ⚔ ⟨ ⟩ ⚲ 爪 ❅ 🅰 ⚱

Dronning Eufemias gate 4 ✉ 0191 – Ⓜ Jernbanetorget   Plan: **D2**
– ☎ 24 10 30 00 – www.thonhotels.no/opera – Closed 24-31 December
480 rm ☐ – ♛1095/2655 NOK ♛♛1195/2755 NOK – 2 suites
• Business • Modern •
Imposing light-stone building in front of the Opera House, close to the sea.
Guest areas are spacious; bedrooms are a split of classic and modern styles but
all are equally well-equipped. The restaurant boasts huge windows and panoramic views; watch the chefs at work in the open kitchen.

Clarion Collection H. Bastion

爪 爪 🅰 ↩ ⚱

Skippergata 7 ✉ 0152 – Ⓜ Jernbanetorget   Plan: **C3**
– ☎ 22 47 77 00 – www.choicehotels.no – Closed Easter and Christmas
99 rm ☐ – ♛1460/2980 NOK ♛♛1460/3180 NOK – 5 suites
• Business • Modern •
Set on the edge of the city, close to the port, this hotel has friendly staff, a cosy
lounge and a charming English-style lobby which offers free snacks. Bedrooms
vary in both their size and furnishings; many have seating areas.

Clarion Collection H. Gabelshus

🌿 爪 爪 ⚱ 🅿️

Gabelsgate 16 ✉ 0272 – ☎ 23 27 65 00   Plan: **A2**
– www.nordicchoicehotels.no – Closed Easter and Christmas
114 rm ☐ – ♛800/2240 NOK ♛♛940/2780 NOK – 1 suite
• Traditional • Business • Classic •
Beautiful ivy-covered house with a peaceful atmosphere, in a smart residential
neighbourhood. The classical wood-furnished lounge has a complimentary all-
day buffet. Charming bedrooms offer a pleasing contrast between old and new.

Saga H. Oslo

⚔ ↩ 🅿️

Eilert Sundtsgate 39 ✉ 0259 – ☎ 22 55 44 90   Plan: **B1**
– www.sagahoteloslo.no – Closed Christmas and Easter
47 rm ☐ – ♛995/2895 NOK ♛♛1095/3495 NOK
• Townhouse • Historic • Grand luxury •
A late Victorian townhouse with a smart, contemporary interior, set in a quiet
city suburb. Most of the bedrooms are spacious: they have bold feature walls,
modern facilities – including coffee machines – and small but stylish shower
rooms. There's a Japanese restaurant in the basement.

Scandic Vulkan

⚔ ⟨ 爪 ❅ 🅰 ↩ ⚱

Maridalsveien 13 ✉ 0178 – ☎ 21 05 71 00   Plan: **D1**
– www.scandichotels.com/vulkan – Closed Christmas and Easter
149 rm ☐ – ♛830/1900 NOK ♛♛1050/2350 NOK
• Business • Chain • Design •
A designer hotel on the site of a former silver mine, next to a great food market.
Modern bedrooms have bold walls and good facilities; the external-
facing rooms have full length windows. The bright, informal restaurant offers
an Italian-influenced menu, and adjoins a trendy bar and deli.

Clarion Collection H. Savoy

↩

Universitetsgata 11 ✉ 0164 – Ⓜ National Theatret   Plan: **C2**
– ☎ 23 35 42 00 – www.nordicchoicehotels.no – Closed 20-27 December
and Easter
93 rm ☐ – ♛940/2440 NOK ♛♛1036/2680 NOK
• Business • Classic •
Centrally located by the National Gallery, in a building dating back to 1850.
Bedrooms are decorated in a mix of classic and contemporary styles; the latter
feature large action photos. They offer complimentary breakfasts and light
meals.
🍴 **restauranteik** – See restaurant listing

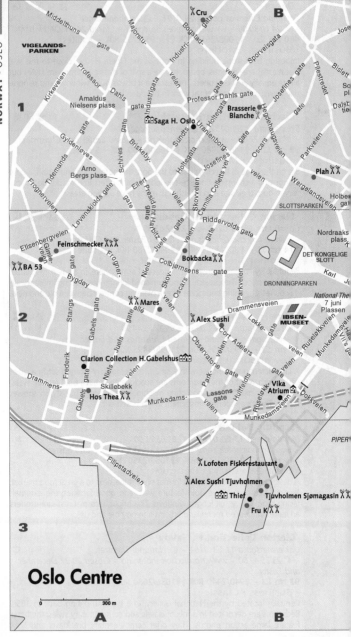

✖ **Cru**
gata

VIGELANDS-
PARKEN

Middelthuns
gate

Majorstu-

Bogstad-

Industri-

Sporvelsgata

Josefines gate

Pilestredet

Bislett

Jose

So
pl

Dalst
tie

A

B

Kirkeveien

Professor
Dahls

gate

Gyldenløves

Tidemands

Frognerveien

Amaldus
Nielsens plass

Arno
Bergs plass

Briskeby-

Schives

Eilert
Sundts-

President Harbitz

gate

gate

Industrigata

Uranienborg

veien

Professor Dahls gate

Holtegata

Josefines

veien

Oscars

Hegdehaugsveien

Parkveien

🏠 **Saga H. Oslo**

**Brasserie
Blanche** ✖

Skovveien

Camilla Colletts vei

Wergelands

Holbe
ga

Plah ✖ ✖

1

Løvenskiolds gate

Riddervolds gate

SLOTTSPARKEN

Elisenbergveien

Gimle-
veien

Feinschmecker ✖ ✖ ✖

Juels

gate

Nordraaks
plass

✖ ✖ **BA 53**

Frogner-

Niels

Shov-

Oscars

gate

Colbjørnsens   gate

● **Bokbacka** ✖ ✖

Parkveien

DET KONGELIGE
SLOTT

DRONNINGPARKEN

Karl Jo

2

Bygdøy

Stangs

Gabels gate

Juels

gate

Niels

alle

✖ ✖ **Mares**

Drammensveien

Lokke-

✖ **Alex Sushi**

Cort Adelers

gate

National The
7 juni
Plassen

**IBSEN-
MUSEET**

Ruseløkkveien

Munkedamsveien

Hills ga

Frederik

Clarion Collection H.Gabelshus 🏠

Observatorie gate

veien

Park-
veien

Drammens-

Gabels gate

Juels
veien

Skillebekk

Hos Thea ✖ ✖

Munkedams-

Lassons
gate

Huitfeldts

gate

Ruseløkk

**Vika
Atrium** 🏠

Dokkveien

Munkedamsveien

PIPER

Filipstadveien

✖ **Lofoten Fiskerestaurant**

✖ **Alex Sushi Tjuvholmen**

🏠 **Thief**

Tjuvholmen Sjømagasin ✖ ✖

Fru K ✖ ✖

3

Oslo Centre

0 ———— 300 m

A

B

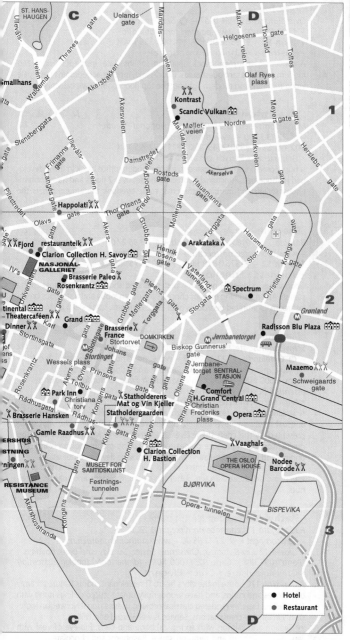

Park Inn

           🔥 AC 🏋️

Ovre Slottsgate 2c ✉ *0157 –* Ⓜ *Stortinget* — Plan: **C2**
– 𝒞 22 40 01 00 – www.parkinn.com/hotel-oslo
118 rm ⊡ – ♦995/3295 NOK ♦♦1095/3395 NOK
• Business • Chain • Functional •

A converted apartment block near Karl Johans Gate. Inside it's bright and modern with pleasant guest areas. Good-sized, functional bedrooms have pale wood furniture and modern lighting; the top floor rooms have balconies.

Vika Atrium

        🛏 🍽 ♨ 🎿 🚗

Munkedamsveien 45 ✉ *0250 –* Ⓜ *National Theatret* — Plan: **B2**
– 𝒞 22 83 33 00 – www.thonhotels.no
102 rm ⊡ – ♦999/2045 NOK ♦♦1195/2695 NOK
• Business • Functional • Modern •

A busy conference hotel located in a large modern office block in the redeveloped harbour area. Functional bedrooms are set over 7 floors and have contemporary styling and marble bathrooms: some overlook the atrium, others the street.

Spectrum

                      🔥

Brugata 7 ✉ *0186 –* Ⓜ *Grønland – 𝒞 23 36 27 00* — Plan: **D2**
– www.thonhotels.no/spectrum – Closed Christmas
151 rm ⊡ – ♦1575/1875 NOK ♦♦1750/2075 NOK
• Business • Functional •

Good value lodge-style hotel in a pedestrianised shopping street, close to the station. An unassuming exterior conceals a modern lobby and a spacious breakfast room. Light-hued bedrooms offer basic comforts; some sleep up to four.

Maaemo (Esben Holmboe Bang)

                    AC

XᵡX
❀❀❀

Schweigaardsgate 15b (entrance via staircase) ✉ *0191* — Plan: **D2**
– Ⓜ *Grønland – 𝒞 22 17 99 69 – www.maaemo.no – Closed Easter, 16-18 May, mid December to mid January and Sunday-Tuesday*
Menu 2600 NOK *– (dinner only and lunch Friday-Saturday) (booking essential) (tasting menu only)*
• Modern cuisine • Design • Fashionable •

A striking, modern restaurant with an intimate, brightly lit interior and an unusual mezzanine-level kitchen; dishes are finished at the table, with some presented by the chefs themselves. Maaemo means 'Mother Earth' and top quality Norwegian produce guides the 20+ course menu; cooking is intricate, original and visually stimulating with some sublime flavour combinations.
→ Oyster emulsion with mussels and dill. Reindeer with preserved plum sauce and artichokes. Brown butter ice cream, molasses and roasted hazelnuts.

Statholdergaarden (Bent Stiansen)

                   🍸 🔄

XᵡX
❀

Rådhusgata 11 (entrance on Kirkegata) ✉ *0151* — Plan: **C3**
– Ⓜ *Stortinget – 𝒞 22 41 88 00 – www.statholdergaarden.no*
– Closed 17 July-8 August, Christmas, Easter, Sunday and bank holidays
Menu 1095 NOK – Carte 925/1080 NOK *– (dinner only) (booking essential)*
• Classic cuisine • Chic • Elegant •

A charming 17C house in the city's heart. Three elegant rooms feature an array of antiques and curios, and have wonderfully ornate stucco ceilings hung with chandeliers. Expertly rendered classical cooking uses seasonal Norwegian ingredients in familiar combinations. Service is well-versed and willing.
→ Scallop and salmon with spring cabbage and ceps. Rib-eye of veal with Jerusalem artichoke and tarragon sauce. Raspberry and chocolate.
Statholderens Mat og Vin Kjeller – See restaurant listing

574

XxX **Feinschmecker** ⚶ 🎫 ✿

Balchensgate 5 ✉ 0265 – ✆ 22 12 93 80 Plan: **A2**
– www.feinschmecker.no – Closed 4 weeks summer, Easter, Christmas and Sunday
Menu 875 NOK – Carte 725/915 NOK – *(dinner only)*
• **Traditional cuisine** • **Classic décor** • **Neighbourhood** •
This long-standing restaurant has a cosy, welcoming atmosphere and a loyal local following, and is run by a charming team. The well-presented dishes are classically based, with French influences. Wine pairings are available.

XX **Kontrast** (Mikael Svenssen) ⴵ 🎫 ✿
✿
Maridalsveien 15 ✉ 0178 – ✆ 21 60 01 01 Plan: **D1**
– www.restaurant-kontrast.no – Closed Christmas, New Year, Easter, last week July- first week August, Sunday and Monday
Menu 795/1450 NOK – Carte 460/630 NOK – *(dinner only)*
• **Scandinavian** • **Design** • **Fashionable** •
A modern restaurant with a stark, semi-industrial feel created by the concrete floor, exposed pipework and open kitchen. Seasonal, organic Norwegian produce is used to create refined, original, full-flavoured dishes whose apparent simplicity often masks their complex nature. Service is well-paced and professional.
→ Scallops with roe emulsion and nasturtium. Salt-baked chicken with meadowsweet gel. Strawberries with rose hip cream and whipped duck eggs.

XX **Festningen** ⚶ ≤ 🛋 ⴵ 🎫 ↯ ✿
Myntgata 9 ✉ 0151 – ✆ 22 83 31 00 Plan: **C3**
– www.festningenrestaurant.no – Closed 19 December-6 January except dinner 31 December, 1 week Easter and Sunday
Menu 315/595 NOK – Carte 615/705 NOK
• **Modern cuisine** • **Brasserie** • **Fashionable** •
A smart, contemporary brasserie with a terrace and lovely views over the water to Aker Brygge; it was once a prison and its name means 'fortress'. The experienced kitchen create unfussy, attractively presented modern Nordic dishes using fresh local produce. The impressive wine list is strong on burgundy.

XX **Bokbacka** ✿
Skovveien 15 ✉ 0257 – ✆ 41 26 01 44 Plan: **A2**
– www.bokbacka.no – Closed Sunday and Monday
Menu 795 NOK – *(dinner only)*
• **Modern cuisine** • **Fashionable** • **Neighbourhood** •
A unique 'food bar' with clean, light styling and fun, idiosyncratic features; seats are arranged around the open kitchen, with only 4 other tables. Many of the theatrically presented dishes on the set omakase-style menu have a story.

XX **Fru K** – Thief Hotel ⴵ 🎫 🚗
Landgangen 1 ✉ 0252 – ✆ 24 00 40 40 Plan: **B3**
– www.thethief.com – Closed Easter, July, Christmas and Sunday
Menu 895/1095 NOK – *(dinner only) (tasting menu only)*
• **Modern cuisine** • **Design** • **Fashionable** •
Chic hotel restaurant, named after Fru Krogh, who tended animals on the Tjuvholmen peninsula long ago. Set 5 and 7 course menus use fine Norwegian ingredients to create tasty dishes. Take in the view from the rooftop 'Foodbar' in summer.

XX **restauranteik** – Clarion Collection H. Savoy 🎫 ✿
🍮
Universitetsgata 11 ✉ 0164 – Ⓜ National Theatret Plan: **C2**
– ✆ 22 36 07 10 – www.restauranteik.no – Closed July, Easter, Christmas, Sunday and Monday
Menu 395 NOK – *(dinner only) (tasting menu only)*
• **Modern cuisine** • **Fashionable** • **Brasserie** •
A contemporary L-shaped dining room in a hotel close to the National Gallery. It's minimalist in style, with colourful artwork, an open kitchen and a glass-walled wine cellar. The weekly 3-5 course set menu comprises inventive international cuisine. Service is efficient and the atmosphere is friendly.

XX **Happolati**

St. Olavs Plass 2 ✉ 0165 – Ⓜ National Theatret
Plan: **C1**
– ℰ 47 97 80 87 – www.happolati.no
– Closed Christmas and Easter
Menu 475/650 NOK – Carte 430/600 NOK
• Asian • Design • Friendly •

This bright, modish restaurant fuses Asian and Nordic styles; its assured cooking uses good quality ingredients and many dishes are designed for sharing. Tightly packed tables and friendly service add to the vibrant ambience.

XX **BA 53**

Bygdoy Allé 53 ✉ 0265 – ℰ 21 42 05 90
Plan: **A2**
– www.ba53.no – Closed Christmas, July and Sunday
Menu 535/875 NOK – Carte 530/730 NOK – (Monday to Friday dinner only)
• Modern cuisine • Fashionable • Neighbourhood •

A daytime coffee shop combines with a moody cocktail bar and a relaxed, softly lit brasserie to create this stylish neighbourhood hotspot. Menus offer a mix of Nordic classics and more modern dishes; four per person is ample.

XX **Ekeberg**

Kongsveien 15 (Southeast: 1 km by Rostockergata, Bispegata amd Geitabru) ✉ 0193 – ℰ 23 24 23 00 – www.ekebergrestauranten.com
– Closed Christmas
Menu 350/470 NOK – Carte 464/649 NOK
• Seafood • Vintage • Design •

A delightfully restored art deco house on the hillside, with charming original fittings, several large terraces and commanding views over the fjords and the city. Cooking is careful, fresh and seasonal; seafood features highly.

XX **Gamle Raadhus**

Nedre Slottsgate 1 ✉ 0151 – Ⓜ Stortinget
Plan: **C3**
– ℰ 22 42 01 07 – www.gamle-raadhus.no – Closed 3 weeks July,
22 December-3 January, Easter and Sunday
Menu 425/469 NOK – Carte 510/705 NOK
• Traditional cuisine • Rustic • Elegant •

Brightly painted house dating from 1641; its charming, antique-filled interior includes a library and an open-fired lounge. Lunch is served in the bar and classical dinners in the traditional dining room. There's also a lovely terrace.

XX **Fjord**

Kristian Augusts Gt. 11 ✉ 0164 – Ⓜ National Theatret
Plan: **C2**
– ℰ 22 98 21 50 – www.restaurantfjord.no – Closed Christmas, Easter,
Sunday and Monday except in December
Menu 445/695 NOK – (dinner only) (booking essential) (tasting menu only)
• Seafood • Design • Fashionable •

A contemporary restaurant opposite the National Gallery. Inside it's dimly lit, with an open kitchen, unusual cobalt blue walls and buffalo horns set into the chandeliers. The 3-5 course menu offers flavoursome seafood dishes.

XX **Dinner**

Stortingsgata 22 ✉ 0161 – Ⓜ National Theatret
Plan: **C2**
– ℰ 23 10 04 66 – www.dinner.no – Closed Christmas, Easter and Sunday lunch
Menu 258/499 NOK – Carte 365/1037 NOK
• Chinese • Design • Elegant •

An intimate restaurant on the central square, close to the National Theatre. A black frosted glass façade masks a smart split-level interior. The kitchen focuses on Sichuan cuisine, with some artfully presented dim sum at lunch.

XX **Nodee Barcode** 🏠 🅰🄲 ⇦

Dronning Eufemais Gate 28 ✉ *0191* Plan: **D3**
*– ⓂJernbanetorget – 𝒞 22 93 34 50 – www.nodee.no – Closed Christmas,
Easter and Sunday lunch*
Menu 240/645 NOK – Carte 345/530 NOK
• Asian • Fashionable • Trendy •
A moody, elegant ground floor restaurant serving an all-encompassing Asian
menu featuring dim sum, sushi and dishes cooked on the Robata grill. There's
a bar and terrace on the 13th floor and on the 14th floor is Nodee Sky, with its
appealing set menu and city views.

XX **Tjuvholmen Sjømagasinet** 🦀 🏠 ⇦

Tjuvholmen Allé 14 ✉ *0251* – 𝒞 *23 89 77 77* Plan: **B3**
– www.sjomagasinet.no – Closed Christmas, Easter and Sunday
Menu 565/655 NOK – Carte 565/835 NOK
• Seafood • Design • Brasserie •
Vast restaurant with three dining rooms, a crab and lobster tank, a superb terrace and a wet fish shop. Its name means 'sea store' and menus are fittingly seafood based. Shellfish is from the nearby dock – the langoustines are fantastic.

XX **Mares** 🅰🄲

Skovveien 1 ✉ *0257* – 𝒞 *22 54 89 80 – www.mares.no* Plan: **A2**
– Closed 12-18 April, 3 July-2 August, 23 December-3 January and Sunday
Menu 485 NOK – Carte 485/705 NOK – *(dinner only) (booking advisable)*
• French • Neighbourhood • Brasserie •
Neighbourhood restaurant with an adjoining deli and fish shop; it's bright and
modern, with white furniture and a slightly industrial feel. Classical French
menus have Spanish and Italian touches – order the fruits de mer 24hrs ahead.

XX **Hos Thea**

Gabelsgate 11 ✉ *0272* – 𝒞 *22 44 68 74* Plan: **A2**
– www.hosthea.no – Closed July, Christmas and Easter
Menu 545 NOK – Carte 665/690 NOK – *(dinner only)*
• Italian • Family • Neighbourhood •
A small, well-established restaurant in a charming residential area. It's decorated
in natural hues and hung with beautiful oils. Menus offer a concise selection of
Mediterranean dishes; start with the delicious homemade bread.

XX **Plah** 🏠 🅰🄲 ⇦

Hegdehaugsveien 22 ✉ *0167* – 𝒞 *22 56 43 00* Plan: **B1**
– www.plah.no – Closed 2 weeks July, Christmas, Easter and Sunday
Menu 695 NOK – Carte 525/695 NOK – *(dinner only)*
• Thai • Neighbourhood • Friendly •
Well-run restaurant offering tasty Thai dishes; Plah means 'fish' and the produce
is from local waters. The tasting and wine menus are good value and service is
knowledgeable. Their next door bar, Ahaan, serves authentic street food.

XX **Theatercaféen** – Continental Hotel 🦀 🕭 🅰🄲 ⇦

Stortingsgaten 24-26 ✉ *0117* – Ⓜ *National Theatret* Plan: **C2**
*– 𝒞 22 82 40 50 – www.theatercafeen.no – Closed Christmas, Easter and
July*
Menu 345/655 NOK – Carte 495/745 NOK
• Traditional cuisine • Luxury • Romantic •
A prestigious Oslo institution in a grand hotel, this charming Viennese 'grand
café' comes with pillars, black banquettes and art nouveau lighting. Fresh
cakes and elaborate lunchtime sandwiches make way for ambitious dinners.

XX **Brasserie Paleo** – Hotel Rosenkrantz 🕭 🅰🄲 ⇦

Rosenkrantz gate 1 ✉ *0159* – Ⓜ *National Theatrer* Plan: **C2**
– 𝒞 23 31 55 80 – www.brasseriepaleo.no – Closed Christmas, Easter and July
Menu 185/495 NOK – Carte 495/605 NOK
• Scandinavian • Trendy • Trendy •
With a name which reflects its philosophy, and a contemporary urban style, this
is not your typical hotel restaurant. Watch the chefs prepare attractive modern
Scandinavian dishes in the open kitchen. Service is professional and friendly.

X **Brasserie Blanche**　　　　　　　　　　　🛜 🅰🅒 ⇔

Josefinesgate 23 ✉ *0352 –* ☏ *23 20 13 10*　　　Plan: **B1**
– www.blanche.no – Closed 3 weeks July, 24 December and Monday
Menu 495 NOK – Carte 339/599 NOK – *(dinner only)*
• French • Cosy • Brasserie •
Cosy French restaurant housed in an 18C building, which was originally a stable
and later spent time as a garage and an interior furnishings store. It has a small
front terrace, a bar decorated with wine boxes and a wall made of corks. The
chef is a Francophile and creates flavoursome classic French dishes.

X **Vaaghals**　　　　　　　　　　　🛜 & 🅰🅒 ⇔

Dronning Eufemias gate 8 (Radhusgaten 30) ✉ *0151*　　Plan: **D3**
– Ⓜ *Jernbanetorget –* ☏ *92 07 09 99 – www.vaaghals.com – Closed 3 last
weeks July, 22 December-3 January, Easter and Sunday*
Menu 650 NOK (dinner) – Carte 455/560 NOK
• Scandinavian • Brasserie • Fashionable •
A bright, contemporary restaurant with an open kitchen and a terrace; located
on the ground floor of one of the modern 'barcode' buildings. Scandinavian
menus feature dry-aged meat; many of the dinner dishes are designed for sharing.

X **Statholderens Mat og Vin Kjeller** – Statholdergaarden

Rådhusgate 11 (entrance from Kirkegata) ✉ *0151*　　Plan: **C3**
– Ⓜ *Stortinget –* ☏ *22 41 88 00 – www.statholdergaarden.no*
*– Closed 9 July-7 August, 23 December-3 January, 19-28 March, 1, 5 and
14-17 May, Sunday and Monday*
Menu 695 NOK – Carte 660/680 NOK – *(dinner only) (booking essential)*
• Norwegian • Rustic • Simple •
The informal sister of Statholdergaarden – set over three rooms in the old vaults
beneath it. One wall of the large entranceway is filled with wine bottles. Choose
from a huge array of small plates or go for the 10 course tasting menu.

X **Brasserie Hansken**　　　　　　　　　　　⇔

Akersgate 2 ✉ *0158 –* Ⓜ *Stortinget –* ☏ *22 42 60 88*　　Plan: **C2**
*– www.brasseriehansken.no – Closed 3 weeks late July-early August,
1 week Easter, 1 week Christmas and Sunday*
Menu 395/595 NOK – Carte 395/695 NOK
• Modern cuisine • Family • Brasserie •
A delightfully traditional brasserie, centrally located by City Hall, with various
charming dining areas and a fantastic terrace. Classical cooking follows the seasons and mixes French and Scandic influences; ingredients are top quality.

X **Cru**　　　　　　　　　　　　　　　　　　🎇

Ingelbrecht, Knudssønsgt 1 ✉ *0365 –* ☏ *23 98 98 98*　　Plan: **B1**
– www.cru.no – Closed July, 23 December-5 January and Sunday
Menu 545/495 NOK – Carte 457/507 NOK – *(dinner only)*
• Norwegian • Wine bar • Trendy •
Upstairs in the rustic restaurant they serve a set 4 course menu, with inventive
British touches and 4 optional extra courses; downstairs in the more informal
wine bar you can enjoy everything from nibbles through to a full à la carte
menu.

X **Arakataka**　　　　　　　　　　　　　🅰🅒 ⇔

Mariboes gate 7 ✉ *0183 –* Ⓜ *Stortinget*　　　Plan: **D2**
– ☏ *23 32 83 00 – www.arakataka.no – Closed July, Christmas and Easter*
Menu 495/565 NOK – Carte 410/510 NOK – *(dinner only) (booking advisable)*
• Norwegian • Fashionable • Friendly •
A smart glass-fronted restaurant with a central food bar, an open kitchen and a
buzzy atmosphere. Choose from a concise menu of seasonal Norwegian small
plates – they recommend 3 savoury dishes plus a dessert per person.

𝕏 **Lofoten Fiskerestaurant**

Stranden 75 ✉ 0250 – 𝒞 22 83 08 08   Plan: **B3**
– www.lofotenfiskerestaurant.no – Closed Christmas
Menu 345/550 NOK – Carte 410/705 NOK
• Seafood • Brasserie • Simple •

A traditional fjord-side restaurant decorated in bright maritime colours and offering lovely views from its large windows and charming terrace. Watch as fresh, simply cooked fish and shellfish are prepared in the semi-open kitchen.

𝕏 **Alex Sushi Tjuvholmen**

Strandpromenaden 11 ✉ 0252 – 𝒞 2243 99 99   Plan: **B3**
– www.alexsushi.no – Closed Easter, Christmas and Sunday
Menu 495/995 NOK – Carte lunch 320/425 NOK
• Sushi • Simple • Neighbourhood •

Set in a fantastic harbourside spot, with a great terrace. The skilful, knowledgeable chefs are surrounded by large scuba diver models. Sushi, sashimi and nigiri feature at lunch, followed by 3 set menus at dinner. The tuna is superb.

𝕏 **Smalhans** ⇔

Waldemar Thranes gate 10A ✉ 0171 – 𝒞 22 69 60 00   Plan: **C1**
– www.smalhans.no – Closed 3 weeks July, Easter, Christmas and Monday
Menu 425/615 NOK – Carte lunch 315/420 NOK
• Traditional • Neighbourhood • Simple •

A sweet neighbourhood café with friendly staff and an urban feel. Coffee and homemade cakes are served in the morning, with a short selection of dishes including soup and a burger on offer between 12pm and 4pm. A daily hot dish is available from 4-6pm, while set menus and sharing plates are served at dinner.

𝕏 **Brasserie France**

Øvre Slottsgate 16 ✉ 0157 – ⓜ Stortinget   Plan: **C2**
– 𝒞 23 10 01 65 – www.brasseriefrance.no – Closed Easter, 23 December-2 January, Sunday and lunch Monday
Menu 320/395 NOK – Carte 470/660 NOK
• French • Brasserie • Traditional décor •

A lively Gallic brasserie in a pedestrianised shopping street, with several private dining rooms. Brasserie classics from bouillabaisse to steak frites feature; for dessert, choose from the 'eat-as-much-as-you-like' pastry trolley.

𝕏 **Alex Sushi** ⇔

Cort Adelers Gate 2 ✉ 0254 – ⓜ National Theatret   Plan: **B2**
– 𝒞 22 43 99 99 – www.alexsushi.no – Closed July, Easter and Christmas
Menu 485 NOK – Carte 195/860 NOK – *(dinner only)*
• Japanese • Design • Minimalist •

A glass-fronted Japanese restaurant and takeaway, with a bright interior made of wood, steel and glass. Sit at the boat-shaped sushi bar to try top quality local sashimi. Half of customers choose the set menus, which offer the best value.

ENVIRONS OF OSLO

AT GREFSEN   North : 10 km by Ring 3

𝕏𝕏 **Grefsenkollen**

Grefsenkollveien 100 ✉ 0490 – 𝒞 22 79 70 60 – www.grefsenkollen.no
– Closed July, Christmas and dinner Sunday-Monday and Easter
Menu 250/845 NOK – Carte lunch 420/600 NOK – *(booking essential at dinner)*
• Norwegian • Romantic • Cosy •

A fairytale chalet in the mountains, with a spacious terrace, a characterful open-fired dining room and lovely views over the city and fjord. Appealing 3 and 5 course dinner menus are well-balanced, intricate and playful – Norwegian ingredients take centre stage. Lunch is light; dinner offers wine pairings.

AT OSLO AIRPORT Northeast : 45 km by E 6 at Gardermoen

Clarion Oslo Airport ♀ 🛏 🕅 🕹 ⇪ 🛜 🅿

Hans Gaarderveg 15 (West: 6 km) ⊠ 2060 – 𝒞 63 94 94 94
– www.clarionosloairport.no
432 rm ⊡ – 🛉1145/1335 NOK 🛉🛉1145/1335 NOK
• Business • Functional •

Typical two-storey Norwegian house, accessed from the airport by a shuttle bus;
it has one of the largest conference capacities in the country. Modern Scandinavian bedrooms come in pale hues. Live music features in the bar and open-fired
lounges, and buffet meals are served in the traditional restaurant.

AT HOLMENKOLLEN Northwest : 10 km by Bogstadveien, Sørkedalsveien and
Holmenkollveien

Holmenkollen Park ⅖ ≼ 🛏 🕅 🕅 🔲 🕹 🔟 ⇪ 🛜 🚗

Kongeveien 26 ⊠ 0787 – Ⓜ Holmenkollen – 𝒞 22 92 20 00
– www.holmenkollenparkhotel.no – Closed 21 December-2 January
336 rm ⊡ – 🛉1049/2099 NOK 🛉🛉1049/2099 NOK
• Traditional • Personalised •

An impressive 1894 red wood building (once a sanatorium for TB patients!),
located beside a world-class ski resort. The interior displays a curious mix of styles, from the classical to the modern; three of the bedrooms have their own saunas.

De Fem Stuer – See restaurant listing

✗✗✗ De Fem Stuer – Holmenkollen Park Hotel ≼ 🕹 🔟 ⇔ 🅿

Kongeveien 26 ⊠ 0787 – Ⓜ Holmenkollen – 𝒞 22 92 27 34
– www.holmenkollenparkhotel.no – Closed 21 December-2 January
Menu 325/395 NOK – Carte 655/885 NOK
• Norwegian • Elegant • Romantic •

A series of five elegant dining rooms in an impressive hotel; three with delightful wood panelling. A buffet lunch is followed by a concise, seasonal à la carte
and a daily set menu. Classical cooking displays French influences.

AT STABEKK Southwest : 9 km by E18

✗✗ Strand 🔟 ⇔ 🅿

Strandalleén 43 ⊠ 1368 – 𝒞 67 53 05 75 – www.strandrestaurant.no
– Closed Christmas, Easter and Monday
Menu 175/625 NOK – Carte 465/625 NOK
• Scandinavian • Traditional décor • Rustic •

An 18C wooden house with a bakery and café, set in a quiet seaside town. The
restaurant is bright and contemporary with an open kitchen and a terrace affording views out over the marina. Classic Scandinavian cooking uses organic produce.

POLAND
POLSKA

WARSAW ●

● Cracow

→ **AREA:**
312 677 km²
(120 725 sq mi).

→ **POPULATION:**
38 593 161 inhabitants.
Density = 123 per km².

→ **CAPITAL:**
Warsaw.

→ **CURRENCY:**
Polish Złoty (zl or PLN).

→ **GOVERNMENT:**
Parliamentary republic (since 1990).
Member of European Union since
2004.

→ **LANGUAGE:**
Polish.

→ **PUBLIC HOLIDAYS:**
New Year's Day (1 Jan); Easter
Monday (late Mar/Apr); Labor Day
(1 May); Constitution Day (3 May);
Pentecost Monday (late May/June);
Corpus Christi (late May/June);
Assumption of the Virgin Mary (15
Aug); All Saints' Day
(1 Nov); Independence Day (11 Nov);
Christmas Day (25 Dec); Boxing Day
(26 Dec).

→ **LOCAL TIME:**
GMT+1 hour in winter and GMT
+2 hours in summer.

→ **CLIMATE:**
Temperate continental with
cold winters and warm summers
(Warsaw: January -2°C; July 20°C).

→ **EMERGENCY:**
Police ✆ **997**;
Medical Assistance ✆ **999**;
Fire Brigade ✆ **998**.
(Dialling **112** within any
EU country will redirect your
call and contact the emergency
services.)

→ **ELECTRICITY:**
230 volts AC, 50Hz; 2 round pin
sockets.

→ **FORMALITIES:**
Travellers from the European Union
(EU), Switzerland, Iceland and
the main countries of North and
South America need a national
identity card or passport (America:
passport required) to visit Poland
for less than three months (tourism
or business purpose). For visitors
from other countries a visa may be
required, in addition to a passport,
especially for those wishing to
stay for longer than three months.
We advise you to check with your
embassy before travelling.

WARSAW
WARSZAWA

Population: 1 714 400

Céline Lecardonnel/Fotolia.com

When UNESCO added Warsaw to its World Heritage list, it was a fitting seal of approval for its inspired rebuild, after eighty per cent of the city was destroyed during World War II. Using plans of the old city, architects painstakingly rebuilt the shattered capital throughout the 1950s, until it became an admirable mirror image of its former self. Now grey communist era apartment blocks sit beside pretty, pastel-coloured aristocratic buildings, their architecture ranging from Gothic to baroque, rococo to secession.

Nestling against the River Vistula, the Old Town was established at the end of the 13C, around what is now the Royal Castle, and a century later the New Town, to the north, began to take shape. To the south of the Old Town runs 'The Royal Route', so named because, from the late middle ages, wealthy citizens built summer residences with lush gardens along these rural thoroughfares. Continue southwards and you're in Lazienki Park with its palaces and pavilions, while to the west lie the more commercial areas of Marshal Street and Solidarity Avenue, once the commercial heart of the city. The northwest of Warsaw was traditionally the Jewish district, until it was destroyed during the war; today it has been redeveloped with housing estates and the sobering Monument to the Ghetto Heroes.

WARSAW IN...

→ **ONE DAY**
Royal Castle, Warsaw History Museum, National Museum, Lazienki Park.

→ **TWO DAYS**
Monument to the Ghetto Heroes, Saxon Gardens, concert at Grand Theatre or Philharmonic Hall.

→ **THREE DAYS**
The Royal Route, Marshal Street, Solidarity Avenue, Wilanow.

ARRIVAL-DEPARTURE

⊞ Warsaw Frederic Chopin Airport is 10km southwest. Bus 175 or 188 takes 20min. Trains run every 10-12min and take 25min. If travelling by taxi, ensure you take one from the rank outside arrivals.

⊞ Warsaw Modlin Airport is 40km northwest. Modlinbus operate a regular service to the Central Station that takes 60min.

GETTING AROUND

If you are visiting the central attractions, go on foot; otherwise, hire a City Bike or take the metro, bus or tram. The RUCH kiosks are often closed in the evenings and at weekends, so it's best to buy tickets in a pack of ten. A flat rate fare for all single journeys applies, and one-day, seven-day and family tickets are also available. The Warsaw Tourist Card is available from tourist information offices; it entitles you to free travel on public transport, free admission to 21 museums, and discounts in some shops, restaurants and leisure centres. (All museums offer free entry on a Sunday.)

CALENDAR HIGHLIGHTS

March-April
Beethoven Easter Festival.

May-September
Chopin concerts in Lazienki Park.

June-July
Mozart Festival.

July-August
Summer Jazz Days.

October
International Film Festival (WIFF), Baroque Opera Festival, Jazz Festival.

November
Piano Festival, Jazz Jamboree.

EATING OUT

The centuries-old traditional cuisine of Warsaw was influenced by neighbouring Russia, Ukraine and Germany, while Jewish dishes were also added to the mix. Over the years there has been a growing sophistication to the cooking and a lighter, more contemporary style has become evident, with time-honoured classics - such as the ubiquitous pierogi (dumplings with various fillings) and the ever-popular breaded pork dish 'bigos' - having been updated with flair. These are accompanied, of course, by chilled Polish vodka, which covers a bewildering range of styles. Warsaw also has a more global side, with everything from stalls selling falafel to restaurants serving Vietnamese, and a large Italian business community has ensured there are a good number of Italian restaurants too. Stylised settings are popular, such as a burghers' houses or vaulted cellars; wherever you eat, check that VAT has been included within the prices (it's not always) and add a ten per cent tip. If it's value for money you're after, head for a Milk Bar, a low priced cafeteria selling traditional dairy-based food.

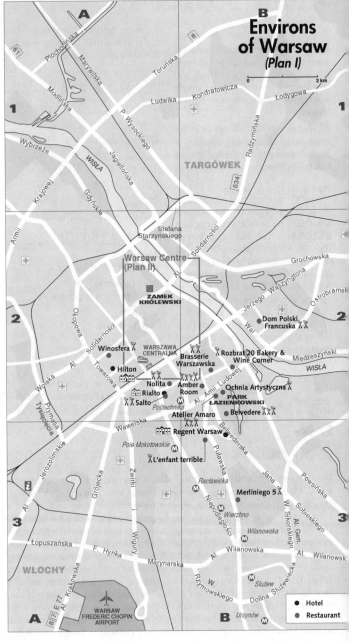

Environs of Warsaw
(Plan I)

0   2 km

TARGÓWEK

Stefana
Starzyńskiego

Warsaw Centre
(Plan II)

ZAMEK
KRÓLEWSKI

Dom Polski,
Francuska

Winosfera

WARSZAWA
CENTRALNA

Brasserie
Warszawska

Rozbrat 20 Bakery &
Wine Corner

Hilton

Nolita

Amber
Room

Ochnia Artystyczna

Rialto

PARK
ŁAZIENKOWSKI

Salto

Atelier Amaro

Belvedere

Regent Warsaw

Pole Mokotowskie

L'enfant terrible

Racławicka

Merliniego 5

Wierzbno

Wilanowska

WŁOCHY

WARSAW
FREDERIC CHOPIN
AIRPORT

Ursynów

● Hotel
● Restaurant

Intercontinental

ul. Emilii Plater 49 ✉ *00 125 –* Ⓜ *Centrum –* ℰ *(22)*   Plan: **C2**
328 8888 – www.warsaw.intercontinental.com
414 rm ☒ – ♦370/1950 PLN ♦♦420/2000 PLN – 21 suites
· Grand Luxury · Business · Modern ·

Striking high-rise hotel in a central location. Smart guest areas include a modern lounge and a clubby bar; bedrooms are large and contemporary. The impressive health and leisure club on the 43rd and 44th floors boasts fantastic views. Informal buffet lunches are served in Downtown, with steaks a speciality in the evening; Platter offers more refined, modern cooking.
Platter by Karol Okrasa – See restaurant listing

Hotel Bristol

ul. Krakowskie Przedmiescie 42-44 ✉ *00 325 –* ℰ *(22)*   Plan: **D1**
551 10 00 – www.hotelbristol.pl
206 rm – ♦550/2700 PLN ♦♦550/2700 PLN – ☒ 130 PLN – 38 suites
· Grand Luxury · Historic · Classic ·

Built in 1901 and set next to the Presidential Palace, this grand, art deco hotel boasts an elegant marble-floored reception and an impressive columned bar. Luxurious bedrooms have a high level of facilities. Unwind in the wine bar or on the terrace. The smart restaurant offers a modern Polish menu.

Regent Warsaw

ul. Belwederska 23 ✉ *00 761 –* ℰ *(22) 558 12 34*   Plan I: **B3**
– www.regent-warsaw.com
246 rm – ♦360/870 PLN ♦♦420/930 PLN – ☒ 85 PLN – 19 suites
· Luxury · Business · Modern ·

Contemporary hotel close to a large park, featuring an impressive open-plan lobby and a glass-roofed lounge-bar. Spacious bedrooms boast top quality furniture, smart bathrooms and a host of cleverly concealed facilities. Split-level Venti Tre offers an extensive Mediterranean menu and wood-fired specialities.

Hilton

ul. Grzybowska 63 ✉ *00 844 –* ℰ *(22) 356 55 55*   Plan I: **A2**
– www.warsaw.hilton.com
314 rm – ♦323/1620 PLN ♦♦377/1620 PLN – ☒ 95 PLN – 10 suites
· Business · Chain · Modern ·

Large, corporate hotel in the business district. The bright atrium houses shops and a lounge-bar; extensive business and leisure facilities include a smart club lounge, a casino and the city's largest event space. Bedrooms are modern and well-equipped. The informal restaurant offers an international menu.

Sheraton

ul. Boleslawa Prusa 2 ✉ *00 493 –* ℰ *(22) 450 6100*   Plan: **D2**
– www.sheraton.pl
350 rm – ♦324/2700 PLN ♦♦324/2700 PLN – ☒ 107 PLN – 15 suites
· Luxury · Business · Classic ·

Spacious hotel on the historic Three Cross Square, with a large open-plan lobby, a smart ballroom, and good conference and leisure facilities. Bedrooms are well-equipped; the top floor Club Rooms are the most contemporary. InAzia offers dishes from China, Thailand, Indonesia, Singapore and Vietnam.

Sofitel Warsaw Victoria

ul. Królewska 11 ✉ *00 065 –* Ⓜ *Świętokrzyska –* ℰ *(22)*   Plan: **C1**
657 80 11 – www.sofitel-victoria-warsaw.com
343 rm – ♦470/1265 PLN ♦♦470/1465 PLN – ☒ 100 PLN – 53 suites
· Business · Luxury · Contemporary ·

Smart hotel by Pilsudski Square, overlooking the Saxon Gardens. Unwind in the lovely spa or the reflective-ceilinged pool. Contemporary guest areas pay homage to the 1970s with geometric designs, and bedrooms are bold, sleek and well-equipped. The delightful brasserie mixes Polish and French cuisine.

POLAND - WARSAW

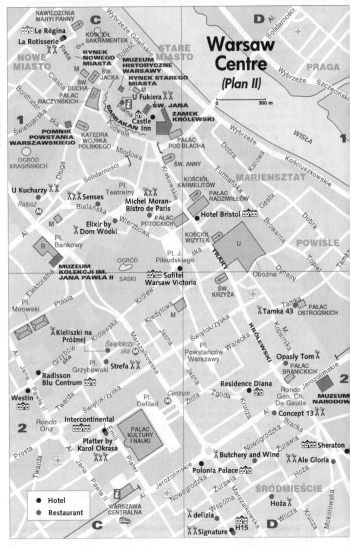

POLAND - WARSAW

Warsaw Centre
(Plan II)

0   300 m

NOWE MIASTO

NAWIEDZENIA MARYI PANNY

Le Régina
La Rotisserie

KOŚCIÓŁ SAKRAMENTEK

Wybrzeże Gdańskie

STARE MIASTO

D

C

Al. Solidarności

PRAGA

Szczecińska

Wybrzeże

RYNEK NOWEGO MIASTA

Freta

ŚW. JACKA

Bolesć

MUZEUM HISTORYCZNE WARSAWY

RYNEK STAREGO MIASTA

PAŁAC RACZYŃSKICH

ŚW. DUCHA

U Fukiera

ŚW. JANA

ZAMEK KRÓLEWSKI

Ciasna

Bonifraterska

Świetojerska

1

POMNIK POWSTANIA WARSZAWSKIEGO

OGRÓD KRASIŃSKICH

Długa

Piwna

Podwale

Castle Inn

BARBAKAN

KATEDRA WOJSKA POLSKIEGO

Miodowa

PAŁAC POD BLACHĄ

ŚW. ANNY

Krakowskie

Dobra

Furmanska

Karowa

WISŁA

Kościuszkowskie

MARIENSZTAT

1

Solidarności

U Kucharzy

Senses

Michel Moran-Bistro de Paris

KOŚCIÓŁ KARMELITÓW

PAŁAC RADZIWIŁŁÓW

Gesta

Dobra

Browarna

Ratusz

PL. Teatralny

Bielańska

Elixir by Dom Wódki

Wierzbowa

PAŁAC POTOCKICH

Hotel Bristol

POWIŚLE

PL. Bankowy

R

OGRÓD

ŚW. ANNY

KOŚCIÓŁ WIZYTEK

U

TRAKI

Dynasy

Topiel

Tamk

MUZEUM KOLEKCJI IM. JANA PAWŁA II

SASKI

PL. J. Piłsudskiego

ska

Sofitel Warsaw Victoria

Oboźna

Elektoralna

PL. Mirowski

Prasia

Krolew

ŚW. KRZYŻA

Kredytowa

Tamka 43

PAŁAC OSTROGSKICH

Tamka

Kieliszki na Próżnej

Królewska

Świętokrzy-ska

Jasna

Świętokrzyska

Warecka

Opasly Tom

M. Kopernika

PAŁAC BRANICKICH

Grzybow-ska

PL. Grzybowski

Strefa

PL. Powstańców Warszawy

Jasna

KRÓLEWSKI

2

Radisson Blu Centrum

Al. Jana

Twarda

Świętokrzyska

Westin

Pawla II

Centrum

M

Zgoda

Złota

Residence Diana

Rondo Gen. Ch. De Gaulle

Krucza

Jerozolimskie

MUZEUM NARODOW

2

Rondo Onz

Intercontinental

Emili

PL. Defilad

Concept 13

Prosta

Platter by Karol Okrasa

PAŁAC KULTURY I NAUKI

Nowogrodzka

Bracka

Żurawia

Sheraton

Twarda

Plater

Butchery and Wine

Ale Gloria

Pawla II

Jerozolimskie

Polonia Palace

Hoża

ŚRÓDMIEŚCIE

WARSZAWA CENTRALNA

Nowogrodzka

Żurawia

Wspólna

Marszałkowska

Hoża

Mokotowska

delizia

Signature

Wilcza

H15

Krucza

C

D

● Hotel

● Restaurant

586

Le Régina
🏨 ⅏ 🎟 ⅏ 🛁

ul. Koscielna 12 ✉ *00 218 –* ☏ *(22) 531 60 00*   Plan: **C1**
– www.mamaisonleregina.com
61 rm – 🛏378/1350 PLN 🛏🛏378/1350 PLN – ☲ 114 PLN – 3 suites
• Luxury • Family • Design •

Charming boutique hotel housed in a neo-18C building, on a peaceful cobbled street close to the castle and Old Town. The décor is cool and understated, with a Mediterranean feel. Subtle design features include room numbers projected onto the floor and hand-painted frescoes on the bedheads. Service is friendly.
La Rotisserie – See restaurant listing

Polonia Palace
⛲ 🎟 🏨 ⅏ 🎟 ⅏ 🛁

al. Jerozolimskie 45 ✉ *00 692 –* Ⓜ *Centrum –* ☏ *(22)*   Plan: **D2**
318 2800 – www.poloniapalace.com
206 rm – 🛏275/760 PLN 🛏🛏275/760 PLN – ☲ 80 PLN – 3 suites
• Business • Family • Contemporary •

Striking hotel dating from 1913, on a busy central street. The elegant interior has a lovely glass-roofed lobby, a popular lounge-bar and a beautifully ornate gilded ballroom. Modern, well-equipped bedrooms come in browns and creams. Formal Strauss offers a large menu of Polish and European cuisine.

Westin
⛲ ⪜ 🎟 🏨 ⅏ 🎟 ⅏ 🛁 🚗

al. Jana Pawla II 21 ✉ *00 854 –* Ⓜ *Świętokrzyska*   Plan: **C2**
– ☏ *(22) 450 80 00 – www.westin.pl*
361 rm – 🛏270/1458 PLN 🛏🛏270/1458 PLN – ☲ 107 PLN – 15 suites
• Luxury • Business • Modern •

An eye-catching modern building on a busy street, featuring a soaring atrium with glass lifts and a wide choice of conference and events rooms. Smart, contemporary bedrooms have good facilities; the top floor Club Rooms are the best. Worldwide ingredients meet Eastern recipes in the restaurant.

Radisson Blu Centrum
⛲ 🎟 🏨 ▣ ⅏ 🎟 ⅏ 🛁 🚗

ul. Grzybowska 24 ✉ *00 132 –* Ⓜ *Świętokrzyska*   Plan: **C2**
– ☏ *(22) 321 88 22 – www.radissonblu.com/hotel-warsaw*
311 rm – 🛏280/2050 PLN 🛏🛏300/2050 PLN – ☲ 104 PLN – 18 suites
• Business • Modern • Design •

Glass-fronted hotel in the business district, boasting state-of-the-art conference facilities and a well-equipped leisure centre. Smart bedrooms come in a choice of 'Maritime', 'Scandinavian' or 'Italian' themes. The all-day brasserie offers modern interpretations of Polish and Mediterranean dishes.

H15
⅏ 🎟 🛁 🚗

ul. Poznańska 15 ✉ *00 680 –* Ⓜ *Politechnika –* ☏ *(22)*   Plan: **D2**
553 87 00 – www.h15ab.com
46 rm – 🛏270/780 PLN 🛏🛏290/780 PLN – ☲ 65 PLN – 30 suites
• Townhouse • Luxury • Contemporary •

Extended townhouse built around a glass quadrangle; once the Russian Embassy and later occupied by the Germans during WWII. Most bedrooms are spacious, bespoke-furnished suites with small kitchenettes and marble-floored bathrooms.
Signature – See restaurant listing

Rialto
🎟 🏨 ⅏ 🎟 ⅏ 🛁 🅿

ul. Wilcza 73 ✉ *00 670 –* Ⓜ *Politechnika –* ☏ *(22)*   Plan I: **A2**
584 87 00 – www.rialto.pl
44 rm – 🛏300/950 PLN 🛏🛏340/1090 PLN – ☲ 85 PLN – 11 suites
• Business • Townhouse • Art déco •

This delightfully converted townhouse dates back to 1906 and its sympathetically refurbished interior still boasts original art deco and art nouveau features. Elegant bedrooms come with a host of facilities and boast beautiful marble-floored bathrooms. There's also a smart bar, a small gym and a sauna.
Salto – See restaurant listing

POLAND - WARSAW

POLAND - WARSAW

Residence Diana
☆ 𝔸𝕂 ⤸
ul Chmielna 13a ✉ *00 021 –* Ⓜ *Centrum –* ℰ *(22)*   Plan: **D2**
505 9100 – www.mamaison.com
46 rm – ♦286/360 PLN ♦♦286/360 PLN – ☲ 57 PLN – 8 suites
• Townhouse • Business • Cosy •

Set in a quiet courtyard off a busy central shopping street, with a spacious
lounge and a smart bar furnished in black wood. Large, modern bedrooms
have small kitchen areas and good facilities; some are duplex or have jacuzzis.
The rustic Italian restaurant specialises in traditional Neapolitan pizzas.

Castle Inn
⩽ ⤸
Plac Zamkowy, ul Swietojanska 2 ✉ *00 288 –* ℰ *(22)*   Plan: **C1**
4250100 – www.castleinn.pl
22 rm – ♦299/399 PLN ♦♦299/599 PLN – ☲ 35 PLN
• Family • Townhouse • Historic •

Small 16C property on a cobbled street in the heart of the Old Town, just a stone's throw from the castle. Bedrooms are unique; designed by local artists, they
range from bohemian to contemporary and come with quirky touches.

XxX Amber Room
🕮 ⇨ 🎋 ⤸ ⇔ 🄿
al Ujazdowskie 13 ✉ *00 567 –* ℰ *(22) 523 66 64*   Plan I: **B2**
*– www.amberroom.pl – Closed Christmas-New Year, Easter and bank
holidays*
Menu 64 PLN (lunch) – Carte 123/415 PLN
• Modern cuisine • Chic • Intimate •

Grand dining room in an attractive villa; home to the exclusive 'Round Table of
Warsaw'. Modern cooking uses top ingredients and has original touches. Service
is attentive and well-paced, and there's a great selection of Krug champagne.

XxX Atelier Amaro (Wojciech Amaro)
& 𝔸𝕂 ⤸ 🄿
ღ   *ul. Agrykola 1* ✉ *00 460 –* ℰ *(22) 6285747*   Plan I: **B2**
*– www.atelieramaro.pl – Closed Easter, Christmas-New Year, 1-16 August,
1 and 11 November and Sunday*
Menu 280/350 PLN – *(dinner only) (booking essential) (tasting menu only)*
• Modern cuisine • Design • Elegant •

An eco-style building on the edge of the park houses this intimate restaurant
with its glass teardrops and tiled concrete sculptures. The menu is called the
'calendar of nature' and showcases foraged herbs and flowers. Ambitious, innovative dishes are full of colour and the Polish spirit matches are a must.
➙ Cucumber with dill and smoked eel. Roe deer with cherries and black
garlic. Blueberry with pine and juniper.

XxX Senses (Andrea Camastra)
𝔸𝕂 ⇔
ღ   *ul. Bielanska 12* ✉ *00 085 –* Ⓜ *Ratusz –* ℰ *(22)*   Plan: **C1**
*331 9697 – www.sensesrestaurant.pl – Closed 2 weeks August, 1-
8 January, Easter, Christmas and Sunday*
Menu 170/550 PLN – *(dinner only) (booking essential) (tasting menu only)*
• Modern cuisine • Elegant • Romantic •

As with the historic building in which it is housed, this formal restaurant connects tradition with modernity. Of the 3 set menus, most opt for the 7 course
dinner to best experience cooking that is innovative, creative and at times
theatrical, but also underpinned by classic Polish flavours.
➙ Sea trout with red caviar, horseradish, lemon and apricot. King crab
goulash with culatello. Raspberries, yoghurt, cherries and rose honey.

XxX Belvedere
🎋 𝔸𝕂 ⤸ ⇔ 🄿
Lazienki Park, ul Agrykoli 1 (Entry from ul Parkowa)   Plan I: **B2**
✉ *00 460 –* ℰ *(22) 55 86 700 – www.belvedere.com.pl – Closed
23 December-3 January*
Menu 67/290 PLN – Carte 139/211 PLN – *(booking essential)*
• Modern cuisine • Chic • Romantic •

An impressive Victorian orangery in Lazienki Park; large arched windows keep it
light despite it being packed with shrubs and trees. Dishes are classic in both
style and presentation. Smartly uniformed staff provide formal service.

XxX **Michel Moran - Bistro de Paris** 　　　　🅰 ⇔ ⇔
Pl. Piłsudskiego 9 ⊠ 00 078 – Ⓜ Ratusz – ℰ (22) 　　Plan: **C1**
826 01 07 – www.restaurantbistrodeparis.com – Closed Easter, Christmas and Sunday
Menu 89 PLN (weekday lunch) – Carte 155/257 PLN
• French • Elegant • Chic •
Smart, marble-floored restaurant at the rear of the Opera House, with striking columns and colourful glass panels. The large menu offers reworked Polish and French dishes, with produce imported from France; the 'Classics' are a hit.

XxX **Platter by Karol Okrasa** – Intercontinental Hotel 　🅰 ⇔ 🚗
ul. Emilii Plater 49 ⊠ 00 125 – Ⓜ Centrum – ℰ (22) 　　Plan: **C2**
328 8730 – www.platter.pl – Closed Saturday lunch and Sunday
Carte 135/245 PLN
• Modern cuisine • Chic • Intimate •
First floor hotel restaurant with smart red and black décor. Menus change with the seasons and offer modern Polish dishes and European classics. Cooking is refined, sophisticated and flavoursome, and relies on native ingredients.

XX **Tamka 43** 　　　　　　　　　　　　 ♿ 🅰 ⇔
ul. Tamka 43 (1st Floor) ⊠ 00 355 – Ⓜ Świętokrzyska 　Plan: **D2**
– ℰ (22) 441 62 34 – www.tamka43.pl – Closed Christmas-New Year and Easter
Menu 59 PLN (weekday lunch) – Carte 88/172 PLN
• Modern cuisine • Design • Fashionable •
Opposite the Chopin Museum, in the building where his archives are kept, is this first floor restaurant with bare brick walls, steel girders and suede-covered pillars. Dishes are original; some are inspired by Chopin's favourite meals!

XX **Brasserie Warszawska** 　　　　　　 🕏 🅰 ⇔ ⇔
🙂 *ul. Górnośląska 24 ⊠ 00 484 – ℰ (22) 628 94 23* 　Plan I: **B2**
– www.brasseriewarszawska.pl – Closed Christmas and Easter
Menu 35/150 PLN – Carte 62/208 PLN
• Modern cuisine • Brasserie • Vintage •
Smart brasserie with a zinc-topped bar, a black and white tiled floor and caricatures of its regulars on the walls. Modern European dishes are executed with care and passion. Meats come from their own butcher's shop and mature steaks are a feature, with a choice of cuts from Poland, Ireland and Australia.

XX **Strefa** 　　　　　　　　　　　　　　 🍴 🅰
ul. Próżna 9 ⊠ 00 107 – Ⓜ Świętokrzyska 　　　Plan: **C2**
– ℰ (22) 255 0850 – www.restauracjastrefa.pl
– Closed 25 December-1 January
Carte 113/183 PLN
• Modern cuisine • Elegant • Intimate •
Sit in the small bar, the neutrally hued restaurant or out on the delightful terrace in the shadow of the church. Modern cooking has a traditional Polish heart – the pierogi in particular are a must-try. Service is professional.

XX **Nolita** 　　　　　　　　　　　　　　 🅰 ⇔
ul. Wilcza 46 ⊠ 00 679 – ℰ (22) 29 20 424 　　　Plan I: **A2**
– www.nolita.pl – Closed 2 weeks August, Christmas-New Year, Easter, Saturday lunch, Sunday and bank holidays
Menu 89 PLN (weekday lunch) – Carte 175/254 PLN – *(booking essential)*
• Modern cuisine • Design • Intimate •
Whitewashed stone and black window blinds are matched inside by a smart monochrome theme, where an open kitchen takes centre stage. Bold, modern dishes feature many flavours and take their influences from across the globe.

XX **AleGloria** 🛱 🗚 ⇔ ⇔

pl. Trzech Krzyzy 3 ✉ *00 535 –* ☏ *(22) 584 70 80*
– www.alegloria.pl – Closed 24-25 December and Easter
Menu 65/150 PLN – Carte 100/210 PLN
Plan: **D2**
• Polish • Traditional décor • Intimate •

Steep steps lead down from a boutique shopping arcade to a spacious restaurant, made up of several charming interconnecting rooms and furnished in white. Hearty, homemade Polish classics are served by a smartly attired team.

XX **Salto** – Rialto Hotel 🕭 🗚

ul. Wilcza 73 ✉ *00 670 –* Ⓜ *Politechnika –* ☏ *(22)*
584 87 00 – www.rialto.pl
Menu 260 PLN – Carte 132/278 PLN
Plan I: **A2**
• Modern cuisine • Intimate • Brasserie •

This plainly decorated dining room sits within an attractive suburban hotel. The chef hails from Argentina and is a fan of all things modern, so you'll find gels, meats cooked in a waterbath and some unusual flavour combinations.

XX **Signature** – H15 Hotel 🕭 🗚

ul. Poznańska 15 ✉ *00 680 –* Ⓜ *Politechnika –* ☏ *(22)*
553 87 55 – www.h15ab.com – Closed Easter, 1-3 May, 25-26 December,
1 January and lunch Saturday-Sunday
Menu 45/150 PLN – Carte 72/227 PLN
Plan: **D2**
• Modern cuisine • Intimate • Bistro •

Black and white photos of old Hollywood Stars hang against white walls in this striking, monochrome hotel restaurant. Cooking is a modern take on traditional Polish recipes and the playful puddings are particularly memorable.

XX **Dom Polski Francuska** 🛱 🗚 ⇔ ⇔

ul. Francuska 11 ✉ *03 906 –* ☏ *(22) 616 24 32*
– www.restauracjadompolski.pl – Closed 24 December
Menu 40 PLN (weekday lunch) – Carte 76/168 PLN
Plan I: **B2**
• Polish • Classic décor • Elegant •

Mediterranean-style villa with attractive gardens and a lovely terrace, in a smart residential area. Various small rooms are set over two floors. Extensive menus offer refined yet hearty dishes; duck and goose are the specialities.

XX **U Kucharzy** 🛱

Państwowego Muzeum Archeologicznego, ul. Długa 52
✉ *00 238 –* Ⓜ *Ratusz –* ☏ *(22) 826 79 36 – www.gessler.pl – Closed*
Christmas, Easter, 31 December and Saturday-Sunday lunch
Menu 25/190 PLN – Carte 67/238 PLN
Plan: **C1**
• Traditional cuisine • Historic • Traditional décor •

'The Cook' is located in a 16C former arsenal and two of the original cannons sit in its large inner courtyard. The day's ingredients are on display in the open kitchen and the chef will often come to the table to carve your meat himself.

XX **Concept 13** 🛱 🕭 🗚 ⇔ ⇔

Vitkac (5th Floor), ul. Bracka 9 ✉ *00 501 –* Ⓜ *Centrum*
– ☏ *(22) 3107373 – www.likusrestauracja.pl – Closed Sunday dinner*
and bank holidays
Menu 55 PLN (weekday lunch) – Carte 107/171 PLN
Plan: **D2**
• Modern cuisine • Design • Fashionable •

Huge restaurant on top of a chic department store, with a wine bar and deli below. Black furnishings, a glass-walled kitchen and a smart terrace feature. Dishes are appealing and well-presented; small plates are the focus at lunch.

XX **U Fukiera** 🛱 🗚 ⇔ ⇔

Rynek Starego Miasta 27 ✉ *00 272 –* ☏ *(22) 831 10 13*
– www.ufukiera.pl – Closed 24-25 and 31 December
Menu 107/172 PLN – Carte 90/206 PLN
Plan: **C1**
• Polish • Traditional décor • Elegant •

Immaculately kept house in the heart of the Old Town, overlooking a historic cobbled square. The fiercely traditional interior comprises several intimate, homely rooms, including a 17C vaulted cellar. Cooking is hearty and classical.

POLAND - WARSAW

XX **La Rotisserie** – Le Régina Hotel
ul. Koscielna 12 ⊠ 00 218 – ℰ (22) 531 60 00 Plan: **C1**
– www.mamaison.com/leregina – Closed dinner 24 December
Carte 150/244 PLN – *(booking essential)*
• Modern cuisine • Chic • Intimate •
A small but stylish hotel restaurant with an arched ceiling, Mediterranean styling and an intimate feel. Refined modern dishes have Polish origins and arrive
attractively presented; the well-travelled chef sources top ingredients.

X **Kieliszki na Próżnej**
ul. Próżnej 12 ⊠ 00 107 – Ⓜ Świętokrzyska – ℰ (501) Plan: **C2**
764 674 – www.kieliszkinaproznej.pl – Closed Christmas
Menu 35 PLN (weekday lunch) – Carte 68/156 PLN – *(bookings advisable at dinner)*
• Modern cuisine • Design • Wine bar •
A huge rack of glasses welcomes you into a parquet-floored room with a striking black & white wildlife mural and zinc ducting. Small growers feature on
the 220-strong wine list and all wines are available by the glass. A concise
menu offers light, modern interpretations of Polish classics; lunch is a steal.

X **Butchery and Wine**
ul. Zurawia 22 ⊠ 00 515 – Ⓜ Centrum – ℰ (22) Plan: **D2**
5023118 – www.butcheryandwine.pl – Closed 1 November, Christmas and Easter
Carte 62/229 PLN – *(booking essential)*
• Meats and grills • Friendly • Trendy •
A keenly run modern bistro in a long, narrow room. The name says it all: staff
wear butcher's aprons, there's a diagram of cuts above the kitchen pass and
the emphasis is on offal and meat – particularly beef – which is served on wooden boards. Wines from around the world provide the perfect match.

X **L'enfant terrible**
ul. Sandomierska 13 (entrance on Rejtana St.) Plan I: **B3**
⊠ 02 567 – Ⓜ Pol Mokotowskie – ℰ (22) 119 57 05 – www.eterrible.pl
– Closed Christmas, Easter, lunch Saturday, Sunday and Monday
Menu 89 PLN (lunch) – Carte 158/185 PLN
• Modern cuisine • Neighbourhood • Romantic •
This delightfully rustic restaurant is owned by a self-taught chef, who picks up
the day's produce on his 40km drive into work. The atmosphere is welcoming
and dishes are modern and well-presented; the sourdough bread is fantastic.

X **Opasły Tom**
ul. Foksal 17 ⊠ 00 372 – Ⓜ Centrum – ℰ (22) Plan: **D2**
621 18 81 – www.kregliccy.eu/opaslytom – Closed 1 November, 24-25 December and Easter
Menu 119/158 PLN – Carte 80/140 PLN
• Polish • Simple • Neighbourhood •
Head past the outside tables, through the front room and on towards the tables
by the kitchen. Good value menus follow the seasons and come under the headings of 'cold', 'hot' and 'sweet'. Dishes are fresh, zingy and full of flavour.

X **ELIXIR by Dom Wódki**
ul. Wierzbowa 9-11 ⊠ 00 094 – Ⓜ Ratusz – ℰ (22) Plan: **C1**
828 22 11 – www.restaurantelixir.pl – Closed Christmas and Easter
Carte 96/143 PLN
• Polish • Wine bar • Fashionable •
A smart, very fashionable bar and restaurant is the setting for this marriage of
modern Polish cuisine and top quality vodkas. The likes of local herring, dumplings and beef tartar are paired with over 250 vodkas from around the world.

591

Hoża

�X☐ ⌨ ⇔

ul. Hoża 25a ✉ *00 521 –* Ⓜ *Centrum –* ✆ *(515)*   Plan: **D2**
*037 001 – www.hoza.warszawa.pl – Closed Good Friday, 11 November
and 25 December*
Carte 66/244 PLN
• Meats and grills • Bistro • Neighbourhood •
The exposed brick walls of this Argentinian steakhouse are painted in striking
colours and its shelves are crammed with red wine. The engaging team offer
good advice and the mature Polish and Argentinian steaks are superbly cooked.

Winosfera

🛜 ⌨ ⇔

ul. Chlodna 31 ✉ *00 867 –* ✆ *(22) 526 25 00*   Plan I: **A2**
*– www.winosfera.pl – Closed Easter, Christmas, Saturday lunch, Sunday
and bank holidays*
Menu 39/49 PLN (weekday lunch) – Carte 102/187 PLN
• Modern cuisine • Design • Trendy •
Found in a former factory on a site where a famed cinema once stood; an
industrial feel remains and they have even incorporated a screening room.
Modern European menus focus on Italy. Select your wine from the well-stocked
shop.

Merliniego 5

🛜 ☐ ⌨

ul. Merliniego 5 ✉ *02 511 –* ✆ *(22) 6460849*   Plan I: **B3**
– www.merliniego5.pl – Closed 25 December and Easter
Menu 175/215 PLN (dinner) – Carte 97/312 PLN – *(booking essential at
dinner)*
• Traditional cuisine • Bistro • Neighbourhood •
Passionately run bistro in the suburbs, with low lighting, exposed brick and dark
wood furnishings. Wide ranging menus offer carefully prepared European classics. Meat lovers should opt for a Polish steak or the steak tasting menu.

delizia

🛜 ☐ ⌨

ul. Hoża 58-60 (entrance on ul. Poznańskiej) ✉ *00 682*   Plan: **D2**
– Ⓜ *Centrum –* ✆ *(22) 622 66 65 – www.delizia.com.pl – Closed 2 weeks
Christmas, Easter, Sunday and bank holidays*
Carte 112/209 PLN – *(booking essential at dinner)*
• Italian • Neighbourhood • Friendly •
An unassuming neighbourhood restaurant where fresh flowers sit on chunky
tables. It's owned by friends and run with the care of a family business. Menus
are concise, with pasta a speciality; fish and cheese are imported from Italy.

Qchnia Artystyczna

🛜 ⌨

ul. Jazdow 2 ✉ *00 467 –* ✆ *(22) 625 76 27*   Plan I: **B2**
– www.qchnia.pl – Closed Christmas, Easter and bank holidays
Carte 82/156 PLN
• Modern cuisine • Fashionable • Simple •
A busy, two-roomed restaurant with simple furnishings, set in a contemporary
art gallery; its terrace looks over the Royal Park. Short daily menus mix Polish
and international influences – dishes are light and full of flavour.

Rozbrat 20 Bakery & Wine Corner

🍴 🛜 ⌨

ul. Rozbrat 20 ✉ *00 447 –* ✆ *(22) 416 6266*   Plan I: **B2**
– www.rozbrat20.com.pl – Closed 25-26 December and 1 November
Menu 35 PLN (weekday lunch) – Carte 56/126 PLN
• Polish • Friendly • Bistro •
A café-cum-bakery-cum-wine-shop with a friendly neighbourhood vibe; the
rear room houses the 200 wines featured on their list. Simple European bistro
dishes include tasty homemade boudin noir at breakfast; the breads are a highlight.

CRACOW
KRAKÓW

Population: 757 430

B. Brillion/MICHELIN

Cracow was deservedly included in the very first UNESCO World Heritage List. Unlike much of Poland, this beautiful old city – the country's capital from the 11C to the 17C – was spared Second World War destruction because the German Governor had his HQ here. So Cracow is still able to boast a hugely imposing market square – the biggest medieval square in Europe – and a hill that's crowned not just with a castle, but a cathedral too. Not far away there's even a glorious chapel made of salt, one hundred metres under the ground.

Cracow is a city famous for its links with Judaism and its Royal Route, but also for its cultural inheritance. During the Renaissance, it became a centre of new ideas that drew the most outstanding writers, thinkers and musicians of the day. It has thousands of architectural monuments and millions of artefacts displayed in its museums and churches; but it's a modern city too, with an eye on the 21C. The heart and soul of Cracow is its old quarter, which received its charter in 1257. It's dominated by the Market Square and almost completely encircled by the Planty gardens. A short way to the south, briefly interrupted by the curving streets of the Okol neighbourhood, is Wawel Hill, and further south from here is the characterful Jewish quarter of Kazimierz. The smart residential areas of Piasek and Nowy Swiat are to the west.

CRACOW IN...

→ **ONE DAY**
St Mary's Church, Cloth Hall, Wawel, main building of National Museum.

→ **TWO DAYS**
Kazimierz, Oskar Schindler's Factory, 'Footsteps of Pope Jean Paul II' tour.

→ **THREE DAYS**
Auschwitz-Birkenau, Wieliczka salt mine.

PRACTICAL INFORMATION

ARRIVAL-DEPARTURE

✈ John Paul II International Airport is 13km west of the city centre. Bus 292 goes to the central bus station. There's a free shuttle to the train station; trains to the centre take 15min. A taxi takes 20min.

GETTING AROUND

The historic city centre is a largely pedestrian precinct, so getting about on foot here is a traffic-free pleasure; the streets in the old quarter are laid out in a grid pattern, which makes orientation even easier. The public transport system is made up of an extensive network of buses and trams – you can use your tickets on both, and there several types available, from 15-minute timed tickets to 7-day passes. Be sure to stamp your ticket upon boarding. The Cracow Tourist Card includes unlimited free travel, as well as free entry to many museums, offers on excursions, and discounts in shops and restaurants; it's valid for 48 or 72 hours.

CALENDAR HIGHLIGHTS

May-June
Film Festival.

June
The Lajkonik Parade, Wianki (flowers floated down the river, music and fireworks).

June-July
Cracow Jewish Culture Festival.

July-August
Festival of Music in Old Cracow.

September
Sacrum Profanum (concerts in post-industrial spaces).

November
Polish Music Festival.

EATING OUT

Even during the communist era, Cracow had a reputation as a good place to eat. In the 1990s, hundreds of new restaurants opened their doors, often in pretty locations with medieval or Renaissance interiors or in intimate cellars. Many Poles go misty-eyed at the thought of Bigos on a cold winter's day; it's a game, sausage and cabbage stew that comes with sauerkraut, onion, potatoes, herbs and spices, and is reputed to get better with reheating on successive days. Pierogi is another favourite: crescent-shaped dumplings which come in either savoury or sweet style. Barszcz is a lemon and garlic flavoured beetroot soup that's invariably good value, while in Kazimierz, specialities include Jewish dumplings - filled with onion, cheese and potatoes - and Berdytchov soup, which imaginatively mixes honey and cinnamon with beef. There are plenty of restaurants specialising in French, Greek, Vietnamese, Middle Eastern, Indian, Italian and Mexican food too. Most restaurants don't close until around midnight and there's no pressure to rush your drinks and leave.

POLAND - CRACOW

Sheraton Grand Krakow

ul. Powisle 7 ✉ *31 101 –* ✆ *(12) 662 10 00*
Plan I: **B2**
– www.sheratongrandkrakow.com
232 rm ☖ – **†**495/1250 PLN **††**575/1330 PLN – 3 suites
• Luxury • Business • Modern •

Well-located international hotel with an impressive glass-roofed atrium and extensive event space in the basement. Bedrooms are luxuriously appointed and well-equipped – some boast river and castle views. Olive offers a popular global menu and Polish specialities, while the sports bar serves a range of pub-style dishes. Start with a drink in the rooftop lounge-bar.

Radisson Blu

ul. Straszewskiego 17 ✉ *31 101 –* ✆ *(12) 618 88 88*
Plan: **E2**
– www.radissonblu.com/hotel-krakow
196 rm ☖ – **†**500/700 PLN **††**600/800 PLN – 7 suites
• Business • Modern •

Purpose-built business hotel by the Planty, not far from the castle and the main square. Bedrooms are spacious and well-appointed: 'City' come in warm red hues and 'Harmony', in cool blues. It has a smart basement fitness centre and an informal dining room offering global dishes and themed weekend buffets.

Grand

ul. Slawkowska 5/7 ✉ *31 014 –* ✆ *(12) 424 08 00*
Plan: **E1**
– www.grand.pl
64 rm ☖ – **†**450/700 PLN **††**550/800 PLN – 9 suites
• Traditional • Luxury • Historic •

Once Duke Czartoryski's palace; now the city's oldest hotel. The classic façade masks a columned lobby and rooms filled with gold leaf, stained glass and antiques. Bedrooms are spacious and the suites are vast, opulent and impressively furnished. The traditional Viennese café offers Polish cuisine.

Stary

ul. Szczepanska 5 ✉ *31 011 –* ✆ *(12) 384 08 08*
Plan: **E1**
– www.stary.hotel.com.pl
78 rm ☖ – **†**490/950 PLN **††**590/1100 PLN – 7 suites
• Luxury • Townhouse • Design •

Behind a traditional townhouse façade, dramatic modern glass and steel structures blend cleverly with 15C features. The contemporary bar and rooftop terrace sit alongside original brick and stonework. Stylish bedrooms boast handmade furniture, impressive marble bathrooms and state-of-the-art lighting.
Trzy Rybki – See restaurant listing

Copernicus

ul. Kanonicza 16 ✉ *31 002 –* ✆ *(12) 424 34 00*
Plan: **E3**
– www.copernicus.hotel.com.pl
29 rm – **†**900 PLN **††**1000/1100 PLN – ☖ 70 PLN – 4 suites
• Luxury • Personalised • Historic •

An elegant townhouse in the castle's shadow, on one of the city's oldest streets. The central atrium has a lounge and a small patio for breakfast and light lunch. Luxurious beamed bedrooms boast handmade furniture and excellent comforts. There's an intimate pool in the medieval cellars and a lovely rooftop terrace.
Copernicus – See restaurant listing

Bonerowski Palace

ul. Św. Jana 1 ✉ *31 013 –* ✆ *(12) 374 13 00*
Plan: **E1**
– www.palacbonerowski.pl
16 rm – **†**700/950 PLN **††**750/1000 PLN – ☖ 75 PLN – 3 suites
• Palace • Historic • Personalised •

A former palace, superbly located on the main square and featuring medieval portals, ornate ceilings, restored polychrome décor and the largest Swarovski chandelier in Europe. Large, antique-furnished bedrooms and chic suites come with marble bathrooms. The restaurant focuses on steaks and fish.

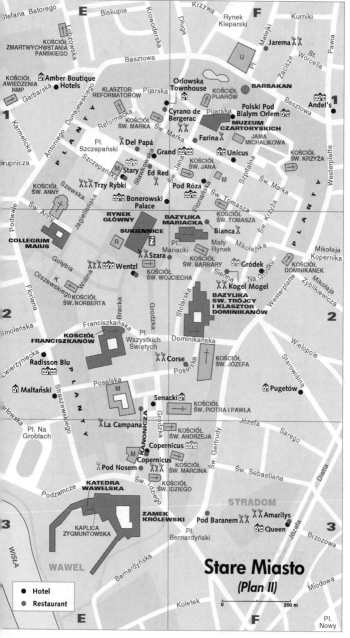

Stare Miasto
(Plan II)

- ● Hotel
- ● Restaurant

Environs of Krakow
(Plan I)

0 — 400 m

KRAKÓW-BALICE

Stare Miasto (Plan II)

ŁOBZÓW

KLEPARZ

Pl. Nowy Kleparz

Yarden

NOWA WIEŚ

PARK KRAKOWSKI

PIASEK

KOŚCIÓŁ ŚW. SZCZEPANA

KOŚCIÓŁ ŚW. JÓZEFA

PARK JORDANA

BŁONIA

Pl. Szczepański

RYNEK GŁÓWNY

SUKIENNICE

COLLEGIUM MAIUS

KOŚCIÓŁ SERCANEK

NOWY ŚWIAT

KOŚCIÓŁ FRANCISZKAN

Kossak

Sheraton Grand Krakow

ZWIERZYNIEC

Pl. Na Stawach

WISŁA

DĘBNIKI

Rynek Dębnicki

Benefis

KOŚCIÓŁ ŚW. STANISŁAWA KOSTKI

Rondo Grunwaldzkie

KATEDRA WAWELSKA

ZAMEK KRÓLEW

KOŚCIÓŁ ŚW. MICH. I STANISŁ

LUDWINÓW

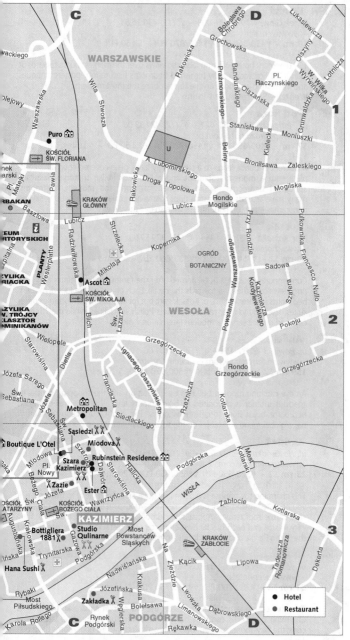

C

WARSZAWSKIE

D

wackiego

olejowy

Warszawska

Wita Stwosza

Rakowicka

Bolesława Chrobrego

Grochowska

Łukasiewicza

W. Wilka Wyrwińskiego

Olszyny

Lotnicza

1

Puro 🏨

KOŚCIÓŁ
SW. FLORIANA

Pawia

KRAKÓW
GŁÓWNY

A. Lubomirskiego

Droga Topolowa

Rakowicka

Prażmowskiego

Bandurskiego

Olszańska

Stanisława

Kielecka

Beliny

Pl.
Raczynskiego

Grunwaldzka

Moniuszki

Bronisława

Zaleskiego

Mogilska

nek
arski

Pl.
Matejki

RBAKAN

Basztowa

Radziwiłłowska

Lubicz

Rondo
Mogilskie

Pułkownika Francesco Nullo

EUM
RTORYSKICH

ziana

PLANTY

Westerplatte

Strzelecka

Mikołaja

Kopernika

OGRÓD
BOTANICZNY

Przy Rondzie

Warszawska

Powstania

Sadowa

Kazimierza Kordylewskiego

Szafera

ZYLIKA
RIACKA

Ascot 🏨

KOŚCIÓŁ
SW. MIKOŁAJA

Blich

Św. Łazarza

WESOŁA

Pokoju

2

ZYLIKA
V. TRÓJCY
LASZTOR
OMINIKANÓW

Wielopole

Dietla

Grzegórzecka

Ignacego Daszyńskiego 90.

Rondo
Grzegórzeckie

Grzegórzecka

Starowiśla

Rzeźnicza

Kotlarska

Józefa Sarego

Sw.
Sebastiana

Metropolitan 🏨

Franciszka

Siedleckiego

Boutique L'Otel

Sw. Sebastiana

Józefa

Miodowa

Pl.
Nowy

Bożego

Sąsiedzi ✗ ✗

Miodova ✗

Szara
Kazimierz ✗ ✗

Rubinstein Residence 🏨

Szeroka

Dajwór

Halicka

Podgórska

Most Kotlarski

WISŁA

Zabłocie

Kotlarska

3

Zazie ✗

Józefa

Ester 🏨

Wawrzyńca

KAZIMIERZ

KRAKÓW
ZABŁOCIE

OŚCIÓŁ SW.
ATARZYNY

Krakowska

KOŚCIÓŁ
BOŻEGO CIAŁA

Studio
Qulinarne

Gazowa

Most
Powstańców
Śląskich

Na Zjeździe

Kącik

Lwowska

Lipowa

Tadeusza Romanowicza

Dekerta

Augustiańska

Bottigliera
1881 ✗

Trynitarska

Podgórska

Nadwiślańska

Krakusa

Zabłocie

Hana Sushi ✗

ińska

Rybaki

Most
Piłsudskiego

Karola Rollego

Józefińska

Zakładka ✗

Węgierska

Bolesawa

Rynek
Podgórski

RęKawka

Limanowskiego

Dąbrowskiego

C

PODGÓRZE

D

● Hotel
● Restaurant

POLAND - CRACOW

Wentzl

Rynek Główny 19 ✉ *31 008 – ℰ (12) 430 26 64* Plan: **E2**
– www.wentzl.pl
18 rm – ♦450/860 PLN ♦♦460/870 PLN – ⊆ 60 PLN
• Luxury • Historic • Elegant •

15C tenement house offering fantastic views over the market square towards St Mary's Basilica. Individually furnished bedrooms feature four-posters, antiques and interesting art: those on the top floor are the most modern.
Wentzl – See restaurant listing

Pod Róza

ul. Florianska 14 ✉ *31 021 – ℰ (12) 424 33 00* Plan: **F1**
– www.podroza.hotel.com.pl
57 rm – ♦400/650 PLN ♦♦450/720 PLN – ⊆ 60 PLN – 4 suites
• Historic • Traditional • Classic •

A discreet entrance leads to a surprisingly large glass-covered courtyard, complete with a modern restaurant and a laid-back Italian trattoria. Classically appointed bedrooms feature silhouette artwork and modern bathrooms; many have jacuzzis. The fourth floor rooms are cosiest and boast city skyline panoramas – the top floor fitness suite shares the view.

Kossak

Plac Kossaka 1 ✉ *31 106 – ℰ (12) 379 59 00* Plan I: **B2**
– www.hotelkossak.pl
60 rm ⊆ – ♦750/800 PLN ♦♦800/860 PLN – 5 suites
• Business • Modern •

Contemporary business hotel named after the famous Polish painter and offering views over the river towards the castle. Each of its well-equipped, modern bedrooms features a piece of Kossak's art; opt for one of the comfortable corner suites. The ground floor restaurant offers Polish specialities, while the 7th floor café and terrace serves a modern international menu.

Andel's

ul. Pawia 3 ✉ *31 154 – ℰ (12) 660 01 00* Plan: **F1**
– www.andelscracow.com – Closed Christmas
159 rm ⊆ – ♦400/880 PLN ♦♦500/970 PLN – 5 suites
• Business • Modern •

An eye-catching modern building by the station and the shopping centre. Its spacious interior is decorated in bold colours and all of the well-equipped bedrooms boast floor to ceiling windows. The bright, curvaceous restaurant has a global menu and tables on the square. Live music features in the chic bar.

Gródek

ul. Na Gródku 4 ✉ *31 028 – ℰ (12) 431 90 30* Plan: **F2**
– www.donimirski.com
23 rm ⊆ – ♦520/650 PLN ♦♦650/850 PLN – 2 suites
• Historic • Townhouse • Elegant •

This charming townhouse is hidden in a quiet side street close to the square. If you need to unwind, seek out the pleasant wood-panelled library bar or grab a seat on the roof terrace. Appealing bedrooms come with good facilities; they vary in size and each has its own character. The restaurant is themed around the South Pacific and serves dishes from across Oceania.

Queen

ul. Józefa Dietla 60 ✉ *31 039 – ℰ (12) 433 33 33* Plan: **F3**
– www.queenhotel.pl
31 rm ⊆ – ♦280/700 PLN ♦♦330/750 PLN – 1 suite
• Business • Design •

This chic boutique hotel sits between the old market square and Kazimierz. Charming bedrooms come in brown and silver and feature the latest mod cons: the 'Sky' rooms look out over the castle and the 3rd floor rooms have balconies.
Amarylis – See restaurant listing

Puro
ul. Ogrodowa 10 ⊠ 31 155 – **Ⓜ** *Krakow Glowny*
– 𝒞 (12) 314 2100 – www.purohotel.pl   Plan I: **C1**
138 rm – **†**300/600 PLN **††**300/600 PLN – ⚏ 50 PLN – 6 suites
• Chain • Modern •
Colour-changing lights illuminate the modern façade and the spacious lobby is decked out with vintage furnishings. Up-to-date bedrooms feature yellow Chesterfield-style headboards, tablet-operated controls and glass bathroom walls decorated with frosted flowers. The restaurant serves an international menu.

Unicus
ul Sw. Marka 20 ⊠ 31 020 – 𝒞 (12) 433 71 11   Plan: **F1**
– www.hotelunicus.pl
35 rm ⚏ – **†**380/700 PLN **††**440/910 PLN
• Business • Townhouse • Modern •
Stylish boutique hotel converted from a row of old tenement houses. Well-appointed bedrooms range in colour from green to gold and boast state-of-the-art shower rooms; Double Deluxes, overlooking Florianska Street, are the best. The bright, barrel-ceilinged basement restaurant serves a modern menu.

Polski Pod Bialym Orlem
ul. Pijarska 17 ⊠ 31 015 – 𝒞 (12) 422 11 44   Plan: **F1**
– www.donimirski.com
60 rm ⚏ – **†**330/390 PLN **††**490/640 PLN – 3 suites
• Historic • Townhouse • Classic •
A traditional hotel overlooking the city walls, with a cosy brick bar dating from the 16C; it's owned by the family of the Czartoryski Princes. Individually styled bedrooms feature tapestries and etchings which reflect the city's heritage.

Senacki
ul. Grodzka 51 ⊠ 31 001 – 𝒞 (12) 422 76 86   Plan: **E2**
– www.hotelsenacki.pl
20 rm ⚏ – **†**750/800 PLN **††**800/860 PLN – 2 suites
• Townhouse • Classic •
Peaceful hotel with an ornate stone façade, set opposite a 17C church on the Royal Way. Bedrooms are bright and modern – those on the upper floors have rooftop views. Buffet breakfasts take place in the hugely atmospheric 13C cellar.

Amber Boutique Hotels
ul. Garbarska 8-10 ⊠ 31 131 – 𝒞 (12) 421 06 06   Plan: **E1**
– www.hotel-amber.pl
38 rm ⚏ – **†**299/544 PLN **††**359/559 PLN
• Townhouse • Modern •
Two traditional townhouses in a residential street, with smart breakfast and fitness rooms. Well-equipped contemporary bedrooms come with complimentary cherry vodka: the 'Design' rooms have feature walls and display local artists' work.

Orlowska Townhouse
ul. Slawkowska 26 ⊠ 31 014 – 𝒞 (12) 429 54 45   Plan: **E1**
– www.orlowskatownhouse.com – Closed Christmas
5 rm – **†**480/580 PLN **††**520/580 PLN – ⚏ 38 PLN
• Historic • Townhouse • Elegant •
17C townhouse on a peaceful central street. Spacious apartment-style bedrooms have small kitchenettes and modern bathrooms, and are furnished in themes including 'Art Deco', 'Poets' and 'Boudoir'. Relax in the intimate piano bar.

POLAND - CRACOW

Yarden
ul Długa 35 ⊠ 31 147 – ℰ *(535) 26 27 55*
Plan I: **B1**
– www.yardenhotel.pl
49 rm � – †180/300 PLN ††260/450 PLN – 4 suites
• Townhouse • Classic •

Modern hotel in a traditional townhouse building, with a tranquil garden hidden behind. Good-sized bedrooms have up-to-date facilities and are furnished with heavy, free-standing wooden furniture; ask for a room with a balcony.

Pugetów
ul. Starowislna 15a ⊠ 31 038 – ℰ *(12) 432 49 50*
Plan: **F2**
– www.donimirski.com
6 rm � – †250/310 PLN ††350/510 PLN – 2 suites
• Historic • Classic • Elegant •

Set in the shadow of Pugetów Palace, in the 19C servants' quarters. With its calm, intimate interior and antique-filled bedrooms, it feels like a private residence. The cosy lounge and breakfast area are in the characterful cellars.

Maltanski
ul. Straszewskiego 14 ⊠ 31 101 – ℰ *(12) 431 00 10*
Plan: **E2**
– www.donimirski.com
16 rm � – †510/590 PLN ††590/650 PLN
• Traditional • Personalised •

Lovely little hotel by the Planty, named after its previous owners, The Knights of Malta. With the castle and square just a stroll away, it makes a great base for exploring. Some of the charming, traditional bedrooms come with patios.

Benefis
ul. Barska 2 ⊠ 30 307 – ℰ *(12) 252 0710*
Plan I: **B3**
– www.hotelbenefis.pl
20 rm � – †240/310 PLN ††280/370 PLN – 6 suites
• Traditional • Modern • Functional •

Small, purpose-built hotel just over the Wisla River, a short walk from town. Bedrooms are modern and surprisingly spacious – most have balconies, and the 4th floor rooms have air con and distant castle views. The smart basement houses a small bar and a simple restaurant serving Polish and Italian cuisine.

Ascot
ul. Radziwillowska 3 ⊠ 31 026 – ℰ *(12) 384 06 06*
Plan I: **C2**
– www.hotelascot.pl
49 rm � – †350/435 PLN ††415/545 PLN
• Business • Traditional • Functional •

Modern hotel located in a residential area, just 5 minutes' walk from town. Bold contemporary art lines the lobby walls and there's a small corner bar. Up-to-date bedrooms come in yellows and reds; those at the front are quieter.

XxX Copernicus – Copernicus Hotel
ul. Kanonicza 16 ⊠ 31 002 – ℰ *(12) 424 34 21*
Plan: **E3**
– www.copernicus.hotel.com.pl
Menu 160/340 PLN – Carte lunch 137/187 PLN – *(booking essential)*
• Modern cuisine • Intimate • Elegant •

Set in the atrium of a charming hotel; an intimate split-level restaurant of less than 10 tables, boasting an ornate hand-painted Renaissance ceiling. 5, 7 and 12 course menus offer well-crafted Polish and European dishes.

XxX Trzy Rybki – Stary Hotel
ul. Szczepanska 5 ⊠ 31 011 – ℰ *(12) 384 08 06*
Plan: **E1**
– www.likusrestauracje.com.pl
Menu 150/200 PLN – Carte 160/180 PLN
• Seafood • Elegant • Design •

An airy two-roomed restaurant in a unique hotel. An impressive vaulted stone ceiling and dramatic flower arrangements dominate. Original modern menus keep seafood to the fore and are accompanied by a superb collection of Italian wines.

XXX **Wentzl** – Wentzl Hotel

Rynek Główny 19 ✉ *31 008 –* ✆ *(12) 4221402* Plan: **E2**
– www.wentzl.pl – Closed 25 December
Carte 106/192 PLN
• Traditional cuisine • Elegant • Chic •

A grand, formal restaurant on the first floor of a 17C hotel, boasting polished parquet floors, a stunning 15C ceiling and a belle époque style. The traditional menu mixes French and Polish influences. Below is a more casual bistro.

POLAND - CRACOW

XX **Szara**

Rynek Główny 6 ✉ *31 042 –* ✆ *(12) 421 66 69* Plan: **E/F2**
– www.szara.pl – Closed 1 November and 24 December
Carte 87/161 PLN
• International • Brasserie • Classic décor •

Well-regarded family-run restaurant on the Grand Square, featuring a lovely terrace, a hand-painted Gothic ceiling and a pleasant brasserie atmosphere. Menus mix Polish, French and Swedish classics; cooking is authentic and hearty.

XX **Kogel Mogel**

ul. Sienna 12 ✉ *31 041 –* ✆ *(12) 426 49 68* Plan: **F2**
– www.kogel-mogel.pl – Closed Easter and Christmas
Carte 69/114 PLN
• Polish • Brasserie • Fashionable •

A smart, lively brasserie; the wine room with its original painted ceiling is a popular spot, as is the enclosed terrace. Extensive menus offer refined, modern versions of classic Polish and Cracovian dishes. Live music is a feature.

XX **Pod Baranem**

ul. Sw. Gertrudy 21 ✉ *31 049 –* ✆ *(12) 429 40 22* Plan: **F3**
– www.podbaranem.com – Closed Easter and 25 December
Menu 50/95 PLN – Carte 60/166 PLN – *(booking essential at dinner)*
• Polish • Neighbourhood • Family •

Traditional family-run restaurant set over 5 rooms, with rug-covered stone floors, homely furnishings and contemporary artwork by Edward Dwurnik. The large menu offers classic Polish cuisine; sharing dishes must be ordered in advance.

XX **Jarema**

Pl. Matejki 5 ✉ *31 157 –* ✆ *(12) 429 36 69* Plan: **F1**
– www.jarema.pl
Menu 35/60 PLN – Carte 50/148 PLN
• Polish • Rustic •

Charming restaurant with a homely feel. Hunting trophies fill the walls and there's live violin and piano music every night. Family recipes are handed down through the generations and focus on dishes from the east of the country.

XX **Amarylis** – Queen Hotel

ul. Józefa Dietla 60 ✉ *31 039 –* ✆ *(12) 433 33 33* Plan: **F3**
– www.queenhotel.pl
Carte 112/140 PLN – *(dinner only)*
• Modern cuisine • Design •

Head down to the hotel's basement and choose from either a traditional brick room or a more modern space furnished in black and white. Cooking mixes of Polish and global influences and dishes are well-presented and full of flavour.

XX **Cyrano de Bergerac**

ul Slawkowska 26 ✉ *31 014 –* ✆ *(12) 411 72 88* Plan: **E1**
– www.cyranodebergerac.pl – Closed Easter, 1 November and Christmas
Carte 95/246 PLN
• Polish • Intimate • Rustic •

Atmospheric restaurant in the barrel-ceilinged cellars of a 17C townhouse. Tapestries, antiques and old implements fill the room, and there's a lovely enclosed terrace to the rear. Refined Polish cooking has French touches.

XX **Corse**

Plan: **F2**

ul Poselska 24 ☒ 31 002 – ✆ (12) 421 62 73
– www.corserestaurant.pl – Closed Easter and Christmas
Carte 60/200 PLN

• Mediterranean cuisine • Traditional décor • Bistro •

Nautically-themed restaurant featuring model ships, paintings of clippers and old ships' lamps. Good-sized menus offer Mediterranean-influenced dishes which use Polish produce; they specialise in seafood but offer more besides.

X **Pod Nosem**

Plan: **E3**

ul. Kanonicza 22 ☒ 31 002 – ✆ (12) 376 00 14
– www.podnosem.com – Closed 24-25 December
Menu 30 PLN (weekday lunch) – Carte 90/145 PLN

• Polish • Cosy • Romantic •

This cosy, characterful restaurant has a medieval feel. The bright ground floor room is hung with tapestries and the white wooden banquettes have tapestry-style seat cushions to match; downstairs is more dimly lit, with a mix of brick and stone walls. Traditional Polish dishes are given a modern touch.

X **Bianca**

Plan: **F2**

Plac Mariacki 2 ☒ 31 042 – ✆ (12) 422 18 71
– www.biancaristorante.pl – Closed Christmas and Easter
Menu 59/150 PLN – Carte 67/128 PLN

• Italian • Bistro • Intimate •

Sit on the small terrace opposite St Mary's Basilica and watch the world go by. Classical menus cover all regions of Italy and the pastas and ragus are freshly made; be sure to try the delicious saltimbocca with its sharp, lemony tang.

X **La Campana**

Plan: **E2**

ul. Kanonicza 7 ☒ 31 002 – ✆ (12) 430 22 32
– www.lacampana.pl – Closed Easter and Christmas
Menu 45/55 PLN – Carte 52/111 PLN

• Italian • Cosy • Rustic •

Discreetly set under an archway; the charming country interior features pine dressers and an olive branch frieze and there's also a beautiful walled garden. The wide-ranging Italian menu features imported produce – the hams are a hit.

X **Farina**

Plan: **F1**

ul. Sw. Marka 16 ☒ 31 018 – ✆ (12) 422 16 80
– www.farina.com.pl – Closed Christmas
Carte 60/238 PLN

• Seafood • Cosy • Friendly •

Pretty little restaurant set over three rooms; all of them cosy and candlelit but each with its own character. Seafood is the speciality, with fish arriving from France several times a week and then cooked whole over salt and herbs.

X **Ed Red**

Plan: **E1**

ul. Skawkowska 3 ☒ 31 014 – ✆ (690) 900 555
– www.edred.pl – Closed Christmas and Easter
Menu 29 PLN (weekday lunch)/120 PLN – Carte 67/245 PLN

• Meats and grills • Rustic • Neighbourhood •

It's all about beef at Ed Red, from roast bone marrow and homemade blood pudding to Polish 21 day dry-aged Limousin steak with béarnaise sauce. Three rustic rooms with reclaimed wooden panels on the walls set the scene perfectly.

X **Del Papá**

Plan: **E1**

ul. Św. Tomasza 6 ☒ 31 014 – ✆ (12) 421 83 43
– www.delpapa.pl – Closed 24-26 December
Menu 24 PLN (weekday lunch) – Carte 65/91 PLN

• Italian • Bistro •

Simple Italian trattoria; dine in the bistro-style room, the characterful Italian 'street' or on the partially covered rear terrace. Menus echo the seasons, offering a good range of honest Italian classics and a fat free selection.

POLAND - CRACOW

Metropolitan

ul Berka Joselewicza 19 ✉ 31 031 – ℰ (12) 442 75 00   Plan: **C2**
– www.hotelmetropolitan.pl
59 rm ☲ – ♦345/795 PLN ♦♦385/835 PLN
• Townhouse • Modern •

A converted 19C townhouse with a smart lobby and a lounge with a central bar. Bold modern décor features throughout; bedrooms come in neutral hues, with a high level of facilities. The informal restaurant serves international fusion dishes. In summer, have breakfast in the enclosed courtyard.

Rubinstein Residence

ul. Szeroka 12 ✉ 31 053 – ℰ (12) 384 00 00   Plan: **C3**
– www.rubinstein.pl
28 rm ☲ – ♦270/430 PLN ♦♦390/560 PLN – 2 suites
• Historic • Townhouse • Personalised •

This pair of restored townhouses is joined by a bright, glass-roofed restaurant and named after Helena Rubinstein, who lived nearby. Well-equipped, characterful bedrooms come with luxurious marble and alabaster bathrooms. It's located in a pleasant square and the roof terrace affords panoramic city views.

Boutique L'Otel

ul. Miodowa 25 ✉ 31 055 – ℰ (12) 633 34 44   Plan: **C3**
– www.apartmenty.oberza.pl – Closed Christmas
18 rm – ♦149/379 PLN ♦♦169/399 PLN – ☲ 25 PLN – 1 suite
• Townhouse • Design •

Delightful former tenement house in the heart of Kazimierz. An impressive staircase leads up to the stylish, individually themed bedrooms which range in design from 'Art Deco' to 'Crystal' and boast smart, modern bathrooms.
Sąsiedzi – See restaurant listing

Ester

ul. Szeroka 20 ✉ 31 053 – ℰ (12) 429 11 88   Plan: **C3**
– www.hotel-ester.krakow.pl – Closed Christmas
32 rm ☲ – ♦250/590 PLN ♦♦280/850 PLN
• Townhouse • Personalised • Cosy •

Cosy little hotel overlooking a pleasant square in the Jewish quarter, with a traditionally furnished interior and bird cages dotted about the place. Comfortable bedrooms are colour themed and boast both baths and showers. The simple café and terrace serves a mix of traditional Polish and Jewish dishes.

XX   **Studio Qulinarne**

ul. Gazowa 4 ✉ 31 060 – ℰ (12) 430 69 14   Plan: **C3**
– www.studioqulinarne.pl – Closed Christmas-New year, Easter, Saturday lunch and Sunday
Menu 210/250 PLN – Carte 130/160 PLN
• International • Neighbourhood •

Passionately run, restyled bus garage with folding glass doors, a cocktail bar and an intimate enclosed terrace. The airy interior features exposed timbers, unusual lighting and black linen. A monthly menu offers well-presented, modern international dishes, and live piano music features later in the week.

 XX   **Szara Kazimierz**

ul. Szeroka 39 ✉ 31 053 – ℰ (12) 429 12 19   Plan: **C3**
– www.szarakazimierz.pl – Closed Christmas
Carte 60/129 PLN
• Polish • Brasserie • Neighbourhood •

Friendly brasserie in a pleasant spot on the square. Sit out the front, on the enclosed rear terrace, or inside, surrounded by photos of Gaultier models. Menus reflect the owners' heritage by mixing Polish and Swedish classics.

X **Sąsiedzi** – Boutique L'Otel 🛜 🛝 ♻
ul. Miodowa 25 ✉ 31 055 – ☏ (12) 654 83 53 Plan: **C3**
– www.oberza.pl – Closed 24-27 December
Carte 50/125 PLN
• Polish • Intimate • Neighbourhood •
With its relaxed, welcoming atmosphere and delightful team, its name, 'Neighbourhood', sums it up well. Dine on the small terrace or in one of several charming cellar rooms. Honest, good value cooking uses old Polish recipes.

X **Bottiglieria 1881** 🕸
ul. Bochenska 5 ✉ 31 061 – ☏ (660) 66 17 56 Plan: **C3**
– www.1881.com.pl – Closed Easter, Christmas-New Year and Monday
Carte 85/133 PLN
• Creative • Wine bar •
This century old cellar is found in the Jewish district. Old wine boxes decorate the room, hand-crafted wood and stone feature and the large cave offers over 100 different wines. The menu is a concise collection of modern dishes.

X **Zazie**
ul. Józefa 34 ✉ 31 056 – ☏ (757) 250 885 Plan: **C3**
– www.zaziebistro.pl – Closed 24-25 December and Easter
Menu 29 PLN (weekday lunch) – Carte 57/86 PLN – (booking essential at dinner)
• French • Bistro •
You'll find this bistro in a corner spot on a pleasant square. Inside it has a lively vibe; ask for a table in the attractive cellar, with its pleasing mix of French memorabilia and brick and stone walls. Great value Gallic dishes range from quiches and gratins to roast duck and beef Bourguignon.

X **Miodova** 🛜 ♻
ul. Szeroka 3 ✉ 31 053 – ☏ (12) 432 5083 Plan: **C3**
– www.miodova.pl – Closed 24-25 December
Carte 78/116 PLN
• Polish • Cosy •
Among a strip of lively restaurants you'll find Miodova, a fashionable restaurant owned by two sisters. It's a comfortable place, with soft sofa-style banquettes and colourful cushions. The menu focuses on regional specialities.

X **Hana Sushi**
ul Weglowa 4 ✉ 31 063 – ☏ (608) 576 255 Plan: **C3**
– www.hanasushi.pl – Closed Monday
Menu 33/150 PLN
• Japanese • Simple •
Hana Sushi is a simple Japanese-style restaurant set slightly off the beaten track. The chef travelled the world working his way up in sushi restaurants, while the sushi master trained in Tokyo. Good value sushi is prepared with finesse.

at PODGÓRZE **PLAN I**

X **Zakladka** 🛜 🅰🅲 🛝 ♻
ul. Józefińska 2 ✉ 30 529 – ☏ (12) 442 74 42 Plan: **C3**
– www.zakladkabistro.pl – Closed 24-25 December
Menu 40/100 PLN – Carte 61/120 PLN
• French • Bistro • Neighbourhood •
Zakladka is set over a footbridge in an old tenement building, and run by a well-known local chef. With chequered floors and red banquettes, the characterful front rooms have a classic bistro feel; the French dishes are equally traditional.

PORTUGAL

PORTUGAL

LISBON

→ **AREA:**
92 391 km² (35 521 sq mi).

→ **POPULATION:**
10 348 648. Density = 112 per km².

→ **CAPITAL:**
Lisbon.

→ **CURRENCY:**
Euro (€).

→ **GOVERNMENT:**
Parliamentary republic (since 1976).
Member of European Union since
1986.

→ **LANGUAGE:**
Portuguese.

→ **PUBLIC HOLIDAYS:**
New Year's Day (1 Jan); Good Friday
(late Mar/Apr); Liberation Day (25
Apr); Labor Day (1 May); Corpus
Christi (late May/June – currently
suspended); Portugal Day (10
June); Assumption of the Virgin
Mary (15 Aug); Republic Day (5 Oct
– currently suspended); All Saints'
Day (1 Nov – currently suspended);
Restoration of Independence Day
(1 Dec – currently suspended);
Immaculate Conception (8 Dec);
Christmas Day (25 Dec).

→ **LOCAL TIME:**
GMT in winter and GMT+1 hour in
summer.

→ **CLIMATE:**
Temperate Mediterranean with
warm winters and hot summers
(Lisbon: January 15°C; July 26°C).

→ **EMERGENCY:**
Police, Medical Assistance and Fire
Brigade ✆ **112**.

→ **ELECTRICITY:**
230 volts AC, 50Hz; 2 round pin
sockets.

→ **FORMALITIES:**
Travellers from the European Union
(EU), Switzerland, Iceland and the
main countries of North and South
America need a national identity
card or passport (America: passport
required) to visit Portugal for less
than three months (tourism or
business purpose). For visitors
from other countries a visa may be
required, in addition to a passport,
especially for those wishing to
stay for longer than three months.
We advise you to check with your
embassy before travelling.

LISBON
LISBOA

Population: 547 733

Alain Rapoport/Fotolia.com

Sitting on the north bank of the River Tagus, beneath huge open skies and surrounded by seven hills, Lisbon boasts an atmosphere that few cities can match. An enchanting walk around the streets has an old-time ambience all of its own, matched only by a jaunt on the trams and funiculars that run up and down the steep hills. At first sight Lisbon is all flaky palaces, meandering alleyways and castellated horizon quarried from medieval stone; but there's a 21C element, too. Slinky new developments line the riverside, linking the old and new in a glorious jumble which spills down the slopes to the water's edge. The views of the water from various vantage points all over Lisbon and the vistas of the 'Straw Sea' – so named because of the golden reflections of the sun – reach out to visitors, along with the sounds of fado, the city's alluring folk music, which conjures up a melancholic yearning.

The compact heart of the city is the Baixa, a flat, 18C grid of streets flanked by the hills. To the west is the elegant commercial district of Chiado and the funky hilltop Bairro Alto, while immediately to the east is Alfama, a tightly packed former Moorish quarter with kasbah-like qualities. North of here is the working-class neighbourhood of Graça and way out west lies the spacious riverside suburb of Belém, while up the river to the east can be found the ultra-modern Parque das Nações.

LISBON IN...

→ **ONE DAY**
Alfama, Castelo São Jorge, Bairro Alto.

→ **TWO DAYS**
Baixa, Calouste Gulbenkian Museum, Parque das Nações.

→ **THREE DAYS**
Museu Nacional de Arte Antiga, Belém.

PRACTICAL INFORMATION

ARRIVAL-DEPARTURE

🛬 Lisbon Portela Airport is 7km north of the town centre. The Metro Red Line takes about 20min. The Aerobus runs every 20-30min.

GETTING AROUND

Lisbon is easy to get around. Four metro lines cover much of the central part of the city and there are six main bus routes and three funiculars. Buses and trams operate every 11-15 minutes; tram routes 15 and 28 serve the main sights. Tickets can be bought as a single fare but it might be worthwhile investing in a 7 Colinas or Viva Viagem Card, which can be loaded with various tickets (which give discounts on standard single fares) or with pre-pay credit for 'zapping'. The 24, 48 or 72 hr Lisboa Card is valid for unlimited travel on public transport and for free or reduced admission to most museums and cultural sites.

CALENDAR HIGHLIGHTS

February
Carnaval.

March
Spring Festival.

April
CCB Music Festival.

June
Festas dos Santos Populares (Feast Days of the Popular Saints), National Day, Lisbon Book Fair, Alkantara Festival (17-day jamboree).

July
Super Bock Super Rock Festival, Almada International Theatre Festival.

November
Arte Lisboa.

EATING OUT

Lisboetas love their local agricultural produce and the cuisine of the region can be characterised by its honesty and simplicity. The city has an age-old maritime tradition and there are a number of fishing ports nearby, so ocean-fresh fish and seafood features in a range of dishes. One thing the locals love in particular is bacalhau (cod), and it's said that in Lisbon, there's a different way to prepare it for every day of the year: it may come oven-baked, slow-cooked or cooked in milk, and it can be served wrapped in cabbage, with tocino belly pork or in a myriad of other ways. While eating in either a humble tasca, a casa de pasto or a restaurante, other specialities to keep an eye out for are clams cooked with garlic and coriander, traditional beef, chicken and sausage stew with vegetables and rice, bean casserole with tocino belly pork, and lamprey eel with rice. Enjoy them with a vinho verde, the wine of the region. A service charge will be included on your bill but it's customary to leave a tip of about ten per cent.

NORTH QUARTER (Plan III)

Old Lisbon
(Plan II)

0   300 m

TEJO

OLD LISBON (Alfama, Castelo de São Jorge, Rossio, Baixa, Chiado, Bairro Alto)

PLAN II

Avenida Palace

🎗 ૯ 🗛 🎗

Plan: **E1**

Rua 1° de Dezembro 123 ⊠ 1200-359
– Ⓜ *Restauradores* – ℰ 213 21 81 00 – www.hotelavenidapalace.pt
66 rm ☑ – ♦165/210 € ♦♦201/247 € – 16 suites
• Business • Classic •

An elegant, prestigious building dating from 1892. This hotel has a magnificent lounge area, delightful English-style bar and well-maintained, classical-style guestrooms.

Pousada de Lisboa

🎗 ૯ 🔲 ૯ 🎗

Plan: **E2**

Praça do Comércio 31 ⊠ 1100-148
– Ⓜ *Terreiro do Paço* – ℰ 218 44 20 01 – www.pousadas.pt
88 rm ☑ – ♦225/410 € ♦♦235/420 € – 2 suites
• Historic building • Historic •

Located in the tourist heart of the city, the property is part of a series of buildings that are listed, national monuments. Attractive lounge furnished with antiques, comfortable guestrooms combining the traditional and the contemporary, as well as a brick-vaulted restaurant offering a modern à la carte menu.

Sofitel Lisbon Liberdade

Av. da Liberdade 127 ✉ *1269-038* – Ⓜ *Avenida*
– 𝒞 *213 22 83 00* – www.sofitel-lisboa.com
Plan: **E1**
151 rm – 🛉160/530 € – 🖵 25 € – 12 suites
• Business • Design •

A good location on one of the city's most prestigious and centrally located avenues. Comfortable public areas with a decor that combines the traditional and contemporary. Friendly service throughout.
Ad Lib – See restaurant listing

Altis Avenida H.

Rua 1º de Dezembro 120 ✉ *1200-360*
Plan: **E1**
– Ⓜ *Restauradores* – 𝒞 *210 44 00 00*
– www.altishotels.com
68 rm 🖵 – 🛉160/250 € 🛉🛉180/270 € – 2 suites
• Townhouse • Cosy •

The hotel's major selling point is its location on the main square, the Praça dos Restauradores. Contemporary guestrooms of differing sizes, some with a small terrace and many with views of the city. The elegant panoramic restaurant is on the seventh floor.

Bairro Alto H.

Praça Luis de Camões 2 ✉ *1200-243* – Ⓜ *Baixa-Chiado*
Plan: **E2**
– 𝒞 *213 40 82 88* – www.bairroaltohotel.com
51 rm 🖵 – 🛉🛉270/440 € – 4 suites
• Luxury • Elegant •

This hotel in the historic centre of Lisbon gives priority to keeping its guestrooms in pristine condition. Contemporary decor, excellent service and a panoramic rooftop terrace. The simply furnished restaurant overlooks the attractive Luís de Camões square.

Internacional Design H.

Rua da Betesga 3 ✉ *1100-090* – Ⓜ *Rossio*
Plan: **E2**
– 𝒞 *213 24 09 90* – www.idesignhotel.com
55 rm 🖵 – 🛉100/450 € 🛉🛉110/460 €
• Townhouse • Design •

In keeping with the hotel name, the decor here is very much designer focused. The guestrooms are on four floors, each with its own style: urban, tribal, zen and pop.

Do Chiado

Rua Nova do Almada 114 ✉ *1200-290*
Plan: **E2**
– Ⓜ *Baixa-Chiado* – 𝒞 *213 25 61 00* – www.hoteldochiado.pt
39 rm 🖵 – 🛉120/240 € 🛉🛉150/300 €
• Townhouse • Functional •

A hotel with well-appointed guestrooms in the heart of the Chiado district. Those on the seventh floor have private balconies with splendid views of the city.

The Beautique H. Figueira

Praça da Figueira 16 ✉ *1100-241* – Ⓜ *Rossio*
Plan: **F2**
– 𝒞 *210 49 29 40* – www.thebeautiquehotels.com
50 rm 🖵 – 🛉95/420 € 🛉🛉110/465 €
• Chain • Design •

A hotel occupying a completely remodelled building, which now boasts a distinct designer look. The intimately styled guestrooms (some with a shower, others a bathtub) are superbly appointed. Enjoy traditional Portuguese cuisine in the hotel restaurant.

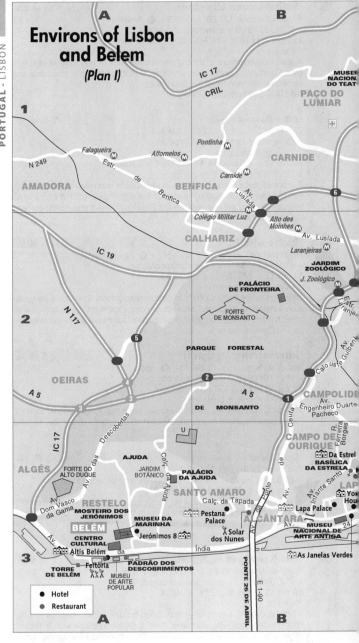

Environs of Lisbon and Belem
(Plan I)

- Hotel
- Restaurant

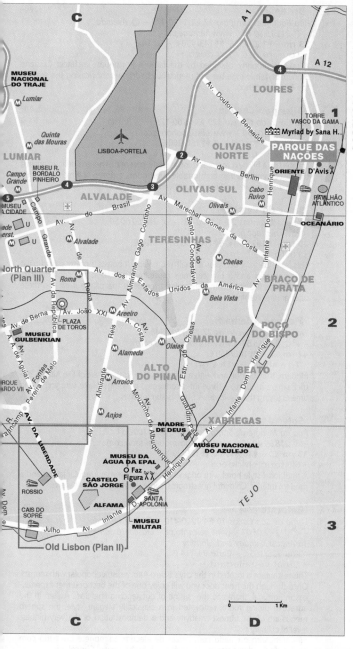

C

D

A 1

A 12

MUSEU NACIONAL DO TRAJE

Lumiar

4

LOURES

TORRE VASCO DA GAMA
Myriad by Sana H...

1

Quinta das Mouras

Av. Doutor A. Bensaúde

OLIVAIS NORTE

PARQUE DAS NAÇÕES

LUMIAR

LISBOA-PORTELA

Av. de Berlim

ORIENTE D'Avis

Campo Grande

MUSEU R. BORDALO PINHEIRO

2

PAVILHÃO ATLÂNTICO

5

4

3

OLIVAIS SUL

Cabo Ruivo

Av. de

Santo

Infante

Dom

Henrique

OCEANÁRIO

MUSEU CIDADE

ALVALADE

Av.

do

Brasil

Av. Marechal Gomes da Costa

Olivais

U

U

Alvalade

TERESINHAS

Av. Gago Coutinho

Av. do Santo Condestável

Chelas

BRAÇO DE PRATA

North Quarter (Plan III)

Roma

Av. de Roma

Av. dos Estados

Unidos

da

América

Bela Vista

POÇO DO BISPO

2

Av. de Berna

Av. João XXI

Areeiro

A. Costa

Chelas

MARVILA

MUSEU GULBENKIAN

Av. da República

PLAZA DE TOROS

Reis

Alameda

Olaias

BEATO

Av. A. de Aguiar

Almirante Reis

ALTO DO PINA

Estr.

Av. Infante Dom Henrique

PARQUE EDUARDO VII

Av. Fontes Pereira de Melo

Arroios

Av. Mouzinho de Albuquerque

Anjos

Gualdim Pais

XABREGAS

MADRE DE DEUS

AV. DA LIBERDADE

R. do Amparo

MUSEU DA ÁGUA DA EPAL

MUSEU NACIONAL DO AZULEJO

O Faz Figura

CASTELO SÃO JORGE

Av. Infante Dom Henrique

ROSSIO

ALFAMA

SANTA APOLONIA

CAIS DO SOPRÉ

Av. 24 de Julho

Av. Infante

MUSEU MILITAR

T E J O

3

Old Lisbon (Plan II)

0   1 Km

C

D

PORTUGAL - LISBON

Britania
                                        🅰🄲
Rua Rodrigues Sampaio 17 ✉ *1150-278 –* Ⓜ *Avenida*   Plan: **E1**
– 𝒞 213 15 50 16 – www.heritage.pt
33 rm – ♦130/450 € ♦♦143/450 € – ☕ 14 €
• Townhouse • Art déco •
A unique property designed by the famous Portuguese architect Cassiano Branco. Stylish lounge-bar and meticulous bedrooms showcasing the spirit of the Art Deco period.

Olissippo Castelo
                               ⬅ & 🅰🄲
Rua Costa do Castelo 120 ✉ *1100-179 –* Ⓜ *Rossio*   Plan: **F1-2**
– 𝒞 218 82 01 90 – www.olissippohotels.com
24 rm ☕ – ♦140/250 € ♦♦150/280 €
• Family • Classic •
Located on a hill next to the San Jorge castle, part of this hotel is built up against the castle ramparts. Very comfortable guestrooms, a dozen of which have their own garden terrace and magnificent views.

Solar do Castelo
                                        ⬙ 🅰🄲
Rua das Cozinhas 2 ✉ *1100-181 – 𝒞 218 80 60 50*   Plan: **F2**
– www.heritage.pt
20 rm – ♦162/450 € ♦♦176/450 € – ☕ 14 €
• Historic • Trendy •
This hotel partially occupies a small 18C palace. It boasts a pretty paved patio with peacocks and a tiny ceramics museum. The classic yet contemporary guestrooms include seven personalised rooms in the palace itself and these offer greater comfort.

Memmo Alfama H.
                                       ⬅ ⛴ 🅰🄲
Travessa das Merceeiras 27 ✉ *1100-348*   Plan: **F2**
– 𝒞 210 49 56 60 – www.memmohotels.com
42 rm ☕ – ♦♦180/450 €
• Townhouse • Design •
Modern, truly unique and with a great location in the heart of the Alfama district, where it occupies three inter-connected buildings. Make sure you spend time enjoying the idyllic views from its sun terraces.

Solar dos Mouros
                                     ⬙ ⬅ 🅰🄲
Rua do Milagre de Santo António 6 ✉ *1100-351*   Plan: **F2**
– 𝒞 218 85 49 40 – www.solardosmouroslisboa.com
13 rm ☕ – ♦109/199 € ♦♦129/299 €
• Historic • Modern •
A traditional-style hotel with original decor, a somewhat irregular layout and a modern interior. Colourful guestrooms, some enjoying excellent views.

Belcanto (José Avillez)

😈😈   *Largo de São Carlos 10* ✉ *1200-410 –* Ⓜ *Baixa-Chiado*   Plan: **E2**
– 𝒞 213 42 06 07 – www.belcanto.pt – Closed 18 January-2 February, 1-16 August, Sunday and Monday
Menu 125/165 € – Carte 94/114 €
• Creative • Elegant •
This restaurant is located in the city's Bairro Alto, a district popular with tourists. Once through the front door you will enjoy one of the best gourmet experiences in Portugal, thanks to the cuisine of outstanding chef José Avillez. In the attractive dining room, renovated in a classically elegant style, the superb menus are of the utmost creativity and a demonstration of the very highest level of culinary skill.
→ Carabineiro grelhado com cinzas de alecrim. Salmonete braseado com molho de fígados e xerém de amêijoas à bulhão pato. Chocolates.

XxX **Tágide** ⩽ AC

Largo da Academia Nacional de Belas Artes 18-20 Plan: **E2**
✉ *1200-005* – Ⓜ *Baixa-Chiado* – ✆ *213 40 40 10*
– www.restaurantetagide.com – Closed Sunday
Carte 40/69 €
• Modern cuisine • Classic décor •
Climb a few steps to Tágide's elegant dining room embellished with spider lamps and attractive azulejo tilework. Updated traditional cuisine and a tapas bar at the entrance.

XX **Alma** (Henrique Sá Pessoa)
⸎ *Anchieta 15* ✉ *1200-023* – Ⓜ *Baixa-Chiado* Plan: **E2**
– ✆ 213 47 06 50 – www.almalisboa.pt – Closed Monday
Menu 60/90 € – Carte 55/76 €
• Creative • Contemporary décor •
An attractive restaurant in the heart of the Chiado district. It occupies an 18C house that was once a warehouse for the famous Bertrand bookshop, the oldest in the world. The modern interior is one of striking contrasts and provides the backdrop for seasonal à la carte options and interesting set menus that encompass traditional, international and more innovative dishes.
→ Escalope de foie gras, maçã, granola, amêndoa, cafe. Salmonete, caldeirada, xerém, salicórnia. Mar e citrinos.

XX **O Faz Figura** ⩽ 🍃 AC

Rua do Paraíso 15-B ✉ *1100-396* – ✆ *218 86 89 81* Plan I: **C3**
– www.fazfigura.com – Closed Monday lunch
Carte 32/58 €
• Modern cuisine • Trendy •
Next to the National Pantheon (Santa Engrácia church), near Alfama. A well-organised operation with classic facilities, in an elegant setting, and traditional cuisine with a creative touch.

XX **Solar dos Presuntos** 🎇 ᴪ AC 🍃

Rua das Portas de Santo Antão 150 ✉ *1150-269* Plan: **E1**
– Ⓜ Avenida – ✆ 213 42 42 53 – www.solardospresuntos.com – Closed August, Christmas, Sunday and Bank Holidays
Carte 33/57 €
• Traditional cuisine • Trendy •
Run by its owners, this pleasant restaurant has an attractive counter of fresh produce on display. Large selection of traditional dishes and seafood specialities, as well as an excellent wine list.

XX **Ad Lib** – Hotel Sofitel Lisbon Liberdade AC

Av. da Liberdade 127 ✉ *1269-038* – Ⓜ *Avenida* Plan: **E1**
– ✆ 213 22 83 50 – www.restauranteadlib.pt
Menu 20/45 € – Carte 37/62 €
• Modern cuisine • Classic décor •
A restaurant with a classic-cum-contemporary decor and lots of personality. In the kitchen the cuisine is a fusion of the best French fare and traditional Portuguese cooking.

X **Mini Bar Teatro** 🍃 ᴪ AC

Rúa António Maria Cardoso 58 ✉ *1200-027* Plan: **E2**
– Ⓜ Baixa-Chiado – ✆ 211 30 53 93 – www.minibar.pt
Menu 39/49 € – Carte approx. 35 € – *(dinner only)*
• Creative • Bistro •
An informal, enticing and relaxed eatery in the Bairro Alto theatre district. Diners are in for a pleasant surprise as the dishes on the menu have been created by José Avillez – Michelin-starred chef at the Belcanto restaurant.

X **100 Maneiras** 🗚

Rua do Teixeira 35 ✉ *1200-459* – ☏ *910 30 75 75*   Plan: **E1**
– www.restaurante100maneiras.com
Menu 60 € *– (dinner only) (tasting menu only)*
· Creative · Simple ·

A small restaurant in a narrow street in the Barrio Alto district. The young chef offers a creative tasting menu, which is fresh, light and imaginatively presented.

X **Chefe Cordeiro** 🗚

Praça do Comércio 20 ✉ *1100-148*   Plan: **E2**
– ⓜ Terreiro do Paço – ☏ *216 08 00 90 – www.chefecordeiro.com – Closed Sunday and Monday*
Menu 14/45 € *– Carte 28/48 €*
· Portuguese · Classic décor ·

Located beneath the arches of the beautiful Praça do Comércio (the centre of tourist activity in Lisbon). The contemporary and colourful interior provides the setting for a menu featuring traditional Portuguese cuisine.

X **Casa de Linhares** 🗚

Beco dos Armazéns do Linho 2 ✉ *1100-037*   Plan: **F2**
– ⓜ Terreiro do Paço – ☏ *910 18 81 18 – www.casadelinhares.com*
Menu 60 € *– Carte 35/45 € – (dinner only) (booking essential)*
· Portuguese · Regional décor ·

This restaurant occupies a Renaissance mansion that has been converted into one of the most popular *Fado* music venues in Lisbon. Impressive menu of traditional Portuguese cuisine.

NORTH QUARTER (Av. da Liberdade, Parque Eduardo VII, Museu Gulbenkian)   **PLAN III**

🏨 **Four Seasons H. Ritz Lisbon** ⬅ 𝄢 ⊕ 🖵 ⅖ 🗚 ⳾ 🚗

Rua Rodrigo da Fonseca 88 ✉ *1099-039*   Plan: **G3**
– ⓜ Marquês de Pombal – ☏ *213 81 14 00 – www.fourseasons.com*
241 rm – ♛♛390/585 € – � 39 € – 41 suites
· Luxury · Classic ·

Experience true pleasure at this luxury hotel where the contemporary look of the building contrasts with the incredibly bright and classically elegant interior. Spacious lounge areas, highly comfortable guestrooms, and an impressive array of beauty treatments.

Varanda – See restaurant listing

🏨 **Porto Bay Liberdade** ✿ 𝄢 🖵 ⅖ 🗚 ⳾ 🚗

Rua Rosa Araújo 8 ✉ *1250-195* – ⓜ *Avenida*   Plan: **G3**
– ☏ 210 01 57 00 – www.portobay.com
95 rm – ♛146/229 € ♛♛157/240 € – � 20 € – 3 suites
· Townhouse · Contemporary ·

This establishment occupies a restored palatial property with a delightfully classic façade and an interior with a contemporary feel. Attractive lobby and well-appointed bedrooms with a classic-modern look, although the standard rooms are a little on the small side. A bistro-style menu is on offer in the restaurant.

🏨 **The Vintage Lisboa** ✿ 𝄢 ⊕ 🖵 ⅖ 🗚 ⳾ 🚗

Rua Rodrigo da Fonseca 2 ✉ *1250-191* – ⓜ *Rato*   Plan: **G3**
– ☏ 210 40 54 00 – www.nauhotels.com
53 rm � – ♛♛130/500 € – 3 suites
· Townhouse · Contemporary ·

Strong attention to detail has resulted in a look that is both personalised and welcoming. The guestrooms are classic yet contemporary in style with top quality fixtures and furnishings. The multi-function restaurant is the setting for breakfast, lunch and dinner.

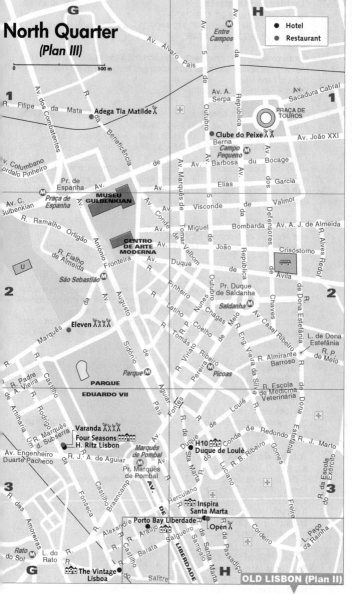

North Quarter
(Plan III)

G

H

● Hotel
● Restaurant

Av. Álvaro Pais

Av. Entre Campos

R. Filipe da Mata

● **Adega Tia Matilde** ⚔

1

Av. dos Combatentes

da Beneficência

Av. A. Serpa

Av. da República

de Outubro

Av. Sacadura Cabral

PRAÇA DE TOUROS

Av. João XXI

1

V. Columbano Bordalo Pinheiro

Av. C. Gulbenkian

Praça de Espanha

Pr. de Espanha

● **Clube do Peixe** ⚔⚔

Berna

Campo Pequeno

Av. Barbosa du Bocage

Elias

MUSEU GULBENKIAN

Av. Marquês de

Visconde de

Garcia

de

dos

Valmor

Av.

R. Ramalho Ortigão

Av.

Miguel

Bombarda

Av. A. J. de Almeida

R. Alves Redol

CENTRO DE ARTE MODERNA

Av. Conde de

Av.

Tomar

de

João

de

Crisóstomo

Ávila

R. Fialho de Almeida

R.

António

Fronteira

Av.

Valbom

de

da República

de

Defensores de

U

São Sebastião Ⓜ

Augusto

Duque

Pinheiro

Pr. Duque de Saldanha

Saldanha

Chaves

Av. Casal Ribeiro

R. de Dona Estefânia

2

Marquês

da

de

Latino

Nunes

Melo

de

L. de Dona Estefânia

R. P. de Melo

● **Eleven** ⚔⚔⚔

Sidónio

de

P. Coelho

R. Viriato

Chagas

R. Almirante Barroso

2

R. Padre A. Vieira

Castilho

R. Marquês d. Subserra

Parque Ⓜ

Parque M

R. Tomás

Ribeiro

Pereira

Picoas Ⓜ

R. Escola de Medicina Veterinária

PARQUE EDUARDO VII

Aguiar

Pais

R. de

Fontes

R. Loulé

de

Redondo

R. da Escola do Exército

Varanda ⚔⚔⚔
Four Seasons 🏨🏨🏨
H. Ritz Lisbon

Av. Engenheiro Duarte Pacheco

R. J. A. de Aguiar

Marquês de Pombal Ⓜ

Pr. Marquês de Pombal

Duque de Sta Maria

● **H10** 🏨🏨
Duque de Loulé

Conde de

R. B. Ribeiro

R. Luciano

Gomes

R. J. Marto

3

R. das Amoreiras

Rodrigo

Marquês

R. J.

Fonseca

Castilho

Braancamp

Av.

Alexandre

Herculano

DE

🏨🏨 **Inspira Santa Marta**

Freire

3

Rato Ⓜ do Sol

L. do Rato

R. Castilho

R. Barata

R. de Santa Marta

● **Porto Bay Liberdade** 🏨

Salgueiro

de

Passadiço

Open ⚔

Cordeiro

L. Paço da Rainha

🏨🏨 **The Vintage Lisboa** ●

G

Salitre

LIBERDADE

Av. DA

H

OLD LISBON (Plan II) ▼

Artilharia

0 ————— 500 m

Inspira Santa Marta

Rua Santa Marta 48 ✉ *1150-297*
Plan: **H3**
– **Ⓜ** *Marqués de Pombal* – ℰ *210 44 09 00* – *www.inspirahotels.com*
89 rm – †**†**99/220 € – ⛶ 14 €
• Townhouse • Modern •
A hotel combining designer features, comfort and a spa. Its aim is to be environmentally sustainable and it has rooms arranged according to the Oriental principles of Feng Shui.
Open – See restaurant listing

H10 Duque de Loulé

Avenida Duque de Loulé 81-83 ✉ *1050-088*
Plan: **H3**
– **Ⓜ** *Marqués de Pombal* – ℰ *213 18 20 00* – *www.h10hotels.com*
84 rm – †100/200 € – ††110/210 € – ⛶ 21 € – 5 suites
• Traditional • Classic •
A hotel with lots of personality, occupying a former convent, from which it has retained the original façade. The splendid interior comes as a delightful surprise with its mix of modernity and traditional Portuguese styling. The focus in the restaurant is very much on native cuisine.

Eleven (Joachim Koerper)

ⓒⓒ

Rua Marquês de Fronteira ✉ *1070-051*
Plan: **G2**
– **Ⓜ** *São Sebastião* – ℰ *213 86 22 11* – *www.restauranteleven.com*
– *Closed Sunday*
Menu 84/160 € – Carte 75/108 €
• Creative • Fashionable •
Housed in a designer-style building above the Amália Rodrigues gardens, this light, airy and modern restaurant boasts splendid views of the Eduardo VII park and the city. Creative gourmet cuisine features on the menu.
→ Barra de Ouro, foie gras de pato, soja, rum, laranja. Trio de porco com tomate, batata, limão confitado e molho de alho. Soufflé de maracujá com gelado de banana.

Varanda – Hotel Four Seasons H. Ritz Lisbon

Rua Rodrigo da Fonseca 88 ✉ *1099-039*
Plan: **G3**
– **Ⓜ** *Marqués de Pombal* – ℰ *213 81 14 00* – *www.fourseasons.com*
Carte 73/115 €
• Modern cuisine • Classic décor •
This restaurant stands out both for its terrace overlooking the Eduardo VII park and for its cuisine, which includes a full buffet and contemporary-style dishes.

Clube do Peixe

Av. 5 de Outubro 180-A ✉ *1050-063*
Plan: **H1**
– **Ⓜ** *Campo Pequeno* – ℰ *217 97 34 34* – *www.clube-do-peixe.com*
Menu 20/45 € – Carte 20/47 €
• Seafood • Classic décor •
A popular local restaurant with an attractive display of fish and seafood at the entrance. The dining room is classic-contemporary in style with the occasional maritime detail in the decor.

Open – Hotel Inspira Santa Marta

Rua Santa Marta 48 ✉ *1150-297* – ℰ *210 44 09 00*
Plan: **H3**
– *www.open.com.pt* – *Closed Saturday lunch, Sunday lunch and Bank Holidays lunch*
Menu 22 € – Carte 21/42 €
• Modern cuisine • Cosy •
A restaurant with a young and relaxed ambience. Healthy, contemporary cooking endeavours to work with organic products as much as possible. Gluten-free dishes are also available.

✗ **Adega Tia Matilde**

Rua da Beneficéncia 77 ✉ *1600-017* – **Ⓜ** *Praça de Espanha* Plan: **G1**
– 𝒞 217 97 21 72 – www.adegatiamatilde.pt – Closed Saturday dinner and Sunday
Menu 22 € – Carte 30/52 €
• Traditional cuisine • Family •
Family-run restaurant with a good local reputation. Spacious dining rooms and tra-
ditional cuisine. The large underground car park makes up for the poor location.

PARQUE DAS NAÇÕES   PLAN I

 Myriad by Sana H.

Cais das Naus, Lote 2.21.01 (Parque das Naçoes) Plan: **D1**
✉ *1990-173* – **Ⓜ** *Oriente* – 𝒞 *211 10 76 00 – www.myriad.pt*
186 rm – 🛏240 € 🛏🛏270 € – ⌸ 30 €
• Business • Modern •
A hotel with a striking look, next to the Vasco de Gama tower. The interior showcases high-level design and functionality with every guestroom overlooking the
river and the impressive terrace. The restaurant offers both Portuguese and
international cuisine.

✗ **D'Avis**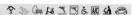

 Av. D. João II 1 (Parque das Naçoes) ✉ *1990-083* Plan: **D1**
– 𝒞 218 68 13 54 – Closed Sunday and Bank Holidays
Carte 20/28 €
• Cuisine from Alentejo • Rustic •
This oasis of rusticity imbued with the spirit of the Alentejo region is in the very
modern setting of the Expo '98 site. The counter at the entrance sells regional
products, while the two cosy dining rooms are decorated with a variety of tradi-
tional and antique objects. Highly authentic Alentejo cuisine.

WEST   PLAN I

 Pestana Palace

Rua Jau 54 ✉ *1300-314* – 𝒞 *213 61 56 00* Plan: **B3**
– www.pestana.com
177 rm ⌸ – 🛏381/472 € 🛏🛏402/494 € – 17 suites
• Palace • Classic •
A beautiful 19C palace decorated in line with the period, with sumptuous lounges, guestrooms featuring an array of decorative detail, and grounds that have
the feel of a botanical garden. In the restaurant, choose from several set menus
at lunchtime and traditional à la carte choices with a modern flair in the evening. A small private room is also available in the old kitchen.

 Lapa Palace

Rua do Pau de Bandeira 4 ✉ *1249-021* – **Ⓜ** *Rato* Plan: **B3**
– 𝒞 213 94 94 94 – www.olissippohotels.com
102 rm ⌸ – 🛏🛏370/430 € – 7 suites
• Grand Luxury • Classic •
A luxurious 19C palace standing on one of the seven hills overlooking Lisbon
and boasting stunning views of the Tagus estuary. The elegant and bright restaurant serves pleasantly updated traditional cuisine. The perfect setting for an
unforgettable stay!

Da Estrela ✿ AK ⇕ 🚗

Rua Saraiva de Carvalho 35 ✉ *1250-242* – **Ⓜ** *Rato* Plan: **B3**
– 𝒞 211 90 01 00 – www.hoteldaestrela.com
13 rm ⌸ – 🛏90/405 € 🛏🛏99/410 € – 6 suites
• Townhouse • Modern •
The hotel's original decor evokes the spirit of the former school that once occupied the building. Hence the combination of old blackboards, tables and coat
racks alongside designer furniture. The multi-function restaurant is used for all
three meal services.

PORTUGAL - LISBON

As Janelas Verdes
  ♿ 🅰🅲

Rua das Janelas Verdes 47 ✉ *1200-690*   Plan: **B3**
– 𝒞 213 96 81 43 – www.heritage.pt
29 rm – ♦143/450 € ♦♦157/450 € – � 14 €
• Traditional • Classic •
This hotel partially occupies an 18C house that is also home to the National Museum of Ancient Art. The hotel has a delightful mix of classic romanticism, warmth, history and personality.

York House
  🍴 🅰🅲 �

Rua das Janelas Verdes 32 ✉ *1200-691*   Plan: **B3**
– 𝒞 213 96 24 35 – www.yorkhouselisboa.com
33 rm – ♦♦90/160 € – ⊔ 15 €
• Historic • Contemporary •
This hotel housed in a 17C Carmelite convent has retained much of its original character. Its renovated interior offers modern comfort and decor. It has two types of guestrooms available, one contemporary and the other more classic in design. The restaurant is striking for its old glazed tiles.

XX
❀

Loco (Alexandre Silva)
  🅰🅲

Rua dos Navegantes 53 ✉ *1250-731* – Ⓜ *Rato*   Plan: **B3**
– 𝒞 213 95 18 61 – www.loco.pt – Closed 1-15 June, 14-22 November and Monday
Menu 70/85 € – *(dinner only) (booking advisable) (tasting menu only)*
• Modern cuisine • Contemporary décor •
Located next to the Basílica da Estrela, Loco has just the one dining room with a surprising design and views of the kitchen. Alexandre Silva, famous for winning the first *Top Chef de Portugal* competition, showcases his cuisine via two enticing and creative tasting menus, which make full use of locally sourced ingredients.
→ Ostra com molho thai, kaffir e chili. Carapau cru com molho de pato. Ravioli de rabo de boi com espuma de alho.

X
❀

Solar dos Nunes
  🅰🅲

Rua dos Lusíadas 68-72 ✉ *1300-372*   Plan: **B3**
– 𝒞 213 64 73 59 – www.solardosnunes.pt
– Closed Sunday
Carte 25/48 €
• Traditional cuisine • Rustic •
This welcoming restaurant stands out for the magnificent mosaic-style floor in the main dining room and its walls covered with appreciative newspaper and magazine reviews. Impressive fish display, as well as a live seafood tank. Traditional Portuguese menu and an excellent wine list.

BELÉM   PLAN I

Altis Belém
  🍴 ≼ 🕭 🌐 🔲 ♿ 🅰🅲 🔈 🚗

Doca do Bom Sucesso ✉ *1400-038* – 𝒞 *210 40 02 00*   Plan: **A3**
– www.altishotels.com
45 rm ⊔ – ♦190/450 € ♦♦210/500 € – 5 suites
• Luxury • Modern •
Luxury and modernity in equal measure! Facilities here include a rooftop chill-out zone, minimalist café and spacious guestrooms, all decorated around the theme of the country's age of discoveries and its cultural exchanges. Enjoy cuisine with a contemporary flair in the bright and elegant restaurant.
❀ **Feitoria** – See restaurant listing

Jerónimos 8 🔥 AC 🔥

Rua dos Jerónimos 8 ✉ *1400-211 – ℰ 213 60 09 00* Plan: **A3**
– www.jeronimos8.com
65 rm 😋 – 🛉130/250 € 🛉🛉150/280 €
• Traditional • Modern •

This comfortable hotel is located next to the Monasterio de Los Jerónimos. It occupies an old building that has been completely renovated with a minimalist feel.

XXX   Feitoria – Hotel Altis Belém 🍴 🍷 🔥 AC 🚗
❀

Doca do Bom Sucesso ✉ *1400-038 – ℰ 210 40 02 08* Plan: **A3**
– www.restaurantefeitoria.com – Closed 1-15 January and Sunday
Menu 80/135 € – Carte 74/91 € – *(dinner only)*
• Modern cuisine • Trendy •

A restaurant of a very high standard, featuring a bar for a pre-dinner drink and a dining room arranged in a contemporary style. The chef offers creative, modern cuisine steeped in tradition, with a focus on high quality products and top-notch presentation.

→ Lula, camarão, amendoim e dashi. Pregado salteado, sardinha e caldeirada. Chocolate, café e azeitona galega.

SPAIN
ESPAÑA

→ **AREA:**
504 645 km² (194 595 sq mi).

→ **POPULATION:**
46 438 422 inhabitants. Density = 92 per km².

→ **CAPITAL:** Madrid.

→ **CURRENCY:**
Euro (€).

→ **GOVERNMENT:**
Constitutional parliamentary monarchy (since 1978). Member of European Union since 1986.

→ **LANGUAGES:**
Spanish (Castilian) but also Catalan in Catalonia, Gallego in Galicia, Euskera in the Basque Country, Valencian in the Valencian Region and Mallorquin in the Balearic Isles.

→ **PUBLIC HOLIDAYS:**
New Year's Day (1 Jan); Epiphany (6 Jan); Good Friday (late Mar/Apr); Labor Day (1 May); Assumption of the Virgin Mary (15 Aug); National Day (12 Oct); All Saints' Day (1 Nov); Constitution Day (6 Dec); Immaculate Conception (8 Dec); Christmas Day (25 Dec). Autonomous communities may replace some dates.

→ **LOCAL TIME:**
GMT+1 hour in winter and GMT +2 hours in summer.

→ **CLIMATE:**
Temperate Mediterranean with mild winters (colder in interior) and sunny, hot summers (Madrid: January 6°C; July 25°C).

→ **EMERGENCY:**
Police ☏ **091**; Medical Assistance and Fire Brigade ☏ **112.** (Dialling **112** within any EU country will redirect your call and contact the emergency services.)

→ **ELECTRICITY:**
230 volts AC, 50Hz; 2 round pin sockets.

→ **FORMALITIES:**
Travellers from the European Union (EU), Switzerland, Iceland and the main countries of North and South America need a national identity card or passport (America: passport required) to visit Spain for less than three months (tourism or business purpose). For visitors from other countries a visa may be required, in addition to a passport, especially for those wishing to stay for longer than three months. We advise you to check with your embassy before travelling.

MADRID

MADRID

Population: 3 165 883

Aidas Zubkonis/Fotolia.com

The renaissance of Madrid has seen it develop as a big player on the world cultural stage, attracting more international music, theatre and dance than it would have dreamed of a few decades ago. The nightlife in Spain's proud capital is second to none and the superb art museums which make up the city's 'golden triangle' have all undergone thrilling reinvention in recent years. This is a city that might think it has some catching up to do: it was only made the capital in 1561 on the whim of ruler, Felipe II. But its position was crucial: slap bang in the middle of the Iberian Peninsula. Ruled by Habsburgs and Bourbons, it soon made a mark in Europe, and the contemporary big wigs of Madrid are now having the same effect – this time with a 21C twist.

The central heart of Madrid is compact, defined by the teeming Habsburg hubs of Puerta del Sol and Plaza Mayor, and the mighty Palacio Real – the biggest official royal residence in the world, with a bewildering three thousand rooms. East of here are the grand squares, fountains and fine museums of the Bourbon District, with its easterly boundary, the Retiro park. West of the historical centre are the capacious green acres of Casa de Campo, while the affluent, regimented grid streets of Salamanca are to the east. Modern Madrid is just to the north, embodied in the grand north-south boulevard Paseo de la Castellana.

MADRID IN...

→ ONE DAY
Puerta del Sol, Plaza Mayor, Palacio Real, Prado.

→ TWO DAYS
Museo Thyssen-Bornemisza, Retiro, Gran Vía, tapas at a traditional taberna.

→ THREE DAYS
Chueca, Malasaña, Centro de Arte Reina Sofía.

PRACTICAL INFORMATION

ARRIVAL-DEPARTURE

✈ Adolfo Suárez Madrid-Barajas Airport is 13km east of the city. Metro Line 8 runs every 4-7min and takes 50min. Commuter rail service C-1 connects T4 with Chamartin and Atocha Railway Stations (frequency 30min); Chamartin for services to the north of Spain and France; Atocha for those to the south.

GETTING AROUND

You can buy single journey tickets, but better value for longer visits is a ten-trip Metrobus ticket, valid on both bus and metro networks, and available from underground stations, bus ticket offices, newsstands and tobacconists. The Tourist Travel Pass is valid from one to seven days for unlimited travel on all public transport in either Zone A or Zone T. A Madrid Card, valid for one, two, three or five day periods, entitles you to travel on all forms of public transport, and grants admission to more than fifty museums. It is also valid for discounts in some nightclubs, shops and restaurants.

CALENDAR HIGHLIGHTS

January
Twelfth Night Procession, Fitur (International Tourism Trade Fair).

February
ARCO (contemporary art fair), Carnaval, Madrid Fusion (gastronomic summit).

April
Día de Cervantes (book fair).

May
Dos de Mayo, Fiesta de San Isidro, Madrid Book Fair.

July-August
Los Veranos de la Villa.

September
Festival de Otoño.

EATING OUT

Madrileños know how to pace themselves. Breakfast is around 8am, lunch 2pm or 3pm, the afternoon begins at 5pm and dinner won't be until 10pm or 11pm. Madrid is the European capital which has best managed to absorb the regional cuisine of the country, largely due to massive internal migration to the city, and it claims to have highest number of bars and restaurants per capita than anywhere else in the world. If you want to tuck into local specialities, you'll find them everywhere around the city. Callos a la Madrileña is Madrid-style tripe, dating back to 1559, while sopas de ajo (garlic soup) is a favourite on cold winter days. Another popular soup (also a main course) is cocido Madrileño, hearty and aromatic and comprised of chickpeas, meat, tocino belly pork, potatoes and vegetables, slowly cooked in a rich broth. To experience the real Madrid dining ambience, get to a traditional taberna in the heart of the old neighbourhood: these are distinguished by a large clock, a carved wooden bar with a zinc counter, wine flasks, marble-topped tables and ceramic tiles.

SPAIN - MADRID

The Westin Palace
☆ ⅃ㄉ ♿ AK ∱⅄ 🚗
pl. de las Cortes 7 ✉ 28014 – Ⓜ *Sevilla*   Plan: **G2**
– ℰ *913 60 80 00 –* www.westin.com
467 rm – ♥♥850/930 € – ⌺ 35 €
• Luxury • Classic •
This elegant, historic building is considered a symbol of the Belle Époque. Its
unusual lounge area is crowned by an expansive Art Nouveau-style glass
atrium. Superb guestrooms furnished in classic-style. Its restaurant, La Rotonda,
offers an international menu.

Villa Real
☆ AK ∱⅄ 🚗
pl. de las Cortes 10 ✉ 28014 – Ⓜ *Sevilla*   Plan: **G2**
– ℰ *914 20 37 67 –* www.hotelvillareal.com
115 rm – ♥♥130/475 € – ⌺ 23 €
• Chain • Personalised •
This hotel displays a valuable collection of Greek and Roman art in many of its
public areas. The comfortable guestrooms are attractively decorated with
mahogany furniture. This informal restaurant with an abundance of natural
light serves cuisine with an international flavour.

Urban
⅃ㄉ ⊐ ♿ AK ∱⅄ 🚗
Carrera de San Jerónimo 34 ✉ 28014 – Ⓜ *Sevilla*
– ℰ *917 87 77 70 –* www.hotelurban.com
96 rm – ♥♥199/600 € – ⌺ 26 €
• Chain • Design •
An avant-garde hotel with high quality furnishings, attractive lighting and
numerous works of art on display. Well-equipped guestrooms pay real attention
to detail.
Cebo – See restaurant listing

Las Letras Gran Vía
⅃ㄉ ♿ AK ∱⅄
Gran Vía 13 ✉ 28013 – Ⓜ *Gran Vía* – ℰ *915 23 79 80*   Plan: **G2**
– www.iberostar.com
109 rm – ♥♥125/365 € – ⌺ 18 €
• Business • Classic •
The hotel's restored façade contrasts sharply with the colourful and contemporary interior. The guestrooms showcase New York-style design, including intimate lighting and even poems on the walls. The modern restaurant, which
almost merges into the lounge-bar, offers à la carte choices and set menus
with an emphasis on traditional cuisine.
Al Trapo – See restaurant listing

Only You H. Madrid
☆ ⅃ㄉ ♿ AK ∱⅄
Barquillo 21 ✉ 28004 – Ⓜ *Chueca* – ℰ *910 05 22 22*   Plan: **G1**
– www.onlyyouhotels.com
120 rm – ♥170/310 € ♥♥220/360 € – ⌺ 22 €
• Business • Design •
A charming hotel occupying a restored 19C palace in the heart of the Chueca
district. Considerable work on the inside has resulted in a modern interior featuring myriad decorative details. It has welcoming guest areas, very well-equipped bedrooms, and a pleasant restaurant.

Dear H.
☆ ⊐ ♿ AK ∱⅄ 🚗
Gran Vía 80 ✉ 28013 – Ⓜ *Plaza de España*   Plan: **E1**
– ℰ *914 12 32 00 –* www.dearhotelmadrid.com
162 rm – ♥♥110/250 € – ⌺ 19 €
• Boutique hotel • Classic •
Occupying a neo-Classical building in a superb location on the Gran Vía – Mad-
rid's equivalent of Broadway. Comfortable, classically furnished guestrooms,
fusion-style cuisine and, above all, superb views from its rooftop terrace.

SPAIN - MADRID

 One Shot Recoletos 04   ♿ 𝕂

Salustiano Olózaga 4 ✉ 28001 – Ⓜ *Banco de España*   Plan: **H2**
– ☏ 911 82 00 70 – www.oneshothotels.com
61 rm ☲ – †159/300 € ††179/350 €
• Business • Contemporary •

This small hotel with an informal air mixes the old and the new. Although small and on the functional side, the guestrooms are embellished with photos by young contemporary artists.

 Posada del Dragón   𐑵 𝕂

Cava Baja 14 ✉ 28005 – Ⓜ *La Latina* – ☏ 911 19 14 24   Plan: **F3**
– www.posadadeldragon.com
27 rm – †79/219 € ††89/239 € – ☲ 12 €
• Historic • Design •

Although it occupies the site of one of the oldest inns in the city, this hotel is a cutting-edge property. It has only retained the framework and 19C courtyard from the original building. The restaurant, which embraces the 'show cooking' concept, occupies what was once the La Antoñita soap factory, from which it takes its name.

XxxX   **La Terraza del Casino** (Paco Roncero)   🥦 🏪 𝕂 ⇔
❀❀   *Alcalá 15-3°* ✉ 28014 – Ⓜ *Sevilla* – ☏ 915 32 12 75   Plan: **G2**
– www.casinodemadrid.es – Closed August, Sunday, Monday and Bank Holidays
Menu 69/148 € – Carte 77/92 €
• Creative • Elegant •

A palatial 19C setting for a restaurant that boasts a more contemporary look nowadays. The chef here offers creative à la carte choices, evident from the starters through to the dessert menu, with everything cooked to perfection. Magnificent terrace!

→ Tarta de ceps con cebolla, bacón al Oporto y costillas de conejo. Gallo, maíz y trufa. Raíces de chocolate.

XxxX   **El Club Allard**   🥦 𝕂 ⇔
❀❀   *Ferraz 2* ✉ 28008 – Ⓜ *Plaza España* – ☏ 915 59 09 39   Plan: **E1**
– www.elcluballard.com – Closed August, Sunday and Monday
Menu 90/120 € – *(tasting menu only)*
• Creative • Classic décor •

A restaurant housed in a listed modernist building, hence the lack of signage outside. The classically elegant interior provides the backdrop for creative, delicately presented cuisine featuring skilful fusions of ingredients and impressive technical ability.

→ Arroz del mar. Lomo de salmonete sobre crema de azafrán y nube de pomelo. Monte Invernal, chocolate, gel de menta y helado de aguacate.

XxX   **Palacio Cibeles**   🏪 ♿ 𝕂
pl. de Cibeles 1-6° ✉ 28014 – Ⓜ *Banco de España*   Plan: **H2**
– ☏ 915 23 14 54 – www.adolfo-palaciodecibeles.com
Menu 50 € – Carte 60/80 €
• Traditional cuisine • Contemporary décor •

The Palacio Cibeles enjoys a marvellous location on the sixth floor of the city's emblematic city hall (Ayuntamiento). In addition to the modern-style dining room, the restaurant has two attractive terraces where guests can dine or simply enjoy a drink. The cooking is of a traditional flavour.

XxX   **Cebo** – Hotel Urban   ♿ 𝕂 ⇔ 🚌
Carrera de San Jerónimo 34 ✉ 28014 – Ⓜ *Sevilla*   Plan: **G2**
– ☏ 917 87 77 70 – www.cebomadrid.com – Closed August, Sunday and Monday
Menu 80 € – Carte 49/66 €
• Creative • Design •

A modern, gastronomic restaurant with a strong designer element. Its bold, creative cuisine, with a clear Catalan influence, is best experienced via its tasting menus.

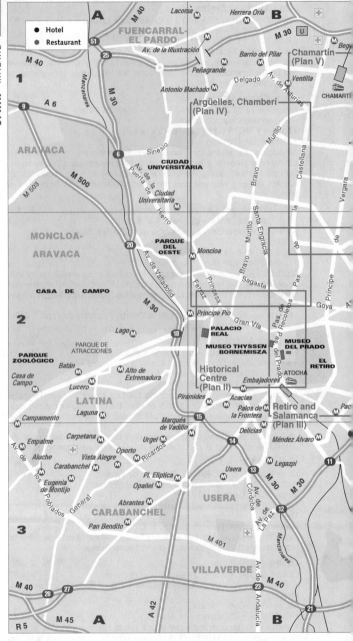

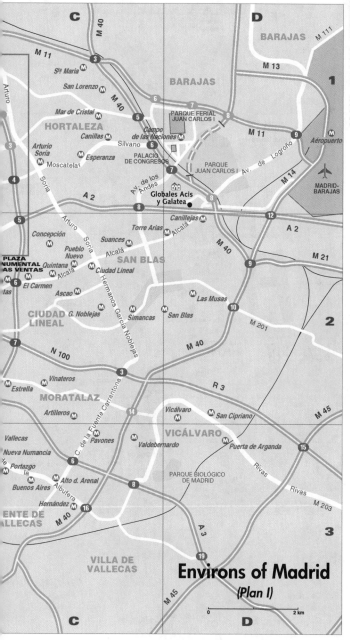

Environs of Madrid
(Plan I)

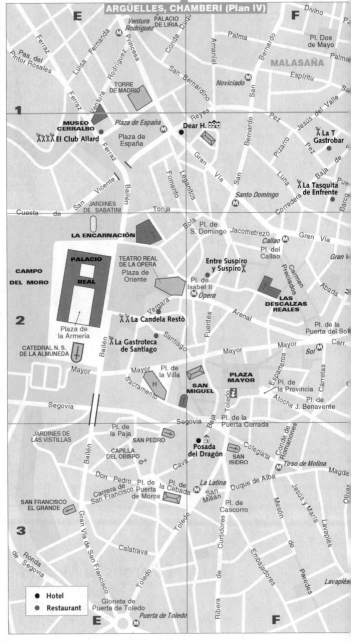

ARGÜELLES, CHAMBERI (Plan IV)

- ● Hotel
- ● Restaurant

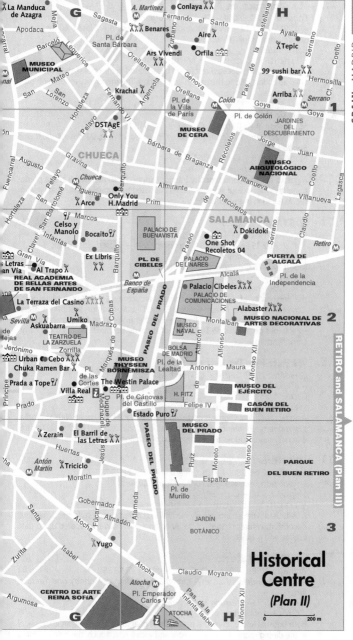

Historical Centre
(Plan II)

0   200 m

631

XxX **La Manduca de Azagra** 🗚

Sagasta 14 ✉ 28004 – Ⓜ *Alonso Martínez* Plan: **G1**
– ☎ *915 91 01 12 – www.lamanducadeazagra.com – Closed August,*
Sunday and Bank Holidays
Carte 35/55 €
• Traditional cuisine • Minimalist •
This spacious, well-located restaurant is decorated in minimalist style with particular attention paid to the design and lighting. The menu focuses on high quality produce.

XxX **Alabaster** ⅙ 🗚 ⇔

Montalbán 9 ✉ 28014 – Ⓜ *Retiro –* ☎ *915 12 11 31* Plan: **H2**
– www.restaurantealabaster.com – Closed Holy Week, 21 days August and
Sunday
Menu 50/70 € – Carte 46/64 €
• Modern cuisine • Trendy •
A gastro-bar and contemporary interior featuring designer detail and a predominantly white colour scheme. It offers updated traditional cuisine that is devoted to Galician ingredients.

XX **DSTAgE** (Diego Guerrero) 🗚 ⇔

❀❀ *Regueros 8 ✉ 28004 –* Ⓜ *Alonso Martínez* Plan: **G1**
– ☎ *917 02 15 86 – www.dstageconcept.com – Closed Holy Week, 1-*
15 August, Saturday and Sunday
Menu 88/118 € – *(tasting menu only)*
• Creative • Trendy •
This restaurant has an urban and industrial look and a relaxed feel that reflects the personality of the chef. The name is an acronym of his core philosophy: 'Days to Smell Taste Amaze Grow & Enjoy'. Discover cuisine that brings disparate cultures, ingredients and flavours together from Spain, Mexico and Japan.
➜ Raviolis de alubias de Tolosa en infusión de berza. El solomillo del carnicero. NiXpero.

XX **El Barril de las Letras** ⅙ 🗚

Cervantes 28 ✉ 28014 – Ⓜ *Antón Martín* Plan: **G3**
– ☎ *911 86 36 32 – www.barrildelasletras.com*
Carte 45/55 €
• Traditional cuisine • Friendly •
A restaurant full of contrasts occupying an old stone-built house with a completely modernised interior, albeit with the occasional exposed brick wall. The traditional menu includes a fair proportion of fish and seafood dishes.

XX **Ex Libris** 🗚

Infantas 29 ✉ 28004 – Ⓜ *Chueca –* ☎ *915 21 28 28* Plan: **G2**
– www.restauranteexlibris.com – Closed August
Menu 12/50 € – Carte 30/46 €
• Traditional cuisine • Elegant •
A restaurant with an attractively maintained contemporary style and an original decor that features pictures of "ex libris" on the walls. Well-prepared up-to-date cuisine and a variety of menus.

XX **La Candela Restò** 🗚

Amnistía 10 ✉ 28013 – Ⓜ *Ópera –* ☎ *911 73 98 88* Plan: **E2**
– www.lacandelaresto.com – Closed Sunday dinner, Monday and Tuesday
lunch
Menu 53/79 € – *(tasting menu only)*
• Creative • Friendly •
Both unusual and unique, this restaurant is guaranteed to make an impression! In the dining room, decorated simply and with a retro touch, the bold cuisine is a fusion of different culinary cultures.

X **Yugo**

San Blas 4 ✉ *28014 –* Ⓜ *Atocha –* ☎ *914 44 90 34* Plan: **G3**
– www.yugothebunker.com – Closed August, Sunday and Monday
Menu 70/100 € *– (tasting menu only)*
• Japanese • Exotic décor •
A highly unusual Japanese restaurant decorated with typical objects from the
homeland alongside recycled materials. Another room in the basement, available for the exclusive use of club members, is known as "The Bunker".

X **La Tasquita de Enfrente** 🆎

Ballesta 6 ✉ *28004 –* Ⓜ *Gran Vía –* ☎ *915 32 54 49* Plan: **F1**
– www.latasquitadeenfrente.com – Closed August and Sunday
Menu 50/65 € *–* Carte 50/70 € *– (booking essential)*
• Traditional cuisine • Family •
Intimate and friendly with a loyal clientele. The chef, who announces the menu
at your table, creates traditional, seasonal cuisine with the occasional contemporary French touch.

X **Entre Suspiro y Suspiro** 🆎

Caños del Peral 3 ✉ *28013 –* Ⓜ *Ópera* Plan: **F2**
– ☎ *915 42 06 44 – www.entresuspiroysuspiro.com – Closed Sunday*
Carte 28/47 €
• Mexican • Friendly •
A good option for those looking to try Mexican cuisine. Behind the discreet
façade you will discover a bright, colourful restaurant. It has a bar at the entrance,
dining rooms spread across two floors and an impressive collection of tequilas!

X **Al Trapo** – Hotel Las Letras Gran Vía ⅗ 🆎

Caballero de Gracia 11 ✉ *28013 –* Ⓜ *Gran Vía* Plan: **G2**
– ☎ *915 24 23 05 – www.altraporestaurante.com – Closed August-*
9 September, Sunday and Monday
Menu 22 € *–* Carte 23/40 €
• Modern cuisine • Trendy •
A bright, modern restaurant with a restrained contemporary decor that includes
bare white tables. The expert knowledge and tutelage of renowned chef Paco
Morales is behind the informal, contemporary cuisine featuring on the enticing
and imaginatively descriptive menu.

X **Krachai** 🆎

Fernando VI-11 ✉ *28004 –* Ⓜ *Alonso Martínez* Plan: **G1**
– ☎ *918 33 65 56 – www.krachai.es – Closed 20 days August and Sunday*
dinner
Menu 14/35 € *–* Carte 25/52 €
• Thai • Oriental décor •
The Krachai is split between two dining rooms, each with attractive lighting and
a contemporary feel. The Thai cuisine on offer is listed on the menu according
to the way it is prepared.

X **La Gastroteca de Santiago** � 🆎

pl. Santiago 1 ✉ *28013 –* Ⓜ *Ópera –* ☎ *915 48 07 07* Plan: **E2**
– www.lagastrotecadesantiago.es – Closed 15-31 August, Sunday dinner
and Monday
Carte 41/65 €
• Modern cuisine • Cosy •
A small, cosy restaurant with two large windows and a modern decor. Friendly
staff, contemporary cuisine and a kitchen that is partially visible to diners.

X **Umiko** 🆎

Los Madrazo 18 ✉ *28014 –* Ⓜ *Sevilla –* ☎ *914 93 87 06* Plan: **G2**
– www.umiko.es – Closed Sunday
Menu 45/120 € *–* Carte 34/47 €
• Japanese • Minimalist •
A fun and different Asian restaurant whose aim is to combine traditional Japanese cuisine with the more traditional cooking of Madrid. The finishing touches
to most of the dishes are added at the bar.

X **Askuabarra** 　　　　　　　　　　　　　　　　　　　AC

Arlabán 7 ⊠ 28014 – Ⓜ Sevilla – ℰ 915 93 75 07 　　Plan: **G2**
– www.askuabarra.com – Closed 2 weeks August, Sunday dinner and Monday
Carte 15/81 €
• Market cuisine • Rustic •
Run by two brothers who have grown up in this profession, hence the value they attach to the use of top-quality products. A modern take on seasonal cuisine, including the house speciality – steak tartare.

X **Zerain** 　　　　　　　　　　　　　　　　　　　AC ⇔

Quevedo 3 ⊠ 28014 – Ⓜ Antón Martín 　　　　　Plan: **G3**
– ℰ 914 29 79 09 – www.restaurante-vasco-zerain-sidreria.es – Closed August and Sunday dinner
Menu 32/36 € – Carte 35/55 €
• Basque • Rustic •
This Basque cider bar is in the heart of Madrid's literary quarter. It has two floors with a welcoming atmosphere and large barrels on display. A typical steakhouse with a focus on grilled meats.

X **Arce** 　　　　　　　　　　　　　　　　　　　　AC ⇔

Augusto Figueroa 32 ⊠ 28004 – Ⓜ Chueca 　　　Plan: **G1**
– ℰ 915 22 04 40 – www.restaurantearce.com – Closed 17-25 April, 15 days August, Monday and Tuesday
Menu 30/70 € – Carte 45/65 €
• Classic cuisine • Classic décor •
A family-run business that prides itself on doing things well, hence the classic cuisine with a focus on quality ingredients and lots of flavour. Extensive à la carte, set menus and the option of half-*raciones*.

X **La T Gastrobar** 　　　　　　　　　　　　　　　AC

Molino del Viento 4 ⊠ 28004 – Ⓜ Noviciado 　　　Plan: **F1**
– ℰ 915 31 14 06 – www.latgastrobar.com – Closed 10-20 August
Menu 25 € – Carte 31/46 €
• Modern cuisine • Trendy •
Welcoming, versatile and informal, with two very different ambiences, both with a meticulous decor and one with views of the kitchen. Top-quality ingredients and dishes that show plenty of refinement.

X **Chuka Ramen Bar** 　　　　　　　　　　　　　　AC

Echegaray 9 ⊠ 28014 – Ⓜ Sevilla – ℰ 640 65 13 46 　Plan: **G2**
– www.chukaramenbar.com – Closed August, Sunday and Monday
Menu 20 € – Carte 25/35 € – *(dinner only except Friday and Saturday)*
• Japanese • Oriental décor •
A bar where the menu features a fusion of Chinese and Japanese cooking. It includes legendary dishes such as the noodle-based Ramen and other more popular street food-style recipes.

X **Triciclo** 　　　　　　　　　　　　　　　　　　AC
☺
Santa María 28 ⊠ 28014 – Ⓜ Antón Martín 　　　Plan: **G3**
– ℰ 910 24 47 98 – www.eltriciclo.es – Closed 15 days February, 15 days July and Sunday
Carte approx. 35 €
• Creative • Bistro •
A restaurant that is on everyone's lips! Triciclo's simplicity is compensated for by a high degree of culinary expertise. This is showcased in well-prepared and attractively presented dishes that encompass personal and traditional, as well as Oriental and fusion influences.

X
(😋)

Tepic

🛖 🅰🅲

Ayala 14 ⊠ 28001 – Ⓜ Goya – ℰ 915 22 08 50   Plan: **H1**
– www.tepic.es
Carte 26/40 €
• Mexican • Rustic •

A Mexican restaurant with its very own character, featuring a rustic yet contemporary space defined by a profusion of wood and a predominance of varying tones of white. High quality cuisine from the homeland alongside an interesting menu of beers, tequila and mezcal.

X

Dokidoki

🅳 🅰🅲 ⇔

Villalar 4 ⊠ 28001 – Ⓜ Retiro – ℰ 917 79 36 49   Plan: **H2**
– www.restaurantedokidoki.es – Closed Holy Week, 15 days August,
Sunday dinner and Monday
Menu 15 € – Carte 40/54 €
• Japanese • Minimalist •

Simplicity and design are the hallmarks of this restaurant where the chef, a passionate fan of Japanese cuisine, offers a menu with two options. One features traditional Japanese dishes and the other is adapted to more European tastes.

💡/

Estado Puro

🛖 🅰🅲

pl. Cánovas del Castillo 4 ⊠ 28014   Plan: **G2**
– Ⓜ Banco de España – ℰ 917 79 30 36
– www.tapasenestadopuro.com
Tapa 4 € **Ración** approx. 13 €
• Modern cuisine • Design •

This gastro-bar with a modern design is in a high-end location between the city's museums and art galleries. The menu covers tapas, *tostas* and *raciones*, all adapted from dishes of the highest quality.

💡/

Bocaito

🅰🅲 ⇔

Libertad 6 ⊠ 28004 – Ⓜ Chueca   Plan: **G2**
– ℰ 915 32 12 19 – www.bocaito.com
– Closed August and Sunday dinner
Tapa 4 € **Ración** approx. 10 €
• Traditional cuisine • Regional décor •

This restaurant is split between two premises which are connected to each other. There are four dining rooms in total, each furnished in rustic Castilian style with a few bullfighting mementoes. Traditional cuisine.

💡/

Prada a Tope

🅰🅲

Príncipe 11 ⊠ 28012 – Ⓜ Sevilla   Plan: **G2**
– ℰ 914 29 59 21 – www.pradaatope.es
– Closed 31 July-14 August
Tapa 5 € **Ración** approx. 12 €
• Traditional cuisine • Rustic •

This restaurant follows the typical decor found throughout this chain. A bar, rustic-style tables and a plethora of wood in the dining room, which is adorned with old photos and typical products from the El Bierzo region.

💡/

Celso y Manolo

🅰🅲

Libertad 1 ⊠ 28004 – Ⓜ Gran Vía – ℰ 915 31 80 79   Plan: **G2**
– www.celsoymanolo.es
Ración approx. 10 €
• Traditional cuisine • Neighbourhood •

A young and informal eatery occupying the site of an old tavern. Extensive ración based menu with an emphasis on natural and organic ingredients.

SPAIN - MADRID

Ritz   ☆ 🖫 ᴋ 🄰🄲 😼

pl. de la Lealtad 5 ✉ *28014*   Plan: I2
– ⓜ Banco de España – ✆ 917 01 67 67
– www.mandarinoriental.com
137 rm – ♛♛275/620 € – ⯊ 35 € – 30 suites
· Grand Luxury · Elegant ·
This internationally prestigious hotel occupies a palatial property from the early 20C. It features beautiful public spaces and sumptuously decorated guestrooms. In the Goya restaurant, endowed with its own inimitable personality, enjoy well-prepared dishes based around a concept that is classical in style.

Villa Magna   ☆ 🖫 ᴋ 🄰🄲 😼 🚗

paseo de la Castellana 22 ✉ *28046 – ⓜ Rubén Darío*   Plan: I1
– ✆ 915 87 12 34 – www.hotelvillamagna.es
120 rm – ♛400/650 € ♛♛650/710 € – ⯊ 42 € – 30 suites
· Luxury · Classic ·
This magnificent hotel boasts a classically elegant lounge area and various categories of guestroom, with the suites on the top floor enjoying the added bonus of a terrace. The enticing food choices include lighter lunch options, one gastronomic restaurant, and another dedicated to a mix of Cantonese and Oriental cuisine.
Tsé Yang – See restaurant listing

Wellington   🖫 ⯊ ᴋ 🄰🄲 😼 🚗

Velázquez 8 ✉ *28001 – ⓜ Retiro – ✆ 915 75 44 00*   Plan: I2
– www.hotel-wellington.com
250 rm – ♛♛176/360 € – ⯊ 30 € – 26 suites
· Luxury · Classic ·
Luxury and tradition go hand-in-hand in this truly emblematic hotel – one that is used by many bullfighters during the city's San Isidro festival. Classically elegant public spaces, a busy English-style bar, plus fully equipped bedrooms.
❀ **Kabuki Wellington** · **Goizeko Wellington** – See restaurant listing

Adler   🄰🄲 🚗

Velázquez 33 ✉ *28001 – ⓜ Velázquez – ✆ 914 26 32 20*   Plan: I2
– www.hoteladler.es
44 rm – ♛♛200/495 € – ⯊ 27 € – 2 suites
· Luxury · Elegant ·
An exclusive and select property with an elegant interior created from materials of the utmost quality. The comfortable guestrooms, all equipped to the very highest level, are worthy of special mention. Small English-style bar, plus a restaurant with its very own character.
niMú – See restaurant listing

Único Madrid   🖫 ᴋ 🄰🄲 😼 🚗

Claudio Coello 67 ✉ *28001 – ⓜ Serrano*   Plan: I1
– ✆ 917 81 01 73 – www.unicohotelmadrid.com
– Closed 7-27 August
43 rm – ♛210 € ♛♛390 € – ⯊ 28 € – 1 suite
· Luxury · Contemporary ·
Behind the attractive classical façade, guests will discover a designer-inspired entrance hall, an elegant public area with several small lounges, and comfortable guestrooms, all featuring a combination of classic and avant-garde decor. A chauffeur-driven service is also available to help you explore the city.
❀❀ **Ramón Freixa Madrid** – See restaurant listing

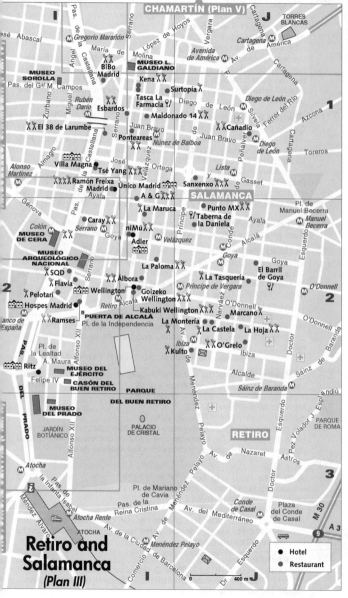

Retiro and Salamanca (Plan III)

CHAMARTÍN (Plan V)

TORRES BLANCAS

SALAMANCA

RETIRO

PARQUE DEL BUEN RETIRO

• Hotel
• Restaurant

0   400 m

Hospes Madrid

pl. de la Independencia 3 ✉ *28001* – 🅜 *Retiro*
– ☎ *914 32 29 11* – *www.hospes.com*
42 rm – 👥 *175/650 €* – 🖙 *28 €* – 5 suites
• Luxury • Contemporary •

The Hospes Madrid occupies a building dating back to 1883. Facilities here include a reception desk located in what was once the carriage entrance, two meeting rooms, and modern guestrooms, many overlooking Alcalá Gate. In the informal restaurant, guests can choose between tapas, raciones and the daily set menu.

Plan: **I2**

Ramón Freixa Madrid – Hotel Único Madrid

Claudio Coello 67 ✉ *28001* – 🅜 *Serrano*
– ☎ *917 81 82 62* – *www.ramonfreixamadrid.com* – *Closed Christmas, Holy Week, August, Sunday, Monday and Bank Holidays*
Menu 95/165 € – Carte 103/130 €
• Creative • Design •

Fronted by a pleasant terrace, this restaurant has a thoroughly modern look and a limited number of tables. In the kitchen, the focus is on impressively consistent cuisine, which is superbly presented and prepared using high quality ingredients.
→ Guisantes lágrima con gamba de Palamós. Cochinillo asado, majado de algas, aceitunas y habitas. Tapón de taninos, frutos salteados y especiados.

Plan: **I1**

Kabuki Wellington (Ricardo Sanz) – Hotel Wellington

Velázquez 6 ✉ *28001* – 🅜 *Retiro* – ☎ *915 77 78 77*
– *www.restaurantekabuki.com* – *Closed Holy Week, 1-21 August, Saturday lunch, Sunday and Bank Holidays*
Menu 93/200 € – Carte 80/128 €
• Japanese • Design •

The group's flagship restaurant boasts a large, contemporary-style dining room on two floors, featuring designer detail and a sushi bar. Japanese cuisine skilfully prepared with top-quality ingredients, accompanied by an exclusive sake menu.
→ Sashimi Wellington. Costillas de wagyu. Texturas de chocolate.

Plan: **I2**

Goizeko Wellington – Hotel Wellington

Villanueva 34 ✉ *28001* – 🅜 *Retiro* – ☎ *915 77 01 38*
– *www.goizekogaztelupe.com* – *Closed Sunday*
Menu 65/69 € – Carte 55/75 €
• Modern cuisine • Classic décor •

The contemporary-classic dining room and the two private rooms have been exquisitely designed. The cuisine on offer is a fusion of traditional, international and creative cooking, and is enriched with a few Japanese dishes.

Plan: **I2**

A y G

Ayala 27 ✉ *28001* – 🅜 *Goya* – ☎ *917 02 62 62*
– *www.aygmadrid.com* – *Closed Sunday*
Menu 45/69 € – Carte 46/65 €
• Peruvian • Minimalist •

A restaurant with an urban feel, offering Peruvian cuisine with Japanese touches, in addition to several signature dishes such as "ají de gallina", "ceviche del amor" and "beso de moza".

Plan: **I1-2**

Sanxenxo

José Ortega y Gasset 40 ✉ *28006* – 🅜 *Núñez de Balboa*
– ☎ *915 77 82 72* – *www.sanxenxo.com.es* – *Closed Holy Week, 15 days August and Sunday dinner*
Carte 45/65 €
• Seafood • Classic décor •

This restaurant serves traditional Galician cuisine based on quality fish and seafood. Covering two floors, the superb dining rooms are decorated with a profusion of granite and wood.

Plan: **J1**

SPAIN - MADRID

XXX **Tsé Yang** – Hotel Villa Magna
paseo de la Castellana 22 ✉ *28046 –* Ⓜ *Rubén Darío*   Plan: I1
– ☎ *914 31 18 18 – www.cafesaigon.es*
Menu 36/63 € – Carte 45/65 €
• Chinese • Oriental décor •
Enjoy the flavours of authentic Cantonese cuisine at this elegantly appointed
Chinese restaurant. It re-creates traditional dishes dating back centuries.

XX **La Paloma**
Jorge Juan 39 ✉ *28001 –* Ⓜ *Príncipe de Vergara*   Plan: I2
– ☎ *915 76 86 92 – www.lapalomarestaurante.es – Closed Holy Week,*
August, Sunday and Bank Holidays
Menu 45 € – Carte 47/79 €
• Classic cuisine • Classic décor •
A professionally run restaurant in an intimate setting. The extensive menu
brings together classic and traditional dishes alongside a selection of daily sug-
gestions and set menus. Signature dishes here include sea urchin, carpaccio of
liver and stuffed pigeon.

XX **Ramsés**
pl. de La Independencia 4 ✉ *28001 –* Ⓜ *Retiro*   Plan: I2
– ☎ *91 435 16 66 – www.ramseslife.com – Closed Monday dinner*
Carte 45/55 €
• Traditional cuisine • Design •
Thanks to its different sections, this design inspired restaurant, decorated by the
famous interior designer Philippe Starck, can turn its hand to numerous events,
from dining to cocktails. High-level cuisine both in terms of concept and technical skill.

XX **El 38 de Larumbe**
paseo de la Castellana 38 ✉ *28006 –* Ⓜ *Rubén Darío*   Plan: I1
– ☎ *915 75 11 12 – www.larumbe.com – Closed 15 days August, Sunday*
dinner and Bank Holidays dinner
Menu 57 € – Carte 45/56 €
• Modern cuisine • Classic décor •
This restaurant has two highly distinct dining areas – one has a gastro-bar feel,
and the other has a more refined setting for à la carte dining. Updated traditional cuisine with the option of ordering half-raciones.

XX **Caray**
Hermosilla 2 ✉ *28001 –* Ⓜ *Colón –* ☎ *914 85 78 01*   Plan: I2
– www.caraymadrid.com
Menu 25 € – Carte 45/56 €
• Traditional cuisine • Elegant •
Attractive, elegant and eclectic, Caray's interior design is a true labour of love.
Updated traditional cuisine accompanied by fine wines from Spain and around
the world.

XX **O grelo**
Menorca 39 ✉ *28009 –* Ⓜ *Ibiza*   Plan: J2
– ☎ *914 09 72 04 – www.restauranteogrelo.com*
– Closed Sunday dinner
Carte 40/65 €
• Galician • Classic décor •
Experience the excellence of traditional Galician cuisine at this restaurant ser-
ving a huge variety of seafood. Having undergone gradual renovation, O grelo
has a more modern look, which includes a reasonably popular gastro-bar, a
main dining room and three private sections.

SPAIN - MADRID

XX · **Maldonado 14** · [AC]

Maldonado 14 ⊠ 28006 – Ⓜ Núñez de Balboa · Plan: I1
– 𝒞 914 35 50 45 – www.maldonado14.com – Closed Holy Week, 1-23 August, Sunday and Bank Holidays dinner
Carte 33/61 €
• Traditional cuisine • Classic décor •
A single dining room on two levels, both featuring a classic decor, quality furnishings and wood floors. The à la carte menu has a traditional feel and includes delicious homely desserts, such as the outstanding apple tart.

XX · **Punto MX** (Roberto Ruiz) · [AC]
ॐ

General Pardiñas 40 ⊠ 28001 – Ⓜ Goya · Plan: J2
– 𝒞 914 02 22 26 – www.puntomx.es
– Closed 23 December - 4 January, Holy Week, 15 days August, Sunday and Monday
Carte 35/60 € – *(booking essential)*
• Mexican • Minimalist •
A Mexican restaurant that steers clear of stereotypes. Both the decor and cuisine are thoroughly modern. Traditional recipes are bolstered by a contemporary technical approach while at the same time adapting to local tastes. Highly interesting combination of Mexican ingredients and others sourced from Spain.
→ Carabinero. Pargo zarandeado a la brasa. Crêpes de cajeta.

XX · **99 sushi bar** · [AC] ⟺

Hermosilla 4 ⊠ 28001 – Ⓜ Serrano – 𝒞 914 31 27 15 · Plan II : H1
– www.99sushibar.com – Closed 1-24 August, Saturday lunch, Sunday and Bank Holidays
Menu 80 € – Carte 40/107 €
• Japanese • Minimalist •
A good restaurant in which to discover the flavours and textures of Japanese cuisine. There is a small bar where sushi is prepared in front of diners, an attractive glass-fronted wine cellar, and a modern dining room featuring typical Japanese decor and furnishings.

XX · **Álbora** · [AC]
ॐ

Jorge Juan 33 ⊠ 28001 – Ⓜ Velázquez · Plan: I2
– 𝒞 917 81 61 97 – www.restaurantealbora.com – Closed 7-27 August and Sunday
Menu 54/74 € – Carte 49/74 €
• Modern cuisine • Design •
An attractive modern setting with two distinct sections: the gastro-bar on the ground floor and the gastronomic restaurant upstairs. Enjoy high level cuisine that makes full use of seasonal ingredients, with some dishes available in smaller half portions.
→ Yema de huevo avainillada con boletus edulis confitados. Rodaballo salvaje con espuma de bloody mary. Torrija al estilo Álbora.

XX · **Ponteareas** · & [AC]

Claudio Coello 96 ⊠ 28005 – Ⓜ Núñez de Balboa · Plan: I1
– 𝒞 915 75 58 73 – www.grupoportonovo.es – Closed 10-29 August, Sunday dinner and Bank Holidays dinner
Menu 60 € – Carte 39/57 €
• Galician • Contemporary décor •
This restaurant with a modern decor offers a tapas bar and an attractive dining room overlooking a garden. Traditional cuisine with Galician roots, as well as good quality fish dishes.

SPAIN - MADRID

Arriba
XX ⊛

AC

Goya 5 (Platea Madrid) ✉ 28001 – Ⓜ *Serrano*   Plan II : **H1**
– ☏ 912 19 23 05 – www.restaurantearriba.com
Carte approx. 35 €
• Traditional cuisine • Design •
An old cinema is the unique setting for this gourmet food hall that includes this restaurant. It occupies the movie hall's balcony with staggered dining sections overlooking the flurry of activity inside the complex. A fun take on traditional and seasonal cuisine.

Esbardos
XX

& AC

Maldonado 4 ✉ 28006 – Ⓜ *Núñez de Balboa*   Plan: **I1**
– ☏ 914 35 08 68 – www.restauranteesbardos.com – Closed Holy Week, August and Sunday dinner
Menu 44/60 € – Carte 35/55 €
• Asturian • Traditional décor •
Esbardos takes its name from an Asturian word meaning 'bear cub', which is appropriate given that the owners own another restaurant called El Oso (The Bear). Typical Asturian cuisine based around top quality products and traditional stews.

niMú – Hotel Adler
XX

AC ⇔ 🚗

Goya 31 ✉ 28001 – Ⓜ *Velázquez – ☏ 914 26 32 25*   Plan: **I2**
– www.nimubistro.com – Closed August
Carte 25/52 €
• Modern cuisine • Design •
This bistro-style restaurant has a striking decor full of charm and character created by interior designer Pascua Ortega. Contemporary menu that includes a choice of raciones.

Cañadío
XX

🍴 AC ⇔

Conde Peñalver 86 ✉ 28005 – Ⓜ *Diego de León*   Plan: **J1**
– ☏ 912 81 91 92 – www.restaurantecanadio.com – Closed August and Sunday dinner
Menu 10/55 € – Carte 31/53 €
• Traditional cuisine • Simple •
The name will ring a bell with those familiar with Santander, given the location of this, the original Cañadío restaurant, on one of the city's most famous squares. Café-bar for tapas, two contemporary dining rooms, and well-prepared traditional cuisine.

La Hoja
XX

AC ⇔

Doctor Castelo 48 ✉ 28009 – Ⓜ *O'Donnell*   Plan: **J2**
– ☏ 914 09 25 22 – www.lahoja.es – Closed August, Sunday dinner and Monday
Carte 45/60 €
• Asturian • Traditional décor •
A reference for Asturian cuisine in Madrid! Two dining rooms with elaborate decor, and another more multi-purpose one dedicated to hunting. The menu features typical bean stews (fabes and verdinas), game and even chicken from the restaurant's own farm... all delicious and in copious portions.

Kena
XX

AC

Diego de León 11 ✉ 28006 – Ⓜ *Núñez de Balboa*   Plan: **I1**
– ☏ 917 25 96 48 – www.kenadeluisarevalo.com – Closed 13-21 August and Sunday
Menu 42/75 € – Carte 50/80 €
• Peruvian • Contemporary décor •
This restaurant is subdivided into three sections and has a contemporary feel. You can follow the evolution of Japanese cooking thanks to its fusion of Japanese culinary techniques with the flavours of Peru.

SPAIN - MADRID

XX **BiBo Madrid**　　　　　　　　　　　　　　　　　　　& ⓀⒸ ⇔

paseo de la Castellana 52 ✉ 28046　　　　　　　　　Plan: I1
– Ⓜ Gregorio Marañón – 𝒸 918 05 25 56 – www.grupodanigarcia.com
Carte 45/60 €
• Modern cuisine • Bistro •

The magic of southern Spain is transported to this restaurant. The striking, light
design inspired by the entrance gateway to the Málaga Fair provides the backdrop for the more informal cuisine of award-winning chef Dani García.

X **Surtopía**　　　　　　　　　　　　　　　　　　　　　　　ⓀⒸ

Núñez de Balboa 106 ✉ 28006 – Ⓜ Núñez de Balboa　　Plan: I1
– 𝒸 915 63 03 64 – www.surtopia.es – Closed Holy Week, 7-27 August,
Sunday, Monday dinner and Tuesday dinner
Menu 35/60 € – Carte 33/44 €
• Andalusian • Fashionable •

A modern restaurant impressively run by its owner who keeps a close on eye on
everything. Traditional Andalucian cuisine with clear culinary influences from
the city of Cádiz.

X **La Maruca**　　　　　　　　　　　　　　　　　　　　🏠 ⓀⒸ ⇔
🙂
Velázquez 54 ✉ 28001 – Ⓜ Velázquez – 𝒸 917 81 49 69　Plan: I2
– www.restaurantelamaruca.com
Carte 24/41 €
• Traditional cuisine • Trendy •

A bright, casual and contemporary restaurant offering high standard, traditional
cuisine. There is a predominance of typical and very reasonably priced Cantab-
rian dishes.

X **La Montería**　　　　　　　　　　　　　　　　　　　　　　ⓀⒸ
🙂
Lope de Rueda 35 ✉ 28009 – Ⓜ Ibiza – 𝒸 915 74 18 12　Plan: J2
– www.lamonteria.es – Closed Sunday dinner
Menu 42 € – Carte 25/39 €
• Traditional cuisine • Simple •

This family-run business has a bar and intimate dining room, which are both
contemporary in feel. The chef creates updated traditional cuisine including
game dishes. Don't leave without trying the monterías (stuffed mussels)!

X **Marcano**　　　　　　　　　　　　　　　　　　　　　　ⓀⒸ ⇔

Doctor Castelo 31 ✉ 28009 – Ⓜ Ibiza – 𝒸 914 09 36 42　Plan: J2
– www.restaurantemarcano.com – Closed Holy Week, 7 days August and
Sunday except December
Carte 40/67 €
• International • Simple •

The cooking here focuses on well-defined flavours. This is demonstrated by the
range of traditional and international dishes, the latter with a European and
Asian twist.

X **Pelotari**　　　　　　　　　　　　　　　　　　　　　　ⓀⒸ ⇔

Recoletos 3 ✉ 28001 – Ⓜ Colón – 𝒸 915 78 24 97　　Plan: I2
– www.pelotari-asador.com – Closed Sunday
Carte 40/55 €
• Basque • Rustic •

This typical Basque eatery specialising in roasted meats is run by its owners,
with one in the kitchen and the other front of house. There are four regional
style dining rooms, two of which can be used as private rooms.

X **Kulto**　　　　　　　　　　　　　　　　　　　　　　　　ⓀⒸ

Ibiza 4 ✉ 28009 – Ⓜ Ibiza – 𝒸 911 73 30 53　　　　Plan: J2
– www.kulto.es – Closed Tuesday
Menu 60/75 € – Carte 40/60 €
• Modern cuisine • Friendly •

This restaurant is pleasant, modern and bright and just a stone's throw from the
Retiro park. Contemporary cuisine that showcases seasonal ingredients and a
fusion of international flavours and influences.

X **Flavia** ⌗ⒶⒸ
Gil de Santivañes 2 ✉ *28001 –* Ⓜ *Colón* Plan: I2
– ℰ *914 93 90 51 – www.flaviamadrid.com*
Menu 17 € – Carte 27/48 €
• Italian • Mediterranean décor •
A modern, urban trattoria laid out on several floors. Good traditional Italian cuisine, always prepared using original ingredients from the homeland.

X **SQD** � ⌗ⒶⒸ ⇔
Villanueva 2 ✉ *28001 –* Ⓜ *Banco de España* Plan: I2
– ℰ *914 35 30 77 – www.sqd.es – Closed 1-21 August, Sunday dinner and*
Monday dinner
Menu 20/50 € – Carte 50/75 €
• Meats and grills • Bistro •
A modern bistro located next to the Museo Arqueológico Nacional. The house speciality is the superb matured beef sourced from either Galicia or France.

X **La Castela** ⌗ⒶⒸ
㋡ *Doctor Castelo 22* ✉ *28009 –* Ⓜ *Ibiza –* ℰ *91 574 00 15* Plan: J2
– www.lacastela.com – closed August and Sunday dinner
Carte 33/45 €
• Traditional cuisine • Traditional décor •
A traditional Madrid style tavern with a tapas bar at the entrance. The menu in the traditional dining room is centred on international cuisine.

X **La Tasquería** ⒶⒸ
㋡ *Duque de Sesto 48* ✉ *28009 –* Ⓜ *Goya* Plan: J2
– ℰ *914 51 10 00 – www.latasqueria.com – Closed 10 days January, 21*
days August, Sunday dinner and Monday
Menu 32 € – Carte 20/36 €
• Spanish • Bistro •
A new-generation tavern (*tasca*) that combines an urban, industrial look with modern, meticulously prepared dishes. There is a particular emphasis on high-quality offal dishes (veal, lamb, pork) served as half-raciones.

Ⓨ/ **Tasca La Farmacia** ⌂ⒶⒸ
Diego de León 9 ✉ *28006 –* Ⓜ *Núñez de Balboa* Plan: I1
– ℰ *915 64 86 52 – www.asadordearanda.com – Closed 15-28 August and*
Sunday
Tapa 4.50 € **Ración** approx. 8 €
• Traditional cuisine • Cosy •
Traditional style tasca, with a beautifully tiled bar adorned with elegant motifs. House specialities include cod and 'zancarrón' (meat on the bone) tapas and snacks.

Ⓨ/ **El Barril de Goya** ⌂ⒶⒸ
Goya 86 ✉ *28009 –* Ⓜ *Goya –* ℰ *915 78 39 98* Plan: J2
– www.elbarrildegoya.com – Closed Sunday dinner
Tapa 6 € **Ración** approx. 14 €
• Seafood • Tapas bar •
A highly renowned seafood restaurant thanks to the extraordinary quality of its ingredients. Away from the sea, its marvellous sliced Iberian ham is equally delicious.

Ⓨ/ **Taberna de la Daniela** ⒶⒸ
General Pardiñas 21 ✉ *28001 –* Ⓜ *Goya* Plan: J2
– ℰ *915 75 23 29 – www.tabernadeladaniela.com*
Tapa 6 € **Ración** approx. 14 €
• Traditional cuisine • Tavern •
A typical taberna in the Salamanca district, with a tiled façade and various dining rooms in which to enjoy a range of tapas. The restaurant is particularly famous for its cocido madrileño (a meat, potato and chickpea stew) that is traditionally eaten in three stages.

XX   **El Barril de Argüelles**   AC

Andrés Mellado 69 ⊠ 28015 – ⓜ *Islas Filipinas*   Plan: **K2**
– ℰ 915 44 36 15 – www.restauranteelbarrildearguelles.com
Carte 35/60 €
• Seafood • Mediterranean décor •

A bar with enticing seafood counters precedes the classic yet contemporary
dining room decorated with a maritime theme. The specialities here are shellfish and octopus, although savoury rice dishes and delicious homemade stews
also feature on the menu.

ℙ/   **El Barril de Argüelles**   AC

Andrés Mellado 69 ⊠ 28015 – ⓜ *Islas Filipinas*   Plan: **K2**
– ℰ 915 44 36 15 – www.grupo-oter.com
Tapa 10 € **Ración** approx. 20 €
• Seafood • Classic décor •

This impressive seafood restaurant has an elegant layout and an extremely
popular bar. Superb fish and shellfish, including octopus and delicious Andalu-
cian-style fresh fish, is served.

🏨   **InterContinental Madrid**   ⇪ ℔ & AC ≴ 🚗

paseo de la Castellana 49 ⊠ 28046   Plan: **L3**
– ⓜ *Gregorio Marañón – ℰ 917 00 73 00*
– www.madrid.intercontinental.com
302 rm – ♥♥180/280 € – ⌿ 32 €
• Grand Luxury • Classic •

A luxury hotel with a classically elegant entrance hall crowned by a cupola and
embellished with a profusion of marble, a pleasant inner patio-terrace, and
guestrooms that stand out for their high levels of comfort. In the restaurant
adjoining the entrance hall-bar, the focus is on an attractive international
menu, with an impressive brunch on Sundays.

🏨   **Hesperia Madrid**   ⇪ ℔ & AC ≴ 🚗

paseo de la Castellana 57 ⊠ 28046   Plan: **L2**
– ⓜ *Gregorio Marañón – ℰ 912 10 88 00*
– www.hesperia-madrid.com
171 rm ⌿ – ♥♥169/259 €
• Luxury • Elegant •

This chain hotel enjoys a superb location on the city's main avenue in a central
business and shopping district. It offers a large choice of elegantly classical
guestrooms and lounges. There is also a variety of dining options including
one restaurant focusing on the flavours of the Mediterranean, and another on
Japanese cooking.
    ❀❀ **Santceloni** – See restaurant listing

🏨   **Orfila**   ⇪ AC ≴ 🚗

Orfila 6 ⊠ 28010 – ⓜ *Alonso Martínez*   Plan II : **H1**
– ℰ 917 02 77 70 – www.hotelorfila.com – Closed August
29 rm – ♥225/325 € ♥♥255/355 € – ⌿ 30 € – 3 suites
• Luxury • Elegant •

This delightfully charming small palace built in the 19C occupies a quiet street
in a central location. It has elegant guestrooms embellished with period furniture. The restaurant has a classic air and serves traditional cuisine as impressive
as its welcoming terrace.

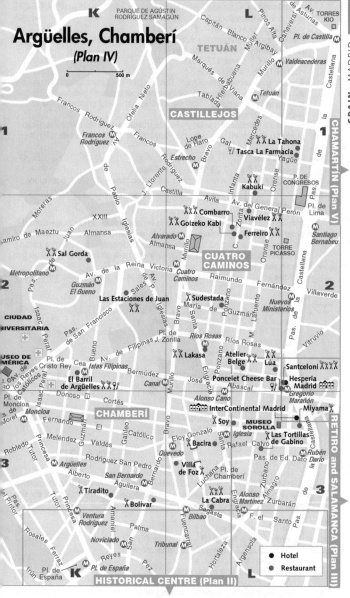

Argüelles, Chamberí
(Plan IV)

0   500 m

PARQUE DE AGUSTÍN
RODRÍGUEZ SAMAGÚN

K   L

TETUÁN

CASTILLEJOS

Francos
Rodríguez

La Tahona
Tasca La Farmacia

Kabuki

P. DE
CONGRESOS
Pl. de
Lima

Combarro
Goizeko Kabi
Viavélez
Ferreiro

Santiago
Bernabeu

CUATRO
CAMINOS

TORRE
PICASSO

Sal Gorda

Metropolitano

Guzmán
El Bueno

Cuatro
Caminos

Las Estaciones de Juan

Sudestada

Nuevos
Ministerios

Villaverde

CIUDAD
UNIVERSITARIA

Ríos Rosas

MUSEO DE
AMÉRICA

Lakasa
Atelier
Belge
Lúa
Santceloni

El Barril
de Argüelles

Poncelet Cheese Bar
Hesperia
Madrid

Pl. de
Moncloa

InterContinental Madrid

Gregorio
Marañón
Miyama

CHAMBERÍ

Soy
MUSEO
SOROLLA
Iglesia
Bacira
Las Tortillas
de Gabino

Argüelles

Villa
de Foz

Rubén
Darío

Tiradito

Bolívar

La Cabra

Ventura
Rodríguez

Bilbao

Alonso
Martínez

Noviciado

Tribunal

Pl. de
España

● Hotel
● Restaurant

K   Pl. de España   L
HISTORICAL CENTRE (Plan II)

SPAIN - MADRID

CHAMARTÍN (Plan V)

RETIRO and SALAMANCA (Plan III)

XXXX **Santceloni** – Hotel Hesperia Madrid   🕸 🗚 ⇔ 🚗

❀❀ *paseo de la Castellana 57* ✉ *28046*   Plan: **L2**
– 🚇 *Gregorio Marañón* – ☏ *912 10 88 40*
– *www.restaurantesantceloni.com* – *Closed Holy Week, August, Saturday lunch, Sunday and Bank Holidays*
Menu 162 € – Carte 117/150 €
• Creative • Elegant •

A great gastronomic experience. This elegant restaurant boasts a superbly arranged classic-contemporary dining room split between two floors. The culinary focus is on updated traditional cuisine that is well presented and comes with a creative touch.

→ Caballa flambeada, caviar y jalea de manzana. Lubina, tomate confitado, pimiento rojo, avellana y sésamo. Panacota de hinojo, aguacate y limón.

XXX **La Cabra**   🗚 ⇔

❀ *Francisco de Rojas 2* ✉ *28010* – 🚇 *Bilbao*   Plan: **L3**
– ☏ *914 45 77 50* – *www.restaurantelacabra.com* – *Closed 1-6 January, Holy Week, August and Sunday*
Menu 50/121 € – Carte 45/65 €
• Modern cuisine • Trendy •

A modern and informal restaurant with various spaces. These range from the tapería, a library-cum-lounge in which to relax after work, and a wine cellar that can also be booked privately. It offers traditional cuisine with a cutting edge, a high level of technical skill, strong emphasis on top quality, and on the whole, seasonal ingredients.

→ Ensalada de cefalópodos. Panceta ahumada y caviar. Yuzu, zanahoria y cilantro.

XXX **Benares**   🗚 ⇔

Zurbano 5 ✉ *28010* – 🚇 *Alonso Martínez*   Plan II : **H1**
– ☏ *913 19 87 16* – *www.benaresmadrid.com* – *Closed 7-21 August and Sunday dinner*
Menu 48/65 € – Carte 45/65 €
• Indian • Classic décor •

A pleasant, well-located restaurant in the same vein as the eponymous London eatery, with the addition of a cocktail bar. A modern take on Indian cuisine.

XX **Las Estaciones de Juan**   🍴 🗚 ⇔

paseo San Francisco de Sales 41 ✉ *28003*   Plan: **K2**
– 🚇 *Guzmán el Bueno* – ☏ *915 98 86 66*
– *www.lascuatroestacionesdejuan.com* – *Closed Sunday dinner*
Menu 30/52 € – Carte 36/57 €
• Traditional cuisine • Classic décor •

A solid performer preparing traditional cuisine with well-prepared ingredients in an impeccable setting combining the traditional and modern. One of the signature dishes is fillet of T-bone steak.

XX **Lúa** (Manuel Domínguez)   🗚 ⇔

❀ *Eduardo Dato 5* ✉ *28003* – 🚇 *Rubén Darío*   Plan: **L2**
– ☏ *913 95 28 53* – *www.restaurantelua.com*
– *Closed Sunday*
Menu 60 € – *(tasting menu only)*
• Modern cuisine • Cosy •

A restaurant that is constantly evolving, with an attractive tapas bar, informal ambience, and a rustic yet contemporary feel. The chef conjures up modern cooking with its roots in his native Galicia. The excellent tasting menu showcases his undoubted skill.

→ Foie mi-cuit sobre empanada de pera y queso San Simón caramelizado. Raya en caldeirada. Cremoso de queso con sopa de violetas.

SPAIN - **MADRID**

XX **Conlaya** 🅰🅲 ⇔
Zurbano 13 ✉ *28010 –* Ⓜ *Alonso Martínez* Plan II : **H1**
– ℰ 91 319 31 16 – www.conlaya.es – Closed August, Sunday and Monday dinner
Menu 35/65 € – Carte 34/52 €
• Classic cuisine • Classic décor •
A touch of Cantabria in the heart of Madrid! Impeccable interior with a traditional ambience, where the regional cuisine is centred around fresh fish straight from the market.

XX **Atelier Belge** 🅰🅲
Bretón de los Herreros 39 ✉ *28003 –* Ⓜ *Alonso Cano* Plan: **L2**
– ℰ 915 45 84 48 – www.atelierbelge.es – Closed 14-20 August, Sunday dinner and Monday
Menu 16/35 € – Carte 42/57 €
• Belgian • Classic décor •
An interesting dining option where you can discover authentic Belgian cuisine with the occasional nod to creativity. Dishes well worth trying include the snails, mussels and the impressive 'Coquelet Brabançonne'!

XX **Lakasa** 🈸 🅰🅲
pl. del Descubridor Diego de Ordás 1 ✉ *28014* Plan: **L2**
– Ⓜ *Rios Rosas – ℰ 915 33 87 15 – www.lakasa.es – Closed Holy Week, Sunday and Monday*
Carte 40/50 €
• Traditional cuisine • Trendy •
A change in location has resulted in a new larger and brighter restaurant with an improved layout. Enjoy tapas and *raciones* at the bar and the very best seasonal cuisine in the main dining room.

XX **Ars Vivendi** 🅰🅲 ⇔
☺ *Zurbano 6* ✉ *28010 –* Ⓜ *Alonso Martínez* Plan II : **H1**
– ℰ 913 10 31 71 – www.restaurantearsvivendi.es – Closed Sunday dinner and Monday
Menu 35/70 € – Carte 35/52 €
• Italian • Cosy •
The life and soul of this restaurant is provided by the couple that own it, with the husband working front-of-house and his wife in charge of the kitchen. Delicious, Italian inspired cuisine that is both creative and attractively presented. The homemade pasta is a feast for the senses!

X **Las Tortillas de Gabino** 🅰🅲
☺ *Rafael Calvo 20* ✉ *28010 –* Ⓜ *Rubén Darío* Plan: **L3**
– ℰ 91 319 75 05 – www.lastortillasdegabino.com – Closed Holy Week, 15 days August, Sunday and Bank Holidays
Carte 25/38 €
• Traditional cuisine • Cosy •
Almost always full every day, this restaurant boasts an entrance hall, two modern dining rooms decorated with wood panelling, and a private dining section. The traditionally inspired menu is complemented by a choice of tortillas which changes through the course of the year.

X **Bolívar** 🅰🅲
☺ *Manuela Malasaña 28* ✉ *28004 –* Ⓜ *San Bernardo* Plan: **K3**
– ℰ 914 45 12 74 – www.restaurantebolivar.com – Closed 1-25 August and Sunday
Menu 30/50 € – Carte 30/45 €
• Traditional cuisine • Family •
A small, family-run restaurant in the city's Malasaña district in which the single dining room is divided into two sections, both with a modern look. Moderately priced traditional cuisine and excellent service.

SPAIN - MADRID

Miyama
%
AC

paseo de la Castellana 45 ⊠ 28013   Plan: **L3**
– Ⓜ Gregorio Marañón – ℰ 913 91 00 26 – www.restaurantemiyama.com
– Closed August, Sunday and Bank Holidays
Carte 40/75 €
• Japanese • Contemporary décor •
A Japanese restaurant that is hugely popular in the city, including with Japanese visitors. An extensive sushi bar and simply laid tables share space in the single dining area. High quality, traditional Japanese cuisine.

Sudestada
%
&. AC

Ponzano 85 ⊠ 28003 – Ⓜ Rios Rosas – ℰ 915 33 41 54   Plan: **L2**
– www.sudestada.eu – Closed Sunday and Monday
Menu 50 € – Carte 40/60 €
• Asian • Trendy •
You can't talk about Sudestada without mentioning chef Estanis Carenzo, the main force behind fashionable ideas such as Street Food. Here Carenzo offers Asian cuisine with a strong Vietnamese focus.

Aire
%
&. AC

Orfila 7 ⊠ 28010 – Ⓜ Alonso Martínez   Plan II : **H1**
– ℰ 911 70 42 28 – www.airerestaurante.com – Closed 20 days August and Sunday dinner
Menu 23/50 € – Carte 24/56 €
• Traditional cuisine • Bistro •
This charming, bistro-style restaurant is the first stage of a unique project. Everything revolves around poultry here (chicken, pigeon, pheasant, goose, partridge etc).

Villa de Foz
%
AC

Gonzálo de Córdoba 10 ⊠ 28010 – Ⓜ Bilbao   Plan: **L3**
– ℰ 914 46 89 93 – www.villadefoz.es – closed August, Sunday dinner and Monday
Menu 18/46 € – Carte 20/44 €
• Galician • Classic décor •
The Villa de Foz has two pleasant dining rooms, both decorated in a style that reflects traditional and contemporary influences. Its à la carte menu of traditional Galician cuisine is enhanced by a fine choice of raciones and home-made desserts.

Soy
%
AC

Viriato 58 ⊠ 28010 – Ⓜ Iglesia – ℰ 914 45 74 47   Plan: **L3**
– www.soypedroespina.com – Closed 15 days August, Saturday lunch, Sunday and Monday dinner
Menu 65 € – Carte 45/60 € – *(booking essential)*
• Japanese • Oriental décor •
This restaurant is simple, intimate and contemporary in style – the perfect setting for the delicious, traditional Japanese cuisine served here. It is not so easy to find, as there is no sign on the building!

Tiradito
%
AC

Conde Duque 13 ⊠ 28015 – Ⓜ San Bernardo   Plan: **K3**
– ℰ 915 41 78 76 – www.tiradito.es – Closed 7 days August, Sunday dinner and Monday
Menu 30/65 € – Carte 31/49 €
• Peruvian • Trendy •
A young and easy-going restaurant serving 100% traditional Peruvian cuisine. Dishes on the menu include ceviches, tiraditos, picoteos and tapas criollas.

SPAIN - MADRID

Ɣ Bacira

Castillo 16 ⊠ 28005 – **Ⓜ** *Iglesia –* ℰ *918 66 40 30*   Plan: **L3**
– www.bacira.es – Closed 23 December-8 January, Sunday dinner and Monday
Menu 14/40 € – Carte 23/47 € – *(booking advisable)*
• International • Classic décor •

Occupying an attractive restaurant with the occasional vintage touch, Bacira is run by its three young co-owners. The emphasis is on fresh fusion cooking inspired by the Mediterranean, the Orient, Japan and Peru (Nikkei cuisine). It is designed for sharing and is served amid a relaxed, informal atmosphere.

Ɣ/ Poncelet Cheese Bar

José Abascal 61 ⊠ 28003 – **Ⓜ** *Gregorio Marañon*   Plan: **L2**
– ℰ 91 399 25 50 – www.ponceletcheesebar.es – Closed Sunday dinner and Monday
Tapa 5 € **Ración** approx. 13 €
• Cheese, fondue and raclette • Design •

An innovative designer space in which everything revolves around the world of cheese. Attractive display cabinets, a bar for tastings, as well as a library specialising in this fine product. Contemporary cuisine and wines by the glass.

XXX Combarro

Reina Mercedes 12 ⊠ 28020 – **Ⓜ** *Nuevos Ministerios*   Plan: **L2**
– ℰ 915 54 77 84 – www.combarro.com – Closed Holy Week, 15 days August and Sunday dinner
Carte 45/60 €
• Seafood • Classic décor •

Galician cuisine with an emphasis on fresh quality produce, including live fish tanks. Public bar, dining on the first floor and a number of rooms in the basement. Classic and elegant in style.

XX Viavélez

av. General Perón 10 ⊠ 28020 – **Ⓜ** *Santiago Bernabeu*   Plan: **L2**
– ℰ 915 79 95 39 – www.restauranteviavelez.com – Closed August, Sunday and Monday lunch in summer, Sunday dinner and Monday the rest of the year
Menu 33/65 € – Carte 38/66 €
• Creative • Trendy •

This tavern-restaurant features a tapas bar at the entrance and a modern and intimate dining room in the basement. Its creative cuisine is based on traditional Asturian recipes.

XX Goizeko Kabi

Comandante Zorita 37 ⊠ 28020 – **Ⓜ** *Alvarado*   Plan: **L2**
– ℰ 915 33 01 85 – www.goizekogaztelupe.es – Closed Sunday dinner
Menu 50/70 € – Carte 50/75 €
• Basque • Contemporary décor •

A fine example of Madrid's more traditional restaurant scene, albeit with a renovated and more contemporary look. Basque cuisine, tapas and dishes perfect for sharing.

XX Kabuki ☸

av. Presidente Carmona 2 ⊠ 28020   Plan: **L1-2**
– **Ⓜ** *Santiago Bernabeu – ℰ 914 17 64 15 – www.restaurantekabuki.com*
– Closed Holy Week, 10-31 August, Saturday lunch, Sunday and Bank Holidays
Menu 70/90 € – Carte 55/80 €
• Japanese • Minimalist •

An intimate Japanese restaurant with a minimalist feel. It has a modern terrace, as well as a kitchen-bar serving a range of dishes, including a wide choice of nigiri sushi. It is best to book ahead as it is often full.
→ Atún picante. Costillas de wagyu. Cremoso de yuzu.

SPAIN - MADRID

XX Ferreiro   🔟 ⇔

Comandante Zorita 32 ✉ 28020 – ⓜ Alvarado   Plan: **L2**
– ℰ 915 53 93 42 – www.restauranteferreiro.com
Menu 30/65 € – Carte 35/57 €
• Traditional cuisine • Classic décor •
Classic-contemporary dining rooms act as a backdrop for traditional cuisine with strong Asturian roots in this restaurant. Extensive menu that is supplemented by a good choice of specials.

XX La Tahona   🏠 🔟 ⇔

Capitán Haya 21 (beside) ✉ 28020 – ⓜ Cuzco   Plan: **L1**
– ℰ 915 55 04 41 – www.asadordearanda.com – Closed 1-26 August and Sunday dinner
Menu 35/50 € – Carte 26/47 €
• Meats and grills • Classic décor •
Part of the El Asador de Aranda chain. La Tahona's dining rooms have a medieval Castillian ambience with a wood fire at the entrance taking pride of place. The suckling lamb (lechazo) is the star dish here!

XX Sal Gorda   🔟

Beatriz de Bobadilla 9 ✉ 28040 – ⓜ Guzmán El Bueno   Plan: **K2**
– ℰ 915 53 95 06 – www.restaurantesalgorda.es – Closed Holy Week, August and Sunday
Menu 35/60 € – Carte 31/51 €
• Classic cuisine • Classic décor •
A compact restaurant with a single dining room decorated in a classic yet contemporary style. The loin of beef cooked in coarse-grained salt (sal gorda) is the house speciality, hence the restaurant name, but is just one of an extensive choice of dishes on the traditional menu.

୨/ Tasca La Farmacia   🔟

Capitán Haya 19 ✉ 28020 – ⓜ Cuzco – ℰ 915 55 81 46   Plan: **L1**
– www.asadordearanda.com – Closed 15-28 August and Sunday
Tapa 4.50 € **Ración** approx. 8 €
• Traditional cuisine • Cosy •
Delightful restaurant decorated with azulejo tiles, stone arches, exposed brickwork, wrought iron lattice windows and an impressive glass ceiling. La Farmacia is famous for its cod dishes.

CHAMARTÍN   PLAN V

🏨 Puerta América   🛗 🔟 ᵴ 🔟 🔟 🚗

av. de América 41 ✉ 28002 – ⓜ Cartagena   Plan: **N3**
– ℰ 917 44 54 00 – www.hotelpuertamerica.com
301 rm ☷ – ⚭120/170 € – 14 suites
• Business • Design •
This colourful and cosmopolitan hotel has a distinct design feel with each of its floors reflecting the creativity of a renowned architect or famous interior designer. Highly original guestrooms with an attractive fitness and well-being space on the top floor.
Lágrimas Negras – See restaurant listing

🏨 NH Eurobuilding   🌂 🛗 🌐 ᵴ 🔟 🔟 🚗

Padre Damián 23 ✉ 28036 – ⓜ Cuzco   Plan: **M2**
– ℰ 913 53 73 00 – www.nh-hotels.com
431 rm – ⚭135/195 € – ☷ 20 €
• Business • Contemporary •
This hotel has a spectacular lobby featuring a hi-tech LED inspired barrel-vaulted ceiling that doubles as the biggest multimedia screen in Europe! Overall, the facilities are spacious with well-equipped contemporary-style guestrooms, a plethora of meeting rooms and myriad lounge areas. The interesting culinary options add an extra dimension.
❀❀❀ **DiverXO** • **99 sushi bar** – See restaurant listing

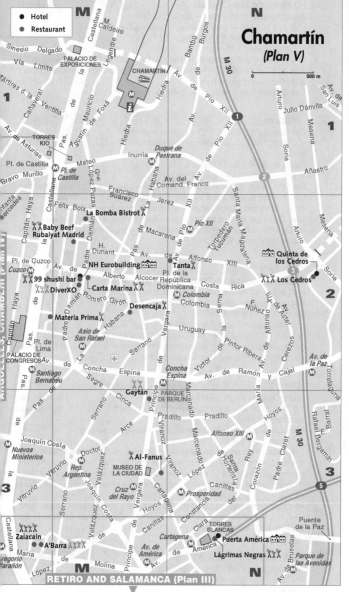

Chamartín
(Plan V)

0   500 m

● Hotel
● Restaurant

M. Caldeiro
Castellana
Legendre
PALACIO DE
EXPOSICIONES
Sinesio   Delgado
Vía   Límite
Mártires d. l. Vía
Cañavera   Ventilla
Av. de Asturias
TORRES
KIO
Pl. de Castilla
Bravo Murillo
Pl. de
Castilla
Mateo
Gral. López Pozas
Castellana
Infanta Mercedes
Félix Boix
Capitán Haya
La Bomba Bistrot ✕
✕✕**Baby Beef**
Rubaiyat Madrid
Pl. de Cuzco
Cuzco Ⓜ
✕✕**99 shushi bar**
✕✕**DiverXO**
Av. de
Haya
Capitán
Pl. de
Lima
PALACIO DE
CONGRESOS
Av.
Pas.
● **Santiago
Bernabéu**
Pas.
de
Serrano
Ⓜ **Nuevos
Ministerios**
Joaquín Costa
Doctor
**Rep.
Argentina**
Serrano
Velázquez
Vitruvio
Vitruvio
Ⓜ
Serrano
Joaquín Costa
✕✕✕✕
Zalacaín
● **A'Barra** ✕✕✕✕
María
Castellana
Gregorio Marañón
Ⓜ
López
Damián
Padre
H.
Dunant
Pas.
de
Macarena
Pío XII
Av.
de
Alberto
Alcocer
NH Eurobuilding 🏨
Romero Girón
Damián
Padre
● **Materia Prima** ✕
**Asio de
San Rafael**
Ⓜ
La
Concha
Serrano
Espina
Santiago
Segre
Cinca
✕✕
Gaytán
Príncipe
Arce
Molina
Príncipe
de Vergara
Velázquez
Joaquín Costa
Canillas
Cruz
del Rayo
Ⓜ
Vergara
Hoyos
de
Canillas
Av. de
América
Bambú
Burgos
Av.
de
Pío XII
CHAMARTÍN
🚉
Hiedra
Av.
de
Pío XII
Ⓜ
Duque de
Pastrana
Inurria
Av. del
Comand. Franco
Habana
Francisco
Suárez
Jerez
XII
Pío XII
Macarena
Av.
de
Alfonso
XIII
República
Dominicana
Ⓜ
Costa
Rica
Ⓜ **Colombia**
Colombia
Serna
F.
Núñez
Uruguay
Vergara
Pintor Ribera
Víctor
de
Ramón
y
Cajal
Concha
Espina
Ⓜ
Tanta ✕
Carta Marina ✕✕
● **Desencaja** ✕
Habana
de
Av.
de
Pío XII
Torpedero
Tucumán
Santa María Magdalena
Costa
Rica
✕✕✕ **Los Cedros**
🏨 **Quinta de
los Cedros**
Av. de Aster
Cerezos
Av.
de
Alfonso
XIII
Arturo
Soria
Mesena
Añastro
M 30
Arturo Julio Dánvila
Mesena
Soria
San Luis
Av. de
Arturo
Soria
Mesena
PARQUE
DE BERLÍN
Pradillo
Viranoz
Pradillo
Alfonso XIII
Hoyos
Rey
de
María
Torrelaguna
Av. de
la Paz
Ⓜ
M 30
Barrio
Rafael Bergamín
L.
✕ **Al-Fanus**
MUSEO DE
LA CIUDAD
Viranoz
López
Cartagena
Canillas
Ⓜ **Prosperidad**
Constancia
Santa
Hortensia
Corazón
Padre
Claret
de
Ⓜ
Puente
de la Paz
Cartagena
Clara
TORRES
BLANCAS
América
Ⓜ
Puerta América 🏨
Lágrimas Negras ✕✕✕
Av. de
Bruselas
N
Parque de
las Avenidas

RETIRO AND SALAMANCA (Plan III)

651

Quinta de los Cedros ⬛ ♨ 🚗

Allendesalazar 4 ✉ *28043 –* 🚇 *Arturo Soria*   Plan: **N2**
– ℰ 915 15 22 00 – www.hotelquintadeloscedros.com
32 rm – ♦83/185 € ♦♦90/220 € – ☝ 15 €
• Traditional • Elegant •
This attractive and surprising modern hotel is surrounded by gardens in the
style of a Tuscan villa. Comfortable guestrooms, including some with a terrace
and others in bungalow style.
Los Cedros – See restaurant listing

A'Barra ♿ ⬛ ♻
⚘
Del Pinar 15 ✉ *28014 –* 🚇 *Gregorio Marañón*   Plan: **M3**
– ℰ 910 21 00 61 – www.restauranteabarra.com – Closed 7-28 August and
Sunday
Menu 65/88 € – Carte 60/80 €
• Traditional cuisine • Design •
Both the decor, featuring a profusion of high-quality wood, and the spacious
layout come as a pleasant surprise. Choose between the calm setting of the
dining room and a large circular bar, which is more geared towards show coo-
king. Elaborate, modern cuisine with an emphasis on choice ingredients.
→ Canelón ibérico. Lengua glaseada con rostí de patata y edamame.
Locura de chocolate.

Zalacaín ♨ ⬛ ♻

Álvarez de Baena 4 ✉ *28006 –* 🚇 *Gregorio Marañón*   Plan: **M3**
– ℰ 915 61 48 40 – www.restaurantezalacain.com – closed Holy Week,
August, Saturday lunch, Sunday and Bank Holidays
Menu 90 € – Carte 75/100 €
• Classic cuisine • Elegant •
Zalacaín is an integral part of Madrid's recent culinary history. It boasts an ele-
gantly classical feel, highly professional service and an extensive à la carte featu-
ring classic Spanish and international cuisine.

DiverXO (David Muñoz) – Hotel NH Eurobuilding ⬛ 🚗
⚘⚘⚘
Padre Damián 23 ✉ *28036 –* 🚇 *Cuzco*   Plan: **M2**
– ℰ 915 70 07 66 – www.diverxo.com – Closed Holy Week, 21 days August,
Sunday and Monday
Menu 165/225 € – (booking essential) (tasting menu only)
• Creative • Design •
This restaurant is an exciting and groundbreaking culinary wonderland, and a
journey into the highly personal world of this chef. To a backdrop of stunning
modern design, enjoy world cuisine that will challenge your palate, intensi-
fying sensations and reaching its apogee in presentation worthy of the finest
canvas.
→ Cigala con bearnesa japonesa, boquerones y zanahorias al vapor. Sandwich crujiente de boquerón y sesamo negro. Chuletón de raya asado con
pimientas del mundo.

Los Cedros – Hotel Quinta de los Cedros 🍴 ⬛ 🚗

Allendesalazar 4 ✉ *28043 –* 🚇 *Arturo Soria*   Plan: **N2**
– ℰ 915 15 22 00 – www.hotelquintadeloscedros.com – Closed Holy Week
and August
Menu 43 € – Carte 36/55 €
• Traditional cuisine • Classic décor •
An excellent restaurant both in terms of its setting and its cuisine, with several
dining areas that include an attractive terrace. Updated classic cuisine with a
focus on top quality ingredients.

SPAIN - MADRID

XxX **Lágrimas Negras** – Hotel Puerta América
av. de América 41 ✉ *28002* – Ⓜ *Cartagena*   Plan: **N3**
– ☎ *917 44 54 05* – *www.hotelpuertamerica.com*
Menu 25/60 € – Carte 33/46 €
• Modern cuisine • Design •
Part of a designer hotel, this restaurant boasts a contemporary look, including
high ceilings and large windows, plus direct access to the terrace. Contemporary cuisine of a very high standard.

XX **Gaytán** (Javier Aranda)   ⚐ 🅰🅲
☼ *Príncipe de Vergara 205 (lateral)* ✉ *28002*   Plan: **M3**
– Ⓜ *Concha Espina* – ☎ *913 48 50 30* – *www.chefjavieraranda.com*
– Closed 5 days Christmas, Holy Week, August, Sunday and Monday
Menu 77/121 € – (tasting menu only)
• Modern cuisine • Minimalist •
This gastronomic restaurant has been designed to cause a stir. The minimalist
interior decor is unexpected, dominated by the presence of original columns
and a large open kitchen, which is the epicentre of activity here. Its different
tasting menus demonstrate an interesting creativity.
→ Ensalada de quisquilla y berberecho. Parpatana de atún rojo. Piña, anís y
melocotón.

XX **Carta Marina**   ⚐ 🅰🅲
Padre Damián 40 ✉ *28036* – Ⓜ *Cuzco*   Plan: **M2**
– ☎ *914 58 68 26* – *www.restaurantecartamarina.com* – Closed Holy
Week, August and Sunday
Menu 45 € – Carte 40/70 €
• Galician • Classic décor •
A true classic! It has attractive summer and winter terraces, a private bar, and
meticulously arranged dining rooms - all featuring a profusion of wood. The
menu remains faithful to traditional Galician ingredients, hence the predomi-
nance of seafood.

XX **99 sushi bar** – Hotel NH Eurobuilding   ⚐ 🅰🅲
Padre Damián 23 ✉ *28036* – Ⓜ *Cuzco*   Plan: **M2**
– ☎ *913 59 38 01* – *www.99sushibar.com* – Closed Sunday dinner
Menu 80 € – Carte 60/75 €
• Japanese • Design •
This restaurant is modern and full of decorative detail. The menu combines tra-
ditional Japanese dishes alongside other recipes blending elements of Spanish
cooking.

XX **Baby Beef Rubaiyat Madrid**   ⚐ ⚐ 🅰🅲
Juan Ramón Jiménez 37 ✉ *28036* – Ⓜ *Cuzco*   Plan: **M2**
– ☎ *91 359 10 00* – *www.rubaiyat.es* – Closed Sunday dinner
Carte 40/60 €
• Meats and grills • Brasserie •
The flavours of São Paulo in the Spanish capital. Meat served here includes Bran-
gus and tropical Kobe beef, although traditional Brazilian dishes also feature,
such as the famous feijoada on Saturdays.

X **Desencaja**   🅰🅲
☺ *paseo de la Habana 84* ✉ *28036* – Ⓜ *Colombia*   Plan: **M2**
– ☎ *914 57 56 68* – *www.dsncaja.com* – Closed Holy Week, August,
Sunday dinner and Monday dinner
Menu 15/50 € – Carte 33/41 €
• Traditional cuisine • Contemporary décor •
An interesting dining option in a resolutely contemporary space with an uncluttered minimalist feel. Trained in some of the country's best restaurants, the chef
here creates traditionally inspired seasonal dishes that are only available to
diners via set menus.

✗ **Tanta**

pl. del Perú 1 ⊠ 28016 – Ⓜ Pío XII – ℰ 913 50 26 26   Plan: **M-N2**
– www.tantamadrid.com
Menu 17/35 € – Carte 35/55 €
• Peruvian • Simple •

Enjoy typical Peruvian dishes such as ceviche, tiraditos, makis, causas and anticuchos in this simple restaurant. It takes its name from the Quechua word for
bread.

✗ **La Bomba Bistrot**

Pedro Mugaruza 5 ⊠ 28036 – Ⓜ Cuzco   Plan: **M2**
*– ℰ 913 50 30 47 – www.labombabistrot.com – Closed 1-24 August,
Sunday dinner and Monday dinner*
Carte 35/50 €
• Traditional cuisine • Bistro •

A welcoming restaurant that tries to recreate the essence of a typical French
bistro. It has an open-view kitchen, pleasing natural light and seasonal home-
style cuisine.

✗ **Materia Prima**

Doctor Fleming 7 ⊠ 28036 – Ⓜ Santiago Bernabeu   Plan: **M2**
– ℰ 913 44 01 77 – www.materia-prima.es
Carte 30/50 €
• Traditional cuisine • Classic décor •

A unique culinary concept where products are displayed as they would be in a
market, which customers then buy at market rates, before being prepared at a
fixed price. Materia Prima's range of fish options is particularly superb.

✗ **Al-Fanus**

Pechuán 6 ⊠ 28002 – Ⓜ Cruz del Rayo   Plan: **M3**
*– ℰ 915 62 77 18 – www.restaurantealfanus.es – Closed Sunday dinner
and Monday dinner*
Menu 21/33 € – Carte 31/46 €
• International • Exotic décor •

If you're unfamiliar with Syrian cuisine, Al-Fanus provides an opportunity to
enjoy the country's best recipes, which are full of subtlety and always loyal to
their Mediterranean roots. Both the decor and the ambience have an Arabian
feel.

PARQUE FERIAL   **PLAN I**

Globales Acis y Galatea

Galatea 6 ⊠ 28042 – Ⓜ Canillejas – ℰ 917 43 49 01   Plan: **D1**
– www.hotelesglobales.com
25 rm – †55/130 € ††66/260 € – ☲ 8 €
• Family • Elegant •

Located in a residential district of the city, this hotel boasts a certain charm, with
its classic yet contemporary guestrooms, with the three boasting a terrace the
pick of the bunch. A dinner option is available to guests staying here, who can
make their choice from a concise set menu.

BARCELONA
BARCELONA

Population: 1 604 555

B. Brillion/MICHELIN

It can't be overestimated how important Catalonia is to the locals of Barcelona: pride in their region of Spain runs deep in the blood. Barcelona loves to mix the traditional with the avant-garde, and this exuberant opening of arms has seen it grow into a pulsating city for visitors. Its rash of theatres, museums and concert halls is unmatched by most other European cities, and many artists and architects, including Picasso, Miró, Dalí, Gaudí and Subirachs, have chosen to live here.

The 19C was a golden period in the city's artistic development, with the growth of the great Catalan Modernism movement, but it was knocked back on its heels after the Spanish Civil War and the rise to power of the dictator Franco, who destroyed hopes for an independent Catalonia. After his death, democracy came to Spain and since then, Barcelona has relished its position as the capital of a restored autonomous region. Go up on the Montjuïc to get a great overview of the city below. Barcelona's atmospheric old town is near the harbour and reaches into the teeming streets of the Gothic Quarter, while the newer area is north of this; its elegant avenues in grid formation making up Eixample. The coastal quarter of Barça has been transformed with the development of trendy Barceloneta. For many, though, the epicentre of this bubbling city is Las Ramblas, scything through the centre of town.

BARCELONA IN...

→ **ONE DAY**
Catedral de Santa Eulalia, Las Ramblas, La Pedrera, Museu Picasso, Sagrada Familia.

→ **TWO DAYS**
Montjuïc, Parc Güell, Nou Camp Stadium, Barceloneta Waterfront, Tibidabo.

→ **THREE DAYS**
Barri Gotic and Palau de la Musica Catalana, Via Laietana, Sitges.

PRACTICAL INFORMATION

ARRIVAL-DEPARTURE

 Barcelona-El Prat Airport is located 13km southwest of the city. The Renfe train (Line R2, suburban train) runs every 30min. The Aerobus runs every 5min.

GETTING AROUND

The Barcelona Card offers three to five days of unlimited travel on the metro and buses, discounts on airport buses and cable cars, reduced entry to museums and attractions and discounts in some restaurants, bars and shops; it is sold at the airport, tourist offices and various other venues. The Articket gives free entry to six museums and galleries over six months and is available from tourist offices. Look out for two tourist buses – the Barcelona City Tour and the Bus Turistic.

CALENDAR HIGHLIGHTS

March
Mobile World Congress.

May
Ciutat Flamenco, Barcelona Guitar Festival.

June
Bicycle Week, Saint John's Day (concerts, dances and bonfires).

September
Fiesta de la Merce (Feast of Our Lady of Mercy).

October
International Jazz Festival, LIBER International Book Fair

October-July
Classical performances at Gran Teatre del Liceu.

EATING OUT

Barcelona has long had a good gastronomic tradition, and geographically it's been more influenced by France and Italy than other Spanish regions. But these days the sensual enjoyment of food has become something of a mainstream religion here. The city has hundreds of tapas bars; a type of cuisine which is very refreshing knocked back with a draught beer. The city's location brings together produce from the land and the sea, with a firm emphasis on seasonality and quality produce. This explains why there are myriad markets in the city, all in great locations. Specialities to look out for include Pantumaca: slices of toasted bread with tomato and olive oil; Escalibada, which is made with roasted vegetables; Esqueixada, a typically Catalan salad, and Crema Catalana, a light custard. One little known facet of Barcelona life is its exquisite chocolate and sweet shops. Two stand out: Fargas, in the Barri Gothic, is the city's most famous chocolate shop, while Cacao Sampaka is the most elegant chocolate store you could ever wish to find.

657

SPAIN - BARCELONA

W Barcelona

☆ ⟨ 🆘 ⛱ ♨ 👓 Ⓐ🆘 ㉔ 🚗
pl. de la Rosa dels Vents 1 (Moll De Llevant) ✉ *08039*   Plan I: **C3**
– ℰ 932 95 28 00 – www.w-barcelona.com
406 rm – 👫299/1025 € – ⌑ 22 € – 67 suites
• Business • Luxury • Design •
This hotel designed by Ricardo Bofill is located in the city's port area. It comprises two glass buildings: one a cube, the other a huge sail rising impressively above the Mediterranean. It has extensive spa facilities. The contemporary looking gastronomic restaurant offers an à la carte menu based around high quality products.
Bravo 24 – See restaurant listing

H1898

☆ ♨ 🆘 ⛱ 👓 ㉔ Ⓐ 🆘 🚗
La Rambla 109 ✉ *08002 –* Ⓜ *Catalunya*   Plan: **F2**
– ℰ 935 52 95 52 – www.hotel1898.com
166 rm – 👫180/450 € – ⌑ 27 € – 3 suites
• Chain • Historic •
The decor in this hotel occupying the former Tabacos de Filipinas headquarters is a mix of the traditional and contemporary. Spa area, guestrooms offering the very best amenities, plus a rooftop solarium with views of the city. This resolutely contemporary restaurant offers an à la carte menu of international dishes.

Mercer H. Barcelona

☆ 🆘 Ⓐ
Lledó 7 ✉ *08002 –* Ⓜ *Jaume I – ℰ 933 10 74 80*   Plan: **G2**
– www.mercerbarcelona.com
27 rm – 👫300/600 € – ⌑ 34 € – 1 suite
• Palace • Historic •
A hotel with lots of history, occupying a palace remodelled by Rafael Moneo but which has retained vestiges of the past, including walls from the Roman city of Barcino. Plenty of artistic detail, superb guestrooms and an attractive rooftop sun terrace.

The Serras

☆ 🆘 🆘 Ⓐ
Passeig de Colom 9 ✉ *08002 –* Ⓜ *Drassanes*   Plan: **G2**
– ℰ 931 69 18 68 – www.hoteltheserrasbarcelona.com
28 rm – 👫300/700 € – ⌑ 26 €
• Luxury • Elegant • Contemporary •
Luxury, practicality and pure lines at this hotel opposite the gigantic Prawn designed by Javier Mariscal. It offers well-equipped guestrooms, a sun terrace on the roof with superb views of the port, and an informal restaurant.

Neri

☆ 🆘 Ⓐ
Sant Sever 5 ✉ *08002 –* Ⓜ *Liceu – ℰ 933 04 06 55*   Plan: **F2**
– www.hotelneri.com
21 rm – 👫250/600 € – ⌑ 27 € – 1 suite
• Historic • Modern •
The modern interior of this hotel occupying an 18C mansion comes as something of a surprise. Library-lounge, designer-inspired guestrooms and a rooftop terrace. In the dining room, embellished with two 12C stone arches, diners can choose from a selection of contemporary Mediterranean cuisine.

España

🆘 Ⓐ ㉔
Sant Pau 9 ✉ *08001 –* Ⓜ *Liceu – ℰ 935 50 00 00*   Plan: **F2**
– www.hotelespanya.com
83 rm – 👫164/347 € – ⌑ 17 €
• Chain • Cosy •
Located right in the heart of the old quarter and easy to find since it occupies a 19C building next to the Liceu. Pleasant lounge area with some historical details, plus comfortable, albeit rather small guestrooms with a contemporary design.
🍴 **Fonda España** – See restaurant listing

Grand H. Central

Via Laietana 30 ⊠ 08003 – Ⓜ *Jaume I*
– 𝒞 932 95 79 00 – www.grandhotelcentral.com
140 rm – ♦♦210/751 € – ⊡ 26 € – 7 suites
• Traditional • Contemporary •

Plan: **F2**

A hotel with a contemporary look and welcoming facilities. Here, guests will find bedrooms with lots of attention to detail, and interesting public spaces such as the rooftop Sky Bar, with a chill- out zone and panoramic pool, the modern City Bar, and the multi-functional The Gallery.

SPAIN - BARCELONA

XxX Torre d'Alta Mar

passeig Joan de Borbó 88 ⊠ 08039 – Ⓜ *Barceloneta*
– 𝒞 932 21 00 07 – www.torredealtamar.com
– Closed 23-27 December, Sunday and Monday lunch
Menu 39/92 € – Carte 70/93 €
• Modern cuisine • Classic décor •

Plan: **H3**

A restaurant whose outstanding feature is its location on top of a 75m-high metal tower. Highly contemporary glass-fronted circular dining room with superb views of the sea, port and city. Traditional à la carte menu featuring contemporary touches.

XX Bravo 24 – Hotel W Barcelona

pl. de la Rosa dels Vents 1 (Moll De Llevant) ⊠ 08039
– 𝒞 932 95 26 36 – www.carlesabellan.com
Menu 90/130 € – Carte 60/80 €
• Traditional cuisine • Fashionable •

Plan I: **C3**

Located on the mezzanine of the W hotel in Barcelona, Bravo 24 has a resolutely contemporary feel, in which wood takes pride of place, plus an attractive summer terrace. Traditionally inspired cuisine enhanced by contemporary touches, plus an impressive array of raciones!

XX Senyor Parellada

L'Argenteria 37 ⊠ 08003 – Ⓜ *Jaume I*
– 𝒞 933 10 50 94 – www.senyorparellada.com
Menu 38/50 € – Carte 30/35 €
• Regional cuisine • Cosy •

Plan: **G2**

An attractive restaurant with a classic-cum-colonial style and various dining rooms in which time seems to have stood still. The highlights are the authentic Catalan cuisine and the small patio with an impressive glass roof.

XX El Cercle

dels Arcs 5-1° ⊠ 08002 – Ⓜ *Liceu – 𝒞 93 624 48 10*
– www.elcerclerestaurant.com
Menu 25/65 € – Carte 33/56 €
• Classic cuisine • Classic décor •

Plan: **F2**

This restaurant is housed in the Reial Cercle Arstístic. It offers different types of cuisine in different dining areas. These range from Japanese specialities to modern Catalan fare.

XX Elx

Moll d'Espanya 5-Maremagnum, Local 9 ⊠ 08039
– Ⓜ *Drassanes – 𝒞 932 25 81 17*
– www.elxrestaurant.com
Menu 35/78 € – Carte 35/45 €
• Traditional cuisine • Trendy •

Plan: **G3**

A restaurant graced with views of the fishing port. Modern dining room and an attractive terrace, where the focus is on fish and a good selection of savoury rice dishes.

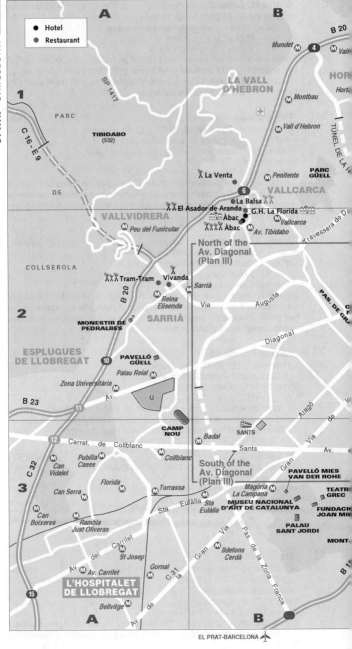

Environs of Barcelona
(Plan I)

0   1 km

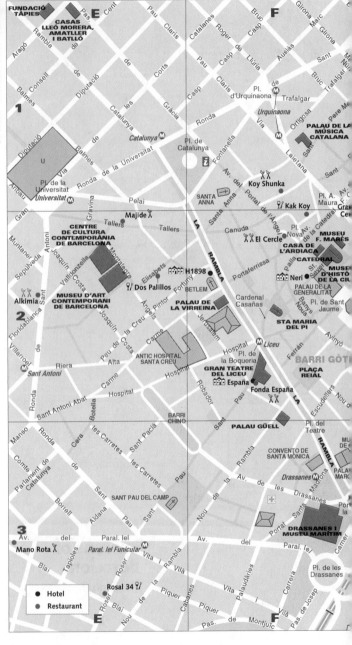

FUNDACIÓ TÀPIES

CASAS LLEÓ MORERA, AMATLLER I BATLLÓ

E

F

1

Aragó

Balmes

Consell

Diputació

Gran

Via

Ronda

Pl. de la Universitat

Universitat Ⓜ

Rambla

de

Claris

Pau

Catalanes

Corts

les

Diputació

de

Catalunya

de

Balmes

de la Universitat

Pelai

Gràcia

Cent

Roger

Casp

de

Pau

Claris

Ronda

Via

Universitat

Catalanes

Bruc

Casp

Llúria

Pl. d'Urquinaona

Urquinaona

Ausias

Sant

Bruc

Girona

Girona

Marc

Ortigosa

Trafalgar

Trafalgar

Pere Mé

PALAU DE LA MÚSICA CATALANA

Laietana

Pl. de Catalunya

Catalunya Ⓜ

Fontanella

Ronda

Muntaner

Sepúlveda

Joaquim

Costa

Valldonzella

Tallers

Majide ✕

Tallers

Tallers

CENTRE DE CULTURA CONTEMPORÀNIA DE BARCELONA

Elisabets

H1898

Dos Palillos

Fortuny

BETLEM

Canuda

LA

RAMBLA

Portal de l'Àngel

SANTA ANNA

Santa Anna

Av. del

Pl. Nova

Av. de la Catedral

Koy Shunka ✕✕

Kak Koy

El Cercle ✕✕

Pl. A. Maura

Gran

Cer

MUSEU F. MARÈS

CASA DE L'ARDIACA

CATEDRAL

MUSE D'HISTÒ DE LA CIU

Alkímia ✕✕

Florida

blanca

Villarroel

de

Riera

Sant Antoni

MUSEU D'ART CONTEMPORANI DE BARCELONA

Joaquim

Àngels

Pintor

Peu

Alta

Montalegre

Costa

de

la

Creu

Carme

Carme

PALAU DE LA VIRREINA

Jerusalem

ANTIC HOSPITAL SANTA CREU

Hospital

Portaferrissa

Cardenal Casañas

Neri

PALAU DE LA GENERALITAT

Banys Nous

Pl. de Sant Jaume

STA MARIA DEL PI

Savier

Pl. de la Boqueria

Liceu Ⓜ

Ferran

Avinyó

BARRI GÒTI

2

Ronda

Sant Antoni Abat

Hospital

Botella

Hospital

Robador

Sant

GRAN TEATRE DEL LICEU

España

Fonda España ✕✕

PLAÇA REIAL

Escudellers

Nou d

LA

3

Manso

Comte

Ronda

de

Parlament de Catalunya

Borrell

Cera

les Carretes

Sant Pacià

Aldana

Pau

Sant

les Carretes

SANT PAU DEL CAMP

Pau

BARRI CHINO

PALAU GÜELL

Rambla

Av.

de

Nou

de

les

Drassanes

CONVENTO DE SANTA MÒNICA

Drassanes Ⓜ

Pl. del Teatre

MU DE (

PALA MAR

RAMBLA

Av. **del** **Paral. lel**

Mano Rota ✕

Blai

Tapioles

Paral. lel Funicular Ⓜ

Roser

Vita i Rambla

Vilà

Rosal 34 ☕

Roser

Blai

Nou

de

Piquer

Cabanes

Vita

Palaudàries

Piquer

de

Montjuïc

Portal

Santa

Drassanes

Av.

del

Paral. lel

DRASSANES I MUSEU MARÍTIM

Pl. de les Drassanes

Carrera

i

Pas. de Josep

Carrer

E

F

● Hotel

● Restaurant

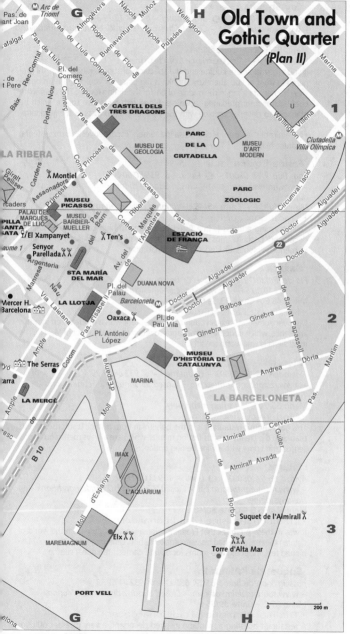

Old Town and Gothic Quarter
(Plan II)

LA RIBERA

Pas. de ant Joan

M Arc de Triomf

Almogàvers Nàpols Muñoz

Roger Buénaventura Nàpols Pujades

Pas. de Lluís Companys

Pl. del Comerç

Portal Nou

Baix Pec Comal

. de t Pere

atafalga

Comerç

Companys

Comerç

Pas.

Princesa de

CASTELL DELS TRES DRAGONS

MUSEU DE GEOLOGIA

Fusina

Picasso

PARC DE LA CIUTADELLA

MUSEU D'ART MODERN

PARC ZOOLOGIC

Wellington

Marina

U

Wellington Villena

M Ciutadella Villa Olímpica

Circumval.lació

Aiguader

Giralt Pelliser

caders

Montiel

Carders

Assaonadors

Princesa

MUSEU PICASSO

Ribera

Comerç

Marques

l'Argentera

Doctor

Aiguader

Aiguader

PALAU DELS MARQUÉS DE LLIÓ

MUSEU BARBIER-MUELLER

PILLA ANTA ATA

T/El Xampanyet

aume 1

Senyor Parellada

STA MARÍA DEL MAR

Ten's

Av. de

ESTACIÓ DE FRANÇA

Doctor

22

Argentina

Nau

Pas. d'Isabel II

Via Laietana

Pl. del Palau

DUANA NOVA

Manesana

LA LLOTJA

Oaxaca

Pl. de Pau Vila

M Barceloneta

Doctor Doctor

Aiguader

Balboa

Ginebra

Pas. de Salvat Papasseit

Mercer H. Barcelona

The Serras

arra

Colom

Ample

d'Espanya

Pl. António López

MUSEU D'HISTÒRIA DE CATALUNYA

MARINA

Ginebra

Andrea

Dòria

Martlim

LA BARCELONETA

Cervera

Almirall

Guiter

ó

Ample

LA MERCÉ

de

esc

B 10

Moll d'Espanya

IMAX

L'AQUÀRIUM

MAREMAGNUM

Elx

PORT VELL

elona

Almirall Aixada

Borbó

Suquet de l'Almirall

Torre d'Alta Mar

0 200 m

SPAIN - BARCELONA

XX   **Koy Shunka** (Hideki Matsuhisa)   🕭 AC

🕸   *Copons 7 ⊠ 08002 –* 🅜 *Urquinaona –* 🕿 *934 12 79 39*   Plan: **F1**
– www.koyshunka.com – Closed Christmas, Holy Week, August, Sunday dinner and Monday
Menu 87/128 € – Carte 65/95 €
• Japanese • Contemporary décor •
If you enjoy Japanese cuisine and the spectacle of superb nigiri and sushi prepared in front of you, then Koy Shunka is the place for you. There is an open-view kitchen standing in the middle of one of the dining rooms. The passionate chef is known for preparing Japanese dishes with a creative touch, which he manages to cleverly combine with the cuisine and products of the Mediterranean.
➜ Chipirones al punto con salsa de ume. "Espardenyes", arroz integral japones. Milhojas.

XX   **Fonda España** – Hotel España   🕭 AC

🕮   *Sant Pau 9 ⊠ 08001 –* 🅜 *Liceu –* 🕿 *935 50 00 00*   Plan: **F2**
– www.hotelespanya.com – Closed Sunday dinner and Bank Holidays dinner
Menu 28/55 € – Carte 35/45 € – (dinner only in August)
• Traditional cuisine • Cosy •
This charming address is in a listed building with high ceilings, a Modernist decor and beautiful mosaics created by the renowned Barcelona architect Domènech i Montaner. Updated traditional cuisine.

X   **Oaxaca**   🍴 🕭 AC

   Pla del Palau 19 ⊠ 08002 – 🅜 *Barceloneta*   Plan: **G2**
– 🕿 *933 19 00 64 – www.oaxacacuinamexicana.com*
Menu 48 € – Carte 33/59 €
• Mexican • Fashionable •
Discover authentic Mexican cuisine in a restaurant with a modern and informal ambience, which nonetheless manages to retain a typical flavour of Mexico. The mezcalería is well worth a visit!

X   **Montiel**   AC ⇔

   Flassaders 19 ⊠ 08003 – 🅜 *Jaume I –* 🕿 *932 68 37 29*   Plan: **G1**
– www.restaurantmontiel.com – Closed 23 January-2 February and Tuesday
Menu 55/70 € – (tasting menu only)
• Modern cuisine • Simple •
This gastronomic restaurant is in the bohemian Born district. It surprises guests thanks to the creativity of its tasting menus, which are always meticulously presented and come with a wine pairing option.

X   **Pitarra**   AC ⇔

   Avinyó 56 ⊠ 08002 – 🅜 *Liceu –* 🕿 *933 01 16 47*   Plan: **G2**
– www.restaurantpitarra.cat – Closed 9-30 August, Sunday and Bank Holidays dinner
Menu 14/55 € – Carte 30/48 €
• Traditional cuisine • Traditional décor •
It was in these premises that Frederic Soler, a leading figure from the world of Catalan theatre, once had his watchmaker's shop. Dining rooms with an old-fashioned feel, including two rooms for private parties. Traditional cuisine.

X   **Suquet de l'Almirall**   🍴 🕭 AC

   passeig Joan de Borbó 65 ⊠ 08003 – 🕿 *932 21 62 33*   Plan: **H3**
– www.suquetdelalmirall.com – Closed Sunday dinner and Monday
Menu 37 € – Carte 39/55 €
• Traditional cuisine • Traditional décor •
A restaurant boasting a maritime inspired decor and a very pleasant outdoor terrace. Extensive menu of traditional cuisine, including a varied selection of fish and rice dishes.

SPAIN - BARCELONA

X **Ten's** 🛱 ㅎ AC

av. Marqués de l'Argentera 11 ⊠ *08003* Plan: **G2**
– **Ⓜ** *Barceloneta* – *℘ 933 19 22 22* – *www.tensbarcelona.com*
Menu 48/62 € – Carte 22/36 €
• Modern cuisine • Fashionable •
A gastro-bar with a thoroughly modern look that is dominated by varying tones
of white. Its concise menu, overseen by the TV chef Jordi Cruz, features tapas
and half portions. These cleverly combine traditional and more cutting-edge
cuisine.

X **Majide** ㅎ AC

Tallers 48 ⊠ *08001* – **Ⓜ** *Universitat* – *℘ 930 16 37 81* Plan: **E2**
– *www.majide.es* – *Closed 7 days Christmas, 21 days August and Monday*
Menu 65 € – Carte 24/55 €
• Japanese • Simple •
A Japanese restaurant that follows the path of the award-winning Koy Shunka,
which is part of the same group. As the kitchen is completely open view, we
recommend a seat at the bar.

ɥ/ **Kak Koy** AC

Ripoll 16 ⊠ *08002* – **Ⓜ** *Urquinaona* – *℘ 933 02 84 14* Plan: **F2**
– *www.kakkoy.com* – *Closed Christmas, Holy Week, August, Monday
dinner and Tuesday*
Tapa 6 € **Ración** approx. 14 €
• Japanese • Cosy •
Japanese cuisine with a Mediterranean influence that has adopted the tapas
and *raciones* concept. The traditional Japanese robata grill takes centre stage
here.

ɥ/ **Dos Palillos** 🛱 AC ✪
✿

Elisabets 9 ⊠ *08001* – **Ⓜ** *Catalunya* – *℘ 933 04 05 13* Plan: **E2**
– *www.dospalillos.com* – *Closed 25 December-9 January, 7-28 August,
Sunday, Monday, Tuesday lunch and Wednesday lunch*
Tapa 8 €
• Asian • Contemporary décor •
A highly original dining option both for its unique "show cooking" concept and
its culinary philosophy. This is centred on the fusion of oriental cuisine and typi-
cally Spanish products. There are two counters for dining, one at the entrance
(no reservations taken and only for à la carte dining), and another further inside,
which has a more gastronomic focus with its tasting menus.
→ Yuba-mochi de soja blanca, verde y negra. Narezushi de lubina salvaje.
"Espardenya" con mentaiko.

ɥ/ **El Xampanyet** AC

Montcada 22 ⊠ *08003* – **Ⓜ** *Jaume I* – *℘ 933 19 70 03* Plan: **G2**
– *Closed 15 days January, Holy Week, August, Sunday dinner and Monday*
Tapa 3.50 € **Ración** approx. 12 €
• Traditional cuisine • Traditional décor •
This old tavern with a long-standing family tradition is decorated with typical
azulejo tiles. Varied selection of tapas with an emphasis on cured meats and
high-quality canned products.

ɥ/ **Rosal 34** AC

Roser 34 ⊠ *08004* – **Ⓜ** *Paral.lel* – *℘ 933 24 90 46* Plan: **E3**
– *www.rosal34.com* – *Closed 5-19 September, Sunday and Monday lunch*
Tapa 5.50 € **Ración** approx. 12 €
• Creative • Rustic •
Rosal 34 is located in an old family wine cellar, where the rustic stonework
blends in with the contemporary decor. Seasonal dishes plus interesting tapas
with a creative touch.

North and South of Av. Diagonal

(Plan III)

0   300 m

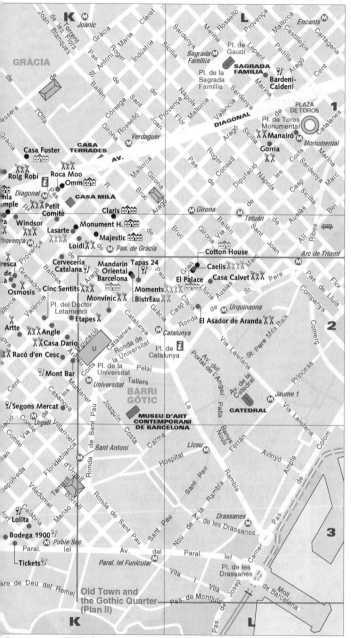

GRÀCIA

Joanic

Pl. de Lepant
Pl. de la Sagrada Família

SAGRADA FAMÍLIA
Sagrada Família

Bardeni-Caldeni

PLAZA DE TOROS
DIAGONAL

Pl. de Toros Monumental

Manairó
Verdaguer

Gorría

Casa Fuster
CASA TERRADES

Roig Robí
Roca Moo
Omm
CASA MILÀ

Diagonal

Petit Comitè

Windsor
Claris
Monument H.

Lasarte
Majestic
Loidi
Pas. de Gràcia

Cotton House

Cerveceria Catalana
Mandarin Oriental Barcelona
Tapas 24

Caelis

El Palace
Casa Calvet

Cinc Sentits
Moments

Osmosis
Monvínic
BistrEau
Urquinaona

Pl. del Doctor Letamendi

El Asador de Aranda

Etapes

Artte
Catalunya

Angle
Ronda de la Universitat
Pl. de Catalunya

Casa Darío
U
Pl. de la Universitat

Racó d'en Cesc
Pelai
Tallers
Universitat

Mont Bar

BARRI GÒTIC

Segons Mercat

MUSEU D'ART CONTEMPORANI DE BARCELONA

Sant Antoni

Liceu

CATEDRAL

Jaume 1

Floridablanca

Lolita
Rambla

Bodega 1900
Poble Sec

Drassanes

Paral.lel

Tickets
Pl. de les Drassanes

Moll de Barcelona

Old Town and the Gothic Quarter (Plan II)

K
L

SPAIN - BARCELONA

Mandarin Oriental Barcelona 🖼 ⊕ 🔲 & ⏲ 🕭
passeig de Gràcia 38-40 ✉ 08007 Plan: **K2**
– Ⓜ *Passeig de Gràcia* – 𝒞 931 51 88 88 – www.mandarinoriental.com
102 rm – 🛏350/550 € – 🏠 45 € – 18 suites
• Luxury • Design •
Experience a fusion of luxury, relaxation and pleasure in a building that once served as a bank. Today, the designer interior is highly innovative and cosmopolitan in feel. It features guestrooms offering high levels of comfort, excellent dining options in the lobby, an attractive patio-terrace, and a laid-back rooftop terrace with great views of the city.
❀❀ **Moments • BistrEau** – See restaurant listing

El Palace 🖼 ⊕ 🔲 & ⏲ 🕭 ⌂
Gran Via de les Corts Catalanes 668 ✉ 08010 Plan: **L2**
– Ⓜ *Urquinaona* – 𝒞 935 10 11 30 – www.hotelpalacebarcelona.com
101 rm – 🛏305/575 € – 🏠 29 € – 24 suites
• Luxury • Classic •
This emblematic hotel occupies a historic building that has been restored to recreate the essence of the golden years of the 1920s. Distinguished lounges and superbly equipped guestrooms, the majority of which are classically elegant in feel with some bathrooms inspired by Roman baths!
❀ **Caelis** – See restaurant listing

Monument H. 🖼 & ⏲ ⌂
passeig de Gracia 75 ✉ 08008 – Ⓜ *Passeig de Gracia* Plan: **K2**
– 𝒞 935 48 20 00 – www.monument-hotel.com
55 rm – 🛏291/528 € – 29 suites
• Grand Luxury • Contemporary •
Occupying an attractive pre-Modernist building with an enviable location just a few metres from Gaudí's famous La Pedrera building. The impressive interior design features a large lobby with a cocktail bar within it, and guestrooms offering high levels of comfort.
❀❀❀ **Lasarte** – See restaurant listing

Majestic 🌿 🖼 🔲 & ⏲ 🕭 ⌂
passeig de Gràcia 68 ✉ 08007 – Ⓜ *Passeig de Gràcia* Plan: **K2**
– 𝒞 934 88 17 17 – www.hotelmajestic.es
272 rm – 🛏249/800 € – 🏠 37 € – 40 suites
• Traditional • Classic •
The Majestic is superbly located and boasts an impressive rooftop terrace with a snack bar and delightful views. It combines excellent service with classic guestrooms offering high levels of comfort. The more functional restaurant alternates between a set menu and à la carte dining in the evening.

Claris 🌿 🖼 🔲 & ⏲ 🕭 ⌂
Pau Claris 150 ✉ 08009 – Ⓜ *Passeig de Gràcia* Plan: **K2**
– 𝒞 934 87 62 62 – www.hotelclaris.com
84 rm – 🛏600/650 € 🛏650/700 € – 🏠 23 € – 40 suites
• Traditional • Modern •
This elegant, stately hotel occupies the former Vedruna palace. It offers a perfect fusion of tradition, cutting-edge design and technology. Impressive archaeological collection. The restaurant of the rooftop offers spectacular views of central Barcelona.

Cotton House 🌿 & 🖼
Gran Vía de les Corts Catalanes 670 ✉ 08010 Plan: **L2**
– Ⓜ *Urquinaona* – 𝒞 934 50 50 45 – www.hotelcottonhouse.com
80 rm – 🛏250/380 € – 🏠 29 € – 3 suites
• Chain • Luxury • Elegant •
As its name suggests, this imposing late-19C building was once the headquarters of the Fundación Textil Algodonera (cotton foundation). Full of character, the hotel offers beautifully kept rooms, albeit some a little on the small side, and creative cuisine based on traditional and international dishes.

Omm   🚴 🔵 🔲 ⚖ 🅰🅲 ⚙ 🚗

Rosselló 265 ✉ *08008 –* Ⓜ *Diagonal – ℰ 934 45 40 00*   Plan: **K1**
– www.hotelomm.com
87 rm – 👫215/480 € – ⊊ 27 € – 4 suites
• Business • Design •
This urban, cutting-edge hotel boasts a spacious lounge area, contemporary bedrooms, and a bar open all day for drinks and informal dining. Other options here include the Ommsession Club with a live DJ, and the rooftop bar with its superb views of the city.
❀ **Roca Moo** – See restaurant listing

 Ohla Eixample   🚴 🔲 ⚖ 🅰🅲 ⚙ 🚗

Corsega 289-291 ✉ *08008 –* Ⓜ *Diagonal*   Plan: **K2-1**
– ℰ 937 37 79 77 – www.ohlaeixample.com
94 rm ⊊ – **👫**240/292 €
• Business • Industrial •
A modern hotel with an industrial aesthetic and a surprising façade, which is even more striking at night thanks to an impressive play of light. Designer inspired guestrooms, an interior terrace and an attractive rooftop and chill-out zone on the roof add to its appeal.
❀ **Xerta** – See restaurant listing

 The Mirror Barcelona   🔲 ⚖ 🅰🅲

Córsega 255 ✉ *08036 –* Ⓜ *Provença – ℰ 932 02 86 86*   Plan: **J2**
– www.themirrorbarcelona.com
63 rm ⊊ – **👫**103/220 €
• Business • Design •
The most striking aspect of this hotel is its design, which will appeal to guests keen on this type of minimalist decor. Everything is dominated by mirrors, the colour white and the use of simple, clean lines.

XxxX **Lasarte** – Hotel Monument H.   🐟 ⚖ 🅰🅲 ↻ 🚗
❀❀❀ *Mallorca 259* ✉ *08008 –* Ⓜ *Passeig de Gràcia*   Plan: **K2**
– ℰ 934 45 32 42 – www.restaurantlasarte.com – Closed 1-9 January, Holy Week, 13 August-4 September, Sunday, Monday and Bank Holidays
Menu 160/195 € – Carte 100/125 €
• Creative • Design •
This impeccable contemporary-style restaurant is constantly changing and has the personal stamp of Martín Berasategui and his team. The original and imaginative cuisine bears the innovative hallmark of the chef, whose creativity is evident in the à la carte options and tasting menus alike.
→ Gamba roja templada sobre un fondo marino, hinojo y mayonesa de su coral. Pichón a la brasa, picadita cítrica de alcaparras, oliva negra, salsa ahumada de zanahoria y galanga. Cacao, ajo negro fermentado, frambuesa y azúcar moscovado.

XxxX **Caelis** (Romain Fornell) – Hotel El Palace   ⚖ 🅰🅲 ↻ 🚗
❀ *Gran Via de les Corts Catalanes 668 (previsto traslado a*   Plan: **L2**
Via Laietana 49) ✉ *08010 –* Ⓜ *Urquinaona – ℰ 935 10 12 05*
– www.caelis.com – Closed Sunday, Monday and Tuesday lunch
Menu 39/132 € – Carte 84/127 €
• Creative • Elegant •
Located inside the Palace Hotel, albeit with its own entrance, Caelis boasts a stylish 19C elegance and undeniable charm in its classically furnished main dining room. Discover its gastronomic creativity through several menus, from which dishes also be ordered individually. A private dining room and attractive cocktail bar are added bonuses.
→ Macarrones en dos servicios, mar y montaña, bogavante y foiegras. Lubina salvaje con velo perfumado al estragón, beurre blanc y guisantes lágrima. Explosión Saint Honoré.

S P A I N - BARCELONA

SPAIN - BARCELONA

XXXX **Moments** – Hotel Mandarin Oriental Barcelona   ⅋ ♿ Ⓚ

ಬಿ ಬಿ *passeig de Gràcia 38-40* ✉ *08007*   Plan: **K2**
– Ⓜ *Passeig de Gràcia* – ℰ *931 51 87 81* – *www.mandarinoriental.com*
– *Closed 17 January-2 February, 22 August-16 September, Sunday and Monday*
Menu 77/166 € – Carte 115/124 €
• Creative • Design •
Accessed via the hotel lobby, Moments stands out for its design, including a private chef's table. Trained in the famous Sant Pau restaurant, Raül Balam conjures up top-notch creative cuisine, which respects flavours, showcases textures and is able to reinterpret tradition through contemporary eyes.
→ Arroz caldoso de colas de gamba. Pluma de cerdo ibérico con bizcocho de avellanas, garbanzos y orejones de melocotón. Terroir de cacao.

XXX **Angle**   ♿ Ⓚ ✿ 🚗

ಬಿ *Aragó 214* ✉ *08011* – Ⓜ *Universitat* – ℰ *932 16 77 77*   Plan: **K2**
– *www.anglebarcelona.com* – *Closed Tuesday and Wednesday*
Menu 75/100 € – *(tasting menu only)*
• Modern cuisine • Minimalist •
Located on the first floor of the Hotel Cram, Angle has a minimalist look dominated by the presence of large white curtains. The creative cooking here demonstrates a high level of technical skill and is influenced by the very best seasonal products. This is in keeping with the philosophy of chef Jordi Cruz who brings inspiration to every dish.
→ Bullabesa de carabinero infusionada con anisados. Espaldita, ventresca y mollejas de cordero con panacota de cabra y toffee salado de setas. Crujiente de galleta con yogur, flores y helado de violetas.

XXX **Casa Calvet**   ♿ Ⓚ ✿

Casp 48 ✉ *08010* – Ⓜ *Urquinaona* – ℰ *934 12 40 12*   Plan: **L2**
– *www.casacalvet.es* – *Closed 7 days August, Sunday, Monday summer and Bank Holidays*
Menu 38/70 € – Carte 48/67 €
• Traditional cuisine • Elegant •
This restaurant occupies a Modernist building designed by Gaudí. It once served as a textile factory and the offices have been converted into private dining rooms. A mix of classic Catalan dishes for à la carte dining alongside good set menus.

XXX **Racó d'en Cesc**   ⅋ 🍴 ♿ Ⓚ ✿

Diputació 201 ✉ *08011* – Ⓜ *Universitat*   Plan: **K2**
– ℰ *934 51 60 02* – *www.elracodencesc.com* – *Closed Holy Week, August, Sunday and Bank Holidays*
Menu 40 € – Carte 40/53 €
• Modern cuisine • Classic décor •
A restaurant with a small terrace, a bistro-style section and a classic dining room, with a different creative Catalan menu in each. A wide choice of craft beers is also available.

XXX **Gaig** (Carles Gaig)   ♿ Ⓚ ✿

ಬಿ *Còrsega 200* ✉ *08036* – Ⓜ *Hospital Clinic*   Plan: **J2**
– ℰ *934 29 10 17* – *www.restaurantgaig.com* – *Closed Holy Week, 10 days August, Sunday dinner, Monday and Bank Holidays dinner*
Menu 68/120 € – Carte 65/95 €
• Modern cuisine • Elegant •
Arranged on two floors, this spacious restaurant exudes elegance and a thoroughly modern feel. The chef here offers a menu divided in two parts, one focusing on traditional dishes, the other on contemporary cuisine. Interesting set menus, select ingredients and superb presentation.
→ Canelones con crema de trufa. Arroz de pichon y setas de Burdeos. Nuestra crema catalana.

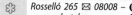

SPAIN - BARCELONA

XxX ✿ **Roca Moo** – Hotel Omm   🍴 ♿ AC ⚑

Rosselló 265 ✉ *08008* – Ⓜ *Diagonal* – ☎ *934 45 40 00*   Plan: **K1**
– www.hotelomm.com – Closed 10 days January, 21 days August, Sunday
and Monday
Menu 49/110 € – Carte 51/77 €
• Creative • Trendy •

A cosmopolitan ambience pervades the café and bright dining room. Contemporary decor defined by skylights and designer details. Signature cuisine, a good combination of flavours and a very original wine list.
→ Nuestro huerto mediterráneo. Raya rallada. Todo el olivo.

XxX **Windsor**   🍴 ☂ ♿ AC ⇔ 🚗

Còrsega 286 ✉ *08008* – Ⓜ *Diagonal* – ☎ *932 37 75 88*   Plan: **K2**
– www.restaurantwindsor.com – Closed 1-10 January, Holy Week, 1-
21 August, Sunday and Bank Holidays
Menu 30/99 € – Carte 48/60 €
• Modern cuisine • Classic décor •

This restaurant, with its updated classic decor, is enhanced by an exquisite terrace and several dining rooms that allow for different configurations. Contemporary Catalan cuisine.

XxX ✿ **Cinc Sentits** (Jordi Artal)   AC

Aribau 58 ✉ *08011* – Ⓜ *Universitat* – ☎ *933 23 94 90*   Plan: **K2**
– www.cincsentits.com – Closed 15 days August, Sunday, Monday and
Bank Holidays
Menu 100/120 € – *(tasting menu only)*
• Creative • Minimalist •

The stylish setting and layout is matched by a truly unique minimalist look, with a predominance of dark tones. You won't find à la carte dishes here as the focus is on enticing set menus that change frequently. Inventive cuisine centred on select Catalan ingredients.
→ Huerto de verduras ecológicas a la parrilla, encurtidas y crudas, con salsa de hierbas. Pichón a la brasa con farsa de su higado, remolacha escabechada y setas. Helado de leche ahumada, crujiente de leche, teja de yogur y dulce de leche casero.

XxX ✿ **Xerta** – Hotel Ohla Eixample   ♿ AC 🚗

Corsega 289 ✉ *08008* – Ⓜ *Diagonal*   Plan: **K2-1**
– ☎ 937 37 90 80 – www.xertarestaurant.com – Closed Sunday and
Monday
Menu 35/98 € – Carte 57/80 €
• Creative • Design •

This restaurant is elegant, contemporary and oozing personality thanks to its striking skylights, vertical garden and large open-view kitchen. Choose from a concise à la carte with a contemporary Mediterranean focus and several set menus. Everything is centred around the very best products from the Ebro delta and fantastic fish sourced from the daily fish market.
→ Arroz cremoso del Delta con ortigas, "espardenyes", mahonesa de algas y salicornia. Anguila del Delta a baja temperatura pero crujiente, con berenjena, miso y ajo negro. Sinfonía de cítricos de Xerta.

XxX **Rías de Galicia**   🍴 ☂ AC

Lleida 7 ✉ *08004* – Ⓜ *Espanya* – ☎ *934 24 81 52*   Plan: **J3**
– www.riasdegalicia.com
Menu 80/120 € – Carte 65/90 €
• Seafood • Classic décor •

This restaurant is run by brothers and located close to the city's exhibition area. It boasts an attractive display cabinet at its entrance, a live fish tank, plus a meticulously arranged dining room decorated in a classic yet contemporary style. The extensive à la carte specialises in Galician fish and shellfish, which is always of the very highest quality.

XXX **Petit Comitè**   🕭 📟 ⇦

passatge de la Concepció 13 ✉ *08007* – Ⓜ *Diagonal*   Plan: **K2**
– ℰ 936 33 76 27 – www.petitcomite.cat
– Closed 8-21 August
Menu 52 € – Carte 36/72 €
• Regional cuisine • Design •
This contemporary restaurant is decorated with lots of dishes. The focus is on local cuisine prepared using Spanish ingredients, including enticing themed daily specials.

XX **Alkimia** (Jordi Vilà)   ✻ 🕭 📟
⧠ *Ronda San Antoni 41, 1° ✉ 08011* – Ⓜ *Universitat*   Plan II : **L2**
– ℰ 932 07 61 15 – www.alkimia.cat – Closed 16 January-5 February, 7 days August, Saturday and Sunday
Menu 98/155 € – Carte 55/85 €
• Modern cuisine • Design •
Alkimia boasts a striking design, with an avant-garde nod to the maritime world and a brand-new "unplugged" concept that complements its main gastronomic dining room. The contemporary cuisine (based around locally sourced ingredients) is sublime, with perfect textures and defined flavours that blend harmoniously together.
→ Raviolis de pollo rustido con crema de queso y su jugo rustido. Langosta en suquet de pan, salsa de jengibre y jerez. Manjar blanco con fruta fresca y vino dulce.

XX **Asador de Aranda**   🕭 📟 ⇦
Londres 94 ✉ 08036 – Ⓜ *Hospital Clínic*   Plan: **L2**
– ℰ 934 14 67 90 – www.asadordearanda.com
– Closed Sunday dinner
Menu 41/50 € – Carte 35/48 €
• Meats and grills • Traditional décor •
This spacious restaurant is decorated in a Castilian style with a wood oven in full view of the dining room. Cooking is traditional, with a particular focus on roast dishes.

XX **Gorría**   📟 ⇦
Diputació 421 ✉ 08013 – Ⓜ *Monumental*   Plan: **L1**
– ℰ 932 45 11 64 – www.restaurantegorria.com – Closed Holy Week, August, Sunday, Monday dinner and Bank Holidays dinner
Carte 30/65 €
• Basque • Rustic •
A well-established Basque restaurant with rustic decor. The excellent menu is complemented by an extensive wine list. Service is attentive.

XX **Pakta**   🕭 📟
⧠ *Lleida 5 ✉ 08004* – Ⓜ *Espanya* – ℰ *936 24 01 77*   Plan: **J3**
– www.pakta.es – Closed Christmas, Holy Week, 3 weeks August, Sunday and Monday
Menu 110 € – *(dinner only except Saturday) (booking essential) (tasting menu only)*
• Peruvian • Design •
A colourful, contemporary and informal restaurant that evokes Peruvian culture. This is evident both in its name (that means 'together' or 'union' in the Quechua language) and its decor with walls and ceilings adorned with striking fabrics. However, the cuisine is very much Japanese, showcasing lots of technical prowess and meticulous presentation. Bookings need to be made online.
→ Makicausa de cangrejo real. Ceviche con leche de tigre de masato. Sashimi de calamar con caviar.

SPAIN - BARCELONA

XX ✿ **Nectari** (Jordi Esteve) ᴬᴷ ⇔

València 28 ✉ 08015 – ⓜ *Tarragona* – ☎ *932 26 87 18* Plan: **J3**
– *www.nectari.es* – *Closed 15 days August and Sunday*
Menu 35/75 € – Carte 53/79 €
• Modern cuisine • Classic décor •
A cosy setting for this completely family-run operation with two small contemporary-style dining rooms and one private area. The owner-chef has put together a menu with a marked Mediterranean bias, enhanced by pleasing creative and innovative touches.
→ Virutas de foie con gelée de Sauternes. San Pedro al estilo Nectari con puerros confitados, espárragos verdes y parmentier de patata. Coulant de chocolate con sorbete cítrico.

XX **Casa Darío** ♿ ᴬᴷ ⇔

Consell de Cent 256 ✉ 08011 – ⓜ *Universitat* Plan: **K2**
– ☎ *934 53 31 35* – *www.casadario.com* – *Closed 1-23 August, Sunday dinner and Monday*
Menu 35 € – Carte 40/75 €
• Galician • Classic décor •
A well-established restaurant with a good reputation for the quality of its ingredients. The restaurant has a private bar, three dining rooms and three private rooms. Galician dishes and seafood are the house specialities.

XX **Monvínic** ⸮ ♿ ᴬᴷ ⇔

Diputació 249 ✉ 08007 – ⓜ *Catalunya* Plan: **K2**
– ☎ *932 72 61 87* – *www.monvinic.com* – *Closed August, Saturday lunch, Sunday and Monday lunch*
Menu 18/75 € – Carte 52/62 €
• Modern cuisine • Wine bar •
This restaurant impresses through its contemporary design and philosophy, with everything revolving around the world of wine. A modern take on traditional cuisine, as well as a splendid wine cellar.

XX **BistrEau** – Hotel Mandarin Oriental Barcelona ♿ ᴬᴷ

passeig de Gràcia 38-40 ✉ 08007 Plan: **K2**
– ⓜ *Passeig de Gràcia* – ☎ *931 51 87 83* – *www.restaurantbistreau.com*
Menu 35/120 € – Carte 45/76 €
• Traditional cuisine • Design •
This is the fiefdom of Ángel León, the so-called 'chef of the sea', in Barcelona. Savour dishes blending the traditional with the creative, and all bearing the stamp of this renowned chef. In the evening, enjoy a unique chef's table experience, limited to just a dozen guests, feasting on a menu faithful to the culinary traditions of his Aponiente restaurant in Andalucia.

XX **Loidi** ♿ ᴬᴷ 🚗

Mallorca 248 ✉ 08008 – ⓜ *Passeig de Gràcia* Plan: **K2**
– ☎ *934 92 92 92* – *www.loidi.com* – *Closed August, Sunday dinner and Bank Holidays dinner*
Menu 29/49 € – *(tasting menu only)*
• Modern cuisine • Friendly •
In this restaurant, the innovative cuisine on offer is light, fast and reasonably priced. Several menus are available, all created under the tutelage of famous chef Martín Berasategui.

XX **Manairó** ♿ ᴬᴷ

Diputació 424 ✉ 08013 – ⓜ *Monumental* Plan: **L1**
– ☎ *932 31 00 57* – *www.manairo.com* – *Closed 1-7 January, Sunday and Bank Holidays*
Menu 40/90 € – Carte 56/75 €
• Creative • Contemporary décor •
A unique restaurant, both in terms of its modern decor and intimate lighting. Contemporary, meticulously presented cuisine with its roots in Catalan cooking.

SPAIN - BARCELONA

X
❀
Hoja Santa (Paco Méndez)   ᕮ AC
av. Mistral 54 ⊠ *08015 –* Ⓜ *Espanya –* ℰ *933 48 21 94*   Plan: **J3**
– www.hojasanta.es – Closed 25 December-8 January, 10-16 April, 7-27 August, Sunday and Monday
Menu 110 € – Carte 56/76 € – *(dinner only except Saturday)*
• Mexican • Design •
Guests can enjoy fine Mexican cuisine at this restaurant named after an indigenous bush. The ambience is relaxed and contemporary, featuring a decor made up of ethnic and colonial details. The enticing combination of flavours and, above all, spicy dishes adapted to a European palate, ensure a thoroughly enjoyable experience.
→ Pipián de pistachos con "espardenya". Mole cenizo de rosas con codorniz de bresse. Maíz, chocolate y cajeta.

X
Mano Rota   AC ⇦
Creus dels Molers 4 ⊠ *08004 –* Ⓜ *Poble Sec*   Plan II : **E3**
– ℰ 931 64 80 41 – www.manorota.com – Closed 13-17 April, 13-31 August, Saturday lunch and Sunday
Menu 18/60 € – Carte 29/53 €
• Modern cuisine • Neighbourhood •
Mano Rota boasts an industrial feel and champions a specific concept: a restaurant with a bar. Its interesting menu includes traditional and contemporary recipes, as well as international dishes from Peru and Japan.

X
Sergi de Meià   ᕮ AC
Aribau 106 ⊠ *08036 –* Ⓜ *Diagonal –* ℰ *931 25 57 10*   Plan: **K2**
– www.restaurantsergidemeia.cat – Closed Sunday and Monday
Menu 22/75 € – Carte 37/50 €
• Regional cuisine • Simple •
The owner-chef unashamedly promotes 100% Catalan cuisine. He rediscovers the flavours of yesteryear and always focuses on organic and locally sourced products.

X
Osmosis   AC
Aribau 100 ⊠ *08036 –* Ⓜ *Diagonal –* ℰ *934 54 52 01*   Plan: **K2**
– www.restauranteosmosis.com – Closed 24-29 December and Sunday
Menu 30/85 € – *(tasting menu only)*
• Modern cuisine • Contemporary décor •
A restaurant with a pleasant, modern ambience arranged over two floors. The contemporary tasting menu, available in both long and short formats, is created using seasonal, market-fresh ingredients.

X
Gresca   AC
Provença 230 ⊠ *08036 –* Ⓜ *Diagonal –* ℰ *934 51 61 93*   Plan: **K2**
– www.gresca.net – Closed 7 days Christmas, Holy Week, 15 days August, Saturday lunch and Sunday
Menu 19/70 € – Carte 37/63 €
• Modern cuisine • Family •
Much talked about in Barcelona thanks to its relaxed atmosphere and friendly service. Find attractive contemporary cuisine including enticing set menus.

X
❀
Disfrutar   ᕮ AC
Villarroel 163 ⊠ *08036 –* Ⓜ *Hospital Clinic*   Plan: **J2**
– ℰ 933 48 68 96 – www.disfrutarbarcelona.com – Closed 7 days November, 7 days March, 1-15 August, Sunday and Monday
Menu 75/135 € – *(tasting menu only)*
• Creative • Design •
Creativity, high technical skill, fantasy and good taste are the hallmarks of the three chefs here. They conjure up a true gastronomic experience via several tasting menus in a simple, contemporary space with an open-view kitchen. The name of the restaurant, which translates as 'enjoy', says it all!
→ Espárragos blancos en escabeche de sauco con anguila y caviar. Pichón a la marroquí. Nuestra tarta al whisky.

X **Espai Kru**   AC ⇔

Lleida 7 ⊠ 08004 – **Ⓜ** *Espanya*   Plan: **J3**
– ℰ 934 23 45 70 – www.espaikru.com
– Closed 15 days August, Sunday dinner and Monday
Menu 60/100 € – Carte 37/70 €
• International • Fashionable •
Located on the first floor of a building, Espai Kru boasts an impressive appearance enhanced by its single space featuring an open-view kitchen, private dining room and cocktail bar. Extensive international and fusion menu, featuring both raw and cooked ingredients.

X **Artte**   &. AC

Muntaner 83C ⊠ 08011 – **Ⓜ** *Universitat*   Plan: **K2**
– ℰ 934 54 90 48 – www.artte.es
– Closed August and Sunday
Menu 16/40 € – Carte 27/45 €
• Mediterranean cuisine • Design •
An unusual bistro that takes its inspiration from the tea rooms of China. Enjoy an artistic-cum-gastronomic experience that extols the virtues of raw, natural foods and vegetarian dishes.

X **Etapes**   ⌂ AC ⇔
⊛
Enrique Granados 10 ⊠ 08007   Plan: **K2**
– ℰ 933 23 69 14 – www.etapes.cat
– Closed Saturday lunch and Sunday dinner
Menu 16 € – Carte 30/42 €
• Modern cuisine • Simple •
An address that is well worth bearing in mind! This small restaurant has a modern yet informal look featuring an elongated dining room with a decor that combines wood, iron and glass. Enjoy contemporary cuisine with an emphasis on meticulous presentation and carefully selected ingredients.

ⓎⅠ **Cervecería Catalana**   ⌂ AC

Mallorca 236 ⊠ 08008 – **Ⓜ** *Diagonal – ℰ 932 16 03 68*   Plan: **K2**
Tapa 4.50 € **Ración** approx. 8 €
• Traditional cuisine • Contemporary décor •
This popular local pub, decorated with racks full of bottles, serves a comprehensive choice of top quality tapas.

ⓎⅠ **Paco Meralgo**   AC ⇔

Muntaner 171 ⊠ 08036 – **Ⓜ** *Hospital Clínic*   Plan: **J2**
– ℰ 934 30 90 27 – www.restaurantpacomeralgo.com
Tapa 5 € **Ración** approx. 10 €
• Traditional cuisine • Mediterranean décor •
The Paco Meralgo has two bars and two separate entrances; although its most impressive feature is its display cabinets filled with fresh, varied, top quality seafood. A private room is also available.

ⓎⅠ **Bodega 1900**   ⌂ AC

Tamarit 91 ⊠ 08015 – **Ⓜ** *Poble Sec – ℰ 933 25 26 59*   Plan: **K3**
– www.bodega1900.com – Closed Christmas, Holy Week, 3 weeks August,
Sunday and Monday
Ración approx. 8 €
• Traditional cuisine • Neighbourhood •
This restaurant has all the charm of an old-fashioned grocery store. The small menu features grilled dishes, Iberian specialities and homemade preserves, all of excellent quality.

SPAIN - BARCELONA

Tickets
                                    🚫 AC

av. del Paral.lel 164 ✉ *08015* – ⓜ *Espanya*   Plan: **K3**
– www.ticketsbar.es – Closed Christmas, Holy Week, 21 days August,
Sunday and Monday
Tapa 8 € **Ración** approx. 15 € – *(dinner only except Saturday) (booking*
essential)
• Creative • Friendly •
A unique restaurant with lots of colour and several bar counters. The innovative
cuisine on offer here, prepared in front of diners, plays homage to the legendary
dishes that were once created at El Bulli. Bookings can only be made via its website.
➜ Mini airbag relleno de espuma de queso manchego. Gofre aéreo de
albahaca y scamorza. Viaje al mundo en 12 ostras.

Mont Bar
                                🐾 🛋 🚫 AC ⇄

Diputació 220 ✉ *08011* – ⓜ *Universitat* – ☏ *933 23 95 90*   Plan: **K2**
– www.montbar.com – Closed 24-26 December and 10-25 January
Tapa 7 € **Ración** approx. 17 €
• Traditional cuisine • Bistro •
This charming and unusual gastro-bar serves traditional cuisine prepared using
top quality ingredients. Friendly and professional service.

Segons Mercat
                                           AC

Gran Via de les Corts Catalanes 552 ✉ *08011*   Plan: **K2**
– ⓜ *Urgell* – ☏ *934 51 16 98 – www.segonsmercat.com*
Tapa 6 € **Ración** approx. 14 €
• Traditional cuisine • Mediterranean décor •
A modern and spacious restaurant with an informal atmosphere. There is a bar
and an elongated dining room decorated with photos and striking wall panels.
Traditional cuisine.

Cañota
                                         🛋 AC

Lleida 7 ✉ *08002* – ⓜ *Espanya* – ☏ *933 25 91 71*   Plan: **J3**
– www.casadetapas.com – Closed Sunday dinner and Monday
Tapa 8 € **Ración** approx. 14 €
• Traditional cuisine • Friendly •
A pleasant and relaxed tapas restaurant that has received the backing of several
famous chefs. Two dining rooms, classically furnished in regional style, and a
terrace, provide the setting for traditional tapas and raciones. Almost everything
on the menu has been designed for sharing!

Tapas 24
                                         🛋 AC

Diputació 269 ✉ *08007* – ⓜ *Passeig de Gràcia*   Plan: **K2**
– ☏ *934 88 09 77 – www.carlesabellan.com*
Tapa 5 € **Ración** approx. 14 €
• Traditional cuisine • Friendly •
A fun tapas restaurant with a long bar where you can see the kitchen team at
work, and where renowned chef Carles Abellan pays homage to traditional
Catalan cuisine. Don't miss the 'Bikini Comerç 24' sandwich!

Lolita
                                           AC

Tamarit 104 ✉ *08015* – ⓜ *Poble Sec* – ☏ *93 424 52 31*   Plan: **K3**
– www.lolitataperia.com – Closed December, Sunday and Monday
Tapa 6 € – *(dinner only except Friday and Saturday)*
• Traditional cuisine • Neighbourhood •
Situated close to the city's exhibition site, this restaurant stands out for its per-
sonalised decor. Traditional tapas created using top quality ingredients.

Atapa-it
                                           AC

Muntaner 146 ✉ *08036* – ⓜ *Hospital Clínic* – ☏ *934 52 07 82* Plan: **J2**
– www.atapait.com – Closed 15 days August, Sunday and Bank Holidays
Tapa 4 € **Ración** approx. 12 €
• Regional cuisine • Bistro •
Contemporary-style restaurant with a small bar and two dining rooms, both
with an informal feel. It serves modern tapas and small dishes that change
depending on market availability.

Ŷ/ **Niño Viejo**

av. Mistral 54 ⊠ 08015 – Ⓜ Poble Sec – ℰ 933 48 21 94   Plan: **J3**
– www.ninoviejo.es – Closed 24 December-8 January, 10-16 April, 7-27 August, Sunday and Monday
Tapa 5 € **Ración** approx. 16 € – *(dinner only except Thursday, Friday and Saturday)*
• Mexican • Exotic décor •
Unusual, lively, colourful and informal – this taco bar with an ethnic feel serves delicious homemade tacos, antojitos and spicy salsas. High quality Mexican cuisine.

SANT MARTÍ PLAN I

Arts

Marina 19 ⊠ 08005 – Ⓜ Ciutadella-Vila Olímpica   Plan: **C2**
– ℰ 932 21 10 00 – www.hotelartsbarcelona.com
397 rm – ♥♥325/495 € – 114 suites
• Luxury • Design •
Superb in every respect. Occupying one of two glass-fronted towers at the Olympic port, the hotel's many selling points include its magnificent views and a stunning, spacious interior including intimate public areas and top-notch guestrooms high on detail. Extensive lounges adorned with works of art and exquisite dining options complete the picture.
❀❀ **Enoteca** • **Arola** – See restaurant listing

Meliá Barcelona Sky

Pere IV-272 ⊠ 08005 – Ⓜ Poblenou – ℰ 933 67 20 70   Plan: **D2**
– www.meliahotels.com
249 rm – ♥90/385 € ♥♥185/438 € – ☐ 18 € – 9 suites
• Business • Design •
The Meliá's main selling points are its modern, designer inspired lobby, lounge bar, and contemporary bedrooms, most enjoying splendid views. The good dining options on offer are complemented by the uniquely decorated restaurant in the lobby with a menu focusing on light and traditional cuisine.
❀ **Dos Cielos** – See restaurant listing

XxX **Enoteca** – Hotel Arts
❀❀
Marina 19 ⊠ 08005 – Ⓜ Ciutadella-Vila Olímpica   Plan: **C2**
– ℰ 934 83 81 08 – www.hotelartsbarcelona.com – Closed 3-11 December, 5-20 March, Sunday and Monday
Menu 170 € – Carte 99/120 €
• Modern cuisine • Mediterranean décor •
The Enoteca boasts a very bright dining room, pure Mediterranean in style and with wine racks providing part of the attractive decor. The perfectly crafted contemporary cuisine has its roots in traditional dishes. It is prepared with top quality ingredients and superb attention to detail.
→ Lenguado y el Mediterráneo. Pichón, sus albóndigas, gelée de patata, salsifí y café. Milhojas de chocolate y café.

XxX **Dos Cielos** (Sergio y Javier Torres) – Hotel Meliá Barcelona Sky
❀
Pere IV-272 ⊠ 08005 – Ⓜ Poblenou   Plan: **D2**
– ℰ 933 67 20 70 – www.doscielos.com
– Closed January, Sunday and Monday
Menu 110 € – Carte 70/95 € – *(dinner only June-15 September)*
• Modern cuisine • Design •
Occupying the 24th floor of the Meliá Barcelona Sky hotel, this restaurant's surprising design includes a kitchen incorporated into the dining room and a steel bar (where guests can also eat), as well as a terrace. Innovative cuisine is constantly striving for new flavours. Superb views of a less-photographed side of Barcelona!
→ Carabineros de Huelva, algas, pepino y ají. Espalda de cabrito lechal, albaricoques, anchoas y migas de pan. Chocolate, whisky y regaliz.

XX **Els Pescadors** 🛋 AC

pl. Prim 1 ✉ *08005* – Ⓜ *Poblenou* – ☏ *932 25 20 18*   Plan: **D2**
– *www.elspescadors.com* – *Closed 23 December-4 January*
Menu 42/78 € – Carte 33/74 €
• Seafood • Trendy •
This restaurant has three dining rooms, one in early-20C café style and two with
a more modern decor. A generous menu based on fish and seafood with rice
dishes and cod to the fore.

XX **Arola** – Hotel Arts 🍸 < 🛋 AC ⇔ 🚗

Marina 19 ✉ *08005* – Ⓜ *Ciutadella-Vila Olímpica*   Plan: **C2**
– ☏ *934 83 80 90* – *www.hotelartsbarcelona.com* – *Closed 1-
30 January, Tuesday and Wednesday*
Carte 65/108 €
• Creative • Trendy •
Modern, urban and informal, including live music sessions with a DJ. Savour a
creative tapas- and ración-based menu either in the dining room or on the
chill-out terrace.

NORTH of AV. DIAGONAL   **PLAN III**

🏨 **Casa Fuster** 🍸 Ló ṫ AC ṡ⅓

passeig de Gràcia 132 ✉ *08008* – Ⓜ *Diagonal*   Plan: **K1**
– ☏ *932 55 30 00* – *www.hotelcasafuster.com*
85 rm – ♦♦198/600 € – � 30 € – 20 suites
• Luxury • Design • Cosy •
A hotel occupying an impressively Modernist-style property with facilities that
include the Café Vienés with live jazz, top-notch guestrooms, and a panoramic
bar on the rooftop terrace. Boasting views of the city's most elegant avenue,
the restaurant offers à la carte dining, complemented by an interesting choice
of set menus.

🏨 **G.H. La Florida** 🍸 ⊗ < 🛋 Ló ⅂ 🖥 ṫ AC ṡ⅓ 🚗

carret. Vallvidrera al Tibidabo 83-93 ✉ *08035*   Plan I: **B2**
– ☏ *932 59 30 00* – *www.hotellaflorida.com*
62 rm ⊆ – ♦♦160/450 € – 8 suites
• Luxury • Chain • Design •
Find charm and avant-garde design on the top of Tibidabo hill, with an interior
created by famous designers and delightful terraces built on different levels. Its
biggest attraction is without doubt the spectacular view of the city from both
the hotel and restaurant.

🏨 **ABaC** AC 🚗

av. del Tibidabo 1 ✉ *08022* – Ⓜ *Av. Tibidabo*   Plan I: **B2**
– ☏ *933 19 66 00* – *www.abacbarcelona.com*
15 rm – ♦♦280/861 € – ⊆ 36 €
• Luxury • Modern •
Enjoy a stay in superb, highly contemporary guestrooms featuring the latest
smart technology and even chromotherapy in the bathrooms. Some spa services are also available.
❀❀ **ABaC** – See restaurant listing

🏨 **Primero Primera** Ló ⅂ ṫ AC 🚗

Doctor Carulla 25-29 ✉ *08017* – Ⓜ *Tres Torres*   Plan: **I1**
– ☏ *934 17 56 00* – *www.primeroprimera.com*
25 rm ⊆ – ♦155/315 € ♦♦165/325 € – 5 suites
• Traditional • Elegant •
This hotel is in a residential district with access via a wide, carriage-style entrance. Attractive spiral staircase leading to eclectic guestrooms, with those
under the eaves the preferred choice.

Pol & Grace   ⚿ AC ♨ 🚗

Guillen Tell 49 ✉ *08006 –* Ⓜ *Plaça Molina*
– ☏ 934 15 40 00 – www.polgracehotel.es   Plan: **J1**
61 rm *–* **♥♥**80/220 € *–* ⬚ 11 €
• Townhouse • Functional •
A cool, urban hotel with functional facilities and a quirky theme for every floor
and room. Located to the north of the city, not far from the Parc Güell, but with
good transport links to the main sights.

XxxX   Via Veneto   🍸 AC ⇔
�☼

Ganduxer 10 ✉ *08021 –* Ⓜ *Hospital Clínic*   Plan: **I2**
– ☏ 932 00 72 44 – www.viavenetorestaurant.com – Closed August,
Saturday lunch and Sunday
Menu 85/125 € *–* Carte 70/100 €
• Classic cuisine • Classic décor •
A famous property in attractive Belle Epoque-style with a dining room laid out
on several levels and a number of private dining areas. Impressively updated
classic menu with game in season and interesting tasting menus. Its wine cellar,
featuring around 1 800 labels, is one of the best in Spain.
➜ "Espardenyes" salteadas con "rossejat" de fideos. Pato asado en su pro-
pio jugo "a la presse". Nuestra torrija con crema de avellanas y helado de
aceite.

XxxX   ABaC *– Hotel ABaC*   🍸 🏠 AC ⇔ 🚗
☼☼

av. del Tibidabo 1 ✉ *08022 –* Ⓜ *Av. Tibidabo*   Plan I: **B2**
– ☏ 933 19 66 00 – www.abacbarcelona.com
Menu 140/170 € *– (tasting menu only)*
• Creative • Design •
A superb culinary experience awaits in the upper reaches of the city. There is a
terrace, designer inspired bar, and a bright, contemporary-style dining room.
ABaC's innovative, technically faultless cuisine is fascinating in its creativity and
pairing of products.
➜ Jugo de cebollas asadas con esferas de scamorza ahumada, nueces y
pieles de naranja. Rodaballo asado, pieles glaseadas y jugo de espinas ahu-
madas con berenjenas yodadas. Infusión helada de chocolate especiado,
rocas de cacao y vainilla, mantequilla y pieles cítricas.

XxX   Hofmann   ⚿ AC ⇔
☼

La Granada del Penedès 14-16 ✉ *08006 –* Ⓜ *Diagonal*   Plan: **J1**
– ☏ 932 18 71 65 – www.hofmann-bcn.com – Closed Christmas, Holy
Week, August, Saturday lunch, Sunday and Bank Holidays
Menu 45/80 € *–* Carte 55/82 €
• Modern cuisine • Classic décor •
The word gastronomy reflects the great passion of May Hofmann, the founder-
chef who set the guidelines to be followed in one of the country's most influential restaurant schools. Her daughter Silvia and the current students continue
her work, producing cuisine that is full of creativity.
➜ Canelón de ternera con foie, crema de queso trufada y teja crujiente de
parmesano. Bogavante a la parrilla con verduras de temporada y salsa
bearnesa. Crujientes templados de vainilla.

XxX   Freixa Tradició   AC
☺

Sant Elíes 22 ✉ *08006 –* Ⓜ *Plaça Molina*   Plan: **J1**
– ☏ 932 09 75 59 – www.freixatradicio.com – Closed Holy Week, 21 days
August, Sunday dinner and Monday
Menu 25/58 € *–* Carte 30/45 €
• Regional cuisine • Design •
Run by the couple that own it, Freixa Tradició has developed into one of the
city's gastronomic institutions since it opened over 30 years ago. In the minima-
list-style dining room you can savour delicious and well-prepared traditional
Catalan cuisine created using a whole host of seasonal ingredients.

XxX **Roig Robí**   🛋 🅰🅒 ⇔

Sèneca 20 ✉ *08006 –* Ⓜ *Diagonal – ℰ 932 18 92 22*   Plan: **K1**
– www.roigrobi.com – Closed 21 days August, Saturday lunch and Sunday
Menu 33/68 € – Carte 45/65 €
• Regional cuisine • Classic décor •
A pleasant restaurant in a classic setting that includes a winter garden-style
dining room laid out around a patio-garden. Traditional Catalan à la carte
dining, set menus and an extensive wine list.

XxX **Tram-Tram**   🛋 🅰🅒 ⇔

Major de Sarrià 121 ✉ *08017 –* Ⓜ *Reina Elisenda*   Plan I: **A2**
– ℰ 932 04 85 18 – www.tram-tram.com – Closed Holy Week, 15 days
August, Sunday dinner, Monday and Bank Holidays
Menu 28/70 € – Carte 40/65 €
• Modern cuisine • Family •
A classically furnished restaurant, the name of which pays homage to this old
form of transport. Updated traditional cuisine with the occasional international
influence, and the option of ordering one of the set menus.

XxX **Botafumeiro**   🅰🅒 ⇔

Gran de Gràcia 81 ✉ *08012 –* Ⓜ *Fontana*   Plan: **J1**
– ℰ 932 18 42 30 – www.botafumeiro.es
Carte approx. 65 €
• Seafood • Classic décor •
Botafumeiro opened its doors in 1975, hence its status as one of Barcelona's
premier seafood restaurants. Galician products are to the fore, along with big
cuts of meat and a variety of platters.

XX **La Balsa**   🛋 ᴋ 🅰🅒

Infanta Isabel 4 ✉ *08022 – ℰ 932 11 50 48*   Plan I: **B1**
– www.labalsarestaurant.com – Closed August, Sunday dinner and
Monday
Menu 20/65 € – Carte 38/56 €
• Mediterranean cuisine • Cosy •
A classic address whose renovation has transformed it into a small architectural
jewel nestled amid a haven of peace and quiet. Good Mediterranean cooking
with a focus on quality products, which you can also enjoy on La Balsa's charming outdoor terraces.

XX **Asador de Aranda**   🛋 🅰🅒 ⇔ 🅿

av. del Tibidabo 31 ✉ *08022 – ℰ 934 17 01 15*   Plan I: **B1-2**
– www.asadordearanda.com – Closed Sunday dinner
Menu 41/50 € – Carte 35/48 €
• Meats and grills • Cosy •
This restaurant occupies the incomparable Casa Roviralta, a Modernist building
also known as El Frare Blanc. The culinary focus here is on typical Castilian cuisine, with a house speciality of roast lamb cooked in a clay oven.

XX **Hisop** (Oriol Ivern)   🅰🅒
ⓢ
passatge de Marimon 9 ✉ *08021 –* Ⓜ *Hospital Clínic*   Plan: **J2**
– ℰ 932 41 32 33 – www.hisop.com – Closed 1-8 January, Saturday lunch,
Sunday and Bank Holidays
Menu 32/61 € – Carte approx. 59 €
• Creative • Minimalist •
Because of its size, this modern restaurant offers guests an intimate dining
experience. Enjoy fresh and creative dishes based around traditional recipes
in the minimalist dining room. Everything is prepared with locally sourced
and seasonal products brought together to produce some interesting combi-
nations.
➜ Gambas de Vilanova con chocolate. Salmonete con mayonesa de
moluscos. Chocolate con pimento amarillo y pimienta Timut.

XX
Mil921 🛱 🗚

Casanova 211 ⊠ 08021 – Ⓜ Hospital Clinic   Plan: **J2**
– ℰ 934 14 34 94 – www.mil921.com – Closed Sunday and Monday dinner
Menu 21/48 € – Carte 36/54 €
• Modern cuisine • Mediterranean décor •
This restaurant is named after the year in which the chef's grandfather was
born. It offers updated traditional cuisine with a nod to old recipes. Make sure
you try the steak tartare (classic or Japanese-style).

X
❀
Céleri (Xavier Pellicer) 🗚

passatge de Marimon 5 ⊠ 08021 – Ⓜ Hospital Clinic   Plan: **J2**
– ℰ 932 52 95 94 – Closed Sunday
Menu 25 € – Carte 36/45 €
• Mediterranean cuisine • Design •
A contemporary eatery occupying the ground floor of the Woki Organic Market.
The focus is on ecological and organic vegetarian cooking in keeping with the
latest raw food concepts, which aim to extract the purest flavours from every
ingredient. In very few restaurants are you likely to see as close up a view of
the kitchen as you are here.
➔ Gazpacho de remolacha, tomate, uva y flores. Coliflor, huevo a 62º,
bacalao y aceite ahumado. Torrija impregnada de leche de arroz y sorbete
de coco.

X
La Venta ← 🛱 🗚 ⇔

pl. Dr. Andreu ⊠ 08035 – ℰ 932 12 64 55   Plan I: **B1**
*– www.laventarestaurant.com – Closed Sunday August and Sunday dinner
rest of the Year*
Menu 44/62 € – Carte 32/50 €
• Catalan • Traditional décor •
A not-to-be-missed experience given its location in the terminus of the Tramvia
Blau tram, with its delightful views of the rooftops of Barcelona. A mix of tradi-
tional, Catalan and Mediterranean cuisine.

X
☺
Vivanda 🛱 🕹 🗚 ⇔

Major de Sarrià 134 ⊠ 08017 – Ⓜ Reina Elisenda   Plan I: **A2**
– ℰ 932 03 19 18 – www.vivanda.cat – Closed Sunday dinner and Monday
Menu 35 € – Carte 28/39 €
• Traditional cuisine • Cosy •
A unique restaurant offering a traditional menu centred around small dishes
(slightly larger than half raciones) advertised as *platos del mes* (dishes of the
month). Attractive tree-shaded terrace and a modern interior combining stan-
dard tables for restaurant dining and bar tables for tapas.

X
Silvestre 🗚 ⇔

Santaló 101 ⊠ 08021 – Ⓜ Muntaner – ℰ 932 41 40 31   Plan: **J1**
*– www.restaurante-silvestre.com – Closed Holy Week, 15 days August,
Saturday dinner July-August,Saturday lunch, Sunday and Bank Holidays*
Menu 25/50 € – Carte 30/40 €
• Traditional cuisine • Cosy •
This restaurant is cosy and welcoming with various private dining areas that add
an intimate feel. Traditional and international cuisine, including appealing fixed
menus and the option of half-raciones for every dish. Try the pig's trotters filled
with cep mushrooms, or the Catalan sausage (butifarra) with port wine... delicious!

𝒴/
Bardeni-Caldeni 🗚

Valencia 454 ⊠ 08013 – Ⓜ Sagrada Familia   Plan: **L1**
– ℰ 932 32 58 11 – www.bardeni.es – Closed August, Sunday and Monday
Tapa 12 €
• Meats and grills • Design •
A restaurant in which meat is very much centre stage. The ambience is that of
an old butcher's shop, enhanced by the exclusive chef's table.

AT SANTA COLOMA de GRAMENET

XX Ca n'Armengol · AC ⇔ 🚗

*Prat de La Riba 1 ☒ 08921 Santa Coloma de Gramenet
– Ⓜ Santa Coloma – 𝒞 933 91 68 55 – www.canarmengol.net – Closed
Holy Week, 2 weeks August, Sunday dinner, Monday and Tuesday dinner*
Menu 11/33 € – Carte 28/48 €

• Traditional cuisine • Classic décor •

A family-run restaurant with a classic ambience. There are two entrances: one
directly through to the old bar, where customers can dine from the set menu,
and the other to the dining rooms and private section reserved for à la carte
dining. Traditionally based cuisine with the option of half-raciones (portions).

XX Lluerna (Víctor Quintillà) · AC ⇔

*Rafael Casanovas 31 ☒ 08921 Santa Coloma de Gramenet
– Ⓜ Santa Coloma – 𝒞 933 91 08 20 – www.lluernarestaurant.com
– Closed 2-14 April, 7-28 August, Sunday and Monday*
Menu 37/72 € – Carte 41/69 €

• Modern cuisine • Fashionable •

A centrally located restaurant well run by the couple that owns it. In the small,
minimalist-style dining room, discover up-to-date cuisine with a solid traditional
base, which you can choose from the à la carte as well as several tasting menus.
The dishes here are perfectly cooked and showcase creativity and meticulous
presentation.

→ Rabo de cerdo ibérico con cohombros. Langostinos de San Carlos salteados con verduras. Crema de arroz con leche y toffee.

VALENCIA
VALÈNCIA

Population: 787 266

Gregory Gerault/hemis.fr

Spain's third largest city offers undeniable character and charm, with unspoilt beaches, numerous museums, amazing nightlife and rip roaring fiestas. The city sits in an enviable position on the Mediterranean coast, with its port and its long golden beach to the east. A mile or so inland is the heart of the city, its beautiful old town; a labyrinth of ancient cobbled streets which pay testament to its rich history, with medieval churches, Renaissance halls of trade and baroque mansions layered on top of an earlier Roman city.

Valencia is the home of paella, and a thriving café scene gives you ample opportunity to tuck into it. The sun shines most of the time here, but if you want shelter there are plenty of museums on hand to offer a cool escape. Culturally, the city has been propelled into the major league in the last few decades. What's taken it there is the exciting City of Arts and Sciences complex, a 21C addition to the city's skyline built within the confines of the Turia River Park; the fabulous nine-mile green space created when the river was diverted after flooding in 1957. This futuristic 'city' draws over four million visitors each year, is made up of four stunning buildings and is home to a science museum, an opera house, an aquarium and an Imax cinema with a planetarium and laserium.

VALENCIA IN...

→ **ONE DAY**
Plaza de la Virgen, La Lonja, Central Market, a trip to the beach.

→ **TWO DAYS**
IVAM (Valencian Institute of Modern Art), City of Arts and Sciences, Carmen district nightlife.

→ **THREE DAYS**
A stroll along the Turia River Park.

PRACTICAL INFORMATION

ARRIVAL-DEPARTURE

🛬 Valencia Airport is 8km west of the city. Metro trains (lines 3 and 5) take about 25min. The Airport bus Number 150, which runs every 26min, takes around 45min.

GETTING AROUND

Valencia has an integrated transport system with metro, buses and trams. Single tickets for the metro, which has six lines, are cheap and can be purchased from station machines or ticket offices. You can buy a one day pass for the metro, trams and buses or, alternatively, a more cost-effective 10-trip pass. Another useful investment is the Valencia Tourist Card, available from tourist offices, hotels, tobacconists and kiosks. It offers free travel on all forms of public transport, as well as discounts in museums, shops, restaurants and on various leisure activities; the cards last for one, two, or three days.

CALENDAR HIGHLIGHTS

January
Epiphany, St Vincent's Day.

March
Las Fallas (the arrival of spring).

April
Semana Santa Marinera (Holy Week).

May
The Crosses of May, Feast of Our Lady of the Forsaken.

June
Corpus Christi.

July
Feria de Julio (July Fair).

August
La Tomatina (battle of the tomatoes) in the village on Buñol.

EATING OUT

Valencia is the city of paella. It was invented here, and this is the place to try it in infinite varieties. For a gargantuan helping, head off to the Las Arenas beach promenade, which is lined with a whole legion of seafood restaurants. On a hot day, the traditional liquid accompaniment is agua de Valencia, a potentially lethal combination of orange juice, Cava and vodka. Most restaurants remain very Spanish in character, and if you're not eating paella, then you'll probably be enjoying tapas, with an emphasis on the excellent local cured hams and cheeses. A little different is the

local delicacy of all i pebre, a mouth-watering meal of stewed eels from the local wetlands, served in a garlic and red pepper sauce. The drink to cool down with is horchata: it's tigernut milk – a mixture of nuts, cinnamon, sugar and water – and is best enjoyed with a doughy cake. Meal times can throw the unwary visitor: lunch is often not served until two in the afternoon, and dinner, in general, is never eaten before nine at night.

Caro H.

企 & AC

Almirante 14 ⊠ *46003 –* ℰ *963 05 90 00*
– www.carohotel.com

Plan: **G1**

25 rm – ♦170/280 € ♦♦180/300 € – ⌸ 22 € – 1 suite

• Luxury • Palace • Minimalist •

A small 19C palace full of fascinating historical interest. Important archaeological remains have been preserved in almost every guestroom, where contemporary urban style sits in harmony with Roman and Moorish artefacts. The restaurant combines perfectly these vestiges of the past with a more modern setting. Contemporary à la carte menu.

Ricard Camarena

AC

Doctor Sumsi 4 (previsto traslado a av. de Burjassot 52)
⊠ *46005 –* Ⓜ *Xàtiva –* ℰ *963 35 54 18*
– www.ricardcamarenarestaurant.com – Closed 1-22 January, Sunday and Monday

Plan: **G3**

Menu 75/105 € – *(tasting menu only)*

• Modern cuisine • Design •

A restaurant boasting a thoroughly modern and meticulous look. There is a unique private section and highly original table that dominates the room from its position opposite the open-view kitchen. The concise choice of daily à la carte choices and the tasting menu demonstrate excellent culinary skill.

→ Ostra valenciana, aguacate y horchata de galanga. Paletilla de cabrito, ensalada de pepino valenciano, yogur y agua de rosas. Mango maduro, curry frio, hierbas y semillas.

Riff (Bernd Knöller)

88 AC

Conde de Altea 18 ⊠ *46005 –* Ⓜ *Colón*
– ℰ *963 33 53 53 – www.restaurante-riff.com – Closed August, Sunday and Monday*

Plan: **H3**

Menu 35/100 € – Carte 55/74 €

• Creative • Design •

This centrally located restaurant has an attractive layout and a carefully styled minimalist look. The owner-chef, who is German but considers himself more of a Valencian, creates innovative cuisine. This is based around seasonal, local ingredients of the highest quality. Interesting set menus.

→ Ostra valenciana y habas. Oreja de cerdo con lentejas negras. Ruibarbo con lichi y rosas.

El Poblet

88 & AC ⟷

Correos 8-1º ⊠ *46002 –* Ⓜ *Colón –* ℰ *961 11 11 06*
– www.elpobletrestaurante.com – Closed Saturday lunch August, Sunday and Tuesday dinner

Plan: **G2**

Menu 50/110 € – Carte 41/57 €

• Creative • Trendy •

In the heart of Valencia, this comfortable restaurant has a contemporary look. It encapsulates the creativity developed in Dénia by the award-winning chef Quique Dacosta. Its extensive à la carte choices are complemented by two interesting and reasonably priced set menus.

→ Cubalibre de foie. Arroz cenizas. Campo de cítricos.

Civera

88 🍴 & AC ⟷

Mosén Femades 10 ⊠ *46002 –* Ⓜ *Colón*
– ℰ *963 52 97 64 – www.marisqueriascivera.com*

Plan: **G3**

Menu 40 € – Carte 35/65 €

• Seafood • Classic décor •

The Civera specialises in fish, seafood and savoury rice dishes. It has a bar with several tables, enticing display cabinets and a dining room with a maritime ambience. Interesting glass-fronted wine cellar.

SPAIN - VALENCIA

XX **El Asador de Aranda**   AK

Félix Pizcueta 8 ⊠ 46004 – **Ⓜ** *Xátiva – ☏ 963 52 97 91*   Plan: **G3**
– www.asadordearanda.net – Closed Sunday dinner
Menu 38 € – Carte 35/45 €
• Traditional cuisine • Classic décor •
Castilian-style furniture, stained glass, coffered ceilings, and an enticing wood-fired oven provide the backdrop to this traditional eatery. Although the speciality is roast suckling pig and lamb, the grilled red meats on offer are also fantastic.

XX **Canyar**   AK ⇔

Segorbe 5 ⊠ 46004 – **Ⓜ** *Bailén – ☏ 963 41 80 82*   Plan: **F3**
– www.canyarrestaurante.com – Closed August and Sunday
Menu 45/73 € – Carte 28/49 €
• Seafood • Classic décor •
The Canyar is somewhat unusual in that it combines old-style decor with modernist detail. It features an astutely selected wine list and high quality fish that arrives daily from Denia.

XX **Lienzo**   AK

🕙 *pl.de Tetuan 18 ⊠ 46003 –* **Ⓜ** *Alameda*   Plan: **G1**
– ☏ 963 52 10 81 – www.restaurantelienzo.com – Closed 14-28 August,
Sunday dinner and Monday
Menu 19/55 € – Carte 35/45 €
• Mediterranean cuisine • Trendy •
Lienzo occupies the ground floor of an elegant building in which the modern layout comes as a surprise. It has two dining rooms separated by a glass-fronted wine cellar and a semi open-view kitchen. Enjoy cuisine with a Mediterranean flavour, a few fusion dishes and several set menus, all of which are highly enticing.

XX **Blanqueries**   AK ⇔

🕙 *Blanqueries 12 (entrada por Padre Huérfanos) ⊠ 46002*   Plan: **F1**
– ☏ 963 91 22 39 – www.blanquerias.com – Closed Holly Week, Sunday
dinner and Monday
Menu 20/27 € – Carte 25/36 €
• Modern cuisine • Minimalist •
This restaurant with a thoroughly cosmopolitan feel is located next to the Torres de Serranos. The interior is dominated by varying tones of white and provides the backdrop for seasonally influenced cuisine with a creative touch.

XX **Eladio**   AK ⇔

Chiva 40 ⊠ 46018 – ☏ 963 84 22 44   Plan I: **B2**
– www.restauranteeladio.es – Closed Holy Week, 5 days August, Sunday
and Monday dinner
Menu 30 € – Carte 25/53 €
• Galician • Classic décor •
This professionally run restaurant boasts a live shellfish tank, a bar, a classically styled dining room and a separate private room. Traditional menu with its roots firmly established in Galician cuisine.

X **Saiti**   AK

🕙 *Reina Doña Germana 4 ⊠ 46005 – ☏ 960 05 41 24*   Plan: **H3**
– www.saiti.es – Closed 15-31 August, Sunday and Monday dinner
Menu 27/50 € – Carte 30/46 €
• Traditional cuisine • Friendly •
A contemporary yet informal bistro-style restaurant in which the kitchen team's ethic focuses on exciting cuisine, hard work and a desire to please. Delicious cooking teeming with interesting combinations is presented in a manner that showcases the quality of ingredients used.

VALENCIA-MANISES

A GODELLA **B** Palmaret

5 Lliria Burjassot-Godella

BORBÒTO

TVV BURJASSOT

V. Andrés E. Burjassot

Campus

Ctra del Pla Fira U St. Joan

del Pou La Granja

CV 31 Benimàmet Empalme Juan XXIII

1 Les Carolines Cantereria Palau de Congressos Av. de Juan XXIII

PATERNA PALACIO DE Florista

CONGRESOS Av.

Campament CV 31 Tavella Camp Garbí Benicalap Trànsits

CV 31 del Túria de Beniferri Av. Dr. Peset Aleixandre

Safor Marxalenes Reus

las Kaymus Avilés Burjassot

Maestro Campanar Reus

Gal Av. Valencianes

MISLATA Av. Rodrigo CAMPANAR Valencia Centre

Mislata-Almassil (Plan II)

San Antonio Av. M. Fernando

2 Ronda Cáuce de Falla Pechina Gran Via de CATEDRA

Mislata Paseo Av. de Pérez el Católico Gran Via

Nou d'Octubre Galdós Ramón y Cajal ESTACIÓN

Ronda 338 Av. del Cid Av. DEL NORTE

XIRIVELLA del Av. del Cid Eladio Carlos

Av. Tres Forques Archiduque Jesús 2 Estacione

Tres Giorgeta

Nuevo Río Picaña Cruces Hospital Martir Av. de

Marginal Patraix

Marginal de Av. de G. Aguilar San

Turia Sant Isidre Vicente Av. del Pianista

V 30 M. Carrasco

Nuevo Ronda

CV 36 Camino València-Sud Ronda

Barranc V 30

3 Picanya V 400

Picanya Paiporta Av. del País

Xiva BENETÚSSER de Madrid Valenciano

PAIPORTA Av. del V 31

Sur Av. Reial SEDAVÍ

A **B**

● Hotel

● Restaurant

688

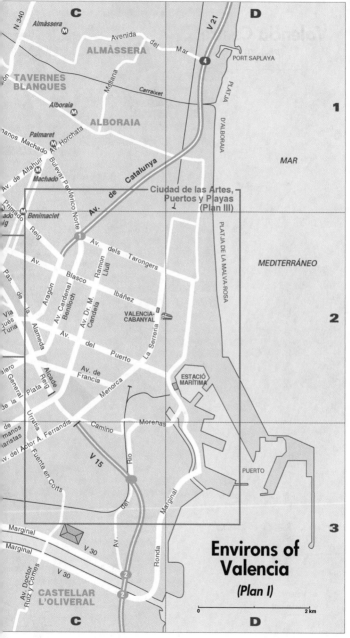

Environs of Valencia
(Plan I)

0   2 km

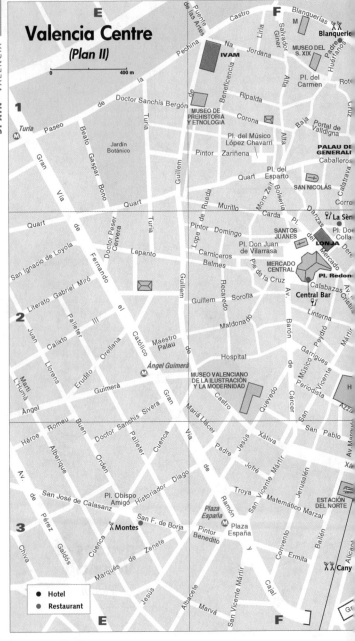

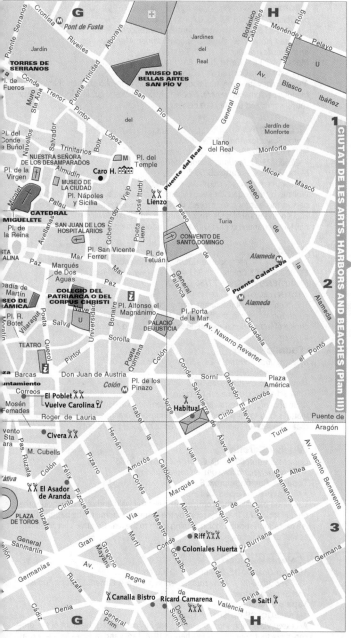

X
🌐

Montes
[AC]

pl. Obispo Amigó 5 ✉ *46007* – Ⓜ *Pl. Espanya*   Plan: **E3**
– ☎ 963 85 50 25 – www.restaurantemontes.com
– Closed Holy Week, August, Sunday dinner, Monday
and Tuesday dinner
Menu 14/23 € – Carte 30/43 €
• Traditional cuisine • Classic décor •
A restaurant with a very traditional feel and lots of loyal customers thanks to its friendly, personalised service. Moderately priced classic cuisine, including tasty soups, stews and savoury rice dishes.

X
🌐

2 Estaciones
🛋 [AC]

Pintor Salvador Abril 28 ✉ *46002*   Plan I: **B2**
– ☎ 963 03 46 70 – www.2estaciones.com
– Closed 23-31 January, Sunday and Monday
Menu 35/48 € – Carte 35/50 €
• Mediterranean cuisine • Bistro •
Well run by the restaurant's two dynamic chefs, who also happen to be the partners in this gastronomic project. Informal bistro ambience with an open-view kitchen and unusual tables made with the legs of old sewing machines. Seasonal, Mediterranean cuisine with a contemporary twist.

X

Habitual
[AC] ⟺

Jorge Juan 19 (Mercado de Colón, planta inferior)   Plan: **H2**
✉ *46004* – Ⓜ *Colón* – ☎ *963 44 56 31 – www.habitual.es*
Menu 18/29 € – Carte 27/56 €
• International • Trendy •
This highly unusual restaurant, part of chef Ricard Camarena's stable, boasts a surprising design in the Modernist Mercado de Colón. Extensive à la carte choice of international and Mediterranean-inspired cuisine.

X

Canalla Bistro
[AC]

Maestro José Serrano 5 ✉ *46003 – ☎ 963 74 05 09*   Plan: **G3**
– www.canallabistro.com
Menu 16/26 € – Carte 26/38 €
• Modern cuisine • Friendly •
A fun and informal restaurant with an open-view kitchen and a decor that partly features crates that were once used to transport oranges. It offers world cuisine that is perfect for sharing and prepared using local ingredients.

🍴

Vuelve Carolina
& [AC]

Correos 8 ✉ *46002* – Ⓜ *Colón – ☎ 963 21 86 86*   Plan: **G2**
– www.vuelvecarolina.com – Closed Sunday
Tapa 4 € **Ración** approx. 9 €
• Creative • Tapas bar •
The wood panelling that completely covers the walls and ceilings provides the unique look here. The large room by the entrance is home to the bar, and there is a more sophisticated looking dining room to the rear. Creative à la carte tapas, as well as two set menus.

🍴

Coloniales Huerta
🛋 [AC]

Maestro Gozalbo 13 ✉ *46005* – Ⓜ *Colón*   Plan: **H3**
– ☎ 963 34 80 09 – www.colonialeshuerta.com – Closed 15 days August
and Sunday dinner
Tapa 6 € **Ración** approx. 14 €
• Traditional cuisine • Cosy •
Accessed via a wine shop, this restaurant has maintained the spirit of the grocery store that opened its doors here in 1916. Tapas and raciones for sharing, as well as attractive menus.

La Sènia

Sènia 2 ✉ 46001 – ✆ 611 49 76 77 Plan: **F2**
– www.tabernalasenia.net
Tapa 7 € **Ración** approx. 14 € – *(dinner only except Friday, Saturday and Sunday)*
• Mediterranean cuisine • Rustic •
Located right in the heart of Valencia, La Sènia has a very clear culinary philosophy: simplicity and quality. This rustic, informal restaurant is a good option if you are looking for contemporary, Mediterranean-style tapas prepared on the spot.

Central Bar

pl. del Mercado ✉ 46001 – ✆ 963 82 92 23 Plan: **F2**
– www.centralbar.es – Closed Sunday
Tapa 3.50 € **Ración** approx. 10 € – *(lunch only)*
• Traditional cuisine • Trendy •
Another property in chef Ricard Camarena's stable, with the added attraction of a location inside the city's impressive central market. Seasonal cuisine, daily suggestions, and delicious baguette-style bocadillos!

CIUDAD DE LAS ARTES – HARBOURS – BEACHES PLAN III

The Westin València

Amadeo de Saboya 16 ✉ 46010 – Ⓜ Alameda Plan: **J1**
– ✆ 963 62 59 00 – www.westinvalencia.com
130 rm – 140/400 € 160/420 € – 24 € – 5 suites
• Luxury • Historic • Classic •
The city's Westin occupies a historic building with an attractive Modernist look. Delightful interior garden, elegant lounges, plus superbly equipped guestrooms, including the spectacular Royal Suite, whose decor is courtesy of the designer Francis Montesinos. Interesting dining options.
Komori – See restaurant listing

Las Arenas

Eugenia Viñes 22 ✉ 46011 Plan: **K2**
– Ⓜ Marina Real Juan Carlos I – ✆ 963 12 06 00
– www.hotelvalencialasarenas.com
243 rm – 150/565 € – 23 € – 10 suites
• Luxury • Business • Classic •
This luxury hotel, located right on the beach, is divided between three buildings and features welcoming public areas, superb meeting rooms, and well-appointed guestrooms. In the elegant Brasserie Sorolla the focus is very much on creative cuisine.

Alejandro del Toro

Amadeo de Saboya 15 ✉ 46010 – Ⓜ Aragón Plan: **J1**
– ✆ 963 93 40 46 – www.restaurantealejandrodeltoro.com – Closed 1-15 September, 24 December-1 January, Sunday dinner and Monday
Menu 24/82 € – Carte 29/51 €
• Creative • Minimalist •
The owner-chef here conjures up creative cuisine in a spacious, minimalist-style dining room with a glass-fronted wine cellar with views through to the kitchen. Alternatively, choose from a more informal menu on the bistro-style terrace.

Vertical

Luis García Berlanga 19 ✉ 46023 – ✆ 963 30 38 00 Plan: **J2**
– www.restaurantevertical.com – Closed Sunday
Menu 50/85 € – *(tasting menu only)*
• Creative • Design •
In addition to its interesting creative cuisine, which is reflected in its gastronomic menus, Vertical stands out for its attractive decor and excellent views from its location on the top floor of the Ilunion Aqua 4 hotel. Contemporary look in the dining room, as well as an unusual chill-out terrace.

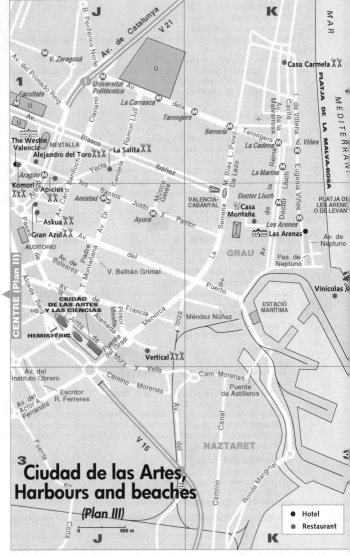

Ciudad de las Artes, Harbours and beaches
(Plan III)

0   500 m

Hotel
Restaurant

SPAIN - VALENCIA

XXX **Komori** – Hotel The Westin València 🛜 ᵫ 🄰🄺 ✿ 🚗

General Gil Dolz ✉ *46010 –* Ⓜ *Alameda* Plan: **J1**
*– ☏ 961 86 62 90 – www.restaurantekomori.com – Closed Holy Week, 15
days August, Saturday lunch, Sunday and Bank Holidays*
Menu 50/70 € – Carte 40/80 €
• Japanese • Minimalist •
A Japanese eatery that follows in the footsteps of the famous Kabuki restaurant
in Madrid, both in terms of its decor and cuisine. The Japanese charcoal grill
here is unique in Spain.

XX **Apicius** 🕸 🄰🄺

Eolo 7 ✉ *46021 –* Ⓜ *Aragón – ☏ 963 93 63 01* Plan: **J1**
*– www.restaurante-apicius.com – Closed Holy Week, August, Saturday
lunch and Sunday*
Menu 25/46 € – Carte 32/53 €
• Modern cuisine • Minimalist •
The single dining room is both spacious and contemporary in feel and the
menus have an emphasis on modern, seasonal cuisine. The extensive wine cellar has a particularly fine selection of German whites.

XX **Vinícolas** ⩽ 🛜 🄰🄺 🄿

Marina Real Juan Carlos I, Local F2 (Marina Sur) Plan: **K2**
✉ *46024 – ☏ 961 10 22 44 – www.vinicolasvalencia.com – Closed
Monday except summer and Sunday dinner*
Menu 35/65 € – Carte 45/78 €
• Traditional cuisine • Minimalist •
An interesting option, given its setting inside a glass cube with a highly minima-
list look. The à la carte menu offers a pleasantly updated take on traditional cui-
sine with a focus on technique, presentation and intense flavours.

XX **Gran Azul** ᵫ 🄰🄺 ✿

🙂 *av. Aragón 12* ✉ *46021 –* Ⓜ *Aragón – ☏ 961 47 45 23* Plan: **J2**
*– www.granazulrestaurante.com – Closed 12-27 August and Sunday
dinner*
Menu 35/65 € – Carte 30/50 €
• Traditional cuisine • Mediterranean décor •
Gran Azul has a contemporary and informal feel. The culinary bias is on savoury
rice and grilled dishes, the latter cooked on a combined Josper grill-oven. The
enticing food display cabinet sets the tone here.

XX **Askua** 🕸 ᵫ 🄰🄺

Felip María Garín 4 ✉ *46021 –* Ⓜ *Aragón* Plan: **J2**
*– ☏ 963 37 55 36 – www.restauranteaskua.com – Closed 3 weeks August,
Sunday and Bank Holidays*
Carte 33/65 €
• Traditional cuisine • Minimalist •
A well-respected restaurant thanks to the quality of its ingredients. In the
modern, brightly decorated dining room the focus is on cuisine full of flavour
prepared using high quality ingredients.

XX **La Salita** 🄰🄺

Séneca 12 ✉ *46021 – ☏ 963 81 75 16* Plan: **J1**
– www.lasalitarestaurante.com – Closed Sunday
Menu 45/64 € – *(tasting menu only)*
• Creative • Cosy •
No mention of La Salita is complete without talking about Begoña Rodrigo, the
winner of Spain's first Top Chef competition. Her tasting menus, focusing on
meticulous presentation and contemporary flavours, continue to surprise
guests.

XX **Casa Carmela** 🏠 Ⓚ ⟷
Isabel de Villena 155 ⊠ *46011 –* ☎ *963 71 00 73*   Plan III : **K1**
– www.casa-carmela.com – Closed Monday
Carte 35/56 € *– (lunch only)*
• **Traditional cuisine** • **Rustic** •
This local institution opened its doors on Malvarrosa beach in 1922. The beautiful glazed Manises tiles provide the perfect backdrop for Casa Carmela's superb paellas.

Ⓨ **Casa Montaña** ⅏ Ⓚ
José Benlliure 69 ⊠ *46011 –* Ⓜ *Maritim Serreria*   Plan: **K2**
– ☎ *963 67 23 14 – www.emilianobodega.com – Closed 24 December-6 January and Sunday dinner*
Tapa 2 € **Ración** approx. 4 €
• **Traditional cuisine** • **Tavern** •
A tavern full of charm dating back to 1836, in which the decor of old barrels and typical decorative detail gives the impression that time has stood still. Choose from an extensive à la carte of tapas options, set menus and an impressive wine list.

AT PALACIO DE CONGRESOS   **PLAN I**

XX **Kaymus** ⅏ Ⓚ ⟷
☺ *av. Maestro Rodrigo 44* ⊠ *46015 –* Ⓜ *Beniferri*   Plan: **B2**
– ☎ *963 48 66 66 – www.kaymus.es – Closed Monday dinner*
Menu 24/59 € *–* Carte 28/40 €
• **Traditional cuisine** • **Design** •
A modern restaurant known for its high quality cuisine, which is prepared simply yet with great finesse. The wine cellar benefits from similar attention to detail.

XX **Tavella** ⅋ Ⓚ ⟷
camino viejo de Líria 93 ⊠ *46015 –* Ⓜ *Beniferri*   Plan: **A1**
– ☎ *635 69 36 56 – www.tavellarestaurant.com – Clased 7-21 August, Sunday dinner and Monday*
Menu 29/49 € *– (tasting menu only)*
• **Traditional cuisine** • **Cosy** •
This restaurant is set in an old family farm accessible via a patio. There are three different ambiences for cuisine that is traditional but with a few Mexican touches, and based around different menus.

SWEDEN
SVERIGE

→ AREA:
449 964 km² (173 731 sq mi).

→ POPULATION:
9 879 066 inhabitants.
Density = 22 per km².

→ CAPITAL:
Stockholm.

→ CURRENCY:
Swedish Krona (Skr or SEK).

→ GOVERNMENT:
Constitutional parliamentary
monarchy (since 1950).
Member of
European Union since 1995.

→ LANGUAGE:
Swedish; many Swedes also speak
good English.

→ PUBLIC HOLIDAYS:
New Year's Day (1 Jan); Epiphany
(6 Jan); Good Friday (late Mar/
Apr); Easter Monday (late Mar/Apr);
Labor Day (1 May); Ascension Day
(May); Whit Sunday (late May/June);
National Day (6 June); Midsummer's
Day (Sat between 20-26 June);
All Saints' Day (1 Nov); Christmas
Day (25 Dec); St Stephen's Day
(26 Dec).

→ LOCAL TIME:
GMT+1 hour in winter and GMT
+2 hours in summer.

→ CLIMATE:
Temperate continental with
cold winters and mild summers
(Stockholm: January -3°C; July 16°C).

→ EMERGENCY:
Police, Medical Assistance and Fire
Brigade ℰ **112** – also on-call doctors
and roadside breakdown service.

→ ELECTRICITY:
230 volts AC, 50Hz; 2 round pin
sockets.

→ FORMALITIES:
Travellers from the European Union
(EU), Switzerland, Iceland and the
main countries of North and South
America need a national identity
card or passport (America: passport
required) to visit Sweden for less
than three months (tourism or
business purpose). For visitors
from other countries a visa may be
required, in addition to a passport,
especially for those wishing to
stay for longer than three months.
We advise you to check with your
embassy before travelling.

STOCKHOLM

Gothenburg

Malmö

STOCKHOLM
STOCKHOLM

Population: 909 637

imagepassion/Fotolia.com

Stockholm is the place to go for clean air, big skies and handsome architecture. And water. One of the great beauties of the city is the amount of water that runs through and around it; it's built on 14 islands, and looks out on 24,000 of them. An astounding two-thirds of the area within the city limits is made up of water, parks and woodland, and there are dozens of little bridges to cross to get from one part of town to another. It's little wonder Swedes appear so calm and relaxed.

It's in Stockholm that the salty waters of the Baltic meet head-on the fresh waters of Lake Mälaren, reflecting the broad boulevards and elegant buildings that shimmer along their edge. Domes, spires and turrets dot a skyline that in the summertime never truly darkens. The heart of the city is the Old Town, Gamla Stan, full of alleyways and lanes little changed from their medieval origins. Just to the north is the modern centre, Norrmalm: a buzzing quarter of shopping malls, restaurants and bars. East of Gamla Stan you reach the small island of Skeppsholmen, which boasts fine views of the waterfront; directly north from here is Östermalm, an area full of grand residences, while southeast you'll find the lovely park island of Djurgården. South and west of Gamla Stan are the two areas where Stockholmers particularly like to hang out, the trendy (and hilly) Södermalm, and Kungsholmen.

STOCKHOLM IN...

→ ONE DAY
Gamla Stan, City Hall, Vasa or Skansen museums, an evening in Södermalm.

→ TWO DAYS
Coffee in Kungsholmen, museums in Skeppsholmen, a stroll around Djurgården.

→ THREE DAYS
Shopping in Norrmalm, boat trip round the archipelago.

PRACTICAL INFORMATION

ARRIVAL-DEPARTURE

✈ Stockholm Arlanda Airport is 40km north of the city. The Arlanda Express train takes 20min to Centralstation and departs every 15min. The airport bus to Cityterminalen takes 40min.

✈ Bromma Stockholm Airport is 7km northwest of the city.

GETTING AROUND

The efficient metro system offers a more direct route than the buses. The No. 7 tram, which runs throughout the summer, takes in quite a few of the main attractions. You can buy single tickets for the bus, tram and metro, but if you're planning to do lots of travelling about the city, you can also get travelcards which cover one or three days. From April-October, city bikes are a cheap way to travel. Purchase a 3-day card, pick up a bike from any of the stands and it's yours for 3 hours.

CALENDAR HIGHLIGHTS

January/February
The Viking Run (ice skating race).

April
Walpurgis Night.

June
Midsummer's Eve celebrations, Stockholm Marathon.

August
Baltic Sea Festival (classical music).

October
Jazz Festival.

November
International Film Festival.

December
Nobel Prize Day.

EATING OUT

Everyone thinks that eating out in Stockholm is invariably expensive, but with a little forward planning it doesn't have to be. In the middle of the day, most restaurants and cafés offer very good value set menus. Keep in mind that, unlike in Southern Europe, the Swedes like to eat quite early, so lunch can often begin at around 11am and dinner may start from 6pm. Picking wild food is a birthright of Swedes, and there's no law to stop you going into forest or field to pick blueberries, cloudberries, cranberries, strawberries, mushrooms and the like. This love of outdoor, natural fare means that Stockholmers have a special bond with menus which relate to the seasons: keep your eyes open for restaurants that feature husmanskost (traditional Swedish dishes), along with huge buffet-style smörgåsbords. These days, however, you might find that your classic meatball, dumpling, herring or gravlax dish comes with a modern twist.

699

SWEDEN - STOCKHOLM

Grand

Södra Blasieholmshamnen 6 ✉ *103 27*   Plan: **C2**
– Ⓜ *Kungsträdgården* – ℰ *(08) 679 35 00* – www.mdghs.com
278 rm ☒ – ♦3600/4200 SEK ♦♦4900/5800 SEK – 34 suites
• Luxury • Historic building • Elegant •

The Grand certainly lives up to its name with its Corinthian columns, handsome panelled bar and impressive spa. Classical bedrooms have marble-decked bathrooms and those at the front have great views over the water to the Old Town. Dining choices include Veranda, with its harbour outlook and smörgåsbords, lively Matbaren and another new restaurant from Mathias Dahlgren which is set to open in 2017.
❀ **Mathias Dahlgren-Matbaren** – See restaurant listing

Sheraton

Tegelbacken 6 ✉ *101 23* – Ⓜ *T-Centralen* – ℰ *(08)*   Plan: **B2**
412 36 02 – www.sheratonstockholm.com
465 rm – ♦1395/5185 SEK ♦♦1395/5185 SEK – ☒ 259 SEK – 29 suites
• Business • Chain • Modern •

This was the first Sheraton to open in Europe, back in 1971, and its unassuming concrete façade is now a listed feature. Bedrooms are smart, spacious and understated, and some overlook Lake Mälaren or the Old Town. The lively restaurant offers international buffet lunches and traditional Swedish dinners.

Nobis

Norrmalmstorg 2-4 ✉ *111 86* – Ⓜ *Östermalmstorg*   Plan: **C2**
– ℰ *(08) 614 10 00* – www.nobishotel.com
201 rm – ♦1890/2290 SEK ♦♦2290/2690 SEK – ☒ 175 SEK – 1 suite
• Historic • Design • Personalised •

It started life as two Royal Palaces and later became a bank (the famous 'Stockholm Syndrome' robbery took place here); now it's a smart hotel with two internal courtyards and spacious bedrooms with clean lines, African wood furnishings and marble bathrooms. Dine on refined Italian cuisine in Caina or more rustic, wholesome dishes in Bakfica, with its pavement terrace.

Haymarket by Scandic

Hötorget 13-15 ✉ *111 57* – Ⓜ *Hötorget* – ℰ *(08)*   Plan: **B2**
517 267 00 – www.scandichotels.com
405 rm ☒ – ♦1050/3200 SEK ♦♦1150/3700 SEK – 16 suites
• Business • Historic building • Art déco •

Built in the 1900s, this former department store sits overlooking the Square, just across from the Concert Hall. Swedish-born Greta Garbo once worked here and the decor, particularly in the bedrooms, gives a nod to the art deco style. There's a small movie theatre, a healthy café-cum-bistro, a European restaurant and an American bar which hosts jazz at weekends.

Elite Eden Park

Sturegatan 22 ✉ *114 36* – Ⓜ *Östermalmstorg* – ℰ *(08)*   Plan: **C1**
5556 2700 – www.elite.se
124 rm ☒ – ♦1300/2850 SEK ♦♦1500/3500 SEK – 1 suite
• Business • Contemporary • Modern •

Smart hotel in a converted office block, designed with the business traveller in mind. Stylish bedrooms boast comfy beds and large showers – some rooms overlook the park and some have small balconies. Choose from an Asian-inspired menu in Miss Voon or traditional British pub dishes in The Bishops Arms.

SWEDEN - STOCKHOLM

Grand Central by Scandic 🏠 ➤ 🕸 & 🕳
Kungsgatan 70 ⊠ *111 20 –* ⓜ *T-Centralen –* ℰ *(08)*   Plan: **B2**
5125 2000 – www.scandichotels.com/grandcentral
391 rm ➤ – ∤1050/3200 SEK ∤∤1150/3700 SEK – 4 suites
• Business • Chain • Contemporary •
The décor of this contemporary hotel ties in with the arts theme of the area and its old Victorian theatre hosts live music and events. Bedrooms range from 'Cozy' (in the windowless basement) to spacious, well-equipped suites. The coffee shop serves snacks and the restaurant Swedish classics.

Radisson Blu Strand 🏠 ➤ 🕸 & 🕳
Nybrokajen 9 ⊠ *103 27 –* ⓜ *Kungsträdgården*   Plan: **C2**
– ℰ *(08) 506 640 00 – www.radissonblu.com/strandhotel-stockholm*
160 rm – ∤1295/2695 SEK ∤∤1395/2995 SEK – ➤ 170 SEK – 11 suites
• Business • Historic building • Contemporary •
This imposing hotel part-dates from the 1912 Olympics and sits in a lively water-side spot overlooking Nybroviken. Bedrooms are a mix of traditional and modern styles; the Tower Suite boasts a roof terrace with stunning city views. Enjoy a mix of local and global dishes in the airy atrium restaurant.

Diplomat 🏠 ➤ 🕸 🕳
Strandvägen 7c ⊠ *114 56 –* ⓜ *Kungsträdgården*   Plan: **C2**
– ℰ *(08) 459 68 00 – www.diplomathotel.com*
129 rm – ∤1750/3950 SEK ∤∤2250/4450 SEK – ➤ 275 SEK – 3 suites
• Traditional • Luxury • Elegant •
Early 20C charm combines with modern furnishings in this art nouveau hotel. Take the old cage lift up to the cosy library, which leads through to a sweet little cocktail bar. Elegant bedrooms come in pastel hues and some have harbour views. T Bar (the old tea salon) serves Scandinavian-inspired brasserie dishes.

Berns 🕸 🕳
Näckströmsgatan 8, Berzelii Park ⊠ *111 47*   Plan: **C2**
– ⓜ *Kungsträdgården –* ℰ *(08) 566 322 00 – www.berns.se*
82 rm – ∤1100/3300 SEK ∤∤1200/3500 SEK – ➤ 195 SEK – 6 suites
• Historic building • Boutique hotel • Design •
In 1863 Heinrich Robert Berns opened Stockholm's biggest concert and party hall on this site and, continuing that tradition, events are a big part of this hotel's business. Bedrooms are modern; some have seating areas or balconies.
Berns Asiatiska – See restaurant listing

Miss Clara by Nobis 🏠 🕸 & 🕳
Sveavägen 48 ⊠ *111 34 –* ⓜ *Hötorget –* ℰ *(08)*   Plan: **B1**
440 67 00 – www.missclarahotel.com
90 rm – ∤1590/2790 SEK ∤∤1690/3190 SEK – ➤ 169 SEK – 2 suites
• Business • Modern • Personalised •
A fashionable hotel in a great location; it used to be a girls' school and its name is that of the former principal. Surprisingly quiet, dark wood bedrooms have good facilities. The atmospheric brasserie offers an international menu with an Italian slant and some classic Swedish specialities.

Ett Hem 🏠 ➤ 🕸
Sköldungagatan 2 ⊠ *114 27 –* ⓜ *Tekniska Högskolan*   Plan: **B1**
– ℰ *(08) 20 05 90 – www.etthem.se*
12 rm ➤ – ∤3900 SEK ∤∤3900/7900 SEK
• Luxury • Design • Classic •
A charming Arts and Crafts townhouse built as a private residence in 1910. It's elegant, understated and makes good use of wood; its name means 'home' and that's exactly how it feels. Bedroom No.6 features an old chimney and No.1 has a four-poster and a huge marble bath. Modern set menus use top seasonal produce and are served in the kitchen, library and orangery.

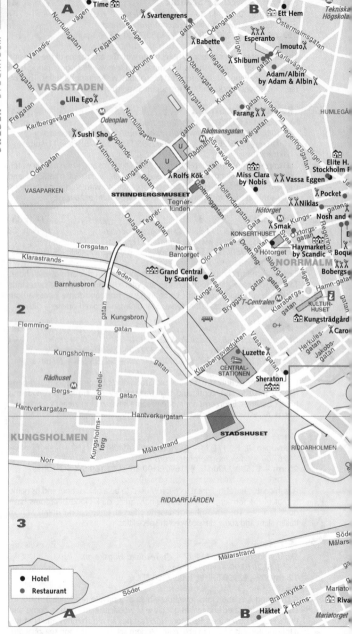

- Hotel
- Restaurant

SWEDEN - STOCKHOLM

A
- Time 🏠

- Svartengrens

Norrtullsvägen
Vanadis-
Dalagatan
Freygatan
Surbrunns-
Sveavägen
Odengatan

- Babette
- Shibumi

Tuleg atan
Birger
Döbelnsgatan
Luntmakargatan

VASASTADEN

1
- Lilla Ego
Karlbergsvägen
- Odenplan
Norrtullsgatan
Upplands-
- Sushi Sho
Västmanna-
Kungstens-

Odengatan

Rådmansgatan
Sveavägen
- Rolfs Kök
- Miss Clara
by Nobis

VASAPARKEN
Drottninggatan
STRINDBERGSMUSEET
Tegnér-
lunden

Tegnér- gatan
Dalagatan

Torsgatan

Klarastrands-

Norra
Bantorget
Barnhusbron
- Grand Central
by Scandic
leden
Kungsgatan

2
Flemming-
Kungsbron
gatan

Kungsholms-
gatan

Rådhuset
Bergs-
gatan
Scheele-

Hantverkargatan
Hantverkargatan
Kungsholms-
torg

KUNGSHOLMEN
Mälarstrand
Norr

RIDDARFJÄRDEN

3
Mälarstrand
Söder

B
- Ett Hem
Östermalmsgatan
- Esperanto
- Imouto
Karlavägen
- Adam/Albin
by Adam & Albin

HUMLEGÅ
- Farang
Tegnérgatan
Regeringsgatan
Birger

Hölländargatan
- Vassa Eggen
- Elite H.
Stockholm
- Pocket
- Niklas
- Nosh and
Kungs- gatan
- Smak
KONSERTHUSET
Oxtorgs-
gatan
- Haymarket
by Scandic
- Boqu
Hötorget
Sveavägen
NORRMALM
- Bobergs
Hamn-gata
Drottning-
gatan
Olof Palmes
Vasagatan
Bryggar-
Klarabergs-
gatan
T-Centralen
**KULTUR-
HUSET**
- Kungsträdgård
- Caro
Herkules-
gatan
Jakobs-
gatan
Vasa-
gatan
- Luzette
Klarabergsviadukten
**CENTRAL-
STATIONEN**
- Sheraton
STADSHUSET
RIDDARHOLMEN

Söde
Mälars
Mariato
- Riva
Mariatorget
Söder
Bränkyrka-
Horns-
- Häktet

A   **B**

702

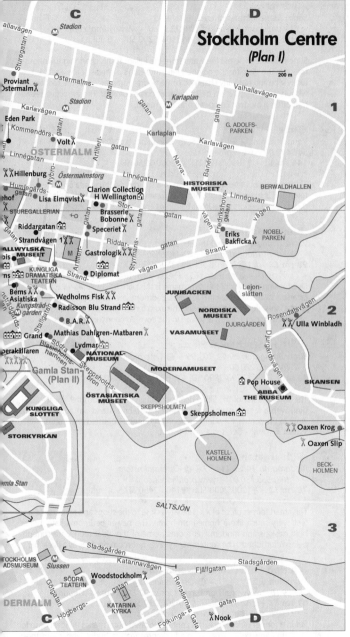

Stockholm Centre
(Plan I)

0   200 m

Stadion

allavägen

Östermalms-
gatan

Karlaplan

Valhallavägen

G. ADOLFS-
PARKEN

1

Sturegatan

Proviant
Östermalm

Stadion

Karlavägen

Eden Park

Kommendörs-
gatan

Östermalms-
gatan

Karlaplan

Karlavägen

Volt

ÖSTERMALM

Linnégatan

Artilleri-
gatan

Narva-
vägen

Banér-
gatan

Hillenburg

Östermalmstorg

Linnégatan

HISTORISKA
MUSEET

BERWALDHALLEN

Humlegårds-
gatan

Clarion Collection
H Wellington

Stor-
gatan

Linnégatan

Fredrikshovs-
gatan

Lisa Elmqvist

STUREGALLERIAN

Brasserie
Bobonne

Specieriet

Eriks
Bakficka

NOBEL-
PARKEN

Riddargatan

Riddar-
gatan

Strandvägen 1

Gastrologik

Styrmans-
gatan

Strand-
vägen

ALLWYLSKA
MUSEET

Diplomat

KUNGLIGA
DRAMATISKA
TEATERN

Artilleri-

JUNIBACKEN

Lejon-
slätten

Berns
Asiatiska

Wedholms Fisk

NORDISKA
MUSEET

Rosendalsvägen

Kungsträd-
gården

Radisson Blu Strand

DJURGÅRDEN

Ulla Winbladh

B.A.R.

VASAMUSEET

Grand

Mathias Dahlgren-Matbaren

Lydmar

Djurgårdsvägen

perakällaren

Blasieholms-
hamnen

NATIONAL-
MUSEET

MODERNAMUSEET

SKANSEN

Gamla Stan
(Plan II)

Södra
Blasieholms-
hamnen

Skeppsholms-
bron

ÖSTASIATISKA
MUSEET

Pop House

ABBA
THE MUSEUM

KUNGLIGA
SLOTTET

SKEPPSHOLMEN

Skeppsholmen

Oaxen Krog

STORKYRKAN

Oaxen Slip

KASTELL-
HOLMEN

BECK-
HOLMEN

mla Stan

SALTSJÖN

3

TOCKHOLMS
ADSMUSEUM

Stadsgården

Slussen

Katarinavägen

Stadsgården

SÖDRA
TEATERN

Woodstockholm

Fjällgatan

Renstiernas Gata

gatan

DERMALM

Högbergs-

Götgatan

KATARINA
KYRKAN

Folkunga-
gata

Nook

Lydmar

⇗ ⇐ ⅍ AC

Södra Blasieholmshamnen 2 ✉ *111 48*
Plan: **C2**
– **M** *Kungsträdgården* – ℰ *(08) 22 31 60* – *www.lydmar.com*
46 rm ⊑ – **♥**2700/3800 SEK **♥♥**3100/5200 SEK – 6 suites
• Townhouse • Personalised • Design •
Superbly located across the water from the Palace is this charming townhouse;
formerly the store for the neighbouring museum's archives. It has a relaxed yet
funky vibe and regularly changing contemporary artwork – and the roof terrace
with its water feature is a delightful spot come summer. The attractive restaurant offers a modern European brasserie menu.

Time

⍲ ⅍ ⅍ ⌘

Vanadisvägen 12 ✉ *113 46* – **M** *Odenplan* – ℰ *(08)*
Plan: **A1**
54 54 73 00 – *www.timehotel.se*
144 rm ⊑ – **♥**1850/2120 SEK **♥♥**2050/2250 SEK
• Business • Modern • Personalised •
This purpose-built business hotel sits in a smart residential area on the edge of
town and is run by a friendly, hands-on team. Bedrooms are bright, airy and of a
good size; Superiors have Juliet balconies and Studios offer long-term lets.

Kungsträdgården

⇗ ⅃⅍ ⍲ AC

Västra Trädgårdsgatan 11b ✉ *10216*
Plan: **B2**
– **M** *Kungsträdgården* – ℰ *(08) 440 6650* – *www.hotelkungstradgarden.se*
98 rm ⊑ – **♥**1090/2890 SEK **♥♥**1350/3250 SEK
• Townhouse • Historic • Personalised •
Overlooking the park of the same name is this part-18C building with a classical
façade and attractive original features. Bedrooms are individually furnished in a
Gustavian-style – it's worth paying the extra for a bigger room. A concise menu
of French-inspired dishes is served in the covered courtyard.

Elite H. Stockholm Plaza

⍲ ⅍ ⅍

Birger Jarlsgatan 29 ✉ *103 95* – **M** *Östermalmstorg*
Plan: **B1**
– ℰ *(08) 566 220 00* – *www.elite.se*
143 rm ⊑ – **♥**1290/2890 SEK **♥♥**1690/3290 SEK – 12 suites
• Business • Chain • Contemporary •
The smaller sister of the Elite Eden Park is this attractive, centrally located buil-
ding with a façade dating from 1884. Bright fabrics stand out against neutral
walls in the compact modern bedrooms; go for one of the corner suites.
Vassa Eggen – See restaurant listing

Riddargatan

⅍

Riddargatan 14 ✉ *114 35* – **M** *Östermalmstorg*
Plan: **C2**
– ℰ *(08) 555 730 00* – *www.profilhotels.com*
78 rm ⊑ – **♥**1200/2000 SEK **♥♥**1400/2450 SEK – 4 suites
• Business • Modern • Personalised •
This smart former office block is situated close to the shops and restaurants, and
feels very much like a home-from-home. The newer bedrooms have bright,
bold designs and modern wet rooms (some of the older rooms are currently
being refurbished). The contemporary breakfast room doubles as a lively bar.

Clarion Collection H. Wellington

⍲ ⅍ ⌘

Storgatan 6 ✉ *114 51* – **M** *Östermalmstorg* – ℰ *(08)*
Plan: **C1**
667 09 10 – *www.wellington.se* – Closed 22 December-4 January
61 rm ⊑ – **♥**820/2420 SEK **♥♥**1420/3220 SEK – 1 suite
• Business • Townhouse • Traditional •
Set in a former office block, this centrally located hotel makes an ideal base for
shopping and sightseeing. Simple bedrooms feature bright fabrics and those
on the top floor have city views. Buffet dinners are included in the price.

SWEDEN - STOCKHOLM

Operakällaren

XxXxX
☺

Operahuset, Karl XII's Torg ✉ *111 86*   Plan: **C2**
– Kungsträdgården – ✆ (08) 676 58 01 – www.operakallaren.se
– Closed 7 July-7 August, 20-21 June, 25-30 December, 1-12 January,
Sunday and Monday
Menu 1050/1550 SEK – *(dinner only)*
• Classic cuisine • Luxury • Historic •

Sweden's most opulent restaurant sits within the historic Opera House, and the
stunning, high-ceilinged room boasts original gilt panelling decorated with frescoes and carvings. Carefully constructed dishes are underpinned by classic techniques. The wine list boasts extensive vintages of the world's great wines.
→ Mackerel with trout roe and browned butter. Saddle and cured fillet of
lamb with artichoke cream. Peach with caramel bavarois and elderflower
granité.

Esperanto (Sayan Isaksson)

XxX
☺

Kungstensgatan 2 (1st Floor) ✉ *114 25*   Plan: **B1**
– Ⓜ Tekniska Högskolan – ✆ (08) 696 23 23
– www.esperantorestaurant.se – Closed Christmas-New Year, Easter,
July and Sunday-Tuesday
Menu 1400/1850 SEK – *(dinner only) (tasting menu only)*
• Creative • Fashionable • Design •

'Esperanto' is a language that crosses frontiers, and the food here has an equally
universal feel. Passionately prepared, original Swedish and Asian dishes feature
a great range of ingredients and have a theatrical element – which is fitting seeing as the restaurant is on the first floor of an old theatre. In one corner there's a
small sushi counter.
→ Silk tofu, buckwheat and langoustine. Pressed beef marrow, potato
water and caviar. Blueberry, milk and horseradish.

Bobergs

XxX
☺

NK Department Store, Hamngatan 18-20 (4th floor)   Plan: **B2**
✉ *111 47* – Ⓜ *Kungsträdgården – ✆ (08) 762 8161*
– www.bobergsmatsal.se – Closed Christmas-New Year, July-mid August
and Sunday
Menu 395 SEK – Carte 405/615 SEK – *(lunch only) (booking advisable)*
• Modern cuisine • Elegant • Classic décor •

Head past the canteen in this historic department store to the elegant birch-
panelled room and ask for a river view. Choose the set business lunch or from
the seasonal à la carte; classic cooking mixes French and Swedish influences.

Gastrologik (Jacob Holmström and Anton Bjuhr)

XX
☺

Artillerigatan 14 ✉ *114 51* – Ⓜ *Östermalmstorg*   Plan: **C2**
– ✆ (08) 66 23 060 – www.gastrologik.se – Closed Christmas, Sunday and
Monday
Menu 1395 SEK – *(dinner only) (booking essential) (surprise menu only)*
• World cuisine • Intimate • Design •

This intimate restaurant is owned by two accomplished young chefs. Cooking is
innovative, flavours are pure and each main ingredient is allowed to shine.
Dishes rely on the latest seasonal ingredients to arrive at the door, so are constantly evolving; the menu isn't presented to you until the end of the meal.
→ Algae-glazed asparagus with grilled butter. Reindeer with matsutake
mushrooms and cabbage. Lovage ice cream, frozen sorrel juice and spruce
tips.

Nosh and Chow

XX

Norrlandsgatan 24 ✉ *111 43* – Ⓜ *Hötorget – ✆ (08)*   Plan: **B2**
503 389 60 – www.noshandchow.se – Closed 24 December, 1 January,
lunch in summer, midsummer, bank holidays and Sunday
Carte 365/790 SEK
• International • Brasserie • Fashionable •

This former bank has been transformed into a glitzy cocktail bar and brasserie
which displays a smart mix of New York and New England styling. Filling dishes
blend French, American and Swedish influences with other global flavours.

SWEDEN - STOCKHOLM

XX Hillenberg

Humlegårdsgatan 14 ⊠ 114 34 – ⓜ Östermalmstorg   Plan: **C1**
– ℰ (08) 519 421 53 – www.hillenberg.se – Closed Saturday lunch and Sunday
Menu 395/675 SEK – Carte 385/835 SEK
• Modern cuisine • Design • Brasserie •
There's a marble bar on each side of this bright, modern restaurant, where the designer's eye for detail is evident. The food reflects the surroundings by being fresh, contemporary, colourful and free from unnecessary frills.

XX Strandvägen 1   🛋 🅰🅺

Strandvägen 1 ⊠ 114 51 – ⓜ Kungsträdgården   Plan: **C2**
– ℰ (08) 663 80 00 – www.strandvagen1.se – Closed 24 December
Carte 425/765 SEK
• International • Design • Elegant •
Sit on the terrace of this modern bistro-style restaurant – a former bank – and watch the boats bobbing up and down in the harbour. Seasonal menus offer generously proportioned, globally inspired dishes with bold flavours.

XX Wedholms Fisk   🅰🅺 ⇔

Nybrokajen 17 ⊠ 111 48 – ⓜ Kungsträdgården   Plan: **C2**
– ℰ (08) 611 78 74 – www.wedholmsfisk.se – Closed 23 December-7 January, midsummer, bank holidays, lunch 26 June-14 August, Saturday lunch and Sunday
Carte 530/1195 SEK – (booking essential)
• Seafood • Intimate • Elegant •
An impressive former auction house set beside the financial institutions on Stockholm's 'Little Wall Street', overlooking the harbour. It's owned by a large fishmonger's which has its own boats; in winter, go for their speciality – turbot.

XX Berns Asiatiska – Berns Hotel   🛋 ⇔

Näckströmsgatan 8, Berzelii Park ⊠ 111 47   Plan: **C2**
– ⓜ Kungsträdgården – ℰ (08) 566 32 67 – www.berns.se
Menu 795 SEK – Carte 399/735 SEK
• Asian • Fashionable • Elegant •
Within the Berns hotel is this stunning rococo ballroom with a terrace overlooking Berzelii Park. The extensive Asian fusion menu covers everything from Chinese to Indian and includes bento boxes, sushi, sharing dishes and weekend brunches.

XX AG   🕸 🅰🅺

Kronobergsgatan 37 (2nd Floor), Kungsholmen (via Flemminggatan A2) ⊠ 112 33 – ⓜ Fridshemsplan – ℰ (08) 410 681 00
– www.restaurangag.se – Closed July, 23-25 June, 24-26 December and Sunday
Carte 335/1285 SEK – (dinner only)
• Meats and grills • Rustic • Fashionable •
An industrial, New York style eatery on the 2nd floor of an old silver factory. Swedish, American and Scottish beef is displayed in huge cabinets and you choose your accompaniments. Expect a great wine list and smooth service.

XX Niklas

Regeringsgatan 66 ⊠ 111 39 – ⓜ Hötorget – ℰ (08)   Plan: **B2**
20 60 10 – www.niklas.se – Closed 24-25 December, 1 January, midsummer, Saturday lunch and Sunday
Carte 330/675 SEK
• Modern cuisine • Fashionable • Bistro •
Contemporary, industrial-style bistro with large blackboard menus on the walls. The owner's extensive travels guide the appealing brasserie menus. You can also try the 'Punk Gastronomy' dinner menu in the adjoining nightclub Weds-Sat.

SWEDEN - STOCKHOLM

XX **Vassa Eggen** – Elite H. Stockholm Plaza   AC
Birger Jarlsgatan 29 ⊠ *103 95* – **Ⓜ** *Östermalmstorg*   Plan: **B1**
– ℰ (08) 21 61 69 – www.vassaeggen.com – Closed midsummer,
Christmas, Saturday lunch and Sunday
Menu 695 SEK – Carte 495/1000 SEK
• Meats and grills • Fashionable • Rustic •
A pleasant bar leads through to a dimly lit hotel dining room where bold art-work hangs on the walls. Hearty Swedish cooking relies on age-old recipes, with a particular focus on meat; whole beasts are butchered and hung on-site.

XX **Farang**   &. AC
Tulegatan 7 ⊠ *113 53* – **Ⓜ** *Rådmansgatan* – ℰ *(08)*   Plan: **B1**
673 74 00 – www.farang.se – Closed July, midsummer, Christmas, Sunday
and Monday
Menu 245/695 SEK – Carte 375/580 SEK
• South East Asian • Minimalist • Fashionable •
The sister of Farang in Helsinki is this vast restaurant with a chic bar. Cooking focuses on southeast Asia and on hot, sweet and sour tastes; dishes are aroma-tic, zingy and colourful. Sharing is encouraged and there's a family atmosphere.

X   **Mathias Dahlgren-Matbaren** – Grand Hotel   &. AC
ॐ *Södra Blasieholmshamnen 6* ⊠ *103 27*   Plan: **C2**
*– **Ⓜ** Kungsträdgården – ℰ (08) 679 35 00 – www.mdghs.com*
– Closed 14 July-8 August, 22 December-10 January, Saturday lunch and
Sunday
Carte 475/835 SEK – *(booking advisable)*
• Modern cuisine • Fashionable • Design •
This popular hotel restaurant is both fun and charmingly run. The open kitchen specialises in flavoursome, well-balanced dishes from an appealing menu divi-ded into the headings 'From our country', 'From other countries' or 'From the plant world'. They keep some seats at the counter for those who haven't boo-ked.
➙ Scandinavian ceviche, horseradish, elderflower and algae. Seared pork, creamy corn and chilli. Baked chocolate, sour cream, toffee ice cream and nuts.

X   **Ekstedt**   ⅏ &.
ॐ *Humlegårdsgatan 17* ⊠ *114 46* – **Ⓜ** *Östermalmstorg*   Plan: **C1**
– ℰ (08) 611 1210 – www.ekstedt.nu – Closed last 2 weeks July, Christmas-New Year, Sunday and Monday
Menu 840/1090 SEK – *(dinner only) (booking essential) (tasting menu only)*
• Meats and grills • Design • Friendly •
An unassuming façade hides a very relaxed, friendly, yet professionally run bras-serie, where ingredients are cooked in a wood-burning oven, over a fire-pit or smoked through a chimney using birch wood. Dishes are inventive but well-balanced – they are given their finishing touches at the stone bar.
➙ Blackened leeks with vendace roe and charcoal-smoked cream. Pike-perch with chanterelles and peas. Wood-fired honey cake with raspberries.

X   **Volt** (Peter Andersson and Fredrik Johnsson)
ॐ *Kommendörsgatan 16* ⊠ *114 48* – **Ⓜ** *Stadion* – ℰ *(08)*   Plan: **C1**
662 34 00 – www.restaurangvolt.se – Closed 4 weeks summer,
Christmas, Sunday and Monday
Menu 585/765 SEK – *(dinner only) (booking essential)*
• Creative • Intimate • Neighbourhood •
An intimate, welcoming restaurant run by a young but experienced team. Coo-king is natural in style, with the largely organic produce yielding clear, bold fla-vours – natural wines also feature. Ingredients are arranged in layers, so that each forkful contains a little of everything; choose 4 or 6 courses.
➙ Grilled beans, oysters and algae. Sweetbread, spring garlic and green strawberries. Blackcurrants and parsnip.

X
ॐ **Imouto**   🔤

Kungstensgatan 2 (1st Floor) ✉ *114 25*   Plan: **B1**
– ⓜ Tekniska Högskolan – ℰ (08) 696 23 23 – www.imouto.se – Closed
Christmas-New Year, Easter, midsummer and Sunday-Tuesday
Menu 1200 SEK – *(dinner only) (booking essential)*
• Sushi • Intimate • Simple •

Its name means 'little sister' and you'll find this 9-seater sushi counter in the corner of Esperanto restaurant. Only an omakase menu is offered, with hot and cold dishes served before the sushi; the rice is from Japan but the fish is mainly from Swedish waters. There are two sittings on Fridays and Saturdays.
→ Soy-glazed langoustine. Turbot with wild garlic oil. Pike-perch sushi.

X
ॐ **Sushi Sho** (Carl Ishizaki)

Upplandsgatan 45 ✉ *113 28 – ⓜ Odenplan – ℰ (08)*   Plan: **A1**
30 30 30 – www.sushisho.se – Closed Christmas-New Year, July,
midsummer, Sunday and Monday
Menu 595 SEK – *(dinner only)*
• Japanese • Neighbourhood • Friendly •

With its white tiled walls and compact counter seating the room couldn't be simpler, but the food is sublime. Meals are served 'omakase' style, with the chef deciding what's best each day and dishes arriving as they're ready. Top quality seafood from local waters features alongside some great egg recipes.
→ Soy-cured egg yolk with okra, tuna and toasted rice. Salmon, sea bass and scallop nigiri. Razor clam with edamame & pea purée, sake and ginger.

X
☺ **Adam/Albin by Adam & Albin**   🔤

Rådmansgatan 16 ✉ *114 25 – ⓜ Tekniska Högskolan*   Plan: **B1**
– ℰ (08) 411 5535 – www.adamalbin.se – Closed Sunday, bank holidays
and restricted opening in summer
Menu 795 SEK – *(dinner only) (booking essential)*
• Modern cuisine • Intimate • Neighbourhood •

Stylish restaurant with Italian marble walls and a mix of individual and communal tables. Following a snack, there are two choices per course. Refined, eye-catching dishes blend the ethos of a Scandic kitchen with global flavours.

X
☺ **Proviant Östermalm**   🔤 ☺

Sturegatan 19 ✉ *114 36 – ⓜ Stadion – ℰ (08) 22 60 50*   Plan: **C1**
– www.proviant.se – Closed 2 weeks Christmas-New Year, 3 weeks
July, and lunch Saturday-Sunday
Menu 295/575 SEK – Carte 455/595 SEK
• Swedish • Bistro • Intimate •

Lively restaurant boasting smart, contemporary décor, a small counter and an adjoining foodstore; located in a chic residential area by Sture Park. Swedish ingredients feature highly – choose from the rustic, classically based dishes on the blackboard, the French-inspired à la carte or the house specialities.

X
☺ **Brasserie Bobonne**

Storgatan 12 ✉ *114 44 – ⓜ Östermalmstorg – ℰ (08)*   Plan: **C1**
660 03 18 – www.bobonne.se – Closed 5 weeks July-August, midsummer,
Christmas, Easter, Sunday and lunch Saturday
Menu 249/550 SEK – Carte 325/615 SEK – *(booking essential)*
• French • Cosy • Bistro •

Sweet little two-roomed restaurant with comfy chairs, period floor tiles and a homely feel. The open-plan kitchen fills the room with pleasant aromas and the blackboard lists tasty, well-balanced dishes crafted from fresh ingredients. Menus are French-inspired, with modern touches and the odd Swedish influence.

X **Lilla Ego** ✣

Västmannag 69 ☒ 113 26 – Ⓜ Odenplan – ℰ (08) Plan: **A1**
*27 44 55 – www.lillaego.com – Closed Christmas, Easter, July Sunday and
Monday*
Carte 495/675 SEK – *(dinner only) (booking essential)*
• Modern cuisine • Friendly • Simple •

One of the hottest tickets in town comes with a pared-down look and a buzzy
vibe; if you haven't booked, try for a counter seat. The two modest chef-owners
have created an appealingly priced menu of robust, satisfying, seasonal dishes.
The 'wrestling' sausage will challenge even the biggest of appetites.

X **Luzette** 🔊 �& AK

Centralstationen, Centralplan 25 ☒ 111 20 Plan: **B2**
– Ⓜ T-Centralen – ℰ (08) 519 316 00 – www.luzette.se
Carte 425/715 SEK
• Swedish • Brasserie • Design •

A modern brasserie and takeaway in the Central train station, inspired by the
grand restaurants of old. Its name means 'light' and refers to the 1920s lumin-
aire designed by Peter Behrens. Swedish cooking features rotisserie specials.

X **Carousel** 🔊 �& AK

Gustav Adolfs Torg 20 ☒ 111 53 – Ⓜ Kungsträdgården Plan: **B2**
*– ℰ (08) 10 27 57 – www.restaurantcarousel.se – Closed 24-26 December,
midsummer and Sunday*
Carte 415/760 SEK
• Swedish • Classic décor • Historic •

Start with a drink under the impressive original ceiling in the bar then sit near
the carousel or out on the terrace. The experienced chefs carefully prepare flavoursome dishes which follow the seasons and have classic Swedish roots.

X **Shibumi** AK

Kungstensgatan 2 ☒ 114 25 – Ⓜ Tekniska Högskolan Plan: **B1**
*– ℰ (08) 696 23 10 – www.shibumi.se – Closed Christmas, Easter,
midsummer, Sunday and Monday*
Carte 245/405 SEK – *(dinner only) (booking advisable)*
• Japanese • Intimate • Minimalist •

This discreet modern restaurant is based on a Japanese izakaya. It's open until
late and comes with an underground buzz – and not just because it's in a basement. Expect plenty of original dishes and a daily changing cocktail list.

X **Svartengrens**

Tulegatan 24 ☒ 113 53 – Ⓜ Tekniska Högskolan Plan: **B1**
*– ℰ (08) 612 65 50 – www.svartengrens.se – Closed Christmas and
midsummer*
Menu 725 SEK – Carte 315/845 SEK – *(dinner only) (booking advisable)*
• Meats and grills • Friendly • Neighbourhood •

The eponymous chef-owner has created a modern bistro specialising in sustainable meat and veg from producers in the archipelago. Along with smoking
and pickling, the dry-ageing is done in-house, and the cuts change daily.

X **Babette** 🔊

Roslagsgatan 6 ☒ 113 55 – Ⓜ Tekniska Högskolan Plan: **B1**
*– ℰ (08) 5090 2224 – www.babette.se – Closed 24-26, 31 December and
June 18-25*
Carte 295/415 SEK – *(dinner only)*
• Modern cuisine • Neighbourhood • Bistro •

You'll feel at home in this modern neighbourhood bistro. Cooking is rustic and
unfussy and the daily selection of small plates and pizzas makes dining flexible.
They limit their bookings so that they can accommodate walk-ins.

SWEDEN - STOCKHOLM

SWEDEN - STOCKHOLM

✗ **Pocket** 🔠 ⇦

Brunnsgatan 1 ⊠ *111 38* – Ⓜ *Östermalmstorg* – ℰ *(08)*　　Plan: **B1**
545 27300 – *www.pontusfrithiof.com* – *Closed July-mid August, Saturday*
lunch, Monday dinner, Sunday and bank holidays
Menu 995 SEK – Carte 325/415 SEK – *(bookings not accepted)*
• Traditional cuisine • Bistro • Simple •

Grab a table in the window of this casual bistro or sit at the counter to watch the
chefs at work. Menus offer French bistro classics with some Swedish influences;
start with a selection of snacks – three are equal to a starter.

✗ **Sturehof** 🕾 🏠 ⅋ 🔠 ⇦

Stureplan 2 ⊠ *114 46* – Ⓜ *Östermalmstorg* – ℰ *(08)*　　Plan: **C1**
40 57 30 – *www.sturehof.com*
Carte 445/895 SEK
• Seafood • Brasserie • Fashionable •

This bustling city institution dates back over a century and is a wonderful mix of
the traditional and the modern. It boasts a buzzing terrace, several marble-topped bars and a superb food court. Classic menus focus on seafood.

✗ **Eriks Bakficka**

Fredrikshovsgatan 4 ⊠ *115 23* – ℰ *(08) 660 15 99*　　Plan: **D2**
– *www.eriks.se* – *Closed mid July to mid August, Christmas, Easter,*
Saturday lunch and Sunday
Carte 420/595 SEK
• Swedish • Bistro •

Set in a residential area close to Djurgårdsbron Bridge and a favourite with the
locals. The bistro-style interior has wood panelling and marble-topped tables.
Simple, unpretentious cooking features Swedish classics and a 'dish of the day'.

✗ **B.A.R.** 🔠

Blasieholmsgatan 4a ⊠ *111 48* – Ⓜ *Kungsträdgården*　　Plan: **C2**
– ℰ *(08) 611 53 35* – *www.restaurangbar.se* – *Closed Christmas-New Year,*
midsummer, lunch July and Sunday
Carte 395/800 SEK
• Seafood • Brasserie • Trendy •

Spacious, canteen-style restaurant with an industrial feel. The wide-ranging
menu changes with each season and offers some interesting side dishes. For
the daily specials, head to the counter and select your meat or fish from the
ice display.

✗ **EAT** 🏠 ⅋

😊 *Jakobsbergsgatan 15* ⊠ *111 44* – Ⓜ *Hötorget* – ℰ *(08)*　　Plan: **B2**
50920300 – *www.eatrestaurant.se* – *Closed Christmas-New Year, lunch*
mid July-mid August, Sunday and lunch Saturday
Menu 440 SEK – Carte 200/585 SEK – *(bookings advisable at dinner)*
• Asian • Brasserie • Fashionable •

Pass the EAT 'Market' fast food outlet in this upmarket shopping mall and head
for the Oriental 'Bistro' with its rich, moody colour scheme and central cocktail
bar. The name stands for 'European Asian Taste' and the Chinese dishes are flavoursome, well-executed and designed for sharing. Opening times can vary.

✗ **Rolfs Kök** 🕾

😊 *Tegnérgatan 41* ⊠ *111 61* – Ⓜ *Rådmansgatan*　　Plan: **B1**
– ℰ *(08) 10 16 96* – *www.rolfskok.se* – *Closed July, 24-26 December,*
midsummer and lunch Saturday-Sunday
Carte 415/700 SEK – *(booking essential)*
• Modern cuisine • Bistro • Rustic •

A popular, buzzy restaurant in a lively commercial district, run by a passionate
chef-owner. The contemporary interior was designed by famous Swedish
artists; sit at the counter to watch the chefs in action. Dishes include homely
Swedish classics and blackboard specials. Every dish has a wine match.

✗ ## Boqueria 🍴 ㄸ

Jakobsbergsgatan 17 ⊠ *111 44 –* Ⓜ *Hötorget –* ✆ *(08)*   Plan: **B2**
307400 – www.boqueria.se – Closed 24-25 December, 1 January and
midsummer
Menu 145 SEK (weekday lunch) – Carte 370/995 SEK
• Spanish • Tapas bar • Fashionable •

A vibrant, bustling tapas restaurant with high-level seating, located in a smart mall. Appealing menus offer tapas and a range of authentic dishes for two or more to share. Sangria and pintxos can be enjoyed in their nearby bar.

✗ ## Speceriet 🅰️🅲

Artillerigatan 14 ⊠ *114 51 –* Ⓜ *Östermalmstorg*   Plan: **C2**
– ✆ *(08) 662 30 60 – www.speceriet.se – Closed Christmas-New Year,*
Sunday, lunch Saturday and Monday
Carte 325/495 SEK
• Classic cuisine • Simple •

The more casual addendum to the Gastrologik restaurant will get you in the mood for sharing. Sit at communal tables and choose from three main dishes at lunchtime and a wider selection of mix and match dishes at dinner.

✗ ## Gro

Sankt Eriksgatan 67 (via Odengatan on Sankt Eriksgatan just before
bridge A1) ⊠ *113 32 –* Ⓜ *Sankt Eriksplan –* ✆ *(08) 643 4222*
– www.grorestaurang.se – Closed July, 23 December-10 January, Sunday
and Monday
Menu 500 SEK – *(dinner only)*
• Modern cuisine • Simple • Friendly •

Formerly a butcher's shop, this is now a simple, relaxed little eatery. Cooking is the chef-owners' take on Swedish classics and uses both traditional and modern techniques; local ingredients, particularly vegetables, play a key role.

✗ ## Zink Grill 🍴

Biblioteksgatan 5 ⊠ *111 46 –* Ⓜ *Östermalmstorg*   Plan: **C2**
– ✆ *(08) 611 42 22 – www.zinkgrill.se – Closed Christmas and midsummer*
Carte 327/633 SEK
• French • Bistro • Traditional décor •

This lively, late night bistro is one of Stockholm's oldest restaurants and the pur-chase of its French zinc bar – dating from 1933 – is how it all began. The Gallic and Italian inspired menu features plenty of charcuterie and grills.

✗ ## Smak 🍴 ㄸ

Oxtorgsgatan 14 ⊠ *104 35 –* Ⓜ *Hötorget –* ✆ *(08)*   Plan: **B2**
22 09 52 – www.restaurangentm.com – Closed Christmas, Easter, Sunday
and lunch Saturday
Menu 400/600 SEK – *(booking essential)*
• Creative • Trendy •

Smak means 'taste' and at dinner you choose 3, 5 or 7 modern small plates according to their flavour (lunch offers express set menus). The large room fea-tures striking brass lamps and the walls are hung with mirrors and tapestries.

✗ ## Lisa Elmqvist

Humlesgårdsgatan 1 ⊠ *114 39 –* Ⓜ *Östermalmstorg*   Plan: **C1**
– ✆ *(08) 553 40410 – www.lisaelmqvist.se – Closed 24 December,*
midsummer, bank holidays and Sunday
Carte 425/1050 SEK
• Seafood • Minimalist •

While the original 19C market hall is being restored, this established family-run restaurant is operating from the temporary marketplace next door. Top quality seafood from the day's catch features in unfussy, satisfying combinations.

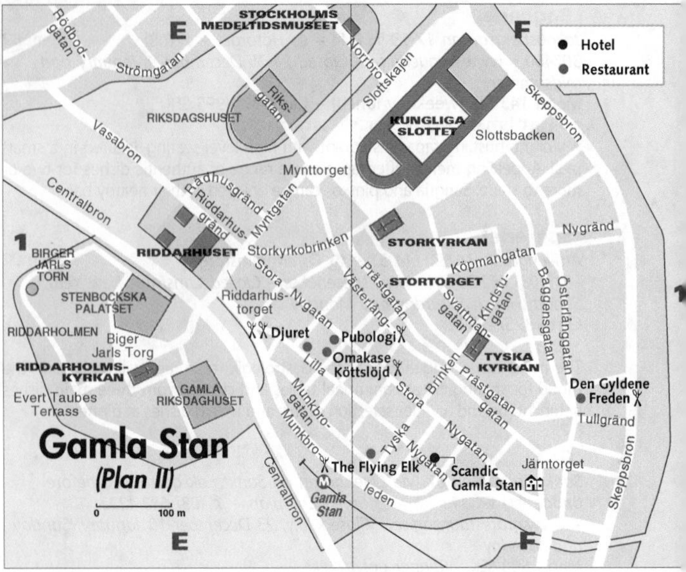

AT GAMLA STAN (OLD STOCKHOLM) — PLAN II

Scandic Gamla Stan

Lilla Nygatan 25 ✉ 111 28 – Ⓜ Gamla Stan – ✆ (08) 517 38 300 – www.scandichotels.se — Plan: **F1**

52 rm ☕ – 🚹845/1908 SEK 🚹🚹1424/2108 SEK

• Townhouse • Historic • Cosy •

A historic townhouse dating from the 17C, located on a cobbled street in the heart of the Old Town. Bedrooms are cosy and decorated in a traditional Swedish style; bathrooms are modern. The roof terrace offers great city views.

Djuret

Lilla Nygatan 5 ✉ 111 28 – Ⓜ Gamla Stan – ✆ (08) 506 400 84 – www.djuret.se – Closed Christmas, July and Sunday — Plan: **E1**

Menu 595 SEK – *(dinner only) (booking essential)*

• Meats and grills • Rustic • Neighbourhood •

It's all about meat here at Djuret. A different beast features on the menu every two weeks – maybe wild boar or reindeer – and there's an excellent selection of wines to accompany. Dine in the 'Meat' room or the 'Trophy' room.

Den Gyldene Freden

Österlånggatan 51 ✉ 10 317 – Ⓜ Gamla Stan – ✆ (08) 24 97 60 – www.gyldenefreden.se – Closed Sunday — Plan: **F1**

Menu 265/470 SEK – Carte 405/775 SEK – *(booking essential)*

• Traditional cuisine • Rustic • Inn •

Built by a vintner in 1722, this historic property is thought to be the city's oldest restaurant. It was bequeathed to the Swedish Academy in 1920 and they continue to meet here weekly. Both the ground floor and the cellar are hugely characterful. Cooking sees refined, modern versions of Swedish classics.

X **Pubologi** 🕸

Stora Nygatan 20 ✉ *111 27 –* Ⓜ *Gamla Stan –* ℰ *(08)* Plan: **E1**
506 400 86 – www.pubologi.se – Closed Christmas-New Year, July and Sunday
Menu 695 SEK – *(dinner only) (booking advisable)*
• Creative • Friendly • Rustic •

A modern, wine-orientated bistro, with one long communal table and several smaller ones; the menus and cutlery are in illuminated drawers in the table. Cooking is fairly elaborate and good use is made of the chargrill.

X **The Flying Elk**

Mälartorget 15 ✉ *111 27 –* Ⓜ *Gamla Stan –* ℰ *(08)* Plan: **F1**
20 85 83 – www.theflyingelk.se – Closed 24-25, 31 December, 1 January and midsummer
Menu 695 SEK – Carte 315/710 SEK – *(dinner only and lunch Saturday and Sunday)*
• Modern cuisine • Inn • Friendly •

A good night out is guaranteed at this lively corner spot, which is modelled on a British pub and has several different bars. Choose from bar snacks, pub dishes with a twist or a popular tasting menu of refined modern classics.

X **Omakase Köttslöjd** 🕸 🅰🅲

Yxsmedsgränd 12 ✉ *111 28 –* Ⓜ *Gamla Stan –* ℰ *(08)* Plan: **E1**
506 400 80 – www.omakasekottslojd.se – Closed Christmas-New Year, July and Sunday-Tuesday
Menu 1195 SEK – *(dinner only) (booking essential) (tasting menu only)*
• Swedish • Cosy • Trendy •

There's plenty of interaction between the chefs and diners at this small restaurant which seats just 16. The chefs pick up to 20 dishes to serve and cooking is an unusual cross between Japanese sushi and home-cured Swedish charcuterie.

AT DJURGÅRDEN PLAN I

🏠 **Pop House** ⚑ 🛏 ♿ 🅰🅲

Djurgårdsvägen 68 ✉ *115 21 –* ℰ *(08) 502 541 40* Plan: **D2**
– www.pophouse.se
49 rm ☲ – 🛏1195/3095 SEK 🛏🛏1295/3295 SEK – 2 suites
• Boutique hotel • Personalised • Minimalist •

Pop House is ideally placed for visitors to the parks and museums of Djurgården. Bypass the queues waiting to enter 'ABBA The Museum', and head up to one of the spacious, simply furnished bedrooms; most have balconies with pleasant views. The small lounge, bar and restaurant are open-plan.

XX **Oaxen Krog** (Magnus Ek) 🕸 ≤ ♿
✿✿ *Beckholmsvägen 26 (off Djurgårdsvägen)* ✉ *115 21* Plan: **D3**
– ℰ *(08) 551 531 05 – www.oaxen.com*
– Closed 21 December-13 January, Easter, midsummer, Sunday-Monday and Tuesday January-March
Menu 1800/2100 SEK – *(dinner only) (booking essential)*
• Creative • Design • Friendly •

This rebuilt boat shed sits in a delightful waterside location. Diners are led through a secret door in Oaxen Slip into an oak-furnished room with a natural, slightly nautical feel. Choose 6 or 10 courses of 'New Nordic' cuisine: beautifully constructed dishes are allied to nature and the seasons – they're delicate and balanced but also offer real depth of flavour.
➔ Turbot with pickled elderflower sauce. Glazed pork with garlic, woodruff and spring onion. Sweet cicely sorbet with milk foam and rhubarb.

713

SWEDEN - STOCKHOLM

XX Ulla Winbladh

🛖 ⇄

Rosendalsvägen 8 ✉ *115 21 –* ℰ *(08) 534 897 01*   Plan: **D2**
– www.ullawinbladh.se – Closed 24-25 December
Menu 515 SEK – Carte 260/625 SEK – *(booking essential)*
• Swedish • Classic décor • Cosy •

Ulla Winbladh was originally built as a steam bakery for the 1897 Stockholm World Fair and is set in charming parkland beside the Skansen open-air museum. Sit on the terrace or in the older, more characterful part of the building. Hearty Swedish dishes include sweet and sour herring and fish roe.

X Oaxen Slip

🛖 ⅙ ⇄

Beckholmsvägen 26 (off Djurgårdsvägen) ✉ *115 21*   Plan: **D3**
– ℰ *(08) 551 53105 – www.oaxen.com – Closed Christmas and New Year*
Carte 265/620 SEK
• Traditional cuisine • Bistro •

A bright, bustling bistro next to the old slipway; try for a spot on the delightful terrace. Light floods the room and boats hang from the girders in a nod to the local shipbuilding industry. The food is wholesome and heartening and features plenty of seafood – whole fish dishes are a speciality.

AT SKEPPSHOLMEN   PLAN I

🏠 Skeppsholmen

✿ 🐾 ≤ 🛏 ℔ ℀ ⅙ 🅰 🎿 ⇄ **P**

Gröna Gången 1 ✉ *111 99 –* ℰ *(08) 407 23 00*   Plan: **D2**
– www.hotelskeppsholmen.se
81 rm ⌸ – ♦1495/2995 SEK ♦♦1495/2995 SEK – 1 suite
• Historic • Design • Personalised •

This 17C hotel is perfect for a peaceful stay close to the city. It's set on a small island beside a beautiful park and was built by the king in 1699 for his soldiers (the conference room was once the officers' mess). White bedrooms have a minimalist style and sea or park views. Menus feature Swedish recipes.

AT SÖDERMALM   PLAN I

🏠 Rival

✿ ⅙ 🎿

Mariatorget 3 ✉ *118 91 –* Ⓜ *Mariatorget –* ℰ *(08)*   Plan: **B3**
545 789 00 – www.rival.se
99 rm – ♦1395/4995 SEK ♦♦1395/4995 SEK – ⌸ 175 SEK – 2 suites
• Boutique hotel • Business • Personalised •

The location is delightful: opposite a beautiful square with gardens and a fountain. It's owned by ABBA's Benny Andersson and the stylish bedrooms come with Swedish movie themes and murals of famous scenes; the 700-seater art deco theatre also hosts regular events and shows. Dine on global dishes either in the bistro or on the balcony; the café is popular for snacks.

X Nook

Åsögatan 176 ✉ *116 32 –* Ⓜ *Medborgarplatsen*   Plan: **D3**
– ℰ *(08) 702 1222 – www.nookrestaurang.se – Closed Christmas, July,*
Sunday and Monday
Menu 380 SEK – Carte 380/430 SEK – *(dinner only) (booking advisable)*
• Modern cuisine • Intimate • Friendly •

This modern restaurant offers great value. Drop into the bar for Asian-influenced snacks or head to the intimately lit dining room with its checkerboard floor for one of two set menus. Creative cooking blends Swedish ingredients with Korean influences; order 3 days ahead for the suckling pig feast.

X **Häktet** 🏠 ⟳

Hornsgatan 82 ✉ *118 21 –* **Ⓜ** *Zinkensdamn – ℰ (08)* Plan: **B3**
84 59 10 – www.haktet.se – Closed 24 and 31 December, 1 January,
midsummer and Sunday
Carte 360/540 SEK *– (dinner only)*
• Modern cuisine • Bistro • Simple •
From 1781-1872 this was a debtors' prison. It has a characterful courtyard terrace and three bars – one in the style of a speakeasy, with a secret door. The
simple bistro at the back serves classic Swedish dishes with a modern edge.

X **Woodstockholm** 🏠 ⟳

Mosebacke Torg 9 ✉ *116 46 –* **Ⓜ** *Slussen – ℰ (08)* Plan: **C3**
36 93 99 – www.woodstockholm.com – Closed Christmas-New Year,
midsummer, Sunday and Monday
Menu 575 SEK – Carte 455/575 SEK *– (dinner only)*
• Modern cuisine • Bistro • Neighbourhood •
A chef-turned-furniture-maker owns this neighbourhood restaurant overlooking the park. Cooking follows a theme which changes every 2 months and
dishes are simple yet full of flavour. In summer, the private room opens as a
wine bar.

AT ARLANDA AIRPORT Northwest : 40 km by Sveavägen and E 4

🏨 **Clarion H. Arlanda Airport** ⚘ ﻟﻌ ﻧ﮺ 🗕 ﻟ 🖾 ﻟ﮶

Tornvägen 2, Sky City (at Terminals 4-5, 1st floor above street level)
✉ *190 45 – ℰ (08) 444 18 00 – www.choice.se/clarion/arlandaairport.se*
414 rm ⌸ – ✝990/2890 SEK ✝✝1190/3090 SEK – 13 suites
• Business • Modern • Functional •
A sleek, corporate hotel next to Terminals 4 and 5, with sound eco-credentials
– they even make honey from their own hives. Relax in the large 'Living
Room' lounge area or in the outside pool, then have dinner in the bistro which
offers a mix of international and Swedish dishes along with runway views.

🏨 **Radisson Blu Sky City** ⚘ ﻟﻌ ﻧ﮺ 🗕 🖾 ﻟ﮶

Sky City (at Terminals 4-5, 2nd floor above street level) ✉ *190 45 – ℰ (08)*
50 67 4000 – www.radissonblu.com/skycityhotel-arlanda
260 rm – ✝1595/2895 SEK ✝✝1595/2895 SEK – ⌸ 150 SEK – 1 suite
• Business • Modern • Functional •
This comfy business hotel enjoys a unique location, looking out over the atrium
of the airport terminal as well as the runway. Well-soundproofed bedrooms
come in three different styles; go for 'Business Class' for more space and amenities. The restaurant serves a blend of Swedish classics and more global dishes.

ENVIRONS OF STOCKHOLM

AT **NORRTULL** North : 2 km by Sveavägen (at beginning of E4)

🏠 **Stallmästaregården** ⚘ ﺩ﮲ ﻟ﮶ **P**

Nortull ✉ *113 47 – ℰ (08) 610 13 00 – www.stallmastaregarden.se*
– Closed 24-30 December
49 rm ⌸ – ✝1495/2995 SEK ✝✝1495/2995 SEK – 3 suites
• Inn • Historic building • Historic •
You can enjoy beautiful views over the water to the Royal Park from this brightly
painted inn, which dates from the 17C. It comprises several buildings set around
a garden courtyard. Cosy bedrooms have a classic style and Oriental touches.
Modern Swedish cuisine is influenced by classic Tore Wretman recipes.

AT **LADUGÅRDSGÄRDET** East : 3 km by Strandvägen

🏠 **Villa Källhagen**   ☆ ⅍ ← 🛏 ⅏ 🆎 ⅍ 🅿

Djurgårdsbrunnsvägen 10 ⊠ *115 27* – ✆ *(08) 665 03 00*
– *www.kallhagen.se*
36 rm ⌕ – ✝1295/2795 SEK ✝✝1495/2995 SEK – 3 suites
• Traditional • Business • Minimalist •
This well-run hotel is a popular place for functions, but with its tranquil
waterside location, it's a hit with leisure guests too. Bedrooms feature four
different colour schemes – inspired by the seasons – and have park or
water views. The modern Swedish menu has a classic edge and comes with
wine pairings.

AT **FJÄDERHOLMARNA ISLAND** East: 25 minutes by boat from Sodermalm,
or 5 minutes from Nacka Strand

XX **Fjäderholmarnas Krog**   ← 🍴 ⅙

Stora Fjäderholmen ⊠ *111 15* – ✆ *(08) 7188 33 55*
– *www.fjaderholmarnaskrog.se* – *Closed 17-28 April, 29 September-
22 November and 22 December-31 March*
Menu 395/495 SEK – Carte 405/880 SEK – *(booking essential)*
• Seafood • Friendly • Rustic •
The location is idyllic and on a sunny day nothing beats a spot on the terrace
watching the ships glide through the archipelago. The airy interior has a
boathouse feel. Classic seafood dishes are replaced by a buffet table at
Christmas.

AT **NACKA STRAND** Southeast : 10 km by Stadsgården or 20 mins by boat
from Nybrokajen

🏨 **Hotel J**   ⅍ ← 🛏 ⅙ 🆎 ⅍ 🅿

Ellensviksvägen 1 ⊠ *131 28* – ✆ *(08) 601 30 00* – *www.hotelj.com*
158 rm ⌕ – ✝1290/2990 SEK ✝✝1290/2990 SEK – 4 suites
• Historic • Design •
This was once the summer house of a local politician and a relaxed atmosphere
still pervades. Maritime knick-knacks feature in the charming guest areas and
bedrooms have a quirky New England style; many overlook the water.
Restaurant J – See restaurant listing

X **Restaurant J** – Hotel J   ← 🍴

Ellensviksvägen 1 ⊠ *131 28* – ✆ *(08) 601 30 25* – *www.hotelj.com*
– *Closed 25-30 December and 1-10 January*
Carte dinner 360/705 SEK
• Swedish • Brasserie •
A short stroll along the waterfront from Hotel J is its long, narrow restaurant.
Huge windows and a lovely terrace make the most of the marina setting (it's
just 20mins from the city by boat). Swedish dishes mix with global fare.

AT **LILLA ESSINGEN** West : 5.5 km by Norr Mälarstrand

XX **Lux Dag för Dag**   ← 🍴 ⅙ 🆎

Primusgatan 116 ⊠ *112 67* – ✆ *(08) 619 01 90* – *www.luxdagfordag.se*
– *Closed 23 December-2 January, 16 July-16 August and Sunday-Monday*
Carte 345/655 SEK
• Modern cuisine • Brasserie • Neighbourhood •
A bright, modern, brasserie-style restaurant in an old waterside Electrolux
factory dating back to 1916. Generously proportioned dishes might look
modern but they have a traditional base; sourcing ingredients locally is para-
mount.

SWEDEN - STOCKHOLM

XX   **Bockholmen**   ⇐ 斎 ✿ **P**

Bockholmsvägen ⊠ *170 78 –* ⓜ *Bergshamra – ✆ (08) 624 22 00
– www.bockholmen.com – Closed 20 December-6 January,
midsummer and lunch October-April*
Carte 290/665 SEK – *(booking essential)*
• Swedish • Traditional décor • Country house •
With charming terraces leading down to the water and an outside bar, this 19C
summer house is the perfect place to relax on a summer's day. It's set on a tiny
island, so opening times vary. Wide-ranging menus include weekend brunch.

XX   **Ulriksdals Wärdshus**   ⇐ 扁 ✿ **P**

*Ulriksdals Slottspark (Northwest: 8 km by Sveavägen and E 18 towards
Norrtälje then take first junction for Ulriksdals Slott)* ⊠ *170 79
–* ⓜ *Bergshamra – ✆ (08) 85 08 15 – www.ulriksdalswardshus.se
– Closed Monday dinner*
Menu 285 SEK (weekday lunch)/485 SEK – Carte 450/745 SEK – *(booking
essential)*
• Traditional cuisine • Inn •
A charming 19C wooden inn located in the park, with traditional winter garden
styling and a lovely wine cellar. Classic Swedish dishes are supplemented by a
smörgåsbord at lunch. Start with drinks on the terrace overlooking the lake.

GOTHENBURG
GÖTEBORG

Kjell Holmner/Göteborg & Co/www.imagebank.sweden.se

Gothenburg is considered to be one of Sweden's friendliest towns, a throwback to its days as a leading trading centre. This is a compact, pretty city whose roots go back four hundred years. It has trams, broad avenues and canals and its centre is boisterous but never feels tourist heavy or overcrowded. Gothenburgers take life at a more leisurely pace than their Stockholm cousins over on the east coast. The mighty shipyards that once dominated the shoreline are now quiet; go to the centre, though, and you find the good-time ambience of Avenyn, a vivacious thoroughfare full of places in which to shop, eat and drink. But for those still itching for a feel of the heavy industry that once defined the place, there's a Volvo museum sparkling with chrome and shiny steel.

The Old Town is the historic heart of the city: its tight grid of streets has grand façades and a fascinating waterfront. Just west is the Vasastan quarter, full of fine National Romantic buildings. Further west again is Haga, an old working-class district which has been gentrified, its cobbled streets sprawling with trendy cafes and boutiques. Adjacent to Haga is the district of Linné, a vibrant area with its elegantly tall 19th century Dutch-inspired buildings. As this is a maritime town, down along the quayside is as good a place to get your bearings as any.

GOTHENBURG IN...

→ **ONE DAY**
The Old Town, Stadsmuseum, The Museum of World Culture.

→ **TWO DAYS**
Liseberg amusement park, The Maritiman, Art Museum, a stroll around Linné.

→ **THREE DAYS**
A trip on a Paddan boat, a visit to the Opera House.

PRACTICAL INFORMATION

ARRIVAL-DEPARTURE

 Landvetter Airport is 25km east of the city. There are regular bus connections to the city centre, including Flygbussarna; payment is by card only and journey time is around 25min.

 City Airport is 15km northwest.

GETTING AROUND

The Gothenburg Card gives you unlimited bus, tram and boat travel within the city and is valid for one, two or three days. It will also guarantee you a sightseeing tour, admission to the Liseberg amusement park, entry to most museums, and discounts in certain shops. Alternatively, buy a 24 or 72 hour credit card style travel pass for unlimited travel on trams, buses and boats. Single tickets are also available. Punts – flat Paddan boats – are a pleasant way to explore this maritime city in summer, gliding past stately canalside buildings.

CALENDAR HIGHLIGHTS

January
International Film Festival.

April
International Science Festival.

June
Match Cup (Sailing),
Midsummer's Eve Celebrations.

July
Gothia Cup (Youth Football).

August
Jazz Festival, Culture Festival.

October
Kulturnatta (Culture Night).

December
Liseberg Christmas Market.

EATING OUT

Gothenburg's oldest food market is called Feskekörka or 'Fish Church'. It does indeed look like a place of worship but its pews are stalls of oysters, prawns and salmon, and where you might expect to find an organ loft, you'll find a restaurant instead. Food – and in particular the piscine variety – is a big reason for visiting Gothenburg. Its restaurants have earned a plethora of Michelin stars, which are dotted all over the compact city. If you're after something a little simpler, head for one of the typical Swedish Konditoris (cafés) – two of the best are Brogyllen and Ahlströms. If you're visiting between December and April, try the traditional cardamom-spiced buns known as 'semla'. The 19C covered food markets, Stora Saluhallen at Kungstorget and Saluhallen Briggen at Nordhemsgatan in Linnestaden, are worth a visit. Also in Kungstorget is the city's most traditional beer hall, Ölhallen 7:an; there are only 6 others in town. Gothenburgers also like the traditional food pairing 'SOS', where herring and cheese are washed down with schnapps.

SWEDEN - GOTHENBURG

Upper House
 ⩽ 🖬 🕙 🕸 ☒ ⛴ 🄰🄲 🅿

Gothia Towers (25th Floor), Mässans Gata 24 ✉ *402 26* — Plan: **D3**
— 𝒞 (031) 708 82 00 — www.upperhouse.se
53 rm � — **†**2890/5390 SEK **††**2890/5390 SEK — 1 suite
• Luxury • Modern •

Set at the top of one of the Gothia Towers; take in the dramatic view from the terrace or from the lovely three-storey spa. Spacious bedrooms are filled with top electronic equipment and Scandic art — the duplex suites are sublime.
🏵 **Upper House** — See restaurant listing

Elite Plaza
 🖬 🕸 🏨 🚗

Västra Hamngatan 3 ✉ *402 22* — 𝒞 *(031) 720 40 40* Plan: **B2**
— www.elite.se — Closed 23-27 December
127 rm ⊻ — **†**1700/2700 SEK **††**2200/4500 SEK — 3 suites
• Luxury • Modern •

Elegant former bank dating back to the 19C, featuring a grand staircase, ornate ceilings and a Venetian-style sitting room. The team are welcoming and service is personalised. Bedrooms seamlessly blend the classical and the modern.
Swea Hof — See restaurant listing

Clarion H. Post
 🕺 ⩽ 🖬 🖻 🕸 ☒ 🄰🄲 🏨 🚗

Drottningtorget 10 ✉ *411 03* — 𝒞 *(031) 61 90 00* Plan: **C2**
— www.clarionpost.se
500 rm ⊻ — **†**1490/2090 SEK **††**1690/2290 SEK — 3 suites
• Historic • Business • Modern •

Stunning neoclassical Post Office from the 1920s; now a modern business hotel with extensive conference facilities. Ask for one of the high-ceilinged bedrooms in the original building. Relax in the rooftop pool, the impressive spa or the cool ground floor bar. Norda is a slick New York style restaurant; vRÅ offers modern Japanese cuisine.
vRÅ — See restaurant listing

Elite Park Avenue
🕺 ⩽ 🖬 🖻 🕸 🄰🄲 🏨 🚗

Kungsportsavenyn 36-38 ✉ *400 15* — 𝒞 *(031) 727 1076* Plan: **C3**
— www.parkavenuecafe.se
317 rm ⊻ — **†**1050/2350 SEK **††**1250/2750 SEK — 9 suites
• Business • Chain • Modern •

Set in a lively location by the Museum of Art, a 1950s building with a stylish interior and spacious, well-equipped bedrooms — the rooftop suites come with balconies. Eat in the English cellar pub; the small Italian eatery-cum-nightclub; or the informal bistro, which mixes French and Swedish cooking.

Avalon
 🕺 🕸 ☒ ⛴ 🄰🄲 🏨 🚗

Kungstorget 9 ✉ *411 17* — 𝒞 *(031) 751 02 00* Plan: **B2**
— www.avalonhotel.se
101 rm ⊻ — **†**1245/2445 SEK **††**1445/2745 SEK — 3 suites
• Business • Modern •

A boutique hotel in a great location near the shops, theatres and harbour. Designer bedrooms have the latest mod cons and come with stylish bathrooms; the penthouse suites have balconies. Relax in the rooftop pool then head for the all-day bistro, which opens onto the piazza and serves international cuisine.

Scandic Rubinen
 🕺 🖬 ⛴ 🏨

Kungsportsavenyn 24 ✉ *400 14* — 𝒞 *(031) 751 54 00* Plan: **C3**
— www.rubybar.se
289 rm ⊻ — **†**790/2290 SEK **††**990/2490 SEK — 3 suites
• Business • Chain • Modern •

Set in the heart of town, on the main street, close to the shops and city sights. Half of the bedrooms are stylish and modern, while the others have a classic Scandic style. Relax in the spa or out beside the lovely rooftop bar with some nibbles or cold meats, then dine overlooking the Avenue.

Radisson Blu Riverside 🏶 ≼ ⯎ ⯑ 🕭 🅰 🔥 🕳

Lindholmspiren 4, Lindholmen Science Park (West: 4 km by Götaälvbron or take free shuttle ferry from Rosenlund 7am-7pm) ✉ *417 56 – ℰ (031) 383 4000 – www.radissonblu.se/riversidehotel-gothenburg.com*

265 rm ⌗ – 🛏1200/2400 SEK 🛏🛏1300/2500 SEK – 7 suites
• Business • Chain • Modern •

Striking waterfront hotel in the Science Park; a regular shuttle bus operates to the city centre. The rooftop wellness complex has a lovely terrace and hot tub. Some of the modern bedrooms afford great river and city views. The open-plan dining area offers a mix of classical and innovative Swedish cuisine.

 Dorsia 🏶 🕭 🅰

Trädgårdsgatan 6 ✉ *411 08 – ℰ (031) 790 10 00*   Plan: **B2**
– www.dorsia.se

37 rm ⌗ – 🛏1950 SEK 🛏🛏2550/6950 SEK
• Townhouse • Family • Art déco •

Exuberant, eccentric, seductive and possibly a little decadent, this townhouse hotel comes with a theatrical belle époque style, where art from the owner's personal collection, fine fabrics and rich colours add to the joie de vivre. The restaurant is equally vibrant and the atmosphere suitably relaxed. The Salon serves small plates from Friday-Sunday.

Dorsia – See restaurant listing

 Pigalle 🏶

Södra Hamngatan 2A ✉ *411 06 – ℰ (031) 802921*   Plan: **B2**
– www.hotelpigalle.se

38 rm ⌗ – 🛏1000/1700 SEK 🛏🛏1700/2600 SEK
• Townhouse • Family • Contemporary •

A top-hatted manager will welcome you to the reception-cum-welcome-bar of this quirky hotel, which is set within the walls of a historic building. The décor is bold and eclectic, with dramatic features and plenty of personality. In the restaurant you can choose to sit at proper tables or on comfy sofas.

 Eggers 🏶 🅰

Drottningtorget 2-4 ✉ *411 03 – ℰ (031) 333 44 44*   Plan: **B2**
– www.hoteleggers.se – Closed 23-26 December

69 rm ⌗ – 🛏1020/1925 SEK 🛏🛏1340/2490 SEK
• Traditional • Classic •

Smart 1859 railway hotel that opened with electricity and telephones in every room. The warm, welcoming interior features old wrought iron, stained glass and period furnishings. The characterful restaurant still has its original wallpaper, and offers Swedish classics and international favourites.

 Novotel Göteborg 🏶 ≼ 🕭 🔥 🅰 🅿

Klippan 1 (Southwest: 3.5 km by Andréeg taking Kiel-Klippan Ö exit, or boat from Rosenlund) ✉ *414 51 – ℰ (031) 720 22 00 – www.novotel.se*

151 rm ⌗ – 🛏990/1910 SEK 🛏🛏1090/2010 SEK – 1 suite
• Chain • Business • Functional •

Close to the foot ferry, a converted waterfront brewery where you can still buy some vintage Porter beers. The clean, bright interior affords views of the Göta Älv river. Bedrooms are spacious and have a Scandic style; pay the extra for a water view. The restaurant offers Swedish and international classics.

 Flora

Grönsakstorget 2 ✉ *411 17 – ℰ (031) 13 86 16*   Plan: **B2**
– www.hotelflora.se – Closed Christmas

65 rm ⌗ – 🛏860/1960 SEK 🛏🛏1190/2240 SEK
• Family • Functional •

This well-located Victorian mid-terrace is nicely run and has a relaxed, funky feel. Bedrooms benefit from high ceilings; ask for one of the newer, designer rooms. The bar-lounge is a popular spot and doubles as the breakfast room.

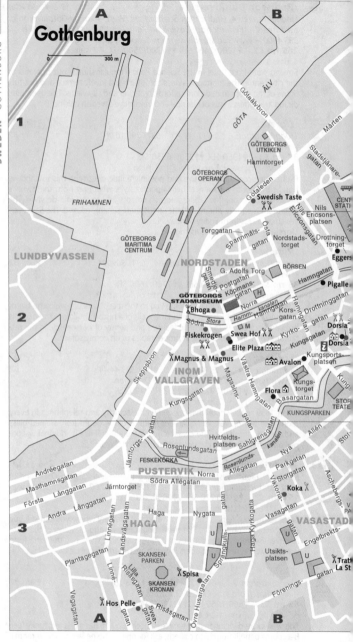

Gothenburg

0 — 300 m

A

B

1

GÖTA ÄLV

Götaälv-bron

GÖTEBORGS UTKIKEN

Hamntorget

GÖTEBORGS OPERAN

Götaleden

● Swedish Taste

FRIHAMNEN

Torggatan

Spannmåls-gatan

Östa gatan

Nordstads-torget

Nils Ericsonsgatan

Nils Ericsons-platsen

CENT STATI

Drottning-torget

GÖTEBORGS MARITIMA CENTRUM

LUNDBYVASSEN

NORDSTADEN

G. Adolfs Torg

BÖRSEN

● Eggers

Smedje gatan

Postgatan

Köpmans-gatan

Hamngatan

● Pigalle

GÖTEBORGS STADMUSEUM

Norra

H

Hamm kanalen

Hamngatan

● Bhoga

Stora

Hamngatan

Kors-gatan

Drottninggatan

Dorsia

Södra

M

Swea Hof

Kyrko-gatan

gatan

Kungsgatan

Dorsia

● Fiskekrogen

Elite Plaza

V;stra Hamngatan

Avalon

Kungsports-platsen

Skeppsbron

Magnus & Magnus

Magasins-gatan

Flora

Kungs-torget

Kung

INOM VALLGRAVEN

Kungsgatan

Basargatan

KUNGSPARKEN

STOR TEATE

Hvitfeldts-platsen

Sahlgrensgatan

Allén

Stor

Järntorgs-gatan

Rosenlundsgatan

kanalen

Nya

Andréegatan

FESKEKÔRKA

Rosenlunds-Allégatan

Parkgatan

Aschebergs-

V PA

Masthamnsgatan

PUSTERVIK

Norra

Storgatan

Viktoria

● Koka

Första Långgatan

Järntorget

Södra Allégatan

gatan

Vasagatan

VASASTADE

Landsvägsgatan

Haga

Nygata

Haga Kyrkogata

Andra Långgatan

HAGA

U

U

Engelbrekts-

3

Plantagegatan

Linné-

SKANSEN-PARKEN

Spränkullsgatan

U

U

Utsikts-platsen

U

Trat La St

Lilla Risåsgatan

SKANSEN KRONAN

Spisa

Övre Husargatan

gatan

Vegagatan

Hos Pelle

Swea-gatan

Risåsgatan

Förenings-

A

B

722

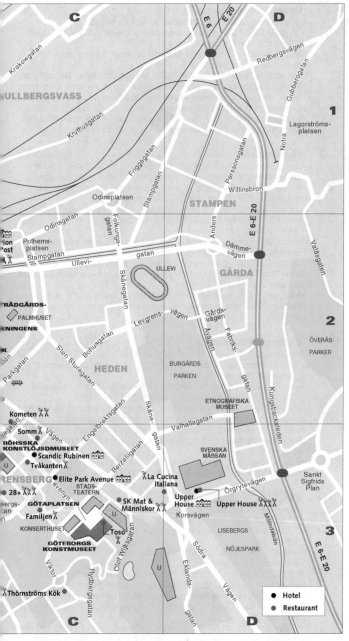

C

D

E 6

E 20

Krakowgatan

ULLBERGSVASS

Kruthusgatan

Redbergsvägen

Gubberogatan

Lagorströms-
platsen

Notra

1

Friggagatan

Stampgatan

Perssonsgatan

Odinsplatsen

Willinsbron

STAMPEN

E 6-E 20

Valåsgatan

ion
Post

Pothems-
platsen

Stampgatan

Odinsgatan

Folkunga-
gatan

Ullevi-   gatan

Anders

Dämme-
vägen

GÅRDA

Skånegatan

ULLEVI

RÄDGÅRDS-

PALMHUSET

Levgrens-   vägen

Gårda-
vägen

Fabriks-

ÖVERÅS-
PARKER

2

ENINGENS

K

Parkgatan

Sten Sturegatan

Bohusgatan

HEDEN

BURGÅRDS
PARKEN

Ävägen

gatan

Kungsbackaleden

Kometen

ETNOGRAFISKA
MUSEET

Engelbrektsgatan

Skåne-

Valhallagatan

Somm

RÖHSSKA
KONSTLÖJSDMUSEET

Scandic Rubinen

Tvåkanten

Berzeligatan

gatan

SVENSKA
MÄSSAN

Sankt
Sigfrids
Plan

RENSBERG

Elite Park Avenue

La Cucina
Italiana

Örgrytevägen

Upper House

28+

avenyn

STADS-
TEATERN

GÖTAPLATSEN

SK Mat &
Människor

Upper
House

Korsvägen

Mölndalsån

E 6-E 20

bergs-
gatan

Familjen

KONSERTHUSET

Toso

LISEBERGS

NÖJESPARK

3

GÖTEBORGS
KONSTMUSEET

Olof Wijksgatan

Viktor

Rydbergsgatan

Södra

Eklanda-

U

Thörnströms Kök

Vägen

gatan

● Hotel

● Restaurant

XxxX
Upper House – Upper House Hotel ❀ ≤ ㊑ Ⓐ㊐

ॐ *Gothia Towers (25th Floor), Mässans Gata 24* ✉ *402 26*   Plan: **D3**
– ℰ (031) 708 82 00 – www.upperhouse.se – Closed 9 July-9 August, 23-
25 December, Sunday and Monday
Menu 1250 SEK *– (dinner only) (booking essential) (tasting menu only)*
• Swedish • Elegant • Chic •

Look out from the 25th floor over 360° of twinkling city lights. Start with 'nib-bles' in the plush bar then watch your bread being cooked over a hot stone. The set menu offers elaborate, visually pleasing, flavourful dishes made with an abundance of fresh, local ingredients. Service is attentive and professional.
→ Quail egg, lemon and dried bleak roe. Courgette flower with sweet-breads and tomato. Cinnamon madeleine with apple butter.

XxX
Sjömagasinet (Gustav Trägårdh) ❀ ≤ ㊟ ㊑ ⇔ Ⓟ

ॐ *Adolf Edelsvärds gata 5, Klippans Kulturreservat 5 (Southwest: 3.5 km by*
Andréeg taking Kiel-Klippan exit (Stena Line), or boat from Rosenlund.
Also evenings and weekends in summer from Lilla Bommens Hamn)
✉ *414 51 – ℰ (031) 775 59 20 – www.sjomagasinet.se*
– Closed 24 December-5 January, Saturday lunch and Sunday
Menu 625/945 SEK *– Carte 675/1225 SEK – (booking essential)*
• Swedish • Rustic • Cosy •

An East India Company warehouse dating from 1775; now a charming split-level restaurant with a lovely terrace and harbour views. Seafood is the strength, with classic Swedish dishes on the 'Wagner' menu and modern Nordic choices on the 'Trägårdh' menu. At lunch they offer a buffet and a concise version of the à la carte.
→ Lobster salad. Steamed turbot with oyster sauce, truffle and potato variations. Dark chocolate brioche, chocolate and peanut crème, sesame ice-cream.

XxX
Thörnströms Kök (Håkan Thörnström) ❀ Ⓐ㊐ ⇔

ॐ *Teknologgatan 3* ✉ *411 32 – ℰ (031) 16 20 66*   Plan: **C3**
– www.thornstromskok.com – Closed 8 July-15 August, 23 December-
5 January, Easter and Sunday
Menu 465 SEK *– Carte 445/760 SEK – (dinner only) (booking essential)*
• Classic cuisine • Neighbourhood • Romantic •

An elegant, long-standing restaurant with a stunning wine cave; set in a quiet residential area and run by a welcoming, knowledgeable team. There's a good choice of menus, including 3 different tasting options. Precise, confi-dent, classically based cooking uses top quality produce to create pronoun-ced flavours.
→ Arctic char with mussels and clams. Sirloin of beef with fermented onion butter. Sorrel mousse, milk foam, red berries and vanilla.

XxX
28+ ❀ Ⓐ㊐ ⇔

ॐ *Götabergsgatan 28* ✉ *411 34*   Plan: **C3**
– ℰ (031) 20 21 61 – www.28plus.se
– Closed 4 July-22 August, Christmas-New Year, Sunday, Monday and
bank holidays
Menu 895 SEK *– Carte 565/655 SEK – (dinner only)*
• Modern cuisine • Chic •

This passionately run basement restaurant has been a Gothenburg institu-tion for over 30 years. Modern cooking showcases prime seasonal ingre-dients, skilfully blending French and Swedish influences to create intricate, flavourful dishes. There's an exceptional cheese selection and an outstan-ding wine list.
→ Sweetbreads with ramsons, morels and cress. Loin of salted cod with fermented garlic gnocchi. Liquorice, lemon, condensed milk and lemon sor-bet.

XX **SK Mat & Människor** (Stefan Karlsson)   ৬. AC
ঞ্চ
Johannebergsgatan 24 ⊠ 412 55 – ℰ (031) 812 580   Plan: **C3**
*– www.skmat.se – Closed 6 weeks summer, 2 weeks Christmas, Sunday
and bank holidays*
Menu 595 SEK – Carte 515/550 SEK – *(dinner only) (booking essential)*
• Swedish • Brasserie • Cosy •
The main focal point of this cosy restaurant is the completely open kitchen; not
only can you watch the chefs at work but they also deliver your food. The effort
put into sourcing and the reverence with which ingredients are treated is commendable and dishes are exciting and packed with flavour.
→ Cured cod with shrimps and elderflower. Swedish strip-loin with parsley
mayonnaise and fried bread. Blueberries with lemon curd and burnt meringue.

XX **Dorsia** – Dorsia Hotel   🛁 🚭 AC ⟺
Trädgårdsgatan 6 ⊠ 411 08 – ℰ (031) 790 10 00   Plan: **B2**
– www.dorsia.se
Menu 185/385 SEK – Carte 595/770 SEK
• Modern cuisine • Exotic décor • Romantic •
A dramatic hotel dining room split over two levels, with gloriously quirky lighting, striking flower arrangements by the owner, and belle époque oil paintings
hanging proudly on the walls. Local fish features highly and puddings are worth
saving room for. Ask for the rare wine book – you'll be impressed!

XX **Fiskekrogen**   🛁 AC ⟺
Lilla Torget 1 ⊠ 411 18 – ℰ (031) 10 10 05   Plan: **B2**
*– www.fiskekrogen.com – Closed Christmas-New Year, midsummer, Easter
and Sunday*
Carte 365/775 SEK – *(dinner only)*
• Seafood • Elegant • Cosy •
A charming seafood restaurant which is set within a columned 1920s Grand
Café and showcases top quality produce. 'Bifångst' is its second smaller dining
area which offers a tasting menu of modern small plates.

XX **Swedish Taste**   ⟺
Sankt Eriksgatan 6 ⊠ 411 05 – ℰ (031) 13 27 80   Plan: **B1**
*– www.swedishtaste.com – Closed 3 July-11 August, Christmas, Saturday
lunch and Sunday*
Menu 315/535 SEK – Carte 520/835 SEK
• Modern cuisine • Fashionable •
A three-storey venture near the Opera House, consisting of a restaurant, a café,
a deli and a cookery school. Lunch is traditional; more elaborate, contemporary dishes follow at dinner. Produce is top quality and flavours are authentic.

XX **Kometen**   🚭
Vasagatan 58 ⊠ 411 37 – ℰ (031) 137988   Plan: **C2**
*– www.restaurangkometen.se – Closed midsummer, 23-27 December and
1 January*
Carte 435/775 SEK – *(booking essential)*
• Scandinavian • Family • Neighbourhood •
The oldest restaurant in town has a classic façade and clubby feel; it opened in
1934 and is now part-owned by celebrated chef Leif Mannerström. Sweden's
culinary traditions are kept alive here in generous, tasty dishes.

XX **Swea Hof** – Elite Plaza Hotel   AC 🚗
Västra Hamngatan 3 ⊠ 404 22 – ℰ (031) 720 40 40   Plan: **B2**
– www.sweahof.se – Closed 23-27 December
Menu 155/260 SEK – Carte 330/1015 SEK
• Modern cuisine • Chic •
Striking hotel restaurant in an impressive glass-enclosed courtyard. Start
with drinks in the bar, then head to the spacious dining room. Fresh, modern
cooking combines French and Scandinavian influences; the lunch menu is concise.

X ✿
Koka
AC

Viktoriagatan 12 ✉ 411 25 – ℰ (031) 701 79 79   Plan: **B3**
– www.restaurangkoka.se – Closed Monday-Tuesday July, Christmas and Sunday
Menu 480/880 SEK – *(dinner only) (tasting menu only)*
• Modern cuisine • Design • Neighbourhood •

An understatedly elegant room with wooden planks on the floors and walls and wooden furniture to match. Choose 3, 5 or 7 courses from the daily set menu; dishes are light and refreshingly playful in their approach and fish features highly. Well-chosen wines and smooth service complete the picture.
→ Mackerel with gooseberries and cress. Pork shoulder, marigold and trout roe. Sorrel, seaweed and raspberry.

X ✿
Bhoga (Gustav Knutsson and Niclas Yngvesson)

Norra Hamngatan 10 ✉ 411 14 – ℰ (031) 13 80 18   Plan: **B2**
– www.bhoga.se – Closed 20 December-10 January, 1-7 August, Sunday and Monday
Menu 600/900 SEK – *(dinner only)*
• Creative • Friendly • Simple •

A chic, contemporary restaurant with an elegant feel, which is passionately run by two well-travelled chefs and their charmingly attentive team. Top quality seasonal ingredients are used in imaginative ways, creating provocative yet harmonious texture and flavour combinations. Wine pairings are original.
→ New potatoes with raspberries, walnuts and marigolds. Roast duck with fermented garlic. Meadowsweet ice cream with blackcurrant and buckwheat.

X ⊛
Somm
❀ AC

Lorensbergsgatan 8 ✉ 411 36 – ℰ (031) 28 28 40   Plan: **C3**
– www.somm.se – Closed July, 23-27 December and 1 January
Menu 395 SEK – Carte 485/585 SEK – *(dinner only)*
• Modern cuisine • Friendly • Cosy •

A simply but warmly decorated neighbourhood bistro, with contemporary artwork and a cosy, friendly feel. Quality seasonal ingredients are used to create tasty modern dishes, which feature on an à la carte and various tasting menus. The wine list offers great choice and the service is charming and professional.

X ⊛
Familjen
❀ ☂ AC

Arkivgatan 7 ✉ 411 34 – ℰ (031) 20 79 79   Plan: **C3**
– www.restaurangfamiljen.se – Closed Christmas and Sunday
Menu 355/455 SEK – Carte 335/575 SEK – *(dinner only) (booking essential)*
• Scandinavian • Vintage • Design •

A lively, friendly eatery divided into three parts: a bar with bench seating and an open kitchen; a bright red room with a characterful cellar and a glass wine cave; and a superb wrap-around terrace. Cooking is good value and portions are generous. There's an appealing wine, beer and cocktail list too.

X
Toso
AC

Götaplatsen ✉ 412 56 – ℰ (031) 787 98 00   Plan: **C3**
– www.toso.nu – Closed Christmas and bank holidays
Menu 530 SEK – Carte 360/525 SEK – *(dinner only)*
• Asian • Bistro • Exotic décor •

There's something for everyone at this modern Asian restaurant, where terracotta warriors stand guard and loud music pumps through the air. Dishes mix Chinese and Japanese influences; start with some of the tempting small plates.

X
Magnus & Magnus
☂

Magasinsgatan 8 ✉ 411 18 – ℰ (031) 13 30 00   Plan: **B2**
– www.magnusmagnus.se – Closed 24-25 December, Sunday and Monday
Menu 555/795 SEK – Carte 585/605 SEK – *(dinner only)*
• Creative • Intimate • Neighbourhood •

A trendy restaurant with a warm, intimate atmosphere, a central bar, an open kitchen and a bright, well-informed team. Modern Nordic cooking has the occasional Asian twist; most diners plump for the set 4 course menu.

✗ ## Hos Pelle

Djupedalsgatan 2 ⊠ *413 07 – 𝒞 (031) 12 10 31*   Plan: **A3**
*– www.hospelle.com – Closed 22-27 December, July, Easter, Saturday
lunch and Sunday*
Menu 465 SEK (dinner) – Carte 290/580 SEK
• Traditional cuisine • Neighbourhood •

An established neighbourhood eatery located close to the castle; you can eat in the wine bar or one of two cosy, rustic dining rooms. Cooking is stout, seasonal and satisfying; the concise set dinner menu has suggested wine pairings.

✗ ## La Cucina Italiana

Skånegatan 33 ⊠ *412 52 – 𝒞 (031) 166 307*   Plan: **C3**
*– www.lacucinaitaliana.nu – Closed Christmas, Easter, midsummer and
Sunday*
Menu 400/700 SEK – Carte 475/730 SEK – *(dinner only) (booking essential)*
• Italian • Friendly •

An intimate and enthusiastically run restaurant consisting of 6 tables. Choose between the à la carte, a 3 course menu and a 6 course surprise tasting 'journey'. The chef-owner regularly travels to Italy to buy cheeses, meats and wines.

✗ ## Tvåkanten

Kungsportsavenyn 27 ⊠ *411 36 – 𝒞 (031) 18 21 15*   Plan: **C3**
*– www.tvakanten.se – Closed Christmas, Easter, midsummer and bank
holidays*
Carte 335/655 SEK
• Traditional cuisine • Brasserie •

Set in a prime corner position on one of the city's most famous streets. A busy bar leads to a cosy cellar-style dining room. Classical menus cover everything from snacks and brunch to more ambitious dishes; there's also a great wine list.

✗ ## Spisa

Övre Husargatan 3 ⊠ *411 22 – 𝒞 (031) 3860610*   Plan: **B3**
– www.spisamatbar.se
Menu 295/495 SEK – Carte 305/445 SEK – *(dinner only)*
• Mediterranean cuisine • Tapas bar •

Contemporary restaurant set a short walk from the city centre in an up-and-coming area and frequented by a lively, sociable crowd. The menu offers tasty sharing plates with French, Spanish and Italian origins. Try a cocktail too!

✗ ## vRÅ – Clarion Hotel Post

Drottningtorget 10 ⊠ *411 03 – 𝒞 (031) 61 90 60*   Plan: **C2**
– www.restaurangvra.se – Closed Sunday, Monday and Friday
Menu 395 SEK – Carte 625/689 SEK – *(dinner only)*
• Japanese • Bistro • Simple •

A modern hotel restaurant run by an attentive, knowledgeable team. Their tagline is 'Swedish ingredients, Japanese flavours' and the produce is top quality. Choose the 8 course set menu or a menu with 3 core dishes which you can add to.

✗ ## Trattoria La Strega

Aschebergsgatan 23b ⊠ *411 25 – 𝒞 (031) 18 15 01*   Plan: **B3**
– www.trattorialastrega.se – Closed July and 24 December-6 January
Menu 500 SEK – Carte 300/520 SEK – *(dinner only) (booking essential)*
• Italian • Friendly • Bistro •

A lively little trattoria in a quiet residential area; run by a charming owner. Sit at a candlelit table to enjoy authentic, boldly flavoured Italian cooking and well-chosen wines. Signature dishes include pasta with King crab ragout.

SWEDEN - GOTHENBURG

AT ERIKSBERG   West : 6 km by Götaälvbron and Lundbyleden, or boat from Rosenlund

 Villan

Sjöportsgatan 2 ⊠ 417 64 – 𝒞 (031) 725 77 77 – www.hotelvillan.com
26 rm ⊊ – ☗1150/1700 SEK ☗☗1400/2100 SEK
• Traditional • Modern •

Characterful wood-clad, family-run house; once home to a shipbuilding manager and later floated over to this location. The stylish interior has smart, clean
lines. Contemporary bedrooms boast good mod cons – No.31 has a sauna and
a TV in the bathroom. The first floor restaurant overlooks the river.

XX   **River Restaurant On The Pier**

Dockepiren ⊠ 417 64 – 𝒞 (031) 51 00 00 – www.riverrestaurant.se
*– Closed 2 weeks January, Christmas, Saturday lunch, Sunday and
Monday*
Menu 400/700 SEK – Carte 400/800 SEK – *(booking advisable)*
• Modern cuisine • Friendly •

A delightful waterfront restaurant overlooking the city and harbour, with a
bright, modern ground floor and an elegant upper level. Come at lunch for an
unfussy set menu or at dinner for a seasonal à la carte of hearty Scandic dishes.

AT LANDVETTER AIRPORT   East : 30 km by Rd 40

 Landvetter Airport Hotel

Flygets Hotellväg ⊠ 438 13 – 𝒞 (031) 97 75 50
– www.landvetterairporthotel.com
186 rm ⊊ – ☗1495/1995 SEK ☗☗1595/2495 SEK – 1 suite
• Business • Modern •

A family-run hotel located just minutes from the airport terminal, in a surprisingly peaceful setting. The light, open interior has a calm air and a fresh Scandic style; bedrooms are sleek and modern. The informal restaurant offers a mix
of Swedish and global dishes, along with a BBQ and grill menu at dinner.

MALMÖ

MALMÖ

Population: 312 400

Michelin

Malmö was founded in the 13C under Danish rule and it wasn't until 1658 that it entered Swedish possession and subsequently established itself as one of the world's biggest shipyards. The building of the 8km long Oresund Bridge in 2000 reconnected the city with Denmark and a year later, the Turning Torso apartment block was built in the old shipyard district, opening up the city to the waterfront. Once an industrial hub, this 'city of knowledge' has impressively green credentials: buses run on natural gas and there are 400km of bike lanes. There's plenty of green space too; you can picnic in Kungsparken or Slottsparken, sit by the lakes in Pildammsparken or pet the farm animals in 'Folkets'.

At the heart of this vibrant city lie three squares: Gustav Adolfs Torg, Stortorget and Lilla Torg, connected by a pedestrianised shopping street. You'll find some of Malmö's oldest buildings in Lilla Torg, along with bustling open-air brasseries; to the west is Scandinavia's oldest surviving Renaissance castle and its beautiful gardens – and beyond that, the 2km Ribersborg Beach with its open-air baths. North is Gamla Väster with its charming houses and galleries, while south is Davidshall, filled with designer boutiques and chic eateries. Further south is Möllevångstorget, home to a throng of reasonably priced Asian and Middle Eastern shops.

MALMÖ IN...

→ **ONE DAY**
Lilla Torg and the Form/Design Centre, Western Harbour.

→ **TWO DAYS**
Modern Museum, Contemporary Art Exhibition at the Konsthall.

→ **THREE DAYS**
Skt Petri Church, an evening at the Malmö Opera.

PRACTICAL INFORMATION

ARRIVAL-DEPARTURE

✈ Sweden's Malmö Sturup Airport is 30km east of the city. The airport bus (Flygbussarna) takes 40min to reach the city centre.

✈ Denmark's Copenhagen Kastrup Airport is 32km northwest of the city. Oresund trains to Malmö Central Station depart every 20min and take 25min.

GETTING AROUND

You must buy your ticket before boarding the bus or train (aside from for the yellow regional buses, where you can pay by card on-board). All ticket machines accept debit/credit cards but very few accept cash. You can buy single, return or 24/72hr tickets; alternatively, purchase a pre-pay reloadable 'jojo' card for a 20% discount on all journeys. Single tickets can also be bought via the Skanetrafiken app and activated upon boarding. 'Around the Sound' tickets offer two days' unlimited travel and discounts for sightseeing, restaurants and hotels. You can complete the circuit in either direction – it includes the train journey over the Oresund Bridge and the ferry crossing from Helsingborg to Helsingor.

CALENDAR HIGHLIGHTS

February
Malmö Games.

March
BUFF Young People's Film Festival.

April
Beer & Whisky Festival, Walpurgis Night.

May
Malmö Garden Show.

June
Sommarscen Malmö (free theatre, concerts and performances).

July
Malmö City Horse Show.

August
Malmö Festival.

September
Malmö Galleries Night, Malmö Chamber Music Festival.

EATING OUT

The gloriously fertile region of Skane puts a wealth of top quality produce on Malmö's doorstep. Dishes rich in dairy and meat – perhaps a little meatier than expected given its waterside proximity – are staple fare and wild herbs and foraged ingredients are the order of the day; wild garlic, asparagus, potatoes and rhubarb are all celebrated here. The locals eat early, so don't be surprised if you're one of just a handful of diners at 1pm or 8pm. The popular social phenomenon 'fika' is a tradition observed by most, preferably several times a day, and involves the drinking of coffee accompanied by something sweet; usually cake or cinnamon buns. Hot meals are popular midday – look out for the great value dagens lunch, which often offers the dish of the day plus salad, bread and water for under 100kr – or for lunch on the run, grab a tunnbrödsrull (sausage and mashed potato in a wrap) from a Korv kiosk. Local delicacies include äggakaka (thick pancakes and bacon), wallenbergare (minced veal patties with mashed potato and peas), marinated herring, eel and goose.

SWEDEN - MALMÖ

 Clarion H. and Congress Malmö Live ⚜ ≤ ℔ 🕸 ㅊ 🆔
Dag Hammarskjölds Torg 2 ✉ *211 18 – ℰ (040) 207500* 🛎 🚗
– www.choicehotels.com Plan II : **E1**
444 rm ⊊ – 🛏1080/2480 SEK 🛏🛏1180/2780 SEK – 2 suites
• Business • Modern • Functional •
The city's second tallest building affords a superb 360° view of the city; choose a bedroom on the upper floors for a view of the Oresund Bridge and Denmark. Kitchen & Table's eclectic menu combines American classics and international influences; enjoy a cocktail in the adjoining Skybar. The ground floor Eatery Social is an informal Mexican-themed restaurant and bar.

 Renaissance ⚜ ℔ ㅊ 🕸 🛎 🚗
Mäster Johansgatan 15 ✉ *211 21 – ℰ (040) 248 500* Plan II : **E1**
– www.renaissancemalmo.se
128 rm ⊊ – 🛏895/2395 SEK 🛏🛏1045/2545 SEK – 1 suite
• Business • Chain • Modern •
A smart hotel on the site of the city's original food market: beamed ceilings and iron columns bring character to the modern interior. Bright, well-equipped bedrooms are quiet considering the hotel's location. There's a colourful bar and a simply furnished restaurant; modern dishes are created using local produce.

 Story Studio Malmo ⚜ ㅊ 🕸 🛎 🚗
Tyfongatan 1 ✉ *211 19 – ℰ (040) 616 52 00* Plan I : **B1**
– www.storyhotels.com – Closed 23-25 December
95 rm ⊊ – 🛏790/2190 SEK 🛏🛏790/2190 SEK
• Chain • Business • Personalised •
The modern, well-equipped bedrooms of this hotel are situated on the 10th-14th floors of a 14 storey building next to the old port, and feature large flat screen TVs and floor to ceiling windows. A ground floor eatery offers French cuisine, while the rooftop restaurant serves Asian-influenced dishes accompanied by a beautiful view over the city and harbour.

 Elite Plaza ℔ 🕸 ㅊ 🕸 🛎 🚗
Gustav Adolfs torg 49 ✉ *211 39 – ℰ (040) 66 44 871* Plan II : **E2**
– www.elite.se
116 rm ⊊ – 🛏977/2450 SEK 🛏🛏1100/2712 SEK – 1 suite
•• Business • Chain • Modern •
Behind the wonderful period façade is a smart, up-to-date corporate hotel. Modern bedrooms are a good size: the best look onto a pretty square; the quietest overlook the inner courtyard. The British-themed bar has a pleasant pavement terrace.

 Mäster Johan 🕸 🛎 🚗
Mäster Johangatan 13 ✉ *211 21 – ℰ (040) 664 64 00* Plan II : **E1**
– www.masterjohan.com
68 rm – 🛏960/2090 SEK 🛏🛏1190/2320 SEK – ⊊ 145 SEK – 10 suites
• Business • Modern • Personalised •
A centrally located hotel, just off the main square, with a relaxed and peaceful air. Stylish, well-proportioned bedrooms have luxurious touches. Enjoy a locally sourced organic breakfast under the atrium's glass roof.

 Mayfair H. Tunneln ⚜ 🛎
Adelgatan 4 ✉ *211 22 – ℰ (040) 10 16 20* Plan II : **E1**
– www.mayfairhotel.se
81 rm ⊊ – 🛏800/1300 SEK 🛏🛏850/2800 SEK
• Townhouse • Historic • Personalised •
An imposing early 17C property steeped in history, with cellars dating back to 1307; enjoy a complimentary coffee in the classical lounge. Bedrooms are spotless and homely; some have a spa bath. Snapphane showcases the latest local, organic ingredients while Malmö Rökeri specialises in smoked produce: both restaurants are overseen by the Vollmer brothers.
Snapphane – See restaurant listing

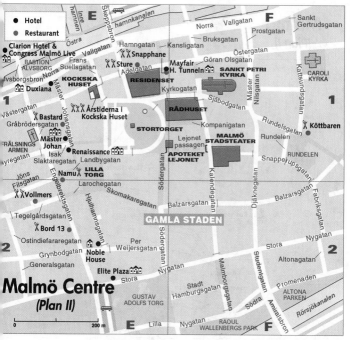

 Duxiana

⚐ 👌 🅰️

Mäster Johansgatan 1 ✉ *211 21*
Plan II : **E1**
– ✆ *(040) 60 77 000*
– *www.hotellinmalmo.com*
22 rm – 🛏️873/2315 SEK 🛏️🛏️1130/2315 SEK – ☕ 70 SEK

• Townhouse • Design • Contemporary •

A well-located boutique hotel; owned by the Dux bed company, who unusually use part of the lobby to showcase their products! Chic, contemporary bedrooms range from compact singles to elegant junior suites with a bath in the room. Staff are friendly and professional. Modern Swedish dishes are served at lunch.

 Park Inn by Radisson Malmö

⚐ 🛏️👌 🔧 🚗

Sjömansgatan 2 ✉ *211 19*
Plan I: **A1**
– ✆ *(040) 628 6000*
– *www.parkinn.com/hotel-malmo*
231 rm ☕ – 🛏️795/1395 SEK 🛏️🛏️795/1395 SEK

• Chain • Functional • Modern •

A good value hotel, well-situated on the Western Harbour beside the World Trade Centre and the Västra Hamnen waterfront. Bedrooms are spacious and well-equipped; the business rooms on the higher floors come with robes and have better views. The Bar & Grill offers easy dining.

733

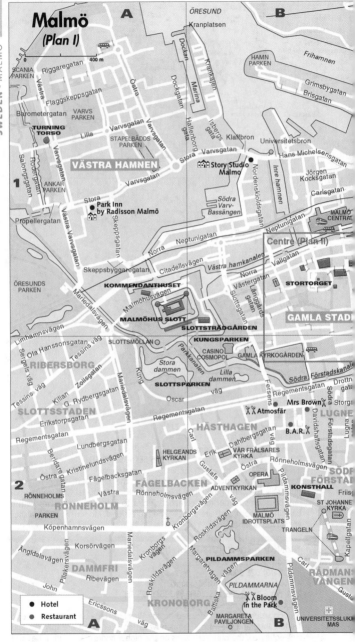

Malmö
(Plan I)

ÖRESUND

Kranplatsen

A

B

SCANIA PARKEN

Riggaregatan

Östra Varvsgatan

Flaggskeppsgatan

Barometergatan

VARVS PARKEN

TURNING TORSO

Lilla Varvsgatan

Varvsgatan

STAPELBÄDDS PARKEN

Dockan

Marina

Hallenborg gata

Isbergs gata

Klaffbron

Kranvägen

HAMN PARKEN

Frihamnen

Grimsbygatan

Brisgatan

Salongsgatan

ANKAR PARKEN

VÄSTRA HAMNEN

Stora Varvsgatan

Story Studio Malmö

Universitetsbron

Hans Michelsensgatan

Jörgen Kocksgatan

Carlsgatan

1

Propellergatan

Västra Varvsgatan

Stora

Park Inn by Radisson Malmö

Skeppsgatan

Södra Varv-Bassängen

Nordenskiöldsgatan

Inre hamnen

MALMÖ CENTRAT

ÖRESUNDS PARKEN

Mariedalsvägen

Norra

Skeppsbyggaregatan

Neptunigatan

Citadellsvägen

Västra hamnkanalen

Vallgatan

Neptunigatan

Centre (Plan II)

KOMMENDANTHUSET

Malmöhusvägen

Norra

Västergatan

Slottsgatan

Ängdårds gatan

STORTORGET

MALMÖHUS SLOTT

SLOTTSTRÄDGÅRDEN

KUNGSPARKEN

GAMLA STAD

Limhamnsvägen

Ola Hanssonsgatan väg

SLOTTSMÖLLAN

Parkkanalen

CASINO COSMOPOL

GAMLA KYRKOGÅRDEN

Södra Förstadskanal

RIBERSBORG

Sergels väg

Tessins gata

Zollsgatan

Kilian

G. Rydbergsgatan

Mariedalsvägen

Kung

Stora dammen

Lilla dammen

Fersens

Regementsgatan

Drottn gate

Södra Storga

Mrs Brown

LUGNE

Tessins väg

Erikstorpsgatan

SLOTTSSTADEN

Oscar

SLOTTSPARKEN

väg

Regementsgatan

Atmosfär

Davidshallsgatan

Förstadsgatan

Lugn

Regementsgatan

Lundbergsgatan

Kristinelundsvägen

Carl

Dahlbergsgatan

HÄSTHAGEN

B.A.R.

SÖDF

FÖRSTA

Beridare gatan

HELGEANDS KYRKAN

Erik

VÅR FRÄLSARES KYRKA

Rönneholmsvägen

Pildammsvägen

Friisg

Östra gatan

Fågelbacksgatan

2

RÖNNEHOLMS PARKEN

Västra

Rönneholmsvägen

FÅGELBACKEN

Gustafs

Östra

OPERA

ADVENTKYRKAN

KONSTHALL

ST JOHANNE KYRKA

Kronborgsvägen

MALMÖ IDROTTSPLATS

TRANGELN

Kapellgatan

Köpenhamnsvägen

Korsörvägen

Mariedalsvägen

Roskildavägen

Margaretavägen

PILDAMMSPARKEN

Pildammsvägen

Carl

RÅDMANS VÄNGEN

Gusta

Änglidalavägen

Pilakervägen

DAMMFRI

Ribevägen

John

Kronborgsvägen

KRONOBORG

Batliska

PILDAMMARNA

Bloom in the Park

MARGARETA PAVILJONGEN

UNIVERSITETSSLUK MAS

Ericssons väg

● Hotel

● Restaurant

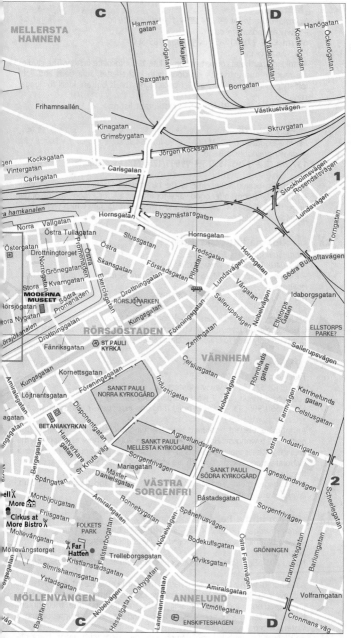

MELLERSTA
HAMNEN

C

D

Hanögatan

Koksgatan

Väderögatan

Kosterögatan

Ockerögatan

Hammar
gatan

Lodgatan

Järkajen

Saxgatan

Borrgatan

Frihamnsallén

Kinagatan

Grimsbygatan

Jörgen Kocksgatan

Carlsgatan

Västkustvägen

Skruvgatan

Kocksgatan

Vintergatan

Carlsgatan

en

Stockholmsvägen

Rosendalsvägen

Torngatan

Lundavägen

1

a hamkanalen

Norra Vallgatan

Östra Tullagatan

Slussgatan

Byggmästaregatan

Östergatan

Drottningtorget

Östra

Noregatan

Grönegatan

Östra

Skansgatan

Förstadsgatan

Hornsgatan

Fredsgatan

Hornsgatan

Hornsgatan

Pilgatan

Lundavägen

Vårgatan

Södra Bulltoftavägen

Stora Kvarngatan

MODERNA
MUSEET

Södra
Promenaden

Exercisgatan

Drottninggatan

RÖRSJÖPARKEN

Sallerupsvägen

Nobelvägen

Idaborgsgatan

Rörsjögatan

Promenaden

Föreningsgatan

Ellstorps
Gatan

ELLSTORPS
PARKE?

Stora Nygatan

Kungsgatan

örsjökanalen

Drottninggatan

RÖRSJÖSTADEN

Zenithgatan

Sallerupsvägen

Fänriksgatan

ST PAULI
KYRKA

VÄRNHEM

Celsiusgatan

Römrhads
gatan

Kungsgatan

Kornettsgatan

Föreningsgatan

Industrigatan

Nobelvägen

Farmvägen

Katrinelunds
gatan

Celsiusgatan

Amiralsgatan

Löjtnantsgatan

SANKT PAULI
NORRA KYRKOGÅRD

Disponentgatan

Hanverkare
gatan

Östra Industrigatan

agatan

BETANIAKYRKAN

St. Knuts väg

Agneslundsvägen

SANKT PAULI
MELLESTA KYRKOGÅRD

Sorgenfrivägen

Agnesluntsvägen

Bergsgatan

Spångatan

Mäster
Danielsgatan

Mariagatan

SANKT PAULI
SÖDRA KYRKOGÅRD

Scheelegatan

2

ell

More

Cirkus at
More Bistro

Monbijougatan

Friisgatan

VÄSTRA
SORGENFRI

Amiralsgatan

Ronnebygatan

Falsterbogatan

Nobelvägen

Båstadsgatan

Spånehusvägen

Sorgenfrivägen

Branteviksgatan

Mollevångsgatan

FOLKETS
PARK

Far i
Hatten

Trelleborgsgatan

Bodekullsgatan

Östra Farmvägen

GRÖNINGEN

Bariumgatan

Möllevångstorget

Kristianstadsgatan

Kiviksgatan

Simrishamnsgatan

Ystadsgatan

MÖLLENVÄNGEN

Bagatan

Nobelvägen

Hasselgatah

Osbygatan

Lantmannagatan

Amiralsgatan

ANNELUND

Vitmöllegatan

ENSKIFTESHAGEN

Volframgatan

Cronmans väg

C

D

735

More

Norra Skolgatan 24 ✉ *214 22 –* ☎ *(040) 655 10 00*   Plan I: **C2**
– www.themorehotel.com
68 rm ⌷ – ♦785/1785 SEK ♦♦985/2785 SEK
· Townhouse · Business · Modern ·
A striking aparthotel converted from a late 19C chocolate factory. The studios are modern and extremely spacious, with kitchenettes, sofa beds and light loft-style living areas. They are let on a nightly basis but are ideal for longer stays.
🍴 **Cirkus at More Bistro** – See restaurant listing

Noble House

Per Weijersgatan 6 ✉ *21134 –* ☎ *(040) 664 30 00*   Plan II : **E2**
– www.hotelnoblehouse.se
137 rm ⌷ – ♦795/1550 SEK ♦♦895/1750 SEK – 2 suites
· Business · Family · Functional ·
A centrally located hotel, close to the bus station. Classically furnished, well-equipped bedrooms offer good value for money; ask for a room on one of the upper floors. There's a cosy lounge and a modern restaurant which serves traditional Swedish dishes.

XxX   Årstiderna i Kockska Huset

Frans Suellsgatan 3 ✉ *211 22*   Plan II : **E1**
– ☎ *(040) 23 09 10 – www.arstiderna.se*
– Closed July, Easter, 24-26 December, Saturday lunch, Sunday and bank holidays
Menu 435/650 SEK – Carte 515/800 SEK
· Traditional · Elegant · Historic ·
Set in softly lit, vaulted cellars, this elegant, formal restaurant is a city institution. Classic cooking proves a match to its surroundings, with local, seasonal ingredients proudly used to create traditional Swedish dishes.

XX   Vollmers (Mats Vollmer)
✿✿

Tegelgårdsgatan 5 ✉ *211 33*   Plan II : **E2**
– ☎ *(040) 57 97 50 – www.vollmers.nu*
– Closed 3 weeks July, 1 week January and Sunday
Menu 650/995 SEK – *(dinner only) (booking essential) (tasting menu only)*
· Creative · Elegant · Intimate ·
An intimate, elegant restaurant with charming, professional service, set in a pretty 19C townhouse. Here the talented Mats Vollmer showcases some of the area's finest seasonal ingredients in set 4, 6 or 8 course menus of intricate and elaborate modern dishes, which are innovative, perfectly balanced and full of flavour.
→ Cabbage, sherry and lardo. Lamb with salsify and liquorice. Rhubarb, lavender and sour cream.

XX   Bloom in the Park (Titti Qvärnström)
✿

Pildammsvägen 17 ✉ *214 66 –* ☎ *(040) 793 63*   Plan I: **B2**
– www.bloominthepark.se – Closed 24 December, Easter, Sunday and bank holidays
Menu 695 SEK – *(dinner only) (booking advisable) (surprise menu only)*
· Creative · Design · Chic ·
A restaurant with a difference: it has no menu and no wine list! Boldly flavoured, eye-catching dishes use imaginative, original combinations of top quality ingredients, including organic herbs and flowers from their greenhouse. It's set in a pretty lakeside lodge and has a stylish interior and a waterside terrace.
→ Weever fish with kohlrabi, lemon and soya. Goat with beans, black olives and tomato chutney. Raspberries with yoghurt and white chocolate.

XX
&3
Sture (Karim Khouani)

Adelgatan 13 ⌂ 211 22 – ℰ 40 12 12 53   Plan II : **E2**
– www.restaurantsture.com – Closed Christmas and 1 January
Menu 950 SEK – *(dinner only) (tasting menu only)*
• French • Friendly • Neighbourhood •

Accomplished chef, Karim Khouani, has brought his exciting blend of French and Scandic cooking from the country into the centre of the city, reinvigorating this culinary institution. Top quality ingredients are used to create inventive, well-balanced and sublimely flavoured dishes.
➔ Foie gras with truffle and cotton candy. Turbot, Oscietra caviar and oyster cream. Pistachio soufflé with griottines.

XX
Snapphane – Mayfair Hotel Tunneln   🅰🄲 ⌾

Adelgatan 4 ⌂ 211 22 – ℰ (040) 15 01 00   Plan II : **E1**
– www.snapphane.nu – Closed 22-26 December, 1 January, Easter and Sunday
Menu 225/495 SEK – *(dinner only) (booking essential)*
• Modern cuisine • Trendy • Intimate •

An elegant, intimate bistro with an open-plan kitchen at its centre. Innovative modern cooking uses top quality ingredients and dishes are well-presented, well-balanced and full of flavour. Service is friendly and professional.

XX
Atmosfär   🍴 ዿ 🅰🄲 ⟷

Fersens väg 4 ⌂ 211 42 – ℰ (040) 12 50 77   Plan I : **B2**
– www.atmosfar.com – Closed Christmas, Saturday lunch and Sunday
Menu 125/350 SEK – Carte 295/395 SEK
• Swedish • Neighbourhood •

A formal yet relaxed eatery on the main road; dine at the bar, in the restaurant or on the pavement terrace. The menu consists of small plates, of which three or four should suffice. Fresh Skåne cooking is delivered with a light touch.

X
☺
Bastard   🍴 🅰🄲

Mäster Johansgatan 11 ⌂ 211 21 – ℰ (040) 12 13 18   Plan II : **E1**
– www.bastardrestaurant.se – Closed Christmas, New Year, Easter, midsummer, Sunday and Monday
Carte 245/355 SEK – *(dinner only) (booking advisable)*
• Modern • Trendy •

Popular with the locals, this is a bustling venue with an edgy, urban vibe. Style-wise, schoolroom meets old-fashioned butcher's, with vintage wood furniture, tiled walls, moody lighting and an open kitchen. Small plates offer nose-to-tail eating with bold, earthy flavours; start with a 'Bastard Plank' to share.

X
☺
Cirkus at More Bistro – More Hotel   🍴 ዿ

Norra Skolgatan 24 ⌂ 214 22 – ℰ (040) 236250   Plan I : **C2**
– www.themorebistro.com – Closed Christmas-New Year, Easter, Saturday lunch and dinner Sunday-Tuesday
Menu 395/595 SEK – Carte 365/550 SEK
• Modern • Bistro • Colourful •

It's housed in a former chocolate factory – now a contemporary aparthotel – and has a name inspired by its resemblance to a 'big top', with its circular shape and coloured drapes which hang around the ceiling. Modern dishes with an international edge use regional ingredients; there's a limited menu at lunch.

X
☺
Namu   🍴 🅰🄲

Landbygatan 5 ⌂ 21134 – ℰ (040) 12 14 90   Plan II : **E1**
– www.namu.nu – Closed 24 December, 2-17 January, Sunday and Monday
Carte 275/400 SEK
• Korean • Friendly • Simple •

Mouthwatering, colourful, zingy food from a past Swedish MasterChef winner blends the authenticity of Korean dishes with a modern Scandinavian touch – and all at prices that won't break the bank. Cookbooks line the shelves and friendly service adds to the lively atmosphere.

SWEDEN - MALMÖ

SWEDEN - MALMÖ

✗ **Bord 13**

Engelbrektsg 13 ✉ *211 33* – ✆ *(042) 58788*　　　　Plan II : **E2**
– *www.bord13.se* – *Closed Christmas, 1 January, Sunday and Monday*
Menu 400/700 SEK – *(dinner only) (tasting menu only)*
• Creative • Wine bar • Friendly •

Sister to B.A.R restaurant, is the bright, spacious and stylish 'Table 13', which offers a set 3 or 6 course menu and a diverse selection of biodynamic wines. Original Nordic cooking has some interesting texture and flavour combinations.

✗ **B.A.R.**

Erik Dahlbergsgatan 3 ✉ *211 48* – ✆ *(040) 17 01 75*　　　Plan I : **B2**
– *www.barmalmo.se* – *Closed Easter, Christmas, Sunday and Monday*
Menu 395 SEK – Carte 340/430 SEK – *(dinner only) (booking advisable)*
• Modern • Wine bar • Neighbourhood •

In trendy Davidshall is this lively wine-bar-cum-restaurant named after its owners, Besnick And Robert. The interesting modern menu tends towards the experimental; expect dishes like Jerusalem artichoke ice cream with hazelnut mayo.

✗ **Far i Hatten**

Folkets Park ✉ *214 37* – ✆ *(040) 615 36 51*　　　　Plan I : **C2**
– *www.farihatten.se* – *Closed Christmas*
Menu 360/520 SEK – *(dinner only and lunch June-August)*
• Swedish • Rustic • Friendly •

This unique restaurant is set in a wooden chalet in the lovely Folkets Park and has a cosy, informal feel, with colourful lights and regular live music in the summer. 4 or 6 course menus list well-presented classics with a creative edge.

✗ **Rebell**

Friisgatan 8B ✉ *211 46* – ✆ *(040) 97 97 35*　　　　Plan I : **C2**
– *www.restaurangrebell.se* – *Closed Christmas, Easter, Saturday lunch and Sunday*
Menu 385 SEK (dinner) – Carte 359/450 SEK
• Modern • Trendy • Bistro •

An informal, contemporary bistro with a stark, simple feel, serving vibrant and tasty modern interpretations of local dishes, with ribs the speciality. A cool soundtrack and locally brewed unfiltered beer add to the fun.

✗ **Mrs Brown**

Storgatan 26 ✉ *211 42* – ✆ *(040) 97 22 50*　　　　Plan I : **B2**
– *www.mrsbrown.se* – *Closed 24 December, Easter, midsummer and Sunday*
Menu 395 SEK – Carte 385/490 SEK – *(dinner only)*
• Traditional • Wine bar • Trendy •

This retro brasserie's bar opens at 3pm for drinks and nibbles, while the kitchen opens at 6pm. Make sure you try one of the cocktails! Well-presented unfussy cooking has a modern edge and showcases the region's ingredients.

✗ **Bistro Stella**

Linnégatan 25, Limhamn (Southwest: 7 km by Limhamnsvägen: bus 4 from Central station) ✉ *216 12* – ✆ *(040) 15 60 40* – *www.bistrostella.se*
– *Closed midsummer, Christmas, Sunday and Monday*
Carte 289/635 SEK – *(dinner only)*
• Modern • Neighbourhood • Pub •

A lively gastropub in a residential area not far from the Oresund Bridge. Its bright, cosy bar sits between two dining rooms and its menu features pub dishes like burgers, fish and chips and charcuterie platters. Cooking is rustic and tasty.

✗ **Köttbaren**

Rundelsgatan ✉ *211 26* – ✆ *(040) 635 89 01*　　　　Plan II : **F1**
– *www.kottbaren.se* – *Closed 15-16 April, 24-25 December, 1 January, Easter and midsummer*
Menu 99/395 SEK – Carte dinner 245/500 SEK
• Meats and grills • Simple • Friendly •

A trendy restaurant with an open kitchen and a relaxed feel, set in the Caroli shopping centre: lunch is a help-yourself buffet, while dinner offers classic Swedish dishes alongside good value, good quality Swedish meats cooked on the grill.

SWITZERLAND
SUISSE, SCHWEIZ, SVIZZERA

→ **AREA:**
41 285 km²
(15 940 sq mi).

→ **CAPITAL:**
Bern (Berne).

→ **POPULATION:**
8 300 000.
Density = 201 per km².

→ **CURRENCY:**
Swiss Franc (CHF).

→ **GOVERNMENT:**
Federation of 26 cantons with
2 assemblies (National Council
and Council of State) forming the
Federal Assembly.

→ **LANGUAGES:**
German (64% of population),
French (20%) and Italian (7%),
are spoken in all administrative
departments, shops, hotels and
restaurants.

→ **PUBLIC HOLIDAYS:**
New Year's Day (1 Jan); Ascension
Day (May); Swiss National Day
(1 Aug); Christmas Day (25 Dec).
All other holidays are decided upon
by each canton, the most popular
being: St Berchtold's Day (2 Jan);
Good Friday (Friday before Easter);
Easter Monday (late Mar/Apr); Whit
Monday (late May/June); Corpus
Christi (late May/June); Assumption
of the Virgin Mary (15 Aug);
All Saints' Day (1 Nov); Immaculate
Conception (8 Dec); St Stephen's
Day (26 Dec).

→ **LOCAL TIME:**
GMT+1 hour in winter and GMT
+2 hours in summer.

→ **CLIMATE**
Temperate continental, varies with
altitude – most of the country has
cold winters and warm summers
(Bern: January 0°C; July 19°C).

→ **EMERGENCY**
Police ☏ **117**; Medical Assistance
☏ **144**; Fire Brigade ☏ **118**.
Anglo-Phone 24hr helpline
☏ **0900 576 444**.
(Dialling **112** within any EU country
will redirect your call and contact
the emergency services.)

→ **ELECTRICITY:**
230 volts AC, 50Hz; 2 round pin
sockets.

→ **FORMALITIES:**
Travellers from the European Union
(EU), Iceland and the main countries
of North and South America need
a national identity card or passport
(America: passport required) to
visit Switzerland for less than
three months (tourism or business
purpose). For visitors from other
countries a visa may be required, in
addition to a passport, especially
for those wishing to stay for longer
than three months. We advise you
to check with your embassy before
travelling.

BERN
BERNE

Population: 140 000

N. Parneix/Fotolia.com

To look at Bern, you'd never believe it to be a capital city. Small and beautifully proportioned, it sits sedately on a spur at a point where the River Aare curves gracefully back on itself. The little city is the best preserved medieval centre north of the Alps – a fact recognised by UNESCO when it awarded Bern World Heritage status – and the layout of the streets has barely changed since the Duke of Zahringen chose the superbly defended site to found the city over 800 years ago. Most of the buildings date from between the 14 and 16C – when Bern was at the height of its power – and the cluster of cobbled lanes, surrounded by ornate sandstone arcaded buildings and numerous fountains and wells, give it the feel of a delightfully overgrown village. (Albert Einstein felt so secure here that while ostensibly employed as a clerk in the Bern patent office he managed to find the time to work out his Theory of Relativity.)

BERN IN...

→ **ONE DAY**
River walk, Old Town (cathedral, clock Tower, arcades), Museum of Fine Arts, cellar fringe theatre.

→ **TWO DAYS**
Zentrum Paul Klee, Einstein's house, Stadttheater.

→ **THREE DAYS**
Bern Museum of History, Swiss Alpine Museum, Rose Garden.

The Old Town stretches eastwards over a narrow peninsula, and is surrounded by the arcing River Aare. The eastern limit of the Old Town is the Nydeggbrücke bridge, while the western end is marked out by the Käfigturm tower, once a city gate and prison. On the southern side of the Aare lies the small Kirchenfeld quarter, which houses some impressive museums, while the capital's famous brown bears are back over the river via the Nydeggbrücke.

PRACTICAL INFORMATION

ARRIVAL-DEPARTURE

✈ Bern Belp International Airport is 9km southeast of the city. The shuttle bus leaves every 30min and takes about 20min.

GETTING AROUND

The Bern Card is well worth investing in. It gives unlimited travel, free admission to museums and gardens, and various reductions around the city. It's available from the Tourist Office, museums and hotels, and is valid for 24hr, 48hr or 72hr.

As Bern is small enough to walk around, it requires no more than a super-efficient bus and tram network. A short cable-railway links the Marzili quarter to the Bundeshaus. You can buy your ticket at the bus or tram stop.

EATING OUT

Bern is a great place to sit and enjoy a meal. Pride of place must go to the good range of alfresco venues in the squares of the old town – popular spots to enjoy coffee and cake. Hiding away in the arcades are many delightful dining choices; some of the best for location alone are in vaulted cellars that breathe historic ambience. If you want to feel what a real Swiss restaurant is like, head for a traditional rustic eatery complete with cow-bells and sample the local dishes like the Berner Platte – a heaving plate of hot and cold meats, served with beans and sauerkraut –

CALENDAR HIGHLIGHTS

February
Carnival.

March
Museums Night.

March-May
International Jazz Festival, Bern Grand Prix (Run).

July
Gurtenfestival (rock music).

August-September
Buskers Bern Street Music festival (series of concerts in the old town).

October
Short Film Festival.

November
Onion Market.

or treberwurst, a sausage poached with fermented grape skins. There's no shortage of international restaurants either, and along with Germany, France and Italy also have their country's cuisine well represented here – it's not difficult to go from rösti to risotto. And, of course, there's always cheese – this is the birthplace of raclette - and tempting chocolates waiting in the wings. A fifteen percent service charge is always added but it's customary to round the bill up.

741

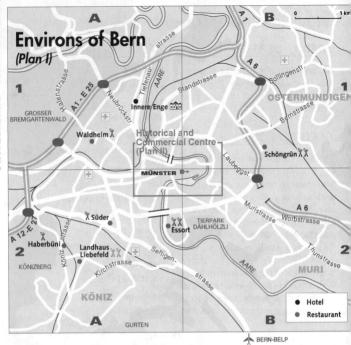

Environs of Bern
(Plan I)

GROSSER
BREMGARTENWALD

Waldheim

Innere/Enge

OSTERMUNDIGEN

Historical and
Commercial Centre
(Plan II)

MÜNSTER

Schöngrün

Süder

Essort

TIERPARK
DÄHLHÖLZLI

A 6   Worbstrasse

MURI

Haberbüni

Landhaus
Liebefeld

KÖNIZBERG

KÖNIZ

GURTEN

● Hotel
● Restaurant

BERN-BELP

HISTORICAL AND COMMERCIAL CENTRE   PLAN II

Bellevue Palace
Kochergasse 3 ⊠ 3011 – ℰ 031 320 45 45   Plan: **D2**
– www.bellevue-palace.ch
128 rm – ♦399/441 CHF ♦♦441/518 CHF – ⊊ 40 CHF – 28 suites
• Grand Luxury • Classic •
This exclusive hotel established in 1913 and sited in the heart of Bern offers first-
class guestrooms and suites and elegant conference facilities in a truly unique
atmosphere. Modern gym with sauna. The comfortable Bellevue Bar serves international cuisine.
VUE • Bellevue Bar – See restaurant listing

Schweizerhof
Bahnhofplatz 11 ⊠ 3001 – ℰ 031 326 80 80   Plan: **C1**
– www.schweizerhof-bern.ch
99 rm – ♦359/389 CHF ♦♦459/519 CHF – ⊊ 45 CHF – 6 suites
• Luxury • Elegant •
Behind the beautifully restored historic façade lies a happy marriage of modern
and classic chic that looks beautiful and provides all the latest technology for
business guests. Those of you in search of charm will love Jack's Brasserie.
Jack's Brasserie – See restaurant listing

Allegro
Kornhausstr. 3 ⊠ 3000 – ℰ 031 339 55 00 – www.allegro-hotel.ch   Plan: **D1**
167 rm – ♦190/390 CHF ♦♦190/450 CHF – ⊊ 26 CHF – 4 suites
• Business • Contemporary •
This lifestyle hotel is ideal for conferences and events, as well as individual
guests. Modern rooms in different categories, plus a beautiful penthouse floor
with its own lounge. One of the restaurants, Il Giardino, serves Italian food.
❀ **Meridiano • Yù** – See restaurant listing

XXXX **VUE** – Hotel Bellevue Palace

Kochergasse 3 ✉ *3011 –* ☎ *031 320 45 45* — Plan: **D2**
– www.bellevue-palace.ch/vue
Menu 78 CHF (weekday lunch) – Carte 65/139 CHF
• Modern cuisine • Classic décor •

Ambitious, contemporary seasonal cuisine with traditional roots is served in this tastefully decorated setting. The terrace affords magnificent views over the Aare.

XXX **Meridiano** – Hotel Allegro

Kornhausstr. 3 ✉ *3000 –* ☎ *031 339 52 45* — Plan: **D1**
– www.allegro-hotel.ch – Closed 1-12 January, 11-26 April, 4-26 July and Saturday lunch, Sunday dinner-Tuesday
Menu 55 CHF (lunch)/165 CHF – Carte 110/135 CHF
• Modern cuisine • Fashionable • Trendy •

You will find the Allegro's culinary flagship right at the top of the hotel where it offers great views, not least from its wonderful terrace. Meanwhile, the food coming out of the open kitchen, made using only the very finest ingredients, is sophisticated and intensely flavoured. The lunchtime menu is shorter but equally good.
→ Gelbflossenmakrele, grüner Spargel, Apfel, Meerrettich-Radislivinaigrette. Greyerzer Saibling, Corne de Gatte, Freilandei. Milchlamm, Schulter und Kotelett, Poivrade, Schafsmilch, Nesseln.

XX **Jack's Brasserie** – Hotel Schweizerhof

Bahnhofplatz 11 ✉ *3001 –* ☎ *031 326 80 80* — Plan: **C1**
– www.schweizerhof-bern.ch
Menu 59/70 CHF – Carte 67/113 CHF
• Classic cuisine • Brasserie •

The restaurant at the Schweizerhof provides an elegant setting, with its attractive decor, pretty alcoves, parquet flooring and stylish lighting. The menu features typical brasserie-style fare, alongside a number of popular classics including the Wiener schnitzel.

X **milles sens - les goûts du monde**

Spitalgasse 38 (Schweizerhofpassage, 1st floor) ✉ *3011* — Plan: **C2**
– ☎ *031 329 29 29 – www.millesens.ch – Closed end July-early August and Sunday; September-April: Saturday lunch, Sunday*
Menu 59 CHF (lunch) – Carte 66/97 CHF
• International • Fashionable •

If you are looking for a lively, modern restaurant, this minimalist-style establishment is for you. The mouthwatering menu promises Aargau chicken tagine, Gurten highland beef duo, and exotic Thai green vegetable curry. At midday there is also an interesting business lunch menu.

X **Kirchenfeld**

Thunstr. 5 ✉ *3005 –* ☎ *031 351 02 78* — Plan: **E2**
– www.kirchenfeld.ch – Closed Sunday-Monday
Menu 75 CHF (dinner) – Carte 57/83 CHF – *(booking advisable)*
• Traditional cuisine • Brasserie •

Eating in this loud and lively restaurant is great fun! Try the flavoursome zander fish served on Mediterranean couscous and one of the sweets, which includes lemon tart and chocolate cake, displayed on the dessert trolley. At lunchtimes the restaurant is full of business people who swear by the daily set menu.

X **Wein & Sein mit Härzbluet**

Münstergasse 50 (at cellar) ✉ *3011 –* ☎ *031 311 98 44* — Plan: **E2**
– www.weinundsein.ch – Closed 1 week March, 2 weeks July and Saturday lunch, Sunday-Monday
Menu 39 CHF (weekday lunch)/98 CHF
• Classic cuisine • Trendy • Rustic •

Venture down the steep steps into the cellar and you will find a friendly and charmingly intimate little restaurant. It serves fresh, flavoursome food with a fine selection of wines and good, professional suggestions. Lunch and small à la carte menus at midday, and a five-course surprise menu in the evenings. Pretty terrace.

Historical and Commercial Centre
(Plan II)

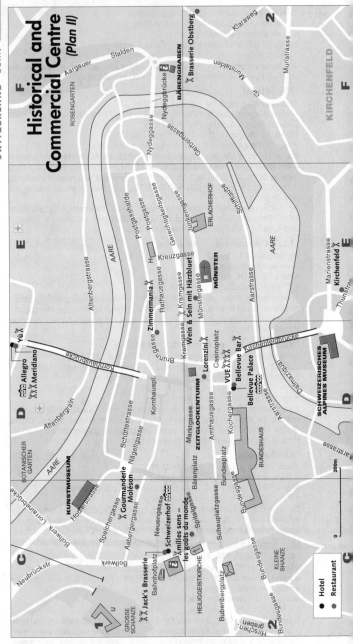

Hotel ●

Restaurant ●

Lorenzini

Hotelgasse 10 ✉ 3011 – ✆ 031 318 50 67 – www.lorenzini.ch Plan: **D2**
Carte 55/98 CHF
• Italian • Friendly •
This attractive Italian restaurant located in the pedestrian zone is tastefully decorated with original paintings. It boasts a formal restaurant on the first floor and a bar, bistro and attractive interior courtyard at ground level.

Bellevue Bar – Hotel Bellevue Palace

Kochergasse 3 ✉ 3011 – ✆ 031 320 45 45 Plan: **D2**
– www.bellevue-palace.ch
Carte 64/110 CHF
• International • Traditional décor •
The sedate charm of this long established grand hotel also extends into the restaurant. Diners, many of whom have travelled from far and wide to get here, can choose from an international menu.

Gourmanderie Moléson

Aarbergergasse 24 ✉ 3011 – ✆ 031 311 44 63 Plan: **C1**
– www.moleson-bern.ch – Closed Christmas-New Year and Saturday lunch, Sunday
Menu 35 CHF (weekday lunch)/77 CHF – Carte 56/92 CHF
• Classic French • Brasserie •
Established in 1865, the Moléson is a lively restaurant located in the centre of Bern. It serves a range of traditional-style dishes from Alsatian flammekueche to multi-course meals.

Yù – Hotel Allegro

Kornhausstr. 3 ✉ 3000 – ✆ 031 339 52 50 Plan: **D1**
– www.allegro-hotel.ch – Closed 9-31 July and Sunday-Monday
Menu 59 CHF – Carte 50/72 CHF – *(dinner only)*
• Chinese • Minimalist •
This restaurant open to the hotel's atrium is one of the most fashionable addresses in town. It exudes stylish Asian cool and serves modern Chinese cuisine.

Zimmermania

Brunngasse 19 ✉ 3011 – ✆ 031 311 15 42 Plan: **D1**
– www.zimmermania.ch – Closed 9 July-7 August and Sunday-Monday; June-September: Saturday lunch
Menu 65 CHF – Carte 41/97 CHF
• Classic French • Traditional décor •
The atmosphere in this cosy, traditionally run restaurant located in a narrow alleyway in the old town is lively and informal.

Brasserie Obstberg

Bantigerstr. 18 ✉ 3006 – ✆ 031 352 04 40 Plan: **F2**
– www.brasserie-obstberg.ch – Closed Saturday lunch, Sunday
Menu 79 CHF (dinner) – Carte 60/84 CHF
• Classic cuisine • Brasserie •
Diners have been coming to Brasserie Obstberg for over 100 years. Today they eat in the lovely, 1930s-style brasserie with its wonderful terrace shaded by mature sweet chestnut trees. The food is fresh and classically French with Swiss influences from the braised lamb shank to the sautéed zander.

ENVIRONS OF BERN — PLAN I

Innere Enge

Engestr. 54 ✉ 3012 – ✆ 031 309 61 11 – www.innere-enge.ch Plan: **A1**
26 rm – †200/370 CHF ††220/370 CHF – ☕ 25 CHF
• Country house • Personalised •
Passionate about jazz, your hosts have created this unique hotel-cum-jazz venue. Many of the rooms are named after famous musicians and decorated with original artefacts. The basement houses a jazz club. Josephine's Brasserie and the historic Park Pavilion offer views over the city.

XX **Landhaus Liebefeld**   🐝 ⇔ 🏡 & ✿ **P**
Schwarzenburgstr. 134 – ℰ 031 971 07 58   Plan: **A2**
– www.landhaus-liebefeld.ch – Closed Sunday
6 rm ⌧ – 🛏180 CHF 🛏🛏290 CHF
Menu 60/133 CHF – Carte 57/111 CHF – *(booking advisable)*
• Classic French • Elegant •
Anywhere you can eat this well in such pleasant surroundings as this former
1671 sheriff's house is bound to attract plenty of regulars. Try the fish soup
– they've been making it from the same recipe for 25 years! The Gaststube serves simpler fare including meatloaf and German noodle dishes. And if you fancy
staying the night, the individually designed rooms are pretty and well furnished.

XX **Essort**   🏡 ✿
Jubiläumstr. 97 ⌧ 3000 – ℰ 031 368 11 11   Plan: **A2**
*– www.essort.ch – Closed 1 week early January, 2 weeks early October,
during Christmas*
Menu 63/105 CHF – Carte 56/86 CHF
• International • Friendly •
In the former US embassy the Lüthi family runs a modern restaurant. It produces international fare in its open kitchen, which is inspired by the owners' countless trips abroad. In summer, dine alfresco at one of the lovely tables laid outside under the mature trees.

XX **Schöngrün**   🏡 & ✿
Monument im Fruchtland 1 (near Paul Klee Centre)   Plan: **B1**
*⌧ 3006 – ℰ 031 359 02 90 – www.restaurants-schoengruen.ch – closed
24-30 December, 17 July-8 August and Sunday dinner-Tuesday*
Menu 38 CHF (lunch)/165 CHF – Carte 59/104 CHF – *(booking advisable)*
• Creative • Fashionable •
This lovely historical villa with its smart, light and airy glazed annexe stands next
to the Paul Klee Centre. The restaurant offers a minimalist interior and a comfortable terrace. A wide range of dishes from the daily special to a set menu is served. It is just a 23min bus ride from the main railway station.

X **Haberbüni**   🐝 🏡 **P**
Könizstr. 175 – ℰ 031 972 56 55 – www.haberbueni.ch   Plan: **A2**
– Closed Saturday lunch and Sunday
Menu 61 CHF (weekday lunch)/105 CHF (dinner)
– Carte 57/83 CHF – *(booking advisable)*
• Modern cuisine • Bourgeois • Cosy •
This warm and welcoming restaurant set in the loft of a large renovated farm-
house or Büni offers ambitious contemporary cuisine and a fine selection of
wines. Shorter midday menu and good business lunch options.

X **Waldheim**   🏡
Waldheimstr. 40 ⌧ 3012 – ℰ 031 305 24 24   Plan: **A1**
– www.waldheim-bern.ch – Closed Saturday lunch, Sunday-Monday
Menu 90 CHF – Carte 41/93 CHF
• Traditional cuisine • Neighbourhood •
This pretty restaurant is panelled in light wood and located in a quiet residential
area. It boasts a healthy number of regulars thanks to the fresh Swiss cuisine (try
the marinated leg of lamb, spit-roasted to a perfect pink) and the friendly service.

X **Süder**   🏡 **P**
Weissensteinstr. 61 ⌧ 3007 – ℰ 031 371 57 67   Plan: **A2**
*– www.restaurant-sueder.ch – Closed 1-10 January, 2 weeks July and
Saturday lunch, Sunday-Monday*
Menu 69 CHF (dinner) – Carte 52/90 CHF
• Swiss • Bourgeois •
This down-to-earth corner restaurant with its lovely wood panelling has many
regulars. They are attracted by the good, honest, fresh Swiss cooking, such as
the veal ragout. In the summer it is no surprise that the tables in the garden
are particularly popular.

GENEVA
GENEVE

Population: 191 557

Kheng Guan Toh/Fotolia.com

In just about every detail except efficiency, Geneva exudes a distinctly Latin feel. It boasts a proud cosmopolitanism, courtesy of a whole swathe of international organisations (dealing with just about every human concern), and of the fact that roughly one in three residents is non-Swiss. Its renowned savoir-vivre challenges that of swishy Zurich, and along with its manicured city parks, it boasts the world's tallest fountain and the world's longest bench. It enjoys cultural ties with Paris and is often called 'the twenty-first arrondissement' – it's also almost entirely surrounded by France.

The River Rhône snakes through the centre, dividing the city into the southern left bank - the old town - and the northern right bank - the 'international quarter' (home to the largest UN office outside New York). The east is strung around the sparkling shores of Europe's largest alpine lake, while the Jura Mountains dominate the right bank, and the Alps form a backdrop to the left bank. Geneva is renowned for its orderliness: the Reformation was born here under the austere preachings of Calvin, and the city has provided sanctuary for religious dissidents, revolutionaries and elopers for at least five centuries. Nowadays, new arrivals tend to be of a more conservative persuasion, as they go their elegant way balancing international affairs alongside *la belle vie*.

GENEVA IN...

→ **ONE DAY**
   St Peter's Cathedral, Maison Tavel, Jet d'Eau, Reformation Wall.

→ **TWO DAYS**
   MAMCO (or Art & History Museum), a lakeside stroll, a trip to Carouge.

→ **THREE DAYS**
   A day in Paquis, including time relaxing at the Bains des Paquis.

PRACTICAL INFORMATION

ARRIVAL-DEPARTURE

Geneva International Airport is 4km northwest of the city. Trains depart every 15min and take 6min. Bus 10 runs every 10min. Pick up a free ticket to the city centre from the machine in the baggage reclaim hall.

GETTING AROUND

Geneva is served by an efficient public transport network which runs like clockwork. There are various timed cards depending on how much travelling you intend to do: for one hour, one day, or 9am-midnight. If you are staying in a hotel, you will receive a Geneva Transport Card, which allows unlimited use of the city's trams, trains, buses and boats. It also offers free admission to many top museums and attractions, plus reductions in some restaurants and shops. The city encourages cycling and from May to October bikes can be borrowed for free. More information from Geneva Tourism on Rue du Mont-Blanc.

CALENDAR HIGHLIGHTS

January
Art Fair.

March
Salon International de l'Automobile.

April
International Exhibition of Inventions.

June-July
Bol d'Or Regatta, Fête de la Musique.

July-August
Fêtes de Genève.

September
Suisse Romande Heritage Days.

December
L'Escalade Procession.

EATING OUT

With the number of international organisations that have set up camp here, this is a place that takes a lot of feeding, so you'll find over 1,000 dining establishments in and around the city. If you're looking for elegance, head to a restaurant overlooking the lake; if your tastes are for home-cooked Sardinian fare, make tracks for the charming Italianate suburb of Carouge; and if you fancy something with an international accent, trendy Paquis has it all at a fair price and on a truly global scale, from Mexican to Moroccan and Jordanian to Japanese. The old town, packed with delightful brasseries and alpine-style chalets, is the place for Swiss staples: you can't go wrong here if you're after a fondue, rustic longeole (pork sausage with cumin and fennel) or a hearty papet vaudois (cream and leek casserole); for a bit of extra atmosphere, head downstairs to a candlelit, vaulted cellar. Although restaurants include a fifteen per cent service charge, it's customary to either round up the bill or give the waiter a five to ten per cent tip.

SWITZERLAND - GENEVA GENÈVE)

Four Seasons Hôtel des Bergues

Quai des Bergues 33 ⊠ 1201 – ℰ 022 908 70 00
– www.fourseasons.com/geneva

Plan: **F3**

95 rm – ♦725/1250 CHF ♦♦725/1250 CHF – ☲ 55 CHF – 20 suites
• Palace • Grand luxury •

With a lovely location at the point where the River Rhône rises from the clear waters of Lake Geneva, this was the first of the great Geneva hotels (1834). It is the very essence of the grand hotel with excellent service and splendid decor (period furniture, marble, fine fabrics, etc). All in all, a superb luxury hotel.
❀ **Il Lago • Izumi** – See restaurant listing

Mandarin Oriental

Quai Turrettini 1 ⊠ 1201 – ℰ 022 909 00 00
– www.mandarinoriental.fr/geneva

Plan: **E3**

189 rm – ♦495/995 CHF ♦♦595/1295 CHF – ☲ 54 CHF – 15 suites
• Luxury • Art déco • Elegant •

Shimmering fabrics, precious woods and marble panelling all contribute to the Art Deco style of this luxurious hotel on the banks of the Rhone. On the seventh floor, the suites have their own private terrace with views of the entire city. Highly comfortable, extremely chic and infinitely elegant.
Rasoi by Vineet • Café Calla – See restaurant listing

Président Wilson

Quai Wilson 47 ⊠ 1211 – ℰ 022 906 66 66
– www.hotelpresidentwilson.com

Plan: **F2**

180 rm – ♦450/1500 CHF ♦♦450/1500 CHF – ☲ 47 CHF – 48 suites
• Grand Luxury • Grand luxury •

A large, modern building on the waterfront, the Président Wilson offers every conceivable comfort. This includes wonderful architectural spaces, beautiful materials, a panoramic pool and a range of restaurants. From the upper floors on the Lake Geneva side, the city pales into insignificance before the wonderful green or snow covered scenery beyond.
❀ **Bayview • L'Arabesque • umami by michel roth** – See restaurant listing

Grand Hôtel Kempinski

Quai du Mont-Blanc 19 ⊠ 1201 – ℰ 022 908 90 81
– www.kempinski.com/geneva

Plan: **F3**

379 rm – ♦490/1500 CHF ♦♦490/1500 CHF – ☲ 50 CHF – 33 suites
• Grand Luxury • Classic •

This contemporary hotel that looks out over the famous fountain and across Lake Geneva offers a wide range of services. The interior is modern but muted. It is full of bars and restaurants, meeting rooms, banqueting suites and shops – offering all the facilities you could ever need!
Le Grill – See restaurant listing

Beau-Rivage

Quai du Mont-Blanc 13 ⊠ 1201 – ℰ 022 716 66 66
– www.beau-rivage.ch

Plan: **F3**

84 rm – ♦510/2890 CHF ♦♦510/2890 CHF – ☲ 47 CHF – 6 suites
• Grand Luxury • Grand luxury •

A truly grand hotel established in the mid-19C. The Beau Rivage entered into the annals of history in 1898 when Empress Elisabeth of Austria passed away in one of its rooms. Its illustrious past is ever present – though never overbearing – in the timeless beauty of its columns and pillars and its marble and stucco work. An elegant refuge from the modern world.
❀ **Le Chat Botté • Patara** – See restaurant listing

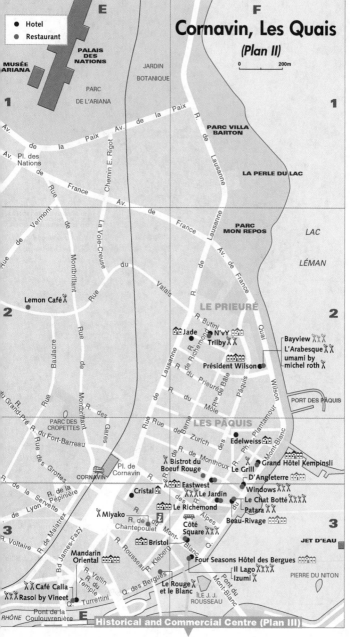

Cornavin, Les Quais

(Plan II)

0   200m

- ● Hotel
- ● Restaurant

PALAIS DES NATIONS

MUSÉE ARIANA

JARDIN BOTANIQUE

PARC DE L'ARIANA

Av. de la Paix

Av. de la Paix

Pl. des Nations

Rue de Vermont

Rue de France

Chemin E. Rigot

La Voie-Creuse

Av. de France

R. de Lausanne

PARC VILLA BARTON

LA PERLE DU LAC

PARC MON REPOS

LAC LÉMAN

Lemon Café X

Rue de Montbrillant

Rue du Valais

LE PRIEURÉ

R. Butini

Jade 🏨

N'vY 🏨

Trilby X

Président Wilson ●

Bayview XXX

L'Arabesque X X

umami by michel roth X

PORT DES PÂQUIS

R. de Lausanne

R. de Richemont

R. du Prieuré

R. de Bâle

R. du Môle

Quai

Wilson

Plantamour

Mont-Blanc

Pâquis

PARC DES CROPETTES

R. du Fort-Barreau

Rue des Gares

Rue de Montbrillant

Pl. de Cornavin

CORNAVIN

LES PÂQUIS

R. de Berne

R. de Zurich

R. de Monthoux

R. des Alpes

Edelweiss 🏨

Grand Hôtel Kempinski 🏨

Le Grill ●

Bistrot du Boeuf Rouge X

D'Angleterre 🏨

Windows XXX

Cristal 🏨

Eastwest 🏨

Le Jardin XXX

Le Richemond 🏨

Le Chat Botté XXXX

Patara XX

Miyako X

R. de Chantepoulet

Côté Square XXX

Beau-Rivage 🏨

R. Rousseau

R. Kléberg

Mont-Blanc

JET D'EAU

Bristol 🏨

Mandarin Oriental 🏨

Bd James-Fazy

R. du Temple

R. Vallin

Q. Turrettini

Café Calla XX

Rasoi by Vineet XXX

Four Seasons Hôtel des Bergues 🏨

Il Lago XXX

Izumi X

Le Rouge et le Blanc X

Pont du Mont-Blanc

ÎLE J. J. ROUSSEAU

PIERRE DU NITON

Q. des Bergues

RHÔNE

Pont de la Coulouvrenière

Historical and Commercial Centre (Plan III)

751

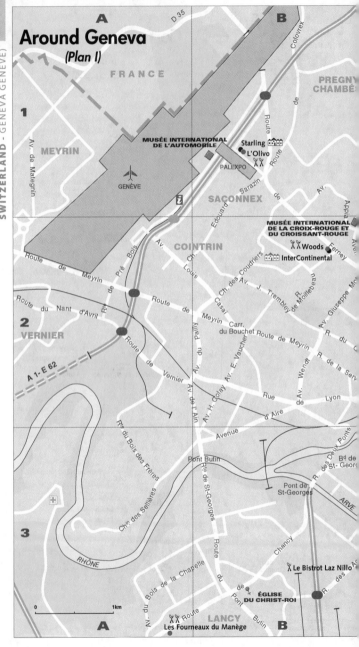

Around Geneva
(Plan I)

A D 35 **B**

Colovrex

FRANCE

PREGNY CHAMBÉ

MEYRIN

Route de

Av. de Mategnin

1

MUSÉE INTERNATIONAL DE L'AUTOMOBILE

Starling

L'Olivo

PALEXPO

GENÈVE

Sarazin

SACONNEX

Appia

Av.

MUSÉE INTERNATIONAL DE LA CROIX-ROUGE ET DU CROISSANT-ROUGE

Edouard

Woods

Ferney

COINTRIN

InterContinental

Route de Meyrin

Ch. des Coudriers

Av. J. Trembley

R. de Mollebeau

de

Av. de Pré-Bois

Louis

Casaï

Ch. du

Av. Giuseppe Mo

Route du Nant d'Avril

Route de

Meyrin Carr. du Bouchet Route de Meyrin

R. du C

2

VERNIER

A 1 - E 62

Route de Vernier

Av. de l'Ain

Av. H. Golay

Av. E. Vaucher

Wendt

R. de la Serv

Rue de Lyon

Av.

d'Aire

Avenue

Rte du Bois des Frères

Pont Butin

Rue de St-Georges

Bd de des St-Georg

Pont de St-Georges

ARVE

3

Chin des Sellières

RHÔNE

Route du

Chancy

Le Bistrot Laz Nillo

R. des A

0 —— 1km

Av. du Bois de la Chapelle

Route de de Pont Butin

ÉGLISE DU CHRIST-ROI

LANCY

Les Fourneaux du Manège

A **B**

SWITZERLAND - GENEVA GENÈVE

752

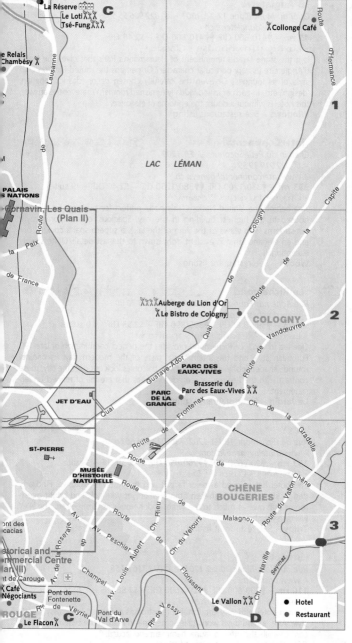

La Réserve C
Le Loti
Tsé-Fung

Collonge Café

e Relais
Chambésy

Lausanne

de

LAC   LÉMAN

Route

Capite

d'Hermance

PALAIS
S NATIONS

rnavin, Les Quais
(Plan II)

Route

la   Paix

Cologny

de France

de

Auberge du Lion d'Or
Le Bistro de Cologny

Quai

COLOGNY

Route   de   Vandœuvres

Gustave-Ador

PARC DES
EAUX-VIVES

Brasserie du
Parc des Eaux-Vives

JET D'EAU

Quai

PARC
DE LA
GRANGE

Frontenex

Ch.   de   la   Gradelle

Route   de

ST-PIERRE

Route

Route

de

MUSÉE
D'HISTOIRE
NATURELLE

Route

CHÊNE
BOUGERIES

Malagnou

Route du Vallon   Chêne

ont des
cacias

Av.   de la   Roseraie

ap

Av.   Peschier

Ch.   Rieu

Ch.   du   Valours

Naville

Seymaz

torical and
mmercial Centre
lan II)
nt de Carouge

Champel

Av.   Louis-Aubert

Florissant

Café
Négociants

Pont de
Fontenette
de

Veyrier

Floissant

Ch.

Le Vallon

ROUGE

Rte

Pont du
Val d'Arve

Rte   de   Vessy

● Hotel

● Restaurant

Le Flacon   C

D'Angleterre

Quai du Mont-Blanc 17 ✉ 1201 – ✆ 022 906 55 55 Plan: **F3**
– www.hoteldangleterre.ch
45 rm – 🚹410/800 CHF 🚹🚹410/800 CHF – ☕48 CHF
• Luxury • Townhouse • Classic •

Is it the stone façade reminiscent of Haussmann's Paris that gives the Hotel d'Angleterre its very particular character? Or perhaps the muted London club style of its lounges? Or even the carefully chosen decor (classic, Venetian, 'design', etc.) in each of its individually furnished rooms? Whatever the answer, this hotel is without a doubt the epitome of elegance.

Windows – See restaurant listing

InterContinental

Chemin du Petit-Saconnex 7 ✉ 1209 Plan I: **B2**
– ✆ 022 919 39 39
– www.intercontinental-geneva.ch
333 rm – 🚹330/1200 CHF 🚹🚹380/1250 CHF – ☕46 CHF – 49 suites
• Chain • Luxury • Elegant •

Just behind the United Nations, this hotel perfect for business travellers is housed in the highest building in the city. Spacious, contemporary-style guestrooms with views of the Jura or the lake, a superb spa, a cocktail bar and an elegance that is evident right down to the last detail. Quite simply exceptional!

Woods – See restaurant listing

Le Richemond

Rue Adhémar-Fabri 8 ✉ 1201 – ✆ 022 715 70 00 Plan: **F3**
– www.dorchestercollection.com
99 rm – 🚹395/890 CHF 🚹🚹395/890 CHF – ☕55 CHF – 10 suites
• Luxury • Historic • Personalised •

Opened in 1863, Le Richemond provides the perfect combination of late-19C European style and the international taste of the modern day. Its original rotunda shaped lobby and wrought iron balconies look out over the city; these contrast with the luxuriously remodelled areas that are full of refined understatement.

Le Jardin – See restaurant listing

N'vY

Rue de Richemont 18 ✉ 1202 – ✆ 022 544 66 66 Plan: **F2**
– www.hotelnvygeneva.com
153 rm – 🚹200/650 CHF 🚹🚹200/650 CHF – ☕30 CHF – 1 suite
• Business • Luxury • Design •

This hotel has enjoyed a major facelift and the result is explosive. Find arty design, super trendy, high-tech fittings wherever you look, and bright guestrooms that owe as much to the writer Jack Kerouac as to street art. The N'vY will take your breath away!

Trilby – See restaurant listing

Bristol

Rue du Mont-Blanc 10 ✉ 1201 – ✆ 022 716 57 58 Plan: **F3**
– www.bristol.ch
110 rm – 🚹290/600 CHF 🚹🚹290/600 CHF – ☕38 CHF – 1 suite
• Business • Functional •

A smart hotel with very comfortable guestrooms decorated in unfussy, classic style. After a hard day's work, take some time to relax in the basement fitness centre which also offers a sauna, hammam and jacuzzi.

Côté Square – See restaurant listing

Eastwest

Rue des Pâquis 6 ✉ *1201*
– ☏ *022 708 17 17*
– *www.eastwesthotel.ch*
37 rm – ❙195/440 CHF ❙❙198/560 CHF
– ☷ 32 CHF – 4 suites

Plan: **F3**

• Townhouse • Contemporary • Cosy •

This pleasant, impeccable hotel is firmly up to date in style with its contemporary furniture, dark tones, occasional splash of colour and open-plan bathrooms. Extremely central location not far from the banks of the river.

Eastwest – See restaurant listing

Jade

Rue Rothschild 55 ✉ *1202* – ☏ *022 544 38 38*
– *www.hoteljadegeneva.com*
47 rm – ❙150/440 CHF ❙❙150/440 CHF – ☷ 18 CHF

Plan: **F2**

• Business • Contemporary •

This hotel is inspired by the ideas of the famous Chinese philosopher Feng Shui and focuses on the circulation of energy. It is decorated with ethnic objects and has a tranquil, Zen-like ambience. An excellent place to rest both body and mind.

Edelweiss

Place de la Navigation 2 ✉ *1201*
– ☏ *022 544 51 51*
– *www.hoteledelweissgeneva.com*
42 rm – ❙150/440 CHF ❙❙150/440 CHF – ☷ 18 CHF

Plan: **F3**

• Business • Cosy • Alpine •

Named after the famous Swiss flower (known as the immortal flower of the snow), this hotel has the typical ambience of a welcoming Swiss chalet. Light wood dominates in the guestrooms, while the restaurant boasts a real ski resort atmosphere, with its live music (every night) and cheese specialities on the menu.

Cristal

Rue Pradier 4 ✉ *1201* – ☏ *022 716 12 21*
– *www.fassbindhotels.ch*
78 rm – ❙140/250 CHF ❙❙170/300 CHF – ☷ 19 CHF

Plan: **E3**

• Business • Design • Minimalist •

A stone's throw from the train station, this Cristal shines brightly. This is firstly thanks to its commitment to the environment, as witnessed by its solar panels and heating supplied by water circulation and airflow. And secondly, by its bright, designer layout dominated by silver and glass.

Le Chat Botté – Hôtel Beau Rivage

Quai du Mont-Blanc 13 ✉ *1201*
– ☏ *022 716 69 20*
– *www.beau-rivage.ch*
– *Closed 9-24 April and Saturday lunch, Sunday*
Menu 60 CHF (weekday lunch)/220 CHF
– Carte 135/198 CHF – *(booking advisable)*

Plan: **F3**

• Modern French • Elegant •

Cannelloni fondant, Swiss veal filet mignon and apple opaline are just some of the top quality dishes served in this restaurant. The skilful chef perfectly illustrates Le Chat Botté's philosophy that industry and knowledge are worth far more than material possessions. Impeccable service and a magnificent terrace overlooking Lake Geneva.

→ Ormeaux de Plouguerneau aux coques et salicornes. Saint-Pierre des côtes bretonnes, citron caviar et yuzu. Volaille du Nant d'Avril laquée au jus de truffes.

SWITZERLAND - GENEVA (GENÈVE)

XxXx · ⊹

Il Lago – Four Seasons Hôtel des Bergues   🏨 🛋 ႕ 🆔

Quai des Bergues 33 ⊠ 1201 – ℰ 022 908 71 10   Plan: **F3**
– www.fourseasons.com/geneva
Menu 78 CHF (lunch)/130 CHF – Carte 105/180 CHF – *(booking essential)*
• Italian • Classic décor • Elegant •
Offering a taste of Italy on Lake Geneva, this restaurant combines a chic decor (superb pilasters and paintings) with elegant Italian cuisine which is light, subtle and fragant. A delightful dining experience!
→ Risotto de homard. Tortelli de fromage, citron et menthe. Cabri laqué au Banyuls, céleri-rave rôti et pomme verte.

XxXx · ⊹

Bayview – Hôtel Président Wilson   🏨 ≤ ႕ 🆔 🚗

Quai Wilson 47 ⊠ 1211 – ℰ 022 906 65 52   Plan: **F2**
– www.hotelpresidentwilson.com – Closed 1-9 January, 16-24 April, 30 July - 29 August and Sunday-Monday
Menu 60 CHF (lunch)/170 CHF – Carte 109/211 CHF
• Modern French • Design • Elegant •
With carefully designed, sober and chic decor and large bay windows facing the lake, this restaurant provides the ideal setting to enjoy elegant cuisine. French classics are reinterpreted with creativity and subtlety, and the carefully produced dishes are chic and contemporary.
→ Ormeau de Plougastel snacké, longeole traditionelle et blanc-manger anisé. Côte de veau fumée minute, petits pois et artichauts violets, crumble thym-citron. Tarte soufflée au chocolat Guanaja 70%.

XxX

Windows – Hôtel D'Angleterre   🏨 ≤ 🆔

Quai du Mont-Blanc 17 ⊠ 1201 – ℰ 022 906 55 14   Plan: **F3**
– www.hoteldangleterre.ch
Menu 59 CHF (weekday lunch) – Carte 79/134 CHF
• Creative French • Elegant • Friendly •
Housed in the Hôtel d'Angleterre, this restaurant offers superb views of Lake Geneva, the Jet d'eau and the mountains in the distance. The menu features delicacies such as scallop carpaccio with lime, avocado tartare and fleur de sel, and half a baked lobster with little gem lettuce and potatoes.

XxX

Rasoi by Vineet – Hôtel Mandarin Oriental   ႕ 🆔 ⇩ 🚗

Quai turrettini 1 ⊠ 1201 – ℰ 022 909 00 00   Plan: **E3**
– www.mandarinoriental.fr/geneva – Closed Sunday-Monday
Menu 65 CHF (lunch)/155 CHF – Carte 85/161 CHF – *(booking advisable)*
• Indian • Cosy •
All the fragrances and colours of Indian cuisine are interpreted here with incredible refinement. Enjoy the cuisine of the sub-continent at its best in this chic and elegant restaurant where you can imagine yourself as a 21C maharaja!

XxX

Le Jardin – Hôtel Le Richemond   🛋 ႕ 🆔 ⇩

Rue Adhémar-Fabri 8 ⊠ 1201 – ℰ 022 715 71 00   Plan: **F3**
– www.dorchestercollection.com – Closed Sunday dinner and Monday, except season
Menu 49 CHF (weekday lunch)/120 CHF – Carte 76/125 CHF
• Modern French • Elegant • Cosy •
This restaurant is situated in the Le Richemond hotel, facing the lake. It serves French cuisine with contemporary flavours and a focus on produce from the region. The terrace is a must in fine weather.

XxX

Côté Square – Hôtel Bristol   🆔

Rue du Mont-Blanc 10 ⊠ 1201 – ℰ 022 716 57 58   Plan: **F3**
– www.bristol.ch – Closed 2-8 January, 14-23 April and Saturday-Sunday
Menu 55 CHF (weekday lunch)/87 CHF – Carte 73/93 CHF
• French • Cosy •
This restaurant has a classic elegance. Wood panelling and paintings add an aristocratic air, enhanced by the occasional notes emanating from the attractive black piano near the bar. On tables covered with immaculately white cloths, enjoy delicious dishes showcasing a variety of textures and flavours.

SWITZERLAND - GENEVA GENÈVE

XX **Café Calla** – Hôtel Mandarin Oriental ≤ & 🖭 ⇔ 🚗

Quai Turrettini 1 ✉ 1201 – ☎ 022 909 00 00 Plan: **E3**
– www.mandarinoriental.fr/geneva
Menu 85 CHF (dinner) – Carte 67/132 CHF
• Mediterranean cuisine • Elegant •
Situated on the lakeside, the Mandarin Oriental's chic brasserie specialises in Mediterranean flavours, offering dishes from all over the region, such as aubergine caviar, chicken and lemon tagine, and Italian-style veal picatta.

XX **Patara** – Hôtel Beau-Rivage ≤ 🛱 🖭 🚗

Quai du Mont-Blanc 13 ✉ 1201 Plan: **F3**
– ☎ 022 731 55 66 – www.patara-geneva.ch
– Closed 2 weeks Christmas-New Year
Menu 49 CHF (lunch)/125 CHF – Carte 67/113 CHF
• Thai • Exotic décor •
Thai specialities served in one of the most beautiful luxury hotels in Geneva. Stylised gold motifs on the walls evoke the exotic ambience of Thailand, while the delicious specialities on the menu add to the sense of discovery.

XX **Trilby** – Hôtel N'vY & 🖭 🚗

Rue de Richemont 18 ✉ 1202 – ☎ 022 544 66 66 Plan: **F2**
– www.hotelnvygeneva.com
Menu 70 CHF – Carte 54/152 CHF
• International • Fashionable • Elegant •
You might want to doff your own trilby as you enter this elegant and welcoming restaurant. The speciality is the outstanding beef, whether it is Scottish (Black Angus), Japanese (Wagyu Kobe) or Swiss (Simmental), accompanied by a choice of original sauces.

XX **L'Arabesque** – Hôtel Président Wilson ≤ & 🖭 🚗

Quai Wilson 47 ✉ 1211 – ☎ 022 906 67 63 Plan: **F2**
– www.hotelpresidentwilson.com
Menu 59 CHF (weekday lunch)/95 CHF – Carte 54/86 CHF
• Lebanese • Elegant •
The attractive decor features gold mosaics, white leather and black lacquerware, evoking the magic of the Orient; in particular the Lebanon, from where the authentic aromas of dishes such as bastorma (dried beef with spices) and houmous (chickpea purée) transport diners to the land of the cedar tree!

XX **Woods** – Hôtel InterContinental ≤ 🛱 & 🖭 🚗

Chemin du Petit-Saconnex 7 ✉ 1209 Plan I: **B2**
– ☎ 022 919 39 39 – www.intercontinental-geneva.ch
– Closed Saturday
Menu 59 CHF (weekday lunch)/68 CHF – Carte 79/124 CHF
• Modern cuisine • Friendly •
This attractive, contemporary-style restaurant is in the InterContinental Hotel. It boasts an attractive wood decor and serves cuisine that is full of flavour.

X **Bistrot du Boeuf Rouge**
😊
Rue Dr. Alfred-Vincent 17 ✉ 1201 Plan: **F3**
– ☎ 022 732 75 37 – www.boeufrouge.ch
– Closed Christmas-2 January, 15 July-13 August, Saturday-Sunday and Bank Holidays
Carte 49/99 CHF – (booking advisable)
• Traditional cuisine • Brasserie • Vintage •
Run by the Farina family for over 20 years, this restaurant serves simple, rustic, yet fresh and tasty cuisine. Dishes include duckling terrine, fera fish from Lake Geneva in a tarragon sauce, and raspberry tart. Attractive, Parisian bistro-style decor.

SWITZERLAND - GENEVA GENÈVE

✗ **umami by michel roth** – Hôtel Président Wilson ≤ ⅋ 🆔 ☜
Quai Wilson 47 ⊠ *1211* – ✆ *022 906 64 52* Plan: **F2**
*– www.hotelpresidentwilson.com – Closed October-April
and Sunday*
Menu 59 CHF (lunch)/95 CHF – Carte 66/90 CHF
• Japanese • Exotic décor • Fashionable •
Dine at this restaurant and you will soon realise that there is far more to Japanese cuisine than sushi and sashimi. Creativity is very much to the fore, with the occasional French influence thrown in for good measure. The maki rolls sautéed with foie gras, green apple and ginger are delicious.

✗ **Le Rouge et le Blanc** 🏠 🆔
Quai des Bergues 27 ⊠ *1201* – ✆ *022 731 15 50* Plan: **E3**
– www.lerougeblanc.ch – Closed 24 December-2 January and Sunday
Carte 54/83 CHF – *(dinner only) (booking advisable)*
• Traditional cuisine • Wine bar •
A good wine selection, rib of beef as the house speciality (for two or three people), plates of tapas that vary according to market availability, and a relaxed and convivial atmosphere. This restaurant makes a good choice for an enjoyable meal out. Open evenings only.

✗ **Lemon Café** 🏠 ☻
Rue du Vidollet 4 ⊠ *1202* – ✆ *022 733 60 24* Plan: **E2**
– www.lemon-cafe.ch – Closed 1-8 January and 24 July-6 August
Menu 52 CHF (lunch) – Carte 49/90 CHF
• Modern French • Simple • Bistro •
At this restaurant the chef delights guests with his travel-inspired dishes. Just some of the options are cod ceviche with a Peruvian flavour, pork spare ribs cooked for 12 hours and served with Maxim's potatoes, and lemon cheesecake.

✗ **Le Grill** – Grand Hôtel Kempinski ≤ ⅋ 🆔 ☻ ☜
Quai du Mont-Blanc 19 ⊠ *1201* – ✆ *022 908 92 20* Plan: **F3**
– www.kempinski.com/geneva
Menu 38 CHF (lunch) – Carte 81/117 CHF
• Meats and grills • Fashionable •
A chic and original restaurant. It offers views of Lake Geneva, as well as of the kitchens, rotisserie and cold rooms where the splendid cuts of meat are stored (300g Parisian entrecôte, beef fillet, rack of lamb, etc). The meat is cooked to perfection and the formula works well.

✗ **Eastwest** – Hôtel Eastwest 🏠 🆔 ☻
Rue des Pâquis 6 ⊠ *1201* – ✆ *022 708 17 07* Plan: **F3**
– www.eastwesthotel.ch
Carte 49/93 CHF – *(booking advisable)*
• International • Design • Cosy •
An attractive Japanese influenced decor and inviting patio contribute to the simple elegance of this restaurant. Provençal vegetables and beef tartare feature on the menu alongside teriyaki sauce and Thai basil.

✗ **Izumi** – Four Seasons Hôtel des Bergues ≤ 🏠 ⅋ 🆔 ☜
Quai des Bergues 33 ⊠ *1201* – ✆ *022 908 75 25* Plan: **F3**
– www.fourseasons.com/geneva – Closed 3 weeks July-August
Menu 65 CHF (lunch)/135 CHF – Carte 78/165 CHF
• Japanese • Elegant • Trendy •
Situated on the top floor of Geneva's leading hotel, this restaurant is bound to surprise and delight you. The Japanese specialities served here are flavoured with the occasional hint of Peru, providing a whole host of striking contrasts which work extremely well. Enjoy your dinner on the terrace while taking in the lovely views of Geneva and the River Rhône below.

X **Miyako** ⇔

Rue Chantepoulet 11 ⊠ 1201 – 𝒞 022 738 01 20   Plan: **E3**
– www.miyako.ch – Closed Sunday
Menu 74/108 CHF – Carte 65/99 CHF
• Japanese • Simple •

This aptly named restaurant (Miyako is the Japanese for heart) plunges you into the heart of Japan. It has tatami flooring, teppanyaki cuisine, fresh fish and attentive service. Arigato!

LEFT BANK   **PLAN III**

 Les Armures 🏆 🕏 AK

Rue du Puits-Saint-Pierre 1 ⊠ 1204 – 𝒞 022 310 91 72   Plan: **H2**
– www.hotel-les-armures.ch
32 rm – †340/545 CHF ††375/720 CHF – � 40 CHF
• Traditional • Historic • Contemporary •

Situated in the heart of the old town, this 17C residence has a certain charm. It has old stone walls and wooden beams, as well as some superb painted ceilings. It is also intimate, romantic and resolutely contemporary in style. Offering a completely different atmosphere, the restaurant is an authentic tavern serving raclettes and fondues.

 De la Cigogne AK 🔐

Place Longemalle 17 ⊠ 1204 – 𝒞 022 818 40 40   Plan: **H1**
– www.relaischateaux.com/cigogne
46 rm ⊑ – †350/560 CHF ††460/675 CHF – 6 suites
• Luxury • Townhouse • Historic •

A cosy, luxurious hotel decorated with pretty prints, antique furniture, paintings and carpets, all of which create a chic, delicate and classic ambience. The sense of comfort and well-being makes it very difficult to leave.
De la Cigogne – See restaurant listing

 Tiffany 🏆 𝄖 🛁 AK 🔐

Rue de l'Arquebuse 20 ⊠ 1204 – 𝒞 022 708 16 16   Plan: **G2**
– www.tiffanyhotel.ch
65 rm – †180/495 CHF ††248/550 CHF – ⊑ 29 CHF
• Traditional • Contemporary • Cosy •

This small, stylish Belle Époque hotel is situated on the edge of the old town. It offers Art Nouveau decor in its lobby and restaurant and Art Deco furnishings in its guestrooms. Pleasant ambience and friendly welcome.

XX **La Bottega** (Francesco Gasbarro) 🏵 AK ⇔
🕸

Rue de La Corraterie 21 – 𝒞 022 736 10 00   Plan: **G2**
– www.labottegatrattoria.com – Closed 23 December-9 January, 1 week Easter, 2 weeks early August and Saturday-Sunday
Menu 50 CHF (weekday lunch)/118 CHF – (booking advisable)
• Italian • Friendly •

There isn't a menu at La Bottega, just a whole heap of inspiration! The chef here presents a re-worked version of Italian cuisine with the help of top-quality Swiss ingredients. The modern, delicious dishes come full of surprises to delight the guests.
→ Ravioli au pigeon et thym. Selle d'agneau et panais. Fraise, basilic et pistache.

XX **Brasserie du Parc des Eaux-Vives** ≤ 🏡 🕹 ⇔

Quai Gustave-Ador 82 ⊠ 1211 – 𝒞 022 849 75 75   Plan I: **D2**
– www.parcdeseauxvives.ch – Closed 1 week mid February
Menu 39 CHF (lunch)/85 CHF – Carte 68/92 CHF
• Modern French • Classic décor •

Situated in the Parc des Eaux-Vives, this beautiful classic-style restaurant occupies a magical setting with long green lawns running down to the lake. The à la carte menu features dishes such as octopus with citrus fruit, local pork chops and veal kidneys in a mustard sauce. Guestrooms with a view of the lake add to the appeal.

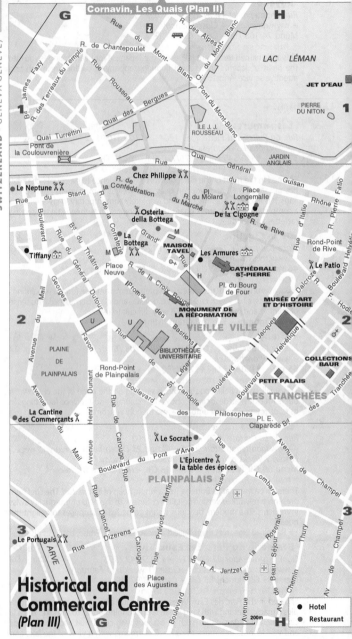

SWITZERLAND – GENEVA GENÈVE

Cornavin, Les Quais (Plan II)

LAC LÉMAN

JET D'EAU

PIERRE DU NITON

Rue du Mont-Blanc

R. de Chantepoulet

Rue Rousseau

Bd James Fazy

R. des Terreaux du Temple

Quai des Bergues

Pont du Mont-Blanc

ÎLE J. J. ROUSSEAU

Quai Turrettini

Pont de la Coulouvrenière

Quai

JARDIN ANGLAIS

Rue

Général

du

Guisan

Rhône

R. Pierre Fatio

Chez Philippe

Le Neptune

R. de la Confédération

Rue du Stand

Boulevard

Rue de la Coratelie

Pl. du Molard

Place Longemalle

De la Cigogne

R. de Rive

Rue d'Italie

Osteria della Bottega

Grand'Rue

La Bottega

MAISON TAVEL

Les Armures

CATHÉDRALE ST-PIERRE

Rond-Point de Rive

Boulevard Helvétique

Le Patio

Tiffany

Bd du Théâtre

Place Neuve

R. de la Croix Rouge

Pl. du Bourg de Four

MUSÉE D'ART ET D'HISTOIRE

R. Hodler

Rue du Général

Georges

Prom. des

MONUMENT DE LA RÉFORMATION

VIEILLE VILLE

R. Jacques

R. Dalcroze

Avenue du Mail

Rue Dutour

Rue de Favon

BIBLIOTHÈQUE UNIVERSITAIRE

des Bastions

Boulevard Helvétique

COLLECTIONS BAUR

PLAINE DE PLAINPALAIS

Rond-Point de Plainpalais

Rue Henri Dunant

Boulevard

R. St-Léger

Boulevard

PETIT PALAIS

LES TRANCHÉES

des Tranchée

La Cantine des Commerçants

R. St-Candolle

des

Philosophes

Pl. E. Claparède

Bd

Avenue du Mail

Le Socrate

Rue d'Arve

Rue

Avenue de Champel

L'Epicentre la table des épices

Boulevard du Pont

Rue de Carouge

Rue Martin

Rue de la Cluse

PLAINPALAIS

Lombard

Rue Dancet

Rue Dizerens

Rue de Carouge

Rue Prévost

de

Roseraie

Thury

Avenue

de Champel

Le Portugais

ARVE

Place des Augustins

R. A. Jentzer

Av. de Beau Séjour

Chemin de

Av. de Champel

Historical and Commercial Centre (Plan III)

G   H

● Hotel
● Restaurant

0   200m

760

XX **Chez Philippe** 🕸 🍴 Ꮣ 🅰🄲
😊 *Rue du Rhône 8 ⊠ 1204 – 𝒞 022 316 16 16*   Plan: **G1**
– www.chezphilippe.ch
Menu 39 CHF – Carte 44/147 CHF
• Meats and grills • Friendly •

Philippe Chevrier, from the Domaine de Châteauvieux, is the brains behind this restaurant inspired by New York steakhouses. Top-quality Swiss meat with delicious seasoning and vegetables ensures that this venture is a resounding success.

XX **De la Cigogne** – Hôtel De la Cigogne   🕸 🍴 🅰🄲 ⇔
Place Longemalle 17 ⊠ 1204 – 𝒞 022 818 40 40   Plan: **H1**
– www.relaischateaux.com/cigogne – Closed Christmas-New Year and Saturday lunch, Sunday
Menu 65/125 CHF – Carte 92/122 CHF
• Modern French • Elegant • Friendly •

This restaurant is sure to please with its intimate atmosphere that is typical of certain hotel restaurants. The classic cuisine includes dishes such as tomato and caper tart and crayfish tails with rocket.

XX **Le Neptune**   🍴
Rue de la Coulouvrenière 38 ⊠ 1204 – 𝒞 022 320 15 05   Plan: **G1**
– www.leneptune.ch – Closed 1 week mid April and Saturday-Sunday
Menu 59/110 CHF – Carte 83/106 CHF
• Modern cuisine • Elegant • Friendly •

Situated in a quiet district on the left bank, this restaurant is run by a chef who is a keen promoter of Alpine cuisine. He carefully selects his suppliers himself, choosing only organic produce and creating dishes that are innovative as well as delicious. In fine weather, enjoy alfresco dining on the small terrace in the inner courtyard.

XX **Le Portugais**   🅰🄲
Boulevard du Pont d'Arve 59 ⊠ 1205 – 𝒞 022 329 40 98   Plan: **G3**
– www.leportugais.ch – Closed July and Sunday-Monday
Menu 46 CHF (lunch)/59 CHF – Carte 45/84 CHF
• Portuguese • Simple •

Many Portuguese have left their mark on history, including famous explorers such as Vasco de Gama and Magellan. However, the only exploring you will be doing in this restaurant is of the culinary variety. Enjoy a choice of excellent fish cooked by an enthusiastic chef and accompanied by good local wine. Friendly, rustic ambience. Obrigado!

X **La Cantine des Commerçants**   🍴 Ꮣ
😊 *Boulevard Carl Vogt 29 ⊠ 1205 – 𝒞 022 328 16 70*   Plan: **G2**
– www.lacantine.ch – Closed Christmas-early January, 2 weeks 13-22 August and Sunday-Monday
Menu 48/65 CHF (dinner) – Carte 56/81 CHF
• French • Design • Fashionable •

A neo-bistro in the old abattoir district of the city, characterised by white and bright green walls, retro decor and a large counter where you can sit and eat. The varied menu is very much in keeping with the times: risotto with gambas and wild herbs, grilled fish and pan-fried fillet of beef.

X **Le Patio**
Boulevard Helvétique 19 ⊠ 1207 – 𝒞 022 736 66 75   Plan: **H2**
– www.lepatiorestaurant.ch – Closed Sunday
Menu 45 CHF (lunch)/60 CHF – Carte 47/108 CHF
• Creative French • Friendly • Bistro •

Philippe Chevrier (chef at the Domaine de Châteauvieux in Satigny) has chosen an original concept here: cuisine that is almost exclusively based on lobster and beef. The menu includes dishes such as lobster tartare and oxtail parmentier, which are fresh, delicious and full of flavour. A highly enjoyable dining experience!

SWITZERLAND - GENEVA GENÈVE

✗ **Le Socrate**   🛖 AC
Rue Micheli-du-Crest 6 ✉ 1205 – ✆ 022 320 16 77   Plan: **H3**
– www.lesocrate.ch – Closed Saturday lunch, Sunday
Carte 48/70 CHF
· Traditional cuisine · Vintage · Friendly ·
A bistro with a delightfully retro dining room adorned with old posters. Sample simple, honest and delicious dishes at tables set close together. A place where good food and conversation are to the fore, in an atmosphere that a certain Greek philosopher would have appreciated!

✗ **L'Epicentre, la table des épices**   🛖
Rue Prévost-Martin 25 ✉ 1205 – ✆ 022 328 14 70   Plan: **G3**
– www.lepicentre.ch – Closed 23 December-8 January, mid August-mid September and Saturday-Sunday
Menu 78/127 CHF – Carte 66/96 CHF
· Creative · Exotic décor · Simple ·
The two chefs at this aptly named restaurant (table des épices means spice table) create fragrant and well-balanced dishes that are full of flavour. They select one or two spices from the 300 varieties that they have bought either in Geneva or abroad as the foundation for each dish. The excellent wine list features mainly natural wines.

✗ **Osteria della Bottega**   🍴
Grand Rue 3 ✉ 1204 – ✆ 022 810 84 51   Plan: **G2**
– www.osteriadellabottega.com – Closed 2 weeks Christmas-New Year, 1 week Easter and Sunday-Monday
Menu 39 CHF (lunch)/70 CHF – Carte 52/82 CHF
· Italian · Friendly · Simple ·
The Bottegas have created a new member of the family, the Osteria. In keeping with its nearby gastronomic sibling, Francesco Gasbarro celebrates the finest products from the Tuscan countryside which he incorporates into recipes of disarming simplicity. A successful venture made even more so by the reasonable prices.

ENVIRONS AND COINTRIN AIRPORT   **PLAN I**

🏨 **La Réserve**
Route de Lausanne 301 – ✆ 022 959 59 59   Plan: **C1**
– www.lareserve.ch
85 rm ⬛ – 🛏550/900 CHF 🛏🛏550/900 CHF – 17 suites
· Grand Luxury · Elegant · Cosy ·
This luxury hotel is a true sanctuary of beauty! Designer Jacques Garcia has used fine materials and dark colours to create guestrooms with an exotic atmosphere and a style that brings to mind an African lodge. Superb spa, access to the lake, boat available for guests – everything seems possible here. Three restaurants offering a vast selection of flavours.
❀ **Tsé Fung** · **Le Loti** – See restaurant listing

🏨 **Starling**   🍴 ℔ 🐟 🚹 AC 🛗 P
Route François-Peyrot 34 – ✆ 022 747 04 00   Plan: **B1**
– www.shgeneva.com
494 rm – 🛏200/400 CHF 🛏🛏200/400 CHF – ⬛ 39 CHF – 2 suites
· Business · Chain · Functional ·
Situated near the airport and Palexpo, this hotel is worthy of the A380, with almost 500 rooms used mainly by business travellers and conference guests. Despite its size, the hotel is anything but impersonal, with attentive staff and numerous leisure facilities (fitness room, well-being centre, restaurants, etc).
L'Olivo – See restaurant listing

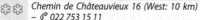

XXXX
ŝ ŝ

Domaine de Châteauvieux (Philippe Chevrier)

Chemin de Châteauvieux 16 (West: 10 km)
– ℰ 022 753 15 11
– www.chateauvieux.ch
– *Closed 2 weeks Christmas-New Year, 1 week during Easter, 2 weeks end July-early August*
13 rm – ♦210/350 CHF ♦♦245/400 CHF – ☷ 20 CHF
Menu 96 CHF (weekday lunch)/290 CHF
– Carte 188/235 CHF – *(booking advisable)*
• Creative • Rustic • Inn •

Off the beaten track, standing above the Geneva countryside and its vineyards, this large traditional house teeming with cachet and individual charm cultivates a true sense of excellence! A culinary technician as much as he is an artist, Philippe Chevrier follows a unique path to unearth truly natural flavours that reconnect with the basics. Delightful rooms for those wishing to stay the night.
➔ Bar de ligne caramélisé, mousseline de betteraves et avocat. Suprême de pigeon des Deux-Sèvres, cuisses confites aux pois chiches. Sucre soufflé et morilles, biscuit noix de pécan, glace aux baies de Genièvre.

XXXX
ŝ

Auberge du Lion d'Or (Thomas Byrne et Gilles Dupont)

Place Pierre-Gautier 5
– ℰ 022 736 44 32
Plan: **D2**
– www.dupont-byrne.ch
– *Closed 24 December-16 January and Saturday-Sunday*
Menu 160/190 CHF – Carte 109/174 CHF
• Modern cuisine • Elegant •

Two heads are often better than one and the two chefs at this restaurant certainly combine their talents to good effect. They offer an excellent choice of produce, original food combinations and cuisine that is full of flavour. Not to mention a romantic view of the lake. A good dining option!
➔ Ravioles gourmandes de crabe royal du Kamchatka et langoustine "Asia". Loup de mer cuit en croûte de sel marin, sauce niçoise. Pomme de ris de veau, bien dorée à la poêle, émulsion de petits pois, croquant aux oignons fumés.
Le Bistro de Cologny – See restaurant listing

XXX
ŝ

Tsé Fung – Hôtel La Réserve

Route de Lausanne 301 – ℰ 022 959 59 59
Plan: **C1**
– www.tsefung.ch
Menu 75 CHF (lunch)/180 CHF – Carte 68/217 CHF
• Chinese • Exotic •

Cantonese – and Chinese cooking in general – can count on Frank Xu to act as its gastronomic ambassador here. His culinary creations are authentic and delicious in equal measure, meticulously prepared with the very best ingredients. His desserts in particular will live long in the memory. Pleasant view of the garden and lake.
➔ Siu Mai de crevette et porc. Canard laqué à la pékinoise en deux services. Soupe de mangue, pomelo et perles de sagou.

XXX

Le Loti – Hôtel La Réserve

Route de Lausanne 301 – ℰ 022 959 59 59
Plan: **C1**
– www.lareserve.ch
Menu 58 CHF (lunch) – Carte 81/128 CHF
• Mediterranean cuisine • Elegant • Intimate •

Named after the travel writer Pierre Loti, this restaurant, with its warm tones and exotic influences, evokes a fascination with other lands. The menu features dishes such as truffle risotto, veal chops, rum baba and chocolate fondant.

XX ⍟ **Le Cigalon** (Jean-Marc Bessire) 🗺 **P**

*Route d'Ambilly 39 (South-East: 5 km by Route de Chêne D3)
– 𝒞 022 349 97 33 – www.le-cigalon.ch – Closed 2 weeks end December-
early January, Easter, 3 weeks mid July-early August and Sunday-Monday*
Menu 54 CHF (weekday lunch)/150 CHF – Carte 94/118 CHF
• Seafood • Elegant •
Judging by the fresh fish on the menu, you would be forgiven for thinking that
the Breton coast lies just outside the doors of this restaurant. Le Cigalon has
specialised in fish and seafood for over 20 years, with delicacies such as fish
soup, scallops and monkfish from Roscoff all featuring on the menu. Table
d'hôte meals for five guests are also available.
➔ Fines tranches de sériole marinées, parfumé à l'huile de crevettes sauvages. La crevette de Myanmar, en finger croustillant, royale coco aux trois
poivres. Bar de ligne rôti sur ses écailles, riz noir vénéré du Piémont.

XX **L'Olivo** – Hôtel Starling 🗺 ⅍ 🄺 ⇔ **P**

Route François-Peyrot 34 – 𝒞 022 747 04 00 Plan: **B1**
*– www.shgeneva.com – Closed Christmas-New Year, Saturday-Sunday and
Bank Holidays*
Menu 43 CHF (lunch) – Carte 70/104 CHF
• Italian • Cosy • Mediterranean décor •
A pleasant restaurant near the airport with a large terrace shaded by olive trees.
The flavours of Italy dominate the menu, which features specialities such as
pasta, risotto, gnocchi with sweet chestnuts, and veal escalopes in a Milanese
sauce.

XX **Les Fourneaux du Manège** 🍽 🗺 ⇔

Route de Chancy 127 – 𝒞 022 870 03 90 Plan: **A3**
*– www.fourneauxdumanege.ch – Closed 23 December-9 January,
1-16 August and Saturday lunch, Sunday dinner-Monday*
Menu 52 CHF (weekday lunch)/118 CHF – Carte 57/123 CHF
• Traditional cuisine • Cosy • Inn •
In this attractive 19C building in the centre of Onex, you will enjoy a warm welcome from a dynamic team. They work mainly with regional produce, in particular the famous fish from Lake Geneva: pike, the salmon-like fera, char
and perch. It is all served with great enthusiasm in the dining room or on the
terrace.

XX **Le Vallon** 🗺 ⇔ **P**

Route de Florissant 182 – 𝒞 022 347 11 04 Plan: **D3**
– www.restaurant-vallon.com – Closed Sunday
Menu 59/84 CHF (dinner) – Carte 58/104 CHF – *(booking advisable)*
• French • Bistro •
This restaurant is a delightful place to eat with its pink façade, green shutters,
wisteria-entwined sign and tree-shaded terrace. The interior decor is typical of
a traditional inn and the menu features classic cuisine.

X ⍟ **Le Flacon** 🗺 ⅍ 🄺 ⇔

Rue Vautier 45 – 𝒞 022 342 15 20 – www.leflacon.ch Plan: **C3**
– Closed Saturday lunch and Sunday-Monday
Menu 75 CHF (lunch)/120 CHF – Carte 90/108 CHF
• Modern cuisine • Design •
An enchanting restaurant where the young chef, only just in his 30s, creates
delicious cuisine from his open-view kitchen. He demonstrates a fine command
of flavour and ingredient combinations, as well as a real eye for detail in his
beautifully presented dishes.
➔ Asperges de Roques-Hautes, citron confit, poutargue et lard blanc.
Volaille du Nant d'Avril, risotto de blette et mousseline de pomme ratte.
Mangue Nam Dok Mai, glace yaourt et lait d'amande.

X
(face icon)
Collonge Café ⌂ & ✿ P

Chemin du Château-de-Bellerive 3 – ℰ 022 777 12 45　　　Plan: **D1**
– www.collonge-cafe.ch – Closed Christmas-New Year, October-May:
Sunday dinner-Monday
Menu 35 CHF (lunch) – Carte 69/103 CHF
• Italian • Friendly • Bistro •

This village inn is now run by Angelo and Viviana Citiulo, previously of La Closerie in Cologny. The couple add just a hint of contemporary style to their Italian dishes, with great results, while the attractive prices certainly pose a challenge to the restaurant's competitors!

X
Café des Négociants 祭 ⌂ ✿

Rue de la Filature 29 – ℰ 022 300 31 30　　　Plan: **C3**
– www.negociants.ch – Closed January-November: Sunday
Menu 29 CHF (lunch)/74 CHF – Carte 45/79 CHF – (booking advisable)
• Classic cuisine • Bistro • Friendly •

This retro-style bistro offers all the pleasures of flavoursome, seasonal cuisine and a wine cellar of gargantuan proportions, accompanied by excellent advice. This combination has more than proved its worth: the restaurant is often fully booked.

X
Le Bistro de Cologny – Restaurant Auberge du Lion d'Or ≼

Place Pierre-Gautier 5 – ℰ 022 736 57 80　　　⌂ & **AC**
– www.dupont-byrne.ch – Closed 24 December-　　　Plan: **D2**
9 January
Carte 70/92 CHF
• Traditional cuisine • Bistro • Inn •

Echoing the success of the gourmet Lion d'Or restaurant, this bistro annexe is much more than an add on, offering delicious dishes such as sole from Brittany and veal fillet with cep mushrooms. The stunning views from the terrace allow diners to make the most of the 'bistronomic' formula at weekends.

X
Le Relais de Chambésy ⌂ P

Place de Chambésy 8 – ℰ 022 758 11 05　　　Plan: **C1**
– www.relaisdechambesy.ch – Closed Sunday, July-August: Saturday lunch,
Sunday
Menu 68 CHF – Carte 56/91 CHF
• Classic French • Rustic • Friendly •

Situated in a quiet village, this old coaching inn continues its tradition of hospitality on the outskirts of Geneva. Classic French cuisine, as well as an attractive terrace surrounded by greenery.

ZURICH
ZÜRICH

Population: 412 200

Mirubi/Fotolia.com

Zurich has a lot of things going for it. A lot of history (2,000 years' worth), a lot of water (two rivers and a huge lake), a lot of beauty and, let's face it, a lot of wealth. It's an important financial and commercial centre, and has a well-earned reputation for good living and a rich cultural life. The place strikes a nice balance – it's large enough to boast some world-class facilities but small enough to hold onto its charm and old-world ambience. The window-shopping here sets it apart from many other European cities – from tiny boutiques and specialist emporiums to a shopping boulevard that's famed across the globe. Although it's not Switzerland's political capital, it's the spiritual one because of its pulsing arts scene: for those who might think the Swiss a bit staid, think again – this is where the nihilistic, anti-art Dada movement began. The attractive Lake Zurich flows northwards into the city, which forms a pleasingly symmetrical arc around it. From the lake, the river Limmat bisects Zurich: on its west bank lies the Old Town, the medieval hub, where the stylishly vibrant Bahnhofstrasse shopping street follows the line of the old city walls. Across the Limmat on the east side is the magnificent twin-towered Grossmünster, while just beyond is the charmingly historic district of Niederdorf and way down south, is the city's largest green space, the Zürichhorn Park.

ZURICH IN...

→ **ONE DAY**
Old Town, Bahnhofstrasse, Zurich West, Grossmünster.

→ **TWO DAYS**
Watch chessplayers on Lindenhof, see Chagall's windows at Fraumünster, Kunsthaus, Cabaret Voltaire, Café Odeon.

→ **THREE DAYS**
Utoquai, Zürichhorn Park, night at the Opera House.

PRACTICAL INFORMATION

ARRIVAL-DEPARTURE

 Zurich International Airport (Kloten) is 10km north of the city. Zürich Hauptbahnhof is the main railway station. Trains run every 10-15min and take 10min.

GETTING AROUND

The public transport system runs like clockwork. The city operates an efficient system on bus, tram, metro, train and boat. You can buy a single ticket, a day ticket or a 9 o'clock Pass. Tickets are available from ticket machines and tourist offices. Remember to validate your ticket at the ticket machine or special orange-coloured machine before boarding. The Zurichcard grants unlimited travel on all public transport (including river and lake boats). It also gives admission to more than forty museums and art collections. The card can be purchased for 24 or 72 hours. Cycling is encouraged here; hire bikes for free from beside the main railway station by leaving ID and a deposit.

EATING OUT

Zurich stands out in Switzerland (along with Geneva) for its top-class restaurants serving international cuisine. Zurich, though, takes the prize when it comes to trendy, cutting-edge places to dine, whether restaurant or bar, whether along the lakeside or in the converted loft of an old factory. In the middle of the day, most locals go for the cheaper daily lunchtime menus, saving themselves for the glories of the evening. The city is host to many traditional, longstanding

CALENDAR HIGHLIGHTS

February-March
Art On Ice, Carnival Procession concluding with the Guggen Monster Concert.

June and July
Zurich Festival.

August
Theatre Spectacle.

September
Weltklasse (Athletics), Zurich International Art Fair.

November
Jazznojazz (music festival).

December
Silvesterlauf (Festive race through the Old Town).

Italian restaurants, but if you want to try something 'totally Zurcher', you can't do any better than tackle geschnetzeltes with rösti: sliced veal fried in butter, simmered with onions and mushrooms, with a dash of white wine and cream, served with hashed brown potatoes. A good place for simple restaurants and bars is Niederdorf, while Zurich West is coming on strong with its twenty-first century zeitgeist diners. It's customary to round up a small bill or leave up to ten percent on a larger one.

767

SWITZERLAND - ZURICH

Ambassador à l'Opéra   🅰🅲 🛋

Falkenstr. 6 ✉ *8008 –* ☏ *044 258 98 98*   Plan: **D3**
– www.ambassadorhotel.ch
45 rm – 🛏295/560 CHF 🛏🛏415/680 CHF – ☑ 33 CHF
• Townhouse • Elegant • Cosy •
This former nobleman's house is now a smart boutique hotel with its own particular style. The comfortable rooms come in all shapes and sizes with some pleasing details. These include excellent beds, Nespresso machines and all the latest technology.
Opera – See restaurant listing

Europe   🅰🅲 🛋

Dufourstr. 4 ✉ *8008 –* ☏ *043 456 86 86*   Plan: **D3**
– www.europehotel.ch
39 rm – 🛏190/380 CHF 🛏🛏250/500 CHF – ☑ 25 CHF – 2 suites
• Historic • Townhouse • Cosy •
A stylish little hotel built between 1898 and 1900 and situated right next to the Opera. The Europe is classically elegant, comfortable and upmarket with a little touch of the 1950s, as well as all the latest technology. No surcharge for room service.
Quaglinos – See restaurant listing

Wellenberg

Niederdorfstr. 10 (at Hirschenplatz) ✉ *8001*   Plan: **D2**
– ☏ *043 888 44 44 – www.hotel-wellenberg.ch*
46 rm ☑ – 🛏235/310 CHF 🛏🛏275/360 CHF – 3 suites
• Business • Contemporary •
The location in the old town is ideal for a city break. Most of the rooms are spacious and some are particularly stylish. There's a fitness park close by and a beauty centre directly opposite.

Florhof   🔥

Florhofgasse 4 ✉ *8001 –* ☏ *044 250 26 26*   Plan: **D2**
– www.hotelflorhof.ch – Closed 24 December-2 January
32 rm ☑ – 🛏185/310 CHF 🛏🛏290/360 CHF
• Townhouse • Elegant • Personalised •
Set in a lovely 18C nobleman's house in the centre of the city, Florhof is a real gem. The atmosphere is pleasantly casual, everything is beautifully kept, and the comfortable, upmarket rooms promise a great night's sleep.
Florhof – See restaurant listing

Marktgasse   🍴 ⅙ 🅰🅲 🔥

Marktgasse 17 ✉ *8001 –* ☏ *044 266 10 10*   Plan: **D2**
– www.marktgassehotel.ch
37 rm – 🛏199/325 CHF 🛏🛏259/435 CHF – ☑ 15 CHF – 2 suites
• Boutique hotel • Historic building • Contemporary •
This boutique hotel is in the centre of the old town. It is housed in a centuries-old listed building full of historical details that give the smart, upmarket, minimalist-style interior a very special ambience. Food options include the fashionable Baltho restaurant and bar serving international cuisine and the Delish Café Take-Out.

Seehof

Seehofstr. 11 ✉ *8008 –* ☏ *044 254 57 57*   Plan: **D3**
– www.seehof.ch – Closed 24-27 December
19 rm ☑ – 🛏180/280 CHF 🛏🛏220/350 CHF – 1 suite
• Business • Contemporary •
Seehof offers an excellent central location tucked away behind the Opera, as well as charming rooms with a sea-faring note. Prettily decorated in welcoming blues and whites, they are simple, modern and very comfortable.

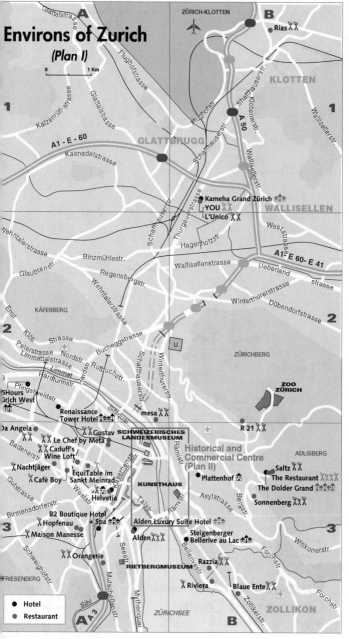

Environs of Zurich
(Plan I)

0   1 Km

A

B

ZÜRICH-KLOTTEN

● Rias ✕✕

Glattalstrasse

KLOTTEN

Flughofstrasse

Katzenrütistrasse

Glattalstrasse

Walliselerstr.

1

A1 - E - 60

Kasnadelstrasse

GLATTBRUGG

Scharhauserstr.

Flughofstr.

Schaffhauserstr.

Klotenerstr.

A 50

Walliselerstr.

1

● Kameha Grand Zürich ▥▥

Wehntalerstrasse

Schaffhauserstr.

Thurgauerstrasse

YOU ✕✕

L'Unico ✕✕

WALLISELLEN

Weststrasse

Binzmühlestr.

Hagerholzstr.

A1- E 60- E 41

Glaubtenstr.

Regensbergstr.

Wallisellenstrasse

Ueberland

strasse

Wehntalerstrasse

Winterthurerstrasse

Dübendorfstrasse

2

KÄFERBERG

Buchegstrasse

Schaffhauserstr.

Winterthurerstr.

U

ZÜRICHBERG

Emil

Klöti

Strasse

Peterstrasse

Nordstr.

Rotbuchstr.

Limmattalstrasse

Hardturmstr.

Limmat

ZOO
ZÜRICHBERG

2

Pfing

5Hours
urich West ▥▥

Renaissance
Tower Hotel ▥▥▥

mesa ✕✕

Da Angela ●
✕✕

✕✕ Gustav

SCHWEIZERISCHES
LANDESMUSEUM

R 21 ✕✕

Badenerstr.

✕✕ Le Chef by Meta

✕✕ Caduff's
Wine Loft

Historical and
Commercial Centre
(Plan II)

ADLISBERG

✕ Nachtjäger

EquiTable im
Sankt Meinrad ✕

Rämistr.

Plattenhof ▥

Saltz ✕✕

The Restaurant ✕✕✕✕

✕ Café Boy

Helvetia ●

Sihlquai

The Dolder Grand ▥▥▥▥

Gutstrasse

Weststr.

KUNSTHAUS

Asylstrasse

Bergstr.

Sonnenberg ✕✕✕

Birmensdorferstr.

B2 Boutique Hotel
+ Spa ▥▥

Alden Luxury Suite Hotel ▥▥

✕ Hopfenau

Talstr.

Steigenberger
● Bellerive au Lac ▥▥

3

✕ Maison Manesse

Alden ✕✕✕

Bellerivestr.

Witikonerstr.

Schweighofstr.

✕✕ Orangerie

Seestr.

Razzia ✕✕

Forchstr.

RIETBERGMUSEUM

FRIESENBERG

✕ Riviera

Blaue Ente ✕✕

Muschelisstr.

Mythenquai

Zollikerstr.

Forchstr.

ZOLLIKON

● Hotel

● Restaurant

Sihl

A 3

ZÜRICHSEE

B

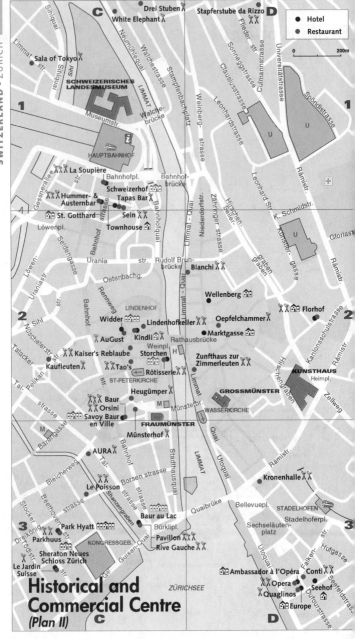

Drei Stuben ✕
White Elephant ✕

Stapferstube da Rizzo ✕✕

C

D

● Hotel
● Restaurant

0 ____ 200m

Sala of Tokyo ✕

SCHWEIZERISCHES
LANDESMUSEUM

1

Museumstr.
Walche-
brücke

HAUPTBAHNHOF

La Soupière ✕✕✕
Bahnhofpl.

Hummer- ✕✕✕
Austernbar
Tapas Bar ✕

Schweizerhof 🏠🏠
Bahnhof-
brücke

St. Gotthard 🏠
Sein ✕✕
Townhouse 🏠

Löwenpl.

Urania   str.
Rudolf Brun-
brücke

Bianchi ✕✕

Oetenbachg.

LINDENHOF

Widder 🏠🏠🏠
Lindenhofkeller ✕✕

Wellenberg 🏠

Oepfelchammer ✕

Marktgasse 🏠

✕✕🏠 Florhof

2

AuGust ✕
Kindli 🏠✕
Rathausbrücke

Kaiser's Reblaube ✕✕
Storchen 🏠🏠
Weinpl.

Zunfthaus zur ✕✕
Zimmerleuten ✕✕

KUNSTHAUS

Kaufleuten ✕
Tao's ✕✕
Rôtisserie ✕✕

ST-PETERKIRCHE

Heugümper ✕

GROSSMÜNSTER

WASSERKIRCHE

Baur ✕✕✕
Orsini ✕✕
Savoy Baur 🏠🏠🏠
en Ville

M

FRAUMÜNSTER
Münsterhof ✕

AURA ✕

Kronenhalle ✕✕

Le Poisson ✕✕

Baur au Lac 🏠🏠🏠

Bellevuepl.

STADELHOFEN
Stadelhoferpl.

Park Hyatt 🏠🏠🏠🏠

3

Parkhuus ✕

Bürklipl.

Pavillon ✕✕✕

Sechseläuten-
platz

Sheraton Neues
Schloss Zürich

Rîve Gauche ✕✕

Le Jardin
Suisse

KONGRESSGEB.

ZÜRICHSEE

Ambassador à l'Opéra 🏠

Conti ✕✕

Opera ✕✕

Seehof 🏠

Quaglinos ✕

Europe 🏠

Historical and
Commercial Centre
(Plan II)

C

D

XX

Stapferstube da Rizzo

Culmannstr. 45 ⊠ 8006 — Plan: **D1**
– ✆ 044 350 11 00
– *www.stapferstube.com*
– *Closed Sunday*
Carte 62/119 CHF
• Italian • Rustic •

Southern Italian Giovanni Rizzo has been calling the shots here at Stapferstube, a well-known Zurich eatery, for some time. As a result, the cooking has a strong Italian feel, as evidenced by the delicious pan-fried squid with garlic, herbs and chilli. The food is served in a friendly, rustic setting and outdoors in summer. Conveniently, the restaurant has its own car park.

XX

Conti

Dufourstr. 1 ⊠ 8008 — Plan: **D3**
– ✆ 044 251 06 66
– *www.bindella.ch*
– *Closed 4 weeks mid July-mid August*
Menu 42/68 CHF
– Carte 58/114 CHF
• Italian • Mediterranean décor •

This restaurant is immediately next to the opera. Find an interior of classical dignity with a lovely high stucco ceiling, an exhibition of paintings, and Italian cuisine.

XX

Bianchi

Limmatquai 82 ⊠ 8001 — Plan: **D2**
– ✆ 044 262 98 44
– *www.ristorante-bianchi.ch*
Carte 48/103 CHF – *(booking advisable)*
• Seafood • Fashionable •

This bright, modern restaurant is located in a quiet spot on the banks of the River Limmat. It serves Mediterranean cuisine and diners are invited to take their pick from the fish and seafood on offer at the generous buffet.

XX

Kronenhalle

Rämistr. 4 ⊠ 8001 — Plan: **D3**
– ✆ 044 262 99 00
– *www.kronenhalle.com*
Carte 60/124 CHF – *(booking advisable)*
• Traditional cuisine • Classic décor •

This building, constructed in 1862, is a Zurich institution located on Bellevue Square. Be sure to take a look at the art collection put together over a period of decades. The atmosphere is traditional, as is the cooking.

XX

Opera – Hotel Ambassador à l'Opéra

Falkenstr. 6 ⊠ 8008 — Plan: **D3**
– ✆ 044 258 98 98
– *www.operarestaurant.ch*
Menu 68/120 CHF (dinner)
– Carte 51/100 CHF
• French • Elegant •

In this modern, elegant restaurant you will find your gaze inevitably wandering to the walls and ceiling to marvel at the opera related decor that fills the room. Fortunately, the food is just as appealing - classic cuisine with an emphasis on fish but also dishes such as saddle of venison and calves' cheeks.

SWITZERLAND - ZURICH

XX **Razzia**
Seefeldstr. 82 ✉ *8008*   Plan: **B3**
– 𝒞 044 296 70 70 – www.razzia-zuerich.ch
– Closed Saturday lunch, Sunday
Menu 59 CHF – Carte 60/103 CHF *– (booking advisable)*
• International • Trendy • Brasserie •
One of Zurich's most fashionable eateries. The small tables arranged in this sty-lish, high-ceilinged former cinema are much in demand. The menu is conside-rable, ranging from red chicken curry to pasta, goose liver and grilled meats.

XX **Florhof** – Hotel Florhof
Florhofgasse 4 ✉ *8001 – 𝒞 044 250 26 26*   Plan: **D2**
– www.hotelflorhof.ch – Closed 24 December-9 January and Saturday lunch, Sunday-Monday
Menu 51 CHF (lunch)/125 CHF – Carte 65/104 CHF
• Mediterranean cuisine • Cosy •
Fancy some flambéed tuna fish sashimi or pan-fried fillet of zander with peas, carrots and ginger, coriander and macadamia nut gremolata? Try for a table on the lovely terrace – a little corner of peace and quiet in the heart of Zürich.

X **Drei Stuben**
Beckenhofstr. 5 ✉ *8006 – 𝒞 044 350 33 00*   Plan: **C1**
– www.dreistuben-zuerich.ch – Closed during Christmas and Saturday lunch, Sunday
Menu 35 CHF (weekday lunch)/65 CHF – Carte 62/115 CHF
• Traditional cuisine • Rustic •
The floors, ceilings and walls here are all done out in rustic wood, lending a comfortable, cosy atmosphere to this restaurant – just what you would expect from a local hostelry with a 300-year-old tradition of serving food. There is also a lovely garden with mature trees. Marco Però and his team cook ambitious, tra-ditional yet contemporary international food.

X **White Elephant**
Neumühlequai 42 ✉ *8006 – 𝒞 044 360 73 22*   Plan: **C1**
– www.whiteelephant.ch
266 rm – ♦395/490 CHF ♦♦395/490 CHF – ☶ 39 CHF – 9 suites
Carte 47/106 CHF
• Thai • Exotic décor •
This restaurant in the Marriott Hotel is a must for fans of authentic Thai cuisine. Made with market fresh produce, the food is authentic and authentically spicy! Whatever you do, don't miss the curries.

X **Quaglinos** – Hotel Europe
Dufourstr. 4 ✉ *8008 – 𝒞 043 456 86 86*   Plan: **D3**
– www.europehotel.ch – Closed 21-26 December
Carte 65/115 CHF
• Classic French • Brasserie •
A lively and authentic Quaglinos brasserie based on the tried and tested bistro formula. It offers typical French savoir vivre and, of course, classic French cuisine including duck foie gras and 'Café de Paris' entrecote.

X **Oepfelchammer**
Rindermarkt 12 (1st floor) ✉ *8001 – 𝒞 044 251 23 36*   Plan: **D2**
– www.oepfelchammer.ch – Closed Sunday-Monday and Bank Holidays
Menu 69/110 CHF – Carte 62/83 CHF
• Traditional cuisine • Rustic • Wine bar •
The poet Gottfried Keller was a regular of the original wine bar. The restaurant serves modern and traditional cuisine in this 19C building.

Baur au Lac   🍴 🖪 ⟨ 🆎 🕍 🚗

Talstr. 1 ✉ *8001 – ℰ 044 220 50 20*   Plan: **C3**
– www.bauraulac.ch
112 rm – 🛏490/570 CHF 🛏🛏680/870 CHF – 🖵 46 CHF – 8 suites
• Grand Luxury • Elegant • Personalised •
Magnificent 19C architecture with luxurious facilities, conscientious management (the second generation of managers from the same family) and plentiful and attentive staff. Some very lovely newer rooms. A terrace leads to the pretty garden.
❀ **Pavillon • Rive Gauche** – See restaurant listing

Park Hyatt   🖪 🕸 ⟨ 🆎 🕍 🚗

Beethoven Str. 21 ✉ *8002 – ℰ 043 883 12 34*   Plan: **C3**
– www.zurich.park.hyatt.ch
134 rm – 🛏490/1050 CHF 🛏🛏490/1200 CHF – 🖵 43 CHF – 4 suites
• Grand Luxury • Contemporary • Elegant •
The Park Hyatt has a large, elegant hall and a lobby area with an entrance to the striking Onyx Bar. It features stylish and modern rooms with lots of space, and a tasteful little spa. The elegant Parkhuus has a show kitchen and a glazed wine cellar on two floors.
Parkhuus – See restaurant listing

Widder   🆎 🕍 🚗

Rennweg 7 ✉ *8001*   Plan: **C2**
– ℰ 044 224 25 26
– www.widderhotel.com
42 rm 🖵 – 🛏490/690 CHF 🛏🛏690/890 CHF – 7 suites
• Luxury • Design • Historic •
Swiss architect Tilla Theus has successfully combined old and new in these nine beautifully restored townhouses in the old city. Historic detail is combined with some lovely one-off decorative pieces. The service is excellent and the Wirtschaft zur Schtund serves tasty Flammkuchen.
❀ **AuGust** – See restaurant listing

Savoy Baur en Ville   ⟨ 🆎 🕍 🚗

Poststr. 12 (at Paradeplatz) ✉ *8001*   Plan: **C2**
– ℰ 044 215 25 25
– www.savoy-zuerich.ch
95 rm 🖵 – 🛏495/690 CHF 🛏🛏690/820 CHF – 9 suites
• Luxury • Classic • Elegant •
The building of this wonderful hotel in 1838 laid the foundations of a long and lasting hotel tradition. Offering first class service in a made-to-measure interior, the upmarket restaurant features unusual Brazilian rock crystal chandeliers and fine table settings. Live piano music in the bar.
Orsini • Baur – See restaurant listing

Storchen   ⟨ ⟨ 🆎 🕍 🚗

Weinplatz 2 (access via Storchengasse 16) ✉ *8001*   Plan: **C2**
– ℰ 044 227 27 27 – www.storchen.ch
66 rm 🖵 – 🛏350/570 CHF 🛏🛏400/840 CHF – 1 suite
• Traditional • Classic • Elegant •
Right on the banks of the River Limmat, this is one of the oldest hotels in the city. Tasteful toile de Jouy fabrics adorn the elegant guestrooms, while the Storchen suite has a roof terrace and lake view. The restaurant's balcony terrace and the 'Barchetta' café in Weinplatz are wonderful.
Rôtisserie – See restaurant listing

Schweizerhof

Bahnhofplatz 7 ✉ 8021 – ℰ 044 218 88 88 — Plan: **C1**
– www.hotelschweizerhof.com
107 rm ⌂ – ♦365/1240 CHF ♦♦515/1240 CHF – 11 suites
• Luxury • Classic •
Established in the 19C, this city hotel with its imposing façade stands at the entrance to the pedestrian zone and is just a few steps from the railway station. It offers excellent service with lots of extras and some particularly comfortable junior suites. Snacks in the Café Gourmet.
La Soupière – See restaurant listing

Sheraton Neues Schloss Zürich

Stockerstr. 17 ✉ 8002 – ℰ 044 286 94 00 — Plan: **C3**
– www.sheraton.com/neuesschloss
60 rm – ♦329 CHF ♦♦329 CHF – ⌂ 39 CHF – 1 suite
• Business • Contemporary •
Just a stone's throw from Lake Zurich, this hotel features straight lines and bright, warm natural tones. The walls of the property are adorned with nice paintings.
Le Jardin Suisse – See restaurant listing

St. Gotthard

Bahnhofstr. 87 ✉ 8021 – ℰ 044 227 77 00 — Plan: **C1**
– www.hotelstgotthard.ch
135 rm – ♦200/350 CHF ♦♦250/500 CHF – ⌂ 34 CHF – 3 suites
• Traditional • Contemporary •
Providing traditional hospitality since 1889, the St Gotthard's guestrooms offer modern elegance in a classical setting. A great location just a stone's throw from the main station. The Manzoni Bar serves excellent coffee.
Hummer- & Austernbar – See restaurant listing

Kindli

Pfalzgasse 1 ✉ 8001 – ℰ 043 888 76 78 – www.kindli.ch — Plan: **C2**
20 rm ⌂ – ♦220/310 CHF ♦♦300/470 CHF
• Traditional • Cosy • Personalised •
For over 500 years pilgrims visited this site; now guests looking for some individuality have taken their place. Although the three single rooms in the eaves don't have en-suites, they do enjoy a lovely view over Zurich. If you want to stay a little longer, try one of the excellent small apartments.
Kindli – See restaurant listing

Townhouse

Schützengasse 7 (5th floor) ✉ 8001 – ℰ 044 200 95 95 — Plan: **C1**
– www.townhouse.ch
25 rm – ♦160/355 CHF ♦♦190/395 CHF – ⌂ 19 CHF
• Townhouse • Classic • Cosy •
The Townhouse is an exclusive hotel in an almost perfect location – just a few steps from the famed Bahnhofstrasse. The furniture and wallpaper will delight enthusiasts of the English style. Breakfast is served in your room or in the bar on the ground floor.

Pavillon – Hotel Baur au Lac

Talstr. 1 ✉ 8001 – ℰ 044 220 50 22 — Plan: **C3**
– www.aupavillon.ch – Closed 15-26 February, 8-22 October and Saturday lunch, Sunday, Bank Holidays
Menu 120/160 CHF – Carte 130/228 CHF
• Classic French • Elegant • Friendly •
Star architect Pierre-Yves Rochon designed the spatial concept of this elegant restaurant. The almost 360° glazed rotunda with its country views is wonderful. Good classic cuisine prepared by Laurent Eperon, with dishes that include roast sea bass with Périgord truffles.
➜ Bar de ligne de Laurent Eperon. Glasierte Kalbshaxe. Yuzu-Basilikum-Parfait, Biskuit mit Orange.

XxX **La Soupière** – Hotel Schweizerhof   🅰️🅒
Bahnhofplatz 7 ⊠ 8021 – 𝒞 044 218 88 40   Plan: **C1**
– www.hotelschweizerhof.com – Closed Saturday lunch, Sunday, July-August: Saturday-Sunday
Menu 79 CHF – Carte 100/122 CHF
• **Market cuisine** • **Elegant** •
An elegant address on the first floor. Warm colours, carefully selected furniture and elegant details set the tone. Serves seasonal, modern cuisine.

XxX **Baur** – Hotel Savoy Baur en Ville   🅰️🅒
Poststr. 12 (at Paradeplatz) ⊠ 8001 – 𝒞 044 215 25 25   Plan: **C2**
– www.savoy-zuerich.ch – Closed Saturday-Sunday
Menu 42 CHF (weekday lunch) – Carte 57/146 CHF
• **Classic French** • **Elegant** • **Chic** •
This restaurant has a stylish, elegant setting that is perfect for Baur's classic French cuisine. Details such as the unusual rock crystal chandeliers together with the luxury fittings and smart table settings set the scene.

XxX **Hummer- & Austernbar** – Hotel St. Gotthard   🅰️🅒
Bahnhofstr. 87 ⊠ 8021 – 𝒞 044 211 76 21   Plan: **C1**
– www.hummerbar.ch
Menu 60 CHF (weekday lunch) – Carte 94/200 CHF
• **Classic French** • **Elegant** • **Cosy** •
A real Zurich institution that first opened its doors in 1935. The elegant interior and signed postcards from celebrities bear witness to the cult status of this restaurant. They serve largely seafood.

XX **Sein** (Martin Surbeck)   🍴🅰️🔄
🕸️ *Schützengasse 5 ⊠ 8001 – 𝒞 044 221 10 65*   Plan: **C1**
– www.zuerichsein.ch – Closed 24 December-3 January, 10-23 April, 16 July-6 August and Saturday-Sunday, mid November-December: Saturday lunch, Sunday
Menu 85 CHF (lunch)/175 CHF – Carte 100/134 CHF
• **Classic French** • **Fashionable** •
You will find a modern note here, not only in the elegant, minimalist-style decor but also in the classic cuisine – made from high quality ingredients without any unnecessary frills. There is also a vegetarian menu. The floor-to-ceiling windows in the restaurant provide an interesting view of the main shopping street outside.
➔ Störcarpaccio mit Kaviar und Sauerrahmsauce. Wachtel-Erbsenrisotto mit roh marinierter Entenleber und Pfefferminze. Geschmorte Toggenburger Kalbs-„Müsli" mit Kartoffelstock, im Öl pochierte Karotten und Zitronenthymian.
🍽️ **Tapas Bar** – See restaurant listing

XX **Lindenhofkeller**   🍴🍴
Pfalzgasse 4 ⊠ 8001 – 𝒞 044 211 70 71   Plan: **C2**
– www.lindenhofkeller.ch – Closed 3 weeks end July-August, 1 week Christmas, Saturday-Sunday and Bank Holidays
Menu 65 CHF (lunch)/135 CHF – Carte 56/133 CHF
• **Classic cuisine** • **Elegant** • **Romantic** •
With its homely romantic touch, this elegant cellar restaurant with wine lounge fits harmoniously into the contemplative old town scene. Classic cooking with modern elements.

XX **Tao's**   🍴🔄
Augustinergasse 3 ⊠ 8001 – 𝒞 044 448 11 22   Plan: **C2**
– www.taos-zurich.ch – Closed Sunday
Carte 58/105 CHF
• **Fusion** • **Exotic décor** • **Elegant** •
A touch of the exotic in the middle of Zurich! Elegant upstairs, a little more informal on the ground floor. Smokers can use Tao's Lounge Bar that offers a Euro-Asian menu. Grilled meats.

XX **Kaiser's Reblaube** 🎐 ✿

Glockengasse 7 ⊠ 8001 – ℰ 044 221 21 20 Plan: **C2**
– www.kaisers-reblaube.ch – Closed 24 July-13 August, January-October:
Saturday lunch, Sunday-Monday and November-December: Saturday
lunch, Sunday
Menu 58 CHF (lunch)/120 CHF – Carte 54/102 CHF
• Classic cuisine • Rustic • Cosy •
Enjoy modern cooking with a traditional influence in this house that was built in
1260 along a small, narrow alley. Comfortable little restaurant on the first-floor
and a wine bar on the ground floor.

XX **Rive Gauche** – Hotel Baur au Lac 🎐 AK P

Talstr. 1 ⊠ 8001 – ℰ 044 220 50 60 – www.agauche.ch Plan: **C3**
– Closed 16 July-13 August
Carte 65/174 CHF
• International • Cosy •
One of the places to be seen in the city centre. The great cosmopolitan interior
attracts a trendy young and young at heart crowd to eat and drink (grilled
meats) but also to see and be seen.

XX **Orsini** – Hotel Savoy Baur en Ville ♿ AK

Poststr. 12 (at Paradeplatz) ⊠ 8001 – ℰ 044 215 25 25 Plan: **C2**
– www.savoy-zuerich.ch
Menu 72 CHF (lunch) – Carte 74/146 CHF
– (booking advisable)
• Italian • Elegant •
This elegant restaurant has been serving classic Italian cuisine for over 30 years.
The sumptuous poppy design on the carpet, repeated in the filigree motif in the
oil paintings on the walls, adds a special touch.

XX **Parkhuus** – Hotel Park Hyatt 🎐 ♿ AK 🚗

Beethoven Str. 21 ⊠ 8002 – ℰ 043 883 10 75 Plan: **C3**
– www.zurich.park.hyatt.ch – Closed Saturday lunch, Sunday
Menu 59 CHF (lunch)/84 CHF – Carte 61/133 CHF
• International • Fashionable •
In keeping with the rest of the hotel, the restaurant is modern and international.
It has a large show kitchen producing creative, contemporary cuisine, as well as
an impressive glazed wine shop accessed via a spiral staircase.

XX **Le Poisson** ⇦ AK 🔐 🔐 P

Claridenstr. 30 ⊠ 8022 – ℰ 044 286 22 22 Plan: **C3**
– www.lepoisson.ch – Closed Saturday lunch, Sunday lunch
62 rm ⌑ – †295/360 CHF ††355/450 CHF
Menu 125 CHF (dinner) – Carte 65/102 CHF
• Seafood • Classic décor •
Fish and seafood take pride of place on the menu at the Glärnischhof's restaurant, from sea bass to bouillabaisse and scallops. The tastefully decorated dining
room is the perfect setting for the food served here, whether you choose one of
the house classics or opt for one of the restaurant's newer dishes.

XX **Rôtisserie** – Hotel Storchen ⇦ 🎐

Weinplatz 2 (access via Storchengasse 16) ⊠ 8001 Plan: **C2**
– ℰ 044 227 21 13 – www.storchen.ch
Menu 90 CHF (dinner) – Carte 75/109 CHF
• Classic French • Cosy •
Take a seat in the tasteful restaurant and marvel first at the wonderful painted
ceiling. Then look out of the window (if you aren't already on the terrace) at the
wonderful views of the River Limmat and the Great Minster.

X
AuGust – Hotel Widder
Rennweg 7 ⊠ 8001 – ℰ 044 224 28 28   Plan: **C2**
– www.au-gust.ch
Carte 55/109 CHF
• Traditional cuisine • Brasserie •
AuGust offers fresh and flavoursome cuisine – including some great terrines and delicious sausages – served in a friendly, classic brasserie atmosphere. The local slow-cooked dishes are also very good.

X
Kaufleuten
Pelikanplatz ⊠ 8001 – ℰ 044 225 33 33   Plan: **C2**
– www.kaufleuten.ch – Closed Sunday lunch
Carte 70/104 CHF
• Market cuisine • Brasserie •
This lively brasserie located in the fashionable venue of the same name is much in demand, not least thanks to its good food. Try the duck ravioli with leek salad or the veal cutlet – sliced for you at your table – before moving on to the club or the bar.

X
Tapas Bar – Restaurant Sein
Schützengasse 5 ⊠ 8001 – ℰ 044 221 10 65   Plan: **C1**
– www.zuerichsein.ch – Closed 24 December-3 January, 10-23 April,
17 July-6 August, Saturday-Sunday and Bank Holidays
Menu 35 CHF – Carte 37/72 CHF
• Modern cuisine • Tapas bar •
This friendly, modern restaurant boasts a light and airy interior and tapas-style food. Try the ravioli with rosemary butter or the Pilze mit Kakaoerde und Mimolette (a mushroom speciality).

X
Heugümper
Waaggasse 4 ⊠ 8001 – ℰ 044 211 16 60   Plan: **C2**
– www.restaurantheuguemper.ch – Closed 24-26 December, 1-
8 January, mid July- mid August and Saturday lunch,Sunday, Februar-
September: Saturday-Sunday
Menu 120 CHF (dinner) – Carte 53/98 CHF
• Fusion • Fashionable • Bistro •
This venerable townhouse in the heart of Zurich serves international cuisine with a Southeast Asian flair. Small lunch menu. Smart modern bistro on the ground floor and an elegant restaurant upstairs.

X
AURA
Bleicherweg 5 ⊠ 8001 – ℰ 044 448 11 44   Plan: **C3**
– www.aura-zurich.ch – Closed Sunday
Carte 48/106 CHF
• Meats and grills • Trendy •
A stylishly urban restaurant, a top-flight events venue, a lounge or a club? AURA is a little bit of each, but above all the place to be for lovers of modern crossover cuisine with a weakness for grilled food – just watch the chefs at work! Located on Paradeplatz in the old stock exchange building.

X
Kindli – Hotel Kindli
Pfalzgasse 1 ⊠ 8001 – ℰ 043 888 76 78 – www.kindli.ch   Plan: **C2**
– Closed Sunday and Bank Holidays
Carte 61/111 CHF – *(booking advisable)*
• Classic French • Inn •
The restaurant's charming character comes in part from its wonderful old wood panelling and the bistro-style, communal arrangement of its beautifully laid tables.

SWITZERLAND - ZURICH

X **Sala of Tokyo** 🛱 AC ⇔

Limmatstr. 29 ✉ *8005 –* ☎ *044 271 52 90* Plan: **C1**
– www.sala-of-tokyo.ch – Closed 3 weeks July-August, 2 weeks Christmas-New Year
Menu 72/195 CHF – Carte 52/128 CHF
• Japanese • Friendly • Exotic décor •

This restaurant has been serving authentic Japanese cuisine for over 30 years. In the air-conditioned Sankaiyaki Room meat is grilled at your table in traditional-style. And of course there is a sushi bar.

X **Le Jardin Suisse** – Hotel Sheraton Neues Schloss Zürich 🛱 AC

Stockerstr. 17 ✉ *8002 –* ☎ *044 286 94 00* Plan: **C3**
– www.sheraton.com/neuesschloss – Closed Saturday lunch, Sunday
Carte 65/99 CHF
• Swiss • Bistro •

A hint of bistro-style pervades this restaurant with its striking exposed stone wall. It offers traditional Swiss specialities that you can enjoy on the terrace (in summer) that skirts round the building.

X **Münsterhof** AC

Münsterhof 6 ✉ *8001 –* ☎ *044 262 33 00* Plan: **C2**
– www.mhof.ch – Closed Christmas and Sunday
Menu 35 CHF (weekday lunch)/91 CHF
– Carte 63/89 CHF – (booking advisable)
• Classic cuisine • Rustic • Friendly •

Set in a historic 11C building, Münsterhof offers a rustic dining room on the ground floor and something a little more elegant upstairs. The menus are the same and include homemade tortellini with veal and Lake Zürich bouillabaisse, not to mention an excellent steak tartare.

ENVIRONS OF ZURICH PLAN I

The Dolder Grand 🌊 ≼ 🛏 🖪 🕸 🐟 🖭 🍴 ᕃ AC 🏋 🚗

Kurhausstr. 65 ✉ *8032 –* ☎ *044 456 60 00* Plan: **B3**
– www.thedoldergrand.com
161 rm – ✦540/740 CHF ✦✦750/1150 CHF – ☷ 48 CHF – 12 suites
• Grand Luxury • Spa and wellness • Contemporary •

The embodiment of exclusivity. Emanating from the 'Curhaus' of 1899 and committed to this tradition just as much as to the requirements of today. The crème de la crème is the 400m² Maestro suite high above Zurich. There are 4000m² of various spa facilities in purist style.
❀❀ **The Restaurant • Saltz** – See restaurant listing

Atlantis 🌊 🖪 🕸 🐟 🖵 🖭 ᕃ AC 🏋 🚗 �︎

Döltschiweg 234 (by Birmensdorferstrasse A3) ✉ *8055 –* ☎ *044 456 55 55*
– www.atlantisbygiardino.com
80 rm ☷ – ✦510/580 CHF ✦✦510/580 CHF – 15 suites
• Luxury • Townhouse • Design •

First opened in 1970, the Atlantis today is a picture of luxury and elegance. You will appreciate the attentive, personal service just as much as the upmarket interior and, of course, the magnificent rural location.
❀❀ **Ecco Zürich • Hide & Seek** – See restaurant listing

Renaissance Tower Hotel 🍴 ≼ 🖪 🕸 ᕃ AC 🏋 🚗

Turbinenstr. 20 ✉ *8005 –* ☎ *044 630 30 30* Plan: **A2**
– www.renaissancezurichtower.com
287 rm – ✦305/500 CHF ✦✦305/500 CHF – ☷ 39 CHF – 13 suites
• Luxury • Business • Contemporary •

The reception area with its smart, minimalist design and contrasting light and dark hues sets the "urban lifestyle" tone which can be seen throughout the hotel, from the bedrooms to the restaurant and the lobby bar. The Executive Club Lounge and 24hr health club and fitness suite on the top floor offer magnificent views.

Alden Luxury Suite Hotel   ♿ AC P

Splügenstr. 2 ✉ *8002 –* ☎ *044 289 99 99*   Plan: **A3**
– www.alden.ch
22 suites – ♦400/1200 CHF ♦♦400/1200 CHF – ☲ 38 CHF
• Luxury • Design •
A great little hotel housed in a magnificent listed building dating back to 1895 with individual, exquisitely designed guestrooms. Non-alcoholic drinks from the mini-bar are included in the price. Two loft suites with a roof terrace.
Alden – See restaurant listing

Kameha Grand Zürich   🛵 ❄ ♿ AC 🏊 🚗

Dufaux-Str. 1 – ☎ *044 525 50 00*   Plan: **B3**
– www.kamehagrandzuerich.com
224 rm – ♦199/469 CHF ♦♦199/469 CHF – ☲ 39 CHF – 21 suites
• Business • Luxury • Design •
A lifestyle hotel set in the middle of the Glattpark. The Kameha Grand is anything but run of the mill with its striking façade, imposing lobby complete with smart bar, and classy, tasteful interior. The service is strikingly straightforward and attentive.
❀ **YOU • L'Unico** – See restaurant listing

B2 Boutique Hotel+Spa   🛵 AC 🚗

Brandschenkenstr. 152 ✉ *8002 –* ☎ *044 567 67 67*   Plan: **A3**
– www.b2boutiquehotels.com
60 rm ☲ **–** ♦310/560 CHF ♦♦340/590 CHF – 8 suites
• Historic • Design •
Housed in a listed brewery building constructed in 1866, this strikingly chic hotel will appeal predominantly to younger guests and architecture enthusiasts. The Bibliothek bar (over 30 000 books) serves small dishes. The thermal bath and spa are particularly impressive (additional charge).

Steigenberger Bellerive au Lac   🏃 ≤ 🛵 ❄ ♿ AC 🏊 🚗

Utoquai 47 ✉ *8008 –* ☎ *044 254 40 00*   Plan: **B3**
– www.zuerich.steigenberger.ch
51 rm – ♦279/459 CHF ♦♦279/459 CHF – ☲ 35 CHF – 1 suite
• Business • Elegant • Contemporary •
This hotel has been extensively renovated and upgraded over recent years. It now offers not only a fine, lakefront location but also comfortable, elegant Art Deco guestrooms with the latest technology and tasteful bathrooms, particularly the Grand Suite with its wonderful roof terrace. The restaurant serves Swiss cuisine with international influences.

25Hours Zürich West   🏃 ❄ ♿ AC 🏊 🚗

Pfingstweidstr. 102 ✉ *8005 –* ☎ *044 577 25 25*   Plan: **A2**
– www.25hours-hotels.com
126 rm – ♦150/350 CHF ♦♦150/350 CHF – ☲ 25 CHF
• Business • Design •
This modern business hotel, in the city's fast-growing development area, is designer Alfredo Häberli's homage to the city of Zurich. The rooms, which come in Platinum, Gold and Silver categories, are brightly coloured, curvaceous and very urban. NENI offers a minimalist feel and Israeli/Oriental cuisine.

Plattenhof   🏃 ♿ 🏊

Plattenstr. 26 ✉ *8032 –* ☎ *044 251 19 10*   Plan: **B3**
– www.plattenhof.ch
37 rm ☲ **–** ♦160/355 CHF ♦♦190/395 CHF
• Business • Design • Minimalist •
This hotel is in a residential quarter on the edge of the city centre. Find distinctly personal service and functional rooms in a modern, plain, designer style. Sento has a bistro atmosphere and serves Italian cuisine.

Helvetia

Stauffacherquai 1 ⊠ *8004 –* ℰ *044 297 99 99*   Plan: **A3**
– www.hotel-helvetia.ch
16 rm – †165/225 CHF ††195/415 CHF – ⊆ 10 CHF
• Townhouse • Cosy • Contemporary •
Your host at the Helvetia is relaxed and friendly, just like his hotel where you will
quickly feel at home. The rooms are charming with their mix of Art Nouveau
and modern touches, as is the restaurant with its stylish upmarket decor and
Swiss/French brasserie-style cuisine.
Helvetia – See restaurant listing

XXXX The Restaurant – Hotel The Dolder Grand
§§ §§   *Kurhausstr. 65* ⊠ *8032 –* ℰ *044 456 60 00*   Plan: **B3**
– www.thedoldergrand.com
*– Closed 121 February-6 March, 25 July-14 August and Saturday lunch,
Sunday-Monday*
Menu 98 CHF (weekday lunch)/298 CHF
– Carte 159/219 CHF – *(booking advisable)*
• Creative • Fashionable • Elegant •
Intense cuisine presented in well-matched, creative combinations with top qua-
lity products combined with skill and flair. The lunchtime taster menu offers
guests the chance to sample an interesting cross-section of dishes from the
main menu. Stylish decor inside and a stunning terrace with a fantastic view
outside.
→ Kaninchen mit Gartenkräutern, Miso, eingelegten Pilzen und grünen
Tomaten. Bretonischer Hummer mit Erdbeeren, Randen, Estragon und
Senf. Kalb mit Morcheln, Emmentaler und Meerrettich.

XXX Ecco Zürich – Hotel Atlantis
§§ §§   *Döltschiweg 234 (by Birmensdorferstrasse A3)* ⊠ *8055 –* ℰ *044 456 55 55*
– www.atlantisbygiardino.ch
Menu 148/204 CHF – *(dinner only and Sunday lunch) (booking essential)*
• Creative • Design • Elegant •
Rolf Fliegauf has now brought the culinary concept from his Ecco restaurants in
Ascona and St Moritz to Zürich. The food is modern, creative and seasonal,
made with great skill from the very best produce. A great asset for the city and
its food lovers.
→ Entenleber, grüner Apfel und Cerealien. Kaisergranat, Blumenkohl und
Mumbai Curry. Mandarine, Kaffeeschokolade und Sauerklee.

XXX Sonnenberg

Hitzigweg 15 ⊠ *8032 –* ℰ *044 266 97 97*   Plan: **B3**
– www.sonnenberg-zh.ch – Closed 1-8 January
Carte 71/159 CHF – *(booking advisable)*
• Classic French • Chic •
A bright, elegant restaurant with attentive table service and an impressive view
over Zurich and the lake. The house specialities are the veal and beef dishes.

XXX Alden – Alden Luxury Suite Hotel

Splügenstr. 2 ⊠ *8002 –* ℰ *044 289 99 99*   Plan: **A3**
– www.alden.ch – Closed Sunday
Menu 49 CHF (weekday lunch) – Carte 66/130 CHF
• Swiss • Elegant •
Clear, straight lines set the tone here and one of the dining rooms has a lovely
stuccoed ceiling, which marries perfectly with the modern look. The Mediterranean cuisine on offer includes fillet of sea bass with wild garlic gnocchi, while at
lunchtime you can enjoy the beef ribs from the trolley.

XX
❀ **mesa**

Weinbergstr. 75 ⊠ 8006 – 𝒞 043 321 75 75   Plan: **A2**
– www.mesa-restaurant.ch – Closed 24 December-10 January, 16 July-
13 August and Saturday lunch, Sunday-Monday
Menu 65 CHF (weekday lunch)/125 CHF
– Carte 80/101 CHF – (booking advisable)
• **Modern cuisine** • **Minimalist** • **Elegant** •

The interior at this restaurant is pleasantly light and bright and the service is relaxed and friendly, attentive and professional. As for the cuisine, you can expect top quality ingredients combined with consummate skill.
➔ Crab Meat Salat, Lattich, Rockefeller-Sauce, grüner Apfel. Ennetbürgner Rinds-Short Rib, Peperoni, Polenta, Mais. Pavlova, Ananas, Mandel.

XX
❀ **YOU** – Hotel Kameha Grand Zürich

Dufaux-Str. 1 – 𝒞 044 525 50 00   Plan: **B3**
– www.kamehagrandzuerich.com – Closed end December-early January,
3 weeks July-August and Saturday lunch, Sunday-Tuesday lunch
Menu 125/180 CHF – Carte 134/164 CHF – *(booking advisable)*
• **Modern cuisine** • **Exotic décor** • **Fashionable** •

The smart, minimalist-style Far Eastern design sets a very particular tone. This is well matched by the classic, modern fare with Far Eastern influences, which is delicate, aromatic and beautifully presented.
➔ Geschmorter Ostsee Aal, mit süss-sauren Randen und Meerrettich. US-Prime-Beef mit fermentierten Perlzwiebeln, Süsskartoffeln und Spinatsalat. Topfen-Soufflé mit Ziegenquark, Pistazie und Shortbread.

XX
☺ **Rias**

Gerbegasse 6 – 𝒞 044 814 26 52 – www.rias.ch – Closed   Plan: **B1**
24 December-early January, mid July-early August, Saturday-Sunday and
Bank Holidays
Menu 49 CHF, 65/125 CHF – Carte 56/110 CHF
• **Country** • **Fashionable** •

Tucked away in one of Kloten's side streets, Rias promises the chance to sample flavoursome food in an appealing contemporary setting. Chef Hansruedi Nef's offerings include dishes such as braised calves' cheeks, slow-cooked beef stew Italian-style and pears in mulled wine with champagne sabayon. You will also find the friendly waiting staff on hand with good wine suggestions (by the glass).

XX
☺ **Da Angela**

Hohlstr. 449 ⊠ 8048 – 𝒞 044 492 29 31   Plan: **A3**
– www.daangela.ch – Closed 24 December-1 January, end July-early
August and Sunday
Carte 62/104 CHF – *(booking advisable)*
• **Italian** • **Traditional décor** •

A very traditional Italian restaurant with a lovely terrace under shady chestnut trees. Homemade pasta is among the dishes prepared from fresh produce.

XX
L'Unico – Hotel Kameha Grand Zürich

Dufaux-Str. 1 – 𝒞 044 525 50 00   Plan: **B3**
– www.kamehagrandzuerich.com – Closed Sunday dinner
Carte 39/125 CHF
• **Italian** • **Trendy** •

L'Unico boasts a number of attractive decorative details including prettily tiled walls and tables, round booths and above you on the ceiling, what is probably the largest pasta plate in the world! As you might expect, fresh pasta such as the brasato ravioli is the focus of the traditional Italian cuisine on offer here.

SWITZERLAND - ZURICH

XX **Gustav** 🛜 ᕕ 🎛 🚗

Gustav-Gull-Platz 5 – 𝒞 044 250 65 00 Plan: **A3**
– www.gustav-zuerich.ch – Closed Sunday
Menu 41 CHF (lunch)/135 CHF – Carte 67/95 CHF
• Italian • Elegant • Fashionable •
Set in an apartment block right next to the main railway station, this elegant restaurant also boasts a café, a bar and a lovely interior courtyard. The Italian food on offer includes turbot and calamari *alla romana* and boned shoulder of veal with polenta.

XX **Caduff's Wine Loft** 🍷 🛜

Kanzleistr. 126 ✉ 8004 – 𝒞 044 240 22 55 Plan: **A3**
– www.wineloft.ch – Closed 24 December-4 January, Saturday lunch and Sunday
Menu 30 CHF (weekday lunch)/125 CHF
– Carte 42/126 CHF – *(booking advisable)*
• Classic French • Trendy •
This fashionable venue has a modern loft atmosphere. As well as the delicious fresh cooking made from quality products, there is an impressive wine selection, with over 2,000 labels on offer.

XX **Blaue Ente** 🛜 ᕕ 🎛 ✧

Seefeldstr. 223 ✉ 8008 – 𝒞 044 388 68 40 Plan: **B3**
– www.blaue-ente.ch – Closed Saturday lunch, Sunday
Carte 52/92 CHF – *(booking advisable)*
• Country • Trendy • Friendly •
Historic industrial architecture outside and a trendy and lively atmosphere (and some fine old machinery) inside. The service is attentive and straightforward while the flavoursome food is made using local produce. The flour even comes from the restaurant's own mill next door. There is a more ambitious evening menu.

XX **Le Chef by Meta** 🎛

Kanonengasse 29 ✉ 8004 – 𝒞 044 240 41 00 Plan: **A3**
– www.restaurant-lechef.ch – Closed 2 weeks end December, 3 weeks July-August and Sunday-Monday
Menu 81/115 CHF – Carte 70/101 CHF
• International • Cosy •
Le Chef manages to be modern yet warm and welcoming thanks to its combination of clean, straight lines, warm wood and purple tones. Meta Hiltebrand offers a range of delicious dishes including roast tomato soup and beef fillet stroganoff.

XX **R21** 🔄 🛎 ⫷ 🛜 ᕕ 🛋 🚗

Orellstr. 21 ✉ 8044 – 𝒞 044 268 35 35 Plan: **B2**
– www.sorellhotels.com
66 rm ⌑ – 🛏220/300 CHF 🛏🛏260/380 CHF   Carte 60/97 CHF
• Market cuisine • Fashionable •
Situated in an attractive, exposed location above Zurich, this restaurant in the Zürichberg Hotel boasts an interesting menu and a simple, modern interior. Enjoy a front row seat as the chefs go about their business in the very impressive show kitchen. Sunday brunch.

XX **Orangerie** 🔄 🛜 🍽 ᕕ 🛋 🚗

Engimattstr. 14 ✉ 8002 – 𝒞 044 284 16 16 Plan: **A3**
– www.engimatt.ch
71 rm ⌑ – 🛏250/400 CHF 🛏🛏290/460 CHF
Menu 53 CHF – Carte 40/98 CHF
• Traditional cuisine • Friendly •
Whether you come here in summer or in winter, you can't escape the feeling that you are close to the stars! The restaurant in the Engimatt Hotel is set in a simply elegant, light and airy winter garden with a lovely terrace. Traditional cuisine.

XX **Saltz** – Hotel The Dolder Grand　　　　　⇐ 🏠 ⚘ 🆎 🚗

Kurhausstr. 65 ✉ *8032 –* ☎ *044 456 60 00*　　　Plan: **B3**
– www.thedoldergrand.com
Carte 83/153 CHF
• International • Fashionable • Friendly •

The original, modern design takes Switzerland as its theme while the international food concentrates on the essentials. The menu includes burrata with datterini tomatoes, hamachi sashimi, sea bass baked in a salt crust or, if you prefer, a dish of *Zürcher Geschnetzeltes* – veal strips in a cream and white wine sauce.

X **Maison Manesse**　　　　　　　　　　　　🕸 🏠

⸙ *Hopfenstr. 2* ✉ *8045 –* ☎ *044 462 01 01*　　　Plan: **A3**
– www.maisonmanesse.ch – Closed Christmas-early January, mid July-early August and Sunday-Monday
Menu 140/160 CHF – *(dinner only) (booking advisable)*
• Creative • Rustic •

One of the hottest places to eat on the Zurich culinary scene, Maison Manesse is as informal as it is unusual. The predominantly white interior is comfortable and rustic, while the cuisine - based on top quality produce - is creative and aromatic. The lunchtime menu features salads, pasta and steaks.
→ Ei, Pilze, Bärlauch. Barramundi, Bier, Hanf. Karotte, Kardamom, Yuzu.

X **EquiTable im Sankt Meinrad**　　　　　　　　🏠

⸙ *Stauffacherstr. 163* ✉ *8004 –* ☎ *043 534 82 77*　　Plan: **A3**
– www.equi-table.ch – Closed 1 week early January, mid July-mid August and Sunday-Monday
Menu 100 CHF (Vegetarian)/180 CHF – *(dinner only) (booking advisable)*
• Modern cuisine • Fashionable •

Just as Sankt Meinrad's parent company deals only in fair trade and organic products, so its kitchen team under Fabian Fuchs uses nothing but the best ingredients in its modern cuisine. The whole experience is rounded off by the friendly service and informal atmosphere.
→ Rhabarber, Avocado, Gurke, Couscous, Frischkäse. Felchen, Mangold, Spargel. Wollschwein, Bergkartoffeln, Bärlauch.

X **Hopfenau**　　　　　　　　　　　　　　　🏠

🏠 *Hopfenstr. 19* ✉ *8045*　　　　　　　　　　　Plan: **A3**
– ☎ *044 211 70 60 – www.hopfenau.ch*
– Closed 23 December-1 January, Saturday lunch, Sunday and Bank Holidays
Menu 40 CHF (lunch) – Carte 51/104 CHF
• Traditional cuisine • Bourgeois •

A really friendly local eatery serving some excellent food, all of which is freshly cooked and delicious to boot. Try the delicious sounding braised shin of beef or Toblerone mousse.

X **Helvetia** – Hotel Helvetia

Stauffacherquai 1 (1st floor) ✉ *8004 –* ☎ *044 297 99 99*　Plan: **A3**
– www.hotel-helvetia.ch
Carte 50/101 CHF
• Traditional cuisine • Cosy •

A floor above the popular and lively bar, Helvetia shares the same wooden floors and panelling and warm, welcoming atmosphere. The friendly and straightforward front-of-house style fits in perfectly here as you sample a delicious crayfish cocktail or fillet of pata negra pork freshly prepared in the kitchen by Francoise Wicki.

✗ ## Nachtjäger ⌂

Badenerstr. 310 ✉ *8004 –* ☏ *043 931 77 90* Plan: **A3**
– www.nachtjaeger.ch – Closed 24 December-2 January, 12 July-
22 August, Sunday-Monday and Bank Holidays
Carte 60/76 CHF – *(dinner only)*
• Market cuisine • Cosy •

This charming little restaurant a little outside the city centre serves "comfort food" – fresh, light cuisine that is highly prized by its guests. The flavoursome fare chalked up on the blackboard includes veal and wheat beer pie and shin of beef with chickpeas and paprika.

✗ ## Café Boy ⌂

Kochstr. 2 ✉ *8004 –* ☏ *044 240 40 24* Plan: **A3**
– www.cafeboy.ch – Closed 2 weeks end December and Saturday-Sunday
Menu 69 CHF (dinner) – Carte 65/93 CHF
• Traditional cuisine • Bistro •

Once the haunt of left-wing political activists, restaurateur Stefan Iseli's Café Boy now serves up the fresh, traditional cuisine of his partner Jann M. Hoffmann in a lively, minimalist bistro setting. Wine is his passion, as you will see when you are given the extensive wine list. Simpler menu at lunchtimes.

✗ ## Riviera ⌂ ♦

Dufourstr. 161 ✉ *8008 –* ☏ *044 422 04 26* Plan: **B3**
– www.enoteca-riviera.ch – Closed 1-10 January, 24 July-14 August and
Saturday lunch, Sunday
Menu 78/122 CHF (dinner) – Carte 61/92 CHF
• Italian • Rustic •

Luca Messina is no newcomer to the Zurich restaurant scene. Riviera's setting is authentically rustic and the cuisine is Italian. It includes homemade pasta and osso buco, as well as an ambitious seasonal tasting menu.

✗ ## Hide & Seek – Hotel Atlantis ⌂ ᵻ Ⓐ ♦ 🚗

Döltschiweg 234 (by Birmensdorferstrasse A3) ✉ *8055 –* ☏ *044 456 55 55*
– www.atlantisbygiardino.ch
Menu 39/49 CHF (lunch) – Carte 57/117 CHF
• International • Chic • Fashionable •

This restaurant with a fusion theme offers a mix of modern European, Middle Eastern and Southeast Asian cuisine and design. The menu includes Thai fishcakes and zander with black quinoa, vanilla carrots and orange *beurre blanc*.

UNITED KINGDOM
UNITED KINGDOM

→ **AREA:**
244 157 km² (94 269 sq mi).

→ **POPULATION:**
65 111 143 inhabitants.
Density = 266 per km².

→ **CAPITAL:** London.

→ **CURRENCY:**
Pound Sterling (£).

→ **GOVERNMENT:**
Constitutional parliamentary
monarchy (since 1707). Member
of European Union since 1973.

→ **LANGUAGE:** English.

→ **PUBLIC HOLIDAYS:**
New Year's Day (1 Jan); Good Friday
(late Mar/Apr); Easter Monday
(late Mar/Apr); Early May Bank
Holiday (first Mon in May); Spring
Bank Holiday (last Mon in May);
Summer Bank Holiday (last Mon
in Aug); Christmas Day (25 Dec);
Boxing Day (26 Dec).

→ **LOCAL TIME:**
GMT in winter and GMT
+1 hour in summer.

→ **CLIMATE:**
Temperate maritime with cool
winters and mild summers
(London: January 3°C; July
17°C), rainfall evenly distributed
throughout the year.

→ **EMERGENCY:**
Police, Medical Assistance, Fire
Brigade ✆ **999** – also used for
Mountain, Cave, Coastguard and
Sea Rescue. (Dialling **112** within
any EU country will redirect your
call and contact the emergency
services.)

Glasgow

Edinburgh

Birmingham

LONDON

→ **ELECTRICITY:**
230 volts AC, 50Hz; 3 flat pin
sockets.

→ **FORMALITIES:**
Travellers from the European
Union (EU), Switzerland, Iceland,
the main countries of North
and South America and some
Commonwealth countries need
a national identity card or passport
(except for Irish nationals; America:
passport required) to visit the
United Kingdom for less than
three months (tourism or business
purpose).
For visitors from other countries
a visa may be required, in addition
to a passport, especially for those
wishing to stay for longer than
three months. We advise you to
check with your embassy before
travelling.

LONDON
LONDON

Population: 8 600 000

Marc Pinter/Fotolia.com

The term 'world city' could have been invented for London. Time zones radiate from Greenwich, global finances zap round the Square Mile and its international restaurants are the equal of anywhere on earth. A stunning diversity of population is testament to the city's famed tolerance; different lifestyles and languages are as much a part of the London scene as cockneys and black cabs. London grew over time in a pretty haphazard way, swallowing up surrounding villages, but retaining an enviable acreage of green 'lungs': a comforting 30 per cent of London's area is made up of open space.

The drama of the city is reflected in its history. From Roman settlement to banking centre to capital of a 19C empire, the city's pulse has never missed a beat; it's no surprise that a dazzling array of theatres, restaurants, museums, markets and art galleries populate its streets. London's piecemeal character has endowed it with distinctly different areas, often breathing down each other's necks. North of Piccadilly lie the playgrounds of Soho and Mayfair, while south is the gentleman's clubland of St James's. On the other side of town are Clerkenwell and Southwark, artisan areas that have been scrubbed down and freshened up. The cool sophistication of Kensington and Knightsbridge is to the west, while a more touristy aesthetic is found in the heaving piazza zone of Covent Garden.

LONDON IN...

→ **ONE DAY**
British Museum, Tower of London, St Paul's Cathedral, Tate Modern.

→ **TWO / THREE DAYS**
National Gallery, London Eye, Natural History Museum, a walk along the Southbank.

→ **THREE DAYS**
Science Museum, Victoria and Albert Museum, National Portrait Gallery.

PRACTICAL INFORMATION

ARRIVAL-DEPARTURE

✈ Heathrow Airport (20mi west). Heathrow Express to Paddington takes 15 min; or take the Piccadilly Line.

✈ Gatwick Airport (28mi south). Gatwick Express to Victoria Station takes 30 min.

✈ Stansted Airport (34mi northeast).

✈ Luton Airport (35mi north).

✈ London City Airport (10mi east).

GETTING AROUND

If you're in London for any period it's worth investing in an Oyster Card, much beloved by locals: these are smartcards with electronically stored pre-pay credit, and they offer good savings on fares. The Underground, known colloquially as the Tube, has 270 stations across the capital and beyond; get yourself a tube map – it's invaluable and also a design classic. Buses can often be the quickest way to travel short distances, especially during the day; or else pick up a 'Boris Bike' from one of the various docking points around the city.

CALENDAR HIGHLIGHTS

February
London Fashion Week.

March
The Boat Race.

April
London Marathon.

May
Chelsea Flower Show.

June
Wimbledon, Trooping the Colour.

August
Notting Hill Carnival.

October
London Film Festival.

November
Lord Mayor's Show.

December
Ice Rinks open across London.

EATING OUT

London is one of the food capitals of the world, where you can eat everything from Turkish to Thai and Polish to Peruvian. Those wishing to sample classic British dishes also have more choice these days as more and more chefs are rediscovering home-grown ingredients, regional classics and traditional recipes. Eating in the capital can be pricey, so check out good value pre- and post-theatre menus, or try lunch at one of the many eateries that drop their prices, but not their standards, in the middle of the day. "Would I were in an alehouse in London! I would give all my fame for a pot of ale and safety", says Shakespeare's Henry V. Samuel Johnson agreed, waxing lyrical upon the happiness produced by a good tavern or inn. Pubs are often open these days from 11am to 11pm (and beyond), so this particular love now knows no bounds, and any tourist is welcome to come along and enjoy the romance. It's not just the cooking that has improved in pubs but wine too; woe betide any establishment in this city that can't distinguish its Gamay from its Grenache.

A

Andaz Liverpool Street		857
Artist Residence		833

B

Baglioni		880
Beaufort		871
The Beaumont		798
Berkeley		828
Bermondsey Square		864
Blakes		877
Brown's		799
Bulgari		852

C

Café Royal		810
The Capital		870
Charlotte Street		837
Chesterfield		799
Chiltern Firehouse		837
Claridge's		798
Connaught		798
Corinthia		833
Covent Garden		847

D

Dean Street Townhouse		810
Dorchester		798
Dorset Square		839
Draycott		870
Dukes		819
Durrants		839

E

Egerton House		870
The Exhibitionist		878

F

45 Park Lane		799
Four Seasons		798

G

The Gore		878
Goring		833
Great Northern H. London		851

H

Halkin		829
Ham Yard		810
Hari		829
Haymarket		819

Hazlitt's		810
Hilton London Bankside		867
Hilton London Heathrow Airport Terminal 5		893
The Hoxton		851

J

Jumeirah Carlton Tower		870

K

K + K George		877
Knightsbridge		871

L

The Lanesborough		829
Langham		837
The Levin		871
The London Edition		837
London Marriott H. County Hall		828
Lord Milner		833

M

Malmaison		884
Mandarin Oriental Hyde Park		852
Marble Arch by Montcalm		840
The Milestone		880
Mondrian London		867
Montcalm London City at The Brewery		858

N

No.11 Cadogan Gardens		871
Number Sixteen		877
No. Ten Manchester Street		840

O

One Aldwych		824

P

The Pelham		877
The Portobello		883

R

Ritz		818
The Rookery		884
Rosewood London		851
Royal Garden		879

S

St James' Court		833

St James's Hotel and Club	🏨	819
St Martins Lane	🏨	824
St Pancras Renaissance	🏨	851
Sanderson	🏨	838
Savoy	🏨	822
Shangri-La	🏨	864
Sofitel	🏨	893
Sofitel London St James	🏨	819
Soho	🏨	810
South Place	🏨	888
Stafford	🏨	819
Sumner	🏨	840

T

Threadneedles	🏨	858
Twenty Nevern Square	🏨	877

W

Waldorf Hilton	🏨	824
The Wellesley	🏨	829
Westbury	🏨	799

Z

Zetter	🏨	888
Zetter Townhouse Marylebone	🏨	838

A

Alain Ducasse		
at The Dorchester	XxXxX ❁❁❁	799
Al Duca	XX	821
The Alfred Tennyson	⌷	833
Alyn Williams		
at The Westbury	XxxX ❁	800
Amaranto	XxX	804
Amaya	XxX ❁	832
Ametsa	XxX ❁	832
Anchor and Hope	⌷ ⓐ	870
Angelus	XX	853
Angler	XX ❁	888
Antico	X	866
Antidote	X	816
Aqua Shard	XX	865
Arabica Bar & Kitchen	X	869
Araki	XX ❁❁❁	804
Archipelago	XX	843
L'Atelier de Joël Robuchon	X ❁	826
L'Autre Pied	XX	841
Avenue	XX	821
A. Wong	X ⓐ	836

B

Babylon	XX	881
Balcon	XX	820
Balthazar	XX	826
Baltic	XX	868
Bandol	X	876
Bao	X ⓐ	818
Baozi Inn	X	817
Barbary	X ⓐ	849
Barbecoa	XX	862
Bar Boulud	XX	853
Barnyard	X ⓐ	850
Barrafina (Adelaide St)	X	826
Barrafina (Drury Ln)	X	826
Barrafina (Soho)	X ❁	813
Barrica	X ⓐ	849
Barshu	X	817
Beast	XX	842
Beijing Dumpling	X	818
Benares	XxX ❁	802
Bentley's	XX	807
Bernardi's	XX	841
Berners Tavern	XX	841
Bibendum	XxX	874
Bibigo	X	816
Bird of Smithfield	X	863
Blanchette	X	815
Bluebird	XX	875
Blueprint Café	X	865
Bob Bob Ricard	XX	812

Bocca di Lupo	X	815
Bo Lang	X	876
Bombay Brasserie	XxxX	878
Bone Daddies	X	817
Bonhams	XX ❁	804
Bonnie Gull	X	846
Le Boudin Blanc	X	809
Boulestin	XX	821
Brasserie Gustave	XX	875
Brasserie Zédel	XX ⓐ	811
Bread Street Kitchen	XX	859
Brumus	XX	822
Butlers Wharf Chop House	X	866

C

Cafe Murano (St James's)	XX	821
Cafe Murano		
(Strand and Covent Garden)	XX	825
Cambio de Tercio	XX	878
Cantina Del Ponte	X	866
Capote y Toros	X	879
Le Caprice	XX	820
Caravan	X	889
Casse Croûte	X	867
Cây Tre	X	817
Céleste	XxxX ❁	832
Ceviche Old St	X	889
Ceviche Soho	X	817
The Chancery	XX ❁	859
Chez Bruce	XX ❁	893
Chiltern Firehouse	XX	842
China Tang	XxX	803
Chiswell Street Dining Rooms	XX	863
Chop Shop	X	822
Chucs Bar and Grill	XX	809
Chutney Mary	XxX	820
Cigala	X	850
Cigalon	XX	862
The Cinnamon Club	XxX	834
Cinnamon Kitchen	XX	862
Cinnamon Soho	X	815
City Social	XxX ❁	858
Clarke's	XX	880
Clerkenwell Kitchen	X	889
Clos Maggiore	XX	825
Clove Club	X ❁	892
Club Gascon	XX ❁	858
Colbert	XX	876
Le Colombier	XX	875
Colony Grill Room	XX	805
Comptoir Gascon	X ⓐ	885
Copita	X ⓐ	814
Corrigan's Mayfair	XxX	803
Coya	XX	807

Cross Keys	🍴🍷	876
Cut	XxX	803

D

Dabbous	X⟡	848
Dean Street Townhouse		
Restaurant	XX	812
Dehesa	X⟡	813
Delaunay	XxX	824
Les Deux Salons	XX	825
Dickie Fitz	XX	843
Dinings	X	846
Dinner		
by Heston Blumenthal	XxX⟡⟡	853
Dishoom	X	828
Dock Kitchen	X	883
Donostia	X	845
Drakes Tabanco	X	849
Duck & Rice	X	815
Duck & Waffle	XX	863

E

Electric Diner	X	884
Elliot's	X⟡	869
Ellory	X⟡	891
Ember Yard	X	814
Enoteca Turi	XX	835
L'Etranger	XX	878

F

Fenchurch	XX	862
Fera at Claridge's	XxX⟡	800
Fischer's	XX	843
Fish Market	X	863
Five Fields	XxX⟡	871
Flat Three	XX	883
Flesh & Buns	X	850
Foley's	X⟡	845
45 Jermyn St	XX	821
Foxlow (Clerkenwell)	X	885
Franco's	XX	821
Frenchie	X	827

G

Galvin Bistrot de Luxe	XX	842
Galvin La Chapelle	XxX⟡	893
Galvin at Windows	XxX⟡	801
Garnier	XX	877
Garrison	🍴🍷	867
Gauthier - Soho	XxX	811
Le Gavroche	XxX⟡⟡	800
Gilbert Scott	XX	852
The Glasshouse	XX⟡	891
Good Earth	XX	876
Goodman Mayfair	XX	808
Gordon Ramsay	XxX⟡⟡⟡	871
The Goring (Dining Room)	XxX⟡	834
Grain Store	X⟡	852
Grand Imperial	XxX	835
Granger & Co. Clerkenwell	X	885
Granger & Co. King's Cross	X	852
Granger & Co. Notting Hill	X	883
Great Queen Street	X⟡	851
Greenhouse	XxX⟡⟡	801
The Grill	XxX	803
Gymkhana	XX⟡	805

H

Hakkasan Hanway Place	XX⟡	848
Hakkasan Mayfair	XX⟡	805
Ham Yard	XX	812
Haozhan	X	815
Harwood Arms	🍴⟡	891
Hawksmoor (City of London)	X	863
Hawksmoor (Knightsbridge)	XX	875
Hawksmoor (Mayfair)	XX	805
Hawksmoor		
(Strand and Covent Garden)	X	827
Heddon Street Kitchen	XX	806
Hedone	XX⟡	890
Hélène Darroze		
at The Connaught	XxxX⟡⟡	800
Hereford Road	X⟡	855
Hix (Soho)	XX	813
Hix Mayfair	XxX	804
Hix Oyster and Chop House	X	885
HKK	XX⟡	892
Honey and Co	X⟡	849
Hoppers	X⟡	816
Hush	XX	808

I

il trillo	XX	875
Imperial China	XxX	811
The Ivy	XxX	824
Ivy Chelsea Garden	XX	874
Ivy Market Grill	XX	826

J

Jinjuu	X	816
José	X⟡	867
José Pizarro	X	863
J. Sheekey	XX	824
J. Sheekey Oyster Bar	X	826
Jugged Hare	🍴🍷	864

K

Kai	XxX⟡	802
Kateh	X⟡	856
Keeper's House	XX	808
Kensington Place	X	882
Kenza	XX	862
Kiku	XX	809
Kitchen Table at Bubbledogs	XX⟡	848
Kitchen W8	XX⟡	880
Kitty Fisher's	X	809
Kouzu	X	836
Koya Bar	X	818
Kurobuta Marble Arch	X	857

L

Lady Ottoline	⏄	851
Latium	XX	841
Launceston Place	XxX	880
Ledbury	XxX ✿✿	883
Les 110 de Taillevent	XX	843
Lima Fitzrovia	X ✿	844
Lima Floral	X	827
Little Social	X	809
Lobos	X	870
Locanda Locatelli	XxX ✿	840
Luc's Brasserie	XX	862
Lurra	XX	841
Lutyens	XxX	858
Lyle's	X ✿	892

M

Mac and Wild	X	845
The Magazine	XX	853
Magdalen	XX	865
Malabar	XX	882
Manchurian Legends	X	818
Marcus	XxxX ✿✿	829
Margaux	X	879
Marianne	XX	854
Masala Grill	XX	874
MASH	XX	813
Massimo	XX	835
Mayfair Chippy	X	810
Maze	XX	806
Maze Grill Mayfair	XX	808
Maze Grill Park Walk	XX	875
Mazi	X	882
Medlar	XX	874
Mele e Pere	X	814
Milos	XxX	820
Min Jiang	XxX	880
The Modern Pantry Clerkenwell	X	889
The Modern Pantry Finsbury Square	XX	888
Momo	XX	806
Mon Plaisir	XX	848
Morito	X ⌂	889
Moro	X	889
Mr Todiwala's Kitchen	XX	893
Murano	XxX ✿	801

N

New St Grill	XX	859
The Ninth	X ✿	849
Noble Rot	X	850
Nobu	XX	808
Nobu Berkeley St	XX	807
Nopi	X	814
Northall	XxX	834

O

Oblix	XX	865
Ognisko	XX	879

(R continued / right column)

Oliver Maki	X	816
Olivo	X	836
Olivocarne	X	836
Olivomare	X	836
100 Wardour St	XX	812
One-O-One	XxX	874
Opera Tavern	X ⌂	827
Opso	X	845
The Orange	⏄	837
Orrery	XxX	840
Osteria Dell' Angolo	XX	835
Ours	XX	878
Outlaw's at The Capital	XX ✿	874
Oxo Tower	XxX	868
Oxo Tower Brasserie	X	869

P

Padella	X ⌂	869
Palomar	X ⌂	814
Park Chinois	XxX	802
Paternoster Chop House	X	864
Percy & Founders	XX	843
La Petite Maison	XX	807
Pétrus	XxX ✿	832
Peyote	X	809
Picture Fitzrovia	X ⌂	845
Picture Marylebone	X	846
Pidgin	X ✿	892
Pied à Terre	XxX ✿	847
Pizarro	X	866
Plum Valley	XX	812
Pollen Street Social	XX ✿	804
Polpetto	X ⌂	814
Polpo at Ape & Bird	X	850
Polpo Covent Garden	X	827
Polpo Smithfield	X	885
Polpo Soho	X	815
Le Pont de la Tour	XxX	865
Portland	X ✿	844
Portman	⏄	846
Portrait	X	822
The Providores	XX	843

Q

Quaglino's	XX	822
Quality Chop House	X	888
Quilon	XxX ✿	834
Quo Vadis	XxX	811

R

Rabbit	X	876
Rabot 1745	XX	868
Red Fort	XxX	811
Refuel	XX	813
Rex Whistler	XX	836
Riding House Café	X	845
Ritz Restaurant	XxXxX ✿	819
Rivea	XX	853
River Café	XX ✿	891
Roast	XX	868

Roka (Aldwych)	XX	825
Roka (Bloomsbury)	XX	848
Roka (Mayfair)	XX	806
Rosa's Soho	X	817
Roux at the Landau	XxX	840
Roux at Parliament Square	XxX	834
Royal China	XX	844
Royal China Club	XX	842
Rules	XX	825

S

St John	X ۞	885
St John Maltby	X	867
Sake No Hana	XX	821
Salt & Honey	X	856
Salt Yard	X ⌂	849
Santini	XxX	835
Sartoria	XxX	803
Sauterelle	XX	859
Scott's	XxX	802
Seven Park Place	XxX ۞	820
Sexy Fish	XX	807
The Shed	X	882
Shoryu	X	822
Six Portland Road	X	883
sixtyone	XX	842
Sketch (The Lecture Room and Library)	XxxX ۞ ۞	800
Sketch (The Gallery)	XX	806
Skylon	XxX	828
Social Eating House	X ۞	813
Social Wine & Tapas	X	844
Sosharu	XX	884
Spring	XX	825
Spuntino	X	816
The Square	XxxX	801
Story	XX ۞	865

T

Talli Joe	X	850
Tamarind	XxX ۞	802
Tapas Brindisa	X	869
Tate Modern (Restaurant)	X	868
Tendido Cero	X	879
10 Greek Street	X	815
Terroirs	X	828
Texture	XX ۞	841
Theo Randall	XX	806

34	XxX	803
Thomas Cubitt	ⓘⓓ	837
Tokimeitē	XX	808
Tonkotsu	X	818
Tredwell's	X	827
Trinity	XX ۞	890
Trishna	X ۞	844
La Trompette	XX ۞	890
28°-50° Fetter Lane	X	864

U

Umu	XxX ۞ ۞	801
UNI	XX	835
Union Street Café	XX	868

V

Vanilla Black	XX	859
Vasco and Piero's Pavilion	XX	812
Veeraswamy	XX ۞	805
Vico	X ⌂	827
Village East	X	866
Vinoteca	X	846
Vivat Bacchus	X	864
Vivat Bacchus London Bridge	X	866

W

The Wallace	XX	842
Well	ⓘⓓ	890
Wild Honey	XX	807
The Wolseley	XxX	820
Wormwood	X	884
Wright Brothers	X	869

Y

Yashin	XX	882
Yashin Ocean House	XX	879
Yauatcha City	XX	859
Yauatcha Soho	XX ۞	811

Z

Zafferano	XxX	832
Zaika	XX	882
Zayane	X	884
Zelman Meats	X	817
Zoilo	X	846
Zuma	XX	853

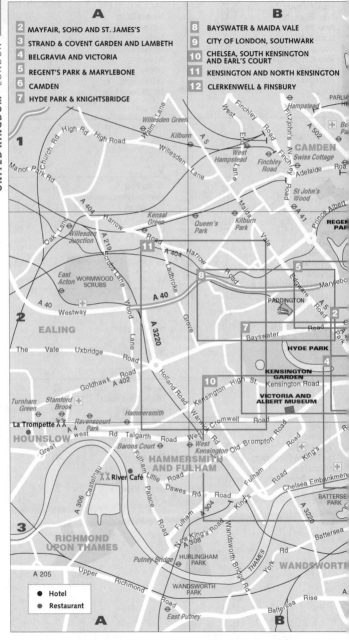

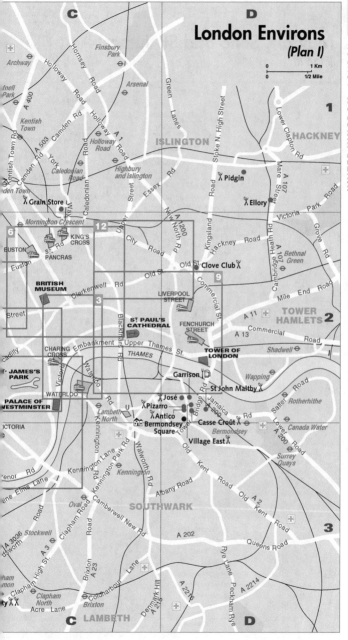

London Environs
(Plan I)

0 _____ 1 Km
0 _____ 1/2 Mile

C **D** **1**

Archway

Inell
Park

Holloway

Hornsey Road

Finsbury
Park

Arsenal

Green Lanes

Lower Clapton Rd

HACKNEY

Kentish
Town

Camden Rd

A 503

Holloway
Road

Holloway Road

A 1

Stoke N. High Street

Mare Street

A 107

Kentish Town Rd

York Way

Camden Rd

Caledonian Road

Caledonian Rd

Highbury
and Islington

New North Rd

Kingsland Road

Hackney Road

A 107

Lower Clapton Rd

Victoria Park Road

Grove Rd

den Town

ISLINGTON

X Pidgin

X Ellory

Grain Store X

Mornington Crescent

Upper Street

Essex Rd

A 200

Bethnal
Green

6 **12** **KING'S
CROSS**

EUSTON
ST.
PANCRAS

Euston

Pancras Rd

City Road

Old St

Old St X Clove Club

Continental St.

Camden High Rd

Bethnal Green Rd

Mile End Road

9

**BRITISH
MUSEUM**

3

Clerkenwell Rd

Blackfriars Rd

LIVERPOOL
STREET

Commercial St.

A 11

**TOWER
HAMLETS** **2**

Street

**ST PAUL'S
CATHEDRAL**

FENCHURCH
STREET

A 13

Commercial

Road

cadilly

CHARING
CROSS

Embankment

Upper Thames St.

**TOWER OF
LONDON**

Shadwell

**-JAMES'S
PARK**

THAMES

Victoria

Waterloo

Garrison

Wapping

Salter Road

Rotherhithe

WATERLOO

St John Maltby X

Rd

**PALACE OF
WESTMINSTER**

Waterloo Rd

X José
X Pizarro
X Antico
Bermondsey
Square

Tower Bridge Rd

Jamaica

A 200

Rd

Canada Water

A 200

ICTORIA

Lambeth
North

Casse Croût X

Bermondsey

Surrey
Quays

Village East X

grenor Rd

Kennington Lane

Kennington Road

Kennington Park Rd

Walworth Rd

Kennington Rd

Albany Road

Old

Kent

Road

Old

A 2

Kent

Road

SOUTHWARK

3

ine Elms Lane

Oval

Clapham Road

Camberwell New Rd

A 202

Rye Lane

Queens Road

Road

A 3036 Stockworth
dsworth

A 3

Brixton
A 23

Coldharbour Lane

Denmark Hill

A 215

A 2216

Peckham Rye

A 2214

ham
mon

ty X X

Clapham
North

Acre Lane

Brixton

C **LAMBETH** **D**

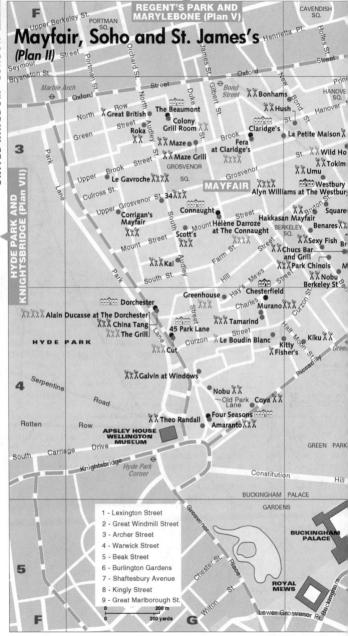

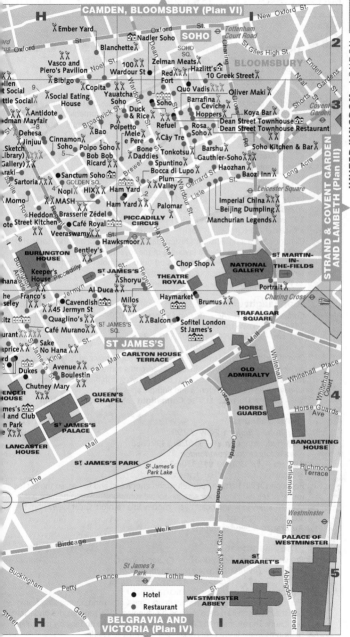

CAMDEN, BLOOMSBURY (Plan VI)

New Oxford St.

Ember Yard
Oxford St.
Tottenham Court Road
St Giles High St.

Nadler Soho
SOHO
SOHO SQ.

BLOOMSBURY

Blanchette

Oxford St.

Endell

Vasco and
Piero's Pavilion
Noel St.
100
Wardour St
Zelman Meats
Hazlitt's
10 Greek Street

Neal Gardens

Shorts

Bibigo

Red
Fort

Copita
Yauatcha
Soho
Quo Vadis
Oliver Maki

Ellen Social
Little Social

Social Eating
House
Duck
& Rice
Soho
Barrafina
Ceviche
Hoppers
Koya Bar

Covent
Garden

Antidote
adman Mayfair

Bao
Refuel
Rosa
Soho
Dean Street Townhouse
Dean Street Townhouse Restaurant

Dehesa
Jinjuu
Cinnamon
Soho
Polpetto
Mele
e Pere
CâMy Tre
Barshu

Sketch
(library)
Gallery)
araki

Polpo Soho
Bob Bob
Ricard
Bone
Daddies
Tonkotsu
Gauthier-Soho
Soho Kitchen & Bar

Bocca di Lupo
Haozhan

Sartoria
Sanctum Soho
GOLDEN SQ.
Plum
Valley
Baozi Inn

Long Acre

Momo
Nopi
HIX
MASH
Ham Yard
Leicester Square

Heddon
ote Street Kitchen
Brasserie Zédel
Café Royal
Ham Yard

Imperial China
Beijing Dumpling
Manchurian Legends

Lisle St.

Veeraswamy
PICCADILLY
CIRCUS
Palomar

Hawksmoor

BURLINGTON
HOUSE
Bentley's

Keeper's
House

ST JAMES'S

Chop Shop
NATIONAL
GALLERY
ST MARTIN-
IN-
THE-FIELDS

hana
Franco's
seley
Al Duca
Shoryu
THEATRE
ROYAL
Portrait

Charing Cross

ltz
45 Jermyn St
Cavendish
Milos
Haymarket
Brumus

TRAFALGAR
SQUARE

urant
Quaglino's
Café Murano
ST JAMES'S
SQ.
Balcon
Sofitel London
St James's

aprice
Sake
No Hana
ST JAMES'S

rd
Dukes
Boulestin
CARLTON HOUSE
TERRACE

Avenue

Whitehall

Chutney Mary
QUEEN'S
CHAPEL
OLD
ADMIRALTY
Whitehall Place

ENCER
HOUSE
mes's
l and Club
n Park
e

St JAMES'S
PALACE
LANCASTER
HOUSE

HORSE
GUARDS

Horse Guards
Ave

Horse Guards

BANQUETING
HOUSE

The Mall
ST JAMES'S PARK
St James's
Park Lake

Parliament

Richmond
Terrace

Birdcage

Walk

Westminster
St.

PALACE OF
WESTMINSTER

Buckingham
France
St James's
Park
Tothill
St.

Storey's Gate

ST
MARGARET'S

Abingdon
Street

Petty

Gate

● Hotel
● Restaurant

WESTMINSTER
ABBEY

BELGRAVIA AND
VICTORIA (Plan IV)

797

MAYFAIR

Dorchester   🕪 🕪 🕪 🕪 🕪 🕪

Park Ln ⊠ *W1K 1QA* – ⓜ *Hyde Park Corner* – ℰ *(020)*   Plan: **G4**
76298888 – *www.dorchestercollection.com*
250 rm – ♦£ 325/925 ♦♦£ 355/995 – � £ 35 – 51 suites
• Grand Luxury • Classic •
One of the capital's iconic properties offering every possible facility and exemplary levels of service. The striking marbled and pillared promenade provides an elegant backdrop for afternoon tea. Bedrooms are eminently comfortable; some overlook Hyde Park. The Grill is for all things British; Alain Ducasse waves Le Tricolore; China Tang celebrates the cuisine of the Orient.
❀❀❀ **Alain Ducasse at The Dorchester • The Grill • China Tang**
– See restaurant listing

Claridge's   ❀ 🕪 🕪 🕪 🕪

Brook St ⊠ *W1K 4HR* – ⓜ *Bond Street* – ℰ *(020)*   Plan: **G3**
76298860 – *www.claridges.co.uk*
197 rm – ♦£ 480/1140 ♦♦£ 480/1140 – � £ 34 – 62 suites
• Grand Luxury • Historic • Classic •
Claridge's has a long, illustrious history dating back to 1812 and this iconic and very British hotel has been a favourite of the royal family over generations. Its most striking decorative feature is its art deco. The hotel also moves with the times, with its modern restaurant Fera proving a perfect fit.
❀ **Fera at Claridge's** – See restaurant listing

Connaught   ❀ 🕪 🕪 🕪 🕪 🕪

Carlos Pl. ⊠ *W1K 2AL* – ⓜ *Bond Street* – ℰ *(020)*   Plan: **G3**
74997070 – *www.the-connaught.co.uk*
121 rm – ♦£ 540/990 ♦♦£ 630/1110 – 25 suites
• Grand Luxury • Townhouse • Classic •
One of London's most famous hotels; restored and renovated but still retaining an elegant British feel. All the luxurious bedrooms come with large marble bathrooms and butler service. There's a choice of two stylish bars and Espelette is an all-day venue for classic French and British dishes.
❀❀ **Hélène Darroze at The Connaught** – See restaurant listing

Four Seasons   🕪 🕪 🕪 🕪 🕪 🕪

Hamilton Pl, Park Ln ⊠ *W1J 7DR*   Plan: **G4**
– ⓜ *Hyde Park Corner* – ℰ *(020) 7499 0888*
– *www.fourseasons.com/london*
193 rm – ♦£ 330/630 ♦♦£ 330/630 – � £ 30 – 33 suites
• Grand Luxury • Business • Modern •
Reopened in 2011 after a huge refurbishment project and has raised the bar for luxury hotels. Striking lobby sets the scene; sumptuous bedrooms have a rich, contemporary look and boast every conceivable comfort. Great views from the stunning rooftop spa.
Amaranto – See restaurant listing

The Beaumont   🕪 🕪 🕪 🕪 🕪

Brown Hart Gdns ⊠ *W1K 6TF* – ⓜ *Bond Street*   Plan: **G3**
– ℰ *(020) 7499 1001* – *www.thebeaumont.com*
73 rm � – ♦£ 435/585 ♦♦£ 435/585 – 10 suites
• Luxury • Art déco • Personalised •
From a 1926 former garage, restaurateurs Chris Corbin and Jeremy King fashioned their first hotel; art deco inspired, it's stunning, stylish and exudes understated luxury. The attention to detail is exemplary, from the undeniably masculine bedrooms to the lively, cool cocktail bar and busy brasserie.
Colony Grill Room – See restaurant listing

UNITED KINGDOM - LONDON

45 Park Lane ⟨ ⫟ 🅟 ⛸ 🄰🄲 🚗
45 Park Ln ⊠ W1K 1PN – Ⓜ *Hyde Park Corner*
– ℰ (020) 7493 4545 – www.45parklane.com
46 rm – ♦£ 495/695 ♦♦£ 495/695 – ⌷ £ 21 – 10 suites

Plan: **G4**

• Luxury • Modern • Elegant •

It was the original site of the Playboy Club and has been a car showroom but now 45 Park Lane has been reborn as The Dorchester's sister hotel. The bedrooms, all with views over Hyde Park, are wonderfully sensual and the marble bathrooms are beautiful.
Cut – See restaurant listing

Westbury ⟨ ⫟ ⛸ 🄰🄲 �
Bond St ⊠ W1S 2YF – Ⓜ *Bond Street*
– ℰ (020) 76297755
– www.westburymayfair.com
246 rm ⌷ – ♦£ 263/599 ♦♦£ 263/599 – 13 suites

Plan: **H3**

• Business • Luxury • Modern •

As stylish now as when it opened in the 1950s. Smart, comfortable bedrooms with terrific art deco inspired suites. Elegant, iconic Polo bar and bright, fresh sushi bar. All the exclusive brands are outside the front door.
❀ **Alyn Williams at The Westbury** – See restaurant listing

Brown's ⫟ ⛸ 🄰🄲 🔊
33 Albemarle St ⊠ W1S 4BP – Ⓜ *Green Park*
– ℰ (020) 7493 6020
– www.roccofortehotels.com
117 rm – ♦£ 420/905 ♦♦£ 420/950 – ⌷ £ 35 – 28 suites

Plan: **H3**

• Luxury • Traditional • Classic •

Opened in 1837 by James Brown, Lord Byron's butler. This urbane and very British hotel with an illustrious past offers a swish bar with Terence Donovan prints, bedrooms in neutral hues and a classic English sitting room for afternoon tea.
Hix Mayfair – See restaurant listing

Chesterfield ⟨ ⛸ 🄰🄲 🔊
35 Charles St ⊠ W1J 5EB – Ⓜ *Green Park*
– ℰ (020) 74912622
– www.chesterfieldmayfair.com
107 rm ⌷ – ♦£ 195/390 ♦♦£ 220/510 – 4 suites

Plan: **G4**

• Townhouse • Traditional • Classic •

An assuredly English feel to this Georgian house. Discreet lobby leads to a clubby bar and wood panelled library. Individually decorated bedrooms, with some antique pieces. Intimate and pretty restaurant.

XxXxX Alain Ducasse at The Dorchester – Dorchester Hotel 🕸
❀❀❀ *Park Ln ⊠ W1K 1QA –* Ⓜ *Hyde Park Corner* ⛸ 🄰🄲 ⇔ 🕙 🚗
– ℰ (020) 76298866

Plan: **G4**

– www.alainducasse-dorchester.com
– Closed 3 weeks August, first week January, 26-30 December, Easter, Saturday lunch, Sunday and Monday
Menu £ 60/95 – *(booking essential)*

• French • Elegant • Luxury •

Elegance, luxury and attention to detail are the hallmarks of Alain Ducasse's London outpost, where the atmosphere is warm and relaxed. The kitchen uses the best seasonal produce, whether British or French, to create visually striking, refined modern dishes. The 'Table Lumière' with its shimmering curtain affords an opulent, semi-private dining experience.
➜ Dorset crab, celeriac and caviar. Simmered halibut with winkles, cockles and razor clams marinière. 'Baba like in Monte Carlo'.

Sketch (The Lecture Room & Library)

XxxX ⵚⵚ

9 Conduit St (1st floor) ⊠ *W1S 2XG* – Ⓜ *Oxford Circus*   Plan: **H3**
– ℰ (020) 76594500 – www.sketch.london – Closed 24 lunch-
31 December, last 2 weeks August, Saturday lunch, Sunday and Monday
Menu £ 35/120 – Carte £ 112/140 – *(booking essential)*
• French • Luxury • Elegant •

Mourad Mazouz and Pierre Gagnaire's 18C funhouse is awash with colour, energy and vim and the luxurious 'Lecture Room & Library' provides the ideal setting for the sophisticated French cooking. Relax and enjoy artfully presented, elaborate dishes that provide many varieties of flavours and textures.
→ Pike soufflé with watercress poached trout and frogs' legs. Organic rack of pork with sage, mango vinegar and seasonal fruit. Pierre Gagnaire's 'grand dessert'.

Hélène Darroze at The Connaught – Connaught Hotel

XxxX ⵚⵚ

Carlos Pl. ⊠ *W1K 2AL* – Ⓜ *Bond Street* – ℰ *(020)*   Plan: **G3**
71078880 – www.the-connaught.co.uk
Menu £ 52/92 – *(booking essential)*
• Modern cuisine • Luxury • Elegant •

From a Solitaire board of 13 marbles, each bearing the name of an ingredient, you choose 5, 7 or 9 (courses); this highlights the quality of produce used. The cooking is lighter these days yet still with the occasional unexpected flavour. The warm service ensures the wood-panelled room never feels too formal.
→ Scallop, tandoori spices, carrot, citrus and coriander. Pigeon with beetroot and foie gras. Savarin Armagnac, rhubarb and ginger.

Le Gavroche (Michel Roux Jnr)

XxxX ⵚⵚ

43 Upper Brook St ⊠ *W1K 7QR* – Ⓜ *Marble Arch*   Plan: **G3**
– ℰ (020) 74080881 – www.le-gavroche.co.uk – Closed Christmas-January,
Saturday lunch, Sunday, Monday and bank holidays
Menu £ 57/128 – Carte £ 67/165 – *(booking essential)*
• French • Intimate • Luxury •

Classical, rich and indulgent French cuisine is the draw at Michel Roux's renowned London institution. The large, smart basement room has a clubby, masculine feel; service is formal and structured but also has charm.
→ Mousseline de homard au champagne et caviar. Côte de veau rôtie, morilles et ail sauvage. Omelette Rothschild.

Fera at Claridge's – Claridge's Hotel

XxxX ⵚ

Brook St ⊠ *W1K 4HR* – Ⓜ *Bond Street* – ℰ *(020)*   Plan: **G3**
7107 8888 – www.feraatclaridges.co.uk
Menu £ 39/110 – Carte £ 53/85 – *(booking advisable)*
• Creative British • Elegant • Luxury •

Earth-father, forager supreme and gastronomic alchemist Simon Rogan brings his wonderfully natural, unforced style of cooking to the capital. The deftly balanced and cleverly textured dishes deliver multi-dimensional layers of flavours and the grand room has been transformed into a thing of beauty.
→ Rose veal tartare with oyster and kohlrabi. Turbot in pine oil, Jerusalem artichoke, oyster mushroom and spring herbs. Meadowsweet cake, celeriac, apple and burnt honey.

Alyn Williams at The Westbury – Westbury Hotel

XxxX ⵚ

37 Conduit St ⊠ *W1S 2YF* – Ⓜ *Bond Street* – ℰ *(020)*   Plan: **H3**
71836426 – www.alynwilliams.com – Closed first
2 weeks January, last 2 weeks August, Sunday and Monday
Menu £ 30/65
• Modern cuisine • Design • Elegant •

Confident, cheery service ensures the atmosphere never strays into terminal seriousness; rosewood panelling and a striking wine display add warmth. The cooking is creative and even playful, but however elaborately constructed the dish, the combinations of flavours and textures always work.
→ Poached foie gras with smoked eel, dulse and mushroom broth. Herdwick lamb with sweetbread kofta, pickled aubergine, feta and cucumber. Caramelised Arctic roll, coffee and vanilla custard millefeuille.

XxxX **The Square** ⌘ ⚹ ◎

6-10 Bruton St. ✉ W1J 6PU – Ⓜ Green Park – ✆ (020) Plan: **H3**
*74957100 – www.squarerestaurant.com – Closed 24-26 December and
Sunday lunch*
Menu £ 40/95
• French • Elegant • Intimate •
It was all change in 2016 when Philip Howard stepped down as chef after 25
years. This smart and sophisticated French restaurant also changed hands and
now belongs to Marlon Abela, whose group includes The Greenhouse.

XxX **Greenhouse** ⌘ ⚹
✿✿ *27a Hay's Mews ✉ W1J 5NY – Ⓜ Hyde Park Corner* Plan: **G4**
*– ✆ (020) 74993331 – www.greenhouserestaurant.co.uk – Closed Saturday
lunch, Sunday and bank holidays*
Menu £ 40/95
• Creative • Fashionable • Elegant •
Chef Arnaud Bignon's cooking is confident, balanced and innovative and uses
the best from Europe's larder; his dishes exude an exhilarating freshness. The
breadth and depth of the wine list is astounding. This is a discreet, sleek and
contemporary restaurant with well-judged service.
→ Orkney scallop with sea urchin, fennel and clementine. Monkfish with
onion, banana, kaffir lime and dukkah. Mananka chocolate with kumquat
and coriander.

XxX **Umu** ⌘ ⚹
✿✿ *14-16 Bruton Pl. ✉ W1J 6LX – Ⓜ Bond Street – ✆ (020)* Plan: **H3**
*74998881 – www.umurestaurant.com – Closed Christmas, New Year,
Saturday lunch, Sunday and bank holidays*
Menu £ 35/155 – Carte £ 57/158
• Japanese • Fashionable • Design •
Stylish, discreet interior using natural materials, with central sushi bar. Extensive
choice of Japanese dishes; choose one of the seasonal kaiseki menus for the full
experience. Over 160 different labels of sake.
→ Cornish line caught squid with Exmoor caviar. Grade 11 Japanese
Wagyu smoked à la minute. Caramel custard with fuki.

XxX **Murano** (Angela Hartnett) ⚹ ⚹
✿ *20 Queen St ✉ W1J 5PP – Ⓜ Green Park – ✆ (020)* Plan: **G4**
74951127 – www.muranolondon.com – Closed Christmas and Sunday
Menu £ 33/65
• Italian • Fashionable • Elegant •
Angela Hartnett's Italian-influenced cooking exhibits an appealing lightness of
touch, with assured combinations of flavours, borne out of confidence in the
ingredients. This is a stylish, elegant room run by a well-organised, professional and friendly team who put their customers at ease.
→ Crab tortellini & bisque with cucumber, turnip and spring onion. Smoked pigeon with orange purée, fennel, pine nuts and pancetta. Pistachio
soufflé with hot chocolate sauce.

XxX **Galvin at Windows** ⪡ ⚹ ⚹
✿ *London Hilton Hotel, 22 Park Ln (28th floor)* Plan: **G4**
*✉ W1K 1BE – Ⓜ Hyde Park Corner – ✆ (020) 72084021
– www.galvinatwindows.com – Closed Saturday lunch and Sunday dinner*
Menu £ 33/70
• Modern cuisine • Friendly • Romantic •
The cleverly laid out room makes the most of the spectacular views across London from the 28th floor. Relaxed service takes the edge off the somewhat corporate atmosphere. The bold cooking uses superb ingredients and the classically based food comes with a pleasing degree of flair and innovation.
→ French asparagus with organic egg and a praline & chickpea tuile. Roast
fillet of halibut with pomme purée, shiitake mushrooms, prawn & dashi
broth. Nougat parfait with banana, muscovado meringues and black pepper ice cream.

XxX ✧

Benares (Atul Kochhar)   ❀ AC ⇔ ⟨◎

12a Berkeley Square House, Berkeley Sq. ✉ *W1J 6BS*   Plan: **H3**
– Ⓜ Green Park – ℰ (020) 76298886 – www.benaresrestaurant.com
– Closed 25 December, 1 January and Sunday lunch
Menu £ 35 (lunch and early dinner) – Carte £ 50/91
• Indian • Chic • Intimate •

No Indian restaurant in London enjoys a more commanding location or expansive interior. Atul Kochhar's influences are many and varied; his spicing is deft and he makes excellent use of British ingredients like Scottish scallops and New Forest venison. The Chef's Table has a window into the kitchen.
→ Pan-seared scallops, broccoli couscous and cauliflower purée. Old Delhi style tandoori chicken, makhani sauce and spring salad. Dark chocolate mousse, passion fruit and hot chocolate sauce.

XxX ✧

Tamarind   AC ⟨◎

20 Queen St. ✉ *W1J 5PR –* Ⓜ *Green Park – ℰ (020)*   Plan: **G4**
76293561 – www.tamarindrestaurant.com – Closed 25-26 December,
1 January and Saturday lunch
Menu £ 22/75 – Carte £ 36/69
• Indian • Chic • Exotic décor •

Makes the best use of its basement location through smoked mirrors, gilded columns and a somewhat exclusive feel. The appealing northern Indian food is mostly traditionally based; kebabs and curries are the specialities, the tandoor is used to good effect and don't miss the carefully judged vegetable dishes.
→ Spiced chickpeas with wheat crisps, yoghurt and tamarind chutney. Lamb simmered with shallots and pickling spices. Cardamom flavoured hung yoghurt.

XxX ✧

Kai   ❀ AC ⇔ ⟨◎

65 South Audley St ✉ *W1K 2QU –* Ⓜ *Hyde Park Corner*   Plan: **G3**
– ℰ (020) 74938988 – www.kaimayfair.co.uk – Closed 25-26 December
and 1 January
Carte £ 39/136 – (booking essential)
• Chinese • Intimate • Chic •

There are a few classics on the menu but Chef Alex Chow's strengths are his modern creations and re-workings of Chinese recipes. His dishes have real depth, use superb produce and are wonderfully balanced. The interior is unashamedly glitzy and the service team anticipate their customers' needs well.
→ Halibut with ginger, spring onions and soy. Kagoshima Wagyu with 7 spice salt and rice balls. Durian and vanilla soufflé with salted caramel.

XxX

Park Chinois   AC ⇔

17 Berkeley St ✉ *W1J 8EA –* Ⓜ *Green Park – ℰ (020)*   Plan: **H3**
3327 8888 – www.parkchinois.com
Carte £ 40/107 – (booking essential)
• Chinese • Exotic décor •

Old fashioned glamour, strikingly rich surroundings, live music and Chinese food combine to great effect at this sumptuously decorated restaurant spread over two floors and created by Alan Yau – one of the UK's most influential restaurateurs.

XxX

Scott's   AC ⇔ ⟨◎

20 Mount St ✉ *W1K 2HE –* Ⓜ *Bond Street – ℰ (020)*   Plan: **G3**
74957309 – www.scotts-restaurant.com – Closed 25-26 December
Carte £ 37/57
• Seafood • Fashionable • Chic •

Scott's is proof that a restaurant can have a long, proud history and still be fashionable, glamorous and relevant. It has a terrific clubby atmosphere and if you're in a two then the counter is a great spot. The choice of prime quality fish and shellfish is impressive.

XxX **Cut** – 45 Park Lane Hotel   🕭 🕭
45 Park Ln ⊠ W1K 1PN – **Ⓜ** *Hyde Park Corner*   Plan: **G4**
– 𝒞 (020) 7493 4545 – www.45parklane.com
Menu £ 29 (weekday lunch) – Carte £ 51/176 – *(booking essential)*
• Meats and grills • Design • Chic •

The first European venture from Wolfgang Puck, the US-based Austrian celebrity chef, is this very slick, stylish and sexy room where glamorous people
come to eat meat. The not-inexpensive steaks are cooked over hardwood and
charcoal and finished off in a broiler.

XxX **34**   🕭 ⇔
34 Grosvenor Sq (entrance on South Audley St)   Plan: **G3**
⊠ W1K 2HD – **Ⓜ** *Marble Arch – 𝒞 (020) 3350 3434*
*– www.34-restaurant.co.uk – Closed 25-26 December, dinner 24 December
and lunch 1 January*
Menu £ 28 (weekday lunch) – Carte £ 34/60
• Meats and grills • Brasserie • Fashionable •

A wonderful mix of art deco styling and Edwardian warmth makes it feel like a
glamorous brasserie. A parrilla grill is used for fish, game and beef – choose
from Scottish dry-aged, US prime, organic Argentinian and Australian Wagyu.

XxX **The Grill** – Dorchester Hotel   🕸 🕭 🕭
Park Ln ⊠ W1S 2XG – **Ⓜ** *Hyde Park Corner – 𝒞 (020)*   Plan: **G4**
76594500 – www.dorchestercollection.com
Menu £ 39 (weekday lunch) – Carte £ 43/89 – *(booking advisable)*
• French • Elegant • Design •

The Grill is relaxed yet formal, with an open kitchen and a striking, hand-blown
Murano glass chandelier as its centrepiece. Grill favourites sit alongside modern
day classics on the menu; sharing dishes are a good choice, as are the speciality
soufflés. Service is smooth and highly professional.

XxX **Corrigan's Mayfair**   🕭 🕭 ⇔
28 Upper Grosvenor St. ⊠ W1K 7EH – **Ⓜ** *Marble Arch*   Plan: **G3**
*– 𝒞 (020) 74999943 – www.corrigansmayfair.com – Closed 25-
30 December, Saturday lunch and bank holidays*
Menu £ 25 (weekday lunch) – Carte £ 32/79
• Modern British • Elegant •

Richard Corrigan's flagship celebrates British and Irish cooking, with game a
speciality. The room is comfortable, clubby and quite glamorous and feels as
though it has been around for years.

XxX **Sartoria**   🕎 🕭 🕭 ⇔
20 Savile Row ⊠ W1S 3PR – **Ⓜ** *Oxford Circus – 𝒞 (020)*   Plan: **H3**
*75347000 – www.sartoria-restaurant.co.uk – Closed 25-
26 December, Saturday lunch, Sunday and bank holidays*
Menu £ 27 (weekday lunch) – Carte £ 26/58
• Italian • Chic • Elegant •

A long-standing feature on Savile Row but now looking much more dapper.
Francesco Mazzei, formerly of L'Anima, hooked up with D&D to take the reins
and the place now feels more energised. There are hints of Calabria but the
menu covers all Italian regions and keeps things fairly classical.

XxX **China Tang** – Dorchester Hotel   🕭 🕭 ⇔
Park Ln ⊠ W1K 1QA – **Ⓜ** *Hyde Park Corner – 𝒞 (020)*   Plan: **G4**
76299988 – www.chinatanglondon.co.uk – Closed 24-25 December
Menu £ 30 (lunch) – Carte £ 28/79
• Chinese • Fashionable • Elegant •

Sir David Tang's atmospheric, art deco-inspired Chinese restaurant, downstairs
at The Dorchester, is always abuzz with activity. Be sure to see the terrific bar,
before sharing the traditional Cantonese specialities.

UNITED KINGDOM - LONDON

UNITED KINGDOM - LONDON

XxX Amaranto – Four Seasons Hotel

Hamilton Pl, Park Ln ⊠ *W1J 7DR*
Plan: **G4**
– ⓜ Hyde Park Corner – ℰ (020) 7319 5206
– www.fourseasons.com/london/dining
Carte £ 28/68
• Italian • Fashionable • Trendy •

It's all about flexibility here, as the Italian-influenced menu is served in the stylish bar, in the comfortable lounge, on the great terrace or in the restaurant, which is decorated in the vivid colours of the amaranth plant.

XxX Hix Mayfair – Brown's Hotel

33 Albemarle St ⊠ *W1S 4BP –* ⓜ *Green Park – ℰ (020)*
Plan: **H3**
75184004 – www.hixmayfair.com
Menu £ 28 (dinner) – Carte £ 33/65
• Traditional British • Traditional décor • Intimate •

This wood-panelled dining room is lightened with the work of current British artists. Mark Hix's well-sourced menu of British classics will appeal to the hunter-gatherer in every man.

XX Araki (Mitsuhiro Araki)
⬡⬡

12 New Burlington St ⊠ *W1S 3BF –* ⓜ *Oxford Circus*
Plan: **H3**
– ℰ (020) 7287 2481 – www.the-araki.com – Closed 27 July-31 August,
Christmas- first week January and Monday
Menu £ 300 – *(dinner only) (booking essential) (tasting menu only)*
• Japanese • Intimate • Minimalist •

Mitsuhiro Araki is one of Japan's great Sushi Masters who closed his Tokyo restaurant to relocate to London because he wanted a fresh challenge. From one of 10 seats at his beautiful cypress counter, watch him deftly prepare Edomae sushi using European seafood. It's very expensive but the different cuts of tuna are stunning and the rice, grown by his father-in-law back in Japan, is also excellent.
→ Sake-steamed abalone with grilled scallop. Tuna tartare with truffle and wasabi. Welsh eel sushi.

XX Pollen Street Social (Jason Atherton)
⬡

8-10 Pollen St ⊠ *W1S 1NQ –* ⓜ *Oxford Circus*
Plan: **H3**
– ℰ (020) 7290 7600 – www.pollenstreetsocial.com – Closed Sunday and
bank holidays
Menu £ 32 (lunch) – Carte £ 60/70 – *(booking essential)*
• Creative • Fashionable • Elegant •

The restaurant where it all started for Jason Atherton when he went solo. Top quality British produce lies at the heart of the menu and the innovative dishes are prepared with great care and no little skill. The room has plenty of buzz, helped along by the 'dessert bar' and views of the kitchen pass.
→ Crab salad with apple, coriander, black garlic, lemon purée and brown crab on toast. Loin and braised neck of lamb with roast artichoke, Merguez sausage, curds & whey. Bitter chocolate pavé with olive biscuit and chocolate ice cream.

XX Bonhams
⬡

101 New Bond St (lower ground floor) (For dinner
Plan: **H3**
entrance via Haunch of Venison Yard off Brook St) ⊠ *W1S 1SR*
– ⓜ Bond Street – ℰ (020) 7468 5868 – www.bonhams.com – Closed
2 weeks August, 24 December-2 January, Saturday-Sunday, dinner
Monday-Tuesday and bank holidays
Menu £ 60 (dinner) – Carte £ 38/68 – *(booking advisable)*
• Modern cuisine • Minimalist • Intimate •

Established in 1793, Bonhams is now one of the world's largest fine art and antique auctioneers. Its restaurant is bright, modern and professionally run. Dishes are elegant and delicate and there is real clarity to the flavours. The wine list has also been very thoughtfully compiled.
→ Pertuis asparagus with soft-boiled egg, confit lemon and trout eggs. Roast Cornish brill with cauliflower couscous and curried mussels. Floating island with sour cherry purée, pistachio anglaise and bitter chocolate sorbet.

XX
£3

Gymkhana
🎧 ⇔ 🐼 📺

42 Albemarle St ✉ *W1S 4JH –* Ⓜ *Green Park – ℰ (020)*　　Plan: **H3**
3011 5900 – www.gymkhanalondon.com – Closed 1-3 January, 25-27 December and Sunday
Menu £ 25 (lunch and early dinner)/80 – Carte £ 25/61 – *(booking essential)*
• Indian • Intimate • Fashionable •
If you enjoy Trishna then you'll love Karam Sethi's Gymkhana – that's if you can get a table. Inspired by Colonial India's gymkhana clubs, the interior is full of wonderful detail and plenty of wry touches; ask to sit downstairs. The North Indian dishes have a wonderful richness and depth of flavour.
→ Kid goat methi keema, salli and pao. Wild muntjac biryani, pomegranate and mint raita. Cardamom and strawberry kheer.

XX
£3

Hakkasan Mayfair
🍸 ᚴ 🎧 ⇔ 📺

17 Bruton St ✉ *W1J 6QB –* Ⓜ *Green Park – ℰ (020)*　　Plan: **H3**
79071888 – www.hakkasan.com – Closed 24-25 December
Menu £ 38 (lunch and early dinner) – Carte £ 34/101 – *(booking essential)*
• Chinese • Minimalist • Trendy •
Less a copy, more a sister to the original; a sister who's just as fun but lives in a nicer part of town. This one has a funky, more casual ground floor to go with the downstairs dining room. You can expect the same extensive choice of top quality, modern Cantonese cuisine; dim sum is a highlight.
→ Jasmine tea-smoked organic pork ribs. Roast silver cod with champagne and honey. Jivara bomb.

XX
£3

Veeraswamy
🎧 ⇔ 🐼 📺

Victory House, 99 Regent St (Entrance on Swallow St.)　　Plan: **H3**
✉ *W1B 4RS –* Ⓜ *Piccadilly Circus – ℰ (020) 77341401*
– www.veeraswamy.com
Menu £ 30 (lunch and early dinner) – Carte £ 40/55
• Indian • Design • Historic •
It may have opened in 1926 but this celebrated Indian restaurant just keeps getting better and better! The classic dishes from across the country are prepared with considerable care by a very professional kitchen. The room is awash with colour and it's run with great charm and enormous pride.
→ Wild tiger prawns, coriander, mint and chilli. Pistachio and almond crusted lamb chops. Caramelised banana kulfi.

XX

Colony Grill Room – The Beaumont Hotel
ᚴ 🎧

Brown Hart Gdns. ✉ *W1K 6TF –* Ⓜ *Bond Street*　　Plan: **G3**
– ℰ (020) 7499 9499 – www.colonygrillroom.com
Carte £ 27/79 – *(booking essential)*
• Traditional British • Brasserie • Fashionable •
Based on 1920s London and New York grill restaurants, The Beaumont's Colony Grill comes with leather booths, striking age-of-speed art deco murals and clever lighting. By making the room and style of service so defiantly old fashioned, Chris Corbin and Jeremy King have created somewhere effortlessly chic.

XX

Hawksmoor
🍸 ᚴ 🎧 🐼

5a Air St ✉ *W1J 0AD –* Ⓜ *Piccadilly Circus – ℰ (020)*　　Plan: **H3**
7406 3980 – www.thehawksmoor.com – Closed 24-26 December
Menu £ 28 (lunch and early dinner) – Carte £ 23/59 – *(booking advisable)*
• Meats and grills • Fashionable • Vintage •
The best of the Hawksmoors is large, boisterous and has an appealing art deco feel. Expect top quality, 35-day aged Longhorn beef but also great seafood, much of which is charcoal grilled. The delightful staff are well organised.

805

XX **Momo**

25 Heddon St. ⊠ W1B 4BH – Ⓜ *Oxford Circus*   Plan: **H3**
– ℰ *(020) 7434 4040 – www.momoresto.com – Closed 25 December and 1 January*
Menu £ 20 (weekday lunch) – Carte £ 28/51
• Moroccan • Exotic décor • Intimate •
An authentic Moroccan atmosphere comes courtesy of the antiques, kilim rugs, Berber artwork, bright fabrics and lanterns – you'll feel you're eating near the souk. Go for the classic dishes: zaalouk, briouats, pigeon pastilla, and tagines with mountains of fluffy couscous.

XX **Sketch (The Gallery)**

9 Conduit St ⊠ W1S 2XG – Ⓜ *Oxford Circus –* ℰ *(020)*   Plan: **H3**
76594500 – www.sketch.london – Closed 25 December
Carte £ 37/80 – *(dinner only) (booking essential)*
• Modern cuisine • Trendy • Intimate •
The striking 'Gallery' has a smart look from India Mahdavi and artwork from David Shrigley. At dinner the room transmogrifies from art gallery to fashionable restaurant, with a menu that mixes the classic, the modern and the esoteric.

XX **Heddon Street Kitchen**

3-9 Heddon St ⊠ W1B 4BE – Ⓜ *Oxford Circus*   Plan: **H3**
– ℰ *(020) 7592 1212*
– www.gordonramsayrestaurants.com/heddon-street-kitchen – Closed 25 December
Menu £ 27 (lunch and early dinner) – Carte £ 30/53
• Modern cuisine • Brasserie • Trendy •
Gordon Ramsay's follow up to Bread Street is spread over two floors and is all about all-day dining: breakfast covers all tastes, there's weekend brunch, and an à la carte offering an appealing range of European dishes executed with palpable care.

XX **Roka**

30 North Audley St ⊠ W1K 6HP – Ⓜ *Bond Street*   Plan: **G3**
– ℰ *(020) 7305 5644 – www.rokarestaurant.com – Closed Christmas-New Year*
Carte £ 24/116
• Japanese • Elegant • Fashionable •
London's third Roka ventured into the rarefied surroundings of Mayfair and the restaurant's seductive looks are a good fit. All the favourites from their modern Japanese repertoire are here, with the robata grill taking centre stage.

XX **Theo Randall**

InterContinental London Park Lane, 1 Hamilton Pl, Park   Plan: **G4**
Ln ⊠ W1J 7QY – Ⓜ *Hyde Park Corner –* ℰ *(020) 73188747*
– www.theorandall.com – Closed Christmas, Easter, Saturday lunch, Sunday dinner and bank holidays
Menu £ 27/33 – Carte £ 40/65
• Italian • Classic décor • Chic •
A lighter, less formal look to the room was unveiled in 2016 to celebrate Theo's 10 years at the InterContinental. The lack of windows and the corporate nature of the hotel have never helped but at least there is now greater synergy between the room and the rustic Italian fare, made with prime ingredients.

XX **Maze**

10-13 Grosvenor Sq ⊠ W1K 6JP – Ⓜ *Bond Street*   Plan: **G3**
– ℰ *(020) 71070000 – www.gordonramsayrestaurants.com/maze*
Menu £ 30 (weekday lunch) – Carte £ 44/76
• Modern cuisine • Fashionable • Design •
This Gordon Ramsay restaurant still offers a glamorous night out, thanks to its great cocktails, effervescent atmosphere and small plates of Asian influenced food. Three or four dishes per person is about the going rate.

XX **Nobu Berkeley St**   AC ⊕

15 Berkeley St. ⊠ W1J 8DY – ⓂGreen Park – ℰ (020)   Plan: **H3**
*72909222 – www.noburestaurants.com – Closed 25 December and Sunday
lunch except December*
Menu £ 40 (lunch) – Carte £ 30/92 – *(booking essential)*
• Japanese • Fashionable • Trendy •
This branch of the glamorous chain is more of a party animal than its elder sibling at The Metropolitan. Start with cocktails then head upstairs for Japanese food with South American influences; try dishes from the wood-fired oven.

XX **Sexy Fish**   AC

Berkeley Sq. ⊠ W1J 6BR – ⓂGreen Park – ℰ (020)   Plan: **H3**
3764 2000 – www.sexyfish.com – Closed 25 December
Carte £ 33/90
• Seafood • Design • Elegant •
Everyone will have an opinion about the name but what's indisputable is that this is a very good looking restaurant, with works by Frank Gehry and Damien Hirst, and a stunning ceiling by Michael Roberts. The fish comes with various Asian influences but don't ignore the meat dishes like the beef rib skewers.

XX **Bentley's**   AC ⇔

11-15 Swallow St. ⊠ W1B 4DG – ⓂPiccadilly Circus   Plan: **H3**
*– ℰ (020) 77344756 – www.bentleys.org – Closed 25 December, 1 January,
Saturday lunch and Sunday*
Menu £ 25 (weekday lunch) – Carte £ 33/76
• Seafood • Traditional décor • Classic décor •
In 2016 this seafood institution celebrated its centenary. It comes in two parts: upstairs is the more formal and smartly dressed Grill, with seafood classics and grilled meats; on the ground floor is the Oyster Bar which is more fun and does a good fish pie.

XX **Coya**   AC ⇔

118 Piccadilly ⊠ W1J 7NW – ⓂHyde Park Corner   Plan: **G4**
*– ℰ (020) 7042 7118 – www.coyarestaurant.com – Closed 24-26 December
and 1 January*
Menu £ 21 (weekday lunch) – Carte £ 33/57 – *(booking advisable)*
• Peruvian • Friendly • Fashionable •
A lively, loud and enthusiastically run basement restaurant that celebrates all things Peruvian, from the people behind Zuma and Roka. Try their ceviche and their skewers, as well as their pisco sours in the fun bar.

XX **Wild Honey**   AC 🍷

12 St George St. ⊠ W1S 2FB – ⓂOxford Circus   Plan: **H3**
*– ℰ (020) 7758 9160 – www.wildhoneyrestaurant.co.uk – Closed 25-
26 December, 1 January and Sunday*
Menu £ 35 (lunch) – Carte £ 39/60
• Modern cuisine • Design • Intimate •
The elegant wood panelling and ornate plasterwork may say 'classic Mayfair institution' but the personable service team keep the atmosphere enjoyably easy-going. The kitchen uses quality British ingredients and a French base but is not afraid of the occasional international flavour.

XX **La Petite Maison**   🍷 AC

54 Brooks Mews ⊠ W1K 4EG – ⓂBond Street   Plan: **H3**
*– ℰ (020) 74954774 – www.lpmlondon.co.uk – Closed Christmas-New
Year*
Carte £ 30/70 – *(booking essential)*
• French • Bistro • Neighbourhood •
A little piece of southern France and Ligurian Italy in Mayfair. The slickly run sister to the Nice original has a buzzy, glamorous feel, with prices to match. Just reading the menus of Mediterranean dishes will improve your tan.

XX **Keeper's House**

Royal Academy of Arts, Burlington House, Piccadilly
Plan: **H3**
✉ *W1J 0BD* – ⓜ *Green Park* – ☏ *(020) 7300 5881*
– www.keepershouse.org.uk – Closed 25-26 December and Sunday
Menu £ 21/26 – Carte £ 27/44
• Modern British • Intimate • Historic •
Built in 1860 and fully restored, this house is part of the Royal Academy. Two
intimate dining rooms are lined with green baize and hung with architectural
casts. The emphasis is on seasonality, freshness and contrasts in textures.

XX **Maze Grill Mayfair**

London Marriott Hotel Grosvenor Square, 10-13
Plan: **G3**
Grosvenor Sq ✉ *W1K 6JP* – ⓜ *Bond Street* – ☏ *(020) 74952211*
– www.gordonramsayrestaurants.com/maze-grill-mayfair
Menu £ 27 (lunch) – Carte £ 29/88
• Meats and grills • Fashionable • Trendy •
Next door to Maze and specialising in steaks cooked on the Josper grill. Expect a
good range of aged meat, including Aberdeen Angus (28 days), Dedham Vale
(31), USDA Prime (36) and Wagyu 9th Grade (49), served on wooden boards.

XX **Goodman Mayfair**

26 Maddox St ✉ *W1S 1QH* – ⓜ *Oxford Circus*
Plan: **H3**
*– ☏ (020) 7499 3776 – www.goodmanrestaurants.com – Closed Sunday
and bank holidays*
Carte £ 28/103 – *(booking essential)*
• Meats and grills • Brasserie • Classic décor •
A worthy attempt at recreating a New York steakhouse; all leather and wood
and macho swagger. Beef is dry or wet aged in-house and comes with a choice
of four sauces; rib-eye the speciality.

XX **Tokimeitē**

23 Conduit St ✉ *W1S 2XS* – ⓜ *Oxford Circus* – ☏ *(020)*
Plan: **H3**
*3826 4411 – www.tokimeite.com – Closed 25 December and Sunday
dinner*
Carte £ 28/136
• Japanese • Chic • Intimate •
Yoshihiro Murata, one of Japan's most celebrated chefs, teamed up with the
Zen-Noh group to open this good looking, intimate restaurant on two floors.
Their aim is to promote Wagyu beef in Europe, so it's understandably the star
of the show.

XX **Hush**

8 Lancashire Ct., Brook St. ✉ *W1S 1EY* – ⓜ *Bond Street*
Plan: **H3**
*– ☏ (020) 76591500 – www.hush.co.uk – Closed 25 December and
1 January*
Carte £ 28/61 – *(booking essential)*
• Modern cuisine • Fashionable • Brasserie •
If there's warmth in the air then tables on the large courtyard terrace are the first
to go. The ground floor serves brasserie classics prepared with care; there's a
stylish cocktail bar upstairs, along with smart private dining rooms.

XX **Nobu**

Metropolitan Hotel, 19 Old Park Ln ✉ *W1Y 1LB*
Plan: **G4**
– ⓜ Hyde Park Corner – ☏ (020) 74474747 – www.noburestaurants.com
Menu £ 30 – Carte £ 24/73 – *(booking essential)*
• Japanese • Fashionable • Minimalist •
Nobu restaurants are now all over the world but this was Europe's first and
opened in 1997. It retains a certain exclusivity and is buzzy and fun. The menu
is an innovative blend of Japanese cuisine with South American influences.

XX **Kiku**   🕭 ᴀᴋ ⇔

17 Half Moon St. ⊠ *W1J 7BE –* Ⓜ *Green Park*   Plan: **H4**
*– ℰ (020) 74994208 – www.kikurestaurant.co.uk – Closed 25-
27 December, 1 January and lunch Sunday and bank holidays*
Menu £ 24 (weekday lunch) – Carte £ 23/78
• Japanese • Neighbourhood • Simple •
For over 35 years this earnestly run, authentically styled, family owned restau-
rant has been providing every style of Japanese cuisine to its homesick Japa-
nese customers, from shabu shabu to sukiyaki, yakitori to teriyaki.

XX **Chucs Bar and Grill**   🕭 ᴀᴋ

30b Dover St. ⊠ *W1S 4NB –* Ⓜ *Green Park – ℰ (020)*   Plan: **H3**
*3763 2013 – www.chucsrestaurant.com – Closed 25-26 and dinner 24 and
31 December, 1 January and bank holidays*
Carte £ 38/59 – *(booking essential)*
• Italian • Elegant • Cosy •
Like the shop to which it's attached, Chucs caters for those who summer on the
Riviera and are not afraid of showing it. It's decked out like a yacht and the con-
cise but not inexpensive menu offers classic Mediterranean dishes.

X **Le Boudin Blanc**   🕭 ᴀᴋ ⇔ ᴏᴣ

5 Trebeck St ⊠ *W1J 7LT –* Ⓜ *Green Park – ℰ (020)*   Plan: **G4**
*74993292 – www.boudinblanc.co.uk – Closed 24-26 December and
1 January*
Menu £ 15 (lunch and early dinner) – Carte £ 28/53
• French • Rustic • Neighbourhood •
Appealing, lively French bistro in Shepherd Market, spread over two floors.
Satisfying French classics and country cooking are the draws, along with
authentic Gallic service. Good value lunch menu.

X **Little Social**   🕭 ᴀᴋ ⇔ 🛇

5 Pollen St ⊠ *W1S 1NE –* Ⓜ *Oxford Circus – ℰ (020)*   Plan: **H3**
7870 3730 – www.littlesocial.co.uk – Closed Sunday and bank holidays
Menu £ 25 (weekday lunch) – Carte £ 33/58 – *(booking essential)*
• French • Bistro • Fashionable •
Jason Atherton's lively French bistro, opposite his Pollen Street Social restaurant,
has a clubby feel and an appealing, deliberately worn look. Service is breezy and
capable and the food is mostly classic with the odd modern twist.

X **Kitty Fisher's**

10 Shepherd Mkt ⊠ *W1J 7QF –* Ⓜ *Green Park*   Plan: **H4**
*– ℰ (0203) 302 1661 – www.kittyfishers.com – Closed Christmas, New
Year, Easter, Sunday and bank holidays*
Menu £ 30 (weekday lunch) – Carte £ 33/54 – *(booking essential)*
• Modern cuisine • Bistro • Cosy •
Warm, intimate and unpretentious restaurant – the star of the show is the wood
grill which gives the dishes added depth. Named after an 18C courtesan, presu-
mably in honour of the profession for which Shepherd Market was once known.

X **Peyote**   🕭 ᴀᴋ ⇔

13 Cork St ⊠ *W1S 3NS –* Ⓜ *Green Park – ℰ (020)*   Plan: **H3**
*7409 1300 – www.peyoterestaurant.com – Closed Saturday lunch and
Sunday*
Menu £ 24 (weekdays) – Carte £ 30/60 – *(booking essential)*
• Mexican • Trendy • Design •
From the people behind Zuma and Roka comes a 'refined interpretation of
Mexican cuisine' at this fun, glamorous spot. There's an exhilarating freshness
to the well-judged dishes; don't miss the great guacamole or the cactus salad.

UNITED KINGDOM - LONDON

✗ **Mayfair Chippy** ⊞ ✿

14 North Audley St ⊠ *W1K 6WE* – Ⓜ *Marble Arch* Plan: **G3**
*– ℰ (020) 7741 2233 – www.eatbrit.com – Closed 25 December and
1 January*
Carte £ 20/35
• Traditional British • Vintage • Traditional décor •
There are chippies, and there is the Mayfair Chippy. Here you can get cocktails,
wine, oysters, starters and dessert but, most significantly, the 'Mayfair Classic'
– fried cod or haddock with chips, tartar sauce, mushy peas and curry sauce.

Soho

 Soho ⭐ ⅙ ⅙ Ⓜ ⅙

4 Richmond Mews ⊠ *W1D 3DH* Plan: **I3**
– Ⓜ Tottenham Court Road – ℰ (020) 7559 3000 – www.sohohotel.com
96 rm – ☗£ 235/340 ☗☗£ 285/540 – ⌚ £ 14 – 7 suites
• Luxury • Personalised • Contemporary •
Stylish and fashionable hotel that mirrors the vibrancy of the neighbourhood.
Boasts two screening rooms, a comfortable drawing room and up-to-the-
minute bedrooms; some vivid, others more muted but all with hi-tech extras.
Refuel – See restaurant listing

 Ham Yard ⅙ ⓂⓂ ⅙ Ⓜ ⅙ 🚗

1 Ham Yard, ⊠ *W1D 7DT* – Ⓜ *Piccadilly Circus* Plan: **I3**
– ℰ (020) 3642 2000 – www.firmdalehotels.com
91 rm – ☗£ 260/380 ☗☗£ 260/380 – ⌚ £ 14 – 2 suites
• Luxury • Business • Elegant •
This stylish hotel from the Firmdale group is set around a courtyard – a haven of
tranquillity in the West End. Each of the rooms is different but all are supremely
comfortable. There's also a great roof terrace, a theatre, a fully stocked library
and bar... and even a bowling alley.
Ham Yard – See restaurant listing

 Café Royal ☗ ⅙ ⓂⓂ ⓂⓂ ⅙ Ⓜ ⅙

68 Regent St ⊠ *W1B 4DY* – Ⓜ *Piccadilly Circus* Plan: **H3**
– ℰ (020) 7406 3333 – www.hotelcaferoyal.com
160 rm – ☗£ 330/500 ☗☗£ 330/600 – ⌚ £ 32 – 16 suites
• Grand Luxury • Palace • Historic •
One of the most famous names of the London social scene for the last 150 years
is now a luxury hotel. The bedrooms are beautiful, elegant and discreet and the
wining and dining options many and varied – they include the gloriously
rococo Oscar Wilde bar, once home to the iconic Grill Room.

 Dean Street Townhouse ⓂK

69-71 Dean St. ⊠ *W1D 3SE* – Ⓜ *Piccadilly Circus* Plan: **I3**
– ℰ (020) 74341775 – www.deanstreettownhouse.com
39 rm – ☗£ 300/450 ☗☗£ 300/550 – ⌚ £ 15
• Townhouse • Classic • Personalised •
In the heart of Soho and where bedrooms range from tiny to bigger; the latter
have roll-top baths in the room. All are well designed and come with a good
range of extras. Cosy ground floor lounge.
Dean Street Townhouse Restaurant – See restaurant listing

⌂ **Hazlitt's** ⓂK

6 Frith St ⊠ *W1D 3JA* – Ⓜ *Tottenham Court Road* Plan: **I3**
– ℰ (020) 74341771 – www.hazlittshotel.com
30 rm – ☗£ 210/235 ☗☗£ 300/650 – ⌚ £ 12
• Townhouse • Traditional • Historic •
Dating from 1718, the former house of essayist and critic William Hazlitt still welcomes many a writer today in its role as a charming townhouse hotel. It has
plenty of character and is warmly run. No restaurant so breakfast in bed really
is the only option – and who is going to object to that?

XxX **Quo Vadis**   🔠 ⇔ 🍷

26-29 Dean St ⊠ *W1D 3LL –* Ⓜ *Tottenham Court Road*   Plan: I3
– 𝒞 (020) 74379585 – www.quovadissoho.co.uk – Closed 25-26 December,
1 January and bank holidays
Menu £ 20 – Carte £ 33/48
• **Traditional British** • **Fashionable** • **Brasserie** •
Owned by the Hart brothers, this Soho institution dates from the 1920s and is as
stylish and handsome as ever. The menu reads like a selection of all your favo-
urite British dishes – game is always a highlight.

XxX **Gauthier - Soho**   🔠 ⇔ 🕊

21 Romilly St ⊠ *W1D 5AF –* Ⓜ *Leicester Square*   Plan: I3
– 𝒞 (020) 74943111 – www.gauthiersoho.co.uk – Closed Monday lunch,
Sunday and bank holidays except Good Friday
Menu £ 18/75
• **French** • **Intimate** • **Neighbourhood** •
Detached from the rowdier elements of Soho is this charming Georgian town-
house, with dining spread over three floors. Alex Gauthier offers assorted
menus of his classically based cooking, with vegetarians particularly well looked
after.

XxX **Red Fort**   🔠 🍷

77 Dean St. ⊠ *W1D 3SH –* Ⓜ *Tottenham Court Road*   Plan: I3
– 𝒞 (020) 74372525 – www.redfort.co.uk – Closed Sunday
Menu £ 15/59 – Carte £ 32/65 – *(bookings advisable at dinner)*
• **Indian** • **Exotic décor** • **Chic** •
A smart, stylish and professionally run Indian restaurant that has been a feature
in Soho since 1983. Cooking is based on the Mughal Court and uses much UK
produce such as Welsh lamb; look out for more unusual choices like rabbit.

XxX **Imperial China**   🔠 ⇔

White Bear Yard, 25a Lisle St ⊠ *WC2H 7BA*   Plan: I3
– Ⓜ *Leicester Square – 𝒞 (020) 7734 3388*
– www.imperialchina-london.com – Closed 25 December
Menu £ 20/36 – Carte £ 16/96 – *(booking advisable)*
• **Chinese** • **Elegant** •
Sharp service and comfortable surroundings are not the only things that set this
restaurant apart: the Cantonese cooking exudes freshness and vitality, whether
that's the steamed dumplings or the XO minced pork with fine beans.

XX   **Yauatcha Soho**   🔠
❀

15 Broadwick St ⊠ *W1F 0DL*   Plan: I3
– Ⓜ *Tottenham Court Road – 𝒞 (020) 74948888 – www.yauatcha.com*
– Closed 25 December
Menu £ 29 (weekday lunch) – Carte £ 18/61
• **Chinese** • **Design** • **Trendy** •
Refined, delicate and delicious dim sum; ideal for sharing in a group. It's over 10
years old yet the surroundings are still as slick and stylish as ever: choose the
lighter, brighter ground floor or the darker, more atmospheric basement.
➔ Scallop shui mai. Kung pao chicken with cashew nut. Chocolate
'pebble'.

XX   **Brasserie Zédel**   🔠
❀

20 Sherwood St ⊠ *W1F 7ED –* Ⓜ *Piccadilly Circus*   Plan: H3
– 𝒞 (020) 7734 4888 – www.brasseriezedel.com – Closed 24-25 December
and 1 January
Menu £ 13/20 – Carte £ 19/41 – *(booking advisable)*
• **French** • **Brasserie** •
A grand French brasserie, which is all about inclusivity and accessibility, in a
bustling subterranean space restored to its original art deco glory. Expect a
roll-call of classic French dishes and some very competitive prices.

UNITED KINGDOM - LONDON

XX **Bob Bob Ricard** [AC]
1 Upper James St ⊠ *W1F 9DF –* Ⓜ *Oxford Circus*   Plan: **H3**
– ℰ *(020) 31451000 – www.bobbobricard.com*
Carte £ 32/87
• Modern cuisine • Vintage • Elegant •
Everyone needs a little glamour now and again and this place provides it. The
room may be quite small but it sees itself as a grand salon – ask for a booth. The
menu is all-encompassing – oysters and caviar to pies and burgers.

XX **100 Wardour St** [AC] ⇔ ⊗
100 Wardour St ⊠ *W1F 0TN*   Plan: **I3**
– Ⓜ *Tottenham Court Road –* ℰ *(020) 7314 4000*
– www.100wardourst.com – Closed 25-26 December
Menu £ 30 (weekday dinner) – Carte £ 17/57
• Modern cuisine • Contemporary décor •
D&D have reinvented the space formerly occupied by Floridita and the original
Marquee Club. At night, head downstairs for cocktails, live music and a modern
menu with Japanese and South American influences. In the daytime stay on
the ground floor for an all-day menu, a bar and a pop-in/plug-in lounge.

XX **Ham Yard** – Ham Yard Hotel   ⛩ & [AC]
1 Ham Yard, ⊠ *W1D 7DT –* Ⓜ *Piccadilly Circus*   Plan: **I3**
– ℰ *(020) 3642 1007 – www.firmdalehotels.com*
Menu £ 20 (dinner) – Carte £ 28/46
• Modern cuisine • Brasserie • Design •
An exuberantly decorated restaurant; start with a cocktail – the bitters and
syrups are homemade with herbs from the hotel's roof garden. The menu
moves with the seasons and the kitchen has the confidence to keep dishes simple.

XX **Dean Street Townhouse Restaurant** – Dean Street Townhouse Hotel
69-71 Dean St. ⊠ *W1D 3SE –* Ⓜ *Piccadilly Circus*   ⛩ [AC] ⊗ ۱۲
– ℰ *(020) 74341775 – www.deanstreettownhouse.com*   Plan: **I3**
Menu £ 29 – Carte £ 29/44 – *(booking essential)*
• Modern British • Brasserie • Elegant •
A Georgian house that's home to a fashionable bar and restaurant which is busy
from breakfast onwards. Appealingly classic British food includes some retro
dishes and satisfying puddings.

XX **Vasco and Piero's Pavilion** [AC] ⇔
15 Poland St ⊠ *W1F 8QE –* Ⓜ *Oxford Circus –* ℰ *(020)*   Plan: **H2**
*7437 8774 – www.vascosfood.com – Closed Saturday lunch, Sunday and
bank holidays*
Menu £ 18 (lunch and early dinner) – Carte £ 25/55 – *(booking essential
at lunch)*
• Italian • Friendly • Neighbourhood •
Regulars and tourists have been flocking to this institution for over 40 years; its
longevity is down to a twice daily changing menu of Umbrian-influenced dishes
rather than the matter-of-fact service or simple decoration.

XX **Plum Valley**   ⇔
20 Gerrard St. ⊠ *W1D 6JQ –* Ⓜ *Leicester Square*   Plan: **I3**
– ℰ *(020) 74944366 – Closed 23-24 December*
Menu £ 38 – Carte £ 19/37
• Chinese • Design •
Its striking black façade makes this modern Chinese restaurant easy to spot in
Chinatown. Mostly Cantonese cooking, with occasional forays into Vietnam and
Thailand; dim sum is the strength.

XX **Refuel** – Soho Hotel   &. AC
4 Richmond Mews ✉ *W1D 3DH*   Plan: I3
– ❶ *Tottenham Court Road* – 𝄞 *(020) 75593007 – www.sohohotel.com*
Menu £ 21/25 – Carte £ 31/54
• Modern British • Fashionable • Brasserie •
At the heart of the cool Soho hotel is their aptly named bar and restaurant. With a menu to suit all moods and wallets, from burgers to Dover sole, and a cocktail list to lift all spirits, it's a fun and bustling spot.

XX **Hix**   AC ⬄ ☕ 🍸
66-70 Brewer St. ✉ *W1F 9UP* – ❶ *Piccadilly Circus*   Plan: H3
– 𝄞 *(020) 72923518 – www.hixsoho.co.uk – Closed 25-26 December*
Menu £ 20 (weekday lunch) – Carte £ 27/65
• Traditional British • Fashionable • Trendy •
The exterior may hint at exclusivity but inside this big restaurant the atmosphere is fun, noisy and sociable. The room comes decorated with the works of eminent British artists. Expect classic British dishes and ingredients.

XX **MASH**   🕸 AC ⬄ ☕
77 Brewer St ✉ *W1F 9ZN* – ❶ *Piccadilly Circus*   Plan: H3
– 𝄞 *(020) 7734 2608 – www.mashsteak.co.uk – Closed 24-26 December and Sunday lunch*
Menu £ 25 – Carte £ 30/94
• Meats and grills • Brasserie • Fashionable •
A team from Copenhagen raised the old Titanic and restored the art deco to create this striking 'Modern American Steak House', offering Danish, Nebraskan and Uruguayan beef. A great bar and slick service add to the grown up feel.

X **Social Eating House**   AC
🕸 *58 Poland St* ✉ *W1F 7NR* – ❶ *Oxford Circus* – 𝄞 *(020)*   Plan: H3
79933251 – www.socialeatinghouse.com – Closed Christmas, Sunday and bank holidays
Menu £ 21 (lunch and early dinner) – Carte £ 39/57 – *(booking advisable)*
• Modern cuisine • Fashionable • Brasserie •
There's something of a Brooklyn vibe to this Jason Atherton restaurant, with its bare brick and raw plastered walls and its speakeasy bar upstairs. It's great fun, very busy and gloriously unstuffy; the menu is an eminently good read, with the best dishes being the simplest ones.
➝ Smoked Lincolnshire eel with salt & vinegar potatoes, macadamia and rock samphire. Rack of Herdwick lamb with confit neck, peas and sheep's ricotta. Chocolate crémeux with salted caramel, mascarpone and almond biscotti.

X **Barrafina**   AC
🕸 *54 Frith St.* ✉ *W1D 3SL* – ❶ *Tottenham Court Road*   Plan: I3
– 𝄞 *(020) 74401456 – www.barrafina.co.uk – Closed bank holidays*
Carte £ 15/34 – *(bookings not accepted)*
• Spanish • Tapas bar • Fashionable •
Be prepared to queue for gaps at the counter at this terrific tapas bar. Wonderfully fresh ingredients allow their natural flavours to shine; the seafood is particularly good. (Moved to Dean St, late 2016.)
➝ Pimientos de padrón. Octopus with capers. Créma Catalana.

X **Dehesa**   🕸 🍽 AC ⬄
🙂 *25 Ganton St* ✉ *W1F 9BP* – ❶ *Oxford Circus* – 𝄞 *(020)*   Plan: H3
74944170 – www.dehesa.co.uk – Closed 25 December
Carte £ 14/36
• Mediterranean cuisine • Tapas bar • Fashionable •
Repeats the success of its sister restaurant, Salt Yard, by offering flavoursome and appealingly priced Spanish and Italian tapas. Busy, friendly atmosphere in appealing corner location. Terrific drinks list too.

✕ **Nopi**   &. 🅰🄲 🕸

21-22 Warwick St. ✉ *W1B 5NE* – Ⓜ *Piccadilly Circus*   Plan: **H3**
– ℰ (020) 74949584 – www.nopi-restaurant.com – Closed 25-26 December
Carte £ 34/48
• Mediterranean cuisine • Design • Fashionable •
The bright, clean look of Yotam Ottolenghi's charmingly run all-day restaurant
matches the fresh, invigorating food. The sharing plates take in the Mediterra-
nean, the Middle East and Asia and the veggie dishes stand out.

✕ **Ember Yard**   🅰🄲 ⇧

60 Berwick St ✉ *W1F 8DX* – Ⓜ *Oxford Circus* – ℰ *(020)*   Plan: **H2**
7439 8057 – www.emberyard.co.uk – Closed 25-26 December and
1 January
Carte £ 20/33 – *(booking advisable)*
• Mediterranean cuisine • Tapas bar • Fashionable •
Those familiar with the Salt Yard Group will recognise the Spanish and Italian
themed menus – but their 4th fun outlet comes with a focus on cooking over
charcoal or wood. There's even a seductive smokiness to some of the cocktails.

✕ **Polpetto**   🅰🄲
🤗
11 Berwick St ✉ *W1F 0PL* – Ⓜ *Tottenham Court Road*   Plan: **I3**
– ℰ (020) 7439 8627 – www.polpetto.co.uk – Closed Sunday
Carte £ 12/18 – *(bookings not accepted at dinner)*
• Italian • Simple • Rustic •
Re-opened by Russell Norman in bigger premises. The style of food is the per-
fect match for this relaxed environment: the small, seasonally inspired Italian
dishes are uncomplicated, appealingly priced and deliver great flavours.

✕ **Copita**   🅰🄲
🤗
27 D'Arblay St ✉ *W1F 8EP* – Ⓜ *Oxford Circus*   Plan: **H3**
– ℰ (020) 7287 7797 – www.copita.co.uk – Closed Sunday and bank
holidays
Carte £ 15/30 – *(bookings not accepted)*
• Spanish • Tapas bar • Rustic •
Perch on one of the high stools or stay standing and get stuck into the daily
menu of small, colourful and tasty dishes. Staff add to the atmosphere and everything on the Spanish wine list comes by the glass or copita.

✕ **Palomar**   &. 🅰🄲
🤗
34 Rupert St ✉ *W1D 6DN* – Ⓜ *Piccadilly Circus*   Plan: **I3**
– ℰ (020) 7439 8777 – www.thepalomar.co.uk – Closed 25-26 December
and Sunday dinner
Carte £ 23/42 – *(booking advisable)*
• World cuisine • Trendy • Cosy •
A hip slice of modern-day Jerusalem in the heart of theatreland, with a zinc kitchen counter running back to an intimate wood-panelled dining room. Like the
atmosphere, the contemporary Middle Eastern cooking is fresh and vibrant.

✕ **Mele e Pere**   🅰🄲 🕸

46 Brewer St ✉ *W1F 9TF* – Ⓜ *Piccadilly Circus* – ℰ *(020)*   Plan: **I3**
7096 2096 – www.meleepere.co.uk – Closed 25-26 December and
1 January
Menu £ 23 (dinner) – Carte £ 23/43
• Italian • Friendly • Neighbourhood •
Head downstairs – the 'apples and pears'? – to a vaulted room in the style of a
homely Italian kitchen, with an appealing vermouth bar. The owner-chef has
worked in some decent London kitchens but hails from Verona so expect
gutsy Italian dishes.

X **Blanchette** 🅰🄲 ⇔
9 D'Arblay St ⊠ *W1F 8DR –* Ⓜ *Oxford Circus –* ℰ *(020)* Plan: **H2**
7439 8100 – www.blanchettesoho.co.uk
Menu £ 20 – Carte £ 14/22 – *(booking essential)*
• French • Simple • Fashionable •
Run by three frères, Blanchette takes French bistro food and gives it the 'small plates' treatment. It's named after their mother – the ox cheek Bourguignon is her recipe. Tiles and exposed brick add to the rustic look.

X **Bocca di Lupo** 🅰🄲 ⇔
12 Archer St ⊠ *W1D 7BB –* Ⓜ *Piccadilly Circus –* ℰ *(020)* Plan: **I3**
77342223 – www.boccadilupo.com – Closed 25 December and 1 January
Carte £ 15/58 – *(booking essential)*
• Italian • Tapas bar •
Atmosphere, food and service are all best when sitting at the marble counter, watching the chefs at work. Specialities from across Italy come in large or small sizes and are full of flavour and vitality. Try also their gelato shop opposite.

X **Polpo Soho** 🅰🄲 ⇔
41 Beak St ⊠ *W1F 9SB –* Ⓜ *Oxford Circus –* ℰ *(020)* Plan: **H3**
7734 4479 – www.polpo.co.uk
Menu £ 25 – Carte £ 12/21 – *(bookings not accepted at dinner)*
• Italian • Tapas bar • Rustic •
A fun and lively Venetian bacaro, with a stripped-down, faux-industrial look. The small plates, from arancini and prosciutto to fritto misto and Cotechino sausage, are so well priced that waiting for a table is worth it.

X **10 Greek Street** 🖧 🅰🄲 ⇔
10 Greek St ⊠ *W1D 4DH –* Ⓜ *Tottenham Court Road* Plan: **I2/3**
– ℰ *(020) 7734 4677 – www.10greekstreet.com – Closed Christmas, Easter and Sunday*
Carte £ 29/67
• Modern cuisine • Bistro • Neighbourhood •
With just 28 seats and a dozen at the counter, the challenge is getting a table at this modishly sparse-looking bistro (no bookings taken at dinner). The chef-owner's blackboard menu comes with Anglo, Mediterranean and Middle Eastern elements.

X **Haozhan** 🅰🄲
8 Gerrard St ⊠ *W1D 5PJ –* Ⓜ *Leicester Square –* ℰ *(020)* Plan: **I3**
74343838 – www.haozhan.co.uk – Closed 24-25 December
Menu £ 14 – Carte £ 15/43
• Chinese • Design •
Interesting fusion-style dishes, with mostly Cantonese but other Asian influences too. Specialities like jasmine ribs or wasabi prawns reveal a freshness that marks this place out from the plethora of Chinatown mediocrity.

X **Cinnamon Soho** 🖧 🅰🄲 🗔
5 Kingly St ⊠ *W1B 5PF –* Ⓜ *Oxford Circus –* ℰ *(020)* Plan: **H3**
7437 1664 – www.cinnamonsoho.com – Closed 1 January
Carte £ 16/33
• Indian • Friendly • Fashionable •
Younger and more fun than its sister the Cinnamon Club. Has a great selection of classic and more modern Indian dishes like Rogan Josh shepherd's pie. High Chai in the afternoon and a pre-theatre menu that's a steal.

X **Duck & Rice** 🅰🄲
90 Berwick St ⊠ *W1F 0QB –* Ⓜ *Tottenham Court Road* Plan: **I3**
– ℰ *(020) 3327 7888 – www.theduckandrice.com*
Carte approx. £ 38
• Chinese • Intimate • Romantic •
Alan Yau is one of our most innovative restaurateurs and once again he's created something different – a modern pub with a Chinese kitchen. Beer is the thing on the ground floor; upstairs is for Chinese favourites and comforting classics.

UNITED KINGDOM - LONDON

X **Antidote**   🏵 🏠

12A Newburgh St ⊠ *W1F 7RR –* Ⓜ *Oxford Circus*   Plan: **H3**
– ℰ (020) 7287 8488 – www.antidotewinebar.com – Closed Sunday
Carte £ 30/41 – *(booking advisable)*
• Modern cuisine • Intimate • Wine bar •
Plates of cheese and charcuterie are the draw in the ground floor wine bar. Upstairs in the dining room you'll find menus focusing on prime, seasonal ingredients accompanied by a wine list specialising in organic and biodynamic wines.

X **Jinjuu**   🆑

15 Kingly St ⊠ *W1B 5PS –* Ⓜ *Oxford Circus – ℰ (020)*   Plan: **H3**
8181 8887 – www.jinjuu.com – Closed 25 December
Menu £ 15 (weekday lunch)/42 – Carte £ 26/86
• Asian • Design • Fashionable •
American-born celebrity chef Judy Joo's first London restaurant is a celebration of her Korean heritage. The vibrant dishes, whether Bibimbap bowls or Ssam platters, burst with flavour and are as enjoyable as the fun surroundings.

X **Hoppers**   🆑
☺
49 Frith St ⊠ *W1D 4SG –* Ⓜ *Tottenham Court Road*   Plan: **I3**
– ℰ (020) 3011 1021 – www.hopperslondon.com – Closed 24-31 December
and 1-3 January.
Carte £ 13/27 – *(bookings not accepted)*
• South Indian • Simple • Rustic •
Street food inspired by the flavours of Tamil Nadu and Sri Lanka features at this fun little spot from the Sethi family (Trishna, Gymkhana). Hoppers are bowl-shaped pancakes made from fermented rice and coconut – ideal with a creamy kari. The 'short eats' are great too, as are the prices, so expect a queue.

X **Oliver Maki**   🆑

33 Dean St ⊠ *W1D 4PW –* Ⓜ *Leicester Square*   Plan: **I3**
– ℰ (020) 7734 0408 – www.olivermaki.co.uk
Carte £ 38/56
• Japanese • Minimalist • Simple •
A small, eagerly run corner restaurant from a group with branches in Kuwait and Bahrain. The modern Japanese food has a more pronounced fusion element than similar types of place – not everything works but the confident kitchen uses good produce.

X **Spuntino**   🆑

61 Rupert St. ⊠ *W1D 7PW –* Ⓜ *Piccadilly Circus*   Plan: **I3**
– www.spuntino.co.uk – Closed dinner 24 December, 25-26, 31 December
and 1 January
Carte £ 14/22 – *(bookings not accepted)*
• North American • Rustic •
Influenced by Downtown New York, with its no-booking policy and industrial look. Sit at the counter and order classics like mac 'n' cheese or mini burgers. The staff, who look like they could also fix your car, really add to the fun.

X **Bibigo**   🆑 ⇔

58-59 Great Marlborough St ⊠ *W1F 7JY*   Plan: **H3**
– Ⓜ *Oxford Circus – ℰ (020) 7042 5225 – www.bibigouk.com*
Menu £ 13 – Carte £ 20/29
• Korean • Friendly • Fashionable •
The enthusiastically run Bibigo represents Korea's largest food company's first foray into the UK market. Watch the kitchen send out dishes such as kimchi, Bossam (simmered pork belly) and hot stone galbi (chargrilled short ribs).

X **Zelman Meats**

2 St Anne's Ct ⊠ W1F 0AZ – ⓜ Tottenham Court Rd   Plan: I2
– ℰ (0207) 437 0566 – www.zelmanmeats.com – Closed bank holidays,
dinner Sunday and lunch Monday
Carte £ 35/49
• Meats and grills • Rustic •

Those clever Goodman people noticed a lack of affordable steakhouses and so opened this fun, semi-industrial space. They serve three cuts of beef: sliced picanha (from the rump), chateaubriand, and a wonderfully smoky short rib.

X **Ceviche Soho**   AC

17 Frith St ⊠ W1D 4RG – ⓜ Tottenham Court Road   Plan: I3
– ℰ (020) 7292 2040 – www.cevicheuk.com/soho
Carte £ 16/27 – (booking essential)
• Peruvian • Friendly • Fashionable •

Based on a Lima Pisco bar, Ceviche is as loud as it is fun. First try the deliriously addictive drinks based on the Peruvian spirit pisco, and then share some thinly sliced sea bass or octopus, along with anticuchos skewers.

X **Cây Tre**   AC

42-43 Dean St ⊠ W1D 4PZ – ⓜ Tottenham Court Road   Plan: I3
– ℰ (020) 7317 9118 – www.caytresoho.co.uk
Menu £ 15/23 – Carte £ 19/30 – (booking advisable)
• Vietnamese • Minimalist •

Bright, sleek and bustling surroundings where Vietnamese standouts include Cha La Lot (spicy ground pork wrapped in betel leaves), slow-cooked Mekong catfish with a well-judged sweet and spicy sauce, and 6 versions of Pho (noodle soup).

X **Rosa's Soho**

48 Dean St ⊠ W1D 5BF – ⓜ Leicester Square – ℰ (020)   Plan: I3
7494 1638 – www.rosasthaicafe.com – Closed 25-26 December
Menu £ 20 – Carte £ 19/25 – (booking advisable)
• Thai • Simple • Friendly •

The worn-in, pared-down look of this authentic Thai café adds to its intimate feel. Signature dishes include warm minced chicken salad and a sweet pumpkin red curry. Tom Yam soup comes with a lovely balance of sweet, sour and spice.

X **Bone Daddies**   AC

31 Peter St ⊠ W1F 0AR – ⓜ Piccadilly Circus – ℰ (020)   Plan: I3
7287 8581 – www.bonedaddies.com – Closed 25 December
Carte £ 16/24 – (bookings not accepted)
• Asian • Fashionable • Neighbourhood •

Maybe ramen is the new rock 'n' roll. The charismatic Aussie chef-owner feels that combinations are endless when it comes to these comforting bowls. Be ready to queue then share a table. It's a fun place, run by a hospitable bunch.

X **Barshu**   AC ⇔

28 Frith St. ⊠ W1D 5LF – ⓜ Leicester Square – ℰ (020)   Plan: I3
72878822 – www.barshurestaurant.co.uk – Closed 24-25 December
Carte £ 27/69 – (booking advisable)
• Chinese • Exotic décor •

The fiery and authentic flavours of China's Sichuan province are the draw here; help is at hand as the menu has pictures. It's decorated with carved wood and lanterns; downstairs is better for groups.

X **Baozi Inn**

25-26 Newport Court ⊠ WC2H 7JS – ⓜ Leicester Square   Plan: I3
– ℰ (020) 72876877 – Closed 24-25 December
Carte £ 15/22 – (bookings not accepted)
• Chinese • Rustic • Simple •

Buzzy, busy little place that's great for a quick bite, especially if you like pork buns, steaming bowls of noodles, a hit of Sichuan fire and plenty of beer or tea. You'll leave feeling surprisingly energised and rejuvenated.

817

UNITED KINGDOM - LONDON

X **Manchurian Legends**   AC

16 Lisle St ⊠ WC2H 7BE – Ⓜ Leicester Square – ℰ (020)   Plan: I3
72876606 – www.manchurianlegends.com – Closed Christmas
Menu £ 16/25 – Carte £ 20/38
• Chinese • Simple • Friendly •
Try specialities from a less familiar region of China: Dongbei, the 'north east'. As
winters there are long, stews and BBQ dishes are popular, as are pickled ingredients and chilli heat. Further warmth comes from the sweet natured staff.

X **Bao**   AC
🍴
53 Lexington St ⊠ W1F 9AS   Plan: H3
– Ⓜ Tottenham Court Road – ℰ (020) 3019 2200 – www.baolondon.com
– Closed Sunday
Carte £ 17/27 – (bookings not accepted)
• Asian • Simple • Cosy •
There are some things in life worth queueing for – and that includes the deli-
cious eponymous buns here at this simple, great value Taiwanese operation.
The classic bao and the confit pork bao are standouts, along with 'small eats'
like trotter nuggets. There's another Bao in Windmill St.

X **Koya Bar**

50 Frith St ⊠ W1D 4SQ – Ⓜ Tottenham Court Road   Plan: I3
– ℰ (020) 74334463 – www.koyabar.co.uk – Closed 24-25 December and
1 January
Carte £ 10/23 – (bookings not accepted)
• Japanese • Simple • Friendly •
A simple, sweet place serving authentic Udon noodles and small plates; they
open early for breakfast. Counter seating means everyone has a view of the
chefs; bookings aren't taken and there is often a queue, but the short wait is
worth it.

X **Beijing Dumpling**   AC

23 Lisle St. ⊠ WC2H 7BA – Ⓜ Leicester Square   Plan: I3
– ℰ (020) 7287 6888 – Closed 24-25 December
Menu £ 18 – Carte £ 10/40
• Chinese • Neighbourhood • Simple •
This relaxed little place serves freshly prepared dumplings of both Beijing and
Shanghai styles. Although the range is not as comprehensive as the name sug-
gests, they do stand out, especially varieties of the famed Siu Lung Bao.

X **Tonkotsu**   AC 🍴

63 Dean St ⊠ W1D 4QG – Ⓜ Tottenham Court Road   Plan: I3
– ℰ (020) 7437 0071 – www.tonkotsu.co.uk
Carte £ 17/26 – (bookings not accepted)
• Japanese • Rustic • Cosy •
Some things are worth queuing for. Good ramen is all about the base stock: 18
hours goes into its preparation here to ensure the bowls of soup and wheat-
based noodles reach a depth of flavour that seems to nourish one's very soul.

ST JAMES'S

🏨 **Ritz**   ♿ AC ♨

150 Piccadilly ⊠ W1J 9BR – Ⓜ Green Park – ℰ (020)   Plan: H4
74938181 – www.theritzlondon.com
136 rm – ♦£ 355/875 ♦♦£ 430/1130 – � £ 35 – 24 suites
• Grand Luxury • Classic • Historic •
World famous hotel, opened in 1906 as a fine example of Louis XVI architecture
and decoration. Elegant Palm Court famed for its afternoon tea. Many of the
lavishly appointed and luxurious rooms and suites overlook the park.
❀ **Ritz Restaurant** – See restaurant listing

Haymarket

1 Suffolk Pl. ⊠ SW1Y 4HX – Ⓜ Piccadilly Circus
– ℰ (020) 74704000 – www.haymarkethotel.com
Plan: I4

50 rm – †£ 230/320 ††£ 230/1395 – ⯑ £ 15 – 3 suites
• Luxury • Personalised • Contemporary •
Smart and spacious hotel in John Nash Regency building, with a stylish blend of modern and antique furnishings. Large, comfortable bedrooms in soothing colours. Impressive basement pool is often used for private parties.
Brumus – See restaurant listing

 Sofitel London St James

6 Waterloo Pl. ⊠ SW1Y 4AN – Ⓜ Piccadilly Circus
– ℰ (020) 77472200 – www.sofitelstjames.com
Plan: I4

183 rm – †£ 240/400 ††£ 240/400 – ⯑ £ 25 – 18 suites
• Luxury • Elegant •
Great location for this international hotel in a Grade II former bank. The triple-glazed bedrooms are immaculately kept; the spa is one of the best around. The bar is inspired by Coco Chanel; the lounge by an English rose garden.
Balcon – See restaurant listing

 Dukes

35 St James's Pl. ⊠ SW1A 1NY – Ⓜ Green Park
– ℰ (020) 74914840 – www.dukeshotel.com
Plan: H4

90 rm – †£ 346/440 ††£ 400/490 – ⯑ £ 24 – 6 suites
• Traditional • Luxury • Classic •
The wonderfully located Dukes has been steadily updating its image over the last few years, despite being over a century old. Bedrooms are now fresh and uncluttered and the atmosphere less starchy. The basement restaurant offers a modern menu, with dishes that are original in look and elaborate in construction.

 Stafford

16-18 St James's Pl. ⊠ SW1A 1NJ – Ⓜ Green Park
– ℰ (020) 7493 0111 – www.thestaffordlondon.com
Plan: H4

104 rm – †£ 350/535 ††£ 350/535 – ⯑ £ 25 – 15 suites
• Luxury • Luxury • Elegant •
Styles itself as a 'country house in the city'; its bedrooms are divided between the main house, converted 18C stables and a more modern mews. Legendary American bar a highlight; traditional British food served in the restaurant.

 St James's Hotel and Club

7-8 Park Pl. ⊠ SW1A 1LS – Ⓜ Green Park – ℰ (020)
73161600 – www.stjameshotelandclub.com
Plan: H4

60 rm – †£ 265/550 ††£ 265/550 – ⯑ £ 23 – 10 suites
• Business • Modern •
1890s house, formerly a private club, in a wonderfully central yet quiet location. Modern, boutique-style interior with over 300 European works of art from the '20s to the '50s. Fine finish to the compact but well-equipped bedrooms.
✿ **Seven Park Place** – See restaurant listing

XxXxX **Ritz Restaurant** – Ritz Hotel

✿

150 Piccadilly ⊠ W1J 9BR – Ⓜ Green Park – ℰ (020)
73002370 – www.theritzlondon.com
Plan: H4

Menu £ 49 (weekday lunch) – Carte £ 72/103
• Classic cuisine • Luxury • Historic •
Thanks to the lavishness of its Louis XVI decoration, there is nowhere grander than The Ritz. The classic cuisine uses extravagant ingredients along with subtle contemporary elements to lift dishes to new heights while still respecting their heritage. The formal service is now more youthful and enthusiastic.
→ Langoustine with broad beans and mint. Loin of lamb with pommes Anna and shallot & herb crust. Custard tart with poached rhubarb and ginger ice cream.

XxX ★ **Seven Park Place** – St James's Hotel and Club   AC ⇔

7-8 Park Pl ⊠ SW1A 1LS – Ⓜ Green Park – ℰ (020)   Plan: **H4**
73161615 – www.stjameshotelandclub.com – Closed Sunday and Monday
Menu £ 32 (weekday lunch)/63 – (booking essential)
• Modern cuisine • Cosy • Fashionable •
William Drabble's cooking is all about the quality of the produce, much of which
comes from the Lake District, and his confident cooking allows natural flavours
to shine. This diminutive restaurant is concealed within the hotel and divided
into two; ask for the warmer, gilded back room.
→ Poached native lobster tail with asparagus and champagne hollandaise.
Griddled fillet of sea bass with salt-baked celeriac, apple and truffle. Victoria
pineapple confit with vanilla and coconut sorbet.

XxX **Chutney Mary**   AC ⇔ 🍸

73 St James's St ⊠ SW1A 1PH – Ⓜ Green Park   Plan: **H4**
– ℰ (020) 7629 6688 – www.chutneymary.com – Closed Sunday
Menu £ 30 (weekday lunch) – Carte £ 35/60
• Indian • Elegant • Design •
After 25 years in Chelsea, one of London's pioneering Indian restaurants
has been establishing itself in a more central position. Spicing is understated;
classics are done well; and some regional dishes have been subtly updated.

XxX **The Wolseley**   AC ⇔ 🍸

160 Piccadilly ⊠ W1J 9EB – Ⓜ Green Park – ℰ (020)   Plan: **H4**
74996996 – www.thewolseley.com – Closed dinner 24 December
Carte £ 22/68 – (booking essential)
• Modern cuisine • Fashionable •
This feels like a grand and glamorous European coffee house, with its pillars
and high vaulted ceiling. Appealing menus offer everything from caviar to a
hot-dog. It's open from early until late and boasts a large celebrity following.

XxX **Milos**   & AC ⇔

1 Regent St ⊠ SW1Y 4NR – Ⓜ Piccadilly Circus   Plan: **I4**
– ℰ (020) 7839 2080 – www.milos.ca – Closed 25 December and Sunday
Menu £ 29/49 – Carte £ 58/130
• Seafood • Elegant • Luxury •
London's branch of this international group of Greek seafood estiatorios makes
the most of the grand listed building it occupies. Choose from the impressive
display of fish flown in daily from Greek waters – and prepare for a sizeable bill.

XX **Balcon** – Sofitel London St James Hotel   AC

8 Pall Mall. ⊠ SW1Y 4AN – Ⓜ Piccadilly Circus   Plan: **I4**
– ℰ (020) 73897820 – www.thebalconlondon.com
Menu £ 20 (lunch) – Carte £ 25/45
• French • Brasserie •
A former banking hall with vast chandeliers and a grand brasserie look. It's open
from breakfast onwards and the menu features French classics like snails and
cassoulet; try the charcuterie from Wales and France.

XX **Le Caprice**   🌿 AC 🍽 🍸

Arlington House, Arlington St. ⊠ SW1A 1RJ   Plan: **H4**
– Ⓜ Green Park – ℰ (020) 76292239 – www.le-caprice.co.uk – Closed 24-
26 December
Menu £ 20 (weekday lunch) – Carte £ 32/65
• Modern cuisine • Fashionable •
For over 35 years Le Caprice's effortlessly sophisticated atmosphere and surroundings have attracted a confident and urbane clientele. The kitchen is well-
practised and capable and there's something for everyone on their catch-all
menu.

XX **Sake No Hana** ⚏

23 St James's ⊠ SW1A 1HA – ⓜ *Green Park –* ✆ *(020)*   Plan: **H4**
7925 8988 – www.sakenohana.com – Closed 25 December and Sunday
Menu £ 31 – Carte £ 22/69

• Japanese • Minimalist • Fashionable •

A modern Japanese restaurant within a Grade II listed '60s edifice – and proof
that you can occasionally find good food at the end of an escalator. As with the
great cocktails, the menu is best enjoyed when shared with a group.

XX **Boulestin** 🍽 ⇄ 🗐

5 St James's St ⊠ SW1A 1EF – ⓜ *Green Park –* ✆ *(020)*   Plan: **H4**
7930 2030 – www.boulestin.com – Closed Sunday and bank holidays
Menu £ 25 – Carte £ 33/60

• French • Elegant • Neighbourhood •

Nearly a century after Xavier Marcel Boulestin opened his eponymous restaurant showcasing 'Simple French Cooking for English Homes', his spirit has
been resurrected at this elegant brasserie, with its lovely courtyard terrace.

XX **Cafe Murano** ⚏ ⇄ 🗐

33 St. James's St ⊠ SW1A 1HD – ⓜ *Green Park*   Plan: **H4**
– ✆ *(0203) 371 5559 – www.cafemurano.co.uk – Closed Sunday dinner*
Menu £ 19 (weekdays)/23 – Carte £ 25/64 – *(booking essential)*

• Italian • Fashionable •

Angela Hartnett and her chef have created an appealing and flexible menu of
delicious North Italian delicacies – the lunch menu is very good value. It's certainly no ordinary café and its popularity means pre-booking is essential.

XX **45 Jermyn St** 🐜 ⚏

45 Jermyn St. ⊠ SW1 6DN – ⓜ *Piccadilly Circus*   Plan: **H4**
– ✆ *(0207) 2054545 – www.45jermynst.com – Closed 25-26 December*
Carte £ 26/66

• Modern British • Brasserie • Elegant •

What was Fortnum & Mason's Fountain restaurant for 60 years is now a bright,
contemporary brasserie. The sodas, coupes and floats pay tribute to its past and
cooking has a strong British element. Prices can be steep but, in contrast, the
well-chosen wine list has very restrained mark-ups.

XX **Franco's** ⚏ 🗐

61 Jermyn St ⊠ SW1Y 6LX – ⓜ *Green Park –* ✆ *(020)*   Plan: **H4**
74992211 – www.francoslondon.com – Closed Sunday and bank holidays
Menu £ 26 – Carte £ 30/60 – *(booking essential)*

• Italian • Traditional décor • Romantic •

Open from breakfast until late, with a café at the front leading into a smart,
clubby restaurant. The menu covers all parts of Italy and includes a popular
grill section and plenty of classics.

XX **Avenue** 🐜 🕭 ⚏ ⇄ 🗐

7-9 St James's St. ⊠ SW1A 1EE – ⓜ *Green Park*   Plan: **H4**
– ✆ *(020) 7321 2111 – www.avenue-restaurant.co.uk – Closed Sunday
dinner and bank holidays*
Menu £ 25 (weekdays) – Carte dinner £ 32/49

• Modern cuisine • Elegant •

Avenue has gone all American, with a smart look from Russell Sage and a contemporary menu inspired by what's cooking in Manhattan. Wine is also made
more of a feature; and, of course, the cocktails at the long, lively bar are great.

XX **Al Duca** ⚏ 🗐

4-5 Duke of York St ⊠ SW1Y 6LA – ⓜ *Piccadilly Circus*   Plan: **H4**
– ✆ *(020) 7839 3090 – www.alduca-restaurant.co.uk – Closed Easter, 25-
26 December, 1 January, Sunday and bank holidays*
Menu £ 17/30

• Italian • Friendly •

Cooking which focuses on flavour continues to draw in the regulars at this
warm and spirited Italian restaurant. Prices are keen when one considers the
central location and service is brisk and confident.

UNITED KINGDOM - LONDON

XX **Quaglino's**   [AC] ⇄ 🖰

16 Bury St ⊠ *SW1Y 6AJ* – **Ⓜ** *Green Park* – 𝒞 *(020)*   Plan: **H4**
79306767 – *www.quaglinos-restaurant.co.uk*
– Closed Easter Monday and Sunday dinner
Menu £ 20 (weekdays)/30 – Carte £ 36/66
• **Modern cuisine** • **Design** •

An updated look, a new bar and live music have added sultriness and energy to
this vast, glamorous and colourful restaurant. The kitchen specialises in contemporary brasserie-style food.

XX **Brumus** – Haymarket Hotel   & [AC] 🖰 🍽

1 Suffolk Pl ⊠ *SW1Y 4HX* – **Ⓜ** *Piccadilly Circus*   Plan: **I4**
– 𝒞 *(020) 74704000* – *www.haymarkethotel.com*
Menu £ 20 – Carte £ 25/61
• **Modern cuisine** • **Fashionable** • **Romantic** •

Pre-theatre dining is an altogether less frenzied activity when you can actually
see the theatre from your table. This is a modern, elegant space with switched-
on staff. Stick to the good value set menu or the 'dish of the day'.

X **Portrait**   ⇐ [AC] 🖰

National Portrait Gallery (3rd floor), St Martin's Pl.   Plan: **I3**
⊠ *WC2H 0HE* – **Ⓜ** *Charing Cross* – 𝒞 *(020) 73122490*
– *www.npg.org.uk/portraitrestaurant* – *Closed 24-26 December*
Menu £ 27 – Carte £ 34/49 – *(lunch only and dinner Thursday-Saturday)*
(booking essential)
• **Modern cuisine** • **Design** •

Set on the top floor of National Portrait Gallery with rooftop local landmark views: a
charming spot to dine or enjoy breakfast or afternoon tea. Carefully prepared
modern European dishes; good value pre-theatre and weekend set menus.

X **Chop Shop**   & [AC] 🖰

66 Haymarket ⊠ *SW1Y 4RF* – **Ⓜ** *Piccadilly Circus*   Plan: **I3**
– 𝒞 *(020) 7842 8501* – *www.chopshopuk.com*
Menu £ 19/35 – Carte £ 24/41
• **Meats and grills** • **Simple** • **Friendly** •

Spread over two floors and with an ersatz-industrial look, this lively spot could
be in Manhattan's Meatpacking district. Start with a cocktail, then order 'jars',
'crocks' or 'planks' of mousses, meatballs and cheeses; then it's the main event
– great steaks and chops.

X **Shoryu**   [AC]

9 Regent St. ⊠ *SW1Y 4LR* – **Ⓜ** *Piccadilly Circus*   Plan: **I4**
– *www.shoryuramen.com* – *Closed 25 December and 1 January*
Carte £ 20/40 – *(bookings not accepted)*
• **Japanese** • **Simple** •

Owned by the Japan Centre opposite and specialising in Hakata tonkotsu
ramen. The base is a milky broth made from pork bones to which is added
hosomen noodles, egg and assorted toppings. Its restorative powers are worth
queuing for. There are a two larger branches in Soho.

STRAND – COVENT GARDEN – LAMBETH   **PLAN III**

STRAND AND COVENT GARDEN

🏨 **Savoy**   🔱 🖾 🔲 & [AC] 🛁 🍽

Strand ⊠ *WC2R 0EU* – **Ⓜ** *Charing Cross* – 𝒞 *(020)*   Plan: **J3**
78364343 – *www.fairmont.com/savoy*
267 rm – 🛏£ 420/1500 🛏🛏£ 420/1500 – � £ 35 – 45 suites
• **Grand Luxury** • **Art déco** • **Elegant** •

A legendary hotel whose luxurious bedrooms and stunning suites come in Edwardian or art deco styles; many also offer a river view. Have tea in the Thames Foyer,
the hotel's heart, or drinks in the famous American Bar or the moodier Beaufort Bar.
Dine in the famous Savoy Grill or in Kaspar's, an informal seafood bar and grill.

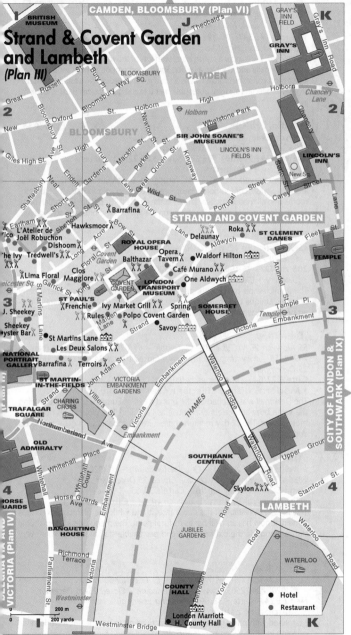

Strand & Covent Garden and Lambeth
(Plan III)

BRITISH MUSEUM

Theobald's

GRAY'S INN FIELD

GRAY'S INN

Russell St.

Bury Pl.

BLOOMSBURY SQ.

CAMDEN

Holborn

Chancery Lane

Great

New

Oxford St.

Bloomsbury Way

Holborn

High

Holborn

Whetstone Park

Chancery

BLOOMSBURY

High

Newton St.

Macklin St.

Parker St.

SIR JOHN SOANE'S MUSEUM

LINCOLN'S INN FIELDS

LINCOLN'S INN

Giles High St.

Shaftesbury

Neal

Endell

Gardens

Drury

Lane

Great Queen St.

Kingsway

Wild St.

New Sq.

Street

Carey

Street

Shorts

St.

Shelton

Bow

St.

Barrafina

Drury

Lane

Portugal

STRAND AND COVENT GARDEN

Fleet

St.

Earlham

L'Atelier de Joël Robuchon

ico

Hawksmoor

Acre

Floral

Roka

Delaunay

Aldwych

ST CLEMENT DANES

TEMPLE

he Ivy

Tredwell's

Dishoom

Long

ROYAL OPERA HOUSE

Covent Garden

Opera

Balthazar

Tavern

Waldorf Hilton

Lima Floral

Clos Maggiore

COVENT GARDEN

Café Murano

One Aldwych

Arundel

elcester Sq.

Garrick St.

King

ST PAUL'S

LONDON TRANSPORT MUSEUM

Spring

SOMERSET HOUSE

Temple Pl.

Temple

J. Sheekey

Frenchie

Ivy Market Grill

Rules

Maiden Lane

Polpo Covent Garden

Strand

Savoy

Victoria

Embankment

Sheekey Oyster Bar

St Martins Lane

Les Deux Salons

NATIONAL PORTRAIT GALLERY

Barrafina

Terroirs

ST MARTIN-IN-THE-FIELDS

John Adam St.

VICTORIA EMBANKMENT GARDENS

Embankment

THAMES

CITY OF LONDON & SOUTHWARK (Plan IX)

Strand

Villiers St.

CHARING CROSS

TRAFALGAR SQUARE

Northumberland

Ave.

Victoria

Embankment

OLD ADMIRALTY

Whitehall

Place

SOUTHBANK CENTRE

Upper Grour

Stamford St.

HORSE GUARDS

Whitehall

Whitehall Court

Horse Guards Ave.

Embankment

Skylon

Waterloo

Road

LAMBETH

BANQUETING HOUSE

Richmond Terrace

Victoria

JUBILEE GARDENS

Road

WATERLOO

Waterloo

Road

Parliament St.

Westminster

Belvedere

COUNTY HALL

York

London Marriott H. County Hall

Westminster Bridge

● Hotel
● Restaurant

0   200 m
    200 yards

VICTORIA (Plan IV)

One Aldwych
令 ℔ ⍟ ☐ � ℀ ⅏ **P**

1 Aldwych ⊠ WC2B 4BZ – **Ⓜ** Temple – *ℰ* (020)   Plan: **J3**
73001000 – www.onealdwych.com
105 rm – †£ 387/770 ††£ 387/770 – ☲ £ 19 – 12 suites
• Grand Luxury • Modern •
Former 19C bank, now a stylish hotel with lots of artwork; the lobby changes its
look seasonally and doubles as a bar. Stylish, contemporary bedrooms with the
latest mod cons; the deluxe rooms and suites are particularly desirable. Impressive leisure facilities. Light, accessible menu at Indigo; modern Basque cooking
in Eneko.

Waldorf Hilton
令 ℔ ⍟ ☐ � ℀ ⅏

Aldwych ⊠ WC2B 4DD – **Ⓜ** Temple – *ℰ* (020)   Plan: **J3**
7836 2400 – www.hilton.co.uk/waldorf
298 rm – †£ 219/599 ††£ 229/609 – ☲ £ 22 – 12 suites
• Historic • Elegant •
Impressive curved and columned façade: an Edwardian landmark in a great
location. Stylish, contemporary bedrooms in calming colours have superb bathrooms and all mod cons. Tea dances in the Grade II listed Palm Court Ballroom.
Stylish 'Homage' is popular for afternoon tea and relaxed brasserie style dining.

St Martins Lane
令 ℔ ℀ ⅏ ⌂

45 St Martin's Ln ⊠ WC2N 3HX – **Ⓜ** Charing Cross
– *ℰ* (020) 7300 5500 – www.morganshotelgroup.com   Plan: **I3**
206 rm ☲ – †£ 199/500 ††£ 199/500 – 2 suites
• Luxury • Design •
The unmistakable hand of Philippe Starck is evident at this most contemporary
of hotels. Unique and stylish, from the starkly modern lobby to the state-of-the-
art bedrooms, which come in a blizzard of white.

Delaunay
℀ ⇔

55 Aldwych ⊠ WC2B 4BB – **Ⓜ** Temple – *ℰ* (020)   Plan: **J3**
74998558 – www.thedelaunay.com – Closed dinner 24 December and
25 December
Carte £ 27/64 – (booking essential)
• Modern cuisine • Elegant • Fashionable •
The Delaunay was inspired by the grand cafés of Europe but, despite sharing
the same buzz and celebrity clientele as its sibling The Wolseley, is not just a
mere replica. The all-day menu is more mittel-European, with great schnitzels
and wieners.

The Ivy
℀ ⇔ ⅋

9 West St ⊠ WC2H 9NE – **Ⓜ** Leicester Square – *ℰ* (020)   Plan: **I3**
7836 4751 – www.the-ivy.co.uk – Closed 25 December
Menu £ 23 (weekday lunch) – Carte £ 30/65
• Traditional British • Fashionable • Classic décor •
This landmark restaurant has had a facelift and while the glamorous clientele
remain, it now has an oval bar as its focal point. The menu offers international
dishes alongside the old favourites and personable staff anticipate your every
need.

J.Sheekey
⍟ ℀

28-32 St Martin's Ct, ⊠ WC2N 4AL – **Ⓜ** Leicester Square   Plan: **I3**
– *ℰ* (020) 7240 2565 – www.j-sheekey.co.uk – Closed 25-26 December
Menu £ 24 – Carte £ 33/69 – (booking essential)
• Seafood • Fashionable •
Festooned with photographs of actors and linked to the theatrical world since
opening in 1890. Wood panels and alcove tables add famed intimacy. Accom-
plished seafood cooking.

XX **Spring**   ♿ 🅰🅺 ⟺

New Wing, Somerset House, Strand (Entrance on   Plan: **J3**
Lancaster Pl) ✉ *WC2R 1LA –* Ⓜ *Temple –* ℰ *(020) 3011 0115*
– www.springrestaurant.co.uk – Closed Sunday dinner
Menu £ 28/32 – Carte £ 40/67 – *(booking advisable)*
• **Italian** • **Fashionable** • **Elegant** •

Spring occupies the 'new wing' of Somerset House that for many years was
inhabited by the Inland Revenue. It's a bright, feminine space under the aegis
of chef Skye Gyngell. Her cooking is Italian-influenced and ingredient-led.

XX **Rules**   🅰🅺 ⟺

35 Maiden Ln ✉ *WC2E 7LB –* Ⓜ *Leicester Square*   Plan: **J3**
– ℰ *(020) 78365314 – www.rules.co.uk – Closed 25-26 December*
Carte £ 36/71 – *(booking essential)*
• **Traditional British** • **Traditional décor** • **Elegant** •

London's oldest restaurant boasts a fine collection of antique cartoons, draw-
ings and paintings. Tradition continues in the menu, specialising in game from
its own estate.

XX **Clos Maggiore**   🏵 🅰🅺 ⟺ 🕸

33 King St ✉ *WC2E 8JD –* Ⓜ *Leicester Square –* ℰ *(020)*   Plan: **J3**
7379 9696 – www.closmaggiore.com – Closed 24-25 December
Menu £ 23 (weekday lunch)/38 – Carte £ 37/66
• **French** • **Classic décor** • **Romantic** •

One of London's most romantic restaurants – but be sure to ask for the enchanting conservatory with its retractable roof. The sophisticated French cooking is
joined by a wine list of great depth. Good value and very popular pre/post
theatre menus.

XX **Roka**   🅰🅺

71 Aldwych ✉ *WC2B 4HN –* Ⓜ *Temple –* ℰ *(020)*   Plan: **J3**
7294 7636 – www.rokarestaurant.com – Closed 25 December
Menu £ 27 – Carte £ 32/58
• **Japanese** • **Fashionable** • **Design** •

This is the fourth and largest Roka in the group. It shares the same stylish look,
efficient service and modern Japanese, although there are some dishes
unique to this branch. Consider the tasting menu for a good all-around experience.

XX **Les Deux Salons**   ♿ 🅰🅺 ⟺ 🕸

40-42 William IV St ✉ *WC2N 4DD –* Ⓜ *Charing Cross*   Plan: **I3**
– ℰ *(020) 7420 2050 – www.lesdeuxsalons.co.uk – Closed 25-26 December
and 1 January*
Menu £ 17 (early dinner) – Carte £ 26/70
• **French** • **Bistro** • **Design** •

Sir Terence Conran took over this handily-placed site in 2015 and injected a tidy
sum into its redesign. On the ground floor is a café, a bistro serving all the
French classics, a bar and an épicerie. Upstairs is a more formal restaurant.

XX **Cafe Murano**   🅰🅺 🕸

36 Tavistock St ✉ *WC2E 7PB –* Ⓜ *Charing Cross*   Plan: **J3**
– ℰ *(020) 7240 3654 – www.cafemurano.co.uk – Closed Sunday dinner*
Menu £ 17 – Carte £ 31/49
• **Italian** • **Neighbourhood** • **Fashionable** •

The second Café Murano is in the heart of Covent Garden, in a space much larger than the St James's original; head for the smart marble-topped counter at
the back. Appealing menu of Northern Italian dishes cooked with care and respect.

XX **Ivy Market Grill** 🛜 ⴵ 🅺 ⟷ 🕸

1 Henrietta St ⌂ WC2E 8PS – Ⓜ Covent Garden   Plan: **J3**
– ☏ (020) 3301 0200 – www.theivymarketgrill.com
Menu £ 21 (early dinner) – Carte £ 25/54
• Traditional British • Design • Brasserie •
Mere mortals can now experience a little of that Ivy glamour by eating here at
the first of their diffusion line. Breakfast, a menu of largely British classics and
afternoon tea keep it busy all day. There's another branch in Chelsea.

XX **Balthazar** ⴵ 🅺 ⟷ 🕸

4-6 Russell St. ⌂ WC2B 5HZ – Ⓜ Covent Garden   Plan: **J3**
– ☏ (020) 3301 1155 – www.balthazarlondon.com – Closed 25 December
Menu £ 18 (weekday lunch) – Carte £ 27/56 – (booking essential)
• French • Brasserie • Classic décor •
Those who know the original Balthazar in Manhattan's SoHo district will find the
London version of this classic brasserie uncannily familiar in looks, vibe and
food. The Franglais menu keeps it simple and the cocktails are great.

X **L'Atelier de Joël Robuchon** 🅺 🕸
❀❀

13-15 West St. ⌂ WC2H 9NE – Ⓜ Leicester Square   Plan: **I3**
– ☏ (020) 70108600 – www.joelrobuchon.co.uk – Closed 25-26 December,
1 January and August bank holiday Monday
Menu £ 38 (lunch and early dinner) – Carte £ 40/90
• French • Elegant • Contemporary décor •
Creative, skilled and occasionally playful cooking; dishes may look delicate but
pack a punch. Ground floor 'Atelier' comes with counter seating and chefs on
view. More structured 'La Cuisine' upstairs and a cool bar above that.
→ Egg cocotte carbonara style with black truffle. Pyrenean milk-fed lamb
cutlets with fresh thyme. Praline custard with hazelnut and white coffee
ice cream.

X **Barrafina** 🅺 ⟷

10 Adelaide St ⌂ WC2N 4HZ – Ⓜ Charing Cross   Plan: **I3**
– ☏ (020) 7440 1456 – www.barrafina.co.uk – Closed Christmas, New Year
and bank holidays
Carte £ 14/34 – (bookings not accepted)
• Spanish • Tapas bar • Trendy •
The second Barrafina is not just brighter than the Soho original – it's bigger too,
so you can wait inside with a drink for counter seats to become available. Try
more unusual tapas like ortiguillas, frit Mallorquin or the succulent meats.

X **Barrafina** 🛜 🅺 ⟷

43 Drury Ln ⌂ WC2B 5AJ – Ⓜ Covent Garden – ☏ (020)   Plan: **J3**
7440 1456 – www.barrafina.co.uk – Closed bank holidays
Carte £ 24/47 – (bookings not accepted)
• Spanish • Tapas bar • Simple •
The third of the Barrafinas is tucked away at the far end of Covent Garden; arrive
early or prepare to queue. Fresh, vibrantly flavoured fish and shellfish dishes are
a real highlight; tortillas y huevos also feature.

X **J. Sheekey Oyster Bar** 🕸

33-34 St Martin's Ct. ⌂ WC2 4AL – Ⓜ Leicester Square   Plan: **I3**
– ☏ (020) 72402565 – www.j-sheekey.co.uk – Closed 25-26 December
Carte £ 25/41
• Seafood • Intimate •
An addendum to J. Sheekey restaurant. Sit at the bar to watch the chefs prepare
the same quality seafood as next door but at slightly lower prices; fish pie and
fruits de mer are the popular choices. Open all day.

X **Frenchie**   ♿ 🅰️🅲

16 Henrietta St ✉ WC2E 8QH – Ⓜ Covent Garden   Plan: J3
– ℰ (020) 7836 4422 – www.frenchiecoventgarden.com – Closed 25-26 December and 1 January
Menu £ 28 *(weekday lunch)* – Carte £ 33/47 *– (booking advisable)*
· Modern cuisine · Bistro · Design ·
A well-run modern-day bistro – younger sister to the Paris original, which shares the name given to chef-owner Greg Marchand when he was head chef at Fifteen. The adventurous, ambitious cooking is informed by his extensive travels.

X **Hawksmoor**   🕸 🅰️🅲 ⇦ 🕸

11 Langley St ✉ WC2H 9JG – Ⓜ Covent Garden   Plan: I3
– ℰ (020) 7420 9390 – www.thehawksmoor.com – Closed 24-26 December
Menu £ 25 *(weekdays)*/28 – Carte £ 25/60
· Meats and grills · Rustic · Brasserie ·
Steaks from Longhorn cattle lovingly reared in North Yorkshire and dry-aged for at least 35 days are the stars of the show. Atmospheric, bustling basement restaurant in former brewery cellars.

X **Tredwell's**   🕸 ♿ 🅰️🅲 🕸

4a Upper St Martin's Ln ✉ WC2H 9EF   Plan: I3
– Ⓜ Leicester Square – ℰ (020) 3764 0840 – www.tredwells.com – Closed 25-26 December, 1 January and Easter Monday
Menu £ 25 *(lunch and early dinner)* – Carte £ 26/51
· Modern British · Brasserie · Fashionable ·
A modern brasserie from Marcus Wareing, with an art deco feel. Cooking is best described as modern English; dishes show a degree of refinement, and a commendable amount of thought has gone into addressing allergen issues.

X **Lima Floral**   🅰️🅲 ⇦ 🕸

14 Garrick St ✉ WC2E 9BJ – Ⓜ Leicester Square   Plan: I3
– ℰ (020) 7240 5778 – www.limalondongroup.com/floral – Closed 26-27 December, 2 January and bank holiday Mondays
Menu £ 18 *(weekdays)* – Carte £ 32/48
· Peruvian · Fashionable · Friendly ·
This second Lima branch has a light and airy feel by day and a cosy, candlelit vibe in the evening; regional Peruvian dishes are served alongside the more popular causa and ceviche. Basement Pisco Bar for Peruvian tapas and Pisco sours.

X   **Vico**   ♿ 🅰️🅲
🙂

1 Cambridge Circus ✉ WC2H 8PA – Ⓜ Leicester Square   Plan: I3
– ℰ (020) 7379 0303 – www.eatvico.com – Closed 25 December and 1 January
Carte £ 23/40
· Italian · Bistro · Simple ·
A relaxed modern-day trattoria with a fountain at its centre and an authentic Gelupo ice cream bar. Authentic Italian dishes are simply cooked, super-fresh and seasonal; generous of portion and vibrant in colour and flavour.

X   **Opera Tavern**   🕸 🅰️🅲
🙂

23 Catherine St. ✉ WC2B 5JS – Ⓜ Covent Garden – ℰ (020)   Plan: J3
7836 3680 – www.operatavern.co.uk – Closed 25 December and 1 January
Carte £ 14/25
· Mediterranean cuisine · Tapas bar · Wine bar ·
Shares the same appealing concept of small plates of Spanish and Italian delicacies as its sisters, Salt Yard and Dehesa. All done in a smartly converted old boozer which dates from 1879; ground floor bar and upstairs dining room.

X **Polpo Covent Garden**   🅰️🅲

6 Maiden Ln. ✉ WC2E 7NA – Ⓜ Leicester Square   Plan: J3
– ℰ (020) 7836 8448 – www.polpo.co.uk – Closed 25-26 December
Carte £ 12/21 *– (bookings not accepted at dinner)*
· Italian · Simple · Trendy ·
First Soho, then Covent Garden got a fun Venetian bacaro. The small plates are surprisingly filling, with delights such as pizzette of white anchovy vying with fennel and almond salad; fritto misto competing with spaghettini and meatballs.

✕ Dishoom 🖼️

Plan: I3

12 Upper St Martin's Ln ✉ *WC2H 9FB*
– Ⓜ *Leicester Square* – ✆ *(020) 7420 9320* – *www.dishoom.com* – *Closed 24 December dinner, 25-26 December and 1-2 January*
Carte £ 13/30 – *(booking advisable)*
• **Indian** • **Exotic** • **Trendy** •
A facsimile of a Bombay café, of the sort opened by Persian immigrants in the early 20C. Try baked roti rolls with chai, vada pav (Bombay's version of the chip butty), a curry or grilled meats. There's another branch in Shoreditch.

✕ Terroirs 🍷 🖼️

Plan: J3

5 William IV St ✉ *WC2N 4DW* – Ⓜ *Charing Cross*
– ✆ *(020) 70360660* – *www.terroirswinebar.com* – *Closed 25-26 December, 1 January, Sunday and bank holidays*
Carte £ 24/37
• **Mediterranean cuisine** • **Wine bar** • **Simple** •
Flavoursome French cooking, with extra Italian and Spanish influences and a thoughtfully compiled wine list. Eat in the lively ground floor bistro/wine bar or in the more intimate cellar, where they also offer some sharing dishes like rib of beef for two.

LAMBETH

🏨 London Marriott H. County Hall ✿ ≤ �'s 🖼️

Plan: J5

Westminster Bridge Rd ✉ *SE1 7PB* – Ⓜ *Westminster*
– ✆ *(020) 79285200* – *www.marriott.co.uk/lonch*
200 rm – ✝£ 420/600 ✝✝£ 600/900 – ☲ £ 22 – 5 suites
• **Business** • **Chain** • **Modern** •
Occupying the historic County Hall building on the banks of the River Thames. Bedrooms are spacious, stylish and modern; many enjoy river and Parliament outlooks. Impressive leisure facilities. World famous views too from wood-panelled Gillray's, which specialises in steaks.

✕✕✕ Skylon 🍷 ≤ 🖼️

Plan: J4

1 Southbank Centre, Belvedere Rd ✉ *SE1 8XX*
– Ⓜ *Waterloo* – ✆ *(020) 76547800* – *www.skylon-restaurant.co.uk*
– *Closed 25 December*
Menu £ 20/28 – Carte £ 27/38
• **Modern cuisine** • **Design** • **Trendy** •
Ask for a window table here at the Royal Festival Hall. Informal grill-style operation on one side, a more formal and expensive restaurant on the other, with a busy cocktail bar in the middle.

BELGRAVIA – VICTORIA   PLAN IV

BELGRAVIA

🏨 Berkeley �'s 🖼️

Plan: G4

Wilton Pl ✉ *SW1X 7RL* – Ⓜ *Knightsbridge* – ✆ *(020) 72356000* – *www.the-berkeley.co.uk*
210 rm – ✝£ 540/750 ✝✝£ 600/870 – ☲ £ 32 – 28 suites
• **Grand Luxury** • **Business** • **Elegant** •
A discreet and very comfortable hotel with an impressive rooftop pool. Opulently decorated, immaculately kept bedrooms; several of the suites have their own balcony. Relax over afternoon tea in the gilded, panelled Collins Room or have a drink in the ice cool Blue Bar.
❀❀ **Marcus** – See restaurant listing

The Lanesborough

Hyde Park Corner ✉ *SW1X 7TA* Plan: **G5**
– Ⓜ Hyde Park Corner – ☎ (020) 72595599
– www.lanesborough.com
93 rm – †£ 500/740 ††£ 500/740 – ☕ £ 38 – 30 suites
• Grand Luxury • Historic • Elegant •
A multi-million pound refurbishment has restored this hotel's Regency splendour; its elegant Georgian-style bedrooms offering bespoke furniture, beautiful fabrics, tablet technologies and 24 hour butler service. Opulent Céleste serves rich French cooking under its domed glass roof.
✿ **Céleste** – See restaurant listing

Halkin

5 Halkin St ✉ *SW1X 7DJ – Ⓜ Hyde Park Corner* Plan: **G5**
– ☎ (020) 73331000
– www.comohotels.com/thehalkin
41 rm – †£ 300/420 ††£ 400/500 – ☕ £ 30 – 6 suites
• Luxury • Townhouse • Elegant •
Opened in 1991 as one of London's first boutique hotels and still looking sharp today. Thoughtfully conceived bedrooms with silk walls and marbled bathrooms; everything at the touch of a button. Abundant Armani-clad staff. Small, discreet bar.
✿ **Ametsa** – See restaurant listing

The Wellesley

11 Knightsbridge ✉ *SW1X 7LY – Ⓜ Hyde Park Corner* Plan: **G4**
– ☎ (020) 7235 3535
– www.thewellesley.co.uk
36 rm – †£ 350/599 ††£ 350/599 – ☕ £ 34 – 14 suites
• Townhouse • Luxury • Art déco •
Stylish, elegant townhouse inspired by the jazz age, on the site of the famous Pizza on the Park. Impressive cigar lounge and bar with a super selection of whiskies and cognacs. Smart bedrooms have full butler service; those facing Hyde Park the most prized. Modern Italian food in the discreet restaurant.

Hari

20 Chesham Pl ✉ *SW1X 8HQ – Ⓜ Knightsbridge* Plan: **G5**
– ☎ (020) 7858 0100 – www.thehari.com
85 rm – †£ 359/599 ††£ 360/660 – ☕ £ 20
• Business • Townhouse • Modern •
An elegant and stylish boutique-style hotel with a relaxed atmosphere and a hint of bohemia. Uncluttered, decently proportioned bedrooms come with oak flooring and lovely marble bathrooms. Italian dishes are served in Pont St restaurant.

XXXX
✿✿

Marcus – Berkeley Hotel

Wilton Pl ✉ *SW1X 7RL – Ⓜ Knightsbridge* Plan: **G4**
– ☎ (020) 72351200 – www.marcus-wareing.com
– Closed Sunday
Menu £ 49/85
• Modern cuisine • Elegant • Intimate •
Marcus Wareing's flagship is elegant, stylish and eminently comfortable, with a relaxed feel and engaging staff who get the tone of the service just right. The menu is flexible and dishes come with a refreshing lack of complication; relying on excellent ingredients and accurate techniques to deliver well-defined flavours.
➜ Salmon with langoustine, buttermilk and quince. Herdwick lamb with onion and anchovy. Pumpkin custard, maple syrup and passion fruit.

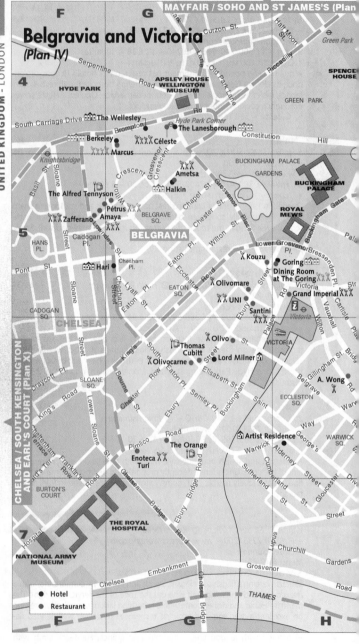

Belgravia and Victoria
(Plan IV)

UNITED KINGDOM - LONDON

CHELSEA / SOUTH KENSINGTON AND EARL'S COURT (Plan X)

F
G
H

4

HYDE PARK

Serpentine

Road

APSLEY HOUSE WELLINGTON MUSEUM

Curzon St.

Half Moon St.

Green Park

Piccadilly

SPENCE HOUSE

GREEN PARK

South Carriage Drive **The Wellesley**

Hyde Park Corner

The Lanesborough

Constitution

Hill

Knightsbridge

Berkeley

XXX **Marcus**

Brompton

XXXX **Céleste**

Grosvenor Crescent

BUCKINGHAM PALACE

GARDENS

BUCKINGHAM PALACE

5

Basil St.

Sloane St.

Crescent

The Alfred Tennyson

XXX **Zafferano**

Pétrus XXX
Amaya

XXX **Ametsa**

Halkin

BELGRAVE SQ.

BELGRAVIA

Chapel St.

Chester St.

Wilton St.

Grosvenor Place

ROYAL MEWS

Buckingham Gate

Pala

HANS PL.

Pont St.

Cadogan Pl.

Lowndes St.

Chesham Pl.

Hari

Lower Grosvenor Pl.

Bressenden Pl.

X **Kouzu**

Str

CADOGAN SQ.

CHELSEA

Chesham Street

Lyall Pl.

Eaton St.

Eaton Pl.

EATON SQ.

Eccleston

Road

X **Olivomare**

XX **UNI**

Goring **Dining Room at The Goring** XXX

Victoria

Grand Imperial XXX

Vauxhall

Victoria

Carlisle

Pla

7

SLOANE SQ.

King's Road

Lower Sloane St.

Bourne St.

Chester St.

Olivocarne

Thomas Cubitt

X **Olivo**

Lord Milner

Elisabeth St.

South Eaton Pl.

Semley Pl.

Ebury

Buckingham

Palace

Road

Saint

George's

Santini XXX

VICTORIA

Belgrave

A. Wong

Rd

ECCLESTON SQ.

WARWICK SQ.

Warw

Rd

Cheltenham

Franklin's

Terrace

Row

Pimlico

Road

The Orange

Enoteca XX
Turi

Ebury Bridge Road

Artist Residence

Warwick

Alderney

Way

Cumberland

Sutherland

St.

Gloucester

Street

Drive

BURTON'S COURT

THE ROYAL HOSPITAL

NATIONAL ARMY MUSEUM

Hospital

Chelsea

Embankment

Chelsea Bridge Road

Ebury Bridge Road

Lupus

Churchill

Grosvenor

Gardens

Road

THAMES

Chelsea Bridge

● Hotel
● Restaurant

F
G
H

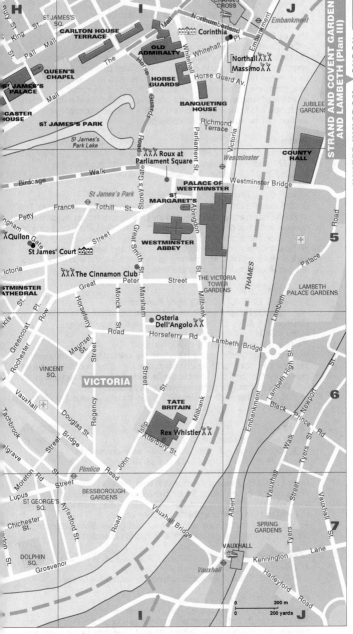

CHARING CROSS

Corinthia

Northall ✗✗✗
Massimo ✗✗

CARLTON HOUSE TERRACE

ST JAMES'S SQ.

King St.

Pall Mall

The Mall

Northumberland Pl.

Embankment

Whitehall

OLD ADMIRALTY

Horse Guards

HORSE GUARDS

Horse Guard Av.

JUBILEE GARDENS

QUEEN'S CHAPEL

ST JAMES'S PALACE

BANQUETING HOUSE

CASTER HOUSE

ST JAMES'S PARK

St James's Park Lake

Richmond Terrace

Victoria

COUNTY HALL

✗✗✗ Roux at Parliament Square

Westminster

Birdcage

Walk

Parliament St.

Westminster Bridge

PALACE OF WESTMINSTER

ST MARGARET'S

Westminster

Petty

France

Tothill St.

St James's Park

Storey's Gate

Abingdon

✗ Quilon

Gate

St James' Court

Great Smith St.

WESTMINSTER ABBEY

Great

✗✗✗ The Cinnamon Club

Peter

Street

THE VICTORIA TOWER GARDENS

St.

LAMBETH PALACE GARDENS

STMINSTER ATHEDRAL

St.

Horseferry

Monck

Marsham

Millbank

THAMES

Palace

Lambeth

Francis

Greencoat

Row

Rochester

Maunsel St.

Street

St. Road

Osteria Dell'Angolo ✗✗

Horseferry Rd

Lambeth Bridge

Lambeth High St.

VINCENT SQ.

VICTORIA

Street

Black

Newport Rd

Prince

Vauxhall

Douglas St.

Regency

Islip St.

TATE BRITAIN

Millbank

Embankment

Walk

Tyers St.

Tachbrook

Bridge

Rex Whistler ✗✗

Vauxhall

elgrave

Moreton Rd

Street

Atterbury St.

John

Lupus

ST GEORGE'S SQ.

Pimlico

Road

Street

Vauxhall

Road

SPRING GARDENS

Chichester St.

Aylesford St.

Road

Vauxhall Bridge

Albert

Tyers

Lane

Vauxhall St.

DOLPHIN SQ.

Grosvenor

BESSBOROUGH GARDENS

VAUXHALL

Kennington

Vauxhall

Harleyford Road

0   200 m
0   200 yards

XxXX
ස
Céleste – The Lanesborough Hotel   ⅃ ㎢ ⅃⊘ 🚗
Hyde Park Corner ⊠ SW1X 7TA – ⓜ Hyde Park Corner   Plan: **G5**
– ℰ (020) 7259 5599 – www.lanesborough.com
Menu £ 29 (lunch) – Carte £ 42/88
· **Creative French** · **Elegant** · **Luxury** ·
The Lanesborough Hotel's restaurant is dressed in opulent Regency clothes; its vast chandeliers, Wedgwood blue friezes and fluted columns giving it a luxurious, formal feel. Classic French cuisine is delivered in an original, modern style; the richness of the dishes reflects the opulence of the décor.
→ Pan-fried langoustine with wild grains and basil-infused broth. Pigeon, petits pois à la Française and potato soufflé. Guanaja chocolate with caramelised cashew nut praline and coffee bean ice cream.

XxX
ස
Pétrus   🍸 ⅃ ㎢ ⇔ ⅃⊘
1 Kinnerton St ⊠ SW1X 8EA – ⓜ Knightsbridge   Plan: **G5**
– ℰ (020) 75921609 – www.gordonramsayrestaurants.com/petrus
– Closed 21-27 December, 1 January and Sunday
Menu £ 38/95
· **French** · **Elegant** · **Fashionable** ·
Gordon Ramsay's Belgravia restaurant is a sophisticated and elegant affair. The service is discreet and professional, and the cooking is rooted in classical techniques but isn't afraid of using influences from further afield. The superb wine list has Château Pétrus going back to 1928.
→ Seared Orkney scallop with braised kombu and bacon & egg sabayon. Rack of Herdwick lamb with pomme purée, artichoke and wild garlic. Coconut parfait with dark chocolate and lime.

XxX
ස
Ametsa – Halkin Hotel   ㎢
5 Halkin St ⊠ SW1X 7DJ – ⓜ Hyde Park Corner   Plan: **G5**
– ℰ (020) 73331234 – www.comohotels.com/thehalkin – Closed 24-
26 December, lunch 31 December, Sunday and lunch Monday
Menu £ 28/110 – Carte £ 58/85
· **Creative** · **Elegant** · **Fashionable** ·
Whilst the father and daughter team from the celebrated Arzak restaurant in San Sebastián are behind it, Ametsa has its own style. Most ingredients are sourced from within the British Isles but the flavours, combinations and colours are typically Basque and the dishes are wonderfully vibrant.
→ Scallops 'at home'. Beef fillet with green tomato. Orange French toast and spinach.

XxX
ස
Amaya   ㎢ ⇔ ⅃⊘
Halkin Arcade, 19 Motcomb St ⊠ SW1X 8JT   Plan: **F5**
– ⓜ Knightsbridge – ℰ (020) 78231166 – www.amaya.biz
Menu £ 24 (weekday lunch) – Carte £ 34/70
· **Indian** · **Design** · **Minimalist** ·
Order a selection of small dishes from the tawa, tandoor or sigri grill and finish with a curry or biryani. Dishes like lamb chops are aromatic and satisfying and the cooking is skilled and consistent. This busy Indian restaurant is bright, colourful and lively; ask for a table by the open kitchen.
→ Flash-grilled rock oysters with coconut and ginger. Slow-roasted leg of baby lamb, cumin and garam masala. 'Passion in chocolate'.

XxX
Zafferano   🍽 ㎢ ⇔
15 Lowndes St ⊠ SW1X 9EY – ⓜ Knightsbridge   Plan: **F5**
– ℰ (020) 72355800 – www.zafferanorestaurant.co.uk – Closed
25 December
Carte £ 36/79 – *(booking essential)*
· **Italian** · **Fashionable** · **Neighbourhood** ·
The immaculately coiffured regulars continue to support this ever-expanding, long-standing and capably run Italian restaurant. They come for the reassuringly familiar, if rather steeply priced dishes from all parts of Italy.

The Alfred Tennyson

10 Motcomb St ⊠ SW1X 8LA – Ⓜ Knightsbridge.   Plan: **G5**
*– ✆ (020) 77306074 – www.thealfredtennyson.co.uk – Closed
25 December*
Carte £ 29/50 – *(booking advisable)*
• **Modern British • Pub • Neighbourhood** •
A cosy, enthusiastically run pub with a busy first-come-first-served ground floor
and a more formal upstairs dining room. Classic dishes have light, modern touches; expect smoked mackerel, duck and venison alongside steaks, burgers and
pies.

VICTORIA

Corinthia

Whitehall Pl. ⊠ SW1A 2BD – Ⓜ Embankment – ✆ (020)   Plan: **J4**
7930 8181 – www.corinthia.com/london
294 rm – ✚£ 342/1140 ✚✚£ 342/1140 – ☲ £ 32 – 23 suites
• **Grand Luxury • Elegant • Contemporary** •
The restored Victorian splendour of this grand, luxurious hotel cannot fail to
impress. Tasteful and immaculately finished bedrooms are some of the largest
in town; suites come with butlers. The stunning spa is over four floors.
Northall • Massimo – See restaurant listing

Goring

15 Beeston Pl ⊠ SW1W 0JW – Ⓜ Victoria – ✆ (020)   Plan: **H5**
7396 9000 – www.thegoring.com
69 rm ☲ – ✚£ 335/615 ✚✚£ 380/710 – 8 suites
• **Luxury • Townhouse • Elegant** •
Under the stewardship of the founder's great grandson, this landmark hotel has
been restored and renovated while maintaining its traditional atmosphere and
pervading sense of Britishness. Expect first class service and immaculate, very
comfortable bedrooms, many of which overlook the garden.
❀ **Dining Room at The Goring** – See restaurant listing

St James' Court

45 Buckingham Gate ⊠ SW1E 6BS – Ⓜ St James's Park   Plan: **H5**
– ✆ (020) 7834 6655 – www.tajhotels.com/stjamescourt
318 rm – ✚£ 198/594 ✚✚£ 198/594 – ☲ £ 21 – 20 suites
• **Luxury • Classic** •
Built in 1897 as serviced accommodation for visiting aristocrats. Behind the
impressive Edwardian façade lies an equally elegant interior. The quietest
bedrooms overlook a courtyard. Relaxed, bright Bistro 51 comes with an international menu; Bank offers brasserie classics in a conservatory.
❀ **Quilon** – See restaurant listing

Artist Residence

52 Cambridge St ⊠ SW1V 4QQ – Ⓜ Victoria – ✆ (020)   Plan: **H6**
79318946 – www.artistresidencelondon.co.uk
10 rm – ✚£ 190/230 ✚✚£ 210/450 – ☲ £ 10
• **Townhouse • Personalised • Contemporary** •
A converted pub made into a comfortable, quirky townhouse hotel, with stylish
bedrooms featuring mini Smeg fridges, retro telephones, reclaimed furniture
and pop art. Cool bar and sitting room beneath the busy Cambridge Street Cafe.

Lord Milner

111 Ebury St ⊠ SW1W 9QU – Ⓜ Victoria – ✆ (020)   Plan: **G6**
78819880 – www.lordmilner.com
11 rm – ✚£ 80/145 ✚✚£ 110/275 – ☲ £ 14
• **Townhouse • Classic** •
A four storey terraced house, with individually decorated bedrooms, three with
four-poster beds and all with smart marble bathrooms. Garden Suite is the best
room; it has its own patio. Breakfast served in your bedroom.

XxX 🕸
Dining Room at The Goring – Goring Hotel   🍴 📶 🔼
15 Beeston Pl ✉ *SW1W 0JW* – Ⓜ *Victoria* – ✆ *(020)*   Plan: **H5**
73969000 – www.thegoring.com – Closed Saturday lunch
Menu £ 45/57
• **Traditional British** • **Elegant** • **Classic décor** •
A paean to all things British and the very model of discretion and decorum – the perfect spot for those who 'like things done properly' but without the stuffiness. The menu is an appealing mix of British classics and lighter, more modern dishes, all prepared with great skill and understanding.
➔ Broth of Cornish squid, plaice and red prawn with roast garlic and saffron. Fallow deer with parsnip, mushroom duxelle, glazed faggot and pine nut. Caramel cream with sea buckthorn jelly, mandarin sorbet and fresh orange.

XxX 🕸
Quilon – St James' Court Hotel   🔼 ✤ 🔟
41 Buckingham Gate ✉ *SW1E 6AF* – Ⓜ *St James's Park*   Plan: **H5**
– ✆ (020) 78211899 – www.quilon.co.uk – Closed 25 December
Menu £ 31/60 – Carte £ 34/67
• **Indian** • **Design** • **Elegant** •
A meal here will remind you how fresh, vibrant, colourful and healthy Indian food can be. Chef Sriram Aylur and his team focus on India's southwest coast, so the emphasis is on seafood and a lighter style of cooking. The room is stylish and comfortable and the service team, bright and enthusiastic.
➔ Lotus stem and colocasia chop with mango and mint. Braised lamb shank with freshly ground herbs. Creamy vermicelli kheer with rose ice cream.

XxX
Roux at Parliament Square   ♿ 🔼 ✤
Royal Institution of Chartered Surveyors, Parliament Sq.   Plan: **I5**
✉ *SW1P 3AD* – Ⓜ *Westminster* – ✆ *(020) 73343737*
– www.rouxatparliamentsquare.co.uk – Closed Saturday, Sunday and bank holidays
Menu £ 35 (weekday lunch)/59 – *(bookings advisable at lunch)*
• **Modern cuisine** • **Elegant** •
Light floods through the Georgian windows of this comfortable restaurant within the offices of the Royal Institute of Chartered Surveyors. Carefully crafted, elaborate and sophisticated cuisine, with some interesting flavour combinations.

XxX
Northall – Corinthia Hotel   ♿ 🔼 🕸
Whitehall Pl. ✉ *WC2N 5AE* – Ⓜ *Embankment* – ✆ *(020)*   Plan: **J4**
7321 3100 – www.thenorthall.co.uk
Menu £ 24/75 – Carte £ 26/73
• **Traditional British** • **Bistro** •
The Corinthia Hotel's British restaurant champions our indigenous produce, and its menu is an appealing document. It occupies two rooms: head for the more modern one with its bar and booths, which is less formal than the other section.

XxX
The Cinnamon Club   ♿ 🔼 ✤ 🔟
30-32 Great Smith St ✉ *SW1P 3BU* – Ⓜ *St James's Park*   Plan: **I5**
– ✆ (020) 7222 2555 – www.cinnamonclub.com – Closed bank holidays
Menu £ 26 (lunch) – Carte £ 31/68
• **Indian** • **Historic** • **Elegant** •
Locals and tourists, business people and politicians – this smart Indian restaurant housed in the listed former Westminster Library attracts them all. The fairly elaborate dishes arrive fully garnished and the spicing is quite subtle.

XXX **Santini** 🛜 AC 😇

29 Ebury St ⊠ SW1W 0NZ – Ⓜ Victoria – 𝒞 (020) Plan: **G5**
7730 4094 – www.santinirestaurant.com – Closed 23-26 December,
1 January and Easter
Carte £ 30/67
• Italian • Fashionable •

Santini has looked after its many immaculately coiffured regulars for over 30 years. The not inexpensive menu of classic Italian dishes is broadly Venetian in style; the daily specials, pasta dishes and desserts are the standout courses.

XXX **Grand Imperial** ♿ AC ⇔

Grosvenor Hotel, 101 Buckingham Palace Rd Plan: **H5**
⊠ SW1W 0SJ – Ⓜ Victoria – 𝒞 (020) 7821 8898
– www.grandimperiallondon.com – Closed 25-26 December
Menu £ 30/60 – Carte £ 20/71
• Chinese • Elegant •

Grand it most certainly is, as this elegant restaurant is in the Grosvenor Hotel's former ballroom. It specialises in Cantonese cuisine, particularly the version found in Hong Kong; steaming and frying are used to great effect.

XX **Massimo** – Corinthia Hotel ♿ AC ⇔

10 Northumberland Ave. ⊠ WC2N 5AE Plan: **J4**
– Ⓜ Embankment – 𝒞 (020) 73213156 – www.corinthia.com/london
– Closed Sunday
Menu £ 30 – Carte £ 28/57
• Italian • Elegant • Fashionable •

Opulent, visually impressive room with an oyster bar on one side. On offer are traditional dishes true to the regions of Italy; seafood dishes stand out. Impressive private dining room comes with its own chef.

XX **Enoteca Turi** 🦐 AC

87 Pimlico Rd ⊠ SW1W 8PU – Ⓜ Sloane Square Plan: **G6**
– 𝒞 (020) 7730 3663 – www.enotecaturi.com – Closed 25-26 December,
1 January, Sunday and bank holiday lunch
Menu £ 26 (lunch) – Carte £ 32/54
• Italian • Neighbourhood •

In 2016 Putney's loss was Pimlico's gain when, after 25 years, Guiseppe and Pamela Turi had to find a new home for their Italian restaurant. They brought their warm hospitality and superb wine list with them, and the chef has introduced a broader range of influences from across the country.

XX **Osteria Dell' Angolo** AC ⇔

47 Marsham St ⊠ SW1P 3DR – Ⓜ St James's Park Plan: **I6**
– 𝒞 (020) 32681077 – www.osteriadellangolo.co.uk – Closed 1-4 January,
Easter, 24-28 December, Saturday lunch, Sunday and bank holidays
Carte £ 32/45 – (booking essential at lunch)
• Italian • Neighbourhood • Brasserie •

At lunch, this Italian opposite the Home Office is full of bustle and men in suits; at dinner it's a little more relaxed. Staff are personable and the menu is reassuringly familiar; homemade pasta and seafood dishes are good.

XX **UNI** AC

18a Ebury St ⊠ SW1W 0LU – Ⓜ Victoria – 𝒞 (020) Plan: **G5**
7730 9267 – www.restaurantuni.com
Carte £ 27/75
• Japanese • Design • Neighbourhood •

Sweet restaurant offering flavoursome Nikkei cuisine, fusing the flavours of Japan and Peru: Nobu without the paparazzi and the prices. Small, stylish and spread across three levels – sit at a table, at the counter or in a cosy cellar alcove.

XX **Rex Whistler**   🕸 ᴸ 🆔

Tate Britain, Millbank ⊠ *SW1P 4RG –* Ⓜ *Pimlico*   Plan: **I6**
– 𝒞 (020) 78878825 – www.tate.org.uk – Closed 24-26 December
Menu £ 31 *– (lunch only)*
• **Traditional British** • **Classic décor** • **Traditional décor** •
The £ 45million renovation of Tate Britain included a freshening up of its restaurant and restoration of Whistler's mural, 'The Expedition in Pursuit of Rare Meats', which envelops the room. The monthly menu is stoutly British and the remarkably priced wine list has an unrivalled 'half bottle' selection.

X **A. Wong**   🍴 🆔
(❀)
70 Wilton Rd ⊠ *SW1V 1DE –* Ⓜ *Victoria – 𝒞 (020)*   Plan: **H6**
7828 8931 – www.awong.co.uk – Closed 23 December-4 January, Sunday and Monday lunch
Menu £ 14 *(weekday lunch)* – Carte £ 22/33 *– (booking essential)*
• **Chinese** • **Friendly** • **Neighbourhood** •
A modern Chinese restaurant with a buzzy ground floor and a sexy basement. Menus are continually evolving and the cooking is light, fresh and well-balanced, with lunchtime dim sum the star of the show. Service is keen, as are the prices.

X **Kouzu**   🆔

21 Grosvenor Gdns ⊠ *SW1 0BD –* Ⓜ *Victoria – 𝒞 (020)*   Plan: **G5**
7730 7043 – www.kouzu.co.uk – Closed 24-25 December, 1 January, Saturday lunch and Sunday
Menu £ 20/85 – Carte £ 27/111
• **Japanese** • **Design** •
Occupying two floors of an attractive 19C Grade II building is this modern Japanese restaurant. Those who know Zuma or Nobu will not only recognise the style of the food but will also find the stylish surroundings familiar.

X **Olivocarne**   🆔

61 Elizabeth St ⊠ *SW1W 9PP –* Ⓜ *Sloane Square*   Plan: **G6**
– 𝒞 (020) 7730 7997 – www.olivorestaurants.com
Menu £ 25 *(weekday lunch)* – Carte £ 30/54
• **Italian** • **Fashionable** • **Neighbourhood** •
Just when you thought Mauro Sanno had this part of town sewn up he opens another restaurant. This one focuses on meat dishes, along with a selection of satisfying Sardinian specialities and is smarter and larger than his others.

X **Olivo**   🆔

21 Eccleston St ⊠ *SW1W 9LX –* Ⓜ *Victoria – 𝒞 (020)*   Plan: **G6**
77302505 – www.olivorestaurants.com – Closed lunch Saturday-Sunday and bank holidays
Menu £ 25 *(weekday lunch)* – Carte £ 31/46 *– (booking essential)*
• **Italian** • **Neighbourhood** • **Bistro** •
Carefully prepared, authentic Sardinian specialities are the highlight at this popular Italian restaurant. Simply decorated in blues and yellows, with an atmosphere of bonhomie.

X **Olivomare**   🍴 🆔

10 Lower Belgrave St ⊠ *SW1W 0LJ –* Ⓜ *Victoria*   Plan: **G5**
– 𝒞 (020) 77309022 – www.olivorestaurants.com – Closed bank holidays
Carte £ 33/44
• **Seafood** • **Design** • **Neighbourhood** •
Expect understated and stylish piscatorial decoration and seafood with a Sardinian base. Fortnightly changing menu, with high quality produce, much of which is available in the deli next door.

Thomas Cubitt

44 Elizabeth St ✉ SW1W 9PA – Ⓜ Sloane Square. Plan: **G6**
– ✆ (020) 77306060 – www.thethomascubitt.co.uk
Carte £ 29/44 – *(booking essential)*
• Modern cuisine • Pub • Intimate •
A pub of two halves: choose the busy ground floor bar with its accessible menu or upstairs for more ambitious, quite elaborate cooking with courteous service and a less frenetic environment.

The Orange

37 Pimlico Rd ✉ SW1W 8NE – Ⓜ Sloane Square. Plan: **G6**
– ✆ (020) 78819844 – www.theorange.co.uk
Carte £ 28/40
• Mediterranean cuisine • Friendly • Neighbourhood •
The old Orange Brewery is as charming a pub as its stucco-fronted façade suggests. Try the fun bar or book a table in the more sedate upstairs room. The menu has a Mediterranean bias; spelt or wheat-based pizzas are a speciality. Bedrooms are stylish and comfortable.

REGENT'S PARK & MARYLEBONE PLAN V

The London Edition

10 Berners St ✉ W1T 3NP – Ⓜ Tottenham Court Road Plan: **H2**
– ✆ (020) 7781 0000 – www.editionhotels.com/london
173 rm – †£ 250/500 ††£ 250/500 – ☕ £ 26 – 9 suites
• Business • Luxury • Design •
Formerly Berners, a classic Edwardian hotel, strikingly reborn through a partnership between Ian Schrager and Marriott – the former's influence most apparent in the stylish lobby and bar. Slick, understated rooms; the best ones have balconies.
Berners Tavern – See restaurant listing

Langham

1c Portland Pl, Regent St ✉ W1B 1JA Plan: **H2**
– Ⓜ Oxford Circus – ✆ (020) 76361000 – www.langhamhotels.com
380 rm – †£ 360/960 ††£ 360/960 – ☕ £ 32 – 24 suites
• Luxury • Palace • Elegant •
Was one of Europe's first purpose-built grand hotels when it opened in 1865. Now back to its best, with its famous Palm Court for afternoon tea, its stylish Artesian bar and bedrooms that are not without personality and elegance.
Roux at The Landau – See restaurant listing

Chiltern Firehouse

1 Chiltern St ✉ W1U 7PA – Ⓜ Baker Street – ✆ (020) 7073 7676 – www.chilternfirehouse.com Plan: **G2**
26 rm – †£ 495/1020 ††£ 495/1020 – ☕ £ 25 – 16 suites
• Townhouse • Historic • Grand luxury •
From Chateau Marmont in LA to The Mercer in New York, André Balazs' hotels are effortlessly cool. For his London entrance, he sympathetically restored and extended a Gothic Victorian fire station. The style comes with an easy elegance; it's an oasis of calm and hardly feels like a hotel at all.
Chiltern Firehouse – See restaurant listing

Charlotte Street

15 Charlotte St ✉ W1T 1RJ – Ⓜ Goodge Street Plan: **I2**
– ✆ (020) 78062000 – www.charlottestreethotel.co.uk
52 rm – †£ 225/470 ††£ 225/470 – ☕ £ 15 – 4 suites
• Grand Luxury • Townhouse • Contemporary •
Stylish interior designed with a charming, understated English feel. Impeccably kept and individually decorated bedrooms. Popular in-house screening room. Colourful restaurant whose terrace spills onto Charlotte Street; grilled meats a highlight.

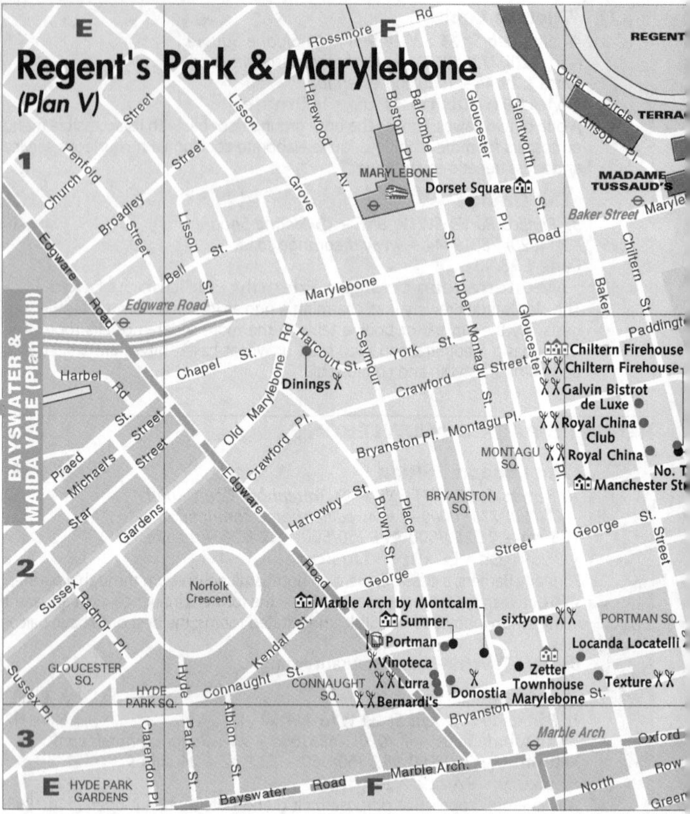
Regent's Park & Marylebone
(Plan V)
E
F
1
2
3
BAYSWATER & MAIDA VALE (Plan VIII)
REGENT
Outer Circle
TERRA
Allsop Pl.
MADAME TUSSAUD'S
Baker Street
Rossmore Rd
Lisson Street
Harewood Av.
Boston Pl.
Balcombe St.
Gloucester Pl.
Glentworth St.
MARYLEBONE
Dorset Square
Penfold Street
Church Street
Broadley Street
Lisson Grove
Bell St.
Edgware Road
Marylebone Road
Chiltern St.
Baker St.
Paddington
Harbel Rd
Chapel St.
Harcourt St.
Old Marylebone Rd
Dinings
Seymour Pl.
York St.
Upper Montagu St.
Crawford St.
Chiltern Firehouse
Galvin Bistrot de Luxe
Royal China Club
Royal China
No. T
Manchester St
Montagu Pl.
MONTAGU SQ.
Bryanston Pl.
Crawford Pl.
Praed St.
Michael's Street
Star Street
Sussex Gardens
Harrowby St.
Brown St.
BRYANSTON SQ.
George St.
Street
Norfolk Crescent
Marble Arch by Montcalm
Sumner
Portman
sixtyone
PORTMAN SQ.
Locanda Locatelli
Radnor Pl.
Kendal St.
Vinoteca
Lurra
Donostia
Zetter Townhouse Marylebone
Texture
GLOUCESTER SQ.
HYDE PARK SQ.
Connaught St.
CONNAUGHT SQ.
Bernardi's
Bryanston St.
Sussex Pl.
Hyde Park St.
Albion St.
Clarendon Pl.
Marble Arch
Oxford
Row
North
Green
HYDE PARK GARDENS
Bayswater Road

Sanderson

50 Berners St ✉ *W1T 3NG* – Ⓜ *Oxford Circus* – ✆ *(020) 73001400* – *www.morganshotelgroup.com* Plan: **H2**

150 rm – 🚹£ 234/538 🚹🚹£ 234/538 – ☕ £ 18

• Luxury • Business • Minimalist •

Originally designed by Philippe Starck and his influence is still evident. The Purple Bar is dark and moody; the Long Bar is bright and stylish. Bedrooms are crisply decorated and come complete with all mod cons.

Zetter Townhouse Marylebone

28-30 Seymour St ✉ *W1H 7JB* – Ⓜ *Marble Arch* – ✆ *(020) 7324 4544* – *www.thezettertownhouse.com* Plan: **F2**

24 rm – 🚹£ 290/480 🚹🚹£ 290/480 – ☕ £ 14

• Townhouse • Elegant • Unique •

A stylish Georgian townhouse, with a sumptuously decorated lounge and cocktail bar and beautifully appointed bedrooms; the best features a roll-top bath on its rootop terrace. Friendly, professional staff and impressive eco credentials.

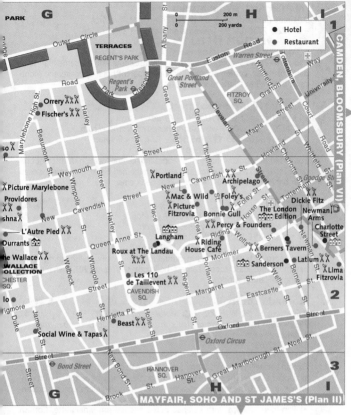

| Hotel | Restaurant |

MAYFAIR, SOHO AND ST JAMES'S (Plan II)

Durrants

26-32 George St ⊠ W1H 5BJ – Ⓜ Bond Street
– ℰ (020) 7935 8131 – www.durrantshotel.co.uk
92 rm – ♦£ 195 ♦♦£ 250/350 – ☲ £ 20 – 4 suites
• Traditional • Business • Classic •
Traditional, privately owned hotel with friendly, long-standing staff. Bedrooms
are now brighter in style but still retain a certain English character. Clubby
dining room for mix of British classics and lighter, European dishes.

Plan: **G2**

Dorset Square

39-40 Dorset Sq ⊠ NW1 6QN – Ⓜ Marylebone
– ℰ (020) 77237874 – www.dorsetsquarehotel.co.uk
38 rm – ♦£ 165/200 ♦♦£ 205/245 – ☲ £ 13
• Townhouse • Business • Contemporary •
Having reacquired this Regency townhouse, Firmdale refurbished it fully before
reopening it in 2012. It has a contemporary yet intimate feel and visiting MCC
members will appreciate the cricketing theme, which even extends to the cocktails in their sweet little basement brasserie.

Plan: **F1**

Marble Arch by Montcalm

31 Great Cumberland Pl ✉ W1H 7TA – Ⓜ Marble Arch – ✆ (020) 7258 0777 – www.themarblearch.co.uk Plan: **F2**

42 rm – †£ 253/374 ††£ 263/374 – ☕ £ 20

• Townhouse • Business • Contemporary •

Bedrooms at this 5-storey Georgian townhouse come with the same high standards of stylish, contemporary design as its parent hotel opposite, the Montcalm, but are just a little more compact.

No. Ten Manchester Street

10 Manchester St ✉ W1U 4DG – Ⓜ Baker Street – ✆ (020) 73175900 – www.tenmanchesterstreethotel.com Plan: **G2**

44 rm – †£ 165/385 ††£ 165/385 – ☕ £ 17 – 9 suites

• Townhouse • Business • Modern •

Converted Edwardian house in an appealing, central location. A discreet entrance leads into a little lounge and an Italian-themed bistro; the semi-enclosed cigar bar is also a feature. Neat, well-kept bedrooms.

Sumner

54 Upper Berkeley St ✉ W1H 7QR – Ⓜ Marble Arch – ✆ (020) 77232244 – www.thesumner.com Plan: **F2**

19 rm ☕ – †£ 160/300 ††£ 160/300

• Townhouse • Business • Personalised •

Two Georgian terrace houses in central location. Comfy, stylish sitting room; basement breakfast room. Largest bedrooms, 101 and 201, benefit from having full-length windows.

Locanda Locatelli (Giorgio Locatelli)

8 Seymour St. ✉ W1H 7JZ – Ⓜ Marble Arch – ✆ (020) 79359088 – www.locandalocatelli.com – Closed 25-26 December and 1 January Plan: **G2**

Carte £ 37/63

• Italian • Fashionable • Elegant •

Giorgio Locatelli's Italian restaurant may be into its second decade but still looks as dapper as ever. The service is smooth and the room was designed with conviviality in mind. The hugely appealing menu covers all regions; unfussy presentation and superb ingredients allow natural flavours to shine.

➜ Pan-fried scallops with celeriac purée and saffron vinaigrette. Cornish red mullet wrapped in Parma ham with fennel and tomato sauce. Gorgonzola panna cotta, chocolate crumble, pear foam and honey ice cream.

Roux at The Landau – Langham Hotel

1c Portland Pl., Regent St. ✉ W1B 1JA – Ⓜ Oxford Circus – ✆ (020) 76361000 – www.rouxatthelandau.com – Closed Saturday lunch and Sunday Plan: **H2**

Menu £ 39 – Carte £ 43/79

• French • Elegant • Design •

Grand, oval-shaped hotel restaurant run under the aegis of the Roux organisation. Classical, French-influenced cooking is the order of the day, but a lighter style of cuisine using the occasional twist is also emerging.

Orrery

55 Marylebone High St ✉ W1U 5RB – Ⓜ Regent's Park – ✆ (020) 7616 8000 – www.orrery-restaurant.co.uk Plan: **G1**

Menu £ 30/55 – *(booking essential)*

• Modern cuisine • Neighbourhood • Design •

These are actually converted stables from the 19C but, such is the elegance and style of the building, you'd never know. Featured is elaborate, modern European cooking; dishes are strong on presentation and come with the occasional twist.

XX   **Texture** (Agnar Sverrisson)   🏵 🏧 ⇔

❁   *34 Portman St ⊠ W1H 7BY –* **Ⓜ** *Marble Arch – 𝒞 (020)*   Plan: **G2**
72240028 – www.texture-restaurant.co.uk – Closed first 2 weeks August,
1 week Easter, Christmas-New Year, Sunday and Monday
Menu £ 29/85 – Carte £ 50/84
• Creative • Design • Fashionable •
Technically skilled but light and invigorating cooking from an Icelandic chef-
owner, who uses ingredients from his homeland. Bright restaurant with high
ceiling and popular adjoining champagne bar. Pleasant service from keen
staff, ready with a smile.
➜ Norwegian king crab with coconut, ginger, lime leaf and lemongrass.
Black Angus rib-eye with ox cheek, horseradish and olive oil béarnaise. Ice-
landic skyr with vanilla ice cream, rye breadcrumbs and Yorkshire rhubarb.

XX   **Lurra**   🛋 🏧

9 Seymour Pl ⊠ W1H 5BA – **Ⓜ** *Marble Arch – 𝒞 (020)*   Plan: **F2**
7724 4545 – www.lurra.co.uk – Closed Monday lunch and Sunday dinner
Carte £ 25/65
• Basque • Design • Neighbourhood •
Its name means 'land' in Basque and reflects their use of the freshest produce,
cooked over a charcoal grill. Choose tasty nibbles or sharing plates like 14 year
old Galician beef, whole grilled turbot or slow-cooked shoulder of lamb.

XX   **Bernardi's**   🏧 ⇔

62 Seymour St ⊠ W1H 5BN – **Ⓜ** *Marble Arch – 𝒞 (020)*   Plan: **F2**
3826 7940 – www.bernardis.co.uk
Menu £ 18 (weekday lunch) – Carte £ 30/42
• Italian • Neighbourhood • Fashionable •
A modern neighbourhood Italian: chic yet relaxed and with a friendly atmosphere. Pop in for breakfast, brunch, lunch, dinner or cicchetti and cocktails;
everything is homemade and dishes are vibrantly flavoured, with a lightness of
touch.

XX   **L'Autre Pied**   🏧 🕎

5-7 Blandford St. ⊠ W1U 3DB – **Ⓜ** *Bond Street*   Plan: **G2**
– 𝒞 (020) 74869696 – www.lautrepied.co.uk – Closed 4 days Christmas,
1 January and Sunday dinner
Menu £ 29/50
• Modern cuisine • Design •
This sibling of Pied à Terre in Charlotte Street has a more relaxed feel and a real
sense of neighbourhood; ask for a table by the window to better enjoy the local
'village' feel. The European-influenced food is modern without being unfamiliar.

XX   **Latium**   🏧

21 Berners St. ⊠ W1T 3LP – **Ⓜ** *Oxford Circus – 𝒞 (020)*   Plan: **H2**
7323 9123 – www.latiumrestaurant.com – Closed 25-26 December,
1 January and lunch Saturday-Sunday
Menu £ 21 (weekdays) – Carte £ 28/42
• Italian • Neighbourhood •
An Italian stalwart with warm, welcoming service, a contemporary look and a
loyal following. The menu focuses on Lazio but travels the length of Italy for
inspiration; 'fatto a casa' is their motto and fresh pasta, their speciality.

XX   **Berners Tavern** – The London Edition Hotel   ♿ 🏧 ⇔

10 Berners St ⊠ WIT 3NP – **Ⓜ** *Tottenham Court Road*   Plan: **H2**
– 𝒞 (020) 7908 7979 – www.bernerstavern.com
Menu £ 25 (lunch) – Carte £ 34/67
• Modern British • Brasserie • Elegant •
What was once a hotel ballroom is now a very glamorous restaurant, with every
inch of wall filled with gilt-framed pictures. Jason Atherton has put together an
appealing, accessible menu and the cooking is satisfying and assured.

XX **Royal China Club**   🔠 🎑

40-42 Baker St ⊠ *W1U 7AJ* – ⓜ *Baker Street* – ℰ *(020)*   Plan: **G2**
7486 3898 – www.royalchinagroup.co.uk – Closed 25-27 December
Carte £ 32/70
• Chinese • Elegant • Romantic •
'The Club' is the glittering bauble in the Royal China chain but along with the luxurious feel of the room comes an appealing sense of calm. Their lunchtime dim sum is very good; at dinner try their more unusual Cantonese dishes.

XX **Galvin Bistrot de Luxe**   🔠 ♿ 🔠 ✥ 🕸

66 Baker St. ⊠ *W1U 7DJ* – ⓜ *Baker Street* – ℰ *(020)*   Plan: **G2**
7935 4007 – www.galvinrestaurants.com – Closed dinner 24 December-
26 December and 1 January
Menu £ 22/24 (weekdays) – Carte £ 33/55
• French • Bistro • Chic •
Firmly established modern Gallic bistro with ceiling fans, globe lights and wood-panelled walls. Satisfying and precisely cooked classic French dishes from the Galvin brothers. The elegant basement cocktail bar adds to the comfy feel.

XX **Chiltern Firehouse** – Chiltern Firehouse Hotel   🔠 🔠 ✥

1 Chiltern St ⊠ *WIU 7PA* – ⓜ *Baker Street* – ℰ *(020)*   Plan: **G2**
7073 7676 – www.chilternfirehouse.com
Carte £ 37/65
• World cuisine • Fashionable • Design •
How appropriate – one of the hottest tickets in town is a converted fire station. The room positively bursts with energy but what makes this celebrity hangout unusual is that the food is rather good. Nuno Mendes' menu is full of vibrant North and South American dishes that are big on flavour.

XX **The Wallace**

Hertford House, Manchester Sq ⊠ *W1U 3BN*   Plan: **G2**
– ⓜ Bond Street – ℰ *(020) 75639505*
– www.peytonandbyrne.co.uk/the-wallace-restaurant/index.html – Closed
24-26 December
Menu £ 23 – Carte £ 31/48 – *(lunch only and dinner Friday-Saturday)*
• Modern British • Friendly •
Large glass-roofed courtyard on the ground floor of Hertford House, home to the splendid Wallace Collection. Menu of Modern British dishes, with plenty to please vegetarians. The ambience is sedate and service is smooth and unruffled.

XX **Beast**   ♿ 🔠

3 Chapel Pl ⊠ *W1G 0BG* – ⓜ *Bond Street* – ℰ *(020)*   Plan: **H2**
7495 1816 – www.beastrestaurant.co.uk – Closed Sunday, lunch Monday-
Wednesday and bank holidays
Carte £ 60/100
• Meats and grills • Elegant • Fashionable •
An underground banquet hall with three exceedingly long tables set for communal dining. Mains include a perfectly cooked hunk of rib-eye steak and a large platter of succulent King crab. Bring a big appetite and a fat wallet.

XX **sixtyone**   ♿ 🔠 ✥

Montcalm Hotel, 61 Upper Berkeley St ⊠ *W1H 7TW*   Plan: **F2**
– ⓜ Marble Arch – ℰ *(020) 7958 3222 – www.montcalm.co.uk – Closed*
Sunday and Monday
Menu £ 25 (lunch and early dinner) – Carte £ 33/84
• Modern British • Elegant • Design •
A joint venture between chef Arnaud Stevens and Searcy's, in a space leased from the Montcalm hotel. The light-filled room is stylish and slick with an eye-catching ceiling display. British cooking is modern and at times quite playful.

XX **Dickie Fitz** 🛋 ⅗ 🆎

48 Newman St ✉ *W1T 1QQ –* Ⓜ *Goodge Street* Plan: **H2**
– 𝒞 (020) 3667 1445 – www.dickiefitz.co.uk – Closed Sunday dinner and bank holiday monday
Carte £ 25/46

• **Modern cuisine** • **Friendly** • **Neighbourhood** •

A light and airy restaurant with soft yellow banquettes and a striking glass-panelled, art deco inspired staircase. Cooking is full of flavour and originality, with a subtle mix of Australian, Pacific and Asian influences.

XX **Percy & Founders** 🛋 ⅗ 🆎 ⇔

1 Pearson Sq, (off Mortimer St) ✉ *W1T 3BF* Plan: **H2**
– Ⓜ *Goodge Street – 𝒞 (020) 3761 0200 – www.percyandfounders.co.uk*
Carte £ 25/49

• **Modern cuisine** • **Brasserie** • **Fashionable** •

Where Middlesex hospital once stood is now a residential development that includes this all-day operation. It's a mix between a smart pub and a modern brasserie and the kitchen brings quite a refined touch to the seasonal menu.

XX **Archipelago** 🆎

53 Cleveland St ✉ *W1T 4JJ –* Ⓜ *Goodge Street* Plan: **H2**
– 𝒞 (020) 76379611 – www.archipelago-restaurant.co.uk
– Closed 24-28 December, Saturday lunch, Sunday and bank holidays
Carte £ 32/46

• **Creative** • **Exotic décor** • **Neighbourhood** •

A true one-off, with eccentric decoration that makes you feel you're in a bazaar. 'Exploring the exotic' is their slogan and the menu reads like an inventory at a safari park; it could include crocodile, zebra and wildebeest.

XX **Fischer's** 🆎

50 Marylebone High St ✉ *W1U 5HN –* Ⓜ *Baker Street* Plan: **G1**
– 𝒞 (020) 7466 5501 – www.fischers.co.uk
– Closed 24-25 December and 1 January
Carte £ 29/47

• **Austrian** • **Brasserie** • **Fashionable** •

An Austrian café and konditorei that summons the spirit of old Vienna, from the owners of The Wolseley et al. Open all day; breakfast is a highlight – the viennoiserie are great. Schnitzels are also good; upgrade to a Holstein.

XX **The Providores** 🆎

109 Marylebone High St. ✉ *W1U 4RX –* Ⓜ *Bond Street* Plan: **G2**
– 𝒞 (020) 7935 6175 – www.theprovidores.co.uk
– Closed 25-26 December
Menu £ 34 (dinner) – Carte £ 35/49

• **Creative** • **Trendy** • **Romantic** •

Packed ground floor for tapas; upstairs for innovative fusion cooking, with spices and ingredients from around the world, including Australasia. Starter-sized dishes at dinner allow for greater choice.

XX **Les 110 de Taillevent** 🍸 🆎

16 Cavendish Sq ✉ *W1G 9DD –* Ⓜ *Oxford Circus* Plan: **H2**
– 𝒞 (020) 3141 6016 – www.les-110-taillevent-london.com – Closed 7-29 August, 25 December and 1 January
Menu £ 30 – Carte £ 35/67

• **French** • **Elegant** • **Design** •

Ornate high ceilings and deep green banquettes create an elegant look for this brasserie deluxe. Dishes are firmly in the French vein and they offer 110 wines by the glass: 4 different pairings for each dish, in 4 different price brackets.

XX **Royal China**   🔲 🏵

24-26 Baker St ✉ *W1U 7AB –* Ⓜ *Baker Street –* 𝒸 *(020)*   Plan: **G2**
74874688 – www.royalchinagroup.co.uk
Menu £ 30 (lunch)/38 – Carte £ 20/74
• Chinese • Exotic décor • Family •
Barbequed meats, assorted soups and stir-fries attract plenty of large groups to
this smart and always bustling Cantonese restaurant. Over 40 different types of
dim sum served during the day.

X **Trishna** (Karam Sethi)   🔲 🔄 🏵
❀
15-17 Blandford St. ✉ *W1U 3DG –* Ⓜ *Baker Street*   Plan: **G2**
– 𝒸 *(020) 79355624 – www.trishnalondon.com – Closed 25-27 December
and 1-3 January*
Menu £ 35 (lunch) – Carte £ 26/46
• Indian • Neighbourhood • Simple •
Double-fronted, modern Indian restaurant dressed in an elegant, understated
style. The coast of southwest India provides the influences and the food is
balanced, satisfying and executed with care – the tasting menus provide a
good all-round experience.
→ Aloo shakarkandi chaat. Bream with green chilli, coriander and smoked
tomato kachumber. Kheer with cardamom, fig, raisin and pistachio.

X **Portland**   🎇 🔲 🔄
❀
113 Great Portland St ✉ *W1W 6QQ*   Plan: **H2**
– Ⓜ *Great Portland Street –* 𝒸 *(020) 7436 3261*
– www.portlandrestaurant.co.uk – Closed Sunday
Carte £ 35/52 – *(booking essential)*
• Modern cuisine • Intimate • Simple •
A no-frills, pared-down restaurant that exudes honesty. One look at the menu
and you know you'll eat well: it twists and turns on a daily basis and the combinations just sound right together. Dishes are crisp and unfussy but with depth
and real understanding – quite something for such a young team.
→ Celeriac and grain risotto, scorched cod cheek and nettle sauce. Cornish
monkfish with courgette, preserved lemon and almond. Steamed chocolate
& ale cake, beer caramel and barley ice cream.

X **Lima Fitzrovia**   🔲 🍵
❀
31 Rathbone Pl ✉ *W1T 1JH –* Ⓜ *Goodge Street*   Plan: **I2**
– 𝒸 *(020) 3002 2640 – www.limalondongroup.com/fitzrovia – Closed
Monday lunch and bank holidays*
Menu £ 25 (lunch and early dinner) – Carte £ 41/53
• Peruvian • Neighbourhood • Exotic décor •
Lima Fitzrovia is one of those restaurants that just makes you feel good about
life – and that's even without the pisco sours. The Peruvian food at this informal,
fun place is the ideal antidote to times of austerity: it's full of punchy, invigorating flavours and fantastically vivid colours.
→ Braised octopus with purple corn and Botija olives. Beef with yellow
potato purée and cow's milk. Dulce de leche ice cream with bee pollen.

X **Social Wine & Tapas**   🎇 🔲

39 James St ✉ *W1U 1DL –* Ⓜ *Bond Street –* 𝒸 *(020)*   Plan: **G2**
7993 3257 – www.socialwineandtapas.com – Closed bank holidays
Menu £ 20 (lunch) – Carte £ 15/36 – *(bookings not accepted)*
• Mediterranean cuisine • Neighbourhood • Trendy •
Another from the Jason Atherton stable, and the name says it all. Urban styling,
with wines on display; sit in the moodily lit basement. A mix of Spanish and
Mediterranean dishes, with some Atherton classics too; desserts are a highlight.

UNITED KINGDOM - LONDON

X · 🏵

Picture Fitzrovia   🗚

110 Great Portland St. ⊠ W1W 6PQ – Ⓜ Oxford Circus   Plan: **H2**
*– ℰ (020) 76377892 – www.picturerestaurant.co.uk – Closed Sunday
and bank holidays*
Menu £ 45 – Carte £ 24/37
· **Modern British · Simple · Vintage ·**
An ex Arbutus and Wild Honey triumvirate have created this cool, great value restaurant. The look may be a little stark but the delightful staff add warmth. The small plates are vibrant and colourful, and the flavours are assured.

X · 🏵

Foley's   🗚

23 Foley St ⊠ W1W 6DU – Ⓜ Goodge Street – ℰ (020)   Plan: **H2**
3137 1302 – www.foleysrestaurant.co.uk – Closed Sunday
Carte £ 23/30 – *(booking advisable)*
· **World cuisine · Neighbourhood · Friendly ·**
Cosy up in one of the ground floor booths or head downstairs to the engine room of this lively, well-run restaurant, with its busy open kitchen and counter seating, and its barrel-vaulted caves for six. Vibrant, original small plates reflect the international spice trail; 3 or 4 dishes will suffice.

X

Riding House Café   🗚 ⇔

43-51 Great Titchfield St ⊠ W1W 7PQ   Plan: **H2**
*– Ⓜ Oxford Circus – ℰ (020) 79270840 – www.ridinghousecafe.co.uk
– Closed 25-26 December*
Carte £ 23/41
· **Modern cuisine · Rustic · Fashionable ·**
It's less a café, more a large, quirkily designed, all-day New York style brasserie and cocktail bar. The small plates have more zing than the main courses. The 'unbookable' side of the restaurant is the more fun part.

X

Mac & Wild   🗚

65 Great Tichfield St ⊠ W1W 7PS – Ⓜ Oxford Circus   Plan: **H2**
– ℰ (020) 7637 0510 – www.macandwild.com – Closed Sunday dinner
Carte £ 23/50
· **Scottish · Friendly · Neighbourhood ·**
The owner of this 'Highland restaurant' is the son of an Ardgay butcher – it is all about their wild venison and top quality game and seafood from Scotland. Don't miss the 'wee plates' like the deliriously addictive haggis pops. There's also a choice of over 100 whiskies.

X

Opso   🛋 ᕕ ⇔

10 Paddington St ⊠ W1U 5QL – Ⓜ Baker Street   Plan: **G1**
*– ℰ (020) 7487 5088 – www.opso.co.uk – Closed 23 December-3 January
and Sunday dinner*
Menu £ 15 (weekday lunch) – Carte £ 17/45
· **Greek · Neighbourhood ·**
A modern Greek restaurant which has proved a good fit for the neighbourhood – and not just because it's around the corner from the Hellenic Centre. It serves small sharing plates that mix the modern with the traditional.

X

Donostia

10 Seymour Pl ⊠ W1H 7ND – Ⓜ Marble Arch – ℰ (020)   Plan: **F2**
*3620 1845 – www.donostia.co.uk – Closed Christmas, Easter and Monday
lunch*
Carte £ 10/37
· **Basque · Tapas bar · Fashionable ·**
The two young owners were inspired by the food of San Sebastiàn to open this pintxos and tapas bar. Sit at the counter for Basque classics like cod with pil-pil sauce, chorizo from the native Kintoa pig and slow-cooked pig's cheeks.

UNITED KINGDOM - LONDON

X **Vinoteca**   🏵 AC

15 Seymour Pl. ⊠ W1H 5BD – ⓜ Marble Arch   Plan: **F2**
– ℰ (020) 7724 7288 – www.vinoteca.co.uk
– Closed Christmas, bank holidays and Sunday dinner
Menu £ 16 (weekday lunch) – Carte £ 21/36 – *(booking advisable)*
• **Modern cuisine** • **Wine bar** • **Neighbourhood** •
Follows the formula of the original: great fun, great wines, gutsy and whole-some food, enthusiastic staff and almost certainly a wait for a table. Influences from sunnier parts of Europe, along with some British dishes.

X **Bonnie Gull**

21a Foley St ⊠ W1W 6DS – ⓜ Goodge Street   Plan: **H2**
– ℰ (020) 7436 0921 – www.bonniegull.com
– Closed 25 December-2 January
Carte £ 22/44 – *(booking essential)*
• **Seafood** • **Simple** • **Traditional décor** •
Sweet Bonnie Gull calls itself a 'seafood shack' – a reference perhaps to its modest beginnings as a pop-up. Start with an order from the raw bar then go for a classic like Cullen skink, a whole Devon cock crab or fish and chips.

X **Picture Marylebone**   AC

19 New Cavendish St ⊠ W1G 9TZ – ⓜ Bond Street   Plan: **G2**
– ℰ (020) 7935 0058 – www.picturerestaurant.co.uk – Closed Sunday and bank holidays
Menu £ 22 (lunch) – Carte £ 27/37
• **Modern British** • **Design** • **Friendly** •
This follow-up to Picture Fitzrovia hit the ground running. The cleverly created à la carte of flavoursome small plates lists 3 vegetable, 3 fish and 3 meat choices, followed by 3 desserts – choose one from each section.

X **Dinings**

22 Harcourt St. ⊠ W1H 4HH – ⓜ Edgware Road   Plan: **F2**
– ℰ (020) 77230666 – www.dinings.co.uk
– Closed Christmas
Carte £ 24/57 – *(booking essential)*
• **Japanese** • **Cosy** • **Simple** •
It's hard not to be charmed by this sweet little Japanese place, with its ground floor counter and basement tables. Its strengths lie with the more creative, con-temporary dishes; sharing is recommended but prices can be steep.

X **Zoilo**   🏵 ⅄ AC ⇔

9 Duke St. ⊠ W1U 3EG – ⓜ Bond Street – ℰ (020)   Plan: **G2**
7486 9699 – www.zoilo.co.uk
Menu £ 10 (weekdays) – Carte £ 20/46
• **Argentinian** • **Friendly** • **Wine bar** •
It's all about sharing so plonk yourself at the counter and discover Argentina's regional specialities. Typical dishes include braised pig head croquettes or grilled scallops with pork belly, and there's an appealing all-Argentinian wine list.

🍺 **Portman**

51 Upper Berkeley St ⊠ W1H 7QW – ⓜ Marble Arch.   Plan: **F2**
– ℰ (020) 7723 8996 – www.theportmanmarylebone.com
Carte £ 25/48
• **Modern cuisine** • **Pub** • **Friendly** •
The condemned on their way to Tyburn Tree gallows would take their last drink here. Now it's an urbane pub with a formal upstairs dining room. The ground floor is more fun for enjoying the down-to-earth menu.

BLOOMSBURY

Covent Garden

10 Monmouth St ⊠ *WC2H 9HB –* Ⓜ *Covent Garden*
– ℰ *(020) 78061000 – www.firmdalehotels.com*
59 rm – ♦£ 230/300 ♦♦£ 300/370 – ⊊ £ 20
· Luxury · Townhouse · Design ·

Plan: I3

Popular with those of a theatrical bent. Boldly designed, stylish bedrooms, with technology discreetly concealed. Boasts a very comfortable first floor oak-panelled drawing room with its own honesty bar. Easy-going menu in Brasserie Max.

Pied à Terre

34 Charlotte St ⊠ *W1T 2NH –* Ⓜ *Goodge Street*
– ℰ *(020) 76361178 – www.pied-a-terre.co.uk – Closed last week*
December-5 January, Saturday lunch, Sunday and bank holidays
Menu £ 38/80 *– (booking essential)*

Plan: I2

· Creative · Elegant · Intimate ·

For over 25 years, David Moore's restaurant has stood apart in Charlotte Street, confident in its abilities and in the loyalty of its regulars. Subtle decorative changes keep it looking fresh and vibrant, while Andrew McFadden delivers refined, creative, flavoursome cooking.

→ Scallop ceviche with cucumber, balsamic and dill. Fallow deer with black pearl curry, smoked bacon and beetroot. Pineapple with kaffir lime and coriander.

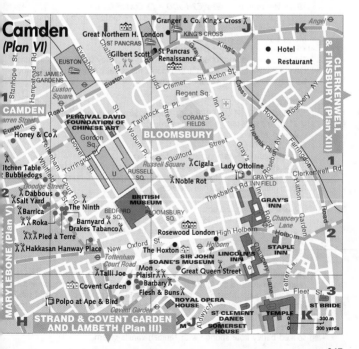

XX   **Hakkasan Hanway Place**   器 AC 🎯
⌘

8 Hanway Pl. ⌂ W1T 1HD – ⓜ Tottenham Court Road   Plan: I2
– ℰ (020) 79277000 – www.hakkasan.com
– Closed 24-25 December
Menu £ 38/128 – Carte £ 32/94
• Chinese • Trendy • Fashionable •

There are now Hakkasans all over the world but this was the original. It has the sensual looks, air of exclusivity and glamorous atmosphere synonymous with the 'brand'. The exquisite Cantonese dishes are prepared with care and consistency by the large kitchen team; lunch dim sum is a highlight.
→ Dim sum platter. Roasted duck with black truffle sauce. Jivara bomb.

XX   **Kitchen Table at Bubbledogs** (James Knappett)   AC
⌘

70 Charlotte St ⌂ W1T 4QG – ⓜ Goodge Street   Plan: H1/2
– ℰ (020) 76377770 – www.kitchentablelondon.co.uk – Closed 1-
14 January, 17 August-2 September, 23-27 December, Sunday and Monday
Menu £ 98 – (dinner only) (booking essential) (tasting menu only)
• Modern cuisine • Fashionable • Neighbourhood •

Fight through the crowds enjoying a curious mix of hotdogs and champagne and head for the curtain – behind it is a counter for 19 diners. Chef-owner James prepares a no-choice menu of around 12 dishes. The produce is exemplary; the cooking has a clever creative edge; and the dishes have real depth.
→ Truffle-roasted Jersey Royals with bacon and crème fraîche. Cornish lobster with chilli, wild garlic and coral foam. Gooseberry and yoghurt parfait with almonds.

XX   **Mon Plaisir**   🍷

19-21 Monmouth St. ⌂ WC2H 9DD – ⓜ Covent Garden   Plan: I3
– ℰ (020) 78367243 – www.monplaisir.co.uk – Closed 25-26 December, Easter Sunday-Monday and Sunday
Menu £ 16/24 – Carte £ 32/46
• French • Family • Bistro •

This proud French institution opened in the 1940s. Enjoy satisfyingly authentic classics in any of the four contrasting rooms, full of Gallic charm; apparently the bar was salvaged from a Lyonnais brothel.

XX   **Roka**   🍴 ᕼ AC

37 Charlotte St ⌂ W1T 1RR – ⓜ Goodge Street   Plan: I2
– ℰ (020) 75806464 – www.rokarestaurant.com
– Closed 25 December
Carte £ 40/70
• Japanese • Fashionable • Design •

Bright, atmospheric interior of teak and oak; bustling and trendy feel. Contemporary touches added to Japanese dishes; try specialities from the on-view Robata grill. Capable and chatty service.

X   **Dabbous** (Ollie Dabbous)   AC
⌘

39 Whitfield St ⌂ W1T 2SF – ⓜ Goodge Street   Plan: I2
– ℰ (020) 7323 1544 – www.dabbous.co.uk – Closed 10 days Christmas-New Year, Easter and Sunday
Menu £ 28/59 – (booking essential)
• Modern cuisine • Design • Neighbourhood •

Still one of the most popular spots in town – the kitchen adopts the 'less is more' approach and the food comes with an elegantly restrained finesse and a bewitching purity. Most have the 7-course menu with its stimulating and sublime combinations of ingredients. The ersatz-industrial room has a simple elegance.
→ Peas with mint. Braised turbot with lemon verbena. Cherry blossom tea-soaked barley flour sponge with Tahitian vanilla cream.

UNITED KINGDOM - LONDON

✗ ✿ **The Ninth** (Jun Tanaka) 🆔

22 Charlotte St ☒ W1T 2NB – Ⓜ *Goodge Street* — Plan: I2
– ℰ *(020) 3019 0880 – www.theninthlondon.com – Closed Christmas-New Year, Sunday and bank holidays*
Menu £ 21 (weekday lunch) – Carte £ 28/47
• Mediterranean cuisine • Brasserie • Fashionable •
Jun Tanaka's first restaurant – the ninth in which he has worked – is this neighbourhood spot with a lively downstairs and more intimate first floor. Cooking uses classical French techniques with a spotlight on the Med; dishes look appealing but the focus is firmly on flavour. Vegetables are a highlight.
➜ Smoked duck breast, caramelised chicory and walnuts. Charcoal-roasted celeriac with smoked almonds and wild garlic. Caramelised lemon tart with fromage frais.

✗ 🙂 **Salt Yard** 🍽 🆔

54 Goodge St. ☒ W1T 4NA – Ⓜ *Goodge Street* — Plan: H2
– ℰ *(020) 76370657 – www.saltyard.co.uk – Closed 25 and dinner 24 and 31 December and 1 January*
Carte £ 17/28
• Mediterranean cuisine • Tapas bar • Intimate •
Ground floor bar and buzzy basement restaurant specialising in good value plates of tasty Italian and Spanish dishes, ideal for sharing; charcuterie a speciality. Super wine list.

✗ 🙂 **Honey & Co** 🆔 🕥

25a Warren St ☒ W1T 5LZ – Ⓜ *Warren Street* — Plan: H1
– ℰ *(020) 73886175 – www.honeyandco.co.uk – Closed 25-26 December and Sunday*
Menu £ 30 – Carte £ 25/31 – *(booking essential)*
• World cuisine • Simple • Neighbourhood •
The husband and wife team at this sweet little café were both Ottolenghi head chefs so expect cooking full of freshness and colour. Influences stretch beyond Israel to the wider Middle East. Open from 8am; packed at night.

✗ 🙂 **Barrica** 🍽 🆔

62 Goodge St ☒ W1T 4NE – Ⓜ *Goodge Street* — Plan: H2
– ℰ *(020) 7436 9448 – www.barrica.co.uk – Closed 25-26 December, 1 January, Sunday and bank holidays*
Carte £ 19/36 – *(booking essential)*
• Spanish • Tapas bar • Friendly •
All the staff at this lively little tapas bar are Spanish, so perhaps it's national pride that makes them run it with a passion lacking in many of their competitors. When it comes to the food, authenticity is high on the agenda.

✗ 🙂 **Barbary** 🆔

16 Neal's Yard ☒ WC2H 9DP – Ⓜ *Covent Garden* — Plan: I3
– www.thebarbary.co.uk – Closed 25-26 December and Monday
Carte £ 22/37 – *(bookings not accepted)*
• World cuisine • Tapas bar • Rustic •
A sultry, atmospheric restaurant from the team behind Palomar: a tiny place with 24 non-bookable seats squeezed around a horseshoe-shaped, zinc-topped counter. The menu of small sharing plates lists dishes from the former Barbary Coast. Service is keen, as are the prices.

✗ **Drakes Tabanco** 🆔

3 Windmill St ☒ W1T 2HY – Ⓜ *Goodge Street –* ℰ *(020)* — Plan: I2
7637 9388 – www.drakestabanco.com – Closed Sunday and bank holidays
Carte £ 22/34
• Spanish • Simple • Rustic •
Taking advantage of our newfound fondness for fino is this simple tabanco, from the people behind nearby Barrica and Copita. The small, Andalusian-inspired tapas menu uses imported produce from Spain alongside British ingredients.

X

Cigala
88 🛱 AK ⇔

54 Lamb's Conduit St. ⊠ WC1N 3LW   Plan: **J1**
*– Ⓜ Russell Square – ℰ (020) 74051717 – www.cigala.co.uk – Closed 25-
26 December, 1 January, Easter Sunday and Monday*
Menu £ 24 (weekdays) – Carte £ 26/39 – *(booking essential)*
• **Spanish** • **Neighbourhood** • **Friendly** •
Longstanding Spanish restaurant, with a lively and convivial atmosphere,
friendly and helpful service and an appealing and extensive menu of classics.
The dried hams are a must and it's well worth waiting the 30 minutes for a
paella.

X

Noble Rot
88 AK

51 Lamb's Conduit St ⊠ WC1N 3NB – Ⓜ Russell Square   Plan: **J1**
*– ℰ (020) 7242 8963 – www.noblerot.co.uk – Closed 25-26 December and
Sunday*
Carte £ 30/43 – *(booking advisable)*
• **Traditional British** • **Rustic** • **Wine bar** •
A wine bar and restaurant from the people behind the wine magazine of the
same name. Unfussy cooking comes with bold, gutsy flavours; expect fish from
the Kent coast as well as classics like terrines, rillettes and home-cured meats.

X

⊛

Barnyard
🛱 AK

18 Charlotte St ⊠ W1T 2LZ – Ⓜ Goodge Street   Plan: **I2**
*– ℰ (020) 7580 3842 – www.barnyard-london.com – Closed 25-
26 December*
Menu £ 21 (lunch) – Carte £ 17/32 – *(bookings not accepted)*
• **Traditional British** • **Rustic** • **Design** •
Dude food prepared with integrity draws the crowds to this fun little place co-
owned by Ollie Dabbous. The food arrives all at once on enamel plates, and
dishes are full of rustic, artery-hardening goodness yet are prepared with precision and care. Just be ready to queue, as it seats fewer than 50.

X

Polpo at Ape & Bird

142 Shaftesbury Ave ⊠ WC2H 8HJ – Ⓜ Leicester Square   Plan: **I3**
– ℰ (020) 7836 3119 – www.polpo.co.uk
Menu £ 25 – Carte £ 12/21 – *(bookings not accepted)*
• **Italian** • **Rustic** • **Simple** •
Even experienced restaurateurs have to sometimes have a rethink. When Rus-
sell Norman found his Ape & Bird pub wasn't working, he simply turned it into
another Polpo. Expect the same style of small plates, just in a bigger place with
a couple of bars.

X

Flesh & Buns
AK 🗔

41 Earlham St ⊠ WC2H 9LX – Ⓜ Leicester Square   Plan: **I3**
– ℰ (020) 7632 9500 – www.fleshandbuns.com – Closed 24-25 December
Menu £ 19 (lunch and early dinner) – Carte £ 21/47 – *(booking advi-
sable)*
• **Asian** • **Trendy** • **Fashionable** •
A loud, fun basement next to the Donmar. There's plenty of Japanese dishes but
star billing goes to the hirata bun – the soft Taiwanese-style steamed pillows of
delight that sandwich your choice of meat or fish filling.

X

Talli Joe
AK ⇔

152-156 Shaftesbury Ave ⊠ WC2H 8HL   Plan: **I3**
*– Ⓜ Covent Garden – ℰ (020) 7836 5400 – www.tallijoe.com – Closed 25-
26 December, 1 January and Sunday*
Carte £ 18/28
• **Indian** • **Fashionable** • **Friendly** •
Talli means 'tipsy' in Hindi and this lively place was inspired by India's dive bars.
Cocktails and tapas-style small plates are the order of the day; some dishes are
old family favourites of the chef, while others have a Western edge.

Lady Ottoline

11a Northington St ⊠ *WC1N 2JF –* Ⓜ *Chancery Lane.*   Plan: J1
– ℰ *(020) 78310008 – www.theladyottoline.com – Closed bank holidays*
Carte £ 26/43

• **Traditional British** • **Cosy** • **Neighbourhood** •

A charmingly traditional feel and a keen sense of history have always defined this classic Victorian pub. Stout British dishes are served in the ground floor bar and the more sedate upstairs dining room.

HOLBORN

Rosewood London   🏋 ⅃🌀 🛎 🎵 🕭 💻 🕭 🚗

252 High Holborn ⊠ *WC1V 7EN –* Ⓜ *Holborn –* ℰ *(020)*   Plan: J2
77818888 – www.rosewoodhotels.com/london
306 rm – ♦£ 378/882 ♦♦£ 378/882 – ☑ £ 20 – 44 suites

• **Historic** • **Luxury** • **Elegant** •

A beautiful Edwardian building that was once the HQ of Pearl Assurance. The styling is very British and the bedrooms are uncluttered and smart. Cartoonist Gerald Scarfe's work adorns the walls of his eponymous bar. A classic brasserie with a menu of British favourites occupies the former banking hall.

The Hoxton   🏋 🕭 💻 🕭

199 - 206 High Holborn ⊠ *WC1V 7BD –* Ⓜ *Holborn*   Plan: J2
– ℰ *(020) 7661 3000 – www.thehoxton.com*
174 rm ☑ – ♦£ 69/299 ♦♦£ 69/299

• **Townhouse** • **Business** • **Contemporary** •

When the room categories are Shoebox, Snug, Cosy and Roomy, you know you're in a hip hotel. A great location and competitive rates plus a retro-style diner, a buzzy lobby and a 'Chicken Shop' in the basement.

Great Queen Street   💻

32 Great Queen St ⊠ *WC2B 5AA –* Ⓜ *Holborn*   Plan: J2
– ℰ *(020) 72420622 – www.greatqueenstreetrestaurant.co.uk – Closed Christmas-New Year, Sunday dinner and bank holidays*
Menu £ 22 (weekday lunch) – Carte £ 21/38 – *(booking essential)*

• **Modern British** • **Rustic** • **Neighbourhood** •

The menu is a model of British understatement and is dictated by the seasons; the cooking, confident and satisfying with laudable prices and generous portions. Lively atmosphere and enthusiastic service. Highlights include the shared dishes like the suet-crusted steak and ale pie for two.

St Pancras Renaissance   ⅃🌀 🛎 🎵 🕭 💻 🕭 🚗

Euston Rd ⊠ *NW1 2AR –* Ⓜ *King's Cross St Pancras*   Plan: J0
– ℰ *(020) 7841 3540 – www.stpancraslondon.com*
245 rm – ♦£ 250/400 ♦♦£ 400/450 – ☑ £ 18 – 10 suites

• **Business** • **Historic** • **Elegant** •

This restored Gothic jewel was built in 1873 as the Midland Grand hotel and reopened in 2011 under the Marriott brand. A former taxi rank is now a spacious lobby and all-day dining is in the old booking office. Luxury suites in Chambers wing; Barlow wing bedrooms are a little more functional.

Gilbert Scott – See restaurant listing

Great Northern H. London   🕭 💻

Pancras Rd ⊠ *N1C 4TB –* Ⓜ *King's Cross St Pancras*   Plan: J0
– ℰ *(020) 3388 0818 – www.gnhlondon.com*
91 rm – ♦£ 249/299 ♦♦£ 249/299 – ☑ £ 25 – 1 suite

• **Historic building** • **Traditional** • **Contemporary** •

Built as a railway hotel in 1854; reborn as a stylish townhouse. Connected to King's Cross' western concourse and just metres from the Eurostar check-in. Bespoke furniture in each of the modern bedrooms, and a pantry on each floor.

XX

Gilbert Scott – St Pancras Renaissance Hotel

Euston Rd ✉ NW1 2AR – Ⓜ King's Cross St Pancras Plan: **J0**
– ✆ (020) 7278 3888 – www.thegilbertscott.co.uk
Menu £ 21 (lunch) – Carte £ 28/61
• Traditional British • Brasserie • Elegant •
Run under the aegis of Marcus Wareing and named after the architect of this Gothic masterpiece, the restaurant has the look of a Grand Salon but the buzz of a brasserie. It celebrates the UK's many regional and historic specialities.

X

Grain Store

Granary Sq, 1-3 Stable St ✉ N1C 4AB Plan: **C2**
– Ⓜ King's Cross St Pancras – ✆ (020) 73244466 – www.grainstore.com
– Closed 24-25 December, 1 January and Sunday dinner
Carte £ 15/35
• Modern cuisine • Rustic • Fashionable •
Big, buzzy 'canteen' from Bruno Loubet and the Zetter hotel people. Eclectic, clever dishes – influenced by Bruno's experiences around the world – are packed with interesting flavours and textures; vegetables often take the lead role.

X

Granger & Co. King's Cross

Stanley Building, 7 Pancras Sq. ✉ N1C 4AG Plan: **J0**
– Ⓜ King's Cross St Pancras
– ✆ (020) 3058 2567 – www.grangerandco.com
– Closed 25-26 December
Carte £ 22/30
• Modern cuisine • Friendly • Neighbourhood •
The third London outpost for Aussie chef Bill Granger is a bright, buzzing place serving small plates, barbecue dishes, and bowls and grains, with plenty of South East Asian flavours. Dishes are vibrant, fresh and uplifting.

HYDE PARK – KNIGHTSBRIDGE PLAN VII

Mandarin Oriental Hyde Park

66 Knightsbridge ✉ SW1X 7LA – Ⓜ Knightsbridge Plan: **F4**
– ✆ (020) 72352000 – www.mandarinoriental.com/london
194 rm – †£ 600/1020 ††£ 600/1020 – ☕ £ 26 – 25 suites
• Grand Luxury • Classic •
The Rosebery, a salon for afternoon tea, is the newest addition to this celebrated hotel which dates from 1889. The luxurious spa now includes a pool; the service is as strong as ever; and the bedrooms, many of which have views of Hyde Park, are spacious and comfortable.
✿✿ **Dinner by Heston Blumenthal • Bar Boulud** – See restaurant listing

Bulgari

171 Knightsbridge ✉ SW7 1DW – Ⓜ Knightsbridge Plan: **F4**
– ✆ (020) 7151 1010 – www.bulgarihotels.com/london
85 rm – †£ 560/790 ††£ 560/790 – ☕ £ 34 – 23 suites
• Luxury • Elegant • Design •
Impeccably tailored hotel making stunning use of materials like silver, mahogany, silk and marble. Luxurious bedrooms with sensual curves, sumptuous bathrooms and a great spa – and there is substance behind the style. Down a sweeping staircase to the Alain Ducasse restaurant.
Rivea – See restaurant listing

XXX
සුසු **Dinner by Heston Blumenthal** – Mandarin Oriental Hyde Park Hotel
66 Knightsbridge, ⊠ SW1X 7LA – Ⓜ Knightsbridge   ⅏ ₥ ⇔
– ℰ (020) 7201 3833 – www.dinnerbyheston.com   Plan: **F4**
– Closed 17-31 October
Menu £ 40 (weekday lunch) – Carte £ 58/121
• **Traditional British** • **Design** • **Fashionable** •
Don't come expecting 'molecular gastronomy' – this is all about respect for, and
a wonderful renewal of, British food, with just a little playfulness thrown in. Each
one of the meticulously crafted and deceptively simple looking dishes comes
with a date relating to its historical provenance.
➜ Mandarin, chicken liver parfait and grilled bread (c.1500). Roast Iberico
pork chop with spelt, ham hock and sauce Robert (c.1820). Tipsy cake
with spit-roast pineapple (c.1810).

XX **Bar Boulud**   ₠ ₥ ⇔
66 Knightsbridge ⊠ SW1X 7LA – Ⓜ Knightsbridge   Plan: **F4**
– ℰ (020) 72352000 – www.mandarinoriental.com/london
Menu £ 19 (weekday lunch) – Carte £ 26/57
• **French** • **Brasserie** • **Fashionable** •
Daniel Boulud's London outpost is fashionable, fun and frantic. His hometown is
Lyon but he built his considerable reputation in New York, so charcuterie, sausa-
ges and burgers are the highlights.

XX **Rivea** – Bulgari Hotel   ⅏ ₠ ₥ ⇔
171 Knightsbridge ⊠ SW7 1DW – Ⓜ Knightsbridge   Plan: **F4**
– ℰ (020) 7151 1025 – www.rivealondon.com
Menu £ 26 (lunch) – Carte £ 39/49
• **Mediterranean cuisine** • **Design** • **Fashionable** •
Elegant basement restaurant where blues and whites make reference to warmer
climes – and also to its sister in St Tropez. Precise, unfussy cooking focuses on the
French and Italian Riviera, with an interesting range of vibrant small plates.

XX **The Magazine**   ⌂ ⌖ ₠ ₥
Serpentine Sackler Gallery, West Carriage Dr, Kensington   Plan: **E4**
Gardens ⊠ W2 2AR – Ⓜ Lancaster Gate – ℰ (020) 7298 7552
– www.magazine-restaurant.co.uk – Closed Monday
Menu £ 24 – Carte £ 26/40 – *(lunch only)*
• **Modern cuisine** • **Design** •
Designed by the late Zaha Hadid, the Serpentine Sackler Gallery comprises a
restored 1805 gunpowder store and a modern tensile extension. The Magazine
is a bright open space with an easy-to-eat menu of dishes whose influences are
largely from within Europe.

XX **Zuma**   ₥
5 Raphael St ⊠ SW7 1DL – Ⓜ Knightsbridge – ℰ (020)   Plan: **F5**
75841010 – www.zumarestaurant.com – Closed 25 December
Carte £ 30/80 – *(booking essential)*
• **Japanese** • **Fashionable** •
Now a global brand but this was the original. The glamorous clientele come for
the striking surroundings, bustling atmosphere and easy-to-share food. Go for
the more modern dishes and those cooked on the robata grill.

BAYSWATER – MAIDA VALE   **PLAN VIII**

XX **Angelus**   ₠ ₥ ⇔
4 Bathurst St ⊠ W2 2SD – Ⓜ Lancaster Gate – ℰ (020)   Plan: **E3**
74020083 – www.angelusrestaurant.co.uk – Closed 24-25 December and
1 January
Menu £ 23 – Carte £ 40/61
• **French** • **Brasserie** • **Neighbourhood** •
Hospitable owner has created an attractive French brasserie within a 19C former pub, with a warm and inclusive feel. Satisfying and honest French cooking
uses seasonal British ingredients.

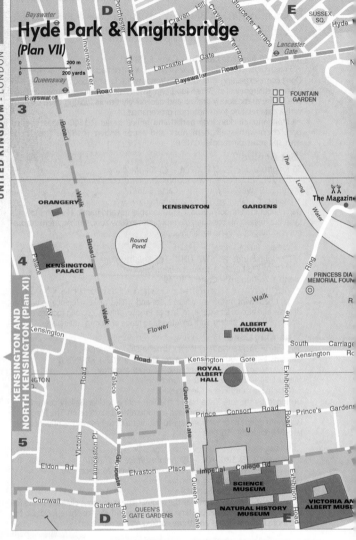

Bayswater

Hyde Park & Knightsbridge
(Plan VII)

0   200 m
0   200 yards

KENSINGTON AND
NORTH KENSINGTON (Plan XI)

FOUNTAIN
GARDEN

ORANGERY

KENSINGTON   GARDENS

The Magazine

Round
Pond

KENSINGTON
PALACE

PRINCESS DIA
MEMORIAL FOUN

Flower

Walk

ALBERT
MEMORIAL

South   Carriage
Kensington   Ro

Kensington   Gore

ROYAL
ALBERT
HALL

Prince   Consort   Road

Prince's   Gardens

Eldon   Rd

Elvaston   Place

Imperial   College   Rd

SCIENCE
MUSEUM

Cornwall

Gardens

QUEEN'S
GATE GARDENS

NATURAL HISTORY
MUSEUM

VICTORIA AN
ALBERT MUSE

XX   **Marianne**

104a Chepstow Rd ⊠ W2 5QS – Ⓜ *Westbourne Park*
– 𝒞 (020) 3675 7750 – www.mariannerestaurant.com – Closed
22 December-5 January , August bank holiday and Monday
Menu £ 35/85 – (dinner only and lunch Friday-Sunday) (booking essential)
(tasting menu only)
• French • Cosy • Intimate •

Plan: **C2**

The eponymous Marianne was a finalist on MasterChef. Her restaurant is a
sweet little place with just 6 tables. Concise daily lunch menu and seasonal tasting menu; cooking is classically based but keeps things quite light.

854

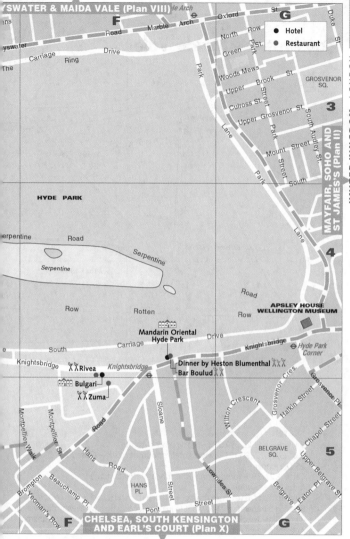

BAYSWATER & MAIDA VALE (Plan VIII)

● Hotel
● Restaurant

HYDE PARK

Serpentine

Mandarin Oriental
Hyde Park

Dinner by Heston Blumenthal
Bar Boulud

Rivea
Bulgari
Zuma

APSLEY HOUSE
WELLINGTON MUSEUM

Hyde Park Corner

BELGRAVE SQ.

HANS PL.

CHELSEA, SOUTH KENSINGTON
AND EARL'S COURT (Plan X)

Hereford Road

3 Hereford Rd ⊠ W2 4AB – Ⓜ Bayswater – ℰ (020)
77271144 – www.herefordroad.org – Closed 24 December-3 January and
August bank holiday   Plan: C2
Menu £ 14 (weekday lunch) – Carte £ 22/32
– (booking essential)

• Traditional British • Neighbourhood • Bistro •

Converted butcher's shop specialising in tasty British dishes without
frills, using first-rate, seasonal ingredients; offal a highlight. Booths for six people
are the prized seats. Friendly and relaxed feel.

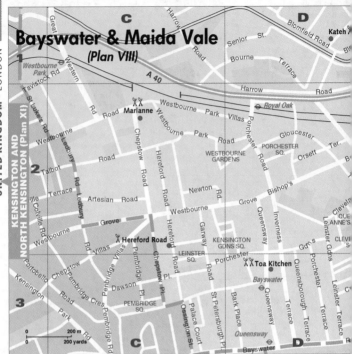

Bayswater & Maida Vale
(Plan VIII)

✗
😊

Kateh

AC

5 Warwick Pl ⊠ W9 2PX – Ⓜ Warwick Avenue   Plan: **D1**
– ℰ (020) 7289 3393 – www.katehrestaurant.co.uk – Closed 25-
26 December
Carte £ 21/39 – *(dinner only and lunch Friday-Sunday)*
(booking essential)
• **Mediterranean cuisine • Neighbourhood • Intimate •**
Booking is imperative if you want to join the locals who have already discovered
what a little jewel they have in the form of this buzzy, busy Persian restaurant.
Authentic stews, expert chargrilling and lovely pastries and teas.

✗

Salt & Honey

AC

28 Sussex Pl ⊠ W2 2TH – Ⓜ Lancaster Gate – ℰ (020)   Plan: **E3**
7706 7900 – www.saltandhoneybistro.com – Closed 25-26 December,
1 January and Monday
Menu £ 15 (weekday lunch) – Carte £ 24/38 – *(bookings advisable at
dinner)*
• **Modern cuisine • Bistro • Neighbourhood •**
A cosy neighbourhood restaurant in a residential area just north of Hyde Park.
Well-priced, colourful, boldly flavoured dishes use the best British ingredients;
expect Mediterranean and Middle Eastern flavours – and plenty of Manuka
honey.

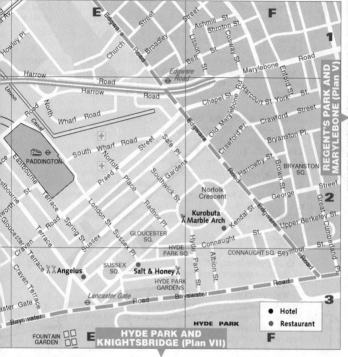

HYDE PARK AND
KNIGHTSBRIDGE (Plan VII)

- Hotel
- Restaurant

X **Kurobuta Marble Arch**   🍴 ⅋ AC

17-20 Kendal St ✉ W2 2AW – Ⓜ Marble Arch – 𝒞 (020)   Plan: **F2**
3475 4158 – www.kurobuta-london.com – Closed 25 December
Carte £ 17/32

• Japanese • Neighbourhood • Fashionable •

The Aussie owner-chef's fun Japanese restaurant was influenced by an izakaya.
The robata grill provides the sticky BBQ pork belly for the pork buns; the black
pepper soft shell crabs fly out of the kitchen; and the yuzu tart is good.

CITY OF LONDON – SOUTHWARK   PLAN IX

CITY OF LONDON

🏨 **Andaz Liverpool Street**   ⅋ ♨ ⅋ AC ⅋

40 Liverpool St ✉ EC2M 7QN – Ⓜ Liverpool Street   Plan: **M2**
– 𝒞 (020) 79611234 – www.andaz.com
267 rm – †£ 173/683 ††£ 189/699 – ⌁ £ 18 – 3 suites

• Business • Design • Contemporary •

A contemporary and stylish interior hides behind the classic Victorian
façade. Bright and spacious bedrooms boast state-of-the-art facilities. Various
dining options include a brasserie specialising in grilled meats, a compact Japanese restaurant and a traditional pub.

Threadneedles

☆ ᴄ AC ᴔ ᴕ

Plan: **M3**

5 Threadneedle St. ⊠ EC2R 8AY – **⓿** *Bank – ℰ (020) 7657 8080 – www.hotelthreadneedles.co.uk*

74 rm – ♦£ 149/599 ♦♦£ 149/599 – ☲ £ 15

• Business • Townhouse • Modern •

A converted bank, dating from 1856, with a smart, boutique feel and a stunning stained-glass cupola in the lounge. Bedrooms are very stylish and individual, featuring Egyptian cotton sheets, iPod docks and thoughtful extras. Spacious bar and restaurant; a striking backdrop to the classical menu.

Montcalm London City at The Brewery

ᴄ AC ᴔ

Plan: **M2**

52 Chiswell St ⊠ EC1Y 4SA – **⓿** *Barbican – ℰ (020) 7614 0100 – www.themontcalmlondoncity.co.uk*

235 rm ☲ – ♦£ 147/400 ♦♦£ 187/500 – 7 suites

• Business • Contemporary • Historic •

The majority of the contemporary rooms are in the original part of the Whitbread Brewery, built in 1714; ask for a quieter one overlooking the courtyard, or one of the 25 found in the 4 restored Georgian townhouses across the road.

Chiswell Street Dining Rooms – See restaurant listing

City Social

⅏ ≲ ᴄ AC ᴕ

Plan: **M3**

Tower 42 (24th floor), 25 Old Broad St ⊠ EC2N 1HQ – **⓿** *Liverpool Street – ℰ (020) 78777703 – www.citysociallondon.com – Closed Sunday and bank holidays*

Carte £ 43/72

• Modern cuisine • Elegant • Design •

Jason Atherton's dark and moody restaurant with an art deco twist, set on the 24th floor of Tower 42; the City views are impressive, especially from tables 10 and 15. The flexible menu is largely European and the cooking manages to be both refined and robust at the same time.

→ Yellowfin tuna tataki with cucumber salad and ponzu dressing. Braised Irish short-rib with celery, watercress and red wine sauce. Chocolate soufflé with orange ice cream.

Lutyens

⅏ AC ᴕ

Plan: **K3**

85 Fleet St. ⊠ EC4Y 1AE – **⓿** *Blackfriars – ℰ (020) 7583 8385 – www.lutyens-restaurant.com – Closed 1 week Christmas-New Year, Saturday, Sunday and bank holidays*

Menu £ 25/33 – Carte £ 30/62

• Modern cuisine • Fashionable •

The unmistakable hand of Sir Terence Conran: timeless and understated good looks mixed with functionality, and an appealing Anglo-French menu with plenty of classics such as fruits de mer and game in season.

Club Gascon (Pascal Aussignac)

⅏ AC

Plan: **L2**

57 West Smithfield ⊠ EC1A 9DS – **⓿** *Barbican – ℰ (020) 76006144 – www.clubgascon.com – Closed Christmas-New Year, Monday lunch, Saturday, Sunday and bank holidays*

Menu £ 35/68 – Carte £ 37/58 – (booking essential)

• French • Intimate • Elegant •

The gastronomy of Gascony and France's southwest are the starting points but the assured and intensely flavoured cooking also pushes at the boundaries. Marble and huge floral displays create suitably atmospheric surroundings.

→ Foie gras terrine with caviar and an oceanic crisp. Lamb with vermouth sauce, mussels and crisp sweetbreads. Scrambled Brillat-Savarin cheese with truffled honey and pistachio.

XX **Yauatcha City**   🛱 ᕼ 🄰🄲 ⇔
Broadgate Circle ⊠ *EC2M 2QS –* ⓜ *Liverpool Street*   Plan: **M2**
– ℰ *(020) 38179880 – www.yauatcha.com – Closed 24 December-*
3 January and bank holidays
Menu £ 29 (weekday lunch) – Carte £ 24/56
• Chinese • Fashionable •
A more corporate version of the stylish Soho original, with a couple of bars and
a terrace at both ends. All the dim sum greatest hits are on the menu but the
chefs have some work to match the high standard found in Broadwick Street.

XX **Bread Street Kitchen**   🄰🄲
10 Bread St ⊠ *EC4M 9AJ –* ⓜ *St Paul's –* ℰ *(020)*   Plan: **L3**
3030 4050 – www.breadstreetkitchen.com
Carte £ 32/57 – *(booking advisable)*
• Modern cuisine • Trendy • Brasserie •
Gordon Ramsay's take on NY loft-style dining comes with a large bar, thumping
music, an open kitchen and enough zinc ducting to kit out a small industrial
estate. For the food, think modern bistro dishes with an element of refinement.

XX **Vanilla Black**   🄰🄲 🄸🄾
17-18 Tooks Ct. ⊠ *EC4A 1LB –* ⓜ *Chancery Lane*   Plan: **K2**
– ℰ *(020) 72422622 – www.vanillablack.co.uk – Closed 2 weeks Christmas*
and bank holidays
Menu £ 27/42 – *(booking essential)*
• Vegetarian • Intimate • Romantic •
A vegetarian restaurant where real thought has gone into the creation of dishes,
which deliver an array of interesting texture and flavour contrasts. Modern techniques are subtly incorporated and while there are some original combinations,
they are well-judged.

XX **New St Grill**   🐝 🛱 ᕼ 🄰🄲
16a New St ⊠ *EC2M 4TR –* ⓜ *Liverpool Street*   Plan: **N2**
– ℰ *(020) 3503 0785 – www.newstreetgrill.com – Closed 25 December-*
3 January except dinner 31 December
Menu £ 27 (lunch and early dinner) – Carte £ 35/69
• Meats and grills • Friendly • Intimate •
D&D converted an 18C warehouse to satisfy our increasing appetite for red
meat. They use Black Angus beef: grass-fed British, aged for 28 days, or corn-
fed American, aged for 40 days. Start with a drink in the Old Bengal Bar.

XX **Sauterelle**   ᕼ ⇔ 🄸🄾
The Royal Exchange ⊠ *EC3V 3LR –* ⓜ *Bank –* ℰ *(020)*   Plan: **M3**
76182483 – www.royalexchange-grandcafe.co.uk – Closed Christmas,
Easter, Saturday, Sunday and bank holidays
Menu £ 25 – Carte £ 32/44
• French • Design •
Impressive location on the mezzanine floor of The Royal Exchange; ask for a
table overlooking the Grand Café which was the original trading floor. A largely
French-inspired contemporary menu makes good use of luxury ingredients.

XX **The Chancery**   🄰🄲 ⇔
9 Cursitor St ⊠ *EC4A 1LL –* ⓜ *Chancery Lane –* ℰ *(020)*
78314000 – www.thechancery.co.uk – Closed 23 December-4 January,   Plan: **K2**
Saturday lunch, Sunday and bank holidays
Menu £ 40/68
• Modern cuisine • Chic • Neighbourhood •
An elegant restaurant that's so close to the law courts you'll assume your fellow
diners are barristers, jurors or the recently acquitted. The menu is appealingly
concise; dishes come with a classical backbone and bold flavours.

UNITED KINGDOM - LONDON

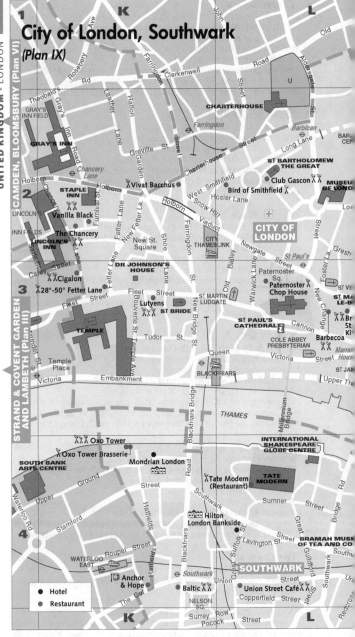

City of London, Southwark

(Plan IX)

| Hotel |
| Restaurant |

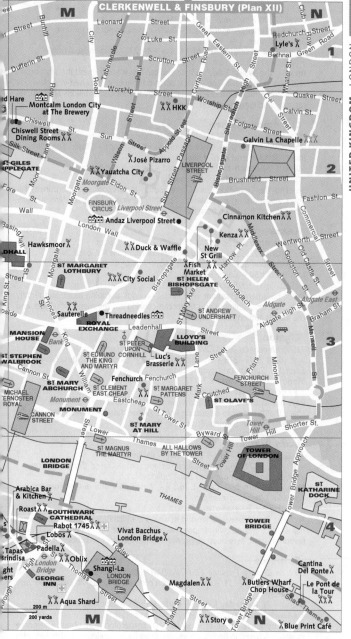

M   N   N   1

Redchurch Street
Lyle's ✗
Leonard   Street
St Luke St.
Scrutton   Street
Bethnal Green Road
Club
Quaker   Street
Calvin St.

Dufferin St.
Bunhill   Row
Tabernacle   St.
City   Road
Paul   Street
Worship   Street
Curtain   Road
Great Eastern St.
High St.
Shoreditch
Wheler St.
Commercial Street

ed Hare
Montcalm London City
at The Brewery
Chiswell   St.
Chiswell Street
Dining Rooms ✗✗
Silk Street
Sun   Street
✗ José Pizarro
Appold Street
✗✗ HKK
Worship St.
Folgate   Street
Galvin La Chapelle ✗✗✗

ST-GILES
IPPLEGATE
Fore   St.
Wall
Moor   Street
✗✗ Yauatcha City
Moorgate Eldon St.
Sun   Street
LIVERPOOL
STREET
Bishopsgate
Brushfield   Street
Fashion St.

Basinghall   Street
FINSBURY
CIRCUS   Liverpool Street
London Wall
Andaz Liverpool Street ●
Liverpool Street ●
Cinnamon Kitchen ✗✗
Kenza ✗✗
Middlesex Street
Wentworth   Street
Old Castle St.
Commercial   Street

DHALL
Hawksmoor ✗
Moorgate
ST MARGARET
LOTHBURY
✗✗ Duck & Waffle
New
St Grill
✗ Fish
Market
✗✗
Harrow Pl.
Goulston   St.
Aldgate   East
Braham St.

Street
St Mary Axe
Houndsditch
Aldgate
Aldgate High St.
Mansell   St.

side
Princes   St.
✗✗ City Social
Bishopsgate
ST HELEN
BISHOPSGATE
ST ANDREW
UNDERSHAFT

Sauterelle
✗✗
● Threadneedles
ROYAL
EXCHANGE
Leadenhall   Street
ST PETER
UPON
CORNHILL
LLOYD'S
BUILDING
Lime   Street
3

MANSION
HOUSE
Bank
King   William   St.
ST EDMUND
THE KING
AND MARTYR
Luc's
Brasserie ✗✗
Friars
Minories
St.

ST STEPHEN
WALBROOK
Cannon   Street
ST MARY
ABCHURCH
ST CLEMENT
EAST CHEAP
Fenchurch   Fenchurch
ST MARGARET
PATTENS
FENCHURCH
STREET
Crutched

MICHAEL
ERNOSTER
ROYAL
CANNON
STREET
Monument ⊖
MONUMENT
Eastcheap
✗✗
Gt Tower St.
ST OLAVE'S
Mark   Lane

ST MARY
AT HILL
Byward St.
Tower
Hill
Shorter St.

LONDON
BRIDGE
Lower   Thames   Street
ST MAGNUS
THE MARTYR
ALL HALLOWS
BY THE TOWER
Tower Hill
Tower
TOWER
OF LONDON
ST
KATHARINE
DOCK

Arabica Bar
& Kitchen ✗
Roast ✗✗
SOUTHWARK
CATHEDRAL
THAMES
Tower Bridge Approach
4

s
Rabot 1745 ✗✗ ✗
Lobos ✗
Vivat Bacchus
London Bridge ✗
TOWER
BRIDGE

Tapas
rindisa
Padella ✗
✗✗ Oblix
London
Bridge
High Street
Cantina
Del Ponte ✗
Le Pont de
la Tour

ght
ers
GEORGE
INN
London Bridge
St Thomas   Street
Shangi-La
LONDON
BRIDGE
Magdalen ✗✗
✗ Butlers Wharf
Chop House
✗✗✗
Shad   Thames

✗✗ Aqua Shard
Tooley   Street
Shand St.
Tower Bridge Road
✗✗ Story ●
✗ Blue Print Café

200 m
200 yards

M   N

XX **Fenchurch** ⩽ 🅴 🅰🅲 ⇌

Level 37, 20 Fenchurch St ⊠ EC3M 3BY Plan: **M3**
– Ⓜ Monument – ℰ (0333) 772 0020 – www.skygarden.london – Closed Sunday dinner
Menu £ 32 (weekday lunch) – Carte £ 44/73 – *(booking advisable)*
• Modern cuisine • Design •
Arrive at the 'Walkie Talkie' early so you can first wander round the Sky Garden and take in the views. The smartly dressed restaurant is housed in a glass box within the atrium. Dishes are largely British; flavour combinations are complementary and ingredients top drawer.

XX **Cinnamon Kitchen** 🍴 🅴 🅰🅲 ⇌ 🗄

9 Devonshire Sq ⊠ EC2M 4YL – Ⓜ Liverpool Street Plan: **N2**
– ℰ (020) 76265000 – www.cinnamon-kitchen.com – Closed Saturday lunch, Sunday and bank holidays
Menu £ 20 (lunch and early dinner) – Carte £ 24/51
• Indian • Trendy • Minimalist •
Sister to The Cinnamon Club. Contemporary Indian cooking, with punchy flavours and arresting presentation. Sprightly service in large, modern surroundings. Watch the action from the Tandoor Bar.

XX **Kenza** 🅰🅲 ⇌

10 Devonshire Sq. ⊠ EC2M 4YP – Ⓜ Liverpool Street Plan: **N2**
– ℰ (020) 79295533 – www.kenza-restaurant.com – Closed 24-25 December, Saturday lunch and bank holidays
Menu £ 30/50 – Carte £ 29/43
• Lebanese • Exotic décor • Design •
Exotic basement restaurant, with lamps, carvings, pumping music and nightly belly dancing. Lebanese and Moroccan cooking are the menu influences and the food is authentic and accurate.

XX **Cigalon** 🅰🅲 ⇌

115 Chancery Ln ⊠ WC2A 1PP – Ⓜ Chancery Lane Plan: **K3**
– ℰ (020) 7242 8373 – www.cigalon.co.uk – Closed Christmas, New Year, Saturday, Sunday and bank holidays
Menu £ 27/35 – Carte £ 31/37
• French • Intimate • Chic •
Pays homage to the food and wine of Provence, in an appropriately bright space that was a once an auction house. All the classics are here, from bouillabaisse to pieds et paquets. Busy bar in the cellar.

XX **Luc's Brasserie** Plan: **M3**

17-22 Leadenhall Mkt ⊠ EC3V 1LR – Ⓜ Bank
– ℰ (020) 76210666 – www.lucsbrasserie.com – Closed Christmas, New Year, Saturday, Sunday and bank holidays
Menu £ 18 (lunch) – Carte £ 26/71 – *(lunch only and dinner Tuesday-Thursday) (booking essential)*
• French • Brasserie • Elegant •
A classic French brasserie looking down on the Victorian splendour of Leadenhall Market and run with impressive efficiency. The menu has all the French favourites you'll ever need, along with steaks in all sizes and chops aplenty.

XX **Barbecoa** 🅰🅲

20 New Change Passage ⊠ EC4M 9AG – Ⓜ St Paul's Plan: **L3**
– ℰ (020) 3005 8555 – www.barbecoa.com – Closed 25-26 December and 1 January
Menu £ 27 (weekday lunch) – Carte £ 33/64 – *(booking essential)*
• Meats and grills • Design • Brasserie •
Set up by Jamie Oliver, to show us what barbecuing is all about. The prime meats, butchered in-house, are just great; go for the pulled pork shoulder with cornbread on the side. By dessert you may be willing to share.

XX **Chiswell Street Dining Rooms** – Montcalm London City Hotel
56 Chiswell St ⊠ *EC1Y 4SA –* Ⓜ *Barbican –* ℰ *(020)*   ᕷ 🅰🅲 🕸
7614 0177 – www.chiswellstreetdining.com – Closed 25-   Plan: **M2**
26 December, 1 January, Saturday and Sunday
Menu £ 38 – Carte £ 31/57
• Modern British • Brasserie • Design •
A Martin brothers' restaurant in a corner spot of the old Whitbread Brewery; it
comes alive in the evening, thanks to its kicking cocktail bar. The menu makes
good use of British produce, especially fish from nearby Billingsgate.

XX **Duck & Waffle**   ≤ ᕷ 🅰🅲 ⇔
Heron Tower (40th floor), 110 Bishopsgate   Plan: **M2**
⊠ *EC2N 4AY –* Ⓜ *Liverpool Street –* ℰ *(020) 3640 7310*
– www.duckandwaffle.com
Carte £ 30/65 – *(booking essential)*
• Modern cuisine • Trendy • Romantic •
The UK's highest restaurant, on the 40th floor of Heron Tower. The menu is
varied and offal is done well – try the crispy pig's ears. It's open 24 hours a day
and offers breakfast, lunch and dinner, as well as brunch at weekends.

X **Bird of Smithfield**   🅰🅲 ⇔
26 Smithfield St ⊠ *EC1A 9LB –* Ⓜ *Farringdon –* ℰ *(020)*   Plan: **L2**
7559 5100 – www.birdofsmithfield.com – Closed Christmas, New Year,
Sunday and bank holidays
Menu £ 18 (lunch and early dinner) – Carte £ 26/46 – *(booking essential)*
• Traditional British • Design • Intimate •
Feels like a private members' club but without the smugness. Five floors of fun
include a cocktail bar, lounge, rooftop terrace and small, friendly restaurant. The
appealing British menu makes good use of the country's larder.

X **Hawksmoor**   🕸 🅰🅲 ⇔
10-12 Basinghall St ⊠ *EC2V 5BQ –* Ⓜ *Bank –* ℰ *(020)*   Plan: **M3**
7397 8120 – www.thehawksmoor.com – Closed 24 December-2 January,
Saturday, Sunday and bank holidays
Menu £ 28 (lunch and early dinner) – Carte £ 23/71 – *(booking essential)*
• Meats and grills • Traditional décor • Brasserie •
Fast and furious, busy and boisterous, this handsome room is the backdrop for
another testosterone filled celebration of the serious business of beef eating.
Nicely aged and rested Longhorn steaks take centre-stage.

X **José Pizarro**   🍽 ᕷ 🅰🅲
36 Broadgate Circle ⊠ *EC2M 1QS –* Ⓜ *Liverpool Street*   Plan: **M2**
– ℰ *(020) 72565333 – www.josepizarro.com – Closed Sunday*
Carte £ 24/31
• Spanish • Tapas bar •
The eponymous chef's third operation is a good fit here: it's well run, flexible
and fairly priced – and that includes the wine list. The Spanish menu is nicely
balanced, with the fish and seafood dishes being the standouts.

X **Fish Market**   🍽 ᕷ 🅰🅲
16b New St ⊠ *EC2M 4TR –* Ⓜ *Liverpool Street*   Plan: **N2**
– ℰ *(020) 3503 0790 – www.fishmarket-restaurant.co.uk – Closed 25-*
26 December, 1 January, Sunday dinner and bank holidays
Menu £ 20 – Carte £ 27/39 – *(booking advisable)*
• Seafood • Friendly •
How to get to the seaside from Liverpool Street? Simply step into this bright fish
restaurant, in an old warehouse of the East India Company, and you'll almost
hear the seagulls. The menu is lengthy and the cooking style classic.

Vivat Bacchus

47 Farringdon St ✉ EC4A 4LL – Ⓜ Farringdon – ✆ (020) 73532648 – www.vivatbacchus.co.uk – Closed Christmas-New Year, Sunday and bank holidays Plan: **K2**

Carte £ 20/45

• Meats and grills • Wine bar • Friendly •

Wine is the star at this bustling City spot: from 4 cellars come 500 labels and 15,000 bottles. The menu complements the wine: steaks, charcuterie, sharing platters and South African specialities feature along with great cheeses.

Paternoster Chop House

Warwick Ct., Paternoster Sq. ✉ EC4M 7DX – Ⓜ St Paul's – ✆ (020) 70299400 – www.paternosterchophouse.co.uk – Closed 26-30 December, 1 January, lunch Saturday and dinner Sunday Plan: **L3**

Menu £ 20 (lunch and early dinner) – Carte £ 28/49

• Traditional British • Brasserie • Trendy •

Appropriately British menu in a restaurant lying in the shadow of St Paul's Cathedral. Large, open room with full-length windows; busy bar attached. Kitchen uses thoughtfully sourced produce.

28°-50° Fetter Lane

140 Fetter Ln ✉ EC4A 1BT – Ⓜ Temple – ✆ (020) 72428877 – www.2850.co.uk – Closed Saturday, Sunday and bank holidays Plan: **K3**

Menu £ 20 (weekday lunch) – Carte £ 26/51

• Modern cuisine • Wine bar • Simple •

From the owner of Texture comes this cellar wine bar and informal restaurant. The terrific wine list is thoughtfully compiled and the grills, cheeses, charcuterie and European dishes are designed to allow the wines to shine.

Jugged Hare

42 Chiswell St ✉ EC1Y 4SA – Ⓜ Barbican. – ✆ (020) 7614 0134 – www.thejuggedhare.com – Closed 25-26 December Plan: **M2**

Carte £ 30/60 – *(booking essential)*

• Traditional British • Pub • Trendy •

Vegetarians may feel ill at ease – and not just because of the taxidermy. The atmospheric dining room, with its open kitchen down one side, specialises in stout British dishes, with meats from the rotisserie a highlight.

Bermondsey

Shangri-La

The Shard, 31 St Thomas St ✉ SE1 9QU – Ⓜ London Bridge – ✆ (020) 7234 8000 – www.shangri-la.com/london Plan: **M4**

202 rm – †£ 350/575 ††£ 350/575 – ☕ £ 32 – 17 suites

• Luxury • Chain • Elegant •

When your hotel occupies floors 34-52 of The Shard, you know it's going to have the wow factor. The pool is London's highest and north-facing bedrooms have the best views. An East-meets-West theme includes the restaurant's menu and afternoon tea when you have a choice of traditional English or Asian.

Bermondsey Square

Bermondsey Sq, Tower Bridge Rd ✉ SE1 3UN – Ⓜ London Bridge – ✆ (020) 7378 2450 – www.bermondseysquarehotel.co.uk Plan: **D2**

90 rm – †£ 99/239 ††£ 99/239 – ☕ £ 11

• Business • Modern • Design •

Cleverly designed hotel in a regenerated square, with subtle '60s influences and a hip feel. Relaxed public areas; well-equipped bedrooms include stylish loft suites.

UNITED KINGDOM - LONDON

XXX **Le Pont de la Tour** 🍴 ≤ 🛋 & ⇔

36d Shad Thames, Butlers Wharf ✉ *SE1 2YE* Plan: **N4**
– ⓜ London Bridge – ℰ (020) 74038403 – www.lepontdelatour.co.uk
– Closed 1 January
Menu £ 20/32 – Carte £ 34/67
• **French • Elegant • Intimate •**
Few restaurants can beat the setting, especially when you're on the terrace with
its breathtaking views of Tower Bridge. For its 25th birthday it got a top-to-toe
refurbishment, resulting in a warmer looking room in which to enjoy the
French-influenced cooking.

XX **Story** (Tom Sellers) & 🅰🅲
✿ *199 Tooley St* ✉ *SE1 2JX –* ⓜ *London Bridge – ℰ (020)* Plan: **N5**
*7183 2117 – www.restaurantstory.co.uk – Closed 2 weeks Christmas-New
Year, Easter, Sunday, Monday lunch and bank holidays*
Menu £ 39 (weekday lunch)/100 – *(booking essential) (tasting menu only)*
• **Modern cuisine • Design • Neighbourhood •**
Tom Sellers offers a 6 or 10 course lunch and a 12 course dinner menu; serving
just 12 tables in what used to be a public toilet and now looks like a Nordic eco-
lodge. Modern techniques and a light touch result in food with a back-to-nature
feel and strong earthy flavours. Dishes are colourful, playful and easy to eat.
➜ Heritage potato cake with shallots. Scallops with ash-roasted cucumber
and dill. Chocolate and lovage.

XX **Magdalen** 🅰🅲
152 Tooley St. ✉ *SE1 2TU –* ⓜ *London Bridge* Plan: **M4**
*– ℰ (020) 74031342 – www.magdalenrestaurant.co.uk – Closed Sunday,
Saturday lunch and bank holidays*
Menu £ 17 (lunch) – Carte £ 29/50
• **Modern British • Neighbourhood •**
The clever sourcing and confident British cooking will leave you satisfied. Add
genial service, an affordable lunch menu and a food-friendly wine list and you
have the favourite restaurant of many.

XX **Oblix** ≤ & 🅰🅲
Level 32, The Shard, 31 St Thomas St. ✉ *SE1 9RY* Plan: **M4**
– ⓜ London Bridge – ℰ (020) 72686700 – www.oblixrestaurant.com
Menu £ 32 (lunch) – Carte £ 29/156
• **Meats and grills • Trendy • Design •**
A New York grill restaurant on the 32nd floor of The Shard; window tables for
two are highly prized. Meats and fish from the rotisserie, grill and Josper oven
are the stars of the show; brunch in the lounge bar at weekends.

XX **Aqua Shard** ≤ 🅰🅲 ⇔
Level 31, The Shard, 31 St Thomas St, ✉ *SE1 9RY* Plan: **M4**
*– ⓜ London Bridge – ℰ (020) 3011 1256 – www.aquashard.co.uk – Closed
25 December*
Menu £ 36 (weekday lunch)/48 – Carte £ 39/79
• **Modern cuisine • Fashionable • Design •**
The Shard's most accessible restaurant covers all bases by serving breakfast,
brunch, lunch, afternoon tea and dinner. If you don't mind queuing, you can
even come just for a drink. The contemporary cooking makes good use of Bri-
tish ingredients and comes with a degree of finesse in flavour and looks.

X **Blueprint Café** ≤
28 Shad Thames, Butlers Wharf ✉ *SE1 2YD* Plan: **N5**
*– ⓜ London Bridge – ℰ (020) 73787031 – www.blueprintcafe.co.uk
– Closed 1 January and Sunday dinner*
Menu £ 25 (weekday lunch) – Carte £ 27/47
• **Modern cuisine • Brasserie • Friendly •**
Retractable, floor to ceiling windows make the most of the river views from this
bright restaurant overlooking the Thames. Cooking is light, seasonally pertinent
and easy to eat and the set menus come with appealing price tags.

X **Village East**   🖭 ⟡

171-173 Bermondsey St ⊠ *SE1 3UW*   Plan: **D2**
*– ⓜ London Bridge – ℰ (020) 7357 6082 – www.villageeast.co.uk – Closed
24-26 December*
Carte £ 27/45
• **Modern cuisine** • **Trendy** • **Neighbourhood** •
Counter dining is the focus in the main room; those celebrating can tuck them-
selves away in a separate bar. Cooking mixes contemporary dishes with Medi-
terranean-inspired plates; the confit turkey leg is the house speciality.

X **Cantina Del Ponte**   ⟨ 🛱

36c Shad Thames, Butlers Wharf ⊠ *SE1 2YE*   Plan: **N4**
*– ⓜ London Bridge – ℰ (020) 74035403 – www.cantina.co.uk – Closed
25 December*
Menu £ 16/23 – Carte £ 28/49
• **Italian** • **Rustic** •
This Italian stalwart offers an appealing mix of classic dishes and reliable favouri-
tes from a sensibly priced menu, in pleasant faux-rustic surroundings. Its plea-
sant terrace takes advantage of its riverside setting.

X **Butlers Wharf Chop House**   ⟨ 🛱 🖭

36e Shad Thames, Butlers Wharf ⊠ *SE1 2YE*   Plan: **N4**
*– ⓜ London Bridge – ℰ (020) 7403 3403
– www.chophouse-restaurant.co.uk – Closed 1 January*
Carte £ 25/60
• **Traditional British** • **Brasserie** • **Simple** •
Grab a table on the terrace in summer and dine in the shadow of Tower Bridge.
Rustic feel to the interior; noisy and fun. The menu focuses on traditional Eng-
lish ingredients and dishes; grilled meats a speciality.

X **Vivat Bacchus London Bridge**   🕸 🛱

4 Hays Ln ⊠ *SE1 2HB* – ⓜ *London Bridge – ℰ (020)*   Plan: **M4**
*72340891 – www.vivatbacchus.co.uk – Closed Christmas-New Year,
Sunday and bank holidays*
Carte £ 20/45
• **Meats and grills** • **Wine bar** • **Friendly** •
Wines from the South African owners' homeland feature strongly and are well-
suited to the meat dishes – the strength here. Choose one of the sharing boards
themed around various countries, like Italian hams or South African BBQ.

X **Pizarro**   🖭 ⟡

194 Bermondsey St ⊠ *SE1 3UW* – ⓜ *Borough*   Plan: **D2**
– ℰ (020) 73789455 – www.josepizarro.com – Closed 24-28 December
Menu £ 35 – Carte £ 25/45
• **Mediterranean cuisine** • **Neighbourhood** • **Simple** •
José Pizarro has a refreshingly simple way of naming his establishments: after
José, his tapas bar, comes Pizarro, a larger restaurant a few doors down. Go for
the small plates, like prawns with piquillo peppers and jamón.

X **Antico**   🖭 🕸

214 Bermondsey St ⊠ *SE1 3TQ* – ⓜ *London Bridge*   Plan: **D2**
*– ℰ (020) 7407 4682 – www.antico-london.co.uk – Closed 24-
26 December, 1 January and Monday*
Menu £ 17 (lunch and early dinner) – Carte £ 25/36
• **Italian** • **Neighbourhood** • **Rustic** •
A former antiques warehouse, with a fun atmosphere. Straightforward Italian
food has its focus on comfort; homemade pasta dishes are a highlight. The
downstairs cocktail bar offers over 80 gins and their own brand of tonic water.

UNITED KINGDOM - LONDON

✗ **Casse Croûte**

109 Bermondsey St ✉ *SE1 3XB* – Ⓜ *London Bridge*   Plan: **D2**
– ℰ (020) 7407 2140 – www.cassecroute.co.uk – Closed Sunday dinner
Carte £ 28/35 – *(booking essential)*
• French • Bistro • Friendly •

Squeeze into this tiny bistro and you'll find yourself transported to rural France.
A blackboard menu offers three choices for each course but new dishes are
added as others run out. The cooking is rustic, authentic and heartening.

✗ **José**   ⅙ 🗚

(☺) *104 Bermondsey St* ✉ *SE1 3UB* – Ⓜ *London Bridge*   Plan: **D2**
*– ℰ (020) 7403 4902 – www.josepizarro.com – Closed 24-
26 December and Sunday dinner*
Carte £ 12/28
• Spanish • Minimalist • Tapas bar •

Standing up while eating tapas feels so right, especially at this snug, lively bar
that packs 'em in like boquerones. The vibrant dishes are intensely flavoured;
five per person should suffice; go for the daily fish dishes from the blackboard.
There's a great list of sherries too.

✗ **St John Maltby**

41 Ropewalk, Maltby St ✉ *SE1 3PA*   Plan I: **D2**
*– Ⓜ London Bridge – ℰ (020) 7553 9844
– www.stjohngroup.uk.com/maltby_street – Closed Christmas, New Year
and Sunday dinner-Tuesday*
Carte £ 31/35 – *(dinner only and lunch Friday-Sunday) (booking advisable)*
• Traditional British • Bistro • Simple •

An austere, industrial-style dining space, tucked under a railway arch in deepest
Bermondsey. Cooking is tasty, satisfying and as British as John Bull and the earthy, original selection of wines are also available to take away.

🍴 **Garrison**   🗚 ⇔

99-101 Bermondsey St ✉ *SE1 3XB* – Ⓜ *London Bridge.*   Plan: **D2**
– ℰ (020) 70899355 – www.thegarrison.co.uk – Closed 25-26 December
Menu £ 24/29 – Carte £ 26/38 – *(booking essential at dinner)*
• Mediterranean cuisine • Pub • Friendly •

Known for its charming vintage look, booths and sweet-natured service, The
Garrison boasts a warm, relaxed vibe. Open from breakfast until dinner, when
a Mediterranean-led menu pulls in the crowds.

SOUTHWARK

🏨 **Mondrian London**   ⛲ ≼ 𝕴𝖟 ⊛ 🐾 🕭 🗚 𝖘𝖆 ⇔ 🛋

20 Upper Ground ✉ *SE1 9PD* – Ⓜ *Southwark* – ℰ (020)   Plan: **K4**
3747 1000 – www.mondrianlondon.com
359 rm – 🛏£ 232 🛏🛏£ 319 – ⌸ £ 16 – 5 suites
• Business • Design • Grand luxury •

The former Sea Containers house now has slick, stylish look evoking the golden
age of the transatlantic liner. Rooms come with a bright splash of colour; Suites
have balconies and Superiors, a river view. Globally influenced small plates in
the smart restaurant, with meat and fish from the grill & clay oven.

🏨 **Hilton London Bankside**   ⛲ 𝕴𝖟 🗖 ⅙ 🗚 𝖘𝖆

2-8 Great Suffolk St ✉ *SE1 0UG* – Ⓜ *Southwark*   Plan: **L4**
– ℰ (020) 3667 5600 – www.londonbankside.hilton.com
292 rm – 🛏£ 230/260 🛏🛏£ 230/260 – ⌸ £ 30 – 30 suites
• Business • Modern •

A sleek, design-led hotel with faux industrial touches; ideally situated for visiting
the attractions of the South Bank. Spacious, contemporary bedrooms are furnished in a minimalist style. Impressive pool in the basement. OXBO serves a range
of British dishes including meats from the Josper grill.

867

UNITED KINGDOM - LONDON

XxX **Oxo Tower**   🕸 ≼ 🏠 **AC** 🛈
Oxo Tower Wharf (8th floor), Barge House St   Plan: **K4**
✉ *SE1 9PH –* **Ⓜ** *Southwark –* 🕽 *(020) 78033888 – www.oxotower.co.uk*
– Closed 25 December
Menu £ 34 (lunch) – Carte £ 41/76
• Modern cuisine • Fashionable • Design •
Set on top of an iconic converted factory and providing stunning views of the
Thames and beyond. Stylish, minimalist interior with huge windows. Expect
quite ambitious, mostly European, cuisine.
Oxo Tower Brasserie – See restaurant listing

XX **Roast**   **AC** 🛈
The Floral Hall, Borough Mkt ✉ *SE1 1TL*   Plan: **M4**
– **Ⓜ** *London Bridge –* 🕽 *(020) 30066111 – www.roast-restaurant.com*
– Closed 25-26 December and 1 January
Menu £ 30/38 – Carte £ 39/69 – *(booking essential)*
• Modern British • Fashionable •
Known for its British food and for promoting UK producers – not surprising con-
sidering the restaurant's in the heart of Borough Market. The 'dish of the day' is
often a highlight; service is affable and there's live music at night.

XX **Baltic**   ♿ ⇔ 🗟
74 Blackfriars Rd ✉ *SE1 8HA –* **Ⓜ** *Southwark –* 🕽 *(020)*   Plan: **K4**
79281111 – www.balticrestaurant.co.uk – Closed 24-26 December
and Monday lunch
Menu £ 18 (weekday lunch)/25 – Carte £ 25/36 – *(bookings advisable at
dinner)*
• World cuisine • Brasserie •
A bright, buzzing restaurant with wooden trussed ceilings, skylights and sleek
styling. The menu specialises in Eastern European food, from Poland, Russia,
Bulgaria and even Siberia. Dumplings and meat dishes stand out – and the vodkas will warm the heart.

XX **Union Street Café**   ♿ **AC** ⇔
47-51 Great Suffolk Street ✉ *SE1 0BS*   Plan: **L4**
– **Ⓜ** *London Bridge –* 🕽 *(020) 7592 7977*
– www.gordonramsayrestaurants.com/union-street-cafe/
Menu £ 20 (weekday lunch) – Carte £ 39/47
• Italian • Trendy • Design •
Occupying a former warehouse, this Gordon Ramsay restaurant has been busy
since day one and comes with a New York feel, a faux industrial look and a basement bar. The Italian menu keeps things simple and stays true to the classics.

XX **Rabot 1745**   🏠 ♿ **AC** ⇔
2-4 Bedal St, Borough Mkt ✉ *SE1 9AL*   Plan: **M4**
– **Ⓜ** *London Bridge –* 🕽 *(020) 73788226 – www.rabot1745.com – Closed*
25-30 December, Sunday and Monday
Carte £ 26/42
• Modern cuisine • Design • Fashionable •
Want something different? How about cocoa cuisine? Rabot 1745 is from the
owners of Hotel Chocolat and is named after their estate in St Lucia. They take
the naturally bitter, spicy flavours of the bean and use them subtly in classically
based dishes. The chocolate mousse dessert is pretty good too!

X **Tate Modern (Restaurant)**   ♿ ⇔
Switch House (9th floor), Tate Modern, Bankside   Plan: **L4**
✉ *SE1 9TG –* **Ⓜ** *Southwark –* 🕽 *(020) 7401 5621 – www.tate.org.uk*
– Closed 24-26 December
Carte £ 27/56 – *(lunch only and dinner Friday-Saturday)*
• Modern British • Design • Brasserie •
A contemporary, faux-industrial style restaurant on the ninth floor of the striking
Switch House extension. Modern menus champion British ingredients; desserts
are a highlight and the wine list interesting and well-priced.

X
(🕸)

Elliot's

12 Stoney St, Borough Market ⊠ *SE1 9AD*   Plan: **L4**
– Ⓜ *London Bridge –* ℰ *(020) 74037436 – www.elliotscafe.com – Closed
Sunday and bank holidays*
Carte £ 19/31 *– (booking advisable)*
• **Modern cuisine** • **Rustic** • **Friendly** •

A lively, unpretentious café which sources its ingredients from Borough Market,
in which it stands. The appealing menu is concise and the cooking is earthy,
pleasingly uncomplicated and very satisfying. Try one of the sharing dishes.

X

Oxo Tower Brasserie   ⇐ 🏠 AC

Oxo Tower Wharf (8th floor), Barge House St   Plan: **K4**
⊠ *SE1 9PH –* Ⓜ *Southwark –* ℰ *(020) 7803 3888 – www.oxotower.co.uk
– Closed 25 December*
Menu £ 30 *(lunch and early dinner) –* Carte £ 27/49
• **Modern cuisine** • **Design** •

Less formal but more fun than the next-door restaurant. Open-plan kitchen produces modern, colourful and easy-to-eat dishes with influences from the Med.
Great views too from the bar.

X
(🕸)

Padella   AC

6 Southwark St, Borough Market ⊠ *SE1 1TQ*   Plan: **M4**
– Ⓜ *London Bridge – www.padella.co – Closed 25-26 December, Sunday
dinner and bank holidays*
Carte £ 14/20 *– (bookings not accepted)*
• **Italian** • **Bistro** • **Simple** •

This lively little sister to Trullo offers a short, seasonal menu where hand-rolled
pasta is the star of the show. Sauces and fillings are inspired by the owners' trips
to Italy and prices are extremely pleasing to the pocket. Sit at the ground floor
counter overlooking the open kitchen.

X

Tapas Brindisa   I⊘

18-20 Southwark St, Borough Market ⊠ *SE1 1TJ*   Plan: **M4**
– Ⓜ *London Bridge –* ℰ *(020) 73578880
– www.brindisatapaskitchens.com*
Carte £ 20/32 *– (bookings not accepted)*
• **Spanish** • **Tapas bar** •

A blueprint for many of the tapas bars that subsequently sprung up over London. It has an infectious energy and the well-priced, robust dishes include Gali-
cian-style hake and black rice with squid; do try the hand-carved Ibérico hams.

X

Wright Brothers

11 Stoney St., Borough Market ⊠ *SE1 9AD*   Plan: **L4**
– Ⓜ *London Bridge –* ℰ *(020) 74039554 – www.thewrightbrothers.co.uk
– Closed bank holidays*
Carte £ 21/87 *– (booking advisable)*
• **Seafood** • **Cosy** • **Traditional décor** •

Originally an oyster wholesaler; now offers a wide range of oysters along with
porter, as well as fruits de mer, daily specials and assorted pies. It fills quickly
and an air of contentment reigns.

X

Arabica Bar & Kitchen   AC I⊘

3 Rochester Walk, Borough Market ⊠ *SE1 9AF*   Plan: **M4**
– Ⓜ *London Bridge –* ℰ *(020) 3011 5151
– www.arabicabarandkitchen.com – Closed 25-27 December and Sunday
dinner*
Menu £ 17/25 *–* Carte £ 17/32 *– (bookings advisable at dinner)*
• **World cuisine** • **Rustic** • **Simple** •

The owner-chef once sold mezze in Borough Market so it's no surprise he
opened his Levantine-inspired restaurant under a railway arch here. This fun,
cavernous place serves sharing plates from Egypt, Syria, Iraq, Jordan and Lebanon.

Lobos

14 Borough High St ✉ SE1 9QG – Ⓜ London Bridge Plan: **M4**
– ✆ (020) 7407 5361 – www.lobostapas.co.uk – Closed 25-26 December and 1 January
Carte £ 14/51
• Spanish • Tapas bar • Rustic •
A dimly lit, decidedly compact tapas bar under the railway arches – sit upstairs to enjoy the theatre of the open kitchen. Go for one of the speciality meat dishes like the leg of slow-roasted Castilian milk-fed lamb.

Anchor & Hope

36 The Cut ✉ SE1 8LP – Ⓜ Southwark. – ✆ (020) 79289898 – www.anchorandhopepub.co.uk – Closed Christmas-New Year, Sunday dinner, Monday lunch and bank holidays Plan: **K4**
Menu £ 15 (weekday lunch) – Carte £ 18/34 – *(bookings not accepted)*
• Modern British • Pub • Rustic •
As popular as ever thanks to its congenial feel and lived-in looks but mostly because of the appealingly seasonal menu and the gutsy, bold cooking that delivers on flavour. No reservations so be prepared to wait at the bar.

CHELSEA – SOUTH KENSINGTON – EARL'S COURT PLAN X

CHELSEA

Jumeirah Carlton Tower

Cadogan Pl ✉ SW1X 9PY – Ⓜ Knightsbridge – ✆ (020) 72351234 – www.jumeirah.com/jct Plan: **F5**
207 rm – †£ 350/835 ††£ 350/835 – ☕ £ 32 – 57 suites
• Business • Modern • Elegant •
Imposing international hotel overlooking a leafy square and just yards from all the swanky boutiques. Well-equipped rooftop health club has great views. Generously proportioned bedrooms boast every conceivable facility.

The Capital

22-24 Basil St. ✉ SW3 1AT – Ⓜ Knightsbridge – ✆ (020) 75895171 – www.capitalhotel.co.uk Plan: **F5**
49 rm – †£ 250/355 ††£ 295/550 – ☕ £ 17 – 1 suite
• Luxury • Traditional • Classic •
This fine, thoroughly British hotel has been under the same private ownership for over 40 years. Known for its discreet atmosphere, conscientious and attentive service and immaculately kept bedrooms courtesy of different designers.
✲ **Outlaw's at The Capital** – See restaurant listing

Draycott

26 Cadogan Gdns ✉ SW3 2RP – Ⓜ Sloane Square – ✆ (020) 77306466 – www.draycotthotel.com Plan: **F6**
35 rm – †£ 192/199 ††£ 378/558 – ☕ £ 22
• Townhouse • Luxury • Personalised •
Charming 19C house with elegant sitting room overlooking tranquil garden for afternoon tea. Bedrooms are individually decorated in a country house style and are named after writers or actors.

Egerton House

17-19 Egerton Terr ✉ SW3 2BX – Ⓜ South Kensington – ✆ (020) 75892412 – www.egertonhousehotel.com Plan: **F5**
28 rm – †£ 295/425 ††£ 295/425 – ☕ £ 29
• Townhouse • Luxury • Classic •
Compact but comfortable townhouse in a very good location, well-maintained throughout and owned by the Red Carnation group. High levels of personal service make the hotel stand out.

Knightsbridge 　　　　　　　　　　　　　　　　　　⟨AC⟩

10 Beaufort Gdns ⊠ *SW3 1PT –* Ⓜ *Knightsbridge* 　　Plan: **F5**
– ℰ *(020) 75846300 – www.knightsbridgehotel.com*
44 rm *–* ♦£ 215/275 ♦♦£ 235/445 *–* ⌣ £ 14
• Luxury • Townhouse • Personalised •

Charming and attractively furnished townhouse in a Victorian terrace, with a
very stylish, discreet feel. Every bedroom is immaculately appointed and has a
style all of its own; fine detailing throughout.

The Levin 　　　　　　　　　　　　　　　　　　　⟨⟩ ⟨AC⟩

28 Basil St. ⊠ *SW3 1AS –* Ⓜ *Knightsbridge –* ℰ *(020)* 　Plan: **F5**
75896286 – www.thelevinhotel.co.uk
12 rm ⌣ *–* ♦£ 248/382 ♦♦£ 255/389
• Townhouse • Classic • Art déco •

Little sister to The Capital next door. Impressive façade, contemporary interior and
comfortable bedrooms in a subtle art deco style, with marvellous champagne mini
bars. Simple dishes served all day down in basement restaurant Le Metro.

No.11 Cadogan Gardens 　　　　　　　　　　　⟨⟩ ⟨⟩ ⟨⟩ ⟨AC⟩

11 Cadogan Gdns ⊠ *SW3 2RJ –* Ⓜ *Sloane Square* 　　Plan: **F6**
– ℰ *(020) 7730 7000 – www.11cadogangardens.com*
56 rm *–* ♦£ 250/370 ♦♦£ 250/370 *–* ⌣ £ 18 *– 7 suites*
• Townhouse • Personalised • Classic •

Townhouse hotel fashioned out of four red-brick houses and exuberantly
dressed in bold colours and furnishings. Theatrically decorated bedrooms vary
in size from cosy to spacious. Intimate basement Italian restaurant with accomplished and ambitious cooking.

Beaufort 　　　　　　　　　　　　　　　　　　　　⟨AC⟩

33 Beaufort Gdns ⊠ *SW3 1PP –* Ⓜ *Knightsbridge* 　　Plan: **F5**
– ℰ *(020) 75845252 – www.thebeaufort.co.uk*
29 rm *–* ♦£ 180/228 ♦♦£ 250/456 *–* ⌣ £ 16
• Traditional • Classic • Personalised •

A vast collection of English floral watercolours adorn this 19C townhouse, set in
a useful location. Modern and co-ordinated rooms. Tariff includes all drinks and
afternoon tea.

Gordon Ramsay 　　　　　　　　　　　　　　　⟨⟩ ⟨AC⟩ ⟨⟩

68-69 Royal Hospital Rd. ⊠ *SW3 4HP* 　　　　　　Plan: **F7**
– Ⓜ *Sloane Square –* ℰ *(020) 73524441*
*– www.gordonramsayrestaurants.com – Closed 21-28 December, Saturday
and Sunday*
Menu £ 65/110 *– (booking essential)*
• French • Elegant • Intimate •

Gordon Ramsay's flagship restaurant is a model of composure and professionalism. The service is discreet and highly polished, yet also warm and reassuring.
The cooking bridges both classical and modern schools and is executed with
considerable poise, a lightness of touch and remarkable attention to detail.
→ Ravioli of lobster with langoustine, salmon, oxalis and wood sorrel.
Dover sole with razor clams, young peas and lemon beurre noisette. Lemo-
nade parfait with honey, bergamot and sheep's milk yoghurt.

Five Fields (Taylor Bonnyman) 　　　　　　　⟨⟩ ⟨⟩ ⟨AC⟩ ⟨⟩

8-9 Blacklands Terr ⊠ *SW3 2SP –* Ⓜ *Sloane Square* 　Plan: **F6**
– ℰ *(020) 7838 1082 – www.fivefieldsrestaurant.com – Closed Christmas-
mid January, first 2 weeks August, Saturday-Sunday and bank holidays*
Menu £ 60 *– (dinner only) (booking essential)*
• Modern cuisine • Neighbourhood • Intimate •

A formally run yet intimate restaurant, with a discreet atmosphere and a warm,
comfortable feel. Modern dishes are skilfully conceived, quite elaborate const-
ructions; attractively presented and packed with flavour. Produce is top-notch
and often comes from the restaurant's own kitchen garden in East Sussex.
→ Veal sweetbread with carrot, apple and tamarind. Herdwick mutton with
green olive, anchovy and baby gem. Ginger, rhubarb and vanilla.

Chelsea, South Kensington and Earl's Court
(Plan X)

HOLLAND PARK

ALBERT MEMORIA

Kensington Road

LEIGHTON HOUSE

High Street Kensington

KENSINGTON SQ.

ROYAL ALBERT HALL

The C

EDWARDES SQ.

X X L'Etranger

Elvaston Pl.

Impa

SCIE MUS

Cornwall Gardens

Queen's

Gardens

Cromwell

The Exhibitionist

Gloucester Road

X X X X Bombay Brasserie

SOUTH KENSINGTON

K + K George

NEVERN SQ.

Earl's Court

EARL'S COURT

X Tendido Cero

Margaux X

Twenty Nevern Square

X X Cambio de Tercio

Capote y Toros

Bromption

Yashin O House X

X X Garnier

THE BOLTONS

Blakes

Maze Grill Park Walk

West Brompton

BROMPTON CEMETERY

X Bandol

il trillo X X

Harwood Arms

Me

Fulham Broadway

Masala Grill X X

WALHAM GREEN

Parsons Green

● Hotel
● Restaurant

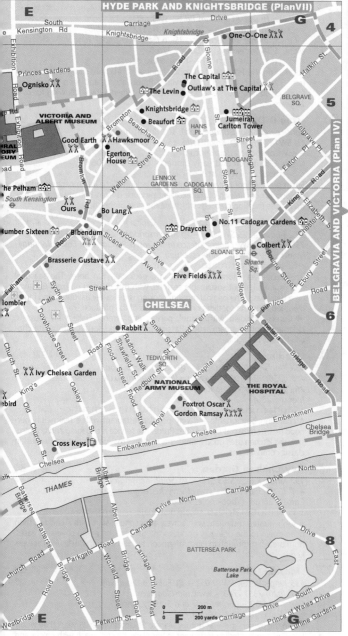

E F G

4

South
Kensington Rd
Carriage   Drive
Knightsbridge   *Knightsbridge*
Sloane
Road

One-O-One 🍴🍴🍴

Halkin St.

Princes Gardens

Ognisko 🍴🍴

The Capital 🏨🏨
The Levin 🏨   Outlaw's at The Capital 🍴🍴

BELGRAVE
SQ.

5

VICTORIA AND
ALBERT MUSEUM

Knightsbridge 🏨
Beaufort 🏨

HANS
PL.

Jumeirah
Carlton Tower 🏨🏨🏨

Belgrave Pl.
Eaton Pl.

Good Earth 🍴🍴 Hawksmoor 🍴
Egerton
House 🏨

Brompton
Beauchamp Pl.
Pont   Street

CADOGAN

Cadogan Lane

King's

Elizabeth

The Pelham 🏨🏨🏨

South Kensington

Ours 🍴🍴

Bo Lang 🍴

Walton   Rd.

LENNOX
GARDENS   CADOGAN
SQ.

Draycott 🏨🏨🏨

St.

Sloane

No.11 Cadogan Gardens 🏨

Chester

Road

Number Sixteen 🏨🏨   Bibendum
🍴🍴

Brasserie Gustave 🍴🍴

Draycott

Cadogan   Ave.

Sloane

Five Fields 🍴🍴🍴

SLOANE SQ.

Colbert 🍴🍴

Lower Sloane St.

Sloane
Sq.

Bourne Street
Ebury   Street

6

Lombier
🍴

Cale
Sydney

Street

CHELSEA

Road   Pimlico

Road

Rabbit 🍴

Smith St.

St Leonard's Terr.

Road   Chelsea   Bridge   Road

7

Ivy Chelsea Garden

ebird

Oakley

Old   Church   St.

King's

Radnor Walk
Shawfield St.
Flood Street
Redburn St.
Flood   St.
Royal

TEDWORTH
SQ.

NATIONAL
ARMY MUSEUM

Hospital

THE ROYAL
HOSPITAL

Foxtrot Oscar 🍴
Gordon Ramsay 🍴🍴🍴

Embankment

Cross Keys 🍺

Embankment   Chelsea

Chelsea
Bridge

Chelsea

North

THAMES

Albert   Bridge

Carriage   Drive   North

Carriage

Drive

8

church Road

Batters

Battersea
Bridge

Parkgate
Road
Worfield Street
Road

Carriage   Drive   West

BATTERSEA PARK

Battersea Park
Lake

South   Drive
Prince of Wales Drive
Lurline Gardens

Westbridge   E   Petworth St.   F   Carriage   G

0 ___ 200 m
0 ___ 200 yards

XXX **Bibendum**   88 AC 🍷

Michelin House, 81 Fulham Rd ⊠ SW3 6RD   Plan: **E6**
– Ⓜ South Kensington – 𝒞 (020) 75815817 – www.bibendum.co.uk
– Closed dinner 24 December, 25-26 December and 1 January
Menu £ 34 (weekdays) – Carte £ 27/63
• French • Design • Fashionable •

Located on the 1st floor of a London landmark – Michelin's former HQ, dating
from 1911. French food comes with a British accent and there's fresh seafood served in the oyster bar below. It's maintained a loyal following for over
20 years.

XXX **One-O-One**   AC

Park Tower Knightsbridge Hotel, 101 Knightsbridge   Plan: **F4**
⊠ SW1X 7RN – Ⓜ Knightsbridge – 𝒞 (020) 72907101
– www.oneoonerestaurant.com
Menu £ 20 (lunch and early dinner) – Carte £ 43/106
• Seafood • Intimate • Friendly •

Smart ground floor restaurant; it might be lacking a little in atmosphere but
the seafood is good. Much of the excellent produce is from Brittany and Norway;
don't miss the King crab legs which are the stars of the show.

XX **Outlaw's at The Capital** - The Capital Hotel   88 AC 🔄 🍷

❀ *22-24 Basil St. ⊠ SW3 1AT – Ⓜ Knightsbridge – 𝒞 (020)*   Plan: **F5**
75911202 – www.capitalhotel.co.uk – Closed Sunday and Easter Monday
Menu £ 29/55 – (booking essential)
• Seafood • Intimate • Elegant •

An elegant yet informal restaurant in a personally run hotel. The seasonal
menus are all about sustainable seafood, with fish shipped up from Cornwall
on a daily basis. The original modern cooking is delicately flavoured and ingredient-led, with the spotlight on the freshness of the produce.
➜ Cured monkfish with fennel, parsley and lemon. Hake with mussels,
cider and clotted cream sauce. Passion fruit tart and sorbet with white chocolate and pistachio.

XX **Medlar**   88 🔄 AC 🔄

438 King's Rd ⊠ SW10 0LJ – Ⓜ South Kensington   Plan: **E7**
– 𝒞 (020) 73491900 – www.medlarrestaurant.co.uk – Closed 24-
26 December and 1 January
Menu £ 28/46
• Modern cuisine • Neighbourhood • Romantic •

A charming, comfortable and very popular restaurant with a real neighbourhood feel, from two alumni of Chez Bruce. The service is engaging and unobtrusive; the kitchen uses good ingredients in dishes that deliver distinct flavours in
classic combinations.

XX **Ivy Chelsea Garden**   🔄 & AC

197 King's Rd ⊠ SW3 5ED – Ⓜ South Kensington   Plan: **E7**
– 𝒞 (020) 3301 0300 – www.theivychelseagarden.com
Carte £ 26/68 – (booking essential)
• Traditional British • Fashionable • Intimate •

A sophisticated restaurant with a lively atmosphere; start with a cocktail, then
head down to the orangery or out to the garden. The menu covers all bases;
from breakfast through to lunch, afternoon tea and dinner, with brunch at weekends.

XX **Masala Grill**   AC 🔄

535 King's Rd ⊠ SW10 0SZ – Ⓜ Fulham Broadway   Plan: **D8**
– 𝒞 (020) 7351 7788 – www.masalagrill.co
Carte £ 24/39 – (dinner only and Sunday lunch)
• Indian • Exotic décor •

When the owners moved Chutney Mary to St James's after 25 years they wisely
installed another Indian restaurant in her place. It's still awash with colour and
vitality but is less expensive and more varied in its influences.

XX **Le Colombier** ⇧

145 Dovehouse St. ⊠ SW3 6LB – Ⓜ *South Kensington*   Plan: **E6**
– ℰ (020) 73511155 – www.le-colombier-restaurant.co.uk
Menu £ 20 (lunch) – Carte £ 34/61
• French • Neighbourhood •
Proudly Gallic corner restaurant in an affluent residential area. Attractive enclosed terrace. Bright and cheerful surroundings and service; traditional French cooking.

XX **Bluebird** Ⓐ ⇧ 🍴

350 King's Rd. ⊠ SW3 5UU – Ⓜ *South Kensington*   Plan: **E7**
– ℰ (020) 75591000 – www.bluebird-restaurant.co.uk
Menu £ 20 (lunch and early dinner) – Carte £ 27/87
• Modern British • Design •
Not just for a night out with friends – with a foodstore, cellar, bakery, café and courtyard there's enough here for a day out too. Big menu to match the big room: everything from British classics to steaks, salads and shellfish.

XX **Hawksmoor** Ⓐ

3 Yeoman's Row ⊠ SW3 2AL – Ⓜ *South Kensington*   Plan: **F5**
*– ℰ (020) 7590 9290 – www.thehawksmoor.com – Closed 24-26 December
and 1 January*
Menu £ 28 (weekday lunch) – Carte £ 26/94
• Meats and grills • Brasserie •
The Hawksmoor people turned to rarefied Knightsbridge for their 5th London branch. Steaks are still the star of the show but here there's also plenty of seafood. Art deco elegance and friendly service compensate for the basement site.

XX **Maze Grill Park Walk** Ⓐ

11 Park Walk ⊠ SW10 0AJ – Ⓜ *South Kensington*   Plan: **D7**
– ℰ (020) 7255 9299
– www.gordonramsayrestaurants.com/maze-grill-park-walk
Carte £ 24/80
• Meats and grills • Fashionable • Neighbourhood •
The site of Aubergine, where it all started for Gordon Ramsay, now specialises in steaks. Dry-aged in-house, the meats are cooked on a fierce bit of kit called a Montague grill. There's another Maze Grill close by in Royal Hospital Road.

XX **Brasserie Gustave** Ⓐ ⇧

4 Sydney St ⊠ SW3 6PP – Ⓜ *South Kensington*   Plan: **E6**
*– ℰ (020) 7352 1712 – www.brasserie-gustave.com – Closed 24-
30 December*
Menu £ 20/28 – Carte £ 32/69
• French • Brasserie • Friendly •
All the traditional French favourites are here, from snails to boeuf Bourguignon and rum baba, all prepared in a way to make Escoffier proud. Studded leather seating and art deco style posters complete the classic brasserie look.

XX **il trillo** 😳 🌳 Ⓐ

4 Hollywood Rd ⊠ SW10 9HY – Ⓜ *Earl's Court*   Plan: **D7**
*– ℰ (020) 3602 1759 – www.iltrillo.net – Closed 10 days August and
1 week Christmas*
Carte £ 33/55 – *(dinner only and lunch Saturday-Sunday)*
• Italian • Friendly • Neighbourhood •
The Bertuccelli family have been making wine and running a restaurant in the Tuscan Hills for over 30 years. Two of the brothers now run this smart local which showcases the produce and wine from their region. Delightful courtyard.

XX **Colbert**   AC
50-52 Sloane Sq ⊠ SW1W 8AX – Ⓜ *Sloane Square*   Plan: **G6**
– 𝒞 (020) 7730 2804 – www.colbertchelsea.com – Closed 25 December
Carte £ 23/54 – *(booking advisable)*
• French • Brasserie • Neighbourhood •
With its posters, chessboard tiles and red leather seats, Colbert bears more than
a passing resemblance to a Parisian pavement café. It's an all-day, every day
operation with French classics from croque monsieur to steak Diane.

XX **Good Earth**   AC 🞉
233 Brompton Rd. ⊠ SW3 2EP – Ⓜ *Knightsbridge*   Plan: **E5**
– 𝒞 (020) 75843658 – www.goodearthgroup.co.uk – Closed 23-
31 December
Carte £ 26/51
• Chinese • Elegant •
The menu might appear predictable but this long-standing Chinese has always
proved a reliable choice in this area. Although there's no particular geographical
bias, the cooking is carefully executed and dishes are authentic.

X **Bandol**   🕸 AC
6 Hollywood Rd ⊠ SW10 9HY – Ⓜ *Earl's Court*   Plan: **D7**
– 𝒞 (020) 7351 1322 – www.barbandol.co.uk – Closed 24-26 December
and 1 January
Menu £ 20 (weekday lunch) – Carte £ 29/52
• Provençal • Design • Intimate •
Stylishly dressed restaurant with a 100 year old olive tree evoking memories of
sunny days spent on the French Riviera. Sharing plates take centre stage on the
Provençal and Niçoise inspired menu; seafood is a highlight.

X **Bo Lang**   AC
100 Draycott Ave ⊠ SW3 3AD – Ⓜ *South Kensington*   Plan: **F6**
– 𝒞 (020) 7823 7887 – www.bolangrestaurant.com
Menu £ 22 (weekday lunch) – Carte £ 25/48
• Chinese • Trendy •
It's all about dim sum at this diminutive Hakkasan wannabe. The kitchen has a
deft touch but stick to the more traditional combinations; come with friends for
the cocktails and to mitigate the effects of some ambitious pricing.

X **Rabbit**
172 King's Rd ⊠ SW3 4UP – Ⓜ *Sloane Square*   Plan: **F6**
– 𝒞 (020) 3750 0172 – www.rabbit-restaurant.com – Closed 22 December-
2 January
Menu £ 14 (weekday lunch)/37 – Carte £ 22/31
• Modern British • Rustic •
The Gladwin brothers have followed the success of The Shed with another similarly rustic and warmly run restaurant. Share satisfying, robustly flavoured plates; game is a real highlight, particularly the rabbit dishes.

🍴 **Cross Keys**   AC
1 Lawrence St ⊠ SW3 5NB – Ⓜ *Sloane Square.*   Plan: **E7**
– 𝒞 (020) 73510686 – www.thecrosskeyschelsea.co.uk – Closed
24 December dinner and 25 December
Carte £ 29/44
• Modern cuisine • Pub • Neighbourhood •
Chelsea's oldest pub, dating from 1708, reopened in 2015 having been saved
from property developers. The place has genuine character and warmth. The
style of cooking is largely contemporary, although there are also dishes for traditionalists.

UNITED KINGDOM - LONDON

EARL'S COURT

K + K George ✿ ⇦ 🖥 🛏 AC 🛎 🚗
1-15 Templeton Pl ⊠ SW5 9NB – Ⓜ Earl's Court Plan: **C6**
– ℰ (020) 75988700 – www.kkhotels.com
154 rm – ♦£ 119/330 ♦♦£ 119/350 – � £ 18
• Business • Modern •

In contrast to its period façade, this hotel's interior is stylish, colourful and contemporary. The hotel is on a quiet street, yet close to the Tube and has a large rear garden where you can enjoy breakfast in summer. Comfortable bar/lounge and a spacious restaurant serving a wide-ranging menu.

Twenty Nevern Square P
20 Nevern Sq. ⊠ SW5 9PD – Ⓜ Earl's Court – ℰ (020) Plan: **C6**
75659555 – www.twentynevernsquare.co.uk
20 rm � – ♦£ 99/249 ♦♦£ 119/299
• Townhouse • Luxury • Personalised •

Privately owned townhouse overlooking an attractive Victorian garden square. It's decorated with original pieces of hand-carved Indonesian furniture; breakfast in a bright conservatory. Some bedrooms have their own terrace.

XX Garnier AC
314 Earl's Court Rd ⊠ SW5 9QB – Ⓜ Earl's Court Plan: **C6**
– ℰ (020) 7370 4536 – www.garnier-restaurant-london.co.uk – Closed
Monday and Tuesday
Menu £ 18/22 – Carte £ 34/55
• French • Neighbourhood • Brasserie •

A wall of mirrors, rows of simply dressed tables and imperturbable service lend an authentic feel to this Gallic brasserie. The extensive menu of comforting French classics is such a good read, you'll find it hard to choose.

SOUTH KENSINGTON

Blakes ✿ 🛏
33 Rowland Gdns ⊠ SW7 3PF – Ⓜ Gloucester Road Plan: **D6**
– ℰ (020) 73706701 – www.blakeshotels.com
45 rm – ♦£ 220/270 ♦♦£ 330/600 – � £ 16 – 8 suites
• Luxury • Design • Contemporary •

Behind the Victorian façade is one of London's first 'boutique' hotels. Dramatic, bold and eclectic décor, with oriental influences and antiques from around the world. Mediterranean dishes in the spacious ground floor restaurant.

The Pelham ✿ 🛏 AC
15 Cromwell Pl ⊠ SW7 2LA – Ⓜ South Kensington Plan: **E6**
– ℰ (020) 7589 8288 – www.pelhamhotel.co.uk
51 rm – ♦£ 180/335 ♦♦£ 260/480 – � £ 18 – 1 suite
• Luxury • Elegant • Personalised •

Great location if you're in town for museum visiting. It's a mix of English country house and city townhouse, with a panelled sitting room and library with honesty bar. Sweet and intimate basement restaurant with Mediterranean menu.

Number Sixteen ⇦ AC
16 Sumner Pl. ⊠ SW7 3EG – Ⓜ South Kensington Plan: **E6**
– ℰ (020) 7589 5232 – www.firmdalehotels.co.uk
41 rm – ♦£ 150/190 ♦♦£ 235/340 – � £ 14
• Townhouse • Luxury • Elegant •

Elegant and delightfully furnished 19C townhouses in smart neighbourhood. Discreet entrance, comfortable sitting room, charming breakfast terrace and pretty little garden at the back. Bedrooms in an English country house style.

⌂

The Exhibitionist
🍴 A/C

8-10 Queensberry Pl ✉ *SW7 2EA – Ⓜ South Kensington* Plan: **E6**
– ✆ (020) 7915 0000 – www.theexhibitionisthotel.com
37 rm – 👤£ 199/239 👥£ 229/319 – ☕ £ 16 – 2 suites
• Townhouse • Elegant • Contemporary •
A funky, design-led boutique hotel fashioned out of several 18C townhouses. The modern artwork changes every few months and the bedrooms are individually furnished – several have their own roof terrace.

⌂

The Gore
🍴 A/C 💼

190 Queen's Gate ✉ *SW7 5EX – Ⓜ Gloucester Road* Plan: **D5**
– ✆ (020) 7584 6601 – www.gorehotel.com
50 rm – 👤£ 275/650 👥£ 275/650 – ☕ £ 15
• Townhouse • Traditional • Classic •
Idiosyncratic, hip Victorian house close to the Royal Albert Hall, whose charming lobby is covered with pictures and prints. Individually styled bedrooms have plenty of character and fun bathrooms. Bright and casual bistro.

🍴🍴🍴🍴

Bombay Brasserie
A/C 🕒

Courtfield Rd. ✉ *SW7 4QH – Ⓜ Gloucester Road* Plan: **D6**
– ✆ (020) 73704040 – www.bombayb.co.uk
– Closed 25 December
Menu £ 25 (weekday lunch) – Carte £ 34/47 – *(bookings advisable at dinner)*
• Indian • Exotic décor • Chic •
Plush new look for this well-run, well-known and comfortable Indian restaurant; very smart bar and conservatory with a show kitchen. More creative dishes now sit alongside the more traditional.

🍴🍴

Ours
♿ A/C ⊡

264 Brompton Rd ✉ *SW3 2AS – Ⓜ South Kensington* Plan: **E6**
– ✆ (020) 7100 2200 – www.restaurant-ours.com – Closed 24-28 December
Menu £ 45/55 – Carte £ 30/69 – *(booking advisable)*
• Modern cuisine • Fashionable • Trendy •
The latest chapter in Tom Sellers' story is this immense restaurant featuring trees, a living plant wall of 1,200 flower pots and a mezzanine level bar-lounge. Modern menu of seasonal, ingredient-led dishes with a fresh, light style.

🍴🍴

L'Etranger
🍇 A/C ⊡

36 Gloucester Rd. ✉ *SW7 4QT – Ⓜ Gloucester Road* Plan: **D5**
– ✆ (020) 75841118 – www.etranger.co.uk
Menu £ 25 (weekdays)/45 – Carte £ 29/61 – *(booking essential)*
• Modern French • Neighbourhood • Romantic •
Eclectic menu mixes French dishes with techniques and flavours from Japanese cooking. Impressive wine and sake lists. Moody and atmospheric room; ask for a corner table.

🍴🍴

Cambio de Tercio
🍇 A/C ⊡

163 Old Brompton Rd. ✉ *SW5 0LJ* Plan: **D6**
– Ⓜ Gloucester Road – ✆ (020) 72448970 – www.cambiodetercio.co.uk
– Closed 2 weeks December and 2 weeks August
Menu £ 45/55 – Carte £ 30/66
• Spanish • Cosy • Family •
A long-standing, ever-improving Spanish restaurant. Start with small dishes like the excellent El Bulli inspired omelette, then have the popular Pluma Iberica. There are super sherries and a wine list to prove there is life beyond Rioja.

XX **Yashin Ocean House**   🛜 ⅛ 𝖠𝖪 ⇄

117-119 Old Brompton Rd ⊠ *SW7 3RN* – 🚇 *Gloucester Road*   Plan: **D6**
– ℰ (020) 7373 3990 – www.yashinocean.com – Closed Christmas
Carte £ 20/86
• Japanese • Chic • Elegant •
The USP of this chic Japanese restaurant is 'head to tail' eating, although, as there's nothing for carnivores, 'fin to scale' would be more precise. Stick with specialities like the whole dry-aged sea bream for the full umami hit.

XX **Ognisko**   🛜 ⇄ 𝖤𝖵

55 Prince's Gate, Exhibition Rd ⊠ *SW7 2PN*   Plan: **E5**
– 🚇 South Kensington – ℰ (020) 7589 0101
– www.ogniskorestaurant.co.uk – Closed 24-26 December and 1 January
Menu £ 22 (lunch and early dinner) – Carte £ 27/37
• Polish • Bistro • Traditional décor •
Ognisko Polskie Club was founded in 1940 in this magnificent townhouse – its restaurant is now open to the public. The gloriously traditional Polish menu celebrates cooking that is without pretence and truly from the heart.

X **Tendido Cero**   𝖠𝖪

174 Old Brompton Rd. ⊠ *SW5 0LJ*   Plan: **D6**
– 🚇 Gloucester Road – ℰ (020) 73703685 – www.cambiodetercio.co.uk
– Closed 2 weeks Christmas-New Year
Menu £ 35 (dinner) – Carte £ 21/51
• Spanish • Tapas bar • Neighbourhood •
It's all about the vibe here at Abel Lusa's tapas bar, just across the road from his Cambio de Tercio restaurant. Colourful surroundings, well-drilled service and a menu of favourites all contribute to the fun and lively atmosphere.

X **Capote y Toros**   🕸 𝖠𝖪

157 Old Brompton Road ⊠ *SW5 0LJ*   Plan: **D6**
– 🚇 Gloucester Road – ℰ (020) 73730567 – www.cambiodetercio.co.uk
– Closed 2 weeks Christmas, Sunday and Monday
Menu £ 30 – Carte £ 20/51 – *(dinner only)*
• Spanish • Tapas bar • Cosy •
Expect to queue at this compact and vividly coloured spot which celebrates sherry, tapas, ham... and bullfighting. Sherry is the star; those as yet unmoved by this most underappreciated of wines will be dazzled by the variety.

X **Margaux**   🕸 𝖠𝖪 ⇄

152 Old Brompton Rd ⊠ *SW5 0BE*   Plan: **D6**
– 🚇 Gloucester Road – ℰ (020) 7373 5753 – www.barmargaux.co.uk
– Closed 24-26 December and 1 January
Menu £ 15 (weekday lunch) – Carte £ 30/52
• Mediterranean cuisine • Trendy • Bistro •
Spain and Italy are the primary influences at this modern bistro. There are classics aplenty alongside more unusual dishes. The wine list provides a good choice of varietals and the ersatz industrial look is downtown Manhattan.

KENSINGTON – NORTH KENSINGTON – NOTTING HILL   PLAN XI

KENSINGTON

 Royal Garden   ⛲ ⇐ 𝖿₆ 𝕸 ⅛ 𝖠𝖪 𝖘𝖠 🅿

2-24 Kensington High St ⊠ *W8 4PT*   Plan: **D4**
– 🚇 High Street Kensington – ℰ (020) 79378000 – www.royalgardenhotel.co.uk
394 rm – ♦£ 190/440 ♦♦£ 240/490 – 🖵 £ 21 – 17 suites
• Business • Luxury • Modern •
A tall, modern hotel with many of its rooms enjoying enviable views over the adjacent Kensington Gardens. All the modern amenities and services, with well-drilled staff. Bright, spacious Park Terrace offers an international menu as well as afternoon tea for which you're accompanied by a pianist.
Min Jiang – See restaurant listing

The Milestone
☆ Ⅰᚷ ⅏ AK

1-2 Kensington Ct ⊠ *W8 5DL*
Plan: **D4**
– Ⓜ *High Street Kensington* – ℰ *(020) 79171000*
– *www.milestonehotel.com*
62 rm ⌂ – ♦£ 348/480 ♦♦£ 400/1000 – 6 suites
• Luxury • Townhouse • Personalised •
Elegant and enthusiastically run hotel with decorative Victorian façade and a very British feel. Charming oak-panelled sitting room is popular for afternoon tea; snug bar in former stables. Meticulously decorated bedrooms offer period detail. Ambitious cooking in discreet Cheneston's restaurant.

Baglioni
Ⅰᚷ AK ㋡

60 Hyde Park Gate ⊠ *SW7 5BB*
Plan: **D4**
– Ⓜ *High Street Kensington* – ℰ *(020) 79378886*
– *www.baglionihotels.com*
67 rm – ♦£ 315/425 ♦♦£ 315/425 – ⌂ £ 26 – 15 suites
• Luxury • Personalised • Classic •
Opposite Kensington Palace and no escaping the fact that this is an Italian owned hotel. The interior is bold and ornate and comes with a certain swagger. Stylish bedrooms have a masculine feel and boast impressive facilities.

Min Jiang – Royal Garden Hotel
≤ AK ㋡

2-24 Kensington High St (10th Floor) ⊠ *W8 4PT*
Plan: **D4**
– Ⓜ *High Street Kensington* – ℰ *(020) 73611988* – *www.minjiang.co.uk*
Menu £ 40/80 – Carte £ 30/98
• Chinese • Elegant • Design •
The cooking at this stylish 10th floor Chinese restaurant covers all provinces, but Cantonese and Sichuanese dominate. Wood-fired Beijing duck is a speciality. The room's good looks compete with the great views of Kensington Gardens.

Launceston Place
AK ㋡

1a Launceston Pl ⊠ *W8 5RL* – Ⓜ *Gloucester Road*
Plan: **D5**
– ℰ *(020) 7937 6912* – *www.launcestonplace-restaurant.co.uk* – *Closed 25-30 December, 1 January, Tuesday lunch and Monday*
Menu £ 30/55 – *(bookings advisable at dinner)*
• Modern cuisine • Neighbourhood • Fashionable •
Few restaurants engender a greater sense of local customer loyalty and proprietorial pride than long-standing Launceston Place. It's formally run but not so much that it impinges on customers' enjoyment. The cooking has a classical French base yet is unafraid to try new things.

Kitchen W8
AK

⁂

11-13 Abingdon Rd ⊠ *W8 6AH*
Plan: **C5**
– Ⓜ *High Street Kensington* – ℰ *(020) 79370120* – *www.kitchenw8.com*
– *Closed 24-26 December and bank holidays*
Menu £ 25 (lunch and early dinner) – Carte £ 35/53
• Modern cuisine • Neighbourhood •
A joint venture between Rebecca Mascarenhas and Philip Howard. Not as informal as the name suggests but still refreshingly free of pomp. The cooking has depth and personality and prices are quite restrained considering the quality of the produce and the kitchen's skill.
→ Salad of veal with charred asparagus, peas and truffle pesto. Fillet of Cornish turbot with St Austell Bay mussels, mousserons, onions and parsley. Passion fruit cream with cured pineapple, lime and mango.

Clarke's
& AK ㋡

124 Kensington Church St ⊠ *W8 4BH*
Plan: **C4**
– Ⓜ *Notting Hill Gate* – ℰ *(020) 72219225* – *www.sallyclarke.com*
– *Closed 2 weeks August, Christmas-New Year, Sunday and bank holidays*
Menu £ 27/39 – Carte £ 41/55 – *(booking advisable)*
• Modern cuisine • Neighbourhood •
Forever popular restaurant that has enjoyed a loyal local following for over 30 years. Sally Clarke uses the freshest seasonal ingredients and her cooking has a famed lightness of touch.

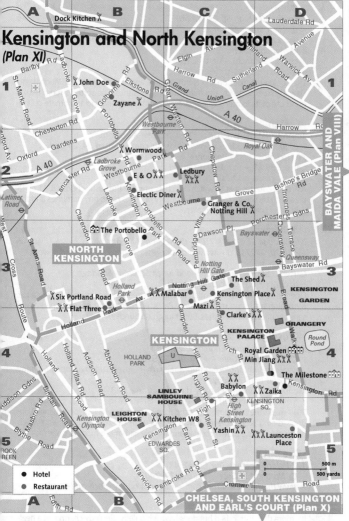

Kensington and North Kensington
(Plan XI)

Legend:
- ● Hotel
- ● Restaurant

CHELSEA, SOUTH KENSINGTON
AND EARL'S COURT (Plan X)

𝕏𝕏 **Babylon**   ← 🅰🄲 ⇔

Plan: **C4**

*The Roof Gardens, 99 Kensington High St (entrance on
Derry St)* ⊠ *W8 5SA –* Ⓜ *High Street Kensington –* 𝒞 *(020) 73683993
– www.roofgardens.virgin.com – Closed 24-30 December, 1-2 January and
Sunday dinner*
Menu £ 28 (lunch) – Carte £ 42/58
• Modern cuisine • Fashionable •
Found on the 7th floor and affording great views of the city skyline and an ama-
zing 1.5 acres of rooftop garden. Stylish modern décor in keeping with the con-
temporary, British cooking.

XX **Zaika**   AK ⑰

1 Kensington High St. ✉ *W8 5NP*   Plan: **D4**
– ⓜ High Street Kensington – ℰ (020) 77956533
*– www.zaikaofkensington.com – Closed 25-26 December, 1 January
and Monday lunch*
Menu £ 22 (lunch) – Carte £ 28/67
• Indian • Exotic décor •
The cooking focuses on the North of India and the influences of Mughal and
Nawabi, so expect rich and fragrantly spiced dishes. The softly-lit room makes
good use of its former life as a bank, with its wood-panelling and ornate ceiling.

XX **Yashin**   AK

1a Argyll Rd. ✉ *W8 7DB –* ⓜ *High Street Kensington*   Plan: **C5**
*– ℰ (020) 79381536 – www.yashinsushi.com – Closed 24, 25 and
31 December and 1 January*
Carte £ 38/89 – *(booking essential)*
• Japanese • Design • Fashionable •
Ask for a counter seat to watch the chefs prepare the sushi; choose 8, 11 or 15
pieces, to be served together. The quality of fish is clear; tiny garnishes and the
odd bit of searing add originality.

XX **Malabar**   AK

27 Uxbridge St. ✉ *W8 7TQ –* ⓜ *Notting Hill Gate*   Plan: **C3**
*– ℰ (020) 77278800 – www.malabar-restaurant.co.uk – Closed 1 week
Christmas*
Carte £ 15/39 – *(dinner only and lunch Saturday-Sunday)*
• Indian • Neighbourhood •
Opened in 1983 in a residential Notting Hill street, but keeps up its appearance,
remaining fresh and good-looking. Balanced menu of carefully prepared and
sensibly priced Indian dishes. Buffet lunch on Sunday.

X **Kensington Place**   AK ⇔

201-209 Kensington Church St. ✉ *W8 7LX*   Plan: **C3**
– ⓜ Notting Hill Gate – ℰ (020) 77273184
*– www.kensingtonplace-restaurant.co.uk – Closed Sunday dinner, Monday
lunch and bank holidays*
Menu £ 20 (lunch and early dinner) – Carte £ 28/47
• Seafood • Neighbourhood • Brasserie •
2017 marks the 30th birthday of this iconic brasserie which helped change London's dining scene forever. Fish is the focus of the fairly priced menu which
mixes classics like prawn cocktail and fish pie with more modern dishes.

X **The Shed**

122 Palace Gardens Terr ✉ *W8 4RT*   Plan: **C3**
– ⓜ Notting Hill Gate – ℰ (020) 7229 4024
– www.theshed-restaurant.com – Closed Monday lunch and Sunday
Carte £ 18/30
• Modern British • Rustic •
It's more than just a shed but does have a higgledy-piggledy charm and a heal-
thy dose of the outdoors. One brother cooks, one manages and the third runs
the farm which supplies the produce for the earthy, satisfying dishes.

X **Mazi**   ⌂

12-14 Hillgate St ✉ *W8 7SR –* ⓜ *Notting Hill Gate*   Plan: **C3**
*– ℰ (020) 72293794 – www.mazi.co.uk – Closed 24-26 December and 1-
2 January*
Menu £ 13 (weekday lunch) – Carte £ 28/54
• Greek • Friendly • Neighbourhood •
It's all about sharing at this simple, bright Greek restaurant where traditional
recipes are given a modern twist to create vibrant, colourful and fresh tasting
dishes. The garden terrace at the back is a charming spot in summer.

NORTH KENSINGTON

The Portobello

22 Stanley Gdns. ⊠ *W11 2NG* – Ⓜ *Notting Hill Gate*   Plan: **B3**
– 𝒞 *(020) 77272777 – www.portobellohotel.com*
21 rm ☲ – †£ 175 ††£ 195/395

• Townhouse • Luxury • Personalised •

An attractive Victorian townhouse in an elegant terrace. Original and theatrical décor. Circular beds, half-testers, Victorian baths: no two bedrooms are the same.

Ledbury (Brett Graham)

127 Ledbury Rd. ⊠ *W11 2AQ* – Ⓜ *Notting Hill Gate*   Plan: **C2**
– 𝒞 *(020) 7792 9090 – www.theledbury.com – Closed 25-26 December, August bank holiday and lunch Monday-Tuesday*
Menu £ 50/95

• Modern cuisine • Neighbourhood • Contemporary décor •

Brett Graham's husbandry skills and close relationship with his suppliers ensure the quality of the produce shines through and flavour combinations linger long in the memory. This smart yet unshowy restaurant comes with smooth and engaging service. Only a tasting menu is served at dinner on weekends.
➔ White beetroot baked in clay with English caviar and smoked & dried eel. Berkshire muntjac with smoked bone marrow, quince and vegetables. Brown sugar tart with stem ginger ice cream.

Flat Three

120-122 Holland Park Ave ⊠ *W11 4UA*   Plan: **B3/4**
– Ⓜ *Holland Park* – 𝒞 *(020) 7792 8987 – www.flatthree.london – Closed 26 December-6 January, 15-26 August, Sunday and Monday*
Menu £ 33 (early dinner) – Carte £ 31/77 – (dinner only and lunch Friday-Saturday)

• Creative • Design • Minimalist •

Basement restaurant blending the cuisines of Scandinavia, Korea and Japan. Not everything works but there's certainly ambition. They make their own soy and miso and serve more foraged ingredients than you'll find in Ray Mears' pocket.

Six Portland Road

6 Portland Rd ⊠ *W11 4LA* – Ⓜ *Holland Park* – 𝒞 *(020)*   Plan: **B3**
7229 3130 – www.sixportlandroad.com – Closed Christmas-New Year, last 2 weeks August, Sunday dinner and Monday
Carte £ 27/56

• French • Neighbourhood • Cosy •

An intimate and personally run neighbourhood restaurant owned by Oli Barker, previously of Terroirs. The menu changes frequently and has a strong French accent; dishes are reassuringly recognisable, skilfully constructed and very tasty.

Dock Kitchen

Portobello Dock, 342-344 Ladbroke Grove ⊠ *W10 5BU*   Plan: **A1**
– Ⓜ *Ladbroke Grove* – 𝒞 *(020) 8962 1610 – www.dockkitchen.co.uk*
– *Closed Christmas, Sunday dinner and bank holidays*
Carte £ 23/38

• Mediterranean cuisine • Design • Trendy •

What started as a 'pop-up' became a permanent feature in this open-plan former Victorian goods yard. The chef's peregrinations inform his cooking, which relies on simple, natural flavours.

Granger and Co. Notting Hill

175 Westbourne Grove ⊠ *W11 2SB* – Ⓜ *Bayswater*   Plan: **C2**
– 𝒞 *(020) 7229 9111 – www.grangerandco.com – Closed August bank holiday weekend and 25-26 December*
Carte £ 23/43 – (bookings not accepted)

• Modern cuisine • Friendly • Fashionable •

When Bill Granger moved from sunny Sydney to cool Notting Hill he opened a local restaurant too. He brought with him that delightful 'matey' service that only Aussies do, his breakfast time ricotta hotcakes and a fresh, zesty menu.

X **Wormwood**

16 All Saints Rd ⊠ W11 1HH – Ⓜ Westbourne Park Plan: **B2**
– ℰ (020) 7854 1808 – www.wormwoodnottinghill.com – Closed
28 August-3 September 24-28 December, 1-2 January, Monday lunch and
Sunday
Carte £ 26/39

• Mediterranean cuisine • Neighbourhood • Friendly •

The look is New England with a Moorish edge and it's named after the primary herb in absinthe; throw in North African dominated Mediterranean food with a creative edge and you have a restaurant doing something a little different.

X **Zayane** AC

91 Golborne Rd ⊠ W10 5NL – Ⓜ Westbourne Park Plan: **B1**
– ℰ (020) 8960 1137 – www.zayanerestaurant.com
Carte £ 27/36

• Moroccan • Neighbourhood • Fashionable •

An intimate neighbourhood restaurant owned by Casablanca-born Meryem Mortell and evoking the sights and scents of North Africa. Carefully conceived dishes have authentic Moroccan flavours but are cooked with modern techniques.

X **Electric Diner** � AC

191 Portobello Rd ⊠ W11 2ED – Ⓜ Ladbroke Grove Plan: **B2**
– ℰ (020) 7908 9696 – www.electricdiner.com – Closed 30-31 August and
25 December
Carte £ 17/34

• Meats and grills • Rustic • Neighbourhood •

Next to the iconic Electric Cinema is this loud, brash and fun all-day operation with an all-encompassing menu; the flavours are as big as the portions. The long counter and red leather booths add to the authentic diner feel.

CLERKENWELL - FINSBURY

CLERKENWELL

🏨 **Malmaison** ⚑ ⅓ AC 🛁

18-21 Charterhouse Sq ⊠ EC1M 6AH – Ⓜ Barbican Plan: **L2**
– ℰ (020) 7012 3700 – www.malmaison.com
97 rm – ♦£ 150/350 ♦♦£ 150/420 – ⚏ £ 15

• Townhouse • Modern • Personalised •

Striking early 20C red-brick building overlooking a pleasant square. Stylish, comfy public areas. Bedrooms in vivid, bold colours, with plenty of extra touches. Modern brasserie with international menu; grilled meats a highlight.

🏨 **The Rookery** AC

12 Peters Ln, Cowcross St ⊠ EC1M 6DS – Ⓜ Farringdon Plan: **L2**
– ℰ (020) 73360931 – www.rookeryhotel.com
33 rm – ♦£ 195/225 ♦♦£ 265/650 – ⚏ £ 12

• Townhouse • Luxury • Personalised •

A row of charmingly restored 18C houses which remain true to their roots courtesy of wood panelling, flagstone flooring, open fires and antique furnishings. Highly individual bedrooms have feature beds and Victorian bathrooms.

XX **Sosharu** AC

63 Clerkenwell Rd ⊠ EC1M 5RR – Ⓜ Farringdon Plan: **K1**
– ℰ (020) 3805 2304 – www.sosharulondon.com – Closed bank holidays
except Good Friday and Sunday
Menu £ 20/30 – Carte £ 29/52

• Japanese • Fashionable • Trendy •

The seventh London restaurant from Jason Atherton and the first serving Japanese food is this bustling operation with a chic, understated style. Six small plates with a large rice pot or a 'classic' between two will do nicely.

X
🕸️

St John

AK ⇄

26 St John St ⊠ *EC1M 4AY –* Ⓜ *Farringdon –* 📞 *(020)* Plan: **L2**
*7251 0848 – www.stjohnrestaurant.com – Closed Christmas-New
Year, Saturday lunch, Sunday dinner and bank holidays*
Carte £ 28/49 – *(booking essential)*
• **Traditional British** • **Minimalist** • **Brasserie** •

A glorious celebration of British fare and a champion of 'nose to tail' eating. Utilitarian surroundings and a refreshing lack of ceremony ensure the food is the focus; it's appealingly simple, full of flavour and very satisfying.
→ Roast bone marrow and parsley salad. Pheasant and trotter pie. Ginger loaf and butterscotch sauce.

X
🐦

Comptoir Gascon

AK

61-63 Charterhouse St. ⊠ *EC1M 6HJ –* Ⓜ *Farringdon* Plan: **K2**
– 📞 *(020) 7608 0851 – www.comptoirgascon.com – Closed Christmas-New
Year, Sunday, Monday and bank holidays*
Menu £ 15 *(weekday lunch)* – Carte £ 21/34 – *(booking essential)*
• **French** • **Bistro** • **Rustic** •

Buzzy restaurant; sister to Club Gascon. Rustic and satisfying specialities from the SW of France include wine, bread, cheese and plenty of duck, with cassoulet and duck rillettes perennial favourites and the duck burger popular at lunch. Great value set 3 course menu. Produce on display to take home.

X

Polpo Smithfield

🏮 AK

3 Cowcross St ⊠ *EC1M 6DR –* Ⓜ *Farringdon. –* 📞 *(020)* Plan: **L2**
*7250 0034 – www.polpo.co.uk – Closed Christmas, New Year and Sunday
dinner*
Carte £ 20/30
• **Italian** • **Friendly** • **Wine bar** •

For his third Venetian-style bacaro, Russell Norman converted an old meat market storage facility; it has an elegantly battered feel. Head first for the Negroni bar downstairs; then over-order tasty, uncomplicated dishes to share.

X

Granger & Co. Clerkenwell

♿ AK

50 Sekforde St ⊠ *EC1R 0HA –* Ⓜ *Farringdon –* 📞 *(020)* Plan: **K1**
7251 9032 – www.grangerandco.com – Closed Sunday dinner
Carte £ 19/40
• **Modern cuisine** • **Family** • **Elegant** •

Aussie food writer and restaurateur Bill Granger's 2nd London branch is a stylish affair. His food is inspired by his travels, with the best dishes being those enlivened with the flavours of SE Asia; his breakfasts are also renowned.

X

Foxlow

♿

69-73 St John St ⊠ *EC1M 4AN –* Ⓜ *Farringdon* Plan: **L2**
– 📞 *(020) 7680 2700 – www.foxlow.co.uk – Closed 24 December-
1 January, Sunday dinner and bank holidays*
Menu £ 18 *(weekdays)* – Carte £ 22/41
• **Meats and grills** • **Neighbourhood** •

From the clever Hawksmoor people comes this fun and funky place where the staff ensure everyone's having a good time. There are steaks available but plenty of other choices with influences from Italy, Asia and the Middle East.

X

Hix Oyster and Chop House

🏮

36-37 Greenhill Rents ⊠ *EC1M 6BN –* Ⓜ *Farringdon* Plan: **L2**
– 📞 *(020) 70171930 – www.hixoysterandchophouse.co.uk – Closed 25-
29 December, Saturday lunch and bank holidays*
Menu £ 10 *(weekday lunch)* – Carte £ 20/58
• **Traditional British** • **Bistro** • **Traditional décor** •

Appropriately utilitarian surroundings put the focus on seasonal and often underused British ingredients. Cooking is satisfying and unfussy, with plenty of oysters and aged beef served on the bone.

Z O D Z O J - Σ O D O Z - X U D Z U

● Hotel
● Restaurant

0

1

2

ISLINGTON

Market
Duncan St.
Row
Nc
Chapel
K
Penton
Street
Vincent
Baron
White
Lion
Street
Donegal St.
Upper
Angel
Colebrooke
Ella
Rodney
St.
Street
St.
Stree
Pentonville
Road
St. John
City
Pentonville
Weston
St.
CLAREMONT
SQ.
Street
Goswell
Road
Amwell
Chadwell
Wakley St.
Penton Rise
King's
Cross
Street
Street
MYDDELTON
SQ.
Arlington Way
Friend
St.
Rawstorne
Road
Acton
St.
Great
Vernon
Rise
PERCY
CIRCUS
Percy
Street
Lloyd St.
River St.
St.
John
Street
Spencer
Street
U
Wharton
Street
Amwell
NORTHAMPTON
SQ.
Ash
LLOYD
SQ.
Wyclif
St.
Seba
Sł
GRANVILLE
SQ.
Baker
Hardwick
Street
St.
Myddelton
Street
Percival
Stre
Cubitt
Street
Lloyd
Margery
Attneave
St.
Yardley
St.
WILMINGTON
SQ. Tysoe St.
Rosebery
Avenue
Street
Cyrus
Farringdon Road
Wren Street
King's Cross Rd
Caravan ●
Exmouth Market
● **Moro** ✕
Skinner
Street
Compton
Agdon St.
Calthorpe
Street
Morito ✕
Corporation
Row
Woodbridge
St.
Phoenix
Place
Mount Pleasant
Quality
Chop House ✕
Bowling Green
Lane
Sans Walk
Seiforde
Street
Gough
Street
Avenue
✕**Clerkenwell**
Kitchen
Farringdon
Clerkenwell
St. John
● **Granger & Co Clerkenwe**
Elm St.
Brownlow Mews
Grays Inn
Nothington
St.
Rosebery
Eyre St.
Hill
Warner St.
Ray St.
Back Hill
Herbal
Hill
Farringdon La.
Road
✕ **The Modern**
Pantry Clerkenwell
● **Well** I
Clerkenwell
St. John's Lane
Great S
Zetter ●
Clerkenwell
John
Street
John St.
Theobald's
Rd
Clerkenwell
Road
Portpool Lane
Leather
Hatton Wall
Saffron
Turnmill
St.
Britton
St.
✕✕
Sosharu
✕**Foxlow**
John
CAMDEN, BLOOMSBURY (Plan VI)
Jockey's Fields
GRAY'S
INN FIELD
GRAY'S
INN
Baldwin's Gardens
Hatton
Cross
St.
Hill
Farringdon
CHARTERHOUS
Polpo Smithfield
The Rookery
Farringdon ⊖
✕
St Jo
Cowcross
S
High
Holborn
Greville
Street
Garden
Street
✕ **Hix Oyster and Chop House** ●
Chancery Lane
STAPLE
INN
High
Holborn
✕ **Comptoir Gascon**
Charterhouse
Farringdon
Street
Street
Smithfield
Malm
LINCOLN'S
INN FIELDS
Chancery
Lane
LINCOLN'S
INN
West
Hosier Lane
Lincoln's
Cursitor St.
Fetter
Lane
New Fetter
Lane
St Andrew St.
Holborn
Snow
Holborn
Viaduct
Hill
Gillspu
Street
K

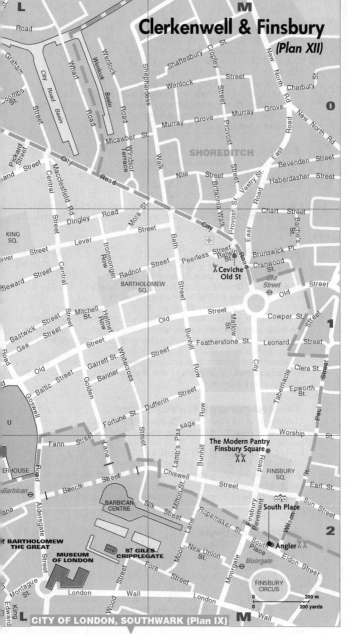

South Place

3 South Pl ⊠ *EC2M 2AF* – Ⓜ *Moorgate* – ☏ *(020)*
35030000 – *www.southplacehotel.com*
Plan: **M2**

80 rm – †£ 185/350 ††£ 185/350 – ☲ £ 17 – 1 suite
• Business • Design • Contemporary •

Restaurant group D&D's first venture into the hotel business is a stylish affair; unsurprising as its interior was designed by Conran & Partners. Bedrooms are a treat for those with an eye for aesthetics and no detail has been forgotten. The ground floor hosts 3 South Place, a bustling bar and grill.
❀ **Angler** – See restaurant listing

Zetter

St John's Sq, 86-88 Clerkenwell Rd. ⊠ *EC1M 5RJ*
– Ⓜ *Farringdon* – ☏ *(020) 7324 4444* – *www.thezetter.com*
Plan: **K1**

59 rm – †£ 150/498 ††£ 150/498 – ☲ £ 14
• Townhouse • Modern • Vintage •

A trendy and discreet converted 19C warehouse with well-equipped bedrooms that come with pleasant touches, such as Penguin paperbacks. The more idiosyncratic Zetter Townhouse across the square is used as an overflow.

Angler – South Place Hotel

❀

3 South Pl ⊠ *EC2M 2AF* – Ⓜ *Moorgate*
– ☏ *(020) 32151260* – *www.anglerrestaurant.com*
Plan: **M2**
– *Closed 26-30 December, Saturday lunch and Sunday*
Menu £ 35 – Carte £ 42/66 – *(booking advisable)*
• Seafood • Elegant • Design •

It's built into the eaves of D&D's South Place hotel, but this 7th floor room feels very much like a stand-alone entity and is bright, elegant and intimate. Fish is the mainstay of the menu; its quality is supreme and the kitchen has a light, yet assured touch.
→ Yellowfin tuna tartare, lime, chilli and avocado. Roast fillet of John Dory with langoustines, mushrooms, truffle and pumpkin. Chocolate fondant with pistachio ice cream.

The Modern Pantry Finsbury Square

14 Finsbury Sq ⊠ *EC2A 1AH* – Ⓜ *Moorgate* – ☏ *(020)*
3696 6565 – *www.themodernpantry.co.uk* – *Closed 25 December and*
Plan: **M2**
Sunday dinner
Menu £ 23 (weekday lunch) – Carte £ 31/47
• World cuisine • Brasserie • Fashionable •

Spacious, elegant dining room on the ground floor of the imposing Alphabeta Building, with a lively bar counter for 'global tapas' and sherry liveners. Extensive menu of internationally influenced dishes; puddings are a highlight.

Quality Chop House

92-94 Farringdon Rd ⊠ *EC1R 3EA* – Ⓜ *Farringdon*
– ☏ *(020) 7278 1452* – *www.thequalitychophouse.com* – *Closed Sunday*
Plan: **K1**
dinner and bank holidays
Menu £ 15 (weekday lunch) – Carte £ 24/44 – *(booking advisable)*
• Traditional British • Cosy • Bistro •

In the hands of owners who respect its history, this 'progressive working class caterer' does a fine job of championing gutsy British grub; game is best but steaks from the butcher next door are also worth ordering. The terrific little wine list has lots of gems. The Grade II listed room, with its trademark booths, has been an eating house since 1869.

UNITED KINGDOM - LONDON

Moro

🏵 🛋 🕭 AC

34-36 Exmouth Mkt ⊠ *EC1R 4QE –* Ⓜ *Farringdon*　　　Plan: **K1**
*– ℰ (020) 78338336 – www.moro.co.uk – Closed dinner 24 December-
2 January, Sunday dinner and bank holidays*
Carte £ 31/43 *– (booking essential)*
• **Mediterranean cuisine** • **Friendly** • **Simple** •

It's the stuff of dreams – pack up your worldly goods, drive through Spain, Portugal, Morocco and the Sahara, and then back in London, open a restaurant and share your love of Moorish cuisine. The wood-fired oven and chargrill fill the air with wonderful aromas and food is vibrant and colourful.

Morito

🛋

32 Exmouth Mkt ⊠ *EC1R 4QE –* Ⓜ *Farringdon*　　　Plan: **K1**
*– ℰ (020) 72787007 – www.morito.co.uk – Closed 24 December-
2 January, Sunday dinner and bank holidays*
Carte £ 14/29 *– (bookings not accepted at dinner)*
• **Spanish** • **Tapas bar** • **Rustic** •

From the owners of next door Moro comes this authentic and appealingly down to earth little tapas bar. Seven or eight dishes between two should suffice but over-ordering is easy and won't break the bank.

Ceviche Old St

AC

2 Baldwin St ⊠ *EC1V 9NU –* Ⓜ *Old Street – ℰ (020)*　　　Plan: **M1**
3327 9463 – www.cevicheuk.com
Menu £ 12 *(weekday lunch) –* Carte £ 17/32
• **Peruvian** • **Brasserie** • **Fashionable** •

Sister to the Soho original is this buzzy Peruvian restaurant in the former Alexandra Trust Dining Rooms, built by tea magnate Sir Thomas Lipton. Start with ceviche and a pisco sour; dishes are easy to eat, vibrant and full of flavour.

The Modern Pantry Clerkenwell

🛋 AC ⇄

47-48 St John's Sq. ⊠ *EC1V 4JJ –* Ⓜ *Farringdon*　　　Plan: **K1**
*– ℰ (020) 75539210 – www.themodernpantry.co.uk – Closed August bank
holiday and 25-26 December*
Carte £ 26/37 *– (booking advisable)*
• **World cuisine** • **Design** • **Bistro** •

Fusion cooking that uses complementary flavours to create vibrant, zesty dishes. The simple, crisp ground floor of this Georgian building has the buzz; upstairs is more intimate. Clued-up service.

Caravan

11-13 Exmouth Market ⊠ *EC1R 4QD –* Ⓜ *Farringdon*　　　Plan: **K1**
*– ℰ (020) 78338115 – www.caravanrestaurants.co.uk – Closed 25,26 and
31 December, 1 January*
Carte £ 26/35 *– (booking advisable)*
• **World cuisine** • **Trendy** • **Neighbourhood** •

A discernible Antipodean vibe pervades this casual eatery, from the laid-back charm of the service to the kitchen's confident combining of unusual flavours. Cooking is influenced by owner's travels – hence the name.

Clerkenwell Kitchen

🛋

27-31 Clerkenwell Cl ⊠ *EC1R 0AT –* Ⓜ *Farringdon*　　　Plan: **K1**
*– ℰ (020) 71019959 – www.theclerkenwellkitchen.co.uk – Closed
Christmas-New Year, Saturday, Sunday and bank holidays*
Carte £ 15/28 *– (lunch only) (booking advisable)*
• **Modern cuisine** • **Friendly** • **Simple** •

The owner of this simple, friendly, tucked away eatery worked with Hugh Fearnley-Whittingstall and is committed to sustainability. Daily changing, well-sourced produce; fresh, flavoursome cooking.

UNITED KINGDOM - LONDON

🍴 **Well**　　　　　　　　　　　　　　　　　　　　　　🛋
180 St John St ✉ EC1V 4JY – Ⓜ Farringdon. – ℰ (020)　　Plan: **L1**
72519363 – www.downthewell.com – Closed 25-26 December
Carte £ 26/41
• **Modern British** • **Pub** • **Neighbourhood** •
This well-supported neighbourhood pub has an intimate basement with sofas
and bright artwork and a ground floor dining room packed with wonky tables.
Seasonal dishes are carefully cooked and full of flavour.

LONDON HEATHROW AIRPORT

GREATER LONDON

CHISWICK

XX **La Trompette**　　　　　　　　　　　　　　　　88 🛋 AK ⇄
⍟ 5-7 Devonshire Rd ✉ W4 2EU – Ⓜ Turnham Green　　Plan I: **A3**
– ℰ (020) 87471836 – www.latrompette.co.uk – Closed 24-26 December
and 1 January
Menu £ 30 (lunch and early dinner)/50 – (booking essential)
• **Modern British** • **Neighbourhood** • **Fashionable** •
Chez Bruce's sister is a delightful neighbourhood restaurant that's now a little
roomier. The service is charming and the food terrific. Dishes at lunch are quite
simple but great value; the cooking at dinner is a tad more elaborate.
➔ Raw scallops with pickled cucumber, kohlrabi and English wasabi.
Shoulder of suckling pig, creamed potato, white sprouting broccoli, chilli
and garlic. Rhubarb crumble soufflé with rhubarb ripple ice cream.

XX **Hedone** (Mikael Jonsson)　　　　　　　　　　　　　AK ⇄
⍟ 301-303 Chiswick High Rd ✉ W4 4HH　　　　　　　Plan: **C4**
– Ⓜ Chiswick Park – ℰ (020) 8747 0377 – www.hedonerestaurant.com
– Closed 2 weeks summer, 2 weeks Christmas-New Year, Sunday and
Monday
Menu £ 45/125 – (dinner only and lunch Friday-Saturday) (booking
essential) (surprise menu only)
• **Modern cuisine** • **Design** • **Friendly** •
Mikael Jonsson, former lawyer turned chef, is not one for complacency, so his
restaurant continues to evolve. The content of his surprise menus is governed
entirely by what ingredients are in their prime – and it is this passion for produce which underpins the superlative and very flavoursome cooking.
➔ Warm Devon crab with velvet crab consommé, hazelnut mayonnaise
and Granny Smith apple. Squab pigeon with chard, olive and coffee-pow-
dered carrots, pigeon jus. Vanilla millefeuille with aged balsamic vinegar.

Clapham Common

XX **Trinity**　　　　　　　　　　　　　　　　　　88 🛋 AK
⍟ 4 The Polygon ✉ SW4 0JG – Ⓜ Clapham Common　　Plan I: **C3**
– ℰ (020) 76221199 – www.trinityrestaurant.co.uk – Closed 24-
30 December and 1-2 January
Menu £ 30 (weekday lunch) – Carte £ 37/52
• **Modern cuisine** • **Fashionable** • **Neighbourhood** •
The cooking at this long-standing, bright and warmly run neighbourhood restaurant is less elaborate than it once was – and it is all the better for it. The focus
remains on the primary ingredient which is given space to shine.
➔ Crispy pig's trotters, sauce gribiche and crackling. Fillet of sea bass with
roast onions, fennel, shrimps and basil. Salted caramel custard tart.

FULHAM

Harwood Arms

🕸 AC

Walham Grove ✉ *SW6 1QP –* Ⓜ *Fulham Broadway.* Plan: **C7**
*– ℰ (020) 73861847 – www.harwoodarms.com – Closed 24-27 December,
1 January and Monday lunch except bank holidays*
Menu £ 36 (weekday lunch)/43 *– (booking essential)*
• Modern British • Pub • Neighbourhood •
Its reputation may have spread like wildfire but this remains a proper, down-to-earth pub that just happens to serve really good food. The cooking is very seasonal, proudly British, full of flavour and doesn't seem out of place in this environment. Service is suitably relaxed and friendly.
➔ Wye Valley asparagus on toast with Cornish crab, watercress and pressed egg. Haunch of Berkshire fallow deer with wild garlic, beetroot and smoked bone marrow. Vanilla custard tart with date and sticky toffee ice cream.

HAMMERSMITH

River Café (Ruth Rogers)

🕸 🍴 ✿

Thames Wharf, Rainville Rd ✉ *W6 9HA* Plan I: **A3**
– Ⓜ *Barons Court – ℰ (020) 73864200 – www.rivercafe.co.uk – Closed
Christmas-New Year, Sunday dinner and bank holidays*
Carte £ 60/82 *– (booking essential)*
• Italian • Fashionable • Design •
It's all about the natural Italian flavours of the superlative ingredients. The on-view kitchen with its wood-fired oven dominates the stylish riverside room; the contagiously effervescent atmosphere is helped along by very charming service.
➔ Chargrilled squid with red chilli and rocket. Wood-roasted veal chop with salsa verde and slow-cooked peas. Chocolate Nemesis.

KEW

The Glasshouse

🕸 AC

14 Station Par. ✉ *TW9 3PZ –* Ⓜ *Kew Gardens – ℰ (020)* Plan: **C4**
*89406777 – www.glasshouserestaurant.co.uk – Closed 24-26 December
and 1 January*
Menu £ 30 (weekday lunch)/50
• Modern cuisine • Fashionable • Neighbourhood •
The Glasshouse is the very model of a modern neighbourhood restaurant and sits in the heart of lovely, villagey Kew. Food is confident yet unshowy – much like the locals – and comes with distinct Mediterranean flavours along with the occasional Asian hint. Service comes with the eagerness of youth.
➔ Duck breast with foie gras parfait, balsamic and beetroot. Loin of lamb with braised shoulder, boulangère potatoes and pea & wild garlic emulsion. Warm custard brioche with roasted apples and tarte Tatin ice cream.

London Fields

Ellory (Matthew Young)

🍴 ᵫ

Netil House, 1 Westgate St ✉ *E8 3RL* Plan I: **D1**
– Ⓜ *London Fields – ℰ (020) 3095 9455 – www.ellorylondon.com – Closed
23 December-3 January, Sunday dinner and Monday*
Carte £ 27/36 *– (dinner only and lunch Friday-Sunday)*
• Modern British • Simple • Neighbourhood •
An unpretentious, stripped back restaurant on the ground floor of Netil House. The menu changes daily and the simply described, modern dishes are original, attractive, perfectly balanced and rich in flavour.
➔ White asparagus, seaweed and trout roe. Turbot with lardo and artichoke. Rhubarb with cow's curd ice cream and tarragon.

X ✸ Pidgin

52 Wilton Way ⊠ E8 1BG – Ⓜ Hackney Central   Plan I: **D1**
– ℰ (020) 7254 8311 – www.pidginlondon.com
– Closed Monday
Menu £ 37 – *(dinner only and lunch Saturday and Sunday) (booking essential) (tasting menu only)*
• **Modern British** • **Neighbourhood** • **Bistro** •
Owners James and Sam previously ran a supper club before opening this delightful little place with its eleven closely packed tables. The no-choice four course menu changes weekly, as does the wine list, and the modern British dishes are easy on the eye, thoughtfully conceived and full of flavour.
→ Fried chicken with caviar, buttermilk and walnut. Cauliflower, juniper, pine and brown butter. Jasmine rice ice cream with apricot and elderflower.

SHOREDITCH

XX ✸ HKK   🕭 🅰🄲 ⇔ 🕅

88 Worship St ⊠ EC2A 2BE – Ⓜ Liverpool Street   Plan: **M2**
– ℰ (020) 3535 1888 – www.hkklondon.com – Closed 25 December and Sunday
Menu £ 35/88 – Carte lunch £ 28/65
• **Chinese** • **Elegant** • **Design** •
Cantonese has always been considered the finest of the Chinese cuisines and here at HKK it is given an extra degree of refinement. Expect classic flavour combinations delivered in a modern way. The room is elegant and graceful; the service smooth and assured.
→ HKK chicken and truffle soup. Cherry wood roast Peking duck. Green apple parfait with cardamom cake and crispy apple noodle.

X ✸ Clove Club (Isaac McHale)   🅰🄲 🕅

380 Old St ⊠ EC1V 9LT – Ⓜ Old Street   Plan: **D2**
– ℰ (020) 77296496 – www.thecloveclub.com
– Closed 2 weeks Christmas-New Year, August bank holiday, Monday lunch and Sunday
Menu £ 65/95 – Carte lunch £ 37/56 – *(bookings advisable at dinner) (tasting menu only)*
• **Modern cuisine** • **Trendy** •
The smart, blue-tiled open kitchen takes centre stage in this sparse room at Shoreditch Town Hall. Set menus showcase expertly sourced produce in dishes that are full of originality, verve and flair – but where flavours are expertly judged and complementary; fish and seafood are a highlight.
→ Raw Orkney scallop, hazelnut, clementine and Périgord truffle. Dry-aged Challans duck in three servings. Warm blood orange, sheep's milk yoghurt mousse and fennel granité.

X ✸ Lyle's (James Lowe)   🅰🄲

Tea Building, 56 Shoreditch High St ⊠ E1 6JJ   Plan: **N1**
– Ⓜ Shoreditch High Street
– ℰ (020) 30115911 – www.lyleslondon.com
– Closed Sunday and bank holidays
Menu £ 49 (dinner) – Carte lunch £ 26/36 – *(set menu only at dinner)*
• **Modern British** • **Simple** •
The young chef-owner is an acolyte of Fergus Henderson and delivers similarly unadulterated flavours from seasonal British produce, albeit from a set menu at dinner. This pared-down approach extends to a room that's high on functionality, but considerable warmth comes from the keen young service team.
→ Gloucester Old Spot, chicory and apple mustard. Dover sole with rape greens and whey butter. Concorde pear with oats.

SPITALFIELDS

XXX **Galvin La Chapelle** 🛱 ৬ 🔀 ⇔
🕸 *35 Spital Sq ⌧ E1 6DY – ⓜ Liverpool Street – ℰ (020)* Plan: **N2**
*7299 0400 – www.galvinrestaurants.com – Closed dinner 25-26 December
and 1 January*
Menu £ 29 (lunch and early dinner) – Carte £ 48/67
• French • Elegant •
The Victorian splendour of St Botolph's Hall, with its vaulted ceiling, arched
windows and marble pillars, lends itself perfectly to its role as a glamorous restaurant. The food is bourgeois French with a sophisticated edge and is bound to
satisfy.
→ Home-cured Shetland salmon with fennel, avocado and ruby grapefruit.
Tagine of Bresse pigeon with couscous and harissa sauce. Tarte Tatin with
crème Normande.

WANDSWORTH

XX **Chez Bruce** (Bruce Poole) 🏵 🔀 ⇔
🕸 *2 Bellevue Rd ⌧ SW17 7EG – ⓜ Tooting Bec – ℰ (020)* Plan: **D5**
*86720114 – www.chezbruce.co.uk – Closed 24-26 December and
1 January*
Menu £ 30/50 – *(booking essential)*
• French • Brasserie • Neighbourhood •
Flavoursome, uncomplicated French cooking with hints of the Mediterranean,
prepared with innate skill; well-organised, personable service and an easy-
going atmosphere – some of the reasons why Chez Bruce remains a favourite
of so many.
→ Fishcake with moules marinière, poached egg and sprouting broccoli.
Rump of veal with leek & bacon sausage, gnocchi, wild garlic and thyme.
Cherry jelly with chocolate mousse and pistachio madeleine.

HEATHROW AIRPORT

🏨 **Sofitel** 🛱 🛦 🕮 🛖 ৬ 🔀 🛱 🚗
Terminal 5, Heathrow Airport ⌧ TW6 2GD Plan: **A4**
– ⓜ Heathrow Terminal 5 – ℰ (020) 87577777
– www.sofitelheathrow.com
605 rm ⌤ – ♦£ 169/350 ♦♦£ 169/450 – 27 suites
• Business • Chain • Contemporary •
Smart and well-run contemporary hotel, designed around a series of atriums,
with direct access to T5. Crisply decorated, comfortable bedrooms with luxurious bathrooms. Choice of restaurant: international or classic French cuisine.

🏨 **Hilton London Heathrow Airport Terminal 5** 🛱 🕮
Poyle Rd, Colnbrook (West : 2.5 mi by A 🛦 🕮 🛖 ৬ 🔀 🚗 🅿
3113) ⌧ SL3 OFF – ℰ (01753) 686860 – www.hilton.com/heathrowt5
350 rm – ♦£ 119/259 ♦♦£ 119/259 – ⌤ £ 21 – 3 suites
• Business • Functional •
A feeling of light and space pervades this modern, corporate hotel. Soundproo-
fed rooms are fitted to a good standard; the spa offers wide-ranging treatments.
Open-plan Gallery for British comfort food.
Mr Todiwala's Kitchen – See restaurant listing

XX **Mr Todiwala's Kitchen** – Hilton London Heathrow Airport Terminal 5 Hotel
Poyle Rd, Colnbrook (West : 2.5 mi by A 3113) ⌧ SL3 OFF 🔀 🅿
*– ℰ (01753) 766482 – www.hilton.com/heathrowterminal5 – Closed
19 December-2 January and Sunday*
Menu £ 45 – Carte £ 28/39 – *(dinner only and lunch Thursday-Saturday)*
• Indian • Individual • Design •
Secreted within the Hilton is Cyrus Todiwala's appealingly stylish, fresh-looking
restaurant. The choice ranges from street food to tandoor dishes, Goan classics
to Parsee specialities; order the 'Kitchen menu' for the full experience.

BIRMINGHAM
BIRMINGHAM

Population: 1 101 360

J. Lorieau/Loop Images/Photononstop

It's hard to visualise Birmingham as an insignificant market town, but England's second city was just such a place throughout much of its history. Then came the boom times of the Industrial Revolution; the town fattening up on the back of the local iron and coal trades. In many people's minds that legacy lives on, the city seen as a rather dour place with shoddy Victorian housing, but 21C Brum has swept away much of its factory grime and polished up its civic face. Its first 'makeover' was over a century ago, when the mayor, Joseph Chamberlain, enlarged the city's boundaries to make it the second largest in the country.

Today it's feeling the benefits of a second modernist surge – a multi-million pound regeneration, typified by shopping arcades and appealing squares; it now boasts more canal miles than Venice and more trees than inhabitants. It's pretty much in the centre of England, surrounded by Stratford-on-Avon in the south and Bridgnorth and Ironbridge in the west, with Wolverhampton and Coventry in its hinterland. Former resident JRR Tolkien would be lost nowadays, with the undulating contours of the flyovers, the self-important muscle of the sporting, conference and exhibition centres – the Barclaycard Arena, the ICC and the NEC – and the trendy makeover of the Bullring and the Gas Street Basin. Perhaps he would feel more at home in the elegant Jewellery Quarter further north.

BIRMINGHAM IN...

→ **ONE DAY**
   The Rag, The Bullring, Birmingham Museum.

→ **TWO DAYS**
   Brindleyplace, a trip on the water-bus to The Mailbox, a cycle ride along the canals.

→ **THREE DAYS**
   Aston hall, take the Shakespeare Express to Stratford.

PRACTICAL INFORMATION

ARRIVAL-DEPARTURE

🛬 Birmingham International Airport is 8 miles east of the city. There's a free AirRail connection to Birmingham International Station every 2min. From there, frequent trains to New St Station take 20min.

GETTING AROUND

There is no central bus station - instead, buses depart from various points all over the city; maps are available from tourist offices, libraries and Network West Midlands. For a single ticket, be sure to have the correct fare ready to pay the driver, as they don't give change. Birmingham New Street Railway Station, located within the Grand Central shopping centre, provides train links all over the country, while Birmingham Snow Hill and Moor Street run mainly local services. The Midland Metro light railway links Snow Hill Station with Wolverhampton.

CALENDAR HIGHLIGHTS

March
St Patrick's Day Parade, Crufts Dog Show.

April
St George's Day Celebration.

May-June
Birmingham Pride.

August
Birmingham International Carnival (Biannual).

October
Comedy Festival.

November
The Motor Show.

EATING OUT

To the southwest of the city is Cadbury World, the UK's only purpose-built visitor centre devoted entirely to chocolate. It's located in the evocative sounding Bourneville area and staff are on hand to tell visitors the history of chocolate and how it's made, but, let's face it, most people go along to get a face full of the stuff. More conventionally, many people who come to Birmingham make for the now legendary area of Sparkbrook, Balsall Heath and Moseley, to the south of the centre. In itself that may not sound too funky, but over the last 30 years or so it's become the area known as the Balti Triangle. The balti was 'officially' discovered in Birmingham in 1976, a full-on dish of aromatic spices, fresh herbs and rich curries, and The Triangle now boasts over 50 establishments dedicated to the dish. For those after something a little more subtle, the city offers a growing number of lively and fashionable restaurants, offering assured and contemporary cuisine.

895

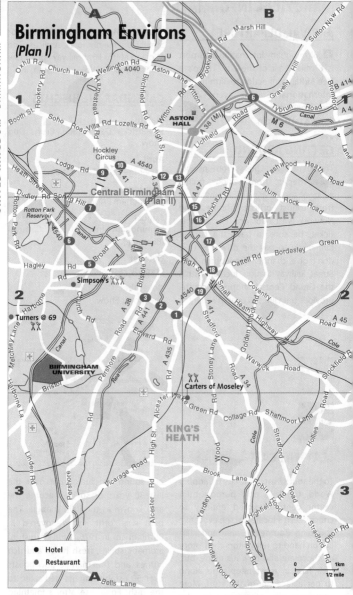

Birmingham Environs
(Plan I)

ASTON HALL

Hockley Circus

Central Birmingham (Plan II)

Rotton Park Reservoir

Simpson's ✕✕✕

Turners @ 69 ✕✕

BIRMINGHAM UNIVERSITY

Carters of Moseley ✕✕

SALTLEY

KING'S HEATH

- ● Hotel
- ● Restaurant

0   1km
0   1/2 mile

Hyatt Regency
2 Bridge St ✉ *B1 2JZ*   Plan: **D2**
– 📞 *(0121) 6431234*
– *www.birmingham.regency.hyatt.com*
319 rm – 🛏£ 95/220 🛏🛏£ 95/220 – 🍽£ 18 – 11 suites
• Business • Luxury • Contemporary •
An eye-catching, mirror-fronted, tower block hotel in a prime city centre location, with a covered link to the International Convention Centre. Spacious bedrooms have floor to ceiling windows and an excellent level of facilities. Aria restaurant, in the atrium, offers modern European menus.

Malmaison
Mailbox, 1 Wharfside St ✉ *B1 1RD* – 📞 *(0121) 2465000*   Plan: **E2**
– *www.malmaison.com*
192 rm 🍽 – 🛏£ 80/250 🛏🛏£ 80/250 – 1 suite
• Business • Luxury • Modern •
A stylish hotel with dark, moody décor, set on the site of the old Royal Mail sorting office next to designer clothing and homeware shops. Bedrooms are spacious and stylish; the Penny Black suite has a mini-cinema and a steam room. Dine from an accessible British menu in the bright, bustling brasserie.

Hotel La Tour
Albert St ✉ *B5 5JE*   Plan: **F2**
– 📞 *(0121) 718 8000*
– *www.hotel-latour.co.uk*
– *Closed 23-30 December*
174 rm – 🛏£ 89/245 🛏🛏£ 89/245 – 🍽£ 18
• Business • Luxury • Modern •
A striking modern building with spacious, stylish guest areas. With their media hubs and TV recording facilities, bedrooms are ideal for business travellers; Superiors come with baths which have TVs mounted above them. The informal chophouse serves an extensive menu of hearty, unfussy classics and steaks.

Hotel Du Vin
25 Church St ✉ *B3 2NR* – 📞 *(0844) 7364 250*   Plan: **E2**
– *www.hotelduvin.com*
66 rm 🍽 – 🛏£ 120/185 🛏🛏£ 130/195
• Business • Luxury • Design •
A characterful former eye hospital with a relaxed, shabby-chic style. Bright bedrooms are named after wine companies and estates; one suite boasts an 8 foot bed, two roll-top baths and a gym. Kick-back in the small cellar pub or comfy champagne bar; the classical bistro has a lively buzz and a French menu.

Hotel Indigo
The Cube ✉ *B1 1PR* – 📞 *(0121) 6432010*   Plan: **E3**
– *www.hotelindigobirmingham.com*
52 rm – 🛏£ 99/200 🛏🛏£ 140/210 – 🍽£ 16
• Business • Chain • Design •
Stylish hotel located on the top three floors of the eye-catching 'Cube' building. Both the appealingly styled guest areas and vividly decorated bedrooms come with floor to ceiling windows. A smart steakhouse serves classic dishes and boasts a champagne bar, a terrace and a view from every table.

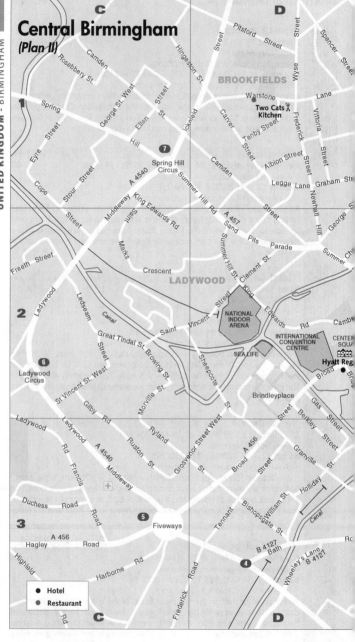

Central Birmingham
(Plan II)

BROOKFIELDS

Two Cats Kitchen

LADYWOOD

NATIONAL INDOOR ARENA

INTERNATIONAL CONVENTION CENTRE

SEA LIFE

CENTER SQUARE

Hyatt Reg

Brindleyplace

Ladywood Circus

Fiveways

- ● Hotel
- ● Restaurant

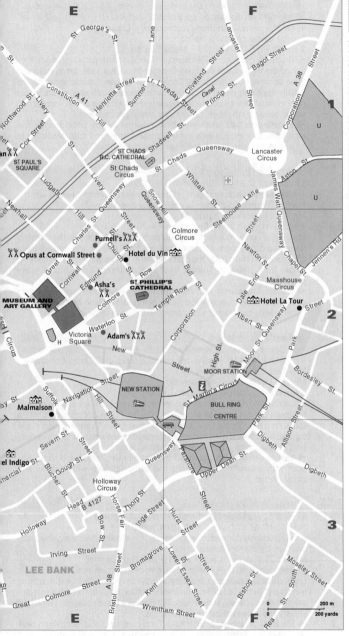

E

F

St. George's Lane

St. George's St.

Northwood St.

Livery

Cox Street

Constitution

A 41

Hill

Henrietta Street

Summer Lr. Loveday Street

Cliveland Street

Lancaster

Bagot Street

Corporation

A 38

Street

1

U

Canal

Princip St.

Shadwell St.

St. Chads Queensway

Lancaster Circus

James Watt Queensway

Aston St.

U

an X X

ST PAUL'S SQUARE

ST CHADS R.C. CATHEDRAL

St Chads Circus

St. Chads

Whittall St.

Steelhouse Lane

Jennen's Rd.

Ludgate

Hill

Livery

Snow Hill Queensway

Charles St. Queensway

Street

Colmore Circus

Newton St.

Masshouse Circus

Newhall

Hill

Purnell's X X X

Church St.

New St.

Hotel du Vin

Bull St.

X X Opus at Cornwall Street

Great

Cornwall St.

Edmund St.

Asha's X X

ST PHILLIP'S CATHEDRAL

Temple Row

Dale End

Hotel La Tour

Street

2

MUSEUM AND ART GALLERY

Colmore St.

Corporation

Albert St. Queensway

Park

St.

Circus

Waterloo St.

Victoria Square

H

Adam's X X X

New Street

High St.

Moor St. Queensway

MOOR STATION

Bordesley St.

Suffolk

Navigation Street

Street

NEW STATION

St. Martin's Circus

Park St.

Allison Street

y St.

Malmaison

Hill Street

BULL RING CENTRE

Digbeth

Severn St.

Bishopsgate St.

Queensway

Upper Dean St.

Digbeth

el Indigo

St.

nercial

Bucklesbury St.

Gough St.

Holloway Circus

Head

B 4127

Horse Fair

Thorp St.

Inge Street

Hurst Street

Street

3

Holloway

Bow St.

Irving Street

Bromsgrove Street

Lower Essex Street

Kent Street

Bishop St.

Moseley Street

LEE BANK

Great

Colmore Street

A 38

Street

Bristol St.

Wrentham Street

Rea St. South

0   200 m

0   200 yards

E

F

UNITED KINGDOM - BIRMINGHAM

❀❀❀ **Simpsons** (Andreas Antona and Luke Tipping) ⇦ 🏦 🏠 ᕂ 🗚
☸ *20 Highfield Rd, Edgbaston ⊠ B15 3DU – 𝒞 (0121)* ⟡ 🕥 **P**
4543434 – www.simpsonsrestaurant.co.uk – Closed Plan: **A2**
Sunday dinner and bank holidays
3 rm ⬚ – **♦**£ 110 **♦♦**£ 110 Menu £ 35/60
• **Modern cuisine** • **Fashionable** • **Contemporary décor** •
Behind the walls of this suburban Georgian house is a sleek dining room and
three contemporary bedrooms. Cooking has a clean, Scandic style and the
visually appealing dishes are packed with flavour. Lunch sees a 2-choice set
price menu; dinner a 4-course set price menu and a tasting option – some courses are served by the chefs. Desserts are satisfyingly traditional.
➜ Sweetbreads with mushroom broth, charred onions, bone marrow and
asparagus. Suckling pig with leeks, aubergine, apple and miso. Madagascan
sugar espuma with Yorkshire rhubarb and gingerbread.

❀❀❀ **Purnell's** (Glynn Purnell) ᕂ 🗚 ⟡
☸ *55 Cornwall St ⊠ B3 2DH – 𝒞 (0121) 2129799* Plan: **E2**
– www.purnellsrestaurant.com – Closed 2 weeks August, 1 week Easter,
1 week Christmas, Saturday lunch, Sunday and Monday
Menu £ 35 (weekday lunch)/88
• **Modern cuisine** • **Design** • **Fashionable** •
Start in the comfy lounge, then head past the wine display to the vibrantly
decorated dining room. Menus range from 3 to 9 courses and some of them
offer swaps so you can try the chef's signature dishes. Sophisticated cooking
ranges from classic to Scandic in style and flavours and textures marry
perfectly.
➜ Chicken liver parfait with red wine braised salsify and sour leaves. Loin
of Balmoral venison, Bordelaise sauce, pommes dauphine and black truffle.
Blood orange curd tartlet with honeycomb, frozen yoghurt and almond.

❀❀❀ **Adam's** (Adam Stokes) ᕂ 🗚
☸ *New Oxford House, 16 Waterloo St ⊠ B2 5UG* Plan: **E2**
– 𝒞 (0121) 643 3745 – www.adamsrestaurant.co.uk – Closed Christmas-
New Year, Sunday and Monday
Menu £ 35/60 – *(booking essential)*
• **Modern cuisine** • **Elegant** • **Design** •
Adam's has moved just around the corner to larger premises. Enjoy a drink in
the smart cocktail bar then move on to the bright, elegant restaurant with a
subtle retro feel. Choose from a concise set menu or an 8 course tasting menu:
top notch produce is used in carefully prepared dishes which have wonderfully
bold complementary flavours and contrasting textures.
➜ Veal sweetbread with air-dried ham, cauliflower, lemon and sorrel. Sea
trout with artichoke, broad beans and garlic. Rhubarb with caramel and
blood orange.

❀❀ **Turners @ 69** (Richard Turner) ᕂ 🗚
☸ *69 High St, Harborne (Southwest : 4 mi. by A 456 and* Plan: **A2**
Norfolk Rd) ⊠ B17 9NS – 𝒞 (0121) 4264440
– www.turnersrestaurantbirmingham.co.uk – Closed Christmas, New Year
and Sunday dinner-Monday
Menu £ 20 (lunch) – Carte £ 30/43 – *(booking essential)*
• **Modern British** • **Neighbourhood** • **Intimate** •
Located in a suburban parade, a busy, smartly furnished restaurant with antique
mirrors and neatly laid tables. Confidently crafted dishes use top quality seasonal ingredients, chosen at their peak. The classically based cooking is refined yet
unfussy and allows natural flavours to shine.
➜ Isle of Wight tomatoes with Innes Farm curd, basil and extra virgin olive
oil. Salt-marsh lamb Wellington with rosemary jelly and lamb jus. Wild
strawberry Arctic roll.

XX   **Carters of Moseley** (Brad Carter)   ♿ 🅰🅲 🛈

⌘   *2c St Mary's Row, Wake Green Rd ⊠ B13 9EZ*   Plan: **B3**
– 𝒞 (0121) 449 8885 – www.cartersofmoseley.co.uk – Closed 1-
18 January, 30 July-16 August, Sunday and Monday
Menu £ 35/75 – *(booking advisable)*
• Modern British • Neighbourhood • Friendly •
Lovely little neighbourhood restaurant with black ash tables and a glass-fronted
cabinet running down one wall. Each dish is made up of three key components
– which can include some unusual ingredients; combinations are well-balanced
and flavours are intense. The young team are friendly and engaging.
→ Orkney scallop with coral roe and pepper dulse. Manx lamb with Jersey
Royals and monk's beard. Goat's yoghurt with pistachio and Alphonso
mango.

XX   **Opus at Cornwall Street**   ♿ 🅰🅲 ⇔ 🛈

54 Cornwall St ⊠ B3 2DE – 𝒞 (0121) 200 2323   Plan: **E2**
– www.opusrestaurant.co.uk – Closed 24 December-3 January, Saturday
lunch, Sunday dinner and bank holidays
Menu £ 20 – Carte £ 26/49
• Modern cuisine • Design • Chic •
Very large and popular restaurant with floor to ceiling windows; enjoy an aperitif in the cocktail bar before dining in the stylish main room or at the chef's table
in the kitchen. Daily changing menu of modern brasserie dishes.

XX   **Lasan**   🅰🅲 🛈

3-4 Dakota Buildings, James St, St Pauls Sq ⊠ B3 1SD   Plan: **E1**
– 𝒞 (0121) 2123664 – www.lasan.co.uk – Closed 25 December
Carte £ 28/45
• Indian • Design • Fashionable •
An industrial-style restaurant in an old Jewellery Quarter art gallery. Original
cooking takes authentic Indian flavours and delivers them in creative modern
combinations; there are some particularly interesting vegetarian choices.

XX   **Asha's**   ♿ 🅰🅲 ⇔ 🛈

12-22 Newhall St ⊠ B3 3LX – 𝒞 (0121) 2002767   Plan: **E2**
– www.ashasuk.co.uk – Closed 26 December, 1 January and lunch
Saturday-Sunday
Menu £ 32 – Carte £ 19/68
• Indian • Exotic décor • Fashionable •
A stylish, passionately run Indian restaurant with exotic décor; owned by renow-
ned artiste/gourmet Asha Bhosle. Extensive menus cover most parts of the Sub-
continent, with everything cooked to order. Tandoori kebabs are a speciality.

X   **Two Cats Kitchen**

27 Warstone Ln ⊠ B18 6JQ – 𝒞 (0121) 212 0070   Plan: **D1**
– www.twocatskitchen.com – Closed 3 weeks Christmas-New Year, Sunday
and Monday
Menu £ 42 – *(dinner only and lunch Friday-Saturday) (booking advisable)*
(tasting menu only)
• Regional cuisine • Simple • Neighbourhood •
Tucked away down an alley in the jewellery quarter is this small restaurant with
exposed brickwork and stained glass windows. The 7 course set menu comprises artistically presented modern dishes of flavoursome New Baltic cuisine.

AT NATIONAL EXHIBITION CENTRE Southeast : 9,5 m. on A 45

XX   **Andy Waters**   ♿ 🅰🅲 🅿

Floor One, Resorts World, Pendigo Way ⊠ B40 1PU – 𝒞 (0201) 273 1238
– www.watersrestaurant.co.uk – Closed 25 December
Menu £ 15 (lunch) – Carte £ 26/48
• Traditional British • Chic • Design •
Unusually set in a shopping centre, beside the cinema, is this comfy, formal restaurant run by an experienced chef – ask for one of the booths. Traditional cooking is given a personal touch; the 2 course lunch menu is good value.

EDINBURGH
EDINBURGH

Population: 495 360

D. Pearson/Agency Jon Arnold Images/age fotostock

The beautiful Scottish capital is laid out on seven, formerly volcanic, hills – a contrast to the modern city, which is elegant, cool and sophisticated. It's essentially two cities in one: the medieval Old Town, huddled around and beneath the crags and battlements of the castle, and the smart Georgian terraces of the New Town, overseen by the 18C architect Robert Adam. You could also say there's now a third element to the equation: the revamped port of Leith, just two miles away.

This is a city that's been attracting tourists since the 19C; and since 1999 it's been the home of the Scottish Parliament, adding a new dimension to its worldwide reputation. It accepts its plaudits with the same ease that it accepts an extra half million visitors at the height of summer, and its status as a UNESCO World Heritage site confirms it as a city that knows how to be both ancient and modern. In the middle is the castle, to the south is the Old Town and to the north is the New Town. There's a natural boundary to the north at the Firth of Forth, while to the south lie the rolling Pentland Hills. Unless you've had a few too many drams, it's just about impossible to get lost here, as prominent landmarks like the Castle, Arthur's Seat and Calton Hill access all areas. Bisecting the town is Princes Street, one side of which invites you to shop, the other, to sit and relax in your own space.

EDINBURGH IN...

→ **ONE DAY**
Calton Hill, Royal Mile, Edinburgh Castle, New Town café, Old Town pub.

→ **TWO DAYS**
Water of Leith, Scottish National Gallery of Modern Art, Leith.

→ **THREE DAYS**
Arthur's Seat, National Museum of Scotland, Holyrood Park, Pentland Hills.

PRACTICAL INFORMATION

ARRIVAL-DEPARTURE

Edinburgh International Airport is 8 miles west of the city centre. There is an Airlink Bus Service to Waverley Bridge every 10min. You can also catch the tram; it takes 35min to reach York Place in the city centre.

GETTING AROUND

There's no underground or tram system, so it might be wise to invest in a DAYticket for the buses; you'll have the freedom of Edinburgh for 24 hours. There are plenty of guided options for looking around: choose from an open-top bus, a walking or cycling tour, or even a ghost tour of the Old Town. All bus tours leave from Waverley Bridge and the hop-on, hop-off nature of the ticket will last 24 hours.

CALENDAR HIGHLIGHTS

March-April
International Science Festival.

July
Jazz and Blues Festival.

August
Edinburgh Festival Fringe (shows, exhibitions, comedy), International Book Festival.

August-September
International Festival (dance, music, theatre), Edinburgh Art Festival.

December
Markets and funfairs, Four-day Hogmanay celebration (torchlight procession, carnival and street party).

EATING OUT

Edinburgh enjoys a varied and interesting restaurant culture so, whatever the occasion, you should find somewhere that fits the bill. The city is said to have more restaurants per head than anywhere in the UK and they vary from lavish establishments in grand hotels to cosy little bistros; you can dine with ghosts in a basement eatery or admire the city from a rooftop table. Scotland's great larder provides much of the produce, and cooking styles range from the innovative and contemporary to the simple and traditional. There are also some good pubs to explore in the old town, and drinking dens also abound in Cowgate and Grassmarket. Further away, in West End, you'll find enticing late-night bars, while the stylish variety, serving cocktails, are more in order in the George Street area of the new town. If you'd rather drink something a little more special then try the 19C Cadenhead's on the Royal Mile – it's the place to go for whiskies and it sells a mindboggling range of rare distillations. The peaty flavoured Laphroaig is a highly recommended dram.

Edinburgh Environs
(Plan I)

FIRTH

CRAMOND

West Shore Rd
West Harbour Rd
Granto

Marine
Drive
West Granton Rd
Ferry Road

Silverknowes Road
Whitehouse Road
B 9085
Pannywell Rd
Road

Cramond Road South
Main St.
Ferry Road
Crewe Road South

A 90 Queensferry Road
Hillhouse Road
Telford Road
A 902

Drum Brae North
B 701
Craigcrook Road
BLACKHALL
Craigleith Rd

Drum Brae South
Clermiston Road
Ravelston Road
A 90 Queensferry Road

Craigs Road
EDINBURGH ZOO
Dykes
SCOTTISH NATIONAL GALLERY OF MODERN ART

St John's Road
MURRAYFIELD

Glasgow Road
A 8 Corstorphine Road
Balgreen Rd
Road
The Dunstane

South gyle Broadway
B 701 Broomhouse Rd
Stenhouse Drive
Gorgie Road
Road
Dalry Rd
Gli

SIGHTHILL
Calder Road
Longstone Rd
Slateford Road
Union Canal
Bia Bistrot
Road

EDINBURGH AIRPORT
A 720
Calder
B 701
Wester Hailes Road
Water of Leith
Colinton Road
Gleniockhart Road
Road

Lanark Road
Gillespie Rd
Colinton Road
Redford Road
Colinton Mains Dri.
B 701
Oxgangs Road
Comiston Road

JUNIPER GREEN
Bonaly Rd
A 720
Comiston Road

● Hotel
● Restaurant

0 ____ 1km
0 ____ 1 mile

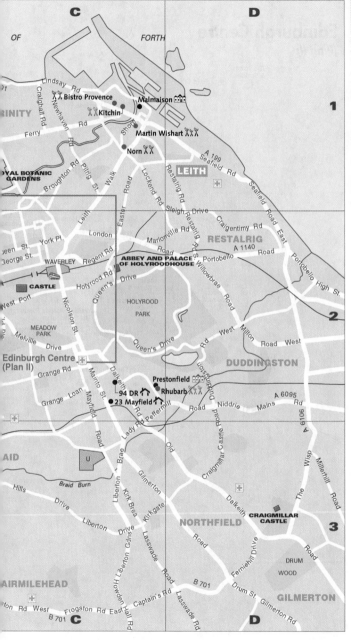

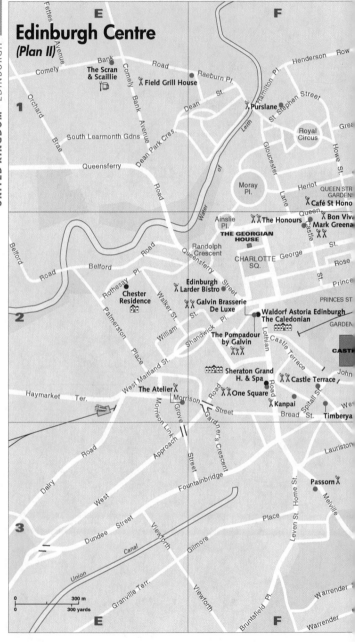

Edinburgh Centre
(Plan II)

Comely   Road

Fettes Avenue

Orchard

Brae

Comely Bank Avenue

Comely Bank

Bank

The Scran & Scaillie

Field Grill House

Raeburn Pl.

Dean St.

Hamilton Pl.

Purslane

St Stephen Street

Henderson Row

Royal Circus

Howe St.

Grea

South Learmonth Gdns

Dean Park Cres.

Water of Leith

Queensferry   Road

Belford

Road

Belford

Rothesay Pl.

Walker St.

Chester Residence

Palmerston Place

William St.

Shandwick Pl.

Queensferry Street

Gloucester Lane

Moray Pl.

Heriot

Ainslie Pl.

The Honours

Café St Hono

Mark Greena

Bon Viv

QUEEN STR GARDEN

Queen St.

Castle

THE GEORGIAN HOUSE

Randolph Crescent

CHARLOTTE SQ.

George St.

Rose St.

Prince

PRINCES ST

Edinburgh Larder Bistro

Galvin Brasserie De Luxe

Waldorf Astoria Edinburgh The Caledonian

GARDEN

The Pompadour by Galvin

Lothian Road

Castle Terrace

CASTL

West Maitland St.

The Atelier

Morrison

Grove

Sheraton Grand H. & Spa

One Square

Castle Terrace

John

Kanpai

Spittal St.

Bread St.

West

Timberya

Haymarket Ter.

Morrison Link

Approach

Gardner's Crescent

Street

Fountainbridge

Lauriston

Leven St.

Home St.

Passorn

Melville

Dalry

Road

West

Dundee Street

Viewforth

Gilmore Place

Canal

Union

Granville Terr.

Viewforth

Bruntsfield

Warrender

Warrender

0 — 300 m
0 — 300 yards

E   F

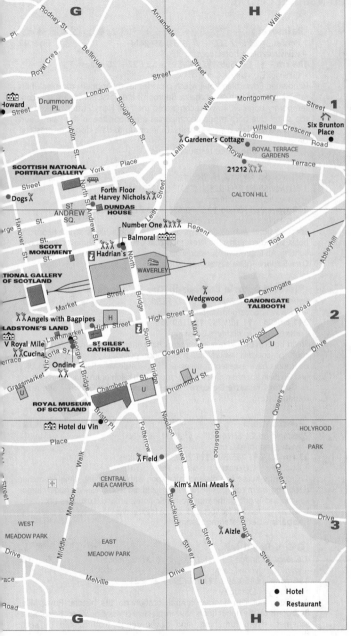

G

H

Rodney St.

Annandale

Walk

1

Royal Cres.

Bellevue

Street

Leith

Howard

Drummond
Pl.

London

Broughton

Street

Montgomery

Street

Street

Hillside

Crescent

Six Brunton
Place

Dublin

St.

Place

London

Road

York

Royal

Terrace

Gardener's Cottage

ROYAL TERRACE
GARDENS

SCOTTISH NATIONAL
PORTRAIT GALLERY

Street

North St. Andrew St.

Leith Street

21212

Terrace

Dogs

Forth Floor
at Harvey Nichols

CALTON HILL

Hanover St.

St.
ANDREW
SQ.

St Andrew St.

DUNDAS
HOUSE

arge

St.

SCOTT
MONUMENT

Number One

Balmoral

Regent

North

Road

Abbeyhill

TIONAL GALLERY
OF SCOTLAND

Hadrian's

WAVERLEY

Street

Bridge

Wedgwood

Canongate

CANONGATE
TALBOOTH

Road

2

Market

High Street

St. Mary's St.

Angels with Bagpipes

High Street

H

South

Cowgate

Holyrood

U

LADSTONE'S LAND

V Royal Mile

Lawnmarket

George IV Bridge

St GILES'
CATHEDRAL

Bridge

U

Terrace

Victoria St.

Ondine

Cucina

U

Drummond St.

Queen's

Grassmarket

Chambers St.

Nicolson Street

ROYAL MUSEUM
OF SCOTLAND

Bristo Pl.

U

HOLYROOD
PARK

Hotel du Vin

Place

Potterrow

Pleasance

Walk

Field

Queen's

Drive

Meadow

CENTRAL
AREA CAMPUS

Kim's Mini Meals

Clerk

Buccleuch

Street

WEST
MEADOW PARK

Street

St. Leonard's Street

Aizle

Drive

Middle

EAST
MEADOW PARK

Drive

3

race

Melville

U

Road

| ● | Hotel |
| ● | Restaurant |

G

H

907

Balmoral

1 Princes St ⊠ EH2 2EQ – ℰ (0131) 5562414
– www.roccofortehotels.com
Plan: **G2**

188 rm – †£ 190/595 ††£ 190/595 – ☑ £ 27 – 20 suites

• Grand Luxury • Chain • Classic •

Renowned Edwardian hotel which provides for the modern traveller whilst retaining its old-fashioned charm. Bedrooms are classical with a subtle contemporary edge; JK Rowling completed the final Harry Potter book in the top suite! Live harp music accompanies afternoon tea in the Palm Court and 'Scotch' offers over 460 malts. Dine on up-to-date dishes or brasserie classics.

❀ **Number One** – See restaurant listing

Sheraton Grand H. & Spa

1 Festival Sq ⊠ EH3 9SR – ℰ (0131) 2299131
– www.sheratonedinburgh.co.uk
Plan: **F2**

269 rm – †£ 170/650 ††£ 170/650 – ☑ £ 22 – 12 suites

• Grand Luxury • Business • Modern •

Spacious hotel with castle views from some rooms. Sleek, stylish bedrooms boast strong comforts, the latest mod cons and smart bathrooms with mood lighting. An impressive four-storey glass cube houses the stunning spa.

One Square – See restaurant listing

Waldorf Astoria Edinburgh The Caledonian

Princes St ⊠ EH1 2AB – ℰ (0131) 222 8888
– www.waldorfastoriaedinburgh.com
Plan: **F2**

241 rm ☑ – †£ 169/759 ††£ 169/759 – 6 suites

• Historic • Luxury • Design •

Smart hotel in the old railway terminus: have afternoon tea on the former forecourt or cocktails where the trains once pulled in. Sumptuous modern bedrooms have excellent facilities; ask for a castle view. Unwind in the UK's first Guerlain spa, then dine in the grand French salon or luxurious brasserie.

❀ **Galvin Brasserie De Luxe • The Pompadour by Galvin** – See restaurant listing

Prestonfield

Priestfield Rd ⊠ EH16 5UT – ℰ (0131) 2257800
– www.prestonfield.com
Plan: **C2**

23 rm ☑ – †£ 295/395 ††£ 295/395 – 5 suites

• Luxury • Country house • Personalised •

17C country house in a pleasant rural spot, with an opulent, dimly lit interior displaying warm colours, fine furnishings and old tapestries – it's hugely atmospheric and is one of the most romantic hotels around. Luxurious bedrooms boast a high level of facilities and service is excellent.

Rhubarb – See restaurant listing

G & V Royal Mile

1 George IV Bridge ⊠ EH1 1AD – ℰ (0131) 2206666
– www.gandvhotel.com
Plan: **G2**

136 rm – †£ 150/390 ††£ 150/390 – ☑ £ 21 – 7 suites

• Luxury • Design •

A striking hotel in a great central location on the historic Royal Mile. Bedrooms on the upper floors have impressive city skyline views. Bold colour schemes, stylish furnishings and clever design features can be seen throughout.

Cucina – See restaurant listing

Howard
☆ ♨ **P**

34 Great King St ✉ *EH3 6QH –* ✆ *(0131) 5573500*   Plan: **G1**
– www.thehoward.com
18 rm �breakfast *–* ♦£ 120/450 ♦♦£ 140/450 *–* 3 suites
• Townhouse • Luxury • Classic •

A series of three Georgian townhouses with many characterful original features still in situ; situated in the heart of the New Town. Bedrooms vary in size and have classic furnishings and a contemporary edge; every room is assigned a butler. Formal dining from modern menus in the elegant restaurant.

Hotel du Vin
☆ ♿ 🅰 ♨

11 Bristo Pl ✉ *EH1 1EZ –* ✆ *(0131) 2474900*   Plan: **G3**
– www.hotelduvin.com/edinburgh
47 rm ⊖ *–* ♦£ 90/300 ♦♦£ 90/300
• Luxury • Design •

Boutique hotel located close to the Royal Mile, featuring unique murals and wine-themed bedrooms furnished with dark wood. Guest areas include a whisky snug and a mezzanine bar complete with glass-fronted cellars and a wine tasting room. The traditional bistro offers classic French cooking.

Chester Residence

9 Rothesay Pl ✉ *EH3 7SL –* ✆ *(0131) 226 2075*   Plan: **E2**
– www.chester-residence.com – Closed 23-26 December
23 suites *–* ♦£ 135/325 ♦♦£ 135/550 *–* ⊖£ 12
• Townhouse • Contemporary • Personalised •

A series of smart Georgian townhouses in a quiet street. The luxurious, individually furnished suites come with kitchens and state-of-the-art facilities including video entry and integrated sound systems; the Mews apartments are the best.

The Dunstane
☆ **P**

4 West Coates ✉ *EH12 5JQ –* ✆ *(0131) 3376169*   Plan: **B2**
– www.thedunstane.co.uk
38 rm ⊖ *–* ♦£ 79/229 ♦♦£ 99/259
• Townhouse • Contemporary • Personalised •

An impressive house which used to be a training centre for the Royal Bank of Scotland. Guest areas retain original Victorian features and the smart bedrooms have designer touches; some are located across a busy road. Small restaurant with a stylish cocktail bar; the menu champions local produce.

Six Brunton Place
♿

6 Brunton Pl ✉ *EH7 5EG –* ✆ *(0131) 6220042*   Plan: **H1**
– www.sixbruntonplace.com
4 rm ⊖ *–* ♦£ 89/159 ♦♦£ 109/199
• Townhouse • Luxury • Contemporary •

This late Georgian townhouse – run by a charming owner – was once home to Frederick Ritchie, who designed the One O'Clock Gun and Time Ball. Inside you'll find flagged floors, columns, marble fireplaces and a cantilevered stone staircase; these contrast with contemporary furnishings and vibrant modern art.

94 DR
P

94 Dalkeith Rd ✉ *EH16 5AF –* ✆ *(0131) 6629265*   Plan: **C2**
– www.94dr.com – Closed 4-18 January and 25-26 December
6 rm ⊖ *–* ♦£ 90/145 ♦♦£ 100/225
• Townhouse • Personalised • Contemporary •

Charming owners welcome you to this very stylish and individual hotel in a Victorian terraced house. Bedrooms are well-equipped, there's a retro lounge with an honesty bar and breakfast is served in the conservatory with its decked terrace.

23 Mayfield

23 Mayfield Gdns ⊠ EH9 2BX – ℰ (0131) 667 5806 Plan: **C2**
– www.23mayfield.co.uk
7 rm ⌂ – †£ 85/165 ††£ 99/189
• **Traditional** • **Classic** • **Personalised** •

Lovingly restored Victorian house with a very welcoming, helpful owner and an outdoor hot tub. Spacious lounge has an honesty bar and a collection of old and rare books. Sumptuous bedrooms come with coordinated soft furnishings, some mahogany features and luxurious bathrooms. Extravagant breakfast choices.

Number One – Balmoral Hotel

1 Princes St ⊠ EH2 2EQ – ℰ (0131) 5576727 Plan: **G2**
– www.roccofortehotels.com – Closed 2 weeks mid-January
Menu £ 75 – *(dinner only)*
• **Modern cuisine** • **Intimate** • **Elegant** •

A stylish, long-standing restaurant with a chic cocktail bar, set in the basement of a grand hotel. Richly upholstered banquettes and red lacquered walls give it a plush, luxurious feel. Cooking is modern and intricate and prime Scottish ingredients are key. Service is professional and has personality.

→ Balmoral smoked salmon with lemon butter, quail's egg and caviar. Roast veal sweetbread with Wye Valley asparagus, morels and madeira sauce. Valrhona chocolate tart '2001', praline and white chocolate.

21212 (Paul Kitching)

3 Royal Terr ⊠ EH7 5AB – ℰ (0345) 2221212 Plan: **H1**
– www.21212restaurant.co.uk – Closed 10 days January, 10 days summer, Sunday and Monday
4 rm ⌂ – †£ 95/295 ††£ 95/295   Menu £ 32/75 – *(booking essential)*
• **Creative** • **Elegant** • **Design** •

Stunningly refurbished Georgian townhouse designed by William Playfair. The glass-fronted kitchen is the focal point of the stylish, high-ceilinged dining room. Cooking is skilful and innovative and features quirky combinations; '21212' reflects the number of dishes per course at lunch – at dinner it's '31313'. Some of the luxurious bedrooms overlook the Firth of Forth.

→ Barley & cardamom, cheese & onion, pimento & mushrooms. Sea bass ratatouille, scallop, caviar and pine nuts. Creamy vanilla rice pudding, kiwi, pears & dill with peanut butter custard.

Rhubarb – Prestonfield Hotel

Priestfield Rd ⊠ EH16 5UT – ℰ (0131) 2251333 Plan: **C2**
– www.prestonfield.com
Menu £ 20/36 – Carte £ 36/70
• **Modern cuisine** • **Elegant** • **Chic** •

Two sumptuous, richly decorated dining rooms set within a romantic 17C country house; so named as this was the first place in Scotland where rhubarb was grown. The concise menu lists modern dishes with some innovative touches and is accompanied by an interesting wine list, with a great selection by the glass.

The Pompadour by Galvin – Waldorf Astoria Edinburgh The Caledonian

Princes St ⊠ EH1 2AB – ℰ (0131) 222 8975
– www.galvinrestaurants.com – Closed 1- Plan: **F2**
16 January, Sunday and Monday
Carte £ 47/67 – *(dinner only and Friday lunch)*
• **French** • **Chic** • **Intimate** •

A grand, first floor hotel restaurant which opened in the 1920s and is modelled on a French salon. Classic Gallic dishes showcase Scottish produce, using techniques introduced by Escoffier, and are executed with a lightness of touch.

XX **Castle Terrace**   ⅙ 🎿 ⒱

33-35 Castle Terr ✉ *EH1 2EL –* ☏ *(0131) 2291222*   Plan: **F2**
– www.castleterracerestaurant.com – Closed Christmas, New Year, 1 week
April, 1 week July, 1 week October, Sunday and Monday
Menu £ 30/65
• Modern cuisine • Intimate • Elegant •
Set in the shadow of the castle is this bright, contemporary restaurant with
hand-painted wallpapers and a mural depicting the Edinburgh skyline. Cooking
is ambitious with a playful element. The wine list offers plenty of choice.

XX **Mark Greenaway**   ⇔ 🍸

69 North Castle St ✉ *EH2 3LJ –* ☏ *(0131) 226 1155*   Plan: **F2**
– www.markgreenaway.com – Closed 25-26 December, 1-2 January,
Sunday and Monday
Menu £ 25 (lunch and early dinner)/66 – Carte £ 38/57 – *(booking advi-*
sable)
• Modern cuisine • Intimate • Romantic •
Smart restaurant located in an old Georgian bank – they store their wine in the
old vault. The well-travelled chef employs interesting texture and flavour combinations. Dishes are modern, ambitious and attractively presented.

XX **The Honours**   ⅙ 🍸

58A North Castle St ✉ *EH2 3LU –* ☏ *(0131) 220 2513*   Plan: **F2**
– www.thehonours.co.uk – Closed 25-26 December, 1-3 January,
Sunday and Monday
Menu £ 23 (lunch and early dinner) – Carte £ 37/70
• Classic cuisine • Brasserie • Fashionable •
Bustling brasserie with a smart, stylish interior and a pleasingly informal atmo-
sphere. Classical brasserie menus have French leanings but always offer some
Scottish dishes too; meats cooked on the Josper grill are popular.

XX **Cucina** – G & V Royal Mile Hotel   🍽 ⅙ ⅙ 🍸

1 George IV Bridge ✉ *EH1 1AD –* ☏ *(0131) 2206666*   Plan: **G2**
– www.gandvhotel.com
Menu £ 19 (lunch) – Carte £ 23/50
• Italian • Design • Fashionable •
A buzzy mezzanine restaurant in a chic hotel, featuring red and blue glass-topped tables and striking kaleidoscope-effect blocks on the walls. Italian dishes
follow the seasons – some are classically based and others are more modern.

XX **One Square** – Sheraton Grand Hotel & Spa   🍽 ⅙ ⅙ ⇔ 🅿

1 Festival Sq ✉ *EH3 9SR –* ☏ *(0131) 2216422*   Plan: **F2**
– www.onesquareedinburgh.co.uk
Menu £ 17 (lunch and early dinner) – Carte £ 28/97
• Traditional cuisine • Classic décor • Brasserie •
So named because it covers one side of the square, this smart hotel restaurant
offers casual dining from an all-encompassing menu, accompanied by views
towards Edinburgh Castle. Its stylish bar stocks over 50 varieties of gin.

XX **Ondine**   ⅙ ⅙ 🍸

2 George IV Bridge (1st floor) ✉ *EH1 1AD –* ☏ *(0131)*   Plan: **G2**
2261888 – www.ondinerestaurant.co.uk – Closed 1 week early January
and 24-26 December
Menu £ 22 (lunch and early dinner) – Carte £ 32/74
• Seafood • Brasserie • Elegant •
Smart, lively restaurant dominated by an impressive horseshoe bar and a crus-
tacean counter. Classic menus showcase prime Scottish seafood in tasty,
straightforward dishes which let the ingredients shine. Service is well-structu-
red.

XX   **Galvin Brasserie De Luxe** – Waldorf Astoria Edinburgh The Caledonian

Princes St ⊠ EH1 2AB – ℰ (0131) 222 8988   ⅋ 🔠 🅿

– www.galvinrestaurants.com   Plan: **F2**

Menu £ 19 – Carte £ 27/50

• French • Brasserie • Chic •

It's accurately described by its name: a simply styled restaurant which looks like a brasserie of old, but with the addition of a smart shellfish counter and formal service. There's an appealing à la carte and a good value two-choice daily set selection; dishes are refined, flavoursome and of a good size.

XX   **Forth Floor at Harvey Nichols**   ⇐ 🏠 ⅋ 🔠 🐾 🕅

30-34 St Andrew Sq ⊠ EH2 2AD – ℰ (0131) 5248350   Plan: **G1**

– www.harveynichols.com – Closed 25 December, 1 January and dinner Sunday-Monday

Menu £ 30 (lunch and early dinner) – Carte £ 34/44

• Modern cuisine • Fashionable • Trendy •

A buzzy fourth floor eatery and terrace offering wonderful rooftop views. Dine on accomplished modern dishes in the restaurant or on old favourites in the all-day bistro. Arrive early and start with a drink in the smart cocktail bar.

XX   **Angels with Bagpipes**   🏠

343 High St, Royal Mile ⊠ EH1 1PW – ℰ (0131)   Plan: **G2**

220 1111 – www.angelswithbagpipes.co.uk – Closed 4-19 January and 24-26 December

Menu £ 20 (lunch) – Carte £ 29/54

• Modern cuisine • Bistro • Design •

Small, stylish restaurant named after the wooden sculpture in St Giles Cathedral, opposite. Dishes are more elaborate than the menu implies; modern interpretations of Scottish classics could include 'haggis, neeps and tattiesgine'.

X   **Timberyard**   🏠 ⅋ 🌣 🕅

10 Lady Lawson St ⊠ EH3 9DS – ℰ (0131) 221 1222   Plan: **F2**

– www.timberyard.co – Closed Christmas, 1 week April, 1 week October, Sunday and Monday

Menu £ 27 (lunch and early dinner)/55 – (booking essential at dinner)

• Modern cuisine • Rustic • Simple •

Trendy warehouse restaurant; its spacious, rustic interior incorporating wooden floors and wood-burning stoves. Scandic-influenced menu offers 'bites', 'small' and 'large' sizes, with some home-smoked dishes and an emphasis on distinct, punchy flavours. Cocktails are made with vegetable purées and foraged herbs.

X   **Aizle**   🕅

107-109 St Leonard's St ⊠ EH8 9QY – ℰ (0131)   Plan: **H3**

662 9349 – www.aizle.co.uk – Closed 1-18 January, 3-18 July, 25-31 December, Monday and Tuesday except in August

Menu £ 45 – (dinner only)

• Modern cuisine • Simple • Neighbourhood •

Modest little suburban restaurant whose name means 'ember' or 'spark'. Well-balanced, skilfully prepared dishes are, in effect, a surprise, as the set menu is presented as a long list of ingredients – the month's 'harvest'.

X   **Passorn**

23-23a Brougham Pl ⊠ EH3 9JU – ℰ (0131) 229 1537   Plan: **F3**

– www.passornthai.com – Closed 25-26 December, 1-2 January, Sunday and Monday lunch

Menu £ 16 (weekday lunch) – Carte £ 24/37 – (booking essential)

• Thai • Friendly • Neighbourhood •

The staff are super-friendly at this extremely popular neighbourhood restaurant, whose name means 'Angel'. Authentic menus feature Thai classics and old family recipes; the seafood dishes are a highlight and presentation is first class. Spices and other ingredients are flown in from Thailand.

X

Dogs

⊕

110 Hanover St (1st Floor) ⊠ *EH2 1DR –* ☏ *(0131) 220 1208*   Plan: **G1**
– www.thedogsonline.co.uk – Closed 25 December and 1 January
Carte £ 12/25

• Traditional cuisine • Bistro • Rustic •

Cosy, slightly bohemian-style eatery on the first floor of a classic Georgian mid-terrace, with two high-ceilinged, shabby chic dining rooms and an appealing bar. Robust, good value comfort food is crafted from local, seasonal produce; dishes such as cock-a-leekie soup and devilled ox livers feature.

X

The Atelier

159 Morrison St ⊠ *EH3 8AG –* ☏ *(0131) 6295040*   Plan: **E2**
– www.theatelierrestaurant.co.uk – Closed 2-3 weeks January, 25-26 December and Monday
Menu £ 18 (lunch) – Carte £ 27/47

• Mediterranean cuisine • Bistro • Neighbourhood •

Attractive little restaurant with bright orange chairs and a stone feature wall. The chef is Polish but his dishes have French and Italian influences; fresh ingredients are prepared with care and cooking has a subtle modern slant.

X

Field Grill House

1-3 Raeburn Pl, Stockbridge ⊠ *EH4 1HU –* ☏ *(0131)*   Plan: **F1**
332 9977 – www.fieldgrillhouse.co.uk – Closed 2 weeks January and Monday
Menu £ 16/17 – Carte £ 25/42

• Meats and grills • Neighbourhood • Friendly •

Large pictures of sheep, pigs, cows and chickens give a clue as to the cooking: the extensive à la carte focuses on grilled meats, with 35-day aged beef sourced from an independent Borders butcher. The set menus are good value.

X

Edinburgh Larder Bistro   🅰🅲 🕎

1a Alva St ⊠ *EH2 4PH –* ☏ *(0131) 225 4599*   Plan: **F2**
– www.edinburghlarder.co.uk – Closed 1 January, Sunday and Monday
Menu £ 15 (lunch and early dinner) – Carte £ 25/36

• Regional cuisine • Bistro • Simple •

Sustainability and provenance are key here: the tables are crafted from scaffold boards, old lobster creels act as lampshades and each month they feature a different local, organic animal on the menu, which is used from nose to tail.

X

Purslane

33a St Stephen St ⊠ *EH3 5AH –* ☏ *(0131) 226 3500*   Plan: **F1**
– www.purslanerestaurant.co.uk – Closed 25-26 December, 1 January and Monday
Menu £ 26 (lunch and early dinner)/38 – *(booking essential)*

• Modern cuisine • Neighbourhood • Rustic •

Set in a residential area, in the basement of a terraced Georgian house; an intimate restaurant of just 7 tables, with wallpaper featuring a pine tree motif. The chef carefully prepares modern dishes using well-practiced techniques.

X

Gardener's Cottage

1 Royal Terrace Gdns ⊠ *EH7 5DX –* ☏ *(0131) 558 1221*   Plan: **H1**
– www.thegardenerscottage.co – Closed Tuesday
Menu £ 50 (dinner) – Carte lunch £ 16/24 – *(bookings advisable at dinner)*

• Traditional cuisine • Rustic • Friendly •

This quirky little eatery was once home to a royal gardener. Two cosy, simply furnished rooms have long communal tables. Lunch is light and dinner offers an 8 course set menu; much of the produce comes from the kitchen garden.

X

Field

41 West Nicholson St ⊠ *EH8 9DB –* ☏ *(0131) 667 7010*   Plan: **G3**
– www.fieldrestaurant.co.uk – Closed Monday
Menu £ 17 (lunch and early dinner) – Carte £ 22/40

• Modern cuisine • Simple • Rustic •

A rustic restaurant run by two young owners, comprising just 8 tables – which are overlooked by a huge canvas of a prized cow. The appealing menu changes slightly each day, offering original modern cooking with a playful element.

X **Bon Vivant** ⚘

55 Thistle St ⊠ *EH2 1DY* – 📞 *(0131) 225 3275*   Plan: **F1**
– *www.bonvivantedinburgh.co.uk* – *Closed 25-26 December and 1 January*
Carte £ 17/35
• **Traditional cuisine** • **Wine bar** • **Cosy** •

A relaxed wine bar in the city backstreets, with a dimly lit interior, tightly packed tables and a cheery, welcoming team. The appealing, twice daily menu has an eclectic mix of influences; start with some of the bite-sized nibbles.

X **Kanpai**

8-10 Grindlay St ⊠ *EH3 9AS* – 📞 *(0131) 228 1602*   Plan: **F2**
– *www.kanpaisushi.co.uk* – *Closed Monday*
Carte £ 13/38
• **Japanese** • **Simple** • **Design** •

Uncluttered, modern Japanese restaurant with a smart sushi bar and cheerful service. Colourful, elaborate dishes have clean, well-defined flavours; the menu is designed to help novices feel confident and experts feel at home.

X **Kim's Mini Meals** ἐ⊟

5 Buccleuch St ⊠ *EH8 9JN* – 📞 *(0131) 6297951*   Plan: **H3**
– *www.kimsminimeals.com*
Carte approx. £ 18 – *(booking essential at dinner)*
• **Korean** • **Simple** • **Friendly** •

A delightfully quirky little eatery filled with bric-a-brac and offering good value, authentic Korean home cooking. Classic dishes like bulgogi, dolsot and jjigae come with your choice of meat or vegetables as the main ingredient.

X **Bia Bistrot** ⊟

19 Colinton Rd ⊠ *EH10 5DP* – 📞 *(0131) 4528453*   Plan: **B2**
– *www.biabistrot.co.uk* – *Closed first week January, 1 week July, Sunday and Monday*
Menu £ 10 (lunch and early dinner) – Carte £ 19/34
• **Classic cuisine** • **Neighbourhood** • **Bistro** •

A simple, good value neighbourhood bistro with a buzzy vibe. Unfussy, flavoursome dishes range in their influences due to the friendly owners' Irish-Scottish and French-Spanish heritages; they are husband and wife and cook together.

X **Café St Honoré**

34 North West Thistle Street Ln. ⊠ *EH2 1EA* – 📞 *(0131)*   Plan: **F1**
2262211 – *www.cafesthonore.com* – *Closed 24-26 December and 1-2 January*
Menu £ 15/23 – Carte £ 28/45 – *(booking essential)*
• **Classic French** • **Bistro** • **Neighbourhood** •

Long-standing French bistro, tucked away down a side street. The interior is cosy, with wooden marquetry, mirrors on the walls and tightly packed tables. Traditional Gallic menus use Scottish produce and they even smoke their own salmon.

X **Wedgwood** ἐἐ

267 Canongate ⊠ *EH8 8BQ* – 📞 *(0131) 5588737*   Plan: **H2**
– *www.wedgwoodtherestaurant.co.uk* – *Closed 2-22 January and 25-26 December*
Menu £ 15 (lunch) – Carte £ 33/53
• **Modern cuisine** • **Friendly** • **Intimate** •

Atmospheric bistro hidden away at the bottom of the Royal Mile. Well-presented dishes showcase produce foraged from the surrounding countryside and feature some original, modern combinations. It's personally run by a friendly team.

🍽 **The Scran & Scallie** ♿ ἐ

1 Comely Bank Rd, Stockbridge ⊠ *EH4 1DT* – 📞 *(0131)*   Plan: **E1**
332 6281 – *www.scranandscallie.com* – *Closed 25 December*
Menu £ 15 (weekday lunch) – Carte £ 23/46 – *(booking advisable)*
• **Traditional British** • **Neighbourhood** • **Family** •

The more casual venture from Tom Kitchin, located in a smart, village-like suburb. It has a wood-furnished bar and a dining room which blends rustic and contemporary décor. Extensive menus follow a 'Nature to Plate' philosophy and focus on the classical and the local.

Malmaison

1 Tower Pl ✉ EH6 7BZ – ✆ (0844) 693 0652 Plan: **C1**
– www.malmaison.com
100 rm – †£ 89/300 ††£ 89/300 – ☕£ 14
• Business • Luxury • Contemporary •
Impressive former seamen's mission located on the quayside; the first of the Malmaison hotels. The décor is a mix of bold stripes and contrasting black and white themes. Comfy, well-equipped bedrooms; one with a four-poster and a tartan roll-top bath. Intimate bar and a popular French brasserie and terrace.

Martin Wishart

54 The Shore ✉ EH6 6RA – ✆ (0131) 5533557 Plan: **C1**
– www.martin-wishart.co.uk – Closed 31 December-18 January, 18-19 October, 25-26 December, Sunday and Monday
Menu £ 29 (weekday lunch)/75 – Carte approx. £ 75 – *(booking essential)*
• Modern cuisine • Elegant • Intimate •
This elegant, modern restaurant is becoming something of an Edinburgh institution. Choose between three 6 course menus – Classic, Seafood and Vegetarian – and a concise à la carte. Top ingredients are used in well-judged, flavourful combinations; dishes are classically based but have elaborate, original touches.
→ Langoustine with kohlrabi, vanilla and passion fruit. Roast breast and pastilla of duck with red cabbage, beetroot, macadamia and redcurrant. Mangaro chocolate dome with banana, yuzu and almond ice cream.

Kitchin (Tom Kitchin)

78 Commercial Quay ✉ EH6 6LX – ✆ (0131) 5551755 Plan: **C1**
– www.thekitchin.com – Closed 23 December-13 January, 4-8 April, 25-29 July, 10-14 October, Sunday and Monday
Menu £ 30 (lunch) – Carte £ 70/87 – *(booking essential)*
• Modern cuisine • Design • Fashionable •
Set in a smart, converted whisky warehouse. 'From nature to plate' is the eponymous chef-owner's motto and the use of natural features like bark wall coverings, alongside the more traditional Harris tweed, reflect his passion for using the freshest and best quality Scottish ingredients. Refined, generously proportioned classic French dishes are packed with vivid flavours.
→ Isle of Cumbrae oysters prepared six ways. Highland hogget with roasted & raw artichoke and black olive. Tomlinson's Farm rhubarb crumble soufflé with vanilla ice cream.

Norn

50-54 Henderson St ✉ EH6 6DE – ✆ (0131) 629 2525 Plan: **C1**
– www.nornrestaurant.com – Closed Sunday-Monday and lunch Tuesday-Wednesday
Menu £ 20/40 – *(booking advisable) (tasting menu only)*
• Modern cuisine • Fashionable • Neighbourhood •
A young couple run this modern restaurant, where the chefs serve the dishes themselves. Creative cooking showcases produce from small Scottish suppliers along with items they have foraged. Lunch is 3 courses and dinner either 4 or 7.

Bistro Provence

88 Commercial St ✉ EH6 6LX – ✆ (0131) 344 4295 Plan: **C1**
– www.bistroprovence.co.uk – Closed 3-15 July and Monday
Menu £ 10/28
• Classic French • Bistro • Friendly •
This converted warehouse brings a taste of France to the cobbled quayside of Leith. It's very personally run by a gregarious owner and a welcoming team, and offers an appealing range of unfussy dishes with Provençal leanings.

GLASGOW
GLASGOW

Population: 598 830

S. Vidler/Prisma/age fotostock

The Clyde played a pivotal role in the original growth of Glasgow: in the 18C as a source of trade with the Americas, and in the 19C as a centre of the world's major shipbuilding industries. During this period many of the imposing buildings on show today were constructed; a testament to the city's wealth. This all changed post-World War II, however, as Glasgow's industry fell into tatters and it gained a troubled, poverty-stricken reputation. But Glasgow is also one of the greatest urban success stories: the 1990 City of Culture award turned its image upside down and since then it has grown immensely as an arts, business and retail centre, and tourists have discovered for themselves its grand Victorian façade and eye-catching riverside milieu.

Cocooned within the curving arm of the M8 motorway, the centre is arranged in a neat grid system – and is home to Glasgow's main cultural venues. The 'Merchant City', just to the east, was the original medieval centre but is now a thriving arts quarter, while the West End – a bohemian district filled with cafés, bars and restaurants – has practically reinvented itself as a town in its own right; it's also where you'll find the Kelvingrove Art Gallery and Museum. Cross the Clyde, to the south, and amongst the sprawling suburbs you come across gems like The Burrell Collection and Charles Rennie Mackintosh's House for an Art Lover.

GLASGOW IN...

→ **ONE DAY**
Kelvingrove Art Gallery, Sauchiehall Street, Glasgow School of Art, West End.

→ **TWO DAYS**
Glasgow Green, Provand's Lordship, Necropolis, Science Centre, trip on the Clyde.

→ **THREE DAYS**
Train journey to the Clyde Valley, Pollok Country Park.

PRACTICAL INFORMATION

ARRIVAL-DEPARTURE

✈ Glasgow International Airport is 8 miles west of the city. The Glasgow Shuttle runs every 10min and takes 25min.

GETTING AROUND

Glasgow has a circular underground system covering the centre and west of the city – to go right round it only takes 24 minutes. You can buy single or return fares as well as all day and 7 day tickets. A good idea on the buses is to buy a FirstDay ticket from your driver; this will let you hop on or off buses right through until midnight. Black cabs are easy to hail all over the city.

CALENDAR HIGHLIGHTS

January
Celtic Connections.

March
Comedy Festival.

June
West End Festival, International Jazz Festival.

July
Merchant City Festival.

August
World Pipe Band Championships.

November
Whisky Live.

EATING OUT

The dreaded legend of the deep-fried Mars bar did no favours for the reputation of the Scottish diet. Don't mention it in Glasgow, though, because in the last decade the place has undergone a gourmet revolution, and these days you can enjoy good food in restaurants from all areas of the world. There are now many establishments specialising in modern Scottish cooking and fish menus have come of age. If you go to the trendy West End or Merchant City quarters you'll find bistros and brasseries that wouldn't be out of place in France or Italy. Glasgow makes the most of the glorious natural larder on its doorstep: spring lamb from the Borders, Perthshire venison, fresh fish and shellfish from the Western Highlands and Aberdeen Angus beef. It's also always had a lot of respect for its liquid refreshment: if you fancy a beer, you can't go far wrong with a pint of Deuchar's, the award-winning 'Bitter & Twisted' or a Dark Island 'imported' from the Orkneys; the locals have taken to real ale from the Scottish regions in a big way.

Hotel du Vin at One Devonshire Gardens   🕭 🐕

1 Devonshire Gdns ✉ *G12 OUX* – ℰ *(0141) 3780385*   Plan: **A1**
– *www.hotelduvin.com*
49 rm – 🛉£ 109/249 🛉🛉£ 109/249 – ⊑ £ 18 – 3 suites
• Townhouse • Luxury • Elegant •

Collection of adjoining townhouses boasting original 19C stained glass, wood panelling and a labyrinth of corridors. Furnished in dark, opulent shades but with a modern, country house air. Luxurious bedrooms; one with a small gym and sauna.
Bistro – See restaurant listing

Blythswood Square   🖪 🕭 🏐 🕭 🖼 🐕

11 Blythswood Sq ✉ *G2 4AD* – ℰ *(0141) 2488888*   Plan: **D2**
– *www.blythswoodsquare.com*
100 rm ⊑ – 🛉£ 120/280 🛉🛉£ 120/280 – 1 suite
• Historic • Luxury • Design •

Stunning property on a delightful Georgian square; once the Scottish RAC HQ. Modern décor contrasts with original fittings. Dark, moody bedrooms have marble bathrooms; the Penthouse Suite features a bed adapted from a snooker table.
Blythswood Square – See restaurant listing

Malmaison   🕭 🐕

278 West George St ✉ *G2 4LL* – ℰ *(0141) 5721000*   Plan: **C2**
– *www.malmaison.com*
72 rm ⊑ – 🛉£ 117/330 🛉🛉£ 129/340 – 8 suites
• Business • Historic • Contemporary •

Impressive-looking former church with moody, masculine décor. Stylish, boldly coloured bedrooms offer good facilities; some are duplex suites. The Big Yin Suite – named after Billy Connolly – has a roll-top bath in the room.
The Honours – See restaurant listing

Grasshoppers   🏠

Caledonian Chambers (6th Floor), 87 Union St   Plan: **D2**
✉ *G1 3TA* – ℰ *(0141) 222 2666* – *www.grasshoppersglasgow.com*
– *Closed 3 days Christmas*
29 rm ⊑ – 🛉£ 75/105 🛉🛉£ 85/125
• Business • Design •

Unusually located, on the 6th floor of the Victorian railway station building; the lounge overlooks what is the largest glass roof in Europe. Stylish, well-designed bedrooms with bespoke Scandinavian-style furnishings and Scottish art. Smart, compact shower rooms. Three course suppers for residents only.

15 Glasgow   🚗 🅿

15 Woodside Pl. ✉ *G3 7QL* – ℰ *(0141) 3321263*   Plan: **C1**
– *www.15glasgow.com*
5 rm ⊑ – 🛉£ 120/150 🛉🛉£ 130/170
• Townhouse • Luxury • Personalised •

Delightful Victorian townhouse set on a quiet square. Characterful original features include mosaic floors and ornate cornicing. Extremely spacious bedrooms boast top quality furnishings and underfloor heating in their bathrooms.

Brian Maule at Chardon d'Or   🖼 ⇔ 🕭 🕅

176 West Regent St. ✉ *G2 4RL* – ℰ *(0141) 2483801*   Plan: **D2**
– *www.brianmaule.com* – *Closed 25 December, 1 January, Sunday and bank holidays*
Menu £ 21 (lunch and early dinner) – Carte £ 45/58
• Modern cuisine • Elegant • Intimate •

Georgian townhouse in the city's heart, with original pillars, ornate carved ceilings and white walls hung with vibrant modern art. Classical cooking with a modern edge; luxurious ingredients and large portions. Friendly, efficient service.

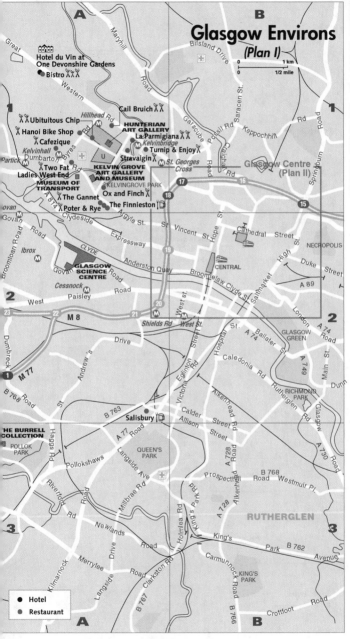

Glasgow Environs
(Plan I)

Hotel du Vin at
One Devonshire Gardens
Bistro

Cail Bruich

Ubiquitous Chip
Hanoi Bike Shop
Cafezique
Kelvinhall
Dumbarto
Ladies West End
MUSEUM OF
TRANSPORT
The Gannet
Poter & Rye

HUNTERIAN
ART GALLERY
La Parmigiana
Kelvinbridge
Turnip & Enjoy
Stravaigin
St. Georges
Cross
KELVIN GROVE
ART GALLERY
AND MUSEUM
KELVINGROVE PARK
Ox and Finch
The Finnieston

Glasgow Centre
(Plan II)

GLASGOW
SCIENCE
CENTRE

Anderston Quay

CENTRAL

NECROPOLIS

Cathedral Street

GLASGOW
GREEN

Salisbury

THE BURRELL
COLLECTION
POLLOK
PARK

QUEEN'S
PARK

RUTHERGLEN

KING'S
PARK

● Hotel
● Restaurant

919

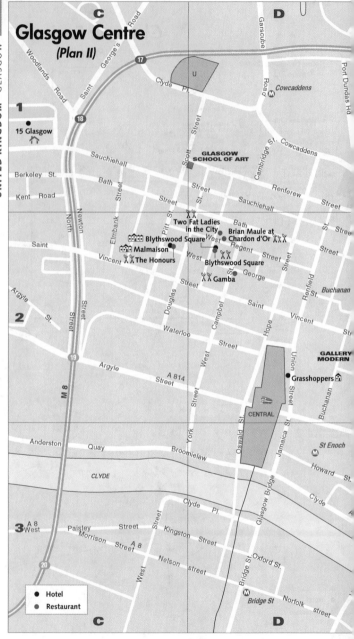

Glasgow Centre
(Plan II)

15 Glasgow

GLASGOW SCHOOL OF ART

Two Fat Ladies in the City
Brian Maule at Chardon d'Or
Blythswood Square
Malmaison
The Honours
Blythswood Square
Gamba

GALLERY MODERN

Grasshoppers

CENTRAL

Cowcaddens

St Enoch

Bridge St

CLYDE

● Hotel
● Restaurant

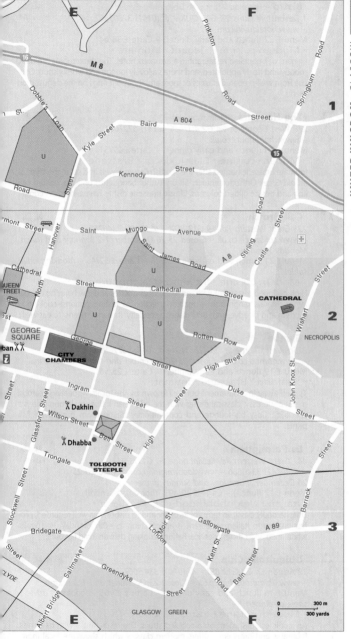

921

XXX **Bistro** – Hotel du Vin at One Devonshire Gardens   ⊗ 占
1 Devonshire Gdns ⊠ *G12 OUX* – ℰ *(0141) 3780385*   Plan: **A1**
– www.hotelduvin.com
Menu £ 22 (lunch and early dinner) – Carte £ 38/64
• Modern cuisine • Elegant • Intimate •
Elegant oak-panelled restaurant in a luxurious hotel. The three rooms are dark, moody and richly appointed, and there's a lovely lounge and whisky snug. Choose from well-prepared classics or more ambitious offerings on the degustation menu.

XX **The Honours** – Malmaison Hotel   占 囲
278 West George St ⊠ *G2 4LL* – ℰ *(0141) 5721001*   Plan: **C2**
– www.thehonours.co.uk
Menu £ 19 (lunch and early dinner) – Carte £ 27/51
• Modern cuisine • Classic décor • Brasserie •
Intimate brasserie named after the Scottish Crown Jewels and set in the crypt of an old Greek Orthodox church. Sit on leather banquettes under a vaulted ceiling and beside gilded columns. Classic brasserie dishes have a modern edge.

XX **Cail Bruich**   囲 ⑩
725 Great Western Rd. ⊠ *G12 8QX* – ℰ *(0141) 3346265*   Plan: **A1**
– www.cailbruich.co.uk – Closed 25-26 December, 1-2 January and lunch Monday-Tuesday
Menu £ 21 (lunch and early dinner)/25 – Carte £ 32/48 – *(booking advisable)*
• Modern cuisine • Intimate • Neighbourhood •
High ceilinged restaurant with red leather banquettes and low hanging copper lamps. Menus range from a market selection to tasting options; cooking is modern and creative, with BBQ dishes a specialty. Its name means 'to eat well'.

XX **Gamba**   🍷
225a West George St. ⊠ *G2 2ND* – ℰ *(0141) 5720899*   Plan: **D2**
– www.gamba.co.uk – Closed 25-26 December and first week January
Menu £ 19 (lunch and early dinner) – Carte £ 25/56
• Seafood • Brasserie • Intimate •
Tucked away in a basement but well-known by the locals. Appealing seafood menu of unfussy, classical dishes with the odd Asian influence; lemon sole is a speciality. Cosy bar-lounge and contemporary dining room hung with fish prints.

XX **La Parmigiana**   囲 🍷
447 Great Western Rd, Kelvinbridge ⊠ *G12 8HH*   Plan: **A1**
– ℰ (0141) 3340686 – www.laparmigiana.co.uk – Closed 25-26 December, 1 January and Sunday dinner
Menu £ 17 (lunch) – Carte £ 30/49 – *(booking essential)*
• Italian • Neighbourhood • Classic décor •
Unashamedly classic in terms of its décor and its dishes, this well-regarded, professionally run Italian restaurant is approaching its 40th birthday. Red walls, white linen and efficient service. Refined cooking delivers bold flavours.

XX **Ubiquitous Chip**   ⊗ 占 囲 🍷
12 Ashton Ln ⊠ *G12 8SJ* – ℰ *(0141) 334 5007*   Plan: **A1**
– www.ubiquitouschip.co.uk – Closed 25 December and 1 January
Menu £ 16 (lunch and early dinner) – Carte £ 29/65 – *(bookings advisable at dinner)*
• Modern cuisine • Bistro • Friendly •
An iconic establishment on a cobbled street. The restaurant – with its ponds, fountains and greenery – offers modern classics which showcase local ingredients, while the mezzanine-level brasserie serves tasty Scottish favourites.

XX **Blythswood Square** – Blythswood Square Hotel &. AC 🕄
11 Blythswood Sq ⊠ G2 4AD – ℰ (0141) 2488888   Plan: **D2**
– www.blythswoodsquare.com
Menu £ 19 (lunch and early dinner) – Carte £ 18/52
• Modern cuisine • Fashionable • Brasserie •
Stylish hotel restaurant in the ballroom of the old RAC building; chic in black
and white, with a zinc-topped bar and Harris Tweed banquettes. Classic menu
with meats from the Josper grill. Desserts showcase the kitchen's ambitious
side.

XX **Two Fat Ladies in the City**   &. 🕄
118a Blythswood St ⊠ G2 4EG – ℰ (0141) 8470088   Plan: **D2**
– www.twofatladiesrestaurant.com
Menu £ 18 (lunch and early dinner) – Carte £ 30/56
• Traditional cuisine • Classic décor • Brasserie •
Intimate restaurant which resembles an old-fashioned brasserie, courtesy of its
wooden floor, banquettes and mirrors. Classically based dishes are straightforward in style, with a modern edge, and fresh Scottish seafood is a feature.

XX **Urban**   AC ⇔ 🕄
23-25 St Vincent Pl. ⊠ G1 2DT – ℰ (0141) 2485636   Plan: **E2**
– www.urbanbrasserie.co.uk – Closed 25 December and 1 January
Menu £ 17 (lunch and early dinner) – Carte £ 22/47
• Traditional British • Brasserie • Classic décor •
Formerly the Bank of England's HQ. The grand dining room has booths, vibrant
artwork and an impressive illuminated glass and wrought iron ceiling. Classic
British dishes feature, along with live music every Friday and Saturday evening.

X **The Gannet**   &. AC
🕄 *1155 Argyle St ⊠ G3 8TB – ℰ (0141) 2042081*   Plan: **A1**
– www.thegannetgla.com – Closed 24-27 December, Sunday dinner and
Monday
Carte £ 28/39
• Modern British • Rustic • Neighbourhood •
This appealingly rustic neighbourhood restaurant makes passionate use of Scotland's larder and as such, the menus are constantly evolving. Classic dishes are
presented in a modern style and they are brought to the table by a charming
team. Exposed stone, untreated wood and corrugated iron all feature.

X **Ox and Finch**   AC ⇔ 🕄
🕄 *920 Sauchiehall St ⊠ G3 7TF – ℰ (0141) 339 8627*   Plan: **A1**
– www.oxandfinch.com – Closed 25-26 December and 1-2 January
Carte £ 16/28
• Modern British • Design • Vintage •
A bright, breezy team run this likeable rustic restaurant, with its tile-backed
open kitchen and wines displayed in a huge metal cage. The Scottish and European small plates will tempt one and all: cooking centres around old favourites
but with added modern twists, and the flavours really shine through.

X **Turnip & Enjoy**
393-395 Great Western Rd ⊠ G4 9HY – ℰ (0141)   Plan: **A1**
334 6622 – www.turnipandenjoy.co.uk – Closed Monday and Tuesday
lunch
Menu £ 17/20 (weekdays) – Carte £ 27/83
• Modern British • Neighbourhood • Rustic •
You can't help but like this sweet neighbourhood restaurant with its sage green
walls and wonderful ceiling mouldings. Service is friendly and the food rustic,
with classical flavours presented in a modern way; desserts are a highlight.

X **Porter & Rye**   🕭   🎿

1131 Argyle St ✉ G3 8ND – ℰ (0141) 572 1212   Plan: **A1**
– www.porterandrye.com – Closed 25 December and 1 January
Carte £ 23/91 – *(booking advisable)*
• Meats and grills • Trendy • Bistro •
Small, well-run loft style operation where wooden floors and exposed bricks
blend with steel balustrades and glass screens. Menus offer creative modern
small plates and a good range of aged Scottish steaks, from onglet to porter-
house.

X **Stravaigin**   🛜 🕭 🎿

😊 *28 Gibson St, ✉ G12 8NX – ℰ (0141) 334 2665*   Plan: **A1**
– www.stravaigin.co.uk – Closed 25 December and 1 January
Carte £ 27/40 – *(booking essential at dinner)*
• International • Simple • Rustic •
Well-run eatery with a relaxed shabby-chic style, a bustling café bar and plenty
of nooks and crannies. Interesting menus uphold the motto 'think global, eat
local', with dishes ranging from carefully prepared Scottish favourites to tasty
Asian-inspired fare. Monthly 'theme' nights range from haggis to tapas.

X **Two Fat Ladies West End**   🗱

88 Dumbarton Rd ✉ G11 6NX – ℰ (0141) 339 1944   Plan: **A1**
*– www.twofatladiesrestaurant.com – Closed 25-26 December and 1-
2 January*
Menu £ 16 (lunch and early dinner) – Carte £ 27/40
• Seafood • Neighbourhood • Bistro •
Quirky neighbourhood restaurant – the first in the Fat Ladies group – with red
velour banquettes, bold blue and gold décor, and a semi open plan kitchen in
the window. Cooking is simple and to the point, focusing on classical fish dishes.

X **Dhabba**   🕭 🎿 🟢

44 Candleriggs ✉ G1 1LE – ℰ (0141) 5531249   Plan: **E3**
– www.thedhabba.com – Closed 25 December and 1 January
Menu £ 10 (weekday lunch) – Carte £ 19/38
• Indian • Fashionable • Colourful •
Stylish restaurant in the heart of the Merchant City. Menus focus on northern
India, with interesting breads and lots of tandoor dishes. Its name refers to a
roadside diner and its walls are decorated with photos of street scenes.

X **Hanoi Bike Shop**   🕭 🎿

8 Ruthven Ln (Off Byres Rd) ✉ G12 9BG – ℰ (0141)   Plan: **A1**
*334 7165 – www.thehanoibikeshop.co.uk – Closed 25 December and
1 January*
Carte £ 18/26
• Vietnamese • Simple • Rustic •
Relaxed Vietnamese café; head to the lighter upstairs room with its fine array of
lanterns. Simple menu of classic Vietnamese dishes including street food like
rice paper summer rolls. Charming, knowledgeable staff offer recommendations.

X **Dakhin**   🕭 🟢

89 Candleriggs ✉ G1 1NP – ℰ (0141) 5532585   Plan: **E2**
– www.dakhin.com – Closed 25 December and 1 January
Menu £ 15 (weekday lunch) – Carte £ 17/34
• South Indian • Simple • Friendly •
It's all about the cooking at this modest, brightly decorated restaurant: authen-
tic, southern Indian dishes might include seafood from Kerala, lamb curry from
Tamil Nadu, and their speciality, dosas – available with a variety of fillings.

X

Cafezique   ♿ AC

66 Hyndland St ⊠ G11 5PT – ℰ (0141) 339 7180   Plan: **A1**
– www.delizique.com – Closed 25-26 December and 1 January
Carte £ 21/28
• Modern cuisine • Bistro • Friendly •

Buzzy eatery with stone walls, wood floors and striking monotone screen prints.
All-day breakfasts and Mediterranean light bites are followed by vibrant dishes
in two sizes at dinner. Many ingredients come from their deli next door.

The Finnieston   ⛱ ♿

1125 Argyle St ⊠ G3 8ND – ℰ (0141) 2222884   Plan: **A1**
– www.thefinniestonbar.com – Closed 25-26 December and 1 January
Carte £ 23/37
• Seafood • Friendly • Cosy •

Small, cosy pub specialising in Scottish seafood and gin cocktails; with an intriguing ceiling, a welcoming fire and lots of booths. Dishes are light, tasty and
neatly presented, relying on just a few ingredients so that flavours are clear.

Salisbury   AC

72 Nithsdale Rd ⊠ G41 2AN – ℰ (0141) 423 0084   Plan: **A2**
– www.thesalisbury.co.uk – Closed 25 December and 1 January
Menu £ 10 (lunch) – Carte £ 23/34
• Modern British • Neighbourhood • Rustic •

A bijou pub on the south side of the city. Its interior is modern and cosy, the
staff are friendly, and the monthly menu has an eclectic mix of Scottish and
international flavours. Local seafood is given an original modern twist.

Europe in maps
and numbers

Eurozone : €

  **EU** + €

 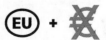 **EU** + ~~€~~

 EU states

Schengen Countries

Area of free movement between member states

 (EU) + Schengen

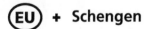

 (EU) + Schengen

 (EU) + Schengen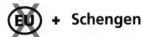

Driving in Europe

The information panels which follow give the principal motoring regulations in force when this guide was prepared for press; an explanation of the symbols is given below, together with some additional notes.

Speed restrictions in kilometres per hour applying to:

 motorways

 dual carriageways

 single carriageways

 urban areas

 Maximum permitted level of alcohol in the bloodstream. This should not be taken as an acceptable level - it is NEVER sensible to drink and drive.

 Whether tolls are payable on motorways and/or other parts of the road network.

 Whether seatbelts are compulsory for the driver and all passengers in both front and back seats.

Whether headlights must be on at all times.

		🛣	🛣	🛣	🏙	🍷	🛣	🦺	◧
AUSTRIA	(A)	130		100	50	0,5	●	●	●
BELGIUM	(B)	120	120	90	50	0,5		●	
CZECH REPUBLIC	(CZ)	130		90	50	0,0	●	●	●
DENMARK	(DK)	130		80	50	0,5		●	●
FINLAND	(FIN)	120		80	50	0,5		●	●
FRANCE	(F)	130	110	90	50	0,5	●	●	
GERMANY	(D)			100	50	0,5		●	●
GREECE	(GR)	130		90	50	0,5		●	
HUNGARY	(H)	130	110	90	50	0,0	●	●	●
IRELAND	(IRL)	120	100	80	50	0,5		●	
ITALY	(I)	130	110	90	50	0,5		●	●
LUXEMBOURG	(L)	130		90	50	0,5		●	
NETHERLANDS	(NL)	130	100	80	50	0,5		●	
NORWAY	(N)	100		80	50	0,2		●	●
POLAND	(PL)	140	120	90	50	0,2		●	●
PORTUGAL	(P)	120	100	90	50	0,5		●	●
SPAIN	(E)	120	120	90	50	0,5		●	●
SWEDEN	(S)	110		70	50	0,2		●	●
SWITZERLAND	(CH)	120	100	80	50	0,5	●	●	
UNITED KINGDOM (Scotland)	(GB)	112	112	96	48	0,8 0,5		●	

●   Compulsory

Distances

(A) AUSTRIA
(AL) ALBANIA
(B) BELGIUM
(BG) BULGARIA
(BIH) BOSNIA-HERZEGOVINA
(BY) BELARUS
(CZ) CZECH REPUBLIC
(CH) SWITZERLAND
(D) GERMANY
(DK) DENMARK
(E) SPAIN
(EST) ESTONIA
(F) FRANCE
(FIN) FINLAND
(GB) UNITED KINGDOM
(GR) GREECE
(H) HUNGARY
(HR) CROATIA
(I) ITALY
(IRL) IRELAND
(L) LUXEMBOURG
(LT) LITHUANIA
(LV) LATVIA
(M) MALTA
(MD) MOLDAVIA
(MK) MACEDONIA (F.Y.R.O.M.)
(MNE) MONTENEGRO
(N) NORWAY
(NL) NETHERLANDS
(P) PORTUGAL
(PL) POLAND
(S) SWEDEN
(RO) ROMANIA
(RUS) RUSSIA
(SRB) SERBIA
(SK) SLOVAK REPUBLIC
(SLO) SLOVENIA
(TR) TURKEY
(UA) UKRAINE

123 : distances by road in kilometers

Glasgow 76 Edinburgh

(IRL)

DUBLIN

673

462 (GB)

Birmingham

202

LONDON BRUSSELS

Rotterdam

114

226

223

401

PARIS

127

Orléans

307

(F)

Gene

154

554

648 620

305

Toulouse 242

293 Montpellier

390

513

619

Barcelona

LISBON 627 MADRID

(P)

(E)

Time zones

Standard Times ahead of or behind Greenwich Mean Time (+ 4.30 variation)

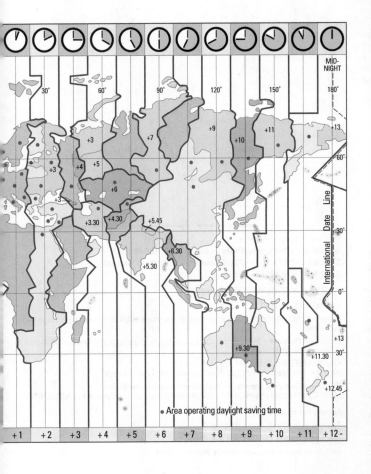

• Area operating daylight saving time

| +1 | +2 | +3 | +4 | +5 | +6 | +7 | +8 | +9 | +10 | +11 | +12 - |

Michelin Travel Partner
Société par actions simplifiées au capital de 11 288 880 EUR
27 Cours de l'Île Seguin - 92100 Boulogne Billancourt (France)
R.C.S. Nanterre 433 677 721

© **Michelin, Propriétaires-Éditeurs**

Dépôt légal : 02-2017

Printed in Italy: 02-2017
Typesetting: JOUVE, Saran (France)
Printing-binding: LEGO Print, Lavis (Italie)
Printed on paper from sustainably managed forests

Our editorial team has taken the greatest care in writing and checking the information in this guide. However, pratical information (administrative formalities, prices, addresses, telephone numbers, Internet addresses, etc) is subject to frequent change and such information should therefore be used for guidance only. It is possible that some of the information in this guide may not be accurate or exhaustive as of the date of publication. Before taking action (in particular in regard to administrative and customs regulations and procedures), you should contact the appropriate of f icial administration. We hereby accept no liability in regard to such information.